THE BEST LAWYERS IN AMERICA

THE BEST LAWYERS IN AMERICA

STEVEN NAIFEH
AND
GREGORY WHITE SMITH
Harvard Law School 1977

1989-1990

WOODWARD/WHITE

New York

Copyright © 1989 by Woodward/White, Inc.
300 Central Park West, New York, NY 10024
All rights reserved. This book, or parts thereof, must not be
reproduced in any form without permission.

Designed by JOEL AVIROM

Library of Congress Cataloging-in-Publication Data

Naifeh, Steven W., 1952–
  The best lawyers in America: 1989–1990 / Steven Naifeh and
Gregory White Smith.
    p. cm.
  ISBN 0-913391-03-4 : $89.00
  1. Lawyers—United States—Directories. 2. Lawyers—Specialties
and specialists—United States—Directories. I. Smith, Gregory White. II. Title.
KF190.N23 1989   89-5296
340′ .025′73—dc19   CIP

PRINTED IN THE UNITED STATES OF AMERICA

We would like to acknowledge our debt to the thousands of attorneys who gave of their time and expertise in the process of compiling these lists.

CONTENTS

ALABAMA	1
ALASKA	20
ARIZONA	27
ARKANSAS	44
CALIFORNIA	51
COLORADO	101
CONNECTICUT	116
DELAWARE	131
DISTRICT OF COLUMBIA	138
FLORIDA	168
GEORGIA	193
HAWAII	209
IDAHO	216
ILLINOIS	220
INDIANA	241
IOWA	256
KANSAS	266
KENTUCKY	278
LOUISIANA	287
MAINE	302
MARYLAND	308
MASSACHUSETTS	317
MICHIGAN	342
MINNESOTA	359
MISSISSIPPI	375

MISSOURI	384
MONTANA	399
NEBRASKA	406
NEVADA	414
NEW HAMPSHIRE	421
NEW JERSEY	428
NEW MEXICO	442
NEW YORK	452
NORTH CAROLINA	519
NORTH DAKOTA	533
OHIO	540
OKLAHOMA	573
OREGON	588
PENNSYLVANIA	598
RHODE ISLAND	624
SOUTH CAROLINA	630
SOUTH DAKOTA	638
TENNESSEE	643
TEXAS	660
UTAH	702
VERMONT	710
VIRGINIA	715
WASHINGTON	739
WEST VIRGINIA	758
WISCONSIN	763
WYOMING	781

INTRODUCTION

Six years and three editions after *The Best Lawyers in America* first appeared, we continue to be gratified by the overwhelmingly favorable response the book has received from both inside and outside the legal community. Many prominent members of the bar, including David Brink of Minneapolis and John Shepherd of St. Louis, both recent past presidents of the American Bar Association, have written to thank us for performing a "needed function" in a reliable, responsible way. Attorneys from all over the country continue to write and call with stories of clients who sought them out or colleagues who referred cases to them through the book. Corporate counsel from *Fortune* 500 companies have written to express their appreciation for what one called an "indispensable resource."

We are proud, therefore, to present *The Best Lawyers in America: 1989-1990*. As those who are familiar with previous editions will see immediately, the new third edition has been thoroughly revised. Most obviously, it is organized by state rather than by field of specialty, a change made in response to many letters, which we hope will make the book even easier to use. The new edition is also larger than ever, due primarily to the addition of several new categories (Appellate Law, Maritime Law, Natural Resources and Environmental Law) and an effort to include lawyers from more communities. Most of the individual lists, in fact, have grown only modestly in size and some have even shrunk. In addition, we have provided subspecialties for corporate lawyers in New York City as well as in the District of Columbia.

Most importantly, every one of the 568 lists that follow has been completely revised on the basis of a new, nationwide survey even more rigorous and comprehensive than those we conducted for previous editions. (See below for a description of the survey process.) The quality of the lists continues to be the backbone of this book, and, more so than ever before, we have bent every effort to ensure that these lists are reliable, accurate, and current.

COMPILING THE THIRD EDITION

We began with the lists from the second edition *as a starting point only*. (For a detailed description of the similar methodology used in the first two editions, see the introduction in either of the earlier volumes.) We placed calls to almost all of the lawyers listed and asked them to nominate the most outstanding attorneys in their area in their specialty. As in the past, we did not attempt to articulate the criteria for judging professional excellence; we left that to the individual attorney. We did, however, routinely couch our inquiry in the following terms: "If you had a close friend or a relative who needed a real estate lawyer (for example), and you couldn't handle the case yourself—for reasons of conflict of interest or time—to whom would you refer them?" All comments, we promised, would remain confidential.

In addition to nominating the lawyers they considered the best in their fields, the respondents were asked to review the names of lawyers already nominated and to suggest deletions. We continued to call lawyers on the lists, adding and removing names, until a clear consensus emerged. Many names received unanimous praise. Others earned mixed assessments. In the latter instance, final decisions were made on a case-by-case basis after additional calls. No name was ever removed from the list on the basis of a single negative vote, nor was any name added to it on the basis of a single nomination.

Because of the favorable attention received by the first two editions, we found our respondents to be even more cooperative than in the past. In 1983, seventy-two of the lawyers we polled refused to cooperate. By 1987, that number had dwindled to nineteen. For this edition, out of thousands of respondents, only five were similarly reticent.

Also because of the book's reputation, lawyers were even more willing than in 1987 to cast negative votes as well as positive ones—an index, we believe, of how seriously they take the voting process. Several of the most famous (or infamous) lawyers in the United States were *not* included on these lists because their colleagues agreed that their national fame did not rest on a foundation of professional excellence.

In the end, we placed approximately 19,000 phone calls and talked with 7,500 attorneys.

In revising the lists, of course, we again faced the most difficult problem: when to delete a name that was listed in the previous edition. *The Best Lawyers in America* is designed to be a current reference work—a picture of the legal profession at a given moment—not a monument to reputations. As a result, we have deleted the names of hundreds of lawyers as part of the revision process. Some, of course, died; others retired or moved into government service. Still others had curtailed their activity to the point where it was no longer appropriate to include them on what is essentially a referral list. The largest group simply did not receive the necessary number of affirmative votes to be included on the list.

In this third edition, we have also continued to make a concerted effort to correct for methodological biases. While the book still tends somewhat to favor older, established lawyers over young but equally capable lawyers (reputations, after all, take time to build), the revised lists include a significantly higher percentage of lawyers under forty than previous lists, especially in relatively new fields such as Environmental Law and Employment Discrimination. We have also continued our effort to include more lawyers from relatively small firms and more lawyers from outside the large commercial centers in each state.

In regard to the problem of how to rank a lawyer who wields considerable political influence in his or her community but is no longer involved in the everyday minutiae of legal work—a problem especially acute in fields like Corporate Law, Real Estate, Labor Law, and Entertainment Law, where a lawyer's ability to make deals is at least as important as his precise command of the law—we have chosen once again to leave the determination of individual cases in the hands of those who cast the votes. As a result, we believe that, for the most part, these lists represent an appropriate mix of successful power-brokers and "lawyers' lawyers."

Even with all these efforts, the current lists continue to represent largely subjective judgments—if not ours, then those of the lawyers we surveyed—and, like all subjective assessments, they are vulnerable to criticism. In the interest of honesty and by way of disclaimer, we should note as we have in previous editions that the lists may tend to reward visibility or popularity over sheer ability. Lawyers who write articles or give lectures are more likely to come to the attention of their colleagues than lawyers who work quietly outside the public eye. This is especially true in fields such as Tax or Trusts and Estates in which lawyers often have little reason to contact one another professionally. In addition, lawyers with agreeable personalities are more likely to be nominated than lawyers who may offend their fellow lawyers while satisfying their clients.

We do not consider any of these possible distortions significant, however, and we remain confident that these lists continue to represent the best possible and certainly the most useful guide to the best lawyers in the United States ever compiled.

THE AUTHORS

Steven Naifeh and Gregory White Smith are both Harvard-trained attorneys. Mr. Naifeh worked briefly for the New York firm of Milbank, Tweed, Hadley & McCloy; Mr. Smith for the San Francisco firm of Morrison & Foerster. Between them, they have written twelve nonfiction books including two *New York Times* non-fiction bestsellers. Mr. Smith has also written a thirteen-part television series on the American Constitution with Archibald Cox.

Please direct all comments or inquiries to Woodward/White, Inc., 300 Central Park West, New York, NY 10024. Telephone: 212-724-7890.

PLEASE NOTE

Within each state, lawyers are listed alphabetically: by category, city, and last name, in that order. "Corporate Law" includes securities, finance, banking, and antitrust. "Family Law" includes divorce, adoption, and child custody. "Bankruptcy Law" includes business reorganization and creditors' rights. "Personal Injury Litigation" includes products liability and medical malpractice.

THE BEST LAWYERS IN AMERICA

ALABAMA

BANKRUPTCY LAW	1
BUSINESS LITIGATION	2
CORPORATE LAW	4
CRIMINAL DEFENSE	6
FAMILY LAW	7
LABOR AND EMPLOYMENT LAW	8
MARITIME LAW	9
NATURAL RESOURCES AND ENVIRONMENTAL LAW	10
PERSONAL INJURY LITIGATION	10
REAL ESTATE LAW	14
TAX AND EMPLOYEE BENEFITS LAW	15
TRUSTS AND ESTATES	18

BANKRUPTCY LAW

Charles L. Denaburg · Najjar, Denaburg, Meyerson, Zarzaur, Max, Wright and Schwartz · 2125 Morris Avenue · Birmingham, AL 35203 · 205-250-8400

Alan D. Levine · Levine & Schilling · 433 Frank Nelson Building · Birmingham, AL 35203 · 205-328-0460

Robert B. Rubin · Sirote, Permutt, McDermott, Slepian, Friend, Friedman, Held & Apolinsky · 2222 Arlington Avenue, South · P.O. Box 55727 · Birmingham, AL 35255 · 205-933-7111

Jerry W. Schoel · Schoel, Ogle and Benton · Watts Building, Third Floor · 2008 Third Avenue North · P.O. Box 1865 · Birmingham, AL 35201-1864 · 205-324-4893

John P. Whittington · Berkowitz, Lefkovits, Isom & Kushner · 1100 Financial Center · Birmingham, AL 35203 · 205-328-0480

George W. Finkbohner, Jr. · Finkbohner, Lawler & Olen · 606 Southtrust Bank Building · P.O. Box 3085 · Mobile, AL 36652 · 205-438-5871

Ronald P. Slepian · Sirote, Permutt, McDermott, Slepian, Friend, Friedman, Held & Apolinsky · One St. Louis Center, Suite 1000 · Mobile, AL 36602 205-432-1671

Charles N. Parnell III · Wood & Parnell · 641 South Lawrence Street · P.O. Box 4189 · Montgomery, AL 36103-4189 · 205-832-4202

BUSINESS LITIGATION

Michael L. Edwards · Balch & Bingham · 505 North 20th Street, Suite 700 · P.O. Box 306 · Birmingham, AL 35201 · 205-251-8100

Edgar M. Elliott III · Rives & Peterson · 1700 Financial Center · Birmingham, AL 35203-2607 · 205-328-8141

Samuel H. Franklin · Bradley, Arant, Rose & White · 1400 Park Place Tower Birmingham, AL 35203 · 205-252-4500

James W. Gewin · Bradley, Arant, Rose & White · 1400 Park Place Tower Birmingham, AL 35203 · 205-252-4500

William C. Knight, Jr. · Burr & Forman · 3000 SouthTrust Tower · Birmingham, AL 35203 · 205-251-3000

Warren B. Lightfoot · (also Appellate) · Bradley, Arant, Rose & White · 1400 Park Place Tower · Birmingham, AL 35203 · 205-252-4500

Crawford S. McGivaren, Jr. · Cabaniss, Johnston, Gardner, Dumas & O'Neal 1900 First National-Southern Natural Building · Birmingham, AL 35203 · 205-252-8800

Hobart A. McWhorter, Jr. · Bradley, Arant, Rose & White · 1400 Park Place Tower · Birmingham, AL 35203 · 205-252-4500

John H. Morrow · Bradley, Arant, Rose & White · 1400 Park Place Tower Birmingham, AL 35203 · 205-252-4500

J. Vernon Patrick, Jr. · Patrick & Lacy · 1201 Financial Center · Birmingham, AL 35203 · 205-323-5665

J. Michael Rediker · Ritchie & Rediker · 312 North 23rd Street · Birmingham, AL 35203 · 205-251-1288

Charles E. Sharp · Sadler, Sullivan, Sharp & Stutts · First National-Southern Natural Building, Suite 1100 · Birmingham, AL 35203 · 205-326-4166

Henry E. Simpson · Lange, Simpson, Robinson & Somerville · 1700 First Alabama Bank Building · 417 North 20th Street · Birmingham, AL 35203 · 205-250-5000

William G. Somerville, Jr. · (Appellate) · Lange, Simpson, Robinson & Somerville · 1700 First Alabama Bank Building · 417 North 20th Street · Birmingham, AL 35203 · 205-250-5000

L. Vastine Stabler, Jr. · Cabaniss, Johnston, Gardner, Dumas & O'Neal · 1900 First National-Southern Natural Building · Birmingham, AL 35203 · 205-252-8800

Louis E. Braswell · Hand, Arendall, Bedsole, Greaves & Johnston · 3000 First National Bank Building · P.O. Box 123 · Mobile, AL 36601 · 205-432-5511

James J. Duffy, Jr. · Inge, Twitty, Duffy, Prince & McKean · First Alabama Bank Building, 13th Floor · 56 St. Joseph Street · P.O. Box 1109 · Mobile, AL 36633 205-433-5441

William H. Hardie, Jr. · Johnstone, Adams, Howard, Bailey & Gordon · Royal St. Francis Building · 104 St. Francis Street · P.O. Box 1988 · Mobile, AL 36633 205-432-7682

Broox G. Holmes · Armbrecht, Jackson, DeMouy, Crowe, Holmes & Reeves 1300 AmSouth Center · P.O. Box 290 · Mobile, AL 36601 · 205-432-6751

John N. Leach, Jr. · Coale, Helmsing, Lyons & Sims · The Laclede Building 150 Government Street · P.O. Box 2767 · Mobile, AL 36652 · 205-432-5521

Champ Lyons, Jr. · (Appellate) · Coale, Helmsing, Lyons, Sims & Leach · The Laclede Building · 150 Government Street · P.O. Box 2767 · Mobile, AL 36652 205-432-5521

Robert C. Black · Hill, Hill, Carter, Franco, Cole & Black · Hill Building, Second Floor · P.O. Box 116 · Montgomery, AL 36195 · 205-834-7600

Robert A. Huffaker · Rushton, Stakley, Johnston & Garrett · 184 Commerce Street · P.O. Box 270 · Montgomery, AL 36195 · 205-834-8480

Oakley Melton, Jr. · (also Appellate) · Melton & Espy · 339 Washington Avenue P.O. Box 1267 · Montgomery, AL 36102 · 205-263-6621

M. Roland Nachman, Jr. · (also Appellate) · Balch & Bingham · The Winter Building · Two Dexter Avenue, Court Square · P.O. Box 78 · Montgomery, AL 36101 · 205-834-6500

Robert D. Segall · Copeland, Franco, Screws & Gill · 444 South Perry Street P.O. Box 347 · Montgomery, AL 36101-0347 · 205-834-1180

Maury D. Smith · Balch & Bingham · The Winter Building · Two Dexter Avenue, Court Square · P.O. Box 78 · Montgomery, AL 36101 · 205-834-6500

Thomas W. Thagard, Jr. · Balch & Bingham · The Winter Building · Two Dexter Avenue, Court Square · P.O. Box 78 · Montgomery, AL 36101 · 205-834-6500

Yetta G. Samford, Jr. · Samford, Denson, Horsley, Pettey, Martin & Barrett · 709 Avenue A · P.O. Box 2345 · Opelika, AL 36803-2345 · 205-745-3504

Sam M. Phelps · Phelps, Owens, Jenkins, Gibson & Fowler · 1201 Greensboro Avenue · Tuscaloosa, AL 35401 · 205-345-5100

CORPORATE LAW

John P. Adams · Bradley, Arant, Rose & White · 1400 Park Place Tower Birmingham, AL 35203 · 205-252-4500

Louis H. Anders, Jr. · Burr & Forman · 3000 SouthTrust Tower · Birmingham, AL 35203 · 205-251-3000

John Bingham · Balch & Bingham · 600 North 18th Street · P.O. Box 306 Birmingham, AL 35201 · 205-251-8100

Thomas Neely Carruthers, Jr. · Bradley, Arant, Rose & White · 1400 Park Place Tower · Birmingham, AL 35203 · 205-252-4500

Richard J. Cohn · Sirote, Permutt, McDermott, Slepian, Friend, Friedman, Held & Apolinsky · 2222 Arlington Avenue, South · P.O. Box 55727 · Birmingham, AL 35255 · 205-933-7111

Fournier J. Gale III · Maynard, Cooper, Frierson & Gale · Watts Building, Twelfth Floor · 2008 Third Avenue North · Birmingham, AL 35203 · 205-252-2889

John E. Grenier · Lange, Simpson, Robinson & Somerville · 1700 First Alabama Bank Building · 417 North 20th Street · Birmingham, AL 35203 · 205-250-5000

William Lyle Hinds, Jr. · Bradley, Arant, Rose & White · 1400 Park Place Tower Birmingham, AL 35203 · 205-252-4500

Harold B. Kushner · Berkowitz, Lefkovits, Isom & Kushner · 1100 Financial Center · Birmingham, AL 35203 · 205-328-0480

Arnold K. Lefkovits · Berkowitz, Lefkovits, Isom & Kushner · 1100 Financial Center · Birmingham, AL 35203 · 205-328-0480

Daniel H. Markstein III · Maynard, Cooper, Frierson & Gale · Watts Building, Twelfth Floor · 2008 Third Avenue North · Birmingham, AL 35203 · 205-252-2889

George F. Maynard · Maynard, Cooper, Frierson & Gale · Watts Building, Twelfth Floor · 2008 Third Avenue North · Birmingham, AL 35203 · 205-252-2889

J. Fred Powell · Burr & Forman · 3000 SouthTrust Tower · Birmingham, AL 35203 · 205-251-3000

J. Michael Rediker · Ritchie & Rediker · 312 North 23rd Street · Birmingham, AL 35203 · 205-251-1288

Joseph G. Stewart · Burr & Forman · 3000 SouthTrust Tower · Birmingham, AL 35203 · 205-251-3000

Robert C. Walthall · Bradley, Arant, Rose & White · 1400 Park Place Tower Birmingham, AL 35203 · 205-252-4500

Charles Larimore Whitaker · Bradley, Arant, Rose & White · 1400 Park Place Tower · Birmingham, AL 35203 · 205-252-4500

John A. Caddell · Caddell & Shanks · 230 East Moulton Street · P.O. Box 1727 Decatur, AL 35602 · 205-353-6401

Marshall J. DeMouy · Armbrecht, Jackson, DeMouy, Crowe, Holmes & Reeves 1300 AmSouth Center · P.O. Box 290 · Mobile, AL 36601 · 205-432-6751

Ramsey McKenney · Hand, Arendall, Bedsole, Greaves & Johnston · 3000 First National Bank Building · P.O. Box 123 · Mobile, AL 36601 · 205-432-5511

J. Manson Murray · Vickers, Riis, Murray and Curran · Merchants National Bank Building, Eighth Floor · P.O. Box 990 · Mobile, AL 36601 · 205-432-9772

E. B. Peebles III · Armbrecht, Jackson, DeMouy, Crowe, Holmes & Reeves 1300 AmSouth Center · P.O. Box 290 · Mobile, AL 36601 · 205-432-6751

CRIMINAL DEFENSE

Albert C. Bowen, Jr. · Beddow, Fullan, Erben & Bowen · 2019 Third Avenue North, Second Floor · Birmingham, AL 35203 · 205-322-7651

William N. Clark · Redden, Mills & Clark · 940 First Alabama Bank Building Birmingham, AL 35203 · 205-322-0457

William M. Dawson, Jr. · Dawson, Ramsey & Mathis · 933 Frank Nelson Building · Birmingham, AL 35203 · 205-323-6171

Arthur Parker · 210 Frank Nelson Building · Birmingham, AL 35203 · 205-324-9517

L. Drew Redden · Redden, Mills & Clark · 940 First Alabama Bank Building Birmingham, AL 35203 · 205-322-0457

Lawrence B. Sheffield, Jr. · Sheffield & Sheffield · 730 Frank Nelson Building Birmingham, AL 35203 · 205-328-1365

Thomas M. Haas · Haas & Knight · 255 St. Francis Street · Mobile, AL 36602 205-432-0457

Barry Hess · Hess, Atchison & Horne · 301 St. Joseph Street · Mobile, AL 36602 205-432-4546

William A. Kimbrough, Jr. · Turner, Onderdonk & Kimbrough · 1359 Dauphin Street · P.O. Box 2821 · Mobile, AL 36652 · 205-432-2855

M. A. Marsal · Seale, Marsal & Seale · 200 Church Street · P.O. Box 1746 Mobile, AL 36633 · 205-432-6685

Dennis N. Balske · Balske & Van Almen · 410 South Perry Street · Montgomery, AL 36104 · 205-263-4700

George L. Beck, Jr. · 22 Scott Street · P.O. Drawer 5019 · Montgomery, AL 36103 · 205-832-4878

David B. Byrne, Jr. · Robison & Belser · 210 Commerce Street, Second Floor P.O. Drawer 1470 · Montgomery, AL 36102 · 205-834-7000

FAMILY LAW

Stephen R. Arnold · Durward and Arnold · City Federal Building, Suite 803 Birmingham, AL 35203 · 205-324-6654

Robert C. Barnett · Barnett, Noble, Hanes, O'Neal & Cotton · City Federal Building, Suite 1600 · 2026 Second Avenue North · Birmingham, AL 35203 205-322-0471

Gerard J. Durward · Durward and Arnold · City Federal Building, Suite 803 Birmingham, AL 35203 · 205-324-6654

James M. Fullan, Jr. · Beddow, Fullan, Erben & Bowen · 2019 Third Avenue North, Second Floor · Birmingham, AL 35203 · 205-322-7651

L. Drew Redden · Redden, Mills & Clark · 940 First Alabama Bank Building Birmingham, AL 35203 · 205-322-0457

Herndon Inge, Jr. · Inge, McMillan, Adams, Coley & Ledyard · SouthTrust Bank Building, 12th Floor · 61 St. Joseph Street · P.O. Box 2345 · Mobile, AL 36652-2345 · 205-433-6506

Albert J. Seale · Seale, Marsal & Seale · 200 Church Street · P.O. Box 1746 Mobile, AL 36633 · 205-432-6685

David B. Byrne, Jr. · Robison & Belser · 210 Commerce Street, Second Floor P.O. Drawer 1470 · Montgomery, AL 36102 · 205-834-7000

John L. Capell III · Capell, Howard, Knabe & Cobbs · 57 Adams Avenue · P.O. Box 2069 · Montgomery, AL 36197 · 205-262-1671

Oakley Melton, Jr. · Melton & Espy · 339 Washington Avenue · P.O. Box 1267 Montgomery, AL 36102 · 205-263-6621

Maury D. Smith · Balch & Bingham · The Winter Building · Two Dexter Avenue, Court Square · P.O. Box 78 · Montgomery, AL 36101 · 205-834-6500

LABOR AND EMPLOYMENT LAW

James Patrick Alexander · (Management) · Bradley, Arant, Rose & White · 1400 Park Place Tower · Birmingham, AL 35203 · 205-252-4500

James U. Blacksher · (Individuals) · 300 North 21st Street · Birmingham, AL 35203 · 205-322-1100

Harold A. Bowron, Jr. · (Management) · Balch & Bingham · 505 North 20th Street, Suite 700 · P.O. Box 306 · Birmingham, AL 35201 · 205-251-8100

Stephen E. Brown · (Management) · Bradley, Arant, Rose & White · 1400 Park Place Tower · Birmingham, AL 35203 · 205-252-4500

John James Coleman, Jr. · (Management) · Bradley, Arant, Rose & White · 1400 Park Place Tower · Birmingham, AL 35203 · 205-252-4500

Jerome A. Cooper · (Labor) · Cooper, Mitch, Crawford, Kuykendall & Whatley · 409 North 21st Street, Suite 201 · Birmingham, AL 35203 · 205-328-9576

John C. Falkenberry · (Labor; Individuals) · Title Building, Fifth Floor · 300 Twenty-First Street North · Birmingham, AL 35203 · 205-322-1100

Sydney F. Frazier, Jr. · (Management) · Cabaniss, Johnston, Gardner, Dumas & O'Neal · 1900 First National-Southern Natural Building · Birmingham, AL 35203 · 205-252-8800

William F. Gardner · (Management) · Cabaniss, Johnston, Gardner, Dumas & O'Neal · 1900 First National-Southern Natural Building · Birmingham, AL 35203 · 205-252-8800

Harry L. Hopkins · (Management) · Lange, Simpson, Robinson & Somerville · 1700 First Alabama Bank Building · 417 North 20th Street · Birmingham, AL 35203 · 205-250-5000

J. Fredric Ingram · (Management) · Burr & Forman · 3000 SouthTrust Tower · Birmingham, AL 35203 · 205-251-3000

Peyton Lacy, Jr. · (Management) · Lange, Simpson, Robinson & Somerville · 1700 First Alabama Bank Building · 417 North 20th Street · Birmingham, AL 35203 · 205-250-5000

George C. Longshore · (Labor) · City Federal Building, Suite 2104 · 2030 Second Avenue North · Birmingham, AL 35203 · 205-323-8504

Charles A. Powell III · (Management) · 2205 Morris Avenue · Birmingham, AL 35203 · 205-251-6666

C. V. Stelzenmuller · (Management) · Burr & Forman · 3000 SouthTrust Tower · Birmingham, AL 35203 · 205-251-3000

Joe R. Whatley, Jr. · (Labor) · Cooper, Mitch, Crawford, Kuykendall & Whatley · 409 North 21st Street, Suite 201 · Birmingham, AL 35203 · 205-328-9576

Robert L. Wiggins, Jr. · (Individuals) · Gordon, Silberman, Wiggins & Childs · 1500 Colonial Bank Building · Birmingham, AL 35203 · 205-328-0640

Willis C. Darby, Jr. · (Management) · Darby & Danner · 200 St. Anthony Street · P.O. Box 2565 · Mobile, AL 36652 · 205-432-2635

J. Cecil Gardner · (Labor) · Lattof & Gardner · First Alabama Bank Building, Ninth Floor · P.O. Box 3066 · Mobile, AL 36652 · 205-432-6691

Brock B. Gordon · (Management) · Johnstone, Adams, Howard, Bailey & Gordon · Royal St. Francis Building · 104 St. Francis Street · P.O. Box 1988 · Mobile, AL 36633 · 205-432-7682

Frank McRight · (Management) · McRight, Jackman, Myrick & Moore · 1100 First Alabama Bank Building · P.O. Box 2846 · Mobile, AL 36652 · 205-432-3444

Gregory B. Stein · (Individuals) · Stein & Brewster · Van Antwerp Building, Suite 405 · 103 Dauphin Street · Mobile, AL 36633-1051 · 205-433-2002

William C. Tidwell III · (Management) · Hand, Arendall, Bedsole, Greaves & Johnston · 3000 First National Bank Building · P.O. Box 123 · Mobile, AL 36601 · 205-432-5511

Bruce J. Downey III · (Management) · Capell, Howard, Knabe & Cobbs · 57 Adams Avenue · P.O. Box 2069 · Montgomery, AL 36197 · 205-262-1671

MARITIME LAW

Joseph M. Allen, Jr. · Johnstone, Adams, Howard, Bailey & Gordon · Royal Saint Francis Building · 104 St. Francis Street · P.O. Box 1988 · Mobile, AL 36633 · 205-432-7682

Rae M. Crowe · Armbrecht, Jackson, DeMouy, Crowe, Holmes & Reeves · 1300 AmSouth Center · P.O. Box 290 · Mobile, AL 36601 · 205-432-6751

Alexander F. Lankford III · Hand, Arendall, Bedsole, Greaves & Johnston · 3000 First National Bank Building · P.O. Box 123 · Mobile, AL 36601 · 205-432-5511

Abram L. Philips, Jr. · Reams, Vollmer, Philips, Killion, Brooks & Schell · The Pillans Building · 3662 Dauphin Street · P.O. Box 8158 · Mobile, AL 36608 · 205-344-4721

W. Boyd Reeves · Armbrecht, Jackson, DeMouy, Crowe, Holmes & Reeves · 1300 AmSouth Center · P.O. Box 290 · Mobile, AL 36601 · 205-432-6751

G. Hamp Uzzelle III · Hand, Arendall, Bedsole, Greaves & Johnston · 3000 First National Bank Building · P.O. Box 123 · Mobile, AL 36601 · 205-432-5511

NATURAL RESOURCES AND ENVIRONMENTAL LAW

William H. Satterfield · Balch & Bingham · The Winter Building · Two Dexter Avenue, Court Square · P.O. Box 78 · Montgomery, AL 36101 · 205-834-6500

Fournier J. Gale III · Maynard, Cooper, Frierson & Gale · Watts Building, 12th Floor · 2008 Third Avenue North · Birmingham, AL 35203 · 205-252-2889

Macbeth Wagnon, Jr. · Bradley, Arant, Rose & White · 1400 Park Place Tower · Birmingham, AL 35203 · 205-252-4500

Conrad P. Armbrecht II · Armbrecht, Jackson, DeMouy, Crowe, Holmes & Reeves · 1300 AmSouth Center · P.O. Box 290 · Mobile, AL 36601 · 205-432-6751

Norton W. Brooker, Jr. · Lyons, Pipes & Cook · Two North Royal Street · P.O. Drawer 2727 · Mobile, AL 36652-2727 · 205-432-4481

Rae M. Crowe · Armbrecht, Jackson, DeMouy, Crowe, Holmes & Reeves · 1300 AmSouth Center · P.O. Box 290 · Mobile, AL 36601 · 205-432-6751

Donald F. Pierce · Hand, Arendall, Bedsole, Greaves & Johnston · 3000 First National Bank Building · P.O. Box 123 · Mobile, AL 36601 · 205-432-5511

PERSONAL INJURY LITIGATION

Frank J. Tipler, Jr. · (Plaintiffs) · Tipler & Tipler · Tipler Building · 218 South Threenotch Street · P.O. Box 1397 · Andalusia, AL 36420 · 205-222-4148

Bibb Allen · (Defendants) · Rives & Peterson · 1700 Financial Center · Birmingham, AL 35203-2607 · 205-328-8141

M. Clay Alspaugh · Hogan, Smith, Alspaugh, Samples & Pratt · 2323 Second Avenue North · Birmingham, AL 35203 · 205-324-5635

Harold A. Bowron, Jr. · (Defendants) · Balch & Bingham · 505 North 20th Street, Suite 700 · P.O. Box 306 · Birmingham, AL 35201 · 205-251-8100

Frank O. Burge, Jr. · (Plaintiffs) · Burge & Wettermark · 1230 First Alabama Bank Building · 417 North 20th Street · Birmingham, AL 35203 · 205-251-9729

Thomas W. Christian · (Defendants) · Rives & Peterson · 1700 Financial Center Birmingham, AL 35203-2607 · 205-328-8141

Edward O. Conerly · (Defendants) · McDaniel, Hall, Conerly & Lusk · 1400 Financial Center · Birmingham, AL 35203 · 205-251-8143

Edgar M. Elliot III · (Defendants) · Rives & Peterson · 1700 Financial Center Birmingham, AL 35203-2607 · 205-328-8141

Clifford Emond, Jr. · (Plaintiffs) · Emond & Vines · 1900 Daniel Building Birmingham, AL 35233 · 205-324-4000

Samuel H. Franklin · (Defendants) · Bradley, Arant, Rose & White · 1400 Park Place Tower · Birmingham, AL 35203 · 205-252-4500

James W. Gewin · (Defendants) · Bradley, Arant, Rose & White · 1400 Park Place Tower · Birmingham, AL 35203 · 205-252-4500

Stephen D. Heninger · (Plaintiffs) · Heninger, Burdge & Vargo · 2021 Third Avenue North, Suite 300 · Birmingham, AL 35203 · 205-322-5153

Warren B. Lightfoot · (Defendants) · Bradley, Arant, Rose & White · 1400 Park Place Tower · Birmingham, AL 35203 · 205-252-4500

Eugene D. Martenson · (Defendants) · Huie, Fernambucq and Stewart · First Alabama Bank Building, Suite 825 · Birmingham, AL 35203 · 205-251-1193

William J. McDaniel · (Defendants) · McDaniel, Hall, Conerly & Lusk · 1400 Financial Center · Birmingham, AL 35203 · 205-251-8143

Crawford S. McGivaren, Jr. · Cabaniss, Johnston, Gardner, Dumas & O'Neal 1900 First National-Southern Natural Building · Birmingham, AL 35203 205-252-8800

Hobart A. McWhorter, Jr. · (Defendants) · Bradley, Arant, Rose & White · 1400 Park Place Tower · Birmingham, AL 35203 · 205-252-4500

John H. Morrow · (Defendants) · Bradley, Arant, Rose & White · 1400 Park Place Tower · Birmingham, AL 35203 · 205-252-4500

Neal C. Newell · (Plaintiffs) · Hare, Wynn, Newell and Newton · City Federal Building, Seventh Floor · Birmingham, AL 35203 · 205-328-5330

Alex W. Newton · (Plaintiffs) · Hare, Wynn, Newell and Newton · City Federal Building, Seventh Floor · Birmingham, AL 35203 · 205-328-5330

W. Lee Pittman · (Plaintiffs) · Pittman, Hooks, Marsh, Dutton & Hollis · Park Place Tower, Suite 800 · 2001 Park Place North · Birmingham, AL 35203 205-322-8880

L. Drew Redden · Redden, Mills & Clark · 940 First Alabama Bank Building · Birmingham, AL 35203 · 205-322-0457

Charles E. Sharp · Sadler, Sullivan, Sharp & Stutts · First National-Southern Natural Building, Suite 1100 · Birmingham, AL 35203 · 205-326-4166

Clarence M. Small, Jr. · (Defendants) · Rives & Peterson · 1700 Financial Center Birmingham, AL 35203-2607 · 205-328-8141

Lanny S. Vines · (Plaintiffs) · Emond & Vines · 1900 Daniel Building · Birmingham, AL 35233 · 205-324-4000

Robert O. Cox · (Defendants) · Poellnitz, Cox & Jones · First National Bank Building · P.O. Box 876 · Florence, AL 35631 · 205-764-0821

James E. Davis, Jr. · (Defendants) · Lanier, Ford, Shaver & Payne · 200 West Court Square · Huntsville, AL 35801 · 205-535-1101

W. Stanley Rodgers · (Defendants) · Lanier, Ford, Shaver & Payne · 200 West Court Square · Huntsville, AL 35801 · 205-535-1101

Richard Bounds · (Plaintiffs) · Cunningham, Bounds, Yance, Crowder & Brown 1601 Dauphin Street · P.O. Box 66705 · Mobile, AL 36600 · 205-471-6191

Robert T. Cunningham, Jr. · (Plaintiffs) · Cunningham, Bounds, Yance, Crowder & Brown · 1601 Dauphin Street · P.O. Box 66705 · Mobile, AL 36600 205-471-6191

James J. Duffy, Jr. · (Defendants) · Inge, Twitty, Duffy, Prince & McKean First Alabama Bank Building, 13th Floor · 56 St. Joseph Street · P.O. Box 1109 Mobile, AL 36633 · 205-433-5441

Broox G. Holmes · (Defendants) · Armbrecht, Jackson, DeMouy, Crowe, Holmes & Reeves · 1300 AmSouth Center · P.O. Box 290 · Mobile, AL 36601 · 205-432-6751

John N. Leach, Jr. · (Defendants) · Coale, Helmsing, Lyons & Sims · The Laclede Building · 150 Government Street · P.O. Box 2767 · Mobile, AL 36652 · 205-432-5521

Jerry A. McDowell · (Defendants) · Hand, Arendall, Bedsole, Greaves & Johnston · 3000 First National Bank Building · P.O. Box 123 · Mobile, AL 36601 · 205-432-5511

W. Boyd Reeves · (Defendants) · Armbrecht, Jackson, DeMouy, Crowe, Holmes & Reeves · 1300 AmSouth Center · P.O. Box 290 · Mobile, AL 36601 · 205-432-6751

Robert C. Black · (Defendants) · Hill, Hill, Carter, Franco, Cole & Black · Hill Building, Second Floor · P.O. Box 116 · Montgomery, AL 36195 · 205-834-7600

Richard H. Gill · Copeland, Franco, Screws & Gill · 444 South Perry Street · P.O. Box 347 · Montgomery, AL 36101-0347 · 205-834-1180

Oakley Melton, Jr. · (Defendants) · Melton & Espy · 339 Washington Avenue · P.O. Box 1267 · Montgomery, AL 36102 · 205-263-6621

Robert D. Segall · Copeland, Franco, Screws & Gill · 444 South Perry Street P.O. Box 347 · Montgomery, AL 36101-0347 · 205-834-1180

Maury D. Smith · Balch & Bingham · The Winter Building · Two Dexter Avenue, Court Square · P.O. Box 78 · Montgomery, AL 36101 · 205-834-6500

Charles A. Stakely · (Defendants) · Rushton, Stakely, Johnston & Garrett · 184 Commerce Street · P.O. Box 270 · Montgomery, AL 36195 · 205-834-8480

Ralph D. Gaines, Jr. · (Defendants) · Gaines, Gaines & Gaines · 127 East North Street · P.O. Box 275 · Talladega, AL 35160 · 205-362-2386

Ernest C. Hornsby · (Plaintiffs) · Hornsby & Schmitt · 213 Barnett Boulevard P.O. Box 606 · Tallassee, AL 36078 · 205-283-6855

Sam M. Phelps · (Defendants) · Phelps, Owens, Jenkins, Gibson & Fowler · 1201 Greensboro Avenue · Tuscaloosa, AL 35401 · 205-345-5100

REAL ESTATE LAW

Charles A. J. Beavers, Jr. · Bradley, Arant, Rose & White · 1400 Park Place Tower · Birmingham, AL 35203 · 205-252-4500

H. Hampton Boles · Balch & Bingham · 505 North 20th Street, Suite 700 · P.O. Box 306 · Birmingham, AL 35201 · 205-251-8100

Douglas P. Corretti · Corretti & Newsom · 1804 Seventh Avenue North · Birmingham, AL 35203 · 205-251-1164

J. Robert Fleenor · Bradley, Arant, Rose & White · 1400 Park Place Tower Birmingham, AL 35203 · 205-252-4500

Frank C. Galloway, Jr. · Cabaniss, Johnston, Gardner, Dumas & O'Neal · 1900 First National-Southern Natural Building · Birmingham, AL 35203 · 205-252-8800

Chervis Isom · Berkowitz, Lefkovits, Isom & Kushner · 1100 Financial Center Birmingham, AL 35203 · 205-328-0480

Randolph H. Lanier · Balch & Bingham · 505 North 20th Street, Suite 700 · P.O. Box 306 · Birmingham, AL 35201 · 205-251-8100

Jerome K. Lanning · Johnston, Barton, Proctor, Swedlaw & Naff · 1100 Park Place Tower · 2001 Park Place · Birmingham, AL 35203 · 205-322-0616

George F. Maynard · Maynard, Cooper, Frierson & Gale · Watts Building, 12th Floor · 2008 Third Avenue North · Birmingham, AL 35203 · 205-252-2889

James L. Permutt · Sirote, Permutt, McDermott, Slepian, Friend, Friedman, Held & Apolinsky · 2222 Arlington Avenue, South · P.O. Box 55727 · Birmingham, AL 35255 · 205-933-7111

J. Fred Powell · Burr & Forman · 3000 SouthTrust Tower · Birmingham, AL 35203 · 205-251-3000

Harold Williams · Balch & Bingham · 505 North 20th Street, Suite 700 · P.O. Box 306 · Birmingham, AL 35201 · 205-251-8100

Stova F. McFadden · McFadden, Lyon, Willoughby & Rouse · 718 Downtowner Boulevard · Mobile, AL 36609 · 205-342-9172

Harold D. Parkman · Hand, Arendall, Bedsole, Greaves & Johnston · 3000 First National Bank Building · P.O. Box 123 · Mobile, AL 36601 · 205-432-5511

Herman B. Franco · Copeland, Franco, Screws & Gill · 444 South Perry Street P.O. Box 347 · Montgomery, AL 36101-0347 · 205-834-1180

Ralph A. Franco · Hill, Hill, Carter, Franco, Cole & Black · Hill Building, Second Floor · P.O. Box 116 · Montgomery, AL 36195 · 205-834-7600

William Inge Hill, Jr. · Hill, Hill, Carter, Franco, Cole & Black · Hill Building, Second Floor · P.O. Box 116 · Montgomery, AL 36195 · 205-834-7600

Rufus M. King · Capell, Howard, Knabe & Cobbs · 57 Adams Avenue · P.O. Box 2069 · Montgomery, AL 36197 · 205-262-1671

TAX AND EMPLOYEE BENEFITS LAW

Louis H. Anders, Jr. · Burr & Forman · 3000 SouthTrust Tower · Birmingham, AL 35203 · 205-251-3000

Harold I. Apolinsky · Sirote, Permutt, McDermott, Slepian, Friend, Friedman, Held & Apolinsky · 2222 Arlington Avenue, South · P.O. Box 55727 · Birmingham, AL 35255 · 205-933-7111

Joseph S. Bluestein · (Employee Benefits) · Sirote, Permutt, McDermott, Slepian, Friend, Friedman, Held & Apolinsky · 2222 Arlington Avenue, South P.O. Box 55727 · Birmingham, AL 35255 · 205-933-7111

Thomas Neely Carruthers, Jr. · Bradley, Arant, Rose & White · 1400 Park Place Tower · Birmingham, AL 35203 · 205-252-4500

Roy J. Crawford · Cabaniss, Johnston, Gardner, Dumas & O'Neal · 1900 First National-Southern Natural Building · Birmingham, AL 35203 · 205-252-8800

C. Fred Daniels · (Employee Benefits) · Dominick, Fletcher, Yeilding, Wood & Lloyd · 2121 Highland Avenue · Birmingham, AL 35205 · 205-939-0033

David S. Dunkle · (Employee Benefits) · Lewis, Martin, Burnett & Dunkle 1900 SouthTrust Tower · Birmingham, AL 35203 · 205-322-8000

William Lyle Hinds, Jr. · Bradley, Arant, Rose & White · 1400 Park Place Tower Birmingham, AL 35203 · 205-252-4500

Robert G. Johnson · (Employee Benefits) · Bradley, Arant, Rose & White · 1400 Park Place Tower · Birmingham, AL 35203 · 205-252-4500

Harold B. Kushner · Berkowitz, Lefkovits, Isom & Kushner · 1100 Financial Center · Birmingham, AL 35203 · 205-328-0480

Arnold K. Lefkovits · Berkowitz, Lefkovits, Isom & Kushner · 1100 Financial Center · Birmingham, AL 35203 · 205-328-0480

J. William Lewis · Lewis, Martin, Burnett & Dunkle · 1900 SouthTrust Tower Birmingham, AL 35203 · 205-322-8000

Edward M. Selfe · Bradley, Arant, Rose & White · 1400 Park Place Tower Birmingham, AL 35203 · 205-252-4500

Robert C. Walthall · Bradley, Arant, Rose & White · 1400 Park Place Tower Birmingham, AL 35203 · 205-252-4500

A. Brand Walton, Jr. · (Employee Benefits) · Burr & Forman · 3000 SouthTrust Tower · Birmingham, AL 35203 · 205-251-3000

J. Gilmer Blackburn · Blackburn and Maloney · 802 Bank Street · P.O. Box 1469 Decatur, AL 35602 · 205-353-7826

Norman W. Harris, Jr. · Harris, Shinn, Phillips & Perry · 214 Johnston Street, SE P.O. Box 1563 · Decatur, AL 35602 · 205-353-7521

G. Porter Brock, Jr. · Hand, Arendall, Bedsole, Greaves & Johnston · 3000 First National Bank Building · P.O. Box 123 · Mobile, AL 36601 · 205-432-5511

Harwell E. Coale, Jr. · Coale, Helmsing, Lyons & Sims · The Laclede Building 150 Government Street · P.O. Box 2767 · Mobile, AL 36652 · 205-432-5521

Stephen G. Crawford · (Employee Benefits) · Hand, Arendall, Bedsole, Greaves & Johnston · 3000 First National Bank Building · P.O. Box 123 · Mobile, AL 36601 · 205-432-5511

Thomas F. Garth · Lyons, Pipes & Cook · Two North Royal Street · Drawer 2727 Mobile, AL 36652-2727 · 205-432-4481

William B. Harvey · (Employee Benefits) · Armbrecht, Jackson, DeMouy, Crowe, Holmes & Reeves · 1300 AmSouth Center · P.O. Box 290 · Mobile, AL 36601 · 205-432-6751

Frederick G. Helmsing · Coale, Helmsing, Lyons & Sims · The Laclede Building 150 Government Street · P.O. Box 2767 · Mobile, AL 36652 · 205-432-5521

J. Jeptha Hill · Hill and Hill · 572 Azalea Road, Suite 101 · P.O. Box 8799 Mobile, AL 36689-0799 · 205-666-1980

J. Thomas Hines, Jr. · Hand, Arendall, Bedsole, Greaves & Johnston · 3000 First National Bank Building · P.O. Box 123 · Mobile, AL 36601 · 205-432-5511

Vivian G. Johnston, Jr. · Hand, Arendall, Bedsole, Greaves & Johnston · 3000 First National Bank Building · P.O. Box 123 · Mobile, AL 36601 · 205-432-5511

F. M. Keeling · Armbrecht, Jackson, DeMouy, Crowe, Holmes & Reeves · 1300 AmSouth Center · P.O. Box 290 · Mobile, AL 36601 · 205-432-6751

Gregory L. Leatherbury, Jr. · (also Employee Benefits) · Hand, Arendall, Bedsole, Greaves & Johnston · 3000 First National Bank Building · P.O. Box 123 Mobile, AL 36601 · 205-432-5511

E. Watson Smith · (also Employee Benefits) · Johnstone, Adams, Howard, Bailey & Gordon · Royal St. Francis Building · 104 St. Francis Street · P.O. Box 1988 Mobile, AL 36633 · 205-432-7682

Henry B. Hardegree · Rushton, Stakely, Johnston & Garrett · 184 Commerce Street · P.O. Box 270 · Montgomery, AL 36195 · 205-834-8480

Gerald W. Hartley · Hill, Hill, Carter, Franco, Cole & Black · Hill Building, Second Floor · P.O. Box 116 · Montgomery, AL 36195 · 205-834-7600

Henry H. Hutchinson · Capell, Howard, Knabe & Cobbs · 57 Adams Avenue P.O. Box 2069 · Montgomery, AL 36197 · 205-262-1671

D. Kyle Johnson · (Employee Benefits) · Capell, Howard, Knabe & Cobbs · 57 Adams Avenue · P.O. Box 2069 · Montgomery, AL 36197 · 205-262-1671

Thomas G. Mancuso · Rushton, Stakely, Johnston & Garrett · 184 Commerce Street · P.O. Box 270 · Montgomery, AL 36195 · 205-834-8480

Alan E. Rothfeder · Kaufman, Rothfeder & Blitz · One Court Square · P.O. Drawer 4540 · Montgomery, AL 36103-4540 · 205-834-1111

James M. Scott · Capell, Howard, Knabe & Cobbs · 57 Adams Avenue · P.O. Box 2069 · Montgomery, AL 36197 · 205-262-1671

Robert D. Thorington · Johnson & Thorington · 504 South Perry Street · P.O. Drawer 1748 · Montgomery, AL 36103 · 205-834-6222

TRUSTS AND ESTATES

Harold I. Apolinsky · Sirote, Permutt, McDermott, Slepian, Friend, Friedman, Held & Apolinsky · 2222 Arlington Avenue, South · P.O. Box 55727 · Birmingham, AL 35255 · 205-933-7111

E. T. Brown, Jr. · Cabaniss, Johnston, Gardner, Dumas & O'Neal · 1900 First National-Southern Natural Building · Birmingham, AL 35203 · 205-252-8800

William Lyle Hinds, Jr. · Bradley, Arant, Rose & White · 1400 Park Place Tower Birmingham, AL 35203 · 205-252-4500

Kirby Sevier · Maynard, Cooper, Frierson & Gale · Watts Building, 12th Floor 2008 Third Avenue North · Birmingham, AL 35203 · 205-252-2889

Leonard Wertheimer III · Wertheimer, McCord, Feld & Hoffman · 2019 Third Avenue North, Third Floor · Birmingham, AL 35203 · 205-252-2100

Paul O. Woodall · Burr & Forman · 3000 SouthTrust Tower · Birmingham, AL 35203 · 205-251-3000

John N. Wrinkle · Bradley, Arant, Rose & White · 1400 Park Place Tower Birmingham, AL 35203 · 205-252-4500

G. Porter Brock, Jr. · Hand, Arendall, Bedsole, Greaves & Johnston · 3000 First National Bank Building · P.O. Box 123 · Mobile, AL 36601 · 205-432-5511

Harwell E. Coale, Jr. · Coale, Helmsing, Lyons & Sims · The Laclede Building 150 Government Street · P.O. Box 2767 · Mobile, AL 36652 · 205-432-5521

Robert M. Galloway · Collins, Galloway & Smith · 3263 Cottage Hill Road · P.O. Box 16629 · Mobile, AL 36616 · 205-476-4493

J. Jeptha Hill · Hill and Hill · 3103 Airport Boulevard, Suite 630 · P.O. Box 16226 Mobile, AL 36616 · 205-478-6031

Lyman F. Holland, Jr. · Hand, Arendall, Bedsole, Greaves & Johnston · 3000 First National Bank Building · P.O. Box 123 · Mobile, AL 36601 · 205-432-5511

Vivian G. Johnston, Jr. · Hand, Arendall, Bedsole, Greaves & Johnston · 3000 First National Bank Building · P.O. Box 123, Drawer C · Mobile, AL 36601 205-432-5511

F. M. Keeling · Armbrecht, Jackson, DeMouy, Crowe, Holmes & Reeves · 1300 AmSouth Center · P.O. Box 290 · Mobile, AL 36601 · 205-432-6751

Gregory L. Leatherbury, Jr. · Hand, Arendall, Bedsole, Greaves & Johnston 3000 First National Bank Building · P.O. Box 123 · Mobile, AL 36601 205-432-5511

Henry B. Hardegree · Rushton, Stakely, Johnston & Garrett · 184 Commerce Street · P.O. Box 270 · Montgomery, AL 36195 · 205-834-8480

Gerald W. Hartley · Hill, Hill, Carter, Franco, Cole & Black · Hill Building, Second Floor · P.O. Box 116 · Montgomery, AL 36195 · 205-834-7600

L. Lister Hill · Capell, Howard, Knabe & Cobbs · 57 Adams Avenue · P.O. Box 2069 · Montgomery, AL 36197 · 205-262-1671

ALASKA

BANKRUPTCY LAW	20
BUSINESS LITIGATION	21
CORPORATE LAW	21
CRIMINAL DEFENSE	22
FAMILY LAW	22
LABOR AND EMPLOYMENT LAW	23
NATURAL RESOURCES AND ENVIRONMENTAL LAW	23
PERSONAL INJURY LITIGATION	24
REAL ESTATE LAW	25
TAX AND EMPLOYEE BENEFITS LAW	25
TRUSTS AND ESTATES	25

BANKRUPTCY LAW

William D. Artus · Artus & Choquette · 629 L Street, Suite 101 · Anchorage, AK 99501 · 907-274-4626

David H. Bundy · Guess & Rudd · 510 L Street, Suite 700 · Anchorage, AK 99501 907-276-5121

David W. Oesting · Davis, Wright & Jones · 550 West Seventh Avenue, Suite 1450 · Anchorage, AK 99501 · 907-276-4488

James D. DeWitt · Guess & Rudd · Key Bank Building, Suite 402 · 100 Cushman Street · P.O. Box 2750 · Fairbanks, AK 99707 · 907-452-8986

BUSINESS LITIGATION

William M. Bankston · Bankston, McCullom & Fossey · 550 West Seventh Avenue, Suite 1800 · Anchorage, AK 99501 · 907-276-1711

John M. Conway · Atkinson, Conway, Bell & Gagnon · 420 L Street, Suite 500 Anchorage, AK 99501 · 907-276-1700

Charles P. Flynn · Burr, Pease & Kurtz · 810 N Street · Anchorage, AK 99501 907-276-6100

Bruce E. Gagnon · Atkinson, Conway, Bell & Gagnon · 420 L Street, Suite 500 Anchorage, AK 99501 · 907-276-1700

Julian L. Mason III · Baily & Mason · 1130 West Sixth Avenue, Suite 100 Anchorage, AK 99501 · 907-276-4331

Winston S. Burbank · Call, Barrett & Burbank · 711 Gaffney Road · Fairbanks, AK 99701 · 907-452-2211

Lloyd I. Hoppner · Hoppner & Paskvan · 714 Fourth Avenue, Suite 301 · P. O. Box 73888 · Fairbanks, AK 99707 · 907-452-1205

William B. Rozell · Faulkner, Banfield, Doogan & Holmes · 302 Gold Street Juneau, AK 99801 · 907-586-2210

CORPORATE LAW

Michael G. Briggs · (also Utilities) · Guess & Rudd · 510 L Street, Suite 700 Anchorage, AK 99501 · 907-276-5121

Ralph E. Duerre · Burr, Pease & Kurtz · 810 N Street · Anchorage, AK 99501 907-276-6100

Bruce E. Gagnon · Atkinson, Conway & Gagnon · 420 L Street, Suite 500 Anchorage, AK 99501 · 907-276-1700

Andrew E. Hoge · (also Utilities) · Hoge and Lekisch · 437 E Street, Suite 500 Anchorage, AK 99501 · 907-276-1726

Roger R. Kemppel · (Utilities) · Kemppel, Huffman & Ginder · 255 East Fireweed Lane, Suite 200 · Anchorage, AK 99503 · 907-277-1604

L. S. Kurtz, Jr. · Burr, Pease & Kurtz · 810 N Street · Anchorage, AK 99501 907-276-6100

Julian L. Mason III · (Utilities) · Baily & Mason · 1130 West Sixth Avenue, Suite 100 · Anchorage, AK 99501 · 907-276-4331

Stanley H. Reitman · Delaney, Wiles, Moore, Hayes, Reitman & Brubaker · 1007 West Third Avenue, Suite 400 · Anchorage, AK 99501 · 907-279-3581

Winston S. Burbank · Call, Barrett & Burbank · 711 Gaffney Road · Fairbanks, AK 99701 · 907-452-2211

CRIMINAL DEFENSE

William P. Bryson · 810 West Second Avenue · Anchorage, AK 99501 · 907-276-8611

Jeffrey M. Feldman · Gilmore & Feldman · 310 K Street, Suite 308 · Anchorage, AK 99501 · 907-279-4506

James D. Gilmore · Gilmore & Feldman · 310 K Street, Suite 308 · Anchorage, AK 99501 · 907-279-4506

Dick L. Madson · 712 Eighth Avenue · Fairbanks, AK 99701 · 907-452-4215

Phillip Paul Weidner · Phillip Paul Weidner & Associates · 330 L Street, Suite 200 · Anchorage, AK 99501 · 907-277-7000

FAMILY LAW

Douglas B. Baily · Baily & Mason · 1130 West Sixth Avenue, Suite 100 · Anchorage, AK 99501 · 907-276-4331

Harry Branson · First National Bank Building, Suite 850 · 425 G Street · Anchorage, AK 99501 · 907-276-7377

Joe M. Huddleston · Hughes, Thorsness, Gantz, Powell & Brundin · 509 West Third Avenue · Anchorage, AK 99501 · 907-274-7522

Timothy M. Lynch · Lynch, Crosby, Molenda & Sisson · Alliance Bank Building, Suite 200 · 601 West Fifth Avenue · Anchorage, AK 99501 · 907-276-3222

John Reese · Reese, Rice and Volland · 211 H Street · Anchorage, AK 99501 · 907-276-5231

LABOR AND EMPLOYMENT LAW

Fred B. Arvidson · (Management) · Hughes, Thorsness, Gantz, Powell & Brundin · 509 West Third Avenue · Anchorage, AK 99501 · 907-274-7522

Charles A. Dunnagan · (Labor) · Jermain, Dunnagan & Owens · 3000 A Street, Suite 300 · Anchorage, AK 99503 · 907-563-8844

Charles P. Flynn · (Management) · Burr, Pease & Kurtz · 810 N Street · Anchorage, AK 99501 · 907-276-6100

Parry E. Grover · (Management) · Davis, Wright & Jones · 550 West Seventh Avenue, Suite 1450 · Anchorage, AK 99501 · 907-276-4488

William K. Jermain · (Labor) · Jermain, Dunnagan & Owens · 3000 A Street, Suite 300 · Anchorage, AK 99503 · 907-563-8844

Thomas R. Lucas · (Management) · Hughes, Thorsness, Gantz, Powell & Brundin · 509 West Third Avenue · Anchorage, AK 99501 · 907-274-7522

Thomas P. Owens, Jr. · (Management) · Owens & Turner · 1500 West 33rd Avenue, Suite 200 · Anchorage, AK 99503-3639 · 907-276-3963

William B. Schendel · (Individuals) · Schendel & Callahan · National Bank Building · 613 Cushman Street · P.O. Box 2137 · Fairbanks, AK 99707 · 907-456-1136

NATURAL RESOURCES AND ENVIRONMENTAL LAW

Thomas E. Meacham · Burr, Pease & Kurtz · 810 N Street · Anchorage, AK 99501 · 907-276-6100

Harris Saxon · Guess & Rudd · 510 L Street, Suite 700 · Anchorage, AK 99501 · 907-276-5121

William B. Rozell · Faulkner, Banfield, Doogan & Holmes · 302 Gold Street · Juneau, AK 99801 · 907-586-2210

PERSONAL INJURY LITIGATION

Douglas B. Baily · Baily & Mason · 1130 West Sixth Avenue, Suite 100 · Anchorage, AK 99501 · 907-276-4331

James J. Delaney, Jr. · (Defendants) · Delaney, Wiles, Hayes, Reitman & Brubaker · 1007 West Third Avenue, Suite 400 · Anchorage, AK 99501 907-279-3581

George N. Hayes · (Defendants) · Delaney, Wiles, Hayes, Reitman & Brubaker 1007 West Third Avenue, Suite 400 · Anchorage, AK 99501 · 907-279-3581

Roger F. Holmes · (Defendants) · Biss & Holmes · 705 Christensen Drive Anchorage, AK 99503 · 907-277-8564

L. Ames Luce · (Plaintiffs) · 1015 West Seventh Avenue · Anchorage, AK 99501 907-276-1191

Theodore M. Pease, Jr. · (Defendants) · Burr, Pease & Kurtz · 810 N Street Anchorage, AK 99501 · 907-276-6100

Eric T. Sanders · (Plaintiffs) · Young & Sanders · 500 L Street, Suite 400 Anchorage, AK 99501 · 907-272-3538

Robert H. Wagstaff · Wagstaff, Pope and Rogers · 912 West Sixth Avenue Anchorage, AK 99501 · 907-277-8611

Joseph L. Young · (Plaintiffs) · Young & Sanders · 500 L Street, Suite 400 Anchorage, AK 99501 · 907-272-3538

Lloyd I. Hoppner · Hoppner & Paskvan · 714 Fourth Avenue, Suite 301 · P.O. Box 73888 · Fairbanks, AK 99707 · 907-452-1205

O. Nelson Parrish · (Plaintiffs) · Parrish Law Office · 536 Fourth Avenue Fairbanks, AK 99701 · 907-456-4070

William B. Rozell · Faulkner, Banfield, Doogan & Holmes · 302 Gold Street Juneau, AK 99801 · 907-586-2210

Burton C. Biss · (Defendants) · Biss & Holmes · Star Route, Box 5111 · Wasilla, AK 99687 · 907-376-5318

REAL ESTATE LAW

William M. Bankston · Bankston, McCullom & Fossey · 550 West Seventh Avenue, Suite 1800 · Anchorage, AK 99501 · 907-276-1711

Peter C. Ginder · Kemppel, Huffman & Ginder · 255 East Fireweed Lane, Suite 200 · Anchorage, AK 99503 · 907-277-1604

Andrew E. Hoge · Hoge and Lekisch · 437 E Street, Suite 500 · Anchorage, AK 99501 · 907-276-1726

Peter A. Lekisch · Hoge and Lekisch · 437 E Street, Suite 500 · Anchorage, AK 99501 · 907-276-1726

Stanley H. Reitman · Delaney, Wiles, Hayes, Reitman & Brubaker · 1007 West Third Avenue, Suite 400 · Anchorage, AK 99501 · 907-279-3581

TAX AND EMPLOYEE BENEFITS LAW

Robert C. Brink · 1625 Tudor Road · Anchorage, AK 99507 · 907-563-2114

Ralph E. Duerre · Burr, Pease & Kurtz · 810 N Street · Anchorage, AK 99501 907-276-6100

Stanley H. Reitman · Delaney, Wiles, Hayes, Reitman & Brubaker · 1007 West Third Avenue, Suite 400 · Anchorage, AK 99501 · 907-279-3581

David G. Shaftel · 425 G Street, Suite 700 · Anchorage, AK 99501 · 907-276-6015

TRUSTS AND ESTATES

Robert C. Brink · 1625 Tudor Road · Anchorage, AK 99507 · 907-563-2114

Trigg T. Davis · Davis & Goerig · 405 West 36th Avenue, Suite 200 · Anchorage, AK 99503 · 907-561-4420

Peter C. Ginder · Kemppel, Huffman & Ginder · 255 East Fireweed Lane, Suite 200 · Anchorage, AK 99503 · 907-277-1604

George E. Goerig, Jr. · Davis & Goerig · 405 West 36th Avenue, Suite 200 Anchorage, AK 99503 · 907-561-4420

Robert L. Manley · Hughes, Thorsness, Gantz, Powell & Brundin · 509 West Third Avenue · Anchorage, AK 99501 · 907-274-7522

Stanley H. Reitman · Delaney, Wiles, Hayes, Reitman & Brubaker · 1007 West Third Avenue, Suite 400 · Anchorage, AK 99501 · 907-279-3581

David G. Shaftel · 425 G Street, Suite 700 · Anchorage, AK 99501 · 907-276-6015

ARIZONA

BANKRUPTCY LAW	27
BUSINESS LITIGATION	28
CORPORATE LAW	30
CRIMINAL DEFENSE	32
FAMILY LAW	33
LABOR AND EMPLOYMENT LAW	33
NATURAL RESOURCES AND ENVIRONMENTAL LAW	35
PERSONAL INJURY LITIGATION	36
REAL ESTATE LAW	38
TAX AND EMPLOYEE BENEFITS LAW	39
TRUSTS AND ESTATES	42

BANKRUPTCY LAW

Edward E. Davis · Davis & Lowe · Security Building, Suite 722 · 234 North Central Avenue · Phoenix, AZ 85004 · 602-253-2882

John J. Dawson · Streich, Lang, Weeks & Cardon · 2100 First Interstate Bank Plaza · P.O. Box 471 · Phoenix, AZ 85001 · 602-229-5200

Richard L. Epling · Brown & Bain · 222 North Central Avenue · P.O. Box 400 · Phoenix, AZ 85001 · 602-257-8777

James M. Marlar · Teilborg, Sanders & Parkes · 3030 North Third Street, Suite 1300 · Phoenix, AZ 85012 · 602-230-5600

Peter J. Rathwell · Snell & Wilmer · 3100 Valley Bank Center · Phoenix, AZ 85073 · 602-257-7211

Gerald K. Smith · Lewis and Roca · First Interstate Bank Building · 100 West Washington Street · Phoenix, AZ 85003 · 602-262-5311

Susan G. Boswell · Streich, Lang, Weeks & Cardon · 23 North Tucson Avenue, Suite 1500 · Tucson, AZ 85701 · 602-628-1419

Joseph R. McDonald · 177 North Church Avenue, Suite 905 · Tucson, AZ 85701 602-792-9220

Lowell E. Rothschild · Mesch, Clark & Rothschild · 259 North Meyer Avenue Tucson, AZ 85701-1090 · 602-624-8886

Clague A. Van Slyke · Bilby & Shoenhair · Citibank Tower, 15th Floor · One South Church Street · P.O. Box 871 · Tucson, AZ 85702 · 602-792-4800

BUSINESS LITIGATION

Robert E. B. Allen · Brown & Bain · 222 North Central Avenue · P.O. Box 400 Phoenix, AZ 85001 · 602-257-8777

Peter D. Baird · Lewis and Roca · First Interstate Bank Building · 100 West Washington Street · Phoenix, AZ 85003 · 602-262-5311

John J. Bouma · Snell & Wilmer · 3100 Valley Bank Center · Phoenix, AZ 85073 602-257-7211

Jack E. Brown · Brown & Bain · 222 North Central Avenue · P.O. Box 400 Phoenix, AZ 85001 · 602-257-8777

George Read Carlock · Ryley, Carlock & Applewhite · The Arizona Bank Building, 26th Floor · 101 North First Avenue · Phoenix, AZ 85003 · 602-258-7701

Harry J. Cavanagh · O'Connor, Cavanagh, Anderson, Westover, Killingsworth & Beshears One East Camelback Road, Suite 1100 · Phoenix, AZ 85012-1656 602-263-2400

Walter Cheifetz · Lewis and Roca · First Interstate Bank Building · 100 West Washington Street · Phoenix, AZ 85003 · 602-262-5311

Daniel Cracchiolo · Burch & Cracchiolo · 702 East Osborn Road · Phoenix, AZ 85014 · 602-274-7611

Donald F. Daughton · Bryan, Cave, McPheeters & Roberts · 2800 North Central Avenue, 21st Floor · Phoenix, AZ 85004 · 602-230-7000

Dan M. Durrant · Streich, Lang, Weeks & Cardon · 2100 First Interstate Bank Plaza · P.O. Box 471 · Phoenix, AZ 85001 · 602-229-5200

Jay Dushoff · Dushoff & McCall · Brookstone Building, Suite 100 · 2025 North Third Street · Phoenix, AZ 85004 · 602-254-3800

Paul F. Eckstein · Brown & Bain · 222 North Central Avenue · P.O. Box 400 Phoenix, AZ 85001 · 602-257-8777

John P. Frank · (Appellate) · Lewis and Roca · First Interstate Bank Building 100 West Washington Street · Phoenix, AZ 85003 · 602-262-5311

Susan M. Freeman · (Appellate) · Lewis and Roca · First Interstate Bank Building 100 West Washington Street · Phoenix, AZ 85003 · 602-262-5311

Philip T. Goldstein · Goldstein, Kingsley & Myres · Professional Arts Building 1110 East McDowell Road · Phoenix, AZ 85006 · 602-254-5581

William S. Hawgood II · Streich, Lang, Weeks & Cardon · 2100 First Interstate Bank Plaza · P.O. Box 471 · Phoenix, AZ 85001 · 602-229-5200

Edwin F. Hendricks · Meyer, Hendricks, Victor, Osborn & Maledon · 2700 North Third Street, Suite 4000 · Phoenix, AZ 85004 · 602-263-8700

Michael J. LaVelle · Allen, Kimerer & LaVelle · 2715 North Third Street Phoenix, AZ 85004 · 602-279-5900

John E. Lundin · Gallagher & Kennedy · 360 East Coronado · Phoenix, AZ 85004 602-250-8500

William J. Maledon · Meyer, Hendricks, Victor, Osborn & Maledon · 2700 North Third Street, Suite 4000 · Phoenix, AZ 85004 · 602-263-8700

Newman R. Porter · Evans, Kitchel & Jenckes · 2600 North Central Avenue, Suite 1900 · Phoenix, AZ 85004-3099 · 602-234-8807

James Powers · Fennemore Craig · Renaissance Building, Suite 2200 · Two North Central Avenue · Phoenix, AZ 85004 · 602-257-8700

Richard A. Segal · Gust, Rosenfeld & Henderson · 3300 Valley Bank Center · 201 North Central Avenue · Phoenix, AZ 85073-3300 · 602-257-7422

Kenneth J. Sherk · Fennemore Craig · Renaissance Building, Suite 2200 · Two North Central Avenue · Phoenix, AZ 85004 · 602-257-8700

Gerald K. Smith · Lewis and Roca · First Interstate Bank Building · 100 West Washington Street · Phoenix, AZ 85003 · 602-262-5311

Paul G. Ulrich · (Appellate) · 3030 North Central Avenue, Suite 1000 · Phoenix, AZ 85012 · 602-248-9465

Philip E. von Ammon · Fennemore Craig · Renaissance Building, Suite 2200 Two North Central Avenue · Phoenix, AZ 85004 · 602-257-8700

Neil Vincent Wake · (Appellate) · Beus, Gilbert, Wake & Morrill · Great American Tower, Suite 1000 · 3200 North Central Avenue · Phoenix, AZ 85012 602-274-8229

Phillip Weeks · Mariscal, Weeks, McIntyre & Friedlander · 201 West Coolidge Street · Phoenix, AZ 85013 · 602-285-5000

Thomas Chandler · Chandler, Tullar, Udall & Redhair · 1700 Arizona Bank Plaza 33 North Stone Avenue · P.O. Box 3069 · Tucson, AZ 85701 · 602-623-4353

David J. Leonard · Leonard & Felker · 155 West Council Street · P.O. Box 191 Tucson, AZ 85702-0191 · 602-622-7733

Robert O. Lesher · Lesher & Borodkin · 3773 East Broadway · Tucson, AZ 85716 602-795-4800

Gerald Maltz · Miller & Pitt · 111 South Church Avenue · Tucson, AZ 85701-1680 · 602-792-3836

Michael J. Meehan · (also Appellate) · Molloy, Jones & Donahue · Arizona Bank Plaza, Suite 2200 · 33 North Stone · P.O. Box 2268 · Tucson, AZ 85702 602-622-3531

John F. Molloy · Molloy, Jones & Donahue · Arizona Bank Plaza, Suite 2200 · 33 North Stone · P.O. Box 2268 · Tucson, AZ 85702 · 602-622-3531

William H. Tinney · Bilby & Shoenhair · Citibank Tower, 15th Floor · One South Church Street · P.O. Box 871 · Tucson, AZ 85702 · 602-792-4800

CORPORATE LAW

Paul R. Madden · Lewis and Roca · 1201 South Alma School Road, Suite 12500 Mesa, AZ 85202 · 602-461-9200

Timothy W. Barton · Jennings, Strouss and Salmon · One Renaissance Square Tower, Suite 1600 · Two North Central Avenue · Phoenix, AZ 85004 602-262-5911

Marriner Cardon · Streich, Lang, Weeks & Cardon · 2100 First Interstate Bank Plaza · P.O. Box 471 · Phoenix, AZ 85001 · 602-229-5200

George Read Carlock · Ryley, Carlock & Applewhite · The Arizona Bank Building, 26th Floor · 101 North First Avenue · Phoenix, AZ 85003 · 602-258-7701

Jon S. Cohen · Snell & Wilmer · 3100 Valley Bank Center · Phoenix, AZ 85073 602-257-7211

Devans Gust · Gust, Rosenfeld & Henderson · 3300 Valley Bank Center · 201 North Central Avenue · Phoenix, AZ 85073-3300 · 602-257-7422

Thomas J. Lang · Streich, Lang, Weeks & Cardon · 2100 First Interstate Bank Plaza · P.O. Box 471 · Phoenix, AZ 85001 · 602-229-5200

Joseph T. Melczer, Jr. · Snell & Wilmer · 3100 Valley Bank Center · Phoenix, AZ 85073 · 602-257-7211

Paul J. Meyer · Meyer, Hendricks, Victor, Osborn & Maledon · 2700 North Third Street, Suite 4000 · Phoenix, AZ 85004 · 602-263-8700

P. Robert Moya · Gaston & Snow · 4722 North 24th Street, Suite 400 · Phoenix, AZ 85016 · 602-468-3600

Frederick H. Rosenfeld · Gust, Rosenfeld & Henderson · 3300 Valley Bank Center · 201 North Central Avenue · Phoenix, AZ 85073-3300 · 602-257-7422

Seymour Sacks · Sacks, Tierney, Kasen & Kerrick · United Bank Tower, 20th Floor · 3300 North Central Avenue · Phoenix, AZ 85012-2576 · 602-279-4900

Morton M. Scult · Lancy, Scult & McVey · 1313 East Osborn, Suite 100 Phoenix, AZ 85014 · 602-266-4747

Charles L. Strouss, Jr. · Jennings, Strouss and Salmon · One Renaissance Square Tower, Suite 1600 · Two North Central Avenue · Phoenix, AZ 85004 602-262-5911

Larry R. Adamson · Fish, Duffield, Miller, Young, Adamson & Alfred · 177 North Church Avenue, Suite 711 · Tucson, AZ 85701 · 602-792-1181

Thomas Chandler · Chandler, Tullar, Udall & Redhair · 1700 Arizona Bank Plaza 33 North Stone Avenue · P.O. Box 3069 · Tucson, AZ 85702 · 602-623-4353

Richard Duffield · Fish, Duffield, Miller, Young, Adamson & Alfred · 177 North Church Avenue, Suite 711 · Tucson, AZ 85701 · 602-792-1181

Eugene C. Gieseler · Bilby & Shoenhair · Citibank Tower, 15th Floor · One South Church Street · P.O. Box 871 · Tucson, AZ 85702 · 602-792-4800

Russell E. Jones · Molloy, Jones & Donahue · Arizona Bank Plaza, Suite 2200 33 North Stone · P.O. Box 2268 · Tucson, AZ 85702 · 602-622-3531

Gordon G. Waterfall · Waterfall, Economidis, Caldwell, Hanshaw & Villamana 5210 East Williams Circle, Suite 800 · Tucson, AZ 85711 · 602-790-5828

CRIMINAL DEFENSE

Michael E. Benchoff · 1400 First Interstate Bank Plaza · 100 West Washington Street · Phoenix, AZ 85003 · 602-254-7174

Larry L. Debus · Debus, Bradford & Kazan · 335 East Palm Lane · Phoenix, AZ 85004 · 602-257-8900

Jordan Green · Lewis and Roca · First Interstate Bank Building · 100 West Washington Street · Phoenix, AZ 85003 · 602-262-5311

Tom Karas · 101 North First Avenue, Suite 2470 · Phoenix, AZ 85003 · 602-271-0115

Michael D. Kimerer · Allen, Kimerer & LaVelle · 2715 North Third Street · P.O. Box 2800 · Phoenix, AZ 85002 · 602-279-5900

Thomas A. Thinnes · 1005 North Second Street · Phoenix, AZ 85004 · 602-257-8408

Robert J. Hirsh · Hirsh, Sherick & Murphy · 177 North Church Avenue, Suite 877 · Tucson, AZ 85701 · 602-884-9630

FAMILY LAW

Jeremy E. Butler · Lewis and Roca · First Interstate Bank Building · 100 West Washington Street · Phoenix, AZ 85003 · 602-262-5311

Philip C. Gerard · O'Connor, Cavanagh, Anderson, Westover, Killingsworth & Beshears · One East Camelback Road, Suite 1100 · Phoenix, AZ 85012-1656 602-263-2400

Jolyon Grant · O'Connor, Cavanagh, Anderson, Westover, Killingsworth & Beshears · One East Camelback Road, Suite 1100 · Phoenix, AZ 85012-1656 602-263-2400

Robert A. Jensen · 3246 North 16th Street · Phoenix, AZ 85016-7192 · 602-264-9081

Brian E. Kelly · O'Connor, Cavanagh, Anderson, Westover, Killingsworth & Beshears · One East Camelback Road, Suite 1100 · Phoenix, AZ 85012-1656 602-263-2400

Sheldon M. Mitchell · Mitchell & Timbanard · 3238 North 16th Street · Phoenix, AZ 85016 · 602-265-1234

Phillip Weeks · Mariscal, Weeks, McIntyre & Friedlander · 201 West Coolidge Street · Phoenix, AZ 85013 · 602-285-5000

Peter Economidis · Waterfall, Economidis, Caldwell, Hanshaw & Villamana · 5210 East Williams Circle, Suite 800 · Tucson, AZ 85711 · 602-790-5828

Leonard Karp · Karp, Stolkin, Weiss & McDonald · Home Federal Tower, Suite 1200 · 32 North Stone Avenue · Tucson, AZ 85701 · 602-882-9705

James L. Stroud · Stompoly & Stroud · United Bank Tower, Suite 1600 · One South Church Avenue · P.O. Box 3017 · Tucson, AZ 85702 · 602-792-2781

David K. Wolfe · Wolfe & Ostapuk · Southwest Savings Building, Suite 300 · 160 North Stone Avenue · Tucson, AZ 85701 · 602-624-8521

LABOR AND EMPLOYMENT LAW

Jon E. Pettibone · (Management) · Lewis and Roca · 1201 South Alma School Road, Suite 12500 · Mesa, AZ 85210 · 602-461-9200

Gerald Barrett · (Labor) · Ward & Keenan · 141 East Palm Lane · Phoenix, AZ 85004 · 602-252-5606

Robert J. Deeny · (Management) · Snell & Wilmer · 3100 Valley Bank Center Phoenix, AZ 85073 · 602-257-7211

Daniel F. Gruender · (Management) · Shimmel, Hill, Bishop & Gruender · 3700 North 24th Street, Suite 200 · Phoenix, AZ 85016 · 602-224-9500

Marty Harper · (Management) · Lewis and Roca · First Interstate Bank Building 100 West Washington Street · Phoenix, AZ 85003 · 602-262-5311

William R. Hayden · (Management) · Snell & Wilmer · 3100 Valley Bank Center Phoenix, AZ 85073 · 602-257-7211

James P. Hendricks · (Management) · Kaplan, Jacobowitz, Byrnes, Rosier & Hendricks · The Merabank Tower, Suite 1500 · 3003 North Central Avenue Phoenix, AZ 85012 · 602-264-3134

Charles F. Jones · (Management) · Jennings, Strouss and Salmon · One Renaissance Square Tower, Suite 1600 · Two North Central Avenue · Phoenix, AZ 85004 · 602-262-5911

Lawrence A. Katz · (Management) · Streich, Lang, Weeks & Cardon · 2100 First Interstate Bank Plaza · P.O. Box 471 · Phoenix, AZ 85001 · 602-229-5200

Michael J. Keenan · (Labor) · Ward & Keenan · 141 East Palm Lane · Phoenix, AZ 85004 · 602-252-5606

Stanley Lubin · (Labor; Individuals) · Law Office of Stanley Lubin · 2700 North Central Avenue, Suite 975 · Phoenix, AZ 85004 · 602-285-4411

Tod F. Schleier · (Individuals) · 3815 North Third Street · Phoenix, AZ 85012 602-277-0157

Ralph B. Sievwright · (Management) · Twitty, Sievwright & Mills · 2702 North Third Street, Suite 4007 · Phoenix, AZ 85004 · 602-248-9424

Anderson D. Ward · (Labor) · Ward & Keenan · 141 East Palm Lane · Phoenix, AZ 85004 · 602-252-5606

Naida B. Axford · (Individuals) · Hocker & Axford · 6601 South Rural Road Tempe, AZ 85283 · 602-897-0990

Peter Johnson · (Management) · Molloy, Jones & Donahue · Arizona Bank Plaza, Suite 2200 · 33 North Stone · P.O. Box 2268 · Tucson, AZ 85702 · 602-622-3531

Max C. Richards · (Management) · Richards & Eisenstein · 4455 South Park Avenue · Tucson, AZ 85714 · 602-889-6324

John A. Robertson · (Management) · Bilby & Shoenhair · Citibank Tower, 15th Floor · One South Church Avenue · P.O. Box 871 · Tucson, AZ 85702 602-792-4800

Armand Salese · (Individuals) · Salese & McCarthy · 124 West Cushing Street Tucson, AZ 85701 · 602-623-0341

Ronald J. Stolkin · (Individuals) · Karp, Stolkin & Weiss · Home Federal Tower, Suite 1200 · 32 North Stone Avenue · Tucson, AZ 85701 · 602-882-9705

NATURAL RESOURCES AND ENVIRONMENTAL LAW

James G. Derouin · Meyer, Hendricks, Victor, Osborn & Maledon · 2700 North Third Street, Suite 4000 · Phoenix, AZ 85004 · 602-263-8700

Fred E. Ferguson, Jr. · (Mining) · Evans, Kitchel & Jenckes · 2600 North Central Avenue, 19th Floor · Phoenix, AZ 85004 · 602-234-2600

Jerry L. Haggard · (Mining) · Evans, Kitchel & Jenckes · 2600 North Central Avenue · Phoenix, AZ 85004-3099 · 602-234-2600

James W. Johnson · (Water) · Fennemore Craig · Renaissance Building, Suite 2200 · Two North Central Avenue · Phoenix, AZ 85004 · 602-257-8700

David P. Kimball III · Evans, Kitchel & Jenckes · 2600 North Central Avenue Phoenix, AZ 85004-3099 · 602-234-2600

Elizabeth Ann Rieke · Jennings, Strouss and Salmon · One Renaissance Square Tower, Suite 1600 · Two North Central Avenue · Phoenix, AZ 85004 602-262-5911

James D. Vieregg · Molloy, Jones & Donahue · Citibank Plaza, Suite 2001 · 4041 North Central Avenue · Phoenix, AZ 85012 · 602-263-7784

John C. Lacy · (Mining) · DeConcini McDonald Brammer Yetwin & Lacy · 2525 East Broadway, Suite 200 · Tucson, AZ 85716 · 602-322-5000

PERSONAL INJURY LITIGATION

Daniel J. Stoops · Mangum, Wall, Stoops & Warden · 222 East Birch Avenue · P.O. Box 10 · Flagstaff, AZ 86002 · 602-774-6664

Michael A. Beale · (Defendants) · Jennings, Strouss and Salmon · One Renaissance Square Tower, Suite 1600 · Two North Central Avenue · Phoenix, AZ 85004 · 602-262-5911

Charles M. Brewer · (Plaintiffs) · 1400 First Interstate Bank Plaza · 100 West Washington Street · Phoenix, AZ 85003 · 602-252-8787

Harry J. Cavanagh · (Defendants) · O'Connor, Cavanagh, Anderson, Westover, Killingsworth & Beshears · One East Camelback Road, Suite 1100 · Phoenix, AZ 85012-1656 · 602-263-2400

Walter Cheifetz · Lewis and Roca · First Interstate Bank Building · 100 West Washington Street · Phoenix, AZ 85003 · 602-262-5311

Daniel Cracchiolo · Burch & Cracchiolo · 702 East Osborn Road · Phoenix, AZ 85014 · 602-274-7611

Philip T. Goldstein · Goldstein, Kingsley & Myres · 1110 East McDowell Road · Phoenix, AZ 85006 · 602-254-5581

Arthur P. Greenfield · (Defendants) · Winston & Strawn · 2300 Great American Tower · 3200 North Central Avenue · Phoenix, AZ 85012 · 602-279-8500

William R. Jones, Jr. · Jones, Skelton & Hochuli · 2702 North Third Street, Suite 3000 · Phoenix, AZ 85004 · 602-263-1700

James J. Leonard, Jr. · (Plaintiffs) · Leonard & Clancy · Luhrs Tower, Sixth Floor · 45 West Jefferson Street · Phoenix, AZ 85003 · 602-258-5749

Frank A. Parks · (Defendants) · Teilborg, Sanders & Parks · Arizona Bank Building, Suite 2900 · 101 North First Avenue · Phoenix, AZ 85003 · 602-251-2700

Warren E. Platt · (Defendants) · Snell & Wilmer · 3100 Valley Bank Center · Phoenix, AZ 85073 · 602-257-7211

Philip A. Robbins · Robbins & Green · 1800 United Bank Building · 3300 North Central Avenue · Phoenix, AZ 85012 · 602-248-7999

Richard A. Segal · (Defendants) · Gust, Rosenfeld & Henderson · 3300 Valley Bank Center · 201 North Central Avenue · Phoenix, AZ 85073-3300 · 602-257-7422

Richard T. Treon · (Plaintiffs) · Treon, Strick, Lucia & Aguirre · 2700 North Central Avenue, Suite 1400 · Phoenix, AZ 85004 · 602-285-4400

John H. Westover · O'Connor, Cavanagh, Anderson, Westover, Killingsworth & Beshears · One East Camelback Road, Suite 1100 · 3003 North Central Avenue · Phoenix, AZ 85012-1656 · 602-263-2400

Elliot G. Wolfe · (Plaintiffs) · Langerman, Begam, Lewis and Marks · 1400 Arizona Title Building · Phoenix, AZ 85003-1787 · 602-254-6071

Philip E. Toci · Toci, Murphy, Lutey & Beck · Elks Building, Third Floor · 117 East Gurley Street · Prescott, AZ 86302-0591 · 602-445-6860

Leonard Everett · (Defendants) · Transamerica Building, Suite 608 · 177 North Church Avenue · Tucson, AZ 85701 · 602-623-1857

Dale Haralson · (Plaintiffs) · Haralson, Kinerk & Morey · 82 South Stone Avenue · Tucson, AZ 85701 · 602-792-4330

Robert Q. Hoyt · (Plaintiffs) · 3501 North Campbell Avenue · Tucson, AZ 85719 · 602-327-6801

William Kimble · (Defendants) · Kimble, Gothreau & Nelson · 700 Great Western Bank Building · 5151 East Broadway · Tucson, AZ 85711 · 602-748-2440

Robert O. Lesher · (Defendants) · Lesher & Borodkin · 3773 East Broadway · Tucson, AZ 85716 · 602-795-4800

Jack Redhair · (Defendants) · Chandler, Tullar, Udall & Redhair · 1700 Arizona Bank Plaza · 33 North Stone Avenue · P.O. Box 3069 · Tucson, AZ 85702 · 602-623-4353

Tom Slutes · (Defendants) · Slutes, Sakrison, Even, Grant & Pelander · 1100 Arizona Bank Plaza · 33 North Stone Avenue · Tucson, AZ 85701-1489 · 602-624-6691

D. B. Udall · (Defendants) · Chandler, Tullar, Udall & Redhair · 1700 Arizona Bank Plaza · 33 North Stone Avenue · P.O. Box 3069 · Tucson, AZ 85702 · 602-623-4353

Thomas A. Zlaket · (Plaintiffs) · Zlaket & Zlaket · 2701 East Speedway, Suite 200 Tucson, AZ 85716 · 602-327-8777

REAL ESTATE LAW

Burton M. Apker · Apker, Apker & Kurtz · 2111 East Highland Avenue, Suite 230 · Phoenix, AZ 85016 · 602-381-0085

Marcia J. Busching · Sacks, Tierney, Kasen & Kerrick · United Bank Tower, 20th Floor · 3300 North Central Avenue · Phoenix, AZ 85012-2576 · 602-279-4900

Marriner Cardon · Streich, Lang, Weeks & Cardon · 2100 First Interstate Bank Plaza · P.O. Box 471 · Phoenix, AZ 85001 · 602-229-5200

Jay Dushoff · Dushoff & McCall · Brookstone Building, Suite 100 · 2025 North Third Street · Phoenix, AZ 85004 · 602-254-3800

James R. Huntwork · Jennings, Strouss and Salmon · One Renaissance Square Tower, Suite 1600 · Two North Central Avenue · Phoenix, AZ 85004 602-262-5911

Robert V. Kerrick · Sacks, Tierney, Kasen & Kerrick · United Bank Tower, 20th Floor · 3300 North Central Avenue · Phoenix, AZ 85012-2576 · 602-279-4900

Thomas J. Lang · Streich, Lang, Weeks & Cardon · 2100 First Interstate Bank Plaza · P.O. Box 471 · Phoenix, AZ 85001 · 602-229-5200

Mark Leibsohn · 201 West Coolidge Avenue · Phoenix, AZ 85013 · 602-234-0800

Lyman A. Manser · Lewis and Roca · First Interstate Bank Building · 100 West Washington Street · Phoenix, AZ 85003 · 602-262-5311

Bruce B. May · Streich, Lang, Weeks & Cardon · 2100 First Interstate Bank Plaza P.O. Box 471 · Phoenix, AZ 85001 · 602-229-5200

Joseph T. Melczer, Jr. · Snell & Wilmer · 3100 Valley Bank Center · Phoenix, AZ 85073 · 602-257-7211

Jay D. Wiley · Snell & Wilmer · 3100 Valley Bank Center · Phoenix, AZ 85073 602-257-7211

Gerald B. Hirsch · 32 North Stone Avenue, Suite 1005 · Tucson, AZ 85701 602-624-9983

James F. Morrow · Streich, Lang, Weeks & Cardon · 1500 Arizona Bank Plaza 33 North Stone Avenue · Tucson, AZ 85701 · 602-628-1419

S. L. Schorr · Lewis and Roca · 5210 East Williams Circle, Suite 600 · Tucson, AZ 85711-4495 · 602-747-9901

Harold C. Warnock · Lesher & Borodkin · 3773 East Broadway · Tucson, AZ 85716 · 602-795-4800

Paul E. Wolf · Miller & Pitt · 111 South Church Avenue · Tucson, AZ 85701-1680 602-792-3836

TAX AND EMPLOYEE BENEFITS LAW

Marvin D. Brody · (Employee Benefits) · 4722 North 24th Street, Court Two, Suite 350 · Phoenix, AZ 85016 · 602-956-5050

John R. Christian · Jennings, Strouss and Salmon · One Renaissance Square Tower, Suite 1600 · Two North Central Avenue · Phoenix, AZ 85004 602-262-5911

Robert D. Collins · 3010 East Camelback Road · Phoenix, AZ 85016 602-954-0281

Anthony V. Ehmann · Ehmann & Hiller · 4722 North 24th Street, Court Two, Suite 350 · Phoenix, AZ 85016 · 602-956-5050

David R. Frazer · Lewis and Roca · First Interstate Bank Building · 100 West Washington Street · Phoenix, AZ 85003 · 602-262-5311

David L. Haga, Jr. · Mohr, Hackett, Pederson, Blakley, Randolph & Haga · 3807 North Seventh Street · Phoenix, AZ 85014 · 602-277-7600

William H. Isaacson · Lewis and Roca · First Interstate Bank Building · 100 West Washington Street · Phoenix, AZ 85003 · 602-262-5311

Edward Jacobson · Snell & Wilmer · 3100 Valley Bank Center · Phoenix, AZ 85073 · 602-257-7211

Leslie T. Jones, Jr. · Jones, Jury, Short & Mast · 722 East Osborn Street, Suite 100 · Phoenix, AZ 85014 · 602-241-0808

Neal Kurn · Fennemore Craig · Renaissance Building, Suite 2200 · Two North Central Avenue · Phoenix, AZ 85004 · 602-257-8700

Stephen E. Lee · Brown & Bain · 222 North Central Avenue · P.O. Box 400 · Phoenix, AZ 85001 · 602-257-8777

David E. Manch · (Employee Benefits) · Lewis and Roca · First Interstate Bank Building · 100 West Washington Street · Phoenix, AZ 85003 · 602-262-5311

Joseph I. McCabe · McCabe & Pietzsch · 300 East Osborn, Suite 2000 · Phoenix, AZ 85012 · 602-264-0800

Joseph T. Melczer, Jr. · Snell & Wilmer · 3100 Valley Bank Center · Phoenix, AZ 85073 · 602-257-7211

Alfred J. Olsen · Olsen-Smith · 3300 Liberty Bank Plaza · 301 East Virginia Avenue · Phoenix, AZ 85004 · 602-258-1411

Michael E. Pietzsch · (Employee Benefits) · McCabe & Pietzsch · 300 East Osborn, Suite 2000 · Phoenix, AZ 85012 · 602-264-0800

Bruce D. Pingree · (Employee Benefits) · Snell & Wilmer · 3100 Valley Bank Center · Phoenix, AZ 85073 · 602-257-7211

Leslie A. Plattner · (Employee Benefits) · Plattner, Schneidman & Schneider · 3010 East Camelback Road · Phoenix, AZ 85016 · 602-957-1872

James Powers · Fennemore Craig · Renaissance Building, Suite 2200 · Two North Central Avenue · Phoenix, AZ 85004 · 602-257-8700

Jay S. Ruffner · Lewis and Roca · First Interstate Bank Building · 100 West Washington Street · Phoenix, AZ 85003 · 602-262-5311

Stephen E. Silver · Burch & Cracchiolo · 702 East Osborn Road · Phoenix, AZ 85014 · 602-274-7611

Howard N. Singer · Meyer, Hendricks, Victor, Osborn & Maledon · 2700 North Third Street, Suite 4000 · Phoenix, AZ 85004 · 602-263-8700

David E. Weiss, Jr. · Streich, Lang, Weeks & Cardon · 2100 First Interstate Bank Plaza · P.O. Box 471 · Phoenix, AZ 85001 · 602-229-5200

John C. Wesley · Gust, Rosenfeld & Henderson · 3300 Valley Bank Center · 201 North Central Avenue · Phoenix, AZ 85073-3300 · 602-257-7422

Stephen S. Case · Case & Bennett · 6740 East Camelback Road, Suite 100 · Scottsdale, AZ 85251 · 602-990-1133

Steven L. Bosse · (Employee Benefits) · O'Connell & Bosse · 1840 East River Road, Suite 100 · Tucson, AZ 85718 · 602-577-8880

Bryan E. Daum · (Employee Benefits) · Bilby & Shoenhair · Citibank Tower, 15th Floor · One South Church Street · P.O. Box 871 · Tucson, AZ 85702 · 602-792-4800

John L. Donahue, Jr. · Molloy, Jones & Donahue · Arizona Bank Plaza, Suite 2200 · 33 North Stone · P.O. Box 2268 · Tucson, AZ 85702 · 602-622-3531

Eugene C. Gieseler · (also Employee Benefits) · Bilby & Shoenhair · Citibank Tower, 15th Floor · One South Church Street · P.O. Box 871 · Tucson, AZ 85702 · 602-792-4800

Roger S. Levitan · Bilby & Shoenhair · Citibank Tower, 15th Floor · One South Church Street · P.O. Box 871 · Tucson, AZ 85702 · 602-792-4800

Terry Marvin · (Employee Benefits) · Dickerman & Nuckolls · 2195 East River Road, Suite 101 · P.O. Box 41570 · Tucson, AZ 85717 · 602-299-2828

Douglas J. Newman · (Employee Benefits) · Karp, Stolkin & Weiss · 32 North Stone Avenue, Suite 1200 · Tucson, AZ 85701 · 602-882-9705

Daniel H. O'Connell · O'Connell & Bosse · 1840 East River Road, Suite 100 · Tucson, AZ 85718 · 602-577-8880

Steven W. Phillips · Hecker, Phillips & Hooker · Rockwell Building · 405 West Franklin Street · P.O. Box 5525 · Tucson, AZ 85703 · 602-882-8912

David W. Richter · Bilby & Shoenhair · Citibank Tower, 15th Floor · One South Church Street · P.O. Box 871 · Tucson, AZ 85702 · 602-792-4800

Daniel C. Turner · (Employee Benefits) · Waterfall, Economidis, Caldwell, Hanshaw & Villamana · 5210 East Williams Circle, Suite 800 · Tucson, AZ 85711 · 602-790-5828

Gordon G. Waterfall · (also Employee Benefits) · Waterfall, Economidis, Caldwell, Hanshaw & Villamana · 5210 East Williams Circle, Suite 800 · Tucson, AZ 85711 · 602-790-5828

TRUSTS AND ESTATES

John R. Christian · Jennings, Strouss and Salmon · One Renaissance Square Tower, Suite 1600 · Two North Central Avenue · Phoenix, AZ 85004 · 602-262-5911

Louis F. Comus, Jr. · Fennemore Craig · Renaissance Building, Suite 2200 · Two North Central Avenue · Phoenix, AZ 85004 · 602-257-8700

Richard H. Elliott · Carson, Messinger, Elliott, Laughlin & Ragan · 1900 United Bank Building · 3300 North Central Avenue · P.O. Box 33907 · Phoenix, AZ 85012 · 602-264-2261

William H. Isaacson · Lewis and Roca · First Interstate Bank Building · 100 West Washington Street · Phoenix, AZ 85003 · 602-262-5311

Neal Kurn · Fennemore Craig · Renaissance Building, Suite 2200 · Two North Central Avenue · Phoenix, AZ 85004 · 602-257-8700

Richard L. Lassen · Jennings, Strouss and Salmon · One Renaissance Square Tower, Suite 1600 · Two North Central Avenue · Phoenix, AZ 85004 · 602-262-5911

Alfred J. Olsen · Olsen-Smith · 3300 Virginia Financial Plaza · 301 East Virginia Avenue · Phoenix, AZ 85004 · 602-258-1411

Robert J. Rosepink · Snell & Wilmer · 3100 Valley Bank Center · Phoenix, AZ 85073 · 602-257-7211

Richard H. Whitney · Gust, Rosenfeld & Henderson · 3300 Valley Bank Center · 201 North Central Avenue · Phoenix, AZ 85073-3300 · 602-257-7422

Stephen S. Case · Case & Bennett · 6740 East Camelback Road, Suite 100 · Scottsdale, AZ 85251 · 602-990-1133

Robert H. Norris · Norris & Adams · 10331 Coggins Drive · Sun City, AZ 85351 · 602-933-8274

Larry R. Adamson · Fish, Duffield, Miller, Young, Adamson & Alfred · 177 North Church Avenue, Suite 711 · Tucson, AZ 85701 · 602-792-1181

John L. Donahue, Jr. · Molloy, Jones & Donahue · Arizona Bank Plaza, Suite 2200 · 33 North Stone · P.O. Box 2268 · Tucson, AZ 85702 · 602-622-3531

G. Eugene Isaak · Miller & Pitt · 111 South Church Avenue · Tucson, AZ 85701-1680 · 602-792-3836

Clark W. Munger · Munger and Munger · 6131 East Grant Road · Tucson, AZ 85712 · 602-721-1900

Daniel H. O'Connell · O'Connell, Wezelman, Poston & Bosse · 1840 East River Road, Suite 100 · Tucson, AZ 85718 · 602-577-8880

William R. Poston · O'Connell, Wezelman, Poston & Bosse · 1840 East River Road, Suite 100 · Tucson, AZ 85718 · 602-577-8880

David W. Richter · Bilby & Shoenhair · Citibank Tower, 15th Floor · One South Church Street · P.O. Box 871 · Tucson, AZ 85702 · 602-792-4800

Paul D. Slosser · Molloy, Jones & Donahue · Arizona Bank Plaza, Suite 2200 · 33 North Stone · P.O. Box 2268 · Tucson, AZ 85702 · 602-622-3531

Harold C. Warnock · Lesher & Borodkin · 3773 East Broadway · Tucson, AZ 85716 · 602-795-4800

Gordon G. Waterfall · Waterfall, Economidis, Caldwell, Hanshaw & Villamana 5210 East Williams Circle, Suite 800 · Tucson, AZ 85711 · 602-790-5828

ARKANSAS

BUSINESS LITIGATION	44
CORPORATE LAW	45
CRIMINAL DEFENSE	45
FAMILY LAW	46
LABOR AND EMPLOYMENT LAW	46
PERSONAL INJURY LITIGATION	47
REAL ESTATE LAW	48
TAX AND EMPLOYEE BENEFITS LAW	49
TRUSTS AND ESTATES	49

BUSINESS LITIGATION

Robert L. Jones, Jr. · Jones, Gilbreath, Jackson & Moll · 401 North Seventh Street · P.O. Box 2023 · Fort Smith, AR 72902 · 501-782-7203

Hillary Rodham Clinton · Rose Law Firm · 120 East Fourth Street · Little Rock, AR 72201 · 501-375-9131

Webster L. Hubbell · Rose Law Firm · 120 East Fourth Street · Little Rock, AR 72201 · 501-375-9131

Alston Jennings, Sr. · Wright, Lindsey & Jennings · 2200 Worthen Bank Building · Little Rock, AR 72201 · 501-371-0808

William H. Sutton · Friday, Eldredge & Clark · 2000 First Commercial Building · Little Rock, AR 72201 · 501-376-2011

William R. Wilson, Jr. · Wilson, Engstrom, Corum & Dudley · 809 West Third Street · P.O. Box 71 · Little Rock, AR 72203 · 501-375-6453

Stephen A. Matthews · Bridges, Young, Matthews, Holmes & Drake · 315 East Eighth Avenue · P.O. Box 7808 · Pine Bluff, AR 71611 · 501-534-5532

James Blair · P.O. Drawer E · Springdale, AR 72764 · 501-756-4000

CORPORATE LAW

Philip S. Anderson · Wright, Lindsay & Jennings · 2200 Worthen Bank Building · Little Rock, AR 72201 · 501-371-0808

Paul B. Benham III · Friday, Eldredge & Clark · 2000 First Commercial Building · Little Rock, AR 72201 · 501-376-2011

Herschel H. Friday · Friday, Eldredge & Clark · 2000 First Commercial Building · Little Rock, AR 72201 · 501-376-2011

H. Maurice Mitchell · Mitchell, Williams, Selig & Tucker · 1000 Savers Federal Building · Capitol Avenue at Spring Street · Little Rock, AR 72201 · 501-376-3151

Robert Shults · Shults, Ray & Kurrus · 1600 Worthen Bank Building · Little Rock, AR 72201 · 501-375-2301

Louis L. Ramsay, Jr. · Ramsay, Cox, Bridgforth, Gilbert, Harrelson & Starling Simmons First National Building, 11th Floor · P.O. Drawer 8509 · Pine Bluff, AR 71611 · 501-535-9000

CRIMINAL DEFENSE

Bobby R. McDaniel · McDaniel & Wells · 400 South Main Street · Jonesboro, AR 72401 · 501-932-5950

William C. McArthur · 300 Spring Building, Room 612 · Little Rock, AR 72201 · 501-376-6173

Richard N. Moore, Jr. · Dodds, Kidd, Ryan & Moore · 313 West Second Street · Little Rock, AR 72201 · 501-375-9901

Samuel A. Perroni · Perroni, Rauls & Looney · 10810 Executive Center Drive · Danville Building, Suite 215 · Little Rock, AR 72211 · 501-227-8999

William R. Wilson, Jr. · Wilson, Engstrom, Corum & Dudley · 809 West Third Street · P.O. Box 71 · Little Rock, AR 72203 · 501-375-6453

FAMILY LAW

Philip E. Dixon · House, Wallace & Jewell · 3800 TCBY Tower Building · Little Rock, AR 72201 · 501-375-9151

Dale Price · Howell, Price, Trice, Basham & Hope · 211 Spring Street · Little Rock, AR 72201 · 501-372-4144

William R. Wilson, Jr. · Wilson, Engstrom, Corum & Dudley · 809 West Third Street · P.O. Box 71 · Little Rock, AR 72203 · 501-375-6453

LABOR AND EMPLOYMENT LAW

Tim Boe · (Management) · Rose Law Firm · 120 East Fourth Street · Little Rock, AR 72201 · 501-375-9131

John L. Burnett · (Labor) · Lavey, Harmon & Burnett · 904 West Second Street Little Rock, AR 72201 · 501-376-2269

Perlesta A. Hollingsworth · (Individuals) · 415 Main Place · Little Rock, AR 72201 · 501-374-3420

Philip E. Kaplan · (Management) · Kaplan, Brewer & Miller · 415 Main Street Little Rock, AR 72201 · 501-372-0400

John T. Lavey · (Labor; Individuals) · Lavey, Harmon & Burnett · 904 West Second Street · Little Rock, AR 72201 · 501-376-2269

Philip K. Lyon · (Management) · Jack, Lyon & Jones · 3400 TCBY Tower Building · Little Rock, AR 72201 · 501-375-1122

James W. Moore · (Management) · Friday, Eldredge & Clark · 2000 First Commercial Building · Little Rock, AR 72201 · 501-376-2011

Richard Quiggle · (Individuals) · 904 West Second Street · P.O. Box 2651 · Little Rock, AR 72203 · 501-375-2963

John W. Walker · (Individuals) · 1723 Broadway · Little Rock, AR 72206 501-374-3758

James E. Youngdahl · (Labor) · Youngdahl & Youngdahl · 2101 South Main Street · P.O. Box 6030 · Little Rock, AR 72216 · 501-376-6355

Jay Thomas Youngdahl · (Labor) · Youngdahl & Youngdahl · 2101 Main Street P.O. Box 6030 · Little Rock, AR 72216 · 501-376-6355

James A. Gilker · (Management) · Gilker & Swan · Highway 71 North · Mountainburg, AR 72946 · 501-783-3109

Marion J. Starling, Jr. · (Management) · Ramsay, Cox, Bridgforth, Gilbert, Harrelson & Starling · Simmons First National Building, 11th Floor · P.O. Drawer 8509 · Pine Bluff, AR 71611 · 501-535-9000

PERSONAL INJURY LITIGATION

Otis H. Turner · (Defendants) · McMillan, Turner & McCorkle · McMillan-Turner Building · 929 Main Street · P.O. Box 607 · Arkadelphia, AR 71923 501-246-2468

H. David Blair · (Plaintiffs) · Blair & Stroud · First South Building, Suite 201 P.O. Box 2135 · Batesville, AR 72503 · 501-793-8350

Ted Boswell · Boswell, Tucker & Brewster · Bryant Center · Bryant, AR 72022 501-847-3031

Robert C. Compton · Compton, Prewett, Thomas & Hickey · 423 North Washington Avenue · El Dorado, AR 71730 · 501-862-3478

Dennis L. Shackleford · (Defendants) · Shackleford, Shackleford & Phillips · 100 East Church Street · P.O. Box 1854 · El Dorado, AR 71731 · 501-862-5523

Sidney P. Davis, Jr. · (Defendants) · Davis, Cox & Wright · 19 East Mountain Street · P.O. Drawer 1688 · Fayetteville, AR 72701 · 501-521-7600

P. H. Hardin · (Defendants) · Hardin, Jesson & Dawson · Rogers Avenue & 16th Street · P.O. Drawer 968 · Fort Smith, AR 72902-0968 · 501-783-6186

Robert L. Jones, Jr. · (Defendants) · Jones, Gilbreath, Jones, Jackson & Moll 401 North Seventh Street · P.O. Box 2023 · Fort Smith, AR 72902 · 501-782-7203

Winslow Drummond · (Plaintiffs) · McMath Law Firm · 711 West Third Street P. O. Box 1470 · Little Rock, AR 72203 · 501-376-3021

Sam Laser · (Defendants) · Laser, Sharp & Mayes · One Spring Street, Suite 300 Little Rock, AR 72201 · 501-376-2981

Sidney S. McMath · (Plaintiffs) · McMath Law Firm · 711 West Third Street P.O. Box 1470 · Little Rock, AR 72201 · 501-376-3021

James M. Moody · (Defendants) · Wright, Lindsey & Jennings · 2200 Worthen Bank Building · Little Rock, AR 72201 · 501-371-0808

William H. Sutton · (Defendants) · Friday, Eldredge & Clark · 2000 First Commercial Building · Little Rock, AR 72201 · 501-376-2011

William R. Wilson, Jr. · Wilson, Engstrom, Corum & Dudley · 809 West Third Street · P.O. Box 71 · Little Rock, AR 72203 · 501-375-6453

Stephen A. Matthews · (Defendants) · Bridges, Young, Matthews, Holmes & Drake · 315 East Eighth Avenue · P.O. Box 7808 · Pine Bluff, AR 71611 501-534-5532

Nicholas H. Patton · (Plaintiffs) · Young, Patton & Folsom · 4122 Texas Boulevard · P.O. Box 1897 · Texarkana, AR 75504 · 501-774-3206

REAL ESTATE LAW

W. Christopher Barrier · Mitchell, Williams, Selig & Tucker · 1000 Savers Federal Building · Capitol Avenue at Spring Street · Little Rock, AR 72201 501-376-3151

George E. Campbell · Rose Law Firm · 120 East Fourth Street · Little Rock, AR 72201 · 501-375-9131

Beresford L. Church, Jr. · Plegge & Church · 1004 Pyramid Place · Little Rock, AR 72201 · 501-374-5612

Darrell D. Dover · House, Wallace & Jewell · 3800 TCBY Tower Building · Little Rock, AR 72201 · 501-375-9151

William L. Terry · Friday, Eldredge & Clark · 2000 First Commercial Building Little Rock, AR 72201 · 501-376-2011

Edward L. Wright, Jr. · Wright, Lindsey & Jennings · 2200 Worthen Bank Building · Little Rock, AR 72201 · 501-371-0808

TAX AND EMPLOYEE BENEFITS LAW

E. Chas. Eichenbaum · Eichenbaum, Scott, Miller, Liles & Heister · Union National Bank Building, Suite 1400 · Little Rock, AR 72201 · 501-376-4531

Byron M. Eiseman, Jr. · Friday, Eldredge & Clark · 2000 First Commercial Building · Little Rock, AR 72201 · 501-376-2011

Gregory B. Graham · Simpson & Graham · 10201 West Markham Street, Suite 300 · P.O. Box 5420 · Little Rock, AR 72215 · 501-221-7100

Joseph B. Hurst, Jr. · (Employee Benefits) · Friday, Eldredge & Clark · 2000 First Commercial Building · Little Rock, AR 72201 · 501-376-2011

W. Wilson Jones · Rose Law Firm · 120 East Fourth Street · Little Rock, AR 72201 · 501-375-9131

Lewis H. Mathis · Friday, Eldredge & Clark · 2000 First Commercial Building Little Rock, AR 72201 · 501-376-2011

A. Wickliffe Nisbet · (Employee Benefits) · Friday, Eldredge & Clark · 2000 First Commercial Building · Little Rock, AR 72201 · 501-376-2011

Thomas L. Overbey · (also Employee Benefits) · 425 North University Avenue · Little Rock, AR 72205-3108 · 501-664-8105

Richard A. Williams · Mitchell, Williams, Selig, Jackson & Tucker · 1000 Savers Federal Building · Capitol Avenue at Spring Street · Little Rock, AR 72201 501-376-3151

Craig H. Westbrook · (Employee Benefits) · Mitchell, Williams, Selig, Jackson & Tucker · 1000 Savers Federal Building · Capitol Avenue at Spring Street · Little Rock, AR 72201 · 501-376-3151

Ted N. Drake · Bridges, Young, Matthews, Holmes & Drake · 315 East Eighth Avenue · P.O. Box 7808 · Pine Bluff, AR 71611 · 501-534-5532

Robert H. Holmes · Bridges, Young, Matthews, Holmes & Drake · 315 East Eighth Avenue · P.O. Box 7808 · Pine Bluff, AR 71611 · 501-534-5532

TRUSTS AND ESTATES

E. Chas. Eichenbaum · Eichenbaum, Scott, Miller, Liles & Heister · Union National Bank Building, Suite 1400 · Little Rock, AR 72201 · 501-376-4531

Byron M. Eiseman, Jr. · Friday, Eldredge & Clark · 2000 First Commercial Building · Little Rock, AR 72201 · 501-376-2011

James E. Harris · Friday, Eldredge & Clark · 2000 First Commercial Building · Little Rock, AR 72201 · 501-376-2011

Richard F. Hatfield · Hatfield & Jordan · First Federal Plaza, Suite 502 · 401 West Capitol · Little Rock, AR 72201 · 501-374-9010

William D. Haught · Wright, Lindsey & Jennings · 2200 Worthen Bank Building · Little Rock, AR 72201 · 501-371-0808

W. Wilson Jones · Rose Law Firm · 120 East Fourth Street · Little Rock, AR 72201 · 501-375-9131

Thomas L. Overbey · 425 North University Avenue · Little Rock, AR 72205-3108 · 501-664-8105

Leonard L. Scott · Eichenbaum, Scott, Miller, Liles & Heister · Union National Bank Building, Suite 1400 · Little Rock, AR 72201 · 501-376-4531

Richard A. Williams · Mitchell, Williams, Selig & Tucker · 1000 Savers Federal Building · Capitol Avenue at Spring Street · Little Rock, AR 72201 · 501-376-3151

J. Gaston Williamson · Rose Law Firm · 120 East Fourth Street · Little Rock, AR 72201 · 501-375-9131

Ted N. Drake · Bridges, Young, Matthews, Holmes & Drake · 315 East Eighth Avenue · P.O. Box 7808 · Pine Bluff, AR 71611 · 501-534-5532

Robert H. Holmes · Bridges, Young, Matthews, Holmes & Drake · 315 East Eighth Avenue · P.O. Box 7808 · Pine Bluff, AR 71611 · 501-534-5532

CALIFORNIA

BANKRUPTCY LAW	51
BUSINESS LITIGATION	54
CORPORATE LAW	60
CRIMINAL DEFENSE	65
ENTERTAINMENT LAW	70
FAMILY LAW	72
LABOR AND EMPLOYMENT LAW	76
MARITIME LAW	80
NATURAL RESOURCES AND ENVIRONMENTAL LAW	81
PERSONAL INJURY LITIGATION	82
REAL ESTATE LAW	88
TAX AND EMPLOYEE BENEFITS LAW	92
TRUSTS AND ESTATES	97

BANKRUPTCY LAW

Henry Cohen · Cohen and Jacobson · Kingsway Building · 1450 Chapin Avenue P.O. Box 231 · Burlingame, CA 94010 · 415-342-6601

Lynn Anderson Koller · Koller & MacConaghy · 2354 Powell Street · Emeryville, CA 94608 · 415-652-5512

Stephen R. Brown · Luce, Forward, Hamilton & Scripps · 4250 Executive Square, Suite 700 · La Jolla, CA 92037 · 619-455-6611

Richard F. Broude · White & Case · Security Pacific Building, 34th Floor · 333 South Hope Street · Los Angeles, CA 90071 · 213-620-7700

Merrill R. Francis · Sheppard, Mullin, Richter & Hampton · 333 South Hope Street, 48th Floor · Los Angeles, CA 90071 · 213-620-1780

Herman L. Glatt · Stutman, Treister & Glatt · 3699 Wilshire Boulevard, Suite 900 Los Angeles, CA 90010 · 213-251-5100

Robert A. Greenfield · Stutman, Treister & Glatt · 3699 Wilshire Boulevard, Suite 900 · Los Angeles, CA 90010 · 213-251-5100

Kenneth N. Klee · Stutman, Treister & Glatt · 3699 Wilshire Boulevard, Suite 900 Los Angeles, CA 90010 · 213-251-5100

Richard B. Levin · Stutman, Treister & Glatt · 3699 Wilshire Boulevard, Suite 900 · Los Angeles, CA 90010 · 213-251-5100

Michael S. Lurey · Latham & Watkins · 555 South Flower Street · Los Angeles, CA 90071 · 213-485-1234

Robert L. Morrison · Lillick McHose & Charles · Citicorp Plaza · 725 South Figueroa · Los Angeles, CA 90017 · 213-488-7100

Richard M. Neiter · Stutman, Treister & Glatt · 3699 Wilshire Boulevard, Suite 900 · Los Angeles, CA 90010 · 213-251-5100

Joel R. Ohlgren · Sheppard, Mullin, Richter & Hampton · 333 South Hope Street, 48th Floor · Los Angeles, CA 90071 · 213-620-1780

Prentice L. O'Leary · Sheppard, Mullin, Richter & Hampton · 333 South Hope Street, 48th Floor · Los Angeles, CA 90071 · 213-620-1780

Ronald S. Orr · Gibson, Dunn & Crutcher · 333 South Grand Avenue · Los Angeles, CA 90071 · 213-229-7000

Lawrence Peitzman · Gendel, Raskoff, Shapiro & Quittner · 1801 Century Park East, Sixth Floor · Los Angeles, CA 90067 · 213-277-5400

Richard T. Peters · Sidley & Austin · 2049 Century Park East, 35th Floor · Los Angeles, CA 90067 · 213-553-8100

Arnold M. Quittner · Gendel, Raskoff, Shapiro & Quittner · 1801 Century Park East, Sixth Floor · Los Angeles, CA 90067 · 213-277-5400

Bernard Shapiro · Gendel, Raskoff, Shapiro & Quittner · 1801 Century Park East, Sixth Floor · Los Angeles, CA 90067 · 213-277-5400

Bruce H. Spector · Stutman, Treister & Glatt · 3699 Wilshire Boulevard, Suite 900 · Los Angeles, CA 90010 · 213-251-5100

Irving Sulmeyer · Sulmeyer, Kupetz, Baumann & Rothman · 300 South Grand Avenue, 14th Floor · Los Angeles, CA 90071 · 213-626-2311

George M. Treister · Stutman, Treister & Glatt · 3699 Wilshire Boulevard, Suite 900 · Los Angeles, CA 90010 · 213-251-5100

J. Ronald Trost · Sidley & Austin · 2049 Century Park East, 35th Floor · Los Angeles, CA 90067 · 213-553-8100

Robert J. White · O'Melveny & Myers · 400 South Hope Street · Los Angeles, CA 90071-2899 · 213-669-6000

Irving J. Kornfield · Kornfield, Paul & Bupp · 1999 Harrison Street, Suite 975 Oakland, CA 94612 · 415-763-1000

Robert L. Ward · 610 Sixteenth Street · Oakland, CA 94612 · 415-834-6400

Steven H. Felderstein · Diepenbrock, Wulff, Plant & Hannegan · 300 Capitol Mall · Sacramento, CA 95814 · 916-444-3910

Robert Ames · Gray, Cary, Ames & Frye · 1700 First Interstate Plaza · 401 B Street · San Diego, CA 92101-4219 · 619-699-2700

Theodore W. Graham · Brobeck, Phleger & Harrison · 225 Broadway, Suite 2100 San Diego, CA 92101 · 619-234-1966

Ralph M. Pray III · Gray, Cary, Ames & Frye · 1700 First Interstate Plaza · 401 B Street · San Diego, CA 92101-4219 · 619-699-2700

Michael H. Ahrens · Bronson, Bronson & McKinnon · Bank of America Center 555 California Street · San Francisco, CA 94104 · 415-986-4200

Peter J. Benvenutti · Heller, Ehrman, White & McAuliffe · 335 Bush Street · San Francisco, CA 94104 · 415-772-6000

Penn Ayers Butler · Murphy, Weir & Butler · 101 California Street, 39th Floor San Francisco, CA 94111 · 415-398-4700

Lawrence Goldberg · Goldberg, Stinnett & McDonald · 44 Montgomery Street, Suite 1700 · San Francisco, CA 94104 · 415-362-5045

John T. Hansen · Thelen, Marrin, Johnson & Bridges · Two Embarcadero Center, Suite 2200 · San Francisco, CA 94111 · 415-392-6320

Frederick D. Holden, Jr. · Brobeck, Phleger & Harrison · Spear Street Tower One Market Plaza · San Francisco, CA 94105 · 415-442-0900

Thomas C. Holman · Pettit & Martin · 101 California Street, 35th Floor · San Francisco, CA 94111 · 415-434-4000

Robert E. Izmirian · Buchalter, Nemer, Fields & Younger · 101 California Street, Suite 2050 · San Francisco, CA 94111-5879 · 415-397-0277

William Kelly · Graham & James · Alcoa Building · One Maritime Plaza, Suite 300 San Francisco, CA 94111 · 415-954-0200

James L. Lopes · Howard, Rice, Nemerovski, Canady, Robertson & Falk · Three Embarcadero Center, Suite 600 · San Francisco, CA 94111 · 415-434-1600

Dennis Montali · Pillsbury, Madison & Sutro · 225 Bush Street · San Francisco, CA 94104 · 415-983-1000

Patrick A. Murphy · Murphy, Weir & Butler · 101 California Street, 39th Floor San Francisco, CA 94111 · 415-398-4700

Harvey S. Schochet · Steefel, Levitt & Weiss · One Embarcadero Center, 29th Floor · San Francisco, CA 94111 · 415-788-0900

Margaret Sheneman · Murphy, Weir & Butler · 101 California Street, 39th Floor San Francisco, CA 94111 · 415-398-4700

Philip S. Warden · Pillsbury, Madison & Sutro · 225 Bush Street · San Francisco, CA 94104 · 415-983-1000

Kenneth J. Campeau · Campeau & Thomas · 55 South Market Street, Suite 1040 San Jose, CA 95113 · 408-295-9555

Harvey W. Hoffman · Bronson, Bronson & McKinnon · 100 B Street, Suite 400 Santa Rosa, CA 95401 · 707-527-8110

BUSINESS LITIGATION

Joseph W. Cotchett · Cotchett & Illston · 840 Malcolm Road, Suite 200 · Burlingame, CA 94010 · 415-342-9000

Robert E. Currie · Latham & Watkins · 650 Town Center Drive, 20th Floor Costa Mesa, CA 92626 · 714-540-1235

Ellis J. Horvitz · (Appellate) · Horvitz Levy & Amerian · 15760 Ventura Boulevard, 18th Floor · Encino, CA 91436 · 818-995-0800

Joseph A. Ball · Ball, Hunt, Hart, Brown and Baerwitz · 211 East Ocean Boulevard, Fifth & Sixth Floors · Long Beach, CA 90802 · 213-435-5631

Samuel A. Keesal, Jr. · Keesal, Young & Logan · 310 Golden Shore · P.O. Box 1730 · Long Beach, CA 90801-1730 · 213-436-9051

Orville A. Armstrong · Baker & McKenzie · 725 South Figueroa Street, 36th Floor · Los Angeles, CA 90017 · 213-629-3000

Leo J. Biegenzahn · Lillick McHose & Charles · Citicorp Plaza · 725 South Figueroa · Los Angeles, CA 90017 · 213-488-7100

Maxwell M. Blecher · Blecher & Collins · 611 West Sixth Street, 28th Floor · Los Angeles, CA 90017 · 213-622-4222

Richard H. Borow · Irell & Manella · 1800 Avenue of the Stars, Suite 900 · Los Angeles, CA 90067 · 213-879-2600

William B. Campbell · Paul, Hastings, Janofsky & Walker · 555 South Flower Street, 22nd Floor · Los Angeles, CA 90071 · 213-489-4000

Richard P. Crane, Jr. · Girardi, Keese and Crane · 1126 Wilshire Boulevard · Los Angeles, CA 90017 · 213-489-5330

Peter Brown Dolan · 333 South Grand Avenue · Los Angeles, CA 90071 · 213-621-9513

Dean C. Dunlavey · Gibson, Dunn & Crutcher · 333 South Grand Avenue · Los Angeles, CA 90071 · 213-229-7000

Daniel Fogel · Fogel, Feldman, Ostrov, Ringer & Klevens · 5900 Wilshire Boulevard, 26th Floor · Los Angeles, CA 90036-5185 · 213-937-6250

Howard I. Friedman · Loeb and Loeb · 1000 Wilshire Boulevard, Suite 1800 Los Angeles, CA 90017 · 213-688-3400

Max L. Gillam · Latham & Watkins · 555 South Flower Street · Los Angeles, CA 90071 · 213-485-1234

Alan N. Halkett · Latham & Watkins · 555 South Flower Street · Los Angeles, CA 90071 · 213-485-1234

C. Stephen Howard · Tuttle & Taylor · 355 South Grand Avenue, 40th Floor Los Angeles, CA 90071 · 213-683-0600

Seth M. Hufstedler · Hufstedler, Miller, Kaus & Beardsley · 355 South Grand Avenue, 45th Floor · Los Angeles, CA 90071-3107 · 213-617-7070

Craig B. Jorgensen · Kindel & Anderson · 555 South Flower Street, 27th Floor Los Angeles, CA 90071 · 213-680-2222

Stuart L. Kadison · Sidley & Austin · 2049 Century Park East, 35th Floor · Los Angeles, CA 90067 · 213-553-8100

Dennis E. Kinnaird · Munger, Tolles & Olson · 355 South Grand Avenue, 35th Floor · Los Angeles, CA 90071 · 213-683-9100

Patrick Lynch · O'Melveny & Myers · 400 South Hope Street · Los Angeles, CA 90071-2899 · 213-669-6000

Ronald L. Olson · Munger, Tolles & Olson · 355 South Grand Avenue, 35th Floor · Los Angeles, CA 90071 · 213-683-9100

John J. Quinn · Kully & Morrolo · 520 South Grand Avenue, Eighth Floor · Los Angeles, CA 90071 · 213-622-0300

Frank Rothman · Skadden, Arps, Slate, Meagher & Flom · 300 South Grand Avenue, 34th Floor · 213-687-5000

Donald C. Smaltz · Morgan, Lewis & Bockius · 801 South Grand Avenue, 20th Floor · Los Angeles, CA 90017 · 213-612-2500

Peter R. Taft · Munger, Tolles & Olson · 355 South Grand Avenue, 35th Floor Los Angeles, CA 90071 · 213-683-9100

Henry C. Thumann · O'Melveny & Myers · 400 South Hope Street · Los Angeles, CA 90071-2899 · 213-669-6000

William W. Vaughn · O'Melveny & Myers · 400 South Hope Street · Los Angeles, CA 90071-2899 · 213-669-6000

Charles S. Vogel · Sidley & Austin · 2049 Century Park East, 35th Floor · Los Angeles, CA 90067 · 213-553-8100

Robert S. Warren · Gibson, Dunn & Crutcher · 333 South Grand Avenue · Los Angeles, CA 90071 · 213-229-7000

Robert L. Winslow · Irell & Manella · 1800 Avenue of the Stars, Suite 900 · Los Angeles, CA 90067 · 213-879-2600

Edwin A. Heafey, Jr. · Crosby, Heafey, Roach & May · 1999 Harrison Street Oakland, CA 94612 · 415-763-2000

Raoul D. Kennedy · Crosby, Heafey, Roach & May · 1999 Harrison Street Oakland, CA 94612 · 415-763-2000

Edmund L. Regalia · Miller, Starr & Regalia · Ordway Building, 16th Floor · One Kaiser Plaza · Oakland, CA 94612 · 415-465-3800

Bruce G. Vanyo · Wilson, Sonsini, Goodrich & Rosati · Two Palo Alto Square Palo Alto, CA 94306 · 415-493-9300

Eugene J. Majeski · Ropers, Majeski, Kohn, Bentley, Wagner & Kane · 1125 Marshall Street · Redwood City, CA 94063 · 415-364-8200

Don C. Brown · Thompson & Colegate · 3610 Fourteenth Street · P.O. Box 1299 Riverside, CA 92502 · 714-682-5550

Enos C. Reid · Reid & Hellyer · 3880 Lemon Street, Fifth Floor · P.O. Box 1300 Riverside, CA 92502-3834 · 714-682-1771

Joseph S. Genshlea · Weintraub Genshlea Hardy Erich & Brown · 2535 Capitol Oaks Drive · Sacramento, CA 95833 · 916-648-9400

Frederick P. Crowell · Gray, Cary, Ames & Frye · 1700 First Interstate Plaza 401 B Street · San Diego, CA 92101-4219 · 619-699-2700

Oscar F. Irwin · Hillyer & Irwin · California First Bank Building, 14th Floor · 530 B Street · San Diego, CA 92101 · 619-234-6121

William S. Lerach · Milberg Weiss Bershad Specthrie & Lerach · 2000 Central Savings Tower · 225 Broadway · San Diego, CA 92101-5050 · 619-231-1058

Gerald L. McMahon · Seltzer Caplan Wilkins & McMahon · 3003-3043 Fourth Avenue · P.O. Box X 33999 · San Diego, CA 92103 · 619-295-3003

David E. Monahan · Gray, Cary, Ames & Frye · 1700 First Interstate Plaza · 401 B Street · San Diego, CA 92101 · 619-699-2700

Robert G. Steiner · Luce, Forward, Hamilton & Scripps · The Bank of California Plaza · 100 West A Street · San Diego, CA 92101 · 619-236-1414

William Alsup · Morrison & Foerster · 345 California Street · San Francisco, CA 94104-2105 · 415-434-7000

David M. Balabanian · McCutchen, Doyle, Brown & Enersen · Three Embarcadero Center · San Francisco, CA 94111 · 415-393-2000

Stephen V. Bomse · Heller, Ehrman, White & McAuliffe · 333 Bush Street · San Francisco, CA 94104 · 415-772-6000

William A. Brockett, Jr. · Keker & Brockett · 807 Montgomery Street · San Francisco, CA 94133 · 415-391-5400

James J. Brosnahan · Morrison & Foerster · 345 California Street · San Francisco, CA 94104-2105 · 415-434-7000

Josef D. Cooper · The Law Offices of Josef D. Cooper · 100 The Embarcadero, Penthouse · San Francisco, CA 94105 · 415-788-3030

E. Judge Elderkin · Brobeck, Phleger & Harrison · Spear Street Tower · One Market Plaza · San Francisco, CA 94105 · 415-442-0900

Jerome B. Falk, Jr. · (also Appellate) · Howard, Rice, Nemerovski, Canady, Robertson & Falk · Three Embarcadero Center, Suite 600 · San Francisco, CA 94111 · 415-434-1600

Frederick P. Furth · Furth, Fahrner, Bluemle & Mason · Furth Building, Suite 1000 · 201 Sansome Street · San Francisco, CA 94104 · 415-433-2070

Melvin R. Goldman · Morrison & Foerster · 345 California Street · San Francisco, CA 94104-2105 · 415-434-7000

Edwin A. Heafey, Jr. · Crosby, Heafey, Roach & May · 333 Bush Street, Suite 2580 · San Francisco, CA 94111 · 415-543-8700

James L. Hunt · McCutchen, Doyle, Brown & Enersen · Three Embarcadero Center · San Francisco, CA 94111 · 415-393-2000

John W. Keker · Keker & Brockett · 807 Montgomery Street · San Francisco, CA 94133 · 415-391-5400

Raoul D. Kennedy · Crosby, Heafey, Roach & May · 333 Bush Street, Suite 2580 · San Francisco, CA 94111 · 415-543-8700

Moses Lasky · Lasky, Haas, Cohler & Munter · 505 Sansome Street, 12th Floor San Francisco, CA 94111-3183 · 415-788-2700

Richard J. Lucas · Orrick, Herrington & Sutcliffe · Transamerica Pyramid · 600 Montgomery Street · San Francisco, CA 94111 · 415-392-1122

John S. Martel · Farella, Braun & Martel · Russ Building, Suite 3000 · 235 Montgomery Street · San Francisco, CA 94104 · 415-954-4400

James E. Merritt · Morrison & Foerster · 345 California Street · San Francisco, CA 94104-2105 · 415-434-7000

Charles O. Morgan, Jr. · 450 Sansome Street, Suite 1310 · San Francisco, CA 94111-3382 · 415-392-2037

M. Laurence Popofsky · Heller, Ehrman, White & McAuliffe · 333 Bush Street San Francisco, CA 94104 · 415-772-6000

Robert D. Raven · Morrison & Foerster · 345 California Street · San Francisco, CA 94104-2105 · 415-434-7000

Paul A. Renne · Cooley, Godward, Castro, Huddleson & Tatum · One Maritime Plaza, 20th Floor · San Francisco, CA 94111 · 415-981-5252

Joseph W. Rogers, Jr. · Rogers, Joseph, O'Donnell & Quinn · 311 California Street · San Francisco, CA 94104 · 415-956-2828

J. Thomas Rosch · McCutchen, Doyle, Brown & Enersen · Three Embarcadero Center · San Francisco, CA 94111 · 415-393-2000

Michael Traynor · Cooley, Godward, Castro, Huddleson & Tatum · One Maritime Plaza, 20th Floor · San Francisco, CA 94111 · 415-981-5252

James P. Kleinberg · McCutchen, Doyle, Brown & Enersen · 55 South Market Street, Suite 1500 · San Jose, CA 95113 · 408-947-8400

Allen J. Ruby · Morgan, Ruby, Teter, Schofield, Franich & Fredkin · 99 Almaden Boulevard, Suite 1000 · San Jose, CA 95113 · 408-288-8288

A. Barry Cappello · Cappello & Foley · 831 State Street · Santa Barbara, CA 93101-3298 · 805-564-2444

CORPORATE LAW

Robert L. Adler · Munger, Tolles & Olson · 355 South Grand Avenue, 35th Floor · Los Angeles, CA 90071 · 213-683-9100

Robert H. Baker · Jones, Day, Reavis & Pogue · 355 South Grand Avenue, Suite 3000 · Los Angeles, CA 90071 · 213-625-3939

Ronald S. Beard · Gibson, Dunn & Crutcher · 333 South Grand Avenue · Los Angeles, CA 90071 · 213-229-7000

Barton Beek · O'Melveny & Myers · 400 South Hope Street · Los Angeles, CA 90071-2899 · 213-669-6000

Richard L. Bernacchi · Irell & Manella · 1800 Avenue of the Stars, Suite 900 · Los Angeles, CA 90067 · 213-879-2600

Andrew E. Bogen · Gibson, Dunn & Crutcher · 333 South Grand Avenue · Los Angeles, CA 90071 · 213-229-7000

David M. Bosko · Sheppard, Mullin, Richter & Hampton · 333 South Hope Street, 48th Floor · Los Angeles, CA 90071 · 213-620-1780

Neal H. Brockmeyer · Kindel & Anderson · 555 South Flower Street, 26th Floor · Los Angeles, CA 90071 · 213-680-2222

Robert E. Carlson · Paul, Hastings, Janofsky & Walker · 555 South Flower Street, 22nd Floor · Los Angeles, CA 90071 · 213-489-4000

Richard Carver · Latham & Watkins · 555 South Flower Street · Los Angeles, CA 90071 · 213-485-1234

Louis M. Castruccio · Irell & Manella · 1800 Avenue of the Stars, Suite 900 · Los Angeles, CA 90067 · 213-879-2600

R. Bradbury Clark · O'Melveny & Myers · 400 South Hope Street · Los Angeles, CA 90071-2899 · 213-669-6000

Michael J. Connell · Paul, Hastings & Janofsky · 555 South Flower Street, 22nd Floor · Los Angeles, CA 90071 · 213-489-4000

John J. Cost · Irell & Manella · 1800 Avenue of the Stars, Suite 900 · Los Angeles, CA 90067 · 213-879-2600

James E. Cross · O'Melveny & Myers · 400 South Hope Street · Los Angeles, CA 90071-2899 · 213-669-6000

Robert E. Denham · Munger, Tolles & Olson · 355 South Grand Avenue, 35th Floor · Los Angeles, CA 90071 · 213-683-9100

Thomas W. Dobson · Latham & Watkins · 555 South Flower Street · Los Angeles, CA 90071 · 213-485-1234

Stanley F. Farrar · Sullivan & Cromwell · 444 South Flower Street, Suite 1200 Los Angeles, CA 90071 · 213-955-8000

William C. Farrer · Hill, Farrer & Burrill · Union Bank Square, 35th Floor · 445 South Figueroa Street · Los Angeles, CA 90071 · 213-620-0460

Ronald L. Fein · Wyman, Bautzer, Kuchel & Silbert · 2049 Century Park East, Suite 1400 · Los Angeles, CA 90067 · 213-556-8000

Robert T. Gelber · Gibson, Dunn & Crutcher · 2029 Century Park East · Los Angeles, CA 90067 · 213-552-8500

William D. Gould · Troy, Casden & Gould · 1801 Century Park East, 16th Floor Los Angeles, CA 90067 · 213-553-4441

Gilbert E. T. Haakh · Baker & McKenzie · 725 South Figueroa Street, 36th Floor Los Angeles, CA 90017 · 213-629-3000

Guido R. Henry, Jr. · Milbank, Tweed, Hadley & McCoy · Manulife Plaza, Suite 1800 · 515 South Figueroa Street · Los Angeles, CA 90071 · 213-688-0200

Grover R. Heyler · Latham & Watkins · 555 South Flower Street · Los Angeles, CA 90071 · 213-485-1234

John D. Hussey · Sheppard, Mullin, Richter & Hampton · 333 South Hope Street, 48th Floor · Los Angeles, CA 90071 · 213-620-1780

Edmund M. Kaufman · Irell & Manella · 1800 Avenue of the Stars, Suite 900 Los Angeles, CA 90067 · 213-879-2600

C. Douglas Kranwinkle · Munger, Tolles & Olson · 355 South Grand Avenue, 35th Floor · Los Angeles, CA 90071 · 213-683-9100

Henry Lesser · Fried, Frank, Harris, Shriver & Jacobson · Citicorp Plaza, Suite 3890 · 725 South Figueroa · Los Angeles, CA 90017 · 213-689-0010

Ronald M. Loeb · Irell & Manella · 1800 Avenue of the Stars, Suite 900 · Los Angeles, CA 90067 · 213-879-2600

Simon M. Lorne · Munger, Tolles & Olson · 355 South Grand Avenue, 35th Floor Los Angeles, CA 90071 · 213-683-9100

Joseph D. Mandel · Tuttle & Taylor · 355 South Grand Avenue, 40th Floor · Los Angeles, CA 90071 · 213-683-0600

Harold Marsh, Jr. · 10920 Wilshire Boulevard, Suite 1000 · Los Angeles, CA 90024 · 213-208-1424

John P. McLoughlin · Latham & Watkins · 555 South Flower Street · Los Angeles, CA 90071 · 213-485-1234

James W. Mercer, Jr. · Hennigan & Mercer · 611 West Sixth Street, 28th Floor Los Angeles, CA 90017 · 213-629-0072

Donn B. Miller · O'Melveny & Myers · 400 South Hope Street · Los Angeles, CA 90071-2899 · 213-669-6000

Gavin Miller · Hufstedler, Miller, Kaus & Beardsley · 355 South Grand Avenue, 45th Floor · Los Angeles, CA 90071-3107 · 213-617-7070

Robert K. Montgomery · Gibson, Dunn & Crutcher · 333 South Grand Avenue Los Angeles, CA 90071 · 213-229-7000

Gary Olson · Latham & Watkins · 555 South Flower Street · Los Angeles, CA 90071 · 213-485-1234

Gerald L. Parsky · Gibson, Dunn & Crutcher · 333 South Grand Avenue · Los Angeles, CA 90071 · 213-229-7000

Thomas B. Pitcher · Gibson, Dunn & Crutcher · 333 South Grand Avenue · Los Angeles, CA 90071 · 213-229-7000

John H. Roney · O'Melveny & Myers · 400 South Hope Street · Los Angeles, CA 90071-2899 · 213-669-6000

Joseph Ryan · O'Melveny & Myers · 400 South Hope Street · Los Angeles, CA 90071-2899 · 213-669-6000

Reade H. Ryan, Jr. · Shearman & Sterling · 725 South Figueroa Street, 21st Floor Los Angeles, CA 90017 · 213-239-0300

Myrl R. Scott · Sheppard, Mullin, Richter & Hampton · 333 South Hope Street, 48th Floor · Los Angeles, CA 90071 · 213-620-1780

Charles V. Thornton · Paul, Hastings, Janofsky & Walker · 555 South Flower Street, 22nd Floor · Los Angeles, CA 90071 · 213-489-4000

Joseph F. Troy · Troy, Casden & Gould · 1801 Century Park East, 16th Floor · Los Angeles, CA 90067 · 213-553-4441

George A. Vandeman · Latham & Watkins · 555 South Flower Street · Los Angeles, CA 90071 · 213-485-1234

Francis M. Wheat · Gibson, Dunn & Crutcher · 333 South Grand Avenue · Los Angeles, CA 90071 · 213-229-7000

Christopher L. Kaufman · Heller, Ehrman, White & McAuliffe · 525 University Avenue, 11th Floor · Palo Alto, CA 94301-1908 · 415-326-7600

Henry P. Massey, Jr. · Wilson, Sonsini, Goodrich & Rosati · Two Palo Alto Square · Palo Alto, CA 94306 · 415-493-9300

William D. Sherman · Morrison & Foerster · 630 Hansen Way · Palo Alto, CA 94304 · 415-354-1500

Lawrence W. Sonsini · Wilson, Sonsini, Goodrich & Rosati · Two Palo Alto Square · Palo Alto, CA 94306 · 415-493-9300

James D. Ward · Thompson & Colegate · 3610 Fourteenth Street · P.O. Box 1299 · Riverside, CA 92502 · 714-682-5550

Joseph S. Genshlea · Weintraub Genshlea Hardy Erich & Brown · 2535 Capitol Oaks Drive · Sacramento, CA 95833 · 916-648-9400

Archie Hefner · Hefner, Stark & Marois · 2710 Gateway Oaks Drive, Suite 300 South · Sacramento, CA 95833 · 916-925-6620

Malcolm S. Weintraub · Weintraub Genshlea Hardy Erich & Brown · 2535 Capitol Oaks Drive · Sacramento, CA 95833 · 916-648-9400

Thomas C. Ackerman, Jr. · Gray, Cary, Ames & Frye · 1700 First Interstate Plaza · 401 B Street · San Diego, CA 92101-4219 · 619-699-2700

John W. Brooks · Luce, Forward, Hamilton & Scripps · The Bank of California Plaza · 110 West A Street · San Diego, CA 92101 · 619-236-1414

Robert G. Copeland · Gray, Cary, Ames & Frye · 1700 First Interstate Plaza · 401 B Street · San Diego, CA 92101-4219 · 619-699-2700

William N. Jenkins · Jenkins & Perry · 1100 Central Savings Tower · 225 Broadway · San Diego, CA 92101 · 619-231-2500

Kenneth M. Poovey · Latham & Watkins · 701 B Street, Suite 2100 · San Diego, CA 92101-8197 · 619-236-1234

John C. Stiska · Brobeck, Phleger & Harrison · 225 Broadway, Suite 2100 · San Diego, CA 92101 · 619-234-1966

Cameron Baker · Pettit & Martin · 101 California Street, 35th Floor · San Francisco, CA 94111 · 415-434-4000

Roland E. Brandel · Morrison & Foerster · 345 California Street · San Francisco, CA 94104-2105 · 415-434-7000

Alexander D. Calhoun, Jr. · Graham & James · Alcoa Building · One Maritime Plaza, Suite 300 · San Francisco, CA 94111 · 415-954-0200

James F. Crafts, Jr. · Orrick, Herrington & Sutcliffe · Transamerica Pyramid · 600 Montgomery Street · San Francisco, CA 94111 · 415-392-1122

Paul L. Davies, Jr. · Pillsbury, Madison & Sutro · 225 Bush Street · San Francisco, CA 94104 · 415-983-1000

Bartley C. Deamer · McCutchen, Doyle, Brown & Enersen · Three Embarcadero Center · San Francisco, CA 94111 · 415-393-2000

Frank E. Farella · Farella, Braun & Martel · Russ Building, 30th Floor · 235 Montgomery Street · San Francisco, CA 94104 · 415-954-4400

Margaret G. Gill · Pillsbury, Madison & Sutro · 225 Bush Street · San Francisco, CA 94104 · 415-983-1000

Michael J. Halloran · Pillsbury, Madison & Sutro · 225 Bush Street · San Francisco, CA 94104 · 415-983-1000

Leslie P. Jay · Orrick, Herrington & Sutcliffe · Transamerica Pyramid · 600 Montgomery Street · San Francisco, CA 94111 · 415-392-1122

John W. Larson · Brobeck, Phleger & Harrison · Spear Street Tower · One Market Plaza · San Francisco, CA 94105 · 415-442-0900

Thomas A. Lee, Jr. · Morrison & Foerster · 345 California Street · San Francisco, CA 94104-2105 · 415-434-7000

Bruce A. Mann · Morrison & Foerster · 345 California Street · San Francisco, CA 94104-2105 · 415-434-7000

Loyd W. McCormick · McCutchen, Doyle, Brown & Enersen · Three Embarcadero Center · San Francisco, CA 94111 · 415-393-2000

David E. Nelson · Morrison & Foerster · 345 California Street · San Francisco, CA 94104-2105 · 415-434-7000

Walter G. Olson · Orrick, Herrington & Sutcliffe · Transamerica Pyramid · 600 Montgomery Street · San Francisco, CA 94111 · 415-392-1122

Denis T. Rice · Howard, Rice, Nemerovski, Canady, Robertson & Falk · Three Embarcadero Center, Suite 600 · San Francisco, CA 94111 · 415-434-1600

Marshall L. Small · Morrison & Foerster · 345 California Street · San Francisco, CA 94104-2105 · 415-434-7000

Thomas Unterman · Morrison & Foerster · 345 California Street · San Francisco, CA 94104-2105 · 415-434-7000

Charles R. Collins · Gibson, Dunn & Crutcher · One Almaden Boulevard, Suite 1000 · San Jose, CA 95113 · 408-998-2000

Jay L. Margulies · Pillsbury, Madison & Sutro · 10 Almaden Boulevard · San Jose, CA 95113 · 408-947-4000

Alan J. Barton · Paul, Hastings, Janofsky & Walker · 1299 Ocean Avenue, Fifth Floor · Santa Monica, CA 90401 · 213-451-1200

CRIMINAL DEFENSE

Bruce I. Hochman · Hochman, Salkin and De Roy · West Tower, Seventh Floor 9100 Wilshire Boulevard · Beverly Hills, CA 90212 · 213-273-1181

Cristina C. Arguedas · Cooper, Arguedas & Cassman · 5900 Hollis Street, Suite N · Emeryville, CA 94608 · 415-654-2000

Penelope M. Cooper · Cooper, Arguedas & Cassman · 5900 Hollis Street, Suite N · Emeryville, CA 94608 · 415-654-2000

Jules F. Bonjour, Jr. · Bonjour, Gough & Thorman · 24301 Southland Drive · Hayward, CA 94545 · 415-785-8400

Philip A. Schnayerson · Garcia & Schnayerson · 225 West Winton Avenue, Suite 208 · Hayward, CA 94544 · 415-782-7580

Marshall W. Krause · (also Appellate) · Krause, Baskin, Grant & Ballantine · 60 East Sir Francis Drake Boulevard · Larkspur, CA 94939 · 415-461-4100

Leslie H. Abramson · 4929 Wilshire Boulevard, Suite 940 · Los Angeles, CA 90010 · 213-933-9002

Harland W. Braun · Two Century Plaza Building, Suite 1800 · 2049 Century Park East · Los Angeles, CA 90067 · 213-277-4777

Douglas Dalton · Dalton & Godfrey · 4525 Wilshire Boulevard, Third Floor · Los Angeles, CA 90010-3886 · 213-933-4945

Max L. Gillam · Latham & Watkins · 555 South Flower Street · Los Angeles, CA 90071 · 213-485-1234

Stanley I. Greenberg · 10960 Wilshire Boulevard, Suite 1225 · Los Angeles, CA 90024 · 213-473-3333

Jan Lawrence Handzlik · 10920 Wilshire Boulevard, Suite 1400 · Los Angeles, CA 90024 · 213-477-7071

Mark O. Heaney · Law Offices of Barry Tarlow · 9119 Sunset Boulevard · Los Angeles, CA 90069 · 213-278-2111

Thomas E. Holliday · Gibson, Dunn & Crutcher · 2029 Century Park East · Los Angeles, CA 90067 · 213-552-8500

Richard H. Kirschner · 10850 Wilshire Boulevard · Los Angeles, CA 90024 · 213-474-6555

Joel Levine · 811 West Seventh Street, 11th Floor · Los Angeles, CA 90017 · 213-622-2635

Michael J. Lightfoot · (also Appellate) · Talcott, Lightfoot, Vandevelde, Woehrle & Sadowsky · 655 South Hope Street, 13th Floor · Los Angeles, CA 90017 · 213-622-4750

Vincent J. Marella · Bird, Marella, Boxer, Wolpert & Matz · 10960 Wilshire Boulevard, 24th Floor · Los Angeles, CA 90024 · 213-312-0300

Edward M. Medvene · Mitchell, Silberberg & Knupp · 11377 West Olympic Boulevard · Los Angeles, CA 90064 · 213-312-2000

Alvin S. Michaelson · Michaelson & Levine · 1900 Avenue of the Stars, Suite 2512 · Los Angeles, CA 90067 · 213-278-4984

Stephen D. Miller · Miller & O'Connell · Biltmore Court, Seventh Floor · 520 South Grand Street · Los Angeles, CA 90071 · 213-627-1900

Robert M. Talcott · Talcott, Lightfoot, Vandevelde, Woehrle & Sadowsky · 655 South Hope Street, 13th Floor · Los Angeles, CA 90017 · 213-622-4750

Barry Tarlow · Law Offices of Barry Tarlow · 9119 Sunset Boulevard · Los Angeles, CA 90069 · 213-278-2111

John D. Vandevelde · Talcott, Lightfoot, Vandevelde, Woehrle & Sadowsky Roosevelt Building, Suite 430 · 727 West Seventh Street · Los Angeles, CA 90017 213-622-4750

Howard L. Weitzman · Wyman, Bautzer, Kuchel & Silbert · 2049 Century Park East, Suite 1400 · Los Angeles, CA 90067 · 213-556-8000

Dennis Roberts · 370 Grand Avenue · Oakland, CA 94610 · 415-465-6363

George W. Porter, Jr. · Covington & Crowe · 1131 West Sixth Street · P.O. Box 1515 · Ontario, CA 91762 · 714-983-9393

Gary C. Scherotter · Heritage Square · 901 Tahquitz Way, Suite C203 · P.O. Box 2224 · Palm Springs, CA 92262 · 619-320-7111

Thomas J. Nolan · Nolan & Parnes · 600 University Avenue · Palo Alto, CA 94301 415-326-2980

Virginia M. Blumenthal · Blumenthal & Lomazow · The Riverside Barrister Building · 3993 Market Street · Riverside, CA 92501 · 714-682-5110

Steven L. Harmon · Bridges and Harmon · Mission Square Plaza, Suite 240 · 3750 University Avenue · Riverside, CA 92501 · 714-682-2760

Gerald D. Polis · 3750 University Avenue, Suite 630 · Riverside, CA 92501 714-684-0131

Clyde M. Blackmon · Blackmon & Drozd · 660 J Street, Suite 260 · Sacramento, CA 95814 · 916-441-0824

Michael S. Sands · 800 Ninth Street, Third Floor · Sacramento, CA 95814 · 916-444-9845

Thomas S. Worthington · Civic Center Building, Suite 101 · 21 West Alisal Street · Salinas, CA 93901 · 408-758-1688

Juanita R. Brooks · 108 Ivy Street · San Diego, CA 92101 · 619-232-8118

John J. Cleary · Cleary & Sevilla · 1010 Second Avenue, Suite 1601 · San Diego, CA 92101-4906 · 619-232-2222

Charles L. Goldberg · Goldberg, Frant & Hall · 303 West A Street · San Diego, CA 92101 · 619-232-6671

Peter J. Hughes · 1010 Second Avenue, Suite 1917 · San Diego, CA 92101 · 619-234-6695

Eugene G. Iredale · 625 Broadway · San Diego, CA 92101 · 619-233-1525

Michael Pancer · 625 Broadway · San Diego, CA 92101 · 619-236-1826

Elisabeth Semel · Semel & Feldman · 225 Broadway, Suite 810 · San Diego, CA 92101 · 619-236-9384

Charles M. Sevilla · Cleary & Sevilla · 1010 Second Avenue, Suite 1601 · San Diego, CA 92101-4906 · 619-232-2222

Milton J. Silverman, Jr. · The Quartermass-Wilde House · 2404 Broadway · San Diego, CA 92102 · 619-231-6611

William A. Brockett, Jr. · Keker & Brockett · 807 Montgomery Street · San Francisco, CA 94133 · 415-391-5400

James J. Brosnahan · Morrison & Foerster · 345 California Street · San Francisco, CA 94104-2105 · 415-434-7000

Gilbert Eisenberg · Filippelli & Eisenberg · 407 Sansome Street · San Francisco, CA 94111 · 415-433-3476

Patrick S. Hallinan · Hallinan & Poplack · 345 Franklin Street · San Francisco, CA 94102 · 415-861-1151

Paul A. Harris · Zaks & Harris · 503 Dolores Street · San Francisco, CA 94110 · 415-863-1531

Susan B. Jordan · Jordan & Osterhoudt · 423 Washington Street, Third Floor · San Francisco, CA 94111 · 415-981-2122

John W. Keker · Keker & Brockett · 807 Montgomery Street · San Francisco, CA 94133 · 415-391-5400

James Larson · Larson and Weinberg · 523 Octavia Street · San Francisco, CA 94102 · 415-431-3472

Ephraim Margolin · (also Appellate) · 240 Stockton Street, Suite 300 · San Francisco, CA 94108 · 415-421-4347

William L. Osterhoudt · Jordan & Osterhoudt · 423 Washington Street, Third Floor · San Francisco, CA 94111 · 415-981-2122

Douglas R. Schmidt · Winslow & Schmidt · 3223 Webster Street · San Francisco, CA 94123 · 415-441-5943

M. Gerald Schwartzbach · McTernan, Stender, Walsh & Schwartzbach · 90 New Montgomery Street, 15th Floor · San Francisco, CA 94105-4505 · 415-777-0313

J. Tony Serra · Serra, Perelson, Anton, Lichter & Daar · 473 Jackson Street · San Francisco, CA 94111 · 415-986-5591

Marcus S. Topel · Topel & Goodman · 832 Sansome Street, Fourth Floor · San Francisco, CA 94111 · 415-421-6140

George G. Walker · 633 Battery, Suite 635 · San Francisco, CA 94111 · 415-421-6911

Doron Weinberg · Larson and Weinberg · 523 Octavia Street · San Francisco, CA 94102 · 415-431-3472

Guyton N. Jinkerson · James Square Building, Suite 190 · 255 North Market Street · San Jose, CA 95110 · 408-297-8555

Allen J. Ruby · Morgan, Ruby, Teter, Schofield, Franich & Fredkin · 99 Almaden Boulevard, Suite 1000 · San Jose, CA 95113 · 408-288-8288

Frank R. Ubhaus · Ubhaus & Collins · 40 South Market Street, Seventh Floor · San Jose, CA 95113 · 408-287-9001

John L. Williams · Manchester & Williams · 150 Almaden Boulevard, Suite 1375 · San Jose, CA 95113 · 408-287-6193

Keith C. Monroe · 1428 North Broadway · Santa Ana, CA 92706 · 714-835-3883

James D. Riddet · Aronson & Riddet · 900 North Broadway, Suite 600 · Santa Ana, CA 92701 · 714-835-8600

Marshall M. Schulman · Schulman & McMillan · 401 Civic Center Drive West, Suite 707 · Santa Ana, CA 92701 · 714-542-3989

Allan H. Stokke · 888 West Santa Ana Boulevard, Suite 200 · Santa Ana, CA 92701-4561 · 714-543-7704

James A. Stotler · 2372 Southeast Bristol Street, Suite A · Santa Ana, CA 92707 714-756-8080

John M. Sink · 1114 State Street · Santa Barbara, CA 93101 · 805-963-4266

Bradley Wm. Brunon · 2600 Colorado Avenue, Suite 440 · Santa Monica, CA 90404 · 213-453-2393

Gerald Chaleff · Chaleff & English · Garden Suite · 1337 Ocean Avenue · Santa Monica, CA 90401 · 213-458-1691

Richard G. Hirsch · Nasatir & Hirsch · 2115 Main Street · Santa Monica, CA 90405 · 213-399-3259

Michael D. Nasatir · Nasatir & Hirsch · 2115 Main Street · Santa Monica, CA 90405 · 213-399-3259

Brian O'Neill · O'Neill & Lysaght · 100 Wilshire Boulevard, Suite 700 · Santa Monica, CA 90401 · 213-451-5700

Victor Sherman · 2115 Main Street · Santa Monica, CA 90405 · 213-399-3259

ENTERTAINMENT LAW

Jay L. Cooper · Cooper, Epstein & Hurewitz · 345 North Maple Drive, Suite 300 · Beverly Hills, CA 90210 · 213-278-1111

Allen E. Susman · Rosenfeld, Meyer & Susman · First Interstate Bank Building, Fourth Floor · 9601 Wilshire Boulevard · Beverly Hills, CA 90210 · 213-858-7700

Eric Weissmann · Weissmann, Wolff, Bergman, Coleman & Silverman · 9665 Wilshire Boulevard, Suite 900 · Beverly Hills, CA 90212 · 213-858-7888

Jacob A. Bloom · Bloom and Dekom · 9255 Sunset Boulevard, 10th Floor · Los Angeles, CA 90069 · 213-278-8622

John G. Branca · Ziffren, Brittenham & Branca · 2121 Avenue of the Stars, 32nd Floor · Los Angeles, CA 90067 · 213-552-3388

Harry M. Brittenham · Ziffren, Brittenham & Branca · 2121 Avenue of the Stars, 32nd Floor · Los Angeles, CA 90067 · 213-552-3388

Donald S. Engel · Engel & Engel · 9200 Sunset Boulevard, Suite 505 · Los Angeles, CA 90069 · 213-550-7178

Bertram Fields · Greenberg, Glusker, Fields, Claman & Machtinger · 1900 Building, 20th Floor · 1900 Avenue of the Stars · Los Angeles, CA 90067 · 213-553-3610

John T. Frankenheimer · Loeb and Loeb · 10100 Santa Monica Boulevard, Suite 2200 · Los Angeles, CA 90067 · 213-282-2000

Barry L. Hirsh · Armstrong, Hirsh & Levine · 1888 Century Park East, Suite 1888 · Los Angeles, CA 90067 · 213-553-0305

Donald S. Passman · Gang, Tyre & Brown · 6400 Sunset Building · Los Angeles, CA 90028 · 213-463-4863

Donald V. Petroni · O'Melveny & Myers · 1800 Century Park East, Suite 600 · Los Angeles, CA 90067 · 213-553-6700

L. Lee Phillips · Manatt, Phelps, Rothenberg & Phillips · Trident Center, East Tower · 11355 Olympic Boulevard · Los Angeles, CA 90064 · 213-312-4000

Bruce M. Ramer · Gang, Tyre & Brown · 6400 Sunset Building · Los Angeles, CA 90028 · 213-463-4863

Charles D. Silverberg · Silverberg, Rosen, Leon and Behr · One Century Plaza, Suite 1900 · 2029 Century Park East · Los Angeles, CA 90067-3088 · 213-277-4500

Payson Wolff · Gang, Tyre & Brown · 6400 Sunset Building · Los Angeles, CA 90028 · 213-463-4863

Kenneth Ziffren · Ziffren, Brittenham & Branca · 2121 Avenue of the Stars, 32nd Floor · Los Angeles, CA 90067 · 213-552-3388

John E. Mason, Jr. · Mason & Gilbert · Wilshire Palisades Building, Penthouse · 1299 Ocean Avenue · Santa Monica, CA 90401 · 213-393-5345

Owen J. Sloane · Wilshire Palisades Building, Penthouse · 1299 Ocean Avenue · Santa Monica, CA 90401 · 213-393-5345

FAMILY LAW

Harry M. Fain · Fain, Kaufman & Young · 121 South Beverly Drive · Beverly Hills, CA 90212 · 213-275-5132

Daniel J. Jaffe · Jaffe & Clemens · 433 North Camden Drive, Suite 1111 · Beverly Hills, CA 90210 · 213-550-0226

David K. Leavitt · 9454 Wilshire Boulevard, Suite 200 · Beverly Hills, CA 90212 · 213-273-3151

Richard C. Berra · Carr, McClellan, Ingersoll, Thompson & Horn · Security Pacific Building · 216 Park Road · P.O. Box 513 · Burlingame, CA 94011-0513 · 415-342-9600

Robert R. Thompson · Carr, McClellan, Ingersoll, Thompson & Horn · Security Pacific Building · 216 Park Road · P.O. Box 513 · Burlingame, CA 94011-0513 · 415-342-9600

S. Michael Love · McDougal, Love, Eckis, Grindle & O'Connor · 460 North Magnolia Street · P.O. Drawer 1466 · El Cajon, CA 92020 · 619-440-4444

Ruth Miller · Davidson, Miller & Digiacinto · 563 Pilgrim Drive, Suite D · Foster City, CA 94404 · 415-574-1215

Stephen A. Kalemkarian · 371 East Bullard Avenue, Suite 115 · Fresno, CA 93710 · 209-435-2525

James E. Sutherland · (Appellate) · 3711 Long Beach Boulevard, Suite 718 · Long Beach, CA 90807 · 213-426-0425

Jerome L. Goldberg · 333 South Grand Avenue, Suite 1880 · Los Angeles, CA 90071 · 213-680-2616

Paul Gutman · 1801 Century Park East, Suite 2211 · Los Angeles, CA 90067 · 213-556-8999

A. David Kagon · Goldman & Kagon · 1801 Century Park East, Suite 2222 · Los Angeles, CA 90067 · 213-552-1707

Gerald E. Lichtig · Lichtig, Ellis and Meyberg · 11111 Santa Monica Boulevard · Los Angeles, CA 90025 · 213-473-8899

Ira H. Lurvey · Lurvey & Shapiro · 2121 Avenue of the Stars, Suite 1550 · Los Angeles, CA 90067 · 213-203-0711

S. David Rosenson · Wasser, Rosenson & Carter · One Century Plaza, Suite 1200 · 2029 Century Park East · Los Angeles, CA 90067 · 213-277-7117

Joseph Taback · 2049 Century Park East, Suite 2310 · Los Angeles, CA 90067 · 213-557-1200

Sorrell Trope · Trope & Trope · 12121 Wilshire Boulevard, Suite 801 · Los Angeles, CA 90025 · 213-879-2726

Dennis M. Wasser · Wasser, Rosenson & Carter · One Century Plaza, Suite 1200 · 2029 Century Park East · Los Angeles, CA 90067 · 213-277-7117

Dennis A. Cornell · Allen, Cornell, Polgar & Proietti · 1640 N Street, Suite 200 · P.O. Box 2184 · Merced, CA 95340 · 209-723-4372

Ronald A. Wagner · Hardin, Cook, Loper, Engel & Bergez · 1999 Harrison Street, 18th Floor · Oakland, CA 94612 · 415-444-3131

Michael E. Wald · Wald, Freedman, Chapman & Bendes · 554 Grand Avenue · Oakland, CA 94610 · 415-444-0560

George H. Norton · Lakin Spears · 285 Hamilton Avenue · P.O. Box 240 · Palo Alto, CA 94301 · 415-328-7000

Lee A. Lopez · Washington Plaza, Suite 411 · 2400 Washington Avenue · P.O. Box 1826 · Redding, CA 96099 · 916-243-1265

O. A. John Goth · Silvestri & Goth · 1000 Marshall Street, Suite B · Redwood City, CA 94063 · 415-367-0442

Francis A. Watson, Jr. · Watson, Hoffe & Barbieri · 3700 Barrett Avenue · Richmond, CA 94805 · 415-237-3700

Michael H. Clepper · 4075 Main Street, Suite 255 · Riverside, CA 92501 · 714-684-5530

Anthony S. Dick · Dick, Wasserman & Wagner · 797 University Avenue · Sacramento, CA 95825 · 916-920-9504

Stephen James Wagner · Dick, Wasserman & Wagner · 797 University Avenue · Sacramento, CA 95825 · 916-920-9504

David L. Wasserman · Dick, Wasserman & Wagner · 797 University Avenue · Sacramento, CA 95825 · 916-920-9504

D. Thomas Woodruff · Woodruff, O'Hair & Posner · 2251 Fair Oakes Boulevard · Sacramento, CA 95825 · 916-920-0211

Gerald L. Barry, Jr. · Mitchell, Keeney, Barry & Pike · 520 West Ash Street, Suite 200 · San Diego, CA 92101 · 619-238-1234

James Edgar Hervey · Hervey and Wood · 1620 Fifth Avenue, Suite 800 · San Diego, CA 92101-2703 · 619-238-1223

Edward B. Huntington · Huntington & Haviland · 1551 Fourth Avenue, Suite 700 · San Diego, CA 92101-3155 · 619-233-9500

John W. Lightner · Lightner and Castro · 3104 Fourth Avenue · San Diego, CA 92103 · 619-291-4500

Gary E. Pike · Mitchell, Keeney, Barry & Pike · 520 West Ash Street, Suite 200 · San Diego, CA 92101 · 619-238-1234

Bonnie Nelson Reading · Seltzer Caplan Wilkins & McMahon · 3003-3043 Fourth Avenue · P.O. Box X 33999 · San Diego, CA 92103 · 619-295-3003

Nordin F. Blacker · 535 Pacific Avenue, First Floor · San Francisco, CA 94133 · 415-397-3222

C. Rick Chamberlin · Stotter, Samuels & Chamberlin · 1735 Franklin Street · San Francisco, CA 94109-3526 · 415-928-5050

Max Gutierrez, Jr. · Brobeck, Phleger & Harrison · Spear Street Tower · One Market Plaza · San Francisco, CA 94105 · 415-442-0900

Pamela E. Pierson · Pierson & Toben · 685 Market Street, Suite 770 · San Francisco, CA 94105 · 415-495-4499

Diana Richmond · 100 The Embarcadero, Suite 260 · San Francisco, CA 94105 · 415-391-3500

Merrill E. Steinberg · Leland, Parachini, Steinberg, Flinn, Matzger & Melnick · 333 Market Street, 27th Floor · San Francisco, CA 94105 · 415-957-1800

Lawrence H. Stotter · Stotter, Samuels & Chamberlin · 1735 Franklin Street San Francisco, CA 94109-3526 · 415-928-5050

Lowell H. Sucherman · Sucherman & Collins · 88 Kearny Street, Suite 1750 · San Francisco, CA 94108 · 415-956-5554

William L. Dok · Dok, Levy & Perrin · 1550 The Alameda, Suite 300 · San Jose, CA 95126 · 408-287-7790

Philip L. Hammer · Hammer and Jacobs · 1960 The Alameda, Suite 140 · San Jose, CA 95126 · 408-243-8200

Hugh T. Thomson · 2060 The Alameda · San Jose, CA 95126 · 408-247-2301

Harry A. Hanson, Jr. · Hanson & Norris · 777 Mariners Island Boulevard, Suite 575 · San Mateo, CA 94404 · 415-571-0600

Verna A. Adams · Adams & Dornan · 633 Fifth Avenue · San Rafael, CA 94901 415-454-8980

Richard F. Barry · Courthouse Square, Suite 350 · 1000 Fourth Street · P.O. Box 1257 · San Rafael, CA 94915 · 415-453-0360

Cecelia D. Lannon · 2022 Fourth Street · San Rafael, CA 94901 · 415-457-0770

John P. McCall · Riede, Rosenberg, McCall & Cahill · Courthouse Square, Suite 500 · 1000 Fourth Street · San Rafael, CA 94901 · 415-454-9880

James K. Batchelor · 829 North Parton Street, Suite 1A · Santa Ana, CA 92701 714-542-2333

David L. Price · 600 West Santa Ana Boulevard, Suite 900 · Santa Ana, CA 92701 714-953-6831

Gertrude D. Chern · Chern, Brenneman & Garcia · 301 East Cook Street, Suite B Santa Maria, CA 93454 · 805-922-4553

James A. Hennenhoefer · 316 South Melrose Drive, Suite 200 · Vista, CA 92083 619-941-2260

Steven D. Hallert · Hallert & Hallert · 710 South Broadway, Suite 312 · Walnut Creek, CA 94596 · 415-933-4033

LABOR AND EMPLOYMENT LAW

Leo Geffner · (Labor) · Taylor, Roth, Bush & Geffner · 3500 West Olive Avenue, Suite 1100 · Burbank, CA 91505 · 818-955-6400

Jay D. Roth · (Labor) · Taylor, Roth, Bush & Geffner · 3500 West Olive Avenue, Suite 1100 · Burbank, CA 91505 · 818-955-6400

John C. McCarthy · (Individuals) · 401 Harvard Avenue · Claremont, CA 91711 714-621-4984

Howard C. Hay · (Management) · Paul, Hastings, Janofsky & Walker · 695 Town Center Drive · Costa Mesa, CA 92626 · 714-641-1100

David C. Larson · (Management) · Rutan & Tucker · Central Bank Tower, Suite 1400 · South Coast Plaza, Town Center · 611 Anton Boulevard · P.O. Box 1950 · Costa Mesa, CA 92628 · 714-641-5100

Joseph Posner · (Individuals) · 16311 Ventura Boulevard, Suite 555 · Encino, CA 91436 · 818-990-1340

James N. Adler · (Management) · Irell & Manella · 1800 Avenue of the Stars, Suite 900 · Los Angeles, CA 90067 · 213-879-2600

Gloria R. Allred · (Individuals) · Allred, Maroko, Goldberg & Ribakoff · 6380 Wilshire Boulevard, Suite 1404 · Los Angeles, CA 90048 · 213-653-6530

Kenneth W. Anderson · (Management) · Gibson, Dunn & Crutcher · 333 South Grand Avenue · Los Angeles, CA 90071 · 213-229-7000

Willard Z. Carr, Jr. · (Management) · Gibson, Dunn & Crutcher · 333 South Grand Avenue · Los Angeles, CA 90071 · 213-229-7000

David A. Cathcart · (Management) · Gibson, Dunn & Crutcher · 333 South Grand Avenue · Los Angeles, CA 90071 · 213-229-7000

Walter Cochran-Bond · (Management) · Proskauer Rose Mendelsohn & Goetz · 2121 Avenue of the Stars, Suite 2700 · Los Angeles, CA 90067-5010 · 213-557-2900

Richard J. Davis, Jr. · (Labor) · Pappy & Davis · 3424 Wilshire Boulevard, 11th Floor · Los Angeles, CA 90017 · 213-385-3071

Robert M. Dohrmann · (Labor) · Schwartz, Steinsapir, Dohrmann & Sommers · 3580 Wilshire Boulevard, Suite 1820 · Los Angeles, CA 90010 · 213-487-5700

William J. Emanuel · (Management) · Morgan, Lewis & Bockius · 801 South Grand Avenue, 20th Floor · Los Angeles, CA 90017 · 213-612-2500

Alan V. Friedman · (Management) · Munger, Tolles & Olson · 355 South Grand Avenue, 35th Floor · Los Angeles, CA 90071 · 213-683-9100

Paul Grossman · (Management) · Paul, Hastings, Janofsky & Walker · 555 South Flower Street, 22nd Floor · Los Angeles, CA 90071 · 213-489-4000

Joseph E. Herman · (Management) · Seyfarth, Shaw, Fairweather & Geraldson 2029 Century Park East, Suite 3300 · Los Angeles, CA 90067 · 213-277-7200

A. Thomas Hunt · (Management) · Proskauer Rose Mendelsohn & Goetz · 2121 Avenue of the Stars, Suite 2700 · Los Angeles, CA 90067-5010 · 213-557-2900

Anthony T. Oliver, Jr. · (Management) · Parker, Milliken, Clark, O'Hara & Samuelian · Security Pacific Plaza, 27th Floor · 333 South Hope Street · Los Angeles, CA 90071 · 213-683-6500

George A. Pappy · (Labor) · Pappy & Davis · 3424 Wilshire Boulevard, 11th Floor Los Angeles, CA 90017 · 213-385-3071

Andrew C. Peterson · (Management) · Paul, Hastings, Janofsky & Walker · 555 South Flower Street, 22nd Floor · Los Angeles, CA 90071 · 213-489-4000

Julius Reich · (Labor) · Reich, Adell & Crost · 501 Shatto Place, Suite 100 · Los Angeles, CA 90020 · 213-386-3860

Glenn Rothner · (Labor) · Reich, Adell & Crost · 501 Shatto Place, Suite 100 Los Angeles, CA 90020 · 213-386-3860

Richard D. Sommers · (Labor) · Schwartz, Steinsapir, Dohrmann & Sommers 3580 Wilshire Boulevard, Suite 1820 · Los Angeles, CA 90010 · 213-487-5700

Laurence D. Steinsapir · (Labor) · Schwartz, Steinsapir, Dohrmann & Sommers 3580 Wilshire Boulevard, Suite 1820 · Los Angeles, CA 90010 · 213-487-5700

William Stewart Waldo · (Management) · Paul, Hastings, Janofsky & Walker 555 South Flower Street, 22nd Floor · Los Angeles, CA 90071 · 213-489-4000

Robert F. Walker · (Management) · Paul, Hastings, Janofsky & Walker · 555 South Flower Street, 22nd Floor · Los Angeles, CA 90071 · 213-489-4000

John S. Welch · (Management) · Latham & Watkins · 555 South Flower Street Los Angeles, CA 90071 · 213-485-1234

Kenneth E. Ristau, Jr. · (Management) · Gibson, Dunn & Crutcher · 800 Newport Center Drive, Suite 700 · P.O. Box 2490 · Newport Beach, CA 92660 714-759-3800

Richard C. White · (Management) · O'Melveny & Myers · Union Bank Building, Suite 1700 · 610 Newport Center Drive · Newport Beach, CA 92660 · 714-760-9600

Laurence P. Corbett · (Management) · Corbett & Kane · Cutter Tower, Suite 500 2200 Powell Street · Oakland, CA 94608 · 415-547-2434

Timothy J. Murphy · (Management) · Crosby, Heafey, Roach & May · 1999 Harrison Street · Oakland, CA 94612 · 415-763-2000

Guy T. Saperstein · (Individuals) · Farnsworth, Saperstein & Seligman · 505 Fourteenth Street, Suite 1150 · Oakland, CA 94612 · 415-763-9800

Brad S. Seligman · (Individuals) · Farnsworth, Saperstein & Seligman · 505 Fourteenth Street, Suite 1150 · Oakland, CA 94612 · 415-763-9800

Paul E. Crost · (Labor) · Reich, Adell & Crost · 1918 West Chapman Avenue, Suite 205 · Orange, CA 92668-2654 · 714-978-6451

Robert W. Bell, Jr. · (Management) · Gray, Cary, Ames & Frye · 1700 First Interstate Plaza · 401 B Street · San Diego, CA 92101-4219 · 619-699-2700

John D. Collins · (Management) · Sheppard, Mullin, Richter & Hampton · 701 B Street, Suite 1000 · San Diego, CA 92101 · 619-239-3669

Brian D. Monaghan · (Individuals) · Monaghan & Metz · First National Bank Building, Suite 1815 · 401 West A Street · San Diego, CA 92101 · 619-231-0059

Josiah L. Neeper · (Management) · Gray, Cary, Ames & Frye · 1700 First Interstate Plaza · 401 B Street · San Diego, CA 92101-4219 · 619-699-2700

Douglas F. Olins · (Labor) · Olins, Foerster & Siegel · 2214 Second Avenue · San Diego, CA 92101 · 619-238-1601

Richard A. Paul · (Management) · Gray, Cary, Ames & Frye · 1700 First Interstate Plaza · 401 B Street · San Diego, CA 92101-4219 · 619-699-2700

Richard D. Prochazka · (Labor) · Prochazka, McGrath & Cortez · 2918 Fifth Avenue · San Diego, CA 92103 · 619-296-7677

James K. Smith · (Management) · Gray, Cary, Ames & Frye · 1700 First Interstate Plaza · 401 B Street · San Diego, CA 92101-4219 · 619-699-2700

Fern M. Steiner · (Labor) · Georgiou & Tosdal · 600 B Street, Suite 1515 · San Diego, CA 92101 · 619-239-7200

Thomas L. Tosdal · (Labor) · Georgiou & Tosdal · 600 B Street, Suite 1515 · San Diego, CA 92101 · 619-239-7200

John L. Anderson · (Labor) · Neyhart, Anderson, Nussbaum, Reilly & Freitas 568 Howard Street · P.O. Box 7426 · San Francisco, CA 94120 · 415-495-4949

Ralph H. Baxter, Jr. · (Management) · Orrick, Herrington & Sutcliffe · Transamerica Pyramid · 600 Montgomery Street · San Francisco, CA 94111 415-392-1122

Duane B. Beeson · (Labor) · Beeson, Tayer & Silbert · 100 Bush Street, Suite 1500 · San Francisco, CA 94104 · 415-986-4060

Marsha S. Berzon · (Labor; Appellate) · Altshuler & Berzon · 177 Post Street, Suite 300 · San Francisco, CA 94108 · 415-421-7151

Gilmore F. Diekmann, Jr. · (Management) · Bronson, Bronson & McKinnon Bank of America Center · 555 California Street · San Francisco, CA 94104 415-986-4200

Alan B. Exelrod · (Individuals) · Cathedral Hill Office Building, Suite 1150 · 1255 Post Street · San Francisco 94109 · 415-673-5902

Wesley J. Fastiff · (Management) · Littler, Mendelson, Fastiff & Tichy · 650 California Street, 20th Floor · San Francisco, CA 94108 · 415-433-1940

Barry S. Jellison · (Labor) · Davis, Cowell & Bowe · 100 Van Ness Street, Ninth Floor · San Francisco, CA 94102 · 415-626-1880

Robert M. Lieber · (Management) · Littler, Mendelson, Fastiff & Tichy · 650 California Street, 20th Floor · San Francisco, CA 94108 · 415-433-1940

John A. McGuinn · (Individuals) · McGuinn, Hillsman & Palefsky · 451 Jackson Street · San Francisco, CA 94111 · 415-421-9292

Stanley H. Neyhart · (Labor) · Neyhart, Anderson, Nussbaum, Reilly & Freitas 568 Howard Street · P.O. Box 7426 · San Francisco, CA 94120 · 415-495-4949

Peter D. Nussbaum · (Labor) · Neyhart, Anderson, Nussbaum, Reilly & Freitas
568 Howard Street · P.O. Box 7426 · San Francisco, CA 94120 · 415-495-4949

Cliff Palefsky · (Individuals) · McGuinn, Hillsman & Palefsky · 451 Jackson Street, Third Floor · San Francisco, CA 94111 · 415-421-9292

James C. Paras · (Management) · Morrison & Foerster · 345 California Street San Francisco, CA 94104-2105 · 415-434-7000

Jonathan H. Sakol · (Management) · McCutchen, Doyle, Brown & Enersen Three Embarcadero Center · San Francisco, CA 94111 · 415-393-2000

Donald S. Tayer · (Labor) · Beeson, Tayer & Silbert · 100 Bush Street, Suite 1500 San Francisco, CA 94104 · 415-986-4060

Victor J. Van Bourg · (Labor) · Van Bourg, Weinberg, Roger & Rosenfeld · 875 Battery Street · San Francisco, CA 94111 · 415-864-4000

Charles E. Voltz · (Management) · Pillsbury, Madison & Sutro · 225 Bush Street San Francisco, CA 94104 · 415-983-1000

Stewart Weinberg · (Labor) · Van Bourg, Weinberg, Roger & Rosenfeld · 875 Battery Street · San Francisco, CA 94111 · 415-864-4000

Raymond L. Wheeler · (Management) · Morrison & Foerster · 345 California Street · San Francisco, CA 94104-2105 · 415-434-7000

M. Kirby C. Wilcox · (Management) · Morrison & Foerster · 345 California Street San Francisco, CA 94104-2105 · 415-434-7000

Nancy L. Abell · (Management) · Paul, Hastings, Janofsky & Walker · 1299 Ocean Avenue, Fifth Floor · Santa Monica, CA 90401 · 213-451-1200

MARITIME LAW

Lawrence D. Bradley, Jr. · Lillick McHose & Charles · Citicorp Plaza · 725 South Figueroa · Los Angeles, CA 90017 · 213-488-7100

Robert E. Coppola · McCutchen, Black, Verleger & Shea · 600 Wilshire Boulevard, Suite 1200 · Los Angeles, CA 90017 · 213-624-2400

Gordon K. Wright · Lillick McHose & Charles · Citicorp Plaza · 725 South Figueroa · Los Angeles, CA 90017 · 213-488-7100

John Allen Flynn · Graham & James · Alcoa Building · One Maritime Plaza, Suite 300 · San Francisco, CA 94111 · 415-954-0200

Thomas D. McCune · Lillick McHose & Charles · Two Embarcadero Center, 26th Floor · San Francisco, CA 94111 · 415-984-8200

Norman B. Richards · McCutchen, Doyle, Brown & Enersen · Three Embarcadero Center · San Francisco, CA 94111 · 415-393-2000

Graydon S. Staring · Lillick McHose & Charles · Two Embarcadero Center, 26th Floor · San Francisco, CA 94111 · 415-984-8200

NATURAL RESOURCES AND ENVIRONMENTAL LAW

Bryant C. Danner · Latham & Watkins · 555 South Flower Street · Los Angeles, CA 90071 · 213-485-1234

Richard J. Denny · McCutchen, Black, Verleger & Shea · 600 Wilshire Boulevard, Suite 1200 · Los Angeles, CA 90017 · 213-624-2400

Betty-Jane Kirwan · McClintock, Kirwan, Benshoof, Rochefort & Weston · 444 South Flower Street, Fifth Floor · Los Angeles, CA 90071 · 213-623-2322

Joel S. Moskowitz · Gibson, Dunn & Crutcher · 333 South Grand Avenue · Los Angeles, CA 90071 · 213-229-7000

M. William Tilden · (Mining) · Gresham, Varner, Savage, Nolan & Tilden · 600 North Arrowhead Avenue, Suite 300 · San Bernardino, CA 92401 · 714-884-2171

David R. Andrews · McCutchen, Doyle, Brown & Enersen · Three Embarcadero Center · San Francisco, CA 94111 · 415-393-2000

Michael R. Barr · Pillsbury, Madison & Sutro · 225 Bush Street · San Francisco, CA 94104 · 415-983-1000

James A. Bruen · Landels, Ripley & Diamond · 450 Pacific Avenue · San Francisco, CA 94133 · 415-788-5000

Ronald C. Hausmann · Tuttle & Taylor · 355 South Grand Avenue, 40th Floor Los Angeles, CA 90071 · 213-683-0600

Robert C. Thompson · Graham & James · Alcoa Building · One Maritime Plaza, Suite 300 · San Francisco, CA 94111 · 415-954-0200

PERSONAL INJURY LITIGATION

Joseph W. Cotchett · (Plaintiffs) · Cotchett & Illston · 840 Malcolm Road, Suite 200 · Burlingame, CA 94010 · 415-342-9000

Herbert Hafif · (Plaintiffs) · 269 West Bonita Avenue · Claremont, CA 91711 · 714-624-1671

William M. Shernoff · (Plaintiffs) · Shernoff, Scott & Bidart · 600 South Indian Hill · Claremont, CA 91711 · 714-621-4935

Marrs A. Craddick · (Defendants) · Craddick, Candland & Conti · 915 San Ramon Valley Boulevard, Suite 260 · P.O. Box 810 · Danville, CA 94526 · 415-838-1100

Robert Roden · (Plaintiffs) · Roden, Ahler and Thompson · 225 East Third Avenue · Escondido, CA 92025 · 619-745-1484

James J. Pagliuso · (Plaintiffs) · 801 North Brand Boulevard · Glendale, CA 91203 818-244-2253

Thomas T. Anderson · (Plaintiffs) · 45-926 Oasis Street · Indio, CA 92201 · 619-347-3364

Joseph E. Thielen · (Plaintiffs) · 3233 East Broadway · Long Beach, CA 90803 213-439-0991

Ried Bridges · (Defendants) · Bonne, Jones, Bridges, Mueller, O'Keefe & Hunt 3699 Wilshire Boulevard, 10th Floor · Los Angeles, CA 90010-2719 · 213-480-1900

Bruce A. Broillet · (Plaintiffs) · Greene, O'Reilly, Broillet, Paul, Simon & Wheeler · 816 South Figueroa Street · Los Angeles, CA 90017 · 213-482-1122

Daniel C. Cathcart · (Plaintiffs) · Magana, Cathcart, McCarthy & Pierry · Gateway West Building, Suite 810 · 1801 Avenue of the Stars · Los Angeles, CA 90067 213-553-6630

Larry R. Feldman · (Plaintiffs) · Fogel, Feldman, Ostrov, Ringer & Klevens 5900 Wilshire Boulevard, 26th Floor · Los Angeles, CA 90036-5185 · 213-937-6250

Thomas V. Girardi · (Plaintiffs) · Girardi, Keese and Crane · 1126 Wilshire Boulevard · Los Angeles, CA 90017 · 213-489-5330

Browne Greene · (Plaintiffs) · Greene, O'Reilly, Broillet, Paul, Simon & Wheeler 816 South Figueroa Street · Los Angeles, CA 90017 · 213-482-1122

David M. Harney · (Plaintiffs) · Harney, Drummond, Garza & Packer · 201 North Figueroa Street, Suite 1300 · Los Angeles, CA 90012-2636 · 213-482-0881

George R. Hillsinger · (Defendants) · Hillsinger and Costanzo · 3055 Wilshire Boulevard, Seventh Floor · Los Angeles, CA 90010 · 213-388-9441

G. Dana Hobart · (Plaintiffs) · 4676 Admiralty Way, Suite 801 · Marina Del Rey, CA 90292 · 213-306-0063

H. Gilbert Jones · (Defendants) · Bonne, Jones, Bridges, Mueller, O'Keefe & Hunt · 801 Civic Center Drive West, Suite 400 · Los Angeles, CA 92701 714-835-1157

Raoul D. Magana · (Plaintiffs) · Magana, Cathcart, McCarthy & Pierry · Gateway West Building, Suite 810 · 1801 Avenue of the Stars · Los Angeles, CA 90067 213-553-6630

James J. McCarthy · (Plaintiffs) · Magana, Cathcart, McCarthy & Pierry · Gateway West Building, Suite 810 · 1801 Avenue of the Stars · Los Angeles, CA 90067 213-553-6630

Wm. Marshall Morgan · (Defendants) · Morgan, Wenzel & McNicholas · TWA Tower, Suite 800 · 1545 Wilshire Boulevard · Los Angeles, CA 90017 213-483-1961

Kenneth N. Mueller · (Defendants) · Bonne, Jones, Bridges, Mueller, O'Keefe & Hunt · 3699 Wilshire Boulevard, 10th Floor · Los Angeles, CA 90010-2719 213-480-1900

David J. O'Keefe · (Defendants) · Bonne, Jones, Bridges, Mueller, O'Keefe & Hunt · 3699 Wilshire Boulevard, 10th Floor · Los Angeles, CA 90010-2719 213-480-1900

Charles B. O'Reilly · (Plaintiffs) · Greene, O'Reilly, Broillet, Paul, Simon & Wheeler · 816 South Figueroa Street · Los Angeles, CA 90017 · 213-482-1122

Timothy L. Walker · (Defendants) · Shield & Smith · 1055 Wilshire Boulevard, 19th Floor · Los Angeles, CA 90017 · 213-482-3010

Lee B. Wenzel · (Defendants) · Morgan, Wenzel & McNicholas · TWA Tower, Suite 800 · 1545 Wilshire Boulevard · Los Angeles, CA 90017 · 213-483-1961

Lewis L. Fenton · (Defendants) · Hoge, Fenton, Jones & Appel · 2801 Monterey-Salinas Highway · P.O. Box 791 · Monterey, CA 93940 · 408-373-1241

Larry Grassini · (Plaintiffs) · Hurley, Grassini and Wrinkle · 11313 Weddington Street · North Hollywood, CA 91601 · 213-877-5422

Edwin A. Heafey, Jr. · (Defendants) · Crosby, Heafey, Roach & May · 1999 Harrison Street · Oakland, CA 94612 · 415-763-2000

Raoul D. Kennedy · (Defendants) · Crosby, Heafey, Roach & May · 1999 Harrison Street · Oakland, CA 94612 · 415-763-2000

Ronald G. Sproat · (Defendants) · Rankin, Sproat & Pollack · 1800 Harrison Street, Suite 1616 · Oakland, CA 94612 · 415-465-3922

John J. Collins · (Defendants) · Collins, Collins, Muir & Traver · 265 North Euclid, Suite 300 · Pasadena, CA 91101 · 818-793-1163

Ned Good · (Plaintiffs) · Law Offices of Ned Good · 70 South Lake Avenue, Suite 600 · Pasadena, CA 91101 · 818-440-0000

George E. Moore · (Plaintiffs) · 350 West Colorado Boulevard, Suite 400 · Pasadena, CA 91105 · 818-440-1111

John M. Bentley · (Defendants) · Ropers, Majeski, Kohn, Bentley, Wagner & Kane · 1125 Marshall Street · Redwood City, CA 94063 · 415-364-8200

Eugene J. Majeski · (Defendants) · Ropers, Majeski, Kohn, Bentley, Wagner & Kane · 1125 Marshall Street · Redwood City, CA 94063 · 415-364-8200

Don C. Brown · (Defendants) · Thompson & Colegate · 3610 Fourteenth Street P.O. Box 1299 · Riverside, CA 92502 · 714-682-5550

Theodore D. Bolling, Jr. · (Defendants) · Bolling, Walter & Gawthrop · 7919 Folsom Boulevard, Suite 300 · P.O. Box 255200 · Sacramento, CA 95865-5200 916-386-0777

Edward Freidberg · (Plaintiffs) · Freidberg Law Corporation · 77 Cadillac Drive, Suite 240 · Sacramento, CA 95825 · 916-929-9060

Morton L. Friedman · (Plaintiffs) · Friedman, Collard & Poswall · 7750 College Town Drive, Suite 300 · Sacramento, CA 95826 · 916-381-9011

John M. Poswall · (Plaintiffs) · Friedman, Collard & Poswall · 7750 College Town Drive, Suite 300 · Sacramento, CA 95826 · 916-381-9011

Leo H. Schuering, Jr. · (Defendants) · Weintraub Genshlea Hardy Erich & Brown · 2535 Capitol Oaks Drive · Sacramento, CA 95833 · 916-648-9400

Florentino Garza · (Plaintiffs) · Garza, Jure & King · Vanir Tower, Suite 800 · 290 North D Street · San Bernardino, CA 92401 · 714-888-0231

William G. Bailey · (Defendants) · McInnis, Fitzgerald, Rees, Sharkey & McIntyre · 1320 Columbia Street · San Diego, CA 92101 · 619-236-1711

Vincent J. Bartolotta, Jr. · (Plaintiffs) · Thorsnes, Bartolotta, McGuire & Padilla Fifth Avenue Financial Center, 11th Floor · 2550 Fifth Avenue · San Diego, CA 92103 · 619-236-9363

Daniel T. Broderick III · (Plaintiffs) · 401 West A Street, Suite 1200 · San Diego, CA 92101 · 619-239-3344

Edward D. Chapin · (Defendants) · Chapin & Brewer · 1010 Second Avenue, Suite 1100 · San Diego, CA 92101 · 619-232-4261

Gordon S. Churchill · (Plaintiffs) · Churchill & Kaplan · 2546 Fourth Avenue San Diego, CA 92103 · 619-233-7241

Patrick R. Frega · (Plaintiffs) · Frega & Tiffany · 1010 Second Avenue, Suite 1906 San Diego, CA 92101 · 619-235-4044

Richard F. Gerry · (Plaintiffs) · Casey, Gerry, Casey, Westbrook, Reed & Hughes · 110 Laurel Street · San Diego, CA 92101 · 619-238-1811

Harvey R. Levine · (Plaintiffs) · Levine, Steinberg & DePasquale · 1200 Third Avenue, Suite 1400 · San Diego, CA 92101 · 619-231-9449

Patrick A. McCormick, Jr. · (Defendants) · McCormick & Royce · The Senator 105 West F Street · San Diego, CA 92101-6085 · 619-231-8802

John F. McGuire · (Plaintiffs) · Thorsnes, Bartolotta, McGuire & Padilla · Fifth Avenue Financial Center, 11th Floor · 2550 Fifth Avenue · San Diego, CA 92103 619-236-9363

James A. McIntyre · (Defendants) · McInnis, Fitzgerald, Rees, Sharkey & McIntyre · 1320 Columbia Street · San Diego, CA 92101 · 619-236-1711

Brian D. Monaghan · (Plaintiffs) · Monaghan & Metz · First National Bank Building, Suite 1815 · 401 West A Street · San Diego, CA 92101 · 619-231-0059

Michael I. Neil · (Defendants) · Hollywood & Neil · 1010 Second Avenue, Suite 1712 · San Diego, CA 92101 · 619-238-1712

T. Michael Reed · (Plaintiffs) · Casey, Gerry, Casey, Westbrook, Reed & Hughes · 110 Laurel Street · San Diego, CA 92101 · 619-238-1811

Douglas R. Reynolds · (Defendants) · 401 West A Street, Suite 2200 · San Diego, CA 92101 · 619-557-7802

Thomas E. Sharkey · (Defendants) · McInnis, Fitzgerald, Rees, Sharkey & McIntyre · 1320 Columbia Street · San Diego, CA 92101 · 619-236-1711

Philip D. Sharp · (Defendants) · Shifflet, Sharp & Walters · 1370 India Street · San Diego, CA 92101-3481 · 619-239-0871

John R. Wingert · (Defendants) · Wingert, Grebing, Anello & Lavoy · Bank of America Plaza, Suite 1750 · 450 B Street · San Diego, CA 92101 · 619-232-8151

Albert R. Abramson · (Plaintiffs) · Abramson & Smith · 44 Montgomery Street, Suite 4211 · San Francisco, CA 94104 · 415-421-7995

Nelson C. Barry · (Defendants) · Bishop, Barry, Howe & Reid · Merchants Exchange Building, 11th Floor · 465 California Street · San Francisco, CA 94104 · 415-421-8550

Ralph W. Bastian, Jr. · (Plaintiffs) · Walkup, Shelby, Bastian, Melodia, Kelly, Echeverria & Link · The Hartford Building, 30th Floor · 650 California Street · San Francisco, CA 94108 · 415-981-7210

David B. Baum · (Plaintiffs) · Townhouse Two · Boston Ship Plaza · San Francisco, CA 94111 · 415-956-5544

Salvatore Bossio · (Defendants) · Hassard, Bonnington, Rogers & Huber · Five Fremont Center, Suite 3400 · 50 Fremont Street · San Francisco, CA 94105 · 415-543-6444

James S. Bostwick · (Plaintiffs) · Bostwick & Tehin · One Lombard, Third Floor · Lombard & Battery at The Embarcadero · San Francisco, CA 94111 · 415-421-5500

Phillip E. Brown · (Plaintiffs) · Hoberg, Finger, Brown, Cox & Molligan · 703 Market Street, Suite 1800 · San Francisco, CA 94103 · 415-543-9464

Robert E. Dryden · (Defendants) · Barfield, Dryden & Ruane · One California Street, Suite 3125 · San Francisco, CA 94111 · 415-362-6715

Edwin W. Green · (Defendants) · Bronson, Bronson & McKinnon · Bank of America Center · 555 California Street · San Francisco, CA 94104 · 415-986-4200

Edwin A. Heafey, Jr. · (Defendants) · Crosby, Heafey, Roach & May · 333 Bush Street, Suite 2580 · San Francisco, CA 94111 · 415-543-8700

Daniel J. Kelly · (Plaintiffs) · Walkup, Shelby, Bastian, Melodia, Kelly, Echeverria & Link · The Hartford Building, 30th Floor · 650 California Street · San Francisco, CA 94108 · 415-981-7210

Raoul D. Kennedy · (Defendants) · Crosby, Heafey, Roach & May · 333 Bush Street, Suite 2580 · San Francisco, CA 94111 · 415-543-8700

Edward J. McFetridge · (Defendants) · St. Clair, Zappettini, McFetridge & Griffin · Russ Building, Suite 635 · 235 Montgomery Street · San Francisco, CA 94104 · 415-421-2462

Paul V. Melodia · (Plaintiffs) · Walkup, Shelby, Bastian, Melodia, Kelly, Echeverria & Link · The Hartford Building, 30th Floor · 650 California Street · San Francisco, CA 94108 · 415-981-7210

Charles O. Morgan, Jr. · 450 Sansome Street, Suite 1310 · San Francisco, CA 94111-3382 · 415-392-2037

James N. Penrod · (Defendants) · Hassard, Bonnington, Rogers & Huber · Five Fremont Center, Suite 3400 · 50 Fremont Street · San Francisco, CA 94105 415-543-6444

Joseph W. Rogers, Jr. · (Defendants) · Rogers, Joseph, O'Donnell & Quinn · 311 California Street, 10th Floor · San Francisco, CA 94104 · 415-956-2828

Gerald C. Sterns · (Plaintiffs) · 280 Utah Street · San Francisco, CA 94103 415-626-1000

Edward A. Hinshaw · (Defendants) · 152 North Third Street, Suite 300 · San Jose, CA 95115 · 408-293-5959

Archie S. Robinson · (Defendants) · Robinson & Wood · 227 North First Street San Jose, CA 95113 · 408-298-7120

Norman W. Saucedo · (Plaintiffs) · Ruocco & Saucedo · River Park Tower, Suite 600 · 333 West San Carlos Street · San Jose, CA 95110 · 408-289-1417

Wylie A. Aitken · (Plaintiffs) · Law Offices of Wylie A. Aitken · 600 West Santa Ana Boulevard, Penthouse Suite · Santa Ana, CA 92701 · 714-834-1424

Arthur N. Hews, Jr. · (Plaintiffs) · 315 West Third Street · Santa Ana, CA 92701 714-541-4331

Robert C. Baker · (Defendants) · Baker, Silberberg & Keener · 2850 Ocean Park Boulevard, Suite 300 · Santa Monica, CA 90405 · 213-399-0900

Marshall Silberberg · (Defendants) · Baker, Silberberg & Keener · 2850 Ocean Park Boulevard, Suite 300 · Santa Monica, CA 90405 · 213-399-0900

Richard D. Aldrich · (Plaintiffs) · 15233 Ventura Boulevard, Suite 512 · Sherman Oaks, CA 91403 · 818-789-6139

Robert L. Anderson · (Defendants) · Anderson, Galloway & Lucchese · 1676 North California Boulevard, Suite 500 · Walnut Creek, CA 94596 · 415-943-6383

Thomas G. Stolpman · (Plaintiffs) · Silver, McWilliams, Stolpman, Mandel & Katzman · 1121 North Avalon Boulevard · Wilmington, CA 90748 · 213-775-7300

REAL ESTATE LAW

M. Rogue Hemley · Latham & Watkins · 650 Town Center Drive, 20th Floor · Costa Mesa, CA 92626 · 714-540-1235

Frederick L. Allen · Allen, Matkins, Leck, Gamble & Mallory · 515 South Figueroa Street, Eighth Floor · Los Angeles, CA 90071 · 213-622-5555

Dennis B. Arnold · Gibson, Dunn & Crutcher · 333 South Grand Avenue · Los Angeles, CA 90071 · 213-229-7000

Stephen Claman · Greenberg, Glusker, Fields, Claman & Machtinger · 1900 Avenue of the Stars, Suite 2000 · Los Angeles, CA 90067 · 213-553-3610

Robert M. Eller · Loeb and Loeb · 1000 Wilshire Boulevard, Suite 1800 · Los Angeles, CA 90017 · 213-688-3400

Frank E. Feder · Loeb and Loeb · 10100 Santa Monica Boulevard, Suite 2200 · Los Angeles, CA 90067 · 213-282-2000

Burton H. Fohrman · Jones, Day, Reavis & Pogue · 355 South Grand Avenue, Suite 3000 · Los Angeles, CA 90071 · 213-625-3939

Louis A. Huskins · Irell & Manella · 1800 Avenue of the Stars, Suite 900 · Los Angeles, CA 90067 · 213-879-2600

Russell L. Johnson · Gibson, Dunn & Crutcher · 333 South Grand Avenue · Los Angeles, CA 90071 · 213-229-7000

Alvin S. Kaufer · Nossaman, Guthner, Knox & Elliott · Union Bank Square, 31st Floor · 445 South Figueroa Street · Los Angeles, CA 90071-1672 · 213-612-7800

Mark L. Lamken · Richards, Watson & Gershon · Security Pacific Plaza, 38th Floor · 333 South Hope Street · Los Angeles, CA 90071 · 213-626-8484

David V. Lee · Latham & Watkins · 555 South Flower Street · Los Angeles, CA 90071 · 213-485-1234

Marvin Leon · Silverberg, Rosen, Leon and Behr · One Century Plaza, Suite 1900 2029 Century Park East · Los Angeles, CA 90067 · 213-277-4500

Richard C. Mallory · Allen, Matkins, Leck, Gamble & Mallory · 515 South Figueroa Street, Eighth Floor · Los Angeles, CA 90071 · 213-622-5555

Michael L. Matkins · Allen, Matkins, Leck, Gamble & Mallory · 515 South Figueroa Street, Eighth Floor · Los Angeles, CA 90071 · 213-622-5555

Michael E. Meyer · Lillick McHose & Charles · Citicorp Plaza, Suite 1200 · 725 South Figueroa Street · Los Angeles, CA 90017-2513 · 213-488-7100

O'Malley M. Miller · Allen, Matkins, Leck, Gamble & Mallory · 515 South Figueroa Street, Eighth Floor · Los Angeles, CA 90071 · 213-622-5555

Phillip R. Nicholson · Cox, Castle & Nicholson · Two Century Plaza, 28th Floor 2049 Century Park East · Los Angeles, CA 90067 · 213-277-4222

Leo J. Pircher · Pircher, Nichols & Meeks · Century City North Building · 10100 Santa Monica Boulevard · Los Angeles, CA 90067 · 213-201-8900

Laurence G. Preble · O'Melveny & Myers · 400 South Hope Street · Los Angeles, CA 90071-2899 · 213-669-6000

Floyd Sayer · Floyd Sayer & Associates · 10960 Wilshire Boulevard · Los Angeles, CA 90024 · 213-477-6001

H. Randall Stoke · Latham & Watkins · 555 South Flower Street · Los Angeles, CA 90071 · 213-485-1234

Herbert J. Strickstein · Two Century Plaza, 12th Floor · 2049 Century Park East Los Angeles, CA 90067 · 213-553-4888

Charles V. Thornton III · Paul, Hastings, Janofsky & Walker · 555 South Flower Street, 22nd Floor · Los Angeles, CA 90071 · 213-489-4000

David H. Vena · Latham & Watkins · 555 South Flower Street · Los Angeles, CA 90071 · 213-485-1234

Richard S. Volpert · Skadden, Arps, Slate, Meagher & Flom · 300 South Grand Avenue, 34th Floor · Los Angeles, CA 90071 · 213-687-5000

Paul R. Walker · Paul, Hastings, Janofsky & Walker · 555 South Flower Street, 22nd Floor · Los Angeles, CA 90071 · 213-489-4000

Alan Wayte · Dewey, Ballantine, Bushby, Palmer & Wood · 333 South Hope Street, 30th Floor · Los Angeles, CA 90071 · 213-626-3399

John W. Whitaker · Lillick McHose & Charles · Citicorp Plaza, Suite 1200 · 725 South Figueroa Street · Los Angeles, CA 90017 · 213-488-7100

Lowell C. Martindale, Jr. · O'Melveny & Myers · Union Bank Building, Suite 1700 · 610 Newport Center Drive · Newport Beach, CA 92660 · 714-760-9600

John R. Simon · Sheppard, Mullin, Richter & Hampton · 4695 MacArthur Court, Seventh Floor · Newport Beach, CA 92660 · 714-752-6400

Ralph C. Wintrode · Gibson, Dunn & Crutcher · 800 Newport Center Drive, Suite 700 · P.O. Box 2490 · Newport Beach, CA 92660 · 714-759-3800

Michael A. Dean · Wendel, Rosen, Black, Dean & Levitan · Clorox Building, Suite 2000 · Oakland City Center · P.O. Box 2047 · Oakland, CA 94604 · 415-834-6600

Harry D. Miller · Miller, Starr & Regalia · Ordway Building, 16th Floor · One Kaiser Plaza · Oakland, CA 94612 · 415-465-3800

Marvin B. Starr · Miller, Starr & Regalia · Ordway Building, 16th Floor · One Kaiser Plaza · Oakland, CA 94612 · 415-465-3800

John V. Diepenbrock · Diepenbrock, Wulff, Plant & Hannegan · 300 Capitol Mall · Sacramento, CA 95814 · 916-444-3910

Archie Hefner · Hefner, Stark & Marois · 2710 Gateway Oaks Drive, Suite 300 South · Sacramento, CA 95833 · 916-925-6620

Sharon D. Roseme · McDonough, Holland & Allen · 555 Capitol Mall, Suite 950 · Sacramento, CA 95814 · 916-444-3900

Thomas C. Ackerman, Jr. · Gray, Cary, Ames & Frye · 1700 First Interstate Plaza · 401 B Street · San Diego, CA 92101 · 619-699-2700

Robert Caplan · Seltzer Caplan Wilkins & McMahon · 3003-3043 Fourth Avenue P.O. Box X 33999 · San Diego, CA 92103 · 619-295-3003

Louis E. Goebel · Goebel, Shensa & Beale · 1202 Kettner Boulevard, Suite 6000 San Diego, CA 92101 · 619-239-2611

E. Ludlow Keeney, Jr. · Mitchell, Keeney, Barry & Pike · 520 West Ash Street, Suite 200 · Columbia at Ash · San Diego, CA 92101 · 619-238-1234

Alex C. McDonald · McDonald, Hecht & Solberg · 1100 Financial Square · 600 B Street · San Diego, CA 92101 · 619-239-3444

Paul I. Meyer · Latham & Watkins · 701 B Street, Suite 2100 · San Diego, CA 92101-8197 · 619-236-1234

Christopher B. Neils · Sheppard, Mullin, Richter & Hampton · 701 B Street, Suite 1000 · San Diego, CA 92101 · 619-239-3669

Alan R. Perry · Jenkins & Perry · 1100 Central Savings Tower · 225 Broadway San Diego, CA 92101 · 619-231-2500

Paul A. Peterson · Peterson, Thelan & Price · California First Bank Building, Suite 2300 · 530 B Street · San Diego, CA 92101 · 619-234-0361

Stephen K. Cassidy · Ellman, Burke & Cassidy · One Ecker Building, Suite 200 Ecker and Stevenson Streets · San Francisco, CA 94105 · 415-777-2727

Robert W. Cheatham · Cheatham & Skovronski · One Montgomery West Tower, Suite 2150 · San Francisco, CA 94104 · 415-986-8600

William K. Coblentz · Coblentz, Cahen, McCabe & Breyer · 222 Kearny Street, Seventh Floor · San Francisco, CA 94108 · 415-391-4800

Stephen A. Cowan · Steefel, Levitt & Weiss · One Embarcadero Center, 29th Floor · San Francisco, CA 94111 · 415-788-0900

Philip E. Diamond · Landels, Ripley & Diamond · 450 Pacific Avenue · San Francisco, CA 94133 · 415-788-5000

Pamela S. Duffy · Coblentz, Cahen, McCabe & Breyer · 222 Kearny Street, Seventh Floor · San Francisco, CA 94108 · 415-391-4800

Howard N. Ellman · Ellman, Burke & Cassidy · One Ecker Building, Suite 200 Ecker and Stevenson Streets · San Francisco, CA 94105 · 415-777-2727

Stephen R. Finn · Brobeck, Phelger & Harrison · Spear Street Tower · One Market Plaza · San Francisco, CA 94105 · 415-442-0900

Robert C. Herr · Pillsbury, Madison & Sutro · 225 Bush Street · San Francisco, CA 94104 · 415-983-1000

Bruce W. Hyman · Landels, Ripley & Diamond · 450 Pacific Avenue · San Francisco, CA 94133 · 415-788-5000

Reverdy Johnson · Pettit & Martin · 101 California Street, 35th Floor · San Francisco, CA 94111 · 415-434-4000

Carlisle B. Lane · Pillsbury, Madison & Sutro · 225 Bush Street · San Francisco, CA 94104 · 415-983-1000

Robert E. Merritt, Jr. · McCutchen, Doyle, Brown & Enersen · Three Embarcadero Center · San Francisco, CA 94111 · 415-393-2000

Noel W. Nellis · Morrison & Foerster · 345 California Street · San Francisco, CA 94104-2105 · 415-434-7000

Susan Jane Passovoy · Coblentz, Cahen, McCabe & Breyer · 222 Kearny Street, Seventh Floor · San Francisco, CA 94108 · 415-391-4800

Robert A. Thompson · Pettit & Martin · 101 California Street, 35th Floor · San Francisco, CA 94111 · 415-434-4000

David M. Van Atta · Graham & James · Alcoa Building · One Maritime Plaza, Suite 300 · San Francisco, CA 94111 · 415-954-0200

Harris W. Seed · Seed, Mackall & Cole · 1006 Santa Barbara Street · P.O. Box 2578 · Santa Barbara, CA 93120 · 805-963-0669

David W. Mitchell · McCutchen, Doyle, Brown & Enersen · Market Post Tower, Suite 1500 · 55 South Market Street · San Jose, CA 95113 · 408-947-8400

TAX AND EMPLOYEE BENEFITS LAW

Bruce I. Hochman · Hochman, Salkin and DeRoy · West Tower, Seventh Floor 9100 Wilshire Boulevard · Beverly Hills, CA 90212 · 213-273-1181

Melvin S. Spears · Ervin, Cohen & Jessup · 9401 Wilshire Boulevard, Ninth Floor Beverly Hills, CA 90212-2974 · 213-273-6333

C. David Anderson · Tuttle & Taylor · 355 South Grand Avenue · Los Angeles, CA 90071 · 213-683-0600

Norman B. Barker · Gibson, Dunn & Crutcher · 333 South Grand Avenue · Los Angeles, CA 90071 · 213-229-7000

S. David Blinn · (Employee Benefits) · Gibson, Dunn & Crutcher · 333 South Grand Avenue · Los Angeles, CA 90071 · 213-229-7000

Richard S. Brawerman · Gibson, Hoffman & Pancione · 1888 Century Park East, Suite 1777 · Los Angeles, CA 90067 · 213-556-4660

James F. Childs, Jr. · Jones, Day, Reavis & Pogue · 355 South Grand Avenue, Suite 3000 · Los Angeles, CA 90071 · 213-624-3939

John R. Cohan · Irell & Manella · 1800 Avenue of the Stars, Suite 900 · Los Angeles, CA 90067 · 213-879-2600

Robert A. DeWitt · Paul, Hastings, Janofsky & Walker · 555 South Flower Street, 22nd Floor · Los Angeles, CA 90071 · 213-489-4000

David E. Gordon · (Employee Benefits) · O'Melveny & Myers · 400 South Hope Street · Los Angeles, CA 90071-2899 · 213-669-6000

Lawrence E. Irell · Irell & Manella · 1800 Avenue of the Stars, Suite 900 · Los Angeles, CA 90067 · 213-879-2600

Philip D. Irwin · O'Melveny & Myers · 400 South Hope Street · Los Angeles, CA 90071-2899 · 213-669-6000

Robert K. Johnson · (Employee Benefits) · Munger, Tolles & Olson · 355 South Grand Avenue, 35th Floor · Los Angeles, CA 90071 · 213-683-9100

James H. Kindel, Jr. · Kindel & Anderson · 555 South Flower Street, 26th Floor Los Angeles, CA 90071 · 213-680-2222

Robert C. Kopple · Mitchel, Silberberg & Knupp · 11377 West Olympic Boulevard · Los Angeles, CA 90064 · 213-312-2000

Dudley M. Lang · McCutchen, Black, Verleger & Shea · 600 Wilshire Boulevard Los Angeles, CA 90017 · 213-624-2400

Arthur Manella · Irell & Manella · 1800 Avenue of the Stars, Suite 900 · Los Angeles, CA 90067 · 213-879-2600

James M. Murphy · Gibson, Dunn & Crutcher · 333 South Grand Avenue · Los Angeles, CA 90071 · 213-229-7000

William R. Nicholas · Latham & Watkins · 555 South Flower Street · Los Angeles, CA 90071 · 213-485-1234

Frederick A. Richman · O'Melveny & Myers · 400 South Hope Street · Los Angeles, CA 90071-2899 · 213-669-6000

Ronald S. Rizzo · (Employee Benefits) · Jones, Day, Reavis & Pogue · 355 South Grand Avenue, Suite 3000 · Los Angeles, CA 90071 · 213-624-3939

John E. Scheifly · Morgan, Lewis & Bockius · 801 South Grand Avenue, Suite 2200 · Los Angeles, CA 90017 · 213-612-2500

Donald R. Spuehler · (Employee Benefits) · O'Melveny & Myers · 400 South Hope Street · Los Angeles, CA 90071-2899 · 213-669-6000

Lawrence M. Stone · Irell & Manella · 1800 Avenue of the Stars, Suite 900 · Los Angeles, CA 90067 · 213-879-2600

Clyde E. Tritt · O'Melveny & Myers · 400 South Hope Street · Los Angeles, CA 90071 · 213-669-6000

John S. Warren · Loeb and Loeb · 1000 Wilshire Boulevard, Suite 1800 · Los Angeles, CA 90017 · 213-688-3400

William P. Wasserman · Loeb and Loeb · 1000 Wilshire Boulevard, Suite 1800 Los Angeles, CA 90017 · 213-688-3400

John S. Welch · (Employee Benefits) · Latham & Watkins · 555 South Flower Street · Los Angeles, CA 90071 · 213-485-1234

Robert L. Whitmire · Kindel & Anderson · 555 South Flower Street, 27th Floor Los Angeles, CA 90071 · 213-680-2222

Werner F. Wolfen · Irell & Manella · 1800 Avenue of the Stars, Suite 900 · Los Angeles, CA 90067 · 213-879-2600

Victor D. Rosen · Wendel, Rosen, Black, Dean & Levitan · Clorox Building, Suite 2000 · Oakland City Center · P.O. Box 2047 · Oakland, CA 94604 415-834-6600

Robert M. Winokur · Crosby, Heafey, Roach & May · 1999 Harrison Street Oakland, CA 94612 · 415-763-2000

James P. Fuller · Fenwick, Davis & West · Two Palo Alto Square, Eighth Floor · Palo Alto, CA 94306 · 415-494-0600

John R. Bonn · Sheppard, Mullin, Richter & Hampton · 701 B Street, Suite 1000 · San Diego, CA 92101 · 619-239-3669

Lawrence S. Branton · (Employee Benefits) · Branton & Wilson · 701 B Street, Suite 1255 · San Diego, CA 92101 · 619-236-1891

George L. Damoose · Procopio, Cory, Hargreaves & Savitch · 530 B Street, Suite 1900 · San Diego, CA 92101 · 619-238-1900

Edward L. Kane · Haskins, Nugent, Newnham, Kane & Zvetina · 1010 Second Avenue, Suite 2200 · San Diego, CA 92101 · 619-236-1323

Richard L. Kintz · Brobeck, Phleger & Harrison · 225 Broadway, Suite 2100 · San Diego, CA 92101 · 619-234-1966

Daniel N. Riesenberg · (Employee Benefits) · Luce, Forward, Hamilton & Scripps · The Bank of California Plaza · 110 West A Street · San Diego, CA 92101 · 619-236-1414

Luther J. Avery · Bancroft, Avery & McAlister · 601 Montgomery Street, Suite 900 · San Francisco, CA 94111 · 415-788-8855

Jeffry A. Bernstein · Coblentz, Cahen, McCabe & Breyer · 222 Kearny Street, Seventh Floor · San Francisco, CA 94108 · 415-391-4800

Robert A. Blum · (Employee Benefits) · Orrick, Herrington & Sutcliffe · Transamerica Pyramid · 600 Montgomery Street · San Francisco, CA 94111 · 415-392-1122

Edward D. Burmeister, Jr. · Baker & McKenzie · Two Embarcadero Center, Suite 2400 · San Francisco, CA 94111 · 415-576-3000

James M. Canty · Pillsbury, Madison & Sutro · 225 Bush Street · San Francisco, CA 94104 · 415-983-1000

Roy E. Crawford · Brobeck, Phleger & Harrison · Spear Street Tower · One Market Plaza · San Francisco, CA 94105 · 415-442-0900

Richard M. Eigner · Pillsbury, Madison & Sutro · 225 Bush Street · San Francisco, CA 94104 · 415-983-1000

Nicholas S. Freud · Kaplan Russin Vecchi & Eytan · 580 California Street, 16th Floor · San Francisco, CA 94104 · 415-421-1100

Joanne M. Garvey · Heller, Ehrman, White & McAuliffe · 333 Bush Street · San Francisco, CA 94104 · 415-772-6000

Richard L. Greene · Greene, Radovsky, Maloney & Share · Spear Street Tower, Suite 3200 · One Market Plaza · San Francisco, CA 94105 · 415-543-1400

William T. Hutton · Howard, Rice, Nemerovski, Canady, Robertson & Falk Three Embarcadero Center, Suite 600 · San Francisco, CA 94111 · 415-434-1600

Thomas F. Kostic · Pettit & Martin · 101 California Street, 35th Floor · San Francisco, CA 94111 · 415-434-4000

Alvin T. Levitt · Steefel, Levitt & Weiss · One Embarcadero Center, 29th Floor San Francisco, CA 94111 · 415-788-0900

Robert C. Livsey · Brobeck, Phleger & Harrison · Spear Street Tower · One Market Plaza · San Francisco, CA 94105 · 415-442-0900

John B. Lowry · McCutchen, Doyle, Brown & Enersen · Three Embarcadero Center · San Francisco, CA 94111 · 415-393-2000

Stephen J. Martin · Pillsbury, Madison & Sutro · 225 Bush Street · San Francisco, CA 94104 · 415-983-1000

T. Neal McNamara · (Employee Benefits) · Pillsbury, Madison & Sutro · 225 Bush Street · San Francisco, CA 94104 · 415-983-1000

Jerry H. Robinson · Heller, Ehrman, White & McAuliffe · 333 Bush Street · San Francisco, CA 94104 · 415-772-6000

Paul J. Sax · Orrick, Herrington & Sutcliffe · Transamerica Pyramid · 600 Montgomery Street · San Francisco, CA 94111 · 415-392-1122

Lawrence B. Silver · Green, Radosky, Maloney & Share · Spear Street Tower, Suite 4200 · One Market Plaza · San Francisco, CA 94104 · 415-543-1400

Hart H. Spiegel · Brobeck, Phleger & Harrison · Spear Street Tower · One Market Plaza · San Francisco, CA 94105 · 415-442-0900

Myron G. Sugarman · Cooley, Godward, Castro, Huddleson & Tatum · One Maritime Plaza, 20th Floor · San Francisco, CA 94111 · 415-981-5252

Thomas D. Terry · (also Employee Benefits) · Morrison & Foerster · 345 California Street · San Francisco, CA 94104-2105 · 415-434-7000

Prentiss Willson, Jr. · Morrison & Foerster · 345 California Street · San Francisco, CA 94104-2105 · 415-434-7000

Cameron W. Wolf, Jr. · Orrick, Herrington & Sutcliffe · Transamerica Pyramid 600 Montgomery Street · San Francisco, CA 94111 · 415-392-1122

Owen G. Fiore · Law Offices of Owen G. Fiore · 101 Park Center Plaza, 13th Floor · San Jose, CA 95113 · 408-257-8545

John F. Hopkins · Hopkins & Carley · 150 Almaden Boulevard, 15th Floor · San Jose, CA 95113 · 408-286-9800

Charles M. Walker · Paul, Hastings, Janofsky & Walker · 1299 Ocean Avenue, Fifth Floor · Santa Monica, CA 90401 · 213-451-1200

TRUSTS AND ESTATES

Theodore J. Cranston · Gray, Cary, Ames & Frye · 1200 Prospect Street, Suite 575 · La Jolla, CA 92037 · 619-454-9101

Robert J. Durham, Jr. · Luce, Forward, Hamilton & Scripps · 4250 Executive Square, Suite 700 · La Jolla, CA 92037 · 619-455-6611

William E. Ferguson · Ferguson, Newburn & Weston · 7777 Fay Avenue, Suite 260 · P.O. Box 1107 · La Jolla, CA 92038 · 619-454-4233

Jonathan G. Blattmachr · Milbank, Tweed, Hadley & McCoy · Manulife Plaza, Suite 1800 · 515 South Figueroa Street · Los Angeles, CA 90071 · 213-688-0200

Theodore E. Calleton · Kindel & Anderson · 555 South Flower Street, 26th Floor Los Angeles, CA 90071 · 213-680-2222

John R. Cohan · Irell & Manella · 1800 Avenue of the Stars, Suite 900 · Los Angeles, CA 90067 · 213-879-2600

Charles A. Collier, Jr. · Irell & Manella · 1800 Avenue of the Stars, Suite 900 Los Angeles, CA 90067 · 213-879-2600

Edmond R. Davis · Brobeck, Phleger & Harrison · 444 South Flower Street, Suite 4300 · Los Angeles, CA 90017 · 213-489-4060

Paul N. Frimmer · Irell & Manella · 1800 Avenue of the Stars, Suite 900 · Los Angeles, CA 90067 · 213-879-2600

Jon J. Gallo · Greenberg, Glusker, Fields, Claman & Machtinger · 1900 Avenue of the Stars, Suite 2000 · Los Angeles, CA 90067 · 213-553-3610

Andrew S. Garb · Loeb and Loeb · 1000 Wilshire Boulevard, Suite 1800 · Los Angeles, CA 90017 · 213-688-3400

Joseph G. Gorman, Jr. · Sheppard, Mullin, Richter & Hampton · 333 South Hope Street, 48th Floor · Los Angeles, CA 90071 · 213-620-1780

Ronald E. Gother · Gibson, Dunn & Crutcher · 333 South Grand Avenue · Los Angeles, CA 90071 · 213-229-7000

Geraldine S. Hemmerling · Armstrong, Hirsch & Levine · 1888 Century Park East, Suite 1888 · Los Angeles, CA 90067 · 213-553-0305

William E. Johnston · Johnson, Bannon, Wohlwend & Johnston · 1800 Avenue of the Stars, Suite 435 · Los Angeles, CA 90067 · 213-552-0175

Solomon M. Kamm · O'Melveny & Myers · 400 South Hope Street · Los Angeles, CA 90071-2899 · 213-669-6000

Edward A. Landry · Musick, Peeler & Garrett · One Wilshire Boulevard, Suite 2000 · Los Angeles, CA 90017 · 213-629-7600

Fred L. Leydorf · Hufstedler, Miller, Kaus & Beardsley · 355 South Grand Avenue, 45th Floor · Los Angeles, CA 90071-3107 · 213-617-7070

Arne S. Lindgren · Latham & Watkins · 555 South Flower Street · Los Angeles, CA 90071 · 213-485-1234

Roy D. Miller · Gibson, Dunn & Crutcher · 333 South Grand Avenue · Los Angeles, CA 90071 · 213-229-7000

Wesley L. Nutten III · Sheppard, Mullin, Richter & Hampton · 333 South Hope Street, 48th Floor · Los Angeles, CA 90071 · 213-620-1780

Byron O. Smith · Adams, Duque & Hazeltine · Pacific Mutual Building, 10th Floor · 523 West Sixth Street · Los Angeles, CA 90014 · 213-620-1240

George E. Stephens, Jr. · Paul, Hastings, Janofsky & Walker · 555 South Flower Street, 22nd Floor · Los Angeles, CA 90071 · 213-489-4000

Stuart P. Tobisman · O'Melveny & Myers · 400 South Hope Street · Los Angeles, CA 90071-2899 · 213-669-6000

David D. Watts · O'Melveny & Myers · 400 South Hope Street · Los Angeles, CA 90071-2899 · 213-669-6000

Harold Weinstock · Weinstock, Manion, Reisman & Shore · 1888 Century Park East, Suite 800 · Los Angeles, CA 90067 · 213-553-8844

Joseph L. Wyatt, Jr. · Hufstedler, Miller, Kaus & Beardsley · 355 South Grand Avenue, 45th Floor · Los Angeles, CA 90071-3107 · 213-617-7070

James D. Devine · Ehrman, Flavin, Devine & Baker · 337 El Dorado Street, Suite 1A2 · P.O. Box 2229 · Monterey, CA 93942 · 408-372-7535

Francis J. Collin, Jr. · Dickenson, Peatman & Fogarty · 809 Coombs Street Napa, CA 94559 · 707-252-7122

John L. McDonnell, Jr. · Fitzgerald, Abbott & Beardsley · 1221 Broadway, 21st Floor · Oakland, CA 94612 · 415-451-3300

William E. Beamer · Gray, Cary, Ames & Frye · 1700 First Interstate Plaza · 401 B Street · San Diego, CA 92101-4219 · 619-699-2700

Edward V. Brennan · Ferris, Brennan & Britton · 1855 First Avenue, Suite 300 San Diego, CA 92101 · 619-233-3131

Stephen L. Newnham · Haskins, Nugent, Newnham, Kane & Zvetina · 1010 Second Avenue, Suite 2200 · San Diego, CA 92101 · 619-236-1323

George E. Olmstead · Glenn, Wright, Jacobs & Schell · 2320 Fifth Avenue, Suite 300 · San Diego, CA, 92101 · 619-239-1211

Margaret Anne Payne · Higgs, Fletcher & Mack · 2000 First National Bank Building · 401 West A Street · San Diego, CA 92101 · 619-236-1551

D. Keith Bilter · Thelen, Marrin, Johnson & Bridges · Two Embarcadero Center, Suite 2200 · San Francisco, CA 94111 · 415-392-6320

Alan D. Bonapart · Bancroft, Avery & McAlister · 601 Montgomery Street, Suite 900 · San Francisco, CA 94111 · 415-788-8855

Raymond G. Ellis · Orrick, Herrington & Sutcliffe · Transamerica Pyramid · 600 Montgomery Street · San Francisco, CA 94111 · 415-392-1122

K. Bruce Friedman · Friedman & Olive · 425 California Street, Suite 2501 · San Francisco, CA 94104 · 415-434-1363

Max Gutierrez, Jr. · Brobeck, Phleger & Harrison · Spear Street Tower · One Market Plaza · San Francisco, CA 94105 · 415-442-0900

William L. Hoisington · Orrick, Herrington & Sutcliffe · Transamerica Pyramid 600 Montgomery Street · San Francisco, CA 94111 · 415-392-1122

Philip Hudner · Pillsbury, Madison & Sutro · 225 Bush Street · San Francisco, CA 94104 · 415-983-1000

Richard S. Kinyon · Morrison & Foerster · 345 California Street · San Francisco, CA 94104-2105 · 415-434-7000

Thomas B. McGuire · Heller, Ehrman, White & McAuliffe · 333 Bush Street San Francisco, CA 94104 · 415-772-6000

Robert A. Mills · McCutchen, Doyle, Brown & Enersen · Three Embarcadero Center · San Francisco, CA 94111 · 415-393-2000

Michael A. Roosevelt · Heller, Ehrman, White & McAuliffe · 333 Bush Street San Francisco, CA 94104 · 415-772-6000

Philip F. Spalding · Cooley, Godward, Castro, Huddleson & Tatum · One Maritime Plaza, 20th Floor · San Francisco, CA 94111-3580 · 415-981-5252

Charles G. Stephenson · Jackson, Tufts, Cole & Black · 650 California Street, 33rd Floor · San Francisco, CA 94108 · 415-433-1950

Edward M. Alvarez · Ferrari, Alvarez, Olsen & Ottoboni · 333 West Santa Clara Street, Suite 700 · San Jose, CA 95113 · 408-280-0535

COLORADO

BANKRUPTCY LAW	101
BUSINESS LITIGATION	102
CORPORATE LAW	103
CRIMINAL DEFENSE	105
FAMILY LAW	106
LABOR AND EMPLOYMENT LAW	106
NATURAL RESOURCES AND ENVIRONMENTAL LAW	108
PERSONAL INJURY LITIGATION	110
REAL ESTATE LAW	111
TAX AND EMPLOYEE BENEFITS LAW	112
TRUSTS AND ESTATES	113

BANKRUPTCY LAW

Ronald M. Martin · Holland & Hart · Holly Sugar Building, Suite 1400 · Chase Stone Center · Colorado Springs, CO 80903 · 719-475-7730

Craig A. Christensen · Sherman & Howard · 633 Seventeenth Street, Suite 3000 · Denver, CO 80202 · 303-297-2900

Edward I. Cohen · 1845 Sherman Street, Suite 600 · Denver, CO 80203 · 303-831-7301

Carl A. Eklund · Roath & Brega · 370 Seventeenth Street, Suite 900 · P.O. Box 5560 T.A. · Denver, CO 80217 · 303-893-5800

Glen E. Keller, Jr. · Davis, Graham & Stubbs · 370 Seventeenth Street, Suite 4700 · P.O. Box 185 · Denver, CO 80201-0185 · 303-892-9400

Stephen E. Snyder · Holme Roberts & Owen · 1700 Broadway · Denver, CO 80290 · 303-861-7000

Harry M. Sterling · Sterling and Miller · 370 Seventeenth Street, Suite 3150 Denver, CO 80202 · 303-893-1000

BUSINESS LITIGATION

James W. Buchanan · Buchanan, Gray, Purvis & Schuetze · The Exeter Building, Suite 501 · 1050 Walnut Street · Boulder, CO 80302 · 303-442-3366

Charles F. Brega · Roath & Brega · 370 Seventeenth Street, Suite 900 · P.O. Box 5560 T.A. · Denver, CO 80217 · 303-893-5800

Peter Breitenstein · Fairfield and Woods · 1700 Lincoln Street, Suite 2400 Denver, CO 80203 · 303-830-2400

Jeffrey A. Chase · Holme Roberts & Owen · 1700 Broadway · Denver, CO 80290 303-861-7000

H. Thomas Coghill · Coghill & Goodspeed · 1430 Colorado State Bank Building 1600 Broadway · Denver, CO 80202 · 303-832-1151

Frederic K. Conover III · Conover, McClearn & Heppenstall · 1775 Sherman Street, Suite 2600 · Denver, CO 80203 · 303-837-9222

William R. Fishman · 303 East 17th Avenue, Suite 800 · Denver, CO 80203 303-863-0060

Walter W. Garnsey, Jr. · Kelly/Haglund/Garnsey & Kahn · 300 Blake Street Building · 1441 Eighteenth Street · Denver, CO 80202 · 303-296-9412

Daniel S. Hoffman · Holme Roberts & Owen · 1700 Broadway · Denver, CO 80290 · 303-861-7000

Edwin S. Kahn · Kelly/Haglund/Garnsey & Kahn · 300 Blake Street Building 1441 Eighteenth Street · Denver, CO 80202 · 303-296-9412

Alex Stephen Keller · Keller, Dunievitz & Johnson · 1050 Seventeenth Street, Suite 2480 · Denver, CO 80265 · 303-571-5302

William C. McClearn · Holland & Hart · 555 Seventeenth Street, Suite 2900 P.O. Box 8749 · Denver, CO 80201 · 303-295-8000

Joseph E. Meyer III · Pendleton & Sabian · 303 East 17th Avenue, Suite 1000 Denver, CO 80203 · 303-839-1204

William E. Murane · Holland & Hart · 555 Seventeenth Street, Suite 2900 · P.O. Box 8749 · Denver, CO 80201 · 303-295-8000

David G. Palmer · Gibson, Dunn & Crutcher · 1801 California Street, Suite 4200 · Denver, CO 80202 · 303-298-7200

Kenneth L. Starr · Holmes & Starr · 717 Seventeenth Street, Suite 2440 · Denver, CO 80202 · 303-292-1500

Roger P. Thomasch · Ballard, Spahr, Andrews & Ingersoll · 1225 Seventh Street, Suite 2300 · Denver, CO 80202 · 303-292-2400

Tucker K. Troutman · Ireland, Stapleton, Pryor & Pascoe · 1675 Broadway, Suite 2600 · Denver, CO 80202 · 303-623-2700

Michael A. Williams · Sherman & Howard · 633 Seventeenth Street, Suite 3000 · Denver, CO 80202-3665 · 303-297-2900

CORPORATE LAW

Robert J. Ahrenholz · Kutak, Rock & Campbell · 2400 ARCO Tower · 707 Seventeenth Street · Denver, CO 80202 · 303-297-2400

H. Gregory Austin · Holland & Hart · 555 Seventeenth Street, Suite 2900 · P.O. Box 8749 · Denver, CO 80201 · 303-295-8000

George W. Bermant · Gibson, Dunn & Crutcher · 1801 California Street, Suite 4200 · Denver, CO 80202 · 303-298-7200

James T. Bunch · Davis, Graham & Stubbs · 370 Seventeenth Street, Suite 4700 · P.O. Box 185 · Denver, CO 80201-0185 · 303-892-9400

David Butler · Holland & Hart · 555 Seventeenth Street, Suite 2900 · P.O. Box 8749 · Denver, CO 80201 · 303-295-8000

Harold S. Bloomenthal · Holme Roberts & Owen · 1700 Broadway, Suite 1800 · Denver, CO 80290 · 303-861-7000

Garth C. Grissom · Sherman & Howard · 633 Seventeenth Street, Suite 3000 · Denver, CO 80202-3665 · 303-297-2900

Cannon Y. Harvey · Holme Roberts & Owen · 1700 Broadway, Suite 1800 · Denver, CO 80290 · 303-861-7000

Hardin Holmes · Holmes & Starr · 717 Seventeenth Street, Suite 2440 · Denver, CO 80202 · 303-292-1500

Dennis M. Jackson · Holland & Hart · 555 Seventeenth Street, Suite 2900 · P.O. Box 8749 · Denver, CO 80201 · 303-295-8000

David R. Johnson · Sherman & Howard · 633 Seventeenth Street, Suite 3000 Denver, CO 80202-3665 · 303-297-2900

John P. Kanouff · Hopper, Kanouff, Smith, Peryam, Terry and Duncan · 1610 Wynkoop Street, Suite 200 · Denver, CO 80202 · 303-892-6003

Francis P. King · Lentz, Evans and King · Lincoln Center Building, Suite 2900 1660 Lincoln Street · Denver, CO 80264 · 303-861-4154

Mark R. Levy · Holland & Hart · 555 Seventeenth Street, Suite 2900 · P.O. Box 8749 · Denver, CO 80201 · 303-295-8000

John G. Lewis · Ireland, Stapleton, Pryor & Pascoe · 1675 Broadway, Suite 2600 Denver, CO 80202 · 303-623-2700

Ernest W. Lohf · Lohf, Shaiman & Ross · 900 Cherry Tower · 950 South Cherry Street · P.O. Box 24188 · Denver, CO 80222 · 303-753-9000

John W. Low · Sherman & Howard · 633 Seventeenth Street, Suite 3000 Denver, CO 80202-3665 · 303-297-2900

James C. Owen, Jr. · Holme Roberts & Owen · 1700 Broadway, Suite 1800 Denver, CO 80290 · 303-861-7000

James L. Palenchar · Kirkland and Ellis · 1999 Broadway, Suite 4000 · Denver, CO 80202 · 303-291-3000

William D. Scheid · Scheid and Horleck · 707 Seventeenth Street, Suite 2800 Denver, CO 80202-3428 · 303-292-4100

Richard G. Wohlgenant · Holme Roberts & Owen · 1700 Broadway, Suite 1800 Denver, CO 80290 · 303-861-7000

Lester R. Woodward · Davis, Graham & Stubbs · 370 Seventeenth Street, Suite 4700 · P.O. Box 185 · Denver, CO 80201-0185 · 303-892-9400

Robert S. Zinn · Davis, Graham & Stubbs · 370 Seventeenth Street, Suite 4700 P.O. Box 185 · Denver, CO 80201-0185 · 303-892-9400

Joseph W. Morrissey, Jr. · Holme Roberts & Owen · 8400 East Prentice Street, Suite 900 · Englewood, CO 80111 · 303-796-7005

CRIMINAL DEFENSE

Daniel C. Hale · Miller, Hale and Harrison · 2305 Broadway · Boulder, CO 80302 · 303-449-2830

Robert Bruce Miller · Miller, Hale and Harrison · 2305 Broadway · Boulder, CO 80302 · 303-449-2830

Theodore A. Borrillo · 5353 West Dartmouth Avenue, Suite 510 · Denver, CO 80227 · 303-985-8888

Charles F. Brega · Roath & Brega · 370 Seventeenth Street, Suite 900 · P.O. Box 5560 T.A. · Denver, CO 80217 · 303-893-5800

Leonard M. Chesler · 1343 Delaware Street · Denver, CO 80204 · 303-893-8933

Lee D. Foreman · Haddon, Morgan & Foreman · 1034 Logan Street · Denver, CO 80203 · 303-831-7364

Walter L. Gerash · Gerash, Robinson & Miranda · 1439 Court Place · Denver, CO 80202 · 303-825-5400

Harold A. Haddon · Haddon, Morgan & Foreman · 1034 Logan Street · Denver, CO 80203 · 303-831-7364

Robert T. McAllister · Martin & McAllister · The Chancery, Suite 1515 · 1120 Lincoln Street · Denver, CO 80203 · 303-830-0566

Larry S. Pozner · Larry Pozner & Associates · 1890 Gaylord Street · Denver, CO 80206 · 303-333-1890

Joseph Saint-Veltri · 1570 Emerson Street · Denver, CO 80218 · 303-832-6777

Daniel J. Sears · Steele Creek Building, Suite 210 · 36 Steele Street · Denver, CO 80206 · 303-322-7700

Daniel T. Smith · Wiggins & Smith · 430 East Seventh Avenue, Suite 200 · Denver, CO 80203 · 303-860-8100

FAMILY LAW

Richard V. Lohman · Susemihl, Lohman, Kent, Carlson & McDermott · 660 Southpointe Court, Suite 210 · Colorado Springs, CO 80906 · 719-579-6500

James T. Bayer · Bayer, Carey & McGee · 1660 Downing Street · Denver, CO 80218 · 303-830-8911

Frederick Epstein · 820 Sixteenth Street · Denver, CO 80202 · 303-571-0771

William L. Hunnicutt · Sherman & Howard · 633 Seventeenth Street, Suite 3000 Denver, CO 80202 · 303-297-2900

Terrance R. Kelly · Kelly/Haglund/Garnsey & Kahn · 300 Blake Street Building 1441 Eighteenth Street · Denver, CO 80202 · 303-296-9412

Lawrence Litvak · 430 East Seventh Avenue · Denver, CO 80203 · 303-837-0757

William J. McCarren · Cogswell and Wehrle · 1700 Lincoln Street, Suite 3500 Denver, CO 80203 · 303-861-2150

Jerry N. Snyder · 1355 South Colorado Boulevard · Denver, CO 80222 303-691-0788

Robert T. Hinds · Robert Hinds & Associates · 1709 West Littleton Boulevard Littleton, CO 80120 · 303-795-1078

LABOR AND EMPLOYMENT LAW

Craig M. Cornish · (Individuals) · Cornish & Dellolio · 431 North Cascade Avenue · Colorado Springs, CO 80903 · 719-475-1204

Walter C. Brauer III · (Labor) · Brauer & Buescher · 1563 Gaylord Street Denver, CO 80206 · 303-333-7751

Thomas B. Buescher · (Labor) · Brauer & Buescher · 1563 Gaylord Street Denver, CO 80206 · 303-333-7751

E. Lee Dale · (Management) · Sherman & Howard · 633 Seventeenth Street, Suite 3000 · Denver, CO 80202-3665 · 303-297-2900

Gregory A. Eurich · (Management) · Holland & Hart · 555 Seventeenth Street, Suite 2900 · P.O. Box 8749 · Denver, CO 80201 · 303-295-8000

Lynn D. Feiger · (Individuals) · Feiger & Hyman · Blake Street Terrace, Suite 520 · 1860 Blake Street · Denver, CO 80202 · 303-292-4200

Joseph M. Goldhammer · (Labor) · Brauer & Buescher · 1563 Gaylord Street Denver, CO 80206 · 303-333-7751

James E. Hautzinger · (Management) · Sherman & Howard · 633 Seventeenth Street, Suite 3000 · Denver, CO 80202-3665 · 303-297-2900

John M. Husband · (Management) · Holland & Hart · 555 Seventeenth Street, Suite 2900 · P.O. Box 8749 · Denver, CO 80201 · 303-295-8000

Jeffrey T. Johnson · (Management) · Holland & Hart · 555 Seventeenth Street, Suite 2900 · P.O. Box 8749 · Denver, CO 80201 · 303-295-8000

Sander N. Karp · (Individuals) · Karp & Dodge · 1100 Stout Street, Suite 470 Denver, CO 80204-2064 · 303-825-3995

Donald P. McDonald · (Labor) · Hornbein, McDonald, Fattor & Hobbs · 1900 Colorado State Bank Building · 1600 Broadway · Denver, CO 80202 303-861-7070

John W. McKendree · (Labor) · McKendree, Toll & Mares · Creswell Mansion 1244 Grant Street · Denver, CO 80203 · 303-861-8906

Robert R. Miller · (Management) · Stettner, Miller and Cohn · Lawrence Street Center, Suite 1000 · 1380 Lawrence Street · Denver, CO 80204 · 303-534-0273

Robert L. Morris · (Management) · Morris, Lower & Sattler · Denver Technological Center, Suite 120 · 7800 East Union Avenue · Denver, CO 80237-2753 303-779-4664

Charles W. Newcom · (Management) · Sherman & Howard · 633 Seventeenth Street, Suite 3000 · Denver, CO 80202-3665 · 303-297-2900

Bruce W. Sattler · (Management) · Holland & Hart · 555 Seventeenth Street, Suite 2900 · P.O. Box 8749 · Denver, CO 80201 · 303-295-8000

William F. Schoeberlein · (Management) · Sherman & Howard · 633 Seventeenth Street, Suite 3000 · Denver, CO 80202-3665 · 303-297-2900

Kenneth R. Stettner · (Management) · Stettner, Miller and Cohn · Lawrence Street Center, Suite 1000 · 1380 Lawrence Street · Denver, CO 80204 303-534-0273

Warren L. Tomlinson · (Management) · Holland & Hart · 555 Seventeenth Street, Suite 2900 · P.O. Box 8749 · Denver, CO 80201 · 303-295-8000

Robert G. Good · (Management) · 5105 DTC Parkway, Suite 202 · Englewood, CO 80111 · 303-773-9889

Earl K. Madsen · (Management) · Bradley, Campbell & Carney · 1717 Washington Avenue · Golden, CO 80401-1994 · 303-278-3300

Kathryn E. Miller · (Management; Individuals) · Miller & Lehrer · 1901 West Littleton Boulevard · Littleton, CO 80120 · 303-798-2525

Robert Truhlar · (Individuals) · Truhlar & Truhlar · 1901 West Littleton Boulevard · Littleton, CO 80120 · 303-794-2404

NATURAL RESOURCES AND ENVIRONMENTAL LAW

Stephen D. Alfers · (Mining) · Davis, Graham & Stubbs · 370 Seventeenth Street, Suite 4700 · P.O. Box 185 · Denver, CO 80201-0185 · 303-892-9400

Howard Lawrence Boigon · (Mining; Oil & Gas) · Davis, Graham & Stubbs · 370 Seventeenth Street, Suite 4700 · P.O. Box 185 · Denver, CO 80201-0185 303-892-9400

Robert T. Connery · Holland & Hart · 555 Seventeenth Street, Suite 2900 · P.O. Box 8749 · Denver, CO 80201 · 303-295-8000

Frank Erisman · Holme Roberts & Owen · 1700 Broadway · Denver, CO 80290 303-861-7000

Terry N. Fiske · (Mining) · Davis, Graham & Stubbs · 370 Seventeenth Street, Suite 4700 · P.O. Box 185 · Denver, CO 80201-0185 · 303-892-9400

Alan J. Gilbert · Sherman & Howard · 633 Seventeenth Street, Suite 3000 Denver, CO 80202-3665 · 303-297-2900

Julia Hook · Holland & Hart · 555 Seventeenth Street, Suite 2900 · P.O. Box 8749 · Denver, CO 80201 · 303-295-8000

Kenneth D. Hubbard · (Mining) · Holland & Hart · 555 Seventeenth Street, Suite 2900 · P.O. Box 8749 · Denver, CO 80201 · 303-295-8000

Henry W. Ipsen · Holme Roberts & Owen · 1700 Broadway · Denver, CO 80290
303-861-7000

Rodney D. Knutson · Knutson, Brightwell & Reeves · 1650 Hudson's Bay Centre
1600 Stout Street · Denver, CO 80202-3133 · 303-825-4877

William R. Marsh · (Mining) · Sherman & Howard · 633 Seventeenth Street,
Suite 3000 · Denver, CO 80202-3665 · 303-297-2900

Harold G. Morris, Jr. · (Mining; Oil & Gas) · Sherman & Howard · 633 Seventeenth Street, Suite 3000 · Denver, CO 80202-3665 · 303-297-2900

Davis O. O'Connor · (Mining; Oil & Gas) · Holland & Hart · 555 Seventeenth
Street, Suite 2900 · P.O. Box 8749 · Denver, CO 80201 · 303-295-8000

William G. Odell · (Oil & Gas) · Poulson, Odell & Peterson · 1775 Sherman
Street, Suite 1400 · Denver, CO 80203 · 303-861-4400

Paul D. Phillips · Holland & Hart · 555 Seventeenth Street, Suite 2900 · P.O. Box
8749 · Denver, CO 80201 · 303-295-8000

James M. Piccone · (Oil & Gas) · Davis, Graham & Stubbs · 370 Seventeenth
Street, Suite 4700 · P.O. Box 185 · Denver, CO 80201-0185 · 303-892-9400

George E. Reeves · Knutson, Brightwell & Reeves · 1650 Hudson's Bay Centre
1600 Stout Street · Denver, CO 80202-3133 · 303-825-4877

Gerald J. Schissler · (Coal) · Holland & Hart · 555 Seventeenth Street, Suite 2900
P.O. Box 8749 · Denver, CO 80201 · 303-295-8000

Don H. Sherwood · (Mining) · Sherman & Howard · 633 Seventeenth Street,
Suite 3000 · Denver, CO 80202-3665 · 303-297-2900

Elizabeth H. Temkin · Davis, Graham & Stubbs · 370 Seventeenth Street, Suite
4700 · P.O. Box 185 · Denver, CO 80201-0185 · 303-892-9400

J. Kemper Will · 1441 Eighteenth Street, Suite 50 · Denver, CO 80202
303-296-8140

PERSONAL INJURY LITIGATION

James W. Buchanan · (Plaintiffs) · Buchanan, Gray, Purvis & Schuetze · The Exeter Building, Suite 501 · 1050 Walnut Street · Boulder, CO 80302 · 303-442-3366

John A. Purvis · Buchanan, Gray, Purvis & Schuetze · The Exeter Building, Suite 501 · 1050 Walnut Street · Boulder, CO 80302 · 303-442-3366

William A. Trine · (Plaintiffs) · Williams, Trine, Greenstein and Griffith · 1435 Arapahoe Avenue · Boulder, CO 80302-6390 · 303-442-0173

Douglas E. Bragg · (Plaintiffs) · Bragg & Dubofsky · Dominion Plaza, North Tower, Suite 1700N · 600 Seventeenth Street · Denver, CO 80202 · 303-571-4030

Charles F. Brega · (Plaintiffs) · Roath & Brega · 370 Seventeenth Street, Suite 900 · P.O. Box 5560 T.A. · Denver, CO 80217 · 303-893-5800

John L. Breit · (Defendants) · Breit, Best, Richman and Bosch · Writer Square, Suite 960 · 1512 Larimer Street · Denver, CO 80202 · 303-573-7777

Arthur H. Downey · (Defendants) · Downey & Gulley · 1200 Cherry Tower · 950 South Cherry Street · Denver, CO 80222 · 303-759-1350

Walter L. Gerash · (Plaintiffs) · Gerash, Robinson, Miller & Miranda · 1439 Court Place · Denver, CO 80202 · 303-825-5400

Daniel S. Hoffman · Holme Roberts & Owen · 1700 Broadway, Suite 1800 · Denver, CO 80290 · 303-861-7000

Joseph C. Jaudon, Jr. · (Defendants) · Long & Jaudon · The Bailey Mansion · 1600 Ogden Street · Denver, CO 80218-1414 · 303-832-1122

Alex Stephen Keller · Keller, Dunievitz & Johnson · 1050 Seventeenth Street, Suite 2480 · Denver, CO 80265 · 303-571-5302

Kenneth N. Kripke · (Plaintiffs) · Kripke, Epstein & Lawrence · Mountain Towers · 4100 East Mississippi Avenue, Suite 710 · Denver, CO 80222 · 303-757-7700

Gerald P. McDermott · (Plaintiffs) · McDermott, Hansen, Anderson & Reilly · 1890 Gaylord Street · Denver, CO 80206-1211 · 303-399-6037

Neil Hillyard · (Plaintiffs) · Branney, Hillyard, Kudla & Lee · 3333 South Bannock, Suite 1000 · Englewood, CO 80110 · 303-761-5600

Irving G. Johnson · (Defendants) · Pryor, Carney and Johnson · Carrara Place, Suite 400 · 6200 South Syracuse Way · P.O. Box 22003 · Englewood, CO 80111-4737 · 303-771-6200

Peter W. Pryor · (Defendants) · Pryor, Carney and Johnson · Carrara Place, Suite 400 · 6200 South Syracuse Way · P.O. Box 22003 · Englewood, CO 80111-4737 303-771-6200

REAL ESTATE LAW

Joel C. Davis · Dietze, Davis and Porter · The Randolph Center, Suite 504 · 1877 Broadway · P.O. Box 1530 · Boulder, CO 80306 · 303-447-1375

Peter C. Dietze · Dietze, Davis and Porter · The Randolph Center, Suite 504 · 1877 Broadway · P.O. Box 1530 · Boulder, CO 80306 · 303-447-1375

Norman Brownstein · Brownstein Hyatt Farber & Madden · 410 Seventeenth Street, 22nd Floor · Denver, CO 80202-4468 · 303-534-6335

Charlton H. Carpenter · Fairfield and Woods · One United Bank Center · 1700 Lincoln Street, Suite 2400 · Denver, CO 80203 · 303-830-2400

Willis V. Carpenter · Carpenter & Klatskin · 1500 Denver Club Building · 518 Seventeenth Street · Denver, CO 80202 · 303-534-6315

James E. Culhane · Davis, Graham & Stubbs · 370 Seventeenth Street, Suite 4700 · P.O. Box 185 · Denver, CO 80201-0185 · 303-892-9400

James L. Cunningham · Sherman & Howard · Stanford Place Three, Suite 700 4382 South Ulster Parkway · Denver, CO 80237 · 303-779-9494

James E. Hegarty · Holland & Hart · 555 Seventeenth Street, Suite 2900 · P.O. Box 8749 · Denver, CO 80201 · 303-295-8000

George M. Hopfenbeck, Jr. · Davis, Graham & Stubbs · 370 Seventeenth Street, Suite 4700 · P.O. Box 185 · Denver, CO 80201-0185 · 303-892-9400

Paul A. Jacobs · Holme Roberts & Owen · 1700 Broadway, Suite 1800 · Denver, CO 80290 · 303-861-7000

Bruce B. Johnson · Otten, Johnson, Robinson, Neff and Ragonetti · 950 Seventeenth Street, Suite 1600 · Denver, CO 80202 · 303-825-8400

Charles E. Rhyne · Gorsuch, Kirgis, Campbell, Walker and Grover · 1401 Seventeenth Street, Suite 1100 · P.O. Box 17180 · Denver, CO 80217 · 303-534-1200

Frank L. Robinson · Otten, Johnson, Robinson, Neff and Ragonetti · 950 Seventeenth Street, Suite 1600 · Denver, CO 80202 · 303-825-8400

W. Dean Salter · Holme Roberts & Owen · 1700 Broadway, Suite 1800 · Denver, CO 80290 · 303-861-7000

Donald E. Spiegleman · Isaacson, Rosenbaum, Spiegleman, Woods, Levy & Snow · 633 Seventeenth Street, Suite 2200 · Denver, CO 80202 · 303-292-5656

Richard G. Wohlgenant · Holme Roberts & Owen · 1700 Broadway, Suite 1800 Denver, CO 80290 · 303-861-7000

TAX AND EMPLOYEE BENEFITS LAW

Michael J. Abramovitz · Abramovitz Merriam & Matthews · 1625 Broadway, Suite 770 · Denver, CO 80202 · 303-592-5404

Cynthia C. Benson · (Employee Benefits) · Sherman & Howard · 633 Seventeenth Street, Suite 3000 · Denver, CO 80202-3665 · 303-297-2900

James E. Bye · Holme Roberts & Owen · 1700 Broadway, Suite 1800 · Denver, CO 80290 · 303-861-7000

Stanley L. Drexler · Drexler & Wald · Western Federal Savings Building, Suite 700 · 210 University Boulevard · Denver, CO 80206 · 303-388-4611

Bruce L. Evans · (Employee Benefits) · Lentz, Evans and King · Lincoln Center Building, Suite 2900 · 1660 Lincoln Street · Denver, CO 80264 · 303-861-4154

Theodore Z. Gelt · Roath & Brega · 370 Seventeenth Street, Suite 900 · P.O. Box 5560 T.A. · Denver, CO 80217 · 303-893-5800

Peter C. Guthery · Wade, Ash, Woods, Hill & Guthery · 360 South Monroe Street, Suite 400 · Denver, CO 80209 · 303-322-8943

Samuel P. Guyton · Holland & Hart · 555 Seventeenth Street, Suite 2900 · P.O. Box 8749 · Denver, CO 80201 · 303-295-8000

Marcia Chadwick Holt · (Employee Benefits) · Davis, Graham & Stubbs · 370 Seventeenth Street, Suite 4700 · P.O. Box 185 · Denver, CO 80201-0185 · 303-892-9400

Francis P. King · Lentz, Evans and King · Lincoln Center Building, Suite 2900 · 1660 Lincoln Street · Denver, CO 80264 · 303-861-4154

Hover T. Lentz · Lentz, Evans and King · Lincoln Center Building, Suite 2900 · 1660 Lincoln Street · Denver, CO 80264 · 303-861-4154

Claude M. Maer, Jr. · Baker & Hostetler · 303 East 17th Avenue, Suite 1100 · Denver, CO 80203 · 303-861-0600

Bruce R. Muir · (Employee Benefits) · Lentz, Evans and King · Lincoln Center Building, Suite 2900 · 1660 Lincoln Street · Denver, CO 80264 · 303-861-4154

Donald J. O'Connor · Davis, Graham & Stubbs · 370 Seventeenth Street, Suite 4700 · P.O. Box 185 · Denver, CO 80201-0185 · 303-892-9400

Robert S. Rich · Davis, Graham & Stubbs · 370 Seventeenth Street, Suite 4700 · P.O. Box 185 · Denver, CO 80201-0185 · 303-892-9400

R. Michael Sanchez · (Employee Benefits) · Sherman & Howard · 633 Seventeenth Street, Suite 3000 · Denver, CO 80202-3665 · 303-297-2900

Joseph H. Thibodeau · Thibodeau and Moats · 155 South Madison Street, Suite 209 · Denver, CO 80209 · 303-320-1250

Robert J. Welter · Holme Roberts & Owen · 1700 Broadway, Suite 1800 · Denver, CO 80290 · 303-861-7000

TRUSTS AND ESTATES

Christopher Brauchli · Brauchli, Snyder, Jevons and Johnson · Continental Building, Suite 405 · 1401 Walnut Street · Boulder, CO 80302 · 303-443-1118

William K. Brown · Holland & Hart · Holly Sugar Building, Suite 1400 · Chase Stone Center · Colorado Springs, CO 80903 · 719-475-7730

Clifton B. Kruse, Jr. · Kruse & Lunch · 350 Holly Sugar Building · Chase Stone Center · Colorado Springs, CO 80903 · 719-473-9911

Walter B. Ash · Wade, Ash, Woods, Hill & Guthery · 360 South Monroe Street, Suite 400 · Denver, CO 80209 · 303-322-8943

Theodore B. Atlass · DeBruyn and Atlass · 2100 East 14th Avenue · Denver, CO 80206 · 303-377-0707

Donald M. Burkhardt · Grant, McHendrie, Haines & Crouse · One United Bank Center, Suite 3000 · 1700 Lincoln Street · Denver, CO 80203 · 303-832-7200

William P. Cantwell · Sherman & Howard · 633 Seventeenth Street, Suite 3000 Denver, CO 80202 · 303-297-2900

Kenneth G. Christianssen · Gorsuch, Kirgis, Campbell, Walker and Grover 1401 Seventeenth Street, Suite 1100 · P.O. Box 17180 · Denver, CO 80217 303-534-1200

Judson W. Detrick · Holme Roberts & Owen · 1700 Broadway, Suite 1800 Denver, CO 80290 · 303-861-7000

J. Michael Farley · Holland & Hart · 555 Seventeenth Street, Suite 2900 · P.O. Box 8749 · Denver, CO 80201 · 303-295-8000

Constance L. Hauver · Sherman & Howard · 633 Seventeenth Street, Suite 3000 Denver, CO 80202-3665 · 303-297-2900

Joseph G. Hodges, Jr. · The Dodge House · 1557 Ogden Street · Denver, CO 80218 · 303-830-8172

Marcia Chadwick Holt · Davis, Graham & Stubbs · 370 Seventeenth Street, Suite 4700 · P.O. Box 185 · Denver, CO 80201-0185 · 303-892-9400

William S. Huff · Holme Roberts & Owen · 1700 Broadway, Suite 1800 · Denver, CO 80290 · 303-861-7000

Hover T. Lentz · Lentz, Evans and King · Lincoln Center Building, Suite 2900 1660 Lincoln Street · Denver, CO 80264 · 303-861-4154

William C. McGehee · Gorsuch, Kirgis, Campbell, Walker and Grover · 1401 Seventeenth Street, Suite 1100 · P.O. Box 17180 · Denver, CO 80217 303-534-1200

Victor Quinn · Cockrell, Quinn & Creighton · Two United Bank Center, Suite 1516 · 1700 Broadway · Denver, CO 80290 · 303-860-7140

L. William Schmidt, Jr. · Moye, Giles, O'Keefe, Vermeire & Gorrell · 1225 Seventeenth Street, 29th Floor · Denver, CO 80202 · 303-292-2900

C. Jean Stewart · Holme Roberts & Owen · 1700 Broadway, Suite 1800 · Denver, CO 80290 · 303-861-7000

James R. Wade · Wade, Ash, Woods, Hill & Guthery · 360 South Monroe Street, Suite 400 · Denver, CO 80209 · 303-322-8943

Lucius E. Woods · Wade, Ash, Woods, Hill & Guthery · 360 South Monroe Street, Suite 400 · Denver, CO 80209 · 303-322-8943

CONNECTICUT

BANKRUPTCY LAW	116
BUSINESS LITIGATION	117
CORPORATE LAW	118
CRIMINAL DEFENSE	120
FAMILY LAW	121
LABOR AND EMPLOYMENT LAW	122
PERSONAL INJURY LITIGATION	124
REAL ESTATE LAW	126
TAX AND EMPLOYEE BENEFITS LAW	127
TRUSTS AND ESTATES	129

BANKRUPTCY LAW

Richard D. Zeisler · Zeisler & Zeisler · 480 Clinton Avenue · Bridgeport, CT 06605 · 203-368-4234

Richard F. Casher · Hebb & Gitlin · One State Street · Hartford, CT 06103 · 203-549-0333

Richard A. Gitlin · Hebb & Gitlin · One State Street · Hartford, CT 06103 · 203-549-0333

Martin W. Hoffman · 410 Asylum Street · Hartford, CT 06103 · 203-525-4287

Harold S. Horwich · Hebb & Gitlin · One State Street · Hartford, CT 06103 · 203-549-0333

Michael E. Riley · Hebb & Gitlin · One State Street · Hartford, CT 06103 · 203-549-0333

Donald Lee Rome · Robinson & Cole · One Commercial Plaza · Hartford, CT 06103-3597 · 203-549-6400

Robert U. Sattin · Reid and Riege · One State Street · Hartford, CT 06103 · 203-278-1150

Howard L. Siegel · Hoberman & Pollack · One State Street · Hartford, CT 06103 203-549-1000

Andrew M. DiPietro, Jr. · DiPietro, Kantrovitz & Brownstein · 64 Grove Street P.O. Drawer 1406 · New Haven, CT 06505 · 203-789-0070

John H. Krick · Greenfield, Krick, Jacobs & Cirillo · 205 Church Street · P.O. Box 1952 · New Haven, CT 06509 · 203-787-6711

BUSINESS LITIGATION

L. Douglas Shrader · Zeldes, Needle & Cooper · 333 State Street · P.O. Box 1740 Bridgeport, CT 06604 · 203-333-9441

Jacob D. Zeldes · Zeldes, Needle & Cooper · 333 State Street · P.O. Box 1740 Bridgeport, CT 06604 · 203-333-9441

Thomas J. Groark, Jr. · Day, Berry & Howard · CityPlace · Hartford, CT 06103-3499 · 203-275-0110

Edward F. Hennessey · Robinson & Cole · One Commercial Plaza · Hartford, CT 06103-3597 · 203-275-8200

Wesley W. Horton · (Appellate) · Moller, Horton & Fineberg · 90 Gillett Street Hartford, CT 06105 · 203-522-8338

Melvin S. Katz · Schatz & Schatz, Ribicoff & Kotkin · 90 State House Square Hartford, CT 06103 · 203-522-3234

James A. Wade · Robinson & Cole · One Commercial Plaza · Hartford, CT 06103-3597 · 203-275-8200

Albert Zakarian · Day, Berry & Howard · CityPlace · Hartford, CT 06103-3499 203-275-0110

J. Daniel Sagarin · Hurwitz & Sagarin · 147 North Broad Street · P.O. Box 112 Milford, CT 06460-0112 · 203-877-6071

William J. Doyle · Wiggin & Dana · 195 Church Street · P.O. Box 1832 · New Haven, CT 06508 · 203-789-1511

Ralph G. Elliot · Tyler, Cooper & Alcorn · 205 Church Street · P.O. Box 1936 New Haven, CT 06509 · 203-789-0700

William F. Gallagher · (Appellate) · Gallagher & Gallagher · 1377 Boulevard P.O. Box 1925 · New Haven, CT 06509 · 203-624-4165

Ira B. Grudberg · Jacobs, Grudberg, Belt & Dow · 350 Orange Street · P.O. Box 606 · New Haven, CT 06503 · 203-772-3100

William R. Murphy · Tyler, Cooper & Alcorn · 205 Church Street · P.O. Box 1936 New Haven, CT 06509 · 203-789-0700

Shaun S. Sullivan · Wiggin & Dana · 195 Church Street · P.O. Box 1832 · New Haven, CT 06508 · 203-789-1511

James R. Fogarty · Epstein & Fogarty · 733 Summer Street · Stamford, CT 06901 203-327-3400

Emanuel Margolis · Wofsey, Rosen, Kweskin & Kuriansky · 600 Summer Street Stamford, CT 06901 · 203-327-2300

John S. McGeeney · Cummings & Lockwood · 10 Stamford Forum · P.O. Box 120 · Stamford, CT 06904 · 203-327-1700

Francis J. McNamara, Jr. · Cummings & Lockwood · 10 Stamford Forum · P.O. Box 120 · Stamford, CT 06904 · 203-327-1700

Lawrence W. Kanaga III · Senie, Stock & LaChance · 125 Main Street · Westport, CT 06880 · 203-226-1223

CORPORATE LAW

David R. Chipman · Gager, Henry & Narkis · Danbury Executive Tower · 30 Main Street · Danbury, CT 06810 · 203-743-6363

Jennifer N. Boyd · Whitman & Ransom · 100 Field Point Road · Greenwich, CT 06830 · 203-869-3800

Morris W. Banks · Sorokin & Sorokin · One Corporate Center · Hartford, CT 06103 · 203-525-6645

William Barnett · Hoberman & Pollack · One State Street · Hartford, CT 06103
203-549-1000

C. Duane Blinn · Day, Berry & Howard · CityPlace · Hartford, CT 06103-3499
203-275-0110

William H. Cuddy · Day, Berry & Howard · CityPlace · Hartford, CT 06103-3499
203-275-0110

Walter M. Fiederowicz · Cummings & Lockwood · CityPlace · 185 Asylum Street
Hartford, CT 06103 · 203-275-6700

Stanford N. Goldman, Jr. · Schatz & Schatz, Ribicoff & Kotkin · One Financial
Plaza · Hartford, CT 06103 · 203-522-3234

F. Lee Griffith, III · Day, Berry & Howard · CityPlace · Hartford, CT 06103-3499
203-275-0110

Timothy L. Largay · Murtha, Cullina, Richter and Pinney · CityPlace · P.O. Box
3197 · Hartford, CT 06103 · 203-240-6000

James I. Lotstein · Cummings & Lockwood · CityPlace · 185 Asylum Street
Hartford, CT 06103 · 203-275-6700

John S. Murtha · Murtha, Cullina, Richter and Pinney · CityPlace · P.O. Box
3197 · Hartford, CT 06103 · 203-240-6000

Geoffrey W. Nelson · Murtha, Cullina, Richter and Pinney · CityPlace · P.O. Box
3197 · Hartford, CT 06103 · 203-240-6000

Willard F. Pinney, Jr. · Murtha, Cullina, Richter and Pinney · CityPlace · P.O.
Box 3197 · Hartford, CT 06103 · 203-240-6000

Sanford L. Rosenberg · Sorokin & Sorokin · One Corporate Center · Hartford,
CT 06103 · 203-525-6645

S. Michael Schatz · Schatz & Schatz, Ribicoff & Kotkin · One Financial Plaza
Hartford, CT 06103 · 203-522-3234

Michael Sudarsky · Murtha, Cullina, Richter and Pinney · CityPlace · P.O. Box
3197 · Hartford, CT 06103 · 203-240-6000

Thomas L. Smith · Robinson & Cole · One Commercial Plaza · Hartford, CT
06103-3597 · 203-275-8200

Alan R. Spier · Robinson & Cole · One Commercial Plaza · Hartford, CT 06103-3597 · 203-275-8200

Bruce G. Temkin · Schatz & Schatz, Ribicoff & Kotkin · One Financial Plaza Hartford, CT 06103 · 203-522-3234

Milton P. DeVane · Tyler, Cooper & Alcorn · 205 Church Street · P.O. Box 1936 New Haven, CT 06509 · 203-789-0700

Irving S. Schloss · Tyler, Cooper & Alcorn · 205 Church Street · P.O. Box 1936 New Haven, CT 06509 · 203-789-0700

Samuel S. Cross · Kelley, Drye & Warren · Six Stamford Forum · Stamford, CT 06901 · 203-324-1400

Harold E. Finn III · Finn Dixon & Herling · One Landmark Square, Suite 600 Stamford, CT 06901 · 203-964-8000

Richard McGrath · Cummings & Lockwood · 10 Stamford Forum · P.O. Box 120 Stamford, CT 06904 · 203-327-1700

Michael L. Widland · Schatz & Schatz, Ribicoff & Kotkin · One Landmark Square · Stamford, CT 06901 · 203-964-0027

David W. Collins · Carmody & Torrance · 50 Leavenworth Street · P.O. Box 1110 Waterbury, CT 06721 · 203-573-1200

Curtis V. Titus · Gager, Henry & Narkis · One Exchange Place · P.O. Box 2480 Waterbury, CT 06722 · 203-597-5100

David R. Levett · Levett, Rockwood & Sanders · 33 Riverside Avenue · Westport, CT 06880 · 203-222-0885

CRIMINAL DEFENSE

Theodore I. Koskoff · Koskoff, Koskoff & Bieder · 350 Fairfield Avenue · P.O. Box 1698 · Bridgeport, CT 06604 · 203-336-4421

Jacob D. Zeldes · Zeldes, Needle & Cooper · 333 State Street · P.O. Box 1740 Bridgeport, CT 06604 · 203-333-9441

F. Mac Buckley · Buckley & Santos · 51 Russ Street · Hartford, CT 06106 203-249-6548

Hubert J. Santos · Buckley & Santos · 51 Russ Street · Hartford, CT 06106 203-249-6548

James A. Wade · Robinson & Cole · One Commercial Plaza · Hartford, CT 06103-3597 · 203-275-8200

J. Daniel Sagarin · Hurwitz & Sagarin · 147 North Broad Street · P.O. Box 112 Milford, CT 06460-0112 · 203-877-6071

Ira B. Grudberg · Jacobs, Grudberg, Belt & Dow · 350 Orange Street · P.O. Box 606 · New Haven, CT 06503 · 203-772-3100

Howard A. Jacobs · Jacobs, Grudberg, Belt & Dow · 350 Orange Street · P.O. Box 606 · New Haven, CT 06503 · 203-772-3100

Hugh F. Keefe · Lynch, Traub, Keefe and Errante · 52 Trumbull Street · P.O. Box 1612 · New Haven, CT 06506 · 203-787-0275

David S. Golub · Silver, Golub & Sandak · 184 Atlantic Street · P.O. Box 389 Stamford, CT 06904 · 203-325-4491

FAMILY LAW

Alfred R. Belinkie · Belinkie & Blawie · 1087 Broad Street · Bridgeport, CT 06604 · 203-368-4201

Michael A. Meyers · Meyers, Breiner & Neufeld · 1087 Broad Street · Bridgeport, CT 06604 · 203-333-9410

Dianne M. Andersen · Andersen & Ferlazzo · 72 North Street · Danbury, CT 06810 · 203-744-2260

Lloyd Cutsumpas · Cutsumpas, Collins, Hannafin, Garamella, Jaber & Tuozzolo 148 Deer Hill Avenue · P.O. Box 440 · Danbury, CT 06813 · 203-744-2150

C. Ian McLachlan · Cummings & Lockwood · Two Greenwich Plaza · Greenwich, CT 06830 · 203-327-1700

Donald J. Cantor · Hyman, Cantor, Seichter & Klau · 60 Washington Street Hartford, CT 06106 · 203-549-6523

Bruce Louden · 99 Pratt Street · Hartford, CT 06103 · 203-246-7200

Gerald A. Roisman · Roisman & McClure · 31 Grand Street · Hartford, CT 06106 203-549-6700

Morton E. Marvin · Marvin, Kennedy, Reese & Hirsch · 258 Elm Street · P.O. Box 1147 · New Canaan, CT 06840 · 203-966-1618

Jeroll R. Silverberg · Silverberg, Marvin & Swaim · 140 Elm Street · New Canaan, CT 06840 · 203-966-9547

Gary I. Cohen · Cohen & Gordon · 59 Elm Street · P.O. Box 1800 · New Haven, CT 06507-1800 · 203-782-9440

James R. Greenfield · Greenfield, Krick, Jacobs & Cirillo · 205 Church Street P.O. Box 1952 · New Haven, CT 06509 · 203-787-6711

Thomas A. Bishop · Susman, Shapiro, Wool, Brennan & Gray · Mariner Square, Suite 240 · Eugene O'Neill Drive · P.O. Box 1591 · New London, CT 06320 203-442-4416

Francis J. Foley III · Brown, Jacobson, Jewett and Laudone · Uncas-Merchants National Bank Building · 22 Courthouse Square · Norwich, CT 06360 · 203-889-3321

Samuel V. Schoonmaker III · Cummings & Lockwood · 10 Stamford Forum P.O. Box 120 · Stamford, CT 06904 · 203-327-1700

Arthur E. Balbirer · Berkowitz & Balbirer · 253 Post Road West · P.O. Box 808 Westport, CT 06881 · 203-226-1001

Gaetano Ferro · Kanowitz and Ferro · 1465 Post Road East · Westport, CT 06880 203-254-3870

LABOR AND EMPLOYMENT LAW

E. Terry Durant · (Management) · Durant, Sabanosh, Nichols & Houston · 855 Main Street · Bridgeport, CT 06601 · 203-366-3438

George N. Nichols · (Management) · Durant, Sabanosh, Nichols & Houston · 855 Main Street · Bridgeport, CT 06601 · 203-366-3438

Brian Clemow · (Management) · Shipman & Goodwin · 799 Main Street · Hartford, CT 06103 · 203-549-4770

Thomas M. Cloherty · (Management) · Murtha, Cullina, Richter and Pinney · CityPlace · P.O. Box 3197 · Hartford, CT 06103 · 203-240-6000

William M. Cullina · (Management) · Murtha, Cullina, Richter and Pinney · CityPlace · P.O. Box 3197 · Hartford, CT 06103 · 203-240-6000

Burton Kainen · (Management) · Siegel, O'Connor, Schiff, Zangari & Kainen · 370 Asylum Street · Hartford, CT 06103 · 203-727-8900

James L. Kestell · (Labor; Individuals) · Kestell, Pogue & Gould · 606 Farmington Avenue · Hartford, CT 06105 · 203-233-9821

Richard D. O'Connor · (Management) · Siegel, O'Connor, Schiff, Zangari & Kainen · 370 Asylum Street · Hartford, CT 06103 · 203-727-8900

Paul W. Orth · (Individuals) · Shipman & Goodwin · 799 Main Street · Hartford, CT 06103 · 203-549-4770

Donald C. Pogue · (Labor) · Kestell, Pogue & Gould · 606 Farmington Avenue · Hartford, CT 06105 · 203-233-9821

Emanuel N. Psarakis · (Management) · Robinson & Cole · One Commercial Plaza · Hartford, CT 06103-3597 · 203-275-8200

Jay S. Siegel · (Management) · Siegel, O'Connor, Schiff, Zangari & Kainen · 370 Asylum Street · Hartford, CT 06103 · 203-727-8900

Felix J. Springer · (Management) · Day, Berry & Howard · CityPlace · Hartford, CT 06103-3499 · 203-275-0100

Albert Zakarian · (Management) · Day, Berry & Howard · CityPlace · Hartford, CT 06103-3499 · 203-275-0100

Joseph D. Garrison · (Individuals) · Garrison, Kahn, Silbert & Arterton · 405 Orange Street · New Haven, CT 06511 · 203-777-4425

David N. Rosen · (Labor; Individuals) · Rosen & Dolan · 400 Orange Street · New Haven, CT 06511 · 203-787-3513

David S. Golub · (Individuals) · Silver, Golub & Sandak · 184 Atlantic Street · P.O. Box 389 · Stamford, CT 06904 · 203-325-4491

William S. Zeman · (Labor) · Zeman & Ellis · 18 North Main Street · West Hartford, CT 06107 · 203-521-4430

Norman Zolot · (Labor) · 264 Amity Road · P.O. Box 3541 · Woodbridge, CT 06525 · 203-397-5346

PERSONAL INJURY LITIGATION

Robert B. Adelman · (Plaintiffs) · Cohen and Wolf · 1115 Broad Street · P.O. Box 1821 · Bridgeport, CT 06601 · 203-368-0211

Arnold Bai · (Defendants) · Bai, Pollock and Dunnigan · The Connecticut Bank & Trust Tower · Bridgeport, CT 06604 · 203-366-7991

Richard A. Bieder · (Plaintiffs) · Koskoff, Koskoff & Bieder · 350 Fairfield Avenue · Bridgeport, CT 06604 · 203-336-4421

Robert J. Cooney · (Defendants) · Williams, Cooney & Sheehy · One Lafayette Circle · Bridgeport, CT 06604 · 203-331-0888

Michael P. Koskoff · (Plaintiffs) · Koskoff, Koskoff & Bieder · 350 Fairfield Avenue · Bridgeport, CT 06604 · 203-336-4421

Theodore I. Koskoff · (Plaintiffs) · Koskoff, Koskoff & Bieder · 350 Fairfield Avenue · Bridgeport, CT 06604 · 203-336-4421

T. Paul Tremont · (Plaintiffs) · Tremont & Sheldon · 64 Lyon Terrace · Bridgeport, CT 06604 · 203-335-5145

Ronald D. Williams · (Defendants) · Williams, Cooney & Sheehy · One Lafayette Circle · Bridgeport, CT 06604 · 203-331-0888

James D. Bartolini · (Plaintiffs) · RisCassi and Davis · 131 Oak Street · P.O. Box 6550 · Hartford, CT 06106 · 203-522-1196

William R. Davis · (Plaintiffs) · RisCassi and Davis · 131 Oak Street · P.O. Box 6550 · Hartford, CT 06106 · 203-522-1196

John R. FitzGerald · (Defendants) · Howard, Kohn, Sprague & FitzGerald · 237 Buckingham Street · P.O. Box 6896, Station A · Hartford, CT 06106 · 203-525-3101

Edward F. Hennessey · Robinson & Cole · One Commercial Plaza · Hartford, CT 06103-3597 · 203-275-8200

Joseph G. Lynch · (Defendants) · Halloran, Sage, Phelon & Hagarty · One Financial Plaza · Hartford, CT 06103 · 203-522-6103

F. Timothy McNamara · 102 Oak Street · Hartford, CT 06106 · 203-249-8458

Hubert J. Santos · (Plaintiffs) · Buckley & Santos · 51 Russ Street · Hartford, CT 06106 · 203-249-6548

John F. Scully · (Defendants) · Cooney, Scully and Dowling · 266 Pearl Street Hartford, CT 06103 · 203-527-1141

Joseph F. Skelley, Jr. · (Defendants) · Skelley, Vinkels, Williams & Rottner · 12 Charter Oak Place · P.O. Box 14890 · Hartford, CT 06114-0890 · 203-246-6891

William J. Doyle · (Defendants) · Wiggin & Dana · 195 Church Street · P.O. Box 1832 · New Haven, CT 06508 · 203-789-1511

Anthony M. Fitzgerald · Carmody & Torrance · 59 Elm Street · P.O. Box 1990 New Haven, CT 06509 · 203-777-5501

Ira B. Grudberg · (Plaintiffs) · Jacobs, Grudberg, Belt & Dow · 350 Orange Street P.O. Box 606 · New Haven, CT 06503 · 203-772-3100

Howard A. Jacobs · (Plaintiffs) · Jacobs, Grudberg, Belt & Dow · 350 Orange Street · P.O. Box 606 · New Haven, CT 06503 · 203-772-3100

Stanley A. Jacobs · (Plaintiffs) · Jacobs & Jacobs · 555 Long Wharf Drive, Suite 13A · New Haven, CT 06511 · 203-777-2300

David W. Skolnick · (Plaintiffs) · Winnick, Skolnick, Rubin & Block · 110 Whitney Avenue · P.O. Box 1755 · New Haven, CT 06510 · 203-772-4400

Shaun S. Sullivan · (Defendants) · Wiggin & Dana · 195 Church Street · P.O. Box 1832 · New Haven, CT 06508 · 203-789-1511

Stephen I. Traub · (Plaintiffs) · Lynch, Traub, Keefe and Errante · 52 Trumbull Street · P.O. Box 1612 · New Haven, CT 06506 · 203-787-0275

Dale Patrick Faulkner · Faulkner & Boyce · 216 Broad Street · P.O. Box 66 New London, CT 06320 · 203-442-9900

Jeffrey B. Sienkiewicz · (Defendants) · Sienkiewicz & Sienkiewicz · Nine South Main Street · P.O. Box 67 · New Milford, CT 06776 · 203-354-1583

Allyn L. Brown, Jr. · (Defendants) · Brown, Jacobson, Jewett and Laudone · Uncas-Merchants National Bank Building · 22 Courthouse Square · Norwich, CT 06360 · 203-889-3321

Wayne G. Tillinghast · (Defendants) · Brown, Jacobson, Jewett and Laudone · Uncas-Merchants National Bank Building · 22 Courthouse Square · Norwich, CT 06360 · 203-889-3321

Richard A. Silver · (Plaintiffs) · Silver, Golub & Sandak · 184 Atlantic Street · P.O. Box 389 · Stamford, CT 06904 · 203-325-4491

REAL ESTATE LAW

Austin K. Wolf · Cohen and Wolf · 1115 Broad Street · P.O. Box 1821 · Bridgeport, CT 06601 · 203-368-0211

Robert J. Birnbaum · Cohn and Birnbaum · One Union Place, Third Floor · Hartford, CT 06103-1409 · 203-549-7230

Gurdon H. Buck · Robinson & Cole · One Commercial Plaza · Hartford, CT 06103-3597 · 203-275-8200

John C. Glezen · Day, Berry & Howard · CityPlace · Hartford, CT 06103-3499 · 203-275-0110

J. Roger Hanlon · Day, Berry & Howard · CityPlace · Hartford, CT 06103-3499 · 203-275-0110

Harold F. Keith · Keith & Aparo · 100 Constitution Plaza · Hartford, CT 06103 · 203-728-0646

H. David Leventhal · Leventhal, Krasow & Roos · One Financial Plaza · Hartford, CT 06103 · 203-549-4100

Michael R. Levin · Levin & D'Agostino · One State Street · Hartford, CT 06103 · 203-527-0400

Mark Oland · Schatz & Schatz, Ribicoff & Kotkin · 90 State House Square · Hartford, CT 06103 · 203-522-3234

I. Milton Widem · Schatz & Schatz, Ribicoff & Kotkin · 90 State House Square · Hartford, CT 06103 · 203-522-3234

Michael Susman · Susman, Duffy & Segaloff · 234 Church Street · P.O. Box 1684 New Haven, CT 06507 · 203-624-9830

David O. Jackson · Pullman, Comley, Bradley & Reeves · 200 Pequot Avenue P.O. Box 510 · Southport, CT 06490 · 203-255-7766

Ronald King · 550 Summer Street · Stamford, CT 06901 · 203-327-1345

Thomas P. Skidd, Jr. · Cummings & Lockwood · 10 Stamford Forum · P.O. Box 120 · Stamford, CT 06904 · 203-327-1700

TAX AND EMPLOYEE BENEFITS LAW

Herbert H. Moorin · (Employee Benefits) · Pullman, Comley, Bradley & Reeves 855 Main Street · Bridgeport, CT 06601 · 203-334-0112

W. Parker Seeley, Jr. · Pullman, Comley, Bradley & Reeves · 855 Main Street Bridgeport, CT 06604 · 203-334-0112

J. Danford Anthony, Jr. · Day, Berry & Howard · CityPlace · Hartford, CT 06103-3499 · 203-275-0100

Frank S. Berall · Copp, Berall & Hempstead · 60 Washington Street · Hartford, CT 06106 · 203-522-2500

Michael L. Coyle · Reid and Riege · One State Street · Hartford, CT 06103 203-278-1150

John T. Del Negro · Murtha, Cullina, Richter and Pinney · CityPlace · P.O. Box 3197 · Hartford, CT 06103 · 203-240-6000

Ira H. Goldman · (Employee Benefits) · Shipman & Goodwin · 799 Main Street Hartford, CT 06103 · 203-549-4770

John J. Jacobson · (Employee Benefits) · Reid and Riege · One State Street Hartford, CT 06103 · 203-278-1150

William R. Judy · (also Employee Benefits) · Reid and Riege · One State Street Hartford, CT 06103 · 203-278-1150

Alex Lloyd · Shipman & Goodwin · 799 Main Street · Hartford, CT 06103 203-549-4770

James B. Lyon · Murtha, Cullina, Richter and Pinney · CityPlace · P.O. Box 3197 Hartford, CT 06103 · 203-240-6000

Charles B. Milliken · (also Employee Benefits) · Shipman & Goodwin · 799 Main Street · Hartford, CT 06103 · 203-549-4770

Raymond J. Payne · (Employee Benefits) · Reid and Riege · One State Street Hartford, CT 06103 · 203-278-1150

Thomas Z. Reicher · (Employee Benefits) · Day, Berry & Howard · CityPlace Hartford, CT 06103-3499 · 203-275-0100

Donald P. Richter · Murtha, Cullina, Richter and Pinney · CityPlace · P.O. Box 3197 · Hartford, CT 06103 · 203-240-6000

John O. Tannenbaum · Robinson & Cole · One Commercial Plaza · Hartford, CT 06103-3597 · 203-275-8200

Richard W. Tomeo · Robinson & Cole · One Commercial Plaza · Hartford, CT 06103-3597 · 203-275-8200

Paul L. Behling · (also Employee Benefits) · Wiggin & Dana · 195 Church Street P.O. Box 1832 · New Haven, CT 06901 · 203-789-1511

Stanley N. Bergman · Bergman, Horowitz & Reynolds · 900 Chapel Street · P.O. Box 426 · New Haven, CT 06502 · 203-789-1320

Newton D. Brenner · Brenner, Saltzman, Wallman & Goldman · 271 Whitney Avenue · P.O. Box 1746 · New Haven, CT 06507 · 203-772-2600

David L. Reynolds · (Employee Benefits) · Bergman, Horowitz, Reynolds & DeSarbo · 900 Chapel Street · P.O. Box 426 · New Haven, CT 06502 203-789-1320

Alan L. Schiff · Siegel, O'Connor, Schiff, Zangari & Kainen · 171 Orange Street P.O. Box 906 · New Haven, CT 06504 · 203-789-0001

Nathan M. Silverstein · Silverstein & Osach · 234 Church Street, Suite 903 · P.O. Box 1727 · New Haven, CT 06507 · 203-865-0121

John F. Strother · (Employee Benefits) · Cummings & Lockwood · 10 Stamford Forum · P.O. Box 120 · Stamford, CT 06904 · 203-327-1700

George G. Vest · Cummings & Lockwood · 10 Stamford Forum · P.O. Box 120 Stamford, CT 06904 · 203-327-1700

Richard A. Hoppe · (also Employee Benefits) · Gager, Henry & Narkis · One Exchange Place · P.O. Box 2480 · Waterbury, CT 06722 · 203-597-5100

TRUSTS AND ESTATES

John S. Mason, Jr. · Mason & Drew · 47 West Main Street · P.O. Box 1180 · Avon, CT 06001 · 203-677-1974

Peter Wilkinson · Marsh, Day & Calhoun · 955 Main Street · Bridgeport, CT 06604 · 203-368-4221

Robert T. Gilhuly · Cummings & Lockwood · Two Greenwich Plaza · Greenwich, CT 06830 · 203-327-1700

R. Regner Arvidson · Robinson & Cole · One Commercial Plaza · Hartford, CT 06103-3597 · 203-275-8200

Frank S. Berall · Copp, Berall & Hempstead · 60 Washington Street · Hartford, CT 06106 · 203-522-2500

James T. Betts · Shipman & Goodwin · 799 Main Street · Hartford, CT 06103 · 203-549-4770

Clifford S. Burdge, Jr. · Reid and Riege · One State Street · Hartford, CT 06103 · 203-278-1150

John M. Donahue · Robinson & Cole · One Commercial Plaza · Hartford, CT 06103-3597 · 203-275-8200

John W. Hincks · Robinson & Cole · One Commercial Plaza · Hartford, CT 06103-3597 · 203-275-8200

Arthur B. Locke · Murtha, Cullina, Richter and Pinney · CityPlace · P.O. Box 3197 · Hartford, CT 06103 · 203-240-6000

Martin Wolman · Day, Berry & Howard · CityPlace · Hartford, CT 06103-3499 · 203-275-0100

Stuyvesant K. Bearns · Shipman & Goodwin · Porter Street · Lakeville, CT 06039 · 203-435-2539

Jeffrey L. Crown · 99 West Main Street · New Britain, CT 06051 · 203-229-6600

Charles C. Kingsley · Wiggin & Dana · 195 Church Street · P.O. Box 1832 · New Haven, CT 06508 · 203-789-1511

James W. Venman · Pullman, Comley, Bradley & Reeves · 200 Pequot Avenue Southport, CT 06490 · 203-255-7766

Ronald O. Dederick · Day, Berry & Howard · One Canterbury Green · Stamford, CT 06901 · 203-977-7300

Gayle Brian Wilhelm · Cummings & Lockwood · 10 Stamford Forum · P.O. Box 120 · Stamford, CT 06904 · 203-327-1700

Warren S. Randall · Halloran, Sage, Phelon & Hagarty · 65 LaSalle Road, Suite 304 · West Hartford, CT 06107 · 203-236-3277

DELAWARE

BANKRUPTCY LAW	131
BUSINESS LITIGATION	132
CORPORATE LAW	133
CRIMINAL DEFENSE	133
FAMILY LAW	134
LABOR AND EMPLOYMENT LAW	134
NATURAL RESOURCES AND ENVIRONMENTAL LAW	134
PERSONAL INJURY LITIGATION	135
REAL ESTATE LAW	135
TAX AND EMPLOYEE BENEFITS LAW	136
TRUSTS AND ESTATES	136

BANKRUPTCY LAW

Patrick Scanlon · Barros, McNamara & Scanlon · State & Loockerman Streets · P.O. Box 1298 · Dover, DE 19903-1298 · 302-734-8400

William L. Witham, Jr. · Prickett, Jones, Elliott, Kristol & Schnee · 26 The Green · Dover, DE 19901 · 302-674-3841

Eric M. Doroshow · Doroshow, Pasquale & Linarducci · 1202 Kirkwood Highway · Wilmington, DE 19805 · 302-998-0100

Richard G. Elliott, Jr. · Richards, Layton & Finger · One Rodney Square · P.O. Box 551 · Wilmington, DE 19899 · 302-658-6541

Eduard F. von Wettberg III · Morris, James, Hitchens & Williams · 1105 North Market Street, 14th Floor · P.O. Box 2306 · Wilmington, DE 19899-2306 · 302-571-6700

Peter J. Walsh · Bayard, Handelman & Murdoch · 1300 Delaware Trust Building
P.O. Box 15130 · Wilmington, DE 19899 · 302-655-5000

BUSINESS LITIGATION

R. Franklin Balotti · Richards, Layton & Finger · One Rodney Square · P.O. Box 551 · Wilmington, DE 19899 · 302-658-6541

Victor F. Battaglia · Biggs and Battaglia · 1206 Mellon Bank Center · 10th and Market Streets · P.O. Box 1489 · Wilmington, DE 19899-1489 · 302-655-9677

Edmund N. Carpenter II · Richards, Layton & Finger · One Rodney Square P.O. Box 551 · Wilmington, DE 19899 · 302-658-6541

Arthur G. Connolly, Jr. · Connolly, Bove, Lodge & Hutz · 1220 Market Street P.O. Box 2207 · Wilmington, DE 19899-2207 · 302-658-9141

Charles S. Crompton, Jr. · Potter Anderson & Corroon · 350 Delaware Trust Building · 902 Market Street · P.O. Box 951 · Wilmington, DE 19899-0951 302-658-6771

Andrew B. Kirkpatrick, Jr. · Morris, Nichols, Arsht & Tunnell · 12th and Market Streets · P.O. Box 1347 · Wilmington, DE 19899-1347 · 302-658-9200

Irving Morris · Morris and Rosenthal · First Federal Plaza, Suite 214 · P.O. Box 1070 · Wilmington, DE 19899-1070 · 302-656-4433

Robert K. Payson · Potter Anderson & Corroon · 350 Delaware Trust Building 902 Market Street · P.O. Box 951 · Wilmington, DE 19899-0951 · 302-658-6771

Charles F. Richards, Jr. · Richards, Layton & Finger · One Rodney Square P.O. Box 551 · Wilmington, DE 19899 · 302-658-6541

A. Gilchrist Sparks III · Morris, Nichols, Arsht & Tunnell · 12th and Market Streets · P.O. Box 1347 · Wilmington, DE 19899-1347 · 302-658-9200

Bruce M. Stargatt · Young, Conaway, Stargatt & Taylor · Rodney Square North, 11th Floor · P.O. Box 391 · Wilmington, DE 19899-0391 · 302-571-6600

E. Norman Veasey · Richards, Layton & Finger · One Rodney Square · P.O. Box 551 · Wilmington, DE 19899 · 302-658-6541

Rodman Ward, Jr. · Skadden, Arps, Slate, Meagher & Flom · One Rodney Square · P.O. Box 636 · Wilmington, DE 19899 · 302-429-9200

CORPORATE LAW

R. Franklin Balotti · Richards, Layton & Finger · One Rodney Square · P.O. Box 551 · Wilmington, DE 19899 · 302-658-6541

Lewis S. Black, Jr. · Morris, Nichols, Arsht & Tunnell · 12th & Market Streets P.O. Box 1347 · Wilmington, DE 19899-1347 · 302-658-9200

Charles S. Crompton, Jr. · Potter Anderson & Corroon · 350 Delaware Trust Building · 902 Market Street · P.O. Box 951 · Wilmington, DE 19899-0951 302-658-6771

Robert K. Payson · Potter Anderson & Corroon · 350 Delaware Trust Building 902 Market Street · P.O. Box 951 · Wilmington, DE 19899-0951 · 302-658-6771

Charles F. Richards, Jr. · Richards, Layton & Finger · One Rodney Square P.O. Box 551 · Wilmington, DE 19899 · 302-658-6541

A. Gilchrist Sparks III · Morris, Nichols, Arsht & Tunnell · 12th & Market Streets · P.O. Box 1347 · Wilmington, DE 19899-1347 · 302-658-9200

Bruce M. Stargatt · Young, Conaway, Stargatt & Taylor · Rodney Square North, 11th Floor · P.O. Box 391 · Wilmington, DE 19899-0391 · 302-571-6600

E. Norman Veasey · Richards, Layton & Finger · One Rodney Square · P.O. Box 551 · Wilmington, DE 19899 · 302-658-6541

CRIMINAL DEFENSE

Sidney Balick · 604 Mellon Bank Center · 10th and Market Streets · Wilmington, DE 19801 · 302-658-4265

Victor F. Battaglia · Biggs and Battaglia · 1206 Mellon Bank Center · 10th and Market Streets · P.O. Box 1489 · Wilmington, DE 19899-1489 · 302-655-9677

Joseph A. Hurley · 1215 King Street · Wilmington, DE 19801 · 302-658-8980

Carl Schnee · Prickett, Jones, Elliott, Kristol & Schnee · 1310 King Street · P.O. Box 1328 · Wilmington, DE 19899-1328 · 302-658-5102

FAMILY LAW

Gerald Z. Berkowitz · Berkowitz, Greenstein, Schagrin & Coonin · 1218 Market Street · Wilmington, DE 19801 · 302-652-3155

Bertram S. Halberstadt · Lindh & Halberstadt · First Federal Plaza, Suite 570 · Wilmington, DE 19801-3564 · 302-652-1196

Michael K. Newell · Bayard, Handelman & Murdoch · 1300 Delaware Trust Building · P.O. Box 15130 · Wilmington, DE 19899 · 302-655-5000

H. Alfred Tarrant, Jr. · Cooch and Taylor · 824 Market Street Mall · P.O. Box 1680 · Wilmington, DE 19899 · 302-652-3641

LABOR AND EMPLOYMENT LAW

Sheldon N. Sandler · (Management) · Young, Conaway, Stargatt & Taylor · Rodney Square North, 11th Floor · P.O. Box 391 · Wilmington, DE 19899-0391 · 302-571-6600

Robert F. Stewart, Jr. · (Management) · Duane, Morris & Heckscher · 1220 Market Building, Suite 7000 · P.O. Box 195 · Wilmington, DE 19899· 302-571-5550

NATURAL RESOURCES AND ENVIRONMENTAL LAW

F. Michael Parkowski · Parkowski, Noble & Guerke · 116 West Water Street · P.O. Box 308 · Dover, DE 19903 · 302-678-3262

Thomas D. Whittington, Jr. · Whittington & Aulgur · Coffee Run Professional Centre · Lancaster Pike & Loveville Road · Hockessin, DE 19707 · 302-239-6100

Henry N. Herndon, Jr. · Morris, James, Hitchens & Williams · 1105 North Market Street, 14th Floor · P.O. Box 2306 · Wilmington, DE 19899-2306 · 302-571-6700

Stephen E. Herrmann · Richards, Layton & Finger · One Rodney Square · P.O. Box 551 · Wilmington, DE 19899 · 302-658-6541

PERSONAL INJURY LITIGATION

Harold Schmittinger · (Plaintiffs) · Schmittinger & Rodriguez · 414 South State Street · Dover, DE 19901 · 302-674-0140

Sidney Balick · (Plaintiffs) · Sidney Balick & Associates · 604 Mellon Bank Center 919 Market Street · Wilmington, DE 19801 · 302-658-4265

Victor F. Battaglia · (Defendants) · Biggs and Battaglia · 1206 Mellon Bank Center · 10th and Market Streets · P.O. Box 1489 · Wilmington, DE 19899-1489 302-655-9677

Ben T. Castle · (Plaintiffs) · Young, Conaway, Stargatt & Taylor · Rodney Square North, 11th Floor · P.O. Box 391 · Wilmington, DE 19899-0391 · 302-571-6600

Mason E. Turner, Jr. · (Defendants) · Prickett, Jones, Elliott, Kristol & Schnee 1310 King Street · P.O. Box 1328 · Wilmington, DE 19899-1328 · 302-658-5102

F. Alton Tybout · Tybout, Redfearn, Casarino & Pell · Bank of Delaware Building, Suite 1110 · 300 Delaware Avenue · P.O. Box 2092 · Wilmington, DE 19801 302-658-6901

Bernard A. van Ogtrop · (Plaintiffs) · Cooch and Taylor · Marine Midland Plaza, Suite 1000 · 824 Market Street Mall · P.O. Box 1680 · Wilmington, DE 19899-1680 · 302-652-3641

REAL ESTATE LAW

Richard P. Beck · Morris, James, Hitchens & Williams · 12th and Market Streets P.O. Box 2306 · Wilmington, DE 19899-2306 · 302-571-6700

Daniel L. Klein · Richards, Layton & Finger · One Rodney Square · P.O. Box 551 Wilmington, DE 19899 · 302-658-6541

Daniel M. Kristol · Prickett, Jones, Elliott, Kristol & Schnee · 1310 King Street P.O. Box 1328 · Wilmington, DE 19899-1328 · 302-658-5102

Richard H. May · Young, Conaway, Stargatt & Taylor · Rodney Square North, 11th Floor · P.O. Box 391 · Wilmington, DE 19899-0391 · 302-571-6600

Donald C. Taylor · Cooch and Taylor · 824 Market Street Mall · P.O. Box 1680 Wilmington, DE 19899 · 302-652-3641

TAX AND EMPLOYEE BENEFITS LAW

Paul H. Boswell, Jr. · Schmittinger & Rodriguez · 414 South State Street · Dover, DE 19901 · 302-674-0140

David J. Garrett · Potter Anderson & Corroon · 350 Delaware Trust Building 902 Market Street · P.O. Box 951 · Wilmington, DE 19899-0951 · 302-658-6771

Johannes R. Krahmer · Morris, Nichols, Arsht & Tunnell · 12th & Market Streets · P.O. Box 1347 · Wilmington, DE 19899-1347 · 302-658-9200

Robert Meyer · Bayard, Handelman & Murdoch · 1300 Delaware Trust Building P.O. Box 15130 · Wilmington, DE 19899 · 302-655-5000

Thomas P. Sweeney · Richards, Layton & Finger · One Rodney Square · P.O. Box 551 · Wilmington, DE 19899 · 302-658-6541

Leonard S. Togman · Potter Anderson & Corroon · 350 Delaware Trust Building 902 Market Street · P.O. Box 951 · Wilmington, DE 19899-0951 · 302-658-6771

Norris P. Wright · Morris, James, Hitchens & Williams · 12th & Market Streets P.O. Box 2306 · Wilmington, DE 19899-2306 · 302-571-6700

TRUSTS AND ESTATES

Paul H. Boswell, Jr. · Schmittinger & Rodriguez · 414 South State Street · Dover, DE 19901 · 302-674-0140

Richard G. Bacon · Richards, Layton & Finger · One Rodney Square · P.O. Box 551 · Wilmington, DE 19899 · 302-658-6541

Robert W. Crowe · Cooch and Taylor · 824 Market Street Mall · P.O. Box 1680 Wilmington, DE 19899 · 302-652-3641

David J. Garrett · Potter Anderson & Corroon · 350 Delaware Trust Building 902 Market Street · P.O. Box 951 · Wilmington, DE 19899-0951 · 302-658-6771

Joseph H. Geoghegan · Potter Anderson & Corroon · 350 Delaware Trust Building · 902 Market Street · P.O. Box 951 · Wilmington, DE 19899-0951 · 302-658-6771

Peter S. Gordon · Williams, Gordon & Martin · One Commerce Center, Suite 600 · 12th & Orange Streets · Wilmington, DE 19899-0511 · 302-575-0873

Henry N. Herndon, Jr. · Morris, James, Hitchens & Williams · 12th and Market Streets · P.O. Box 2306 · Wilmington, DE 19899-2306 · 302-571-6700

F. Edmund Lynch · Bayard, Handelman & Murdoch · 1300 Delaware Trust Building · P.O. Box 15130 · Wilmington, DE 19899 · 302-655-5000

Joanna Reiver · Schlusser, Reiver, Hughes & Sisk · 1700 West 14th Street Wilmington, DE 19806 · 302-655-8181

Thomas P. Sweeney · Richards, Layton & Finger · One Rodney Square · P.O. Box 551 · Wilmington, DE 19899 · 302-658-6541

Norris P. Wright · Morris, James, Hitchens & Williams · 12th and Market Streets P.O. Box 2306 · Wilmington, DE 19899-2306 · 302-571-6700

DISTRICT OF COLUMBIA

BANKRUPTCY LAW	138
BUSINESS LITIGATION	139
CORPORATE LAW	146
CRIMINAL DEFENSE	152
FAMILY LAW	155
LABOR AND EMPLOYMENT LAW	156
NATURAL RESOURCES AND ENVIRONMENTAL LAW	159
PERSONAL INJURY LITIGATION	161
REAL ESTATE LAW	161
TAX AND EMPLOYEE BENEFITS LAW	163
TRUSTS AND ESTATES	166

BANKRUPTCY LAW

Nelson Deckelbaum · Deckelbaum & Ogens · 1140 Connecticut Avenue, NW Washington, DC 20036 · 202-223-1474

Francis P. Dicello · Hazel, Thomas, Beckhorn and Hanes · 1575 I Street, NW, Suite 600 · Washington, DC 20005 · 202-898-0010

Charles A. Docter · Docter & Docter · 1325 G Street, NW, Suite 700 · Washington, DC 20005 · 202-628-6800

Murray Drabkin · Cadwalader, Wickersham & Taft · 1333 New Hampshire Avenue, NW, Suite 700 · Washington, DC 20036 · 202-862-2200

Roger Frankel · Lerch, Early, Roseman & Frankel · 923 Fifteenth Street, NW Washington, DC 20005 · 202-293-5494

Richard H. Gins · Gins & Seeber · 2021 L Street, NW, Suite 200 · Washington, DC 20036 · 202-785-9123

Bruce Goldstein · Zuckerman, Spaeder, Goldstein, Taylor & Kolker · 1201 Connecticut Avenue, NW, Suite 1200 · Washington, DC 20036 · 202-778-1800

William J. Perlstein · Wilmer, Cutler & Pickering · 2445 M Street, NW · Washington, DC 20037-1420 · 202-663-6000

Roger M. Whelan · Verner, Liipfert, Bernhard, McPherson and Hand · 901 Fifteenth Street, NW, Suite 700 · Washington, DC 20005 · 202-371-6000

BUSINESS LITIGATION

Howard Adler, Jr. · (Antitrust) · Davis, Graham & Stubbs · 1200 Nineteenth Street, NW, Suite 500 · Washington, DC 20036 · 202-822-8660

Kenneth C. Anderson · (Antitrust) · Squire, Sanders & Dempsey · 1201 Pennsylvania Avenue, NW · P.O. Box 407 · Washington, DC 20044 · 202-626-6600

Harvey M. Applebaum · (Antitrust; International Trade) · Covington & Burling 1201 Pennsylvania Avenue, NW · P.O. Box 7566 · Washington, DC 20044 202-662-6000

John W. Barnum · (Antitrust; Securities; Transportation) · White & Case · 1747 Pennsylvania Avenue, NW · Washington, DC 20006 · 202-872-0013

Robert T. Basseches · (Transportation) · Shea & Gardner · 1800 Massachusetts Avenue, NW, Suite 800 · Washington, DC 20036 · 202-828-2000

David Booth Beers · Shea & Gardner · 1800 Massachusetts Avenue, NW, Suite 800 · Washington, DC 20036 · 202-828-2000

Richard W. Beckler · (Complex Fraud; Securities) · Fulbright & Jaworski · 1150 Connecticut Avenue, NW · Washington, DC 20036 · 202-452-6800

Alexander E. Bennett · (Government Contract) · Arnold & Porter · Thurman Arnold Building · 1200 New Hampshire Avenue, NW · Washington, DC 20036 202-872-6700

Robert S. Bennett · Dunnells, Duvall, Bennett & Porter · 2100 Pennsylvania Avenue, Fourth Floor · Washington, DC 20037 · 202-861-1400

Judah Best · (Appellate; Securities) · Debevoise & Plimpton · 555 Thirteenth Street, NW, Suite 1100 East · Washington, DC 20004 · 202-383-8000

Peter K. Bleakley · Arnold & Porter · Thurman Arnold Building · 1200 New Hampshire Avenue, NW · Washington, DC 20036 · 202-872-6700

Timothy J. Bloomfield · (Antitrust) · Dunnells, Duvall, Bennett & Porter · 2100 Pennsylvania Avenue, Fourth Floor · Washington, DC 20037 · 202-861-1400

John Bodner, Jr. · (Antitrust) · Howrey & Simon · 1730 Pennsylvania Avenue, NW, Suite 900 · Washington, DC 20006-4793 · 202-783-0800

Charles N. Brower · (International) · White & Case · 1747 Pennsylvania Avenue, NW, Suite 500 · Washington, DC 20006 · 202-872-0013

Thomas W. Brunner · (Antitrust; Environmental; Insurance) · Wiley, Rein & Fielding · 1776 K Street, NW · Washington, DC 20006-2359 · 202-429-7000

Donald T. Bucklin · Squire, Sanders & Dempsey · 1201 Pennsylvania Avenue, NW · P.O. Box 407 · Washington, DC 20044 · 202-626-6600

Plato Cacheris · (RICO) · Dunnells, Duvall, Bennett & Porter · 2100 Pennsylvania Avenue, Fourth Floor · Washington, DC 20037 · 202-861-1400

Vincent H. Cohen · Hogan & Hartson · Columbia Square · 555 Thirteenth Street, NW · Washington, DC 20004-1109 · 202-637-5600

Richard T. Colman · Howrey & Simon · 1730 Pennsylvania Avenue, NW, Suite 900 · Washington, DC 20006-4793 · 202-783-0800

Aubrey M. Daniel III · (Antitrust; Products Liability) · Williams & Connolly · Hill Building · 839 Seventeenth Street, NW · Washington, DC 20006 · 202-331-5000

Sidney Dickstein · Dickstein, Shapiro & Morin · 2101 L Street, NW, Suite 900 Washington, DC 20037 · 202-785-9700

Richard O. Duvall · Dunnells, Duvall, Bennett & Porter · 2100 Pennsylvania Avenue, Fourth Floor · Washington, DC 20037 · 202-861-1400

Timothy B. Dyk · (FCC; First Amendment) · Wilmer, Cutler & Pickering · 2445 M Street, NW · Washington, DC 20037 · 202-663-6000

Milton Eisenberg · (Government Contract) · Fried, Frank, Harris, Shriver & Jacobson · 1001 Pennsylvania Avenue, NW, Suite 800 · Washington, DC 20004-3505 · 202-639-7000

Richard J. Favretto · (Antitrust; RICO; Securities) · Mayer, Brown & Platt · 2000 Pennsylvania Avenue, NW, Suite 6500 · Washington, DC 20006 · 202-463-2000

Donald L. Flexner · Crowell & Moring · 1001 Pennsylvania Avenue, NW Washington, DC 20004-2505 · 202-624-2500

Richard J. Flynn · (Antitrust; Regulated Industries) · Sidley & Austin · 1722 I Street, NW · Washington, DC 20006 · 202-429-4000

Paul L. Friedman · White & Case · 1747 Pennsylvania Avenue, NW · Washington, DC 20006 · 202-872-0013

Vincent J. Fuller · Williams & Connolly · Hill Building · 839 Seventeenth Street, NW · Washington, DC 20006 · 202-331-5000

William L. Gardner · Morgan, Lewis & Bockius · 1800 M Street, NW, Suite 800N · Washington, DC 20036 · 202-467-7000

Robert J. Geniesse · (Administrative) · Debevoise & Plimpton · 555 Thirteenth Street, NW, Suite 1100 East · Washington, DC 20004 · 202-383-8000

Jamie S. Gorelick · (Financial Institutions; Procurement Fraud; Securities; White Collar Criminal) · Miller, Cassidy, Larroca & Lewin · 2555 M Street, NW, Suite 500 · Washington, DC 20037 · 202-293-6400

Joseph M. Hassett · Hogan & Hartson · Columbia Square · 555 Thirteenth Street, NW · Washington, DC 20004-1109 · 202-637-5600

John D. Hawke, Jr. · (Banking) · Arnold & Porter · Thurman Arnold Building 1200 New Hampshire Avenue, NW · Washington, DC 20036 · 202-872-6700

Michael J. Henke · (Administrative; Antitrust) · Vinson & Elkins · 1455 Pennsylvania Avenue, NW, Suite 700 · Washington, DC 20004 · 202-639-6500

Richard A. Hibey · Anderson, Hibey, Nauheim & Blair · 1708 New Hampshire Avenue, NW · Washington, DC 20009 · 202-483-1900

Harry Huge · (Securities) · Rogovin, Huge & Schiller · 1250 Twenty-Fourth Street, NW, Suite 700 · Washington, DC 20037-1124 · 202-467-8300

David B. Isbell · (Accounting) · Covington & Burling · 1201 Pennsylvania Avenue, NW · P.O. Box 7566 · Washington, DC 20044 · 202-662-6000

William H. Jeffress, Jr. · (Antitrust; Banking) · Miller, Cassidy, Larroca & Lewin 2555 M Street, NW, Suite 500 · Washington, DC 20037 · 202-293-6400

Joel I. Klein · Onek, Klein & Farr · 2550 M Street, NW, Suite 350 · Washington, DC 20037 · 202-775-0184

Daniel F. Kolb · (Accounting; Antitrust; Securities) · Davis Polk & Wardwell 1575 I Street, NW, Suite 400 · Washington, DC 20005 · 202-789-7100

Abe Krash · (Antitrust) · Arnold & Porter · Thurman Arnold Building · 1200 New Hampshire Avenue, NW · Washington, DC 20036 · 202-872-6700

Lawrence J. Latto · (Insurance; Securites) · Shea & Gardner · 1800 Massachusetts Avenue, NW, Suite 800 · Washington, DC 20036 · 202-828-2000

Nathan Lewin · (Appellate) · Miller, Cassidy, Larroca & Lewin · 2555 M Street, NW, Suite 500 · Washington, DC 20037 · 202-293-6400

Richard C. Lowery · Wiley, Rein & Fielding · 1776 K Street, NW · Washington, DC 20006-2359 · 202-429-7000

Michael J. Madigan · Akin, Gump, Strauss, Hauer & Feld · 1333 New Hampshire Avenue, NW, Suite 400 · Washington, DC 20036 · 202-887-4000

Arthur F. Mathews · (Commodities; Foreign Corrupt Practices Act; RICO; Securities) · Wilmer, Cutler & Pickering · 2445 M Street, NW · Washington, DC 20037 · 202-663-6000

Daniel K. Mayers · (Antitrust; Appellate; Media) · Wilmer, Cutler & Pickering · 2445 M Street, NW · Washington, DC 20037 · 202-663-6000

William E. McDaniels · (Libel & Slander; Medical Malpractice; Products Liablity) · Williams & Connolly · Hill Building · 839 Seventeenth Street, NW Washington, DC 20006 · 202-331-5000

Bruce L. McDonald · Wiley, Rein & Fielding · 1776 K Street, NW · Washington, DC 20006-2359 · 202-429-7000

Hugh M. McIntosh · (Energy; Commercial; Corporate Finance; Real Estate Finance) · Vinson & Elkins · 1455 Pennsylvania Avenue, NW, Suite 700 · Washington, DC 20004 · 202-639-6500

R. Bruce McLean · (Energy) · Akin, Gump, Strauss, Hauer & Feld · 1333 New Hampshire Avenue, NW, Suite 400 · Washington, DC 20036 · 202-887-4000

James E. Merritt · Morrison & Foerster · 2000 Pennsylvania Avenue, NW, Suite 5500 · Washington, DC 20006 · 202-887-1500

Charles A. Miller · (Administrative; Health & Welfare; Transportation) · Covington & Burling · 1201 Pennsylvania Avenue, NW · P.O. Box 7566 · Washington, DC 20044 · 202-662-6000

Herbert J. Miller, Jr. · Miller, Cassidy, Larroca & Lewin · 2555 M Street, NW, Suite 500 · Washington, DC 20037 · 202-293-6400

Ralph J. Moore, Jr. · (Railway) · Shea & Gardner · 1800 Massachusetts Avenue, NW, Suite 800 · Washington, DC 20036 · 202-828-2000

Hugh P. Morrison, Jr. · (Antitrust) · Cahill Gordon & Reindel · 1990 K Street, NW · Washington, DC 20006 · 202-862-8900

David C. Murchison · (Antitrust) · Howrey & Simon · 1730 Pennsylvania Avenue, NW, Suite 900 · Washington, DC 20006-4793 · 202-783-0800

Irvin B. Nathan · (Antitrust; RICO; Securities) · Arnold & Porter · Thurman Arnold Building · 1200 New Hampshire Avenue, NW · Washington, DC 20036 · 202-872-6700

Peter J. Nickles · Covington & Burling · 1201 Pennsylvania Avenue, NW · P.O. Box 7566 · Washington, DC 20044 · 202-662-6000

John E. Nolan, Jr. · Steptoe & Johnson · 1330 Connecticut Avenue, NW Washington, DC 20036 · 202-429-3000

Theodore B. Olson · (Appellate; Commercial; Constitutional; Media) · Gibson, Dunn & Crutcher · 1050 Connecticut Avenue, NW, Suite 900 · Washington, DC 20036 · 202-955-8500

Roberts B. Owen · (Antitrust; International) · Covington & Burling · 1201 Pennsylvania Avenue, NW · P.O. Box 7566 · Washington, DC 20044 · 202-662-6000

Thomas E. Patton · (Antitrust; Securities) · Schnader, Harrison, Segal & Lewis 1111 Nineteenth Street, NW, Suite 1000 · Washington, DC 20036 · 202-463-2900

Richard M. Phillips · (Securities) · Kirkpatrick & Lockhart · 1800 M Street, NW, South Lobby, Suite 900 · Washington, DC 20036 · 202-778-9000

Harvey L. Pitt · (Securities) · Fried, Frank, Harris, Shriver & Jacobson · 1001 Pennsylvania Avenue, NW, Suite 800 · Washington, DC 20004-2505 · 202-639-7000

Stephen J. Pollak · (Antitrust; Appellate; Civil Rights; Government Regulations; Labor) · Shea & Gardner · 1800 Massachusetts Avenue, NW, Suite 800 · Washington, DC 20036 · 202-828-2000

E. Barrett Prettyman, Jr. · (Appellate) · Hogan & Hartson · Columbia Square 555 Thirteenth Street, NW · Washington, DC 20004-1109 · 202-637-5600

A. Raymond Randolph · (Appellate) · Pepper, Hamilton & Scheetz · 1300 Nineteenth Street, NW · Washington, DC 20036 · 202-828-1200

Bert W. Rein · Wiley, Rein & Fielding · 1776 K Street, NW · Washington, DC 20006-2359 · 202-429-7000

Daniel A. Rezneck · (Appellate) · Arnold & Porter · Thurman Arnold Building 1200 New Hampshire Avenue, NW · Washington, DC 20036 · 202-872-6700

James Robertson · (Commercial; Products Liability) · Wilmer, Cutler & Pickering · 2445 M Street, NW · Washington, DC 20037 · 202-663-6000

Charles F. C. Ruff · (RICO; Securities) · Covington & Burling · 1201 Pennsylvania Avenue, NW · P.O. Box 7566 · Washington, DC 20044 · 202-662-6000

Stephen H. Sachs · (Commercial; White Collar Criminal) · Wilmer, Cutler & Pickering · 2445 M Street, NW · Washington, DC 20037 · 202-663-6000

Stephen M. Sacks · Arnold & Porter · Thurman Arnold Building · 1200 New Hampshire Avenue, NW · Washington, DC 20036 · 202-872-6700

Robert N. Sayler · (Administrative) · Covington & Burling · 1201 Pennsylvania Avenue, NW · P.O. Box 7566 · Washington, DC 20044 · 202-662-6000

John H. Schafer III · (Antitrust; Securities) · Covington & Burling · 1201 Pennsylvania Avenue, NW · P.O. Box 7566 · Washington, DC 20044 · 202-662-6000

Lawrence H. Schwartz · Cooter & Gell · 1201 New York Avenue, NW, Suite 1000 · Washington, DC 20005 · 202-289-5638

William H. Schweitzer · (Election) · Baker & Hostetler · 1050 Connecticut Avenue, NW, Suite 1100 · Washington, DC 20036 · 202-861-1500

David I. Shapiro · Dickstein, Shapiro & Morin · 2101 L Street, NW, Suite 900 Washington, DC 20037 · 202-785-9700

James E. Sharp · Sharp, Green & Lankford · 1785 Massachusetts Avenue, NW, Fourth Floor · Washington, DC 20036 · 202-745-1700

John H. Shenefield · (Antitrust) · Morgan, Lewis & Bockius · 1800 M Street, NW, Suite 800N · Washington, DC 20036 · 202-467-7000

Stephen N. Shulman · (Claims Against Government; Equal Employment) · Cadwalader, Wickersham & Taft · 1333 New Hampshire Avenue, NW, Suite 700 Washington, DC 20036 · 202-862-2200

Deanne C. Siemer · Wilmer, Cutler & Pickering · 2445 M Street, NW · Washington, DC 20037 · 202-663-6000

Earl J. Silbert · Schwalb, Donnenfeld, Bray & Silbert · 1025 Thomas Jefferson Street, Third Floor · Washington, DC 20007 · 202-965-7910

Allen R. Snyder · (Appellate; Commercial; Constitutional) · Hogan & Hartson · Columbia Square · 555 Thirteenth Street, NW · Washington, DC 20004-1109 · 202-637-5600

William W. Taylor III · Zuckerman, Spaeder, Goldstein, Taylor & Kolker · 1201 Connecticut Avenue, NW, Suite 1200 · Washington, DC 20036 · 202-778-1800

Steven M. Umin · Williams & Connolly · Hill Building · 839 Seventeenth Street, NW · Washington, DC 20006 · 202-331-5000

John Vanderstar · (Antitrust; Appellate; Constitutional) · Covington & Burling · 1201 Pennsylvania Avenue, NW · P.O. Box 7566 · Washington, DC 20044 · 202-662-6000

John W. Vardaman, Jr. · (Environmental) · Williams & Connolly · Hill Building · 839 Seventeenth Street, NW · Washington, DC 20006 · 202-331-5000

James H. Wallace, Jr. · (Antitrust; Franchising; Patent) · Wiley, Rein & Fielding · 1776 K Street, NW · Washington, DC 20006-2359 · 202-429-7000

David N. Webster · (Criminal Defendants; Products Liability) · Nussbaum, Owen & Webster · One Thomas Circle, NW, Suite 200 · Washington, DC 20005 · 202-833-8900

Robert L. Weinberg · (RICO) · Williams & Connolly · Hill Building · 839 Seventeenth Street, NW · Washington, DC 20006 · 202-331-5000

Richard J. Wertheimer · (Antitrust; Securities) · Arnold & Porter · Thurman Arnold Building · 1200 New Hampshire Avenue, NW · Washington, DC 20036 · 202-872-6700

Howard P. Willens · Wilmer, Cutler & Pickering · 2445 M Street, NW · Washington, DC 20037 · 202-663-6000

Elroy H. Wolff · (Antitrust; Trade Regulations) · Sidley & Austin · 1722 I Street, NW · Washington, DC 20006 · 202-429-4000

Paul Martin Wolff · (Banking; First Amendment; Securities) · Williams & Connolly · Hill Building · 839 Seventeenth Street, NW · Washington, DC 20006 202-331-5000

CORPORATE LAW

Clifford J. Alexander · (Banking; Broker-Dealer; Investment Adviser; Investment Companies; Securities) · Kirkpatrick & Lockhart · 1800 M Street, NW Washington, DC 20036 · 202-778-9000

Charles E. Allen · (Savings Institutions) · Hogan & Hartson · Columbia Square 555 Thirteenth Street, NW · Washington, DC 20004-1109 · 202-637-5600

Robert A. Altman · (Banking; Finance; Food & Drug) · Clifford & Warnke · 815 Connecticut Avenue, NW, 12th Floor · Washington, DC 20006 · 202-828-4200

Donald I. Baker · (Antitrust; Banking) · Sutherland, Asbill & Brennan · 1275 Pennsylvania Avenue, NW, Suite 800 · Washington, DC 20004 · 202-383-0100

Edward A. Benjamin · (Securities) · Ropes & Gray · 1001 Pennsylvania Avenue, NW, Suite 1200 South · Washington, DC 20004 · 202-626-3900

Alan J. Berkeley · (Securities) · Kirkpatrick & Lockhart · 1800 M Street, NW Washington, DC 20036 · 202-778-9000

John Bodner, Jr. · (Antitrust) · Howrey & Simon · 1730 Pennsylvania Avenue, NW, Suite 900 · Washington, DC 20006-4793 · 202-783-0800

Brooksley Born · Arnold & Porter · Thurman Arnold Building · 1200 New Hampshire Avenue, NW · Washington, DC 20036 · 202-872-6700

Charles N. Brower · (International) · White & Case · 1747 Pennsylvania Avenue, NW, Suite 500 · Washington, DC 20006 · 202-872-0013

David N. Brown · (Mergers & Acquisitions; Securities) · Covington & Burling 1201 Pennsylvania Avenue, NW · P.O. Box 7566 · Washington, DC 20044 202-662-6000

Joseph A. Califano, Jr. · Dewey, Ballantine, Bushby, Palmer & Wood · 1775 Pennsylvania Avenue, NW · Washington, DC 20006 · 202-862-1000

Stuart F. Carwile · Wiley, Rein & Fielding · 1776 K Street, NW · Washington, DC 20006-2359 · 202-429-7000

Richard W. Cass · Wilmer, Cutler & Pickering · 2445 M Street, NW · Washington, DC 20037 · 202-663-6000

George L. Christopher · Kirkpatrick & Lockhart · 1800 M Street, NW, South Lobby, Suite 900 · Washington, DC 20036 · 202-778-9000

Clark M. Clifford · Clifford & Warnke · 815 Connecticut Avenue, NW, 12th Floor · Washington, DC 20006 · 202-828-4200

Calvin H. Cobb, Jr. · (Securities & Related Litigation) · Steptoe & Johnson · 1330 Connecticut Avenue, NW · Washington, DC 20036 · 202-429-3000

Louis R. Cohen · Wilmer, Cutler & Pickering · 2445 M Street, NW · Washington, DC 20037 · 202-663-6000

William T. Coleman, Jr. · (Antitrust; International Trade; Mergers & Acquisitions) · O'Melveny & Meyers · 555 Thirteenth Street, NW, Suite 500 West Washington, DC 20004 · 202-383-5300

Myron P. Curzan · Arnold & Porter · Thurman Arnold Building · 1200 New Hampshire Avenue, NW · Washington, DC 20036 · 202-872-6700

Lloyd N. Cutler · (Antitrust; International) · Wilmer, Cutler & Pickering · 2445 M Street, NW · Washington, DC 20037 · 202-663-6000

Nelson Deckelbaum · (Business Reorganization) · Deckelbaum & Ogens · 1140 Connecticut Avenue, NW · Washington, DC 20036 · 202-223-1474

Edward E. Dyson · (International) · Baker & McKenzie · 815 Connecticut Avenue, NW, Suite 1100 · Washington, DC 20006 · 202-452-7000

Peter D. Ehrenhaft · (International Transactions; Technology Transfers) · Bryan, Cave, McPheeters & McRoberts · 1015 Fifteenth Street, NW, Suite 1000 · Washington, DC 20005-2689 · 202-289-6100

Anthony F. Essaye · (International Banking) · Rogers & Wells · 1737 H Street, NW · Washington, DC 20006 · 202-331-7760

Kenneth R. Feinberg · (Administrative) · Kaye, Scholer, Fierman, Hays & Handler · 901 Fifteenth Street, NW, Suite 1100 · Washington, DC 20005 202-682-3500

Lloyd H. Feller · (Securities) · Morgan, Lewis & Bockius · 1800 M Street, NW, Suite 800N · Washington, DC 20036 · 202-467-7000

Ralph C. Ferrara · (Securities) · Debevoise & Plimpton · 555 Thirteenth Street, NW, Suite 1100 East · Washington, DC 20004 · 202-383-8000

James F. Fitzpatrick · (Administrative; Legislative Proceedings) · Arnold & Porter · Thurman Arnold Building · 1200 New Hampshire Avenue, NW · Washington, DC 20036 · 202-872-6700

Howard I. Flack · (Savings Institutions) · Hogan & Hartson · Columbia Square 555 Thirteenth Street, NW · Washington, DC 20004-1109 · 202-637-5600

George C. Freeman, Jr. · (Administrative; Energy; Environmental) · Hunton & Williams · 2000 Pennsylvania Avenue, NW · P.O. Box 19230 · Washington, DC 20036 · 202-955-1500

Milton V. Freeman · (Securities) · Arnold & Porter · Thurman Arnold Building 1200 New Hampshire Avenue, NW · Washington, DC 20036 · 202-872-6700

Daniel M. Gribbon · Covington & Burling · 1201 Pennsylvania Avenue, NW P.O. Box 7566 · Washington, DC 20044 · 202-662-6000

John D. Hawke, Jr. · (Banking) · Arnold & Porter · Thurman Arnold Building 1200 New Hampshire Avenue, NW · Washington, DC 20036 · 202-872-6700

Michael S. Helfer · (Banking) · Wilmer, Cutler & Pickering · 2445 M Street, NW Washington, DC 20037 · 202-663-6000

Robert E. Herzstein · (International Trade and Investment) · Arnold & Porter Thurman Arnold Building · 1200 New Hampshire Avenue, NW · Washington, DC 20036 · 202-872-6700

Carla Anderson Hills · (Antitrust; Government Regulation) · Weil, Gotshal & Manges · 1615 L Street, NW, Suite 700 · Washington, DC 20036 · 202-682-7000

William M. Isaac · (Banking) · Arnold & Porter · Three Lafayette Centre, Suite 850 · 1155 Twenty-First Street, NW · Washington, DC 20036 · 202-872-6700

Robert E. Jordan III · (Antitrust; Petroleum) · Steptoe & Johnson · 1330 Connecticut Avenue, NW · Washington, DC 20036 · 202-429-3000

Miles W. Kirkpatrick · (Antitrust) · Morgan, Lewis & Bockius · 1800 M Street, NW, Suite 800N · Washington, DC 20036 · 202-467-7000

Michael R. Klein · (SEC Investigations; Securities) · Wilmer, Cutler & Pickering 2445 M Street, NW · Washington, DC 20037 · 202-663-6000

Abe Krash · (Antitrust) · Arnold & Porter · Thurman Arnold Building · 1200 New Hampshire Avenue, NW · Washington, DC 20036 · 202-872-6700

Stuart J. Land · (Food & Drug) · Arnold & Porter · Thurman Arnold Building 1200 New Hampshire Avenue, NW · Washington, DC 20036 · 202-872-6700

Dennis J. Lehr · (Banking) · Hogan & Hartson · Columbia Square · 555 Thirteenth Street, NW · Washington, DC 20004-1109 · 202-637-5600

Arnold M. Lerman · (Administrative; Antitrust; Banking) · Wilmer, Cutler & Pickering · 2445 M Street, NW · Washington, DC 20037 · 202-663-6000

Alan B. Levenson · (Securities) · Fulbright & Jaworski · 1150 Connecticut Avenue, NW · Washington, DC 20036 · 202-452-6800

Dennis G. Lyons · Arnold & Porter · Thurman Arnold Building · 1200 New Hampshire Avenue, NW · Washington, DC 20036 · 202-872-6700

Stanley J. Marcuss · (International) · Milbank, Tweed, Hadley & McCloy · 1825 I Street, NW, Suite 900 · Washington, DC 20006 · 202-835-7500

Daniel H. Margolis · (Antitrust) · McGuire, Woods, Battle & Boothe · 1627 I Street, NW, Suite 1000 · Washington, DC 20006 · 202-857-1700

David B. H. Martin, Jr. · (Banking; Mergers & Acquisitions; Securities) · Hogan & Hartson · Columbia Square · 555 Thirteenth Street, NW · Washington, DC 20004-1109 · 202-637-5600 6858

Paul J. Mason · (Securities) · Sutherland, Asbill & Brennan · 1275 Pennsylvania Avenue, NW, Suite 800 · Washington, DC 20004 · 202-383-0100

Neal S. McCoy · (Securities) · Skadden, Arps, Slate, Meagher & Flom · 1440 New York Avenue, NW · Washington, DC 20005 · 202-371-7000

Allan S. Mostoff · (Financial Institutions; Investment Companies & Advisers; Securities) · Dechert Price & Rhoads · 1500 K Street, NW, Suite 400 · Washington, DC 20005 · 202-626-3300

Cantwell Faulkner Muckenfuss III · (Banking; Financial Institutions) · Gibson, Dunn & Crutcher · 1050 Connecticut Avenue, NW, Suite 900 · Washington, DC 20036 · 202-955-8500

John F. Olson · (Securities) · Gibson, Dunn & Crutcher · 1050 Connecticut Avenue, NW, Suite 900 · Washington, DC 20036 · 202-955-8500

Neal D. Peterson · (Banking; Financial Institutions) · Peterson, Engberg & Peterson · 1730 M Street, NW, Suite 907 · Washington, DC 20036 · 202-296-0360

Richard M. Phillips · (Securities) · Kirkpatrick & Lockhart · 1800 M Street, NW, South Lobby, Suite 900 · Washington, DC 20036 · 202-778-9000

Robert Pitofsky · (Antitrust) · Arnold & Porter · Thurman Arnold Building · 1200 New Hampshire Avenue, NW · Washington, DC 20036 · 202-872-6700

Harvey L. Pitt · (Securities) · Fried, Frank, Harris, Shriver & Jacobson · 1001 Pennsylvania Avenue, NW, Suite 800 · Washington, DC 20004-2505 · 202-639-7000

John G. Reed · (Securities) · White & Case · 1747 Pennsylvania Avenue, NW Washington, DC 20006 · 202-872-0013

George B. Reid, Jr. · (Leveraged Buyouts; Mergers & Acquisitions; Securities Regulations) · Covington & Burling · 1201 Pennsylvania Avenue, NW · P.O. Box 7566 · Washington, DC 20044 · 202-662-6000

William D. Rogers · (International) · Arnold & Porter · Thurman Arnold Building 1200 New Hampshire Avenue, NW · Washington, DC 20036 · 202-872-6700

William P. Rogers · (International) · Rogers & Wells · 1737 H Street, NW Washington, DC 20006 · 202-331-7760

Peter J. Romeo · (Securities) · Hogan & Hartson · Columbia Square · 555 Thirteenth Street, NW · Washington, DC 20004-1109 · 202-637-5600

James J. Rosenhauer · Hogan & Hartson · Columbia Square · 555 Thirteenth Street, NW · Washington, DC 20004-1109 · 202-637-5600

Douglas E. Rosenthal · (Antitrust; International) · Sutherland, Asbill & Brennan 1275 Pennsylvania Avenue, NW, Suite 800 · Washington, DC 20004 · 202-383-0100

Eugene T. Rossides · (International Trade; Legislative) · Rogers & Wells · 1737 H Street, NW · Washington, DC 20006 · 202-331-7760

Marcus A. Rowden · (Energy; High Technology; International) · Fried, Frank, Harris, Shriver & Jacobson · 1001 Pennsylvania Avenue, NW, Suite 800 · Washington, DC 20004-2505 · 202-639-7000

Richard H. Rowe · Proskauer Rose Goetz & Mendelsohn · 2001 L Street, NW, Suite 400 · Washington, DC 20036 · 202-466-7300

Henry P. Sailer · (Trade Regulation) · Covington & Burling · 1201 Pennsylvania Avenue, NW · P.O. Box 7566 · Washington, DC 20044 · 202-662-6000

Frank P. Saponaro, Jr. · (Energy; Public Utilities) · Morgan, Lewis & Bockius · 1800 M Street, NW, Suite 800N · Washington, DC 20036 · 202-467-7000

James H. Schropp · (Securities) · Fried, Frank, Harris, Shriver & Jacobson · 1001 Pennsylvania Avenue, NW, Suite 800 · Washington, DC 20004-2505 · 202-639-7000

Joe Sims · (Antitrust) · Jones, Day, Reavis & Pogue · Metropolitan Square, Suite 700 · 655 Fifteenth Street, NW · Washington, DC 20005-5701 · 202-879-3939

Michael N. Sohn · (Administrative; Antitrust; Trade Regulations) · Arnold & Porter · Thurman Arnold Building · 1200 New Hampshire Avenue, NW · Washington, DC 20036 · 202-872-6700

A. A. Sommer, Jr. · (Securities) · Morgan, Lewis & Bockius · 1800 M Street, NW, Suite 800N · Washington, DC 20036 · 202-467-7000

Richard A. Steinwurtzel · Fried, Frank, Harris, Shriver & Jacobson · 1001 Pennsylvania Avenue, NW, Suite 800 · Washington, DC 20004-2505 · 202-639-7000

Samuel A. Stern · (International) · Dickstein, Shapiro & Morin · 2101 L Street, NW, Suite 900 · Washington, DC 20037 · 202-785-9700

John R. Stevenson · (International Arbitrations) · Sullivan & Cromwell · 1701 Pennsylvania Avenue, NW · Washington, DC 20006 · 202-956-7500

Walter Sterling Surrey · (International) · Jones, Day, Reavis & Pogue · Metropolitan Square, Suite 700 · Washington, DC 20005 · 202-682-4000

William E. Swope · Jones, Day, Reavis & Pogue · Metropolitan Square, Suite 700 · 655 Fifteenth Street, NW · Washington, DC 20005-5701 · 202-879-3939

Thomas P. Vartanian · (Financial Institutions Transactions; Mergers & Acquisitions) · Fried, Frank, Harris, Shriver & Jacobson · 1001 Pennsylvania Avenue, NW, Suite 800 · Washington, DC 20004-2505 · 202-639-7000

G. Duane Vieth · Arnold & Porter · Thurman Arnold Building · 1200 New Hampshire Avenue, NW · Washington, DC 20036 · 202-872-6700

Robert L. Wald · (Antitrust) · Pepper, Hamilton & Scheetz · 1300 Nineteenth Street, NW · Washington, DC 20036 · 202-828-1200

Peter J. Wallison · (Banking; Finance) · Gibson, Dunn & Crutcher · 1050 Connecticut Avenue, NW, Suite 900 · Washington, DC 20036 · 202-955-8500

Alan S. Ward · (Antitrust) · Baker & Hostetler · 1050 Connecticut Avenue, NW, Suite 1100 · Washington, DC 20036 · 202-861-1500

Paul C. Warnke · (Administrative; Antitrust; International Trade) · Clifford & Warnke · 815 Connecticut Avenue, NW, 12th Floor · Washington, DC 20006 202-828-4200

Mark A. Weiss · (Banking; Financial Institutions) · Covington & Burling · 1201 Pennsylvania Avenue, NW · P.O. Box 7566 · Washington, DC 20044· 202-662-6000

Richard E. Wiley · (Telecommunications) · Wiley, Rein & Fielding · 1776 K Street, NW · Washington, DC 20006-2359 · 202-429-7000

Wesley S. Williams, Jr. · (Banking) · Covington & Burling · 1201 Pennsylvania Avenue, NW · P.O. Box 7566 · Washington, DC 20044 · 202-662-6000

J. Roger Wollenberg · (Telecommunications) · Wilmer, Cutler & Pickering 2445 M Street, NW · Washington, DC 20037 · 202-663-6000

CRIMINAL DEFENSE

Raymond Banoun · Arent, Fox, Kintner, Plotkin & Kahn · Washington Square 1050 Connecticut Avenue, NW · Washington, DC 20036-5339 · 202-857-6000

Richard W. Beckler · Fulbright & Jaworski · 1150 Connecticut Avenue, NW Washington, DC 20036 · 202-452-6800

Robert S. Bennett · Dunnells, Duvall, Bennett & Porter · 2100 Pennsylvania Avenue, Fourth Floor · Washington, DC 20037 · 202-861-1400

Richard Ben-Veniste · Ben-Veniste & Shernoff · 1667 K Street, NW, Suite 405 Washington, DC 20006 · 202-331-8700

Judah Best · (also Appellate) · Debevoise & Plimpton · 555 Thirteenth Street, NW, Suite 1100 East · Washington, DC 20004 · 202-383-8000

John M. Bray · Schwalb, Donnenfeld, Bray & Silbert · 1025 Thomas Jefferson Street, NW, Suite 300 East · Washington, DC 20007 · 202-965-7910

Donald T. Bucklin · Squire, Sanders & Dempsey · 1201 Pennsylvania Avenue, NW · P.O. Box 407 · Washington, DC 20044 · 202-626-6600

Plato Cacheris · Dunnells, Duvall, Bennett & Porter · 2100 Pennsylvania Avenue, Fourth Floor · Washington, DC 20037 · 202-861-1400

Aubrey M. Daniel III · Williams & Connolly · Hill Building · 839 Seventeenth Street, NW · Washington, DC 20006 · 202-331-5000

John M. Dowd · Heron, Burchette, Ruckert & Rothwell · 1025 Thomas Jefferson Street, NW · Washington, DC 20007 · 202-337-7700

Gerald A. Feffer · Williams & Connolly · Hill Building · 839 Seventeenth Street, NW · Washington, DC 20006 · 202-331-5000

Hamilton P. Fox III · Dewey, Ballantine, Bushby, Palmer & Wood · 1775 Pennsylvania Avenue, NW, Suite 600 · Washington, DC 20006 · 202-862-1000

Paul L. Friedman · White & Case · 1747 Pennsylvania Avenue, NW · Washington, DC 20006 · 202-872-0013

Vincent J. Fuller · Williams & Connolly · Hill Building · 839 Seventeenth Street, NW · Washington, DC 20006 · 202-331-5000

William J. Garber · 301 I Street, NW · Washington, DC 20001 · 202-638-4667

Brian P. Gettings · Cohen, Gettings, Alper & Dunham · 1201 Pennsylvania Avenue, NW, Suite 821 · Washington, DC 20004 · 202-628-7944

Seymour Glanzer · Dickstein, Shapiro & Morin · 2101 L Street, NW, Suite 900 · Washington, DC 20037 · 202-785-9700

Thomas C. Green · Sharp, Green & Lankford · 1785 Massachusetts Avenue, NW, Fourth Floor · Washington, DC 20036 · 202-745-1700

Richard A. Hibey · Anderson, Hibey, Nauheim & Blair · 1708 New Hampshire Avenue, NW · Washington, DC 20009 · 202-483-1900

William G. Hundley · Akin, Gump, Strauss, Hauer & Feld · 1333 New Hampshire Avenue, NW, Suite 400 · Washington, DC 20036 · 202-887-4000

William H. Jeffress, Jr. · Miller, Cassidy, Larroca & Lewin · 2555 M Street, NW, Suite 500 · Washington, DC 20037 · 202-293-6400

Nathan Lewin · (also Appellate) · Miller, Cassidy, Larroca & Lewin · 2555 M Street, NW, Suite 500 · Washington, DC 20037 · 202-293-6400

Arthur F. Mathews · Wilmer, Cutler & Pickering · 2445 M Street, NW · Washington, DC 20037 · 202-663-6000

William E. McDaniels · Williams & Connolly · Hill Building · 839 Seventeenth Street, NW · Washington, DC 20006 · 202-331-5000

Herbert J. Miller, Jr. · Miller, Cassidy, Larroca & Lewin · 2555 M Street, NW, Suite 500 · Washington, DC 20037 · 202-293-6400

R. Stan Mortenson · Miller, Cassidy, Larroca & Lewin · 2555 M Street, NW, Suite 500 · Washington, DC 20037 · 202-293-6400

R. Kenneth Mundy · 1155 Fifteenth Street, NW, Suite 1004 · Washington, D. C. 20005 · 202-223-4470

Robert F. Muse · Stein, Mitchell & Mezines · 1100 Connecticut Avenue, NW, 11th Floor · Washington, DC 20036 · 202-737-7777

Irvin B. Nathan · Arnold & Porter · Thurman Arnold Building · 1200 New Hampshire Avenue, NW · Washington, DC 20036 · 202-872-6700

David Povich · Williams & Connolly · Hill Building · 839 Seventeenth Street, NW · Washington, DC 20006 · 202-331-5000

A. Raymond Randolph · (also Appellate) · Pepper, Hamilton & Scheetz · 1300 Nineteenth Street, NW · Washington, DC 20036 · 202-828-1200

Carl S. Rauh · Dunnells, Duvall, Bennett & Porter · 2100 Pennsylvania Avenue, NW, Fourth Floor · Washington, DC 20037 · 202-861-1400

Daniel A. Rezneck · Arnold & Porter · Thurman Arnold Building · 1200 New Hampshire Avenue, NW · Washington, DC 20036 · 202-872-6700

Kenneth M. Robinson · 301 I Street, NW · Washington, DC 20001 · 202-347-6100

Charles F. C. Ruff · Covington & Burling · 1201 Pennsylvania Avenue, NW P.O. Box 7566 · Washington, DC 20044 · 202-662-6000

James E. Sharp · Sharp, Green & Lankford · 1785 Massachusetts Avenue, NW, Fourth Floor · Washington, DC 20036 · 202-745-1700

Earl J. Silbert · Schwalb, Donnenfeld, Bray & Silbert · 1025 Thomas Jefferson Street, Third Floor · Washington, DC 20007 · 202-965-7910

Jacob A. Stein · (also Appellate) · Stein, Mitchell & Mezines · 1100 Connecticut Avenue, NW, 11th Floor · Washington, DC 20036 · 202-737-7777

Brendan V. Sullivan, Jr. · Williams & Connolly · Hill Building · 839 Seventeenth Street, NW · Washington, DC 20006 · 202-331-5000

William W. Taylor III · Zuckerman, Spaeder, Goldstein, Taylor & Kolker · 1201 Connecticut Avenue, NW, Suite 1200 · Washington, DC 20036 · 202-778-1800

John W. Vardaman, Jr. · Williams & Connolly · Hill Building · 839 Seventeenth Street, NW · Washington, DC 20006 · 202-331-5000

Robert L. Weinberg · Williams & Connolly · Hill Building · 839 Seventeenth Street, NW · Washington, DC 20006 · 202-331-5000

Howard P. Willens · Wilmer, Cutler & Pickering · 2445 M Street, NW · Washington, DC 20037 · 202-663-6000

Roger E. Zuckerman · Zuckerman, Spaeder, Goldstein, Taylor & Kolker · 1201 Connecticut Avenue, NW, Suite 1200 · Washington, DC 20036 · 202-778-1800

FAMILY LAW

Sanford K. Ain · Sherman, Meehan & Curtin · 1900 M Street, NW, Suite 601 Washington, DC 20036 · 202-331-7120

Rita M. Bank · Klores, Feldesman & Tucker · 2001 L Street, NW, Suite 300 Washington, DC 20036 · 202-466-8960

Pamela Borland Forbes · Klores, Feldesman & Tucker · 2001 L Street, NW, Suite 300 · Washington, DC 20036 · 202-466-8960

Daniel G. Grove · Keck, Mahin & Cate · 1730 Pennsylvania Avenue, Suite 350 Washington, DC 20006-4706 · 202-347-7006

Armin U. Kuder · Kuder, Temple, Smollar & Heller · 1015 Twentieth Street, NW, Suite 200 · Washington, DC 20036 · 202-331-7522

Charles H. Mayer · Shapiro & Mayer · 1707 H Street, NW, Suite 805 · Washington, DC 20006 · 202-331-0991

Sidney S. Sachs · Sachs, Greenebaum & Tayler · 1140 Connecticut Avenue, NW, Suite 900 · Washington, DC 20036 · 202-828-8200

Daniel E. Schultz · Sherman, Meehan & Curtin · 1900 M Street, NW, Suite 601 Washington, DC 20036 · 202-331-7120

Peter R. Sherman · Sherman, Meehan & Curtin · 1900 M Street, NW, Suite 601 Washington, DC 20036 · 202-331-7120

Marna Susan Tucker · Klores, Feldesman & Tucker · 2001 L Street, NW, Suite 300 · Washington, DC 20036 · 202-466-8960

Hal Witt · Witt, Nolan & Bindeman · 1140 Connecticut Avenue, NW, Suite 600 Washington, DC 20036 · 202-296-3333

LABOR AND EMPLOYMENT LAW

Robert M. Baptiste · (Labor) · Baptiste & Wilder · 1919 Pennsylvania Avenue, NW · Washington, DC 20006 · 202-223-0723

David S. Barr · (Labor) · Barr, Peer & Cohen · 1620 I Street, NW, Suite 603 Washington, DC 20006 · 202-223-1900

Hugh J. Beins · (Labor) · Beins, Axelrod & Osborne · 2033 K Street, NW, Suite 300 · Washington, DC 20006 · 202-429-1900

Elliot Bredhoff · (Labor) · Bredhoff & Kaiser · 1000 Connecticut Avenue, NW, Suite 1300 · Washington, DC 20036 · 202-833-9340

Charles I. Cohen · (Management) · Vedder, Price, Kaufman, Kammholz & Day 1919 Pennsylvania Avenue, NW, Suite 500 · Washington, DC 20006 · 202-828-5000

George H. Cohen · (Labor) · Bredhoff & Kaiser · 1000 Connecticut Avenue, NW, Suite 1300 · Washington, DC 20036 · 202-833-9340

Laurence J. Cohen · (Labor) · Sherman, Dunn, Cohen, Leifer & Counts · 1125 Fifteenth Street, NW, Suite 801 · Washington, DC 20005 · 202-785-9300

Robert J. Connerton · (Labor) · Connerton, Ray & Simon · 1920 L Street, NW, Fourth Floor · Washington, DC 20036 · 202-466-6790

William J. Curtin · (Management) · Morgan, Lewis & Bockius · 1800 M Street, NW, Suite 800N · Washington, DC 20036 · 202-467-7000

Robert B. Fitzpatrick · (Individuals) · Fitzpatrick, Verstegen & Cashdan · Spring Valley Center, Suite 400 · 4801 Massachusetts Avenue, NW · Washington, DC 20016-2087 · 202-364-8710

Laurence E. Gold · (Labor) · Connerton, Ray & Simon · 1920 L Street, NW, Fourth Floor · Washington, DC 20036 · 202-466-6790

Robert C. Gombar · (Management) · Jones, Day, Reavis & Pogue · 1450 G Street, NW · Washington, DC 20005-2088 · 202-879-3939

Michael H. Gottesman · (Labor) · Bredhoff & Kaiser · 1000 Connecticut Avenue, NW, Suite 1300 · Washington, DC 20036 · 202-833-9340

Isaac N. Groner · (Labor) · Cole and Groner · 1615 L Street, NW, Suite 1000 Washington, DC 20036 · 202-331-8888

Richard C. Hotvedt · (Management) · Morgan, Lewis & Bockius · 1800 M Street, NW, Suite 800N · Washington, DC 20036 · 202-467-7000

Harry Huge · (Individuals) · Rogovin, Huge & Schiller · 1250 Twenty-Fourth Street, NW, Suite 700 · Washington, DC 20037-1124 · 202-467-8300

John S. Irving, Jr. · (Management) · Kirkland & Ellis · 655 Fifteenth Street, NW Washington, DC 20005 · 202-879-5000

George W. Johnston · (Management) · Venable, Baetjer, Howard & Civiletti 1301 Pennsylvania Avenue, NW, Suite 1200 · Washington, DC 20004 · 202-783-4300

George Kaufmann · (Labor) · Dickstein, Shapiro & Morin · 2101 L Street, NW, Suite 900 · Washington, DC 20037 · 202-785-9700

William J. Kilberg · (Management) · Gibson, Dunn & Crutcher · 1050 Connecticut Avenue, NW, Suite 900 · Washington, DC 20036 · 202-955-8500

Richard Kirschner · (Labor) · Kirschner, Weinberg & Dempsey · 1615 L Street, NW, Suite 1360 · Washington, DC 20036 · 202-775-5900

Andrew M. Kramer · (Management) · Jones, Day, Reavis & Pogue · Metropolitan Square, Suite 700 · 655 Fifteenth Street, NW · Washington, DC 20005-5701 202-879-3939

Ian D. Lanoff · Bredhoff & Kaiser · 1000 Connecticut Avenue, NW, Suite 1300 Washington, DC 20036 · 202-833-9340

John A. McGuinn · (Management) · Porter, Wright, Duff & Hasley · International Square · 1825 I Street, NW, Suite 300 · Washington, DC 20006-5486 202-293-8600

Peter G. Nash · (Management) · Ogletree, Deakins, Nash, Smoak and Stewart 2400 N Street, NW, Fifth Floor · Washington, DC 20037 · 202-887-0855

Charles P. O'Connor · (Management) · Morgan, Lewis & Bockius · 1800 M Street, NW, Suite 800N · Washington, DC 20036 · 202-467-7000

William W. Osborne, Jr. · (Labor) · Beins, Axelrod & Osborne · 2033 K Street, NW, Suite 300 · Washington, DC 20006 · 202-429-1900

Frank Petramalo, Jr. · (Labor) · Gordon & Barnett · 1133 Twenty-First Street, NW, Suite 450 · Washington, DC 20036 · 202-833-3400

Jerome Powell · (Management) · Reed Smith Shaw & McClay · 1150 Connecticut Avenue, NW · Washington, DC 20036 · 202-457-6100

Thomas J. Quigley · (Management) · Squire, Sanders & Dempsey · 1201 Pennsylvania Avenue, NW · P.O. Box 407 · Washington, DC 20044 · 202-626-6600

T. Timothy Ryan, Jr. · (Management) · Pierson, Ball & Dowd · Ring Building 1200 Eighteenth Street, NW · Washington, DC 20036 · 202-331-8566

Steven J. Sacher · (Management) · Johnson & Swanson · Columbia Square Building, Suite 660 West · 555 Thirteenth Street, NW · Washington, DC 20004 202-383-8760

Arthur M. Schiller · (Labor) · Newman & Newell · 21 Dupont Circle, NW, Suite 401 · Washington, DC 20036 · 202-857-5659

Stanley R. Strauss · (Management) · Vedder, Price, Kaufman, Kammholz & Day 1919 Pennsylvania Avenue, NW, Suite 500 · Washington, DC 20006 · 202-828-5000

Stephen E. Tallent · (Management) · Gibson, Dunn & Crutcher · 1050 Connecticut Avenue, NW, Suite 900 · Washington, DC 20036 · 202-955-8500

Carl L. Taylor · (Management) · Johnson & Swanson · Columbia Square Building, Suite 660 West · 555 Thirteenth Street, NW · Washington, DC 20004 · 202-383-8760

Michael A. Taylor · (Management) · Ogletree, Deakins, Nash, Smoak and Stewart · 2400 N Street, NW, Fifth Floor · Washington, DC 20037 · 202-887-0855

Robert T. Thompson · (Management) · Thompson, Mann and Hutson · 1730 Pennsylvania Avenue, NW, Suite 1250 · Washington, DC 20006 · 202-783-1900

Dennis H. Vaughn · (Management) · Paul, Hastings, Janofsky & Walker · 1050 Connecticut Avenue, NW, 12th Floor · Washington, DC 20036-5331 · 202-223-9000

Carl W. Vogt · (Management) · Fulbright & Jaworski · 1150 Connecticut Avenue, NW · Washington, DC 20036 · 202-452-6800

Lawrence T. Zimmerman · (Management) · 2300 N Street, NW, Suite 600 · Washington, DC 20037 · 202-663-9013

NATURAL RESOURCES AND ENVIRONMENTAL LAW

Lynn R. Coleman · Skadden, Arps, Slate, Meagher & Flom · 1440 New York Avenue, NW · Washington, DC 20005 · 202-371-7000

Andrea Bear Field · Hunton & Williams · 2000 Pennsylvania Avenue, NW · P.O. Box 19230 · Washington, DC 20036 · 202-955-1500

Theodore L. Garrett · Covington & Burling · 1201 Pennsylvania Avenue, NW P.O. Box 7566 · Washington, DC 20044 · 202-662-6000

Carroll L. Gilliam · (Natural Gas) · Grove, Jaskiewicz, Gilliam and Cobert · 1730 M Street, NW, Suite 501 · Washington, DC 20036 · 202-296-2900

J. Hovey Kemp · (Oil & Gas) · Davis, Graham & Stubbs · 1200 Nineteenth Street, NW, Suite 500 · Washington, DC 20036 · 202-822-8660

Angus Macbeth · Sidley & Austin · 1722 I Street, NW · Washington, DC 20006 202-429-4000

Barry L. Malter · Breed, Abbott & Morgan · International Square, Suite 1000 1875 I Street, NW · Washington, DC 20006 · 202-466-1100

Hugh M. McIntosh · (Oil & Gas) · Vinson & Elkins · 1455 Pennsylvania Avenue, NW, Suite 700 · Washington, DC 20004 · 202-639-6500

David E. Menotti · Perkins Coie · 1110 Vermont Avenue, NW, Suite 1200 Washington, DC 20005 · 202-887-9030

Rush Moody, Jr. · (Gas Pipelines) · Akin, Gump, Strauss, Hauer & Feld · 1333 New Hampshire Avenue, NW, Suite 400 · Washington, DC 20036 · 202-887-4000

James W. Moorman · Cadwalader, Wickersham & Taft · 1333 New Hampshire Avenue, NW, Suite 700 · Washington, DC 20036 · 202-862-2200

Frederick Moring · (Natural Gas) · Crowell & Moring · 1001 Pennsylvania Avenue, NW · Washington, DC 20004-2505 · 202-624-2500

Jerome C. Muys · (Public Lands; Water) · Will & Muys · 1825 I Street, NW, Suite 920 · Washington, DC 20006 · 202-429-4344

William F. Pedersen, Jr. · Perkins Coie · 1110 Vermont Avenue, NW, Suite 1200 Washington, DC 20005 · 202-887-9030

John R. Quarles, Jr. · Morgan, Lewis & Bockius · 1800 M Street, NW, Suite 800N · Washington, DC 20036 · 202-467-7000

Stephen D. Ramsey · Sidley & Austin · 1722 I Street, NW · Washington, DC 20006 · 202-429-4000

James A. Rogers · Skadden, Arps, Slate, Meagher & Flom · 1440 New York Avenue, NW · Washington, DC 20005 · 202-371-7000

Steven Schatzow · Morgan, Lewis & Bockius · 1800 M Street, NW, Suite 800N Washington, DC 20036 · 202-467-7000

John T. Smith II · Covington & Burling · 1201 Pennsylvania Avenue, NW · P.O. Box 7566 · Washington, DC 20044 · 202-662-6000

Richard G. Stoll, Jr. · Freedman, Levy, Kroll & Simonds · 1050 Connecticut Avenue, NW, Suite 825 · Washington, DC 20036-5366 · 202-457-5100

Steven A. Tasher · Donovan Leisure Newton & Irvine · 1850 K Street, NW, Suite 1200 · Washington, DC 20006 · 202-862-4700

Allan J. Topol · Covington & Burling · 1201 Pennsylvania Avenue, NW · P.O. Box 7566 · Washington, DC 20044 · 202-662-6000

Thomas H. Truitt · Piper & Marbury · 1200 Nineteenth Street, NW · Washington, DC 20036 · 202-861-3900

William A. White · (Coal) · Dechert Price & Rhoads · 1500 K Street, NW Washington, DC 20005 · 202-626-3300

PERSONAL INJURY LITIGATION

Richard Ben-Veniste · (Plaintiffs) · Ben-Veniste & Shernoff · 1667 K Street, NW, Suite 405 · Washington, DC 20006 · 202-331-8700

Vincent H. Cohen · (Defendants) · Hogan & Hartson · Columbia Square · 555 Thirteenth Street, NW · Washington, DC 20004-1109 · 202-637-5600

Milton Heller · (Plaintiffs) · Solar Building, Suite 300 · 1000 Sixteenth Street, NW Washington, DC 20036 · 202-737-4300

John F. Mahoney, Jr. · (Defendants) · Mahoney, Hogan, Heffler & Heald · 777 Fourteenth Street, NW, Suite 600 · Washington, DC 20005 · 202-347-6161

Gerard E. Mitchell · (Plaintiffs) · Stein, Mitchell & Mezines · 1100 Connecticut Avenue, NW, 11th Floor · Washington, DC 20036 · 202-737-7777

Joseph D. Montedonico · (Defendants) · Donahue, Ehrmantraut and Montedonico · 1605 New Hampshire Avenue, NW · Washington, DC 20009 · 202-797-0700

Robert F. Muse · (Plaintiffs) · Stein, Mitchell & Mezines · 1100 Connecticut Avenue, NW, 11th Floor · Washington, DC 20036 · 202-737-7777

Jack H. Olender · (Plaintiffs) · Jack H. Olender and Associates · One Farragut Square South, 11th Floor · 1634 I Street, NW · Washington, DC 20006 202-879-7777

Jacob A. Stein · (Plaintiffs) · Stein, Mitchell & Mezines · 1100 Connecticut Avenue, NW, 11th Floor · Washington, DC 20036 · 202-737-7777

David N. Webster · Nussbaum, Owen & Webster · One Thomas Circle, NW, Suite 200 · Washington, DC 20005 · 202-833-8900

REAL ESTATE LAW

Sanford K. Ain · Sherman, Meehan & Curtin · 1900 M Street, NW, Suite 601 Washington, DC 20036 · 202-331-7120

George H. Beuchert, Jr. · Stohlman, Beuchert, Egan & Smith · 1775 Pennsylvania Avenue, NW, Suite 400 · Washington, DC 20006 · 202-452-1775

C. Richard Beyda · Grossberg, Yochelson, Fox & Beyda · 1707 H Street, NW, Suite 300 · Washington, DC 20006 · 202-298-7600

Myron P. Curzan · Arnold & Porter · Thurman Arnold Building · 1200 New Hampshire Avenue, NW · Washington, DC 20036 · 202-872-6700

Jeffry R. Dwyer · Morrison & Foerster · 2000 Pennsylvania Avenue, NW, Suite 5500 · Washington, DC 20006 · 202-887-1500

Herbert M. Franklin · Lane and Edson · 2300 M Street, NW · Washington, DC 20037 · 202-955-9600

Joseph M. Fries · Arent, Fox, Kintner, Plotkin & Kahn · Washington Square 1050 Connecticut Avenue, NW · Washington, DC 20036-5339 · 202-857-6000

Norman M. Glasgow, Sr. · Wilkes, Artis, Hedrick & Lane · 1666 K Street, NW, Suite 1100 · Washington, DC 20006-2359 · 202-457-7800

Solomon Grossberg · Grossberg, Yochelson, Fox & Beyda · 1707 H Street, NW, Suite 300 · Washington, DC 20006 · 202-298-7600

Albert L. Ledgard, Jr. · Wilkes, Artis, Hedrick & Lane · 1666 K Street, NW, Suite 1100 · Washington, DC 20006-2359 · 202-457-7800

R. Robert Linowes · Linowes & Blocher · 655 Fifteenth Street, NW, Suite 400 Washington, DC 20005 · 202-872-9080

Leonard S. Melrod · Melrod, Redman & Gartlan · 1801 K Street, NW, Suite 1100 Washington, DC 20006 · 202-822-5300

David M. Osnos · Arent, Fox, Kintner, Plotkin & Kahn · Washington Square 1050 Connecticut Avenue, NW · Washington, DC 20036-5339 · 202-857-6000

Stephen W. Porter · Dunnells, Duvall, Bennett & Porter · 2100 Pennsylvania Avenue, Fourth Floor · Washington, DC 20037 · 202-861-1400

Whayne S. Quin · Wilkes, Artis, Hedrick & Lane · 1666 K Street, NW, Suite 1100 · Washington, DC 20006-2359 · 202-457-7800

Stefan F. Tucker · Tucker, Flyer, Sanger & Lewis · 1615 L Street, NW, Suite 400 Washington, DC 20036 · 202-452-8600

TAX AND EMPLOYEE BENEFITS LAW

Donald C. Alexander · Cadwalader, Wickersham & Taft · 1333 New Hampshire Avenue, NW, Suite 700 · Washington, DC 20036 · 202-862-2200

Mac Asbill, Jr. · Sutherland, Asbill & Brennan · 1275 Pennsylvania Avenue, Suite 800 · Washington, DC 20004 · 202-383-0100

Dennis P. Bedell · Miller & Chevalier · Metropolitan Square, Suite 900 · 655 Fifteenth Street, NW · Washington, DC 20005 · 202-626-5800

Mortimer M. Caplin · Caplin & Drysdale · One Thomas Circle, NW, Suite 1100 Washington, DC 20005 · 202-862-5000

John E. Chapoton · Vinson & Elkins · Willard Office Building, Suite 700 · 1455 Pennsylvania Avenue · Washington, DC 20004 · 202-639-6500

Sheldon S. Cohen · Morgan, Lewis & Bockius · 1800 M Street, NW, Suite 800N Washington, DC 20036 · 202-467-7000

H. Stewart Dunn, Jr. · Ivins, Phillips & Barker · 1700 Pennsylvania Avenue, NW, Suite 600 · Washington, DC 20006 · 202-393-7600

Gerald A. Feffer · Williams & Connolly · Hill Building · 839 Seventeenth Street, NW · Washington, DC 20006 · 202-331-5000

Kenneth W. Gideon · Fried, Frank, Harris, Shriver & Jacobson · 1001 Pennsylvania Avenue, NW, Suite 800 · Washington, DC 20004-2505 · 202-639-7000

Martin D. Ginsburg · Fried, Frank, Harris, Shriver & Jacobson · 1001 Pennsylvania Avenue, NW, Suite 800 · Washington, DC 20004-2505 · 202-639-7000

Jay W. Glasmann · Ivins, Phillips & Barker · 1700 Pennsylvania Avenue, NW, Suite 600 · Washington, DC 20006 · 202-393-7600

Fred T. Goldberg, Jr. · Skadden, Arps, Slate, Meagher & Flom · 1440 New York Avenue, NW · Washington, DC 20005 · 202-371-7000

Michael S. Gordon · (Employee Benefits) · 1747 Pennsylvania Avenue, NW Washington, DC 20006 · 202-223-8576

Erwin N. Griswold · Jones, Day, Reavis & Pogue · Metropolitan Square, Suite 600 · 655 Tenth Street, NW · Washington, DC 20005-5701 · 202-879-3939

Joseph H. Guttentag · Arnold & Porter · Thurman Arnold Building · 1200 New Hampshire Avenue, NW · Washington, DC 20036 · 202-872-6700

Don V. Harris, Jr. · Covington & Burling · 1201 Pennsylvania Avenue, NW · P.O. Box 7566 · Washington, DC 20044 · 202-662-6000

Lawrence J. Hass · (Employee Benefits) · Akin, Gump, Strauss, Hauer & Feld 1333 New Hampshire Avenue, NW, Suite 400 · Washington, DC 20036 202-887-4000

Edward J. Hawkins · Squire, Sanders & Dempsey · 1201 Pennsylvania Avenue, NW · P.O. Box 407 · Washington, DC 20044 · 202-626-6600

James P. Holden · Steptoe & Johnson · 1330 Connecticut Avenue, NW · Washington, DC 20036 · 202-429-3000

John B. Jones, Jr. · Covington & Burling · 1201 Pennsylvania Avenue, NW · P.O. Box 7566 · Washington, DC 20044 · 202-662-6000

A. Carl Kaseman III · Piper & Marbury · 1200 Nineteenth Street, NW · Washington, DC 20036 · 202-861-3900

William J. Kilberg · (Employee Benefits) · Gibson, Dunn & Crutcher · 1050 Connecticut Avenue, NW, Suite 900 · Washington, DC 20036 · 202-955-8500

Jerome Kurtz · Paul, Weiss, Rifkind, Wharton & Garrison · 1615 L Street, NW, Suite 1300 · Washington, DC 20036 · 202-223-7300

F. David Lake, Jr. · Wilmer, Cutler & Pickering · 2445 M Street, NW · Washington, DC 20037 · 202-663-6000

Stuart M. Lewis · (Employee Benefits) · Silverstein and Mullens · 1776 K Street, NW · Washington, DC 20006 · 202-452-7989

Jerome B. Libin · Sutherland, Asbill & Brennan · 1275 Pennsylvania Avenue, Suite 800 · Washington, DC 20004 · 202-383-0100

Phillip L. Mann · Miller & Chevalier · Metropolitan Square, Suite 900 · 655 Fifteenth Street · Washington, DC 20005 · 202-626-5700

Louis T. Mazawey · (Employee Benefits) · Groom and Nordberg · 1775 Pennsylvania Avenue, NW · Washington, DC 20006 · 202-857-0620

William S. McKee · King & Spalding · 1730 Pennsylvania Avenue, NW, Suite 1200 · Washington, DC 20006 · 202-737-0500

Ralph J. Moore, Jr. · Shea & Gardner · 1800 Massachusetts Avenue, NW · Washington, DC 20036 · 202-828-2000

Cono R. Namorato · Caplin & Drysdale · One Thomas Circle, NW, Suite 1100 · Washington, DC 20005 · 202-862-5000

John S. Nolan · Miller & Chevalier · Metropolitan Square, Suite 900 · 655 Fifteenth Street, NW · Washington, DC 20005 · 202-626-5800

James T. O'Hara · Jones, Day, Reavis & Pogue · Metropolitan Square · 655 Tenth Street, NW · Washington, DC 20005-5701 · 202-879-3939

C. Frederick Oliphant III · (Employee Benefits) · Miller & Chevalier · Metropolitan Square, Suite 900 · 655 Fifteenth Street, NW · Washington, DC 20005 · 202-626-5800

Gary G. Quintiere · (Employee Benefits) · Morgan, Lewis & Bockius · 1800 M Street, NW, Suite 800N · Washington, DC 20036 · 202-467-7000

Lipman Redman · Melrod, Redman & Gartlan · 1801 K Street, NW, Suite 1100 · Washington, DC 20006 · 202-822-5300

Theodore E. Rhodes · (Employee Benefits) · Steptoe & Johnson · 1330 Connecticut Avenue, NW · Washington, DC 20036 · 202-429-3000

Mikel M. Rollyson · Davis Polk & Wardwell · 1575 I Street, NW, Suite 400 · Washington, DC 20005 · 202-789-7100

H. David Rosenbloom · Caplin & Drysdale · One Thomas Circle, NW, Suite 1100 · Washington, DC 20005 · 202-862-5000

Stanford G. Ross · Arnold & Porter · Thurman Arnold Building · 1200 New Hampshire Avenue, NW · Washington, DC 20005 · 202-872-6700

Steven J. Sacher · (Employee Benefits) · Johnson & Swanson · Columbia Square Building, Suite 660 West · 555 Thirteenth Street, NW · Washington, DC 20004 · 202-383-8760

K. Peter Schmidt · (Employee Benefits) · Arnold & Porter · Thurman Arnold Building · 1200 New Hampshire Avenue, NW · Washington, DC 20036 · 202-872-6700

Stuart E. Seigel · Williams & Connolly · Hill Building · 839 Seventeenth Street, NW · Washington, DC 20006 · 202-331-5000

Larry E. Shapiro · (Employee Benefits) · Lee, Toomey & Kent · 1200 Eighteenth Street, NW, Eighth Floor · Washington, DC 20036 · 202-457-8500

Leonard L. Silverstein · Silverstein and Mullens · 1776 K Street, NW · Washington, DC 20006 · 202-452-7989

Richard W. Skillman · (Employee Benefits) · Caplin & Drysdale · One Thomas Circle, NW, Suite 1100 · Washington, DC 20005 · 202-862-5000

William L. Sollee · (Employee Benefits) · Ivins, Phillips & Barker · 1700 Pennsylvania Avenue, NW, Suite 600 · Washington, DC 20006 · 202-393-7600

Thomas A. Troyer · Caplin & Drysdale · One Thomas Circle, NW, Suite 1100 Washington, DC 20005 · 202-862-5000

Stefan F. Tucker · Tucker, Flyer, Sanger & Lewis · 1615 L Street, NW, Suite 400 Washington, DC 20036 · 202-452-8600

John M. Vine · (Employee Benefits) · Covington & Burling · 1201 Pennsylvania Avenue, NW · P.O. Box 7566 · Washington, DC 20044 · 202-662-6000

K. Martin Worthy · Hopkins, Sutter, Hamel & Park · 888 Sixteenth Street, NW Washington, DC 20006 · 202-835-8000

TRUSTS AND ESTATES

Doris D. Blazek · Covington & Burling · 1201 Pennsylvania Avenue, NW · P.O. Box 7566 · Washington, DC 20044 · 202-662-6000

Fenton J. Burke · Dewey, Ballantine, Bushby, Palmer & Wood · 1775 Pennsylvania Avenue, NW, Suite 200 · Washington, DC 20006 · 202-862-1000

Earl M. Colson · Arent, Fox, Kintner, Plotkin & Kahn · Washington Square 1050 Connecticut Avenue, NW · Washington, DC 20036-5339 · 202-857-6000

Michael F. Curtin · Sherman, Meehan & Curtin · 1900 M Street, NW, Suite 601 Washington, DC 20036 · 202-331-7120

Sara-Ann Determan · Hogan & Hartson · Columbia Square · 555 Thirteenth Street, NW · Washington, DC 20004-1109 · 202-637-5600

Richard H. Mayfield · Craighill, Mayfield & McCally · 4910 Massachusetts Avenue, NW, Suite 215 · Washington, DC 20016 · 202-364-4242

Nancy K. Mintz · Arnold & Porter · Thurman Arnold Building · 1200 New Hampshire Avenue, NW · Washington, DC 20036 · 202-872-6700

Shirley D. Peterson · Steptoe & Johnson · 1330 Connecticut Avenue, NW · Washington, DC 20036 · 202-429-3000

FLORIDA

BANKRUPTCY LAW	**168**
BUSINESS LITIGATION	**170**
CORPORATE LAW	**172**
CRIMINAL DEFENSE	**173**
FAMILY LAW	**176**
LABOR AND EMPLOYMENT LAW	**177**
MARITIME LAW	**180**
NATURAL RESOURCES AND ENVIRONMENTAL LAW	**181**
PERSONAL INJURY LITIGATION	**182**
REAL ESTATE LAW	**186**
TAX AND EMPLOYEE BENEFITS LAW	**188**
TRUSTS AND ESTATES	**190**

BANKRUPTCY LAW

Patrick A. Barry · Blackwell Walker Fascell & Hoehl · Barnett Bank Building, Suite 1210 · One East Broward Boulevard · Fort Lauderdale, FL 33305 · 305-728-9000

Jeffrey H. Beck · Ruden, Barnett, McClosky, Smith, Schuster & Russell · NCNB Plaza, Penthouse B · 110 East Broward Boulevard · P.O. Box 1900 · Fort Lauderdale, FL 33302 · 305-764-6660

Reggie David Sanger · Shoemaker & Sanger · 208 Southeast Ninth Street · Fort Lauderdale, FL 33316 · 305-463-8547

Stephen D. Busey · Smith & Hulsey · 1800 Florida National Bank Tower · 225 Water Street · P.O. Box 53315 · Jacksonville, FL 32201-3315 · 904-359-7700

Scott L. Baena · Stroock & Stroock & Lavan · Southeast Financial Center, Suite 3300 · 200 South Biscayne Boulevard · Miami, FL 33131-2385 · 305-358-9900

John H. Genovese · Stroock & Stroock & Lavan · Southeast Financial Center, Suite 3300 · 200 South Biscayne Boulevard · Miami, FL 33131-2385 · 305-358-9900

John W. Kozyak · Kozyak Tropin & Throckmorton · Southeast Financial Center, Suite 2850 · 200 South Biscayne Boulevard · Miami, FL 33131-2335 · 305-372-1800

Timothy J. Norris · Weil, Gotshal & Manges · 701 Brickell Avenue · Miami, FL 33131 · 305-577-3100

Lawrence M. Schantz · Schantz, Schatzman, Aaronson & Berlin · Southeast Financial Center, Suite 3650 · 200 South Biscayne Boulevard · Miami, FL 33131 305-371-3100

Robert A. Schatzman · Schantz, Schatzman, Aaronson & Berlin · Southeast Financial Center, Suite 3650 · 200 South Biscayne Boulevard · Miami, FL 33131 305-371-3100

Irving M. Wolff · Holland & Knight · 1200 Brickell Avenue · P.O. Box 015441 Miami, FL 33131 · 305-374-8500

Jules S. Cohen · 808 North Mills Avenue · Orlando, FL 32803 · 407-896-4493

Michael G. Williamson · Maguire, Voorhis & Wells · Two South Orange Plaza P.O. Box 633 · Orlando, FL 32802 · 407-843-4421

Leonard H. Gilbert · Carlton, Fields, Ward, Emmanuel, Smith & Cutler · One Harbor Place · 777 South Harbour Island Drive · P.O. Box 3239 · Tampa, FL 33601 · 813-223-7000

Douglas P. McClurg · Holland & Knight · 400 North Ashley Drive, Suite 2300 P.O. Box 1288 · Tampa, FL 33601 · 813-227-8500

Harley E. Riedel II · Stichter & Riedel · 100 Madison Street · P.O. Drawer 2802 Tampa, FL 33601 · 813-229-0144

Don M. Stichter · Stichter & Riedel · 100 Madison Street · P.O. Drawer 2802 Tampa, FL 33601 · 813-229-0144

Charles M. Tatelbaum · Kass, Hodges & Massari · 1505 North Florida Avenue Tampa, FL 33601 · 813-229-0900

William Knight Zewadski · Trenam, Simmons, Kemker, Scharf, Barkin, Frye & O'Neill · Barnett Plaza, Suite 2700 · 101 East Kennedy Boulevard · P.O. Box 1102 Tampa, FL 33602 · 813-223-7474

Daniel L. Bakst · Ackerman, Bakst, Gundlach, Lauer & Zwickel · Northbridge Centre, 15th Floor · 515 North Flagler Drive · P.O. Drawer 3948 · West Palm Beach, FL 33402 · 407-655-4500

BUSINESS LITIGATION

Ruben M. Garcia · Las Olas Isles Building, Suite 300 · 1700 East Las Olas Boulevard · Fort Lauderdale, FL 33301 · 305-462-4600

John F. Corrigan · 500 North Ocean Street · Jacksonville, FL 32202 904-353-8295

John A. De Vault III · Bedell, Dittmar, De Vault & Pillans · The Bedell Building 101 East Adams Street · Jacksonville, FL 32202 · 904-353-0211

C. Harris Dittmar · Bedell, Dittmar, De Vault & Pillans · The Bedell Building 101 East Adams Street · Jacksonville, FL 32202 · 904-353-0211

Steven A. Werber · Commander Legler Werber Dawes Sadler & Howell · 200 Laura Street · P.O. Box 240 · Jacksonville, FL 32202 · 904-359-2000

James L. Armstrong III · Smathers & Thompson · 2400 Miami Center · 201 South Biscayne Boulevard · Miami, FL 33131 · 305-379-6523

Hugo L. Black, Jr. · Kelly, Black, Black, Byrne & Beasley · 1400 Alfred I. du Pont Building · 169 East Flagler Street · Miami, FL 33131 · 305-358-5700

Sam Daniels · (Appellate) · Daniels and Hicks · 100 North Biscayne Boulevard, 24th Floor · Miami, FL 33132 · 305-374-8171

Barry R. Davidson · Coll Davidson Carter Smith Salter & Barkett · 3200 Miami Center · 201 South Biscayne Boulevard · Miami, FL 33131 · 305-373-5200

Joel D. Eaton · (Appellate) · Podhurst, Orseck, Parks, Josefsberg, Eaton, Meadow & Olin · City National Bank Building, Suite 800 · 25 West Flagler Street Miami, FL 33130 · 305-358-2800

Bruce W. Greer · Greer, Homer, Cope & Bonner · 100 Southeast Second Street, Suite 3400 · Miami, FL 33131 · 305-350-5100

Mark Hicks · (Appellate) · Daniels and Hicks · 100 North Biscayne Boulevard, 24th Floor · Miami, FL 33132 · 305-374-8171

Robert C. Josefsberg · Podhurst, Orseck, Parks, Josefsberg, Eaton, Meadow & Olin · City National Bank Building, Suite 800 · 25 West Flagler Street · Miami, FL 33130 · 305-358-2800

James J. Kenny · Kenny Nachwalter & Seymour · 400 Miami Center · 201 South Biscayne Boulevard · Miami, FL 33131 · 305-358-8151

Michael Nachwalter · Kenny Nachwalter & Seymour · 400 Miami Center · 201 South Biscayne Boulevard · Miami, FL 33131 · 305-358-8151

Aaron Podhurst · Podhurst, Orseck, Parks, Josefsberg, Eaton, Meadow & Olin · City National Bank Building, Suite 800 · 25 West Flagler Street · Miami, FL 33130 · 305-358-2800

Gerald F. Richman · Floyd Pearson Richman Greer Weil Zack & Brumbaugh · 175 Northwest First Avenue, 26th Floor · Miami, FL 33128 · 305-373-4000

David L. Ross · Greenberg, Traurig, Hoffman, Lipoff, Rosen & Quentel · 1221 Brickell Avenue · Miami, FL 33131 · 305-579-0500

Richard Caldwell Smith · Coll Davidson Carter Smith Salter & Barkett · 3200 Miami Center · 201 South Biscayne Boulevard · Miami, FL 33131 · 305-373-5200

Herbert Stettin · AmeriFirst Building, Suite 2215 · One Southeast Third Avenue · Miami, FL 33131 · 305-373-3353

Parker Davidson Thomson · (Appellate) · Thomson Bohrer Werth & Razook · Southeast Financial Center, Suite 4900 · 200 South Biscayne Boulevard · Miami, FL 33131-2363 · 305-350-7200

Darryl M. Bloodworth · Dean, Mead, Egerton, Bloodworth, Capouano & Bozarth · 250 North Orange Avenue, Suite 1200 · P.O. Box 2346 · Orlando, FL 32802 · 407-841-1200

Gregory A. Presnell · Akerman, Senterfitt & Eidson · CNA Tower, 17th Floor · 255 South Orange Avenue · P.O. Box 231 · Orlando, FL 32802 · 407-843-7860

H. Edward Moore, Jr. · Moore, Hill & Westmoreland · Sun Bank Tower, Ninth Floor · 220 West Garden Street · P.O. Box 1792 · Pensacola, FL 32598-1792 · 904-434-3541

Julian D. Clarkson · (Appellate) · Holland & Knight · Barnett Bank Building, Suite 600 · P.O. Drawer 810 · Tallahassee, FL 32302 · 904-224-7000

Marvin E. Barkin · Trenam, Simmons, Kemker, Scharf, Barkin, Frye & O'Neill · Barnett Plaza, Suite 2700 · 101 East Kennedy Boulevard · P.O. Box 1102 · Tampa, FL 33601 · 813-223-7474

William C. Frye · Trenam, Simmons, Kemker, Scharf, Barkin, Frye & O'Neill · Barnett Plaza, Suite 2700 · 101 East Kennedy Boulevard · P.O. Box 1102 · Tampa, FL 33601 · 813-223-7474

Thomas C. MacDonald, Jr. · Shackleford, Farrior, Stallings & Evans · East Kennedy Boulevard, Suite 1400 · P.O. Box 3324 · Tampa, FL 33601 · 813-273-5000

Sylvia H. Walbolt · Carlton, Fields, Ward, Emmanuel, Smith & Cutler · One Harbor Place · 777 South Harbour Island Drive · P.O. Box 3239 · Tampa, FL 33601 · 813-223-7000

Larry A. Klein · (Appellate) · Klein & Beranek · Flagler Center, Suite 503 · 501 South Flagler Drive · West Palm Beach, FL 33401 · 407-659-5455

Sidney A. Stubbs, Jr. · Jones, Foster, Johnston & Stubbs · Flagler Center Tower · 505 South Flagler Drive · P.O. Drawer E · West Palm Beach, FL 33402-3475 · 407-659-3000

CORPORATE LAW

William H. Adams III · Mahoney Adams Milam Surface & Grimsley · Barnett Bank Building · 100 Laura Street · P.O. Box 4099 · Jacksonville, FL 32201 · 904-354-1100

Kenneth M. Kirschner · Kirschner, Main, Petrie & Graham · 10 West Adams Street · Jacksonville, FL 32202 · 904-354-4141

Mitchell W. Legler · Commander Legler Werber Dawes Sadler & Howell · 200 Laura Street · Jacksonville, FL 32202 · 904-359-2000

Luther F. Sadler, Jr. · Commander Legler Werber Dawes Sadler & Howell · 200 Laura Street · Jacksonville, FL 32202 · 904-359-2000

William O. E. Henry · Holland & Knight · 800 North Magnolia Avenue, Penthouse A · P.O. Box 1526 · Orlando, FL 32802 · 407-425-8500

Cesar L. Alvarez · Greenberg, Traurig, Hoffman, Lipoff, Rosen & Quentel 1221 Brickell Avenue · Miami, FL 33131 · 305-579-0500

James W. Beasley, Jr. · Tew Jorden Schulte & Beasley · Barnett Building, 22nd Floor · 701 Brickell Avenue · Miami, FL 33131-2395 · 305-371-2600

Bowman Brown · Shutts & Bowen · Edward Ball Building Miami Center, Suite 1500 · 201 South Biscayne Boulevard · Miami, FL 33131 · 305-358-6300

Jerry B. Crockett · Steel Hector & Davis · 4000 Southeast Financial Center · 200 South Biscayne Boulevard · Miami, FL 33131-2398 · 305-577-2800

Larry J. Hoffman · Greenberg, Traurig, Hoffman, Lipoff, Rosen & Quentel 1221 Brickell Avenue · Miami, FL 33131 · 305-579-0500

Thomas R. McGuigan · Steel Hector & Davis · 4000 Southeast Financial Center 200 South Biscayne Boulevard · Miami, FL 33131-2398 · 305-577-2800

Noel H. Nation · Baker & McKenzie · Barnett Building, Suite 1600 · 701 Brickell Avenue · Miami, FL 33131 · 305-789-8900

Charles Edison Harris · Smith, Mackinnon, Mathews, Harris & Christiansen CNA Tower, Suite 850 · 255 South Orange Avenue · P.O. Box 2254 · Orlando, FL 32802-2254 · 407-843-7300

Warren J. Frazier · Shackleford, Farrior, Stallings & Evans · 501 East Kennedy Boulevard, Suite 1400 · P.O. Box 3324 · Tampa, FL 33601 · 813-273-5000

Michael L. Jamieson · Holland & Knight · 400 North Ashley Drive, Suite 2300 P.O. Box 1288 · Tampa, FL 33601 · 813-227-8500

Richard M. Leisner · Trenam, Simmons, Kemker, Scharf, Barkin, Frye & O'Neill · Barnett Plaza, Suite 2700 · 101 East Kennedy Boulevard · P.O. Box 1102 Tampa, FL 33601 · 813-223-7474

Robert C. Rasmussen · Glenn, Rasmussen, Fogarty, Merryday & Russo · Ashley Tower, Suite 1300 · 100 South Ashley Drive · P.O. Box 3333 · Tampa, FL 33601-3333 · 813-229-3333

CRIMINAL DEFENSE

Joseph G. Donahey, Jr. · Tanney, Forde, Donahey, Eno & Tanney · 13584 Forty-Ninth Street North, Suite A · Clearwater, FL 33520 · 813-576-6270

Edward A. Carhart · 717 Ponce de Leon Boulevard, Suite 331 · Coral Gables, FL 33134 · 305-445-1122

J. David Bogenschutz · Kay and Bogenschutz · 633 Southeast Third Avenue, Suite 4F · Fort Lauderdale, FL 33301 · 305-764-0033

Bruce M. Lyons · Lyons and Sanders · 600 Northeast Third Avenue · Fort Lauderdale, FL 33304-2689 · 305-467-8700

Bruce S. Rogow · Nova University Law Center · 3100 Southwest Ninth Avenue Fort Lauderdale, FL 33315 · 305-524-2465

Bruce E. Wagner · 1520 Southeast Third Avenue · Fort Lauderdale, FL 33316 305-467-2602

Bruce A. Zimet · One Financial Plaza, Suite 2612 · Fort Lauderdale, FL 33394 305-764-7081

Larry G. Turner · Turner, Kurrus & Griscti · 204 West University Avenue, Suite 6 P.O. Box 508 · Gainesville, FL 32602 · 904-375-4460

Edward M. Booth · Booth and Arnold · 1301 Gulf Life Drive · Jacksonville, FL 32207 · 904-399-5400

Henry M. Coxe III · Coxe & Schemer · 424 East Monroe Street · Jacksonville, FL 32202 · 904-356-2389

Albert J. Datz · Datz, Jacobson & Lembcke · Independent Square, Suite 2902 One Independent Drive · Jacksonville, FL 32202 · 904-355-5467

C. Harris Dittmar · Bedell, Dittmar, De Vault & Pillans · The Bedell Building 101 East Adams Street · Jacksonville, FL 32202 · 904-353-0211

William J. Sheppard · Sheppard & White · 215 Washington Street · Jacksonville, FL 32202 · 904-356-9661

F. Lee Bailey · Bailey, Gerstein, Rashkind & Dresnick · 4770 Biscayne Boulevard, Suite 950 · Miami, FL 33137 · 305-573-4400

Donald I. Bierman · Bierman, Shohat & Loewy · 175 Northwest Avenue, Suite 1730 · Miami, FL 33128 · 305-358-7000

Roy E. Black · Black & Furci · Miami Center, Suite 1300 · 201 South Biscayne Boulevard · Miami, FL 33131 · 305-371-6421

Irwin J. Block · Fine Jacobson Schwartz Nash Block & England · 100 Southeast Second Street · Miami, FL 33131 · 305-577-4050

Jack M. Denaro · Dadeland Square, Suite 504 · 7700 North Kendall · Miami, FL 33156 · 305-274-9550

Richard E. Gerstein · Bailey, Gerstein, Rashkind & Dresnick · 4770 Biscayne Boulevard, Suite 950 · Miami, FL 33137 · 305-573-4400

Joel Hirschhorn · 2766 Douglas Road · Miami, FL 33133 · 305-445-5320

James J. Hogan · 2400 South Dixie Highway, Suite 200 · Miami, FL 33133 305-854-8989

Robert C. Josefsberg · Podhurst, Orseck, Parks, Josefsberg, Eaton, Meadow & Olin · City National Bank Building, Suite 800 · 25 West Flagler Street · Miami, FL 33130 · 305-358-2800

Theodore Klein · Fine Jacobson Schwartz Nash Block & England · 100 Southeast Second Street · Miami, FL 33131 · 305-577-4050

Albert J. Krieger · 1899 South Bayshore Drive · Miami, FL 33133 · 305-854-0050

E. David Rosen · New World Tower, Suite 2910 · 100 North Biscayne Boulevard Miami, FL 33132 · 305-377-3737

Edward R. Shohat · Bierman, Shohat & Loewy · 175 Northwest Avenue, Suite 1730 · Miami, FL 33128 · 305-358-7000

Neal R. Sonnett · Sonnett, Sale & Kuehne · Atico Building, Fifth Floor · 200 Southeast First Street · Miami, FL 33131 · 305-358-7477

James M. Russ · Tinker Building · 18 West Pine Street · Orlando, FL 32801 407-849-6050

E. C. Deeno Kitchen · Kitchen & High · 1102 North Gadsden Street · P.O. Box 1854 · Tallahassee, FL 32302 · 904-561-6219

Murray M. Wadsworth · Wadsworth & Davis · 203 North Gadsden Street, Suite One · P.O. Box 10529 · Tallahassee, FL 32302-2529 · 904-224-9037

Ronald K. Cacciatore · 600 North Florida Avenue, Suite 1535 · 412 East Madison Street · Tampa, FL 33602 · 813-223-4831

Barry A. Cohen · Cohen and Reback · 100 Twiggs Street, Suite 4000 · Tampa, FL 33602 · 813-225-1655

Gary R. Trombley · Winkles, Trombley, Kynes & Markman · 707 North Franklin Street, 10th Floor · P.O. Box 3356 · Tampa, FL 33602 · 813-229-7918

FAMILY LAW

Brenda M. Abrams · Abrams & Abrams · 3341 Cornelia Drive · Coconut Grove, FL 33133 · 305-858-8828

Alan J. Rubinstein · 2126 First Street · P.O. Box 368 · Fort Myers, FL 33902 813-332-3400

A. Matthew Miller · Miller, Schwartz & Miller · 4040 Sheridan Street · Hollywood, FL 33021 · 305-962-2000

James Fox Miller · Miller, Schwartz & Miller · 4040 Sheridan Street · Hollywood, FL 33021 · 305-962-2000

Edward M. Booth · Booth and Arnold · 1301 Gulf Life Drive · Jacksonville, FL 32207 · 904-399-5400

Albert J. Datz · Datz, Jacobson & Lembcke · Independent Square, Suite 2902 Jacksonville, FL 32202 · 904-355-5467

Elliot Zisser · Zisser, Robison, Spohrer & Wilner · 624 Ocean Street · Jacksonville, FL 32202 · 904-354-8455

Harold Peter Barkas · 600 Concord Building · Miami, FL 33130 · 305-374-0565

Marsha B. Elser · 1575 Courthouse Tower · 44 West Flagler Street · Miami, FL 33130 · 305-577-0090

Melvyn B. Frumkes · Frumkes and Greene · 100 North Biscayne Boulevard Miami, FL 33132 · 305-371-5600

Maurice Jay Kutner · 28 West Flagler Street, 12th Floor · Miami, FL 33130-1801 305-377-9411

Ray H. Pearson · Floyd Pearson Richman Greer Weil Zack & Brumbaugh · 175 Northwest First Avenue, 26th Floor · Miami, FL 33128 · 305-373-4000

Eleanor L. Schockett · 717 Ingraham Building · 25 Southeast Second Avenue Miami, FL 33131 · 305-374-3533

Burton Young · Young, Stern & Tannenbaum · 17071 West Dixie Highway P.O. Box 600 550 · North Miami Beach, FL 33160 · 305-945-1851

Michael R. Walsh · 326 North Fern Creek Avenue · Orlando, FL 32803 407-896-9431

David H. Levin · Levin, Middlebrooks, Mabie, Thomas, Mayes & Mitchell Seville Tower · 226 South Palafox Street · P.O. Box 12308 · Pensacola, FL 32581 904-435-7000

Arthur D. Ginsburg · Icard, Merrill, Cullis, Timm, Furen & Ginsburg · 2033 Main Street, Suite 600 · Sarasota, FL 34237 · 813-366-8100

Robert W. Fields · Garcia & Fields · 101 East Kennedy Boulevard, Suite 2560 Tampa, FL 33602 · 813-222-8500

Stephen W. Sessums · Sessums & Mason · 307 South Magnolia Avenue · Tampa, FL 33606 · 813-251-9200

James P. O'Flarity · 215 Fifth Street, Suite 108 · West Palm Beach, FL 33401 407-659-4666

Donald J. Sasser · 310 Okeechobee Boulevard · P.O. Drawer M · West Palm Beach, FL 33402 · 407-659-5174

Ria Simon · Jones, Foster, Johnston & Stubbs · 505 South Flagler Drive, Suite 1100 · West Palm Beach, FL 33401 · 407-659-3000

LABOR AND EMPLOYMENT LAW

Rodney W. Smith · (Labor; Individuals) · 409 Northeast First Street · P.O. Box 628 · Alachua, FL 32615 · 904-462-4005

Neil Chonin · (Individuals) · Chonin & Sher · 304 Palermo Avenue · Coral Gables, FL 33134 · 305-443-5125

William H. Andrews · (Management) · Coffman, Coleman, Andrews & Groggan 2065 Herschel Street · P.O. Box 40089 · Jacksonville, FL 32203 · 904-389-5161

Daniel R. Coffman, Jr. · (Management) · Coffman, Coleman, Andrews & Groggan · 2065 Herschel Street · P.O. Box 40089 · Jacksonville, FL 32203 · 904-389-5161

Patrick D. Coleman · (Management) · Coffman, Coleman, Andrews & Groggan 2065 Herschel Street · P.O. Box 40089 · Jacksonville, FL 32203 · 904-389-5161

Guy O. Farmer II · (Management) · Foley & Lardner · 200 West Forsythe Street, Suite 1700 · P.O. Box 1290 · Jacksonville, FL 32201-1290 · 904-356-2029

Michael K. Grogan · (Management) · Coffman, Coleman, Andrews & Groggan 2065 Herschel Street · P.O. Box 40089 · Jacksonville, FL 32203 · 904-389-5161

John F. Kattman · (Labor) · Kattman, Eshelman & MacLennan · 1920 San Marco Boulevard · Jacksonville, FL 32207 · 904-398-1229

Lacy Mahon, Jr. · (Labor) · Lacy Mahon, Jr. & Mark H. Mahon · Blackstone Building, Suite 1120 · 233 East Bay Street · Jacksonville, FL 32202 · 904-354-3526

Michael W. Casey III · (Management) · Muller, Mintz, Kornreich, Caldwell, Casey, Crosland & Bramnick · Southeast Financial Center, Suite 3600 · 200 South Biscayne Boulevard · Miami, FL 33131-2338 · 305-358-5500

Elizabeth J. du Fresne · (Individuals) · Steel Hector & Davis · 4000 Southeast Financial Center, 41st Floor · Miami, FL 33131 · 305-577-2855

Joseph Z. Fleming · (Management) · 620 Ingraham Building · 25 Southeast Second Avenue · Miami, FL 33131 · 305-373-0791

Peter J. Hurtgen · (Management) · Morgan, Lewis & Bockius · 5300 Southeast Financial Center · 200 South Biscayne Boulevard · Miami, FL 33131 · 305-579-0300

Jesse S. Hogg · (Management) · Hogg, Allen, Ryce, Norton & Blue · 121 Majorca, Third Floor · Miami, FL 33134 · 305-445-7801

Joseph H. Kaplan · (Labor) · Kaplan, Sicking & Bloom · 1951 Northwest 17th Avenue · P.O. Box 520337 · Miami, FL 33152 · 305-325-1661

David V. Kornreich · (Management) · Muller, Mintz, Kornreich, Caldwell, Casey, Crosland & Bramnick · Southeast Financial Center, Suite 3600 · 200 South Biscayne Boulevard · Miami, FL 33131-2338 · 305-358-5500

Ira J. Kurzban · (Individuals) · Kurzban Kurzban and Weinger · Plaza 2650, Second Floor · 2650 Southwest 27th Avenue · Miami, FL 33133 · 305-444-0060

David M. Lipman · (Individuals) · Lipman & Weisberg · 5901 Southwest 74th Street, Suite 304 · Miami, FL 33143 · 305-662-2600

George F. Lynch · (Management) · Squire, Sanders & Dempsey · 3000 Miami Center · 201 South Biscayne Boulevard · Miami, FL 33131 · 305-577-8700

Robert A. Sugarman · (Labor) · Sugarman & Susskind · 5959 Blue Lagoon Drive, Suite 150 · Miami, FL 33126 · 305-264-2121

Howard S. Susskind · (Labor) · 5959 Blue Lagoon Drive, Suite 150 · Miami, FL 33126 · 305-264-2121

Robert E. Weisberg · (Individuals) · Lipman & Weisberg · 5901 Southwest 74th Street, Suite 304 · Miami, FL 33143 · 305-662-2600

James G. Brown · (Management) · Richeson and Brown · 135 North Magnolia Avenue · P.O. Box 3006 · Orlando, FL 32802 · 407-425-7755

Norman F. Burke · (Management) · Foley & Lardner, van den Berg, Gay, Burke, Wilson & Arkin · 111 North Orange Avenue · P.O. Box 2193 · Orlando, FL 32802-2193 · 407-423-7656

Richard A. DuRose · (Management) · Smith & Schnacke · One Dupont Center, Suite 1300 · 390 North Orange Avenue · P.O. Box 4961 · Orlando, FL 32802 407-839-6000

Joseph Egan, Jr. · (Labor) · Egan, Lev & Siwica · 918 Lucerne Terrace · Orlando, FL 32806 · 407-422-1400

Thomas C. Garwood, Jr. · (Management) · Garwood & McKenna · 322 East Pine Street · P.O. Box 60 · Orlando, FL 32801 · 407-841-9496

Tobe M. Lev · Egan, Lev & Siwica · 918 Lucerne Terrace · Orlando, FL 32806 407-422-1400

Thomas J. Pilacek · (Labor; Individuals) · Pilacek & Cohen · 1516 East Hillcrest Street, Suite 204 · Orlando, FL 32803 · 407-894-1888

Leo P. Rock, Jr. · (Management) · Gray, Harris and Robinson · Southeast Bank Building, Suite 1200 · 201 East Pine Street · P.O. Box 3068 · Orlando, FL 32802 407-843-8880

Thomas W. Brooks · (Labor; Individuals) · Meyer, Brooks & Cooper · 911 East Park Avenue · Tallahasee, FL 32301 · 904-681-9343

John-Edward Alley · (Management) · Alley and Alley · 205 Brush Street · P.O. Box 1427 · Tampa, FL 33601 · 813-229-6481

James M. Blue · (Management) · Hogg, Allen, Ryce, Norton & Blue · 111 Parker Street, Suite 200 · Tampa, FL 33606 · 813-251-1210

John J. Chamblee, Jr. · (Labor) · Chamblee, Miles & Grizzard · 202 Cardy Street Tampa, FL 33606 · 813-251-4542

John E. Dinkel III · (Management) · MacFarland, Ferguson, Allison & Kelly · 215 Madison Street · P.O. Box 1531 · Tampa, FL 33602 · 813-223-2411

Thomas M. Gonzalez · (Management) · Thompson, Sizemore & Gonzalez · The Plaza on the Mall, Suite 838 · 201 East Kennedy Boulevard · P.O. Box 639 Tampa, FL 33601 · 813-273-0050

Frank E. Hamilton, Jr. · (Labor) · Frank Hamilton & Associates · 2620 West Kennedy Boulevard · Tampa, FL 33609 · 813-879-9842

Paul A. Saad · (Management) · Carlton, Fields, Ward, Emmanuel, Smith & Cutler · One Harbor Place · 777 South Harbour Island Drive · P.O. Box 3239 Tampa, FL 33601 · 813-223-7000

William E. Sizemore · (Management) · Thompson, Sizemore & Gonzalez · The Plaza on the Mall, Suite 838 · 201 East Kennedy Boulevard · P.O. Box 639 Tampa, FL 33601 · 813-273-0050

Harrison C. Thompson, Jr. · (Management) · Thompson, Sizemore & Gonzalez The Plaza on the Mall, Suite 838 · 201 East Kennedy Boulevard · P.O. Box 639 Tampa, FL 33601 · 813-273-0050

Peter W. Zinober · (Management) · Zinober & Burr · First Union Bank Building, Suite 1206 · 501 East Kennedy Boulevard · Tampa, FL 33602 · 813-224-9004

MARITIME LAW

James F. Moseley · Taylor, Moseley & Joyner · 501 West Bay Street · Jacksonville, FL 32202 · 904-356-1306

G. Morton Good · Kelley Drye and Warren · Miami Center, Suite 2400 · 201 South Biscayne Boulevard · Miami, FL 33131 · 305-379-6523

Frank J. Marston · Fowler, White, Burnett, Hurley, Banick & Strickroot · Courthouse Center, 11th Floor · 175 Northwest First Avenue · Miami, FL 33128-1817 305-358-6550

David G. Hanlon · Shackleford, Farrior, Stallings & Evans · East Kennedy Boulevard, Suite 1400 · P.O. Box 3324 · Tampa, FL 33601 · 813-273-5000

Brendan P. O'Sullivan · Fowler, White, Gillen, Boggs, Villareal and Banker · 501 East Kennedy Boulevard, Suite 1700 · P.O. Box 1438 · Tampa, FL 33601 813-228-7411

Roger A. Vaughan, Jr. · (Plaintiffs) · Wagner, Cunningham, Vaughan & McLaughlin · 708 Jackson Street (Corner of Jefferson) · Tampa, FL 33602 813-223-7421

Dewey R. Villareal, Jr. · Fowler, White, Gillen, Boggs, Villareal and Banker · 501 East Kennedy Boulevard, Suite 1700 · P.O. Box 1438 · Tampa, FL 33601 813-228-7411

NATURAL RESOURCES AND ENVIRONMENTAL LAW

Donald C. McClosky · Ruden, Barnett, McClosky, Smith, Schuster & Russell NCNB Building, Penthouse B · 110 East Broward Boulevard · P.O. Box 1900 Fort Lauderdale, FL 33302 · 305-764-6660

Frank X. Friedmann, Jr. · Rogers, Towers, Bailey, Jones & Gay · 1300 Gulf Life Drive · Jacksonville, FL 32207 · 904-398-3911

Alan S. Gold · Greenberg, Traurig, Hoffman, Lipoff, Rosen & Quentel · 1221 Brickell Avenue · Miami, FL 33131 · 305-579-0500

Anthony J. O'Donnell, Jr. · (Plaintiffs) · Akerman, Senterfitt & Eidson · 801 Brickell Avenue, 24th Floor · Miami, FL 33131 · 305-374-5600

Stanley B. Price · Fine Jacobson Schwartz Nash Block & England · 100 Southeast Second Street · Miami, FL 33131 · 305-577-4000

Clifford A. Schulman · Greenberg, Traurig, Hoffman, Lipoff, Rosen & Quentel 1221 Brickell Avenue · Miami, FL 33131 · 305-579-0500

Robert H. Traurig · Greenberg, Traurig, Hoffman, Lipoff, Rosen & Quentel 1221 Brickell Avenue · Miami, FL 33131 · 305-579-0500

Robert J. Pleus, Jr. · Smathers, Pleus, Adams, Fassett & Divine · 940 Highland Avenue · P.O. Box 2747 · Orlando, FL 32802 · 407-422-8116

John G. Fletcher II · 7600 Red Road, Suite 115 · Miami, FL 33143 · 305-665-7521

Wade L. Hopping · Hopping Boyd Green & Sams · First Florida Bank Building, Suite 420 · P.O. Box 6526 · Tallahassee, FL 32314 · 904-222-7500

Joseph W. Landers, Jr. · Landers & Parsons · 310 West College Avenue, Third Floor · P.O. Box 271 · Tallahassee, FL 32302 · 904-681-0311

Robert M. Rhodes · Steel, Hector & Davis · 310 West College Avenue, Second Floor · Tallahassee, FL 32301-1848 · 904-222-4192

Gary P. Sams · Hopping Boyd Green & Sams · First Florida Bank Building, Suite 420 · P.O. Box 6526 · Tallahassee, FL 32314 · 904-222-7500

Roger D. Schwenke · Carlton, Fields, Ward, Emmanuel, Smith & Cutler · One Harbor Place · 777 South Harbour Island Drive · P.O. Box 3239 · Tampa, FL 33601 · 813-223-7000

William R. Boose III · Boose Casey Ciklin Lubitz Martens McBane & O'Connell Northbridge Tower I, 19th Floor · 515 North Flagler Drive · West Palm Beach, FL 33401 · 407-832-5900

PERSONAL INJURY LITIGATION

Rex Conrad · (Defendants) · Conrad, Scherer & James · 633 South Federal Highway · P.O. Box 14723 · Fort Lauderdale, FL 33302 · 305-462-5500

Joseph S. Kashi · (Defendants) · Conrad, Scherer & James · 633 South Federal Highway · P.O. Box 14723 · Fort Lauderdale, FL 33302 · 305-462-5500

Jon E. Krupnick · (Plaintiffs) · Krupnick, Campbell, Malone and Roselli · 700 Southeast Third Avenue · Fort Lauderdale, FL 33316 · 305-763-8181

Sheldon J. Schlesinger · (Plaintiffs) · 1212 Southeast Third Avenue · Fort Lauderdale, FL 33316 · 305-467-8800

Dianne Jay Weaver · (Plaintiffs) · Weaver, Weaver, Lardin & Petrie · 500 Southeast Sixth Street · P.O. Box 14663 · Fort Lauderdale, FL 33302-4663 · 305-763-2511

Robert J. Beckham · (Plaintiffs) · Beckham, McAliley & Schulz · Independent Square, Suite 3131 · One Independent Drive · Jacksonville, FL 32202 904-354-9022

James E. Cobb · (Defendants) · Mathews, Osborne, McNatt & Cobb · 1500 American Heritage Life Building · 11 East Forsyth Street · Jacksonville, FL 32202 904-354-0624

William C. Gentry · (Plaintiffs) · Gentry & Phillips · Six East Bay Street, Suite 400 · P.O. Box 837 · Jacksonville, FL 32201 · 904-356-4100

James C. Rinaman, Jr. · (Defendants) · Marks, Gray, Conroy & Gibbs · 800 Southeast Bank Building · 1200 Gulf Life Drive · P.O. Box 447 · Jacksonville, FL 32201 · 904-398-0900

Sammy Cacciatore · (Plaintiffs) · Nance, Cacciatore and Sisserson · 525 North Harbor City Boulevard · Melbourne, FL 32935 · 407-254-8416

James C. Blecke · (Appellate) · 19 West Flagler Street · Miami, FL 33130 305-358-5999

Henry Burnett · (Defendants) · Fowler, White, Burnett, Hurley, Banick & Strickroot · City National Bank Building, Fifth Floor · 25 West Flagler Street Miami, FL 33130 · 305-358-6550

Bill Colson · (Plaintiffs) · Colson, Hicks & Eidson · Southeast Financial Center, 54th Floor · 200 South Biscayne Boulevard · Miami, FL 33131-2310 · 305-373-5400

Joel D. Eaton · (Appellate) · Podhurst, Orseck, Parks, Josefsberg, Eaton, Meadow & Olin · City National Bank Building, Suite 800 · 25 West Flagler Street Miami, FL 33130 · 305-358-2800

David C. Goodwin · (Defendants) · Morgan Lewis & Bockius · 5300 Southeast Financial Center · 200 South Biscayne Boulevard · Miami, FL 33131-2339 305-579-0300

William M. Hicks · (Plaintiffs) · Colson, Hicks & Eidson · Southeast Financial Center, 54th Floor · 200 South Biscayne Boulevard · Miami, FL 33131-2310 305-373-5400

Edward A. Moss · Anderson, Moss, Russo, Gievers & Cohen · New World Tower, Suite 2300 · 100 North Biscayne Boulevard · Miami, FL 33132 305-358-5171

Robert L. Parks · Podhurst, Orseck, Parks, Josefsberg, Eaton, Meadow & Olin · City National Bank Building, Suite 800 · 25 West Flagler Street · Miami, FL 33130 · 305-358-2800

Aaron Podhurst · Podhurst, Orseck, Parks, Josefsberg, Eaton, Meadow & Olin · City National Bank Building, Suite 800 · 25 West Flagler Street · Miami, FL 33130 · 305-358-2800

Stanley M. Rosenblatt · (Plaintiffs) · Concord Building, 11th & 12th Floors · 66 West Flagler Street · Miami, FL 33130 · 305-374-6131

Murray Sams, Jr. · (Plaintiffs) · Sams, Ward, Yanowitch, Spiegel & Alger · 700 Concord Building · 66 West Flagler Street · Miami, FL 33130 · 305-374-3181

J. B. Spence · (Plaintiffs) · Spence, Payne, Masington, Grossman & Needle · 2950 Southwest 27th Avenue, Suite 300 · Miami, FL 33133 · 305-447-0641

Larry S. Stewart · (Plaintiffs) · Stewart Tilghman Fox & Bianchi · 44 West Flagler Street, Suite 1900 · Miami, FL 33130-1808 · 305-358-6644

Joe N. Unger · (Appellate) · 66 West Flagler Street · Miami, FL 33130 · 305-374-5500

Michael Maher · (Plaintiffs) · Maher, Overchuck and Langa · 90 East Livingston Street, Suite 200 · Orlando, FL 32801 · 407-849-6510

Fredric G. Levin · (Plaintiffs) · Levin, Middlebrooks, Mabie, Thomas, Mayes & Mitchell · Seville Tower · 226 South Palafox Street · P.O. Box 12308 · Pensacola, FL 32581 · 904-435-7000

Lefferts L. Mabie, Jr. · (Plaintiffs) · Levin, Middlebrooks, Mabie, Thomas, Mayes & Mitchell · Seville Tower · 226 South Palafox Street · P.O. Box 12308 Pensacola, FL 32581 · 904-435-7000

Alan C. Sundberg · (Appellate) · Carlton, Fields, Ward, Emmanuel, Smith & Cutler · One Harbor Place · 777 South Harbour Island Drive · P.O. Box 3239 Tampa, FL 33601 · 813-223-7000

Robert E. Banker · (Defendants) · Fowler, White, Gillen, Boggs, Villareal and Banker · 501 East Kennedy Boulevard, Suite 1700 · P.O. Box 1438 · Tampa, FL 33601 · 813-228-7411

Anthony W. Cunningham · (Plaintiffs) · Wagner, Cunningham, Vaughan & McLaughlin · 708 Jackson Street (Corner of Jefferson) · Tampa, FL 33602 813-223-7421

T. Paine Kelly, Jr. · (Defendants) · MacFarland, Ferguson, Allison & Kelly · 215 Madison Street · P.O. Box 1531 · Tampa, FL 33602 · 813-223-2411

Roger A. Vaughan, Jr. · (Plaintiffs) · Wagner, Cunningham, Vaughan & McLaughlin · 708 Jackson Street (Corner of Jefferson) · Tampa, FL 33602 813-223-7421

F. William Wagner · (Plaintiffs) · Wagner, Cunningham, Vaughan & McLaughlin 708 Jackson Street (Corner of Jefferson) · Tampa, FL 33602 · 813-223-7421

C. Steven Yerrid · Stagg, Hardy & Yerrid · One Tampa City Center, Suite 2600 Tampa, FL 33602 · 813-223-4456

Theodore Babbitt · (Plaintiffs) · Babbitt and Hazouri · 1801 Australian Avenue South · P.O. Drawer 024426 · West Palm Beach, FL 33402 · 407-684-2500

John R. Beranek · (Appellate) · Klein & Beranek · Flagler Center, Suite 503 · 501 South Flagler Drive · West Palm Beach, FL 33401 · 407-659-5455

Edna L. Caruso · (Appellate) · Barrister's Building, Suite 4B · 1615 Forum Place West Palm Beach, FL 33401 · 407-686-8010

Al J. Cone · (Plaintiffs) · Cone, Wagner, Nugent, Johnson, Roth & Romano · 505 South Flagler Drive, Suite 200-300 · P.O. Box 3466 · West Palm Beach, FL 33402 407-655-5200

Fred A. Hazouri · (Plaintiffs) · Babbitt and Hazouri · 1801 Australian Avenue South · P.O. Drawer 024426 · West Palm Beach, FL 33402 · 407-832-0800

Larry A. Klein · (Appellate) · Klein & Beranek · Flagler Center, Suite 503 · 501 South Flagler Drive · West Palm Beach, FL 33401 · 407-659-5455

Lake Lytal, Jr. · (Plaintiffs) · Lytal & Reiter · 515 North Flagler Drive, 10th Floor P.O. Box 024466 · West Palm Beach, FL 33402 · 407-655-1990

Robert M. Montgomery, Jr. · (Plaintiffs) · Montgomery, Searcy and Denney 2139 Palm Beach Lakes Boulevard · P.O. Drawer 3626 · West Palm Beach, FL 33402 · 407-686-6300

Joseph J. Reiter · (Plaintiffs) · Lytal & Reiter · 515 North Flagler Drive, 10th Floor · P.O. Box 024466 · West Palm Beach, FL 33402 · 407-655-1990

Christian D. Searcy, Sr. · (Plaintiffs) · Montgomery, Searcy and Denney · 2139 Palm Beach Lakes Boulevard · P.O. Drawer 3626 · West Palm Beach, FL 33402 407-686-6300

REAL ESTATE LAW

Donald C. McClosky · Ruden, Barnett, McClosky, Smith, Schuster & Russell · The North Carolina National Bank Building · 110 East Broward Boulevard · P.O. Box 1900 · Fort Lauderdale, FL 33302 · 305-764-6660

Charles E. Commander III · Commander Legler Werber Dawes Sadler & Howell · 200 Laura Street · P.O. Box 240 · Jacksonville, FL 32202 · 904-359-2000

David M. Foster · Rogers, Towers, Bailey, Jones & Gay · 1300 Gulf Life Drive · Jacksonville, FL 32207 · 904-398-3911

Robert O. Mickler · Martin, Ade, Birchfield & Mickler · 3000 Independent Square · One Independent Drive · P.O. Box 59 · Jacksonville, FL 32201 · 904-354-2050

James S. Taylor · Ulmer, Murchison, Ashby & Taylor · First Union Bank Building · 200 West Forsyth Street · P.O. Box 479 · Jacksonville, FL 32201 · 904-354-5652

Henry M. Kittleson · Holland & Knight · 92 Lake Wire Drive · P.O. Box 32092 · Lakeland, FL 33802 · 813-682-1161

Lawrence Godofsky · Greenberg, Traurig, Hoffman, Lipoff, Rosen & Quentel · 1221 Brickell Avenue · Miami, FL 33131 · 305-579-0500

Matthew B. Gorson · Greenberg, Traurig, Hoffman, Lipoff, Rosen & Quentel · 1221 Brickell Avenue · Miami, FL 33131 · 305-579-0500

Burton A. Hartman · Squire, Sanders & Dempsey · 3000 Miami Center · 201 South Biscayne Boulevard · Miami, FL 33131 · 305-577-8700

David S. Kenin · Greenberg, Traurig, Hoffman, Lipoff, Rosen & Quentel · 1221 Brickell Avenue · Miami, FL 33131 · 305-579-0500

Robert E. Livingston · Patton & Kanner · 150 Southeast Second Avenue, Third Floor · Miami, FL 33131 · 305-373-5761

Albert D. Quentel · Greenberg, Traurig, Hoffman, Lipoff, Rosen & Quentel · 1221 Brickell Avenue · Miami, FL 33131 · 305-579-0500

Donald S. Rosenberg · Rosenberg & Reisman · 2600 AmeriFirst Building · One Southeast Third Avenue · Miami, FL 33131 · 305-358-2600

Morris Rosenberg · Rosenberg & Reisman · 2600 AmeriFirst Building · One Southeast Third Avenue · Miami, FL 33131 · 305-358-2600

Robert H. Traurig · Greenberg, Traurig, Hoffman, Lipoff, Rosen & Quentel 1221 Brickell Avenue · Miami, FL 33131 · 305-579-0500

Leo Rose, Jr. · Therrel Baisden & Meyer Weiss · Sun Bank/Miami, Suite 600 1111 Lincoln Road · Miami Beach, FL 33139 · 305-672-1921

Harry B. Smith · Ruden, Barnett, McClosky & Smith · Barnett Bank Building, Suite 1900 · 701 Brickell Avenue · Miami Beach, FL 33131 · 305-789-2700

John F. Lowndes · Lowndes, Drosdick, Doster, Kantor & Reed · 215 North Eola Drive · P.O. Box 2809 · Orlando, FL 32802 · 407-843-4600

James K. Rush · Anderson & Rush · 322 East Central Boulevard · P.O. Box 2288 Orlando, FL 32802 · 305-849-0020

Patrick G. Emmanuel · Emmanuel, Sheppard & Condon · 30 South Spring Street P.O. Box 1271 · Pensacola, FL 32596 · 904-433-6581

Anthony S. Battaglia · Battaglia, Ross, Hastings and Dicus · 980 Tyrone Boulevard · P.O. Box 41100 · Saint Petersburg, FL 33743 · 813-381-2300

Joseph B. Cofer · Carlton, Fields, Ward, Emmanuel, Smith & Cutler · One Harbor Place · 777 South Harbour Island Drive · P.O. Box 3239 · Tampa, FL 33601 · 813-223-7000

Thomas N. Henderson III · Hill, Ward & Henderson · 101 East Kennedy Boulevard, Suite 3700 · P.O. Box 2231 · Tampa, FL 33601 · 813-221-3900

Stephen J. Mitchell · Annis, Mitchell, Cockey, Edwards & Roehn · One Tampa City Center Building, Suite 2100 · P.O. Box 3433 · Tampa, FL 33601 · 813-229-3321

James M. Reed · Reed & Black · 101 East Kennedy Boulevard, Suite 3650 · P.O. Box 438 · Tampa, FL 33601-0438 · 813-221-3330

Leslie D. Scharf · Trenam, Simmons, Kemker, Scharf, Barkin, Frye & O'Neill Barnett Plaza, Suite 2700 · 101 East Kennedy Boulevard · P.O. Box 1102 · Tampa, FL 33601 · 813-223-7474

Marvin S. Rosen · Honigman Miller Schwartz & Cohn · 1655 Palm Beach Lakes Boulevard, Suite 600 · West Palm Beach, FL 33401 · 407-683-3400

TAX AND EMPLOYEE BENEFITS LAW

Bruce H. Bokor · Johnson, Blakely, Pope, Bokor, Ruppel & Burns · 911 Chestnut Street · P.O. Box 1368 · Clearwater, FL 33517 · 813-461-1818

Charles P. Sacher · (Employee Benefits) · Walton Lantaff Schroeder & Carson Gables International Plaza, Suite 1101 · 2655 Le Jeune Road · Coral Gables, FL 33134 · 305-379-6411

Donald R. Tescher · Tescher & Milstein · 2100 Ponce de Leon Boulevard, Penthouse · Coral Gables, FL 33134 · 305-444-0383

James B. Davis · (Employee Benefits) · Greaton and Davis · 2601 East Oakland Park Boulevard, Suite 601 · P.O. Box 9027 · Fort Lauderdale, FL 33310 · 305-561-0313

Louis J. Dereuil · Isley & Dereuil · 1040 Bayview Drive, Suite 424 · Fort Lauderdale, FL 33304 · 305-564-7525

Michael L. Trop · (Employee Benefits) · Kopelowitz, Atlas, Pearlman & Trop · 700 Southeast Third Avenue, Suite 300 · Fort Lauderdale, FL 33316 · 305-463-3173

Kenneth G. Anderson · Gulf Life Tower, Suite 2540 · Jacksonville, FL 32207 · 904-399-8000

Fred H. Steffey · Southpoint Building, Suite 300 · 6620 Southpoint Drive South · Jacksonville, FL 32216 · 904-739-0037

John D. Armstrong · Mershon, Sawyer, Johnston, Dunwody & Cole · Southeast Financial Center, Suite 4500 · 200 South Biscayne Boulevard · Miami, FL 33131-2387 · 305-358-5100

Michael J. Canan · (Employee Benefits) · Steel Hector & Davis · 4000 Southeast Financial Center · 200 South Biscayne Boulevard · Miami, FL 33131-2398 · 305-577-2800

Edward Heilbronner · (Employee Benefits) · Paul, Landy, Beily & Harper · 200 Southeast First Street, 12th Floor · Miami, FL 33131 · 305-358-9300

Robert F. Hudson, Jr. · Baker & McKenzie · Barnett Bank Building, Suite 1600 · 701 Brickell Avenue · Miami, FL 33131 · 305-371-4064

Martin Kalb · Greenberg, Traurig, Hoffman, Lipoff, Rosen & Quentel · 1221 Brickell Avenue · Miami, FL 33131 · 305-579-0500

Joel J. Karp · Paul, Landy, Beily & Harper · 200 Southeast First Street, 12th Floor · Miami, FL 33131 · 305-358-9300

Shepard King · Steel Hector & Davis · 4000 Southeast Financial Center · 200 South Biscayne Boulevard · Miami, FL 33131-2398 · 305-577-2800

Norman H. Lipoff · Greenberg, Traurig, Hoffman, Lipoff, Rosen & Quentel · 1221 Brickell Avenue · Miami, FL 33131 · 305-579-0500

Robert E. Muraro · Thomson Bohrer Werth & Razook · 4900 Southeast Financial Center · 200 South Biscayne Boulevard · Miami, FL 33131 · 305-350-7200

Martin J. Nash · Fine Jacobson Schwartz Nash Block & England · One CenTrust Financial Center · 100 Southeast Second Street · Miami, FL 33131 · 305-577-4000

Henry H. Raattama, Jr. · Mershon, Sawyer, Johnston, Dunwody & Cole · Southeast Financial Center, Suite 4500 · 200 South Biscayne Boulevard · Miami, FL 33131-2387 · 305-358-5100

Benjamin S. Schwartz · Fine Jacobson Schwartz Nash Block & England · One CenTrust Financial Center · 100 Southeast Second Street · Miami, FL 33131 · 305-577-4000

Byron L. Sparber · Squire, Sanders & Dempsey · 3000 Miami Center · 201 South Biscayne Boulevard · Miami, FL 33131 · 305-577-8700

Samuel C. Ullman · Smathers & Thompson · 2400 Miami Center · 201 South Biscayne Boulevard · Miami, FL 33131 · 305-379-6523

Andrew H. Weinstein · Holland & Knight · 1200 Brickell Avenue · P.O. Box 015441 · Miami, FL 33131 · 305-374-8500

Charles H. Egerton · Dean, Mead, Egerton, Bloodworth, Capouano & Bozarth · 250 North Orange Avenue, Suite 1200 · Orlando, FL 32801 · 407-841-1200

Robert W. Mead, Jr. · Dean, Mead, Egerton, Bloodworth, Capouano & Bozarth · 250 North Orange Avenue, Suite 1200 · Orlando, FL 32801 · 407-841-1200

Michael D. Annis · Annis, Mitchell, Cockey, Edwards & Roehn · One Tampa City Center Building, Suite 2100 · P.O. Box 3433 · Tampa, FL 33601 · 813-229-3321

Leslie J. Barnett · Barnett, Bolt & Kirkwood · 100 Twiggs Street · P.O. Box 3287 · Tampa, FL 33602 · 813-223-5551

Joseph D. Edwards · (Employee Benefits) · Annis, Mitchell, Cockey, Edwards & Roehn · One Tampa City Center Building, Suite 2100 · P.O. Box 3433 · Tampa, FL 33601 · 813-229-3321

Albert C. O'Neill, Jr. · Trenam, Simmons, Kemker, Scharf, Barkin, Frye & O'Neill · Barnett Plaza, Suite 2700 · 101 East Kennedy Boulevard · P.O. Box 1102 Tampa, FL 33601 · 813-223-7474

Frederick M. Rothenberg · (Employee Benefits) · Fowler, White, Gillen, Boggs, Villareal and Banker · 501 East Kennedy Boulevard, Suite 1700 · P.O. Box 1438 Tampa, FL 33601 · 813-228-7411

Stanley W. Rosenkranz · Shear, Newman, Hahn & Rosenkranz · 201 East Kennedy Boulevard, Suite 1000 · P.O. Box 2378 · Tampa, FL 33601 813-228-8530

Ronald J. Russo · (also Employee Benefits) · Glenn, Rasmussen, Fogerty, Merryday & Russo · Ashley Tower, Suite 1300 · 100 South Ashley Drive · P.O. Box 3333 · Tampa, FL 33601-3333 · 813-229-3333

Sherwin P. Simmons · Trenam, Simmons, Kemker, Scharf, Barkin, Frye & O'Neill · Barnett Plaza, Suite 2700 · 101 East Kennedy Boulevard · P.O. Box 1102 Tampa, FL 33601 · 813-223-7474

Jerald David August · One Clearlake Centre, Suite 1111 · 250 Australian Avenue South · West Palm Beach, FL 33401 · 407 835-9600

TRUSTS AND ESTATES

Robert D. Chapin · Chapin & Armstrong · 1201 Northeast Eighth Street · Delray Beach, FL 33444 · 407-272-1225

Rohan Kelley · 3365 Galt Ocean Drive · Fort Lauderdale, FL 33308 · 305-563-1400

John G. Grimsley · Mahoney Adams Milam Surface & Grimsley · Barnett Bank Building · 100 Laura Street · P.O. Box 4099 · Jacksonville, FL 32201 · 904-354-1100

Fred H. Steffey · Southpoint Building, Suite 300 · 6620 Southpoint Drive South Jacksonville, FL 32216 · 904-739-0037

Norman J. Benford · Greenberg, Traurig, Hoffman, Lipoff, Rosen & Quentel 1221 Brickell Avenue · Miami, FL 33131 · 305-579-0500

Atwood Dunwody · Mershon, Sawyer, Johnston, Dunwody & Cole · Southeast Financial Center, Suite 4500 · 200 South Biscayne Boulevard · Miami, FL 33131-2387 · 305-358-5100

Robert D. W. Landon II · Mershon, Sawyer, Johnston, Dunwody & Cole Southeast Financial Center, Suite 4500 · 200 South Biscayne Boulevard · Miami, FL 33131-2387 · 305-358-5100

Samuel S. Smith · Ruden, Barnett, McClosky, Smith, Schuster & Russell Barnett Bank Tower, Suite 1900 · 701 Brickell Avenue · Miami, FL 33131 305-789-2700

Wilson Smith · Dadeland Towers, Suite 515 · 9200 South Dadeland Boulevard Miami, FL 33156 · 305-662-5852

Paul M. Stokes · Smathers & Thompson · 2400 Miami Center · 201 South Biscayne Boulevard · Miami, FL 33131 · 305-379-6523

Bruce Stone · Holland & Knight · 1200 Brickell Avenue · P.O. Box 015441 Miami, FL 33101 · 305-374-8500

Robert A. White · Mershon, Sawyer, Johnston, Dunwody & Cole · Southeast Financial Center, Suite 4500 · 200 South Biscayne Boulevard · Miami, FL 33131-2387 · 305-358-5100

Robert D. W. Landon II · Mershon, Sawyer, Johnston, Dunwody & Cole · 600 Fifth Avenue South · Naples, FL 33940 · 813-262-7302

William S. Belcher · Belcher & Fleece · Courthouse Square, Suite 301 · 600 First Avenue North · P.O. Box 330 · St. Petersburg, FL 33731 · 813-822-3941

Charles E. Early · Early & Early · Barnett Building, Suite 920 · 1390 Main Street Sarasota, FL 33577 · 813-366-2707

Leslie J. Barnett · Barnett, Bolt & Kirkwood · 100 Twiggs Street · P.O. Box 3287 Tampa, FL 33602 · 813-223-5551

John Arthur Jones · Holland & Knight · 400 North Ashley Drive, Suite 2300 P.O. Box 1288 · Tampa, FL 33601 · 813-227-8500

Edward F. Koren · Holland & Knight · 400 North Ashley Drive, Suite 2300 · P.O. Box 1288 · Tampa, FL 33601 · 813-227-8500

Roger O. Isphording · Isphording, Korp, Payne, Muirhead, Haworth & White 333 South Tamiami Trail · P.O Box 1614 · Venice, FL 33595 · 813-488-7751

James G. Pressly, Jr. · Gunster, Yoakley, Criser & Stewart · Phillips Point · 777 South Flagler Drive, Suite 500 · West Palm Beach, FL 33401-6194 · 407-655-1980

A. Obie Stewart · Gunster, Yoakley, Criser & Stewart · Phillips Point · 777 South Flagler Drive, Suite 500 · West Palm Beach, FL 33401-6194 · 407-655-1980

GEORGIA

BANKRUPTCY LAW	193
BUSINESS LITIGATION	194
CORPORATE LAW	196
CRIMINAL DEFENSE	198
ENTERTAINMENT LAW	199
FAMILY LAW	199
LABOR AND EMPLOYMENT LAW	200
NATURAL RESOURCES AND ENVIRONMENTAL LAW	201
PERSONAL INJURY LITIGATION	201
REAL ESTATE LAW	203
TAX AND EMPLOYEE BENEFITS LAW	205
TRUSTS AND ESTATES	207

BANKRUPTCY LAW

R. Neal Batson · Alston & Bird · Citizens & Southern National Bank Building, Suite 1200 · 35 Broad Street · Atlanta, GA 30335 · 404-586-1500

C. David Butler · Alston & Bird · Citizens & Southern National Bank Building, Suite 1200 · 35 Broad Street · Atlanta, GA 30335 · 404-586-1500

Charles E. Campbell · Hicks, Maloof & Campbell · 101 Marietta Tower, Suite 3401 · Atlanta, GA 30335 · 404-588-1100

Christopher L. Carson · Hansell & Post · 3300 First Atlanta Tower · Atlanta, GA 30383 · 404-581-8000

Ezra H. Cohen · Troutman, Sanders, Lockerman & Ashmore · Candler Building, Suite 1400 · 127 Peachtree Street, NE · Atlanta, GA 30043 · 404-658-8000

C. Edward Dobbs · Parker, Hudson, Rainer & Dobbs · 1200 Carnegie Building 133 Carnegie Way · Atlanta, GA 30303 · 404-523-5300

Robert E. Hicks · Hicks, Maloof & Campbell · 101 Marietta Tower, Suite 3401 Atlanta, GA 30335 · 404-588-1100

Alfred S. Lurey · Kilpatrick & Cody · 100 Galleria Parkway, NW · Atlanta, GA 30339 · 404-956-2600

Joel B. Piassick · Smith, Gambrell & Russell · 2400 First Atlanta Tower · Atlanta, GA 30383-2501 · 404-656-1800

Samuel J. Zusmann, Jr. · Small & White · 2970 Peachtree Road, NW, Suite 400 P.O. Box 53483 · Atlanta, GA 30355 · 404-237-0071

Jerome L. Kaplan · Arnall Golden & Gregory · 582 Walnut Street · Macon, GA 30201 · 912-745-3344

BUSINESS LITIGATION

Byron R. Attridge · King & Spalding · 2500 Trust Company Tower · Atlanta, GA 30303 · 404-572-4600

Griffin B. Bell · King & Spalding · 2500 Trust Company Tower · Atlanta, GA 30303 · 404-572-4600

Emmet J. Bondurant II · Bondurant, Mixson & Elmore · 3900 IBM Tower · 1201 West Peachtree Street, NW · Atlanta, GA 30309 · 404-881-4100

Nickolas P. Chilivis · Chilivis & Grindler · 3127 Maple Drive, NE · Atlanta, GA 30305 · 404-233-4171

John J. Dalton · Troutman, Sanders, Lockerman & Ashmore · Candler Building, Suite 1400 · 127 Peachtree Street, NE · Atlanta, GA 30043 · 404-658-8000

J. D. Fleming, Jr. · Sutherland, Asbill & Brennan · 3100 First Atlanta Tower Atlanta, GA 30383 · 404-658-8700

G. Conley Ingram · Alston & Bird · 100 Galleria Parkway, Suite 1200 · Atlanta, GA 30339 · 404-955-8400

Frank C. Jones · King & Spalding · 2500 Trust Company Tower · Atlanta, GA 30303 · 404-572-4600

Frank Love, Jr. · Powell, Goldstein, Frazer & Murphy · 900 Circle 75 Parkway, Suite 800 · Atlanta, GA 30339 · 404-951-5800

John T. Marshall · Powell, Goldstein, Frazer & Murphy · The Citizens and Southern National Bank Building, 11th Floor · 35 Broad Street · Atlanta, GA 30335 · 404-572-6600

Earle B. May, Jr. · Alston & Bird · Citizens and Southern National Bank Building, Suite 1200 · 35 Broad Street · Atlanta, GA 30335 · 404-586-1500

Eugene G. Partain · Powell, Goldstein, Frazer & Murphy · The Citizens and Southern National Bank Building, 11th Floor · 35 Broad Street · Atlanta, GA 30335 · 404-572-6600

C. B. Rogers · Rogers & Hardin · Peachtree Center, 2700 Cain Tower · 229 Peachtree Street, NE · Atlanta, GA 30303 · 404-522-4700

Sidney O. Smith, Jr. · Alston & Bird · Citizens and Southern National Bank Building, Suite 1200 · 35 Broad Street · Atlanta, GA 30335 · 404-586-1500

Trammell E. Vickery · Hansell & Post · 3300 First Atlanta Tower · Atlanta, GA 30383-3101 · 404-581-8000

Wyck A. Knox, Jr. · Knox & Zacks · First Union Bank Building, Suite 1400 · 699 Broad Street · P.O. Box 2043 · Augusta, GA 30903 · 404-724-2622

Robert C. Norman · Hull, Towill, Norman & Barrett · Trust Company Bank Building, Seventh Floor · P.O. Box 1564 · Augusta, GA 30913 · 404-722-4481

W. G. Scrantom, Jr. · Page, Scrantom, Harris & Chapman · 1043 Third Avenue P.O. Box 1199 · Columbus, GA 31994 · 404-324-0251

E. Freeman Leverett · Heard, Leverett & Phelps · 25 Thomas Street · P.O. Drawer 399 · Elberton, GA 30635 · 404-283-2651

Walter C. Hartridge · Bouhan, Williams & Levy · The Armstrong House · 447 Bull Street · P.O. Box 2139 · Savannah, GA 31498 · 912-236-2491

Malcolm R. Maclean · Hunter, Maclean, Exley & Dunn · 200 East St. Julian Street · P.O. Box 9848 · Savannah, GA 31412 · 912-236-0261

John B. Miller · Miller, Simpson & Tatum · Trust Company Bank Building, Suite 400 · 33 Bull Street · P.O. Box 1567 · Savannah, GA 31498 · 912-233-5722

CORPORATE LAW

H. H. Perry, Jr. · Perry, Walters & Lippitt · 409 North Jackson Street · P.O. Box 527 · Albany, GA 31703 · 912-432-7438

Miles J. Alexander · Kilpatrick & Cody · The Equitable Building, Suite 3100 100 Peachtree Street · Atlanta, GA 30043 · 404-572-6500

David S. Baker · Powell, Goldstein, Frazer & Murphy · 900 Circle 75 Parkway, Suite 800 · Atlanta, GA 30339 · 404-951-5800

George L. Cohen · Sutherland, Asbill & Brennan · 3100 First Atlanta Tower Atlanta, GA 30303 · 404-658-8700

F. Dean Copeland · Alston & Bird · Citizens & Southern National Bank Building, Suite 1200 · 35 Broad Street · Atlanta, GA 30335 · 404-586-1500

Tench C. Coxe · Troutman, Sanders, Lockerman & Ashmore · Candler Building, Suite 1400 · 127 Peachtree Street, NE · Atlanta, GA 30043 · 404-658-8000

F. T. Davis, Jr. · Long, Aldridge & Norman · 1900 Rhodes-Haverty Building · 134 Peachtree Street, NW · Atlanta, GA 30043 · 404-527-4000

William E. Eason, Jr. · Kilpatrick & Cody · The Equitable Building, Suite 3100 100 Peachtree Street · Atlanta, GA 30043 · 404-572-6500

Bradley Hale · King & Spalding · 2500 Trust Company Tower · Atlanta, GA 30303 · 404-572-4600

Edward J. Hardin · Rogers & Hardin · Peachtree Center, 2700 Cain Tower · 229 Peachtree Street, NE · Atlanta, GA 30303 · 404-522-4700

Edward J. Hawie · King & Spalding · 2500 Trust Company Tower · Atlanta, GA 30303 · 404-572-4600

John D. Hopkins · King & Spalding · 2500 Trust Company Tower · Atlanta, GA 30303 · 404-572-4600

Paul L. Hudson, Jr. · Parker, Hudson, Rainer & Dobbs · 1200 Carnegie Building 133 Carnegie Way · Atlanta, GA 30303 · 404-523-5300

Elliott Goldstein · Powell, Goldstein, Frazer & Murphy · The Citizens & Southern National Bank Building, 11th Floor · 35 Broad Street · Atlanta, GA 30335 404-572-6600

Harry C. Howard · King & Spalding · 2500 Trust Company Tower · Atlanta, GA 30303 · 404-572-4600

McChesney Hill Jeffries · Hansell & Post · 3300 First Atlanta Tower · Atlanta, GA 30383-3101 · 404-581-8000

Clay C. Long · Long, Aldridge & Norman · 1900 Rhodes-Haverty Building · 134 Peachtree Street, NW · Atlanta, GA 30043 · 404-527-4000

Sidney J. Nurkin · Powell, Goldstein, Frazer & Murphy · 400 Perimeter Center Terrace, Suite 1050 · 35 Broad Street · Atlanta, GA 30346 · 404-399-2800

Barry Phillips · Kilpatrick & Cody · The Equitable Building, Suite 3100 · 100 Peachtree Street · Atlanta, GA 30043 · 404-572-6500

Robert M. Royalty · Sutherland, Asbill & Brennan · 3100 First Atlanta Tower Atlanta, GA 30303 · 404-658-8700

Harold L. Russell · Smith, Gambrell & Russell · 2400 First Atlanta Tower · Two Peachtree Street, NE · Atlanta, GA 30383-2501 · 404-656-1800

James M. Sibley · King & Spalding · 2500 Trust Company Tower · Atlanta, GA 30303 · 404-572-4600

Nathaniel G. Slaughter III · Slaughter & Virgin · 400 Colony Square, Suite 1110 1201 Peachtree Street, NE · Atlanta, GA 30361 · 404-897-1110

James L. Smith III · Trotter, Smith & Jacobs · 400 Colony Square, Suite 2100 1201 Peachtree Street · Atlanta, GA 30361 · 404-881-0500

Michael H. Trotter · Trotter, Smith & Jacobs · 400 Colony Square, Suite 2100 1201 Peachtree Street · Atlanta, GA 30361 · 404-881-0500

Neil L. Williams, Jr. · Alston & Bird · Citizens & Southern National Bank Building, Suite 1200 · 35 Broad Street · Atlanta, GA 30335 · 404-586-1500

James H. Wilson, Jr. · Sutherland, Asbill & Brennan · 3100 First Atlanta Tower Atlanta, GA 30303 · 404-658-8700

Forrest L. Champion, Jr. · Champion & Champion · 1030 Second Avenue Columbus, GA 31901 · 404-324-4477

Albert W. Stubbs · Hatcher, Stubbs, Land, Hollis & Rothschild · 500 The Corporate Center · P.O. Box 2707 · Columbus, GA 31993-5699 · 404-324-0201

John D. Comer · Sell & Melton · 1414 Charter Medical Building · P.O. Box 229 · Macon, GA 31297-2899 · 912-746-8521

Edward J. Harrell · Martin, Snow, Grant & Napier · 240 Third Street · P.O. Box 1606 · Macon, GA 31202-1606 · 912-743-7051

Albert P. Reichert · Anderson, Walker & Reichert · Trust Company Bank Building, Suite 404 · Macon, GA 31298-0399 · 912-743-8651

G. Boone Smith III · Smith & Hawkins · 230 Third Avenue · P.O. Box 6495 · Macon, GA 31208 · 912-743-4436

Thomas S. Gray, Jr. · Oliver Maner & Gray · 218 West State Street · P.O. Box 10186 · Savannah, GA 31412 · 912-236-3311

CRIMINAL DEFENSE

Edward D. Tolley · Cook, Noell, Tolley & Aldridge · 304 East Washington Street · P.O. Box 1927 · Athens, GA 30603 · 404-549-6111

Nickolas P. Chilivis · Chilivis & Grindler · 3127 Maple Drive, NE · Atlanta, GA 30305 · 404-233-4171

Robert G. Fierer · Fierer & Westby · 152 Nassau Street, NW · Atlanta, GA 30303 · 404-688-5500

Jerome J. Froelich, Jr. · McKenney & Froelich · The Standard Building, Eighth Floor · 92 Luckie Street, NW · Atlanta, GA 30303 · 404-522-9200

Edward T. M. Garland · The Garland Firm · 92 Luckie Street, NW · Atlanta, GA 30303 · 404-577-2225

John R. Martin · Martin & Wilkes · 44 Broad Street · 504 Grant Building · Atlanta, GA 30303 · 404-522-0400

Frank K. Martin · The Joseph House · 828 Broadway · P.O. Box 1436 · Columbus, GA 31902-1436 · 404-324-7371

William T. Moore, Jr. · Oliver Maner & Gray · 218 West State Street · P.O. Box 10186 · Savannah, GA 31412 · 912-236-3311

Bobby Lee Cook · Cook & Palmour · 128 South Commerce Street · P.O. Box 370 · Summerville, GA 30747 · 404-857-3421

J. Converse Bright · Blackburn, Bright & Edwards · 1008 North Patterson Street · P.O. Box 579 · Valdosta, GA 31603-0579 · 912-247-0800

ENTERTAINMENT LAW

Joel A. Katz · Katz & Cherry · 5775 Peachtree Dunwoody Road, NE, Suite B130 · Atlanta, GA 30342 · 404-252-6600

FAMILY LAW

Edward E. Bates, Jr. · Hurt, Richardson, Garner, Todd & Cadenhead · 999 Peachtree Street, NE, Suite 1400 · Atlanta, GA 30309 · 404-870-6000

A. Paul Cadenhead · Hurt, Richardson, Garner, Todd & Cadenhead · 999 Peachtree Street, NE, Suite 1400 · Atlanta, GA 30309 · 404-870-6000

Harry L. Cashin, Jr. · Cashin & Morton · 2100 Peachtree Center, Cain Tower · 229 Peachtree Street, NE · Atlanta, GA 30303 · 404-522-8100

Baxter L. Davis · Davis, Matthews & Quigley · Lenox Towers II, 14th Floor · 3400 Peachtree Road, NE · Atlanta, GA 30326 · 404-261-3900

Harry P. Hall, Jr. · Westmoreland & Hall · 10 Piedmont Center, Suite 500 · 3495 Piedmont Road, NE · Atlanta, GA 30305 · 404-365-9090

Barry B. McGough · Frankel, Hardwick, Tanenbaum, Fink & Clark · 359 East Paces Ferry Road, NE · Atlanta, GA 30305 · 404-266-2930

C. Wilbur Warner, Jr. · Warner, Mayoue & Ryals · 100 Galleria Parkway, NW, Suite 1300 · Atlanta, GA 30339-3183 · 404-951-2700

B. Seth Harp, Jr. · Harp & Smith · 936 Second Avenue · P.O. Box 1172 · Columbus, GA 31902 · 404-323-2761

M. T. Simmons, Jr. · Simmons, Warren & Szczecko · 850 First National Bank Building · Decatur, GA 30030 · 404-378-1711

Kice H. Stone · Stone, Christian & Peterman · Great Southern Federal Building, Suite 230 · 484 Mulberry Street · P.O. Box 107 · Macon, GA 31202-0107 · 912-741-0060

Lawrence B. Custer · Custer, Hill & Clark · 241 Washington Avenue · P.O. Box 1224 · Marietta, GA 30061 · 404-429-8300

LABOR AND EMPLOYMENT LAW

Duane C. Aldrich · (Management) · Kilpatrick & Cody · The Equitable Building, Suite 3100 · 100 Peachtree Street · Atlanta, GA 30043 · 404-572-6500

Lovic A. Brooks, Jr. · (Management) · Constangy, Brooks & Smith · 2400 The 230 Building · 230 Peachtree Street, NW · Atlanta, GA 30303 · 404-525-8622

Thomas H. Christopher · (Management) · Kilpatrick & Cody · The Equitable Building, Suite 3100 · 100 Peachtree Street · Atlanta, GA 30043 · 404-572-6500

Homer L. Deakins · (Management) · Ogletree, Deakins, Nash, Smoak and Stewart · IBM Tower, Suite 3800 · 1201 West Peachtree Street · Atlanta, GA 30309 404-881-1300

James D. Fagan · (Labor) · Stanford, Fagan & Giolito · 1401 Peachtree Street, NE, Suite 238 · Atlanta, GA 30309 · 404-897-1000

John Randall Goldthwaite, Jr. · (Labor) · 1372 Peachtree Street, NE, Suite 203 Atlanta, GA 30309 · 404-872-2889

E. Reginald Hancock · (Management) · Smith, Currie & Hancock · 2600 Peachtree Center, Harris Tower · 233 Peachtree Street, NE · Atlanta, GA 30043-6601 · 404-521-3800

Margie Pitts Hames · (Individuals) · 794 Juniper Street · Atlanta, GA 30308 · 404-577-7952

C. Lash Harrison · (Management) · Ford & Harrison · 600 Peachtree at the Circle Building · 1275 Peachtree Street, NE · Atlanta, GA 30309 · 404-888-3800

Harris Jacobs · (Labor) · Jacobs and Langford · The Equitable Building, Suite 1000 · 100 Peachtree Street, NW · Atlanta, GA 30303 · 404-522-4280

Dana E. McDonald · (Individuals) · 141 Walton Street, NW · Atlanta, GA 30303 404-581-1900

Mary Ann B. Oakley · (Individuals) · Oakley & Bonner · Carnegie Way, Suite 508 Atlanta, GA 30303 · 404-223-5250

William B. Paul · (Management) · Clark, Paul, Hoover & Mallard · One Midtown Plaza · 1360 Peachtree Street, NE · Atlanta, GA 30309-3214 · 404-874-7500

Erle Phillips · (Management) · Fisher & Phillips · 1500 Resurgens Plaza · 945 East Paces Ferry Road · Atlanta, GA 30326 · 404-231-1400

Frank Barry Shuster · (Labor) · Blackburn, Shuster, King & King · 6735 Peachtree Industrial Boulevard, Suite 235 · Atlanta, GA 30360 · 404-441-1526

Morgan C. Stanford · (Labor) · Stanford, Fagan & Giolito · 1401 Peachtree Street, NE, Suite 238 · Atlanta, GA 30309 · 404-897-1000

James W. Wimberly, Jr. · (Management) · Wimberly, Lawson, Cobb & Leggio Lenox Towers, Suite 1750 · 3400 Peachtree Road, NE · Atlanta, GA 30326 404-365-0900

NATURAL RESOURCES AND ENVIRONMENTAL LAW

David S. Baker · Powell, Goldstein, Frazer & Murphy · 900 Circle 75 Parkway, Suite 800 · Atlanta, GA 30339 · 404-951-5800

J. D. Fleming, Jr. · Sutherland, Asbill & Brennan · 3100 First Atlanta Tower Atlanta, GA 30383 · 404-658-8700

Edward W. Killorin · (Timber) · Killorin & Killorin · 11 Piedmont Center, Suite 825 · Atlanta, GA 30305 · 404-365-0825

James S. Stokes · Alston & Bird · 100 Galleria Parkway, Suite 1200 · Atlanta, GA 30339 · 404-955-8400

PERSONAL INJURY LITIGATION

Gary B. Blasingame · (Defendants) · Blasingame, Burch, Garrard & Bryant · 440 College Avenue North · P.O. Box 832 · Athens, GA 30603 · 404-353-3433

William Q. Bird · (Plaintiffs) · Bird & Associates · 14 Seventeenth Street, Suite Five · Atlanta, GA 30309 · 404-873-4696

Nickolas P. Chilivis · Chilivis & Grindler · 3127 Maple Drive, NE · Atlanta, GA 30305 · 404-233-4171

Foy R. Devine · (Plaintiffs) · Devine & Morris · 2931 Piedmont Road, NE Atlanta, GA 30305 · 404-233-4141

Joe C. Freeman, Jr. · Freeman & Hawkins · 2800 First Atlanta Tower · Atlanta, GA 30383 · 404-522-0856

George W. Hart · (Defendants) · Hart & Sullivan · One Midtown Plaza, Suite 800 1360 Peachtree Street, NE · Atlanta, GA 30309 · 404-870-8000

Paul M. Hawkins · (Plaintiffs) · Freeman & Hawkins · 2800 First Atlanta Tower Atlanta, GA 30383 · 404-522-0856

William C. Lanham · (Plaintiffs) · Johnson & Ward · 2100 The Equitable Building 100 Peachtree Street, NE · Atlanta, GA 30303 · 404-524-5626

Frank Love, Jr. · Powell, Goldstein, Frazer & Murphy · 900 Circle 75 Parkway, Suite 800 · Atlanta, GA 30339 · 404-951-5800

William H. Major · Heyman and Sizemore · 1940 The Equitable Building · 100 Peachtree Street, NE · Atlanta, GA 30303 · 404-521-2268

Thomas William Malone · (Plaintiffs) · 2957 Claremont Road, Suite 250 · P.O. Box 49406 · Atlanta, GA 30359 · 404-325-8855

John T. Marshall · Powell, Goldstein, Frazer & Murphy · The Citizens & Southern National Bank Building, 11th Floor · 35 Broad Street · Atlanta, GA 30335 404-572-6600

Edgar A. Neely, Jr. · (Defendants) · Neely & Player · Hass-Howell Building · 75 Poplar Street · Atlanta, GA 30303-2122 · 404-681-2600

Albert H. Parnell · (Defendants) · Freeman & Hawkins · 2800 First Atlanta Tower · Atlanta, GA 30383 · 404-522-0856

Andrew M. Scherffius · (Plaintiffs) · 999 Peachtree Street, NE, Suite 1600 · P.O. Box 7890 · Atlanta, GA 30357 · 404-874-4115

Ben L. Weinberg, Jr. · (Defendants) · Long, Weinberg, Ansley and Wheeler · 999 Peachtree Street, NE · Atlanta, GA 30309 · 404-876-2700

Sidney F. Wheeler · (Defendants) · Long, Weinberg, Ansley and Wheeler · 999 Peachtree Street, NE · Atlanta, GA 30309 · 404-876-2700

Thomas R. Burnside, Jr. · (Plaintiffs) · Burnside, Wall & Daniel · 454 Greene Street · P.O. Box 2125 · Augusta, GA 30903 · 404-722-0768

Gould B. Hagler · (Defendants) · Fulcher, Hagler, Reed, Obenshain, Hanks & Harper · 520 Greene Street · P.O. Box 1477 (13) · Augusta, GA 30913 · 404-724-0171

Wallace E. Harrell · (Defendants) · Gilbert, Whittle, Harrell, Scarlett & Skelton First Federal Plaza, Suite 200 · Brunswick, GA 31521 · 912-265-6700

David H. Tisinger · Tisinger, Tisinger, Vance & Greer · 100 Wagon Yard Plaza P.O. Box 2069 · Carrollton, GA 30117 · 404-834-4467

James E. Butler, Jr. · (Plaintiffs) · Butler, Wooten, Overby & Cheeley · 1500 Second Avenue · P.O. Box 2766 · Columbus, GA 31902 · 404-322-1990

C. Neal Pope · (Plaintiffs) · Pope, Kellogg, McGlamry, Kilpatrick & Morrison 720 Broadway · P.O. Box 2128 · Columbus, GA 31902-2128 · 404-324-0050

W. G. Scrantom, Jr. · Page, Scrantom, Harris & Chapman · 1043 Third Avenue P.O. Box 1199 · Columbus, GA 31994 · 404-324-0251

Charles H. Hyatt · (Plaintiffs) · 201 Trust Building · Decatur, GA 30030 404-378-3635

Charles M. Jones · (Plaintiffs) · Jones, Osteen, Jones & Arnold · 206 East Court Street · P.O. Box 800 · Hinesville, GA 31313 · 912-876-0111

Cubbedge Snow, Jr. · (Defendants) · Martin, Snow, Grant & Napier · 240 Third Street · P.O. Box 1606 · Macon, GA 31202-1606 · 912-743-7051

Robert M. Brinson · (Defendants) · Brinson, Askew & Berry · Omberg House 615 West First Street · P.O. Box 5513 · Rome, GA 30161 · 404-291-8853

Kirk M. McAlpin · (Defendants) · 32 East Bay Street · P.O. Box 10027 · Savannah, GA 31412 · 912-232-8962

Frank W. Seiler · Bouhan, Williams & Levy · The Armstrong House · 447 Bull Street · P.O. Box 2139 · Savannah, GA 31498 · 912-236-2491

REAL ESTATE LAW

John G. Aldridge · Long, Aldridge & Norman · Two Concourse Parkway, Suite 750 · Atlanta, GA 30328-5347 · 404-527-4000

L. Travis Brannon, Jr. · Hansell & Post · 3300 First Atlanta Tower · Atlanta, GA 30383-3101 · 404-581-8000

David Lee Coker · King & Spalding · 2500 Trust Company Tower · Atlanta, GA 30303 · 404-572-4600

A. James Elliott · Alston & Bird · 100 Galleria Parkway, Suite 1200 · Atlanta, GA 30339 · 404-955-8400

Robert G. Holt · Holt, Ney, Zatcoff & Wasserman · 100 Galleria Parkway, Suite 600 · Atlanta, GA 30339 · 404-956-9600

Clay C. Long · Long, Aldridge & Norman · 1900 Rhodes-Haverty Building · 134 Peachtree Street, NW · Atlanta, GA 30043 · 404-527-4000

Julian D. Nealey · Hansell & Post · 3300 First Atlanta Tower · Atlanta, GA 30383-3101 · 404-581-8000

James M. Ney · Holt, Ney, Zatcoff & Wasserman · 100 Galleria Parkway, Suite 600 · Atlanta, GA 30339 · 404-956-9600

William R. Patterson · Sutherland, Asbill & Brennan · 333 Peachtree Road, NE Atlanta, GA 30326 · 404-266-7200

William F. Stevens · Long, Aldridge & Norman · Atlanta Financial South Tower, Suite 420 · Two Concourse Parkway · Atlanta, GA 30328-5347 · 404-527-4000

W. Joseph Thompson · Powell, Goldstein, Frazer & Murphy · 900 Circle 75 Parkway, Suite 800 · Atlanta, GA 30339 · 404-951-5800

James H. Wildman · King & Spalding · 2500 Trust Company Tower · Atlanta, GA 30303 · 404-572-4600

Sanford H. Zatcoff · Holt, Ney, Zatcoff & Wasserman · 100 Galleria Parkway, Suite 600 · Atlanta, GA 30339 · 404-956-9600

William W. Shearouse, Jr. · Friedman, Haslam, Weiner, Ginsberg, Shearouse & Weitz · 14 East State Street · P.O. Box 10105 · Savannah, GA 31412-0305 · 912-233-2251

Charles L. Sparkman · Oliver Maner & Gray · 218 West State Street · P.O. Box 10186 · Savannah, GA 31412 · 912-236-3311

TAX AND EMPLOYEE BENEFITS LAW

Harold E. Abrams · Kilpatrick & Cody · 100 Galleria Parkway, Suite 1750 · Atlanta, GA 30339 · 404-956-2600

Herschel M. Bloom · King & Spalding · 2500 Trust Company Tower · Atlanta, GA 30303 · 404-572-4600

Jerold N. Cohen · Sutherland, Asbill & Brennan · 3100 First Atlanta Tower · Atlanta, GA 30383 · 404-658-8700

Philip C. Cook · Alston & Bird · Citizens & Southern National Bank Building, Suite 1200 · 35 Broad Street · Atlanta, GA 30335 · 404-586-1500

Frazer Durrett, Jr. · Alston & Bird · Citizens & Southern National Bank Building, Suite 1200 · 35 Broad Street · Atlanta, GA 30335 · 404-586-1500

Michael J. Egan · Sutherland, Asbill & Brennan · 3100 First Atlanta Tower · Atlanta, GA 30383 · 404-658-8700

Charles E. Elrod, Jr. · (Employee Benefits) · Elrod & Thompson · 1500 Peachtree Center, South Tower · 225 Peachtree Street, NE · Atlanta, GA 30303 · 404-659-1500

Robert M. Fink · Troutman, Sanders, Lockerman & Ashmore · Candler Building, Suite 1400 · 127 Peachtree Street, NE · Atlanta, GA 30043 · 404-658-8000

Stephen F. Gertzman · Sutherland, Asbill & Brennan · 3100 First Atlanta Tower · Atlanta, GA 30383 · 404-658-8700

James K. Hasson, Jr. · Sutherland, Asbill & Brennan · 3100 First Atlanta Tower · Atlanta, GA 30383 · 404-658-8700

Lee H. Henkel, Jr. · Troutman, Sanders, Lockerman & Ashmore · Candler Building, Suite 1400 · 127 Peachtree Street, NE · Atlanta, GA 30043 · 404-658-8000

Robert H. Hishon · Hishon & Ranney · 200 Galleria Parkway, Suite 1500 · Atlanta, GA 30339 · 404-984-4000

William L. Kinzer · Powell, Goldstein, Frazer & Murphy · The Citizens & Southern National Bank Building, 11th Floor · 35 Broad Street · Atlanta, GA 30335 · 404-572-6600

Don Kohla · (Employee Benefits) · King & Spalding · 2500 Trust Company Tower · Atlanta, GA 30303 · 404-572-4600

Harry V. Lamon, Jr. · (Employee Benefits) · Hurt, Richardson, Garner, Todd & Cadenhead · 1400 Peachtree Place Tower · 999 Peachtree Street, NE · Atlanta, GA 30309 · 404-870-6000

James H. Landon · (Employee Benefits) · Hansell & Post · 3300 First Atlanta Tower · Atlanta, GA 30383 · 404-581-8000

Oliver C. Murray, Jr. · Hansell & Post · 3300 First Atlanta Tower · Atlanta, GA 30383 · 404-581-8000

William R. Patterson · Sutherland, Asbill & Brennan · Atlanta Financial South Tower, Suite 420 · 3333 Peachtree Road, NE · Atlanta, GA 30326 · 404-266-7200

Randolph W. Thrower · Sutherland, Asbill & Brennan · 3100 First Atlanta Tower Atlanta, GA 30383 · 404-658-8700

John A. Wallace · King & Spalding · 2500 Trust Company Tower · Atlanta, GA 30303 · 404-572-4600

Michael G. Wasserman · Holt, Ney, Zatcoff & Wasserman · 100 Galleria Parkway, Suite 600 · Atlanta, GA 30339 · 404-956-9600

James H. Wilson, Jr. · Sutherland, Asbill & Brennan · 3100 First Atlanta Tower Atlanta, GA 30383 · 404-658-8700

Walter H. Wingfield · (Employee Benefits) · Sutherland, Asbill & Brennan · 3100 First Atlanta Tower · Atlanta, GA 30383 · 404-658-8700

Robert G. Woodward · King & Spalding · 2500 Trust Company Tower · Atlanta, GA 30303 · 404-572-4600

J. Quentin Davidson, Jr. · Davidson & Calhoun · The Joseph House · 828 Broadway · P.O. Box 2828 · Columbus, GA 31994-1599 · 404-327-2552

Morton A. Harris · Page, Scrantom, Harris & Chapman · 1043 Third Avenue P.O. Box 1199 · Columbus, GA 31994 · 404-324-0251

Albert P. Reichert, Jr. · Anderson, Walker & Reichert · Trust Company Bank Building, Suite 404 · Macon, GA 31298-0399 · 912-743-8651

David H. Dickey · Oliver Maner & Gray · 218 West State Street · P.O. Box 10186 Savannah, GA 31412 · 912-236-3311

Henry M. Dunn, Jr. · Hunter, Maclean, Exley & Dunn · 200 East St. Julian Street · P.O. Box 9848 · Savannah, GA 31412 · 912-236-0261

Julian R. Friedman · Oliver Maner & Gray · 218 West State Street · P.O. Box 10186 · Savannah, GA 31412 · 912-236-3311

Mark M. Silvers, Jr. · Hunter, Maclean, Exley & Dunn · Castle Building, Third Floor · 200 East St. Julian Street · P.O. Box 9848 · Savannah, GA 31412 912-236-0261

TRUSTS AND ESTATES

Larry V. McLeod · Erwin, Epting, Gibson & McLeod · Citizens & Southern National Bank Building, Eighth Floor · P.O. Box 8108 · Athens, GA 30603 404-549-9400

Frazer Durrett, Jr. · Alston & Bird · Citizens & Southern National Bank Building, Suite 1200 · 35 Broad Street · Atlanta, GA 30335 · 404-586-1500

Robert G. Edge · Alston & Bird · 100 Galleria Parkway, Suite 1200 · Atlanta, GA 30339 · 404-955-8400

Michael J. Egan · Sutherland, Asbill & Brennan · 3100 First Atlanta Tower Atlanta, GA 30383 · 404-658-8700

William Joseph Linkous, Jr. · Powell, Goldstein, Frazer & Murphy · The Citizens and Southern National Bank Building, 11th Floor · 35 Broad Street · Atlanta, GA 30335 · 404-572-6600

Joseph C. Miller · Rogers & Hardin · Peachtree Center, 2700 Cain Tower · 229 Peachtree Street, NE · Atlanta, GA 30303 · 404-522-4700

Wayne R. Vason · Troutman, Sanders, Lockerman & Ashmore · Candler Building, Suite 1400 · 127 Peachtree Street, NE · Atlanta, GA 30043 · 404-658-8000

John A. Wallace · King & Spalding · 2500 Trust Company Tower · Atlanta, GA 30303 · 404-572-4600

Benjamin T. White · Alston & Bird · 100 Galleria Parkway, Suite 1200 · Atlanta, GA 30339 · 404-955-8400

Larry J. White · Sutherland, Asbill & Brennan · 3100 First Atlanta Tower Atlanta, GA 30383 · 404-658-8700

John D. Comer · Sell & Melton · 1414 Charter Medical Building · P.O. Box 229 Macon, GA 31297-2899 · 912-746-8521

Albert P. Reichert · Anderson, Walker & Reichert · Trust Company Bank Building, Suite 404 · Macon, GA 31298-0399 · 912-743-8651

Julian R. Friedman · Oliver Maner & Gray · 218 West State Street · P.O. Box 10186 · Savannah, GA 31412 · 912-236-3311

John E. Simpson · Miller, Simpson & Tatum · Trust Company Bank Building, Suite 400 · 33 Bull Street · P.O. Box 1567 · Savannah, GA 31498 · 912-233-5722

HAWAII

BANKRUPTCY LAW	209
BUSINESS LITIGATION	210
CORPORATE LAW	210
CRIMINAL DEFENSE	211
FAMILY LAW	211
LABOR AND EMPLOYMENT LAW	212
PERSONAL INJURY LITIGATION	212
REAL ESTATE LAW	213
TAX AND EMPLOYEE BENEFITS LAW	214
TRUSTS AND ESTATES	215

BANKRUPTCY LAW

R. Charles Bocken · Damon, Key, Char & Bocken · Pauahi Tower, Suite 1600 · 1001 Bishop Street · Honolulu, HI 96813 · 808-531-8031

William H. Dodd · Chun, Kerr & Dodd · Amfac Building, 14th Floor · 700 Bishop Street · Honolulu, HI 96813 · 808-531-6575

James N. Duca · Kessner, Duca & Maki · Central Pacific Plaza, 19th Floor · 220 South King Street · Honolulu, HI 96813 · 808-522-1900

Don Jeffrey Gelber · Gelber & Gelber · Hawaii Building, Suite 1400 · 745 Fort Street · Honolulu, HI 96813 · 808-524-0155

James A. Wagner · Wagner, Watson & DiBianco · Mauka Tower, Suite 2480 · 737 Bishop Street · Honolulu, HI 96813 · 808-533-1872

BUSINESS LITIGATION

Martin Anderson · Goodsill Anderson Quinn & Stifel · Bancorp Tower · Financial Plaza of the Pacific · P.O. Box 3196 · Honolulu, HI 96801 · 808-547-5600

James S. Campbell · Cades Schutte Fleming & Wright · 1000 Bishop Street P.O. Box 939 · Honolulu, HI 96808 · 808-521-9200

William H. Dodd · Chun, Kerr & Dodd · Amfac Building, 14th Floor · 700 Bishop Street · Honolulu, HI 96813 · 808-531-6575

Wallace S. Fujiyama · Fujiyama, Duffy & Fujiyama · Pauahi Tower, Suite 2700 Bishop Square · 1001 Bishop Street · Honolulu, HI 96813 · 808-536-0802

Edward A. Jaffe · Cades Schutte Fleming & Wright · 1000 Bishop Street · P.O. Box 939 · Honolulu, HI 96808 · 808-521-9200

Paul A. Lynch · Case & Lynch · 2600 Grosvenor Center, Mauka Tower · 737 Bishop Street · Honolulu, HI 96813 · 808-547-5400

Dennis E. W. O'Connor · Hoddick, Reinwald, O'Connor & Marrack · 2400 PRI Tower, Grosvenor Center · P.O. Box 3199 · Honolulu, HI 96801 · 808-524-8350

CORPORATE LAW

James W. Boyle · Carlsmith, Wichman, Case, Mukai & Ichiki · Pacific Tower, Suite 2200 · 1001 Bishop Street · P.O. Box 656 · Honolulu, HI 96809 · 808-523-2500

Daniel H. Case · Case & Lynch · 2600 Grosvenor Center, Mauka Tower · 737 Bishop Street · Honolulu, HI 96813 · 808-547-5400

James H. Case · Carlsmith, Wichman, Case, Mukai & Ichiki · Pacific Tower, Suite 2200 · 1001 Bishop Street · P.O. Box 656 · Honolulu, HI 96809 · 808-523-2500

Marshall M. Goodsill · Goodsill Anderson Quinn & Stifel · Bancorp Tower Financial Plaza of the Pacific · P.O. Box 3196 · Honolulu, HI 96801-3196 808-547-5600

Michael P. Porter · Cades Schutte Fleming & Wright · 1000 Bishop Street · P.O. Box 939 · Honolulu, HI 96808 · 808-521-9200

E. Gunner Schull · Cades Schutte Fleming & Wright · 1000 Bishop Street · P.O. Box 939 · Honolulu, HI 96808 · 808-521-9200

Hugh Shearer · Goodsill Anderson Quinn & Stifel · Bancorp Tower · Financial Plaza of the Pacific · P.O. Box 3196 · Honolulu, HI 96801 · 808-547-5600

CRIMINAL DEFENSE

John S. Edmunds · Edmunds, Verga, Van Etten & O'Brien · Davies Pacific Center, Suite 2104 · 841 Bishop Street · Honolulu, HI 96813 · 808-524-2000

Brook Hart · Hart & Wolff · Melim Building, Suite 610 · 333 Queen Street Honolulu, HI 96813 · 808-526-0811

Matthew S. K. Pyun, Jr. · 615 Piikoi Street, Suite 1601 · Honolulu, HI 96814 808-524-1633

Philip H. Lowenthal · Lowenthal, August, Graham & Seitz · 2261 Aupuni Street Wailuku, HI 96793 · 808-242-5000

FAMILY LAW

William C. Darrah · Douthit & Darrah · 547 Halekauwila Street, Suite 105 Honolulu, HI 96813 · 808-531-7232

Durell Douthit · Douthit & Darrah · 547 Halekauwila Street, Suite 105 · Honolulu, HI 96813 · 808-531-7232

Geoffrey Hamilton · Char Hamilton Campbell & Thom · Grosvenor Center, Mauka Tower, Suite 2100 · 737 Bishop Street · Honolulu, HI 96813 · 808-524-3824

Charles T. Kleintop · Stirling & Kleintop · 900 Fort Street Mall, Suite 1650 Honolulu, HI 96813 · 808-524-5183

Thomas L. Stirling, Jr. · Stirling & Kleintop · 900 Fort Street Mall, Suite 1650 Honolulu, HI 96813 · 808-524-5183

LABOR AND EMPLOYMENT LAW

Jared H. Jossem · (Management) · Torkildson, Katz, Jossem, Fonseca, Jaffe & Moore · Amfac Building, 15th Floor · 700 Bishop Street · Honolulu, HI 96813 808-521-1051

Robert S. Katz · (Management) · Torkildson, Katz, Jossem, Fonseca, Jaffe & Moore · Amfac Building, 15th Floor · 700 Bishop Street · Honolulu, HI 96813 808-521-1051

James A. King · (Labor) · King, Nakamura & Chun-Hoon · 900 Fort Street Mall Honolulu, HI 96813 · 808-521-8041

Jeffrey S. Portnoy · (Individuals) · Cades Schutte Fleming & Wright · 1000 Bishop Street · P.O. Box 939 · Honolulu, HI 96808 · 808-521-9200

Alvin T. Shim · (Labor) · Shim, Sigal, Tam & Naito · 333 Queen Street, Suite 900 Honolulu, HI 96813 · 808-524-5803

Herbert R. Takahashi · (Labor; Individuals) · 547 Halekauwila Street, Room 206 Honolulu, HI 96813 · 808-526-3003

Raymond M. Torkildson · (Management) · Torkildson, Katz, Jossem, Fonseca, Jaffe & Moore · Amfac Building, 15th Floor · 700 Bishop Street · Honolulu, HI 96813 · 808-521-1051

PERSONAL INJURY LITIGATION

Edmund Burke · (Defendants) · Burke, Sakai, McPheeters, Bordner & Gilardy 3100 Mauka Tower · Grosvenor Center · 737 Bishop Street · Honolulu, HI 96813 808-523-9833

James E. Duffy, Jr. · Fujiyama, Duffy & Fujiyama · Pauahi Tower, Suite 2700 Bishop Square · 1001 Bishop Street · Honolulu, HI 96813 · 808-536-0802

John S. Edmunds · (Plaintiffs) · Edmunds, Verga, Van Ettan & O'Brien · Davies Pacific Center, Suite 2104 · 841 Bishop Street · Honolulu, HI 96813 · 808-524-2000

David L. Fairbanks · (Plaintiffs) · Cronin, Fried, Sekiya, Kekina & Fairbanks 1900 Davies Pacific Center · 841 Bishop Street · Honolulu, HI 96813 · 808-524-1433

Wallace S. Fujiyama · Fujiyama, Duffy & Fujiyama · Pauahi Tower, Suite 2700 Bishop Square · 1001 Bishop Street · Honolulu, HI 96813 · 808-536-0802

Burnham H. Greeley · (Defendants) · Greeley, Walker & Kowen · Pauahi Tower, Suite 1300 · 1001 Bishop Street · Honolulu, HI 96813 · 808-526-2211

Bert T. Kobayashi, Jr. · (Defendants) · Kobayashi, Watanabe, Sugita, Kawashima & Goda · Hawaii Building, Eighth Floor · 745 Fort Street · Honolulu, HI 96813 808-544-8300

Ronald D. Libkuman · Libkuman, Ventura, Ayabe, Chong & Nishimoto · 3000 Grosvenor Center · 737 Bishop Street · Honolulu, HI 96813 · 808-537-6119

David C. Schutter · (Plaintiffs) · Schutter & Glickstein · Kawaiahao Plaza, Penthouse Suite 618 · 567 South King Street · Honolulu, HI 96813 · 808-524-4600

Gerald Y. Sekiya · (Plaintiffs) · Cronin, Fried, Sekiya, Kekina & Fairbanks · 1900 Davies Pacific Center · 841 Bishop Street · Honolulu, HI 96813 · 808-524-1433

Raymond J. Tam · (Plaintiffs) · Shim, Tam & Kirimitsu · 333 Queen Street, Suite 900 · Honolulu, HI 96813 · 808-524-5803

James F. Ventura · Libkuman, Ventura, Ayabe, Chong & Nishimoto · 3000 Grosvenor Center · 737 Bishop Street · Honolulu, HI 96813 · 808-537-6119

James Krueger · (Plaintiffs) · 2065 Main Street · P.O. Box T · Wailuku, Maui, HI 96793 · 808-244-7444

REAL ESTATE LAW

Clinton R. Ashford · Ashford & Wriston · Title Guaranty Building, Sixth Floor 235 Queen Street · P.O. Box 131 · Honolulu, HI 96810 · 808-524-4787

Robert B. Bunn · Cades Schutte Fleming & Wright · 1000 Bishop Street · P.O. Box 939 · Honolulu, HI 96808 · 808-521-9200

Daniel H. Case · Case, Kay & Lynch · 2600 Grosvenor Center · Mauka Tower 737 Bishop Street · Honolulu, HI 96813 · 808-547-5400

Edward Y. C. Chun · Chun, Kerr & Dodd · Amfac Building, 14th Floor · 700 Bishop Street · Honolulu, HI 96813 · 808-531-6575

C. Jepson Garland · Goodsill Anderson Quinn & Stifel · Bancorp Tower · Financial Plaza of the Pacific · P.O. Box 3196 · Honolulu, HI 96801 · 808-547-5600

John Jubinsky · Ashford & Wriston · Title Guaranty Building, Sixth Floor · 235 Queen Street · P.O. Box 131 · Honolulu, HI 96810 · 808-524-4787

Douglas E. Prior · Cades Schutte Fleming & Wright · 1000 Bishop Street · P.O. Box 939 · Honolulu, HI 96808 · 808-521-9200

Dwight M. Rush · Rush, Moore, Craven & Stricklin · Hawaii Building, 20th Floor 745 Fort Street · Honolulu, HI 96813 · 808-521-0400

Donald E. Scearce · Cades Schutte Fleming & Wright · 1000 Bishop Street · P.O. Box 939 · Honolulu, HI 96808 · 808-521-9200

TAX AND EMPLOYEE BENEFITS LAW

James P. Conahan · (Employee Benefits) · Carlsmith, Wichman, Case, Mukai & Ichiki · Pacific Tower, Suite 2200 · 1001 Bishop Street · P.O. Box 656 · Honolulu, HI 96809 · 808-523-2500

H. Mitchell D'Olier · Goodsill Anderson Quinn & Stifel · Bancorp Tower Financial Plaza of the Pacific · P.O. Box 3196 · Honolulu, HI 96801-3196 808-547-5600

Roger H. Epstein · Cades Schutte Fleming & Wright · 1000 Bishop Street · P.O. Box 939 · Honolulu, HI 96808 · 808-521-9200

Roger W. Fonseca · (Employee Benefits) · Torkildson, Katz, Jossem, Fonseca, Jaffe & Moore · Amfac Building, 15th Floor · 700 Bishop Street · Honolulu, HI 96813 · 808-521-1051

Stephen M. Gelber · Gelber & Gelber · Hawaii Building, Suite 1400 · 745 Fort Street · Honolulu, HI 96813 · 808-524-0155

Mervyn S. Gerson · Gerson, Grekin & Wynhoff · Pacific Tower, Suite 780 · 1001 Bishop Street · Honolulu, HI 96813 · 808-524-4800

George G. Grubb · Carlsmith, Wichman, Case, Mukai & Ichiki · Pacific Tower, Suite 2200 · 1001 Bishop Street · P.O. Box 656 · Honolulu, HI 96809 · 808-523-2500

Michael A. Shea · Goodsill Anderson Quinn & Stifel · Bancorp Tower · Financial Plaza of the Pacific · P.O. Box 3196 · Honolulu, HI 96801-3196 · 808-547-5600

TRUSTS AND ESTATES

A. Singleton Cagle · Cades Schutte Fleming & Wright · 1000 Bishop Street · P.O. Box 939 · Honolulu, HI 96808 · 808-521-9200

C. F. Damon, Jr. · Damon, Key, Char & Bocken · Pauahi Tower, Suite 1600 1001 Bishop Street · Honolulu, HI 96813 · 808-531-8031

Robert Williams Hastings II · Torkildson, Katz, Jossem, Fonseca, Jaffe & Moore Amfac Building, 15th Floor · 700 Bishop Street · Honolulu, HI 96813 · 808-521-1051

Robert G. Hite · Goodsill Anderson Quinn & Stifel · Bancorp Tower · Financial Plaza of the Pacific · P.O. Box 3196 · Honolulu, HI 97801-3196 · 808-547-5600

David C. Larsen · Cades Schutte Fleming & Wright · 1000 Bishop Street · P.O. Box 939 · Honolulu, HI 96808 · 808-521-9200

Elliot H. Loden · 2990 Grosvenor Center · 737 Bishop Street · Honolulu, HI 96813 · 808-524-8099

Arthur B. Reinwald · Hoddick, Reinwald, O'Connor & Marrack · 2400 PRI Tower, Grosvenor Center · P.O. Box 3199 · Honolulu, HI 96801 · 808-524-8350

James L. Starshak · Carlsmith, Wichman, Case, Mukai & Ichiki · Pacific Tower, Suite 2200 · 1001 Bishop Street · P.O. Box 656 · Honolulu, HI 96809 808-523-2500

IDAHO

BANKRUPTCY LAW	216
BUSINESS LITIGATION	216
CORPORATE LAW	217
CRIMINAL DEFENSE	217
FAMILY LAW	217
LABOR AND EMPLOYMENT LAW	218
NATURAL RESOURCES AND ENVIRONMENTAL LAW	218
PERSONAL INJURY LITIGATION	218
REAL ESTATE LAW	218
TAX AND EMPLOYEE BENEFITS LAW	219
TRUSTS AND ESTATES	219

BANKRUPTCY LAW

R. Michael Southcombe · Clemons, Cosho & Humphrey · 815 West Washington Street · Boise, ID 83702 · 208-344-7811

Terry L. Myers · Givens, McDevitt, Pursley, Webb & Buser · Park Place, Suite 200 · 277 North Sixth Street · P.O. Box 2720 · Boise, ID 83701 · 208-342-6571

BUSINESS LITIGATION

Carl P. Burke · Elam, Burke and Boyd · First Interstate Bank Building, Suite 1010 · 702 West Idaho Street · P.O. Box 1559 · Boise, ID 83701 · 208-343-5454

Jess B. Hawley, Jr. · Hawley Troxell Ennis & Hawley · One Capitol Center, Seventh Floor · P.O. Box 1617 · Boise, ID 83701 · 208-344-6000

Chas. F. McDevitt · Givens, McDevitt, Pursley, Webb & Buser · Park Place, Suite 200 · 277 North Sixth Street · P.O. Box 2720 · Boise, ID 83701 · 208-342-6571

Louis F. Racine, Jr. · Racine, Olson, Nye, Cooper & Budge · Center Plaza · P.O. Box 1391 · Pocatello, ID 83201 · 208-232-6101

CORPORATE LAW

Carl P. Burke · Elam, Burke and Boyd · First Interstate Bank Building, Suite 1010 702 West Idaho Street · P.O. Box 1559 · Boise, ID 83701 · 208-343-5454

Jess B. Hawley, Jr. · Hawley Troxell Ennis & Hawley · One Capital Center, Seventh Floor · P.O. Box 1617 · Boise, ID 83701 · 208-344-6000

Chas. F. McDevitt · Givens, McDevitt, Pursley, Webb & Buser · Park Place, Suite 200 · 277 North Sixth Street · P.O. Box 2720 · Boise, ID 83701 208-342-6571

Louis F. Racine, Jr. · Racine, Olson, Nye, Cooper & Budge · Center Plaza · P.O. Box 1391 · Pocatello, ID 83201 · 208-232-6101

CRIMINAL DEFENSE

Thomas A. Mitchell · 316 Elder Building · Coeur d'Alene, ID 83814 · 208-664-8111

FAMILY LAW

Paul J. Buser · Givens, McDevitt, Pursley, Webb & Buser · Park Place, Suite 200 277 North Sixth Street · P.O. Box 2720 · Boise, ID 83701 · 208-342-6571

Louis H. Cosho · Clemons, Cosho & Humphrey · 815 West Washington Street Boise, ID 83702 · 208-344-7811

Stanley W. Welsh · Clemons, Cosho & Humphrey · 815 West Washington Street Boise, ID 83702 · 208-344-7811

LABOR AND EMPLOYMENT LAW

Fred Joseph Hahn · (Management) · Holden, Kidwell, Hahn & Crapo · Idaho First National Bank Building · P.O. Box 129 · Idaho Falls, ID 83402 · 208-523-0620

NATURAL RESOURCES AND ENVIRONMENTAL LAW

Kent W. Foster · (Mining; Water) · Holden, Kidwell, Hahn & Crapo · Idaho First National Bank Building, Third Floor · 330 Shoup Avenue · P.O. Box 50130 · Idaho Falls, ID 83405 · 208-523-0620

Thomas G. Nelson · (Water) · Nelson, Rosholt, Robertson, Tolman & Tucker · 142 Third Avenue North · P.O. Box 1906 · Twin Falls, ID 83303 · 208-734-0700

PERSONAL INJURY LITIGATION

Peter J. Boyd · (Defendants) · Elam, Burke and Boyd · First Interstate Bank Building, Suite 1010 · 702 West Idaho Street · P.O. Box 1559 · Boise, ID 83701 · 208-343-5454

Carl P. Burke · (Defendants) · Elam, Burke and Boyd · First Interstate Bank Building, Suite 1010 · 702 West Idaho Street · P.O. Box 1559 · Boise, ID 83701 · 208-343-5454

Louis F. Racine, Jr. · Racine, Olson, Nye, Cooper & Budge · Center Plaza · P.O. Box 1391 · Pocatello, ID 83201 · 208-232-6101

John C. Hepworth · (Plaintiffs) · Hepworth, Nungester, Felton & Lezamiz · 133 Shoshone Street North · P.O. Box 389 · Twin Falls, ID 83303-0389 · 208-734-7510

REAL ESTATE LAW

M. Neil Newhouse · Hawley Troxell Ennis & Hawley · One Capital Center, Seventh Floor · P.O. Box 1617 · Boise, ID 83701 · 208-344-6000

Kenneth L. Pursley · Givens, McDevitt, Pursley, Webb & Buser · Park Place, Suite 200 · 277 North Sixth Street · P.O. Box 2720 · Boise, ID 83701 · 208-342-6571

TAX AND EMPLOYEE BENEFITS LAW

Robert S. Erickson · Hawley Troxell Ennis & Hawley · One Capital Center, Seventh Floor · P.O. Box 1617 · Boise, ID 83701 · 208-344-6000

Stephen E. Martin · Holden, Kidwell, Hahn & Crapo · Idaho First National Bank Building, Third Floor · 330 Shoup Avenue · P.O. Box 50130 · Idaho Falls, ID 83405 · 208-523-0620

Gayle A. Sorenson · (Employee Benefits) · Holden, Kidwell, Hahn & Crapo Idaho First National Bank Building · P.O. Box 129 · Idaho Falls, ID 83402 208-523-0620

Philip E. Peterson · 318 Fifth Street · Lewiston, ID 83501 · 208-885-6422

TRUSTS AND ESTATES

Stephen E. Martin · Holden, Kidwell, Hahn & Crapo · Idaho First National Bank Building, Third Floor · 330 Shoup Avenue · P.O. Box 50130 · Idaho Falls, ID 83405 · 208-523-0620

Philip E. Peterson · 318 Fifth Street · Lewiston, ID 83501 · 208-885-6422

Edward D. Ahrens · White, Ahrens, Peterson & Perry · 104 Ninth Avenue South P.O. Box 247 · Nampa, ID 83653-0247 · 208-466-9272

ILLINOIS

BANKRUPTCY LAW	220
BUSINESS LITIGATION	221
CORPORATE LAW	223
CRIMINAL DEFENSE	228
FAMILY LAW	229
LABOR AND EMPLOYMENT LAW	230
MARITIME LAW	232
NATURAL RESOURCES AND ENVIRONMENTAL LAW	232
PERSONAL INJURY LITIGATION	233
REAL ESTATE LAW	234
TAX AND EMPLOYEE BENEFITS LAW	236
TRUSTS AND ESTATES	239

BANKRUPTCY LAW

H. Bruce Bernstein · Sidley & Austin · One First National Plaza · Chicago, IL 60603 · 312-853-7000

Milton L. Fisher · Mayer, Brown & Platt · 190 South La Salle Street · Chicago, IL 60603 · 312-782-0600

Malcolm M. Gaynor · Schwartz Cooper Kolb & Gaynor · Two First National Plaza, Suite 1100 · Chicago, IL 60603 · 312-726-0845

Louis W. Levit · Levit and Mason · 135 South La Salle Street, Suite 1525 Chicago, IL 60603 · 312-263-5100

David N. Missner · Schwartz Cooper Kolb & Gaynor · Two First National Plaza, Suite 1100 · Chicago, IL 60603 · 312-726-0845

Gerald F. Munitz · Winston & Strawn · One First National Plaza, Suite 5000 Chicago, IL 60603 · 312-558-5600

Norman H. Nachman · Winston & Strawn · One First National Plaza, Suite 5000 Chicago, IL 60603 · 312-558-5600

A. Bruce Schimberg · Sidley & Austin · One First National Plaza · Chicago, IL 60603 · 312-853-7000

J. Robert Stoll · Mayer, Brown & Platt · 190 South La Salle Street · Chicago, IL 60603 · 312-782-0600

Allan G. Sweig · Altheimer & Gray · 333 West Wacker Drive, Suite 2600 Chicago, IL 60606 · 312-750-6750

Neal L. Wolf · Ross & Hardies · 150 North Michigan Avenue · Chicago, IL 60601-7567 · 312-558-1000

Clyde Meachum · Meachum & Meachum · 110 North Vermilion Street · Danville, IL 61832 · 217-442-1390

Joel A. Kunin · Carr, Korein, Kunin, Schlichter & Montroy · 412 Missouri Avenue East St. Louis, IL 62201 · 618-274-0434

BUSINESS LITIGATION

Fred H. Bartlit, Jr. · Kirkland & Ellis · 200 East Randolph Drive · Chicago, IL 60601 · 312-861-2000

Frank Cicero, Jr. · Kirkland & Ellis · 200 East Randolph Drive · Chicago, IL 60601 · 312-861-2000

Michael W. Coffield · Coffield Ungaretti Harris & Slavin · 3500 Three First National Plaza · Chicago, IL 60602 · 312-977-4400

Edward L. Foote · Winston & Strawn · One First National Plaza, Suite 5000 Chicago, IL 60603 · 312-558-5600

Thomas A. Foran · Foran, Wiss & Schultz · 30 North La Salle Street, Suite 3000 Chicago, IL 60602 · 312-368-8330

Kevin M. Forde · (Appellate) · 111 West Washington Street, Suite 1100 · Chicago, IL 60602 · 312-726-5015

William J. Harte · 111 West Washington Street, Suite 1100 · Chicago, IL 60602 · 312-726-5015

Reuben L. Hedlund · Latham & Watkins · Sears Tower, Suite 5800 · Chicago, IL 60606 · 312-876-7700

William R. Jentes · Kirkland & Ellis · 200 East Randolph Drive · Chicago, IL 60601 · 312-861-2000

Donald G. Kempf, Jr. · Kirkland & Ellis · 200 East Randolph Drive · Chicago, IL 60601 · 312-861-2000

Kael B. Kennedy · Matkov, Salzman, Madoff & Gunn · 100 West Monroe Street, Suite 1500 · Chicago, IL 60603 · 312-332-0777

Francis J. McConnell · Kovar, Nelson, Brittain & Sledz · 140 South Dearborn Street, Suite 500 · Chicago, IL 60603 · 312-726-9131

Francis D. Morrissey · (Appellate) · Baker & McKenzie · Prudential Plaza, 28th Floor · Chicago, IL 60601 · 312-861-8000

Patrick W. O'Brien · Mayer, Brown & Platt · 190 South La Salle Street · Chicago, IL 60603 · 312-782-0600

Richard J. Phelan · Phelan, Pope & John · 180 North Wacker Drive · Chicago, IL 60606 · 312-621-0700

Earl E. Pollock · Sonnenschein Carlin Nath & Rosenthal · Sears Tower, Suite 8000 · 233 South Wacker Drive · Chicago, IL 60606 · 312-876-8000

Lowell E. Sachnoff · Sachnoff Weaver & Rubenstein · 30 South Wacker Drive, Suite 2900 · Chicago, IL 60606 · 312-207-1000

Thomas P. Sullivan · Jenner & Block · One IBM Plaza · Chicago, IL 60611 · 312-222-9350

Philip W. Tone · Jenner & Block · One IBM Plaza · Chicago, IL 60611 · 312-222-9350

Howard J. Trienens · Sidley & Austin · One First National Plaza · Chicago, IL 60603 · 312-853-7000

Dan K. Webb · Winston & Strawn · One First National Plaza, Suite 5000 · Chicago, IL 60603 · 312-558-5600

H. Blair White · Sidley & Austin · One First National Plaza · Chicago, IL 60603 312-853-7000

Max E. Wildman · Wildman, Harrold, Allen & Dixon · One IBM Plaza, Suite 3000 · Chicago, IL 60611 · 312-222-0400

CORPORATE LAW

Jean Allard · Sonnenschein Carlin Nath & Rosenthal · Sears Tower, Suite 8000 233 South Wacker Drive · Chicago, IL 60606 · 312-876-8000

J. Trent Anderson · Mayer, Brown & Platt · 190 South La Salle Street · Chicago, IL 60603 · 312-782-0600

James G. Archer · Sidley & Austin · One First National Plaza · Chicago, IL 60603 312-853-7000

Cameron S. Avery · Bell, Boyd & Lloyd · Three First National Plaza, Suite 3200 70 West Madison Street · Chicago, IL 60602 · 312-372-1121

Frank E. Babb · McDermott, Will & Emery · 111 West Monroe Street · Chicago, IL 60603 · 312-372-2000

Harold S. Barron · Seyfarth, Shaw, Fairweather & Geraldson · 55 East Monroe Street, Suite 4200 · Chicago, IL 60603 · 312-346-8000

Robert L. Berner, Jr. · Baker & McKenzie · Prudential Plaza, 28th Floor Chicago, IL 60601 · 312-861-8000

H. Bruce Bernstein · Sidley & Austin · One First National Plaza · Chicago, IL 60603 · 312-853-7000

Robert L. Bevan · Hopkins & Sutter · Three First National Plaza · Chicago, IL 60602 · 312-558-6600

John H. Bitner · Bell, Boyd & Lloyd · Three First National Plaza, Suite 3200 70 West Madison Street · Chicago, IL 60602 · 312-372-1121

John C. Blew · Bell, Boyd & Lloyd · Three First National Plaza, Suite 3200 · 70 West Madison Street · Chicago, IL 60602 · 312-372-1121

Bruce L. Bower · Winston & Strawn · One First National Plaza, Suite 5000 Chicago, IL 60603 · 312-558-5600

James J. Brennan · Sidley & Austin · One First National Plaza · Chicago, IL 60603 · 312-853-7000

Milton H. Cohen · Schiff Hardin & Waite · 7200 Sears Tower · 233 South Wacker Drive · Chicago, IL 60606 · 312-876-1000

Peter P. Coladarci · Chapman and Cutler · 111 West Monroe Street, Suite 1400 Chicago, IL 60603 · 312-845-3000

Thomas A. Cole · Sidley & Austin · One First National Plaza · Chicago, IL 60603 312-853-7000

Dale E. Colling · Mayer, Brown & Platt · 190 South La Salle Street · Chicago, IL 60603 · 312-782-0600

Dewey B. Crawford · Gardner, Carton & Douglas · Quaker Tower, 33rd Floor 321 North Clark Street · Chicago, IL 60610-4795 · 312-644-3000

Charles F. Custer · Vedder, Price, Kaufman & Kammholz · 115 South La Salle Street, 30th Floor · Chicago, IL 60603 · 312-781-2200

Wilbur C. Delp, Jr. · Sidley & Austin · One First National Plaza · Chicago, IL 60603 · 312-853-7000

Edwin R. Dunn · Baker & McKenzie · Prudential Plaza, 28th Floor · Chicago, IL 60601 · 312-861-8000

Paul H. Dykstra · Gardner, Carton & Douglas · Quaker Tower, 33rd Floor · 321 North Clark Street · Chicago, IL 60610-4795 · 312-644-3000

Joseph S. Ehrman · Sidley & Austin · One First National Plaza · Chicago, IL 60603 · 312-853-7000

Jay Erens · Hopkins & Sutter · Three First National Plaza · Chicago, IL 60602 312-558-6600

C. Curtis Everett · Bell, Boyd & Lloyd · Three First National Plaza, Suite 3200 70 West Madison Street · Chicago, IL 60602 · 312-372-1121

Ronald H. Filler · Vedder, Price, Kaufman & Kammholz · 115 South La Salle Street, 30th Floor · Chicago, IL 60603 · 312-781-2200

Neil Flanagin · Sidley & Austin · One First National Plaza · Chicago, IL 60603 312-853-7000

Raymond I. Geraldson · Seyfarth, Shaw, Fairweather & Geraldson · 55 East Monroe Street, Suite 4200 · Chicago, IL 60603 · 312-346-8000

Francis J. Gerlits · Kirkland & Ellis · 200 East Randolph Drive · Chicago, IL 60601 · 312-861-2000

Norman M. Gold · Altheimer & Gray · 333 West Wacker Drive, Suite 2600 Chicago, IL 60606 · 312-750-6750

Stanford J. Goldblatt · Hopkins & Sutter · Three First National Plaza · Chicago, IL 60602 · 312-558-6600

Stuart L. Goodman · Schiff Hardin & Waite · 7200 Sears Tower · 233 South Wacker Drive · Chicago, IL 60606 · 312-876-1000

R. James Gormley · Bell, Boyd & Lloyd · Three First National Plaza, Suite 3200 70 West Madison Street · Chicago, IL 60602 · 312-372-1121

Milton H. Gray · Altheimer & Gray · 333 West Wacker Drive, Suite 2600 Chicago, IL 60606 · 312-750-6750

Warren F. Grienenberger · Gardner, Carton & Douglas · Quaker Tower, 33rd Floor · 321 North Clark Street · Chicago, IL 60610-4795 · 312-644-3000

Victor E. Grimm · Bell, Boyd & Lloyd · Three First National Plaza, Suite 3200 70 West Madison Street · Chicago, IL 60602 · 312-372-1121

Frederick Hartman · Schiff Hardin & Waite · 7200 Sears Tower · 233 South Wacker Drive · Chicago, IL 60606 · 312-876-1000

Robert A. Helman · Mayer, Brown & Platt · 190 South La Salle Street · Chicago, IL 60603 · 312-782-0600

James P. Hemmer · Bell, Boyd & Lloyd · Three First National Plaza, Suite 3200 70 West Madison Street · Chicago, IL 60602 · 312-372-1121

Leo Herzel · Mayer, Brown & Platt · 190 South La Salle Street · Chicago, IL 60603 · 312-782-0600

Glen E. Hess · Kirkland & Ellis · 200 East Randolph Drive · Chicago, IL 60601 312-861-2000

James D. Johnson · Sidley & Austin · One First National Plaza · Chicago, IL 60603 · 312-853-7000

Andrew R. Laidlaw · Seyfarth, Shaw, Fairweather & Geraldson · 55 East Monroe Street, Suite 4200 · Chicago, IL 60603 · 312-346-8000

Jack S. Levin · Kirkland & Ellis · 200 East Randolph Drive · Chicago, IL 60601 312-861-2000

Julius Lewis · Sonnenschein Carlin Nath & Rosenthal · Sears Tower, Suite 8000 233 South Wacker Drive · Chicago, IL 60606 · 312-876-8000

Donald G. Lubin · Sonnenschein Carlin Nath & Rosenthal · Sears Tower, Suite 8000 · 233 South Wacker Drive · Chicago, IL 60606 · 312-876-8000

H. George Mann · McDermott, Will & Emery · 111 West Monroe Street Chicago, IL 60603 · 312-372-2000

Charles R. Manzoni, Jr. · Gardner, Carton & Douglas · Quaker Tower, 33rd Floor · 321 North Clark Street · Chicago, IL 60610-4795 · 312-644-3000

Jeremiah Marsh · Hopkins & Sutter · Three First National Plaza · Chicago, IL 60602 · 312-558-6600

John T. McCarthy · Bell, Boyd & Lloyd · Three First National Plaza, Suite 3200 70 West Madison Street · Chicago, IL 60602 · 312-372-1121

John H. McDermott · McDermott, Will & Emery · 111 West Monroe Street Chicago, IL 60603 · 312-372-2000

Harrold E. McKee · Mayer, Brown & Platt · 190 South La Salle Street · Chicago, IL 60603 · 312-782-0600

Stanley H. Meadows · McDermott, Will & Emery · 111 West Monroe Street Chicago, IL 60603 · 312-372-2000

Peter H. Merlin · Gardner, Carton & Douglas · Quaker Tower, 33rd Floor · 321 North Clark Street · Chicago, IL 60610-4795 · 312-644-3000

Howard C. Michaelsen, Jr. · McDermott, Will & Emery · 111 West Monroe Street · Chicago, IL 60603 · 312-372-2000

Maurice J. Miller · Sidley & Austin · One First National Plaza · Chicago, IL 60603 · 312-853-7000

Paul J. Miller · Sonnenschein Carlin Nath & Rosenthal · Sears Tower, Suite 8000 233 South Wacker Drive · Chicago, IL 60606 · 312-876-8000

Allan B. Muchin · Katten, Muchin & Zavis · 525 West Monroe Street, Suite 1600 · Chicago, IL 60606-3693 · 312-902-5200

Charles W. Mulaney, Jr. · Skadden, Arps, Slate, Meagher & Flom · 333 West Wacker Drive · Chicago, IL 60606 · 312-407-0700

Cordell J. Overgaard · Hopkins & Sutter · Three First National Plaza · Chicago, IL 60602 · 312-558-6600

Gerald M. Penner · Katten, Muchin & Zavis · 525 West Monroe Street, Suite 1600 · Chicago, IL 60606-3693 · 312-902-5200

William O. Petersen · Vedder, Price, Kaufman & Kammholz · 115 South La Salle Street, 30th Floor · Chicago, IL 60603 · 312-781-2200

Michael E. Phenner · Hopkins & Sutter · Three First National Plaza · Chicago, IL 60602 · 312-558-6600

Edward G. Proctor · Hinshaw, Culbertson, Moelmann, Hoban & Fuller · 222 North La Salle Street, Suite 300 · Chicago, IL 60601-1081 · 312-704-3000

J. Arden Rearick · Winston & Strawn · One First National Plaza, Suite 5000 · Chicago, IL 60603 · 312-558-5600

James M. Reum · Hopkins & Sutter · Three First National Plaza · Chicago, IL 60602 · 312-558-6600

Thomas A. Reynolds, Jr. · Winston & Strawn · One First National Plaza, Suite 5000 · Chicago, IL 60603 · 312-558-5600

James T. Rhind · Bell, Boyd & Lloyd · Three First National Plaza, Suite 3200 · 70 West Madison Street · Chicago, IL 60602 · 312-372-1121

Burton R. Rissman · Schiff Hardin & Waite · 7200 Sears Tower · 233 South Wacker Drive · Chicago, IL 60606 · 312-876-1000

Richard M. Rosenberg · Mayer, Brown & Platt · 190 South La Salle Street · Chicago, IL 60603 · 312-782-0600

Harold D. Shapiro · Sonnenschein Carlin Nath & Rosenthal · Sears Tower, Suite 8000 · 233 South Wacker Drive · Chicago, IL 60606 · 312-876-8000

Keith Shay · Schiff Hardin & Waite · 7200 Sears Tower · 233 South Wacker Drive · Chicago, IL 60606 · 312-876-1000

Frederick B. Thomas · Mayer, Brown & Platt · 190 South La Salle Street · Chicago, IL 60603 · 312-782-0600

Kenneth I. Vaughan · Chapman and Cutler · 111 West Monroe Street, Suite 1400 · Chicago, IL 60603 · 312-845-3000

Norman Waite, Jr. · Winston & Strawn · One First National Plaza, Suite 5000 · Chicago, IL 60603 · 312-558-5600

Priscilla A. Walter · Gardner, Carton & Douglas · Quaker Tower, 33rd Floor · 321 North Clark Street · Chicago, IL 60610-4795 · 312-644-3000

Herbert S. Wander · Katten, Muchin & Zavis · 525 West Monroe Street, Suite 1600 · Chicago, IL 60606-3693 · 312-902-5200

Wayne W. Whalen · Skadden, Arps, Slate, Meagher & Flom · 333 West Wacker Drive · Chicago, IL 60606 · 312-407-0700

Joseph E. Wyse · Seyfarth, Shaw, Fairweather & Geraldson · 55 East Monroe Street, Suite 4200 · Chicago, IL 60603 · 312-346-8000

Robert A. Yolles · Jones, Day, Reavis & Pogue · 222 West Washington Street, 26th Floor · Chicago, IL 60606 · 312-782-3939

CRIMINAL DEFENSE

Samuel Forbes Adam · 53 West Jackson Street, Suite 1430 · Chicago, IL 60604 · 312-236-5543

William A. Barnett · 135 South La Salle Street, Suite 808 · Chicago, IL 60603 · 312-726-4480

Thomas M. Breen · 221 North La Salle Street, Suite 2100 · Chicago, IL 60601 · 312-346-2550

George J. Cotsirilos · Cotsirilos & Crowley · 33 North Dearborn Street · Chicago, IL 60602 · 312-263-0345

John Powers Crowley · Cotsirilos & Crowley · 33 North Dearborn Street · Chicago, IL 60602 · 312-263-0345

Thomas D. Decker · Thomas D. Decker & Associates · 135 South La Salle Street, Suite 1527 · Chicago, IL 60603 · 312-263-4180

Edward M. Genson · Genson, Steinback and Gillespie · 53 West Jackson Boulevard, Suite 1420 · Chicago, IL 60604 · 312-726-9015

Royal B. Martin, Jr. · Silets and Martin · 140 South Dearborn Street, 15th Floor Chicago, IL 60603 · 312-263-5800

George J. Murtaugh, Jr. · 100 West Monroe Street, Suite 1800 · Chicago, IL 60603 · 312-781-0940

Michael B. Nash · Nash and Nash · 53 West Jackson Boulevard, Suite 615 Chicago, IL 60604 · 312-922-8980

Harvey M. Silets · Silets and Martin · 140 South Dearborn Street, 15th Floor Chicago, IL 60603 · 312-263-5800

Robert M. Stephenson · (also Appellate) · Cotsirilos & Crowley · 33 North Dearborn Street · Chicago, IL 60602 · 312-263-0345

James R. Streicker · Cotsirilos & Crowley · 33 North Dearborn Street · Chicago, IL 60602 · 312-263-0345

Thomas P. Sullivan · Jenner & Block · One IBM Plaza · Chicago, IL 60611 · 312-222-9350

Patrick A. Tuite · Tuite, Mejia & Giacchetti · 105 West Adams Street, 31st Floor Chicago, IL 60603 · 312-641-1022

Dan K. Webb · Winston & Strawn · One First National Plaza, Suite 5000 Chicago, IL 60603 · 312-558-5600

FAMILY LAW

Miles N. Beermann · Beermann, Swerdlove, Woloshin, Barezky & Berkson · 69 West Washington Street, Room 600 · Chicago, IL 60602 · 312-621-9700

Arthur M. Berman · Kirsh, Berman & Hoffenberg · 120 West Madison Street Chicago, IL 60602 · 312-782-3020

Muller Davis · Davis, Friedman, Zavett, Kane & MacRae · The Marquette Building, Suite 1600 · 140 South Dearborn Street · Chicago, IL 60603 · 312-782-2220

Owen L. Doss · Doss, Puchalski & Keenan · 20 North Wacker Drive · Chicago, IL 60606 · 312-726-3060

Joseph N. Du Canto · Schiller, Du Canto and Fleck · 200 North La Salle Street, Suite 2700 · Chicago, IL 60601 · 312-641-5560

James H. Feldman · Jenner & Block · One IBM Plaza · Chicago, IL 60611 · 312-222-9350

Charles J. Fleck · Schiller, Du Canto and Fleck · 200 North La Salle Street, Suite 2700 · Chicago, IL 60601 · 312-641-5560

James T. Friedman · Davis, Friedman, Zavett, Kane & MacRae · The Marquette Building, Suite 1600 · 140 South Dearborn Street · Chicago, IL 60603 · 312-782-2220

Sanford Kirsh · Kirsh, Berman & Hoffenberg · 120 West Madison Street · Chicago, IL 60602 · 312-782-3020

Bernard B. Rinella · Rinella and Rinella · One North La Salle Street, Suite 3400 Chicago, IL 60602 · 312-236-5454

Donald C. Schiller · Schiller, Du Canto and Fleck · 200 North La Salle Street, Suite 2700 · Chicago, IL 60601 · 312-641-5560

Errol Zavett · Davis, Friedman, Zavett, Kane & MacRae · The Marquette Building, Suite 1600 · 140 South Dearborn Street · Chicago, IL 60603 · 312-782-2220

Harold G. Field · Harold G. Field & Associates · 126 South County Farm Road, Suite 2B · Wheaton, IL 60187 · 312-665-5800

H. Joseph Gitlin · Gitlin & Burns · 111 Dean Street · Woodstock, IL 60098 815-338-0021

LABOR AND EMPLOYMENT LAW

Lester Asher · (Labor) · Asher, Pavalon, Gittler and Greenfield · Two North La Salle Street, Suite 1200 · Chicago, IL 60602 · 312-263-1500

Charles Barnhill, Jr. · (Individuals) · Davis, Barnhill & Galland · 14 West Erie Street · Chicago, IL 60610 · 312-751-1170

Stuart Bernstein · (Management) · Mayer, Brown & Platt · 190 South La Salle Street · Chicago, IL 60603 · 312-782-0600

Sherman M. Carmell · (Labor) · Carmell, Charone, Widmer & Mathews · 39 South La Salle Street, Suite 1110 · Chicago, IL 60603 · 312-236-8033

Sheldon M. Charone · (Labor) · Carmell, Charone, Widmer & Mathews · 39 South La Salle Street, Suite 1110 · Chicago, IL 60603 · 312-236-8033

R. Theodore Clark, Jr. · (Management) · Seyfarth, Shaw, Fairweather & Geraldson · 55 East Monroe Street, Suite 4200 · Chicago, IL 60603 · 312-346-8000

Gilbert A. Cornfield · (Labor) · Cornfield and Feldman · 343 South Dearborn Street, 13th Floor · Chicago, IL 60604-3852 · 312-922-2800

Eugene Cotton · (Labor) · Cotton, Watt, Jones & King · One IBM Plaza, Suite 4750 · 330 North Wabash Avenue · Chicago, IL 60611 · 312-467-0590

Lawrence D. Ehrlich · (Management) · Borovsky, Ehrlich & Kronenberg · 205 North Michigan Avenue, 41st Floor · Chicago, IL 60601 · 312-861-0800

Gilbert Feldman · (Labor) · Cornfield and Feldman · 343 South Dearborn Street, 13th Floor · Chicago, IL 60604-3852 · 312-922-2800

James C. Franczek, Jr. · Vedder, Price, Kaufman & Kammholz · 115 South La Salle Street, 30th Floor · Chicago, IL 60603 · 312-781-2200

Marvin Gittler · (Labor) · Asher, Pavalon, Gittler and Greenfield · Two North La Salle Street, Suite 1200 · Chicago, IL 60602 · 312-263-1500

Irving M. Friedman · (Labor) · Katz, Friedman, Schur & Eagle · Seven South Dearborn, Suite 1734 · Chicago, IL 60603 · 312-263-6330

Joseph M. Jacobs · (Labor) · Jacobs, Burns, Sugarman & Orlove · 201 North Wells Street, Suite 1900 · Chicago, IL 60606 · 312-372-1646

Theophil C. Kammholz · (Management) · Vedder, Price, Kaufman & Kammholz · 115 South La Salle Street, 30th Floor · Chicago, IL 60603 · 312-781-2200

Harold A. Katz · (Labor) · Katz, Friedman, Schur & Eagle · Seven South Dearborn Street, Suite 1734 · Chicago, IL 60603 · 312-263-6330

Richard W. Laner · (Management) · Laner, Muchin, Dombrow and Becker · 350 North Clark Street · Chicago, IL 60610-4798 · 312-467-9800

Kenneth T. Lopatka · (Management) · Jenner & Block · One IBM Plaza · Chicago, IL 60611 · 312-222-9350

George J. Matkov, Jr. · (Management) · Matkov, Salzman & Madoff · 100 West Monroe Street, Suite 1500 · Chicago, IL 60603-1906 · 312-332-0777

Richard L. Marcus · (Management) · Sonnenschein Carlin Nath & Rosenthal Sears Tower, Suite 8000 · 233 South Wacker Drive · Chicago, IL 60606 312-876-8000

Thomas R. Meites · (Individuals) · Meites, Frackman & Mulder · 135 South La Salle Street · Chicago, IL 60603 · 312-263-0272

Edward B. Miller · (Management) · Pope, Ballard, Shepard & Fowle · 69 West Washington Street · Chicago, IL 60602 · 312-630-4200

Richard D. Ostrow · (Management) · Seyfarth, Shaw, Fairweather & Geraldson 55 East Monroe Street, Suite 4200 · Chicago, IL 60603 · 312-346-8000

MARITIME LAW

Warren J. Marwedel · Tribler & Marwedel · 230 West Monroe Street, Suite 220 Chicago, IL 60606 · 312-368-1262

Theodore C. Robinson · Ray, Robinson, Hanninen & Carle · 135 South La Salle Street, Suite 1916 · Chicago, IL 60603 · 312-726-2905

Michael A. Snyder · Snyder & Gerard · Three First National Plaza, Suite 1250 Chicago, IL 60602 · 312-580-0710

NATURAL RESOURCES AND ENVIRONMENTAL LAW

Percy L. Angelo · Mayer, Brown & Platt · 190 South La Salle Street · Chicago, IL 60603 · 312-782-0600

Thomas M. McMahon · Sidley & Austin · One First National Plaza · Chicago, IL 60603 · 312-853-7000

Sheldon A. Zabel · Schiff Hardin & Waite · 7200 Sears Tower · 233 South Wacker Drive · Chicago, IL 60606 · 312-876-1000

PERSONAL INJURY LITIGATION

William C. Murphy · Murphy, Hupp, Foote, Mielke and Kinnally · North Island Center · P.O. Box 1327 · Aurora, IL 60507 · 312-844-0056

Jerome Mirza · (Plaintiffs) · Jerome Mirza and Associates · 705 East Washington Street · P.O. Box 308 · Bloomington, IL 61701-0186 · 309-827-8011

Thomas F. Bridgman · (Defendants) · Baker & McKenzie · Prudential Plaza, Suite 2800 · Chicago, IL 60601 · 312-861-8000

Michel A. Coccia · (Defendants) · Baker & McKenzie · Prudential Plaza, Suite 2800 · Chicago, IL 60601 · 312-861-8000

Robert J. Cooney, Sr. · (Plaintiffs) · Robert J. Cooney & Associates · 77 West Washington Street · Chicago, IL 60602 · 312-236-6166

Philip H. Corboy · (Plaintiffs) · Corboy & Demetrio · 33 North Dearborn Street, Suite 630 · Chicago, IL 60602 · 312-346-3191

Thomas A. Demetrio · (Plaintiffs) · Corboy & Demetrio · 33 North Dearborn Street, Suite 630 · Chicago, IL 60602 · 312-346-3191

James T. Demos · (Plaintiffs) · Demos & Burke · 33 North Dearborn Street, Suite 826 · Chicago, IL 60602 · 312-263-4388

Richard G. French · (Defendants) · French Rogers Kezelis & Kominiarek · 33 North Dearborn Street, Suite 1800 · Chicago, IL 60602 · 312-782-0634

John D. Hayes · (Plaintiffs) · Hayes & Power · Three First National Plaza, Suite 3910 · Chicago, IL 60602 · 312-236-9381

Al Hofeld · (Plaintiffs) · Hofeld and Schaffner · 33 North Dearborn Street, Suite 1600 · Chicago, IL 60602 · 312-372-4250

Harold L. Jacobson · (Defendants) · Lord, Bissell & Brook · Harris Bank Building, Suites 3200-3600 · 115 South La Salle Street · Chicago, IL 60603 · 312-443-0700

William V. Johnson · (Defendants) · Johnson, Cusack & Bell · 211 West Wacker Drive, Suite 1800 · Chicago, IL 60606 · 312-372-0770

John J. Kennelly · (Plaintiffs) · John J. Kennelly & Associates · 111 West Washington Street, Suite 1449 · Chicago, IL 60602 · 312-346-3546

William D. Maddux · (Plaintiffs) · William D. Maddux & Associates · One North La Salle Street, Suite 3800 · Chicago, IL 60602 · 312-782-2525

C. Barry Montgomery · (Defendants) · Williams and Montgomery · 20 North Wacker Drive, Suite 2100 · Chicago, IL 60606 · 312-443-3200

Richard E. Mueller · (Defendants) · Lord, Bissell & Brook · Harris Bank Building, Suites 3200-3600 · 115 South La Salle Street · Chicago, IL 60603 · 312-443-0700

Nat P. Ozmon · (Plaintiffs) · Anesi, Ozmon, Lewin & Associates · 188 West Randolph Street, Suite 1600 · Chicago, IL 60601 · 312-372-3822

Joseph A. Power, Jr. · (Plaintiffs) · Hayes & Power · Three First National Plaza, Suite 3910 · Chicago, IL 60602 · 312-236-9381

Neil K. Quinn · (Defendants) · Pretzel & Stouffer · One South Wacker Drive, Suite 2500 · Chicago, IL 60606 · 312-346-1973

Leonard M. Ring · (Plaintiffs) · Leonard M. Ring and Associates · 111 West Washington Street, Suite 1333 · Chicago, IL 60602 · 312-332-1765

Thomas F. Tobin · (Defendants) · Baker & McKenzie · Prudential Plaza, Suite 2800 · Chicago, IL 60601 · 312-861-8000

Max Wildman · (Defendants) · Wildman, Harrold, Allen & Dixon · One IBM Plaza, Suite 3000 · Chicago, IL 60611 · 312-222-0400

Rex Carr · (Plaintiffs) · Carr, Korein, Kunin, Schlichter & Montroy · 412 Missouri Avenue · East St. Louis, IL 62201 · 618-274-0434

Frederick W. Allen · (Plaintiffs) · Allen & Clark · Savings Center Tower, Suite 1810 · 411 Hamilton Boulevard · Peoria, IL 61602 · 309-674-2164

Thomas F. Londrigan · (Plaintiffs) · Londrigan, Potter & Randle · 1227 South Seventh Street · Springfield, IL 62703 · 217-544-9823

REAL ESTATE LAW

Frank C. Bernard · Sonnenschein Carlin Nath & Rosenthal · Sears Tower, Suite 8000 · 233 South Wacker Drive · Chicago, IL 60606 · 312-876-8000

Martin K. Blonder · Rosenthal and Schanfield · Mid Continental Plaza, Suite 4620 · 55 East Monroe Street · Chicago, IL 60603 · 312-236-5622

Charles L. Edwards · Rudnick & Wolfe · 203 North La Salle Street, 18th Floor · Chicago, IL 60602 · 312-368-4000

Livingston Fairbank, Jr. · Rudnick & Wolfe · 203 North La Salle Street, 18th Floor · Chicago, IL 60602 · 312-368-4000

Fred I. Feinstein · McDermott, Will & Emery · 111 West Monroe Street · Chicago, IL 60603 · 312-372-2000

Norman Geis · Greenberger, Krauss & Jacobs · 180 North La Salle Street, Suite 2700 · Chicago, IL 60601 · 312-346-1300

Jerome H. Gerson · Rudnick & Wolfe · 203 North La Salle Street, 18th Floor · Chicago, IL 60602 · 312-368-4000

David Glickstein · Greenberger, Krauss & Jacobs · 180 North La Salle Street, Suite 2700 · Chicago, IL 60601 · 312-346-1300

Robert H. Goldman · Rudnick & Wolfe · 203 North La Salle Street, 18th Floor · Chicago, IL 60602 · 312-368-4000

Donald J. Gralen · Sidley & Austin · One First National Plaza · Chicago, IL 60603 · 312-853-7000

Ernest Greenberger · Greenberger, Krauss & Jacobs · 180 North La Salle Street, Suite 2700 · Chicago, IL 60601 · 312-346-1300

Wayne R. Hannah, Jr. · Sonnenschein Carlin Nath & Rosenthal · Sears Tower, Suite 8000 · 233 South Wacker Drive · Chicago, IL 60606 · 312-876-8000

Thomas C. Homburger · Bell, Boyd & Lloyd · Three First National Plaza, Suite 3200 · 70 West Madison Street · Chicago, IL 60602 · 312-372-1121

Paul Homer · Rudnick & Wolfe · 203 North La Salle Street, 18th Floor · Chicago, IL 60202 · 312-368-4000

Maurice Jacobs · Greenberger, Krauss & Jacobs · 180 North La Salle Street, Suite 2700 · Chicago, IL 60601 · 312-346-1300

Howard E. Kane · Rudnick & Wolfe · 203 North La Salle Street, 18th Floor · Chicago, IL 60602 · 312-368-4000

Michael S. Kurtzon · Miller, Shakman, Nathan & Hamilton · 208 South La Salle Street, Suite 1200 · Chicago, IL 60604 · 312-263-3700

David E. Malfar · 77 West Washington Street · Chicago, IL 60602 · 312-726-8200

Ronald S. Miller · Miller, Shakman, Nathan & Hamilton · 208 South La Salle Street, Suite 1200 · Chicago, IL 60604 · 312-263-3700

Frank A. Reichelderfer · Wilson & McIlvaine · 135 South La Salle Street, Suite 2300 · Chicago, IL 60603 · 312-263-1212

Alfred M. Rogers, Jr. · Mayer, Brown & Platt · 190 South La Salle Street Chicago, IL 60603 · 312-782-0600

Lester Rosen · Rosenthal and Schanfield · Mid Continental Plaza, Suite 4620 · 55 East Monroe Street · Chicago, IL 60603 · 312-236-5622

Merwin S. Rosenberg · Rudnick & Wolfe · 203 North La Salle Street, 18th Floor Chicago, IL 60602 · 312-368-4000

Paul D. Rudnick · Rudnick & Wolfe · 203 North La Salle Street, 18th Floor Chicago, IL 60602 · 312-368-4000

Stanton Schuman · Foss, Schuman, Drake & Barnard · 11 South La Salle Street, Suite 1100 · Chicago, IL 60603 · 312-782-2610

Perry J. Snyderman · Rudnick & Wolfe · 203 North La Salle Street, 18th Floor Chicago, IL 60602 · 312-368-4000

William R. Theiss · Kirkland & Ellis · 200 East Randolph Drive · Chicago, IL 60601 · 312-861-2000

Brian Meltzer · Keck, Mahin & Cate · 1699 East Woodfield Road, Suite 206 Schaumburg, IL 60173 · 312-330-1200

TAX AND EMPLOYEE BENEFITS LAW

Melvin S. Adess · Kirkland & Ellis · 200 East Randolph Drive · Chicago, IL 60601 312-861-2000

Robert H. Aland · Baker & McKenzie · Prudential Plaza, Suite 3200 · Chicago, IL 60601 · 312-861-8000

Sheldon I. Banoff · Katten, Muchin & Zavis · 525 West Monroe, Suite 1600 Chicago, IL 60606-3693 · 312-902-5200

Frank V. Battle, Jr. · Sidley & Austin · One First National Plaza · Chicago, IL 60603 · 312-853-7000

Michael G. Beemer · Vedder, Price, Kaufman & Kammholz · 115 South La Salle Street, 30th Floor · Chicago, IL 60603 · 312-781-2200

Theodore Berger · Miller, Shakman, Nathan & Hamilton · 208 South La Salle Street, Suite 1200 · Chicago, IL 60604 · 312-263-3700

Stephen S. Bowen · Latham & Watkins · Sears Tower, Suite 5800 · Chicago, IL 60606 · 312-876-7700

Patrick J. Caraher · (Employee Benefits) · McDermott, Will & Emery · 111 West Monroe Street · Chicago, IL 60603 · 312-372-2000

Lawrence M. Dubin · Hopkins & Sutter · Three First National Plaza · Chicago, IL 60602 · 312-558-6600

Bradford L. Ferguson · Hopkins & Sutter · Three First National Plaza · Chicago, IL 60602 · 312-558-6600

Sheldon I. Fink · Sonnenschein Carlin Nath & Rosenthal · Sears Tower, Suite 8000 · 233 South Wacker Drive · Chicago, IL 60606 · 312-876-8000

Louis S. Freeman · Sonnenschein Carlin Nath & Rosenthal · Sears Tower, Suite 8000 · 233 South Wacker Drive · Chicago, IL 60606 · 312-876-8000

William C. Golden · Sidley & Austin · One First National Plaza · Chicago, IL 60603 · 312-853-7000

Arthur I. Gould · Mayer, Brown & Platt · 190 South La Salle Street · Chicago, IL 60603 · 312-782-0600

Crane C. Hauser · Winston & Strawn · One First National Plaza, Suite 5000 Chicago, IL 60603 · 312-558-5600

Frederic W. Hickman · Hopkins & Sutter · Three First National Plaza · Chicago, IL 60602 · 312-558-6600

George B. Javaras · Kirkland & Ellis · 200 East Randolph Drive · Chicago, IL 60601 · 312-861-2000

Burton W. Kanter · Neal, Gerber & Eisenberg · 208 South La Salle Street, Ninth Floor · Chicago, IL 60604 · 312-269-8000

Jared Kaplan · Keck, Mahin & Cate · 8300 Sears Tower · 233 South Wacker Drive · Chicago, IL 60606-6589 · 312-876-3400

Stanton A. Kessler · Mayer, Brown & Platt · 190 South La Salle Street · Chicago, IL 60603 · 312-782-0600

Howard G. Krane · Kirkland & Ellis · 200 East Randolph Drive · Chicago, IL 60601 · 312-861-2000

Herbert W. Krueger · (Employee Benefits) · Mayer, Brown & Platt · 190 South La Salle Street · Chicago, IL 60603 · 312-782-0600

Milton A. Levenfeld · Levenfeld, Eisenberg, Janger, Glassberg & Samotny · 33 West Monroe Street, 21st Floor · Chicago, IL 60603 · 312-346-8380

Jack S. Levin · Kirkland & Ellis · 200 East Randolph Drive · Chicago, IL 60601 312-861-2000

Richard L. Menson · (Employee Benefits) · Gardner, Carton & Douglas · Quaker Tower, 33rd Floor · 321 North Clark Street · Chicago, IL 60610-4795 · 312-644-3000

Timothy M. Mlsna · (Employee Benefits) · Kirkland & Ellis · 200 East Randolph Drive · Chicago, IL 60601 · 312-861-2000

William L. Morrison · Gardner, Carton & Douglas · Quaker Tower, 33rd Floor 321 North Clark Street · Chicago, IL 60610-4795 · 312-644-3000

Alan D. Nesburg · (Employee Benefits) · McDermott, Will & Emery · 111 West Monroe Street · Chicago, IL 60603 · 312-372-2000

John K. O'Connor · Lord, Bissell & Brook · Harris Bank Building, Suites 3200-3600 · 115 South La Salle Street · Chicago, IL 60603 · 312-443-0700

Arthur S. Rollin · Skadden, Arps, Slate, Meagher & Flom · 333 West Wacker Drive · Chicago, IL 60606 · 312-407-0700

Edward C. Rustigan · Mayer, Brown & Platt · 190 South La Salle Street · Chicago, IL 60603 · 312-782-0600

Roger C. Siske · (Employee Benefits) · Sonnenschein Carlin Nath & Rosenthal Sears Tower, Suite 8000 · 233 South Wacker Drive · Chicago, IL 60606 312-876-8000

Samuel C. Thompson, Jr. · Schiff Hardin & Waite · 7200 Sears Tower · 233 South Wacker Drive · Chicago, IL 60606 · 312-876-1000

Douglas H. Walter · Bell, Boyd & Lloyd · Three First National Plaza, Suite 3200 70 West Madison Street · Chicago, IL 60602 · 312-782-3939

TRUSTS AND ESTATES

Ivan A. Elliott, Jr. · Conger & Elliott · Farm Bureau Building · Carmi, IL 62821 618-382-4187

Frederick G. Acker · McDermott, Will & Emery · 111 West Monroe Street · Chicago, IL 60603 · 312-372-2000

Roy M. Adams · Schiff Hardin & Waite · 7200 Sears Tower · 233 South Wacker Drive · Chicago, IL 60606 · 312-876-1000

W. Timothy Baetz · McDermott, Will & Emery · 111 West Monroe Street · Chicago, IL 60603 · 312-372-2000

Larry D. Berning · Sidley & Austin · One First National Plaza · Chicago, IL 60603 · 312-853-7000

Arthur W. Brown, Jr. · Altheimer & Gray · 333 West Wacker Drive, Suite 2600 Chicago, IL 60606 · 312-750-6750

Leon Bud Feldman · Jenner & Block · One IBM Plaza · Chicago, IL 60611 · 312-222-9350

Donald A. Gillies · Altheimer & Gray · 333 West Wacker Drive, Suite 2600 Chicago, IL 60606 · 312-750-6750

Donald A. Glassberg · Levenfeld, Eisenberg, Janger, Glassberg & Samotny · 33 West Monroe Street, 21st Floor · Chicago, IL 60603 · 312-346-8380

Howard M. McCue III · Mayer, Brown & Platt · 190 South La Salle Street · Chicago, IL 60603 · 312-782-0600

Franklin W. Nitikman · McDermott, Will & Emery · 111 West Monroe Street Chicago, IL 60603 · 312-372-2000

James M. Trapp · McDermott, Will & Emery · 111 West Monroe Street · Chicago, IL 60603 · 312-372-2000

William C. Weinsheimer · Hopkins & Sutter · Three First National Plaza
Chicago, IL 60602 · 312-558-6600

James N. Zartman · Chapman and Cutler · 111 West Monroe Street, Suite 1300
Chicago, IL 60603 · 312-845-3000

Jerold I. Horn · 515 Jefferson Bank Building · Peoria, IL 61602 · 309-676-2778

INDIANA

BANKRUPTCY LAW	241
BUSINESS LITIGATION	242
CORPORATE LAW	244
CRIMINAL DEFENSE	246
FAMILY LAW	247
LABOR AND EMPLOYMENT LAW	248
NATURAL RESOURCES AND ENVIRONMENTAL LAW	249
PERSONAL INJURY LITIGATION	249
REAL ESTATE LAW	251
TAX AND EMPLOYEE BENEFITS LAW	252
TRUSTS AND ESTATES	254

BANKRUPTCY LAW

William A. Thorne · Thorne, Grodnik & Ransel · 228 West High Street · Elkhart, IN 46516-3176 · 219-294-7473

Howard B. Sandler · Beckman, Lawson, Sandler, Snyder & Federoff · 2110 Fort Wayne National Bank Building · 110 West Berry Street · Fort Wayne, IN 46802 · 219-422-2561

Jerald I. Ancel · Ancel, Miroff & Frank · Two Market Square Center, Suite 1000 · P.O. Box 44219 · Indianapolis, IN 46244 · 317-634-1245

Steven H. Ancel · Ancel & Dunlap · Market Square Center, Suite 1770 · Indianapolis, IN 46204 · 317-634-9052

Sigmund J. Beck · Bamberger & Feibleman · 500 Union Federal Building · 45 North Pennsylvania Street · Indianapolis, IN 46204 · 317-639-5151

James E. Carlberg · Klineman, Rose, Wolf and Wallack · 2130 Indiana National Bank Tower · One Indiana Square · Indianapolis, IN 46204 · 317-639-4141

James M. Carr · Baker & Daniels · 108 North Pennsylvania, Suite 810 · Indianapolis, IN 46204 · 317-237-4535

John R. Carr, Jr. · Buschmann, Carr & Meyer · 1015 Merchants Plaza, East Tower · 101 West Washington Street · Indianapolis, IN 46204 · 317-636-5511

David H. Kleiman · Dann Pecar Newman Talesnick & Kleiman · One American Square, Suite 2300 · P.O. Box 82008 · Indianapolis, IN 46282 · 317-632-3232

James A. Knauer · Kroger, Gardis & Regas · 700 Guaranty Building · 20 North Meridian Street · Indianapolis, IN 46204-3059 · 317-634-6328

Elliott D. Levin · Rubin & Levin · 500 Marott Center · 342 Massachusetts Avenue · Indianapolis, IN 46204-2161 · 317-634-0300

Stanley Talesnick · Dann Pecar Newman Talesnick & Kleiman · One American Square, Suite 2300 · P.O. Box 82008 · Indianapolis, IN 46282 · 317-632-3232

BUSINESS LITIGATION

John L. Carroll · Johnson, Carroll & Griffith · 2230 West Franklin Street · P.O. Box 6016 · Evansville, IN 47712-0016 · 812-425-4466

Leonard E. Eilbacher · Hunt, Suedhoff, Borror & Eilbacher · 900 Paine Webber Building · 803 South Calhoun Street · Fort Wayne, IN 46802-2399 · 219-423-1311

Edward L. Murphy, Jr. · Livingston, Dildine, Haynie & Yoder · 1400 One Summit Square · Fort Wayne, IN 46802 · 219-423-9411

Richard E. Steinbronn · Barnes & Thornburg · One Summit Square, Suite 600 · Fort Wayne, IN 46802 · 219-423-9440

Frederick F. Eichhorn, Jr. · Eichhorn, Eichhorn & Link · 200 Russell Street · P.O. Box 6328 · Hammond, IN 46325-6328 · 219-931-0560

David C. Jensen · Eichhorn, Eichhorn & Link · 200 Russell Street · P.O. Box 6328 · Hammond, IN 46325-6328 · 219-931-0560

Frederick H. Link · Eichhorn, Eichhorn & Link · 200 Russell Street · P.O. Box 6328 · Hammond, IN 46325-6328 · 219-931-0560

Terrill Albright · Baker & Daniels · 108 North Pennsylvania, Suite 810 · Indianapolis, IN 46204 · 317-237-4535

William C. Barnard · (also Appellate) · Sommer & Barnard · 54 Monument Circle, Ninth Floor · Indianapolis, IN 46204 · 317-639-5400

Virgil L. Beeler · (also Appellate) · Baker & Daniels · 108 North Pennsylvania, Suite 810 · Indianapolis, IN 46204 · 317-237-4535

Jerry P. Belknap · Barnes & Thornburg · 1313 Merchants Bank Building · 11 South Meridian Street · Indianapolis, IN 46204 · 317-638-1313

Theodore R. Boehm · (also Appellate) · Baker & Daniels · 108 North Pennsylvania, Suite 810 · Indianapolis, IN 46204 · 317-237-4535

Joe C. Emerson · Baker & Daniels · 108 North Pennsylvania, Suite 810 · Indianapolis, IN 46204 · 317-237-4535

Samuel A. Fuller · Lewis, Kappes, Fuller & Eads · One American Square, Suite 1210 · Indianapolis, IN 46282 · 317-639-1210

John W. Houghton · Barnes & Thornburg · 1313 Merchants Bank Building · 11 South Meridian Street · Indianapolis, IN 46204 · 317-638-1313

Arthur P. Kalleres · Ice Miller Donadio & Ryan · One American Square · P.O. Box 82001 · Indianapolis, IN 46282-0002 · 317-236-2100

Donald E. Knebel · Barnes & Thornburg · 1313 Merchants Bank Building · 11 South Meridian Street · Indianapolis, IN 46204 · 317-638-1313

James A. McDermott · (also Appellate) · Barnes & Thornburg · 1313 Merchants Bank Building · 11 South Meridian Street · Indianapolis, IN 46204 · 317-638-1313

Lee B. McTurnan · Hackman, McClarnon & McTurnan · 1900 One Indiana Square · Indianapolis, IN 46204 · 317-636-5401

Hugh E. Reynolds, Jr. · Locke, Reynolds, Boyd & Weisell · One Indiana Square, 21st Floor · Indianapolis, IN 46204 · 317-639-5534

Christopher G. Scanlon · Baker & Daniels · 108 North Pennsylvania, Suite 810 · Indianapolis, IN 46204 · 317-237-4535

Geoffrey Segar · Ice Miller Donadio & Ryan · One American Square · P.O. Box 82001 · Indianapolis, IN 46282-0002 · 317-236-2100

Evan E. Steger · Ice Miller Donadio & Ryan · One American Square · P.O. Box 82001 · Indianapolis, IN 46282-0002 · 317-236-2100

Stephen W. Terry, Jr. · Baker & Daniels · 108 North Pennsylvania, Suite 810 · Indianapolis, IN 46204 · 317-237-4535

William P. Wooden · Wooden McLaughlin & Sterner · 909 Merchants Plaza East Tower · Indianapolis, IN 46204 · 317-639-6151

Russell H. Hart · Stuart & Branigin · 801 The Life Building · P.O. Box 1010 · Lafayette, IN 47902 · 317-423-1561

James V. McGlone · Stuart & Branigin · 801 The Life Building · P.O. Box 1010 · Lafayette, IN 47902 · 317-423-1561

J. Lee McNeely · McNeely, Sanders and Stephenson · 611 South Harrison Street · P.O. Box 457 · Shelbyville, IN 46176 · 317-392-3619

Robert J. Konopa · Butler, Simeri, Konopa & Laderer · One Michiana Square, Suite 300 · 100 East Wayne Street · South Bend, IN 46601 · 219-233-3303

Richard W. Morgan · Barnes & Thornburg · 600 First Source Bank Building · 100 North Michigan Street · South Bend, IN 46601 · 219-233-1171

Franklin A. Morse II · Barnes & Thornburg · 600 First Source Bank Building · 100 North Michigan Street · South Bend, IN 46601 · 219-233-1171

John T. Mulvihill · Barnes & Thornburg · 600 First Source Bank Building · 100 North Michigan Street · South Bend, IN 46601 · 219-233-1171

James H. Pankow · Jones, Obenchain, Ford, Pankow & Lewis · 1800 Valley American Bank Building · P.O. Box 4577 · South Bend, IN 46634-4577 · 219-233-1194

Thomas H. Singer · (Plaintiffs) · Law Offices of Thomas H. Singer · 205 First Bank Building, Third Floor · South Bend, IN 46601 · 219-232-4747

CORPORATE LAW

Philip L. Carson · Baker & Daniels & Shoaff · 2400 Fort Wayne National Bank Building · P.O. Box 12709 · Fort Wayne, IN 46864 · 219-424-8000

Miles C. Gerberding · Barnes & Thornburg · One Summit Square, Suite 600 Fort Wayne, IN 46802 · 219-423-9440

David Haist · Barnes & Thornburg · One Summit Square, Suite 600 · Fort Wayne, IN 46802 · 219-423-9440

Robert T. Hoover · Baker & Daniels & Shoaff · 2400 Fort Wayne National Bank Building · P.O. Box 12709 · Fort Wayne, IN 46864 · 219-424-8000

Thomas M. Shoaff · Baker & Daniels & Shoaff · 2400 Fort Wayne National Bank Building · P.O. Box 12709 · Fort Wayne, IN 46864 · 219-424-8000

James A. Aschleman · Baker & Daniels · 108 North Pennsylvania, Suite 810 Indianapolis, IN 46204 · 317-237-4535

Robert S. Ashby · Barnes & Thornburg · 1313 Merchants Bank Building · 11 South Meridian Street · Indianapolis, IN 46204 · 317-638-1313

Leonard J. Betley · Ice Miller Donadio & Ryan · One American Square · P.O. Box 82001 · Indianapolis, IN 46282-0002 · 317-236-2100

John D. Cochran · Baker & Daniels · 108 North Pennsylvania, Suite 810 Indianapolis, IN 46204 · 317-237-4535

Richard E. Deer · Barnes & Thornburg · 1313 Merchants Bank Building · 11 South Meridian Street · Indianapolis, IN 46204 · 317-638-1313

Richard M. Leagre · Leagre & Barnes · 9100 Keystone Crossing, Suite 800 · P.O. Box 40609 · Indianapolis, IN 46240-0609 · 317-843-1655

Thomas M. Lofton · Baker & Daniels · 108 North Pennsylvania, Suite 810 Indianapolis, IN 46204 · 317-237-4535

Michael P. Lucas · Barnes & Thornburg · 1313 Merchants Bank Building · 11 South Meridian Street · Indianapolis, IN 46204 · 317-638-1313

Bruce A. Polizotto · Ice Miller Donadio & Ryan · One American Square · P.O. Box 82001 · Indianapolis, IN 46282-0002 · 317-236-2100

Robert H. Reynolds · Barnes & Thornburg · 1313 Merchants Bank Building · 11 South Meridian Street · Indianapolis, IN 46204 · 317-638-1313

Robert D. Risch · Ice Miller Donadio & Ryan · One American Square · P.O. Box 82001 · Indianapolis, IN 46282-0002 · 317-236-2100

Jack R. Snyder · Ice Miller Donadio & Ryan · One American Square · P.O. Box 82001 · Indianapolis, IN 46282-0002 · 317-236-2100

James A. Strain · Barnes & Thornburg · 1313 Merchants Bank Building · 11 South Meridian Street · Indianapolis, IN 46204 · 317-638-1313

Charles M. Boynton · Doran, Manion, Boynton, Kamm & Esmont · 202 South Michigan Avenue, Room 725 · South Bend, IN 46601 · 219-233-6117

John A. Burgess · Barnes & Thornburg · 600 First Source Bank Building · 100 North Michigan Street · South Bend, IN 46601 · 219-233-1171

G. Burt Ford · Jones, Obenchain, Ford, Pankow & Lewis · 1800 Valley American Bank Building · P.O. Box 4577 · South Bend, IN 46634-4577 · 219-233-1194

Edward J. Gray · Barnes & Thornburg · 600 First Source Bank Building · 100 North Michigan Street · South Bend, IN 46601 · 219-233-1171

Warren E. McGill · Barnes & Thornburg · 600 First Source Bank Building · 100 North Michigan Street · South Bend, IN 46601 · 219-233-1171

Nelson J. Vogel, Jr. · Barnes & Thornburg · 600 First Source Bank Building · 100 North Michigan Street · South Bend, IN 46601 · 219-233-1171

CRIMINAL DEFENSE

Jeffrey A. Lockwood · Schuyler, Eisele & Lockwood · 217 American Federal Building · 100 West 11th Street · Anderson, IN 46016 · 317-643-3300

Tom G. Jones · Jones, Loveall & Johnson · 150 North Main Street · Franklin, IN 46131 · 317-736-7174

Robert W. Hammerle · Allen, Baratz, Conway & Hammerle · 301 Massachusetts Avenue, Suite 200 · Indianapolis, IN 46204 · 317-635-6567

Richard Kammen · McClure, McClure & Kammen · 235 North Delaware · Indianapolis, IN 46204 · 317-632-6341

J. Richard Kiefer · Safrin, Kiefer & McGoff · 8900 Keystone Crossing, Suite 1000 · Indianapolis, IN 46240 · 317-848-1000

Owen M. Mullin · 116 North Delaware Street · Indianapolis, IN 46204 · 317-639-1391

Don A. Tabbert · Tabbert & Ford · Indiana National Bank Tower, Suite 2580 · One Indiana Square · Indianapolis, IN 46204 · 317-639-5444

James H. Voyles, Jr. · Ober, Symmes, Cardwell, Voyles & Zahn · 300 Consolidated Building · 115 North Pennsylvania Street · Indianapolis, IN 46204 · 317-632-4463

Nick J. Thiros · Cohen & Thiros · Gainer Bank Center, Suite 899 · 8585 Broadway · Merrillville, IN 46410 · 219-769-1600

FAMILY LAW

Andrew C. Mallor · Mallor, Grodner & Bohrer · 1011 North Walnut Street · P.O. Box 1426 · Bloomington, IN 47402 · 812-336-0200

John D. Proffitt · Campbell, Kyle & Proffitt · 650 East Carmel Drive, Suite 400 · Carmel, IN 46032 · 317-846-6514

John M. Howard, Jr. · Howard & Lawson · 110 South Washington Street · Danville, IN 46122 · 317-745-6471

James A. Buck · Buck, Berry, Landau & Breunig · 302 North Alabama Street · Indianapolis, IN 46204 · 317-638-3333

Franklin I. Miroff · Ancel, Miroff & Frank · Two Market Square Center, Suite 1000 · P.O. Box 44219 · Indianapolis, IN 46244 · 317-634-1245

Marvin H. Mitchell · Mitchell Hurst Jacobs & Dick · 152 East Washington Street · Indianapolis, IN 46204 · 317-636-0808

Molly P. Rucker · Rucker and Cheerva · 520 Merchants Bank Building · Indianapolis, IN 46204 · 317-637-3011

James P. Seidensticker, Jr. · Bose McKinney & Evans · 1100 First Indiana Building · 11 North Pennsylvania Street · Indianapolis, IN 46204 · 317-637-5353

Wilson S. Stober · Baker & Daniels · 810 Fletcher Trust Building · Indianapolis, IN 46204 · 317-237-4535

LABOR AND EMPLOYMENT LAW

Ernest M. Beal, Jr. · (Individuals) · 9009 Coldwater Road, Suite 300 · Fort Wayne, IN 46825 · 219-489-2833

Herbert C. Snyder, Jr. · (Management) · Barnes & Thornburg · One Summit Square, Suite 600 · Fort Wayne, IN 46802 · 219-423-9440

Robert K. Bellamy · (Management) · Barnes & Thornburg · 1313 Merchants Bank Building · 11 South Meridian Street · Indianapolis, IN 46204 · 317-638-1313

S. R. Born II · (Management) · Ice Miller Donadio & Ryan · One American Square · P.O. Box 82001 · Indianapolis, IN 46282-0002 · 317-236-2100

Belle Choate · (Individuals) · Choate Visher & Haith · 151 North Delaware Street, Suite 740 · Indianapolis, IN 46204 · 317-634-3113

Leland B. Cross, Jr. · (Management) · Ice Miller Donadio & Ryan · One American Square · P.O. Box 82001 · Indianapolis, IN 46282-0002 · 317-236-2100

Frederick W. Dennerline III · (Labor) · Fillenwarth, Dennerline, Groth & Baird 1213 North Arlington Avenue, Suite 204 · Indianapolis, IN 46219 · 317-353-9363

Edward J. Fillenwarth, Jr. · (Labor) · Fillenwarth, Dennerline, Groth & Baird 1213 North Arlington Avenue, Suite 204 · Indianapolis, IN 46219 · 317-353-9363

William R. Groth · (Labor) · Fillenwarth, Dennerline, Groth & Baird · 1213 North Arlington Avenue, Suite 204 · Indianapolis, IN 46219 · 317-353-9363

Raymond J. Hafsten, Jr. · (Individuals) · 615 Merchants Bank Building · 11 South Meridian Street · Indianapolis, IN 46204 · 317-635-2244

Robert E. Highfield · (Management) · Barnes & Thornburg · 1313 Merchants Bank Building · 11 South Meridian Street · Indianapolis, IN 46204 · 317-638-1313

Martin J. Klaper · (Management) · Ice Miller Donadio & Ryan · One American Square · P.O. Box 82001 · Indianapolis, IN 46282-0002 · 317-236-2100

Barry A. Macey · (Labor; Individuals) · Segal & Macey · 445 North Pennsylvania Street · Indianapolis, IN 46204 · 317-637-2345

Michael R. Maine · (Management) · Baker & Daniels · 108 North Pennsylvania, Suite 810 · Indianapolis, IN 46204 · 317-237-4535

David W. Miller · (Management) · Baker & Daniels · 108 North Pennsylvania, Suite 810 · Indianapolis, IN 46204 · 317-237-4535

Alan T. Nolan · (Management) · Ice Miller Donadio & Ryan · One American Square · P.O. Box 82001 · Indianapolis, IN 46282-0002 · 317-236-2100

Richard E. Parker · (Management) · Ice Miller Donadio & Ryan · One American Square · P.O. Box 82001 · Indianapolis, IN 46282-0002 · 317-236-2100

William E. Roberts · (Management) · Barnes & Thornburg · 1313 Merchants Bank Building · 11 South Meridian Street · Indianapolis, IN 46204 · 317-638-1313

Jack H. Rogers · (Management) · Barnes & Thornburg · 1313 Merchants Bank Building · 11 South Meridian Street · Indianapolis, IN 46204 · 317-638-1313

Susan B. Tabler · (Management) · Ice Miller Donadio & Ryan · One American Square · P.O. Box 82001 · Indianapolis, IN 46282-0002 · 317-236-2100

George J. Zazas · (Management) · Barnes & Thornburg · 1313 Merchants Bank Building · 11 South Meridian Street · Indianapolis, IN 46204 · 317-638-1313

Daniel W. Rudy · (Management) · Barnes & Thornburg · 600 First Source Bank Building · 100 North Michigan Street · South Bend, IN 46601 · 219-233-1171

NATURAL RESOURCES AND ENVIRONMENTAL LAW

W. C. Blanton · Ice Miller Donadio & Ryan · One American Square · P.O. Box 82001 · Indianapolis, IN 46282-0002 · 317-236-2100

G. Daniel Kelley, Jr. · (also Coal) · Ice Miller Donadio & Ryan · One American Square · P.O. Box 82001 · Indianapolis, IN 46282-0002 · 317-236-2100

Bryan G. Tabler · Barnes & Thornburg · 1313 Merchants Bank Building · 11 South Meridian Street · Indianapolis, IN 46204 · 317-638-1313

PERSONAL INJURY LITIGATION

John T. Sharpnack · (Defendants) · Sharpnack, Bigley, David & Rumple · 321 Washington Street · P.O. Box 310 · Columbus, IN 47202-0310 · 812-372-1553

Charles L. Berger · (Plaintiffs) · Berger and Berger · 313 Main Street · Evansville, IN 47708 · 812-425-8101

Sydney L. Berger · (Plaintiffs) · Berger and Berger · 313 Main Street · Evansville, IN 47708 · 812-425-8101

William E. Borror · (Defendants) · Hunt, Suedhoff, Borror & Eilbacher · 900 Paine Webber Building · 803 South Calhoun Street · Fort Wayne, IN 46802-2399 219-423-1311

John M. Clifton, Jr. · (Defendants) · Barrett & McNagny · 215 East Barry Street P.O. Box 2263 · Fort Wayne, IN 46801-2263 · 219-423-9551

Sherrill Wm. Colvin · (Plaintiffs) · Snouffer, Haller & Colvin · 2000 Fort Wayne Bank Building · Fort Wayne, IN 46802-2375 · 219-424-2000

Edward L. Murphy, Jr. · (Defendants) · Livingston, Dildine, Haynie & Yoder 1400 One Summit Square · Fort Wayne, IN 46802 · 219-423-9411

Tom G. Jones · (Plaintiffs) · Jones, Loveall & Johnson · 150 North Main Street Franklin, IN 46131 · 317-736-7174

Frederick H. Link · (Defendants) · Eichhorn, Eichhorn & Link · 200 Russell Street · P.O. Box 6328 · Hammond, IN 46325-6328 · 219-931-0560

Ralph A. Cohen · (Defendants) · Ice Miller Donadio & Ryan · One American Square · P.O. Box 82001 · Indianapolis, IN 46282-0002 · 317-236-2100

James V. Donadio · (Defendants) · Ice Miller Donadio & Ryan · One American Square · P.O. Box 82001 · Indianapolis, IN 46282-0002 · 317-236-2100

James R. Fisher · (Defendants) · Ice Miller Donadio & Ryan · One American Square · P.O. Box 82001 · Indianapolis, IN 46282-0002 · 317-236-2100

F. Boyd Hovde · (Plaintiffs) · Townsend, Hovde & Montross · 230 East Ohio Street · Indianapolis, IN 46204 · 317-637-1521

William W. Hurst · (Plaintiffs) · Mitchell Hurst Jacobs & Dick · 152 East Washington Street · Indianapolis, IN 46204 · 317-636-0808

William V. Hutchens · (Defendants) · Locke, Reynolds, Boyd & Weisell · One Indiana Square, 21st Floor · Indianapolis, IN 46204 · 317-639-5534

Lloyd H. Milliken, Jr. · (Defendants) · Locke, Reynolds, Boyd & Weisell · One Indiana Square, 21st Floor · Indianapolis, IN 46204 · 317-639-5534

W. Scott Montross · (Plaintiffs) · Townsend, Hovde & Montross · 230 East Ohio Street · Indianapolis, IN 46204 · 317-637-1521

Geoffrey Segar · (Defendants) · Ice Miller Donadio & Ryan · One American Square · P.O. Box 82001 · Indianapolis, IN 46282-0002 · 317-236-2100

Gordon E. Tabor · (Plaintiffs) · Tabor, Fels & Tabor · 141 East Ohio Street, Suite 200 · Indianapolis, IN 46204 · 317-236-9000

John F. Townsend, Jr. · (Plaintiffs) · Townsend, Hovde & Montross · 230 East Ohio Street · Indianapolis, IN 46204 · 317-637-1521

Harry A. Wilson, Jr. · (Plaintiffs) · Wilson & Kehoe · 850 Fort Wayne Avenue P.O. Box 1317 · Indianapolis, IN 46206 · 317-632-7393

Louis Buddy Yosha · (Plaintiffs) · Townsend, Yosha & Cline · 2220 North Meridian Street · Indianapolis, IN 46208 · 317-925-9200

John A. Young · (Defendants) · Young, Cochran & Reese · 630 Century Building 36 South Pennsylvania Street · Indianapolis, IN 46204 · 317-633-4200

Roger L. Pardieck · (Plaintiffs) · Pardieck & Gill · 100 North Chestnut Street P.O. Box 608 · Seymour, IN 47274 · 812-523-8686

John E. Doran · (Defendants) · Doran, Manion, Boynton, Kamm & Esmont · 202 South Michigan Avenue, Room 725 · South Bend, IN 46601 · 219-233-6117

James H. Pankow · (Defendants) · Jones, Obenchain, Ford, Pankow & Lewis 1800 Valley American Bank Building · P.O. Box 4577 · South Bend, IN 46634-4577 · 219-233-1194

Thomas H. Singer · (Plaintiffs) · Law Offices of Thomas H. Singer · 205 First Bank Building, Third Floor · South Bend, IN 46601 · 219-232-4747

Max E. Goodwin · (Plaintiffs) · Mann, Chaney, Johnson, Goodwin & Williams Sixth and Ohio Streets, NW · P.O. Box 1643 · Terre Haute, IN 47808 · 812-232-0107

REAL ESTATE LAW

W. Jack Schroeder · 307 Union Federal Building · Evansville, IN 47708 · 812-423-0073

Robert T. Hoover · Baker & Daniels & Shoaff · 2400 Fort Wayne Bank Building P.O. Box 12709 · Fort Wayne, IN 46864 · 219-424-8000

Douglas E. Miller · Barrett & McNagny · Lincoln Bank Tower, Third Floor P.O. Box 2263 · Fort Wayne, IN 46801-2263 · 219-423-9551

John A. Grayson · Ice Miller Donadio & Ryan · One American Square · P.O. Box 82001 · Indianapolis, IN 46282-0002 · 317-236-2100

Tom Charles Huston · Barnes & Thornburg · 1313 Merchants Bank Building · 11 South Meridian Street · Indianapolis, IN 46204 · 317-638-1313

William F. LeMond · LeMond, Carson, Yockey, Pehler & Caplin · 600 Union Federal Building · Indianapolis, IN 46204-3180 · 317-635-4500

Norman R. Newman · Dann Pecar Newman Talesnick & Kleiman · One American Square, Suite 2300 · P.O. Box 82008 · Indianapolis, IN 46282 · 317-632-3232

Philip A. Nicely · Bose McKinney & Evans · 1100 First Indiana Building · 11 North Pennsylvania Avenue · Indianapolis, IN 46204 · 317-637-5353

Philip D. Pecar · Dann Pecar Newman Talesnick & Kleiman · One American Square, Suite 2300 · P.O. Box 82008 · Indianapolis, IN 46282 · 317-632-3232

Charles E. Wilson · Ice Miller Donadio & Ryan · One American Square · P.O. Box 82001 · Indianapolis, IN 46282-0002 · 317-236-2100

Thomas R. McCully · Stuart & Branigin · 801 The Life Building · P.O. Box 1010 Lafayette, IN 47902 · 317-423-1561

Bruce R. Bancroft · Barnes & Thornburg · 600 First Source Bank Building · 100 North Michigan Street · South Bend, IN 46601 · 219-233-1171

Charles M. Boynton · Doran, Manion, Boynton, Kamm & Esmont · 202 South Michigan Avenue, Room 725 · South Bend, IN 46601 · 219-233-6117

Richard W. Morgan · Barnes & Thornburg · 600 First Source Bank Building · 100 North Michigan Street · South Bend, IN 46601 · 219-233-1171

TAX AND EMPLOYEE BENEFITS LAW

George N. Bewley, Jr. · (Employee Benefits) · Bewley & Koday · 2006 Fort Wayne National Bank Building · 110 West Berry Street · Fort Wayne, IN 46802 219-424-0566

Miles C. Gerberding · Barnes & Thornburg · One Summit Square, Suite 600 · Fort Wayne, IN 46802 · 219-423-9440

David Haist · Barnes & Thornburg · One Summit Square, Suite 600 · Fort Wayne, IN 46802 · 219-423-9440

N. Thomas Horton II · (Employee Benefits) · Barrett & McNagny · 215 East Berry Street · P.O. Box 2263 · Fort Wayne, IN 46801-2263 · 219-423-9551

Stephen J. Williams · Shambaugh, Kast, Beck & Williams · 1900 Lincoln Bank Tower · Fort Wayne, IN 46802-2405 · 219-423-1430

Toni Sue Ax · (Employee Benefits) · Barnes & Thornburg · 1313 Merchants Bank Building · 11 South Meridian Street · Indianapolis, IN 46204 · 317-638-1313

Donald P. Bennett · Baker & Daniels · 108 North Pennsylvania, Suite 810 · Indianapolis, IN 46204 · 317-237-4535

Leonard J. Betley · Ice Miller Donadio & Ryan · One American Square · P.O. Box 82001 · Indianapolis, IN 46282-0002 · 317-236-2100

Mary Beth Braitman · (Employee Benefits) · Ice Miller Donadio & Ryan · One American Square · P.O. Box 82001 · Indianapolis, IN 46282-0002 · 317-236-2100

Donald W. Buttrey · McHale, Cook & Welch · 1122 Chamber of Commerce Building · Indianapolis, IN 46204 · 317-634-7588

Francina A. Dlouhy · Baker & Daniels · 108 North Pennsylvania, Suite 810 · Indianapolis, IN 46204 · 317-237-4535

Daniel H. FitzGibbon · Barnes & Thornburg · 1313 Merchants Bank Building · 11 South Meridian Street · Indianapolis, IN 46204 · 317-638-1313

Robert E. Johnson · Krieg DeVault Alexander & Capehart · 2800 Indiana National Bank Tower · One Indiana Square · Indianapolis, IN 46204 · 317-636-4341

James D. Kemper · (Employee Benefits) · Ice Miller Donadio & Ryan · One American Square · P.O. Box 82001 · Indianapolis, IN 46282-0002 · 317-236-2100

Marc W. Sciscoe · (Employee Benefits) · Baker & Daniels · 108 North Pennsylvania, Suite 810 · Indianapolis, IN 46204 · 317-237-4535

Barton T. Sprunger · Ice Miller Donadio & Ryan · One American Square · P.O. Box 82001 · Indianapolis, IN 46282-0002 · 317-236-2100

Larry J. Stroble · Barnes & Thornburg · 1313 Merchants Bank Building · 11 South Meridian Street · Indianapolis, IN 46204 · 317-638-1313

Donald G. Sutherland · Ice Miller Donadio & Ryan · One American Square · P.O. Box 82001 · Indianapolis, IN 46282-0002 · 317-236-2100

Brian J. Lake · (Employee Benefits) · Barnes & Thornburg · 600 First Source Bank Building · 100 North Michigan Street · South Bend, IN 46601 · 219-233-1171

Richard B. Urda, Jr. · (Employee Benefits) · The Urda Professional Corporation · 311 First Interstate Bank Building · South Bend, IN 46601 · 219-234-2161

Nelson J. Vogel, Jr. · Barnes & Thornburg · 600 First Source Bank Building · 100 North Michigan Street · South Bend, IN 46601 · 219-233-1171

TRUSTS AND ESTATES

James M. Barrett III · Barrett & McNagny · 215 East Berry Street · P.O. Box 2263 · Fort Wayne, IN 46801-2263 · 219-423-9551

Philip S. Cooper · Busby, Austin, Cooper & Farr · 407-418 Anderson Bank Building · P.O. Box 390 · Anderson, IN 46015-0390 · 317-644-2891

Donald W. Jurgemeyer · 325 Washington Street · P.O. Box 624 · Columbus, IN 47202-0624 · 812-372-0205

Miles C. Gerberding · Barnes & Thornburg · One Summit Square, Suite 800 · Fort Wayne, IN 46802 · 219-423-9440

Stephen J. Williams · Shambaugh, Kast, Beck & Williams · 1900 Lincoln Bank Tower · Fort Wayne, IN 46802-2405 · 219-423-1430

Robert S. Ashby · Barnes & Thornburg · 1313 Merchants Bank Building · 11 South Meridian Street · Indianapolis, IN 46204 · 317-638-1313

Arthur W. Banta · Krieg DeVault Alexander & Capehart · 2800 Indiana National Bank Tower · One Indiana Square · Indianapolis, IN 46204 · 317-636-4341

Charles F. Cremer, Jr. · Cremer & Hobbs · Two Market Square Center, Suite 915 · Indianapolis, IN 46204 · 317-636-8182

Francis J. Feeney, Jr. · Feeney & Ward · 1014 Circle Tower Building · Indianapolis, IN 46204 · 317-639-9501

Kristin G. Fruehwald · Barnes & Thornburg · 1313 Merchants Bank Building · 11 South Meridian Street · Indianapolis, IN 46204 · 317-638-1313

G. Weldon Johnson · Johnson, Hall and Lawhead · 8900 Keystone Crossing, Suite 940 · Indianapolis, IN 46240-2112 · 317-848-5808

Robert A. Lichtenauer · 8125 Knue Road, Suite 133 · Indianapolis, IN 46250 317-845-1988

James F. Matthews · Hill, Fulwider, McDowell, Funk & Matthews · One Indiana Square, Suite 2335 · Indianapolis, IN 46204 · 317-634-2955

Russell Jay Ryan, Jr. · Hackman, McClarnon & McTurnan · One Indiana Square, Suite 1900 · Indianapolis, IN 46204 · 317-636-5401

Shirley A. Shideler · Barnes & Thornburg · 1313 Merchants Bank Building · 11 South Meridian Street · Indianapolis, IN 46204 · 317-638-1313

Jerome M. Strauss · Ice Miller Donadio & Ryan · One American Square · P.O. Box 82001 · Indianapolis, IN 46282-0002 · 317-236-2100

Gordon D. Wishard · Hackman, McClarnon & McTurnan · One Indiana Square, Suite 1900 · Indianapolis, IN 46204 · 317-636-5401

John A. Burgess · Barnes & Thornburg · 600 First Source Bank Building · 100 North Michigan Street · South Bend, IN 46601 · 219-233-1171

G. Burt Ford · Jones, Obenchain, Ford, Pankow & Lewis · 1800 Valley American Bank Building · P.O. Box 4577 · South Bend, IN 46634-4577 · 219-233-1194

Edward J. Gray · Barnes & Thornburg · 600 First Source Bank Building · 100 North Michigan Street · South Bend, IN 46601 · 219-233-1171

Warren E. McGill · Barnes & Thornburg · 600 First Source Bank Building · 100 North Michigan Street · South Bend, IN 46601 · 219-233-1171

IOWA

BANKRUPTCY LAW	256
BUSINESS LITIGATION	257
CORPORATE LAW	257
CRIMINAL DEFENSE	258
FAMILY LAW	259
LABOR AND EMPLOYMENT LAW	259
PERSONAL INJURY LITIGATION	260
REAL ESTATE LAW	262
TAX AND EMPLOYEE BENEFITS LAW	263
TRUSTS AND ESTATES	264

BANKRUPTCY LAW

Larry G. Gutz · Moyer & Bergman · Commerce Exchange Building, Suite 315 · 2720 First Avenue, NE · P.O. Box 1943 · Cedar Rapids, IA 52406 · 319-366-7331

Carroll J. Reasoner · Shuttleworth & Ingersoll · 500 Merchants National Bank Building · P.O. Box 2107 · Cedar Rapids, IA 52406 · 319-365-9461

Harry R. Terpstra · Terpstra Law Offices · 830 Higley Building · Cedar Rapids, IA 52401 · 319-364-2467

C. R. Hannan · Perkins, Sacks, Hannan, Reilly & Petersen · 215 South Main Street · P.O. Box 1016 · Council Bluffs, IA 51502-1016 · 712-328-1575

Thomas L. Flynn · Wimer, Hudson, Flynn & Neugent · 222 Equitable Building · Des Moines, IA 50309 · 515-244-4201

Donald F. Neiman · Neiman, Neiman, Stone & Spellman · 1119 High Street · Des Moines, IA 50308-2674 · 515-282-9247

A. Frank Baron · Baron, Sar, Wenell, Lohr & Jarman · 750 Pierce Street · Sioux City, IA 51102 · 712-277-1015

BUSINESS LITIGATION

David M. Elderkin · Elderkin, Pirnie, von Lackum & Elderkin · 700 Higley Building · P.O. Box 1968 · Cedar Rapids, IA 52406 · 319-362-2137

Patrick M. Roby · Shuttleworth & Ingersoll · 500 Merchants National Bank Building · P.O. Box 2107 · Cedar Rapids, IA 52406-2107 · 319-365-9461

Robert V. P. Waterman · Lane & Waterman · 600 Davenport Bank Building · Davenport, IA 52801 · 319-324-3246

Lex Hawkins · Hawkins & Norris · 2801 Fleur Drive · Des Moines, IA 50321 · 515-288-6532

H. Richard Smith · Ahlers, Cooney, Dorweiler, Haynie, Smith & Allbee · 100 Court Avenue, Suite 600 · Des Moines, IA 50309 · 515-243-7611

Maurice B. Nieland · Kindig, Beebe, Rawlings, Nieland, Probasco & Killinger · 300 Toy National Bank Building · Sioux City, IA 51101 · 712-277-2373

John J. Greer · Greer, Nelson, Montgomery, Barry & Bovee · Professional Building · P.O. Box 7038 · Spencer, IA 51301 · 712-262-1150

David J. Dutton · Mosier, Thomas, Beatty, Dutton, Braun & Staack · 3151 Brockway Road · P.O. Box 810 · Waterloo, IA 50704 · 319-234-4471

CORPORATE LAW

F. James Bradley · Bradley & Riley · First Corporate Place · 100 First Street, SW · Cedar Rapids, IA 52404 · 319-363-0101

Thomas M. Collins · Shuttleworth & Ingersoll · 500 Merchants National Bank Building · P.O. Box 2107 · Cedar Rapids, IA 52406 · 319-365-9461

Darrel A. Morf · Simmons, Perrine, Albright & Ellwood · 1200 Merchants National Bank Building · Cedar Rapids, IA 52401 · 319-366-7641

Carroll J. Reasoner · Shuttleworth & Ingersoll · 500 Merchants National Bank Building · P.O. Box 2107 · Cedar Rapids, IA 52406-2107 · 319-365-9461

David W. Belin · Belin Harris Helmick Tesdell Lamson McCormick · 2000 Financial Center · Seventh & Walnut Streets · Des Moines, IA 50309 · 515-243-7100

Donald J. Brown · Davis, Hockenberg, Wine, Brown, Koehn & Shors · 2300 Financial Center · 666 Walnut Street · Des Moines, IA 50309 · 515-243-2300

A. Arthur Davis · Davis, Hockenberg, Wine, Brown, Koehn & Shors · 2300 Financial Center · 666 Walnut Street · Des Moines, IA 50309 · 515-243-2300

L. Call Dickinson, Jr. · Dickinson, Throckmorton, Parker, Mannheimer & Raife 1600 Hub Tower · Des Moines, IA 50309 · 515-244-2600

Edgar F. Hansell · Nyemaster, Goode, McLaughlin, Emery & O'Brian · 1900 Hub Tower · Des Moines, IA 50309 · 515-283-3100

Jeffrey E. Lamson · Belin Harris Helmick Tesdell Lamson McCormick · 2000 Financial Center · Seventh & Walnut Streets · Des Moines, IA 50309 · 515-243-7100

Milton O. Riepe · Gamble, Riepe, Webster, Davis & Green · 2600 Ruan Center 666 Grand Avenue · Des Moines, IA 50309 · 515-243-6251

Harley Allen Whitfield · Whitfield, Musgrave & Eddy · 1300 First Interstate Bank Building · Des Moines, IA 50309 · 515-288-6041

Marvin S. Berenstein · Berenstein, Vriezelaar, Moore, Moser & Tigges · 300 Commerce Building · P.O. Box 1557 · Sioux City, IA 51102 · 712-252-3226

Marvin J. Klass · Klass, Hanks, Stoos & Carter · Jackson Plaza, Suite 300 · Fourth and Jackson Streets · P.O. Box 327 · Sioux City, IA 51102 · 712-252-1866

W. Louis Beecher · Beecher, Beecher, Holmes & Rathert · Court Square Building, Suite 300 · 620 Lafayette Street · P.O. Box 178 · Waterloo, IA 50704 319-234-1766

Steven A. Weidner · Swisher & Cohrt · 528 West Fourth Street · P.O. Box 1200 Waterloo, IA 50704 · 319-232-6555

CRIMINAL DEFENSE

William L. Kutmus · Kutmus & Pennington · 620 Fleming Building · 218 Sixth Avenue · Des Moines, IA 50309 · 515-288-3339

Raymond Rosenberg · The Rosenberg Law Firm · 1010 Insurance Exchange Building · 505 Fifth Avenue · Des Moines, IA 50309 · 515-243-7600

Lawrence F. Scalise · Scalise, Scism, Sandre & Uhl · 2910 Grand Avenue · Des Moines, IA 50312 · 515-282-2910

Leon F. Spies · Mellon & Spies · 411 Iowa State Bank & Trust Building · Iowa City, IA 52240 · 319-337-4193

Gary E. Wenell · Baron, Sar, Wenell, Lohr & Jarman · 750 Pierce Street · Sioux City, IA 51102 · 712-277-1015

FAMILY LAW

Robert M. Jilek · Simmons, Perrine, Albright & Ellwood · 1200 Merchants National Bank Building · Cedar Rapids, IA 52401 · 319-366-7641

Harlan Hockett · 605 Midland Financial Building · Des Moines, IA 50309 515-243-1188

Roger J. Hudson · Wimer, Hudson, Flynn & Neugent · 222 Equitable Building Des Moines, IA 50309 · 515-244-4201

Thomas P. Hyland · Hyland, Laden & Pearson · 3232 Hubbell Avenue · Des Moines, IA 50317 · 515-262-9595

James M. Meade · 6963 University Avenue · Des Moines, IA 50311 · 515-274-1429

Patricia A. Shoff · Davis, Hockenberg, Wine, Brown, Koehn & Shors · 2300 Financial Center · 666 Walnut Street · Des Moines, IA 50309 · 515-243-2300

Sharon A. Mellon · Mellon & Spies · 411 Iowa State Bank & Trust Building Iowa City, IA 52240 · 319-337-4193

Patricia A. McGivern · Clark, Butler, Walsh & McGivern · River Plaza Building, Suite 400 · 10 West Fourth Street · P.O. Box 596 · Waterloo, IA 50704 319-234-5701

LABOR AND EMPLOYMENT LAW

John R. Carpenter · (Management) · Simmons, Perrine, Albright & Ellwood 1200 Merchants National Bank Building · Cedar Rapids, IA 52401 · 319-366-7641

John C. Barrett · (Individuals) · Barrett & Trott · 910 Equitable Building · Des Moines, IA 50309 · 515-244-4474

Neil A. Barrick · (Labor) · Fairmont Plaza Building, Suite 102 · 2525 East Euclid Avenue · Des Moines, IA 50317 · 515-265-2333

Mark W. Bennett · (Individuals) · Babich, Bennett, Nickerson & Newlin · 100 Court Avenue, Suite 403 · Des Moines, IA 50309 · 515-244-4300

John R. Phillips · (Management) · Nyemaster, Goode, McLaughlin, Emery & O'Brian · 1900 Hub Tower · Des Moines, IA 50309 · 515-283-3100

Kathleen A. Reimer · (Individuals) · Rogers, Reavely, Shinkle & Reimer · 100 Court Avenue, Suite 203 · Des Moines, IA 50309 · 515-244-7126

Charles W. McManigal · (Management) · Laird, Burington, Heiny, McManigal, Walters & Winga · 300 American Federal Building · 10 First Street, NW · P.O. Box 1567 · Mason City, IA 50401-8567 · 515-423-5154

Harry H. Smith · (Labor) · Smith & Smith · 632-640 Badgerow Building · Sioux City, IA 51101 · 712-255-8094

MacDonald Smith · (Labor) · Smith & Smith · 632-640 Badgerow Building Sioux City, IA 51101 · 712-255-8094

Leon R. Shearer · (Management) · Shearer, Hintze & Templer · 437 Colony Park Building · 3737 Woodland Avenue · West Des Moines, IA 50265 · 515-225-3737

PERSONAL INJURY LITIGATION

David M. Elderkin · Elderkin, Pirnie, von Lackum & Elderkin · 700 Higley Building · P.O Box 1968 · Cedar Rapids, IA 52406 · 319-362-2137

Ralph W. Gearhart · (Defendants) · Shuttleworth & Ingersoll · 500 Merchants National Bank Building · P.O. Box 2107 · Cedar Rapids, IA 52406 · 319-365-9461

Patrick M. Roby · (Defendants) · Shuttleworth & Ingersoll · 500 Merchants National Bank Building · P.O. Box 2107 · Cedar Rapids, IA 52406-2107 319-365-9461

James R. Snyder · (Defendants) · Simmons, Perrine, Albright & Ellwood · 1200 Merchants National Bank Building · Cedar Rapids, IA 52401 · 319-366-7641

Robert C. Tilden · (Defendants) · Simmons, Perrine, Albright & Ellwood · 1200 Merchants National Bank Building · Cedar Rapids, IA 52401 · 319-366-7641

Peter J. Peters · 233 Pearl Street · P.O. Box 938 · Council Bluffs, IA 51502 · 712-328-3157

Philip J. Willson · (Defendants) · Smith, Peterson, Beckman & Willson · 370 Midlands Mall · P.O. Box 249 · Council Bluffs, IA 51502 · 712-328-1833

Robert A. Van Vooren · Lane & Waterman · 700 Davenport Bank Building · Davenport, IA 52801 · 319-324-3246

Robert V. P. Waterman · (Defendants) · Lane & Waterman · 700 Davenport Bank Building · Davenport, IA 52801 · 319-324-3246

Kent M. Forney · (Defendants) · Bradshaw, Fowler, Proctor & Fairgrave · Des Moines Building, 11th Floor · Des Moines, IA 50309-2464 · 515-243-4191

Lex Hawkins · (Plaintiffs) · Hawkins & Norris · 2801 Fleur Drive · Des Moines, IA 50321 · 515-288-6532

Verne Lawyer · (Plaintiffs) · Fleming Building, Fourth Floor · Des Moines, IA 50309 · 515-288-2213

Ross H. Sidney · (Defendants) · Grefe & Sidney · 2222 Grand Avenue · P.O. Box 10434 · Des Moines, IA 50306 · 515-245-4300

H. Richard Smith · (Defendants) · Ahlers, Cooney, Dorweiler, Haynie, Smith & Allbee · 100 Court Avenue, Suite 600 · Des Moines, IA 50309 · 515-243-7611

LeRoy R. Voigts · (Defendants) · Nyemaster, Goode, McLaughlin, Emery & O'Brien · 1900 Hub Tower · Des Moines, IA 50309 · 515-283-3100

William C. Fuerste · Fuerste, Carew, Coyle, Juergens & Sudmeier · 200 Security Building · Dubuque, IA 52001 · 319-556-4011

Francis Fitzgibbons · Fitzgibbons Brothers · 108 North Seventh Street · P.O. Box 496 · Estherville, IA 51334 · 712-362-7215

James P. Hayes · (Plaintiffs) · Meardon, Sueppel, Downer & Hayes · 122 South Linn Street · Iowa City, IA 52240 · 319-338-9222

Marvin F. Heidman · Eidsmoe, Heidman, Redmond, Fredregill, Patterson & Schatz · Home Federal Building, Suite 200 · 701 Pierce Street · P.O. Box 3086 · Sioux City, IA 51102 · 712-255-8838

William J. Rawlings · Kindig, Beebe, Rawlings, Nieland, Probasco & Killinger · 300 Toy National Bank Building · Sioux City, IA 51101 · 712-277-2373

John J. Greer · Greer, Nelson, Montgomery, Barry & Bovee · Professional Building · P.O. Box 7038 · Spencer, IA 51301 · 712-262-1150

David J. Dutton · Mosier, Thomas, Beatty, Sutton, Braun & Staack · 3151 Brockway Road · P.O. Box 810 · Waterloo, IA 50704 · 319-234-4471

Edward J. Gallagher, Jr. · Gallagher, Langlas & Gallagher · Law Building · 405 East Fifth Street · P.O. Box 2615 · Waterloo, IA 50704 · 319-233-6163

Eldon R. McCann · (Defendants) · Swisher & Cohrt · 528 West Fourth Street · P.O. Box 1200 · Waterloo, IA 50704 · 319-232-6555

REAL ESTATE LAW

LeRoy H. Redfern · Redfern, McKinley, Mason & Dieter · 315 Clay Street · P.O. Box 627 · Cedar Falls, IA 50613 · 319-277-6830

David W. Kubicek · Simmons, Perrine, Albright & Ellwood · 1200 Merchants National Bank Building · Cedar Rapids, IA 52401 · 319-366-7641

Stephen J. Petosa · Petosa, Petosa & Boecker · 205 American Federal Building · 601 Grand Avenue · Des Moines, IA 50309 · 515-282-8161

Richard E. Ramsay · Davis, Hockenberg, Wine, Brown, Koehn & Shors · 2300 Financial Center · 666 Walnut Street · Des Moines, IA 50309 · 515-243-2300

John B. Anderson · Corbett, Anderson, Corbett & Daniels · 400 Security Bank Building · P.O. Box 3527 · Sioux City, IA 51102 · 712-277-1261

George F. Madsen · Marks & Madsen · United Federal Plaza Building, Suite 303 · P.O. Box 3226 · Sioux City, IA 51102 · 712-258-1200

W. Louis Beecher · Beecher, Beecher, Holmes & Rathert · Court Square Building, Suite 300 · 620 Lafayette Street · P.O. Box 178 · Waterloo, IA 50704 · 319-234-1766

George D. Keith · Martin, Nutting, Miller, Keith & Pedersen · Sycamore 501 Building, Suite 710 · P.O. Box 2158 · Waterloo, IA 50704 · 319-235-9212

TAX AND EMPLOYEE BENEFITS LAW

J. Scott Bogguss · (also Employee Benefits) · Moyer & Bergman · Commerce Exchange Building, Third Floor · 2720 First Avenue, NE · P.O. Box 1943 · Cedar Rapids, IA 52406 · 319-366-7331

Michael P. Donohue · Moyer & Bergman · Commerce Exchange Building, Third Floor · 2720 First Avenue, NE · P.O. Box 1943 · Cedar Rapids, IA 52406 · 319-366-7331

Gary J. Streit · (also Employee Benefits) · Shuttleworth & Ingersoll · 500 Merchants National Bank Building · P.O. Box 2107 · Cedar Rapids, IA 52406-2107 319-365-9461

Gene H. Snapp, Jr. · (Employee Benefits) · 525 Davenport Bank Building Davenport, IA 52801 · 319-322-7917

Donald J. Brown · Davis, Hockenberg, Wine, Brown, Koehn & Shors · 2300 Financial Center · 666 Walnut Street · Des Moines, IA 50309 · 515-243-2300

Bruce I. Campbell · Davis, Hockenberg, Wine, Brown, Koehn & Shors · 2300 Financial Center · 666 Walnut Street · Des Moines, IA 50309 · 515-243-2300

Frank J. Carroll · Davis, Hockenberg, Wine, Brown, Koehn & Shors · 2300 Financial Center · 666 Walnut Street · Des Moines, IA 50309 · 515-243-2300

David C. Craig · (Employee Benefits) · Brown, Winick, Graves, Donnelly, Baskerville & Schoenebaum · Two Ruan Center, Suite 1100 · 601 Locust Street · Des Moines, IA 50309 · 515-283-2076

John V. Donnelly · Brown, Winick, Graves, Donnelly, Baskerville & Shoenebaum · Two Ruan Center, Suite 1100 · 601 Locust Street · Des Moines, IA 50309 515-283-2076

Terry C. Hancock · (Employee Benefits) · Bradshaw, Fowler, Proctor & Fairgrave Des Moines Building, 11th Floor · Des Moines, IA 50309-2464 · 515-243-4191

James R. Monroe · 2115 Forest · P.O. Box 4904 · Des Moines, IA 50306 · 515-244-0652

Burns Mossman · Nyemaster, Goode, McLaughlin, Emery & O'Brien · 1900 Hub Tower · Des Moines, IA 50309 · 515-283-3100

John H. Raife · Dickinson, Throckmorton, Parker, Mannheimer & Raife · 1600 Hub Tower · Des Moines, IA 50309 · 515-244-2600

R. Craig Shives · (Employee Benefits) · Nyemaster, Goode, McLaughlin, Emery & O'Brien · 1900 Hub Tower · Des Moines, IA 50309 · 515-283-3100

William S. Smith · Smith, Schneider & Stiles · 4717 Grand Avenue · Des Moines, IA 50312 · 515-274-2345

Jon L. Staudt · Belin Harris Helmick Tesdell Lamson McCormick · 2000 Financial Center · Seventh & Walnut Streets · Des Moines, IA 50309 · 515-243-7100

Drew R. Tillotson · Nyemaster, Goode, McLaughlin, Emery & O'Brien · 1900 Hub Tower · Des Moines, IA 50309 · 515-283-3100

Marvin Winick · Brown, Winick, Graves, Donnelly, Baskerville & Schoenebaum Two Ruan Center, Suite 1100 · 601 Locust Street · Des Moines, IA 50309 515-283-2076

David D. Crumley · Stark, Crumley & Jacobs · Warden Plaza · Fort Dodge, IA 50501 · 515-576-7558

Maurice E. Stark · Stark, Crumley & Jacobs · Warden Plaza · Fort Dodge, IA 50501 · 515-576-7558

William V. Phelan · Phelan, Tucker, Boyle & Mullen · 321 East Market · P.O. Box 2150 · Iowa City, IA 52244 · 319-354-1104

Marvin S. Berenstein · Berenstein, Vriezelaar, Moore, Moser & Tigges · 300 Commerce Building · P.O. Box 1557 · Sioux City, IA 51102 · 712-252-3226

Orville W. Bloethe · 702 Third Street · Victor, IA 52347 · 319-647-3121

John D. Hintze · (also Employee Benefits) · Shearer, Hintze & Templer · 437 Colony Park Building · 3737 Woodland Avenue · West Des Moines, IA 50265 515-225-3737

TRUSTS AND ESTATES

LeRoy H. Redfern · Redfern, McKinley, Mason & Dieter · 315 Clay Street · P.O. Box 627 · Cedar Falls, IA 50613 · 319-277-6830

F. James Bradley · Bradley & Riley · First Corporate Place · 100 First Street, SW Cedar Rapids, IA 52404 · 319-363-0101

Darrel A. Morf · Simmons, Perrine, Albright & Ellwood · 1200 Merchants National Bank Building · Cedar Rapids, IA 52401 · 319-366-7641

Jack W. Peters · Stuart, Tinley, Peters, Thorn, Smits & Sens · 310 West Kanesville Boulevard, Second Floor · P.O. Box 398 · Council Bluffs, IA 51502 712-322-4033

Robert C. Reimer · Reimer, Lohman & Reitz · 25 South Main Street · Denison, IA 51442 · 712-263-4627

Bruce I. Campbell · Davis, Hockenberg, Wine, Brown, Koehn & Shors · 2300 Financial Center · 666 Walnut Street · Des Moines, IA 50309 · 515-243-2300

Charles E. Harris · Belin Harris Helmick Tesdell Lamson McCormick · 2000 Financial Center · Des Moines, IA 50309 · 515-243-7100

J. Edward Power · Bradshaw, Fowler, Proctor & Fairgrave · Des Moines Building, 11th Floor · Des Moines, IA 50309-2464 · 515-243-4191

William V. Phelan · Phelan, Tucker, Boyle & Mullen · 321 East Market · P.O. Box 2150 · Iowa City, IA 52244 · 319-354-1104

Harold R. Winston · Winston, Reuber & Swanson · 119 Second Street, NW Mason City, IA 50401 · 515-423-1913

John B. Anderson · Corbett, Anderson, Corbett & Daniels · 400 Security Bank Building · P.O. Box 3527 · Sioux City, IA 51102 · 712-277-1261

Marvin S. Berenstein · Berenstein, Vriezelaar, Moore, Moser & Tigges · 300 Commerce Building · P.O. Box 1557 · Sioux City, IA 51102 · 712-252-3226

Orville W. Bloethe · 702 Third Street · Victor, IA 52347 · 319-647-3121

Richard G. Zellhoefer · Zellhoefer Law Firm · The Chicago Central Building, Suite 507 · P.O. Box 477 · Waterloo, IA 50704 · 319-291-4045

KANSAS

BANKRUPTCY LAW	266
BUSINESS LITIGATION	267
CORPORATE LAW	268
CRIMINAL DEFENSE	269
FAMILY LAW	270
LABOR AND EMPLOYMENT LAW	270
NATURAL RESOURCES AND ENVIRONMENTAL LAW	271
PERSONAL INJURY LITIGATION	272
REAL ESTATE LAW	274
TAX AND EMPLOYEE BENEFITS LAW	274
TRUSTS AND ESTATES	276

BANKRUPTCY LAW

Chris W. Henry · McDowell, Rice & Smith · 600 Security Bank Building · Kansas City, KS 66101 · 913-621-5400

Thomas M. Mullinix III · Evans & Mullinix · Tower State Bank Building · 1314 North 38th Street · Kansas City, KS 66102 · 913-621-1200

F. Stannard Lentz · Lentz & Clark · 5818 Reeds Road · P.O. Box 1704 · Mission, KS 66222-0704 · 913-384-2464

John T. Flannagan · 300A South Clairborne, Suite Three · P.O. Box 2011 · Olathe, KS 66061 · 913-782-7040

Michael H. Berman · 4121 West 83rd Street, Suite 265 · P.O. Box 8010 · Prairie Village, KS 66208 · 913-649-1555

Robert L. Baer · Cosgrove, Webb & Oman · Bank IV Tower, Suite 1100 · One Townsite Plaza · Topeka, KS 66603 · 913-235-9511

Jan M. Hamilton · Hamilton, Peterson, Tipton & Keeshan · 1206 West 10th Street · Topeka, KS 66604-1291 · 913-233-1903

Dale L. Somers · Eidson, Lewis, Porter & Haynes · 1300 Merchants National Bank Building · Topeka, KS 66612 · 913-233-2332

David C. Adams · Morris, Laing, Evans, Brock & Kennedy · 200 West Douglas Street, Fourth Floor · Wichita, KS 67202 · 316-262-2671

Donald W. Bostwick · Adams, Jones, Robinson and Malone · 600 Market Centre 155 North Market Street · P.O. Box 1034 · Wichita, KS 67201 · 316-265-8591

J. Eric Engstrom · Fleeson, Gooing, Coulson & Kitch · 1600 Kansas State Bank Building · 125 North Market Street · P.O. Box 997 · Wichita, KS 67201 316-267-7361

Christopher J. Redmond · Redmond, Redmond & Nazar · 331 East Douglas Street · Wichita, KS 67202-3405 · 316-262-8361

BUSINESS LITIGATION

John J. Jurcyk, Jr. · McAnany, Van Cleave & Phillips · 707 Minnesota Avenue, Fourth Floor · P.O. Box 1398 · Kansas City, KS 66117 · 913-371-3838

George A. Lowe · Lowe, Farmer, Bacon & Roe · Colonial Building · 110 West Loula · P.O. Box 580 · Olathe, KS 66061 · 913-782-0422

Roger D. Stanton · Stinson, Mag & Fizzell · 7500 West 110th Street · Overland Park, KS 66210 · 913-451-8600

Charles D. McAtee · Eidson, Lewis, Porter & Haynes · 1300 Merchants National Bank Building · Topeka, KS 66612 · 913-233-2332

Donald Patterson · Fisher, Patterson, Sayler & Smith · 400 Bank IV Tower · P.O. Box 949 · Topeka, KS 66601 · 913-232-7761

Richard C. Hite · Kahrs, Nelson, Fanning, Hite & Kellogg · 200 West Douglas Street, Suite 630 · Wichita, KS 67202-3089 · 316-265-7761

Robert L. Howard · Foulston, Siefkin, Powers & Eberhardt · 700 Fourth Financial Center · Broadway at Douglas · Wichita, KS 67202 · 316-267-6371

Joseph W. Kennedy · Morris, Laing, Evans, Brock & Kennedy · 200 West Douglas Street, Fourth Floor · Wichita, KS 67202 · 316-262-2671

W. Robert Martin · Martin, Pringle, Oliver, Wallace & Swartz · 300 Page Court 220 West Douglas Street · Wichita, KS 67202 · 316-265-9311

Donald R. Newkirk · Fleeson, Gooing, Coulson & Kitch · 1600 Kansas State Bank Building · 125 North Market Street · P.O. Box 997 · Wichita, KS 67201 316-267-7361

Gerald Sawatzky · Foulston, Siefkin, Powers & Eberhardt · 700 Fourth Financial Center · Broadway at Douglas · Wichita, KS 67202 · 316-267-6371

Mikel L. Stout · Foulston, Siefkin, Powers & Eberhardt · 700 Fourth Financial Center · Broadway at Douglas · Wichita, KS 67202 · 316-267-6371

John P. Woolf · Triplett, Woolf & Garretson · 800 Centre City Plaza · 151 North Main Street · Wichita, KS 67202 · 316-265-5700

CORPORATE LAW

William P. Trenkle, Jr. · Mangan, Dalton, Trenkle, Rebein and Doll · 208 West Spruce Street · Dodge City, KS 67801 · 316-227-8126

Webster L. Golden · Stevens, Brand, Lungstrum, Golden & Winter · 502 First National Bank Tower · P.O. Box 1200 · Lawrence, KS 66044 · 913-843-0811

Charles S. (Terry) Arthur III · Arthur, Green, Arthur, Conderman & Stutzman 201-203 Union National Bank Tower · P.O. Box 248 · Manhattan, KS 66502 913-537-1345

C. Maxwell Logan · Shook, Hardy & Bacon · 40 Corporate Woods, Suite 650 9401 Indian Creek Parkway · P.O. Box 25128 · Overland Park, KS 66225 913-451-6060

Alson R. Martin · Shook, Hardy & Bacon · 40 Corporate Woods, Suite 650 · 9401 Indian Creek Parkway · P.O. Box 25128 · Overland Park, KS 66225 · 913-451-6060

Thomas W. Van Dyke · Linde Thomson Langworthy Kohn & Van Dyke · 9300 Metcalf, Suite 1000 · Overland Park, KS 66212 · 913-649-4900

Robert E. Edmonds · Goodell, Stratton, Edmonds & Palmer · 215 East Eighth Avenue · Topeka, KS 66603-3999 · 913-233-0593

H. Philip Elwood · Goodell, Stratton, Edmonds & Palmer · 215 East Eighth Avenue · Topeka, KS 66603-3999 · 913-233-0593

James D. Waugh · Cosgrove, Webb & Oman · Bank IV Tower, Suite 1100 · One Townsite Plaza · Topeka, KS 66603 · 913-235-9511

Stanley G. Andeel · Foulston, Siefkin, Powers & Eberhardt · 700 Fourth Financial Center · Broadway at Douglas · Wichita, KS 67202 · 316-267-6371

William M. Cobb · Bever, Dye, Mustard & Belin · 713 First National Bank Building · Wichita, KS 67202 · 316-263-8294

Benjamin C. Langel · Foulston, Siefkin, Powers & Eberhardt · 700 Fourth Financial Center · Broadway at Douglas · Wichita, KS 67202 · 316-267-6371

Willard B. Thompson · Fleeson, Gooing, Coulson & Kitch · 1600 Kansas State Bank Building · 125 North Market Street · P.O. Box 997 · Wichita, KS 67201 316-267-7361

Thomas C. Triplett · Triplett, Woolf & Garretson · 800 Centre City Plaza · 151 North Main Street · Wichita, KS 67202 · 316-265-5700

Gerrit H. Wormhoudt · Fleeson, Gooing, Coulson & Kitch · 1600 Kansas State Bank Building · 125 North Market Street · P.O. Box 997 · Wichita, KS 67201 316-267-7361

CRIMINAL DEFENSE

James L. Eisenbrandt · Morris & Larson · 6900 College Boulevard, Suite 800 Overland Park, KS 66211 · 913-345-1233

Mark L. Bennett, Jr. · Bennett, Dillon & Callahan · 1605 Southwest 37th Street Topeka, KS 66611 · 913-267-5063

Robert D. Hecht · Scott, Quinlan & Hecht · 3301 Van Buren · Topeka, KS 66611 913-267-0040

Jack Focht · Focht, Hughey, Hund & Calvert · Brooker Plaza, Suite 300 · 807 North Waco · Wichita, KS 67203 · 316-269-9055

Stephen M. Joseph · Joseph, Robison & Anderson · 209 East William, Suite 800 Wichita, KS 67202 · 316-262-0667

Daniel E. Monnat · Monnat & Spurrier · 321 East William, Suite 603 · Wichita, KS 67202 · 316-264-2800

Charles A. O'Hara · O'Hara, O'Hara & Tousley · 1502 North Broadway · Wichita, KS 67214 · 316-263-5601

Stephen E. Robison · Joseph, Robison & Anderson · 209 East William Street, Suite 800 · Wichita, KS 67202 · 316-262-0667

Craig Shultz · Shultz & Webb · 205 East Central · Wichita, KS 67202 · 316-269-2284

FAMILY LAW

J. Bradley Short · 11100 Ash, Suite 200 · Leawood, KS 66211 · 913-491-4400

Joe L. Norton · Watson, Ess, Marshall & Enggas · 130 North Cherry Street · P.O. Box 550 · Olathe, KS 66061 · 913-782-2350

Ray L. Borth · Morris, Larson, King & Stamper · 6900 College Boulevard, Eighth Floor · Overland Park, KS 66210 · 913-345-1233

John H. Johntz, Jr. · Payne & Jones · Commerce Terrace, Suite 200 · College Boulevard at King · P.O. Box 25625 · Overland Park, KS 66225 · 913-469-4100

T. Bradley Manson · Payne & Jones · Commerce Terrace, Suite 200 · College Boulevard at King · P.O. Box 25625 · Overland Park, KS 66225 · 913-469-4100

Linda D. Elrod · Washburn University Law School · 1700 College Avenue · Topeka, KS 66621 · 913-295-6300

Stephen J. Blaylock · Woodard, Blaylock, Hernandez, Pilgreen & Roth · Riverfront Place · 833 North Waco · P.O. Box 127 · Wichita, KS 67201 · 316-263-4958

Donald E. Lambdin · Lambdin & Kluge · 830 North Main · P.O. Box 454 · Wichita, KS 67201 · 316-265-3285

LABOR AND EMPLOYMENT LAW

John J. Blake · (Labor) · Blake & Uhlig · 475 New Brotherhood Building · Eighth & State Avenues · Kansas City, KS 66101 · 913-321-8884

Joseph W. Moreland · (Labor) · Blake & Uhlig · 475 New Brotherhood Building Eighth & State Avenues · Kansas City, KS 66101 · 913-321-8884

William G. Haynes · (Management) · Eidson, Lewis, Porter & Haynes · 1300 Merchants National Bank Building · Topeka, KS 66612 · 913-233-2332

Arthur E. Palmer · (Management) · Goodell, Stratton, Edmonds & Palmer · 215 East Eighth Avenue · Topeka, KS 66603-3999 · 913-233-0593

Fred W. Phelps, Jr. · (Individuals) · 1414 South Topeka Boulevard · P.O. Box 1886 · Topeka, KS 66601 · 913-233-4162

Margie J. Phelps · (Individuals) · 1414 South Topeka Boulevard · P.O. Box 1886 · Topeka, KS 66601 · 913-233-4162

W. Stanley Churchill · (Management) · Martin, Churchill, Overman, Hill & Cole 500 North Market Street · Wichita, KS 67214 · 316-263-3200

William H. Dye · (Management) · Foulston, Siefkin, Powers & Eberhardt · 700 Fourth Financial Center · Broadway at Douglas Street · Wichita, KS 67202 316-267-6371

Thomas E. Hammond · (Labor) · Render & Kamas · 700 Riverview Building · 345 Riverview Street · P.O. Box 47370 · Wichita, KS 67201 · 316-267-2212

Marvin J. Martin · (Management) · Martin, Churchill, Overman, Hill & Cole 500 North Market Street · Wichita, KS 67214 · 316-263-3200

Robert N. Partridge · (Management) · Foulston, Siefkin, Powers & Eberhardt 700 Fourth Financial Center · Broadway at Douglas Street · Wichita, KS 67202 316-267-6371

Stephen B. Plummer · (Individuals) · Rumsey, Richey & Plummer · 1041 North Waco Street · Wichita, KS 67203 · 316-262-4481

NATURAL RESOURCES AND ENVIRONMENTAL LAW

Ralph R. Brock · (Oil & Gas) · Morris, Laing, Evans, Brock & Kennedy · 200 West Douglas Street, Fourth Floor · Wichita, KS 67202 · 316-262-2671

Kenneth W. Pringle · Martin, Pringle, Oliver, Wallace & Swartz · 300 Page Court 220 West Douglas Street · Wichita, KS 67202 · 316-265-9311

Randall K. Rathbun · (Plaintiffs) · Depew, Gillen & Rathbun · 621 First National Bank Building · Wichita, KS 67202 · 316-265-9621

Gerald Sawatzky · Foulston, Siefkin, Powers & Eberhardt · 700 Fourth Financial Center · Broadway at Douglas · Wichita, KS 67202 · 316-267-6371

PERSONAL INJURY LITIGATION

Jack E. Dalton · Mangan, Dalton, Trenkle, Rebein and Doll · 208 West Spruce Street · Dodge City, KS 67801 · 316-227-8126

John J. Jurcyk, Jr. · (Defendants) · McAnany, Van Cleave & Phillips · 707 Minnesota Avenue, Fourth Floor · P.O. Box 1398 · Kansas City, KS 66117 · 913-371-3838

Donald W. Vasos · (Plaintiffs) · Vasos, Kugler & Dickerson · 10 Cambridge Place, Suite 200 · 10 East Cambridge Circle Drive · Kansas City, KS 66103 · 913-342-3100

Gene H. Sharp · Neubauer, Sharp, McQueen, Dreiling & Morain · 419 North Kansas Street · P.O. Box 2619 · Liberal, KS 67905-2619 · 316-624-2548

Victor A. Bergman · (Plaintiffs) · Shamberg, Johnson, Bergman & Goldman 4551 West 107th Street, Suite 355 · Overland Park, KS 66207 · 913-642-0600

Lynn R. Johnson · (Plaintiffs) · Shamberg, Johnson, Bergman & Goldman · 4551 West 107th Street, Suite 355 · Overland Park, KS 66207 · 913-642-0600

Frank Saunders, Jr. · (Defendants) · Wallace, Saunders, Austin, Brown & Enochs · 10111 Santa Fe Drive · P.O. Box 12290 · Overland Park, KS 66212 · 913-888-1000

John E. Shamberg · (Plaintiffs) · Shamberg, Johnson, Bergman & Goldman 4551 West 107th Street, Suite 355 · Overland Park, KS 66207 · 913-642-0600

Thomas E. Sullivan · (Plaintiffs) · Commerce Plaza, Suite 900 · 7300 West 110th Street · Overland Park, KS 66210 · 913-451-1981

Charles S. Fisher, Jr. · (Plaintiffs) · Fisher, Heck and Cavanaugh · 1321 Topeka Avenue · P.O. Box 1677 · Topeka, KS 66601 · 913-354-7621

Jerry R. Palmer · (Plaintiffs) · Palmer, Marquardt & Snyder · Columbian Building, Suite 102 · 112 West Sixth · Topeka, KS 66603 · 913-233-1836

Donald Patterson · (Defendants) · Fisher, Patterson, Sayler & Smith · 400 Bank IV Tower · P.O. Box 949 · Topeka, KS 66601 · 913-232-7761

Eugene B. Ralston · (Plaintiffs) · Eugene B. Ralston & Associates · 2913 Southwest Maupin Lane · P.O. Box 4837 · Topeka, KS 66604 · 913-273-8002

Gene E. Schroer · (Plaintiffs) · Schroer, Rice · 115 East Seventh Street · Topeka, KS 66603 · 913-357-0333

Wayne T. Stratton · (Defendants) · Goodell, Stratton, Edmonds & Palmer · 215 East Eighth Avenue · Topeka, KS 66603-3999 · 913-233-0593

Wesley A. Weathers · Weathers & Riley · 4848 Southwest 21st Street · P.O. Box 67209 · Topeka, KS 66667 · 913-273-2020

Arden J. Bradshaw · (Plaintiffs) · Post, Syrios & Bradshaw · Occidental Plaza, Suite 204 · 300 North Main Street · Wichita, KS 67202 · 316-267-6391

Richard C. Hite · (Defendants) · Kahrs, Nelson, Fanning, Hite & Kellogg · 200 West Douglas Street, Suite 630 · Wichita, KS 67202-3089 · 316-265-7761

H. E. Jones · (Defendants) · Herschberger, Patterson, Jones & Roth · 600 Hardage Center North · 100 South Main Street · Wichita, KS 67202 · 316-263-7583

Albert L. Kamas · (Plaintiffs) · Render & Kamas · 700 Riverview Building · 345 Riverview · P.O. Box 47370 · Wichita, KS 67201 · 316-267-2212

Darrell D. Kellogg · (Defendants) · Kahrs, Nelson, Fanning, Hite & Kellogg · 200 West Douglas Street, Suite 630 · Wichita, KS 67202-3089 · 316-265-7761

Gerald L. Michaud · (Plaintiffs) · Michaud & Hutton · Building 1200 · 8100 East 22nd Street North · P.O. Box 2757 · Wichita, KS 67201-2757 · 316-686-3404

Bradley Post · (Plaintiffs) · Post, Syrios & Bradshaw · Occidental Plaza, Suite 204 300 North Main Street · Wichita, KS 67202 · 316-267-6391

Mikel L. Stout · (Defendants) · Foulston, Siefkin, Powers & Eberhardt · 700 Fourth Financial Center · Broadway at Douglas · Wichita, KS 67202 · 316-267-6371

Darrell L. Warta · (Defendants) · Foulston, Siefkin, Powers & Eberhardt · 700 Fourth Financial Center · Broadway at Douglas · Wichita, KS 67202 · 316-267-6371

REAL ESTATE LAW

Stephen T. Adams · Blackwell Sanders Matheny Weary & Lombardi · 40 Corporate Woods, Suite 1200 · 9401 Indian Creek Parkway · P.O. Box 25388 Overland Park, KS 66225 · 913-345-8400

Jack N. Fingersh · Brown, Koralchik & Fingersh · Corporate Woods, Building 40, Suite 1100 · 9401 Indian Creek Parkway · P.O. Box 25550 · Overland Park, KS 66225 · 913-451-8500

Gerald L. Goodell · Goodell, Stratton, Edmonds & Palmer · 215 East Eighth Avenue · Topeka, KS 66603-3999 · 913-233-0593

Philip L. Bowman · Adams, Jones, Robinson and Malone · Market Center, Suite 600 · 155 North Market Street · P.O. Box 1034 · Wichita, KS 67201 · 316-265-8591

Phillip S. Frick · Foulston, Siefkin, Powers & Eberhardt · 700 Fourth Financial Center · Broadway at Douglas · Wichita, KS 67202 · 316-267-6371

Willard B. Thompson · Fleeson, Gooing, Coulson & Kitch · 1600 Kansas State Bank Building · 125 North Market Street · P.O. Box 997 · Wichita, KS 67201 · 316-267-7361

TAX AND EMPLOYEE BENEFITS LAW

Philip D. Ridenour · Ridenour and Knobbe · 109 West Avenue A · P.O. Box 808 Cimarron, KS 67835 · 316-855-3492

William P. Trenkle, Jr. · Mangan, Dalton, Trenkle, Rebein and Doll · 208 West Spruce Street · Dodge City, KS 67801 · 316-227-8126

Martin B. Dickinson, Jr. · Barber, Emerson, Springer, Zinn & Murray · Massachusetts Street at South Park · P.O. Box 666 · Lawrence, KS 66044 · 913-843-6600

Richard L. Zinn · Barber, Emerson, Springer, Zinn & Murray · Massachusetts Street at South Park · P.O. Box 666 · Lawrence, KS 66044 · 913-843-6600

Charles S. (Terry) Arthur III · Arthur, Green, Arthur, Conderman & Stutzman 201-203 Union National Bank Tower · P.O. Box 248 · Manhattan, KS 66502 913-537-1345

George F. Crawford · Morrison, Hecker, Curtis, Kuder & Parrish · Corporate Woods, Suite 520 · Building 14 · 8717 West 110th Street · Overland Park, KS 66210-2192 · 913-345-2700

C. Maxwell Logan · Shook, Hardy & Bacon · 40 Corporate Woods, Suite 650 · 9401 Indian Creek Parkway · P.O. Box 25128 · Overland Park, KS 66225 · 913-451-6060

Alson R. Martin · (also Employee Benefits) · Shook, Hardy & Bacon · 40 Corporate Woods, Suite 650 · 9401 Indian Creek Parkway · P.O. Box 25128 · Overland Park, KS 66225 · 913-451-6060

Thomas J. Kennedy · Kennedy Berkley Yarnevich & Williamson · United Building, Seventh Floor · P.O. Box 2567 · Salina, KS 67402-2567 · 913-825-4674

Peter L. Peterson · (also Employee Benefits) · Clark, Mize & Linville · 129 South Eighth Street · P.O. Box 380 · Salina, KS 67402-0380 · 913-823-6325

Barney J. Heeney, Jr. · Schroeder, Heeney, Groff and Coffman · Capitol Tower, Suite 408 · 400 Southwest Eighth Avenue · Topeka, KS 66603-3956 · 913-234-3461

Henry L. Hiebert · 117 Southeast Sixth Street · P.O. Box 2758 · Topeka, KS 66601 · 913-232-5688

Donald J. Horttor · Cosgrove, Webb & Oman · Bank IV Tower, Suite 1100 · One Townsite Plaza · Topeka, KS 66603 · 913-235-9511

R. Austin Nothern · Eidson, Lewis, Porter & Haynes · 1300 Merchants National Bank Building · Topeka, KS 66612 · 913-233-2332

Jeffrey L. Ungerer · Davis, Wright, Unrein, Hummer & McCallister · The Davis Building · 3715 Southwest 29th Street · P.O. Box 4385 · Topeka, KS 66604 913-273-4220

Stanley G. Andeel · Foulston, Siefkin, Powers & Eberhardt · 700 Fourth Financial Center · Broadway at Douglas Street · Wichita, KS 67202 · 316-267-6371

William M. Cobb · Bever, Dye, Mustard & Belin · 713 First National Bank Building · Wichita, KS 67202 · 316-263-8294

James P. Rankin · (Employee Benefits) · Foulston, Siefkin, Powers & Eberhardt 700 Fourth Financial Center · Broadway at Douglas Street · Wichita, KS 67202 316-267-6371

R. Chris Robe · (Employee Benefits) · Bever, Dye, Mustard & Belin · 713 First National Bank Building · Wichita, KS 67202 · 316-263-8294

Harvey Sorensen · Foulston, Siefkin, Powers & Eberhardt · 700 Fourth Financial Center · Broadway at Douglas Street · Wichita, KS 67202 · 316-267-6371

Willard B. Thompson · Fleeson, Gooing, Coulson & Kitch · 1600 Kansas State Bank Building · 125 North Market Street · P.O. Box 997 · Wichita, KS 67201 316-267-7361

Thomas C. Triplett · Triplett, Woolf & Garretson · 800 Centre City Plaza · 151 North Main Street · Wichita, KS 67202 · 316-265-5700

TRUSTS AND ESTATES

William P. Trenkle, Jr. · Mangan, Dalton, Trenkle, Rebein and Doll · 208 West Spruce Street · Dodge City, KS 67801 · 316-227-8126

Martin B. Dickinson, Jr. · Barber, Emerson, Springer, Zinn & Murray · Massachusetts Street at South Park · P.O. Box 666 · Lawrence, KS 66044 · 913-843-6600

Webster L. Golden · Stevens, Brand, Lungstrum, Golden & Winter · 502 First National Bank Tower · P.O. Box 1200 · Lawrence, KS 66044 · 913-843-0811

Charles S. (Terry) Arthur III · Arthur, Green, Arthur, Conderman & Stutzman 201-203 Union National Bank Tower · P.O. Box 248 · Manhattan, KS 66502 913-537-1345

Nancy Schmidt Roush · Shook, Hardy & Bacon · 40 Corporate Woods, Suite 650 9401 Indian Creek Parkway · P.O. Box 25128 · Overland Park, KS 66225 · 913-451-6060

Peter L. Peterson · Clark, Mize & Linville · 129 South Eighth Street · P.O. Box 380 · Salina, KS 67402-0380 · 913-823-6325

Murray F. Hardesty · Hardesty & Woolpert · 2201 West 29th Street · P.O. Box 5514 · Topeka, KS 66605 · 913-266-4595

Donald J. Horttor · Cosgrove, Webb & Oman · Bank IV Tower, Suite 1100 · One Townsite Plaza · Topeka, KS 66603 · 913-235-9511

E. Gene McKinney · McKinney & McKinney · 517 Capitol Federal Building · 700 Kansas Avenue · Topeka, KS 66603 · 913-233-1321

R. Austin Nothern · Eidson, Lewis, Porter & Haynes · 1300 Merchants National Bank Building · Topeka, KS 66612 · 913-233-2332

Stanley G. Andeel · Foulston, Siefkin, Powers & Eberhardt · 700 Fourth Financial Center · Broadway at Douglas Street · Wichita, KS 67202 · 316-267-6371

Linda K. Constable · Foulston, Siefkin, Powers & Eberhardt · 700 Fourth Financial Center · Broadway at Douglas Street · Wichita, KS 67202 · 316-267-6371

Richard C. Harris · Foulston, Siefkin, Powers & Eberhardt · 700 Fourth Financial Center · Broadway at Douglas Street · Wichita, KS 67202 · 316-267-6371

Willard B. Thompson · Fleeson, Gooing, Coulson & Kitch · 1600 Kansas State Bank Building · 125 North Market Street · P.O. Box 997 · Wichita, KS 67201 316-267-7361

Thomas C. Triplett · Triplett, Woolf & Garretson · 800 Centre City Plaza · 151 North Main Street · Wichita, KS 67202 · 316-265-5700

KENTUCKY

BANKRUPTCY LAW	278
BUSINESS LITIGATION	279
CORPORATE LAW	280
CRIMINAL DEFENSE	281
FAMILY LAW	281
LABOR AND EMPLOYMENT LAW	281
NATURAL RESOURCES AND ENVIRONMENTAL LAW	282
PERSONAL INJURY LITIGATION	283
REAL ESTATE LAW	284
TAX AND EMPLOYEE BENEFITS LAW	285
TRUSTS AND ESTATES	286

BANKRUPTCY LAW

W. Thomas Bunch · Bunch & Brock · Security Trust Building, Suite 805 · P.O. Box 2086 · Lexington, KY 40507 · 606-254-5522

Joseph M. Scott, Jr. · Stoll, Keenon & Park · 1000 First Security Plaza · Lexington, KY 40507-1380 · 606-231-3000

Jerry D. Truitt · Sturgill, Turner and Truitt · 155 East Main Street · Lexington, KY 40507 · 606-255-8581

John W. Ames · Goldberg & Simpson · 2800 First National Tower · Louisville, KY 40202 · 502-589-4440

John P. Reisz · Greenebaum, Boone, Treitz, Maggiolo, Reisz & Brown · 2700 First National Tower · Louisville, KY 40202 · 502-589-4100

David T. Stosberg · Wyatt, Tarrant & Combs · 2700 Citizens Plaza · Louisville, KY 40202 · 502-589-5235

BUSINESS LITIGATION

John David Cole · Cole, Broderick, Minton, Moore & Thornton · Phoenix Place 921 College Street · P.O. Box 1869 · Bowling Green, KY 42101 · 502-781-6650

William E. Johnson · Johnson, Judy, Stoll, Keenon & Park · 326 West Main Street · Frankfort, KY 40601 · 502-875-5544

Charles L. Calk · Gess Mattingly Saunier & Atchison · 201 West Short Street Lexington, KY 40507-1269 · 606-255-2344

C. Kilmer Combs · Wyatt, Tarrant & Combs · Lexington Financial Center · 250 West Main Street · Lexington, KY 40507 · 606-233-2012

C. Gibson Downing · 1999 Richmond Road, Suite 2B · Lexington, KY 40502 606-268-2869

Harry B. Miller, Jr. · Miller, Griffin & Marks · Security Trust Building, Suite 700 Lexington, KY 40507 · 606-255-6676

James Park, Jr. · Brown, Todd & Heyburn · 2700 Lexington Financial Center Lexington, KY 40507-1634 · 606-233-4068

O. Grant Bruton · Middleton & Reutlinger · 2500 Brown & Williamson Tower Louisville, KY 40202-3410 · 502-584-1135

K. Gregory Haynes · Wyatt, Tarrant & Combs · 2600 Citizens Plaza · Louisville, KY 40202 · 502-589-5235

Marvin J. Hirn · Hirn, Reed, Harper & Eisinger · 2450 Meidinger Tower Louisville, KY 40202 · 502-585-2450

Sheryl G. Snyder · Wyatt, Tarrant & Combs · 2600 Citizens Plaza · Louisville, KY 40202 · 502-589-5235

Kenneth J. Tuggle · Brown, Todd & Heyburn · 1600 Citizens Plaza · Louisville, KY 40202 · 502-589-5400

Lively M. Wilson · Stites & Harbison · 600 West Main Street · Louisville, KY 40202 · 502-587-3400

Edgar A. Zingman · Wyatt, Tarrant & Combs · 2600 Citizens Plaza · Louisville, KY 40202 · 502-589-5235

Morton J. Holbrook, Jr. · Holbrook, Wible, Sullivan & Helmers · 100 Saint Ann Building · P.O. Box 727 · Owensboro, KY 42302 · 502-926-4000

CORPORATE LAW

John G. Atchison, Jr. · Gess Mattingly Saunier & Atchison · 201 West Short Street · Lexington, KY 40507-1269 · 606-255-2344

Lawrence K. Banks · Greenebaum Doll & McDonald · 1400 Vine Center Tower P.O. Box 1808 · Lexington, KY 40593 · 606-231-8500

C. Gibson Downing · 1999 Richmond Road, Suite 2B · Lexington, KY 40502 606-268-2869

Lawrence E. Forgy, Jr. · Stoll, Keenon & Park · 1000 First Security Plaza Lexington, KY 40507-1380 · 606-231-3000

James A. Kegley · Greenebaum Doll & McDonald · 1400 Vine Center Tower P.O. Box 1808 · Lexington, KY 40593 · 606-231-8500

James Park, Jr. · Brown, Todd & Heyburn · 2700 Lexington Financial Center Lexington, KY 40507-1634 · 606-233-4068

Stewart E. Conner · Wyatt, Tarrant & Combs · 2800 Citizens Plaza · Louisville, KY 40202 · 502-589-5235

Gordon B. Davidson · Wyatt, Tarrant & Combs · 2700 Citizens Plaza · Louisville, KY 40202 · 502-589-5235

Ivan M. Diamond · Greenebaum Doll & McDonald · 3300 First National Tower Louisville, KY 40202 · 502-589-4200

A. Robert Doll · Greenebaum Doll & McDonald · 3300 First National Tower Louisville, KY 40202 · 502-589-4200

Irwin J. Eisinger · Hirn, Reed, Harper & Eisinger · 2450 Meidinger Tower Louisville, KY 40202 · 502-585-2450

Edwin H. Perry · Greenebaum Doll & McDonald · 3300 First National Tower Louisville, KY 40202 · 502-589-4200

R. James Straus · Brown, Todd & Heyburn · 1600 Citizens Plaza · Louisville, KY 40202 · 502-589-5400

Rucker Todd · Brown, Todd & Heyburn · 1600 Citizens Plaza · Louisville, KY 40202 · 502-589-5400

James S. Welch · Ogden & Robertson · 1200 One Riverfront Plaza · Louisville, KY 40202 · 502-582-1601

CRIMINAL DEFENSE

William E. Johnson · Johnson, Judy, Stoll, Keenon & Park · 326 West Main Street · Frankfort, KY 40601 · 502-875-6000

James A. Shuffett · Shuffett and Shuffett · 403 Security Trust Building · Short & Mill Streets · Lexington, KY 40507-1292 · 606-252-5794

Frank E. Haddad, Jr. · Kentucky Home Life Building, Fifth Floor · Louisville, KY 40202 · 502-583-4881

FAMILY LAW

Glen S. Bagby · Brock, Brock & Bagby · 190 Market Street · Lexington, KY 40507 606-255-7795

Harry B. Miller, Jr. · Miller, Griffin & Marks · Security Trust Building, Suite 700 Lexington, KY 40507 · 606-255-6676

Natalie S. Wilson · Gess Mattingly Saunier & Atchison · 201 West Short Street Lexington, KY 40507-1269 · 606-255-2344

Virginia C. Burbank · First Trust Centre · Fifth and Market Streets, Suite 600 North · Louisville, KY 40202 · 502-589-5257

William P. Mulloy, Sr. · Mulloy, Walz, Wetterer, Fore & Schwartz · 200 South Fifth Street · Louisville, KY 40202 · 502-589-5250

LABOR AND EMPLOYMENT LAW

Allen P. Dodd III · (Individuals) · Dodd & Dodd · 621 West Main Street Louisville, KY 40202 · 502-584-1108

Jon L. Fleischaker · (Management) · Wyatt, Tarrant & Combs · 2700 Citizens Plaza · Louisville, KY 40202 · 502-589-5235

James C. Hickey · (Individuals) · Ewen, MacKenzie & Peden · 650 Starks Building · Louisville, KY 40202 · 502-589-1110

D. Patton Pelfrey · (Management) · Brown, Todd & Heyburn · 1600 Citizens Plaza · Louisville, KY 40202 · 502-589-5400

Alton D. Priddy · (Labor) · Hardy, Logan, Priddy & Cotton · 604 Republic Building · 429 West Muhammad Ali Boulevard · Louisville, KY 40202 · 502-569-2740

Raymond L. Sales · (Labor) · Segal, Isenberg, Sales, Stewart & Cutler · Marion E. Taylor Building, Third Floor · 312 Fourth Avenue · Louisville, KY 40202 502-568-5600

Herbert L. Segal · (Labor) · Segal, Isenberg, Sales, Stewart & Cutler · Marion E. Taylor Building, Third Floor · 312 Fourth Avenue · Louisville, KY 40202 502-568-5600

James U. Smith III · (Management) · Smith and Smith · 400 North First Trust Centre · 200 South Fifth Street · Louisville, KY 40202 · 502-587-0761

Matthew Ryan Westfall · (Management) · Westfall, Talbott & Woods · 501 South Second Street · Louisville, KY 40202 · 502-584-7722

NATURAL RESOURCES AND ENVIRONMENTAL LAW

George L. Seay, Jr. · Wyatt, Tarrant & Combs · McClure Building, Suite 200 308 West Main Street · P.O. Box 495 · Frankfort, KY 40602 · 502-223-2104

Joseph J. Zaluski · Wyatt, Tarrant & Combs · McClure Building, Suite 200 · 308 West Main Street · P.O. Box 495 · Frankfort, KY 40602 · 502-223-2104

Maxwell P. Barret, Jr. · Stoll, Keenon & Park · 1000 First Security Plaza Lexington, KY 40507-1380 · 606-231-3000

Lloyd R. Cress · Greenebaum Doll & McDonald · 1400 Vine Center Tower · P.O. Box 1808 · Lexington, KY 40593 · 606-231-8500

Marcus P. McGraw · Greenebaum Doll & McDonald · 1400 Vine Center Tower P.O. Box 1808 · Lexington, KY 40593 · 606-231-8500

Donald H. Vish · Wyatt, Tarrant & Combs · Lexington Financial Center · 250 West Main Street · Lexington, KY 40507 · 606-233-2012

PERSONAL INJURY LITIGATION

John David Cole · (Defendants) · Cole, Broderick, Minton, Moore & Thornton Phoenix Place · 921 College Street · P.O. Box 1869 · Bowling Green, KY 42101 502-781-6650

Mark G. Arnzen · (Defendants) · Robinson, Arnzen, Parry & Wentz · 600 Greenup Street · Covington, KY 41012-0472 · 606-431-6100

John L. Spalding · (Defendants) · Spalding & Hannah · Professional Arts Building · 333 Madison Avenue · Covington, KY 41011 · 606-291-4646

Philip Taliaferro III · (Plaintiffs) · Taliaferro & Mann · 120 West Fifth Street · P.O. Box 468 · Covington, KY 41012-0468 · 606-291-9900

E. Andre Busald · (Plaintiffs) · Busald Funk Zevely · 226 Main Street · Florence, KY 41042 · 606-371-3600

Uhel O. Barrickman · (Defendants) · Richardson, Barrickman, Dickinson & Ropp · New Farmers National Bank Building · P.O. Box 358 · Glasgow, KY 42141 502-651-2116

W. T. Adkins · (Defendants) · Boehl Stopher Graves & Deindoerfer · 444 West Second Street · Lexington, KY 40508 · 606-252-6721

William R. Garmer · (Plaintiffs) · Savage, Garmer & Elliott · 300 West Short Street · Lexington, KY 40507 · 606-254-9351

Deddo G. Lynn · (Defendants) · Hays, Moss and Lynn · 267 West Short Street · Lexington, KY 40507 · 606-253-0523

Peter Perlman · (Plaintiffs) · 388 South Broadway · Lexington, KY 40508 · 606-253-3919

Joe C. Savage · (Plaintiffs) · Savage, Garmer & Elliott · 300 West Short Street · Lexington, KY 40507 · 606-254-9351

Robert J. Turley · (Plaintiffs) · Turley & Moore · Limestone Building, Second Floor · 134 North Limestone Street · Lexington, KY 40507 · 606-252-1705

John T. Ballantine · (Defendants) · Ogden & Robertson · 1200 One Riverfront Plaza · Louisville, KY 40202 · 502-582-1601

Charles J. Cronan IV · (Defendants) · Stites & Harbison · 600 West Main Street Louisville, KY 40202 · 502-587-3400

Frank P. Doheny, Jr. · (Defendants) · Woodward, Hobson & Fulton · 2500 First National Tower · Louisville, KY 40202 · 502-585-3321

Frederick C. Dolt · (Plaintiffs) · 310 Starks Building · Louisville, KY 40202 502-587-6554

Larry B. Franklin · (Plaintiffs) · Franklin and Hance · First National Tower, 23rd Floor · 101 South Fifth Street · Louisville, KY 40202 · 502-582-2270

William D. Grubbs · (Defendants) · Woodward, Hobson & Fulton · 2500 First National Tower · Louisville, KY 40202 · 502-585-3321

William O. Guethlein · (Defendants) · Boehl Stopher Graves & Deindoerfer 2300 One Riverfront Plaza · Louisville, KY 40202 · 502-589-5980

Armer H. Mahan, Jr. · (Defendants) · Lynch, Cox, Gilman & Mahan · 1800 Meidinger Tower · Louisville, KY 40202 · 502-582-2429

William R. Patterson, Jr. · (Plaintiffs) · Landrum, Shouse & Patterson · Republic Building, 11th Floor · Fifth and Ali Streets · Louisville, KY 40202 · 502-589-7616

Edward H. Stopher · (Defendants) · Boehl Stopher Graves & Deindoerfer · 2300 One Riverfront Plaza · Louisville, KY 40202 · 502-589-5980

Gary M. Weiss · (Plaintiffs) · Weiss, Karp & Roseberry · 304 West Liberty Street, Suite 210 · Louisville, KY 40202 · 502-589-6650

Lively M. Wilson · (Defendants) · Stites & Harbison · 600 West Main Street Louisville, KY 40202 · 502-587-3400

Frank V. Benton III · (Defendants) · Benton, Benton & Luedeke · 18 North Fort Thomas Avenue · Newport, KY 41075 · 606-781-2345

REAL ESTATE LAW

Michael L. Ades · Greenebaum Doll & McDonald · 1400 Vine Center Tower P.O. Box 1808 · Lexington, KY 40593 · 606-231-8500

Gary W. Barr · Stoll, Keenon & Park · 1000 First Security Plaza · Lexington, KY 40507-1380 · 606-231-3000

Charles Richard Doyle · Gess Mattingly Saunier & Atchison · 201 West Short Street · Lexington, KY 40507-1269 · 606-255-2344

James T. Hodge · Wyatt, Tarrant & Combs · Lexington Financial Center · 250 West Main Street · Lexington, KY 40507 · 606-233-2012

William M. Lear, Jr. · Stoll, Keenon & Park · 1000 First Security Plaza · Lexington, KY 40507-1380 · 606-231-3000

Foster Ockerman · Martin, Ockerman & Brabant · 200 North Upper Street Lexington, KY 40507 · 606-254-4401

Mark B. Davis, Jr. · Brown, Todd & Heyburn · 1600 Citizens Plaza · Louisville, KY 40202 · 502-589-5400

Michael M. Fleishman · Greenebaum Doll & McDonald · 3300 First National Tower · Louisville, KY 40202 · 502-589-4200

Alfred S. Joseph III · Stites & Harbison · 600 West Main Street · Louisville, KY 40202 · 502-587-3400

John S. Osborn, Jr. · Wyatt, Tarrant & Combs · 2700 Citizens Plaza · Louisville, KY 40202 · 502-589-5235

Michael G. Shaikun · Greenebaum Doll & McDonald · 3300 First National Tower · Louisville, KY 40202 · 502-589-4200

TAX AND EMPLOYEE BENEFITS LAW

Charles R. Hembree · Kincaid, Wilson, Schaeffer & Hembree · Kincaid Towers, Suite 500 · Lexington, KY 40507 · 606-253-6411

Charles Fassler · Greenebaum Doll & McDonald · 3300 First National Tower Louisville, KY 40202 · 502-589-4200

G. Alexander Hamilton · (Employee Benefits) · Wyatt, Tarrant & Combs · 2800 Citizens Plaza · Louisville, KY 40202 · 502-589-5235

Laramie L. Leatherman · Greenebaum Doll & McDonald · 3300 First National Tower · Louisville, KY 40202 · 502-589-4200

Thomas J. Luber · Wyatt, Tarrant & Combs · 2800 Citizens Plaza · Louisville, KY 40202 · 502-589-5235

Joseph C. Oldham · (Employee Benefits) · Ogden & Robertson · 1200 One Riverfront Plaza · Louisville, KY 40202 · 502-582-1601

Ivan J. Schell · (Employee Benefits) · Ewen, MacKenzie & Peden · 650 Starks Building · Louisville, KY 40202 · 502-589-1110

Rucker Todd · Brown, Todd & Heyburn · 1600 Citizens Plaza · Louisville, KY 40202 · 502-589-5400

TRUSTS AND ESTATES

John G. Atchison, Jr. · Gess Mattingly Saunier & Atchison · 201 West Short Street · Lexington, KY 40507-1269 · 606-255-2344

John T. Bondurant · Brown, Todd & Heyburn · 1600 Citizens Plaza · Louisville, KY 40202 · 502-589-5400

James L. Coorssen · Barnett & Alagia · The Fifth Avenue Building · 444 South Fifth Street · Louisville, KY 40202 · 502-585-4131

John R. Cummins · Greenebaum Doll & McDonald · 3300 First National Tower Louisville, KY 40202 · 502-589-4200

Gerald F. Greenwell · Brown, Todd & Heyburn · 1600 Citizens Plaza · Louisville, KY 40202 · 502-589-5400

Martin S. Weinberg · Greenebaum Doll & McDonald · 3300 First National Tower · Louisville, KY 40202 · 502-589-4200

LOUISIANA

BANKRUPTCY LAW	287
BUSINESS LITIGATION	288
CORPORATE LAW	289
CRIMINAL DEFENSE	290
FAMILY LAW	291
LABOR AND EMPLOYMENT LAW	291
MARITIME LAW	292
NATURAL RESOURCES AND ENVIRONMENTAL LAW	293
PERSONAL INJURY LITIGATION	294
REAL ESTATE LAW	297
TAX AND EMPLOYEE BENEFITS LAW	298
TRUSTS AND ESTATES	300

BANKRUPTCY LAW

David S. Rubin · Kantrow, Spaht, Weaver & Blitzer · City Plaza, Suite 300 · 445 North Boulevard · P.O. Box 2997 · Baton Rouge, LA 70821-2997 · 504-383-4703

William E. Steffes · Steffes & Macmurdo · 10311 Jefferson Highway, #A-2 Baton Rouge, LA 70809 · 504-291-5857

Douglas S. Draper · Friend, Wilson & Draper · 1335 First National Bank of Commerce Building · New Orleans, LA 70112 · 504-581-9595

Edward M. Heller · Bronfin, Heller, Steinberg & Berins · 2500 Poydras Center 650 Poydras Street · New Orleans, LA 70130 · 504-568-1888

R. Patrick Vance · Jones, Walker, Waechter, Poitevent, Carrere & Denegre Place St. Charles · 201 St. Charles Avenue · New Orleans, LA 70170 · 504-582-8000

James Robert Jeter · Cook, Yancey, King & Galloway · 1700 Commercial National Tower · 333 Texas Street · Shreveport, LA 71101-3621 · 318-221-6277

BUSINESS LITIGATION

Robert E. Barkley, Jr. · Sessions, Fishman, Rosenson, Boisfontaine, Nathan & Winn · Place St. Charles · 201 St. Charles Avenue · New Orleans, LA 70170 504-582-1500

Curtis R. Boisfontaine · Sessions, Fishman, Rosenson, Boisfontaine, Nathan & Winn · Place St. Charles · 201 St. Charles Avenue · New Orleans, LA 70170 504-582-1500

Gene W. Lafitte · Liskow & Lewis · One Shell Square, 50th Floor · New Orleans, LA 70139 · 504-581-7979

Charles W. Lane III · Jones, Walker, Waechter, Poitevent, Carrere & Denegre Place St. Charles · 201 St. Charles Avenue · New Orleans, LA 70170 · 504-582-8000

John M. McCollam · Gordon, Arata, McCollam, Stuart & Duplantis · Place St. Charles, Suite 4000 · 201 St. Charles Avenue · New Orleans, LA 70170 · 504-582-1111

Benjamin R. Slater, Jr. · Monroe & Lemann · Place St. Charles, Suite 3300 · 201 St. Charles Avenue · New Orleans, LA 70170 · 504-586-1900

Walter C. Thompson, Jr. · Sessions, Fishman, Rosenson, Boisfontaine, Nathan & Winn · Place St. Charles · 201 St. Charles Avenue · New Orleans, LA 70170 504-582-1500

Phillip A. Wittmann · Stone, Pigman, Walther, Wittmann & Hutchinson · 546 Carondelet Street · New Orleans, LA 70130-3588 · 504-581-3200

Sidney E. Cook · Cook, Yancey, King & Galloway · 1700 Commercial National Tower · 333 Texas Street · Shreveport, LA 71101-3621 · 318-221-6277

Joseph W. Milner · Blanchard, Walker, O'Quinn & Roberts · First National Bank Tower, 15th Floor · P.O. Drawer 1126 · Shreveport, LA 71163 · 318-221-6858

Billy R. Pesnell · Hargrove, Guyton, Ramey and Barlow · First Federal Plaza, Seventh Floor · P.O. Box B · Shreveport, LA 71161-0010 · 318-227-1113

Robert G. Pugh · Pugh and Pugh · 330 Marshall Street, Suite 1200 · Shreveport, LA 71101 · 318-227-2270

CORPORATE LAW

Michael H. Rubin · Rubin, Curry, Colvin & Joseph · One American Place, Suite 1400 · Baton Rouge, LA 70825-0001 · 504-383-1400

Anthony J. Correro III · Jones, Walker, Waechter, Poitevent, Carrere & Denegre Place St. Charles · 201 St. Charles Avenue · New Orleans, LA 70170 · 504-582-8000

George Denegre · Jones, Walker, Waechter, Poitevent, Carrere & Denegre Place St. Charles · 201 St. Charles Avenue · New Orleans, LA 70170 · 504-582-8000

Louis Y. Fishman · Sessions, Fishman, Rosenson, Boisfontaine, Nathan & Winn Place St. Charles · 201 St. Charles · New Orleans, LA 70170 · 504-582-1500

Paul M. Haygood · Phelps, Dunbar, Marks, Claverie & Sims · Texaco Center, 30th Floor · 400 Poydras Street · New Orleans, LA 70130 · 504-566-1311

Campbell C. Hutchinson · Stone, Pigman, Walther, Wittmann & Hutchinson 546 Carondelet Street · New Orleans, LA 70130-3588 · 504-581-3200

Guy C. Lyman, Jr. · Milling, Benson, Woodward, Hillyer, Pierson & Miller LL&E Tower, Suite 2300 · 909 Poydras Street · New Orleans, LA 70112-1017 504-569-7000

L. Richards McMillan II · Jones, Walker, Waechter, Poitevent, Carrere & Denegre · Place St. Charles · 201 St. Charles Avenue · New Orleans, LA 70170 504-582-8000

Charles A. Snyder · Milling, Benson, Woodward, Hillyer, Pierson & Miller LL&E Tower, Suite 2300 · 909 Poydras Street · New Orleans, LA 70112-1017 504-569-7000

Walter B. Stuart IV · Gordon, Arata, McCollam, Stuart & Duplantis · Place St. Charles · 201 St. Charles Avenue, Suite 4000 · New Orleans, LA 70170 · 504-582-1111

Ewell P. Walther, Jr. · Stone, Pigman, Walther, Wittmann & Hutchinson · 546 Carondelet Street · New Orleans, LA 70130-3588 · 504-581-3200

John D. Wogan · Monroe & Lemann · Place St. Charles, Suite 3300 · 201 St. Charles Avenue · New Orleans, LA 70170 · 504-586-1900

Richard P. Wolfe · Monroe & Lemann · Place St. Charles, Suite 3300 · 201 St. Charles Avenue · New Orleans, LA 70170 · 504-586-1900

CRIMINAL DEFENSE

Camille F. Gravel, Jr. · Gravel & Brady · 711 Washington Street · P.O. Box 1792 Alexandria, LA 71309 · 318-487-4501

J. Michael Small · One Centre Court, Suite 201 · P.O. Box 1470 · Alexandria, LA 71309 · 318-487-8963

Lewis O. Unglesby · Unglesby & Barrios · 246 Napoleon Street · Baton Rouge, LA 70802 · 504-387-0120

Risley C. Triche · Triche, Sternfels & Nail · 307 Levee Street · P.O. Drawer 339 Napoleonville, LA 70390 · 504-369-6168

F. Irvin Dymond · Dymond, Crull & Castaing · First National Bank of Commerce Building, Suite 707 · New Orleans, LA 70112 · 504-581-7700

Michael S. Fawer · Fawer & Zatzkis · 530 Natchez Street · New Orleans, LA 70130 · 504-525-1500

Robert Glass · Glass & Reed · 338 Lafayette Street · New Orleans, LA 70130 504-581-9065

John R. Martzell · Martzell, Thomas & Bickford · 338 Lafayette Street · New Orleans, LA 70130 · 504-581-9065

Julian R. Murray, Jr. · Murray, Braden, Gonzalez & Richardson · 612 Gravier Street · New Orleans, LA 70130 · 504-581-2000

John Wilson Reed · Glass & Reed · 338 Lafayette Street · New Orleans, LA 70130 · 504-581-9065

L. Edwin Greer · Peatross, Greer & Frazier · Hutchinson Building, Suite 404 P.O. Box 404 · Shreveport, LA 71162 · 318-222-0202

Wellborn Jack, Jr. · 101 Milam Street · Shreveport, LA 71101 · 318-227-9637

FAMILY LAW

Robert L. Cole · Cole, Guidry, Prather & Forrest · 405 West Main Street · Lafayette, LA 70501 · 318-232-6183

Dudley D. Flanders · Flanders and Flanders · 600 Loyola Avenue, Suite 201 · New Orleans, LA 70113 · 504-586-1441

Robert C. Lowe · Lowe, Stein, Hoffman & Allweiss · 650 Poydras Street, Suite 2450 · New Orleans, LA 70130 · 504-581-2450

Philip R. Riegel, Jr. · First National Bank of Commerce Building · 210 Baronne Street, Suite 620 · New Orleans, LA 70112 · 504-522-0126

Hani E. Dehan · Love, Rigby, Dehan, Love & McDaniel · Johnson Building, Sixth Floor · P.O. Box 1835 · Shreveport, LA 71166 · 318-226-1880

Kenneth Rigby · Love, Rigby, Dehan, Love & McDaniel · Johnson Building, Sixth Floor · P.O. Box 1835 · Shreveport, LA 71166 · 318-226-1880

H. F. Sockrider, Jr. · Sockrider, Bolin & Anglin · 327 Crockett Street · Shreveport, LA 71101 · 318-221-5503

LABOR AND EMPLOYMENT LAW

William R. D'Armond · Kean, Miller, Hawthorne, D'Armond, McCowan & Jarman · One American Place, 22nd Floor · Baton Rouge, LA 70825 · 504-387-0999

G. Michael Pharis · (Management) · Taylor, Porter, Brooks & Phillips · Louisiana National Bank Building, Eighth Floor · P.O. Drawer 2471 · Baton Rouge, LA 70821-2471 · 504-387-3221

Jerry L. Gardner, Jr. · (Labor; Individuals) · Gardner, Robein and Healey · 2540 Severn Avenue, Suite 400 · Metairie, LA 70002 · 504-885-9994

Louis L. Robein, Jr. · (Labor; Individuals) · Gardner, Robein and Healey · 2540 Severn Avenue, Suite 400 · Metairie, LA 70002 · 504-885-9994

Meyer H. Gertler · (Individuals) · Gertler and Gertler · 127-129 Carondelet Street · New Orleans, LA 70130 · 504-581-6411

Steven Hymowitz · (Management) · McCalla, Thompson, Pyburn & Ridley · Poydras Center, Suite 2800 · 650 Poydras Street · P.O. Box 50639 · New Orleans, LA 70130 · 504-524-2499

Leslie L. Inman · (Management) · Kullman, Inman, Bee and Downing · 615 Howard Avenue · P.O. Box 60118 · New Orleans, LA 70160 · 504-524-4162

Frederick S. Kullman · (Management) · Kullman, Inman, Bee and Downing 615 Howard Avenue · P.O. Box 60118 · New Orleans, LA 70160 · 504-524-4162

D. Andrew Lang · (Management) · McGlinchy, Stafford, Mintz, Cellini & Lang 643 Magazine Street · New Orleans, LA 70130-3477 · 504-586-1200

Robert K. McCalla · (Management) · McCalla, Thompson, Pyburn & Ridley Poydras Center, Suite 2800 · 650 Poydras Street · P.O. Box 50639 · New Orleans, LA 70130 · 504-524-2499

A. Richard Gear · Cook, Yancey, King & Galloway · 1700 Commercial National Tower · 333 Texas Street · Shreveport, LA 71101-3621 · 318-221-6277

MARITIME LAW

Leonard Fuhrer · (Plaintiffs) · Fuhrer, Flournoy, Hunter & Morton · 900 Foisy Avenue · P.O. Box 1270 · Alexandria, LA 71301 · 318-487-9858

Paul H. Due · (Plaintiffs) · Due, Smith & Caballero · 8201 Jefferson Highway Baton Rouge, LA 70809 · 504-929-7481

John Allen Bernard · Onebane, Donohoe, Bernard, Torian, Diaz, McNamara & Abell · 102 Versailles Boulevard, Suite 600 · P.O. Drawer 3507 · Lafayette, LA 70502 · 318-237-2660

James R. Nieset · Plauche, Smith & Nieset · 1123 Pithon Street · P.O. Drawer 1705 · Lake Charles, LA 70602 · 318-436-0522

Donald R. Abaunza · Liskow & Lewis · One Shell Square, 50th Floor · New Orleans, LA 70139 · 504-581-7979

Robert B. Acomb, Jr. · Jones, Walker, Waechter, Poitevent, Carrere & Denegre Place St. Charles · 201 St. Charles Avenue · New Orleans, LA 70170 · 504-582-8000

Edward S. Bagley · Terriberry, Carroll & Yancey · 3100 Energy Centre · 1100 Poydras Street · New Orleans, LA 70163 · 504-523-6451

John A. Bolles · Terriberry, Carroll & Yancey · 3100 Energy Centre · 1100 Poydras Street · New Orleans, LA 70163 · 504-523-6451

Wood Brown III · Montgomery, Barnett, Brown, Read, Hammond & Mintz · 3200 Energy Centre · 1100 Poydras Street · New Orleans, LA 70163 · 504-585-3200

Eldon E. Fallon · Kierr, Gainsburgh, Benjamin, Fallon, David & Ates · 1718 First National Bank of Commerce Building · New Orleans, LA 70112 · 504-522-2304

Warren M. Faris · Faris, Ellis, Cutrone & Gilmore · 1207 Whitney Building · New Orleans, LA 70130 · 504-581-6373

George Frilot · Lemle, Kelleher, Kohlmeyer, Dennery, Hunley, Moss & Frilot · Pan-American Life Center, 21st Floor · 601 Poydras Street · New Orleans, LA 70130-6097 · 504-586-1241

Samuel C. Gainsburgh · (Plaintiffs) · Kierr, Gainsburgh, Benjamin, Fallon, David & Ates · 1718 First National Bank of Commerce Building · New Orleans, LA 70112 · 504-522-2304

John B. Gooch, Jr. · Montgomery, Barnett, Brown, Read, Hammond & Mintz · 3200 Energy Centre · 1100 Poydras Street · New Orleans, LA 70163 · 504-585-3200

John Phelps Hammond · Montgomery, Barnett, Brown, Read, Hammond & Mintz · 3200 Energy Centre · 1100 Poydras Street · New Orleans, LA 70163 · 504-585-3200

George W. Healey III · Phelps, Dunbar, Marks, Claverie & Sims · Texaco Center, 30th Floor · 400 Poydras Street · New Orleans, LA 70130 · 504-566-1311

John W. Sims · Phelps, Dunbar, Marks, Claverie & Sims · Texaco Center, 30th Floor · 400 Poydras Street · New Orleans, LA 70130 · 504-566-1311

NATURAL RESOURCES AND ENVIRONMENTAL LAW

Lawrence E. Donohoe, Jr. · Onebane, Donohoe, Bernard, Torian, Diaz, McNamara & Abell · 102 Versailles Boulevard, Suite 600 · P.O. Drawer 3507 · Lafayette, LA 70502 · 318-237-2660

Daniel Ryan Sartor, Jr. · Snellings, Breard, Sartor, Inabnett & Trascher · 1503 North 19th Street · P.O. Box 2055 · Monroe, LA 71207-2055 · 318-387-8000

Gene W. Lafitte · Liskow & Lewis · One Shell Square, 50th Floor · New Orleans, LA 70139 · 504-581-7979

John M. McCollam · Gordon, Arata, McCollam & Duplantis · Place St. Charles, Suite 4000 · 201 St. Charles Avenue · New Orleans, LA 70170-0001 · 504-582-1111

Ray A. Barlow · Hargrove, Guyton, Ramey & Barlow · First Federal Plaza, Seventh Floor · P.O. Box B · Shreveport, LA 71161-0010 · 318-227-1113

Robert Roberts III · Blanchard, Walker, O'Quinn & Roberts · First National Bank Tower, 15th Floor · P.O. Drawer 1126 · Shreveport, LA 71163 · 318-221-6858

PERSONAL INJURY LITIGATION

Leonard Fuhrer · (Plaintiffs) · Fuhrer, Flournoy, Hunter & Morton · 900 Foisy Avenue · P.O. Box 1270 · Alexandria, LA 71301 · 318-487-9858

Howard B. Gist, Jr. · (Defendants) · Gist, Methvin, Hughes & Munsterman · 803 Johnston Street · P.O. Box 1871 · Alexandria, LA 71309-1871 · 318-448-1632

LeDoux R. Provosty, Jr. · (Defendants) · Provosty, Sadler & deLaunay · Hibernia Bank Building, Eighth Floor · P.O. Drawer 1791 · Alexandria, LA 71309-1791 318-445-3631

Paul H. Due · (Plaintiffs) · Due, Smith & Caballero · 8201 Jefferson Highway Baton Rouge, LA 70809 · 504-929-7481

Robert J. Vandaworker · (Defendants) · Taylor, Porter, Brooks & Phillips · LNB Building, Eighth Floor · 451 Florida Street · P.O. Drawer 2471 · Baton Rouge, LA 70821-2471 · 504-387-3221

James E. Diaz, Sr. · (Defendants) · Onebane, Donohoe, Bernard, Torian, Diaz, McNamara & Abell · 102 Versailles Boulevard, Suite 600 · P.O. Drawer 3507 Lafayette, LA 70502 · 318-237-2660

Patrick A. Juneau, Jr. · (Defendants) · Juneau, Judice, Hill & Adley · 926 Coolidge Boulevard · Lafayette, LA 70503 · 318-235-2405

Anthony D. Moroux · (Plaintiffs) · Moroux, Domengeaux & Davis · 201 West Main Street · Lafayette, LA 70502 · 318-233-6168

John G. Torian II · (Defendants) · Onebane, Donohoe, Bernard, Torian, Diaz, McNamara & Abell · 102 Versailles Boulevard, Suite 600 · P.O. Drawer 3507 Lafayette, LA 70502 · 318-237-2660

Bob F. Wright · (Plaintiffs) · Domengeaux & Wright · 556 Jefferson Street, Suite 500 · P.O. Box 3668 · Lafayette, LA 70502-3668 · 318-233-3033

William B. Baggett, Sr. · (Plaintiffs) · Baggett, McCall & Burgess · 3006 Country Club Road · Lake Charles, LA 70605 · 318-478-8888

Thomas M. Bergstedt · (Defendants) · Scofield, Bergstedt, Gerard, Mount & Veron · 1114 Ryan Street · P.O. Drawer 3028 · Lake Charles, LA 70602 · 318-433-9436

A. Lane Plauche · (Defendants) · Plauche, Smith & Nieset · 1123 Pithon Street P.O. Drawer 1705 · Lake Charles, LA 70602 · 318-436-0522

John B. Scofield · (Defendants) · Scofield, Bergstedt, Gerard, Mount & Veron 1114 Ryan Street · P.O. Drawer 3028 · Lake Charles, LA 70602 · 318-433-9436

Philippi P. St. Pee · Francipane, Regan & St. Pee · 3324 North Causeway Boulevard · Metairie, LA 70002 · 504-837-2456

Lawrence K. Burleigh · (Plaintiffs) · Guarisco Shopping Center · 907 Seventh Street · P.O. Box 2625 · Morgan City, LA 70381 · 504-384-1910

Gerard F. Thomas, Jr. · Thomas & Dunahoe · 137 Trudeau Street · P.O. Box 548 Natchitoches, LA 71457 · 318-352-6455

Robert B. Acomb, Jr. · (Defendants) · Jones, Walker, Waechter, Poitevent, Carrere & Denegre · Place St. Charles · 201 St. Charles Avenue · New Orleans, LA 70170 · 504-582-8000

Henry B. Alsobrook, Jr. · (Defendants) · Adams and Reese · 4500 One Shell Square · New Orleans, LA 70139 · 504-581-3234

Wood Brown III · Montgomery, Barnett, Brown, Read, Hammond & Mintz 3200 Energy Centre · 1100 Poydras Street · New Orleans, LA 70163 · 504-585-3200

Alvin R. Christovich, Jr. · (Defendants) · Christovich and Kearney · Pan American Life Center, Suite 2300 · 601 Poydras Street · New Orleans, LA 70130 504-561-5700

William K. Christovich · (Defendants) · Christovich and Kearney · Pan American Life Center, Suite 2300 · 601 Poydras Street · New Orleans, LA 70130 · 504-561-5700

Robert M. Contois, Jr. · (Defendants) · Jones, Walker, Waechter, Poitevent, Carrere & Denegre · Place St. Charles · 201 St. Charles Avenue · New Orleans, LA 70170 · 504-582-8000

Eldon E. Fallon · (Plaintiffs) · Kierr, Gainsburgh, Benjamin, Fallon, David & Ates · 1718 First National Bank of Commerce Building · New Orleans, LA 70112 504-522-2304

Samuel C. Gainsburgh · (Plaintiffs) · Kierr, Gainsburgh, Benjamin, Fallon, David & Ates · 1718 First National Bank of Commerce Building · New Orleans, LA 70112 · 504-522-2304

Frederick J. Gisevius, Jr. · (Plaintiffs) · 615 Richards Building · New Orleans, LA 70112 · 504-581-4282

Russ M. Herman · (Plaintiffs) · Herman, Herman, Katz & Cotlar · 820 O'Keefe Avenue · New Orleans, LA 70113 · 504-581-4892

H. Martin Hunley, Jr. · (Defendants) · Lemle, Kelleher, Kohlmeyer, Dennery, Hunley, Moss & Frilot · Pan-American Life Center, 21st Floor · 601 Poydras Street · New Orleans, LA 70130-6097 · 504-586-1241

Frank E. Lamothe III · (Plaintiffs) · Lamothe & Hamilton · Pan American Life Center, Suite 2411 · 601 Poydras Street · New Orleans, LA 70130 · 504-566-1805

Robert E. Leake, Jr. · (Defendants) · Leake & Andersson · 1700 Energy Centre 1100 Poydras Street · New Orleans, LA 70163 · 504-585-7500

Harvey J. Lewis · (Plaintiffs) · Lewis & Kullman · 2615 Pan American Life Center 601 Poydras Street · New Orleans, LA 70130 · 504-588-1500

John R. Martzell · (Plaintiffs) · Martzell, Thomas & Bickford · 338 Lafayette Street · New Orleans, LA 70130 · 504-581-9065

Dermot S. McGlinchey · (Defendants) · McGlinchey, Stafford, Mintz, Cellini & Lang · 643 Magazine Street · New Orleans, LA 70130-3477 · 504-586-1200

Stephen B. Murray · (Plaintiffs) · Murray Law Firm · 650 Poydras Street, Suite 1450 · New Orleans, LA 70130 · 504-525-8100

John J. Weigel · Jones, Walker, Waechter, Poitevent, Carrere & Denegre · Place St. Charles · 201 St. Charles Avenue · New Orleans, LA 70170 · 504-582-8000

Lawrence D. Wiedemann · (Plaintiffs) · Wiedemann & Fransen · 821 Baronne Street · P.O. Box 30648 · New Orleans, LA 70190-0648 · 504-581-6180

Thomas J. Wyllie · (Defendants) · Adams and Reese · 4500 One Shell Square · New Orleans, LA 70139 · 504-581-3234

Leslie J. Schiff · Sandoz, Sandoz & Schiff · 137 West Landry Street · P.O. Drawer 900 · Opelousas, LA 70570 · 318-942-9771

A. Kennon Goff III · Goff and Goff · 612 North Vienna Street · P.O. Box 2050 · Ruston, LA 71273-2050 · 318-255-1760

Troy E. Bain · (Plaintiffs) · 1540 Irving Place · Shreveport, LA 71101 · 318-221-0076

Sidney E. Cook · (Defendants) · Cook, Yancey, King & Galloway · 1700 Commercial National Tower · 333 Texas Street · Shreveport, LA 71101-3621 · 318-221-6277

Herschel E. Richard, Jr. · (Defendants) · Cook, Yancey, King & Galloway · 1700 Commercial National Tower · 333 Texas Street · Shreveport, LA 71101-3621 · 318-221-6277

Charles W. Salley · (Defendants) · Lunn, Irion, Johnson, Salley & Carlisle · 500 Slattery Building · P.O. Box 1534 · Shreveport, LA 71165-1534 · 318-222-0665

REAL ESTATE LAW

Donald E. Bradford · Two United Plaza, Suite 900 · 8550 United Plaza Boulevard · Baton Rouge, LA 70809 · 504-924-7124

H. Edwin McGlasson, Jr. · Voorhies & Labbe · Arcadiana National Bank Building, Fourth Floor · 700 St. John Street · P.O. Box 3527 · Lafayette, LA 70502 · 318-232-9700

Philip deV. Claverie · Phelps, Dunbar, Marks, Claverie & Sims · Texaco Center, 30th Floor · 400 Poydras Street · New Orleans, LA 70130 · 504-566-1311

Julian H. Good · Lemle, Kelleher, Kohlmeyer, Dennery, Hunley, Moss & Frilot · Pan-American Life Center, 21st Floor · 601 Poydras Street · New Orleans, LA 70130-6097 · 504-586-1241

Mitchell W. Herzog · Shushan, Meyer, Jackson, McPherson & Herzog · 1010 Common Street, Suite 1500 · New Orleans, LA 70112 · 504-581-9444

Henry F. O'Connor, Jr. · Steeg and O'Connor · Place St. Charles · 201 St. Charles Avenue, Suite 3201 · New Orleans, LA 70170 · 504-582-1199

Louis G. Shushan · Shushan, Meyer, Jackson, McPherson & Herzog · 1010 Common Street, Suite 1500 · New Orleans, LA 70112 · 504-581-9444

Moise S. Steeg, Jr. · Steeg and O'Connor · Place St. Charles · 201 St. Charles Avenue, Suite 3201 · New Orleans, LA 70170 · 504-582-1199

Ewell P. Walther, Jr. · Stone, Pigman, Walther, Wittmann & Hutchinson · 546 Carondelet Street · New Orleans, LA 70130-3588 · 504-581-3200

Hugh T. Ward · Peters, Ward, Bright & Hennessy · The First National Bank Tower, Suite 1000 · 400 Texas Street · P.O. Box 91 · Shreveport, LA 71161 318-221-0684

TAX AND EMPLOYEE BENEFITS LAW

John C. Blackman IV · (also Employee Benefits) · Jones, Walker, Waechter, Poitevent, Carrere & Denegre · One American Place · P.O. Box 1267 · Baton Rouge, LA 70821 · 504-343-4465

Robert R. Casey · Jones, Walker, Waechter, Poitevent, Carrere & Denegre · One American Place · P.O. Box 1267 · Baton Rouge, LA 70821 · 504-343-4465

Carey J. Messina · Kean, Miller, Hawthorne, D'Armond, McCowan & Jarman · One American Place, 22nd Floor · P.O. Box 3513 · Baton Rouge, LA 70821 · 504-387-0999

Robert C. Schmidt · (Employee Benefits) · 10935 Perkins Road · P.O. Box 80317 Baton Rouge, LA 70898 · 504-767-7093

Robert Lee Curry III · Theus, Grisham, Davis & Leigh · 1600 Lamy Lane · P.O. Drawer 4768 · Monroe, LA 71211-4768 · 318-388-0100

Paul K. Kirkpatrick, Jr. · Hudson, Potts & Bernstein · Ouachita National Bank Building, 10th Floor · P.O. Drawer 3008 · Monroe, LA 71210 · 318-388-4400

Jane E. Armstrong · (Employee Benefits) · Phelps, Dunbar, Marks, Claverie & Sims · Texaco Center, 30th Floor · 400 Poydras Street · New Orleans, LA 70130 504-566-1311

Hilton S. Bell · (Employee Benefits) · Milling, Benson, Woodward, Hillyer, Pierson & Miller · LL&E Tower, Suite 2300 · 909 Poydras Street · New Orleans, LA 70112-1017 · 504-569-7000

Edward B. Benjamin, Jr. · Jones, Walker, Waechter, Poitevent, Carrere & Denegre · Place St. Charles · 201 St. Charles Avenue · New Orleans, LA 70170 504-582-8000

William C. Gambel · Milling, Benson, Woodward, Hillyer, Pierson & Miller LL&E Tower, Suite 2300 · 909 Poydras Street · New Orleans, LA 70112-1017 504-569-7000

Michael E. Guarisco · Guarisco, Weiler & Cordes · 2660 Poydras Center · 650 Poydras Street · New Orleans, LA 70130 · 504-524-2944

Thomas C. Keller · Jones, Walker, Waechter, Poitevent, Carrere & Denegre Place St. Charles · 201 St. Charles Avenue · New Orleans, LA 70170 · 504-582-8000

Thomas B. Lemann · Monroe & Lemann · Place St. Charles, Suite 3300 · 201 St. Charles Avenue · New Orleans, LA 70170 · 504-586-1900

Edward F. Martin · (Employee Benefits) · Jones, Walker, Waechter, Poitevent, Carrere & Denegre · Place St. Charles · 201 St. Charles Avenue · New Orleans, LA 70170 · 504-582-8000

Max Nathan, Jr. · Sessions, Fishman, Rosenson, Boisfontaine, Nathan & Winn Place St. Charles · 201 St. Charles Avenue · New Orleans, LA 70170 · 504-582-1500

Rudolph R. Ramelli · (Employee Benefits) · Jones, Walker, Waechter, Poitevent, Carrere & Denegre · Place St. Charles · 201 St. Charles Avenue · New Orleans, LA 70170 · 504-582-8000

Jerome J. Reso, Jr. · Baldwin & Haspel · 1100 Poydras Street, 22nd Floor · New Orleans, LA 70163-0800 · 504-581-1711

H. Paul Simon · Simon, Peragine, Smith & Redfearn · Energy Centre, 30th Floor 1100 Poydras Street · New Orleans, LA 70163-3000 · 504-569-2030

Quintin T. Hardtner III · Hargrove, Guyton, Ramey and Barlow · First Federal Plaza, Seventh Floor · P.O. Box B · Shreveport, LA 71161-0010 · 318-227-1113

J. Edgerton Pierson, Jr. · Blanchard, Walker, O'Quinn & Roberts · First National Bank Tower, 15th Floor · P.O. Drawer 1126 · Shreveport, LA 71163 · 318-221-6858

Cecil E. Ramey, Jr. · Hargrove, Guyton, Ramey and Barlow · First Federal Plaza, Seventh Floor · P.O. Box B · Shreveport, LA 71161-0010 · 318-227-1113

Donald P. Weiss · Wiener, Weiss, Madison & Howell · First Federal Plaza, Third Floor · 505 Travis Street · Shreveport, LA 71101 · 318-226-9100

TRUSTS AND ESTATES

Sidney M. Blitzer, Jr. · Kantrow, Spaht, Weaver & Blitzer · City Plaza, Suite 300 445 North Boulevard · P.O. Box 2997 · Baton Rouge, LA 70821-2997 · 504-383-4703

Gerald Le Van · Le Van & Ray · Four United Plaza, Second Floor · 8555 United Plaza Boulevard · Baton Rouge, LA 70809 · 504-925-2282

Ben R. Miller, Jr. · Kean, Miller, Hawthorne, D'Armond, McCowan & Jarman · One American Place, 22nd Floor · Baton Rouge, LA 70825 · 504-387-0999

H. Edwin McGlasson, Jr. · Voorhies & Labbe · Acadiana National Bank Building, Fourth Floor · 700 St. John Street · P.O. Box 3527 · Lafayette, LA 70502 · 318-232-9700

William E. Shaddock · Stockwell, Sievert, Viccellio, Clements & Shaddock · One Lakeside Plaza · P.O. Box 2900 · Lake Charles, LA 70601 · 318-436-9491

John C. Blackman IV · Jones, Walker, Waechter, Poitevent, Carrere & Denegre · One American Place · P.O. Box 1267 · Baton Rouge, LA 70821 · 504-343-4465

Robert Lee Curry III · Theus, Grisham, Davis & Leigh · 1600 Lamy Lane · P.O. Drawer 4768 · Monroe, LA 71211-4768 · 318-388-0100

Paul K. Kirkpatrick, Jr. · Hudson, Potts & Bernstein · Ouachita National Bank Building, 10th Floor · P.O. Drawer 3008 · Monroe, LA 71210 · 318-388-4400

D. R. Sartor, Jr. · Snellings, Breard, Sartor, Inabnett & Trascher · 1503 North 19th Street · P.O. Box 2055 · Monroe, LA 71207-2055 · 318-387-8000

Edward B. Benjamin, Jr. · Jones, Walker, Waechter, Poitevent, Carrere & Denegre · Place St. Charles · 201 St. Charles Avenue · New Orleans, LA 70170 · 504-582-8000

Thomas B. Lemann · Monroe & Lemann · Place St. Charles, Suite 3300 · 201 St. Charles Avenue · New Orleans, LA 70170 · 504-586-1900

Edward F. Martin · Jones, Walker, Waechter, Poitevent, Carrere & Denegre · Place St. Charles · 201 St. Charles Avenue · New Orleans, LA 70170 · 504-582-8000

Joel A. Mendler · Baldwin & Haspel · 1100 Poydras Street, 22nd Floor · New Orleans, LA 70163-0800 · 504-581-1711

Max Nathan, Jr. · Sessions, Fishman, Rosenson, Boisfontaine, Nathan & Winn · Place St. Charles · 201 St. Charles Avenue · New Orleans, LA 70170 · 504-582-1500

Paul O. H. Pigman · Stone, Pigman, Walther, Wittmann & Hutchinson · 546 Carondelet Street · New Orleans, LA 70130-3588 · 504-581-3200

Jerome J. Reso, Jr. · Baldwin & Haspel · 1100 Poydras Street, 22nd Floor · New Orleans, LA 70163-0800 · 504-581-1711

H. Paul Simon · Simon, Peragine, Smith & Redfearn · Energy Centre, 30th Floor · 1100 Poydras Street · New Orleans, LA 70163-3000 · 504-569-2030

Quintin T. Hardtner III · Hargrove, Guyton, Ramey & Barlow · First Federal Plaza, Seventh Floor · P.O. Box B · Shreveport, LA 71161-0010 · 318-227-1113

T. Haller Jackson, Jr. · Tucker, Jeter, Jackson and Hickman · 405 Edwards Street, Suite 905 · Shreveport, LA 71101-3146 · 318-425-7764

Stuart D. Lunn · Smitherman, Lunn, Chastain & Hill · Commercial National Bank Building, Suite 800 · 333 Texas Street · Shreveport, LA 71101-3673 · 318-227-1990

J. Edgerton Pierson, Jr. · Blanchard, Walker, O'Quin & Roberts · First National Bank Tower, 15th Floor · P.O. Drawer 1126 · Shreveport, LA 71163 · 318-221-6858

Cecil E. Ramey, Jr. · Hargrove, Guyton, Ramey & Barlow · First Federal Plaza, Seventh Floor · P.O. Box B · Shreveport, LA 71161-0010 · 318-227-1113

Donald P. Weiss · Wiener, Weiss, Madison & Howell · First Federal Plaza, Third Floor · 505 Travis Street · Shreveport, LA 71101 · 318-226-9100

Jacques L. Wiener, Jr. · Wiener, Weiss, Madison & Howell · First Federal Plaza, Third Floor · 505 Travis Street · Shreveport, LA 71101 · 318-226-9100

MAINE

BANKRUPTCY LAW	302
BUSINESS LITIGATION	303
CORPORATE LAW	303
CRIMINAL DEFENSE	304
FAMILY LAW	304
LABOR AND EMPLOYMENT LAW	305
NATURAL RESOURCES AND ENVIRONMENTAL LAW	305
PERSONAL INJURY LITIGATION	306
REAL ESTATE LAW	306
TAX AND EMPLOYEE BENEFITS LAW	306
TRUSTS AND ESTATES	306

BANKRUPTCY LAW

Louis H. Kornreich · Gross, Minsky, Mogul & Singal · One Merchants Plaza · P.O. Box 917 · Bangor, ME 04401 · 207-942-4644

Daniel Amory · Drummond Woodsum Plimpton & MacMahon · 245 Commercial Street · Portland, ME 04101 · 207-772-1941

Andrew A. Cadot · Perkins, Thompson, Hinckley & Keddy · One Canal Plaza · P.O. Box 426 · Portland, ME 04112-0426 · 207-774-2635

Gerald S. Cope · Cope and Cope · 415 Congress Street, Suite 300 · Portland, ME 04101 · 207-772-7491

George J. Marcus · Pierce, Atwood, Scribner, Allen, Smith & Lancaster · One Monument Square · Portland, ME 04101 · 207-773-6411

Gregory A. Tselikis · Bernstein, Shur, Sawyer and Nelson · 100 Middle Street, Sixth Floor · P.O. Box 9729 · Portland, ME 04101 · 207-774-1200

P. Benjamin Zuckerman · Verrill & Dana · Two Canal Plaza · P.O. Box 586 Portland, ME 04112 · 207-774-4000

BUSINESS LITIGATION

Charles H. Abbott · Skelton, Taintor & Abbott · 95 Main Street · P.O. Box 3200 Auburn, ME 04210 · 207-784-1371

Lewis V. Vafiades · Vafiades, Brountas & Kominsky · One Merchants Plaza · P.O. Box 919 · Bangor, ME 04401 · 207-947-6915

Jack H. Simmons · Berman, Simmons & Goldberg · 129 Lisbon Street · P.O. Box 961 · Lewiston, ME 04240 · 207-784-3576

Ralph I. Lancaster, Jr. · Pierce, Atwood, Scribner, Allen, Smith & Lancaster One Monument Square · Portland, ME 04101 · 207-773-6411

Gerald F. Petruccelli · Petruccelli & Cox · 50 Monument Square · Portland, ME 04101 · 207-775-0200

Jotham D. Pierce, Jr. · Pierce, Atwood, Scribner, Allen, Smith & Lancaster · One Monument Square · Portland, ME 04101 · 207-773-6411

Peter J. Rubin · Bernstein, Shur, Sawyer and Nelson · 100 Middle Street, Sixth Floor · P.O. Box 9729 · Portland, ME 04101 · 207-774-1200

CORPORATE LAW

Bruce A. Coggeshall · Pierce, Atwood, Scribner, Allen, Smith & Lancaster · One Monument Square · Portland, ME 04101 · 207-773-6411

Joseph L. Delafield III · Drummond Woodsum Plimpton & MacMahon · 245 Commercial Street · Portland, ME 04101 · 207-772-1941

Gordon F. Grimes · Bernstein, Shur, Sawyer and Nelson · 100 Middle Street, Sixth Floor · P.O. Box 9729 · Portland, ME 04101 · 207-774-1200

Leonard M. Nelson · Bernstein, Shur, Sawyer and Nelson · 100 Middle Street, Sixth Floor · P.O. Box 9729 · Portland, ME 04101 · 207-774-1200

Jeremiah D. Newbury · Pierce, Atwood, Scribner, Allen, Smith & Lancaster One Monument Square · Portland, ME 04101 · 207-773-6411

Peter B. Webster · Verrill & Dana · Two Canal Plaza · P.O. Box 586 · Portland, ME 04112 · 207-774-4000

Owen W. Wells · Perkins, Thompson, Hinckley & Keddy · One Canal Plaza P.O. Box 426 · Portland, ME 04112-0426 · 207-774-2635

Harold E. Woodsum, Jr. · Drummond Woodsum Plimpton & MacMahon · 245 Commercial Street · Portland, ME 04101 · 207-772-1941

CRIMINAL DEFENSE

George Z. Singal · Gross, Minsky, Mogul & Singal · One Merchants Plaza · P.O. Box 917 · Bangor, ME 04401 · 207-942-4644

Jack H. Simmons · Berman, Simmons & Goldberg · 129 Lisbon Street · P.O. Box 961 · Lewiston, ME 04240 · 207-784-3576

Peter J. DeTroy III · Norman, Hanson & DeTroy · 415 Congress Street, Fifth Floor · P.O. Box 4600 DTS · Portland, ME 04112 · 207-774-7000

Ralph I. Lancaster, Jr. · Pierce, Atwood, Scribner, Allen, Smith & Lancaster One Monument Square · Portland, ME 04101 · 207-773-6411

Daniel G. Lilley · 377 Fore Street · P.O. Box 4803 DTS · Portland, ME 04112 207-774-6206

Peter J. Rubin · Bernstein, Shur, Sawyer and Nelson · 100 Middle Street, Sixth Floor · P.O. Box 9729 · Portland, ME 04101 · 207-774-1200

FAMILY LAW

Roger J. Katz · Lipman & Katz · 72 Winthrop Street · Augusta, ME 04330 207-622-3711

Susan R. Kominsky · Vafiades, Brountas & Kominsky · One Merchants Plaza P.O. Box 919 · Bangor, ME 04401 · 207-947-6915

Robert A. Laskoff · 103 Park Street · P.O. Box 7206 · Lewiston, ME 04240 207-786-3173

Sumner Thurman Bernstein · Bernstein, Shur, Sawyer and Nelson · 100 Middle Street, Sixth Floor · P.O. Box 9729 · Portland, ME 04101 · 207-774-1200

Phyllis G. Givertz · Givertz, Lunt & Hambley · 408 Fore Street · P.O. Box 4801 · Portland, ME 04112 · 207-772-8373

Barry Zimmerman · Kelly, Remmel & Zimmerman · 53 Exchange Street · Portland, ME 04101 · 207-775-1020

LABOR AND EMPLOYMENT LAW

Herbert H. Bennett · (Management) · Herbert H. Bennett & Associates · 121 Middle Street · Portland, ME 04101-4104 · 207-773-4775

Peter H. Jacobs · (Management) · Pierce, Atwood, Scribner, Allen, Smith & Lancaster · One Monument Square · Portland, ME 04101 · 207-773-6411

S. Mason Pratt, Jr. · (Management) · Pierce, Atwood, Scribner, Allen, Smith & Lancaster · One Monument Square · Portland, ME 04101 · 207-773-6411

Howard T. Reben · (Individuals) · Sunenblick, Reben, Benjamin & March · 97 India Street · Portland, ME 04101 · 207-772-5496

Patrick N. McTeague · (Labor) · McTeague, Higbee, Libner, Reitman, MacAdam & Case · Four Union Park · P.O. Box 5000 · Topsham, ME 04086 · 207-725-5581

NATURAL RESOURCES AND ENVIRONMENTAL LAW

Clifford H. Goodall · Dyer, Goodall & Larouche · 45 Memorial Circle · Augusta, ME 04330 · 207-622-3693

Jeffrey A. Thaler · (Plaintiffs) · Berman, Simmons & Goldberg · 129 Lisbon Street · P.O. Box 961 · Lewiston, ME 04240 · 207-784-3576

Daniel E. Boxer · Pierce, Atwood, Scribner, Allen, Smith & Lancaster · One Monument Square · Portland, ME 04101 · 207-773-6411

Kenneth F. Gray · Pierce, Atwood, Scribner, Allen, Smith & Lancaster · One Monument Square · Portland, ME 04101 · 207-773-6411

E. Stephen Murray · Murray, Plumb & Murray · 75 Pearl Street · Portland, ME 04101 · 207-773-5651

PERSONAL INJURY LITIGATION

George Z. Singal · Gross, Minsky, Mogul & Singal · One Merchants Plaza · P.O. Box 917 · Bangor, ME 04401 · 207-942-4644

Lewis V. Vafiades · (Defendants) · Vafiades, Brountas & Kominsky · One Merchants Plaza · P.O. Box 919 · Bangor, ME 04401 · 207-947-6915

Jack H. Simmons · (Defendants) · Berman, Simmons & Goldberg · 129 Lisbon Street · P.O. Box 961 · Lewiston, ME 04240 · 207-784-3576

Ralph I. Lancaster, Jr. · Pierce, Atwood, Scribner, Allen, Smith & Lancaster One Monument Square · Portland, ME 04101 · 207-773-6411

Peter J. Rubin · Bernstein, Shur, Sawyer and Nelson · 100 Middle Street, Sixth Floor · P.O. Box 9729 · Portland, ME 04101 · 207-774-1200

REAL ESTATE LAW

David Plimpton · Drummond Woodsum Plimpton & MacMahon · 245 Commercial Street · Portland, ME 04101 · 207-772-1941

Louis A. Wood · Verrill & Dana · Two Canal Plaza · P.O. Box 586 · Portland, ME 04112 · 207-774-4000

TAX AND EMPLOYEE BENEFITS LAW

Craig W. Friedrich · Bernstein, Shur, Sawyer and Nelson · 100 Middle Street, Sixth Floor · P.O. Box 9729 · Portland, ME 04101 · 207-774-1200

William C. Smith · Pierce, Atwood, Scribner, Allen, Smith & Lancaster · One Monument Square · Portland, ME 04101 · 207-773-6411

Thomas J. Van Meer · Verrill & Dana · Two Canal Plaza · P.O. Box 586 · Portland, ME 04112 · 207-774-4000

TRUSTS AND ESTATES

Richard P. LeBlanc · Bernstein, Shur, Sawyer and Nelson · 100 Middle Street, Sixth Floor · P.O. Box 9729 · Portland, ME 04101 · 207-774-1200

William C. Smith · Pierce, Atwood, Scribner, Allen, Smith & Lancaster · One Monument Square · Portland, ME 04101 · 207-773-6411

Thomas J. Van Meer · Verrill & Dana · Two Canal Plaza · P.O. Box 586 · Portland, ME 04112 · 207-774-4000

Robert B. Williamson, Jr. · Verrill & Dana · Two Canal Plaza · P.O. Box 586 · Portland, ME 04112 · 207-774-4000

MARYLAND

BANKRUPTCY LAW	308
BUSINESS LITIGATION	309
CORPORATE LAW	309
CRIMINAL DEFENSE	310
FAMILY LAW	310
LABOR AND EMPLOYMENT LAW	311
MARITIME LAW	312
NATURAL RESOURCES AND ENVIRONMENTAL LAW	313
PERSONAL INJURY LITIGATION	313
REAL ESTATE LAW	314
TAX AND EMPLOYEE BENEFITS LAW	315
TRUSTS AND ESTATES	315

BANKRUPTCY LAW

Nathan B. Feinstein · Piper & Marbury · 36 South Charles Street · Baltimore, MD 21201 · 301-539-2530

Richard M. Kremen · Semmes, Bowen & Semmes · 250 West Pratt Street · Baltimore, MD 21201 · 301-539-5040

Harvey M. Lebowitz · Frank, Bernstein, Conaway & Goldman · 300 East Lombard Street · Baltimore, MD 21202 · 301-625-3500

George W. Liebmann · Eight West Hamilton Street · Baltimore, MD 21201 · 301-752-5887

Roger Frankel · Lerch, Early, Roseman & Frankel · Three Bethesda Metro Center, 10th Floor · Bethesda, MD 20814 · 301-986-1300

Alan S. Kerxton · 4550 Montgomery Avenue, Suite 775N · Bethesda, MD 20814
301-951-1500

Richard H. Gins · Gins & Seeber · 451 Hungerford Drive, Suite 505 · Rockville, MD 20850 · 301-762-9123

BUSINESS LITIGATION

George Beall · Miles & Stockbridge · 10 Light Street · Baltimore, MD 21202
301-727-6464

Francis B. Burch, Jr. · Piper & Marbury · 36 South Charles Street · Baltimore, MD 21201 · 301-539-2530

Benjamin R. Civiletti · Venable, Baetjer and Howard · 1800 Mercantile Bank & Trust Building · Two Hopkins Plaza · Baltimore, MD 21201 · 301-244-7400

George A. Nilson · Piper & Marbury · 36 South Charles Street · Baltimore, MD 21201 · 301-539-2530

Wilbur D. Preston, Jr. · Whiteford, Taylor & Preston · Signet Tower, Suite 1400 Seven Saint Paul Street · Baltimore, MD 21202 · 301-347-8700

Shale D. Stiller · Frank, Bernstein, Conaway & Goldman · 300 East Lombard Street · Baltimore, MD 21202 · 301-625-3500

James J. Cromwell · Frank, Bernstein, Conaway & Goldman · 6701 Democracy Boulevard, Suite 600 · Bethesda, MD 20817 · 301-897-8282

CORPORATE LAW

Lowell R. Bowen · Miles & Stockbridge · 10 Light Street · Baltimore, MD 21202
301-727-6464

Andre W. Brewster · Piper & Marbury · 36 South Charles Street · Baltimore, MD 21201 · 301-539-2530

Edward Owen Clarke, Jr. · Piper & Marbury · 36 South Charles Street · Baltimore, MD 21201 · 301-539-2530

Decatur H. Miller · Piper & Marbury · 36 South Charles Street · Baltimore, MD 21201 · 301-539-2530

Roger D. Redden · (Utilities) · Piper & Marbury · 36 South Charles Street · Baltimore, MD 21201 · 301-539-2530

L. P. Scriggins · Piper & Marbury · 36 South Charles Street · Baltimore, MD 21201 · 301-539-2530

Shale D. Stiller · Frank, Bernstein, Conaway & Goldman · 300 East Lombard Street · Baltimore, MD 21202 · 301-625-3500

Alan D. Yarbro · Venable, Baetjer and Howard · 1800 Mercantile Bank & Trust Building · Two Hopkins Plaza · Baltimore, MD 21201 · 301-244-7400

CRIMINAL DEFENSE

Benjamin R. Civiletti · Venable, Baetjer and Howard · 1800 Mercantile Bank & Trust Building · Two Hopkins Plaza · Baltimore, MD 21201 · 301-244-7400

Marvin J. Garbis · Melnicove, Kaufman, Weiner, Smouse & Garbis · 36 South Charles Street · Baltimore, MD 21201 · 301-332-8500

Andrew Jay Graham · Kramon & Graham · Sun Life Building, Charles Center 20 South Charles Street · Baltimore, MD 21201 · 301-752-6030

H. Russell Smouse · Melnicove, Kaufman, Weiner, Smouse & Garbis · 36 South Charles Street · Baltimore, MD 21201 · 301-332-8500

James P. Ulwick · Kramon & Graham · Sun Life Building, Charles Center · 20 South Charles Street · Baltimore, MD 21201 · 301-752-6030

Arnold M. Weiner · Melnicove, Kaufman, Weiner, Smouse & Garbis · 36 South Charles Street · Baltimore, MD 21201 · 301-332-8500

Russell J. White · White & Karceski · 300 East Joppa Road, Suite 1110 · Towson, MD 21204 · 301-583-1325

FAMILY LAW

Bruce A. Kaufman · Rosenthal & Kaufman · 1212 Blaustein Building · One North Charles Street · Baltimore, MD 21201 · 301-752-5678

Beverly Anne Groner · Groner and Groner · Air Rights Plaza III, Suite 403N 4550 Montgomery Avenue · Bethesda, MD 20814 · 301-657-2828

Walter W. Johnson, Jr. · 8701 Georgia Avenue, Suite 700 · Silver Spring, MD 20910 · 301-587-2090

LABOR AND EMPLOYMENT LAW

Herbert J. Belgrad · (Labor) · Kaplan, Heyman, Greenberg, Engelman & Belgrad · Charles & Redwood Streets · 20 South Charles Street · Baltimore, MD 21201 · 301-539-6967

C. Christopher Brown · (Individuals) · Brown & Goldstein · Maryland Bar Center, Suite 300 · 520 West Fayette Street · Baltimore, MD 21201 · 301-659-0717

Jana Howard Carey · (Management) · Venable, Baetjer and Howard · 1800 Mercantile Bank & Trust Building · Two Hopkins Plaza · Baltimore, MD 21201 301-244-7400

Leonard E. Cohen · (Management) · Frank, Bernstein, Conaway & Goldman 300 East Lombard Street · Baltimore, MD 21202 · 301-625-3500

A. Samuel Cook · (Management) · Venable, Baetjer and Howard · 1800 Mercantile Bank & Trust Building · Two Hopkins Plaza · Baltimore, MD 21201 · 301-244-7400

Warren M. Davison · (Management) · Littler, Mendelson, Fastiff & Tichy · The World Trade Center, Suite 1653 · Baltimore, MD 21202 · 301-528-9545

Stephen W. Godoff · (Individuals) · Godoff & Zimmerman · 14 West Madison Street · Baltimore, MD 21201 · 301-539-0717

Stephen D. Langhoff · (Individuals) · 17 Commerce Street, Second Floor · Baltimore, MD 21202 · 301-332-1010

N. Peter Lareau · (Management) · Venable, Baetjer and Howard · 1800 Mercantile Bank & Trust Building · Two Hopkins Plaza · Baltimore, MD 21201 · 301-244-7400

Joseph K. Pokempner · (Management) · Whiteford, Taylor & Preston · Seven Saint Paul Street, Suite 1400 · Baltimore, MD 21202 · 301-347-8700

William J. Rosenthal · (Management) · Shawe & Rosenthal · Sun Life Building Charles Center · Baltimore, MD 21201 · 301-752-1040

Earle K. Shawe · (Management) · Shawe & Rosenthal · Sun Life Building Charles Center · Baltimore, MD 21201 · 301-752-1040

Larry M. Wolf · (Management) · Whiteford, Taylor & Preston · Seven Saint Paul Street, Suite 1400 · Baltimore, MD 21202 · 301-347-8700

Cosimo C. Abato · (Labor) · Abato, Rubenstein & Abato · 2360 West Joppa Road, Suite 308 · Lutherville, MD 21093 · 301-321-0990

Bernard W. Rubenstein · (Labor) · Abato, Rubenstein & Abato · 2360 West Joppa Road, Suite 308 · Lutherville, MD 21093 · 301-321-0990

Joel A. Smith · (Labor) · Abato, Rubenstein & Abato · 2360 West Joppa Road, Suite 308 · Lutherville, MD 21093 · 301-321-0990

MARITIME LAW

William R. Dorsey III · Semmes, Bowen & Semmes · 250 West Pratt Street Baltimore, MD 21201 · 301-539-5040

Francis J. Gorman · Semmes, Bowen & Semmes · 250 West Pratt Street Baltimore, MD 21201 · 301-539-5040

Donald C. Greenman · Ober, Kaler, Grimes & Shriver · 1600 Maryland National Bank Building · 10 Light Street · Baltimore, MD 21202 · 301-685-1120

Manfred W. Leckszas · Ober, Kaler, Grimes & Shriver · 1600 Maryland National Bank Building · 10 Light Street · Baltimore, MD 21202 · 301-685-1120

Charles E. Quandt · Niles, Barton & Wilmer · Legg Mason Tower, Suite 1400 111 South Calvert Street · Baltimore, MD 21202 · 301-783-6300

Kieron F. Quinn · Quinn, Ward and Kershaw · 113 West Monument Street Baltimore, MD 21201 · 301-685-6700

David W. Skeen · Wright, Constable & Skeen · 20 South Charles Street, Third Floor · Baltimore, MD 21201 · 301-539-5541

M. Hamilton Whitman, Jr. · Ober, Kaler, Grimes & Shriver · 1600 Maryland National Bank Building · 10 Light Street · Baltimore, MD 21202 · 301-685-1120

NATURAL RESOURCES AND ENVIRONMENTAL LAW

Robert G. Smith · Venable, Baetjer and Howard · 1800 Mercantile Bank & Trust Building · Two Hopkins Plaza · Baltimore, MD 21201 · 301-244-7400

Thomas H. Truitt · Piper & Marbury · 36 South Charles Street · Baltimore, MD 21201 · 301-539-2530

PERSONAL INJURY LITIGATION

Paul D. Bekman · Israelson, Salsbury, Clements & Bekman · Jefferson Building, Suite 600 · Charles and Fayette Streets · Baltimore, MD 21202 · 301-539-6633

Randall C. Coleman · (Defendants) · Ober, Kaler, Grimes & Shriver · 1600 Maryland National Bank Building · 10 Light Street · Baltimore, MD 21202 301-685-1120

Marvin Ellin · (Plaintiffs) · Ellin and Baker · 1101 St. Paul Street, Second Floor Baltimore, MD 21202 · 301-727-1787

James M. Gabler · (Plaintiffs) · Sandbower, Gabler & O'Shaughnessy · 22 East Fayette Street, Fifth Floor · Baltimore, MD 21202 · 301-576-0762

M. King Hill, Jr. · (Defendants) · Smith, Somerville & Case · 100 Light Street, Sixth Floor · Baltimore, MD 21202 · 301-727-1164

Max R. Israelson · (Plaintiffs) · Israelson, Salsbury, Clements & Bekman · Jefferson Building, Suite 600 · Charles and Fayette Streets · Baltimore, MD 21202 301-539-6633

John E. Sandbower III · Sandbower, Gabler & O'Shaughnessy · 22 East Fayette Street, Fifth Floor · Baltimore, MD 21202 · 301-576-0762

Donald E. Sharpe · (Defendants) · Piper & Marbury · 36 South Charles Street Baltimore, MD 21201 · 301-539-2530

William B. Whiteford · (Defendants) · Whiteford, Taylor & Preston · Signet Tower, Suite 1400 · Seven Saint Paul Street · Baltimore, MD 21202 · 301-347-8700

James J. Cromwell · (Defendants) · Frank, Bernstein, Conaway & Goldman 6701 Democracy Boulevard, Suite 600 · Bethesda, MD 20817 · 301-897-8282

Thomas A. Farrington · (Defendants) · 9200 Basil Court, Suite 204 · Landover, MD 20785 · 301-322-4000

Albert D. Brault · (Defendants) · Brault, Graham, Scott & Brault · 101 South Washington Street · Rockville, MD 20850 · 301-424-1060

William A. Ehrmantraut · (Defendants) · Donahue, Ehrmantraut and Montedonico · 110 North Washington Street, Fifth Floor · Rockville, MD 20850 301-424-3900

Francis J. Ford · (Defendants) · Ford & O'Neill · 17 West Jefferson Street Rockville, MD 20850 · 301-279-2000

George W. Shadoan · (Plaintiffs) · Shadoan and Michael · 108 Park Avenue Rockville, MD 20850 · 301-762-5150

Bayard Z. Hochberg · (Plaintiffs) · Hochberg, Chiarello, Costello & Dowell · 528 East Joppa Road · Towson, MD 21204 · 301-823-2922

George W. White, Jr. · (Plaintiffs) · White, Mindel, Clarke & Hill · 29 West Susquehanna Avenue, Suite 600 · Towson, MD 21204 · 301-828-1050

Charles E. Channing, Jr. · (Defendants) · Sasscer, Clagett, Channing & Bucher 14803 Pratt Street · P.O. Box 550 · Upper Marlboro, MD 20772 · 301-627-5500

REAL ESTATE LAW

Charles T. Albert · Piper & Marbury · 36 South Charles Street · Baltimore, MD 21201 · 301-539-2530

Ronald P. Fish · Frank, Bernstein, Conaway & Goldman · 300 East Lombard Street · Baltimore, MD 21202 · 301-625-3500

Morton P. Fisher, Jr. · Frank, Bernstein, Conaway & Goldman · 300 East Lombard Street · Baltimore, MD 21202 · 301-625-3500

David H. Fishman · Gordon, Feinblatt, Rothman, Hoffberger & Hollander Garrett Building · 233 East Redwood Street · Baltimore, MD 21202 · 301-576-4000

Edward J. Levin · Piper & Marbury · 36 South Charles Street · Baltimore, MD 21201 · 301-539-2530

Russell Ronald Reno, Jr. · Venable, Baetjer and Howard · 1800 Mercantile Bank & Trust Building · Two Hopkins Plaza · Baltimore, MD 21201 · 301-244-7400

TAX AND EMPLOYEE BENEFITS LAW

Bryson L. Cook · Venable, Baetjer and Howard · 1800 Mercantile Bank & Trust Building · Two Hopkins Plaza · Baltimore, MD 21201 · 301-244-7400

Marvin J. Garbis · Melnicove, Kaufman, Weiner, Smouse & Garbis · 36 South Charles Street · Baltimore, MD 21201 · 301-332-8500

Lawrence M. Katz · Piper & Marbury · 36 South Charles Street · Baltimore, MD 21201 · 301-539-2530

Shale D. Stiller · Frank, Bernstein, Conaway & Goldman · 300 East Lombard Street · Baltimore, MD 21202 · 301-625-3500

TRUSTS AND ESTATES

Albert S. Barr III · Village Square I, Suite 127 · Village of Cross Keys · Baltimore, MD 21210 · 301-435-8787

Max E. Blumenthal · Frank, Bernstein, Conaway & Goldman · 300 East Lombard Street · Baltimore, MD 21202 · 301-625-3500

Stanard T. Klinefelter · Piper & Marbury · 36 South Charles Street · Baltimore, MD 21201 · 301-539-2530

Alexander I. Lewis III · Venable, Baetjer and Howard · 1800 Mercantile Bank & Trust Building · Two Hopkins Plaza · Baltimore, MD 21201 · 301-244-7400

A. MacDonough Plant · Semmes, Bowen & Semmes · 250 West Pratt Street · Baltimore, MD 21201 · 301-539-5040

C. Van Leuven Stewart · Venable, Baetjer and Howard · 1800 Mercantile Bank & Trust Building · Two Hopkins Plaza · Baltimore, MD 21201 · 301-244-7400

Robert M. Thomas · Venable, Baetjer and Howard · 1800 Mercantile Bank & Trust Building · Two Hopkins Plaza · Baltimore, MD 21201 · 301-244-7400

George E. Thomsen · McKenney, Thomsen and Burke · 1723 Munsey Building · Baltimore, MD 21202 · 301-539-2595

W. Shepherdson Abell · Furey, Doolan & Abell · Penthouse One · 8401 Connecticut Avenue · Chevy Chase, MD 20815 · 301-652-6880

Ralph J. Moore, Jr. · Shea and Gardner · 358 Hungerford Court · Rockville, MD 20850 · 301-424-4602

MASSACHUSETTS

BANKRUPTCY LAW	317
BUSINESS LITIGATION	319
CORPORATE LAW	322
CRIMINAL DEFENSE	324
ENTERTAINMENT LAW	327
FAMILY LAW	327
LABOR AND EMPLOYMENT LAW	329
NATURAL RESOURCES AND ENVIRONMENTAL LAW	332
PERSONAL INJURY LITIGATION	332
REAL ESTATE LAW	335
TAX AND EMPLOYEE BENEFITS LAW	337
TRUSTS AND ESTATES	340

BANKRUPTCY LAW

Mark N. Berman · Hutchins & Wheeler · 101 Federal Street · Boston, MA 02110 · 617-951-6600

Henry J. Boroff · 15 Court Square · Boston, MA 02108 · 617-227-7030

Paul P. Daley · Hale and Dorr · 60 State Street · Boston, MA 02109 · 617-742-9100

Peter A. Fine · Choate, Hall & Stewart · Exchange Place · 53 State Street · Boston, MA 02109 · 617-227-5020

Frederick G. Fisher, Jr. · Hale and Dorr · 60 State Street · Boston, MA 02109 · 617-742-9100

Robert M. Gargill · Choate, Hall & Stewart · Exchange Place · 53 State Street · Boston, MA 02109 · 617-227-5020

Daniel M. Glosband · Goodwin, Procter & Hoar · Exchange Place · Boston, MA 02109 · 617-570-1000

Richard L. Levine · Hill & Barlow · One International Place · 100 Oliver Street · Boston, MA 02110 · 617-439-3555

William F. Macauley · Craig and Macauley · 600 Atlantic Avenue · Boston, MA 02210 · 617-367-9500

William F. McCarthy · Ropes & Gray · 225 Franklin Street · Boston, MA 02110 · 617-423-6100

Richard E. Mikels · Mintz, Levin, Cohn, Ferris, Glovsky and Popeo · One Financial Center · Boston, MA 02111 · 617-542-6000

Charles P. Normandin · Ropes & Gray · 225 Franklin Street · Boston, MA 02110 · 617-423-6100

Michael J. Pappone · Goodwin, Procter & Hoar · Exchange Place · Boston, MA 02109 · 617-570-1000

Mark N. Polebaum · Hale and Dorr · 60 State Street · Boston, MA 02109 · 617-742-9100

Barry M. Portnoy · Sullivan & Worcester · One Post Office Square · Boston, MA 02109 · 617-338-2800

Jon D. Schneider · Goodwin, Procter & Hoar · Exchange Place · Boston, MA 02109 · 617-570-1000

Robert Somma · Goldstein & Manello · 265 Franklin Street · Boston, MA 02110 · 617-439-8900

C. Hall Swaim · Hale and Dorr · 60 State Street · Boston, MA 02109 · 617-742-9100

John L. Whitlock · Palmer & Dodge · One Beacon Street, 22nd Floor · Boston, MA 02108 · 617-227-4400

Eugene B. Berman · Kamberg, Berman & Gold · 31 Elm Street · P.O. Box 2439 · Springfield, MA 01101-2439 · 413-781-1300

Joseph B. Collins · Hendel, Collins & Newton · 101 State Street · Springfield, MA 01103 · 413-734-6411

Philip J. Hendel · Hendel, Collins & Newton · 101 State Street · Springfield, MA 01103 · 413-734-6411

Irving D. Labovitz · Cooley, Shrair, Alpert, Labovitz and Dambrov · 1380 Main Street, Fifth Floor · Springfield, MA 01103 · 413-781-0750

J. Robert Seder · Seder & Chandler · Burnside Building · 339 Main Street Worcester, MA 01608 · 508-757-7721

George W. Tetler III · Bowditch & Dewey · 311 Main Street · Worcester, MA 01608 · 508-791-3511

Jack L. Wolfson · Wolfson, Dodson, Keenan & Cotton · 390 Main Street, Suite 1000 · Worcester, MA 01608 · 508-791-8181

BUSINESS LITIGATION

Samuel Adams · Warner & Stackpole · 28 State Street · Boston, MA 02109 617-725-1400

Edward J. Barshak · Sugarman, Rogers, Barshak & Cohen · 33 Union Street Boston, MA 02108-2406 · 617-227-3030

Thomas D. Burns · Burns & Levinson · 50 Milk Street · Boston, MA 02109 617-451-3300

Robert A. Cesari · Cesari and McKenna · Union Wharf East · Boston, MA 02109 617-523-8100

Earle C. Cooley · Cooley, Manion, Moore & Jones · Russia Wharf West · 530 Atlantic Avenue · Boston, MA 02210 · 617-542-3700

John J. Curtin, Jr. · Bingham, Dana & Gould · 150 Federal Street · Boston, MA 02110 · 617-951-8000

Harry T. Daniels · Hale and Dorr · 60 State Street · Boston, MA 02109 · 617-742-9100

Jerome P. Facher · Hale and Dorr · 60 State Street · Boston, MA 02109 · 617-742-9100

Robert E. Fast · Hale and Dorr · 60 State Street · Boston, MA 02109 · 617-742-9100

Francis H. Fox · Bingham, Dana & Gould · 150 Federal Street · Boston, MA 02110 · 617-951-8000

Paul B. Galvani · Ropes & Gray · 225 Franklin Street · Boston, MA 02111 · 617-423-6100

David A. Garbus · Brown, Rudnick, Freed & Gesmer · One Financial Center, 18th Floor · Boston, MA 02111 · 617-330-9000

Jerome Gotkin · Widett, Slater & Goldman · 60 State Street · Boston, MA 02109 617-227-7200

John M. Harrington, Jr. · Ropes & Gray · 225 Franklin Street · Boston, MA 02111 · 617-423-6100

Samuel Hoar · Goodwin, Procter & Hoar · Exchange Place · Boston, MA 02109 617-570-1000

Michael B. Keating · Foley, Hoag & Eliot · One Post Office Square · Boston, MA 02109 · 617-482-1390

Joel A. Kozol · Friedman & Atherton · 28 State Street, 19th Floor · Boston, MA 02109 · 617-227-5540

James B. Lampert · Hale and Dorr · 60 State Street · Boston, MA 02109 · 617-742-9100

Daniel O. Mahoney · Palmer & Dodge · One Beacon Street · Boston, MA 02108 617-227-4400

Gael Mahony · Hill & Barlow · One International Place · 100 Oliver Street Boston, MA 02110 · 617-439-3555

A. Lane McGovern · Ropes & Gray · 225 Franklin Street · Boston, MA 02111 617-423-6100

George A. McLaughlin, Jr. · The McLaughlin Brothers · 44 School Street Boston, MA 02108 · 617-523-7165

William G. Meserve · Ropes & Gray · 225 Franklin Street · Boston, MA 02111 617-423-6100

Robert J. Muldoon, Jr. · Sherin and Lodgen · 100 Summer Street · Boston, MA 02110 · 617-426-5720

Martin J. O'Donnell · Cesari and McKenna · Union Wharf East · Boston, MA 02109 · 617-523-8100

Blair L. Perry · Hale and Dorr · 60 State Street · Boston, MA 02109 · 617-742-9100

R. Robert Popeo · Mintz, Levin, Cohn, Ferris, Glovsky and Popeo · One Financial Center · Boston, MA 02111 · 617-542-6000

Richard W. Renehan · Hill & Barlow · One International Place · 100 Oliver Street Boston, MA 02110 · 617-439-3555

Jeffrey B. Rudman · Hale and Dorr · 60 State Street · Boston, MA 02109 617-742-9100

Stanley H. Rudman · Rubin and Rudman · 50 Rose Wharf · Boston, MA 02110 617-330-7000

James D. St. Clair · Hale and Dorr · 60 State Street · Boston, MA 02109 617-742-9100

Thomas J Sartory · Goulston & Storrs · 400 Atlantic Avenue · Boston, MA 02210-2206 · 617-482-1776

Marshall Simonds · Goodwin, Procter & Hoar · Exchange Place · Boston, MA 02109 · 617-570-1000

Joseph D. Steinfield · Hill & Barlow · One International Place · 100 Oliver Street Boston, MA 02110 · 617-439-3555

J. Owen Todd · Hale and Dorr · 60 State Street · Boston, MA 02109 · 617-742-9100

Allan van Gestel · Goodwin, Procter & Hoar · Exchange Place · Boston, MA 02109 · 617-570-1000

Richard K. Donahue · Donahue & Donahue · 21 George Street · Lowell, MA 01852 · 508-458-6887

Charles K. Bergin, Jr. · Robinson Donovan Madden & Barry · Valley Bank Tower, Suite 1400 · 1500 Main Street · Springfield, MA 01115 · 413-732-2301

Frederick S. Pillsbury · Doherty, Wallace, Pillsbury and Murphy · 1414 Main Street · Springfield, MA 01144 · 413-733-3111

John D. Ross, Jr. · Ross & Ross · 101 State Street, Suite 701-705 · Springfield, MA 01103 · 413-736-2725

Michael G. Angelini · Bowditch & Dewey · 311 Main Street · Worcester, MA 01608 · 508-791-3511

Burton Chandler · Seder & Chandler · Burnside Building · 339 Main Street Worcester, MA 01608 · 508-757-7721

Charles B. Swartwood III · Mountain, Dearborn & Whiting · 370 Main Street, Seventh Floor · Worcester, MA 01608 · 508-756-2423

Seymour Weinstein · Weinstein, Bernstein & Burwick · 370 Main Street, Suite 1150 · Worcester, MA 01608 · 508-756-4393

CORPORATE LAW

Constantine Alexander · Nutter, McClennen & Fish · One International Place, 15th Floor · Boston, MA 02110-2699 · 617-439-2000

Norman B. Asher · Hale and Dorr · 60 State Street · Boston, MA 02109 · 617-742-9100

John E. Beard · Ropes & Gray · 225 Franklin Street · Boston, MA 02110 · 617-423-6100

Norman A. Bikales · Sullivan & Worcester · One Post Office Square · Boston, MA 02109 · 617-338-2800

Paul P. Brountas · Hale and Dorr · 60 State Street · Boston, MA 02109 · 617-742-9100

Truman S. Casner · Ropes & Gray · 225 Franklin Street · Boston, MA 02110 617-423-6100

F. Douglas Cochrane · Ropes & Gray · 225 Franklin Street · Boston, MA 02110 617-423-6100

John F. Cogan, Jr. · Hale and Dorr · 60 State Street · Boston, MA 02109 617-742-9100

Donald J. Evans · Goodwin, Procter & Hoar · Exchange Place · Boston, MA 02109 · 617-570-1000

Champe A. Fisher · Ropes & Gray · 225 Franklin Street · Boston, MA 02110 617-423-6100

Richard E. Floor · Goodwin, Procter & Hoar · Exchange Place · Boston, MA 02109 · 617-570-1000

Donald W. Glazer · Ropes & Gray · 225 Franklin Street · Boston, MA 02110 617-423-6100

William M. Glovsky · Mintz, Levin, Cohn, Ferris, Glovsky and Popeo · One Financial Center · Boston, MA 02111 · 617-542-6000

Gordon B. Greer · Bingham, Dana & Gould · 150 Federal Street · Boston, MA 02110 · 617-951-8000

Irving J. Helman · Nutter, McClennen & Fish · One International Place, 15th Floor · Boston, MA 02110-2699 · 617-439-2000

Stanley Keller · Palmer & Dodge · One Beacon Street · Boston, MA 02108 617-227-4400

Anthony J. Medaglia, Jr. · Hutchins & Wheeler · 101 Federal Street · Boston, MA 02110 · 617-951-6600

Andrew L. Nichols · Choate, Hall & Stewart · Exchange Place · 53 State Street Boston, MA 02109 · 617-227-5020

Kenneth J. Novack · Mintz, Levin, Cohn, Ferris, Glovsky and Popeo · One Financial Center · Boston, MA 02111 · 617-542-6000

Robert L. Nutt · Ropes & Gray · 225 Franklin Street · Boston, MA 02110 617-423-6100

Everett H. Parker · Bingham, Dana & Gould · 150 Federal Street · Boston, MA 02110 · 617-951-8000

Paul R. Rugo · Goodwin, Procter & Hoar · Exchange Place · Boston, MA 02109 617-570-1000

Ernest J. Sargeant · Ropes & Gray · 225 Franklin Street · Boston, MA 02110 617-423-6100

Richard W. Southgate · Ropes & Gray · 225 Franklin Street · Boston, MA 02110 617-423-6100

Richard J. Testa · Testa, Hurwitz & Thibeault · Exchange Place · 53 State Street · Boston, MA 02109 · 617-367-7500

George W. Thibeault · Testa, Hurwitz & Thibeault · Exchange Place · 53 State Street · Boston, MA 02109 · 617-367-7500

Edward J. Barry · Robinson Donovan Madden & Barry · Valley Bank Tower, Suite 1400 · 1500 Main Street · Springfield, MA 01115 · 413-732-2301

Paul S. Doherty · Doherty, Wallace, Pillsbury and Murphy · 1414 Main Street · Springfield, MA 01144 · 413-733-3111

Ronald P. Weiss · Bulkley, Richardson and Gelinas · BayBank Tower, Suite 2700 · 1500 Main Street · P.O. Box 15507 · Springfield, MA 01115 · 413-781-2820

Michael G. Angelini · Bowditch & Dewey · 311 Main Street · Worcester, MA 01608 · 508-791-3511

Burton Chandler · Seder & Chandler · Burnside Building · 339 Main Street · Worcester, MA 01608 · 508-757-7721

Phillip S. Davis · Fletcher, Tilton & Whipple · 370 Main Street · Worcester, MA 01608 · 508-798-8621

David L. Lougee · Mirick, O'Connell, DeMallie & Lougee · 1700 Mechanics Bank Tower · Worcester Center · Worcester, MA 01608 · 508-799-0541

Thomas R. Mountain · Mountain, Dearborn & Whiting · 370 Main Street, Seventh Floor · Worcester, MA 01608 · 508-756-2423

J. Robert Seder · Seder & Chandler · Burnside Building · 339 Main Street · Worcester, MA 01608 · 508-757-7721

CRIMINAL DEFENSE

Gerald Alch · 11 Beacon Street · Boston, MA 02108 · 617-227-9852

F. Lee Bailey · Bailey & Fishman · 66 Long Wharf · Boston, MA 02110 · 617-723-1980

Joseph J. Balliro, Sr. · Balliro, Mondano & Balliro · Three Arlington Street · Boston, MA 02116 · 617-227-5822

Earle C. Cooley · Cooley, Manion, Moore & Jones · Russia Wharf West · 530 Atlantic Avenue · Boston, MA 02210 · 617-542-3700

Albert F. Cullen, Jr. · Cullen & Wall · 141 Tremont Street, Seventh Floor · Boston, MA 02111 · 617-482-8650

Francis J. DiMento · DiMento & Sullivan · 100 State Street · Boston, MA 02109 · 617-523-5253

Thomas E. Dwyer, Jr. · Dwyer & Collora · 400 Atlantic Avenue · Boston, MA 02110 · 617-357-9202

Nancy Gertner · Silverglate, Gertner, Fine & Good · 89 Broad Street, 14th Floor · Boston, MA 02110 · 617-542-6663

Andrew H. Good · Silverglate, Gertner, Fine & Good · 89 Broad Street, 14th Floor · Boston, MA 02110 · 617-542-6663

William P. Homans, Jr. · Homans, Hamilton, Dahmen & Marshall · One Court Street · Boston, MA 02108 · 617-523-3716

Albert L. Hutton, Jr. · Six Beacon Street · Boston, MA 02108 · 617-227-1111

J. Albert Johnson · Johnson, Mee & May · Eight Whittier Place · Boston, MA 02114 · 617-227-8900

Robert D. Keefe · Hale and Dorr · 60 State Street · Boston, MA 02109 · 617-742-9100

Joseph S. Oteri · Oteri, Weinberg & Lawson · 75 Blossom Court · Boston, MA 02114 · 617-227-3700

Harvey A. Silverglate · Silverglate, Gertner, Fine & Good · 89 Broad Street, 14th Floor · Boston, MA 02110 · 617-542-6663

Paul T. Smith · 265 Franklin Street, Suite 900 · Boston, MA 02110 · 617-439-9220

James D. St. Clair · Hale and Dorr · 60 State Street · Boston, MA 02109 · 617-742-9100

Max D. Stern · Stern & Shapiro · 80 Boylston Street · Boston, MA 02116 · 617-542-0663

James J. Sullivan, Jr. · DiMento & Sullivan · 100 State Street · Boston, MA 02109 · 617-523-5253

John Wall · Cullen & Wall · 141 Tremont Street, Seventh Floor · Boston, MA 02111 · 617-482-8650

Martin G. Weinberg · Oteri, Weinberg & Lawson · 75 Blossom Court · Boston, MA 02114 · 617-227-3700

Thomas F. McEvilly · McEvilly & Curley · 48 West Street · Leominster, MA 01453 · 508-534-3556

Barry M. Haight · Buckley, Haight, Muldoon, Jubinville & Gilligan · 480 Adams Street · Milton, MA 01286 · 617-698-5700

Martin Kenneth Leppo · Leppo & Traini · 490 North Main Street · Randolph, MA 02368 · 617-742-1213

Anthony M. Traini · Leppo & Traini · 490 North Main Street · Randolph, MA 02368 · 617-742-1213

Thomas C. Troy · 270 Main Street · Reading, MA 01867 · 617-942-1800

William M. Bennett · Bennett & Jennings · 1248 Main Street · Springfield, MA 01103 · 413-737-7349

Efrem A. Gordon · 101 State Street, Room 410 · Springfield, MA 01103 · 413-737-4316

John M. Thompson · Thompson, Thompson & Jacobson · 94 State Street · Springfield, MA · 413-781-4343

Peter L. Ettenberg · Rotman, Gould & Ettenberg · 370 Main Street · Worcester, MA 01608 · 508-752-6733

Conrad W. Fisher · Fisher, Mandell & Newlands · 47 Harvard Street · Worcester, MA 01609-2876 · 508-791-3466

Andrew L. Mandell · Fisher, Mandell & Newlands · 47 Harvard Street · Worcester, MA 01609-2876 · 508-791-3466

Michael M. Monopoli · 94 Highland Street · Worcester, MA 01609 · 508-754-2229

James G. Reardon · Reardon & Reardon · One Exchange Place · Worcester, MA 01608 · 508-754-1111

ENTERTAINMENT LAW

Bob Wolfe · Bob Wolfe Associates · 4575 Prudential Tower · Boston, MA 02199 · 617-437-1212

FAMILY LAW

Jacob M. Atwood · Atwood & Cherny · 211 Commonwealth Avenue · Boston, MA 02116 · 617-262-6400

Shirley D. Bayle · Young & Bayle · 60 State Street · Boston, MA 02109 · 617-227-9490

Ruth R. Budd · Hemenway & Barnes · 60 State Street · Boston, MA 02109 · 617-227-7940

Barry J. Connelly · Connelly & Norton · 204 Union Wharf · Boston, MA 02109 · 617-367-0600

James R. DeGiacomo · Roche, Carens & DeGiacomo · One Post Office Square · Boston, MA 02109 · 617-451-9300

George M. Ford · Burns & Levinson · 50 Milk Street · Boston, MA 02109 · 617-451-3300

Weld S. Henshaw · Choate, Hall & Stewart · Exchange Place · 53 State Street · Boston, MA 02109 · 617-227-7566

Monroe L. Inker · White, Inker, Aronson · One Washington Mall · Boston, MA 02108 · 617-367-7700

Norman I. Jacobs · Esdaile, Barrett & Esdaile · 75 Federal Street · Boston, MA 02110 · 617-482-0333

Paul M. Kane · McGrath & Kane · Four Longfellow Place · Boston, MA 02114 · 617-523-5600

Haskell A. Kassler · Kassler & Feuer · 85 Devonshire Street · Boston, MA 02109 · 617-227-4800

Robert J. Kates · Widett, Slater & Goldman · 60 State Street · Boston, MA 02109 · 617-227-7200

David H. Lee · Bowser & Lee · 399 Boylston Street, Suite 1200 · Boston, MA 02116 · 617-266-6262

Robert F. McGrath · McGrath & Kane · Four Longfellow Place · Boston, MA 02114 · 617-523-5600

W. Hugh M. Morton · Hill & Barlow · One International Place · 100 Oliver Street · Boston, MA 02110 · 617-439-3555

John J. Norton · Connelly & Norton · 343 Commercial Street · 204 Union Wharf · Boston, MA 02109 · 617-367-0600

Lawrence T. Perera · Hemenway & Barnes · 60 State Street, Eighth Floor · Boston, MA 02109 · 617-227-7940

Paul P. Perocchi · Brown, Rudnick, Freed & Gesmer · One Financial Center, 18th Floor · Boston, MA 02111 · 617-330-9000

Samuel S. Robinson · Peabody & Arnold · 50 Rowes Wharf · Boston, MA 02110 · 617-951-2100

J. Owen Todd · Hale and Dorr · 60 State Street · Boston, MA 02109 · 617-742-9100

Margaret S. Travers · Taylor, Anderson & Travers · 75 Federal Street · Boston, MA 02110 · 617-654-8200

John P. White, Jr. · White, Inker, Aronson · One Washington Mall · Boston, MA 02108 · 617-367-7700

Ronald A. Witmer · Hale and Dorr · 60 State Street · Boston, MA 02109 · 617-742-9100

Jason J. Cohen · Cohen & Gaffin · Court Square Building · 615 Concord Street · P.O. Box 886 · Framingham, MA 01701 · 508-872-6565

Paul A. Cataldo · Bachner, Roche and Cataldo · 55 West Central Street · P.O. Box 267 · Franklin, MA 02038 · 508-528-2400

Harvey Beit · Beit, Stevens & O'Flaherty · 104 State Street · Newburyport, MA 01950 · 508-462-4416

Efrem A. Gordon · 101 State Street, Room 410 · Springfield, MA 01103 · 413-737-4316

Samuel A. Marsella · Doherty, Wallace, Pillsbury and Murphy · 1414 Main Street · Springfield, MA 01144 · 413-733-3111

Peter Roth · Bulkley, Richardson and Gelinas · BayBank Tower, Suite 2700 · 1500 Main Street · P.O. Box 15507 · Springfield, MA 01115 · 413-781-2820

Gerald E. Norman · Norman & Ricci · Worcester Plaza, 18th Floor · 446 Main Street · Worcester, MA 01608 · 508-752-7548

LABOR AND EMPLOYMENT LAW

Michael R. Brown · (Management) · Goldstein & Manello · 265 Franklin Street · Boston, MA 02110 · 617-439-8900

John A. Canavan, Jr. · (Management) · Nutter, McClennen & Fish · One International Place, 15th Floor · Boston, MA 02110-2699 · 617-439-2000

Louis Chandler · (Management) · Stoneman, Chandler & Miller · 99 High Street · Boston, MA 02110 · 617-542-6789

Richard W. Coleman · (Labor) · Segal, Roitman & Coleman · 11 Beacon Street · Boston, MA 02108 · 617-742-0208

Glenn E. Dawson · (Management) · 101 Tremont Street · Boston, MA 02108 · 617-338-9828

Allan W. Drachman · (Management) · Deutsch Williams Brooks DeRensis Holland & Drachman · 99 Summer Street · Boston, MA 02110-1235 · 617-951-2300

David B. Ellis · (Management) · Foley, Hoag & Eliot · One Post Office Square · Boston, MA 02109 · 617-482-1390

Michael A. Feinberg · (Labor) · Feinberg & Feld · 33 Broad Street · Boston, MA 02109 · 617-227-1976

Arthur J. Flamm · (Labor) · Flamm & Birmingham · 50 Congress Street · Boston, MA 02109 · 617-720-3888

Murray S. Freeman · (Management) · Nutter, McClennen & Fish · One International Place, 15th Floor · Boston, MA 02110-2699 · 617-973-9700

Nancy Gertner · (Individuals) · Silverglate, Gertner, Fine & Good · 89 Broad Street, 14th Floor · Boston, MA 02110 · 617-542-6663

Alvin M. Glazerman · (Management) · Edwards & Angell · 101 Federal Street Boston, MA 02110 · 617-439-4444

Albert L. Goldman · (Labor) · Angoff, Goldman, Manning, Pyle, Wanger & Hiatt · 44 School Street · Boston, MA 02108 · 617-723-5500

James T. Grady · (Labor) · Grady and Dwyer · One Center Plaza, Suite 260 Boston, MA 02108 · 617-723-9777

Jonathan P. Hiatt · (Labor) · Angoff, Goldman, Manning, Pyle, Wanger & Hiatt · 44 School Street · Boston, MA 02108 · 617-723-5500

Alan Kaplan · (Management) · Morgan, Brown & Joy · One Boston Place Boston, MA 02108 · 617-523-6666

Henry M. Kelleher · (Management) · Foley, Hoag & Eliot · One Post Office Square · Boston, MA 02109 · 617-482-1390

Harold L. Lichten · (Individuals) · Angoff, Goldman, Manning, Pyle, Wanger & Hiatt · 44 School Street · Boston, MA 02108 · 617-723-5500

Joan A. Lukey · (Individuals) · Hale and Dorr · 60 State Street · Boston, MA 02109 · 617-742-9100

Harold N. Mack · (Management) · Morgan, Brown & Joy · One Boston Place Boston, MA 02108 · 617-523-6666

Robert D. Manning · (Labor) · Angoff, Goldman, Manning, Pyle, Wanger & Hiatt · 44 School Street · Boston, MA 02108 · 617-723-5500

John F. McMahon, Jr. · (Labor) · Angoff, Goldman, Manning, Pyle, Wanger & Hiatt · 44 School Street · Boston, MA 02108 · 617-723-5500

Alan S. Miller · (Management) · Stoneman, Chandler & Miller · 99 High Street Boston, MA 02110 · 617-542-6789

Thomas L. P. O'Donnell · (Management) · Ropes & Gray · 225 Franklin Street Boston, MA 02110 · 617-423-6100

Stephen B. Perlman · (Management) · Ropes & Gray · 225 Franklin Street Boston, MA 02110 · 617-423-6100

Warren H. Pyle · (Labor; Individuals) · Angoff, Goldman, Manning, Pyle, Wanger & Hiatt · 44 School Street · Boston, MA 02108 · 617-723-5500

Nelson G. Ross · (Management) · Ropes & Gray · 225 Franklin Street · Boston, MA 02110 · 617-423-6100

Mark E. Schreiber · (Individuals) · 11 Beacon Street · Boston, MA 02108 617-720-1310

Robert M. Segal · (Labor) · Segal, Roitman & Coleman · 11 Beacon Street Boston, MA 02108 · 617-742-0208

Donald J. Siegel · (Labor) · Segal, Roitman & Coleman · 11 Beacon Street Boston, MA 02108 · 617-742-0208

Ira Sills · (Labor) · Segal, Roitman & Coleman · 11 Beacon Street · Boston, MA 02108 · 617-742-0208

Jerome H. Somers · (Management) · Goodwin, Procter & Hoar · Exchange Place Boston, MA 02109 · 617-570-1000

Arthur L. Stevenson · (Management) · Goodwin, Procter & Hoar · Exchange Place · Boston, MA 02109 · 617-570-1000

E. David Wanger · (Labor) · Angoff, Goldman, Manning, Pyle, Wanger & Hiatt 44 School Street · Boston, MA 02108 · 617-723-5500

Arthur P. Menard · (Management) · 29 Admiral's Way · Chelsea, MA 02150 617-889-2200

John D. O'Reilly III · (Management) · O'Reilly & Grosso · 1300A Worcester Road Framingham, MA 01701 · 508-875-1220

Alan J. McDonald · (Labor) · McDonald, Noonan and Kaplan · One Gateway Center · Newton, MA 02158 · 617-965-8116

Nathan S. Paven · (Labor) · Nathan S. Paven & Associates · 40 Wollaston Avenue P.O. Box 88 · Quincy, MA 02170 · 617-472-0480

Ralph F. Abbott, Jr. · (Management) · Skoler, Abbott, Hayes & Presser · One Monarch Place, Suite 2000 · Springfield, MA 01144 · 413-737-4753

Frederick L. Sullivan · (Management) · Sullivan & Hayes · BayBank Tower, Suite 1712 · 1500 Main Street · P.O. Box 15668 · Springfield, MA 01115 · 413-736-4538

Michael G. Angelini · (Management) · Bowditch & Dewey · 311 Main Street Worcester, MA 01608 · 508-791-3511

James E. Wallace, Jr. · (Management) · Bowditch & Dewey · 311 Main Street Worcester, MA 01608 · 508-791-3511

Robert Weihrauch · (Management) · Weihrauch & Coblentz · 19 Norwich Street Worcester, MA 01608 · 508-752-7549

NATURAL RESOURCES AND ENVIRONMENTAL LAW

Laurie Burt · Foley, Hoag & Eliot · One Post Office Square · Boston, MA 02109 617-482-1390

Susan M. Cooke · Goodwin, Procter & Hoar · Exchange Place · Boston, MA 02109 · 617-570-1000

Michael P. Last · Gaston & Snow · One Federal Street · Boston, MA 02110 617-426-4600

Gregor I. McGregor · (also Plaintiffs) · McGregor, Shea & Doliner · 18 Tremont Street, Suite 900 · Boston, MA 02108 · 617-227-7289

Anton T. Moehrke · 283 Dartmouth Street · Boston, MA 02116 · 617-266-5700

Mary K. Ryan · Nutter, McClennen & Fish · One International Place, 15th Floor Boston, MA 02110-2699 · 617-439-2000

Jan R. Schlichtmann · (Plaintiffs) · Schlichtmann, Conway, Crowley & Hugo 171 Milk Street · Boston, MA 02109 · 617-423-9777

PERSONAL INJURY LITIGATION

J. Norman O'Connor · (Defendants) · Donovan & O'Connor · One Commercial Place · Adams, MA 01220 · 413-743-3200

Samuel Adams · (Defendants) · Warner & Stackpole · 28 State Street · Boston, MA 02109 · 617-725-1400

Charles F. Barrett · (Defendants) · Nutter, McClennen & Fish · One International Place, 15th Floor · Boston, MA 02110-2699 · 617-439-2000

Charles W. Barrett, Jr. · (Plaintiffs) · Esdaile, Barrett & Esdaile · 75 Federal Street · Boston, MA 02110 · 617-482-0333

Edward J. Barshak · (Defendants) · Sugarman, Rogers, Barshak & Cohen · 33 Union Street · Boston, MA 02108-2406 · 617-227-3030

Leo V. Boyle · (Plaintiffs) · Meehan, Boyle & Cohen · 85 Devonshire Street · Boston, MA 02109 · 617-523-8300

Thomas D. Burns · (Defendants) · Burns & Levinson · 50 Milk Street · Boston, MA 02109 · 617-451-3300

Thomas E. Cargill, Jr. · (Plaintiffs) · Cargill, Masterman & Culbert · One Lewis Wharf · Boston, MA 02110 · 617-227-0400

Thomas E. Connolly · (Plaintiffs) · Connolly & Leavis · 168 Milk Street · Boston, MA 02109 · 617-742-1700

Earle C. Cooley · Cooley, Manion, Moore & Jones · Russia Wharf West · 530 Atlantic Avenue · Boston, MA 02210 · 617-542-3700

William J. Dailey, Jr. · (Defendants) · Sloane & Walsh · 10 Tremont Street · Boston, MA 02108 · 617-523-6010

J. Newton Esdaile · (Plaintiffs) · Esdaile, Barrett & Esdaile · 75 Federal Street · Boston, MA 02110 · 617-482-0333

James N. Esdaile, Jr. · (Plaintiffs) · Esdaile, Barrett & Esdaile · 75 Federal Street · Boston, MA 02110 · 617-482-0333

John J. C. Herlihy · Herlihy and O'Brien · 133 Federal Street · Boston, MA 02110 · 617-426-6100

Samuel Hoar · (Defendants) · Goodwin, Procter & Hoar · Exchange Place · Boston, MA 02109 · 617-570-1000

Raymond J. Kenney, Jr. · (Defendants) · Martin, Magnuson, McCarthy & Kenney · 133 Portland Street · Boston, MA 02114 · 617-227-3240

James F. Meehan · Meehan, Boyle & Cohen · 85 Devonshire Street · Boston, MA 02109 · 617-523-8300

Michael E. Mone · (Plaintiffs) · Esdaile, Barrett & Esdaile · 75 Federal Street · Boston, MA 02110 · 617-482-0333

John J. O'Brien · (Defendants) · Herlihy and O'Brien · 133 Federal Street · Boston, MA 02110 · 617-426-6100

Lionel H. Perlo · (Defendants) · Ficksman & Conley · 28 State Street, Suite 2015
Boston, MA 02109 · 617-720-1515

Charles P. Reidy III · (Defendants) · Martin, Magnuson, McCarthy & Kenney
133 Portland Street · Boston, MA 02114 · 617-227-3240

Camille Francis Sarrouf · (Plaintiffs) · Sarrouf, Tarricone & Flemming · 95
Commercial Wharf · Boston, MA 02110 · 617-227-5800

Marshall Simonds · (Defendants) · Goodwin, Proctor & Hoar · Exchange Place
Boston, MA 02109 · 617-570-1000

Abner R. Sisson · (Plaintiffs) · Sisson, Bloomenthal and Allen · One Bromfield
Street · Boston, MA 02108 · 617-451-8100

Neil Sugarman · (Plaintiffs) · Sugarman and Sugarman · 141 Tremont Street
Boston, MA 02111 · 617-542-1000

Paul R. Sugarman · (Plaintiffs) · Sugarman and Sugarman · 141 Tremont Street
Boston, MA 02111 · 617-542-1000

Edward M. Swartz · (Plaintiffs) · Swartz & Swartz · 10 Marshall Street · Boston,
MA 02108 · 617-742-1900

Albert P. Zabin · (Plaintiffs) · Schneider, Reilly, Zabin & Costello · One Center
Plaza, Suite 200 · Boston, MA 02108 · 617-227-7500

Thomas F. Burke · (Plaintiffs) · Burke and Smith · 49 Slocum Road · Dartmouth,
MA 02747 · 508-993-1743

Richard K. Donahue · Donahue & Donahue · 21 George Street · Lowell, MA
01852 · 508-458-6887

Charles R. Desmarais · (Defendants) · 446 County Street · New Bedford, MA
02740 · 508-999-2341

David A. McLaughlin · McLaughlin & Folan · 448 County Street · New Bedford,
MA 02740 · 508-992-9800

James L. Allen · Allen, Dusel, Murphy & Fennell · 101 State Street · Springfield,
MA 01103 · 413-732-2147

Charles K. Bergin, Jr. · Robinson Donovan Madden & Barry · Valley Bank
Tower, Suite 1400 · 1500 Main Street · Springfield, MA 01115 · 413-732-2301

Edward L. Donnellan · (Defendants) · Keyes and Donnellan · Northeast Savings Building · 1243 Main Street · Springfield, MA 01103 · 413-781-6540

Gerard L. Pelligrini · Pelligrini & Seely · 21 Stockbridge Street · Springfield, MA 01103 · 413-785-5307

Frederick S. Pillsbury · (Defendants) · Doherty, Wallace, Pillsbury and Murphy 1414 Main Street · Springfield, MA 01144 · 413-733-3111

John D. Ross, Jr. · Ross & Ross · 101 State Street, Suite 701-705 · Springfield, MA 01103 · 413-736-2725

William E. Bernstein · (Plaintiffs) · Weinstein, Bernstein & Burwick · 370 Main Street, Suite 1150 · Worcester, MA 01608 · 508-756-4393

John F. Keenan · (Plaintiffs) · Wolfson, Dodson, Keenan & Cotton · 390 Main Street, Suite 1000 · Worcester, MA 01608 · 508-791-8181

Gerard R. Laurence · (Defendants) · Milton, Laurence & Dixon · 825 Mechanics Bank Tower · Worcester, MA 01608 · 508-791-6386

Philip J. MacCarthy · (Defendants) · MacCarthy Pojani and Hurley · 446 Main Street · Worcester, MA 01608 · 508-798-2480

James G. Reardon · (Plaintiffs) · Reardon & Reardon · One Exchange Place Worcester, MA 01608 · 508-754-1111

Berge C. Tashjian · (Defendants) · Tashjian, Simsarian & Wickstrom · 370 Main Street · Worcester, MA 01608 · 508-756-1578

Seymour Weinstein · (Plaintiffs) · Weinstein, Bernstein & Burwick · 370 Main Street, Suite 1150 · Worcester, MA 01608 · 508-756-4393

John A. Wickstrom · (Defendants) · Tashjian, Simsarian & Wickstrom · 370 Main Street · Worcester, MA 01608 · 508-756-1578

REAL ESTATE LAW

Stephen Carr Anderson · Rackemann, Sawyer & Brewster · One Financial Center · Boston, MA 02111 · 617-542-2300

Norman T. Byrnes · Gaston & Snow · One Federal Street · Boston, MA 02110 617-426-4600

Howard E. Cohen · Mintz, Levin, Cohn, Ferris, Glovsky and Popeo · One Financial Center · Boston, MA 02111 · 617-542-6000

A. Jeffrey Dando · Goodwin, Procter & Hoar · Exchange Place · Boston, MA 02109 · 617-570-1000

Robert C. Davis · Hale and Dorr · 60 State Street · Boston, MA 02109 · 617-742-9100

John K. Dineen · Gaston Snow & Ely Bartlett · One Federal Street · Boston, MA 02110 · 617-426-4600

Steven S. Fischman · Goulston & Storrs · 400 Atlantic Avenue · Boston, MA 02210-2206 · 617-482-1776

Peter D. Gens · Brown, Rudnick, Freed & Gesmer · One Financial Center, 18th Floor · Boston, MA 02111 · 617-330-9000

Joseph W. Haley · Goodwin, Procter & Hoar · Exchange Place · Boston, MA 02109 · 617-570-1000

John D. Hamilton, Jr. · Hale and Dorr · 60 State Street · Boston, MA 02109 617-742-9100

Thomas Kaplan · Goulston & Storrs · 400 Atlantic Avenue · Boston, MA 02210-2206 · 617-482-1776

Jordon P. Krasnow · Goulston & Storrs · 400 Atlantic Avenue · Boston, MA 02210-2206 · 617-482-1776

Stephen P. Lindsay · Ropes & Gray · 225 Franklin Street · Boston, MA 02110 617-423-6100

Richard H. Lovell · Rackemann, Sawyer & Brewster · One Financial Center Boston, MA 02111 · 617-542-2300

Vincent P. McCarthy · Hale and Dorr · 60 State Street · Boston, MA 02109 617-742-9100

Phillip J. Nexon · Goulston & Storrs · 400 Atlantic Avenue · Boston, MA 02210-2206 · 617-482-1776

John A. Pike · Ropes & Gray · 225 Franklin Street · Boston, MA 02110 617-423-6100

David P. Ries · Goodwin, Procter & Hoar · Exchange Place · Boston, MA 02109 617-570-1000

Alan W. Rottenberg · Goulston & Storrs · 400 Atlantic Avenue · Boston, MA 02210-2206 · 617-482-1776

Philip D. Stevenson · Hale and Dorr · 60 State Street · Boston, MA 02109 617-742-9100

Elliot M. Surkin · Hill & Barlow · One International Place · 100 Oliver Street · Boston, MA 02110 · 617-439-3555

Robert Tuchmann · Hale and Dorr · 60 State Street · Boston, MA 02109 617-742-9100

Peter Van · Fine & Ambrogne · Exchange Place · Boston, MA 02109 · 617-367-0100

Herbert W. Vaughan · Hale and Dorr · 60 State Street · Boston, MA 02109 617-742-9100

A. Craig Brown · Doherty, Wallace, Pillsbury and Murphy · 1414 Main Street · Springfield, MA 01144 · 413-733-3111

Michael S. Ratner · Bacon, Wilson, Ratner, Cohen, Salvage, Fialky & Fitzgerald · 95 State Street, Suite 1100 · Springfield, MA 01103 · 413-781-0560

Stephen A. Shatz · Shatz, Schwartz and Fentin · 1441 Main Street, Suite 1100 · Springfield, MA 01103 · 413-737-1131

Austin W. Keane · Bowditch & Dewey · 311 Main Street · Worcester, MA 01608 508-791-3511

TAX AND EMPLOYEE BENEFITS LAW

David R. Andelman · Lourie & Cutler · 60 State Street · Boston, MA 02109 617-742-6720

Thomas W. Anninger · (Employee Benefits) · Mintz, Levin, Cohn, Ferris, Glovsky and Popeo · One Financial Center · Boston, MA 02111 · 617-542-6000

David J. Blattner, Jr. · Ropes & Gray · 225 Franklin Street · Boston, MA 02110 617-423-6100

Kingsbury Browne, Jr. · Hill & Barlow · One International Place · 100 Oliver Street · Boston, MA 02110 · 617-439-3555

John J. Cleary · (Employee Benefits) · Goodwin, Procter & Hoar · Exchange Place · Boston, MA 02109 · 617-570-1000

Frederic G. Corneel · Sullivan & Worcester · One Post Office Square · Boston, MA 02109 · 617-338-2800

Andrew H. Cox · (Employee Benefits) · Ropes & Gray · 225 Franklin Street Boston, MA 02110 · 617-423-6100

Howard A. Cubell · Goodwin, Procter & Hoar · Exchange Place · Boston, MA 02109 · 617-570-1000

Michael M. Davis · Sullivan & Worcester · One Post Office Square · Boston, MA 02109 · 617-338-2800

David M. Donaldson · Ropes & Gray · 225 Franklin Street · Boston, MA 02110 617-423-6100

M. Gordon Ehrlich · Bingham, Dana & Gould · 150 Federal Street · Boston, MA 02110 · 617-951-8000

Marion R. Fremont-Smith · Choate, Hall & Stewart · Exchange Place · 53 State Street · Boston, MA 02109 · 617-227-5020

Russell A. Gaudreau, Jr. · (Employee Benefits) · Ropes & Gray · 225 Franklin Street · Boston, MA 02110 · 617-423-6100

Richard W. Giuliani · Hale and Dorr · 60 State Street · Boston, MA 02109 617-742-9100

Edward L. Glazer · Goodwin, Procter & Hoar · Exchange Place · Boston, MA 02109 · 617-570-1000

Richard M. Harter · (Employee Benefits) · Bingham, Dana & Gould · 150 Federal Street · Boston, MA 02110 · 617-951-8000

Frederick D. Herberich · Gaston & Snow · One Federal Street · Boston, MA 02110 · 617-426-4600

Jerome S. Hertz · Mintz, Levin, Cohn, Ferris, Glovsky and Popeo · One Financial Center · Boston, MA 02111 · 617-542-6000

Edward F. Hines, Jr. · Choate, Hall & Stewart · Exchange Place · 53 State Street · Boston, MA 02109 · 617-227-5020

James R. Hopkins · Fine & Ambrogne · Exchange Place · Boston, MA 02109 · 617-367-0100

Daniel D. Levenson · Lourie & Cutler · 60 State Street · Boston, MA 02109 · 617-742-6720

Harry K. Mansfield · Ropes & Gray · 225 Franklin Street · Boston, MA 02110 · 617-423-6100

Paul R. McDaniel · Hill & Barlow · One International Place · 100 Oliver Street · Boston, MA 02110 · 617-439-3555

Robert J. McDonough · Widett, Slater & Goldman · 60 State Street · Boston, MA 02109 · 617-227-7200

Robert J. McGee · Palmer & Dodge · One Beacon Street · Boston, MA 02108 · 617-227-4400

Michael E. Mooney · Nutter, McClennen & Fish · Federal Reserve Plaza · One International Place, 15th Floor · Boston, MA 02210 · 617-973-9700

Wilson C. Piper · Ropes & Gray · 225 Franklin Street · Boston, MA 02110 · 617-423-6100

David L. Raish · (Employee Benefits) · Ropes & Gray · 225 Franklin Street · Boston, MA 02110 · 617-423-6100

Leonard Schneidman · Foley, Hoag & Eliot · One Post Office Square · Boston, MA 02109 · 617-482-1390

Walter G. Van Dorn · Powers & Hall · 100 Franklin Street · Boston, MA 02110 · 617-357-1500

Paul S. Doherty · Doherty, Wallace, Pillsbury and Murphy · 1414 Main Street · Springfield, MA 01144 · 413-733-3111

Richard M. Gaberman · Gaberman & Parish · 32 Hampden Street · Springfield, MA 01103 · 413-781-5066

Robert E. Murphy · Doherty, Wallace, Pillsbury and Murphy · 1414 Main Street · Springfield, MA 01144 · 413-733-3111

Ronda G. Parish · (Employee Benefits) · Gaberman & Parish · 32 Hampden Street Springfield, MA 01103 · 413-781-5066

Raymond T. Mahon · Bowditch & Dewey · 311 Main Street · Worcester, MA 01608 · 508-791-3511

Andrew B. O'Donnell · Mirick, O'Connell, DeMallie & Lougee · 1700 Mechanics Bank Tower · Worcester, MA 01608 · 508-799-0541

TRUSTS AND ESTATES

Thomas H. Belknap · Hill & Barlow · One International Place · 100 Oliver Street Boston, MA 02110 · 617-439-3555

W. Lincoln Boyden · Ropes & Gray · 225 Franklin Street · Boston, MA 02110 617-423-6100

Marion R. Fremont-Smith · Choate, Hall & Stewart · Exchange Place · 52 State Street · Boston, MA 02109 · 617-227-5020

Alfred W. Fuller · Ropes & Gray · 225 Franklin Street · Boston, MA 02110 617-423-6100

Louis H. Hamel, Jr. · Hale and Dorr · 60 State Street · Boston, MA 02109 617-742-9100

William F. Kehoe · Gaston & Snow · One Federal Street · Boston, MA 02110 617-426-4600

Francis S. Moulton, Jr. · Bingham, Dana & Gould · 150 Federal Street · Boston, MA 02110 · 617-951-8000

William J. Pechilis · Goodwin, Procter & Hoar · Exchange Place · Boston, MA 02109 · 617-570-1000

Lawrence T. Perera · Hemenway & Barnes · 60 State Street · Boston, MA 02109 617-227-7940

John A. Perkins · Palmer & Dodge · One Beacon Street · Boston, MA 02108 617-227-4400

Robert C. Pomeroy · Goodwin, Procter & Hoar · Exchange Place · Boston, MA 02109 · 617-570-1000

Hanson S. Reynolds · Foley, Hoag & Eliot · One Post Office Square · Boston, MA 02109 · 617-482-1390

Nicholas U. Sommerfeld · Gaston & Snow · One Federal Street · Boston, MA 02110 · 617-426-4600

Augustus W. Soule, Jr. · Sullivan & Worcester · One Post Office Square · Boston, MA 02109 · 617-338-2800

Jonathan Strong · Hill & Barlow · One International Place · 100 Oliver Street Boston, MA 02110 · 617-439-3555

Philip H. Suter · Sullivan & Worcester · One Post Office Square · Boston, MA 02109 · 617-338-2800

James G. Wheeler · Hutchins & Wheeler · 101 Federal Street · Boston, MA 02110 617-951-6600

Paul S. Doherty · Doherty, Wallace, Pillsbury and Murphy · 1414 Main Street Springfield, MA 01144 · 413-733-3111

Richard M. Gaberman · Garberman & Parish · 32 Hampden Street · Springfield, MA 01103 · 413-781-5066

Robert E. Murphy · Doherty, Wallace, Pillsbury and Murphy · 1414 Main Street Springfield, MA 01144 · 413-733-3111

Gordon H. Wentworth · Robinson Donovan Madden & Barry · Valley Bank Tower, Suite 1400 · 1500 Main Street · Springfield, MA 01115 · 413-732-2301

Burton Chandler · Seder & Chandler · Burnside Building · 339 Main Street Worcester, MA 01608 · 508-757-7721

Richard W. Dearborn · Mountain, Dearborn & Whiting · 370 Main Street, Seventh Floor · Worcester, MA 01608 · 508-756-2423

Thomas R. Mountain · Mountain, Dearborn & Whiting · 370 Main Street, Seventh Floor · Worcester, MA 01608 · 508-756-2423

Sumner B. Tilton, Jr. · Fletcher, Tilton & Whipple · 370 Main Street · Worcester, 01608 · 508-798-8621

MICHIGAN

BANKRUPTCY LAW	342
BUSINESS LITIGATION	343
CORPORATE LAW	345
CRIMINAL DEFENSE	347
FAMILY LAW	348
LABOR AND EMPLOYMENT LAW	349
NATURAL RESOURCES AND ENVIRONMENTAL LAW	351
PERSONAL INJURY LITIGATION	352
REAL ESTATE LAW	353
TAX AND EMPLOYEE BENEFITS LAW	355
TRUSTS AND ESTATES	357

BANKRUPTCY LAW

Stanley B. Bernstein · Dickinson, Wright, Moon, Van Dusen & Freeman · 800 First National Building · Detroit, MI 48226 · 313-223-3500

I. William Cohen · Hertzberg, Jacob and Weingarten · Buhl Building, 15th Floor Detroit, MI 48226 · 313-961-6400

Jonathan S. Green · Jaffe, Snider, Raitt & Heuer · 1800 First National Building Detroit, MI 48226 · 313-961-8380

Stuart E. Hertzberg · Hertzberg, Jacob and Weingarten · Buhl Building, 15th Floor · Detroit, MI 48226 · 313-961-6400

Louis P. Rochkind · Jaffe, Snider, Raitt & Heuer · 1800 First National Building Detroit, MI 48226 · 313-961-8380

Barbara Rom · Hertzberg, Jacob and Weingarten · Buhl Building, 15th Floor Detroit, MI 48226 · 313-961-6400

Ronald L. Rose · Dykema & Gossett · 400 Renaissance Center, 35th Floor · Detroit, MI 48243 · 313-568-6800

Lawrence K. Snider · Jaffe, Snider, Raitt & Heuer · 1800 First National Building · Detroit, MI 48226 · 313-961-8380

Sheldon S. Toll · Honigman Miller Schwartz & Cohn · 2290 First National Building · Detroit, MI 48226 · 313-256-7800

Herbert N. Weingarten · Hertzberg, Jacob and Weingarten · Buhl Building, 15th Floor · Detroit, MI 48226 · 313-961-6400

Timothy J. Curtin · Varnum, Riddering, Schmidt & Howlett · 171 Monroe Avenue, NW, Suite 800 · Grand Rapids, MI 49503 · 616-459-4186

James A. Engbers · Miller, Johnson, Snell & Cummiskey · 800 Calder Plaza Building · Grand Rapids, MI 49503 · 616-459-8311

James B. Frakie · Day, Sawdey, Flaggert & Porter · Old Kent Center · 200 Monroe Avenue, Suite 300 · Grand Rapids, MI 49503 · 616-774-8121

Jeffrey R. Hughes · Varnum, Riddering, Schmidt & Howlett · 171 Monroe Avenue, NW, Suite 800 · Grand Rapids, MI 49503 · 616-459-4186

Robert W. Sawdey · Day, Sawdey, Flaggert & Porter · Old Kent Center · 200 Monroe Avenue, Suite 300 · Grand Rapids, MI 49503 · 616-774-8121

Robert H. Skilton III · Warner, Norcross & Judd · 900 Old Kent Building · One Vandenberg Center · Grand Rapids, MI 49503 · 616-459-6121

Wallace M. Handler · Snyder & Handler · 1365 American Center · 27777 Frank Road · Southfield, MI 48034 · 313-352-1900

BUSINESS LITIGATION

Richard G. Smith · Smith & Brooker · 703 Washington Avenue · P.O. Box X-921 · Bay City, MI 48707-0921 · 517-892-2595

Carl H. von Ende · Miller, Canfield, Paddock and Stone · Pinehurst Office Center, Suite 100 · 1400 North Woodward · P.O. Box 2014 · Bloomfield Hills, MI 48303-2014 · 313-645-5000

Lawrence G. Campbell · Dickinson, Wright, Moon, Van Dusen & Freeman · 800 First National Building · Detroit, MI 48226 · 313-223-3500

Laurence D. Connor · Dykema & Gossett · 400 Renaissance Center, 35th Floor Detroit, MI 48243 · 313-568-6800

Robert G. Cutler · Dykema & Gossett · 400 Renaissance Center, 35th Floor Detroit, MI 48243 · 313-568-6800

Eugene Driker · Barris, Sott, Denn & Driker · 211 West Fort Street, 15th Floor Detroit, MI 48226 · 313-965-9725

Robert A. Fineman · Honigman Miller Schwartz & Cohn · 2290 First National Building · Detroit, MI 48226 · 313-256-7800

Norman Hyman · Honigman Miller Schwartz & Cohn · 2290 First National Building · Detroit, MI 48226 · 313-256-7800

Philip J. Kessler · Butzel Long Gust Klein & Van Zile · 1650 First National Building · Detroit, MI 48226 · 313-963-8142

Kenneth J. McIntyre · Dickinson, Wright, Moon, Van Dusen & Freeman · 800 First National Building · Detroit, MI 48226 · 313-223-3500

Richard E. Rassel · Butzel Long Gust Klein & Van Zile · 1650 First National Building · Detroit, MI 48226 · 313-963-8142

James K. Robinson · Honigman Miller Schwartz & Cohn · 2290 First National Building · Detroit, MI 48226 · 313-256-7800

William A. Sankbeil · Kerr, Russell and Weber · Comerica Building, Suite 2100 Detroit, MI 48226 · 313-961-0200

William M. Saxton · Butzel Long Gust Klein & Van Zile · 1650 First National Building · Detroit, MI 48226 · 313-963-8142

Theodore Souris · Bodman, Longley & Dahling · 100 Renaissance Center, 34th Floor · Detroit, MI 48243 · 313-259-7777

W. Gerald Warren · Dickinson, Wright, Moon, Van Dusen & Freeman · 800 First National Building · Detroit, MI 48226 · 313-223-3500

Donald S. Young · Dykema & Gossett · 400 Renaissance Center, 35th Floor Detroit, MI 48243 · 313-568-6800

Irwin M. Alterman · Kaufman & Payton · 30833 Northwestern Highway, Suite 200 · Farmington Hills, MI 48018 · 313-626-5000

Richard B. Baxter · Dykema & Gossett · 200 Oldtown Riverfront Building · 248 Louis Campau Promenade, NW · Grand Rapids, MI 49503 · 616-776-7500

James S. Brady · Miller, Johnson, Snell & Cummiskey · 800 Calder Plaza Building · Grand Rapids, MI 49503 · 616-459-8311

Grant J. Gruel · Gruel, Mills, Nims and Pylman · 50 Monroe Place, Suite 700 West · Grand Rapids, MI 49503 · 616-235-5500

William K. Holmes · Warner, Norcross & Judd · 900 Old Kent Building · One Vandenberg Center · Grand Rapids, MI 49503 · 616-459-6121

Thomas J. McNamara · Warner, Norcross & Judd · 900 Old Kent Building · One Vandenberg Center · Grand Rapids, MI 49503 · 616-459-6121

L. Roland Roegge · Smith, Haughey, Rice & Roegge · 200 Calder Plaza Building 250 Monroe Avenue, NW · Grand Rapids, MI 49503 · 616-774-8000

Michael F. Cavanaugh · Fraser Trebilcock Davis & Foster · 1000 Michigan National Tower · Lansing, MI 48933 · 517-482-5800

John L. Collins · Foster, Swift, Collins & Coey · 313 South Washington Square Lansing, MI 48933 · 517-372-8050

Webb A. Smith · Foster, Swift, Collins & Coey · 313 South Washington Square Lansing, MI 48933 · 517-372-8050

Theodore W. Swift · Foster, Swift, Collins & Coey · 313 South Washington Square · Lansing, MI 48933 · 517-372-8050

CORPORATE LAW

Chris L. McKenney · Conlin, McKenney & Philbrick · 700 City Center Building Ann Arbor, MI 48104 · 313-761-9000

Bruce D. Birgbauer · Miller, Canfield, Paddock and Stone · 2500 Comerica Building · 211 West Fort Street · Detroit, MI 48226 · 313-963-6420

David A. Ettinger · Honigman Miller Schwartz & Cohn · 2290 First National Building · Detroit, MI 48226 · 313-256-7800

Fred W. Freeman · Dickinson, Wright, Moon, Van Dusen & Freeman · 800 First National Building · Detroit, MI 48226 · 313-223-3500

Richard B. Gushee · Miller, Canfield, Paddock and Stone · 2500 Comerica Building · 211 West Fort Street · Detroit, MI 48226 · 313-963-6420

Verne C. Hampton II · Dickinson, Wright, Moon, Van Dusen & Freeman · 800 First National Building · Detroit, MI 48226 · 313-223-3500

Edward C. Hanpeter · Dykema & Gossett · 400 Renaissance Center, 35th Floor · Detroit, MI 48243 · 313-568-6800

Ira J. Jaffe · Jaffe, Snider, Raitt & Heuer · 1800 First National Building · Detroit, MI 48226 · 313-961-8380

Cyril Moscow · Honigman Miller Schwartz & Cohn · 2290 First National Building · Detroit, MI 48226 · 313-256-7800

Martin C. Oetting · Hill, Lewis, Adams, Goodrich & Tait · 100 Renaissance Center, 32nd Floor · Detroit, MI 48243 · 313-259-3232

George E. Parker III · Miller, Canfield, Paddock and Stone · 2500 Comerica Building · 211 West Fort Street · Detroit, MI 48226 · 313-963-6420

Asher Rabinowitz · Honigman Miller Schwartz & Cohn · 2290 First National Building · Detroit, MI 48226 · 313-256-7800

Richard D. Rohr · Bodman, Longley & Dahling · 100 Renaissance Center, 34th Floor · Detroit, MI 48243 · 313-259-7777

Alan E. Schwartz · Honigman Miller Schwartz & Cohn · 2290 First National Building · Detroit, MI 48226 · 313-256-7800

Brian Sullivan · Dykema & Gossett · 400 Renaissance Center, 35th Floor · Detroit, MI 48243 · 313-568-6800

Richard C. Van Dusen · Dickinson, Wright, Moon, Van Dusen & Freeman · 800 First National Building · Detroit, MI 48226 · 313-223-3500

Frank K. Zinn · Dykema & Gossett · 400 Renaissance Center, 35th Floor · Detroit, MI 48243 · 313-568-6800

Conrad A. Bradshaw · Warner, Norcross & Judd · 900 Old Kent Building · One Vandenberg Center · Grand Rapids, MI 49503 · 616-459-6121

R. Malcolm Cumming · Warner, Norcross & Judd · 900 Old Kent Building · One Vandenberg Center · Grand Rapids, MI 49503 · 616-459-6121

James N. DeBoer, Jr. · Varnum, Riddering, Schmidt & Howlett · 171 Monroe Avenue, NW, Suite 800 · Grand Rapids, MI 49503 · 616-459-4186

Paul K. Gaston · Warner, Norcross & Judd · 900 Old Kent Building · One Vandenberg Center · Grand Rapids, MI 49503 · 616-459-6121

David M. Hecht · Hecht & Cheney · Frey Building, Sixth Floor · Grand Rapids, MI 49503 · 616-458-1300

Donald L. Johnson · Varnum, Riddering, Schmidt & Howlett · 171 Monroe Avenue, NW, Suite 800 · Grand Rapids, MI 49503 · 616-459-4186

Hugh H. Makens · Warner, Norcross & Judd · 900 Old Kent Building · One Vandenberg Center · Grand Rapids, MI 49503 · 616-459-6121

Charles E. McCallum · Warner, Norcross & Judd · 900 Old Kent Building · One Vandenberg Center · Grand Rapids, MI 49503 · 616-459-6121

Daniel C. Molhoek · Varnum, Riddering, Schmidt & Howlett · 171 Monroe Avenue, NW, Suite 800 · Grand Rapids, MI 49503 · 616-459-4186

John R. Nichols · Law, Weathers & Richardson · 500 Union Bank Building Grand Rapids, MI 49503 · 616-459-1171

Gordon J. Quist · Miller, Johnson, Snell & Cummiskey · 800 Calder Plaza Building · Grand Rapids, MI 49503 · 616-459-8311

Ronald R. Pentecost · Fraser Trebilcock Davis & Foster · 1000 Michigan National Tower · Lansing, MI 48933 · 517-482-5800

Peter S. Sheldon · Dickinson, Wright, Moon, Van Dusen & Freeman · 215 South Washington Square, Suite 200 · Lansing, MI 48933 · 517-371-1730

John J. Slavin · Freud, Markus, Slavin & Galgan · 100 East Big Beaver Road, Suite 900 · Troy, MI 48083 · 313-528-3223

CRIMINAL DEFENSE

Robert S. Harrison · Robert S. Harrison & Associates · 6735 Telegraph Road, Suite 350 · Birmingham, MI 48010 · 313-540-5900

David F. DuMouchel · 1930 Buhl Building · Detroit, MI 48226 · 313-962-0100

Neil H. Fink · Evans & Luptak · 2500 Buhl Building · Detroit, MI 48226 · 313-963-9625

James K. Robinson · Honigman Miller Schwartz & Cohn · 2290 First National Building · Detroit, MI 48226 · 313-256-7800

Leo A. Farhat · Farhat, Story & Kraus · Corporate Place, Suite 300 · 1111 Michigan Avenue · East Lansing, MI 48823 · 517-351-3700

Dennis C. Kolenda · Varnum, Riddering, Schmidt & Howlett · 171 Monroe Avenue, NW, Suite 800 · Grand Rapids, MI 49503 · 616-459-4186

FAMILY LAW

Thomas H. Green · Conner, Harbour & Green · 325 East Eisenhower Parkway, Suite Two · Ann Arbor, MI 48108 · 313-761-2314

Henry Baskin · 30200 Telegraph Road · Birmingham, MI 48010 · 313-642-5500

Hanley M. Gurwin · Hill, Lewis, Adams, Goodrich & Tate · 255 South Woodward Avenue, Suite 205 · Birmingham, MI 48011 · 313-642-9692

Norman N. Robbins · 30400 Telegraph Road · Birmingham, MI 48010 · 313-647-5530

Frederick G. Buesser, Jr. · Buesser, Buesser, Blank, Lynch, Fryhoff & Graham · 4190 Telegraph Road, Suite 201 · Bloomfield Hills, MI 48013 · 313-642-7880

Frederick G. Buesser III · Buesser, Buesser, Blank, Lynch, Fryhoff & Graham · 4190 Telegraph Road, Suite 201 · Bloomfield Hills, MI 48013 · 313-642-7880

John F. Schaefer · Williams, Schaefer, Ruby & Williams · 525 North Woodward Avenue, Suite 1200 · Bloomfield Hills, MI 48013 · 313-642-0333

Carole L. Chiamp · Chiamp & Wenger · 3610 Cadillac Tower · Detroit, MI 48226 · 313-961-5660

Kenneth E. Prather · Prather, Harrington & Foley · 3800 Penobscot Building · Detroit, MI 48226-4220 · 313-962-7722

Jeptha W. Schureman · Schureman, Frakes, Glass & Wulfmeier · 440 East Congress, Fourth Floor · Detroit, MI 48226 · 313-961-1500

Robert J. Barnard, Jr. · Barnard, Smith & Burness · 249 Cooley Street · Kalamazoo, MI 49007 · 616-349-3700

LABOR AND EMPLOYMENT LAW

Charles E. Keller · (Management) · Keller, Thoma, Schwarze, Schwarze, DuBay & Katz · 100 West Long Lake Road, Suite 122 · Bloomfield Hills, MI 48013 313-647-3114

Brian S. Ahearn · (Management) · Stringari, Fritz, Kreger, Ahearn, Bennett and Hunsinger · 650 First National Building · Detroit, MI 48226 · 313-961-6474

Robert J. Battista · (Management) · Butzel Long Gust Klein & Van Zile · 1650 First National Building · Detroit, MI 48226 · 313-963-8142

Kathleen L. Bogas · (Individuals) · Sachs, Nunn, Kates, Kadushin, O'Hare, Helveston & Waldman · 1000 Farmer Street · Detroit, MI 48226 · 313-965-3464

John F. Brady · (Management) · Riley and Roumell · Ford Building, Seventh Floor · Detroit, MI 48226-3986 · 313-962-8255

Richard J. Fritz · (Management) · Stringari, Fritz, Kreger, Ahearn, Bennett and Hunsinger · 650 First National Building · Detroit, MI 48226 · 313-961-6474

Deborah L. Gordon · (Individuals) · Stark & Gordon · 1600 Ford Building Detroit, MI 48226 · 313-962-3784

Gordon A. Gregory · (Labor) · Gregory, Van Lopik, Moore & Jeakle · 2042 First National Building · Detroit, MI 48226 · 313-964-5600

Ronald R. Helveston · (Labor) · Sachs, Nunn, Kates, Kadushin, O'Hare, Helveston & Waldman · 1000 Farmer Street · Detroit, MI 48226 · 313-965-3464

Thomas G. Kienbaum · (Management) · Dickinson, Wright, Moon, Van Dusen & Freeman · 800 First National Building · Detroit, MI 48226 · 313-223-3500

John Corbett O'Meara · (Management) · Dickinson, Wright, Moon, Van Dusen & Freeman · 800 First National Building · Detroit, MI 48226 · 313-223-3500

Michael L. Pitt · (Individuals) · Kelman, Loria, Downing, Schneider & Simpson · 2300 First National Building · 660 Woodward Avenue · Detroit, MI 48226 · 313-961-7363

Ronald J. Reosti · (Individuals) · Ronald Reosti & Associates · 925 Ford Building · Detroit, MI 48226 · 313-962-2770

John R. Runyan, Jr. · (Individuals) · Sachs, Nunn, Kates, Kadushin, O'Hare, Helveston & Waldman · 1000 Farmer Street · Detroit, MI 48226 · 313-965-3464

Theodore Sachs · (Labor) · Sachs, Nunn, Kates, Kadushin, O'Hare, Helveston & Waldman · 1000 Farmer Street · Detroit, MI 48226 · 313-965-3464

Ronald J. Santo · (Management) · Dykema & Gossett · 400 Renaissance Center, 35th Floor · Detroit, MI 48243 · 313-568-6800

William M. Saxton · (Management) · Butzel Long Gust Klein & Van Zile · 1650 First National Building · Detroit, MI 48226 · 313-963-8142

Sheldon J. Stark · (Individuals) · Stark & Gordon · 1600 Ford Building · Detroit, MI 48226 · 313-962-3784

Robert M. Vercruysse · (Management) · Butzel Long Gust Klein & Van Zile · 1650 First National Building · Detroit, MI 48226 · 313-963-8142

Eugene Alkema · (Management) · Varnum, Riddering, Schmidt & Howlett · 171 Monroe Avenue, NW, Suite 800 · Grand Rapids, MI 49503 · 616-459-4186

Jack R. Clary · (Management) · Clary, Nantz, Wood, Hoffius, Rankin & Cooper · 500 Calder Plaza, Suite 500 · 250 Monroe Avenue, NW · Grand Rapids, MI 49503 · 616-459-9487

Michael L. Fayette · (Labor) · Pinsky, Smith, Fayette, Soet & Hulswit · 1515 McKay Tower · Grand Rapids, MI 49503 · 616-451-8496

Norman E. Jabin · (Management) · Miller, Johnson, Snell & Cummiskey · 800 Calder Plaza Building · Grand Rapids, MI 49503 · 616-459-8311

H. Rhett Pinsky · (Individuals) · Pinsky, Smith, Fayette, Soet & Hulswit · 1515 McKay Tower · Grand Rapids, MI 49503 · 616-451-8496

Kent J. Vana · (Management) · Varnum, Riddering, Schmidt & Howlett · 171 Monroe Avenue, NW, Suite 800 · Grand Rapids, MI 49503 · 616-459-4186

Carl E. Ver Beek · (Management) · Varnum, Riddering, Schmidt & Howlett · 171 Monroe Avenue, NW, Suite 800 · Grand Rapids, MI 49503 · 616-459-4186

Thomas P. Hustoles · (Management) · Miller, Canfield, Paddock and Stone · 444 West Michigan Avenue · Kalamazoo, MI 49007 · 616-381-7030

Darryl R. Cochrane · (Labor) · McCroskey, Feldman, Cochrane & Brock · 1440 Peck Street · P.O. Box 27 · Muskegon, MI 49443 · 616-726-4861

Donald J. Veldman · (Management) · Warner, Norcross & Judd · 801 West Norton · Muskegon, MI 49441 · 616-739-2297

James A. White · (Labor) · White, Beekman, Przybylowicz, Schneider & Baird · 2214 University Park Drive, Suite 200 · Okemos, MI 48864 · 517-349-7744

J. Douglas Korney · (Labor) · Levin, Levin, Garvett and Dill · 3000 Town Center, Suite 1800 · Southfield, MI 48075 · 313-352-8200

Samuel C. McKnight · (Labor) · Klimist, McKnight, Sale & McClow · 26211 Central Park Boulevard, Suite 614 · Southfield, MI 48076 · 313-354-9650

Bruce A. Miller · (Labor) · Miller, Cohen, Martens & Ice · 17117 West Nine Mile, Suite 1400 · Southfield, MI 48075 · 313-559-2110

NATURAL RESOURCES AND ENVIRONMENTAL LAW

Jeffrey K. Haynes · (Plaintiffs) · Vanderkloot & Haynes · 860 West Long Lake Road, Suite 300 · P.O. Box 980 · Bloomfield Hills, MI 48013 · 313-540-8388

Joseph M. Polito · Honigman Miller Schwartz & Cohn · 2290 First National Building · Detroit, MI 48226 · 313-256-7800

Herbert G. Sparrow III · Dickinson, Wright, Moon, Van Dusen & Freeman · 800 First National Building · Detroit, MI 48226 · 313-223-3500

David L. Tripp · Dykema & Gossett · 400 Renaissance Center, 35th Floor · Detroit, MI 48243 · 313-568-6800

John W. Voelpel · Honigman Miller Schwartz & Cohn · 2290 First National Building · Detroit, MI 48226 · 313-256-7800

Peter W. Steketee · 660 Cascade West Parkway, SE, Suite 65 · Grand Rapids, MI 49506 · 616-949-6551

Michael L. Robinson · Warner, Norcross & Judd · Comerica Bank Building · 801 West Norton Avenue · Muskegon, MI 49441 · 616-739-2297

PERSONAL INJURY LITIGATION

Richard G. Smith · (Defendants) · Smith & Brooker · 703 Washington Avenue P.O. Box X-921 · Bay City, MI 48707-0921 · 517-892-2595

Kenneth B. McConnell · (Plaintiffs) · 2000 North Woodward Avenue, Suite 100 Bloomfield Hills, MI 48013 · 313-645-1710

George J. Bedrosian · (Plaintiffs) · Goodman, Eden, Millender & Bedrosian Cadillac Tower, 30th Floor · Detroit, MI 48226 · 313-965-0050

William D. Booth · (Defendants) · Plunkett, Cooney, Rutt, Watters, Stanczyk & Pedersen · 900 Marquette Building · Detroit, MI 48226 · 313-965-3900

Lawrence S. Charfoos · (Plaintiffs) · Charfoos & Christensen · Penobscot Building, 40th Floor · Detroit, MI 48226 · 313-963-8080

David W. Christensen · (Plaintiffs) · Charfoos & Christensen · Penobscot Building, 40th Floor · Detroit, MI 48226 · 313-963-8080

David J. Cooper · (Defendants) · Garan, Lucow, Miller, Seward, Cooper & Becker · 1000 Woodbridge Place · Detroit, MI 48207-3192 · 313-446-1530

Daniel L. Garan · (Defendants) · Garan, Lucow, Miller, Seward, Cooper & Becker · 1000 Woodbridge Place · Detroit, MI 48207-3192 · 313-446-1530

Richard M. Goodman · (Plaintiffs) · 1394 East Jefferson Street · Detroit, MI 48207 · 313-567-6165

John A. Kruse · (Defendants) · Harvey, Kruse, Westen & Milan · 1590 First National Bank Building · Detroit, MI 48226 · 313-964-3100

Richard J. McClear · (Defendants) · Dykema & Gossett · 400 Renaissance Center, 35th Floor · Detroit, MI 48243 · 313-568-6800

John E. S. Scott · (Defendants) · Dickinson, Wright, Moon, Van Dusen & Freeman · 800 First National Building · Detroit, MI 48226 · 313-223-3500

Richard B. Baxter · Dykema & Gossett · 200 Oldtown Riverfront Building · 248 Louis Campau Promenade, NW · Grand Rapids, MI 49503 · 616-776-7500

Grant J. Gruel · Gruel, Mills, Nims and Pylman · 50 Monroe Place, Suite 700 West · Grand Rapids, MI 49503 · 616-235-5500

Thomas J. McNamara · (Defendants) · Warner, Norcross & Judd · 900 Old Kent Building · One Vandenberg Center · Grand Rapids, MI 49503 · 616-459-6121

William G. Reamon, Sr. · (Plaintiffs) · Waters Building, Suite 200-C · Grand Rapids, MI 49503 · 616-774-2377

William J. Waddell · 180 Monroe Avenue, NW, Suite 4000 · Grand Rapids, MI 49503 · 616-235-7737

John L. Collins · (Defendants) · Foster, Swift, Collins & Coey · 313 South Washington Square · Lansing, MI 48933 · 517-372-8050

William N. Kritselis · (Plaintiffs) · Church, Kritselis, Wyble & Robinson · 3939 Capitol City Boulevard · Lansing, MI 48906-9962 · 517-323-4770

George T. Sinas · (Plaintiffs) · Sinas, Dramis, Brake, Boughton, McIntyre & Reisig · 520 Seymour Avenue · Lansing, MI 48933-1192 · 517-372-7780

Cassius E. Street, Jr. · (Plaintiffs) · Street & Grua · 2401 East Grand River Lansing, MI 48912 · 517-487-8300

Stanley S. Schwartz · (Plaintiffs) · Sommers, Schwartz, Silver & Schwartz · 2000 Town Center, Suite 900 · Southfield, MI 48075 · 313-355-0300

William J. Weinstein · (Plaintiffs) · Weinstein, Gordon and Hoffman · 18411 West Twelve Mile Road · Southfield, MI 48076 · 313-443-1500

Dean A. Robb · (Plaintiffs) · Robb, Messing & Palmer · 420 East Front Street P.O. Box 1132 · Traverse City, MI 49684 · 616-947-2462

REAL ESTATE LAW

Robert E. Gilbert · Miller, Canfield, Paddock and Stone · 101 North Main Street, Seventh Floor · Ann Arbor, MI 48104 · 313-663-2445

Stephen A. Bromberg · Butzel Long Gust Klein & Van Zile · 32270 Telegraph Road, Suite 200 · Birmingham, MI 48010 · 313-258-1616

Gary A. Taback · Taback and Hall · 31000 Telegraph Road, Suite 200 · Birmingham, MI 48101 · 313-642-7330

Robert S. Bolton · Butzel, Keidan, Simon, Myers & Graham · 300 East Long Lake Road, Suite 200 · Bloomfield Hills, MI 48013 · 313-644-5100

Stephen E. Dawson · Dickinson, Wright, Moon, Van Dusen & Freeman · 525 North Woodward Avenue · P.O. Box 509 · Bloomfield Hills, MI 48013 · 313-646-4300

William T. Myers · Dykema & Gossett · 505 North Woodward Avenue, Suite 3000 · Bloomfield Hills, MI 48013 · 313-540-0700

Richard E. Rabbideau · Dykema & Gossett · 505 North Woodward Avenue, Suite 3000 · Bloomfield Hills, MI 48013 · 313-540-0700

John E. Amerman · Honigman Miller Schwartz & Cohn · 2290 First National Building · Detroit, MI 48226 · 313-256-7800

William G. Barris · Barris, Sott, Denn & Driker · 211 West Fort Street, 15th Floor · Detroit, MI 48226 · 313-965-9725

Maurice S. Binkow · Honigman Miller Schwartz & Cohn · 2290 First National Building · Detroit, MI 48226 · 313-256-7800

James W. Draper · Dykema & Gossett · 400 Renaissance Center, 35th Floor · Detroit, MI 48243 · 313-568-6800

William B. Dunn · Clark, Klein & Beaumont · 1600 First Federal Building · 1001 Woodward Avenue · Detroit, MI 48226 · 313-965-8300

Russell A. McNair, Jr. · Dickinson, Wright, Moon, Van Dusen & Freeman · 800 First National Building · P.O. Box 509 · Detroit, MI 48226 · 313-223-3500

Peter A. Nathan · Hertzberg, Jacob and Weingarten · Buhl Building, 15th Floor · Detroit, MI 48226 · 313-961-6400

Stephen G. Palms · Miller, Canfield, Paddock and Stone · 2500 Comerica Building · 211 West Fort Street · Detroit, MI 48226 · 313-963-6420

Allen Schwartz · Miller, Canfield, Paddock and Stone · 2500 Comerica Building · 211 West Fort Street · Detroit, MI 48226 · 313-963-6420

James M. Tervo · Dickinson, Wright, Moon, Van Dusen & Freeman · 800 First National Building · Detroit, MI 48226 · 313-223-3500

William J. Zousmer · Honigman Miller Schwartz & Cohn · 2290 First National Building · Detroit, MI 48226 · 313-256-7800

Jack M. Bowie · McShane & Bowie · 540 Old Kent Building · Grand Rapids, MI 49503 · 616-774-0641

James R. Brown · Mika, Meyers, Beckett & Jones · 200 Ottawa Street, NW, Suite 700 · Grand Rapids, MI 49503 · 616-459-3200

John G. Cameron, Jr. · Warner, Norcross & Judd · 900 Old Kent Building · One Vandenberg Center · Grand Rapids, MI 49503 · 616-459-6121

Robert L. Nelson · Dykema & Gossett · 200 Oldtown Riverfront Building · 248 Louis Campau Promenade, NW · Grand Rapids, MI 49503 · 616-776-7500

Sheldon P. Winkelman · Honigman Miller Schwartz & Cohn · 2290 First National Building · Detroit, MI 48226 · 313-256-7800

Douglas J. Austin · Fraser Trebilcock Davis & Foster · 1000 Michigan National Tower · Lansing, MI 48933 · 517-482-5800

Robert J. McCullen · Foster, Swift, Collins & Coey · 313 South Washington Square · Lansing, MI 48933 · 517-372-8050

TAX AND EMPLOYEE BENEFITS LAW

Robert B. Stevenson · (Employee Benefits) · First National Bank Building, Suite 902 · 201 South Main Street · Ann Arbor, MI 48104-2105 · 313-747-7050

Louis W. Kasischke · Dykema & Gossett · 505 North Woodward Avenue, Suite 3000 · Bloomfield Hills, MI 48013 · 313-540-0700

Samuel J. McKim III · Miller, Canfield, Paddock and Stone · Pinehurst Office Center, Suite 100 · 1400 North Woodward Avenue · P.O. Box 2014 · Bloomfield Hills, MI 48303-2014 · 313-645-5000

Ward Randol, Jr. · (Employee Benefits) · Dickinson, Wright, Moon, Van Dusen & Freeman · 525 North Woodward Avenue · P.O. Box 509 · Bloomfield Hills, MI 48013 · 313-646-4300

Robert G. Buydens · (Employee Benefits) · Clark, Klein & Beaumont · 1600 First Federal Building · 1001 Woodward Avenue · Detroit, MI 48226 · 313-965-8300

Joseph F. Dillon · Raymond & Dillon · 400 Renaissance Center, Suite 2370 · Detroit, MI 48243 · 313-259-7700

John H. Eggertsen · (Employee Benefits) · Honigman Miller Schwartz & Cohn · 2290 First National Building · Detroit, MI 48226 · 313-256-7800

E. James Gamble · Dykema & Gossett · 400 Renaissance Center, 35th Floor · Detroit, MI 48243 · 313-568-6800

Eugene A. Gargaro, Jr. · Dykema & Gossett · 400 Renaissance Center, 35th Floor · Detroit, MI 48243 · 313-568-6800

Miles Jaffe · Honigman Miller Schwartz & Cohn · 2290 First National Building · Detroit, MI 48226 · 313-256-7800

Joseph F. Maycock, Jr. · (Employee Benefits) · Miller, Canfield, Paddock and Stone · 2500 Comerica Building · 211 West Fort Street · Detroit, MI 48226 · 313-963-6420

David M. Rosenberger · (Employee Benefits) · Dykema & Gossett · 400 Renaissance Center, 35th Floor · Detroit, MI 48243 · 313-568-6800

Sherill Siebert · (Employee Benefits) · Honigman Miller Schwartz & Cohn · 2290 First National Building · Detroit, MI 48226 · 313-256-7800

Stevan Uzelac · Miller, Canfield, Paddock and Stone · 2500 Comerica Building · 211 West Fort Street · Detroit, MI 48226 · 313-963-6420

Lawrence R. Van Til · Van Til, Kasiborski & Ronayne · 400 Renaissance Center, Suite 500 · Detroit, MI 48243 · 313-259-2250

James C. Bruinsma · (Employee Benefits) · Miller, Johnson, Snell & Cummiskey · 800 Calder Plaza Building · Grand Rapids, MI 49503 · 616-459-8311

Stephen R. Kretschman · Warner, Norcross & Judd · 900 Old Kent Building · One Vandenberg Center · Grand Rapids, MI 49503 · 616-459-6121

John W. McNeil · Miller, Johnson, Snell & Cummiskey · 800 Calder Plaza Building · Grand Rapids, MI 49503 · 616-459-8311

J. Lee Murphy · Miller, Johnson, Snell & Cummiskey · 800 Calder Plaza Building · Grand Rapids, MI 49503 · 616-459-8311

Roger H. Oetting · Warner, Norcross & Judd · 900 Old Kent Building · One Vandenberg Center · Grand Rapids, MI 49503 · 616-459-6121

Vernon P. Saper · (Employee Benefits) · Warner, Norcross & Judd · 900 Old Kent Building · One Vandenberg Center · Grand Rapids, MI 49503 · 616-459-6121

George L. Whitfield · (Employee Benefits) · Warner, Norcross & Judd · 900 Old Kent Building · One Vandenberg Center · Grand Rapids, MI 49503 · 616-459-6121

Allan J. Claypool · Foster, Swift, Collins & Coey · 313 South Washington Square · Lansing, MI 48933 · 517-372-8050

Stephen I. Jurmu · (Employee Benefits) · Foster, Swift, Collins & Coey · 313 South Washington Square · Lansing, MI 48933 · 517-372-8050

Peter S. Sheldon · Dickinson, Wright, Moon, Van Dusen & Freeman · 215 South Washington Square, Suite 200 · Lansing, MI 48933 · 517-371-1730

J. D. Hartwig · Hartwig, Crow & Jones · 206 Court Street · P.O. Box 6 · St. Joseph, MI 49085 · 616-983-0615

Marcus Plotkin · Plotkin, Yolles, Siegel, Schultz & Polk · 2000 Town Center, Suite 600 · Southfield, MI 48075 · 313-354-3200

TRUSTS AND ESTATES

Susan S. Westerman · Stein, Moran & Westerman · 320 North Main Street · Ann Arbor, MI 48104 · 313-769-6838

E. James Gamble · Dykema & Gossett · 400 Renaissance Center, 35th Floor · Detroit, MI 48243 · 313-568-6800

Raymond T. Huetteman, Jr. · Dykema & Gossett · 400 Renaissance Center, 35th Floor · Detroit, MI 48243 · 313-568-6800

Robert B. Joslyn · Joslyn, Keydel, Wallace & Joslyn · 2211 Comerica Building · Detroit, MI 48226 · 313-964-4181

Frederick R. Keydel · Joslyn, Keydel, Wallace & Joslyn · 2211 Comerica Building · Detroit, MI 48226 · 313-964-4181

George D. Miller, Jr. · Bodman, Longley & Dahling · 100 Renaissance Center, 34th Floor · Detroit, MI 48243 · 313-259-7777

Douglas J. Rasmussen · Clark, Klein & Beaumont · 1600 First Federal Building · 1001 Woodward Avenue · Detroit, MI 48226 · 313-965-8300

Robert Donald Brower, Jr. · Miller, Johnson, Snell & Cummiskey · 800 Calder Plaza Building · Grand Rapids, MI 49503 · 616-459-8311

Dirk C. Hoffius · Varnum, Riddering, Schmidt & Howlett · 171 Monroe Avenue, NW, Suite 800 · Grand Rapids, MI 49503 · 616-459-4186

Fredric A. Sytsma · Varnum, Riddering, Schmidt & Howlett · 171 Monroe Avenue, NW, Suite 800 · Grand Rapids, MI 49503 · 616-459-4186

W. Michael Van Haren · Warner, Norcross & Judd · 900 Old Kent Building · One Vandenberg Center · Grand Rapids, MI 49503 · 616-459-6121

Allan J. Claypool · Foster, Swift, Collins & Coey · 313 South Washington Square · Lansing, MI 48933 · 517-372-8050

Joe C. Foster, Jr. · Fraser Trebilcock Davis & Foster · 1000 Michigan National Tower · Lansing, MI 48933 · 517-482-5800

John N. Seaman · MacLean, Seaman, Laing & Guilford · Michigan National Tower, 19th Floor · Lansing, MI 48933 · 517-372-0930

Everett R. Zack · Fraser Trebilcock Davis & Foster · 1000 Michigan National Tower · Lansing, MI 48933 · 517-482-5800

James A. Kendall · Currie & Kendall · 6024 Eastman Road · P.O. Box 1846 · Midland, MI 48641 · 517-839-0300

Michael W. Irish · Culver, Lague & McNally · 500 Terrace Plaza · P.O. Box 389 · Muskegon, MI 49443 · 616-725-8148

John Harvey Martin · Landman, Latimer, Clink & Robb · 400 Terrace Plaza · P.O. Box 1488 · Muskegon, MI 49443 · 616-722-2671

J. D. Hartwig · Hartwig, Crow & Jones · 206 Court Street · St. Joseph, MI 49085 · 616-983-0615

James E. Beall · Stark, Reagan & Finnerty · 1111 West Long Lake Road, Suite 202 · Troy, MI 48098 · 313-641-9955

MINNESOTA

BANKRUPTCY LAW	359
BUSINESS LITIGATION	360
CORPORATE LAW	362
CRIMINAL DEFENSE	363
FAMILY LAW	364
LABOR AND EMPLOYMENT LAW	365
NATURAL RESOURCES AND ENVIRONMENTAL LAW	366
PERSONAL INJURY LITIGATION	367
REAL ESTATE LAW	369
TAX AND EMPLOYEE BENEFITS LAW	370
TRUSTS AND ESTATES	372

BANKRUPTCY LAW

James L. Baillie · Fredrikson & Byron · 1100 International Centre · 900 Second Avenue South · Minneapolis, MN 55402 · 612-347-7000

Richard D. Holper · Robins, Zelle, Larson & Kaplan · 1800 International Centre · 900 Second Avenue South · Minneapolis, MN 55402-3394 · 612-349-8500

William I. Kampf · Fredrikson & Byron · 1100 International Centre · 900 Second Avenue South · Minneapolis, MN 55402 · 612-347-7000

James H. Levy · Levy & Miller · 570 Towle Building · 330 Second Avenue South · Minneapolis, MN 55401 · 612-332-5933

Melvin I. Orenstein · Lindquist & Vennum · 4200 IDS Center · 80 South Eighth Street · Minneapolis, MN 55402 · 612-371-3211

Howard A. Patrick · Robins, Zelle, Larson & Kaplan · 1800 International Centre · 900 Second Avenue South · Minneapolis, MN 55402-3394 · 612-349-8500

Paul J. Scheerer · Dorsey & Whitney · 2200 First Bank Place East · Minneapolis, MN 55402 · 612-340-2600

BUSINESS LITIGATION

John J. Killen · Johnson, Killen, Thibodeau & Seiler · 811 Norwest Center Duluth, MN 55802 · 218-722-6331

Lawrence C. Brown · Faegre & Benson · 2300 Multifoods Tower · 33 South Sixth Street · Minneapolis, MN 55402-3694 · 612-371-5300

Tyrone P. Bujold · Robins, Zelle, Larson & Kaplan · 1800 International Centre 900 Second Avenue South · Minneapolis, MN 55402-3394 · 612-349-8500

Gordon G. Busdicker · Faegre & Benson · 2300 Multifoods Tower · 33 South Sixth Street · Minneapolis, MN 55402-3694 · 612-371-5300

Peter Dorsey · Dorsey & Whitney · 2200 First Bank Place East · Minneapolis, MN 55402 · 612-340-2600

Harold D. Field, Jr. · Leonard, Street and Deinard · 150 South Fifth Street, Suite 2300 · Minneapolis, MN 55402 · 612-335-1500

John D. French · Faegre & Benson · 2300 Multifoods Tower · 33 South Sixth Street · Minneapolis, MN 55402-3694 · 612-371-5300

Terence M. Fruth · Fruth & Anthony · 1350 International Centre · 900 Second Avenue South · Minneapolis, MN 55402 · 612-349-6969

Craig W. Gagnon · Oppenheimer Wolff and Donnelly · 45 South Seventh Street Minneapolis, MN 55402 · 612-344-9300

Edward M. Glennon · Lindquist & Vennum · 4200 IDS Center · 80 South Eighth Street · Minneapolis, MN 55402 · 612-371-3211

Elliot S. Kaplan · Robins, Zelle, Larson & Kaplan · 1800 International Centre 900 Second Avenue South · Minneapolis, MN 55402-3394 · 612-349-8500

Timothy D. Kelly · Fruth & Anthony · 1350 International Centre · 900 Second Avenue South · Minneapolis, MN 55402 · 612-349-6969

Dale I. Larson · Robins, Zelle, Larson & Kaplan · 1800 International Centre · 900 Second Avenue South · Minneapolis, MN 55402-3394 · 612-349-8500

John D. Levine · Dorsey & Whitney · 2200 First Bank Place East · Minneapolis, MN 55402 · 612-340-2600

James B. Loken · Faegre & Benson · 2300 Multifoods Tower · 33 South Sixth Street · Minneapolis, MN 55402-3694 · 612-371-5300

Clay R. Moore · Mackall, Crounse & Moore · 1600 TCF Tower · 121 South Eighth Street · Minneapolis, MN 55402 · 612-333-1341

Jerome B. Pederson · Fredrikson & Byron · 1100 International Centre · 900 Second Avenue South · Minneapolis, MN 55402 · 612-347-7000

Charles W. Quaintance, Jr. · Maslon Edelman Borman & Brand · Eighth and Nicollet Mall · Minneapolis, MN 55402 · 612-339-8015

Robert A. Schwartzbauer · Dorsey & Whitney · 2200 First Bank Place East Minneapolis, MN 55402 · 612-340-2600

Robert J. Sheran · (Appellate) · Lindquist & Vennum · 4200 IDS Center · 80 South Eighth Street · Minneapolis, MN 55402 · 612-371-3211

Daniel R. Shulman · Gray, Plant, Mooty, Mooty & Bennett · 3400 City Center 33 South Sixth Street · Minneapolis, MN 55402 · 612-343-2800

James S. Simonson · Gray, Plant, Mooty, Mooty & Bennett · 3400 City Center 33 South Sixth Street · Minneapolis, MN 55402 · 612-343-2800

Jan Stuurmans · Stuurmans & Karan · 600 Title Insurance Building · 400 Second Avenue South · Minneapolis, MN 55401 · 612-339-5581

Thomas W. Tinkham · Dorsey & Whitney · 2200 First Bank Place East · Minneapolis, MN 55402 · 612-340-2600

Robert R. Dunlap · Dunlap, Keith, Finseth, Berndt & Sandberg · 505 Marquette Bank Building · P.O. Box 549 · Rochester, MN 55903 · 507-288-9111

Ronald L. Seeger · Michaels Seeger Rosenblad & Arnold · Norwest Bank Building, Suite 550 · 21 First Street Southwest · Rochester, MN 55902 · 507-288-7755

John A. Cochrane · Cochrane & Bresnahan · 24 East Fourth Street · St. Paul, MN 55101-1099 · 612-298-1950

David C. Forsberg · Briggs and Morgan · West 2200 First National Bank Building St. Paul, MN 55101 · 612-291-1215

Elmer B. Trousdale · Oppenheimer Wolff and Donnelly · 1700 First Bank Building · St. Paul, MN 55101 · 612-227-7271

Eugene M. Warlich · Doherty, Rumble & Butler · 2800 Minnesota World Trade Center · St. Paul, MN 55101 · 612-291-9353

CORPORATE LAW

David L. Boehnen · Dorsey & Whitney · 2200 First Bank Place East · Minneapolis, MN 55402 · 612-340-2600

Michael E. Bress · Dorsey & Whitney · 2200 First Bank Place East · Minneapolis, MN 55402 · 612-340-2600

Kenneth L. Cutler · Dorsey & Whitney · 2200 First Bank Place East · Minneapolis, MN 55402 · 612-340-2600

Stanley Efron · Henson & Efron · 1200 Title Insurance Building · Minneapolis, MN 55401 · 612-339-2500

Gerald T. Flom · Faegre & Benson · 2300 Multifoods Tower · 33 South Sixth Street · Minneapolis, MN 55402-3694 · 612-371-5300

John D. French · Faegre & Benson · 2300 Multifoods Tower · 33 South Sixth Street · Minneapolis, MN 55402-3694 · 612-371-5300

James A. Halls · Faegre & Benson · 2300 Multifoods Tower · 33 South Sixth Street · Minneapolis, MN 55402-3694 · 612-371-5300

John S. Hibbs · Dorsey & Whitney · 2200 First Bank Place East · Minneapolis, MN 55402 · 612-340-2600

Samuel L. Kaplan · Kaplan, Strangis and Kaplan · 555 Pillsbury Center · 200 South Sixth Street · Minneapolis, MN 55402 · 612-375-1138

Richard G. Lareau · Oppenheimer Wolff and Donnelly · 45 South Seventh Street Minneapolis, MN 55402 · 612-344-9300

Keith A. Libbey · Fredrikson & Byron · 1100 International Centre · 900 Second Avenue South · Minneapolis, MN 55402 · 612-347-7000

Gerald E. Magnuson · Lindquist & Vennum · 4200 IDS Center · 80 South Eighth Street · Minneapolis, MN 55402 · 612-371-3211

Lee R. Mitau · Dorsey & Whitney · 2200 First Bank Place East · Minneapolis, MN 55402 · 612-340-2600

Morris M. Sherman · Leonard, Street and Deinard · 150 South Fifth Street, Suite 2300 · Minneapolis, MN 55402 · 612-335-1500

Roger V. Stageberg · Lommen, Nelson, Cole & Stageberg · 1100 TCF Tower 121 South Eighth Street · Minneapolis, MN 55402 · 612-339-8131

Ralph Strangis · Kaplan, Strangis and Kaplan · 555 Pillsbury Center · 200 South Sixth Street · Minneapolis, MN 55402 · 612-375-1138

Burt E. Swanson · Briggs and Morgan · 2400 IDS Center · Minneapolis, MN 55402 · 612-339-0661

Richard G. Swanson · Dorsey & Whitney · 2200 First Bank Place East · Minneapolis, MN 55402 · 612-340-2600

William A. Whitlock · Dorsey & Whitney · 2200 First Bank Place East · Minneapolis, MN 55402 · 612-340-2600

Alan J. Willensky · Dorsey & Whitney · 2200 First Bank Place East · Minneapolis, MN 55402 · 612-340-2600

Frank Hammond · Briggs and Morgan · West 2200 First National Bank Building St. Paul, MN 55101 · 612-291-1215

Lawrence J. Hayes · Maun, Green, Hayes, Simon, Johanneson and Brehl · 332 Hamm Building · St. Paul, MN 55102 · 612-224-7300

Thomas E. Rohricht · Doherty, Rumble & Butler · 2800 Minnesota World Trade Center · St. Paul, MN 55101 · 612-291-9333

Eugene M. Warlich · Doherty, Rumble & Butler · 2800 Minnesota World Trade Center · St. Paul, MN 55101 · 612-291-9333

Sherman Winthrop · Winthrop & Weinstine · 1800 Conwed Tower · 444 Cedar Street · St. Paul, MN 55101 · 612-292-8110

CRIMINAL DEFENSE

Robert E. Lucas · Lucas & Carlson · 404 Central Avenue North · Duluth, MN 55807 · 218-624-3671

Joseph S. Friedberg · Commerce At The Crossings, Suite 205 · 250 Second Avenue, South · Minneapolis, MN 55401 · 612-339-8626

Bruce Hartigan · 100 South Fifth Street, Suite 2160 · Minneapolis, MN 55402 · 612-333-2404

William J. Mauzy · 701 Fourth Avenue South, Suite 1710 · Minneapolis, MN 55415 · 612-340-9108

Ronald I. Meshbesher · Meshbesher, Singer & Spence · 1616 Park Avenue Minneapolis, MN 55404 · 612-339-9121

Jack S. Nordby · Meshbesher, Singer & Spence · 1616 Park Avenue · Minneapolis, MN 55404 · 612-339-9121

Phillip S. Resnick · Resnick & Bartsh · 510 Lumber Exchange Building · Minneapolis, MN 55402 · 612-339-0411

Douglas W. Thomson · Thomson & Ellis · 345 St. Peter Street, Suite 300 · St. Paul, MN 55102 · 612-227-0856

FAMILY LAW

Jack S. Jaycox · 400 Southgate Office Plaza · 5001 West 80th Street · Bloomington, MN 55437 · 612-835-6300

James H. Hennessy · Moss & Barnett · 1200 Pillsbury Center · 200 South Sixth Street · Minneapolis, MN 55402 · 612-339-8551

Robert F. Henson · Henson & Efron · 1200 Title Insurance Building · Minneapolis, MN 55401 · 612-339-2500

A. Larry Katz · Katz, Davis, Manka & Haugan · 4830 IDS Center · 80 South Eighth Street · Minneapolis, MN 55402 · 612-333-1671

Edward L. Winer · Moss & Barnett · 1200 Pillsbury Center · 200 South Sixth Street · Minneapolis, MN 55402 · 612-339-8551

Robert H. Zalk · Fredrikson & Byron · 1100 International Centre · 900 Second Avenue South · Minneapolis, MN 55402 · 612-347-7000

Lawrence D. Downing · O'Brien, Ehrick, Wolf, Deaner & Downing · 611 Marquette Bank Building · P.O. Box 968 · Rochester, MN 55903 · 507-289-4041

Richard D. Goff · Goff, Kaplan & Wolf · 2200 American National Bank Building · St. Paul, MN 55101 · 612-222-6341

William E. Haugh, Jr. · Collins, Buckley, Sauntry and Haugh · West 1100 First National Bank Building · 332 Minnesota Street · St. Paul, MN 55101 · 612-227-0611

LABOR AND EMPLOYMENT LAW

Don L. Bye · (Labor) · Halverson, Watters, Bye, Downs & Maki · 700 Providence Building · Duluth, MN 55802 · 218-727-6833

Emery W. Bartle · (Management) · Dorsey & Whitney · 2200 First Bank Place East · Minneapolis, MN 55402 · 612-340-2600

Dale E. Beihoffer · (Management) · Faegre & Benson · 2300 Multifoods Tower · 33 South Sixth Street · Minneapolis, MN 55402-3694 · 612-371-5300

Gregg M. Corwin · (Labor) · West Parkdale Building, Suite 430 · 1660 South Highway 100 · Minneapolis, MN 55416 · 612-544-7774

Terence M. Fruth · (Management) · Fruth & Anthony · 1350 International Centre · 900 Second Avenue South · Minneapolis, MN 55402 · 612-349-6969

Stephen D. Gordon · (Labor) · Gordon-Miller-O'Brien · 1208 Plymouth Building · 12 South Sixth Street · Minneapolis, MN 55402 · 612-333-5831

Kathleen M. Graham · (Individuals) · Leonard, Street and Deinard · 150 South Fifth Street, Suite 2300 · Minneapolis, MN 55402 · 612-335-1500

David R. Hols · (Management) · Felhaber, Larson, Fenlon and Vogt · 1935 Piper Jaffray Tower · 220 Ninth Street · Minneapolis, MN 55402 · 612-339-6321

John J. McGirl, Jr. · (Management) · Doherty, Rumble & Butler · 3750 IDS Tower · 80 South Eighth Street · Minneapolis, MN 55402 · 612-340-5555

Richard A. Miller · (Labor) · Gordon-Miller-O'Brien · 1208 Plymouth Building · 12 South Sixth Street · Minneapolis, MN 55402 · 612-333-5831

Roger A. Peterson · (Labor) · Peterson, Engberg & Peterson · 700 Title Insurance Building · Minneapolis, MN 55401 · 612-338-6743

James M. Samples · (Management) · Faegre & Benson · 2300 Multifoods Tower · 33 South Sixth Street · Minneapolis, MN 55402-3694 · 612-371-5300

Paul C. Sprenger · (Individuals) · Sprenger, Olson & Shutes · 325 Ridgewood Avenue · Minneapolis, MN 55403 · 612-871-8910

John C. Zwakman · (Management) · Dorsey & Whitney · 2200 First Bank Place East · Minneapolis, MN 55402 · 612-340-2600

Edward J. Bohrer · (Management) · Felhaber, Larson, Fenlon and Vogt · 900 Meritor Tower · 444 Cedar Street · St. Paul, MN 55101 · 612-222-6321

Michael J. Galvin, Jr. · (Management) · Briggs and Morgan · West 2200 First National Bank Building · St. Paul, MN 55101 · 612-291-1215

Roger A. Jensen · (Labor) · Peterson, Bell, Converse & Jensen · 2100 American National Bank Building · St. Paul, MN 55101 · 612-224-4703

Thomas P. Kane · (Management) · Oppenheimer Wolff and Donnelly · 1700 First Bank Building · St. Paul, MN 55101 · 612-227-7271

Eric R. Miller · (Labor) · Oppenheimer Wolff and Donnelly · 1700 First Bank Building · St. Paul, MN 55101 · 612-227-7271

James C. O'Neill · (Individuals) · 425 Hamm Building · St. Paul, MN 55102 · 612-222-7463

Thomas M. Vogt · (Management) · Felhaber, Larson, Fenlon and Vogt · 900 Meritor Tower · 444 Cedar Street · St. Paul, MN 55101 · 612-222-6321

NATURAL RESOURCES AND ENVIRONMENTAL LAW

Charles K. Dayton · (Logging) · Leonard, Street and Deinard · 150 South Fifth Street, Suite 2300 · Minneapolis, MN 55402 · 612-335-1500

Raymond A. Haik · Popham, Haik, Schnobrich & Kaufman · 3300 Piper Jaffray Tower · 222 South Ninth Street · Minneapolis, MN 55402 · 612-333-4800

John H. Herman · (Logging) · Leonard, Street and Deinard · 150 South Fifth Street, Suite 2300 · Minneapolis, MN 55402 · 612-335-1500

James B. Loken · Faegre & Benson · 2300 Multifoods Tower · 33 South Sixth Street · Minneapolis, MN 55402-3694 · 612-371-5300

Brian B. O'Neill · (Plaintiffs) · Faegre & Benson · 2300 Multifoods Tower · 33 South Sixth Street · Minneapolis, MN 55402-3694 · 612-371-5300

PERSONAL INJURY LITIGATION

Romaine R. Powell · Powell, Lang & Schueppert · 713 Beltrami Avenue · Bemidji, MN 56601 · 218-751-5650

Richard L. Pemberton · Rufer & Hefte · Law Office Building · Fergus Falls, MN 56537 · 218-736-5493

Robert M. Austin · (Defendants) · Austin & Roth · 715 Cargill Building · Northstar Center · Minneapolis, MN 55402 · 612-332-4273

Richard A. Bowman · (Defendants) · Bowman and Brooke · Midwest Plaza West, Suite 600 · 801 Nicollet Mall · Minneapolis, MN 55402 · 612-339-8682

Tyrone P. Bujold · (Plaintiffs) · Robins, Zelle, Larson & Kaplan · 1800 International Centre · 900 Second Avenue South · Minneapolis, MN 55402-3394 · 612-349-8500

Michael V. Ciresi · (Plaintiffs) · Robins, Zelle, Larson & Kaplan · 1800 International Centre · 900 Second Avenue South · Minneapolis, MN 55402-3394 612-349-8500

Phillip A. Cole · (Defendants) · Lommen, Nelson, Cole & Stageberg · 1100 TCF Tower · Minneapolis, MN 55402 · 612-339-8131

William T. Egan · (Defendants) · Rider, Bennett, Egan & Arundel · 2500 First Bank Place West · Minneapolis, MN 55402 · 612-340-7951

James L. Fetterly · (Plaintiffs) · Fetterly & Gordon · 808 Nicollet Mall, Suite 800 Minneapolis, MN 55402 · 612-333-2003

David F. Fitzgerald · (Defendants) · Rider, Bennett, Egan & Arundel · 2500 First Bank Place West · Minneapolis, MN 55402 · 612-340-7951

James Fitzmaurice · (Defendants) · Faegre & Benson · 2300 Multifoods Tower 33 South Sixth Street · Minneapolis, MN 55402-3694 · 612-371-5300

William D. Flaskamp · (Defendants) · Meagher, Geer, Markham, Anderson, Adamson, Flaskamp & Brennan · 4200 Multifoods Tower · Minneapolis, MN 55402 · 612-338-0661

Ludwig B. Gartner, Jr. · (Defendants) · Faegre & Benson · 2300 Multifoods Tower · 33 South Sixth Street · Minneapolis, MN 55402-3694 · 612-371-5300

Richard G. Hunegs · (Plaintiffs) · DeParcq, Perl, Hunegs, Rudquist & Koenig 608 Second Avenue South, Room 565 · Minneapolis, MN 55402 · 612-339-4511

James R. Schwebel · (Plaintiffs) · Schwebel, Goetz & Sieben · 5120 IDS Center 80 South Eighth Street · Minneapolis, MN 55402 · 612-333-8361

Mark N. Stageberg · (Defendants) · Lommen, Nelson, Cole & Stageberg · 1100 TCF Tower · Minneapolis, MN 55402 · 612-339-8131

Lynn G. Truesdell III · (Defendants) · Bassford, Heckt, Lockhart, Truesdell & Briggs · 3550 Multifoods Tower · Minneapolis, MN 55402-3787 · 612-333-3000

Gunder D. Gunhaus · (Defendants) · Gunhaus, Grinnell, Klinger, Swenson & Guy · 512 Center Avenue · P.O. Box 1077 · Moorehead, MN 56560-1077 · 218-236-6462

C. Allen Dosland · (Defendants) · Gislason, Dosland, Hunter and Malecki · State and Center Streets · New Ulm, MN 56073 · 507-354-3111

Robert R. Dunlap · (Defendants) · Dunlap, Keith, Finseth, Berndt & Sandberg 505 Marquette Bank Building · P.O. Box 549 · Rochester, MN 55903 · 507-288-9111

Richard R. Quinlivan · (Defendants) · Quinlivan, Sherwood, Spellacy & Tarvestad · Norwest Center, Sixth Floor · 400 First Street South · P.O. Box 1619 · St. Cloud, MN 56302 · 612-251-1414

Thomas M. Conlin · (Defendants) · Murnane, Conlin, White, Brandt & Hoffman One Capital Centre Plaza, Suite 1400 · Wabasha at Sixth Street · St. Paul, MN 55102 · 612-227-9411

John F. Eisberg · (Plaintiffs) · Robins, Zelle, Larson & Kaplan · 1500 Amhoist Tower · 345 Saint Peter Street · St. Paul, MN 55102-1638 · 612-224-5884

Boyd H. Ratchye · (Defendants) · Doherty, Rumble & Butler · 2800 Minnesota World Trade Center · 30 East Seventh Street · St. Paul, MN 55101 · 612-291-9333

Russell M. Spence · (Plaintiffs) · Meshbesher, Singer & Spence · 2020 Amhoist Tower · St. Paul, MN 55102 · 612-227-0799

Robert T. White · (Defendants) · Murnane, Conlin, White, Brandt & Hoffman · One Capital Centre Plaza, Suite 1400 · Wabasha at Sixth Street · St. Paul, MN 55102 · 612-227-9411

REAL ESTATE LAW

Allan E. Mulligan · Larkin, Hoffman, Daly & Lindgren · Northwestern Financial Center, Suite 1500 · 7900 Xerxes Avenue South · Bloomington, MN 55431 · 612-835-3800

William M. Burns · Hanft, Fride, O'Brien, Harries, Swelbar & Burns · 1000 First Bank Place · Duluth, MN 55802 · 218-722-4766

Paul J. Lokken · Hanft, Fride, O'Brien, Harries, Swelbar & Burns · 1000 First Bank Place · Duluth, MN 55802 · 218-722-4766

William G. Bale · Hillstrom & Bale · 607 Marquette Avenue, Suite 10 · Minneapolis, MN 55402 · 612-332-8063

Philip F. Boelter · Dorsey & Whitney · 2200 First Bank Place East · Minneapolis, MN 55402 · 612-340-2600

John T. Candell · Hagerty & Candell · 701 Fourth Avenue, Suite 1700 · Minneapolis, MN 55415 · 612-349-9000

John R. Carroll · Best and Flanagan · 3500 IDS Center · Minneapolis, MN 55402 · 612-339-7121

John S. Crouch · Gray, Plant, Mooty, Mooty & Bennett · 3400 City Center · 33 South Sixth Street · Minneapolis, MN 55402 · 612-343-2800

Stephen J. Davis · 3910 Multifoods Tower · 33 South Sixth Street · Minneapolis, MN 55402 · 612-341-0300

James B. Druck · Halpern & Druck · 1709 Northstar West Building · Minneapolis, MN 55402 · 612-339-7666

James A. Dueholm · Faegre & Benson · 2300 Multifoods Tower · 33 South Sixth Street · Minneapolis, MN 55402-3694 · 612-371-5300

Thomas S. Erickson · Dorsey & Whitney · 2200 First Bank Place East · Minneapolis, MN 55402 · 612-340-2600

Charles S. Ferrell · Faegre & Benson · 2300 Multifoods Tower · 33 South Sixth Street · Minneapolis, MN 55402-3694 · 612-371-5300

Duane E. Joseph · Dorsey & Whitney · 2200 First Bank Place East · Minneapolis, MN 55402 · 612-340-2600

Richard H. Massopust · Oppenheimer Wolff and Donnelly · 45 South Seventh Street, Suite 3400 · Minneapolis, MN 55402 · 612-344-9300

Thomas M. Mayerle · Faegre & Benson · 2300 Multifoods Tower · 33 South Sixth Street · Minneapolis, MN 55402-3694 · 612-371-5300

Melvin R. Mooty · Gray, Plant, Mooty, Mooty & Bennett · 3400 City Center · 33 South Sixth Street · Minneapolis, MN 55402 · 612-343-2800

Paul H. Ravich · Robins, Zelle, Larson & Kaplan · 1800 International Centre · 900 Second Avenue South · Minneapolis, MN 55402-3394 · 612-349-8500

Frederic T. Rosenblatt · Leonard, Street and Deinard · 150 South Fifth Street, Suite 2300 · Minneapolis, MN 55402 · 612-335-1500

Robert J. Silverman · Dorsey & Whitney · 2200 First Bank Place East · Minneapolis, MN 55402 · 612-340-2600

John W. Thiel · Gray, Plant, Mooty, Mooty & Bennett · 3400 City Center · 33 South Sixth Street · Minneapolis, MN 55402 · 612-343-2800

Mark W. Westra · Fabyanske, Svoboda, Westra & Davis · International Center 11, Suite 1150 · 920 Second Avenue South · Minneapolis, MN 55402 · 612-338-0115

Charles R. Haynor · Briggs and Morgan · 2400 IDS Center · St. Paul, MN 55402 612-339-0661

TAX AND EMPLOYEE BENEFITS LAW

Paul J. Lokken · Hanft, Fride, O'Brien, Harries, Swelbar & Burns · 1000 First Bank Place · Duluth, MN 55802 · 218-722-4766

James H. Stewart · Fryberger, Buchanan, Smith & Frederick · 700 Lonsdale Building · Duluth, MN 55802 · 218-722-0861

David R. Brennan · Faegre & Benson · 2300 Multifoods Tower · 33 South Sixth Street · Minneapolis, MN 55402-3694 · 612-371-5300

Don D. Carlson · (Employee Benefits) · Dorsey & Whitney · 2200 First Bank Place East · Minneapolis, MN 55402 · 612-340-2600

Jack W. Carlson · Thomsen, Nybeck, Johnson, Bouquet, Van Valkenburg, Ohmstad & Smith · 3300 Edinborough Way, Suite 600 · Minneapolis, MN 55435 612-835-7000

Hubert V. Forsier · (Employee Benefits) · Faegre & Benson · 2300 Multifoods Tower · 33 South Sixth Street · Minneapolis, MN 55402-3694 · 612-371-5300

Gene N. Fuller · Larkin, Hoffman, Daly & Lindgren · Piper Jaffray Tower, Suite 2000 · 222 South Ninth Street · Minneapolis, MN 55402 · 612-338-6610

Bruce D. Grussing · (Employee Benefits) · Gray, Plant, Mooty, Mooty & Bennett 3400 City Center · 33 South Sixth Street · Minneapolis, MN 55402 · 612-343-2800

George E. Harding · (Employee Benefits) · Faegre & Benson · 2300 Multifoods Tower · 33 South Sixth Street · Minneapolis, MN 55402-3694 · 612-371-5300

William H. Hippee, Jr. · Dorsey & Whitney · 2200 First Bank Place East · Minneapolis, MN 55402 · 612-340-2600

John S. Jagiela · Oppenheimer Wolff and Donnelly · 3400 Plaza VII · 45 South Seventh Street · Minneapolis, MN 55402 · 612-344-9300

Judith Dowdle Lindquist · (Employee Benefits) · Gray, Plant, Mooty, Mooty & Bennett · 3400 City Center · 33 South Sixth Street · Minneapolis, MN 55402 612-343-2800

James W. Littlefield · Hart, Bruner & O'Brien · 1221 Nicollet Mall, Seventh Floor · Minneapolis, MN 55403 · 612-332-1431

Phillip H. Martin · Dorsey & Whitney · 2200 First Bank Place East · Minneapolis, MN 55402 · 612-340-2600

John M. Nichols · (Employee Benefits) · Gray, Plant, Mooty, Mooty & Bennett 3400 City Center · 33 South Sixth Street · Minneapolis, MN 55402 · 612-343-2800

Burton G. Ross · Ross, Faulken & Rosenblatt · 4000 Piper Jaffray Tower · 222 South Ninth Street · Minneapolis, MN 55402 · 612-338-0888

Clinton A. Schroeder · Gray, Plant, Mooty, Mooty & Bennett · 3400 City Center 33 South Sixth Street · Minneapolis, MN 55402 · 612-343-2800

Bruce J. Shnider · Dorsey & Whitney · 2200 First Bank Place East · Minneapolis, MN 55402 · 612-340-2600

John K. Steffen · Faegre & Benson · 2300 Multifoods Tower · 33 South Sixth Street · Minneapolis, MN 55402-3694 · 612-371-5300

John W. Windhorst, Jr. · Dorsey & Whitney · 2200 First Bank Place East · Minneapolis, MN 55402 · 612-340-2600

Kimball J. Devoy · Doherty, Rumble & Butler · 2800 Minnesota World Trade Center · 30 East Seventh Street · St. Paul, MN 55101 · 612-291-9333

Jerome A. Geis · Briggs and Morgan · West 2200 First National Bank Building · St. Paul, MN 55101 · 612-291-1215

John P. Schmidtke · (Employee Benefits) · Oppenheimer Wolff and Donnelly 1700 First Bank Building · St. Paul, MN 55101 · 612-227-7271

TRUSTS AND ESTATES

Richard R. Burns · Hanft, Fride, O'Brien, Harries, Swelbar & Burns · 1000 First Bank Place · Duluth, MN 55802 · 218-722-4766

Mark T. Signorelli · Brown, Andrew, Hallenbeck, Signorelli & Zallar · Alworth Building, Suite 300 · Duluth, MN 55802 · 218-722-1764

Edward M. Arundel · Rider, Bennett, Egan & Arundel · 2500 First Bank Place West · Minneapolis, MN 55402 · 612-340-7951

John P. Byron · Fredrikson & Byron · 1100 International Centre · 900 Second Avenue South · Minneapolis, MN 55402 · 612-347-7000

Robert L. Crosby · Best and Flanagan · 3500 IDS Center · Minneapolis, MN 55402 · 612-339-7121

Patrick F. Flaherty · Moss & Barnett · 1200 Pillsbury Center · 200 South Sixth Street · Minneapolis, MN 55402 · 612-339-8551

John E. Harris · Faegre & Benson · 2300 Multifoods Tower · 33 South Sixth Street · Minneapolis, MN 55402-3694 · 612-371-5300

Edward G. Heilman · Faegre & Benson · 2300 Multifoods Tower · 33 South Sixth Street · Minneapolis, MN 55402-3694 · 612-371-5300

Larry R. Henneman · Rider, Bennett, Egan & Arundel · 2500 First Bank Place West · Minneapolis, MN 55402 · 612-340-7951

Larry W. Johnson · Dorsey & Whitney · 2200 First Bank Place East · Minneapolis, MN 55402 · 612-340-2600

Sidney Kaplan · Mackall, Crounse & Moore · 1600 TCF Tower · 121 South Eighth Street · Minneapolis, MN 55402 · 612-333-1341

Faith L. Ohman · Dorsey & Whitney · 2200 First Bank Place East · Minneapolis, MN 55402 · 612-340-2600

John L. Powers · Fredrikson & Byron · 1100 International Centre · 900 Second Avenue South · Minneapolis, MN 55402 · 612-347-7000

Raymond A. Reister · Dorsey & Whitney · 2200 First Bank Place East · Minneapolis, MN 55402 · 612-340-2600

Richard C. Schmoker · Faegre & Benson · 2300 Multifoods Tower · 33 South Sixth Street · Minneapolis, MN 55402-3694 · 612-371-5300

Robert A. Stein · Gray, Plant, Mooty, Mooty & Bennett · 3400 City Center · 33 South Sixth Street · Minneapolis, MN 55402 · 612-343-2800

Robert J. Struyk · Dorsey & Whitney · 2200 First Bank Place East · Minneapolis, MN 55402 · 612-340-2600

Robert G. Weber · Fredrikson & Byron · 1100 International Centre · 900 Second Avenue South · Minneapolis, MN 55402 · 612-347-7000

John R. Wicks · Dorsey & Whitney · 340 First National Bank Building · P.O. Box 848 · Rochester, MN 55902 · 507-288-3156

Steve A. Brand · Briggs and Morgan · West 2200 First National Bank Building · St. Paul, MN 55101 · 612-291-1215

Robert L. Bullard · Oppenheimer Wolff and Donnelly · West 1700 First Bank Building · St. Paul, MN 55101 · 612-227-7271

Terence N. Doyle · Briggs and Morgan · West 2200 First National Bank Building · St. Paul, MN 55101 · 612-291-1215

John L. Hannaford · Doherty, Rumble & Butler · 2800 Minnesota World Trade Center · 30 East Seventh Street · St. Paul, MN 55101 · 612-291-9333

John C. Johanneson · Maun, Green, Hayes, Simon, Johanneson and Brehl · 332 Hamm Building · St. Paul, MN 55102 · 612-224-7300

John J. McNeely · Briggs and Morgan · West 2200 First National Bank Building · St. Paul, MN 55101 · 612-291-1215

Cole Oehler · Briggs and Morgan · West 2200 First National Bank Building · St. Paul, MN 55101 · 612-291-1215

Lehan J. Ryan · Oppenheimer Wolff and Donnelly · 1700 First Bank Building · St. Paul, MN 55101 · 612-227-7271

McNeil V. Seymour, Jr. · Briggs and Morgan · West 2200 First National Bank Building · St. Paul, MN 55101 · 612-291-1215

Richard A. Wilhoit · Doherty, Rumble & Butler · 2800 Minnesota World Trade Center · 30 East Seventh Street · St. Paul, MN 55101· 612-291-9333

MISSISSIPPI

BANKRUPTCY LAW	375
BUSINESS LITIGATION	376
CORPORATE LAW	376
CRIMINAL DEFENSE	378
FAMILY LAW	378
LABOR AND EMPLOYMENT LAW	378
NATURAL RESOURCES AND ENVIRONMENTAL LAW	379
PERSONAL INJURY LITIGATION	380
REAL ESTATE LAW	381
TAX AND EMPLOYEE BENEFITS LAW	382
TRUSTS AND ESTATES	382

BANKRUPTCY LAW

Jefferson C. Bell · 216 West Pine Street · Hattiesburg, MS 39401 · 601-582-5011

Richard T. Bennett · Bennett, Lotterhos, Sulser & Wilson · 200 North State Street · P.O. Box 98 · Jackson, MS 39205 · 601-944-0466

Robert W. King · King & Spencer · Court Square South Building · 429 Tombigbee Street · P.O. Box 123 · Jackson, MS 39205 · 601-948-1547

Robert G. Nichols, Jr. · Unifirst Federal Savings Building · Jackson, MS 39201 · 601-354-4057

James W. O'Mara · Butler, Snow, O'Mara, Stevens & Cannada · Deposit Guaranty Plaza, 17th Floor · P.O. Box 22567 · Jackson, MS 39205 · 601-948-5711

Pat H. Scanlon · Young, Scanlon and Sessums · 2000 Deposit Guaranty Plaza · Jackson, MS 39201 · 601-948-6100

BUSINESS LITIGATION

Fred C. DeLong, Jr. · Campbell, DeLong, Hagwood, Wade & Stuart · 923 Washington Avenue · P.O. Box 1856 · Greenville, MS 38701 · 601-335-6011

W. Joel Blass · Mize, Thompson & Blass · Gulf National Bank Building, Suite 310 · P.O. Box 160 · Gulfport, MS 39502 · 601-863-2612

Rowland W. Heidelberg · Heidelberg, Sutherland and McKenzie · The 301 West Pine Building · P.O. Box 1070 · Hattiesburg, MS 39401 · 601-545-8180

Frank D. Montague, Jr. · Montague, Pittman & Schwartz · 525 Main Street · P.O. Drawer 1975, · Hattiesburg, MS 39401 · 601-544-1234

Alex A. Alston, Jr. · Thomas, Price, Alston, Jones & Davis · 121 North State Street · P.O. Drawer 1532 · Jackson, MS 39215-1532 · 601-948-6882

Lawrence J. Franck · Butler, Snow, O'Mara, Stevens & Cannada · 1700 Deposit Guaranty Plaza, 17th Floor · P.O. Box 22567 · Jackson, MS 39205 · 601-948-5711

William F. Goodman, Jr. · Watkins & Eager · 120 North Congress Street, Suite 800 · P.O. Box 650 · Jackson, MS 39205 · 601-948-6470

George P. Hewes III · Brunini, Grantham, Grower & Hewes · 1400 Trustmark Building · P.O. Drawer 119 · Jackson, MS 39205 · 601-948-3101

Alan W. Perry · Forman, Perry, Watkins, Krutz & McNamara · One Jackson Place, Suite 1200 · P.O. Box 22608 · Jackson, MS 39225-2608 · 601-969-6011

Thomas D. Bourdeaux · Bourdeaux and Jones · 505 Twenty-First Avenue · P.O. Box 2009 · Meridian, MS 39301 · 601-693-2393

CORPORATE LAW

Fred C. DeLong, Jr. · Campbell, DeLong, Hagwood, Wade & Stuart · 923 Washington Avenue · P.O. Box 1856 · Greenville, MS 38701 · 601-335-6011

W. Joel Blass · Mize, Thompson & Blass · Gulf National Bank Building, Suite 310 · P.O. Box 160 · Gulfport, MS 39501 · 601-863-2612

Charles R. Galloway · Galloway & Galloway · 1300 Twenty-Fifth Avenue, Suite 204 · P.O. Drawer 4248 · Gulfport, MS 39502 · 601-864-1170

George E. Morse · White & Morse · One Hancock Plaza, Suite 1209 · P.O. Drawer 100 · Gulfport, MS 39501 · 601-863-9821

James F. McKenzie · Heidelberg, Sutherland and McKenzie · The 301 West Pine Building · P.O. Box 1070 · Hattiesburg, MS 39401 · 601-545-8180

Frank D. Montague, Jr. · Montague, Pittman & Schwartz · 525 Main Street P.O. Box 1975 · Hattiesburg, MS 39401 · 601-544-1234

Leigh B. Allen III · Brunini, Grantham, Grower & Hewes · 1400 Trustmark Building · P.O. Drawer 119 · Jackson, MS 39205 · 601-948-3101

Robert C. Cannada · Butler, Snow, O'Mara, Stevens & Cannada · Deposit Guaranty Plaza, 17th Floor · P.O. Box 22567 · Jackson, MS 39205 · 601-948-5711

William O. Carter, Jr. · Wise Carter Child & Caraway · 600 Heritage Building Congress at Capitol · P.O. Box 651 · Jackson, MS 39205 · 601-354-2385

George R. Fair · Watkins & Eager · 120 North Congress Street, Suite 800 · P.O. Box 650 · Jackson, MS 39205 · 601-948-6470

E. Clifton Hodge, Jr. · Phelps, Dunbar, Marks, Claverie & Sims · Mirror Lake Plaza, Suite 1400 · 2829 Lakeland Drive · P.O. Box 55507 · Jackson, MS 39216 601-939-3895

William Steene Painter · Watkins Ludlam & Stennis · Deposit Guaranty Plaza, 20th Floor · 633 North State Street · P.O. Box 427 · Jackson, MS 39205 601-949-4900

Edward A. Wilmesherr · Butler, Snow, O'Mara, Stevens & Cannada · Deposit Guaranty Plaza, 17th Floor · P.O. Box 22567 · Jackson, MS 39205 · 601-948-5711

Thomas D. Bourdeaux · Bourdeaux and Jones · 505 Twenty-First Avenue · P.O. Box 2009 · Meridian, MS 39301 · 601-693-2393

F. M. Bush III · Mitchell, McNutt, Bush, Lagrone & Sams · 316 Court Street P.O. Box 466 · Tupelo, MS 38802-0648 · 601-842-3871

Fred M. Bush, Jr. · Mitchell, McNutt, Bush, Lagrone & Sams · 316 Court Street P.O. Box 466 · Tupelo, MS 38802-0648 · 601-842-3871

CRIMINAL DEFENSE

John Booth Farese · Farese, Farese & Farese · P.O. Box 98 · Ashland, MS 38603
601-224-6211

Boyce Holleman · 1913 Fifteenth Street · P.O. Drawer 1030 · Gulfport, MS 39502
601-863-3142

Weaver E. Gore, Jr. · 616 Unifirst Federal Savings Building · P.O. Box 186 Jackson, MS 39205 · 601-354-4057

William Sebastian Moore · 499 South President Street · Jackson, MS 39201
601-969-1222

Thomas E. Royals · Royals, Hartung & Davis · Eastover Bank Building, Suite 1225 · P.O. Box 864 · Jackson, MS 39205 · 601-948-7777

FAMILY LAW

Joseph R. Meadows · Meadows & Riley · 1720 Twenty-Third Avenue · P.O. Drawer 550 · Gulfport, MS 39501 · 601-864-4511

James A. Becker, Jr. · Watkins & Eager · 120 North Congress Street, Suite 800 P.O. Box 650 · Jackson, MS 39205 · 601-948-6470

L. C. James · 105 North State Street · Jackson, MS 39201 · 601-354-0797

LABOR AND EMPLOYMENT LAW

Danny E. Cupit · (Labor; Individuals) · Cupit & Maxey · 304 North Congress Street · P.O. Box 22666 · Jackson, MS 39205 · 601-355-1553

Louis A. Fuselier · (Management) · Fuselier, Ott, McKee & Walker · 2100 Deposit Guaranty Plaza · Jackson, MS 39201 · 601-948-2226

John L. Maxey II · (Labor; Individuals) · Cupit & Maxey · 304 North Congress Street · P.O. Box 22666 · Jackson, MS 39205 · 601-355-1553

M. Curtiss McKee · (Management) · Fuselier, Ott, McKee & Walker · 2100 Deposit Guaranty Plaza · Jackson, MS 39201 · 601-948-2226

Kenneth E. Milam · (Management) · Miller, Milam & Moeller · State and Capitol Streets · P.O. Box 3439 · Jackson, MS 39225-3439 · 601-948-3131

Armin J. Moeller · (Management) · Miller, Milam & Moeller · State and Capitol Streets · P.O. Box 3439 · Jackson, MS 39225-3439 · 601-948-3131

Emile C. Ott · (Management) · Fuselier, Ott, McKee & Walker · 2100 Deposit Guaranty Plaza · Jackson, MS 39201 · 601-948-2226

NATURAL RESOURCES AND ENVIRONMENTAL LAW

Alex A. Alston, Jr. · (Plaintiffs) · Thomas, Price, Alston, Jones & Davis · 121 North State Street · P.O. Drawer 1532 · Jackson, MS 39215-1532 · 601-948-6882

Thomas R. Crews · Thompson, Alexander & Crews · Thompson Building · 118 North Congress Street · P.O. Box 410 · Jackson, MS 39205 · 601-948-4831

Martha W. Gerald · Gerald, Brand, Watters, Cox & Hemleben · 317 East Capitol Street · P.O. Box 158 · Jackson, MS 39205 · 601-948-3030

John M. Grower · Brunini, Grantham, Grower & Hewes · 1400 Trustmark Building · P.O. Drawer 119 · Jackson, MS 39205 · 601-948-3101

Scott P. Hemleben · (Oil & Gas) · Gerald, Brand, Watters, Cox & Hemleben · 317 East Capitol Street · P.O. Box 158 · Jackson, MS 39205 · 601-948-3030

Otis Johnson, Jr. · (Oil & Gas) · Heidelberg, Woodliff & Franks · Capital Towers, Suite 1400 · Jackson, MS 39201 · 601-948-3800

John Land McDavid · (Oil & Gas) · McDavid, Noblin & West · 200 Security Centre North, Suite 1000 · 210 South Lamar Street · Jackson, MS 39201 601-948-3305

Jefferson D. Stewart · Brunini, Grantham, Grower & Hewes · 1400 Trustmark Building · P.O. Drawer 119 · Jackson, MS 39205 · 601-948-3101

Glenn G. Taylor · (Oil & Gas) · Copeland Cook Taylor & Bush · Capital Towers Building, Suite 112 · 125 South Congress Street · P.O. Drawer 2132 · Jackson, MS 39225-2132 · 601-354-0123

William Marion Smith · Adams, Forman, Truly, Smith & Bramlette · 409 Franklin Street · P.O. Box 1307 · Natchez, MS 39120 · 601-442-6495

PERSONAL INJURY LITIGATION

Charles M. Merkel · (Plaintiffs) · Merkel & Cocke · 30 Delta Avenue · P.O. Box 1388 · Clarksdale, MS 38614 · 601-627-9641

William J. Threadgill · (Defendants) · Threadgill, Smith, Sanders & Jolly · 215 Fifth Street North · P.O. Box 1366 · Columbus, MS 39701 · 601-328-2316

Fred C. DeLong, Jr. · (Defendants) · Campbell, DeLong, Hagwood, Wade & Stuart · 923 Washington Avenue · P.O. Box 1856 · Greenville, MS 38701 601-335-6011

Harry R. Allen · (Defendants) · Bryan, Nelson, Allen, Schroeder and Cobb · 1201 Thirty-First Avenue · P.O. Drawer 4108 · Gulfport, MS 39502 · 601-864-4011

Rae Bryant · (Defendants) · Bryant, Stennis & Colingo · 2223 Fourteenth Street P.O. Box 10 · Gulfport, MS 39501 · 601-863-6101

Boyce Holleman · 1913 Fifteenth Street · P.O. Drawer 1030 · Gulfport, MS 39502 601-863-3142

Rowland W. Heidelberg · (Defendants) · Heidelberg, Sutherland and McKenzie The 301 West Pine Building · P.O. Box 1070 · Hattiesburg, MS 39401 601-545-8180

Curtis E. Coker · (Defendants) · Daniel, Coker, Horton and Bell · 111 East Capitol Building, Suite 600 · P.O. Box 1084 · Jackson, MS 39205 · 601-969-7607

James P. Cothren · (Plaintiffs) · Cothren & Pittman · 410 South Presidents Street P.O. Box 22985 · Jackson, MS 39201 · 601-948-6151

Joe H. Daniel · (Defendants) · Daniel, Coker, Horton and Bell · 111 East Capitol Building, Suite 600 · P.O. Box 1084 · Jackson, MS 39205 · 601-969-7607

Lawrence J. Franck · (Defendants) · Butler, Snow, O'Mara, Stevens & Cannada Deposit Guaranty Plaza, 17th Floor · P.O. Box 22567 · Jackson, MS 39205 601-948-5711

William F. Goodman, Jr. · (Defendants) · Watkins & Eager · 120 North Congress Street, Suite 800 · P.O. Box 650 · Jackson, MS 39205 · 601-948-6470

Lee Davis Thames · (Defendants) · Butler, Snow, O'Mara, Stevens & Cannada Deposit Guaranty Plaza, 17th Floor · P.O. Box 22567 · Jackson, MS 39205 601-948-5711

Ernest W. Graves · (Defendants) · Gibbes, Graves, Mullins, Bullock & Ferris · 1107 West Sixth Street · P.O. Box 1409 · Laurel, MS 39441-1409 · 601-649-8611

Leonard B. Melvin, Jr. · (Plaintiffs) · Melvin & Melvin · 424 Sawmill Road · P.O. Box 142 · Laurel, MS 39441 · 601-426-6306

Thomas D. Bourdeaux · (Defendants) · Bourdeaux and Jones · 505 Twenty-First Avenue · P.O. Box 2009 · Meridian, MS 39301 · 601-693-2393

Walter W. Eppes, Jr. · (Defendants) · Eppes, Watts & Shannon · 4805 Poplar Springs Drive · P.O. Box 3787 · Meridian, MS 39303-3787 · 601-483-3968

Jack F. Dunbar · Holcomb, Dunbar, Connell, Chaffin & Willard · Courthouse Square · 1217 Jackson Avenue · P.O. Box 707 · Oxford, MS 38655 · 601-234-9775

Grady F. Tollison, Jr. · Tollison and Alexander · 103 North Lamar Avenue · P.O. Box 1216 · Oxford, MS 38655 · 601-234-7070

L. F. Sams, Jr. · (Defendants) · Mitchell, McNutt, Bush, Lagrone & Sams · 316 Court Street · P.O. Drawer 648 · Tupelo, MS 38802-0648 · 601-842-3871

William H. Liston · (Plaintiffs) · Liston, Gibson & Lancaster · 128 North Quitman Avenue · P.O. Box 645 · Winona, MS 38967 · 601-283-2132

REAL ESTATE LAW

Charles K. Pringle · 415 Vieux Marche · P.O. Box 211 · Biloxi, MS 39533 · 601-374-1747

Walter Rayford Jones · Jones, Jones & Jones · 1605 Twenty-Third Avenue · P.O. Box 4227 · Gulfport, MS 39501 · 601-864-8965

James F. McKenzie · Heidelberg, Sutherland and McKenzie · The 301 West Pine Building · P.O. Box 1070 · Hattiesburg, MS 39401 · 601-545-8180

Bobby L. Covington · Taylor, Covington & Smith · 315 Tombigee Street · Jackson, MS 39201 · 601-961-4861

Henry M. Kendall · Trustmark National Bank, Suite 537 · 248 East Capitol Street · P.O. Box 330 · Jackson, MS 39205 · 601-353-2797

William C. Smith, Jr. · Taylor, Covington & Smith · 315 Tombigee Street · Jackson, MS 39201 · 601-961-4861

Jim B. Tohill · Watkins, Ludlam & Stennis · 633 North State Street · P.O. Box 427 · Jackson, MS 39205 · 601-949-4900

TAX AND EMPLOYEE BENEFITS LAW

Paul M. Newton · Newton and Hoff · 2416 Fourteenth Street · P.O. Box 910 · Gulfport, MS 39501 · 601-863-8827

D. Carl Black, Jr. · (also Employee Benefits) · Butler, Snow, O'Mara, Stevens & Cannada · Deposit Guaranty Plaza, 17th Floor · P.O. Box 22567 · Jackson, MS 39205 · 601-948-5711

James K. Dossett, Jr. · Dossett, Goode, Barnes and Broom · Security Centre North, Suite 900 · 200 Lamar Street · P.O. Box 2449 · Jackson, MS 39225-2449 · 601-948-3160

David B. Grishman · Watkins Ludlam & Stennis · 633 North State Street · P.O. Box 427 · Jackson, MS 39205 · 601-949-4900

C. Delbert Hosemann, Jr. · (Employee Benefits) · Phelps, Dunbar, Marks, Claverie & Sims · Mirror Lake Plaza, Suite 1400 · 2829 Lakeland Drive · P.O. Box 55507 · Jackson, MS 39216 · 601-939-3895

Warren V. Ludlam, Jr. · Watkins Ludlam & Stennis · 633 North State Street · P.O. Box 427 · Jackson, MS 39205 · 601-949-4900

Lauch M. Magruder, Jr. · Magruder, Montgomery & Brocato · 1800 Deposit Guaranty Plaza · Jackson, MS 39201 · 601-354-5504

Hugh C. Montgomery, Jr. · Magruder, Montgomery & Brocato · 1800 Deposit Guaranty Plaza · Jackson, MS 39201 · 601-354-5504

TRUSTS AND ESTATES

Edward P. Connell · Holcomb, Dunbar, Connell, Chaffin & Willard · 152 Delta Avenue · P.O. Box 368 · Clarksdale, MS 38614 · 601-627-2241

Paul M. Newton · Newton and Hoff · 2416 Fourteenth Street · P.O. Box 910 · Gulfport, MS 39501 · 601-863-8827

Leigh B. Allen III · Brunini, Grantham, Grower & Hewes · 1400 Trustmark Building · P.O. Drawer 119 · Jackson, MS 39205 · 601-948-3101

D. Carl Black, Jr. · Butler, Snow, O'Mara, Stevens & Cannada · Deposit Guaranty Plaza, 17th Floor · P.O. Box 22567 · Jackson, MS 39205 · 601-948-5711

William O. Carter, Jr. · Wise Carter Child & Caraway · 600 Heritage Building Congress at Capitol · P.O. Box 651 · Jackson, MS 39205 · 601-354-2385

Lauch M. Magruder, Jr. · Magruder, Montgomery, Brocato & Hoseman · 1800 Deposit Guaranty Plaza · Jackson, MS 39201 · 601-354-5504

Jay A. Travis III · Butler, Snow, O'Mara, Stevens & Cannada · Deposit Guaranty Plaza, 17th Floor · P.O. Box 22567 · Jackson, MS 39205 · 601-948-5711

F. M. Bush III · Mitchell, McNutt, Bush, Lagrone & Sams · 105 Front Street P.O. Drawer 648 · Tupelo, MS 38802-0648 · 601-842-3871

MISSOURI

BANKRUPTCY LAW	384
BUSINESS LITIGATION	385
CORPORATE LAW	386
CRIMINAL DEFENSE	388
FAMILY LAW	388
LABOR AND EMPLOYMENT LAW	389
MARITIME LAW	391
NATURAL RESOURCES AND ENVIRONMENTAL LAW	391
PERSONAL INJURY LITIGATION	392
REAL ESTATE LAW	393
TAX AND EMPLOYEE BENEFITS LAW	395
TRUSTS AND ESTATES	397

BANKRUPTCY LAW

Arthur B. Federman · Linde Thompson Langworthy Kohn & Van Dyke · 2700 City Center Square · 12th & Baltimore · P.O. Box 26010 · Kansas City, MO 64196-6010 · 816-474-6420

James C. Mordy · Morrison, Hecker, Curtis, Kuder & Parrish · 1700 Bryant Building · 1102 Grand Avenue · Kansas City, MO 64106-2370 · 816-842-5910

Michael R. Rosen · Berman, DeLeve, Kuchan & Chapman · Home Savings Building, Suite 600 · 1006 Grand Avenue · Kansas City, MO 64106 · 816-471-5900

Mendel Small · Spencer, Fane, Britt & Browne · 1400 Commerce Bank Building 1000 Walnut Street · Kansas City, MO 64106-2140 · 816-474-8100

R. Pete Smith · McDowell, Rice & Smith · 12 Wyandotte Plaza, Suite 1300 · 120 West 12th Street · Kansas City, MO 64105 · 816-221-5400

Steven Goldstein · Husch, Eppenberger, Donohue, Cornfeld & Jenkins · The Boatmen's Tower, 13th Floor · 100 North Broadway · St. Louis, MO 63102 314-421-4800

David A. Lander · Thompson & Mitchell · One Mercantile Center, Suite 3400 St. Louis, MO 63101 · 314-421-4800

Lloyd A. Palans · Gallop, Johnson & Neuman · 101 South Hanley Road, Suite 1600 · St. Louis, MO 63105 · 314-862-1200

Gregory D. Willard · Bryan, Cave, McPheeters & McRoberts · 500 North Broadway · St. Louis, MO 63102-2186 · 314-231-8600

BUSINESS LITIGATION

Spencer Brown · Deacy & Deacy · 1000 Bryant Building · 1102 Grant Avenue Kansas City, MO 64106 · 816-421-4000

Reed O. Gentry · Field, Gentry, Benjamin & Robertson · 600 East 11th Street Kansas City, MO 64106 · 816-842-6031

John M. Kilroy · Shughart, Thomson & Kilroy · 12 Wyandotte Plaza, Suite 1800 120 West 12th Street · Kansas City, MO 64105 · 816-421-3355

William H. Sanders · Blackwell Sanders Matheny Weary & Lombardi · Two Pershing Square · 2300 Main Street, Suite 1100 · Kansas City, MO 64108 816-274-6800

R. Lawrence Ward · Shughart, Thomson & Kilroy · 12 Wyandotte Plaza, Suite 1800 · 120 West 12th Street · Kansas City, MO 64105 · 816-421-3355

Robert Smith Allen · Lewis & Rice · 611 Olive Street, 14th Floor · St. Louis, MO 63101 · 314-444-7600

John J. Cole · Armstrong, Teasdale, Kramer, Vaughan & Schlafley · 611 Olive Street, Suite 1900 · St. Louis, MO 63101 · 314-621-5070

Henry D. Menghini · Evans & Dixon · Marquette Building, 16th Floor · 314 North Broadway · St. Louis, MO 63102-2093 · 314-621-7755

William A. Richter · Peper, Martin, Jensen, Maichel and Hetlage · 720 Olive Street, 24th Floor · St. Louis, MO 63101 · 314-421-3850

Veryl L. Riddle · Bryan, Cave, McPheeters & McRoberts · 500 North Broadway St. Louis, MO 63102-2186 · 314-231-8600

John C. Shepherd · Shepherd, Sandberg & Phoenix · One City Centre, Suite 1500 · St. Louis, MO 63101 · 314-231-3332

Thomas E. Wack · Bryan, Cave, McPheeters & McRoberts · 500 North Broadway St. Louis, MO 63102-2186 · 314-231-8600

W. Stanley Walch · Thompson & Mitchell · One Mercantile Center, Suite 3400 St. Louis, MO 63101 · 314-231-7676

Thomas C. Walsh · Bryan, Cave, McPheeters & McRoberts · 500 North Broadway · St. Louis, MO 63102-2186 · 314-231-8600

CORPORATE LAW

John R. Bancroft · Morrison, Hecker, Curtis, Kuder & Parrish · 1700 Bryant Building · 1102 Grand Avenue · Kansas City, MO 64106-2370 · 816-842-5910

Thomas I. Gill · Smith, Gill, Fisher & Butts · One Kansas City Place, 36th Floor 1200 Main Street · Kansas City, MO 64105 · 816-474-7400

William A. Hirsch · Morrison, Hecker, Curtis, Kuder & Parrish · 1700 Bryant Building · 1102 Grand Avenue · Kansas City, MO 64106-2370 · 816-842-5910

Basil W. Kelsey · (Utilities) · Spencer, Fane, Britt & Browne · 1400 Commerce Bank Building · 1000 Walnut Street · Kansas City, MO 64106-2140 · 816-474-8100

Robert P. Lyons · Spencer, Fane, Britt & Browne · 1400 Commerce Bank Building · 1000 Walnut Street · Kansas City, MO 64106-2140 · 816-474-8100

John F. Marvin · Watson, Ess, Marshall & Enggas · 1010 Grand Avenue · Kansas City, MO 64106-2271 · 816-842-3132

Howard H. Mick · Stinson, Mag & Fizzell · 920 Main Street · P.O. Box 19251 Kansas City, MO 64141 · 816-842-8600

Richard N. Nixon · Stinson, Mag & Fizzell · 920 Main Street · P.O. Box 19251 Kansas City, MO 64141 · 816-842-8600

William M. Stapleton · Lathrop, Koontz & Norquist · 2600 Mutual Benefit Life Building · 2345 Grand Avenue · Kansas City, MO 64108 · 816-842-0820

Daniel C. Weary · Blackwell Sanders Matheny Weary & Lombardi · Two Pershing Square, Suite 1100 · 2300 Main Street · Kansas City, MO 64108 · 816-274-6800

Ralph G. Wrobley · Stinson, Mag & Fizzell · 920 Main Street · P.O. Box 19251 Kansas City, MO 64141 · 816-842-8600

Charles C. Allen, Jr. · Lewis & Rice · 611 Olive Street, 14th Floor · St. Louis, MO 63101 · 314-444-7600

Thomas V. Connelly · Bryan, Cave, McPheeters & McRoberts · 500 North Broadway · St. Louis, MO 63102-2186 · 314-231-8600

John J. Goebel · Bryan, Cave, McPheeters & McRoberts · 500 North Broadway St. Louis, MO 63102-2186 · 314-231-8600

Edward B. Greensfelder · Greensfelder, Hemker, Wiese, Gale & Chappelow 1800 Equitable Building · Ten South Broadway · St. Louis, MO 63102 · 314-241-9090

William G. Guerri · Thompson & Mitchell · One Mercantile Center, Suite 3400 St. Louis, MO 63101 · 314-231-7676

George A. Jensen · Peper, Martin, Jensen, Maichel and Hetlage · 720 Olive Street, 24th Floor · St. Louis, MO 63101 · 314-421-3850

Don G. Lents · Bryan, Cave, McPheeters & McRoberts · 500 North Broadway St. Louis, MO 63102-2186 · 314-231-8600

John V. Lonsberg · Bryan, Cave, McPheeters & McRoberts · 500 North Broadway · St. Louis, MO 63102-2186 · 314-231-8600

Walter L. Metcalfe, Jr. · Bryan, Cave, McPheeters & McRoberts · 500 North Broadway · St. Louis, MO 63102-2186 · 314-231-8600

Paul F. Pautler · Thompson & Mitchell · One Mercantile Center, Suite 3400 · St. Louis, MO 63101 · 314-231-7676

Robert L. Sweney · Bryan, Cave, McPheeters & McRoberts · 500 North Broadway · St. Louis, MO 63102-2186 · 314-231-8600

David F. Ulmer · Thompson & Mitchell · One Mercantile Center, Suite 3400 · St. Louis, MO 63101 · 314-231-7676

W. Stanley Walch · Thompson & Mitchell · One Mercantile Center, Suite 3400 St. Louis, MO 63101 · 314-231-7676

Bruce E. Woodruff · Armstrong, Teasdale, Kramer, Vaughan & Schlafley · 611 Olive Street, Suite 1900 · St. Louis, MO 63101 · 314-621-5070

CRIMINAL DEFENSE

Charles A. Shaw · 225 South Meramec, Suite 324T · Clayton, MO 63105 · 314-725-9700

Robert C. Welch · Paden, Welch, Martin & Albano · Law Building · 311 West Kansas Avenue · Independence, MO 64050 · 816-836-8000

Robert Beaird · Quinn, Peebles, Beaird & Cardarella · 1104 Oak Street · Kansas City, MO 64106 · 816-471-3100

Robert G. Duncan · Duncan, Coulson & Schloss · 2800-B Kendallwood Parkway Kansas City, MO 64119 · 816-455-0555

Gerald M. Handley · Speck and Handley · 1125 Grand Avenue, Suite 1804 Kansas City, MO 64106 · 816-471-7145

David W. Russell · Koenigsdorf, Wyrsch & Ramsey · Home Savings Building, Suite 1050 · 1006 Grand Avenue · Kansas City, MO 64106 · 816-221-0080

James R. Wyrsch · Koenigsdorf, Wyrsch & Ramsey · Home Savings Building, Suite 1050 · 1006 Grand Avenue · Kansas City, MO 64106 · 816-221-0080

Irl B. Baris · 611 Olive Street, Suite 2020 · St. Louis, MO 63101 · 314-231-1312

Lawrence J. Fleming · Popkin & Stern · 8182 Maryland Avenue, 15th Floor · St. Louis, MO 63105 · 314-862-0900

Norman S. London · 1600 Boatmen's Tower · 100 North Broadway · St. Louis, MO 63102 · 314-231-8700

Donald L. Wolff · Wolff & Mass · 8019 Forsyth · St. Louis, MO 63105 · 314-725-8019

FAMILY LAW

Jack Cochran · Cochran, Oswald, Barton, McDonald & Graham · One Jefferson Place · P.O. Box 550 · Blue Springs, MO 64015 · 816-229-8121

Gina M. Graham · Cochran, Oswald, Barton, McDonald & Graham · One Jefferson Place · P.O. Box 550 · Blue Springs, MO 64015 · 816-229-8121

Roger P. Krumm · Krumm & Shryock · 14 West Fifth Street · Fulton, MO 65251 · 314-642-9183

Michael S. J. Albano · Paden, Welch, Martin & Albano · Law Building · 311 West Kansas Avenue · Independence, MO 64050 · 816-836-8000

John W. Dennis, Jr. · Paden, Welch, Martin & Albano · Law Building · 311 West Kansas Avenue · Independence, MO 64050 · 816-836-8000

Robert C. Paden · Paden, Welch, Martin & Albano · Law Building · 311 West Kansas Avenue · Independence, MO 64050 · 816-836-8000

Lori J. Levine · Carson, Coil, Riley, McMillin, Levine and Veit · 211 East Capitol Avenue · P.O. Box 235 · Jefferson City, MO 65102 · 314-636-2177

Regina Keelan Bass · Thayer, Bernstein & Bass · 8900 Ward Parkway, Suite 210 · Kansas City, MO 64114 · 816-444-8030

Charlotte P. Thayer · Thayer, Bernstein & Bass · 8900 Ward Parkway, Suite 210 · Kansas City, MO 64114 · 816-444-8030

David B. Lacks · Love, Lacks & Paule · Pierre Laclede Building, Suite 680 · 7701 Forsyth Boulevard · St. Louis, MO 63105-1893 · 314-863-4100

Merle L. Silverstein · Rosenblum, Goldenhersh, Silverstein & Zafft · 7777 Bonhomme, Suite 1414 · St. Louis, MO 63105 · 314-726-6868

Charles P. Todt · Charles P. Todt & Associates · 212 South Meramec · St. Louis, MO 63105 · 314-862-5520

John A. Turcotte, Jr. · Diekemper, Hammond, Shinners, Turcotte and Larrew · 7730 Carondelet Avenue · St. Louis, MO 63105 · 314-727-1015

Robert C. Fields · 221 Woodruff Building · 333 Jefferson Street · Springfield, MO 65806 · 417-831-1505

LABOR AND EMPLOYMENT LAW

Jerome A. Diekemper · (Labor) · Diekemper, Hammond & Shinners · 7730 Carondelet Avenue, Suite 222 · Clayton, MO 63105 · 314-727-1015

David Achtenberg · (Individuals) · Achtenberg & Achtenberg · Mark Twain Plaza Bank Building, Suite 200 · 4901 Main Street · Kansas City, MO 64112-2634 · 816-753-1050

Arthur A. Benson II · (Individuals) · Benson & McKay · 1430 Commerce Tower · 911 Main Street · Kansas City, MO 64105 · 816-842-7603

Allan L. Bioff · (Management) · Watson, Ess, Marshall & Enggas · 1010 Grand Avenue · Kansas City, MO 64106-2271 · 816-842-3132

Clifton L. Elliott · (Management) · Smith, Gill, Fisher & Butts · One Kansas City Place, 35th Floor · 1200 Main Street · Kansas City, MO 64105 · 816-474-7400

Michael D. Gordon · (Labor) · Jolley, Walsh, Hager & Gordon · 204 West Linwood Boulevard · Kansas City, MO 64111 · 816-561-3755

William A. Jolley · (Labor) · Jolley, Walsh, Hager & Gordon · 204 West Linwood Boulevard · Kansas City, MO 64111 · 816-561-3755

Jack L. Whitacre · (Management) · Spencer, Fane, Britt & Browne · 1400 Commerce Bank Building · 1000 Walnut Street · Kansas City, MO 64106-2140 · 816-474-8100

James R. Willard · (Management) · Spencer, Fane, Britt & Browne · 1400 Commerce Bank Building · 1000 Walnut Street · Kansas City, MO 64106-2140 · 816-474-8100

Alan I. Berger · (Management) · McMahon, Berger, Hanna, Linihan, Cody & McCarthy · 2730 North Ballas Road, Suite 200 · St. Louis, MO 63131 · 314-567-7350

James K. Cook · (Labor) · Schuchat, Cook & Werner · Shell Building, Suite 250 · 1221 Locust Street · St. Louis, MO 63103 · 314-621-2626

Dennis C. Donnelly · (Management) · Bryan, Cave, McPheeters & McRoberts · 500 North Broadway · St. Louis, MO 63012-2186 · 314-231-8600

Bruce S. Feldacker · (Labor) · 705 Olive Street, Suite 500 · St. Louis, MO 63101 · 314-231-2970

Ronald K. Fisher · (Management) · Harris, Dowell & Fisher · 15400 South Outer Highway 40, Suite 202 · St. Louis, MO 63017 · 314-532-0300

Louis Gilden · (Individuals) · 317 North 11th Street, Suite 1220 · St. Louis, MO 63101 · 314-241-6607

Michael J. Hoare · (Individuals) · 314 North Broadway · St. Louis, MO 63102
314-241-7961

Fred Leicht · (Management) · Armstrong, Teasdale, Kramer, Vaughan & Schlafley · 611 Olive Street, Suite 1900 · St. Louis, MO 63101 · 314-621-5070

Ned O. Lemkemeier · (Management) · Bryan, Cave, McPheeters & McRoberts 500 North Broadway · St. Louis, MO 63012-2186 · 314-231-8600

Morris J. Levin · (Labor) · Levin and Weinhaus · 906 Olive Street, Suite 900 · St. Louis, MO 63101 · 314-621-8363

Glenn L. Moller · (Management) · Lashly, Baer & Hamel · 714 Locust Street St. Louis, MO 63101 · 314-621-2939

Daniel J. Sullivan · (Management) · Lewis & Rice · 611 Olive Street, 14th Floor St. Louis, MO 63101 · 314-444-7600

Charles A. Werner · (Labor) · Schuchat, Cook & Werner · Shell Building, Suite 250 · 1221 Locust Street · St. Louis, MO 63103 · 314-621-2626

MARITIME LAW

Michael D. O'Keefe · Thompson & Mitchell · One Mercantile Center, Suite 3400 St. Louis, MO 63101 · 314-421-4800

Elmer Price · Goldstein & Price · 1300 Paul Brown Building · 818 Olive Street St. Louis, MO 63101 · 314-421-0710

NATURAL RESOURCES AND ENVIRONMENTAL LAW

Robert L. Driscoll · Stinson, Mag & Fizzell · 920 Main Street · P.O. Box 19251 Kansas City, MO 64141 · 816-842-8600

Stephen J. Owens · Stinson, Mag & Fizzell · 920 Main Street · P.O. Box 19251 Kansas City, MO 64141 · 816-842-8600

James T. Price · Spencer, Fane, Britt & Browne · 1400 Commerce Bank Building 1000 Walnut Street · Kansas City, MO 64106-2140 · 816-474-8100

Nicholas C. Gladding · Husch, Eppenberger, Donohue, Cornfeld & Jenkins · The Boatmen's Tower, 13th Floor · 100 North Broadway · St. Louis, MO 63102 · 314-421-4800

Lewis C. Green · (Plaintiffs) · Green, Hennings & Henry · Marquette Building, Suite 1830 · 314 North Broadway · St. Louis, MO 63102 · 314-231-4181

Robert M. Lucy · Bryan, Cave, McPheeters & McRoberts · 500 North Broadway · St. Louis, MO 63102-2186 · 314-231-8600

Edwin L. Noel · Armstrong, Teasdale, Kramer, Vaughan & Schlafley · 611 Olive Street, Suite 1900 · St. Louis, MO 63101 · 314-621-5070

PERSONAL INJURY LITIGATION

Raymond C. Lewis, Jr. · (Defendants) · Smith, Lewis, Beckett & Powell · Haden Building · 901 East Broadway · Columbia, MO 65201-4894 · 314-443-3141

Lyman Field · Field, Gentry, Benjamin & Robertson · 600 East 11th Street · Kansas City, MO 64106 · 816-842-6031

Max W. Foust · (Plaintiffs) · Morris & Foust · 2390 City Center Square · 12th & Baltimore · P.O. Box 26490 · Kansas City, MO 64196 · 816-474-6050

Reed O. Gentry · (Defendants) · Field, Gentry, Benjamin & Robertson · 600 East 11th Street · Kansas City, MO 64106 · 816-842-6031

John M. Kilroy · (Defendants) · Shughart, Thomson & Kilroy · 12 Wyandotte Plaza, Suite 1800 · 120 West 12th Street · Kansas City, MO 64105 · 816-421-3355

Patrick McLarney · (Defendants) · Shook, Hardy & Bacon · One Kansas City Place, 31st Floor · 1200 Main Street · Kansas City, MO 64105 · 816-474-6550

Larry L. McMullen · (Defendants) · Blackwell Sanders Matheny Weary & Lombardi · Two Pershing Square, Suite 1100 · 2300 Main Street · Kansas City, MO 64108 · 816-274-6800

William H. Sanders · (Defendants) · Blackwell Sanders Matheny Weary & Lombardi · Two Pershing Square, Suite 1100 · 2300 Main Street · Kansas City, MO 64108 · 816-274-6800

Lantz Welch · (Plaintiffs) · 2930 City Center Square · 1100 Main · P.O. Box 26250 · Kansas City, MO 64196 · 816-421-1600

Paul S. Brown · (Defendants) · Brown, James & Rabbitt · 705 Olive Street, Suite 1100 · St. Louis, MO 63101 · 314-421-3400

Eugene K. Buckley · (Defendants) · Evans & Dixon · Marquette Building, 16th Floor · 314 North Broadway · St. Louis, MO 63102 · 314-621-7755

Ben Ely, Jr. · (Defendants) · Kortenhof & Ely · 1015 Locust Street, Suite 300 St. Louis, MO 63101 · 314-621-5757

Robert C. Ely · (Defendants) · Louderman Building, Suite 700 · 317 North 11th Street · St. Louis, MO 63101 · 314-421-0216

William W. Evans · (Defendants) · Evans & Dixon · Marquette Building, 16th Floor · 314 North Broadway · St. Louis, MO 63102 · 314-621-7755

Theodore Hoffman · (Plaintiffs) · 1015 Locust Street, Suite 1134 · St. Louis, MO 63101 · 314-241-1020

James E. Hullverson · (Plaintiffs) · Hullverson, Hullverson & Frank · 1010 Market Street, Suite 1550 · St. Louis, MO 63101 · 314-421-2313

Thomas C. Hullverson · (Plaintiffs) · Hullverson, Hullverson & Frank · 1010 Market Street, Suite 1550 · St. Louis, MO 63101 · 314-421-2313

Joseph M. Kortenhof · (Defendants) · Kortenhof & Ely · 1015 Locust Street, Suite 300 · St. Louis, MO 63101 · 314-621-5757

Daniel T. Rabbitt · (Defendants) · Brown, James & Rabbitt · 705 Olive Street, Suite 1100 · St. Louis, MO 63101 · 314-421-3400

John C. Shepherd · Shepherd, Sandberg & Phoenix · One City Centre, Suite 1500 · St. Louis, MO 63101 · 314-231-3332

Don B. Sommers · (Plaintiffs) · Paul Brown Building, Suite 1630 · 818 Olive Street · St. Louis, MO 63101 · 314-436-2088

Thomas Strong · (Plaintiffs) · Strong & Wooddell · 901 East Battlefield · Springfield, MO 65807 · 417-887-4300

REAL ESTATE LAW

Sherwin L. Epstein · Sherwin L. Epstein & Associates · Home Savings Bank Building, Suite 1700 · 1006 Grand Avenue · Kansas City, MO 64106 · 816-421-6200

Larrie C. Hindman · Morrison, Hecker, Curtis, Kuder & Parrish · 1700 Bryant Building · 1102 Grand Avenue · Kansas City, MO 64106-2370 · 816-842-5910

James M. Jenkins · Husch, Eppenberger, Donohue, Cornfeld & Jenkins · 2500 City Center Square · 12th & Baltimore · P.O. Box 26006 · Kansas City, MO 64196 816-421-4800

Michael G. O'Flaherty · Stinson, Mag & Fizzell · 920 Main Street · P.O. Box 19251 · Kansas City, MO 64141 · 816-842-8600

Richard W. Scarritt · Spencer, Fane, Britt & Browne · 1400 Commerce Bank Building · 1000 Walnut Street · Kansas City, MO 64106-2140 · 816-474-8100

Stephen K. Taylor · Watson, Ess, Marshall & Enggas · 1010 Grand Avenue Kansas City, MO 64106-2271 · 816-842-3132

Fred E. Arnold · Thompson & Mitchell · One Mercantile Center, Suite 3400 · St. Louis, MO 63101 · 314-231-7676

Donald U. Beimdiek · Armstrong, Teasdale, Kramer, Vaughan & Schlafley · 611 Olive Street, Suite 1900 · St. Louis, MO 63101 · 314-621-5070

John A. Blumenfeld · Blumenfeld, Sandweiss, Marx, Tureen, Ponfil & Kaskowitz · 168 North Meramec Avenue, Fourth Floor · St. Louis, MO 63105 314-863-0800

Robert S. Goldenhersh · Rosenblum, Goldenhersh, Silverstein & Zafft · 7777 Bonhomme Street, Suite 1400 · St. Louis, MO 63105 · 314-726-6868

Harvey A. Harris · The Stolar Partnership · Lammert Building, Seventh Floor 911 Washington Avenue · St. Louis, MO 63101 · 314-231-2800

Richard A. Hetlage · Peper, Martin, Jensen, Maichel and Hetlage · 720 Olive Street, 24th Floor · St. Louis, MO 63101 · 314-421-3850

Robert O. Hetlage · Peper, Martin, Jensen, Maichel and Hetlage · 720 Olive Street, 24th Floor · St. Louis, MO 63101 · 314-421-3850

Andrew S. Love, Jr. · Bryan, Cave, McPheeters & McRoberts · 500 North Broadway · St. Louis, MO 63102-2186 · 314-231-8600

George V. Meisel · Bryan, Cave, McPheeters & McRoberts · 500 North Broadway St. Louis, MO 63102-2186 · 314-231-8600

Jerome M. Rubenstein · Bryan, Cave, McPheeters & McRoberts · 500 North Broadway · St. Louis, MO 63102-2186 · 314-231-8600

Shulamith Simon · Husch, Eppenberger, Donohue, Cornfeld & Jenins · The Boatmen's Tower, 13th Floor · 100 North Broadway · St. Louis, MO 63102 · 314-421-4800

Walter J. Taylor · Lewis & Rice · 611 Olive Street, 14th Floor · St. Louis, MO 63101 · 314-444-7600

TAX AND EMPLOYEE BENEFITS LAW

Thomas C. Graves · (Employee Benefits) · Morrison, Hecker, Curtis, Kuder & Parrish · 1700 Bryant Building · 1102 Grand Avenue · Kansas City, MO 64106-2370 · 816-842-5910

Ronald L. Langstaff · Spencer, Fane, Britt & Browne · 1400 Commerce Bank Building · 1000 Walnut Street · Kansas City, MO 64106-2140 · 816-474-8100

Ross W. Lillard · (Employee Benefits) · Stinson, Mag & Fizzell · 920 Main Street P.O. Box 19251 · Kansas City, MO 64141 · 816-842-8600

Robert P. Lyons · Spencer, Fane, Britt & Browne · 1400 Commerce Bank Building · 1000 Walnut Street · Kansas City, MO 64106-2140 · 816-474-8100

Morton Y. Rosenberg · Stinson, Mag & Fizzell · 920 Main Street · P.O. Box 19251 · Kansas City, MO 64141 · 816-842-8600

Sylvan Siegler · Margolin and Kirwan · 1000 United Missouri Bank Building · 928 Grand Avenue · Kansas City, MO 64106 · 816-842-7080

Myron E. Sildon · (also Employee Benefits) · Sildon & Kroeker · 2800 City Center Square · 1100 Main Street · Kansas City, MO 64105 · 816-474-7777

Perry M. Toll · (Employee Benefits) · Shughart, Thomson & Kilroy · 12 Wyandotte Plaza, Suite 1800 · 120 West 12th Street · Kansas City, MO 64105 · 816-421-3355

Daniel C. Weary · Blackwell Sanders Matheny Weary & Lombardi · Two Pershing Square, Suite 1100 · 2300 Main Street · Kansas City, MO 64108 · 816-274-6800

Stanley P. Weiner · Shook, Hardy & Bacon · One Kansas City Place, 31st Floor 1200 Main Street · Kansas City, MO 64105 · 816-474-6550

John P. Williams · (Employee Benefits) · Blackwell Sanders Matheny Weary & Lombardi · Two Pershing Square, Suite 1100 · 2300 Main Street · Kansas City, MO 64108 · 816-274-6800

Charles M. Babington III · (Employee Benefits) · Thompson & Mitchell · One Mercantile Center, Suite 3400 · St. Louis, MO 63101 · 314-231-7676

Harold G. Blatt · (Employee Benefits) · Bryan, Cave, McPheeters & McRoberts · 500 North Broadway · St. Louis, MO 63102-2186 · 314-231-8600

Lawrence Brody · Bryan, Cave, McPheeter & McRoberts · 500 North Broadway · St. Louis, MO 63102-2186 · 314-231-8600

Edward J. Buchholz · Bryan, Cave, McPheeter & McRoberts · 500 North Broadway · St. Louis, MO 63102-2186 · 314-231-8600

Dave L. Cornfeld · Husch, Eppenberger, Donohue, Cornfeld & Jenkins · The Boatmen's Tower, 13th Floor · 100 North Broadway · St. Louis, MO 63102 · 314-421-4800

William D. Crampton · Bryan, Cave, McPheeter & McRoberts · 500 North Broadway · St. Louis, MO 63102-2186 · 314-231-8600

Joseph P. Giljum · Kohn, Shands, Elbert, Gianoulakis & Giljum · 411 North Seventh Street, Suite 1215 · St. Louis, MO 63101 · 314-241-3963

Paul G. Griesemer · (Employee Benefits) · Peper, Martin, Jensen, Maichel and Hetlage · 720 Olive Street, 24th Floor · St. Louis, MO 63101 · 314-421-3850

Warren L. Maichel · Peper, Martin, Jensen, Maichel and Hetlage · 720 Olive Street, 24th Floor · St. Louis, MO 63101 · 314-421-3850

Joan M. Newman · (Employee Benefits) · Lewis & Rice · 611 Olive Street, 14th Floor · St. Louis, MO 63101 · 314-444-7600

Michael N. Newmark · Gallop, Johnson & Neuman · 101 South Hanley Road, Suite 1600 · St. Louis, MO 63105 · 314-862-1200

Edward W. Rataj · (Employee Benefits) · Bryan, Cave, McPheeters & McRoberts · 500 North Broadway · St. Louis, MO 63102-2186 · 314-231-8600

Douglas D. Ritterskamp · (Employee Benefits) · Bryan, Cave, McPheeters & McRoberts · 500 North Broadway · St. Louis, MO 63102-2186 · 314-231-8600

Llewellyn Sale III · (Employee Benefits) · Husch, Eppenberger, Donohue, Cornfeld & Jenkins · The Boatmen's Tower, 13th Floor · 100 North Broadway · St. Louis, MO 63102 · 314-421-4800

TRUSTS AND ESTATES

Byron A. Stewart, Jr. · Constance, Stewart & Cook · 501 West Lexington Avenue Independence, MO 64050 · 816-833-1800

Peter W. Brown · Husch, Eppenberger, Donohue, Cornfeld & Jenkins · 2500 City Center Square · 12th & Baltimore · P.O. Box 26006 · Kansas City, MO 64196 816-421-4800

Donald H. Chisholm · Stinson, Mag & Fizzell · 920 Main Street · P.O. Box 19251 · Kansas City, MO 64141 · 816-842-8600

John C. Davis · Stinson, Mag & Fizzell · 920 Main Street · P.O. Box 19251 · Kansas City, MO 64141 · 816-842-8600

George R. Haydon, Jr. · Watson, Ess, Marshall & Enggas · 1010 Grand Avenue · Kansas City, MO 64106-2271 · 816-842-3132

Roger T. Hurwitz · Morrison, Hecker, Curtis, Kuder & Parrish · 1700 Bryant Building · 1102 Grand Avenue · Kansas City, MO 64106-2370 · 816-842-5910

Guy A. Magruder, Jr. · Van Osdol, Magruder, Erickson and Redmond · 515 Commerce Trust Building · Kansas City, MO 64106 · 816-421-0644

Maurice J. O'Sullivan, Jr. · Lathrop, Koontz & Norquist · 2600 Mutual Benefit Life Building · 2345 Grand Avenue · Kansas City, MO 64108 · 816-842-0820

Edward A. Setzler · Spencer, Fane, Britt & Browne · 1400 Commerce Bank Building · 1000 Walnut Street · Kansas City, MO 64106-2140 · 816-474-8100

Sylvan Siegler · Margolin and Kirwan · 1000 United Missouri Bank Building · 928 Grand Avenue · Kansas City, MO 64106 · 816-842-7080

Myron E. Sildon · Sildon & Kroeker · 2800 City Center Square · 1100 Main Street Kansas City, MO 64105 · 816-474-7777

David L. West · Blackwell Sanders Matheny Weary & Lombardi · Two Pershing Square, Suite 1100 · 2300 Main Street · Kansas City, MO 64108 · 816-274-6800

Richard D. Woods · Shook, Hardy & Bacon · One Kansas City Place, 31st Floor 1200 Main Street · Kansas City, MO 64105 · 816-474-6550

Lawrence Brody · Bryan, Cave, McPheeters & McRoberts · 500 North Broadway St. Louis, MO 63102-2186 · 314-231-8600

Dave L. Cornfeld · Husch, Eppenberger, Donohue, Cornfeld & Jenkins · The Boatmen's Tower, 13th Floor · 100 North Broadway · St. Louis, MO 63102 314-421-4800

John E. Dooling, Jr. · Greensfelder, Hemker, Wiese, Gale & Chappelow · 1800 Equitable Building · Ten South Broadway · St. Louis, MO 63102 · 314-241-9090

Milton Greenfield, Jr. · Greenfield, Davidson & Ward · 1516 Chemical Building 721 Olive Street · St. Louis, MO 63101 · 314-241-5735

Lawrence P. Katzenstein · Husch, Eppenberger, Donohue, Cornfeld & Jenkins The Boatmen's Tower, 13th Floor · 100 North Broadway · St. Louis, MO 63102 314-421-4800

Michael D. Mulligan · Lewis & Rice · 611 Olive Street, 14th Floor · St. Louis, MO 63101 · 314-444-7600

Kathleen R. Sherby · Bryan, Cave, McPheeters & McRoberts · 500 North Broadway · St. Louis, MO 63102-2186 · 314-231-8600

Franklin F. Wallis · Bryan, Cave, McPheeters & McRoberts · 500 North Broadway · St. Louis, MO 63102-2186 · 314-231-8600

MONTANA

BANKRUPTCY LAW	399
BUSINESS LITIGATION	400
CORPORATE LAW	400
CRIMINAL DEFENSE	401
LABOR AND EMPLOYMENT LAW	401
NATURAL RESOURCES AND ENVIRONMENTAL LAW	402
PERSONAL INJURY LITIGATION	402
REAL ESTATE LAW	404
TAX AND EMPLOYEE BENEFITS LAW	404
TRUSTS AND ESTATES	405

BANKRUPTCY LAW

Joel E. Guthals · Wright, Tolliver & Guthals · Windsor Court · 10 North 27th Street · P.O. Box 1977 · Billings, MT 59103 · 406-245-3071

Charles W. Hingle · Dorsey & Whitney · 401 North 31st Street · P.O. Box 7188 · Billings, MT 59103 · 406-252-3800

Sherry Scheel Matteucci · Crowley, Haughey, Hanson, Toole & Dietrich · 500 Transwestern Plaza II · 490 North 31st Street · P.O. Box 2529 · Billings, MT 59103 · 406-252-3441

Sidney R. Thomas · Moulton, Bellingham, Longo & Mather · 200 Securities Building · P.O. Box 2545 · Billings, MT 59103-2545 · 406-248-7731

Arthur G. Matteucci · Matteucci & Falcon · Norwest Bank Building, Suite 400 · 21 Third Street North · P.O. Box 151 · Great Falls, MT 59403 · 406-727-5740

Harold V. Dye · Milodragovich, Dale & Dye · Sunstone Building · 620 High Park Way · P.O. Drawer R · Missoula, MT 59806 · 406-728-1455

Donald MacDonald IV · Connell, Beers & MacDonald · 234 East Pine · P.O. Box 7307 · Missoula, MT 59807 · 406-728-8796

BUSINESS LITIGATION

George Dalthorp · Crowley, Haughey, Hanson, Toole & Dietrich · 500 Transwestern Plaza II · 490 North 31st Street · P.O. Box 2529 · Billings, MT 59103 406-252-3441

A. Clifford Edwards · Anderson, Edwards & Molloy · 1601 Lewis Avenue, Suite 206 · P.O. Box 21497 · Billings, MT 59104 · 406-248-7521

Stephen H. Foster · Holland & Hart · 175 North 27th Street, Suite 1400 · Billings, MT 59101 · 406-252-2166

James H. Goetz · (Appellate) · Goetz, Madden & Dunn · 35 North Grand Avenue Bozeman, MT 59715 · 406-587-0618

Urban L. Roth · Poore, Roth & Robinson · 1341 Harrison Avenue · P.O. Box 3328 Butte, MT 59701-4898 · 406-782-1223

John D. Stephenson, Jr. · Jardine, Stephenson, Blewett & Weaver · First National Bank Building, Seventh Floor · P.O. Box 2269 · Great Falls, MT 59403 406-727-5000

Ronald F. Waterman · Gough, Shanahan, Johnson & Waterman · 301 First National Bank Building · P.O. Box 1715 · Helena, MT 59624 · 406-442-8560

Sam E. Haddon · Boone, Karlberg and Haddon · Central Square, Suite 301 · 201 West Main Street · Missoula, MT 59802-4497 · 406-543-6646

William Evan Jones · Garlington, Lohn & Robinson · 199 West Pine · P.O. Box 7909 · Missoula, MT 59807-7909 · 406-728-1200

Sherman V. Lohn · Garlington, Lohn & Robinson · 199 West Pine · P.O. Box 7909 · Missoula, MT 59807-7909 · 406-728-1200

CORPORATE LAW

John M. Dietrich · Crowley, Haughey, Hanson, Toole & Dietrich · 500 Transwestern Plaza II · 490 North 31st Street · P.O. Box 2529 · Billings, MT 59103 406-252-3441

Gerald F. Krieg · Crowley, Haughey, Hanson, Toole & Dietrich · 500 Transwestern Plaza II · 490 North 31st Street · P.O. Box 2529 · Billings, MT 59103 · 406-252-3441

Ward A. Shanahan · Gough, Shanahan, Johnson & Waterman · 301 First National Bank Building · P.O. Box 1715 · Helena, MT 59624 · 406-442-8560

Thomas H. Boone · Boone, Karlberg & Haddon · Central Square, Suite 301 · 201 West Main Street · Missoula, MT 59802-4497 · 406-543-6646

Harry A. Haines · Worden, Thane & Haines · 3203 Russell Street · P.O. Box 4747 · Missoula, MT 59806 · 406-721-3400

Sherman V. Lohn · Garlington, Lohn & Robinson · 199 West Pine · P.O. Box 7909 · Missoula, MT 59807-7909 · 406-728-1200

CRIMINAL DEFENSE

Charles F. Moses · Moses Law Firm · The Terrace · 300 North 25th Street · P.O. Box 2533 · Billings, MT 59103 · 406-248-7702

Gregory A. Jackson · Jackson & Rice · Arcade Building, Suite 3D · Helena, MT 59601 · 406-443-2140

W. William Leaphart · Leaphart Law Firm · One Last Chance Gulch, Suite Six · Helena, MT 59601 · 406-442-4930

LABOR AND EMPLOYMENT LAW

Donald C. Robinson · (Management) · Poore, Roth & Robinson · 1341 Harrison Avenue · P.O. Box 3328 · Butte, MT 59701-4898 · 406-782-1223

Benjamin W. Hilley · (Labor; Individuals) · Hilley & Loring · 121 Fourth Street North, Suite 2G · Great Falls, MT 59401 · 406-761-3100

Tom L. Lewis · (Individuals) · Regnier, Lewis, Boland and Roberts · 725 Third Avenue North · P.O. Box 2325 · Great Falls, MT 59403 · 406-761-5595

D. Patrick McKittrick · (Labor) · 410 Central Avenue · Great Falls, MT 59401 · 406-727-4041

James M. Regnier · (Individuals) · Regnier, Lewis, Boland and Roberts · 725 Third Avenue North · P.O. Box 2325 · Great Falls, MT 59403 · 406-761-5595

Jeremy G. Thane · (Management) · Worden, Thane & Haines · 3203 Russell Street · P.O. Box 4747 · Missoula, MT 59806 · 406-721-3400

NATURAL RESOURCES AND ENVIRONMENTAL LAW

James H. Goetz · (Plaintiffs) · Goetz, Madden & Dunn · 35 North Grand Avenue Bozeman, MT 59715 · 406-587-0618

William H. Bellingham · Moulton, Bellingham, Longo & Mather · 200 Securities Building · P.O. Box 2545 · Billings, MT 59103-2545 · 406-248-7731

Louis R. Moore · Crowley, Haughey, Hanson, Toole & Dietrich · 500 Transwestern Plaza II · 490 North 31st Street · P.O. Box 2529 · Billings, MT 59103 406-252-3441

Ted J. Doney · (Water) · Doney & Thorson · 314 North Last Chance Gulch Helena, MT 59601 · 406-443-7018

Robert G. Anderson · (Oil & Gas) · Anderson, Beatty & Lee · 153 Main Street P.O. Drawer D · Shelby, MT 59474 · 406-434-5518

PERSONAL INJURY LITIGATION

Wade J. Dahood · (Plaintiffs) · Knight, Dahood, McLean & Everett · P.O. Box 727 · Anaconda, MT 59711 · 406-563-3424

Gene Huntley · (Plaintiffs) · 204 South First Street, West · P.O. Box 760 · Baker, MT 59313 · 406-778-2831

Richard W. Anderson · (Plaintiffs) · Anderson, Edwards & Molloy · 1601 Lewis Avenue, Suite 206 · P.O. Box 21497 · Billings, MT 59104 · 406-248-7521

William H. Bellingham · (Defendants) · Moulton, Bellingham, Longo & Mather 200 Securities Building · P.O. Box 2545 · Billings, MT 59103-2545 · 406-248-7731

Richard F. Cebull · (Defendants) · Anderson, Brown, Gerbase, Cebull, Fulton, Harman & Ross · 315 North 24th Street · P.O. Drawer 849 · Billings, MT 59103-0849 · 406-248-2611

A. Clifford Edwards · (Plaintiffs) · Anderson, Edwards & Molloy · 1601 Lewis Avenue, Suite 206 · P.O. Box 1049 · Billings, MT 59103 · 406-248-7521

Jack Ramirez · (Defendants) · Crowley, Haughey, Hanson, Toole & Dietrich 500 Transwestern Plaza II · 490 North 31st Street · P.O. Box 2529 · Billings, MT 59103 · 406-252-3441

Bruce R. Toole · (Defendants) · Crowley, Haughey, Hanson, Toole & Dietrich 500 Transwestern Plaza II · 490 North 31st Street · P.O. Box 2529 · Billings, MT 59103 · 406-252-3441

Urban L. Roth · Poore, Roth & Robinson · 1341 Harrison Avenue · P.O. Box 3328 Butte, MT 59701-4898 · 406-782-1223

John C. Hoyt · (Plaintiffs) · Hoyt & Blewett · 501 Second Avenue North · P.O. Box 2807 · Great Falls, MT 59403 · 406-761-1960

Tom L. Lewis · (Plaintiffs) · Regnier, Lewis & Boland · 725 Third Avenue North P.O. Box 2325 · Great Falls, MT 59403 · 406-761-5595

James M. Regnier · (Plaintiffs) · Regnier, Lewis & Boland · 725 Third Avenue North · P.O. Box 2325 · Great Falls, MT 59403 · 406-761-5595

P. Keith Keller · (Defendants) · Keller, Reynolds, Drake, Sternhagen and Johnson · 38 South Last Chance Gulch · Helena, MT 59601 · 406-442-0230

Stuart L. Kellner · (Defendants) · Hughes, Kellner, Sullivan & Alke · 406 Fuller Avenue · P.O. Box 1166 · Helena, MT 59624 · 406-442-3690

Sam E. Haddon · (Defendants) · Boone, Karlberg & Haddon · Central Square, Suite 301 · 201 West Main Street · Missoula, MT 59802-4497 · 406-543-6646

William Evans Jones · (Defendants) · Garlington, Lohn & Robinson · 199 West Pine · P.O. Box 7909 · Missoula, MT 59807-7909 · 406-728-1200

Sherman V. Lohn · (Defendants) · Garlington, Lohn & Robinson · 199 West Pine P.O. Box 7909 · Missoula, MT 59807-7909 · 406-728-1200

Larry E. Riley · (Defendants) · Garlington, Lohn & Robinson · 199 West Pine P.O. Box 7909 · Missoula, MT 59807-7909 · 406-728-1200

Terry N. Trieweiler · (Plaintiffs) · Trieweiler Law Firm · 233 Second Street Whitefish, MT 59937 · 406-862-4597

REAL ESTATE LAW

Richard W. Josephson · Josephson and Fredricks · 115 West Second Avenue · Big Timber, MT 59011 · 406-932-5440

John M. Dietrich · Crowley, Haughey, Hanson, Toole & Dietrich · 500 Transwestern Plaza II · 490 North 31st Street · P.O. Box 2529 · Billings, MT 59103 · 406-252-3441

Gareld F. Krieg · Crowley, Haughey, Hanson, Toole & Dietrich · 500 Transwestern Plaza II · 490 North 31st Street · P.O. Box 2529 · Billings, MT 59103 · 406-252-3441

Leonard A. Schulz · Schulz, Davis & Warren · 122 East Glendale · P.O. Box 28 · Dillon, MT 59725 · 406-683-2363

Harry A. Haines · Worden, Thane & Haines · 3203 Russell Street · P.O. Box 4747 · Missoula, MT 59806 · 406-721-3400

Robert M. Knight · Knight, Maclay & Maser · 300 Glacier Building · 111 North Higgins Avenue · P.O. Box 8957 · Missoula, MT 59807 · 406-721-5440

TAX AND EMPLOYEE BENEFITS LAW

David L. Johnson · Crowley, Haughey, Hanson, Toole & Dietrich · 500 Transwestern Plaza II · 490 North 31st Street · P.O. Box 2529 · Billings, MT 59103 · 406-252-3441

Myles J. Thomas · Crowley, Haughey, Hanson, Toole & Dietrich · 500 Transwestern Plaza II · 490 North 31st Street · P.O. Box 2529 · Billings, MT 59103 · 406-252-3441

Thomas F. Topel · Dorsey & Whitney · 1200 First Interstate Center · P.O. Box 7188 · Billings, MT 59103 · 406-252-3800

Dale Forbes · Church, Harris, Johnson & Williams · Norwest Bank Building, Third Floor · P.O. Box 1645 · Great Falls, MT 59403 · 406-761-3000

John R. Kline · Arcade Building, Suite 35 · 111 North Last Chance Gulch · P.O. Box 1705 · Helena, MT 59624 · 406-442-8950

Harry A. Haines · Worden, Thane & Haines · 3203 Russell Street · P.O. Box 4747 · Missoula, MT 59806 · 406-721-3400

John R. McInnis · Garlington, Lohn & Robinson · 199 West Pine · P.O. Box 7909 Missoula, MT 59807-7090 · 406-728-1200

TRUSTS AND ESTATES

John M. Dietrich · Crowley, Haughey, Hanson, Toole & Dietrich · 500 Transwestern Plaza II · 490 North 31st Street · P.O. Box 2529 · Billings, MT 59103 406-252-3441

Myles J. Thomas · Crowley, Haughey, Hanson, Toole & Dietrich · 500 Transwestern Plaza II · 490 North 31st Street · P.O. Box 2529 · Billings, MT 59103 406-252-3441

Thomas F. Topel · Dorsey & Whitney · 1200 First Interstate Center · P.O. Box 7188 · Billings, MT 59103 · 406-252-3800

Dale Forbes · Church, Harris, Johnson & Williams · Norwest Bank Building, Third Floor · P.O. Box 1645 · Great Falls, MT 59403 · 406-761-3000

John R. Kline · Arcade Building, Suite 35 · 111 North Last Chance Gulch · P.O. Box 1705 · Helena, MT 59624 · 406-442-8950

George D. Goodrich · Garlington, Lohn & Robinson · 199 West Pine · P.O. Box 7909 · Missoula, MT 59807-7909 · 406-728-1200

John R. McInnis · Garlington, Lohn & Robinson · 199 West Pine · P.O. Box 7909 Missoula, MT 59807-7909 · 406-728-1200

NEBRASKA

BANKRUPTCY LAW	406
BUSINESS LITIGATION	407
CORPORATE LAW	407
CRIMINAL DEFENSE	408
FAMILY LAW	408
LABOR AND EMPLOYMENT LAW	409
PERSONAL INJURY LITIGATION	409
REAL ESTATE LAW	410
TAX AND EMPLOYEE BENEFITS LAW	411
TRUSTS AND ESTATES	412

BANKRUPTCY LAW

Joseph H. Badami · Badami and Radke · 1235 N Street, Suite 402 · Lincoln, NE 68508 · 402-473-6464

Harry D. Dixon, Jr. · Dixon & Dixon · One First National Center, Suite 1900 16th & Dodge Streets · Omaha, NE 68102 · 402-345-3900

Paul F. Festersen · 510 Service Life Building · 19th & Farnam Streets · Omaha, NE 68102 · 402-344-3400

Jerrold L. Strasheim · Baird, Holm, McEachen, Pedersen, Hamann & Strasheim 1500 Woodmen Tower · Omaha, NE 68102 · 402-344-0500

Steven C. Turner · Baird, Holm, McEachen, Pedersen, Hamann & Strasheim 1500 Woodmen Tower · Omaha, NE 68102 · 402-344-0500

BUSINESS LITIGATION

M. J. "Jim" Bruckner · Bruckner, O'Gara, Keating, Sievers & Hendry · 530 South 13th Street, Suite A · Lincoln, NE 68508 · 402-475-8230

Fredric H. Kauffman · Cline, Williams, Wright, Johnson & Oldfather · First National Bank Building, Suite 1900 · Lincoln, NE 68508 · 402-474-6900

William G. Campbell · Kutak Rock & Campbell · The Omaha Building · 1650 Farnam Street · Omaha, NE 68102 · 402-346-6000

Charles F. Gotch · Cassem, Tierney, Adams, Gotch & Douglas · 8805 Indian Hills Drive, Suite 300 · Omaha, NE 68114 · 402-345-9924

Joseph K. Meusey · Fraser, Stryker, Veach, Vaughn, Meusey, Olson, Boyer & Bloch · 500 Electric Building · Omaha, NE 68102 · 402-341-6000

CORPORATE LAW

Warren C. Johnson · Cline, Williams, Wright, Johnson & Oldfather · First National Bank Building, Suite 1900 · Lincoln, NE 68508 · 402-474-6900

Theodore L. Kessner · Crosby, Guenzel, Davis, Kessner & Kuester · 400 Lincoln Benefit Life Building · 134 South 13th Street · Lincoln, NE 68508 · 402-475-5131

Robert J. Routh · Knudsen, Berkheimer, Richardson & Endacott · 1000 NBC Center · Lincoln, NE 68508 · 402-475-7011

James W. Brown · Brown & Brown · 1700 Woodmen Tower · Omaha, NE 68102 402-346-5010

Thomas R. Burke · Kennedy, Holland, DeLacy & Svoboda · Kennedy Holland Building · 10306 Regency Parkway Drive · Omaha, NE 68114 · 402-397-0203

Deryl F. Hamann · Baird, Holm, McEachen, Pedersen, Hamann & Strasheim · 1500 Woodmen Tower · Omaha, NE 68102 · 402-344-0500

Howard J. Kaslow · Abrahams, Kaslow & Cassman · 8712 West Dodge Road, Suite 300 · Omaha, NE 68114 · 402-392-1250

Edmund D. McEachen · Baird, Holm, McEachen, Pedersen, Hamann & Strasheim · 1500 Woodmen Tower · Omaha, NE 68102 · 402-344-0500

Stephen T. McGill · McGill, Parsonage & Lanphier · 10010 Regency Circle, Suite 300 · Omaha, NE 68114 · 402-397-9988

Harold L. Rock · Kutak Rock & Campbell · The Omaha Building · 1650 Farnam Street · Omaha, NE 68102 · 402-346-6000

Bruce C. Rohde · McGrath, North, Mullin & Kratz · One Central Park Plaza, Suite 1100 · Omaha, NE 68102 · 402-341-3070

CRIMINAL DEFENSE

Kirk E. Naylor, Jr. · 1111 Lincoln Mall, Suite 300 · Lincoln, NE 68508 · 402-474-5529

J. William Gallup · Gallup, Schaefer & Slowiaczek · 1001 Farnum on The Mall Omaha, NE 68102 · 402-341-0700

J. Joseph McQuillan · Walentine, O'Toole, McQuillan & Gordon · 11301 Davenport Street · Omaha, NE 68154 · 402-330-6300

FAMILY LAW

Paul E. Galter · Bauer, Galter & O'Brien · 811 South 13th Street · Lincoln, NE 68508 · 402-475-0811

Susan Jacobs · Healey, Wieland, Kluender, Atwood, Jacobs & Geier · 1141 H Street · P.O. Box 83104 · Lincoln, NE 68501-3104 · 402-476-2847

Con M. Keating · Bruckner, O'Gara, Keating, Sievers & Hendry · 530 South 13th Street, Suite A · Lincoln, NE 68508 · 402-475-8230

Albert L. Feldman · Harris, Feldman Law Offices · Westmark Plaza, Suite 200 10707 Pacific Street · Omaha, NE 68114 · 402-397-1200

Steven J. Lustgarten · Lustgarten and Roberts · 477 Continental Building · 209 South 19th Street · Omaha, NE 68102 · 402-346-1920

Warren S. Zweiback · Zweiback, Flaherty, Betterman & Lamberty · Bozell & Jacobs Plaza, Suite 100 · 10250 Regency Circle · Omaha, NE 68114 · 402-397-1140

LABOR AND EMPLOYMENT LAW

Steven D. Burns · (Individuals) · Burns & Grenier · 3400 O Street · P.O. Box 30333 · Lincoln, NE 68503-0333 · 402-474-1513

Thom K. Cope · (Individuals) · Bailey, Polsky, Cada, Todd & Cope · Cooper Plaza Building, Suite 400 · 211 North 12th Street · Lincoln, NE 68508 402-476-8877

William A. Harding · (Management) · Nelson & Harding · 500 The Atrium · 1200 N Street · P.O. Box 82028 · Lincoln, NE 68501-2028 · 402-475-6761

Theodore L. Kessner · (Labor) · Crosby, Guenzel, Davis, Kessner & Kuester 400 Lincoln Benefit Life Building · 134 South 13th Street · Lincoln, NE 68508 402-475-5131

Mark Maguire · (Labor; Individuals) · Crosby, Guenzel, Davis, Kessner & Kuester · 400 Lincoln Benefit Life Building · 134 South 13th Street · Lincoln, NE 68508 · 402-475-5131

Dale E. Bock · (Management) · Taylor, Connolly, Kluver & Bock · 940 Commercial Federal Tower · 2120 South 72nd Street · Omaha, NE 68124 · 402-391-3712

Thomas F. Dowd · (Labor) · Dowd, Fahey & Dinsmore · 1905 Harney Street, Suite 710 · Omaha, NE 68102 · 402-341-2020

Dean G. Kratz · (Management) · McGrath, North, Mullin & Kratz · One Central Park Plaza, Suite 1100 · Omaha, NE 68102 · 402-341-3070

Roger J. Miller · (Management) · McGrath, North, Mullin & Kratz · One Central Park Plaza, Suite 1100 · Omaha, NE 68102 · 402-341-3070

George C. Rozmarin · (Management) · Fraser, Stryker, Veach, Vaughn, Meusey, Olson, Boyer & Bloch · 500 Electric Building · Omaha, NE 68102 · 402-341-6000

David D. Weinberg · (Labor) · Weinberg & Weinberg · 8901 Indian Hills Drive, Suite One · Omaha, NE 68114 · 402-397-0999

PERSONAL INJURY LITIGATION

M. J. "Jim" Bruckner · (Plaintiffs) · Bruckner, O'Gara, Keating, Sievers & Hendry · 530 South 13th Street, Suite A · Lincoln, NE 68508 · 402-475-8230

Fredric H. Kauffman · (Defendants) · Cline, Williams, Wright, Johnson & Oldfather · First National Bank Building, Suite 1900 · Lincoln, NE 68508 · 402-474-6900

Daniel D. Jewell · (Defendants) · Jewell, Gatz, Collins & Dreier · 105 South Second Street · P.O. Box 1367 · Norfolk, NE 68701 · 402-371-4844

John T. Carpenter · (Plaintiffs) · Miller, Carpenter, Rowen, Fitzgerald & Coe · The Law Building, Suite 200 · 500 South 18th Street · Omaha, NE 68102 · 402-341-0994

Charles F. Gotch · (Defendants) · Cassem, Tierney, Adams, Gotch & Douglas · 8805 Indian Hills Drive, Suite 300 · Omaha, NE 68114 · 402-390-0300

Joseph K. Meusey · (Defendants) · Fraser, Stryker, Veach, Vaughn, Meusey, Olson, Boyer & Bloch · 500 Electric Building · Omaha, NE 68102 · 402-341-6000

Robert Paul Chaloupka · (Plaintiffs) · Van Steenberg, Brower, Chaloupka, Mullin & Holyoke · 1904 First Avenue · P.O. Box 1204 · Scottsbluff, NE 69361 · 308-635-3161

Francis L. Winner · (Defendants) · Winner, Nichols, Douglas, Kelly & Arfmann · 105 East 16th Street · P.O. Box 419 · Scottsbluff, NE 69361 · 308-632-7191

REAL ESTATE LAW

Thomas J. Fitchett · Pierson, Fitchett, Hunzeker, Blake & Loftis · 530 South 13th Street, Suite B · Lincoln, NE 68508 · 402-476-7621

William H. Coates · Abrahams, Kaslow & Cassman · 8712 West Dodge Road, Suite 300 · Omaha, NE 68114 · 402-392-1250

Richard E. Croker · Croker, Huck & McReynolds · Commercial Federal Tower, Suite 1250 · 2120 South 72nd Street · Omaha, NE 68124 · 402-391-6777

William A. Day, Jr. · Gross, Welch, Vinardi, Kauffman & Day · 800 Commercial Federal Tower · 2120 South 72nd Street · Omaha, NE 68124 · 402-392-1500

John H. Fullenkamp · Walsh, Fullencamp & Doyle · 11440 West Center Road · Omaha, NE 68144 · 402-334-0700

Robert J. Huck · Croker, Huck & McReynolds · Commercial Federal Tower, Suite 1250 · 2120 South 72nd Street · Omaha, NE 68124 · 402-391-6777

TAX AND EMPLOYEE BENEFITS LAW

M. Douglas Deitchler · Baylor, Evnen, Curtiss, Grimit & Witt · 1200 American Charter Center · 206 South 13th Street · Lincoln, NE 68508 · 402-475-1075

David A. Ludtke · Rembolt Ludtke Parker & Berger · Century House, Suite 102 1201 Lincoln Mall · Lincoln, NE 68508 · 402-475-5100

L. Bruce Wright · (Employee Benefits) · Cline, Williams, Wright, Johnson & Oldfather · First National Bank Building, Suite 1900 · Lincoln, NE 68508 · 402-474-6900

Charles E. Wright · Cline, Williams, Wright, Johnson & Oldfather · First National Bank Building, Suite 1900 · Lincoln, NE 68508 · 402-474-6900

Donald H. Kelley · Kelley, Scritsmier, Moore & Byrne · 221 West Second Street P.O. Box 1669 · North Platte, NE 69103-1669 · 308-532-7110

William A. Day, Jr. · Gross, Welch, Vinardi, Kauffman & Day · 800 Commercial Federal Tower · 2120 South 72nd Street · Omaha, NE 68124 · 402-392-1500

Howard Fredrick Hahn · Gross, Welch, Vinardi, Kauffman & Day · 800 Commercial Federal Tower · 2120 South 72nd Street · Omaha, NE 68124 · 402-392-1500

Deryl F. Hamann · Baird, Holm, McEachen, Pedersen, Hamann & Strasheim · 1500 Woodmen Tower · Omaha, NE 68102 · 402-344-0500

David L. Hefflinger · McGrath, North, Mullin & Kratz · One Central Park Plaza, Suite 1100 · Omaha, NE 68102 · 402-341-3070

T. Geoffrey Lieben · (also Employee Benefits) · Fitzgerald, Schorr, Barmettler & Brennan · 1000 Woodmen Tower · Omaha, NE 68102 · 402-342-5550

Kent O. Littlejohn · Baird, Holm, McEachen, Pedersen, Hamann & Strasheim · 1500 Woodmen Tower · Omaha, NE 68102 · 402-344-0500

William E. Mooney, Jr. · Schmid, Mooney & Frederick · 1800 First National Center · 16th and Dodge Streets · Omaha, NE 68102 · 402-341-7100

John E. North · McGrath, North, Mullin & Kratz · One Central Park Plaza, Suite 1100 · Omaha, NE 68102 · 402-341-3070

Gary W. Radil · (Employee Benefits) · Baird, Holm, McEachen, Pedersen, Hamann & Strasheim · 1500 Woodmen Tower · Omaha, NE 68102 · 402-344-0500

Arden J. Rupiper · (Employee Benefits) · Schmid, Mooney & Frederick · 1800 First National Center · 16th and Dodge Streets · Omaha, NE 68102 · 402-341-7100

Charles A. Schorr · Fitzgerald, Schorr, Barmettler & Brennan · 1000 Woodmen Tower · Omaha, NE 68102 · 402-342-5550

TRUSTS AND ESTATES

M. Douglas Deitchler · Baylor, Evnen, Curtiss, Grimit & Witt · 1200 American Charter Center · 206 South 13th Street · Lincoln, NE 68508 · 402-475-1075

Thomas J. Fitchett · Pierson, Fitchett, Hunzeker, Blake & Loftis · 530 South 13th Street, Suite B · Lincoln, NE 68508 · 402-476-7621

David A. Ludtke · Rembolt Ludtke Parker & Berger · Century House, Suite 102 1201 Lincoln Mall · Lincoln, NE 68508 · 402-475-5100

Charles E. Wright · Cline, Williams, Wright, Johnson & Oldfather · First National Bank Building, Suite 1900 · Lincoln, NE 68508 · 402-474-6900

Donald H. Kelley · Kelley, Scritsmier, Moore & Byrne · 221 West Second Street P.O. Box 1669 · North Platte, NE 69103-1669 · 308-532-7110

Thomas R. Burke · Kennedy, Holland, DeLacy & Svoboda · Kennedy Holland Building · 10306 Regency Parkway Drive · Omaha, NE 68114 · 402-397-0203

William A. Day, Jr. · Gross, Welch, Vinardi, Kauffman & Day · 800 Commercial Federal Tower · 2120 South 72nd Street · Omaha, NE 68124 · 402-392-1500

Deryl F. Hamann · Baird, Holm, McEachen, Pedersen, Hamann & Strasheim 1500 Woodmen Tower · Omaha, NE 68102 · 402-344-0500

David L. Hefflinger · McGrath, North, Mullin & Kratz · One Central Park Plaza, Suite 1100 · Omaha, NE 68102 · 402-341-3070

Michael D. Jones · Ellick & Jones · 8805 Indian Hills Drive, Suite 280 · Omaha, NE 68114 · 402-390-0390

T. Geoffrey Lieben · Fitzgerald, Schorr, Barmettler & Brennan · 1000 Woodmen Tower · Omaha, NE 68102 · 402-342-5550

William E. Mooney, Jr. · Schmid, Mooney & Frederick · 1800 First National Center · 16th & Dodge Streets · Omaha, NE 68102 · 402-341-7100

John E. North · McGrath, North, Mullin & Kratz · One Central Park Plaza, Suite 1100 · Omaha, NE 68102 · 402-341-3070

Charles A. Schorr · Fitzgerald, Schorr, Barmettler & Brennan · 1000 Woodmen Tower · Omaha, NE 68102 · 402-342-5550

NEVADA

BANKRUPTCY LAW	414
BUSINESS LITIGATION	415
CORPORATE LAW	415
CRIMINAL DEFENSE	416
FAMILY LAW	416
LABOR AND EMPLOYMENT LAW	417
NATURAL RESOURCES AND ENVIRONMENTAL LAW	417
PERSONAL INJURY LITIGATION	417
REAL ESTATE LAW	418
TAX AND EMPLOYEE BENEFITS LAW	419
TRUSTS AND ESTATES	420

BANKRUPTCY LAW

Gerald M. Gordon · Wiener, Waldman, Gordon & Silver · Chicago Title Building, Suite 801 · 701 East Bridger Avenue · Las Vegas, NV 89101 · 702-382-9666

William L. McGimsey · 601 East Charleston Boulevard · Las Vegas, NV 89104 · 702-382-9948

Sallie Bernard Armstrong · Hale, Lane, Peek, Dennison and Howard · Valley Bank Plaza, Suite 650 · 50 West Liberty Street · P.O. Box 3237 · Reno, NV 89505 · 702-786-7900

Janet L. Chubb · 290 South Arlington Avenue, Suite 100 · Reno, NV 89501 · 702-322-3811

Richard W. Horton · Lionel Sawyer & Collins · 50 West Liberty Street, Suite 1100 · Reno, NV 89501 · 702-788-8666

Cheryl A. Skigin · Gibson & Skigin · 1695 Meadowood Lane, Suite 200 · Reno, NV 89502 · 702-829-2666

BUSINESS LITIGATION

Morton R. Galane · First Interstate Bank Building, Suite 1100 · 302 East Carson Avenue · Las Vegas, NV 89101 · 702-382-3290

Paul Hejmanowski · Lionel Sawyer & Collins · 1700 Valley Bank Plaza Building 300 South Fourth Street · Las Vegas, NV 89101 · 702-383-8888

Samuel S. Lionel · Lionel Sawyer & Collins · 1700 Valley Bank Plaza Building 300 South Fourth Street · Las Vegas, NV 89101 · 702-383-8888

Stephen L. Morris · Lionel Sawyer & Collins · 1700 Valley Bank Plaza Building 300 South Fourth Street · Las Vegas, NV 89101 · 702-383-8888

Paul A. Bible · Bible, Santini, Hoy, Miller & Trachok · 232 Court Street · Reno, NV 89501-1808 · 702-786-8000

C. Robert Cox · Walther, Key, Maupin, Oats, Cox, Lee & Klaich · Lakeside Professional Plaza, Suite 200 · 3500 Lakeside Court · Reno, NV 89509 · 702-827-2000

David W. Hagen · Guild, Hagen & Clark · 102 Rolf Way · P.O. Box 2838 · Reno, NV 89505 · 702-786-2366

Richard W. Horton · Lionel Sawyer & Collins · 50 West Liberty Street, Suite 1100 · Reno, NV 89501 · 702-788-8666

J. Stephen Peek · Hale, Lane, Peek, Dennison and Howard · Valley Bank Plaza, Suite 650 · 50 West Liberty Street · P.O. Box 3237 · Reno, NV 89505 702-786-7900

John C. Renshaw · Vargas & Bartlett · 201 West Liberty Street · P.O. Box 281 Reno, NV 89504 · 702-786-5000

CORPORATE LAW

Charles W. Deaner · Deaner, Deaner & Scann · 720 South Fourth Street, Suite 300 · Las Vegas, NV 89101 · 702-382-6911

Samuel S. Lionel · Lionel Sawyer & Collins · 1700 Valley Bank Plaza Building 300 South Fourth Street · Las Vegas, NV 89101 · 702-383-8888

John D. O'Brien · 1009 Valley Bank Plaza, Suite 1009 · 300 South Fourth Street Las Vegas, NV 89101 · 702-382-5222

Robert C. Anderson · Anderson & Pearl · 241 Ridge Street, Suite 300 · P.O. Box 21150 · Reno, NV 89515 · 702-348-5000

Edward Everett Hale · Hale, Lane, Peek, Dennison and Howard · Valley Bank Plaza, Suite 650 · 50 West Liberty Street · P.O. Box 3237 · Reno, NV 89505 702-786-7900

F. DeArmond Sharp · Hawkins & Sharp · Security Bank Building, Suite 416 One East Liberty Street · P.O. Box 750 · Reno, NV 89504 · 702-786-4646

CRIMINAL DEFENSE

Dominic P. Gentile · First Interstate Bank Building, Sixth Floor · 302 East Carson Avenue · Las Vegas, NV 89101 · 702-386-0066

Oscar B. Goodman · Goodman, Terry, Stein & Quintana · 520 South Fourth Street · Las Vegas, NV 89101-6593 · 702-384-5563

Richard A. Wright · Wright Shinehouse & Stewart · First Interstate Bank Building, Third Floor · 302 East Carson Avenue · Las Vegas, NV 89101 · 702-386-5054

C. Frederick Pinkerton · 543 Plumas Street · Reno, NV 89509 · 702-322-7553

Jerome M. Polaha · 450 Marsh Avenue · P.O. Box 3556 · Reno, NV 89505 702-786-5344

FAMILY LAW

George M. Dickerson · Dickerson, Dickerson & Lieberman · 330 South Third Street, Suite 1130 · Las Vegas, NV 89101 · 702-388-8600

Ronald J. Logar · 243 South Sierra Street · Reno, NV 89501 · 702-786-5040

Harry B. Swanson · Swanson & Capurro · One East First Street, Suite 1100 Reno, NV 89501 · 702-329-8686

LABOR AND EMPLOYMENT LAW

Frederic I. Berkley · (Labor) · Gang & Berkley · 415 South Sixth Street, Suite 101 · Las Vegas, NV 89101 · 702-385-3761

Kevin C. Efroymson · (Management) · 2915 West Charleston Boulevard, Suite Nine · Las Vegas, NV 89102 · 702-870-9601

Gregory J. Kamer · (Management) · Building D, Suite 208 · 2300 Paseo del Prado · Las Vegas, NV 89102 · 702-364-1014

Daniel Marks · (Individuals) · John Peter Lee · Valley Bank Plaza, Suite 1500 · 300 South Fourth Street · Las Vegas, NV 89101 · 702-382-4044

Richard S. Segerblom · (Individuals) · 324 South Third Street · Las Vegas, NV 89101 · 702-384-1044

NATURAL RESOURCES AND ENVIRONMENTAL LAW

Jack E. Hull · Vaughn, Hull & Copenhaver · 530 Idaho Street · P.O. Box 1420 · Elko, NV 89801 · 702-738-4031

John C. Miller · Bible, Hoy, Miller, Trachok & Wadhams · Blohm Building, Suite 201 · Elko, NV 89801 · 702-738-8064

Earl M. Hill · Hill Cassas de Lipkau and Erwin · Holcomb Professional Building, Suite 300 · 333 Holcomb Avenue · P.O. Box 2790 · Reno, NV 89505 · 702-323-1601

PERSONAL INJURY LITIGATION

William S. Barker · (Defendants) · Barker, Gillock, Koning, Brown & Early · 430 South Third Street · Las Vegas, NV 89101 · 702-386-1086

Drake DeLanoy · (Defendants) · Beckley, Singleton, DeLanoy, Jemison & List · 411 East Bonneville Avenue · Las Vegas, NV 89101 · 702-385-3373

Allan R. Earl · (Plaintiffs) · Galatz, Earl, Catalano & Smith · 710 South Fourth Street · Las Vegas, NV 89101 · 702-386-0000

Morton R. Galane · (Plaintiffs) · First Interstate Bank Building, Suite 1100 · 302 East Carson Avenue · Las Vegas, NV 89101 · 702-382-3290

Neil G. Galatz · (Plaintiffs) · Galatz, Earl, Catalano & Smith · 710 South Fourth Street · Las Vegas, NV 89101 · 702-386-0000

Gerald I. Gillock · (Defendants) · Barker, Gillock, Koning, Brown & Early · 430 South Third Street · Las Vegas, NV 89101 · 702-386-1086

David Goldwater · 1000 First National Bank Building · Las Vegas, NV 89101 · 702-385-5266

Rex A. Jemison · (Defendants) · Beckley, Singleton, DeLanoy, Jemison & List · 411 East Bonneville Avenue · Las Vegas, NV 89101 · 702-385-3373

James F. Pico · (Defendants) · Miles, Pico & Mitchell · 2000 South Eastern Avenue · Las Vegas, NV 89104 · 702-457-9099

William O. Bradley · (Plaintiffs) · Bradley & Drendel · 401 Flint Street · Reno, NV 89501 · 702-329-2273

John Squire Drendel · (Plaintiffs) · Bradley & Drendel · 401 Flint Street · Reno, NV 89501 · 702-329-2273

C. James Georgeson · (Defendants) · Shamberger, Georgeson, McQuaid & Thompson · 100 West Grove Street, Suite 500 · P.O. Box 3257 · Reno, NV 89509 · 702-827-6440

Peter Chase Neumann · (Plaintiffs) · 136 Ridge Street · Reno, NV 89501 · 702-786-3750

Eugene J. Wait, Jr. · (Defendants) · 305 West Moana Lane, Suite D · P.O. Box 719 · Reno, NV 89504-0719 · 702-827-5500

REAL ESTATE LAW

Michael E. Buckley · Jones, Jones, Close & Brown · Valley Bank Plaza, Suite 700 · 300 South Fourth Street · Las Vegas, NV 89101-6026 · 702-385-4202

Charles W. Deaner · Deaner, Deaner & Scann · 720 South Fourth Street, Suite 300 · Las Vegas, NV 89101 · 702-382-6911

Barry Stephen Goold · Gibson Law Office · 617 Valley Bank Plaza · 300 South Fourth Street · Las Vegas, NV 89101 · 702-386-0030

Jodi E. Raizin · Sully, Lenhard & Raizin · Valley Bank Plaza, Suite 1515 · 300 South Fourth Street · Las Vegas, NV 89101 · 702-384-3500

Jeffrey P. Zucker · Lionel Sawyer & Collins · 1700 Valley Bank Plaza Building 300 South Fourth Street · Las Vegas, NV 89101 · 702-383-8888

Edward Everett Hale · Hale, Lane, Peek, Dennison and Howard · Valley Bank Plaza, Suite 650 · 50 West Liberty Street · P.O. Box 3237 · Reno, NV 89505 702-786-7900

David R. Hoy · Bible, Santini, Hoy, Miller & Trachok · 232 Court Street · Reno, NV 89501-1808 · 702-786-8000

F. DeArmond Sharp · Hawkins & Sharp · Security Bank Building, Suite 416 One East Liberty Street · P.O. Box 750 · Reno, NV 89504 · 702-786-4646

TAX AND EMPLOYEE BENEFITS LAW

Patricia L. Brown · (also Employee Benefits) · Beckley, Singleton, Delanoy, Jemison & List · 803 South Sixth Street · P.O. Box 1420 · Las Vegas, NV 89101 702-384-4404

Jeffrey L. Burr · 1900 East Flamingo Road, Suite 252 · Las Vegas, NV 89119 702-369-9919

Douglas M. Edwards · (also Employee Benefits) · Edwards, Kolesar, Toigo & Sewell · Nevada Savings Financial Center, Suite 380 · 3320 West Sahara Avenue Las Vegas, NV 89102 · 702-362-7800

A. Kent Greene · (Employee Benefits) · Clark, Greene & Associates · 5606 South Eastern Avenue · Las Vegas, NV 89119 · 702-736-1844

Robert C. Anderson · Anderson & Pearl · 241 Ridge Street, Suite 300 · P.O. Box 21150 · Reno, NV 89515 · 702-348-5000

L. Robert LeGoy, Jr. · (Employee Benefits) · Walther, Key, Maupin, Oats, Cox, Lee & Klaich · Lakeside Professional Plaza, Suite 200 · 3500 Lakeside Court Reno, NV 89509 · 702-827-2000

Ernest J. Maupin III · Walther, Key, Maupin, Oats, Cox, Lee & Klaich · Lakeside Professional Plaza, Suite 200 · 3500 Lakeside Court · Reno, NV 89509 702-827-2000

G. Barton Mowry · Walther, Key, Maupin, Oats, Cox, Lee & Klaich · Lakeside Professional Plaza, Suite 200 · 3500 Lakeside Court · Reno, NV 89509 · 702-827-2000

Andrew Pearl · Anderson & Pearl · 241 Ridge Street, Suite 300 · P.O. Box 21150 · Reno, NV 89515 · 702-348-5000

TRUSTS AND ESTATES

Patricia L. Brown · Beckley, Singleton, Delanoy, Jemison & List · 803 South Sixth Street · P.O. Box 1420 · Las Vegas, NV 89101 · 702-384-4404

Jeffrey L. Burr · 1900 East Flamingo Road, Suite 252 · Las Vegas, NV 89119 · 702-369-9919

Charles William Johnson · Johnson & Rushforth · 530 South Fourth Street · Las Vegas, NV 89101 · 702-384-2830

Layne T. Rushforth · Johnson & Rushforth · 530 South Fourth Street · Las Vegas, NV 89101 · 702-384-2830

Ernest J. Maupin III · Walther, Key, Maupin, Oats, Cox, Lee & Klaich · Lakeside Professional Plaza, Suite 200 · 3500 Lakeside Court · Reno, NV 89509 · 702-827-2000

G. Barton Mowry · Walther, Key, Maupin, Oats, Cox, Lee & Klaich · Lakeside Professional Plaza, Suite 200 · 3500 Lakeside Court · Reno, NV 89509 · 702-827-2000

Andrew Pearl · Anderson & Pearl · 241 Ridge Street, Suite 300 · P.O. Box 21150 · Reno, NV 89515 · 702-348-5000

NEW HAMPSHIRE

BANKRUPTCY LAW	**421**
BUSINESS LITIGATION	**421**
CORPORATE LAW	**422**
CRIMINAL DEFENSE	**423**
FAMILY LAW	**424**
LABOR AND EMPLOYMENT LAW	**424**
PERSONAL INJURY LITIGATION	**424**
REAL ESTATE LAW	**425**
TAX AND EMPLOYEE BENEFITS LAW	**426**
TRUSTS AND ESTATES	**426**

BANKRUPTCY LAW

Daniel J. Callaghan · Devine, Millimet, Stahl & Branch · 111 Amherst Street · P.O. Box 719 · Manchester, NH 03105 · 603-669-1000

Daniel W. Sklar · Sheehan, Phinney, Bass & Green · Hampshire Plaza · 1000 Elm Street · Manchester, NH 03101 · 603-668-0300

Mark W. Vaughn · Devine, Millimet, Stahl & Branch · 111 Amherst Street · P.O. Box 719 · Manchester, NH 03105 · 603-669-1000

J. Michael Deasy · Deasy & Dwyer · 60 Main Street · Nashua, NH 03060 · 603-595-9700

BUSINESS LITIGATION

Richard B. Couser · Orr and Reno · One Eagle Square · P.O. Box 709 · Concord, NH 03301-0709 · 603-224-2381

Charles G. Douglas III · (Appellate) · McSwiney, Jones, Semple & Douglas · Eight Center Street · Concord, NH 03301 · 603-224-1989

Martin L. Gross · (Appellate) · Sulloway Hollis & Soden · Nine Capitol Street · P.O. Box 1256 · Concord, NH 03301 · 603-224-2341

Ronald L. Snow · Orr and Reno · One Eagle Square · P.O. Box 709 · Concord, NH 03301-0709 · 603-224-2381

Frederic K. Upton · (Appellate) · Upton, Sanders and Smith · Ten Centre Street · Concord, NH 03301 · 603-224-7791

W. Wright Danenbarger · Wiggin & Nourie · The Parish House · Franklin & Market Streets · P.O. Box 808 · Manchester, NH 03105 · 603-669-2211

E. Donald Dufresne · Devine, Millimet, Stahl & Branch · 111 Amherst Street · P.O. Box 719 · Manchester, NH 03105 · 603-669-1000

Jack B. Middleton · McLane, Graf, Raulerson & Middleton · 40 Stark Street · P.O. Box 326 · Manchester, NH 03105 · 603-625-6464

James R. Muirhead · McLane, Graf, Raulerson & Middleton · 40 Stark Street · P.O. Box 326 · Manchester, NH 03105 · 603-625-6464

Thomas H. Richards · Sheehan, Phinney, Bass & Green · Hampshire Plaza · 1000 Elm Street · Manchester, NH 03101 · 603-668-0300

Eugene M. Van Loan, III · Wadleigh, Starr, Peters, Dunn & Chiesa · 95 Market Street · Manchester, NH 03101 · 603-669-4140

CORPORATE LAW

Charles F. Lahey · Orr and Reno · One Eagle Square · P.O. Box 709 · Concord, NH 03301-0709 · 603-224-2381

Charles F. Sheridan, Jr. · Sulloway Hollis & Soden · Nine Capitol Street · P.O. Box 1256 · Concord, NH 03301 · 603-224-2341

T. William Bigelow · Wiggin & Nourie · The Parish House · Franklin & Market Streets · P.O. Box 808 · Manchester, NH 03105 · 603-669-2211

Robert E. Dastin · Sheehan, Phinney, Bass & Green · Hampshire Plaza · 1000 Elm Street · Manchester, NH 03101 · 603-668-0300

Charles A. DeGrandpre · McLane, Graf, Raulerson & Middleton · 40 Stark Street · P.O. Box 326 · Manchester, NH 03105 · 603-625-6464

John S. Holland · Devine, Millimet, Stahl & Branch · 111 Amherst Street · P.O. Box 719 · Manchester, NH 03105 · 603-669-1000

Joseph A. Millimet · Devine, Millimet, Stahl & Branch · 111 Amherst Street P.O. Box 719 · Manchester, NH 03105 · 603-669-1000

John R. Monson · Wiggin & Nourie · The Parish House · Franklin & Market Streets · P.O. Box 808 · Manchester, NH 03105 · 603-669-2211

Alan L. Reische · Sheehan, Phinney, Bass & Green · Hampshire Plaza · 1000 Elm Street · Manchester, NH 03101 · 603-668-0300

Robert A. Raulerson · McLane, Graf, Raulerson & Middleton · 40 Stark Street P.O. Box 326 · Manchester, NH 03105 · 603-625-6464

Norman H. Stahl · Devine, Millimet, Stahl & Branch · 111 Amherst Street · P.O. Box 719 · Manchester, NH 03105 · 603-669-1000

William C. Tucker · Wadleigh, Starr, Peters, Dunn & Chiesa · 95 Market Street Manchester, NH 03101 · 603-669-4140

Chester H. Lopez, Jr. · Hamblett & Kerrigan · One Indian Head Plaza · P.O. Box 868X · Nashua, NH 03061 · 603-883-5501

CRIMINAL DEFENSE

Steven M. Gordon · Shaheen, Cappiello, Stein & Gordon · Five Green Street Concord, NH 03301 · 603-228-1109

Robert A. Stein · Shaheen, Cappiello, Stein & Gordon · Five Green Street Concord, NH 03301 · 603-228-1109

William E. Brennan · Brennan Professional Association · 85 Brook Street Manchester, NH 03104 · 603-668-8300

Cathy J. Green · (also Appellate) · 108 Bay Street · Manchester, NH 03104 603-669-7603

Richard B. McNamara · Wiggin & Nourie · The Parish House · Franklin & Market Streets · P.O. Box 808 · Manchester, NH 03105 · 603-669-2211

FAMILY LAW

Charles G. Douglas III · McSwiney, Jones, Semple & Douglas · Eight Center Street · Concord, NH 03301 · 603-224-1989

L. Jonathan Ross · Wiggin & Nourie · The Parish House · Franklin & Market Streets · P.O. Box 808 · Manchester, NH 03105 · 603-669-2211

LABOR AND EMPLOYMENT LAW

Edward M. Kaplan · (Management; Individuals) · Sulloway Hollis & Soden Nine Capitol Street · P.O. Box 1256 · Concord, NH 03301 · 603-224-2341

Edward E. Shumaker III · (Management) · Gallagher, Callahan & Gartrell · 214 North Main Street · P.O. Box 1415 · Concord, NH 03301 · 603-228-1181

Richard E. Galway, Jr. · (Management) · Devine, Millimet, Stahl & Branch · 111 Amherst Street · P.O. Box 719 · Manchester, NH 03105 · 603-669-1000

Alan Hall · (Management) · Wadleigh, Starr, Peters, Dunn & Chiesa · 95 Market Street · Manchester, NH 03101 · 603-669-4140

Robert A. Wells · (Individuals) · McLane, Graf, Raulerson & Middleton · 40 Stark Street · P.O. Box 326 · Manchester, NH 03105 · 603-625-6464

PERSONAL INJURY LITIGATION

Edward M. Kaplan · (Plaintiffs) · Sulloway Hollis & Soden · Nine Capitol Street P.O. Box 1256 · Concord, NH 03301 · 603-224-2341

Ernest T. Smith III · (Plaintiffs) · Upton, Sanders and Smith · Ten Centre Street Concord, NH 03301 · 603-224-7791

Ronald L. Snow · (Defendants) · Orr and Reno · One Eagle Square · P.O. Box 709 · Concord, NH 03301-0709 · 603-224-2381

Dort S. Bigg · Wiggin & Nourie · The Parish House · Franklin & Market Streets P.O. Box 808 · Manchester, NH 03105 · 603-669-2211

John T. Broderick, Jr. · (Defendants) · Devine, Millimet, Stahl & Branch · 111 Amherst Street · P.O. Box 719 · Manchester, NH 03105 · 603-669-1000

W. Wright Danenbarger · (Defendants) · Wiggin & Nourie · The Parish House Franklin & Market Streets · P.O. Box 808 · Manchester, NH 03105 · 603-669-2211

E. Donald Dufresne · (Defendants) · Devine, Millimet, Stahl & Branch · 111 Amherst Street · P.O. Box 719 · Manchester, NH 03105 · 603-669-1000

John E. Friberg · (Defendants) · Wadleigh, Starr, Peters, Dunn & Chiesa · 95 Market Street · Manchester, NH 03101 · 603-669-4140

Jack B. Middleton · (Plaintiffs) · McLane, Graf, Raulerson & Middleton · 40 Stark Street · P.O. Box 326 · Manchester, NH 03105 · 603-625-6464

David L. Nixon · (Plaintiffs) · Brown and Nixon · 80 Merrimack Street · Manchester, NH 03101 · 603-669-8080

William S. Orcutt · (Defendants) · Wiggin & Nourie · The Parish House Franklin & Market Streets · P.O. Box 808 · Manchester, NH 03105 · 603-669-2211

Philip G. Peters · (Defendants) · Wadleigh, Starr, Peters, Dunn & Chiesa · 95 Market Street · Manchester, NH 03101 · 603-669-4140

L. Jonathan Ross · (Defendants) · Wiggin & Nourie · The Parish House Franklin & Market Streets · P.O. Box 808 · Manchester, NH 03105 · 603-669-2211

Joseph M. Kerrigan · (Defendants) · Hamblett & Kerrigan · One Indian Head Plaza · P.O. Box 868X · Nashua, NH 03061 · 603-883-5501

James John Kalled · (Plaintiffs) · Route 171 · Courthouse Square · Ossipee, NH 03864 · 603-539-2218

REAL ESTATE LAW

Donald E. Gartrell · Gallagher, Callahan & Gartrell · 214 North Main Street P.O. Box 1415 · Concord, NH 03301 · 603-228-1181

John B. Pendleton · Gallagher, Callahan and Gartrell · 214 North Main Street P.O. Box 1415 · Concord, NH 03301 · 603-228-1181

Eaton W. Tarbell, Jr. · Sulloway Hollis & Soden · Nine Capitol Street · P.O. Box 1256 · Concord, NH 03301 · 603-224-2341

John J. Ryan · Casassa and Ryan · 459 Lafayette Road · Hampton, NH 03842 603-926-6336

Norman H. Stahl · Devine, Millimet, Stahl & Branch · 111 Amherst Street · P.O. Box 719 · Manchester, NH 03105 · 603-669-1000

William C. Tucker · Wadleigh, Starr, Peters, Dunn & Chiesa · 95 Market Street · Manchester, NH 03101 · 603-669-4140

TAX AND EMPLOYEE BENEFITS LAW

David F. Conley · Sulloway Hollis & Soden · Nine Capitol Street · P.O. Box 1256 · Concord, NH 03301 · 603-224-2341

Douglas R. Chamberlain · (Employee Benefits) · Wiggin & Nourie · The Parish House · Franklin & Market Streets · P.O. Box 808 · Manchester, NH 03105 · 603-669-2211

Alan P. Cleveland · (Employee Benefits) · Sheehan, Phinney, Bass & Green · Hampshire Plaza · 1000 Elm Street · Manchester, NH 03101 · 603-668-0300

John S. Holland · Devine, Millimet, Stahl & Branch · 111 Amherst Street · P.O. Box 719 · Manchester, NH 03105 · 603-669-1000

Wayne T. Murray · Sheehan, Phinney, Bass & Green · Hampshire Plaza · 1000 Elm Street · Manchester, NH 03101 · 603-668-0300

William V. A. Zorn · McLane, Graf, Raulerson & Middleton · 40 Stark Street · P.O. Box 326 · Manchester, NH 03105 · 603-625-6464

TRUSTS AND ESTATES

David F. Conley · Sulloway Hollis & Soden · Nine Capitol Street · P.O. Box 1256 · Concord, NH 03301 · 603-224-2341

Malcolm McLane · Orr and Reno · One Eagle Square · P.O. Box 709 · Concord, NH 03301-0709 · 603-224-2381

Joseph S. Ransmeier · Ransmeier & Spellman · One Capitol Street · P.O. Box 1378 · Concord, NH 03301 · 603-228-0477

George R. Hanna · Faulkner, Plaut, Hanna, Zimmerman & Freund · 91 Court Street · P.O. Box 527 · Keene, NH 03431-0527 · 603-352-3630

Charles A. DeGrandpre · McLane, Graf, Raulerson & Middleton · 40 Stark Street · P.O. Box 326 · Manchester, NH 03105 · 603-625-6464

John S. Holland · Devine, Millimet, Stahl & Branch · 111 Amherst Street · P.O. Box 719 · Manchester, NH 03105 · 603-669-1000

Richard A. Morse · Sheehan, Phinney, Bass & Green · Hampshire Plaza · 1000 Elm Street · Manchester, NH 03101 · 603-668-0300

William V. A. Zorn · McLane, Graf, Raulerson & Middleton · 40 Stark Street P.O. Box 326 · Manchester, NH 03105 · 603-625-6464

NEW JERSEY

BANKRUPTCY LAW	428
BUSINESS LITIGATION	429
CORPORATE LAW	430
CRIMINAL DEFENSE	432
FAMILY LAW	433
LABOR AND EMPLOYMENT LAW	434
NATURAL RESOURCES AND ENVIRONMENTAL LAW	437
PERSONAL INJURY LITIGATION	437
REAL ESTATE LAW	438
TAX AND EMPLOYEE BENEFITS LAW	439
TRUSTS AND ESTATES	440

BANKRUPTCY LAW

Arthur J. Abramowitz · Davis, Reberkenny & Abramowitz · 499 Cooper Landing Road · P.O. Box 5459 · Cherry Hill, NJ 08002 · 609-667-6000

Neil A. Kleinberg · Kleinberg, Moroney, Masterson & Schachter · The Common 225 Millburn Avenue · Millburn, NJ 07041 · 201-467-3900

Myron S. Lehman · Lehman, Wasserman & Jurista · The Common · 225 Millburn Avenue · Millburn, NJ 07041 · 201-467-2700

Nathan Ravin · Ravin, Greenberg & Zackin · 101 Eisenhower Parkway · Roseland, NJ 07068 · 201-226-1500

Arthur Teich · Teich, Groh and Frost · 691 State Highway 33 · Trenton, NJ 08619 609-394-3161

BUSINESS LITIGATION

Morrill J. Cole · Cole, Schotz, Bernstein, Meisel & Forman · Court Plaza, North 25 Main Street · Hackensack, NJ 07602-0800 · 201-489-3000

Paul A. Rowe · Greenbaum, Rowe, Smith, Ravin, Davis & Bergstein · Metro Corporate Campus · 99 Wood Avenue South · Iselin, NJ 08830 · 201-549-5600

Thomas F. Campion · Shanley & Fisher · 131 Madison Avenue · Morristown, NJ 07960-1979 · 201-285-1000

Clyde A. Szuch · Pitney, Hardin, Kipp & Szuch · 163 Madison Avenue, CN 1945 Morristown, NJ 07960 · 201-623-1980

Clive S. Cummis · Sills Cummis Zuckerman Radin Tischman Epstein & Gross 33 Washington Street · Newark, NJ 07102-3179 · 201-643-3232

Michael R. Griffinger · Crummy, Del Deo, Dolan, Griffinger & Vecchione · One Gateway Center · Newark, NJ 07102-5311 · 201-622-2235

Eugene M. Haring · McCarter & English · Four Gateway Center · 100 Mulberry Street · Newark, NJ 07102-4096 · 201-622-4444

Joseph E. Irenas · McCarter & English · Four Gateway Center · 100 Mulberry Street · Newark, NJ 07102-4096 · 201-622-4444

Frederick B. Lacey · LeBoeuf, Lamb, Leiby & MacRae · One Gateway Center, Suite 603 · Newark, NJ 07102 · 201-643-8000

John L. McGoldrick · McCarter & English · Four Gateway Center · 100 Mulberry Street · Newark, NJ 07102-4096 · 201-622-4444

William B. McGuire · Tompkins, McGuire & Wachenfeld · Four Gateway Center 100 Mulberry Street · Newark, NJ 07102 · 201-622-3000

H. Curtis Meanor · Podvey, Sachs, Meanor & Catenacci, Suite 2504 · One Gateway Center · Newark, NJ 07102-5311 · 201-622-4702

Donald A. Robinson · Robinson, Wayne & LaSala · One Gateway Center Newark, NJ 07102-5311 · 201-621-7900

Albert G. Besser · Hannoch Weisman · Four Becker Farm Road · Roseland, NJ 07068 · 201-535-5300

Robert J. Del Tufo · Hannoch Weisman · Four Becker Farm Road · Roseland, NJ 07068 · 201-535-5300

Adrian M. Foley, Jr. · Connell, Foley & Geiser · 85 Livingston Avenue · Roseland, NJ 07068 · 201-535-0500

Irwin I. Kimmelman · Kimmelman, Wolff & Samson · 280 Corporate Center Five Becker Farm Road · Roseland, NJ 07068 · 201-740-0500

Laurence B. Orloff · Orloff, Lowenbach, Stifelman & Siegel · 101 Eisenhower Parkway · Roseland, NJ 07068 · 201-622-6200

Ronald M. Sturtz · Hannoch Weisman · Four Becker Farm Road · Roseland, NJ 07068 · 201-535-5300

Frederic K. Becker · Wilentz, Goldman & Spitzer · 90 Woodbridge Center Drive P.O. Box 10 · Woodbridge, NJ 07095 · 201-636-8000

CORPORATE LAW

Philip L. Chapman · Klein, Chapman, Greenburg, Henkoff & Siegel · 935 Allwood Road · P.O. Box 2048 · Clifton, NJ 07015 · 201-777-8900

Alan E. Davis · Greenbaum, Rowe, Smith, Ravin, Davis & Bergstein · Metro Corporate Campus · 99 Wood Avenue South · Iselin, NJ 08830 · 201-549-5600

Allen Ravin · Greenbaum, Rowe, Smith, Ravin, Davis & Bergstein · Metro Corporate Campus · 99 Wood Avenue South · Iselin, NJ 08830 · 201-549-5600

John A. Aiello · Giordano, Halleran & Ciesla · 270 State Highway #35 · P.O. Box 190 · Middletown, NJ 07748 · 201-741-3900

Thomas J. Bitar · Dillon, Bitar & Luther · 53 Maple Avenue · P.O. Box 398 Morristown, NJ 07960 · 201-539-3100

Thomas E. Colleton, Jr. · Riker, Danzig, Scherer, Hyland & Perretti · Headquarters Plaza · One Speedwell Avenue · Morristown, NJ 07960-1981 · 201-538-0800

Robert Fischer III · Riker, Danzig, Scherer, Hyland & Perretti · Headquarters Plaza · One Speedwell Avenue · Morristown, NJ 07960-1981 · 201-538-0800

William D. Hardin · Pitney, Hardin, Kipp & Szuch · 163 Madison Avenue, CN 1945 · Morristown, NJ 07960-1945 · 201-267-3333

Robert P. Hazlehurst Jr. · Pitney, Hardin, Kipp & Szuch · 163 Madison Avenue, CN 1945 · Morristown, NJ 07960-1945 · 201-267-3333

Joseph H. Kott · Pitney, Hardin, Kipp & Szuch · 163 Madison Avenue, CN 1945 Morristown, NJ 07960-1945 · 201-267-3333

Joseph Lunin · Pitney, Hardin, Kipp & Szuch · 163 Madison Avenue, CN 1945 Morristown, NJ 07960-1945 · 201-267-3333

Bart J. Colli · McCarter & English · Four Gateway Center · 100 Mulberry Street Newark, NJ 07102-4096 · 201-622-4444

Joseph E. Irenas · McCarter & English · Four Gateway Center · 100 Mulberry Street · Newark, NJ 07102-4096 · 201-622-4444

Steven H. Knee · Stryker, Tams & Dill · 33 Washington Street · Newark, NJ 07102 · 201-624-9300

Todd M. Poland · McCarter & English · Four Gateway Center · 100 Mulberry Street · Newark, NJ 07102-4096 · 201-622-4444

Peter H. Ehrenberg · Lowenstein, Sandler, Kohl, Fisher & Boylan · 65 Livingston Avenue · Roseland, NJ 07068 · 201-992-8700

Ellen B. Kulka · Hannoch Weisman · Four Becker Farm Road · Roseland, NJ 07068 · 201-535-5300

Ralph M. Lowenbach · Orloff, Lowenbach, Stifelman & Siegel · 101 Eisenhower Parkway · Roseland, NJ 07068 · 201-622-6200

Alan V. Lowenstein · Lowenstein, Sandler, Kohl, Fisher & Boylan · 65 Livingston Avenue · Roseland, NJ 07068 · 201-992-8700

John R. MacKay 2nd · Lowenstein, Sandler, Kohl, Fisher & Boylan · 65 Livingston Avenue · Roseland, NJ 07068 · 201-992-8700

Richard M. Sandler · Lowenstein, Sandler, Kohl, Fisher & Boylan · 65 Livingston Avenue · Roseland, NJ 07068 · 201-992-8700

John D. Schupper · Lowenstein, Sandler, Kohl, Fisher & Boylan · 65 Livingston Avenue · Roseland, NJ 07068 · 201-992-8700

Bruce D. Shoulson · Lowenstein, Sandler, Kohl, Fisher & Boylan · 65 Livingston Avenue · Roseland, NJ 07068 · 201-992-8700

Peter D. Hutcheon · Norris, McLaughlin & Marcus · 1081 Route 22 · P.O. Box 1018 · Sommerville, NJ 08876-1018 · 201-722-0700

Frederic K. Becker · Wilentz, Goldman & Spitzer · 90 Woodbridge Center Drive P.O. Box 10 · Woodbridge, NJ 07095 · 201-636-8000

Stuart A. Hoberman · Wilentz, Goldman & Spitzer · 90 Woodbridge Center Drive · P.O. Box 10 · Woodbridge, NJ 07095 · 201-636-8060

CRIMINAL DEFENSE

Edwin J. Jacobs, Jr. · Jacobs, Todd & Bruso · 1125 Pacific Avenue · Atlantic City, NJ 08401 · 609-348-1125

Carl D. Poplar · Poplar & Florio · Building One, Suite C · 1010 Kings Highway South · Cherry Hill, NJ 08034 · 609-795-5560

Miles Feinstein · 66 Mt. Prospect Avenue · Clifton, NJ 07011 · 201-779-1124

Joseph A. Hayden, Jr. · Hayden and Perle · 80 River Street · Hoboken, NJ 07030 201-795-9681

Roger A. Lowenstein · Dickinson, Creighton & Lowenstein · 51 Newark Street Hoboken, NJ 07030 · 201-659-6969

Leonard Meyerson · Miller, Hochman, Meyerson & Schwartz · 955 West Side Avenue · Jersey City, NJ 07306 · 201-333-9000

Dino D. Bliablias · Stein, Bliablias, McGuire & Pantages · Eisenhower Plaza II, Second Floor · 354 Eisenhower Parkway · P.O. Box 460 · Livingston, NJ 07039 201-992-1100

Francis J. Hartman · 300 Chester Avenue · Moorestown, NJ 08057 · 609-267-5030

Thomas R. Ashley · Ashley & Charles · 24 Commerce Street · Newark, NJ 07102 201-623-0501

Raymond A. Brown · Brown & Brown · Gateway One, Suite 300 · Newark, NJ 07102 · 201-622-1846

Michael A. Querques · 433 Central Avenue · Orange, NJ 07050 · 201-673-1400

Matthew P. Boylan · Lowenstein, Sandler, Kohl, Fisher & Boylan · 65 Livingston Avenue · Roseland, NJ 07068 · 201-992-8700

Justin P. Walder · Walder, Sondak, Berkeley & Brogan · Five Becker Farm Road · Roseland, NJ 07068 · 201-992-5300

Theodore V. Wells, Jr. · Lowenstein, Sandler, Kohl, Fisher & Boylan · 65 Livingston Avenue · Roseland, NJ 07068 · 201-992-8700

Robert F. Novins · Novins, York, DeVincens & Pentony · 202 Main Street, CN 2032 · Toms River, NJ 08753 · 201-349-7100

Michael Critchley · Critchley & Roche · 354 Main Street · West Orange, NJ 07052 · 201-731-9831

Michael D'Alessio, Jr. · 20 Northfield Avenue · West Orange, NJ 07052 · 201-736-1500

Harvey Weissbard · Weissbard & Wiewiorka · 20 Northfield Avenue · West Orange, NJ 07052 · 201-731-9770

FAMILY LAW

Richard J. Feinberg · Feinberg, Dee & Feinberg · 554 Broadway · Bayonne, NJ 07002 · 201-339-5500

Harold M. Savage, Sr. · Savage & Savage · 103 B Troy Towers · Bloomfield, NJ 07003 · 201-743-0900

Gardner B. Miller · Miller & Lawless · The Canfield Office Park · 882 Pompton Avenue · Cedar Grove, NJ 07009 · 201-239-1040

Thomas S. Forkin · Forkin & McShane · 750 North Kings Highway · Cherry Hill, NJ 08034 · 609-779-8500

Arthur Rose · Rose & De Fuccio · 35 Essex Street · Hackensack, NJ 07601 · 201-488-7800

Lee M. Hymerling · Archer & Greiner · One Centennial Square · Haddonfield, NJ 08033 · 609-795-2121

Gary N. Skoloff · Skoloff & Wolfe · 293 Eisenhower Parkway · Livingston, NJ 07039 · 201-992-0900

Anne W. Elwell · Elwell and Crane · 38 Park Street · Montclair, NJ 07042 201-783-3390

Sheldon M. Simon · 555 Speedwell Avenue · Morris Plains, NJ 07950 201-538-2266

Barry I. Croland · Stern, Steiger, Croland, Tanenbaum & Schielke · One Mack Centre Drive · Paramus, NJ 07652 · 201-262-9400

Bernard H. Hoffman · Hoffman and Schreiber · 199 Broad Street · P.O. Drawer 789 · Red Bank, NJ 07701 · 201-842-7272

Edward S. Snyder · Three Becker Farm Road · Roseland, NJ 07068 · 201-994-4442

Frank A. Louis · Pogarsky & Louis · 213 Washington Street · P.O. Box 461 Tom's River, NJ 08753-0461 · 201-349-0600

Theodore Sager Meth · Meth & Woehling · 50 Elmer Street · Westfield, NJ 07090 · 201-232-7831

David M. Wildstein · Wilentz, Goldman & Spitzer · 90 Woodbridge Center Drive P.O. Box 10 · Woodbridge, NJ 07095 · 201-636-8000

LABOR AND EMPLOYMENT LAW

Steven R. Cohen · Selikoff & Cohen · (Labor; Individuals) · 1101 Kings Highway North, Suite G102 · Cherry Hill, NJ 08034 · 609-482-1990

Robert F. O'Brien · (Labor) · Tomar, Seliger, Simonoff, Adourian & O'Brien · 41 South Haddon Avenue · Haddonfield, NJ 08033 · 609-429-1100

David Seliger · (Labor) · Tomar, Seliger, Simonoff, Adourian & O'Brien · 41 South Haddon Avenue · Haddonfield, NJ 08033 · 609-429-1100

Howard S. Simonoff · (Labor; Individuals) · Tomar, Seliger, Simonoff, Adourian & O'Brien · 41 South Haddon Avenue · Haddonfield, NJ 08033 · 609-429-1100

Steven W. Suflas · (Management) · Archer & Greiner · One Centennial Square Haddonfield, NJ 08033 · 609-795-2121

Edward A. Cohen · (Labor) · Schneider, Cohen, Solomon, Leder & Montalbano 591 Summit Avenue · Jersey City, NJ 07306 · 201-656-8241

Bruce D. Leder · (Labor) · Schneider, Cohen, Solomon, Leder & Montalbano 591 Summit Avenue · Jersey City, NJ 07306 · 201-656-8241

Paul A. Montalbano · (Labor) · Schneider, Cohen, Solomon, Leder & Montalbano · 591 Summit Avenue · Jersey City, NJ 07306 · 201-656-8241

Zachary Schneider · (Labor) · Schneider, Cohen, Solomon, Leder & Montalbano 591 Summit Avenue · Jersey City, NJ 07306 · 201-656-8241

David S. Solomon · (Labor) · Schneider, Cohen, Solomon, Leder & Montalbano 591 Summit Avenue · Jersey City, NJ 07306 · 201-656-8241

S. Joseph Fortunato · (Management) · Pitney, Hardin, Kipp & Szuch · 163 Madison Avenue, CN 1945 · Morristown, NJ 07960-1945 · 201-267-3333

Francis X. Dee · (Management) · Carpenter, Bennett & Morrissey · Gateway Three · 100 Mulberry Street · Newark, NJ 07102 · 201-622-7711

Ronald H. De Maria · (Management) · De Maria, Ellis & Hunt · 744 Broad Street, 32nd Floor · Newark, NJ 07102 · 201-623-1699

H. Reed Ellis · (Management) · De Maria, Ellis & Hunt · 744 Broad Street, 32nd Floor · Newark, NJ 07102 · 201-623-1699

Angelo J. Genova · (Management) · De Maria, Ellis & Hunt · 744 Broad Street, 32nd Floor · Newark, NJ 07102 · 201-623-1699

Albert G. Kroll · (Labor) · Zazzali, Zazzali & Kroll · Gateway One · Newark, NJ 07102 · 201-623-1822

Craig H. Livingston · (Labor; Individuals) · Ball, Tykulsker & Livingston · 108 Washington Street · Newark, NJ 07102 · 201-622-4545

Thomas L. Morrissey · (Management) · Carpenter, Bennett & Morrissey · Gateway Three · 100 Mulberry Street · Newark, NJ 07102 · 201-622-7711

Sidney Reitman · (Labor) · Reitman, Parsonnet, Maisel & Duggan · 744 Broad Street · Newark, NJ 07102 · 201-622-8347

Denise Reinhardt · (Individuals) · Reinhardt & Schachter · 744 Broad Street, #3101 · Newark, NJ 07102 · 201-623-1600

Donald A. Romano · (Management) · Carpenter, Bennett & Morrissey · Gateway Three · 100 Mulberry Street · Newark, NJ 07102 · 201-622-7711

Edward F. Ryan · (Management) · Carpenter, Bennett & Morrissey · Gateway Three · 100 Mulberry Street · Newark, NJ 07102 · 201-622-7711

Paul Schachter · (Individuals) · Reinhardt & Schachter · 744 Broad Street, #3101 Newark, NJ 07102 · 201-623-1600

James R. Zazzali · (Labor) · Zazzali, Zazzali & Kroll · Gateway One · Newark, NJ 07102 · 201-623-1822

Jerold E. Glassman · (Management) · Grotta, Glassman & Hoffman · 75 Livingston Avenue · Roseland, NJ 07068 · 201-992-4800

Marvin M. Goldstein · (Management) · Grotta, Glassman & Hoffman · 75 Livingston Avenue · Roseland, NJ 07068 · 201-992-4800

Harold L. Hoffman · (Management) · Grotta, Glassman & Hoffman · 75 Livingston Avenue · Roseland, NJ 07068 · 201-992-4800

Desmond Massey · (Management) · Grotta, Glassman & Hoffman · 75 Livingston Avenue · Roseland, NJ 07068 · 201-992-4800

Stephen A. Ploscowe · (Management) · Grotta, Glassman & Hoffman · 75 Livingston Avenue · Roseland, NJ 07068 · 201-992-4800

Vincent J. Apruzzese · (Management) · Apruzzese, McDermott, Mastro & Murphy · Independence Plaza · 500 Morris Avenue · Springfield, NJ 07081 · 201-467-1776

Francis A. Mastro · (Management) · Apruzzese, McDermott, Mastro & Murphy Independence Plaza · 500 Morris Avenue · Springfield, NJ 07081 · 201-467-1776

James F. Murphy · (Management) · Apruzzese, McDermott, Mastro & Murphy Independence Plaza · 500 Morris Avenue · Springfield, NJ 07081 · 201-467-1776

Howard A. Goldberger · (Labor) · Goldberger & Finn · 81 Northfield Avenue West Orange, NJ 07052 · 201-731-0500

Nancy Erika Smith · (Individuals) · Kiernan & Smith · 100 Executive Drive West Orange, NJ 07052 · 201-736-7033

NATURAL RESOURCES AND ENVIRONMENTAL LAW

Lewis Goldshore · Goldshore & Wolf · 2683 Main Street · P.O. Box 6820 · Lawrenceville, NJ 08648 · 609-896-1660

Theodore A. Schwartz · Schwartz Tobia & Stanziale · 22 Crestmont Road Montclair, NJ 07042 · 201-746-6000

William H. Hyatt, Jr. · Pitney, Hardin, Kipp & Szuch · 163 Madison Avenue, CN 1945 · Morristown, NJ 07960 · 201-623-1980

A. Patrick Nucciarone · Hannoch Weisman · Four Becker Farm Road · Roseland, NJ 07068 · 201-535-5300

Michael L. Rodburg · Lowenstein, Sandler, Kohl, Fisher & Boylan · 65 Livingston Avenue · Roseland, NJ 07068 · 201-992-8700

Steven J. Picco · Picco Mack Kennedy Jaffe Perrella & Yoskin · 240 West State Street · Trenton, NJ 08608 · 609-393-0621

Michael Gordon · Gordon, Gordon & Haley · 80 Main Street · West Orange, NJ 07052 · 201-736-0094

David B. Farer · Farer, Siegal & Fersko · 425 North Avenue East · P.O. Box H Westfield, NJ 07091 · 201-789-8550

PERSONAL INJURY LITIGATION

Gerald B. O'Connor · (Plaintiffs) · O'Connor & Rhatican · 383 Main Street Chatham, NJ 07928 · 201-635-2210

Joseph H. Kenney · Kenney & Kearney · 220 Lake Drive East, Suite 210 · P.O. Box 5034 · Cherry Hill, NJ 08034 · 609-779-7000

David A. Parker · (Defendants) · Parker, McCay & Criscuolo · Three Greentree Centre, Suite 401 · Route 73 & Greentree Road · Marlton, NJ 08053 · 609-267-2850

Myron J. Bromberg · Porzio, Bromberg & Newman · 163 Madison Avenue Morristown, NJ 07960-1997 · 201-538-4006

Thomas F. Campion · (Defendants) · Shanley & Fisher · 131 Madison Avenue Morristown, NJ 07960-1979 · 201-285-1000

Raymond M. Tierney, Jr. · (Defendants) · Shanley & Fisher · 131 Madison Avenue · Morristown, NJ 07960-1979 · 201-285-1000

John M. Blume · (Plaintiffs) · Blume, Vasquez, Goldfaden, Berkowitz, Oliveras & Donnelly · Five Commerce Street, Fourth Floor · Newark, NJ 07102 201-622-1881

John E. Keale · (Defendants) · Carpenter, Bennett & Morrissey · Gateway Three 100 Mulberry Street · Newark, NJ 07102 · 201-622-7711

Frederick B. Lacey · (Defendants) · LeBoeuf, Lamb, Leiby & MacRae · One Gateway Center, Suite 603 · Newark, NJ 07102 · 201-643-8000

John L. McGoldrick · (Defendants) · McCarter & English · Four Gateway Center 100 Mulberry Street · Newark, NJ 07102-4096 · 201-622-4444

William B. McGuire · (Defendants) · Tompkins, McGuire & Wachenfeld · Four Gateway Center · 400 Mulberry Street · Newark, NJ 07102 · 201-622-3000

H. Curtis Meanor · (Defendants) · Podvey, Sachs, Meanor & Catenacci · One Gateway Center, Suite 2504 · Newark, NJ 07102-5311 · 201-662-4702

Carl Greenberg · Budd Larner Kent Gross Picillo Rosenbaum Greenberg & Sade 150 John F. Kennedy Parkway, CN 1000 · Short Hills, NJ 07078-0999 · 201-379-4800

David R. Gross · Budd Larner Kent Gross Picillo Rosenbaum Greenberg & Sade 150 John F. Kennedy Parkway, CN 1000 · Short Hills, NJ 07078-0999 · 201-379-4800

Burchard V. Martin · (Defendants) · Martin, Crawshaw & Mayfield · Sentry Office Plaza · 216 Haddon Avenue, Suite 320 · P.O. Box 358 · Westmont, NJ 08108 · 609-858-0900

Morris Brown · (Plaintiffs) · Wilentz, Goldman & Spitzer · 90 Woodbridge Center Drive · P.O. Box 10 · Woodbridge, NJ 07095 · 201-636-8000

REAL ESTATE LAW

Edward M. Schotz · Cole, Schotz, Bernstein, Meisel & Forman · Court Plaza North · 25 Main Street · Hackensack, NJ 07601-7015 · 201-489-3000

Robert S. Greenbaum · Greenbaum, Rowe, Smith, Ravin, Davis & Bergstein · Metro Corporate Campus · 99 Wood Avenue South · Iselin, NJ 08830 · 201-549-5600

Wendell A. Smith · Greenbaum, Rowe, Smith, Ravin, Davis & Bergstein · Metro Corporate Campus · 99 Wood Avenue South · Iselin, NJ 08830 · 201-549-5600

Lawrence B. Mink · Clapp & Eisenberg · 80 Park Plaza · Newark, NJ 07102 · 201-642-3900

George C. Witte, Jr. · McCarter & English · Four Gateway Center · 100 Mulberry Street · Newark, NJ 07102-4096 · 201-622-4444

Martin E. Dollinger · Dollinger & Dollinger · 365 West Passaic Street · Rochelle Park, NJ 07662 · 201-368-0640

Edward S. Radzely · Kimmelman, Wolff & Samson · 280 Corporate Center · Five Becker Farm Road · Roseland, NJ 07068 · 201-740-0500

George Y. Sodowick · Brach, Eichler, Rosenberg, Silver, Bernstein, Hammer & Gladstone · 101 Eisenhower Parkway · Roseland, NJ 07068 · 201-228-5700

Joseph LeVow Steinberg · Lowenstein, Sandler, Kohl, Fisher & Boylan · 65 Livingston Avenue · Roseland, NJ 07068 · 201-992-8700

H. Harding Brown · Epstein, Epstein, Brown & Bosek · 505 Morris Avenue · P.O. Box 705 · Springfield, NJ 07081 · 201-467-4444

TAX AND EMPLOYEE BENEFITS LAW

Emmanuel Liebman · 409 East Marlton Pike · Cherry Hill, NJ 08034 · 609-795-8600

William T. Knox IV · (Employee Benefits) · Herold and Haines · 645 Martinsville Road · P.O. Box 266 · Liberty Corner, NJ 07938 · 201-647-1022

Peter C. Aslanides · McCarter & English · Four Gateway Center · 100 Mulberry Street · Newark, NJ 07102-4096 · 201-622-4444

Laurence Reich · Carpenter, Bennett, & Morrissey · Gateway Three · 100 Mulberry Street · Newark, NJ 07102 · 201-622-7711

Paul I. Rosenberg · Fox and Fox · 570 Broad Street · Newark, NJ 07102 · 201-622-3624

Stephen G. Siegel · McCarter & English · Four Gateway Center · 100 Mulberry Street · Newark, NJ 07102-4096 · 201-622-4444

Howard Denburg · (Employee Benefits) · Lowenstein, Sandler, Kohl, Fisher & Boylan · 65 Livingston Avenue · Roseland, NJ 07068 · 201-992-8700

Arnold Fisher · Lowenstein, Sandler, Kohl, Fisher & Boylan · 65 Livingston Avenue · Roseland, NJ 07068 · 201-992-8700

Benedict M. Kohl · Lowenstein, Sandler, Kohl, Fisher & Boylan · 65 Livingston Avenue · Roseland, NJ 07068 · 201-992-8700

Stephen P. Lichtstein · (Employee Benefits) · Hannoch Weisman · Four Becker Farm Road · Roseland, NJ 07068 · 201-535-5300

Milton H. Stern · Hannoch Weisman · Four Becker Farm Road · Roseland, NJ 07068 · 201-535-5300

Leonard J. Witman · (Employee Benefits) · Brach, Eichler, Rosenberg, Silver, Bernstein, Hammer & Gladstone · 101 Eisenhower Parkway · Roseland, NJ 07068 201-228-5700

Joel A. Wolff · Kimmelman, Wolff & Samson · 280 Corporate Center · Five Becker Farm Road · Roseland, NJ 07068 · 201-740-0500

TRUSTS AND ESTATES

Peter E. Driscoll · Archer & Greiner · One Centennial Square · Haddonfield, NJ 08033 · 609-795-2121

John Barker · Pitney, Hardin, Kipp & Szuch · 163 Madison Avenue, CN 1945 Morristown, NJ 07960-1945 · 201-267-3333

Sidney G. Dillon · Dillon, Bitar & Luther · 53 Maple Avenue · P.O. Box 398 Morristown, NJ 07960 · 201-539-3100

Richard Kahn · Dillon, Bitar & Luther · 53 Maple Avenue · P.O. Box 398 Morristown, NJ 07960 · 201-539-3100

Shirley A. O'Neill · Riker, Danzig, Scherer, Hyland & Perretti · Headquarters Plaza · One Speedwell Avenue · Morristown, NJ 07960-1981 · 201-538-0800

George A. Aguilar · Stryker, Tams & Dill · 33 Washington Street · Newark, NJ 07102 · 201-624-9300

Rodney N. Houghton · McCarter & English · Four Gateway Center · 100 Mulberry Street · Newark, NJ 07102-4096 · 201-622-4444

Stephen G. Siegel · McCarter & English · Four Gateway Center · 100 Mulberry Street · Newark, NJ 07102-4096 · 201-622-4444

Howard G. Wachenfeld · Tompkins, McGuire & Wachenfeld · Four Gateway Center · 100 Mulberry Street · Newark, NJ 07102 · 201-622-3000

Bernard S. Berkowitz · Hannoch Weisman · Four Becker Farm Road · Roseland, NJ 07068 · 201-535-5300

Arnold Fisher · Lowenstein, Sandler, Kohl, Fisher & Boylan · 65 Livingston Avenue · Roseland, NJ 07068 · 201-992-8700

Joseph E. Imbriaco · Young, Rose and Millspaugh · 65 Livingston Avenue · Roseland, NJ 07068 · 201-994-7777

Benedict M. Kohl · Lowenstein, Sandler, Kohl, Fisher & Boylan · 65 Livingston Avenue · Roseland, NJ 07068 · 201-992-8700

Gordon A. Millspaugh, Jr. · Young, Rose and Millspaugh · 65 Livingston Avenue Roseland, NJ 07068 · 201-994-7777

Ashley Steinhart · Hannoch Weisman · Four Becker Farm Road · Roseland, NJ 07068 · 201-535-5300

Richard F. Lert · Wilentz, Goldman & Spitzer · 90 Woodbridge Center Drive P.O. Box 10 · Woodbridge, NJ 07095 · 201-636-8000

NEW MEXICO

BANKRUPTCY LAW	442
BUSINESS LITIGATION	442
CORPORATE LAW	444
CRIMINAL DEFENSE	445
FAMILY LAW	445
LABOR AND EMPLOYMENT LAW	446
NATURAL RESOURCES AND ENVIRONMENTAL LAW	447
PERSONAL INJURY LITIGATION	448
REAL ESTATE LAW	449
TAX AND EMPLOYEE BENEFITS LAW	450
TRUSTS AND ESTATES	451

BANKRUPTCY LAW

Paul M. Fish · Modrall, Sperling, Roehl, Harris & Sisk · Sunwest Bank Building, Suite 1000 · 500 Fourth Street, NW · P.O. Box 2168 · Albuquerque, NM 87102 · 505-848-1800

Robert A. Johnson · Kemp, Smith, Duncan & Hammond · 200 Lomas Boulevard, NW, Suite 700 · P.O. Box 1276 · Albuquerque, NM 87103 · 505-247-2315

James S. Starzynski · Rodey, Dickason, Sloan, Akin & Robb · 20 First Plaza, Suite 700 · Third & Tijeras, NW · P.O. Box 1888 · Albuquerque, NM 87103 · 505-765-5900

BUSINESS LITIGATION

Peter J. Adang · Modrall, Sperling, Roehl, Harris & Sisk · Sunwest Building · 500 Fourth Street, NW · P.O. Box 2168 · Albuquerque, NM 87103 · 505-848-1800

Frank H. Allen, Jr. · Modrall, Sperling, Roehl, Harris & Sisk · Sunwest Bank Building · 500 Fourth Street, NW · P.O. Box 2168 · Albuquerque, NM 87103 505-848-1800

John R. Cooney · Modrall, Sperling, Roehl, Harris & Sisk · Sunwest Bank Building · 500 Fourth Street, NW · P.O. Box 2168 · Albuquerque, NM 87103 505-848-1800

William S. Dixon · Rodey, Dickason, Sloan, Akin & Robb · 20 First Plaza, Suite 700 · Third & Tijeras, NW · P.O. Box 1888 · Albuquerque, NM 87103 · 505-765-5900

Bruce Hall · Rodey, Dickason, Sloan, Akin & Robb · 20 First Plaza, Suite 700 Third & Tijeras, NW · P.O. Box 1888 · Albuquerque, NM 87103 · 505-765-5900

C. LeRoy Hansen · Civerolo, Hansen and Wolf · 500 Marquette, NW, Suite 1400 P.O. Drawer 887 · Albuquerque, NM 87103 · 505-842-8255

Robert A. Johnson · Kemp, Smith, Duncan & Hammond · 200 Lomas Boulevard, NW, Suite 700 · P.O. Box 1276 · Albuquerque, NM 87103 · 505-247-2315

Eric D. Lanphere · Lanphere, McBride & Gross · City Centre Building, Suite 200W · 6400 Uptown Boulevard, NE · Albuquerque, NM 87110 · 505-881-3333

Marshall G. Martin · Poole, Tinnin & Martin · 219 Central, NW, Suite 700 · P.O. Box 1769 · Albuquerque, NM 87103 · 505-842-8155

Russell Moore · Keleher & McLeod · Public Service Building · 414 Silver Avenue, SW · P.O. Drawer AA · Albuquerque, NM 87103 · 505-842-6262

Norman S. Thayer, Jr. · Sutin, Thayer & Browne · 6501 Americas Parkway, NE, 10th Floor · 600 First Plaza · P.O. Box 35130 · Albuquerque, NM 87176 · 505-842-8200

Rex D. Throckmorton · Rodey, Dickason, Sloan, Akin & Robb · 20 First Plaza, Suite 700 · Third & Tijeras, NW · P.O. Box 1888 · Albuquerque, NM 87103 · 505-765-5900

Harold L. Hensley, Jr. · Hinkle, Cox, Eaton, Coffield & Hensley · United Bank Plaza, Suite 700 · P.O. Box 10 · Roswell, NM 88201 · 505-622-6510

Stuart D. Shanor · Hinkle, Cox, Eaton, Coffield & Hensley · United Bank Plaza, Suite 700 · P.O. Box 10 · Roswell, NM 88201 · 505-622-6510

J. E. Gallegos · The Gallegos Law Firm · 300 Paseo de Peralta, Suite 100 · Santa Fe, NM 87501 · 505-983-6686

Seth D. Montgomery · Montgomery & Andrews · 325 Paseo de Peralta · P.O. Box 2307 · Santa Fe, NM 87504-2307 · 505-982-3873

CORPORATE LAW

Mark K. Adams · Rodey, Dickason, Sloan, Akin & Robb · 20 First Plaza, Suite 700 · Third & Tijeras, NW · P.O. Box 1888 · Albuquerque, NM 87103 505-765-5900

Richard K. Barlow · Chappell & Barlow · 2125 Louisiana Boulevard, NE, Suite 3500 · Albuquerque, NM 87110 · 505-889-3636

Graham Browne · Sutin, Thayer & Browne · 6501 Americas Parkway, NE, 10th Floor · 600 First Plaza · P.O. Box 35130 · Albuquerque, NM 87176 · 505-842-8200

Dale Wallace Ek · Modrall, Sperling, Roehl, Harris & Sisk · Sunwest Bank Building · 500 Fourth Street, NW · P.O. Box 2168 · Albuquerque, NM 87103 505-848-1800

Dennis J. Falk · Modrall, Sperling, Roehl, Harris & Sisk · Sunwest Bank Building 500 Fourth Street, NW · P.O. Box 2168 · Albuquerque, NM 87103 · 505-848-1800

Robert G. Heyman · Sutin, Thayer & Browne · 6501 Americas Parkway, NE, 10th Floor · 600 First Plaza · P.O. Box 35130 · Albuquerque, NM 87176 505-842-8200

William B. Keleher · Keleher & McLeod · Public Service Building · 414 Silver Avenue, SW · P.O. Drawer AA · Albuquerque, NM 87103 · 505-842-6262

Henry A. Kelly · Poole, Tinnin & Martin · 219 Central, NW, Suite 700 · P.O. Box 1769 · Albuquerque, NM 87103 · 505-842-8155

Dennis M. McCary · Dines & McCary · City Centre Building, Suite 233W · 6400 Uptown Boulevard, NE · Albuquerque, NM 87110 · 505-889-4050

Charles L. Moore · Keleher & McLeod · Public Service Building · 414 Silver Avenue, SW · P.O. Drawer AA · Albuquerque, NM 87103 · 505-842-6262

Robert C. Poole · Poole, Tinnin & Martin · 219 Central, NW, Suite 700 · P.O. Box 1769 · Albuquerque, NM 87103 · 505-842-8155

Robert M. St. John · Rodey, Dickason, Sloan, Akin & Robb · 20 First Plaza, Suite 700 · Third & Tijeras, NW · P.O. Box 1888 · Albuquerque, NM 87103 505-765-5900

William C. Schaab · Rodey, Dickason, Sloan, Akin & Robb · 20 First Plaza, Suite 700 · Third & Tijeras, NW · P.O. Box 1888 · Albuquerque, NM 87103 505-765-5900

Daniel A. Sisk · Modrall, Sperling, Roehl, Harris & Sisk · Sunwest Bank Building 500 Fourth Street, NW · P.O. Box 2168 · Albuquerque, NM 87103 · 505-848-1800

Charles I. Wellborn · Modrall, Sperling, Roehl, Harris & Sisk · Sunwest Bank Building · 500 Fourth Street, NW · P.O. Box 2168 · Albuquerque, NM 87103 505-848-1800

CRIMINAL DEFENSE

James L. Brandenburg · Brandenburg & Brandenburg · 715 Tijeras, NW · Albuquerque, NM 87102 · 505-842-5924

Charles W. Daniels · Freedman, Boyd & Daniels · 20 First Plaza, Suite 212 Albuquerque, NM 87102 · 505-842-9960

Nancy Hollander · Freedman, Boyd & Daniels · 20 First Plaza, Suite 212 Albuquerque, NM 87102 · 505-842-9960

Ronald Edwin Koch · 503 Slate Avenue, NW · Albuquerque, NM 87102 505-247-2972

Randi McGinn · 420 Central Southwest, Suite 200 · Albuquerque, NM 87102 505-843-6161

Ray Twohig · 420 Central, SW · Albuquerque, NM 87102 · 505-843-6223

Mark H. Donatelli · Rothstein, Bailey, Bennett, Daly & Donatelli · 136 Grant Avenue · P.O. Box 8180 · Santa Fe, NM 87504-8180 · 505-988-8004

Robert R. Rothstein · Rothstein, Bailey, Bennett, Daly & Donatelli · 136 Grant Avenue · P.O. Box 8180 · Santa Fe, NM 87504-8180 · 505-988-8004

FAMILY LAW

Jan B. Gilman · Atkinson & Kelsey · 1300 First Interstate Building · P.O. Drawer 1126 · Albuquerque, NM 87103 · 505-842-6111

David H. Kelsey · Atkinson & Kelsey · 1300 First Interstate Building · P.O. Drawer 1126 · Albuquerque, NM 87103 · 505-842-6111

Sandra Morgan Little · Atkinson & Kelsey · 1300 First Interstate Building · P.O. Drawer 1126 · Albuquerque, NM 87103 · 505-842-6111

Joseph J. Mullins · Rodey, Dickason, Sloan, Akin & Robb · 20 First Plaza, Suite 700 · Third & Tijeras, NW · P.O. Box 1888 · Albuquerque, NM 87103 505-765-5900

Betty Read · 801 Tijeras Avenue, NW · Albuquerque, NM 87102 · 505-247-9933

Barbara L. Shapiro · Poole, Tinnin & Martin · 219 Central, NW, Suite 700 · P.O. Box 1769 · Albuquerque, NM 87103 · 505-842-8155

David L. Walther · P.O. Box 1592 · Santa Fe, NM 87504 · 505-984-0097

LABOR AND EMPLOYMENT LAW

John W. Boyd · (Individuals) · Freedman, Boyd & Daniels · 20 First Plaza, Suite 212 · Albuquerque, NM 87102 · 505-842-9960

Duane C. Gilkey · (Management) · Rodey, Dickason, Sloan, Akin & Robb · 20 First Plaza, Suite 700 · Third & Tijeras, NW · P.O. Box 1888 · Albuquerque, NM 87103 · 505-765-5900

Eric Isbell-Sirotkin · (Individuals) · 901 Silver, SW · Albuquerque, NM 87102 505-843-6581

Roland B. Kool · (Labor) · Kool, Kool, Bloomfield & Hollis · 1516 San Pedro Boulevard, NE · Albuquerque, NM 87110 · 505-266-7841

K. Lee Peifer · (Labor; Individuals) · Freedman, Boyd & Daniels · 20 First Plaza, Suite 212 · Albuquerque, NM 87102 · 505-842-9960

Robert C. Poole · (Management) · Poole, Tinnin & Martin · 219 Central, NW, Suite 700 · P.O. Box 1769 · Albuquerque, NM 87103 · 505-842-8155

Robert P. Tinnin, Jr. · (Management) · Poole, Tinnin & Martin · 219 Central, NW, Suite 700 · P.O. Box 1769 · Albuquerque, NM 87103 · 505-842-8155

NATURAL RESOURCES AND ENVIRONMENTAL LAW

Mark K. Adams · Rodey, Dickason, Sloan, Akin & Robb · 20 First Plaza, Suite 700 · Third & Tijeras, NW · P.O. Box 1888 · Albuquerque, NM 87103 505-765-5900

Clifford K. Atkinson · (Water) · Modrall, Sperling, Roehl, Harris & Sisk · Sunwest Bank Building, Suite 1000 · 500 Fourth Street, NW · P.O. Box 2168 Albuquerque, NM 87102 · 505-848-1800

Larry P. Ausherman · (Mining) · Modrall, Sperling, Roehl, Harris & Sisk Sunwest Bank Building, Suite 1000 · 500 Fourth Street, NW · P.O. Box 2168 Albuquerque, NM 87102 · 505-848-1800

Lynn H. Slade · (Indian Affairs; Oil & Gas) · Modrall, Sperling, Roehl, Harris & Sisk · Sunwest Bank Building, Suite 1000 · 500 Fourth Street, NW · P.O. Box 2168 · Albuquerque, NM 87102 · 505-848-1800

Lester K. Taylor · (Oil & Gas) · Nordhaus, Haltom, Taylor, Taradish & Frye · 500 Marquette Avenue, NW, Suite 1050 · Albuquerque, NM 87102 · 505-243-4275

A. J. Losee · (Oil & Gas) · Losee & Carson · 300 American Home Building · P.O. Drawer 239 · Artesia, NM 88210 · 505-746-3508

Grove T. Burnett · (Plaintiffs) · Route 1 · P.O. Box 9A · Glorieta, NM 87535 505-757-8408

Sim B. Christy IV · (Oil & Gas) · 920 United Bank Plaza · 400 North Pennsylvania Avenue · P.O. Box 569 · Roswell, NM 88201 · 505-625-2021

Don M. Fedric · (Oil & Gas) · Hunker-Fedric · Hinkle Building, Suite 210 · P.O. Box 1837 · Roswell, NM 88201 · 505-622-2700

Richard N. Carpenter · (Mining) · Stephenson, Carpenter, Crout & Olmstead 141 East Palace Avenue · P.O. Box 669 · Santa Fe, NM 87504 · 505-982-4611

William F. Carr · (Oil & Gas) · Campbell & Black · 110 North Guadalupe · P.O. Box 2208 · Santa Fe, NM 87504-2208 · 505-988-4421

John B. Draper · (Water) · Montgomery & Andrews · 325 Paseo de Peralta · P.O. Box 2307 · Santa Fe, NM 87504-2307 · 505-982-3873

Richard A. Simms · (Water) · 300 Galisteo, Suites 204-206 · P.O. Box 280 · Santa Fe, NM 87504 · 505-983-3880

PERSONAL INJURY LITIGATION

William H. Carpenter · (Plaintiffs) · Carpenter & Goldberg · 1600 University Boulevard, Suite B · Albuquerque, NM 87102 · 505-243-1336

Stephen Durkovich · (Plaintiffs) · 412 Eleventh Street, NW · Albuquerque, NM 87102 · 505-247-2367

Bruce Hall · Rodey, Dickason, Sloan, Akin & Robb · 20 First Plaza, Suite 700 Third & Tijeras, NW · P.O. Box 1888 · Albuquerque, NM 87103 · 505-765-5900

Kenneth L. Harrigan · (Defendants) · Modrall, Sperling, Roehl, Harris & Sisk Sunwest Bank Building · 500 Fourth Street, NW · P.O. Box 2168 · Albuquerque, NM 87103 · 505-848-1800

Charles B. Larrabee · (Defendants) · Rodey, Dickason, Sloan, Akin & Robb · 20 First Plaza, Suite 700 · Third & Tijeras, NW · P.O. Box 1888 · Albuquerque, NM 87103 · 505-765-5900

W. Robert Lasater, Jr. · (Defendants) · Rodey, Dickason, Sloan, Akin & Robb 20 First Plaza, Suite 700 · Third & Tijeras, NW · P.O. Box 1888 · Albuquerque, NM 87103 · 505-765-5900

Robert G. McCorkle · (Defendants) · Rodey, Dickason, Sloan, Akin & Robb · 20 First Plaza, Suite 700 · Third & Tijeras, NW · P.O. Box 1888 · Albuquerque, NM 87103 · 505-765-5900

Ranne B. Miller · (Defendants) · Miller, Stratvert, Torgerson & Schlenker · 200 Lomas Boulevard, NW, Ninth Floor · P.O. Box 25687 · Albuquerque, NM 87125 505-842-1950

James C. Ritchie · (Defendants) · Rodey, Dickason, Sloan, Akin & Robb · 20 First Plaza, Suite 700 · Third & Tijeras, NW · P.O. Box 1888 · Albuquerque, NM 87103 · 505-765-5900

William E. Snead · (Plaintiffs) · Ortega and Snead · 201 Twelfth Street, NW P.O. Box 2226 · Albuquerque, NM 87103 · 505-842-8177

Wayne C. Wolf · (Defendants) · Civerolo, Hansen and Wolf · 500 Marquette, NW, Suite 1400 · P.O. Drawer 887 · Albuquerque, NM 87103 · 505-842-8255

Lowell Stout · (Plaintiffs) · Stout & Stout · 218 West Lea · P.O. Box 716 · Hobbs, NM 88240 · 505-393-1555

Harold L. Hensley, Jr. · Hinkle, Cox, Eaton, Coffield & Hensley · United Bank Plaza, Suite 700 · P.O. Box 10 · Roswell, NM 88201 · 505-622-6510

Russell D. Mann · (Defendants) · Atwood, Malone, Mann & Turner · Sunwest Centre · P.O. Drawer 700 · Roswell, NM 88201 · 505-622-6221

Bob F. Turner · (Defendants) · Atwood, Malone, Mann & Turner · Sunwest Centre · P.O. Drawer 700 · Roswell, NM 88201 · 505-622-6221

Matias A. Zamora · (Plaintiffs) · 444 Galisteo Street, Suite E · P.O. Box 1117 Santa Fe, NM 87504-1117 · 505-982-4449

REAL ESTATE LAW

Bill Chappell, Jr. · Chappell & Barlow · 2125 Louisiana Boulevard, NE, Suite 3500 · Albuquerque, NM 87110 · 505-889-3636

Dale Wallace Ek · Modrall, Sperling, Roehl, Harris & Sisk · Sunwest Bank Building · 500 Fourth Street, NW · P.O. Box 2168 · Albuquerque, NM 87103 · 505-848-1800

Patrick W. Hurley · Keleher & McLeod · Public Service Building · 414 Silver Avenue, SW · P.O. Drawer AA · Albuquerque, NM 87103 · 505-842-6262

Donald L. Jones · Sutin, Thayer & Browne · 6501 Americas Parkway, NE, 10th Floor · 600 First Plaza · P.O. Box 35130 · Albuquerque, NM 87176 · 505-842-8200

William B. Keleher · Keleher & McLeod · Public Service Building · 414 Silver Avenue, SW · P.O. Drawer AA · Albuquerque, NM 87103 · 505-842-6262

Dennis M. McCary · Dins & McCary · City Center Building, Suite 233W · 6400 Uptown Boulevard, NE · Albuquerque, NM 87110 · 505-889-4050

John A. Myers · Cole & Myers · 6400 Uptown Boulevard, NE, Suite 300 West · Albuquerque, NM 87110 · 505-889-4040

Charles P. Price III · Sutin, Thayer & Browne · 6501 Americas Parkway, NE, 10th Floor · 600 First Plaza · P.O. Box 35130 · Albuquerque, NM 87176 · 505-842-8200

John P. Salazar · Rodey, Dickason, Sloan, Akin & Robb · 20 First Plaza, Suite 700 · Third & Tijeras, NW · P.O. Box 1888 · Albuquerque, NM 87103 · 505-765-5900

Gene C. Walton · Rodey, Dickason, Sloan, Akin & Robb · 20 First Plaza, Suite 700 · Third & Tijeras, NW · P.O. Box 1888 · Albuquerque, NM 87103 505-765-5900

Bruce E. Wiggins · Sutin, Thayer & Browne · 6501 Americas Parkway, NE, 10th Floor · 600 First Plaza · P.O. Box 35130 · Albuquerque, NM 87176 · 505-842-8200

John P. Burton · Rodey, Dickason, Sloan, Akin & Robb · Marcy Plaza, Suite 101 123 East Marcy Street · P.O. Box 1357 · Santa Fe, NM 87501 · 505-984-0100

TAX AND EMPLOYEE BENEFITS LAW

Richard K. Barlow · Chappell & Barlow · 2125 Louisiana Boulevard, NE, Suite 3500 · Albuquerque, NM 87110 · 505-889-3636

John E. Heer III · (Employee Benefits) · Modrall, Sperling, Roehl, Harris & Sisk Sunwest Bank Building · 500 Fourth Street, NW · P.O. Box 2168 · Albuquerque, NM 87103 · 505-848-1800

John D. Laflin · Laflin, Lieuwen, Tucker & Kay · American Federal Savings Building, Suite 330 · 2400 Louisiana Boulevard, NE · Albuquerque, NM 87110 505-883-0679

John Lieuwen · (also Employee Benefits) · Laflin, Lieuwen, Tucker & Kay American Federal Savings Building, Suite 330 · 2400 Louisiana Boulevard, NE Albuquerque, NM 87110 · 505-883-0679

Dennis D. Meridith · Moses, Dunn, Beckley, Espinosa & Tuthill · 612 First Street, NW · Albuquerque, NM 87102 · 505-843-9440

Julie P. Neerken · (Employee Benefits) · Poole, Tinnin & Martin · 219 Central, NW, Suite 700 · P.O. Box 1769 · Albuquerque, NM 87103 · 505-842-8155

James M. Parker · (Employee Benefits) · Modrall, Sperling, Roehl, Harris & Sisk Sunwest Bank Building · 500 Fourth Street, NW · P.O. Box 2168 · Albuquerque, NM 87103 · 505-848-1800

Charles L. Saunders, Jr. · Kemp, Smith, Duncan & Hammond · 200 Lomas Boulevard, NW, Suite 700 · P.O. Box 1276 · Albuquerque, NM 87103 · 505-247-2315

Thomas Smidt II · Kemp, Smith, Duncan & Hammond · 200 Lomas Boulevard, NW, Suite 700 · P.O. Box 1276 · Albuquerque, NM 87103 · 505-247-2315

Patricia Tucker · Laflin, Lieuwen, Tucker & Kay · American Federal Savings Building, Suite 330 · 2400 Louisiana Boulevard, NE · Albuquerque, NM 87110 · 505-883-0679

Curtis W. Schwartz · Modrall, Sperling, Roehl, Harris & Sisk · 119 East Marcy, Suite 200 · Santa Fe, NM 87504 · 505-988-8039

TRUSTS AND ESTATES

Suzanne M. Barker · Poole, Tinnin & Martin · 219 Central, NW, Suite 700 · P.O. Box 1769 · Albuquerque, NM 87103 · 505-842-8155

Richard K. Barlow · Chappell & Barlow · 2125 Louisiana Boulevard, NE, Suite 3500 · Albuquerque, NM 87110 · 505-889-3636

John D. Laflin · Laflin, Lieuwen, Tucker & Kay · American Federal Savings Building, Suite 330 · 2400 Louisiana Boulevard, NE · Albuquerque, NM 87110 · 505-883-0679

John Lieuwen · Laflin, Lieuwen, Tucker & Kay · American Federal Savings Building, Suite 330 · 2400 Louisiana Boulevard, NE · Albuquerque, NM 87110 · 505-883-0679

Dennis D. Meridith · Moses, Dunn, Beckley, Espinosa & Tuthill · 612 First Street, NW · Albuquerque, NM 87102 · 505-843-9440

Kendall O. Schlenker · Miller, Stratvert, Torgerson & Schlenker · Cavan Building, Suite 1100 · 500 Marquette, NW · P.O. Box 25687 · Albuquerque, NM 87125 · 505-842-1950

Thomas Smidt II · Kemp, Smith, Duncan & Hammond · 200 Lomas Boulevard NW, Suite 700 · P.O. Box 1276 · Albuquerque, NM 87103 · 505-247-2315

NEW YORK

BANKRUPTCY LAW	452
BUSINESS LITIGATION	455
CORPORATE LAW	462
CRIMINAL DEFENSE	481
ENTERTAINMENT LAW	485
FAMILY LAW	486
LABOR AND EMPLOYMENT LAW	490
MARITIME LAW	496
NATURAL RESOURCES AND ENVIRONMENTAL LAW	499
PERSONAL INJURY LITIGATION	499
REAL ESTATE LAW	504
TAX AND EMPLOYEE BENEFITS LAW	507
TRUSTS AND ESTATES	513

BANKRUPTCY LAW

Donald G. Hatt · 11 North Pearl Street · Albany, NY 12207 · 518-463-1189

William M. McCarthy · McCarthy and Evanick · 60 South Swan Street · Albany, NY 12210 · 518-434-6141

Carl L. Bucki · Moot & Sprague · 2300 Main Place Tower · Buffalo, NY 14202 · 716-845-5200

Harold P. Bulan · Goldstein, Navagh, Bulan & Chiari · Rand Building, Suite 1440 · Buffalo, NY 14203 · 716-854-1332

William H. Gardner · Hodgson, Russ, Andrews, Woods & Goodyear · 1800 One M&T Plaza · Buffalo, NY 14203 · 716-856-4000

William E. Lawson · Aaron, Dautch, Sternberg & Lawson · 500 Convention Tower · Buffalo, NY 14202 · 716-854-3015

Donald P. Sheldon · 200 Olympic Towers · 300 Pearl Street · Buffalo, NY 14202 716-842-6009

Robert M. Spaulding · Phillips, Lytle, Hitchcock, Blaine & Huber · 3400 Marine Midland Center · Buffalo, NY 14203 · 716-847-8400

Michael L. Cook · Skadden, Arps, Slate, Meagher & Flom · 919 Third Avenue New York, NY 10022 · 212-735-3000

Michael J. Crames · Levin & Weintraub & Crames · 225 Broadway · New York, NY 10007 · 212-962-3300

Denis F. Cronin · Wachtell, Lipton, Rosen & Katz · 299 Park Avenue · New York, NY 10171 · 212-371-9200

Ronald DeKoven · Shearman & Sterling · 599 Lexington Avenue · New York, NY 10022 · 212-848-4000

Chaim J. Fortgang · Wachtell, Lipton, Rosen & Katz · 299 Park Avenue · New York, NY 10171 · 212-371-9200

Marcia Landweber Goldstein · Weil, Gotshal & Manges · 767 Fifth Avenue New York, NY 10153 · 212-310-8000

Henry L. Goodman · Zalkin, Rodin & Goodman · 750 Third Avenue · New York, NY 10017 · 212-682-6900

George A. Hahn · Hahn & Hessen · Empire State Building, Suite 3700 · 350 Fifth Avenue · New York, NY 10118 · 212-736-1000

Marvin E. Jacob · Weil, Gotshal & Manges · 767 Fifth Avenue · New York, NY 10153 · 212-310-8000

John J. Jerome · Milbank, Tweed, Hadley & McCloy · One Chase Manhattan Plaza · New York, NY 10005 · 212-530-5000

Alan W. Kornberg · Milbank, Tweed, Hadley & McCloy · One Chase Manhattan Plaza · New York, NY 10005 · 212-530-5000

Lillian E. Kraemer · Simpson Thacher & Bartlett · 425 Lexington Avenue · New York, NY 10017 · 212-455-2000

Robert H. MacKinnon · Shearman & Sterling · 599 Lexington Avenue · New York, NY 10022 · 212-848-4000

Alan B. Miller · Weil, Gotshal & Manges · 767 Fifth Avenue · New York, NY 10153 · 212-310-8000

Harvey R. Miller · Weil, Gotshal & Manges · 767 Fifth Avenue · New York, NY 10153 · 212-310-8000

Herbert P. Minkel, Jr. · Fried, Frank, Harris, Shriver & Jacobson · One New York Plaza · New York, NY 10004-1980 · 212-820-8000

Harold S. Novikoff · Wachtell, Lipton, Rosen & Katz · 299 Park Avenue · New York, NY 10171 · 212-371-9200

Barry G. Radick · Milbank, Tweed, Hadley & McCloy · One Chase Manhattan Plaza · New York, NY 10005 · 212-530-5000

Leonard M. Rosen · Wachtell, Lipton, Rosen & Katz · 299 Park Avenue · New York, NY 10171 · 212-371-9200

Robert J. Rosenberg · Latham & Watkins · 885 Third Avenue, Suite 1000 · New York, NY 10022 · 212-906-1200

Myron Trepper · Levin & Weintraub & Crames · 225 Broadway · New York, NY 10007 · 212-962-3300

Joel B. Zweibel · Kramer, Levin, Nessen, Kamin & Frankel · 919 Third Avenue New York, NY 10022 · 212-715-9100

Warren H. Heilbronner · Mousaw, Vigdor, Reeves, Heilbronner & Kroll · 600 First Federal Plaza · Rochester, NY 14614 · 716-325-2500

C. Bruce Lawrence · Suter Doyle Kesselring Lawrence & Werner · 950 Crossroads Building · Two State Street · Rochester, NY 14614 · 716-325-6446

Louis A. Ryen · Lacy, Katzen, Ryen & Mittleman · The Granite Building · 130 East Main Street · Rochester, NY 14604 · 716-454-5650

William S. Thomas, Sr. · Nixon, Hargrave, Devans & Doyle · Lincoln First Tower · Rochester, NY 14603 · 716-546-8000

Richard P. Vullo · Weinstein, Vullo & Miller · One Exchange Street, Suite 900 Rochester, NY 14614 · 716-325-3175

John R. Weider · Harter, Secrest & Emery · 700 Midtown Tower · Rochester, NY 14604 · 716-232-6500

Michael J. Balanoff · Grass, Balanoff, Costa & Whitelaw · One Lincoln Center, 12th Floor · Syracuse, NY 13202 · 315-472-7832

Harold P. Goldberg · Goldberg, Harding & Talev · 217 South Salina Street · Syracuse, NY 13202 · 315-422-6191

Peter L. Hubbard · Menter, Rudin & Trivelpiece · 500 South Salina Street, Suite 500 · Syracuse, NY 13202-3300 · 315-474-7541

Edward M. Zachary · Menter, Rudin & Trivelpiece · 500 South Salina Street, Suite 500 · Syracuse, NY 13202-3300 · 315-474-7541

BUSINESS LITIGATION

John T. DeGraff, Jr. · DeGraff, Foy, Conway, Holt-Harris and Mealey · 90 State Street · Albany, NY 12207 · 518-462-5301

Carroll J. Mealey · DeGraff, Foy, Conway, Holt-Harris and Mealey · 90 State Street · Albany, NY 12207 · 518-462-5301

Alexander C. Cordes · Phillips, Lytle, Hitchcock, Blaine & Huber · 3400 Marine Midland Center · Buffalo, NY 14203 · 716-847-8400

David K. Floyd · Phillips, Lytle, Hitchcock, Blaine & Huber · 3400 Marine Midland Center · Buffalo, NY 14203 · 716-847-8400

Victor T. Fuzak · Hodgson, Russ, Andrews, Woods & Goodyear · 1800 One M&T Plaza · Buffalo, NY 14203 · 716-856-4000

Frank T. Gaglione · Saperston & Day · Goldome Center, One Fountain Plaza · Buffalo, NY 14203-1486 · 716-856-5400

Richard F. Griffin · Moot & Sprague · 2300 Main Place Tower · Buffalo, NY 14202 · 716-845-5200

Richard E. Moot · Moot & Sprague · 2300 Main Place Tower · Buffalo, NY 14202 · 716-845-5200

H. Kenneth Schroeder, Jr. · Hodgson, Russ, Andrews, Woods & Goodyear · 1800 One M&T Plaza · Buffalo, NY 14203 · 716-856-4000

John H. Stenger · Jaeckle, Fleischman & Mugel · 800 Norstar Building · 12 Fountain Plaza · Buffalo, NY 14202 · 716-856-0600

Floyd Abrams · Cahill Gordon & Reindel · 80 Pine Street · New York, NY 10005 212-701-3000

Michael F. Armstrong · Barrett Smith Simon & Armstrong · 26 Broadway · New York, NY 10004 · 212-422-8180

Jack C. Auspitz · Morrison & Foerster · 415 Madison Avenue · New York, NY 10017 · 212-355-4415

Stephen M. Axinn · Skadden, Arps, Slate, Meagher & Flom · 919 Third Avenue New York, NY 10022 · 212-371-6000

Thomas D. Barr · Cravath, Swaine & Moore · One Chase Manhattan Plaza · New York, NY 10005 · 212-422-3000

Arnold Bauman · Shearman & Sterling · Citicorp Building, 32nd Floor · 153 East 53rd Street · New York, NY 10022 · 212-848-4000

Dennis J. Block · Weil, Gotshal & Manges · 767 Fifth Avenue · New York, NY 10153 · 212-310-8000

David Boies · Cravath, Swaine & Moore · One Chase Manhattan Plaza · New York, NY 10005 · 212-422-3000

Edward Brodsky · Spengler Carlson Gubar Brodsky & Frischling · 280 Park Avenue · New York, NY 10017 · 212-286-4000

Melvyn L. Cantor · Simpson Thacher & Bartlett · 425 Lexington Avenue · New York, NY 10017 · 212-455-2000

Michael A. Cardozo · Proskauer Rose Goetz & Mendelsohn · 300 Park Avenue New York, NY 10022 · 212-909-7000

Marc P. Cherno · Fried, Frank, Harris, Shriver & Jacobson · One New York Plaza New York, NY 10004-1980 · 212-820-8000

Arthur H. Christy · Christy & Viener · 620 Fifth Avenue · New York, NY 10020 212-399-9200

Merrell E. Clark, Jr. · Winthrop, Stimson, Putnam & Roberts · 40 Wall Street New York, NY 10005 · 212-943-0700

Robert Stephan Cohen · Morrison Cohen & Singer · 110 East 59th Street · New York, NY 10022 · 212-593-0100

Donald J. Cohn · Webster & Sheffield · 237 Park Avenue · New York, NY 10017 · 212-808-6000

Michael A. Cooper · Sullivan & Cromwell · 125 Broad Street · New York, NY 10004 · 212-558-4000

Edward N. Costikyan · Paul, Weiss, Rifkind, Wharton & Garrison · 1285 Avenue of the Americas · New York, NY 10019 · 212-373-3000

Louis A. Craco · Willkie Farr & Gallagher · One Citicorp Center · 153 East 53rd Street · New York, NY 10022 · 212-935-8000

Thomas F. Curnin · Cahill Gordon & Reindel · 80 Pine Street · New York, NY 10005 · 212-701-3000

Paul J. Curran · Kaye, Scholer, Fierman, Hays & Handler · 425 Park Avenue · New York, NY 10022 · 212-407-8000

Raymond L. Falls, Jr. · Cahill Gordon & Reindel · 80 Pine Street · New York, NY 10005 · 212-701-3000

Peter M. Fishbein · Kaye, Scholer, Fierman, Hays & Handler · 425 Park Avenue · New York, NY 10022 · 212-407-8000

Robert B. Fiske, Jr. · Davis Polk & Wardwell · One Chase Manhattan Plaza · New York, NY 10005 · 212-530-4000

Joseph M. Fitzpatrick · Fitzpatrick, Cella, Harper & Scinto · 277 Park Avenue · New York, NY 10172 · 212-758-2400

Peter E. Fleming Jr. · Curtis, Mallet-Prevost, Colt & Mosle · 101 Park Avenue · New York, NY 10178 · 212-696-6000

David L. Foster · Willkie Farr & Gallagher · One Citicorp Center · 153 East 53rd Street · New York, NY 10022 · 212-935-8000

Marvin E. Frankel · Kramer, Levin, Nessen, Kamin & Frankel · 919 Third Avenue · New York, NY 10022 · 212-715-9100

Victor S. Friedman · Fried, Frank, Harris, Shriver & Jacobson · One New York Plaza · New York, NY 10004-1980 · 212-820-8000

Barry H. Garfinkel · Skadden, Arps, Slate, Meagher & Flom · 919 Third Avenue
New York, NY 10022 · 212-371-6000

Milton S. Gould · Shea & Gould · 1251 Avenue of the Americas · New York, NY 10020 · 212-827-3000

Oliver F. Green · Paul, Hastings, Janofsky & Walker · Nine West 57th Street
New York, NY 10019 · 212-832-6100

Michael D. Hess · White & Case · 1155 Avenue of the Americas · New York, NY 10036 · 212-819-8200

Alan J. Hruska · Cravath, Swaine & Moore · One Chase Manhattan Plaza · New York, NY 10005 · 212-422-3000

John Roscoe Hupper · Cravath, Swaine & Moore · One Chase Manhattan Plaza
New York, NY 10005 · 212-422-3000

Jacob Imberman · Proskauer Rose Goetz & Mendelsohn · 300 Park Avenue
New York, NY 10022 · 212-909-7000

William E. Jackson · Milbank, Tweed, Hadley & McCloy · One Chase Manhattan Plaza · New York, NY 10005 · 212-530-5538

Lewis A. Kaplan · Paul, Weiss, Rifkind, Wharton & Garrison · 1285 Avenue of the Americas · New York, NY 10019 · 212-373-3000

Edmund H. Kerr · Cleary, Gottlieb, Steen & Hamilton · One State Street Plaza
New York, NY 10004 · 212-344-0600

Allen Kezsbom · Fried, Frank, Harris, Shriver & Jacobson · One New York Plaza
New York, NY 10004-1980 · 212-820-8000

Henry L. King · Davis Polk & Wardwell · One Chase Manhattan Plaza · New York, NY 10005 · 212-530-4000

T. Barry Kingham · Curtis, Mallet-Prevost, Colt & Mosle · 101 Park Avenue
New York, NY 10178 · 212-696-6000

David Klingsberg · Kaye, Scholer, Fierman, Hays & Handler · 425 Park Avenue
New York, NY 10022 · 212-407-8000

Daniel J. Kornstein · Kornstein Veisz & Wexler · 757 Third Avenue · New York, NY 10017 · 212-418-8600

Frederick B. Lacey · LeBoeuf, Lamb, Leiby & MacRae · 520 Madison Avenue New York, NY 10022 · 212-715-8000

Martin N. Leaf · Leaf Sternklar & Drogin · 440 Park Avenue South · New York, NY 10016 · 212-685-8400

Daniel P. Levitt · Kramer, Levin, Nessen, Kamin & Frankel · 919 Third Avenue New York, NY 10022 · 212-715-9100

Arthur L. Liman · Paul, Weiss, Rifkind, Wharton & Garrison · 1285 Avenue of the Americas · New York, NY 10019 · 212-373-3000

Sanford M. Litvack · Dewey, Ballantine, Bushby, Palmer & Wood · 140 Broadway, 46th Floor · New York, NY 10005 · 212-820-1100

Martin London · Paul, Weiss, Rifkind, Wharton & Garrison · 1285 Avenue of the Americas · New York, NY 10019 · 212-373-3000

William J. Manning · Simpson Thacher & Bartlett · 425 Lexington Avenue · New York, NY 10017 · 212-455-2000

Denis McInerney · Cahill Gordon & Reindel · 80 Pine Street · New York, NY 10005 · 212-701-3000

Ira M. Millstein · Weil, Gotshal & Manges · 767 Fifth Avenue · New York, NY 10153 · 212-310-8000

Michael W. Mitchell · Skadden, Arps, Slate, Meagher & Flom · 919 Third Avenue · New York, NY 10022 · 212-371-6000

Peter H. Morrison · Morrison Cohen & Singer · 110 East 59th Street · New York, NY 10022 · 212-593-0100

Maurice N. Nessen · Kramer, Levin, Nessen, Kamin & Frankel · 919 Third Avenue · New York, NY 10022 · 212-715-9100

Bernard W. Nussbaum · Wachtell, Lipton, Rosen & Katz · 299 Park Avenue New York, NY 10171-0149 · 212-371-9200

Otto G. Obermaier · Obermaier, Morvillo & Abramowitz · 1120 Avenue of the Americas, Suite 1500 · New York, NY 10036 · 212-221-1414

Sheldon Oliensis · Kaye, Scholer, Fierman, Hays & Handler · 425 Park Avenue New York, NY 10022 · 212-407-8000

Norman S. Ostrow · Grand & Ostrow · 641 Lexington Avenue · New York, NY 10022 · 212-832-3611

Barrington D. Parker, Jr. · Morrison & Foerster · 415 Madison Avenue · New York, NY 10017 · 212-355-4415

Daniel A. Pollack · Pollack & Kaminsky · 61 Broadway, Suite 2500 · New York, NY 10006 · 212-952-0330

Philip C. Potter, Jr. · Davis Polk & Wardwell · One Chase Manhattan Plaza New York, NY 10005 · 212-530-4000

Sheldon Raab · Fried, Frank, Harris, Shriver & Jacobson · One New York Plaza New York, NY 10004-1980 · 212-820-8000

James W. Rayhill · Carter, Ledyard & Milburn · Two Wall Street · New York, NY 10005 · 212-732-3200

Roy L. Reardon · Simpson Thacher & Bartlett · 425 Lexington Avenue · New York, NY 10017 · 212-455-2000

Edward J. Reilly · Milbank, Tweed, Hadley & McCloy · One Chase Manhattan Plaza · New York, NY 10005 · 212-530-5000

George D. Reycraft · Cadwalader, Wickersham & Taft · 100 Maiden Lane · New York, NY 10038 · 212-504-6000

Robert S. Rifkind · Cravath, Swaine & Moore · One Chase Manhattan Plaza New York, NY 10005 · 212-422-3000

Stanley D. Robinson · Kaye, Scholer, Fierman, Hays & Handler · 425 Park Avenue · New York, NY 10022 · 212-836-8000

Asa Rountree · Debevoise & Plimpton · 875 Third Avenue · New York, NY 10022 · 212-909-6000

Allen G. Schwartz · Proskauer Rose Goetz & Mendelsohn · 300 Park Avenue New York, NY 10022 · 212-909-7000

Marvin Schwartz · Sullivan & Cromwell · 125 Broad Street · New York, NY 10004 212-558-4000

Jerome G. Shapiro · Hughes Hubbard & Reed · One Wall Street · New York, NY 10005 · 212-709-7000

Leon Silverman · Fried, Frank, Harris, Shriver & Jacobson · One New York Plaza · New York, NY 10004 · 212-820-8000

Robert J. Sisk · Hughes Hubbard & Reed · One Wall Street · New York, NY 10005 · 212-709-7000

Eugene P. Souther · Seward & Kissel · Wall Street Plaza · 88 Pine Street · New York, NY 10005 · 212-412-4100

Gordon B. Spivack · Coudert Brothers · 200 Park Avenue · New York, NY 10166 · 212-880-4400

Alvin M. Stein · Parker Chapin Flattau & Klimpl · 1211 Avenue of the Americas · New York, NY 10036 · 212-704-6000

Stephen R. Steinberg · Reavis & McGrath · 345 Park Avenue · New York, NY 10154 · 212-486-9500

Jay Topkis · Paul, Weiss, Rifkind, Wharton & Garrison · 1285 Avenue of the Americas · New York, NY 10019 · 212-373-3000

Harold R. Tyler, Jr. · Patterson, Belknap, Webb & Tyler · 30 Rockefeller Center · New York, NY 10112 · 212-541-4000

Herbert M. Wachtell · Wachtell, Lipton, Rosen & Katz · 299 Park Avenue · New York, NY 10171-0149 · 212-371-9200

Gerald Walpin · Rosenman & Colin · 575 Madison Avenue · New York, NY 10022 · 212-940-8800

Stephen A. Weiner · Winthrop, Stimson, Putnam & Roberts · 40 Wall Street · New York, NY 10005 · 212-943-0700

Melvyn I. Weiss · Milberg Weiss Bershad Specthrie & Lerach · One Pennsylvania Plaza · New York, NY 10119 · 212-594-5300

George Weisz · Cleary, Gottlieb, Steen & Hamilton · One State Street Plaza · New York, NY 10004 · 212-344-0600

William E. Willis · Sullivan & Cromwell · 125 Broad Street · New York, NY 10004 · 212-558-4000

William Lent Dorr · Harris, Beach, Wilcox, Rubin and Levey · 130 East Main Street · Rochester, NY 14604 · 716-232-4440

Edward H. Fox · Harris, Beach, Wilcox, Rubin and Levey · 130 East Main Street Rochester, NY 14604 · 716-232-4440

David M. Lascell · Nixon, Hargrave, Devans & Doyle · Lincoln First Tower Rochester, NY 14603 · 716-546-8000

Anthony R. Palermo · Harter, Secrest & Emery · 700 Midtown Tower · Rochester, NY 14604 · 716-232-6500

Kenneth A. Payment · Harter, Secrest & Emery · 700 Midtown Tower · Rochester, NY 14604 · 716-232-6500

John J. Dee · Bond, Schoeneck & King · One Lincoln Center, 18th Floor · Syracuse, NY 13202-1355 · 315-422-0121

George H. Lowe · Bond, Schoeneck & King · One Lincoln Center, 18th Floor · Syracuse, NY 13202-1355 · 315-422-0121

Kevin M. Reilly · Mackenzie Smith Lewis Michell & Hughes · 600 Onondaga Savings Bank Building · Syracuse, NY 13202 · 315-474-7571

Carter H. Strickland · Mackenzie Smith Lewis Michell & Hughes · 600 Onondaga Savings Bank Building · Syracuse, NY 13202 · 315-474-7571

E. Stewart Jones, Jr. · 28 Second Street · Troy, NY 12181 · 518-274-5820

Henry G. Miller · Clark, Gagliardi & Miller · Inns of Court Building · 99 Court Street · White Plains, NY 10601 · 914-946-8900

CORPORATE LAW

John A. Beach · Bond, Schoeneck & King · 111 Washington Avenue · Albany, NY 12210-2280 · 518-462-7421

John E. Holt-Harris, Jr. · DeGraff, Foy, Conway, Holt-Harris and Mealey · 90 State Street · Albany, NY 12207 · 518-462-5301

Ronald S. Krolick · Krolick and DeGraff · Three City Square · Albany, NY 12207 518-465-2333

Michael Whiteman · Whiteman Osterman & Hanna · One Commerce Plaza Albany, NY 12260 · 518-449-7600

Frederick G. Attea · Phillips, Lytle, Hitchcock, Blaine & Huber · 3400 Marine Midland Center · Buffalo, NY 14203 · 716-847-8400

John C. Barber, Jr. · Hodgson, Russ, Andrews, Woods & Goodyear · 1800 One M&T Plaza · Buffalo, NY 14203 · 716-856-4000

Donald S. Day · Saperston & Day · Goldome Center, One Fountain Plaza · Buffalo, NY 14203-1486 · 716-856-5400

Arnold B. Gardner · Kavinoky & Cook · 120 Delaware Avenue · Buffalo, NY 14202 · 716-856-9234

Alvin M. Glick · Falk & Siemer · Main Place Tower, Suite 1900 · Buffalo, NY 14202 · 716-852-6670

Waldron S. Hayes, Jr. · Phillips, Lytle, Hitchcock, Blaine & Huber · 3400 Marine Midland Center · Buffalo, NY 14203 · 716-847-8400

Richard E. Heath · Hodgson, Russ, Andrews, Woods & Goodyear · 1800 One M&T Plaza · Buffalo, NY 14203 · 716-856-4000

William I. Schapiro · Jaeckle, Fleischmann & Mugel · 800 Norstar Building · 12 Fountain Plaza · Buffalo, NY 14202-2222 · 716-856-0600

Robert O. Swados · Cohen Swados Wright Hanifin Bradford & Brett · 70 Niagara Street · Buffalo, NY 14202 · 716-856-4600

George M. Zimmermann · Albrecht, Maguire, Heffern & Gregg · 2100 Empire Tower · Buffalo, NY 14202 · 716-853-1521

J. Robert LaPann · LaPann, Reardon, Morris, FitzGerald and Firth · One Broad Street Plaza · P.O. Box 2069 · Glens Falls, NY 12801 · 518-792-5894

Roger S. Aaron · (Mergers & Acquisitions) · Skadden, Arps, Slate, Meagher & Flom · 919 Third Avenue · New York, NY 10022 · 212-735-3000

George B. Adams, Jr. · (Finance; International) · Debevoise & Plimpton · 875 Third Avenue · New York, NY 10022 · 212-909-6000

Richard Marlow Allen · (Bankruptcy; Project Finance) · Cravath, Swaine & Moore · One Chase Manhattan Plaza · New York, NY 10005 · 212-422-3000

Neil T. Anderson · Sullivan & Cromwell · 125 Broad Street · New York, NY 10004 · 212-558-4000

Alan Appelbaum · Cleary, Gottlieb, Steen & Hamilton · One State Street Plaza New York, NY 10004 · 212-344-0600

James M. Asher · (Finance; Mergers & Acquisitions; Securities) · Rogers & Wells Pan Am Building · 200 Park Avenue · New York, NY 10166 · 212-878-8000

Peter A. Atkins · (Mergers & Acquisitions; Securities) · Skadden, Arps, Slate, Meagher & Flom · 919 Third Avenue · New York, NY 10022 · 212-735-3000

Gerald S. Backman · Weil, Gotshal & Manges · 767 Fifth Avenue · New York, NY 10153 · 212-310-8000

Martin Balsam · (Securities) · Kramer, Levin, Nessen, Kamin & Frankel · 919 Third Avenue · New York, NY 10022 · 212-715-9100

Stephen E. Banner · (Mergers & Acquisitions; Securities) · Simpson Thacher & Bartlett · 425 Lexington Avenue · New York, NY 10017 · 212-455-2000

David E. Baudler · (Banking; Finance; Mergers & Acquisitions) · Morrison & Foerster · 415 Madison Avenue · New York, NY 10017 · 212-355-4415

Richard I. Beattie · (Leveraged Buyouts; Mergers & Acquisitions) · Simpson Thacher & Bartlett · 425 Lexington Avenue · New York, NY 10017 · 212-455-2000

Melvin Leonard Bedrick · Cravath, Swaine & Moore · One Chase Manhattan Plaza · New York, NY 10005 · 212-422-3000

Louis Begley · (International; Mergers & Acquisitions) · Debevoise & Plimpton 875 Third Avenue · New York, NY 10022 · 212-909-6000

John W. Belash · (Mutual Funds; Securities) · Gordon, Hurwitz, Butowsky, Weitzen, Shalov & Wein · 101 Park Avenue · New York, NY 10178 · 212-557-8000

Joshua M. Berman · Kramer, Levin, Nessen, Kamin & Frankel · 919 Third Avenue · New York, NY 10022 · 212-715-9100

David W. Bernstein · (Finance; Mergers & Acquisitions; Securities) · Rogers & Wells · Pan Am Building · 200 Park Avenue · New York, NY 10166 · 212-878-8000

Kenneth J. Bialkin · (Corporate Finance; Mergers & Acquisitions; Securities Regulations) · Skadden, Arps, Slate, Meagher & Flom · 919 Third Avenue · New York, NY 10022 · 212-735-3000

Eugene L. Bondy, Jr. · Rogers & Wells · Pan Am Building · 200 Park Avenue New York, NY 10166 · 212-878-8000

Arthur M. Borden · (Securities) · Rosenman & Colin · 575 Madison Avenue New York, NY 10022 · 212-940-8800

Ronald E. Brackett · (Finance; Mergers & Acquisitions; Securities) · Rogers & Wells · Pan Am Building · 200 Park Avenue · New York, NY 10166 · 212-878-8000

Floyd E. Brandow, Jr. · (Securities Regulation) · Milbank, Tweed, Hadley & McCloy · One Chase Manhattan Plaza · New York, NY 10005 · 212-530-5000

Meredith M. Brown · (Mergers & Acquisitions) · Debevoise & Plimpton · 875 Third Avenue · New York, NY 10022 · 212-909-6000

F. Sedgwick Browne · (Insurance; Reinsurance) · Lord, Day & Lord, Barrett Smith · 25 Broadway · New York, NY 10004 · 212-344-8480

David Owen Brownwood · (Banking; Securities) · Cravath, Swaine & Moore · One Chase Manhattan Plaza · New York, NY 10005 · 212-422-3000

Barry R. Bryan · (Finance; International) · Debevoise & Plimpton · 875 Third Avenue · New York, NY 10022 · 212-909-6000

Samuel Coles Butler · (International; Mergers & Acquisitions; Securities) · Cravath, Swaine & Moore · One Chase Manhattan Plaza · New York, NY 10005 · 212-422-3000

Robert Carswell · (Banking) · Shearman & Sterling · 599 Lexington Avenue · New York, NY 10022 · 212-848-4000

Seymour H. Chalif · Kaye, Scholer, Fierman, Hays & Handler · 425 Park Avenue · New York, NY 10022 · 212-836-8000

David B. Chapnick · (Mergers & Acquisitions; Securities) · Simpson Thacher & Bartlett · 425 Lexington Avenue · New York, NY 10017 · 212-455-2000

Michael A. Chapnick · (Bank Finance for Lenders; Government Securities) · Lord, Day & Lord, Barrett Smith · 25 Broadway · New York, NY 10004 · 212-344-8480

Jonathan M. Clark · (Securities) · Davis Polk & Wardwell · One Chase Manhattan Plaza · New York, NY 10005 · 212-530-4000

George M. Cohen · (International Banking & Finance) · Cleary, Gottlieb, Steen & Hamilton · One State Street Plaza · New York, NY 10004 · 212-344-0600

H. Rodgin Cohen · (Banking) · Sullivan & Cromwell · 125 Broad Street · New York, NY 10004 · 212-558-4000

Jerome Alan Cohen · (Chinese) · Paul, Weiss, Rifkind, Wharton & Garrison 1285 Avenue of the Americas · New York, NY 10019 · 212-373-3000

C. Payson Coleman, Jr. · (Aviation Finance; International; Securities) · Winthrop, Stimson, Putnam & Roberts · 40 Wall Street · New York, NY 10005 · 212-943-0700

Martin A. Coleman · Rubin Baum Levin Constant & Friedman · 30 Rockefeller Center, 29th Floor · New York, NY 10112 · 212-698-7700

Faith Colish · 63 Wall Street · New York, NY 10005 · 212-509-5300

Sydney M. Cone III · (Finance; International) · Cleary, Gottlieb, Steen & Hamilton · One State Street Plaza · New York, NY 10004 · 212-344-0600

Thomas E. Constance · (Securities) · Shea & Gould · 1251 Avenue of the Americas · New York, NY 10020 · 212-827-3000

Stephen H. Cooper · Weil, Gotshal & Manges · 767 Fifth Avenue · New York, NY 10153 · 212-310-8000

Laurence E. Cranch · (Finance; Mergers & Acquisitions; Securities) · Rogers & Wells · Pan Am Building · 200 Park Avenue · New York, NY 10166 · 212-878-8000

Benjamin Field Crane · (Finance; Mergers & Acquisitions) · Cravath, Swaine & Moore · One Chase Manhattan Plaza · New York, NY 10005 · 212-422-3000

Ronald F. Daitz · (Finance; Mergers & Acquisitions; Securities) · Weil, Gotshal & Manges · 767 Fifth Avenue · New York, NY 10153 · 212-310-8000

John S. D'Alimonte · Willkie Farr & Gallagher · One Citicorp Center · 153 East 53rd Street · New York, NY 10022 · 212-935-8000

Stephen J. Dannhauser · (Finance; Mergers & Acquisitions; Restructurings; Securities) · Weil, Gotshal & Manges · 767 Fifth Avenue · New York, NY 10153 · 212-310-8000

Peter H. Darrow · (Finance; Securities) · Cleary, Gottlieb, Steen & Hamilton · One State Street Plaza · New York, NY 10004 · 212-344-0600

Edward S. Davis · (International; Securities) · Hughes Hubbard & Reed · 330 Madison Avenue · New York, NY 10017 · 212-856-4500

Joseph Diamond · (Banking; Financial Services) · Skadden, Arps, Slate, Meagher & Flom · 919 Third Avenue · New York, NY 10022 · 212-735-3000

Robert E. Dineen, Jr. · (Banking; Securities) · Shearman & Sterling · 599 Lexington Avenue · New York, NY 10022 · 212-848-4000

Peter R. Douglas · (International; Mergers & Acquisitions) · Davis Polk & Wardwell · One Chase Manhattan Plaza · New York, NY 10005 · 212-530-4000

W. Leslie Duffy · Cahill Gordon & Reindel · 80 Pine Street · New York, NY 10005 · 212-701-3000

John T. Dunne · Kaye, Scholer, Fierman, Hays & Handler · 425 Park Avenue · New York, NY 10022 · 212-836-8000

Cornelius J. Dwyer, Jr. · (Finance; International) · Shearman & Sterling · 599 Lexington Avenue · New York, NY 10022 · 212-848-4000

Klaus Eppler · (Mergers & Acquisitions; Securities) · Proskauer Rose Goetz & Mendelsohn · 300 Park Avenue · New York, NY 10022 · 212-909-7000

Jeffrey M. Epstein · (Banking; Finance) · Kaye, Scholer, Fierman, Hays & Handler · 425 Park Avenue · New York, NY 10022 · 212-836-8000

William M. Evarts, Jr. · (Mergers & Acquisitions; Securities) · Winthrop, Stimson, Putnam & Roberts · 40 Wall Street · New York, NY 10005 · 212-943-0700

Robert H. Falk · (Leveraged Buyouts; Securities) · Skadden, Arps, Slate, Meagher & Flom · 919 Third Avenue · New York, NY 10022 · 212-735-3000

Peter M. Fass · (Public Syndications of Real Estate) · Kaye, Scholer, Fierman, Hays & Handler · 425 Park Avenue · New York, NY 10022 · 212-836-8000

Gerald Feller · Kaye, Scholer, Fierman, Hays & Handler · 425 Park Avenue · New York, NY 10022 · 212-836-8000

Allen Finkelson · Cravath, Swaine & Moore · One Chase Manhattan Plaza · New York, NY 10005 · 212-422-3000

Fred N. Fishman · Kaye, Scholer, Fierman, Hays & Handler · 425 Park Avenue · New York, NY 10022 · 212-836-8000

Arthur Fleischer, Jr. · (Mergers & Acquisitions) · Fried, Frank, Harris, Shriver & Jacobson · One New York Plaza · New York, NY 10004 · 212-820-8000

Joseph H. Flom · (Mergers & Acquisitions) · Skadden, Arps, Slate, Meagher & Flom · 919 Third Avenue · New York, NY 10022 · 212-735-3000

James H. Fogelson · (Mergers & Acquisitions) · Wachtell, Lipton, Rosen & Katz 299 Park Avenue · New York, NY 10171-0149 · 212-371-9200

Blaine V. Fogg · (Mergers & Acquisitions) · Skadden, Arps, Slate, Meagher & Flom · 919 Third Avenue · New York, NY 10022 · 212-735-3000

John C. Fontaine · (International; Securities) · Hughes Hubbard & Reed · One Wall Street · New York, NY 10005 · 212-709-7000

George J. Forsyth · Milbank, Tweed, Hadley & McCloy · One Chase Manhattan Plaza · New York, NY 10005 · 212-530-5000

Stephen Fraidin · (Mergers & Acquisitions) · Fried, Frank, Harris, Shriver & Jacobson · One New York Plaza · New York, NY 10004 · 212-820-8000

Arthur H. Fredston · (Finance; International; Mergers & Acquisitions) · Winthrop, Stimson, Putnam & Roberts · 40 Wall Street · New York, NY 10005 212-943-0700

James C. Freund · (Mergers & Acquisitions) · Skadden, Arps, Slate, Meagher & Flom · 919 Third Avenue · New York, NY 10022 · 212-735-3000

Robert L. Friedman · (Mergers & Acquisitions) · Simpson Thacher & Bartlett 425 Lexington Avenue · New York, NY 10017 · 212-455-2000

Stanley J. Friedman · (Securities) · Shereff, Friedman, Hoffman & Goodman 919 Third Avenue · New York, NY 10022 · 212-758-9500

James J. Fuld · (Finance; Securities) · Proskauer Rose Goetz & Mendelsohn · 300 Park Avenue · New York, NY 10022 · 212-909-7000

Herbert L. Galant · (Finance; Mergers & Acquisitions; Securities) · Fried, Frank, Harris, Shriver & Jacobson · One New York Plaza · New York, NY 10004 212-820-8000

Sean J. Geary · (Capital Markets) · White & Case · 1155 Avenue of the Americas New York, NY 10036 · 212-819-8200

Thomas Gilroy · (International; Mergers & Acquisitions; Securities) · Hughes Hubbard & Reed · One Wall Street · New York, NY 10005 · 212-709-7000

Michael Harper Goff · (Corporate Finance; Investment) · Debevoise & Plimpton · 875 Third Avenue · New York, NY 10022 · 212-909-6000

Michael B. Goldberg · (Leveraged Buyouts) · Skadden, Arps, Slate, Meagher & Flom · 919 Third Avenue · New York, NY 10022 · 212-735-3000

William W. Golub · (Corporate Reorganization; Securities) · Rosenman & Colin · 575 Madison Avenue · New York, NY 10022 · 212-940-8800

Stephen Allen Grant · (International; Mergers & Acquisitions; Securities) · Sullivan & Cromwell · 125 Broad Street · New York, NY 10004 · 212-558-4000

David G. Gray · (Bank Regulations) · Simpson Thacher & Bartlett · 425 Lexington Avenue · New York, NY 10017 · 212-455-2000

Gilson B. Gray III · (Banking; International) · Hughes Hubbard & Reed · One Wall Street · New York, NY 10005 · 212-709-7000

Robert W. Gray · Winthrop, Stimson, Putnam & Roberts · 40 Wall Street · New York, NY 10005 · 212-943-0700

Michael Gruson · (Banking; International) · Shearman & Sterling · 599 Lexington Avenue · New York, NY 10022 · 212-848-4000

William A. Hagan, Jr. · (Banking) · Shea & Gould · 1251 Avenue of the Americas · New York, NY 10020 · 212-827-3000

Peter R. Haje · (Finance; Mergers & Acquisitions; Securities) · Paul, Weiss, Rifkind, Wharton & Garrison · 1285 Avenue of the Americas · New York, NY 10019 · 212-373-3000

Joseph W. Halliday · (Banking) · Skadden, Arps, Slate, Meagher & Flom · 919 Third Avenue · New York, NY 10022 · 212-735-3000

Joseph Daniel Hansen · (Finance; Mergers & Acquisitions; Securities) · Kaye, Scholer, Fierman, Hays & Handler · 425 Park Avenue · New York, NY 10022 · 212-836-8000

David W. Heleniak · (Mergers & Acquisitions) · Shearman & Sterling · 599 Lexington Avenue · New York, NY 10022 · 212-848-4000

Edwin Heller · (Securities) · Fried, Frank, Harris, Shriver & Jacobson · One New York Plaza · New York, NY 10004 · 212-820-8000

Dennis S. Hersch · (Mergers & Acquisitions) · Davis Polk & Wardwell · One Chase Manhattan Plaza · New York, NY 10005 · 212-530-4000

Seymour Hertz · (Mergers & Acquisitions; Public & Private Finance; Securities) Paul, Weiss, Rifkind, Wharton & Garrison · 1285 Avenue of the Americas · New York, NY 10019 · 212-373-3000

Robert B. Hiden, Jr. · (Commodities) · Sullivan & Cromwell · 125 Broad Street New York, NY 10004 · 212-558-4000

William E. Hirschberg · (Banking; Finance) · Shearman & Sterling · 599 Lexington Avenue · New York, NY 10022 · 212-848-4000

Robert B. Hodes · Willkie Farr & Gallagher · One Citicorp Center · 153 East 53rd Street · New York, NY 10022 · 212-935-8000

Joel S. Hoffman · Simpson Thacher & Bartlett · 425 Lexington Avenue · New York, NY 10017 · 212-455-2000

Lawrence J. Hohlt · (Banking; International) · Hughes Hubbard & Reed · One Wall Street · New York, NY 10005 · 212-709-7000

G. Malcolm Holderness · (Corporate Finance; Insurance Industry; Mergers & Acquisitions) · Milbank, Tweed, Hadley & McCloy · One Chase Manhattan Plaza New York, NY 10005 · 212-530-5000

Arne Hovdesven · (Securities) · Shearman & Sterling · 599 Lexington Avenue New York, NY 10022 · 212-848-4000

David M. Huggin · (Banking) · Sullivan & Cromwell · 125 Broad Street · New York, NY 10004 · 212-558-4000

John Francis Hunt · (Finance) · Cravath, Swaine & Moore · One Chase Manhattan Plaza · New York, NY 10005 · 212-422-3000

James B. Hurlock · (International Financial Transactions) · White & Case · 1155 Avenue of the Americas · New York, NY 10036 · 212-819-8200

Jerome E. Hyman · (Aviation; Securities) · Cleary, Gottlieb, Steen & Hamilton One State Street Plaza · New York, NY 10004 · 212-344-0600

Michael Iovenko · (Banking; Insurance) · Hughes Hubbard & Reed · One Wall Street · New York, NY 10005 · 212-709-7000

Allen I. Isaacson · (International Financial Institutions; Mergers & Acquisitions) Fried, Frank, Harris, Shriver & Jacobson · One New York Plaza · New York, NY 10004 · 212-820-8000

Arnold S. Jacobs · (Corporate; Finance; Securities) · 1251 Avenue of the Americas · New York, NY 10020 · 212-827-3000

Arthur P. Jacobs · (Mergers & Acquisitions) · Weil, Gotshal & Manges · 767 Fifth Avenue · New York, NY 10153 · 212-310-8000

Stephen E. Jacobs · Weil, Gotshal & Manges · 767 Fifth Avenue · New York, NY 10153 · 212-310-8000

Douglas W. Jones · Milbank, Tweed, Hadley & McCloy · One Chase Manhattan Plaza · New York, NY 10005 · 212-530-5000

Richard D. Kahn · (Finance; Non-Profit Organizations; Securities) · Debevoise & Plimpton · 875 Third Avenue · New York, NY 10022 · 212-909-6000

Lewis A. Kaplan · (Antitrust; Mergers & Acquisitions) · Paul, Weiss, Rifkind, Wharton & Garrison · 1285 Avenue of the Americas · New York, NY 10019 212-373-3000

Peter Karasz · (International; Oil & Gas; Mergers & Acquisitions) · Cleary, Gottlieb, Steen & Hamilton · One State Street Plaza · New York, NY 10004 212-344-0600

Roberta S. Karmel · (Securities; Securities & Banking Regulation) · Kelley Drye & Warren · 101 Park Avenue · New York, NY 10178 · 202-808-7800

Richard D. Katcher · (Mergers & Acquisitions; Securities) · Wachtell, Lipton, Rosen & Katz · 299 Park Avenue · New York, NY 10171-0149 · 212-371-9200

George A. Katz · (Mergers & Acquisitions) · Wachtell, Lipton, Rosen & Katz 299 Park Avenue · New York, NY 10171-0149 · 212-371-9200

Stuart Z. Katz · (Mergers & Acquisitions) · Fried, Frank, Harris, Shriver & Jacobson · One New York Plaza · New York, NY 10004 · 212-820-8000

Ed Kaufmann · (International; Securities) · Hughes Hubbard & Reed · One Wall Street · New York, NY 10005 · 212-709-7000

Peter L. Keane · Lord, Day & Lord, Barrett Smith · 25 Broadway · New York, NY 10004 · 212-344-8480

Howard S. Kelberg · (Finance; Securities) · Winthrop, Stimson, Putnam & Roberts · 40 Wall Street · New York, NY 10005 · 212-943-0700

George C. Kern, Jr. · Sullivan & Cromwell · 250 Park Avenue · New York, NY 10177 · 212-558-4000

Jerome H. Kern · Shea & Gould · 1251 Avenue of the Americas · New York, NY 10020 · 212-827-3000

B. Robbins Kiessling · Cravath, Swaine & Moore · One Chase Manhattan Plaza New York, NY 10005 · 212-422-3000

Fredric J. Klink · (Finance; Mergers & Acquisitions; Securities) · Loeb and Loeb 230 Park Avenue, 20th Floor · New York, NY 10169 · 212-692-4800

Immanuel Kohn · (Corporate Reorganizations & Financing Transactions; Mergers & Acquisitions) · Cahill Gordon & Reindel · 80 Pine Street · New York, NY 10005 · 212-701-3000

Roy M. Korins · (General Commercial; International) · Esanu Katsky Korins & Siger · 500 Fifth Avenue, 37th Floor · New York, NY 10110-0266 · 212-391-2424

Morris J. Kramer · (Mergers & Acquisitions) · Skadden, Arps, Slate, Meagher & Flom · 919 Third Avenue · New York, NY 10022 · 212-735-3000

Sanford Krieger · (Mergers & Acquisitions) · Fried, Frank, Harris, Shriver & Jacobson · One New York Plaza · New York, NY 10004 · 212-820-8000

William C. F. Kurz · Winthrop, Stimson, Putnam & Roberts · 40 Wall Street New York, NY 10005 · 212-943-0700

Dennis W. LaBarre · (Financial Institutions; Project Finance) · Jones, Day, Reavis & Pogue · 599 Lexington Avenue · New York, NY 10022 · 212-326-3939

W. Loeber Landau · (Finance; Mergers & Acquisitions; Securities) · Sullivan & Cromwell · 250 Park Avenue · New York, NY 10177 · 212-558-4000

Robert Todd Lang · (Mergers & Acquisitions; Securities) · Weil, Gotshal & Manges · 767 Fifth Avenue · New York, NY 10153 · 212-310-8000

Martin N. Leaf · Leaf Sternklar & Drogin · 440 Park Avenue South · New York, NY 10016 · 212-685-8400

Lawrence Lederman · (Finance; Mergers & Acquisitions; Securities) · Wachtell, Lipton, Rosen & Katz · 299 Park Avenue · New York, NY 10171-0149 · 212-371-9200

Edwin Deane Leonard · (Mergers & Acquisitions) · Davis Polk & Wardwell · One Chase Manhattan Plaza · New York, NY 10005 · 212-530-4000

Joseph H. Levie · (Banking; Finance) · Rogers & Wells · Pan Am Building · 200 Park Avenue · New York, NY 10166 · 212-878-8000

Ezra G. Levin · (Banking; Mergers & Acquisitions; Securities) · Kramer, Levin, Nessen, Kamin & Frankel · 919 Third Avenue · New York, NY 10022 · 212-715-9100

Victor I. Lewkow · (Mergers & Acquisitions) · Cleary, Gottlieb, Steen & Hamilton · One State Street Plaza · New York, NY 10004 · 212-344-0600

Albert F. Lilley · (Corporate Governance; Public Utility Finance; Securities Regulation) · Milbank, Tweed, Hadley & McCloy · One Chase Manhattan Plaza New York, NY 10005 · 212-530-5000

George N. Lindsay · (International; Mergers & Acquisitions) · Debevoise & Plimpton · 875 Third Avenue · New York, NY 10022 · 212-909-6000

Martin Lipton · Wachtell, Lipton, Rosen & Katz · 299 Park Avenue · New York, NY 10171-0149 · 212-371-9200

Francis D. Logan · (Banking) · Milbank, Tweed, Hadley & McCloy · One Chase Manhattan Plaza · New York, NY 10005 · 212-530-5000

Bevis Longstreth · (Finance; Securities) · Debevoise & Plimpton · 875 Third Avenue · New York, NY 10022 · 212-909-6000

George Theodore Lowy · (International; Mergers & Acquisitions; Securities) Cravath, Swaine & Moore · One Chase Manhattan Plaza · New York, NY 10005 212-422-3000

John J. Madden · (Mergers & Acquisitions) · Shearman & Sterling · 599 Lexington Avenue · New York, NY 10022 · 212-848-4000

Matthew J. Mallow · (Corporate Finance) · Skadden, Arps, Slate, Meagher & Flom · 919 Third Avenue · New York, NY 10022 · 212-735-3000

Edgar M. Masinter · (Banking; Securities) · Simpson Thacher & Bartlett · 425 Lexington Avenue · New York, NY 10017 · 212-455-2000

John E. Massengale · (Corporate Finance; Mergers & Acquisitions; Securities) Paul, Weiss, Rifkind, Wharton & Garrison · 1285 Avenue of the Americas · New York, NY 10019 · 212-373-3000

William B. Matteson · (International; Mergers & Acquisitions) · Debevoise & Plimpton · 875 Third Avenue · New York, NY 10022 · 212-909-6000

John J. McAtee, Jr. · (Mergers & Acquisitions) · Davis Polk & Wardwell · One Chase Manhattan Plaza · New York, NY 10005 · 212-530-4000

David A. McCabe · (International; Securities) · Shearman & Sterling · 599 Lexington Avenue · New York, NY 10022 · 212-848-4000

Willis McDonald IV · (Mergers & Acquisitions; Securities) · White & Case · 1155 Avenue of the Americas · New York, NY 10036 · 212-819-8200

John J. McNally · (Mergers & Acquisitions; Securities) · White & Case · 1155 Avenue of the Americas · New York, NY 10036 · 212-819-8200

Walter G. McNeill · (Structured Finance) · Skadden, Arps, Slate, Meagher & Flom · 919 Third Avenue · New York, NY 10022 · 212-735-3000

John E. Merow · Sullivan & Cromwell · 125 Broad Street · New York, NY 10004 212-558-4000

Ricardo A. Mestres, Jr. · (Mergers & Acquisitions; Securities) · Sullivan & Cromwell · 125 Broad Street · New York, NY 10004 · 212-558-4000

Roger M. Milgrim · (Intellectual Property; Licensing) · Milgrim Thomajan Jacobs & Lee · The Chrysler Building · 405 Lexington Avenue · New York, NY 10174 212-867-6660

Clyde Mitchell · White & Case · 1155 Avenue of the Americas · New York, NY 10036 · 212-819-8200

Franklin H. Moore, Jr. · (Securities) · Shearman & Sterling · 599 Lexington Avenue · New York, NY 10022 · 212-848-4000

Francis J. Morison · (International; Securities) · Davis Polk & Wardwell · One Chase Manhattan Plaza · New York, NY 10005 · 212-530-4000

Morton Moskin · White & Case · 1155 Avenue of the Americas · New York, NY 10036 · 212-819-8200

James F. Munsell · Cleary, Gottlieb, Steen & Hamilton · One State Street Plaza · New York, NY 10004 · 212-344-0600

Jiro Murase · (Banking; International; Mergers & Acquisitions) · Marks Murase & White · 400 Park Avenue · New York, NY 10022 · 212-832-3333

William O. Murphy · (Banking) · Simpson Thacher & Bartlett · 425 Lexington Avenue · New York, NY 10017 · 212-455-2000

Toby S. Myerson · (Banking; Finance; Mergers & Acquisitions) · Paul, Weiss, Rifkind, Wharton & Garrison · 1285 Avenue of the Americas · New York, NY 10019 · 212-373-3000

Andre W. G. Newburg · (International; Securities) · Cleary, Gottlieb, Steen & Hamilton · One State Street Plaza · New York, NY 10004 · 212-344-0600

Bruce W. Nichols · (Banking) · Davis Polk & Wardwell · One Chase Manhattan Plaza · New York, NY 10005 · 212-530-4000

Matthew Nimetz · (International Transactions; Mergers & Acquisitions) · Paul, Weiss, Rifkind, Wharton & Garrison · 1285 Avenue of the Americas · New York, NY 10019 · 212-373-3000

Bernard William Nimkin · (Corporate Finance; Mergers & Acquisitions; Securities) · Kaye, Scholer, Fierman, Hays & Handler · 425 Park Avenue · New York, NY 10022 · 212-836-8000

Jack H. Nusbaum · (Mergers & Acquisitions) · Willkie Farr & Gallagher · One Citicorp Center · 153 East 53rd Street · New York, NY 10022 · 212-935-8000

Robert S. O'Hara, Jr. · (Banking; Finance; Mergers & Acquisitions) · Milbank, Tweed, Hadley & McCloy · One Chase Manhattan Plaza · New York, NY 10005 · 212-530-5000

Roger B. Oresman · Milbank, Tweed, Hadley & McCloy · One Chase Manhattan Plaza · New York, NY 10005 · 212-530-5000

David G. Ormsby · Cravath, Swaine & Moore · One Chase Manhattan Plaza · New York, NY 10005 · 212-422-3000

Alan H. Paley · (Mergers & Acquisitions; Venture Capital) · Debevoise & Plimpton · 875 Third Avenue · New York, NY 10022 · 212-909-6000

Joel I. Papernik · (Mergers & Acquisitions; Securities) · Shea & Gould · 1251 Avenue of the Americas · New York, NY 10020 · 212-827-3000

Guy Paschal · (Finance; Investment) · Debevoise & Plimpton · 875 Third Avenue · New York, NY 10022 · 212-909-6000

Roswell B. Perkins · (Mergers & Acquisitions; Securities) · Debevoise & Plimpton · 875 Third Avenue · New York, NY 10022 · 212-909-6000

Donaldson C. Pillsbury · (Banking; International) · Davis Polk & Wardwell · One Chase Manhattan Plaza · New York, NY 10005 · 212-530-4000

Samuel F. Pryor III · (International; Securities) · Davis Polk & Wardwell · One Chase Manhattan Plaza · New York, NY 10005 · 212-530-4000

Frank C. Puleo · (Banking; Federal Securities Laws) · Milbank, Tweed, Hadley & McCloy · One Chase Manhattan Plaza · New York, NY 10005 · 212-530-5000

Leonard V. Quigley · (International; Mergers & Acquisitions; Securities Financings) · Paul, Weiss, Rifkind, Wharton & Garrison · 1285 Avenue of the Americas · New York, NY 10019 · 212-373-3000

Edward S. Reid · (Mergers & Acquisitions; Securities) · Davis Polk & Wardwell · One Chase Manhattan Plaza · New York, NY 10005 · 212-530-4000

John J. Roche · (Banking) · Shearman & Sterling · 599 Lexington Avenue · New York, NY 10022 · 212-848-4000

William P. Rogers · (International) · Rogers & Wells · Pan Am Building · 200 Park Avenue · New York, NY 10166 · 212-878-8000

Robert Rosenman · Cravath, Swaine & Moore · One Chase Manhattan Plaza · New York, NY 10005 · 212-422-3000

Michael A. Ross · (Banking) · Shearman & Sterling · 599 Lexington Avenue · New York, NY 10022 · 212-848-4000

Peter D. Rowntree · (International Banking) · Milbank, Tweed, Hadley & McCloy · One Chase Manhattan Plaza · New York, NY 10005 · 212-530-5000

Ernest Rubenstein · (Mergers & Acquisitions) · Paul, Weiss, Rifkind, Wharton & Garrison · 1285 Avenue of the Americas · New York, NY 10019 · 212-373-3000

Frederic A. Rubinstein · (Venture Capital) · Kelley Drye & Warren · 101 Park Avenue · New York, NY 10178 · 202-808-7800

John S. Russell, Jr. · Winthrop, Stimson, Putnam & Roberts · 40 Wall Street · New York, NY 10005 · 212-943-0700

Howard Schneider · (Commodities & Securities Regulation; International) Rosenman & Colin · 575 Madison Avenue · New York, NY 10022 · 212-940-8800

Paul S. Schreiber · (Investment Companies & Advisers) · Kramer, Levin, Nessen, Kamin & Frankel · 919 Third Avenue · New York, NY 10022 · 212-715-9100

Thomas G. Schueller · (Mergers & Acquisitions; Securities) · Hughes Hubbard & Reed · One Wall Street · New York, NY 10005 · 212-709-7000

Stephen J. Schulte · (Mergers & Acquisitions) · Schulte Roth & Zabel · 900 Third Avenue · New York, NY 10022 · 212-758-0404

Terrance W. Schwab · (Banking) · Kelley Drye & Warren · 101 Park Avenue New York, NY 10178 · 202-808-7800

George M. Shapiro · (Banking; Private International Trade) · Proskauer Rose Goetz & Mendelsohn · 300 Park Avenue · New York, NY 10022 · 212-909-7000

Isaac Shapiro · (International Commercial Transactions) · Skadden, Arps, Slate, Meagher & Flom · 919 Third Avenue, 46th Floor · New York, NY 10022 · 212-371-6000

Michael P. Shumaecker · (Banking; Finance) · Winthrop, Stimson, Putnam & Roberts · 40 Wall Street · New York, NY 10005 · 212-943-0700

Sidney J. Silberman · Kaye, Scholer, Fierman, Hays & Handler · 425 Park Avenue · New York, NY 10022 · 212-836-8000

Joseph R. Siphron · Milbank, Tweed, Hadley & McCloy · One Chase Manhattan Plaza · New York, NY 10005 · 212-530-5000

David V. Smalley · (Finance; Securities) · Debevoise & Plimpton · 875 Third Avenue · New York, NY 10022 · 212-909-6000

Bradley Y. Smith · (Banking) · Davis Polk & Wardwell · One Chase Manhattan Plaza · New York, NY 10005 · 212-530-4000

Theodore C. Sorensen · (International Business Transactions) · Paul, Weiss, Rifkind, Wharton & Garrison · 1285 Avenue of the Americas · New York, NY 10019 · 212-373-3000

Lee B. Spence, Jr. · (Securities) · Gibson, Dunn & Crutcher · 200 Park Avenue, 47th Floor · New York, NY 10166 · 212-351-4000

Allan G. Sperling · Cleary, Gottlieb, Steen & Hamilton · One State Street Plaza · New York, NY 10004 · 212-344-0600

Richard D. Spizzirri · (Limited Partnerships; Mergers & Acquisitions; Research & Development Finance) · Davis Polk & Wardwell · One Chase Manhattan Plaza · New York, NY 10005 · 212-530-4000

Benjamin F. Stapleton · (Mergers & Acquisitions) · Sullivan & Cromwell · 125 Broad Street · New York, NY 10004 · 212-558-4000

Richard A. Stark · (Mergers & Acquisitions; Securities Offerings) · Milbank, Tweed, Hadley & McCloy · One Chase Manhattan Plaza · New York, NY 10005 · 212-530-5000

Alan Clements Stephenson · (Mergers & Acquisitions) · Wasserstein & Perella & Co. · 31 West 52nd Street · New York, NY 10019 · 212-969-2700

Ned B. Stiles · (Finance; Mergers & Acquisitions; Securities) · Cleary, Gottlieb, Steen & Hamilton · One State Street Plaza · New York, NY 10004 · 212-344-0600

David P. Stone · Weil, Gotshal & Manges · 767 Fifth Avenue · New York, NY 10153 · 212-310-8000

Milton G. Strom · (Securities) · Skadden, Arps, Slate, Meagher & Flom · 919 Third Avenue · New York, NY 10022 · 212-735-3000

David W. Swanson · White & Case · 1155 Avenue of the Americas · New York, NY 10036 · 212-819-8200

John C. Taylor III · (Leveraged Buyouts; Mergers & Acquisitions) · Paul, Weiss, Rifkind, Wharton & Garrison · 1285 Avenue of the Americas · New York, NY 10019 · 212-373-3000

Arbie R. Thalacker · (International Joint Ventures; Mergers & Acquisitions; Securities) · Shearman & Sterling · 599 Lexington Avenue · New York, NY 10022 · 212-848-4000

Allen L. Thomas · Paul, Weiss, Rifkind, Wharton & Garrison · 1285 Avenue of the Americas · New York, NY 10019 · 212-373-3000

Robert M. Thomas, Jr. · (International; Finance; Securities) · Sullivan & Cromwell · 125 Broad Street · New York, NY 10004 · 212-558-4000

Judith R. Thoyer · Paul, Weiss, Rifkind, Wharton & Garrison · 1285 Avenue of the Americas · New York, NY 10019 · 212-373-3000

Robert L. Tortoriello · (Banking) · Cleary, Gottlieb, Steen & Hamilton · One State Street Plaza · New York, NY 10004 · 212-344-0600

Cyrus R. Vance · (Antitrust) · Simpson Thacher & Bartlett · 425 Lexington Avenue · New York, NY 10017 · 212-455-2000

Charles H. Vejvoda · (Banking; Creditors' Rights) · Winthrop, Stimson, Putnam & Roberts · 40 Wall Street · New York, NY 10005 · 212-943-0700

Stephen R. Volk · (Mergers & Acquisitions) · Shearman & Sterling · 599 Lexington Avenue · New York, NY 10022 · 212-848-4000

Mark A. Walker · (International Business Transactions; International Finance; Sovereign Debt Restructuring) · Cleary, Gottlieb, Steen & Hamilton · One State Street Plaza · New York, NY 10004 · 212-344-0600

Duane D. Wall · (Banking; International Finance) · White & Case · 1155 Avenue of the Americas · New York, NY 10036 · 212-819-8200

Robert D. Webster · (Banking; International) · Winthrop, Stimson, Putnam & Roberts · 40 Wall Street · New York, NY 10005 · 212-943-0700

Peter H. Weil · (Asset-Based Lending; Corporate Finance; Reorganizations) Kaye, Scholer, Fierman, Hays & Handler · 425 Park Avenue · New York, NY 10022 · 212-836-8000

Stephen K. West · Sullivan & Cromwell · 125 Broad Street · New York, NY 10004 212-558-4000

John W. White · Cravath, Swaine & Moore · One Chase Manhattan Plaza · New York, NY 10005 · 212-422-3000

Charles S. Whitman III · (International; Securities) · Davis Polk & Wardwell One Chase Manhattan Plaza · New York, NY 10005 · 212-530-4000

Peter Whitridge Williams · (Banking; Finance) · Rogers & Wells · Pan Am Building · 200 Park Avenue · New York, NY 10166 · 212-878-8000

Thomas A. Williams · Milbank, Tweed, Hadley & McCloy · One Chase Manhattan Plaza · New York, NY 10005 · 212-530-5000

William J. Williams, Jr. · (Finance) · Sullivan & Cromwell · 125 Broad Street New York, NY 10004 · 212-558-4000

Paul H. Wilson, Jr. · (Business; Securities) · Debevoise & Plimpton · 875 Third Avenue · New York, NY 10022 · 212-909-6000

James Ronald Wolfe · (Lease Finance; Project Finance) · Simpson Thacher & Bartlett · 425 Lexington Avenue · New York, NY 10017 · 212-455-2000

Jacob J. Worenklein · (Project Finance & Development) · Milbank, Tweed, Hadley & McCloy · One Chase Manhattan Plaza · New York, NY 10005 · 212-530-5000

Cecil Wray, Jr. · (Finance; Securities) · Debevoise & Plimpton · 875 Third Avenue · New York, NY 10022 · 212-909-6000

William F. Wynne, Jr. · (Mergers & Acquisitions) · White & Case · 1155 Avenue of the Americas · New York, NY 10036 · 212-819-8200

John Edward Young · Cravath, Swaine & Moore · One Chase Manhattan Plaza New York, NY 10005 · 212-422-3000

Julian W. Atwater · Nixon, Hargrave, Devans & Doyle · Lincoln First Tower Rochester, NY 14603 · 716-546-8000

Thomas E. Clement · Nixon, Hargrave, Devans & Doyle · Lincoln First Tower Rochester, NY 14603 · 716-546-8000

B. G. Staffan Lundback · Nixon, Hargrave, Devans & Doyle · Lincoln First Tower · Rochester, NY 14603 · 716-546-8000

Thomas A. Solberg · Harter, Secrest & Emery · 700 Midtown Tower · Rochester, NY 14604 · 716-232-6500

Alan J. Underberg · Underberg & Kessler · 1800 Lincoln First Tower · Rochester, NY 14604 · 716-258-2800

Justin L. Vigdor · Mousaw, Vigdor, Reeves, Heilbronner & Kroll · 600 First Federal Plaza · Rochester, NY 14614 · 716-325-2500

John A. Beach · Bond, Schoeneck & King · One Lincoln Center, 18th Floor Syracuse, NY 13202-1355 · 315-422-0121

Charles T. Beeching, Jr. · Bond, Schoeneck & King · One Lincoln Center, 18th Floor · Syracuse, NY 13202-1355 · 315-422-0121

Carter B. Chase · Hiscock & Barclay · Financial Plaza · P.O. Box 4878 · Syracuse, NY 13221 · 315-422-2131

Donald A. Denton · Hancock & Estabrook · One Mony Plaza, 14th Floor · 100 Madison Street · Syracuse, NY 13202-2791 · 315-471-3151

George S. Deptula · Hiscock & Barclay · Financial Plaza · P.O. Box 4878 Syracuse, NY 13221 · 315-422-2131

James R. McVety · Hancock & Estabrook · One Mony Plaza, 14th Floor · 100 Madison Street · P.O. Box 4976 · Syracuse, NY 13221-4976 · 315-471-3151

Lynn H. Smith · Lombardi, Devorsetz, Stinziano & Smith · 555 East Genesee Street · Syracuse, NY 13202 · 315-471-2244

Edward M. Zachary · Menter, Rudin & Trivelpiece · 500 South Salina Street, Suite 500 · Syracuse, NY 13202 · 315-474-7541

Ivan Serchuk · Serchuk Wolfe & Zelermyer · 81 Main Street · White Plains, NY 10601 · 914-761-2100

CRIMINAL DEFENSE

Stephen R. Coffey · O'Connell and Aronowitz · 100 State Street, Eighth Floor Albany, NY 12207 · 518-462-5601

William J. Dreyer · Dreyer, Kinsella, Boyajian & Tuttle · 75 Columbia Street Albany, NY 12210 · 518-463-7784

Harold J. Boreanaz · Boreanaz, Baker & Humann · 736 Brisbane Building Buffalo, NY 14203 · 716-854-5800

Paul J. Cambria, Jr. · Lipsitz, Green, Fahringer, Roll, Schuller & James · One Niagara Square · Buffalo, NY 14202 · 716-849-1333

John W. Condon, Jr. · Condon, La Tona, Pieri & Dillon · 300 Statler Towers Buffalo, NY 14202 · 716-856-2183

Terrence M. Connors · Connors & Vilardo · Old City Court Building · 42 Delaware Avenue, Suite 710 · Buffalo, NY 14202 · 716-852-5533

Joel L. Daniels · 444 Statler Towers · Buffalo, NY 14202 · 716-856-5140

Herbert L. Greenman · Lipsitz, Green, Fahringer, Roll, Schuller & James · One Niagara Square · Buffalo, NY 14202 · 716-849-1333

Joseph M. La Tona · Condon, La Tona, Pieri & Dillon · 300 Statler Towers · Buffalo, NY 14202 · 716-856-2183

Mark J. Mahoney · Bermingham, Cook & Mahoney · 1620 Statler Towers · Buffalo, NY 14202-3066 · 716-854-6800

Joseph V. Sedita · Moot & Sprague · 2300 Empire Tower · Buffalo, NY 14202 · 716-845-5200

Elkan Abramowitz · Obermaier, Morvillo & Abramowitz · 1120 Avenue of the Americas, Suite 1500 · New York, NY 10036 · 212-221-1414

Stanley S. Arkin · 600 Third Avenue · New York, NY 10016 · 212-869-1450

Michael F. Armstrong · Barrett Smith Simon & Armstrong · 26 Broadway · New York, NY 10004 · 212-422-8180

Herald Price Fahringer · Lipsitz, Green, Fahringer, Roll, Schuller & James · 540 Madison Avenue · New York, NY 10022 · 212-751-1330

Robert B. Fiske, Jr. · Davis Polk & Wardwell · One Chase Manhattan Plaza · New York, NY 10005 · 212-530-4000

Peter E. Fleming Jr. · Curtis, Mallet-Prevost, Colt & Mosle · 101 Park Avenue · New York, NY 10178 · 212-696-6000

Jay Goldberg · 250 Park Avenue, 14th Floor · New York, NY 10177-0077 · 212-983-6000

Paul R. Grand · Grand & Ostrow · 641 Lexington Avenue · New York, NY 10022 · 212-832-3611

Frederick P. Hafetz · Goldman & Hafetz · 60 East 42nd Street, Suite 950 · New York, NY 10165 · 212-682-7000

Jack S. Hoffinger · Hoffinger Friedland Dobrish Bernfeld & Hasen · 110 East 59th Street · New York, NY 10022-1392 · 212-421-4000

Robert Kasanof · Law Firm of Robert Kasanof · 767 Third Avenue · New York, NY 10017 · 212-355-6505

Stephen E. Kaufman · 277 Park Avenue · New York, NY 10172 · 212-826-0820

Michael Kennedy · 148 East 78th Street · New York, NY 10021 · 212-737-0400

James M. LaRossa · LaRossa, Mitchell & Ross · 41 Madison Avenue · New York, NY 10010 · 212-696-9700

Andrew M. Lawler · 220 East 42nd Street · New York, NY 10017 · 212-687-8850

Gerald B. Lefcourt · 148 East 78th Street · New York, NY 10021 · 212-737-0400

Jack T. Litman · Litman, Asche, Lupkin & Gioiella · 45 Broadway Atrium · New York, NY 10006 · 212-809-4500

Peter H. Morrison · Morrison Cohen & Singer · 110 East 59th Street · New York, NY 10022 · 212-593-0100

Robert G. Morvillo · Obermaier, Morvillo & Abramowitz · 1120 Avenue of the Americas, Suite 1500 · New York, NY 10036 · 212-221-1414

Gary P. Naftalis · Kramer, Levin, Nessen, Kamin & Frankel · 919 Third Avenue New York, NY 10022 · 212-715-9100

Gustave H. Newman · 641 Lexington Avenue · New York, NY 10022 · 212-308-7900

Otto G. Obermaier · Obermaier, Morvillo & Abramowitz · 1120 Avenue of the Americas, Suite 1500 · New York, NY 10036 · 212-221-1414

Norman S. Ostrow · Grand & Ostrow · 641 Lexington Avenue · New York, NY 10022 · 212-832-3611

Jed S. Rakoff · Mudge Rose Guthrie Alexander & Ferdon · 180 Maiden Lane New York, NY 10038 · 212-510-7000

Jules Ritholz · Kostelanetz & Ritholz · 80 Pine Street · New York, NY 10005 212-422-4030

Paul K. Rooney · 26 Broadway · New York, NY 10004 · 212-269-4420

Edward M. Shaw · Stillman, Friedman & Shaw · 521 Fifth Avenue · New York, NY 10175 · 212-661-4100

Charles A. Stillman · Stillman, Friedman & Shaw · 521 Fifth Avenue · New York, NY 10175 · 212-661-4100

Patrick M. Wall · 36 West 44th Street, Suite 1313 · New York, NY 10036 212-840-7188

John R. Wing · Weil, Gotshal & Manges · 767 Fifth Avenue · New York, NY 10153 · 212-310-8000

Lawrence J. Andolina · Jesserer, Andolina & Lamb · 510 Wilder Building Rochester, NY 14614 · 716-325-6700

Charles F. Crimi · Crimi & Crimi · One East Main Street · Rochester, NY 14614 716-325-2830

Michael T. DiPrima · 30 West Broad Street, Room 404 · Rochester, NY 14614 716-454-2930

Felix V. Lapine · 17 East Main Street, Suite 500 · Rochester, NY 14614 · 716-454-6690

David A. Murante · Eight Exchange Street · Rochester, NY 14614 · 716-232-6830

Norman A. Palmiere · Palmiere & Pellegrino · 13 South Fitzhugh Street · Rochester, NY 14614 · 716-232-6144

John R. Parrinello · Redmond & Parrinello · 400 Executive Office Building Rochester, NY 14614 · 716-454-2321

Karl F. Salzer · Gough, Skipworth, Petralia, Summers, Eves & Trevett · 1020 Reynolds Arcade · 16 East Main Street · Rochester, NY 14614 · 716-454-2181

John F. Speranza · 19 West Main Street · Rochester, NY 14614 · 716-454-1500

Joseph E. Fahey · Wiles & Fahey · 1010 State Tower Building · Syracuse, NY 13202 · 315-474-4648

Edward F. Gerber · University Building, Suite 631 · 120 East Washington Street Syracuse, NY 13202 · 315-472-4484

Emil M. Rossi · The Hills Building · 217 Montgomery Street · Syracuse, NY 13202 · 315-471-0126

P. R. Shanahan · R. J. & P. R. Shanahan · Onondaga County Savings Bank Building · Syracuse, NY 13202 · 315-474-1267

E. Stewart Jones, Jr. · 28 Second Street · Troy, NY 12181 · 518-274-5820

ENTERTAINMENT LAW

Richard L. Barovick · Loeb and Loeb · 230 Park Avenue · New York, NY 10169 · 212-692-4800

John F. Breglio · Paul, Weiss, Rifkind, Wharton & Garrison · 1285 Avenue of the Americas · New York, NY 10019 · 212-373-3000

Alvin Deutsch · Linden and Deutsch · 320 Park Avenue, Second Floor · New York, NY 10022 · 212-758-1100

Michael P. Frankfurt · Frankfurt, Garbus, Klein & Selz · 488 Madison Avenue, Ninth Floor · New York, NY 10022 · 212-980-0120

Leonard Franklin · Franklin, Weinrib, Rudell & Vassallo · 488 Madison Avenue, Eighth Floor · New York, NY 10022 · 212-935-5500

Martin Garbus · Frankfurt, Garbus, Klein & Selz · 488 Madison Avenue, Ninth Floor · New York, NY 10022 · 212-980-0120

Paul Gitlin · Ernst, Cane, Berner & Gitlin · Seven West 51st Street · New York, NY 10019 · 212-586-1640

Allen J. Grubman · Grubman, Indursky & Schindler · 575 Madison Avenue, Suite 600 · New York, NY 10022 · 212-888-6600

Arthur J. Klein · Frankfurt, Garbus, Klein & Selz · 488 Madison Avenue, Ninth Floor · New York, NY 10022 · 212-980-0120

Victor A. Kovner · Lankenau Kovner & Bickford · 30 Rockefeller Plaza · New York, NY 10112-0150 · 212-489-8230

Thomas M. Lewyn · Simpson Thacher & Bartlett · 425 Lexington Avenue · New York, NY 10017 · 212-455-2000

Paul G. Marshall · Marshall Morris Wattenberg & Platt · 130 West 57th Street New York, NY 10019 · 212-582-1122

Robert H. Montgomery, Jr. · Paul, Weiss, Rifkind, Wharton & Garrison · 1285 Avenue of the Americas · New York, NY 10019 · 212-373-3000

E. Gabriel Perle · Proskauer Rose Goetz & Mendelsohn · 300 Park Avenue · New York, NY 10022 · 212-909-7000

Harriet F. Pilpel · Weil, Gotshal & Manges · 767 Fifth Avenue · New York, NY 10153 · 212-310-8000

Michael I. Rudell · Franklin, Weinrib, Rudell & Vassallo · 488 Madison Avenue, Eighth Floor · New York, NY 10022 · 212-935-5500

Paul Sawyer · Phillips, Nizer, Benjamin, Krim & Ballon · 40 West 57th Street · New York, NY 10019 · 212-977-9700

Paul D. Schindler · Grubman, Indursky & Schindler · 575 Madison Avenue, Suite 600 · New York, NY 10022 · 212-888-6600

Paul J. Sherman · Pryor, Cashman, Sherman & Flynn · 410 Park Avenue · New York, NY 10022 · 212-421-4100

Lee N. Steiner · Loeb and Loeb · 230 Park Avenue · New York, NY 10169 · 212-692-4800

Robert G. Sugarman · Weil, Gotshal & Manges · 767 Fifth Avenue · New York, NY 10153 · 212-310-8000

Nancy F. Wechsler · Linden and Deutsch · 320 Park Avenue, Second Floor · New York, NY 10022 · 212-758-1100

FAMILY LAW

Stanley A. Rosen · McNamee, Lochner, Titus & Williams · 75 State Street · P.O. Box 459 · Albany, NY 12201-0459 · 518-434-3136

Sanford Soffer · 90 State Street · Albany, NY 12207-1765 · 518-436-7634

Bruno Colapietro · Chernin & Gold · Bache Building · 71 State Street · P.O. Box 1563 · Binghamton, NY 13902 · 607-723-9581

Donald M. Sukloff · Bernstein, Gitlitz & Sukloff · Key Bank Building · 59-61 Court Street, Sixth Floor · State Street Entrance · Binghamton, NY 13901 · 607-723-7913

Saul Edelstein · 26 Court Street · Brooklyn, NY 11242 · 718-875-3550

Grace Marie Ange · Ange & Gordon · 560 Statler Towers · Buffalo, NY 14202 · 716-854-8888

Paul Ivan Birzon · Birzon, Zakia, Stapell, Rosa, Olena & Davis · 360 Statler Towers · Buffalo, NY 14202 · 716-847-6060

William J. Cunningham, Jr. · 37 Franklin Street · Buffalo, NY 14202 · 716-856-7177

Peter J. Fiorella, Jr. · Fiorella, Aman & Vance · The Wickwire Mansion · 877 Delaware Avenue · Buffalo, NY 14209 · 716-882-3333

Mark G. Hirschorn · Siegel, Kelleher & Kahn · 426 Franklin Street · Buffalo, NY 14212 · 716-881-5800

Paul D. Pearson · Hodgson, Russ, Andrews, Woods & Goodyear · 1800 One M&T Plaza · Buffalo, NY 14203 · 716-856-4000

Herbert M. Siegel · Siegel, Kelleher & Kahn · 426 Franklin Street · Buffalo, NY 14212 · 716-881-5800

David G. Stiller · Heimerl, Stiller, Keenan & Longo · 1566 Statler Towers Buffalo, NY 14202 · 716-854-5063

Leonard Swagler · 704 Statler Towers · Buffalo, NY 14202 · 716-856-3315

Michael B. Atkins · Taylor, Atkins & Ostrow · 200 Garden City Plaza · Garden City, NY 11530 · 516-877-1800

Joel R. Brandes · 200 Garden City Plaza · Garden City, NY 11530 · 516-746-6995

Willard H. DaSilva · 585 Stewart Avenue · Garden City, NY 11530 · 516-222-0700

Stephen Gassman · 600 Old Country Road · Garden City, NY 11530 · 516-228-9181

Michael J. Ostrow · Taylor, Atkins & Ostrow · 200 Garden City Plaza · Garden City, NY 11530 · 516-877-1800

Leo Dikman · Dikman, Dikman and Botter · 161-10 Jamaica Avenue · Jamaica, NY 11432 · 718-739-4830

Michael Dikman · Dikman, Dikman and Botter · 161-10 Jamaica Avenue · Jamaica, NY 11432 · 718-739-4830

Kenneth Koopersmith · Koopersmith, Feigenbaum & Potruch · 3000 Marcus Avenue, Suite 3W7 · Lake Success, NY 11042 · 516-354-0800

Stephen W. Schlissel · Ruskin, Schlissel, Moscou, Evans & Faltischek · 170 Old Country Road · Mineola, NY 11501 · 516-248-9500

Eleanor Breitel Alter · Rosenman & Colin · 575 Madison Avenue · New York, NY 10022 · 212-940-8800

Alvin Ashley · Colton, Hartnick, Yamin & Sheresky · 79 Madison Avenue · New York, NY 10016 · 212-532-5100

Robert Stephan Cohen · Morrison Cohen & Singer · 110 East 59th Street · New York, NY 10022 · 212-593-0100

Robert Z. Dobrish · Hoffinger Friedland Dobrish Bernfeld & Hasen · 110 East 59th Street · New York, NY 10022-1392 · 212-421-4000

Joan L. Ellenbogen · Ellenbogen & Goldstein · 888 Seventh Avenue · New York, NY 10106 · 212-245-3260

Myrna Felder · The Firm of Raoul Lionel Felder · 437 Madison Avenue · New York, NY 10022 · 212-832-3939

Raoul Lionel Felder · The Firm of Raoul Lionel Felder · 437 Madison Avenue · New York, NY 10022 · 212-832-3939

Samuel G. Fredman · Fink, Weinberger, Fredman, Berman & Lowell · 551 Fifth Avenue · New York, NY 10176 · 212-682-0546

William C. Herman · Rosenthal, Herman & Mantel · 310 Madison Avenue, Suite 2024 · New York, NY 10017 · 212-972-8911

Kenneth D. Kemper · Kessler & Kemper · Two Dag Hammerskjold Plaza, Suite 1402 · New York, NY 10017 · 212-371-3710

Stanford G. Lotwin · Tenzer, Greenblatt, Fallon & Kaplan · 405 Lexington Avenue · New York, NY 10174 · 212-573-4300

Julia Perles · Phillips, Nizer, Benjamin, Krim & Ballon · 40 West 57th Street · New York, NY 10019 · 212-977-9700

Stanley Plesent · Squadron, Ellenoff, Plesent & Lehrer · 551 Fifth Avenue · New York, NY 10017 · 212-661-6500

Miriam M. Robinson · Finkelstein & Robinson · 350 Fifth Avenue · New York, NY 10118 · 212-594-9050

Rona J. Shays · Rosenthal & Shays · 276 Fifth Avenue · New York, NY 10001 · 212-684-1700

Norman M. Sheresky · Colton, Hartnick, Yamin & Sheresky · 79 Madsion Avenue · New York, NY 10016 · 212-532-5100

Sanford S. Dranoff · Ferraro Rogers Dranoff Greenbaum Goldstein & Miller · One Blue Hill Plaza, Suite 900 · P.O. Box 1629 · Pearl River, NY 10965-8629 · 914-735-7100

Perry Satz · Satz and Kirshon · 309 Mill Street · Poughkeepsie, NY 12601 · 914-454-4040

Brian J. Barney · Pauley & Barney · 215 Times Square Building · 45 Exchange Street · Rochester, NY 14614 · 716-232-1411

S. Gerald Davidson · Davidson, Fink, Cook and Gates · 900 First Federal Plaza · Rochester, NY 14614 · 716-546-6448

Joel J. Goldman · Kaman, Berlove, Marafioti, Jacobstein & Goldman · 13 South Fitzhugh Street, Suite 400 · Rochester, NY 14614 · 716-325-7440

Lewis J. Gould · Gould & Peck · 45 Exchange Street · Rochester, NY 14614 · 716-546-3065

Gregory J. Mott · Davidson, Fink, Cook and Gates · 900 First Federal Plaza · Rochester, NY 14614 · 716-546-6448

Joan de R. O'Byrne · 19 West Main Street · Rochester, NY 14614 · 716-546-3340

Raymond J. Pauley · Pauley & Barney · 215 Times Square Building · 45 Exchange Street · Rochester, NY 14614 · 716-232-1411

Gerard R. Gemmette · 19 Front Street · Schenectady, NY 12305 · 518-370-4187

Bruce G. Behrins · 1492 Victory Boulevard · Staten Island, NY 10301 · 718-447-5540

Edward B. Alderman · Alderman and Alderman · Empire Building, Suite 555 · 472 South Salina Street · Syracuse, NY 13202 · 315-422-8131

Anthony J. Di Caprio, Jr. · Di Caprio & Di Caprio · 503 Myrtle Street · Syracuse, NY 13204 · 315-468-1109

Gary L. Orenstein · 818 State Tower Building · 109 South Warren Street · Syracuse, NY 13202 · 315-422-8185

Timothy M. Tippins · 102 Third Street · Troy, NY 12180 · 518-271-0707

Henry S. Berman · Fink, Weinberger, Fredman, Berman & Lowell · 81 Main Street · White Plains, NY 10601 · 914-761-7550

Samuel G. Fredman · Fink, Weinberger, Fredman, Berman & Lowell · 81 Main Street · White Plains, NY 10601 · 914-761-7550

LABOR AND EMPLOYMENT LAW

Edward L. Bookstein · (Management) · Kohn, Bookstein & Karp · 90 State Street · Albany, NY 12207 · 518-449-8810

Bruce C. Bramley · (Labor) · Pozefsky, Pozefsky & Bramley · 90 State Street · Albany, NY 12207 · 518-434-2622

Richard C. Heffern · (Management) · Bond, Schoeneck & King · 111 Washington Avenue · Albany, NY 12210 · 518-462-7421

Melvin H. Osterman, Jr. · (Management) · Whiteman Osterman & Hanna · One Commerce Plaza · Albany, NY 12260 · 518-449-7600

William Pozefsky · (Labor) · Pozefsky, Pozefsky & Bramley · 90 State Street · Albany, NY 12207 · 518-434-2622

Richard R. Rowley · (Labor; Individuals) · Rowley, Forrest and O'Donnell · 90 State Street · Albany, NY 12207 · 518-434-6187

Frank A. Nemia · (Management) · Twining, Nemia, Hill & Steflik · 53 Front Street · Binghamton, NY 13905 · 607-772-1700

Amy Gladstein · (Labor; Individuals) · Gladstein, Reis & Meginniss · 26 Court Street, Suite 1304 · Brooklyn, NY 11242 · 718-858-9131

Walter M. Meginniss · (Labor; Individuals) · Gladstein, Reis & Meginniss · 26 Court Street, Suite 1304 · Brooklyn, NY 11242 · 718-858-9131

Jeremy V. Cohen · (Management) · Flaherty, Cohen, Grande, Randazzo & Doren · 135 Delaware Avenue, Suite 210 · Buffalo, NY 14202 · 716-853-7262

John F. Donovan · (Management) · Phillips, Lytle, Hitchcock, Blaine & Huber 3400 Marine Midland Center · Buffalo, NY 14203 · 716-847-8400

Robert A. Doren · (Management) · Flaherty, Cohen, Grande, Randazzo & Doren 135 Delaware Avenue, Suite 210 · Buffalo, NY 14202 · 716-853-7262

E. Joseph Giroux, Jr. · (Labor) · 1828 Liberty Building · Buffalo, NY 14202 716-853-6300

Genuino J. Grande · (Management) · Flaherty, Cohen, Grande, Randazzo & Doren · 135 Delaware Avenue, Suite 210 · Buffalo, NY 14202 · 716-853-7262

David E. Hall · (Management) · Hodgson, Russ, Andrews, Woods & Goodyear 1800 One M&T Plaza · Buffalo, NY 14203 · 716-856-4000

Ronald L. Jaros · (Labor) · Lipsitz, Green, Fahringer, Roll, Schuller & James One Niagara Square · Buffalo, NY 14202 · 716-849-1333

Richard Lipsitz · (Labor) · Lipsitz, Green, Fahringer, Roll, Schuller & James One Niagara Square · Buffalo, NY 14202 · 716-849-1333

Randall M. Odza · (Management) · Jaeckle, Fleischmann & Mugel · 800 Norstar Building · 12 Fountain Plaza · Buffalo, NY 14202 · 716-856-0600

Edward G. Piwowarczyk · (Management) · Jaeckle, Fleischmann & Mugel · 800 Norstar Building · 12 Fountain Plaza · Buffalo, NY 14202 · 716-856-0600

Joseph L. Randazzo · (Management) · Flaherty, Cohen, Grande, Randazzo & Doren · 135 Delaware Avenue, Suite 210 · Buffalo, NY 14202 · 716-853-7262

Eugene W. Salisbury · (Labor) · Lipsitz, Green, Fahringer, Roll, Schuller & James · One Niagara Square · Buffalo, NY 14202 · 716-849-1333

James N. Schmit · (Management) · Damon & Morey · 1600 Main Place Tower Buffalo, NY 14202 · 716-856-5500

W. James Schwan · Wyssling, Schwan & Montgomery · 1230 Delaware Avenue Buffalo, NY 14209 · 716-882-2243

Brian J. Troy · (Management) · Jaeckle, Fleischmann & Mugel · 800 Norstar Building · 12 Fountain Plaza · Buffalo, NY 14202 · 716-865-0600

Robert M. Walker · (Management) · Hodgson, Russ, Andrews, Woods & Goodyear · 1800 One M&T Plaza · Buffalo, NY 14203 · 716-856-4000

Martin F. Idzik · (Management) · Phillips, Lytle, Hitchcock, Blaine & Huber · 307 Chase Lincoln First Bank Building · P.O. Box 1279 · Jamestown, NY 14702-1279 · 716-664-3906

Albert X. Bader, Jr. · (Management) · Simpson Thacher & Bartlett · 425 Lexington Avenue · New York, NY 10017 · 212-455-2000

Charles G. Bakaly, Jr. · (Management) · O'Melveny & Myers · 153 East 53rd Street, 53rd Floor · New York, NY 10022-4611 · 212-326-2000

L. Robert Batterman · (Management) · Proskauer Rose Goetz & Mendelsohn · 300 Park Avenue · New York, NY 10022 · 212-909-7000

Warren J. Bennia · (Individuals) · 220 East 54th Street · New York, NY 10022 · 212-688-0101

Michael I. Bernstein · (Management) · Benetar Isaacs Bernstein & Schair · 950 Third Avenue · New York, NY 10022 · 212-753-8900

Diane S. Blank · (Individuals) · Blank & Blank · 342 East 78th Street · New York, NY 10021-2232 · 212-535-8800

John D. Canoni · (Management) · Townley & Updike · Chrysler Building · 405 Lexington Avenue · New York, NY 10174 · 212-682-4567

Eugene T. D'Ablemont · (Management) · Kelley Drye & Warren · 101 Park Avenue · New York, NY 10178 · 212-808-7800

Marvin Dicker · (Management) · Proskauer Rose Goetz & Mendelsohn · 300 Park Avenue · New York, NY 10022 · 212-909-7000

Eugene G. Eisner · (Labor) · Eisner & Levy · 113 University Place, Eighth Floor · New York, NY 10003 · 212-473-1122

Sheldon Engelhard · (Labor) · Vladeck, Waldman, Elias & Engelhard · 1501 Broadway · New York, NY 10036 · 212-354-8330

Allen I. Fagin · (Management) · Proskauer Rose Goetz & Mendelsohn · 300 Park Avenue · New York, NY 10022 · 212-909-7000

Leonard N. Flamm · (Individuals) · Hockert & Flamm · 880 Third Avenue · New York, NY 10022 · 212-752-3380

Eugene S. Friedman · (Labor) · Friedman, Levy-Warren & Moss · 1500 Broadway, Suite 2303 · New York, NY 10036-4015 · 212-354-4500

Howard L. Ganz · (Management) · Proskauer Rose Goetz & Mendelsohn · 300 Park Avenue · New York, NY 10022 · 212-909-7000

Janice Goodman · (Individuals) · 500 Fifth Avenue, Suite 5530 · New York, NY 10110 · 212-869-1940

Kenneth E. Gordon · (Labor; Individuals) · Gordon & Gordon · Three Park Avenue, 28th Floor · New York, NY 10016 · 212-725-3700

Ronald M. Green · (Management) · Epstein, Becker & Green · 250 Park Avenue, 14th Floor · New York, NY 10177 · 212-370-9800

Jerold D. Jacobson · (Management) · Summit, Rovins & Feldesman · 445 Park Avenue · New York, NY 10022 · 212-702-2200

Mark A. Jacoby · (Management) · Weil, Gotschal & Manges · 767 Fifth Avenue New York, NY 10153 · 212-310-8000

Alan S. Jaffe · (Management) · Proskauer Rose Goetz & Mendelsohn · 300 Park Avenue · New York, NY 10022 · 212-909-7000

Jerome B. Kauff · (Management) · Dretzin, Kauff, McClain & McGuire · 950 Third Avenue, 15th Floor · New York, NY 10022 · 212-644-1010

Saul G. Kramer · (Management) · Proskauer Rose Goetz & Mendelsohn · 300 Park Avenue · New York, NY 10022 · 212-909-7000

William A. Krupman · (Management) · Jackson, Lewis, Schnitzler & Krupman 261 Madison Avenue · New York, NY 10016 · 212-697-8200

Richard A. Levy · (Labor) · Eisner & Levy · 113 University Place, Eighth Floor New York, NY 10003 · 212-473-1122

Everett E. Lewis · (Labor) · Lewis, Greenwald, Kennedy & Lewis · 232 West 40th Street · New York, NY 10018 · 212-382-0029

Leonard Liebowitz · (Labor) · Liebowitz & DuBrul · Three East 54th Street, Suite 1200 · New York, NY 10022 · 212-593-3310

Jerome B. Lurie · (Labor) · Cohn, Glickstein & Lurie · 1370 Avenue of the Americas · New York, NY 10019 · 212-757-4000

Martin J. Oppenheimer · (Management) · Proskauer Rose Goetz & Mendelsohn 300 Park Avenue · New York, NY 10022 · 212-909-7000

Wayne N. Outten · (Individuals) · Lankenau Kovner & Bickford · 30 Rockefeller Plaza · New York, NY 10112-0150 · 212-489-8230

Peter M. Panken · (Management) · Parker Chapin Flattau & Klimpl · 1211 Avenue of the Americas · New York, NY 10036 · 212-704-6000

Bertrand B. Pogrebin · (Management) · Rains & Pogrebin · 425 Park Avenue New York, NY 10022 · 212-980-3560

Gregory I. Rasin · (Management) · Jackson, Lewis, Schnitzler & Krupman · 261 Madison Avenue · New York, NY 10016 · 212-697-8200

Eric Rosenfeld · (Management) · Seyfarth, Shaw, Fairweather & Geraldson · 757 Third Avenue · New York, NY 10017 · 212-715-9000

Stanley Schair · (Management) · Benetar Isaacs Bernstein & Schair · 950 Third Avenue, Sixth Floor · New York, NY 10022 · 212-753-8900

Martin C. Seham · (Management) · Seham, Klein & Zelman · 485 Madison Avenue, 15th Floor · New York, NY 10022 · 212-935-6020

Martin N. Silberman · (Individuals) · 396 Broadway, Suite 200 · New York, NY 10013 · 212-219-2100

Edward Silver · (Management) · Proskauer Rose Goetz & Mendelsohn · 300 Park Avenue · New York, NY 10022 · 212-909-7000

Bruce H. Simon · (Labor) · Cohen, Weiss and Simon · 330 West 42nd Street New York, NY 10036 · 212-563-4100

I. Philip Sipser · (Labor) · Sipser, Weinstock, Harper & Dorn · 380 Madison Avenue · New York, NY 10017 · 212-867-2100

Lewis M. Steel · (Individuals) · Steel, Bellman & Levine · 351 Broadway · New York, NY 10013 · 212-925-7400

Jerome Y. Sturm · (Labor) · Sturm & Perl · 21 East 40th Street · New York, NY 10016 · 212-685-8487

Judith P. Vladeck · (Labor; Individuals) · Vladeck, Waldman, Elias & Engelhard 1501 Broadway · New York, NY 10036 · 212-354-8330

Jay W. Waks · (Management) · Kaye, Scholer, Fierman, Hays & Handler · 425 Park Avenue · New York, NY 10023 · 212-836-8000

Seymour M. Waldman · (Labor) · Vladeck, Waldman, Elias & Engelhard · 1501 Broadway · New York, NY 10036 · 212-354-8330

Henry Weiss · (Labor) · Cohen, Weiss and Simon · 330 West 42nd Street · New York, NY 10036 · 212-563-4100

Richard N. Chapman · (Management) · Harris, Beach, Wilcox, Rubin and Levey Granite Building · 130 East Main Street · Rochester, NY 14604 · 716-232-4440

Thomas G. Dignan · (Management) · Nixon, Hargrave, Devans & Doyle · Lincoln First Tower · Rochester, NY 14603 · 716-546-8000

Michael T. Harren · (Labor; Individuals) · Chamberlain, D'Amanda, Oppenheimer and Greenfield · 1600 Crossroads Building · Two State Street · Rochester, NY 14614 · 716-232-3730

Carl R. Krause · (Management) · Harris, Beach, Wilcox, Rubin and Levey Granite Building · 130 East Main Street · Rochester, NY 14604 · 716-232-4440

Emmelyn S. Logan-Baldwin · (Individuals) · 171 State Street · Rochester, NY 14614 · 716-232-2292

Gerald L. Paley · (Management) · Phillips, Lytle, Hitchcock, Blaine & Huber 1400 First Federal Plaza · Rochester, NY 14614 · 716-238-2000

Susan Robfogel · (Management) · Nixon, Hargrave, Devans & Doyle · Lincoln First Tower · Rochester, NY 14603 · 716-546-8000

Jules L. Smith · Blitman and King · The Fitch Building, Suite 200 · 315 Alexander Street · Rochester, NY 14614 · 716-232-5600

Eugene D. Ulterino · (Management) · Nixon, Hargrave, Devans & Doyle Lincoln First Tower · Rochester, NY 14603 · 716-546-8000

Franklin H. Goldberger · (Management) · Ogletree, Deakins, Nash, Smoak and Stewart · 215 State Street · Schenectady, NY 12305 · 518-374-4029

William L. Bergan · (Management) · Bond, Schoeneck & King · One Lincoln Center, 16th Floor · Syracuse, NY 13202-1355 · 315-422-0121

Earl P. Boyle · (Labor) · Boyle, Wittenburg & Cantone · University Building, Suite 920 · 120 East Washington Street · Syracuse, NY 13202 · 315-422-2208

W. Carroll Coyne · (Management) · Hancock & Estabrook · One Mony Plaza, 14th Floor · 100 Madison Street · P.O. Box 4976 · Syracuse, NY 13221-4976 315-471-3151

Tracy H. Ferguson · (Management) · Bond, Schoeneck & King · One Lincoln Center, 16th Floor · Syracuse, NY 13202-1355 · 315-422-0121

Bernard T. King · (Labor) · Blitman and King · The 500 Building, Suite 1100 500 South Salina Street · Syracuse, NY 13202 · 315-422-7111

Robert W. Kopp · (Management) · Bond, Schoeneck & King · One Lincoln Center, 16th Floor · Syracuse, NY 13202-1355 · 315-422-0121

James R. LaVaute · (Labor) · Blitman and King · The 500 Building, Suite 1100 500 South Salina Street · Syracuse, NY 13202 · 315-422-7111

Raymond W. Murray, Jr. · (Management) · Bond, Schoeneck & King · One Lincoln Center, 16th Floor · Syracuse, NY 13202-1355 · 315-422-0121

Philip D. Tobin · (Labor) · 65 Main Street · Tuckahoe, NY 10707 · 914-779-5703

Patrick L. Vaccaro · (Management) · Johnson, Lewis, Schnitzler & Krupman One North Broadway · White Plains, NY 10601 · 914-328-0404

MARITIME LAW

Richard G. Ashworth · Haight, Gardner, Poor & Havens · 195 Broadway, 24th Floor · New York, NY 10007 · 212-341-7000

Richard B. Barnett · Haight, Gardner, Poor & Havens · 195 Broadway, 24th Floor New York, NY 10007 · 212-341-7000

R. Glenn Bauer · Haight, Gardner, Poor & Havens · 195 Broadway, 24th Floor New York, NY 10007 · 212-341-7000

Arthur J. Blank, Jr. · Hill, Betts & Nash · One World Trade Center, Suite 5215 New York, NY 10048 · 212-839-7000

Richard H. Brown, Jr. · Kirlin, Campbell & Keating · 14 Wall Street, 23rd Floor New York, NY 10005 · 212-732-5520

Raymond J. Burke, Jr. · Burke & Parsons · 1114 Avenue of the Americas, 34th Floor · New York, NY 10036 · 212-354-3800

Francis X. Byrn · Haight, Gardner, Poor & Havens · 195 Broadway, 24th Floor New York, NY 10007 · 212-341-7000

J. Edwin Carey · Hill, Rivkins, Carey, Loesberg, O'Brien & Mulroy · 21 West Street · New York, NY 10006 · 212-825-1000

Stephen K. Carr · Haight, Gardner, Poor & Havens · 195 Broadway, 24th Floor New York, NY 10007 · 212-341-7000

Michael Marks Cohen · Burlingham Underwood & Lord · One Battery Park Plaza, 25th Floor · New York, NY 10004 · 212-422-7585

M. E. DeOrchis · DeOrchis & Partners · 71 Broadway, Suite 2000 · New York, NY 10006 · 212-425-9797

Vincent M. DeOrchis · DeOrchis & Partners · 71 Broadway, Suite 2200 · New York, NY 10006 · 212-425-9797

Steve C. Dune · Cadwalader, Wickersham & Taft · 100 Maiden Lane · New York, NY 10038 · 212-504-6000

Emery W. Harper · Lord, Day & Lord, Barrett Smith · 25 Broadway, Eighth Floor · New York, NY 10004 · 212-344-8480

Nicholas J. Healy · Healy & Baillie · 29 Broadway, 25th Floor · New York, NY 10006 · 212-943-3980

Franklin G. Hunt · Lord, Day & Lord, Barrett Smith · 25 Broadway, Eighth Floor New York, NY 10004 · 212-344-8480

Douglas A. Jacobsen · Bigham Englar Jones & Houston · 14 Wall Street · New York, NY 10005-2140 · 212-732-4646

Edward C. Kalaidjian · Thacher Proffitt & Wood · Two World Trade Center, 39th Floor · New York, NY 10048 · 212-912-7400

Marshall P. Keating · Kirlin, Campbell & Keating · 14 Wall Street, 23rd Floor New York, NY 10005 · 212-732-5520

John D. Kimball · Healy & Baillie · 29 Broadway, 25th Floor · New York, NY 10006 · 212-943-3980

Alan S. Loesberg · Hill, Rivkins, Carey, Loesberg, O'Brien & Mulroy · 21 West Street · New York, NY 10006 · 212-825-1000

Herbert M. Lord · Burlingham Underwood & Lord · One Battery Park Plaza, 25th Floor · New York, NY 10004 · 212-422-7585

David L. Maloof · Donovan Maloof Walsh & Repetto · 161 William Street · New York, NY 10038-2681 · 212-964-3553

Elliott B. Nixon · Burlingham Underwood & Lord · One Battery Park Plaza, 25th Floor · New York, NY 10004 · 212-422-7585

David A. Nourse · Nourse & Bowles · One Exchange Plaza at 55 Broadway · New York, NY 10006 · 212-952-6200

Francis J. O'Brien · Hill, Rivkins, Carey, Loesberg, O'Brien & Mulroy · 21 West Street · New York, NY 10006 · 212-825-1000

Gordon W. Paulsen · Healy & Baillie · 29 Broadway, 25th Floor · New York, NY 10006 · 212-943-3980

John G. Poles · Poles, Tublin, Patestides & Stratakis · 46 Trinity Place, Fifth Floor · New York, NY 10006 · 212-943-0110

Richard E. Repetto · Donovan Maloof Walsh & Repetto · 161 William Street New York, NY 10038-2681 · 212-964-3553

J. Bond Smith · Lord, Day & Lord, Barrett Smith · 25 Broadway, Eighth Floor New York, NY 10004 · 212-344-8480

Richard H. Sommer · Kirlin, Campbell & Keating · 14 Wall Street, 23rd Floor New York, NY 10005 · 212-732-5520

Bernard J. Tansey · Mendes & Mount · Three Park Avenue · New York, NY 10016 · 212-951-2200

Charles L. Trowbridge · Walker & Corsa · 40 Wall Street · New York, NY 10005 212-344-4700

Melvin J. Tublin · Poles, Tublin, Patestides & Stratakis · 46 Trinity Place, Fifth Floor · New York, NY 10006 · 212-943-0110

Sheldon A. Vogel · Thacher Proffitt & Wood · Two World Trade Center, 39th Floor · New York, NY 10048 · 212-912-7400

Kenneth H. Volk · Burlingham Underwood & Lord · One Battery Park Plaza, 25th Floor · New York, NY 10004 · 212-422-7585

Donald M. Waesche, Jr. · Waesche, Sheinbaum & O'Regan · 120 Broadway, Suite 1825 · New York, NY 10271-0156 · 212-227-3550

Hollis M. Walker, Jr. · Walker & Corsa · 40 Wall Street · New York, NY 10005 · 212-344-4700

Richard H. Webber · Hill, Rivkins, Carey, Loesberg, O'Brien & Mulroy · 21 West Street · New York, NY 10006 · 212-825-1000

NATURAL RESOURCES AND ENVIRONMENTAL LAW

Donald W. Stever · Sidley & Austin · 520 Madison Avenue, Fifth Floor · New York, NY 10022 · 212-418-2100

Steven A. Tasher · Donovan Leisure Newton & Irvine · 30 Rockefeller Plaza · New York, NY 10112 · 212-632-3000

PERSONAL INJURY LITIGATION

Morris J. Bloomberg · (Plaintiffs) · The Bloomberg Firm · 109 State Street · Albany, NY 12207 · 518-434-1121

James S. Carter · (Defendants) · Carter, Conboy, Bardwell, Case and Blackmore · 74 Chapel Street · Albany, NY 12207 · 518-465-3484

Stephen R. Coffey · (Plaintiffs) · O'Connell and Aronowitz · 100 State Street, Eighth Floor · Albany, NY 12207 · 518-462-5601

John T. DeGraff, Jr. · (Plaintiffs) · DeGraff, Foy, Conway, Holt-Harris and Mealey · 90 State Street · Albany, NY 12207 · 518-462-5301

Richard M. Gershon · (Defendants) · Thorn & Gershon · 19 Aviation Road · Albany, NY 12205 · 518-459-8971

Earl S. Jones, Jr. · (Defendants) · Maynard, O'Connor & Smith · 80 State Street · Albany, NY 12207 · 518-465-3553

John K. Powers · (Plaintiffs) · Powers & Santola · 600 Broadway · Albany, NY 12207 · 518-465-5995

John W. Tabner · (Plaintiffs) · Tabner and Laudato · 26 Computer Drive West · P.O. Box 12605 · Albany, NY 12212-2605 · 518-459-9000

Lee S. Michaels · (Plaintiffs) · 71 South Street · P.O. Box 308 · Auburn, NY 13021 · 315-253-3293

Calrton F. Thompson · (Defendants) · Levene, Gouldin & Thompson · 902 Press Building · P.O. Box F-1706 · Binghamton, NY 13902 · 607-772-9200

Joseph M. Irom · (Plaintiffs) · Irom & Wittels · 349 East 149th Street · Bronx, NY 10451 · 212-665-0220

Paul W. Beltz · (Plaintiffs) · 36 Church Street · Buffalo, NY 14202 · 716-852-0111

John F. Canale · (Defendants) · Canale, Madden and Burke · 43 Court Street, Suite 530 · Buffalo, NY 14202 · 716-853-7100

Alexander C. Cordes · (Defendants) · Phillips, Lytle, Hitchcock, Blaine & Huber · 3400 Marine Midland Center · Buffalo, NY 14203 · 716-847-8400

David K. Floyd · (Defendants) · Phillips, Lytle, Hitchcock, Blaine & Huber 3400 Marine Midland Center · Buffalo, NY 14203 · 716-847-8400

George M. Gibson · (Defendants) · Damon & Morey · 1600 Main Place Tower Buffalo, NY 14202 · 716-856-5500

Richard F. Griffin · (Defendants) · Moot & Sprague · 2300 Main Place Tower Buffalo, NY 14202 · 716-845-5200

Sheldon Hurwitz · (Defendants) · Hurwitz & Fine · 1400 Liberty Building Buffalo, NY 14202 · 716-853-6100

Philip H. Magner, Jr. · (Plaintiffs) · Magner, Love & Morris · 1725 Statler Towers Buffalo, NY 14202 · 716-856-8480

James S. McAskill · (Defendants) · Damon & Morey · 1600 Main Place Tower Buffalo, NY 14202 · 716-856-5500

Samuel R. Miserendino · (Plaintiffs) · Miserendino, Krull & Foley · 964 Ellicott Square Building · Buffalo, NY 14203 · 716-854-1002

William S. Reynolds · (Defendants) · O'Shea, Reynolds, Napier, Quinn & Cummings · 181 Franklin Street · Buffalo, NY 14202 · 716-853-6341

Daniel T. Roach · (Defendants) · Maloney, Gallup, Roach, Brown & McCarthy 1620 Liberty Building · Buffalo, NY 14202 · 716-852-0400

Terry D. Smith · (Plaintiffs) · Smith, Keller, Hayes & Miner · 1212 Chemical Bank Building · 69 Delaware Avenue · Buffalo, New York 14202 · 716-855-3611

Emmet J. Agoglia · McCoy, Agoglia, Beckett & Fassberg · 80 East Old Country Road · Mineola, NY 11501 · 516-741-2422

Marvin V. Ausubel · (Defendants) · Fried, Frank, Harris, Shriver & Jacobson One New York Plaza · New York, NY 10004-1980 · 212-820-8000

Francis P. Bensel · (Defendants) · Martin, Clearwater & Bell · 220 East 42nd Street · New York, NY 10017 · 212-697-3122

Sheila L. Birnbaum · (Defendants) · Skadden, Arps, Slate, Meagher & Flom 919 Third Avenue · New York, NY 10022 · 212-735-3000

John J. Bower · (Defendants) · Bower and Gardner · 110 East 59th Street · New York, NY 10022 · 212-751-2900

Robert L. Conason · (Plaintiffs) · Gair, Gair & Conason · 80 Pine Street · New York, NY 10005 · 212-943-1090

Joseph M. Costello · (Defendants) · Costello & Shea · 50 Broadway · New York, NY 10004 · 212-483-9600

Peter E. De Blasio · (Plaintiffs) · 233 Broadway, 43rd Floor · New York, NY 10279 212-732-2620

Stanley D. Friedman · (Defendants) · McAloon, Friedman & Mandell · 116 John Street, 29th Floor · New York, NY 10038 · 212-732-8700

Theodore H. Friedman · (Plaintiffs) · Friedman & Eisenstein · 325 Broadway New York, NY 10007 · 212-619-1690

John Gardner · (Defendants) · Bower and Gardner · 110 East 59th Street · New York, NY 10022 · 212-751-2900

Richard Godosky · Weiss, Molod, Berkowitz & Godosky · 12 East 41st Street New York, NY 10017 · 212-213-8500

Peter James Johnson · Leahey & Johnson · 120 Wall Street, Suite 2220 · New York, NY 10005 · 212-269-7308

Gunther H. Kilsch · (Defendants) · McAloon, Friedman & Mandell · 116 John Street, 29th Floor · New York, NY 10038 · 212-732-8700

Norman J. Landau · (Plaintiffs) · Landau & Miller · 233 Broadway · New York, NY 10279 · 212-962-7545

Martin N. Leaf · Leaf Sternklar & Drogin · 440 Park Avenue South · New York, NY 10016 · 212-685-8400

Harry H. Lipsig · (Plaintiffs) · Lipsig, Sullivan & Liapakis · 100 Church Street New York, NY 10007 · 212-732-9000

Roger P. McTiernan · (Defendants) · Barry, McTiernan & Moore · 22 Cortlandt Street, Ninth Floor · New York, NY 10007 · 212-964-4270

David G. Miller · (Plaintiffs) · Gair, Gair & Conason · 80 Pine Street · New York, NY 10005 · 212-943-1090

Donald Miller · (Plaintiffs) · Landau & Miller · 233 Broadway · New York, NY 10279 · 212-962-7545

Thomas A. Moore · (Plaintiffs) · Kramer, Dillof, Tessel, Duffy & Moore · 233 Broadway, 45th Floor · New York, NY 10279 · 212-267-4177

Luke M. Pittoni · (Defendants) · Heidell, Pittoni, Murphy & Bach · 100 Park Avenue, 35th Floor · New York, NY 10017 · 212-683-2224

Fred Queller · (Plaintiffs) · Queller, Fisher, Bower & Wisotsky · 110 Wall Street New York, NY 10005 · 212-422-3600

Ivan S. Schneider · (Plaintiffs) · Schneider, Kleinick & Weitz · 11 Park Place, 10th Floor · New York, NY 10007 · 212-962-1780

John A. Schultz · (Defendants) · Herzfeld & Rubin · 40 Wall Street · New York, NY 10005 · 212-344-0680

Harold L. Schwab · (Defendants) · Lester Schwab Katz & Dwyer · 120 Broadway New York, NY 10271 · 212-964-6611

Robert G. Sullivan · (Plaintiffs) · Lipsig, Sullivan & Liapakis · 100 Church Street New York, NY 10007 · 212-732-9000

George G. van Setter · (Defendants) · Martin, Clearwater & Bell · 220 East 42nd Street · New York, NY 10017 · 212-697-3122

Edwin N. Weidman · (Plaintiffs) · 150 Broadway · New York, NY 10038 · 212-349-4123

Harvey Weitz · (Plaintiffs) · Schneider, Kleinick & Weitz · 11 Park Place, 10th Floor · New York, NY 10007 · 212-962-1780

Angelo G. Faraci · (Plaintiffs) · Faraci, Guadagnino, Lange & Johns · 45 Exchange Street · Rochester, NY 14614 · 716-325-5150

Alexander Geiger · (Plaintiffs) · Geiger and Rothenberg · 825 Times Square Building · 45 Exchange Street · Rochester, NY 14614 · 716-232-1946

David M. Lascell · (Defendants) · Nixon, Hargrave, Devans & Doyle · Lincoln First Tower · Rochester, NY 14603 · 716-546-8000

James C. Moore · (Defendants) · Harter, Secrest & Emery · 700 Midtown Tower · Rochester, NY 14604 · 716-232-6500

Anthony R. Palermo · (Defendants) · Harter, Secrest & Emery · 700 Midtown Tower · Rochester, NY 14604 · 716-232-6500

Norman A. Palmiere · (Plaintiffs) · Palmiere & Pellegrino · 13 South Fitzhugh Street · Rochester, NY 14614 · 716-232-6144

David Rothenberg · (Plaintiffs) · Geiger and Rothenberg · 825 Times Square Building · 45 Exchange Street · Rochester, NY 14614 · 716-232-1946

Robert T. Skipworth · (Defendants) · Gough, Skipworth, Petralia, Summers, Eves & Trevett · 1020 Reynolds Arcade · 16 East Main Street · Rochester, NY 14614 · 716-454-2181

Jeffrey M. Wilkens · (Defendants) · Osborn, Reed, Van de Vate and Burke · Watts Building, Fourth Floor · 47 South Fitzhugh Street · Rochester, NY 14614 · 716-454-6480

S. Paul Battaglia · (Defendants) · Bond, Schoeneck & King · One Lincoln Center, 17th Floor · Syracuse, NY 13202-1355 · 315-422-0121

Irwin Birnbaum · (Plaintiffs) · Birnbaum & Rojas · 108 West Jefferson Street, Suite 300 · Syracuse, NY 13202 · 315-422-0246

John C. Cherundolo · (Plaintiffs) · Cherundolo, Bottar & Del Duchetto · 407 South Warren Street, Suite 400 · Syracuse, NY 13202 · 315-422-3466

John J. Dee · (Plaintiffs) · Bond, Schoeneck & King · One Lincoln Center, 17th Floor · Syracuse, NY 13202-1355 · 315-422-0121

Paul M. Hanrahan · (Defendants) · Hancock & Estabrook · One Mony Plaza, 14th Floor · 100 Madison Street · P.O. Box 4976 · Syracuse, NY 13221-4976 315-471-3151

William F. Lynn · (Plaintiffs) · 1001 Onondaga Savings Bank Building · Syracuse, NY 13202 · 315-474-1267

Charles M. Manheim · (Defendants) · Sugarman, Wallace, Manheim & Schoenwald · 499 South Warren Street · Syracuse, NY 13202 · 315-422-1203

Laurence F. Sovik · (Defendants) · Smith, Sovik, Kendrick, Schwarzer & Sugnet 300 Empire Building · 472 South Salina Street · Syracuse, NY 13202-2473 315-474-2911

E. Stewart Jones, Jr. · 28 Second Street · Troy, NY 12181 · 518-274-5820

Henry G. Miller · (Plaintiffs) · Clark, Gagliardi & Miller · Inns of Court Building 99 Court Street · White Plains, NY 10601 · 914-946-8900

REAL ESTATE LAW

Lawrence F. Anito, Jr. · Helm, Shapiro, Anito & Aldrich · 111 Washington Avenue · Albany, NY 12210 · 518-465-7563

Harold C. Hanson · Hinman, Straub, Pigors & Manning · 121 State Street Albany, NY 12207 · 518-436-0751

Edward J. Trombly · Hiscock & Barclay · One Keycorp Plaza, Suite 1100 Albany, NY 12207 · 518-434-2163

Peter J. Battaglia · Williams, Stevens, McCarville & Frizzell · 1920 Liberty Building · Buffalo, NY 14202 · 716-856-2112

Marvin R. Baum · 1400 Statler Towers · Buffalo, NY 14202 · 716-847-8800

George R. Grasser · Phillips, Lytle, Hitchcock, Blaine & Huber · 3400 Marine Midland Center · Buffalo, NY 14203 · 716-847-8400

Gerard R. Haas · Phillips, Lytle, Hitchcock, Blaine & Huber · 3400 Marine Midland Center · Buffalo, NY 14203 · 716-847-8400

Franklin Pack · Pack, Hartman, Ball & Huckabone · 230 Brisbane Building Buffalo, NY 14203 · 716-856-9533

Raymond F. Roll, Jr. · Lipsitz, Green, Fahringer, Roll, Schuller & James · One Niagara Square · Buffalo, NY 14202 · 716-849-1333

Jack Adelman · Cadwalader, Wickersham & Taft · 100 Maiden Lane · New York, NY 10038 · 212-504-6000

Steven M. Alden · Debevoise & Plimpton · 875 Third Avenue · New York, NY 10022 · 212-909-6000

Alan J. B. Aronsohn · Robinson, Silverman, Pearce, Aronsohn & Berman · 230 Park Avenue · New York, NY 10169 · 212-687-0400

Franklin L. Bass · Fried, Frank, Harris, Shriver & Jacobson · One New York Plaza · New York, NY 10004-1980 · 212-820-8000

Leonard Boxer · Stroock & Stroock & Lavan · Seven Hanover Square · New York, NY 10004 · 212-806-5400

John D. Cohen · Tenzer, Greenblatt, Fallon & Kaplan · The Chrysler Building 405 Lexington Avenue · New York, NY 10174 · 212-573-4300

Robert M. Feely · Shearman & Sterling · Citicorp Center · 153 East 53rd Street New York, NY 10022 · 212-848-4000

Charles A. Goldstein · Shea & Gould · 1251 Avenue of the Americas · New York, NY 10020 · 212-827-3000

Philip H. Hedges · White & Case · 1155 Avenue of the Americas · New York, NY 10036 · 212-819-8200

Samuel W. Ingram, Jr. · Shea & Gould · 1251 Avenue of the Americas · New York, NY 10020 · 212-827-3000

William M. Kufeld · Carb, Luria, Glassner, Cook & Kufeld · 529 Fifth Avenue New York, NY 10017 · 212-986-3131

Anthony B. Kuklin · Paul, Weiss, Rifkind, Wharton & Garrison · 1285 Avenue of the Americas · New York, NY 10019 · 212-373-3000

Walter F. Leinhardt · Paul, Weiss, Rifkind, Wharton & Garrison · 1285 Avenue of the Americas · New York, NY 10019 · 212-373-3000

Samuel H. Lindenbaum · Rosenman & Colin · 575 Madison Avenue · New York, NY 10022 · 212-940-8800

Sydney A. Luria · Carb, Luria, Glassner, Cook & Kufeld · 529 Fifth Avenue New York, NY 10017 · 212-986-3131

Peter L. Malkin · Wien, Malkin & Bettex · Lincoln Building · 60 East 42nd Street, 48th Floor · New York, NY 10165 · 212-687-8700

Melvin Michaelson · Kaye, Scholer, Fierman, Hays & Handler · 425 Park Avenue New York, NY 10022 · 212-407-8000

Benjamin F. Needell · Skadden, Arps, Slate, Meagher & Flom · 919 Third Avenue · New York, NY 10022 · 212-371-6000

John C. Nelson · Milbank, Tweed, Hadley & McCloy · One Chase Manhattan Plaza · New York, NY 10005 · 212-530-5000

Benet Polikoff, Jr. · Rosenman & Colin · 575 Madison Avenue · New York, NY 10022 · 212-940-8800

David Alan Richards · Sidley & Austin · 520 Madison Avenue · New York, NY 10022 · 212-418-2100

Paul E. Roberts · Morgan, Lewis & Bockius · 101 Park Avenue · New York, NY 10178 · 212-309-6000

Martin S. Saiman · Kaye, Scholer, Fierman, Hays & Handler · 425 Park Avenue New York, NY 10022 · 212-407-8000

Flora Schnall · Milbank, Tweed, Hadley & McCloy · One Chase Manhattan Plaza · New York, NY 10005 · 212-530-5000

Gerald N. Schrager · Dreyer and Traub · 101 Park Avenue · New York, NY 10178 212-661-8800

Alvin Silverman · Wien, Malkin & Bettex · Lincoln Building · 60 East 42nd Street, 48th Floor · New York, NY 10165 · 212-687-8700

Donald H. Siskind · Rosenman & Colin · 575 Madison Avenue · New York, NY 10022 · 212-940-8800

Neil Underberg · Whitman & Ransom · 200 Park Avenue, 27th Floor · New York, NY 10166 · 212-351-3000

John E. Zuccotti · Brown & Wood · One World Trade Center · New York, NY 10048 · 212-839-5300

John E. Blyth · Harter, Secrest & Emery · 700 Midtown Tower · Rochester, NY 14604 · 716-232-6500

Richard A. Calabrese · Elliott, Stern & Calabrese · One East Main Street Rochester, NY 14614 · 716-232-4724

John B. Hood · Nixon, Hargrave, Devans & Doyle · Lincoln First Tower Rochester, NY 14603 · 716-546-8000

Frank B. Iacovangelo · Gallo & Iacovangelo · 80 West Main Street, Suite 200 Rochester, NY 14614 · 716-454-7145

Charles E. Littlefield · Harris, Beach, Wilcox, Rubin and Levey · 130 East Main Street · Rochester, NY 14604 · 716-232-4440

Thomas P. Moonan · Harris, Beach, Wilcox, Rubin and Levey · 130 East Main Street · Rochester, NY 14604 · 716-232-4440

William D. Smith · Harter, Secrest & Emery · 700 Midtown Tower · Rochester, NY 14604 · 716-232-6500

Stephen L. Johnson · Bond, Schoeneck & King · One Lincoln Center, 17th Floor · Syracuse, NY 13202-1355 · 315-422-0121

C. Daniel Shulman · Shulman Law Offices · 500 South Salina Street, Suite 1020 · Syracuse, NY 13202 · 315-424-8944

Gregory R. Thornton · Hancock & Estabrook · One Mony Plaza, 14th Floor · 100 Madison Street · P.O. Box 4976 · Syracuse, NY 13221-4976 · 315-471-3151

Charles H. Umbrecht, Jr. · Hancock & Estabrook · One Mony Plaza, 14th Floor · 100 Madison Street · P.O. Box 4976 · Syracuse, NY 13221-4976 · 315-471-3151

TAX AND EMPLOYEE BENEFITS LAW

Richard V. D'Alessandro · 69 Columbia Street · Albany, NY 12207 · 518-449-1421

Robert E. Helm · (Employee Benefits) · Helm, Shapiro, Anito & Aldrich · 111 Washington Avenue · Albany, NY 12210 · 518-465-7563

Dianne Bennett · (also Employee Benefits) · Hodgson, Russ, Andrews, Woods & Goodyear · 1800 One M&T Plaza · Buffalo, NY 14203 · 716-856-4000

Irving D. Brott, Jr. · (Employee Benefits) · Phillips, Lytle, Hitchcock, Blaine & Huber · 3400 Marine Midland Center · Buffalo, NY 14203 · 716-847-8400

Richard F. Campbell · Hodgson, Russ, Andrews, Woods & Goodyear · 1800 One M&T Plaza · Buffalo, NY 14203 · 716-856-4000

Paul R. Comeau · Hodgson, Russ, Andrews, Woods & Goodyear · 1800 One M&T Plaza · Buffalo, NY 14203 · 716-856-4000

Richard E. Heath · Hodgson, Russ, Andrews, Woods & Goodyear · 1800 One M&T Plaza · Buffalo, NY 14203 · 716-856-4000

Donald C. Lubick · Hodgson, Russ, Andrews, Woods & Goodyear · 1800 One M&T Plaza · Buffalo, NY 14203 · 716-856-4000

Albert R. Mugel · Jaeckle, Fleischmann & Mugel · 800 Norstar Building · 12 Fountain Plaza · Buffalo, NY 14202 · 716-856-0600

Daniel R. Sharpe · (Employee Benefits) · Hodgson, Russ, Andrews, Woods & Goodyear · 1800 One M&T Plaza · Buffalo, NY 14203 · 716-856-4000

M. Bernard Aidinoff · Sullivan & Cromwell · 125 Broad Street · New York, NY 10004 · 212-558-4000

Richard C. Blake · Simpson Thacher & Bartlett · 425 Lexington Avenue · New York, NY 10017 · 212-455-2000

David H. Brockway · Dewey, Ballantine, Bushby, Palmer & Wood · 140 Broadway, 45th Floor · New York, NY 10005 · 212-820-1100

Herbert L. Camp · Cravath, Swaine & Moore · One Chase Manhattan Plaza New York, NY 10005 · 212-422-3000

Peter C. Canellos · Wachtell, Lipton, Rosen & Katz · 299 Park Avenue · New York, NY 10171-0149 · 212-371-9200

Walter C. Cliff · Cahill Gordon & Reindel · 80 Pine Street · New York, NY 10005 212-701-3000

Richard G. Cohen · Winthrop, Stimson, Putnam & Roberts · 40 Wall Street New York, NY 10005 · 212-943-0700

Dale S. Collinson · Willkie Farr & Gallagher · One Citicorp Center · 153 East 53rd Street · New York, NY 10022 · 212-935-8000

Kenneth C. Edgar, Jr. · (Employee Benefits) · Simpson Thacher & Bartlett · 425 Lexington Avenue · New York, NY 10017 · 212-455-2000

James S. Eustice · Kronish, Lieb, Weiner & Hellman · 1345 Avenue of the Americas · New York, NY 10105 · 212-841-6000

Peter L. Faber · Kaye, Scholer, Fierman, Hays & Handler · 425 Park Avenue New York, NY 10022 · 212-836-8000

Arthur A. Feder · Fried, Frank, Harris, Shriver & Jacobson · One New York Plaza New York, NY 10004 · 212-820-8000

M. Carr Ferguson · Davis Polk & Wardwell · One Chase Manhattan Plaza · New York, NY 10005 · 212-530-4000

Robert C. Fleder · (Employee Benefits) · Paul, Weiss, Rifkind, Wharton & Garrison · 1285 Avenue of the Americas · New York, NY 10019 · 212-373-3000

Frederick Gelberg · Moses & Singer · 1271 Avenue of the Americas, 45th Floor New York, NY 10020 · 212-246-3700

Sanford H. Goldberg · Roberts & Holland · 30 Rockefeller Plaza · New York, NY 10112 · 212-903-8700

Harold R. Handler · Simpson Thacher & Bartlett · 425 Lexington Avenue · New York, NY 10017 · 212-455-2000

Gordon D. Henderson · Weil, Gotshal & Manges · 767 Fifth Avenue · New York, NY 10022 · 212-310-8000

Richard Joseph Hiegel · Cravath, Swaine & Moore · One Chase Manhattan Plaza New York, NY 10005 · 212-422-3000

Robert A. Jacobs · Milbank, Tweed, Hadley & McCloy · One Chase Manhattan Plaza · New York, NY 10005 · 212-530-5000

Arthur Kalish · Paul, Weiss, Rifkind, Wharton & Garrison · 1285 Avenue of the Americas · New York, NY 10019 · 212-373-3000

Sherwin Kamin · Kramer, Levin, Nessen, Kamin & Frankel · 919 Third Avenue New York, NY 10022 · 212-715-9100

Lydia E. Kess · Davis Polk & Wardwell · One Chase Manhattan Plaza · New York, NY 10005 · 212-530-4000

Charles I. Kingson · Willkie Farr & Gallagher · One Citicorp Center · 153 East 53rd Street · New York, NY 10022 · 212-935-8000

Edward D. Kleinbard · Cleary, Gottlieb, Steen & Hamilton · One State Street Plaza · New York, NY 10004 · 212-344-0600

Boris Kostelanetz · Kostelanetz & Ritholz · 80 Pine Street · New York, NY 10005 212-422-4030

William N. Kravitz · (Employee Benefits) · Skadden, Arps, Slate, Meagher & Flom · 919 Third Avenue · New York, NY 10022 · 212-735-3000

Arthur H. Kroll · (Employee Benefits) · Patterson, Belknap, Webb & Tyler · 30 Rockefeller Plaza · New York, NY 10112 · 212-698-2500

James Patrick Lawton · (Employee Benefits) · Davis Polk & Wardwell · One Chase Manhattan Plaza · New York, NY 10005 · 212-530-4000

Richard M. Leder · Richard O. Loengard, Jr. · Fried, Frank, Harris, Shriver & Jacobson · One New York Plaza · New York, NY 10004 · 212-820-8000

Thomas S. Monfried · (Employee Benefits) · Willkie Farr & Gallagher · One Citicorp Center · 153 East 53rd Street · New York, NY 10022 · 212-935-8000

Michael J. Nassau · (Employee Benefits) · Kramer, Levin, Nessen, Kamin & Frankel · 919 Third Avenue · New York, NY 10022 · 212-715-9100

Stuart I. Odell · Dewey, Ballantine, Bushby, Palmer & Wood · 140 Broadway, 44th Floor · New York, NY 10005 · 212-820-1280

James M. Peaslee · Cleary, Gottlieb, Steen & Hamilton · One State Street Plaza New York, NY 10004 · 212-344-0600

Howard Pianko · (Employee Benefits) · Hughes Hubbard & Reed · One Wall Street · New York, NY 10005 · 212-709-7000

Robert H. Preiskel · Fried, Frank, Harris, Shriver & Jacobson · One New York Plaza · New York, NY 10004 · 212-820-8000

Richard C. Pugh · Cleary, Gottlieb, Steen & Hamilton · One State Street Plaza New York, NY 10004 · 212-344-0600

John C. Richardson · LeBoeuf, Lamb, Leiby & MacRae · 520 Madison Avenue New York, NY 10022 · 212-715-8000

Jules Ritholz · Kostelanetz & Ritholz · 80 Pine Street · New York, NY 10005 212-422-4030

James R. Rowen · Shearman & Sterling · Citicorp Center · 153 East 53rd Street New York, NY 10022 · 212-848-4000

Hugh Rowland, Jr. · Debevoise & Plimpton · 875 Third Avenue · New York, NY 10022 · 212-909-6000

Stanley I. Rubenfeld · Shearman & Sterling · Citicorp Center · 153 East 53rd Street · New York, NY 10022 · 212-848-4000

David Sachs · White & Case · 1155 Avenue of the Americas · New York, NY 10036 · 212-819-8200

Irving Salem · Latham & Watkins · 885 Third Avenue, Suite 1000 · New York, NY 10022-4802 · 212-906-1200

Leslie B. Samuels · Cleary, Gottlieb, Steen & Hamilton · One State Street Plaza New York, NY 10004 · 212-344-0600

Donald Schapiro · Chadbourne & Parke · 30 Rockefeller Plaza · New York, NY 10112 · 212-408-5100

Ruth G. Schapiro · Proskauer Rose Goetz & Mendelsohn · 300 Park Avenue New York, NY 10022 · 212-909-7000

Michael L. Schler · Cravath, Swaine & Moore · One Chase Manhattan Plaza New York, NY 10005 · 212-422-3000

Susan P. Serota · (Employee Benefits) · Winthrop, Stimson, Putnam & Roberts 40 Wall Street · New York, NY 10005 · 212-943-0700

Mayer Siegel · (Employee Benefits) · Fried, Frank, Harris, Shriver & Jacobson One New York Plaza · New York, NY 10004 · 212-820-8000

Jesse G. Silverman, Jr. · Roberts & Holland · 30 Rockefeller Plaza · New York, NY 10112 · 212-903-8700

Robert J. Stokes · (Employee Benefits) · Cravath, Swaine & Moore · One Chase Manhattan Plaza · New York, NY 10005 · 212-422-3000

A. Richard Susko · (Employee Benefits) · Cleary, Gottlieb, Steen & Hamilton One State Street Plaza · New York, NY 10004 · 212-344-0600

Willard B. Taylor · Sullivan & Cromwell · 125 Broad Street · New York, NY 10004 · 212-558-4000

David R. Tillinghast · Hughes Hubbard & Reed · One Wall Street · New York, NY 10005 · 212-709-7000

B. Cary Tolley · Hunton & Williams · 100 Park Avenue · New York, NY 10017 · 212-309-1000

David E. Watts · Dewey, Ballantine, Bushby, Palmer & Wood · 140 Broadway · New York, NY 10005 · 212-820-1100

Philip S. Winterer · Debevoise & Plimpton · 875 Third Avenue · New York, NY 10022 · 212-909-6000

Alfred D. Youngwood · Paul, Weiss, Rifkind, Wharton & Garrison · 1285 Avenue of the Americas · New York, NY 10019 · 212-373-3000

Victor Zonana · Arnold & Porter · 65 East 55th Street, 31st Floor · 425 Park Avenue · New York, NY 10022 · 212-750-5050

Richard S. Fischer · (Employee Benefits) · Nixon, Hargrave, Devans & Doyle · Lincoln First Tower · Rochester, NY 14603 · 716-546-8000

Sherman F. Levey · Harris, Beach, Wilcox, Rubin and Levey · 130 East Main Street · Rochester, NY 14604 · 716-232-4440

E. Parker Brown II · Hancock & Estabrook · One Mony Plaza, 14th Floor · 100 Madison Street · P.O. Box 4976 · Syracuse, NY 13221-4976 · 315-471-3151

Stephen H. Cohen · (Employee Benefits) · Scolaro, Shulman, Cohen, Lawler & Burnstein · 1064 James Street · Syracuse, NY 13203 · 315-471-8111

Gary R. Germain · Bond, Schoeneck & King · One Lincoln Center, 17th Floor · Syracuse, NY 13202-1355 · 315-422-0121

Clayton H. Hale, Jr. · Mackenzie Smith Lewis Michell & Hughes · 600 Onondaga Savings Bank Building · P.O. Box 4967 · Syracuse, NY 13221 · 315-474-7571

Richard D. Hole · (Employee Benefits) · Bond, Schoeneck & King · One Lincoln Center, 18th Floor · Syracuse, NY 13202-1355 · 315-422-0121

Robert V. Hunter · Hunter & Hartnett · The Clinton Exchange, Suite 106 · Four Clinton Square · Syracuse, NY 13202-1075 · 315-476-0532

Richard S. Scolaro · Scolaro, Shulman, Cohen, Lawler & Burnstein · 1064 James Street · Syracuse, NY 13203 · 315-471-8111

George C. Shattuck · Bond, Schoeneck & King · One Lincoln Center, 17th Floor Syracuse, NY 13202-1355 · 315-422-0121

TRUSTS AND ESTATES

James B. Ayers · DeGraff, Foy, Conway, Holt-Harris and Mealey · 90 State Street Albany, NY 12207 · 518-462-5301

Thomas E. Dolin · Hiscock & Barclay · One Keycorp Plaza, Suite 1100 · Albany, NY 12207 · 518-434-2163

William S. Haase · McNamee, Lochner, Titus & Williams · 75 State Street · P.O. Box 459 · Albany, NY 12201 · 518-434-3136

Albert Hessberg II · Hiscock & Barclay · One Keycorp Plaza, Suite 1100 · Albany, NY 12207 · 518-434-2163

Albert A. Manning · Hinman, Straub, Pigors & Manning · 121 State Street Albany, NY 12207 · 518-436-0751

Timothy B. Thornton · McNamee, Lochner, Titus & Williams · 75 State Street P.O. Box 459 · Albany, NY 12201-0459 · 518-434-3136

Richard P. Wallace · Martin, Shudt, Wallace, DiLorenzo & Copps · 146 Washington Avenue · Albany, NY 12210 · 518-449-5100

John P. McLane · Boyle, Anderson, Lipski, McLane & Lynch · 120 Genesee Street · P.O. Box 578 · Auburn, NY 13021 · 315-253-0326

Thomas M. Barney · Phillips, Lytle, Hitchcock, Blaine & Huber · 3400 Marine Midland Center · Buffalo, NY 14203 · 716-847-8400

Gordon A. MacLeod · Hodgson, Russ, Andrews, Woods & Goodyear · 1800 One M&T Plaza · Buffalo, NY 14203 · 716-856-4000

Albert R. Mugel · Jaeckle, Fleischmann & Mugel · 800 Norstar Building · 12 Fountain Plaza · Buffalo, NY 14202-2222 · 716-856-0600

Stephen M. Newman · Hodgson, Russ, Andrews, Woods & Goodyear · 1800 One M&T Plaza · Buffalo, NY 14203 · 716-856-4000

Arthur M. Sherwood · Phillips, Lytle, Hitchcock, Blaine & Huber · 3400 Marine Midland Center · Buffalo, NY 14203 · 716-847-8400

Mal L. Barasch · Rosenman & Colin · 575 Madison Avenue · New York, NY 10022 · 212-940-8800

Christine Beshar · Cravath, Swaine & Moore · One Chase Manhattan Plaza · New York, NY 10005 · 212-422-3000

Herbert H. Chaice · Patterson, Belknap, Webb & Tyler · 30 Rockefeller Plaza · New York, NY 10112 · 212-698-2500

Donald C. Christ · Sullivan & Cromwell · 250 Park Avenue · New York, NY 10177 · 212-558-4000

Henry Christensen III · Sullivan & Cromwell · 250 Park Avenue · New York, NY 10177 · 212-558-4000

Carolyn C. Clark · Milbank, Tweed, Hadley & McCloy · One Chase Manhattan Plaza · New York, NY 10005 · 212-530-5000

Richard B. Covey · Carter, Ledyard & Milburn · Two Wall Street · New York, NY 10005 · 212-732-3200

George DeSipio · Cleary, Gottlieb, Steen & Hamilton · One State Street Plaza · New York, NY 10004 · 212-344-0600

James F. Dolan · Davis Polk & Wardwell · 499 Park Avenue, 24th Floor · New York, NY 10022 · 212-688-7771

Bernard Finkelstein · Paul, Weiss, Rifkind, Wharton & Garrison · 1285 Avenue of the Americas · New York, NY 10019 · 212-373-3000

Alexander D. Forger · Milbank, Tweed, Hadley & McCloy · One Chase Manhattan Plaza · New York, NY 10005 · 212-530-5000

Michael I. Frankel · Carter, Ledyard & Milburn · Two Wall Street, 15th Floor · New York, NY 10005 · 212-732-3200

Bernard H. Greene · Paul, Weiss, Rifkind, Wharton & Garrison · 1285 Avenue of the Americas · New York, NY 10019 · 212-373-3000

Dan T. Hastings · Milbank, Tweed, Hadley & McCloy · One Chase Manhattan Plaza · New York, NY 10005 · 212-530-5000

Philip J. Hirsch · Proskauer Rose Goetz & Mendelsohn · 300 Park Avenue · New York, NY 10022 · 212-909-7000

Linda B. Hirschshon · Gilbert, Segall and Young · 430 Park Avenue, 11th Floor New York, NY 10022 · 212-644-4000

Philip G. Hull · Winthrop, Stimson, Putnam & Roberts · 40 Wall Street · New York, NY 10005 · 212-943-0700

Jane B. Jacobs · Patterson, Belknap, Webb & Tyler · 30 Rockefeller Plaza · New York, NY 10112 · 212-698-2500

Mildred E. Kalik · Simpson Thacher & Bartlett · 425 Lexington Avenue · New York, NY 10017 · 212-455-2000

Joseph Kartiganer · Simpson Thacher & Bartlett · 425 Lexington Avenue · New York, NY 10017 · 212-455-2000

Charles L. Kramer · McLaughlin & Stern, Ballen and Ballen · 122 East 42nd Street · New York, NY 10168 · 212-867-2500

Theodore A. Kurz · Debevoise & Plimpton · 875 Third Avenue · New York, NY 10022 · 212-909-6000

Paul C. Lambert · Breed, Abbott & Morgan · Citicorp Center, 56th Floor · 153 East 53rd Street · New York, NY 10022 · 212-888-0800

James Woodman Lloyd · Davis Polk & Wardwell · One Chase Manhattan Plaza New York, NY 10005 · 212-530-4000

Ira H. Lustgarten · Willkie Farr & Gallagher · One Citicorp Center · 153 East 53rd Street · New York, NY 10022 · 212-935-8000

Jerome A. Manning · Stroock & Stroock & Lavan · Seven Hanover Square · New York, NY 10004 · 212-806-5400

Carlyn S. McCaffrey · Weil, Gotshal & Manges · 767 Fifth Avenue · New York, NY 10153 · 212-310-8000

Lawrence Newman · Kaye, Scholer, Fierman, Hays & Handler · 425 Park Avenue New York, NY 10022 · 212-407-8000

David C. Oxman · Davis Polk & Wardwell · 499 Park Avenue, 24th Floor · New York, NY 10022 · 212-668-7771

William Parsons, Jr. · Davis Polk & Wardwell · One Chase Manhattan Plaza · New York, NY 10005 · 212-530-4000

Richard Henry Pershan · LeBoeuf, Lamb, Leiby & MacRae · 520 Madison Avenue · New York, NY 10022 · 212-715-8000

Samuel S. Polk · Milbank, Tweed, Hadley & McCloy · One Chase Manhattan Plaza · New York, NY 10005 · 212-530-5000

Barbara Paul Robinson · Debevoise & Plimpton · 875 Third Avenue · New York, NY 10022 · 212-909-6000

Edward S. Schlesinger · 630 Third Avenue · New York, NY 10017 · 212-682-3540

Sanford J. Schlesinger · Shea & Gould · 1251 Avenue of the Americas · New York, NY 10020 · 212-827-3000

Arthur D. Sederbaum · Leaf, Sternklar & Drogin · 440 Park Avenue South · New York, NY 10016 · 212-685-8400

Michael V. Sterlacci · Winthrop, Stimson, Putnam & Roberts · 40 Wall Street · New York, NY 10005 · 212-943-0700

Lawrence B. Thompson · Emmet, Marvin & Martin · 48 Wall Street · New York, NY 10005 · 212-422-2974

Charles W. Ufford, Jr. · Skadden, Arps, Slate, Meagher & Flom · 919 Third Avenue · New York, NY 10022 · 212-735-3000

Carroll L. Wainwright, Jr. · Milbank, Tweed, Hadley & McCloy · One Chase Manhattan Plaza · New York, NY 10005 · 212-530-5000

William B. Warren · Dewey, Ballantine, Bushby, Palmer & Wood · 140 Broadway · New York, NY 10005 · 212-820-1100

James B. Welles, Jr. · Debevoise & Plimpton · 875 Third Avenue · New York, NY 10022 · 212-909-6000

Douglas F. Williamson, Jr. · Winthrop, Stimson, Putnam & Roberts · 40 Wall Street · New York, NY 10005 · 212-943-0700

E. Lisk Wyckoff, Jr. · Kelley Drye & Warren · 600 Fifth Avenue, 18th Floor · New York, NY 10020 · 212-808-7800

William D. Zabel · Schulte, Roth & Zabel · 900 Third Avenue · New York, NY 10022 · 212-758-0404

Henry S. Ziegler · Shearman & Sterling · Citicorp Center · 153 East 53rd Street New York, NY 10022 · 212-848-8000

Crandall Melvin, Jr. · The Melvin Law Firm · 6834 Buckley Road · North Syracuse, NY 13212 · 315-451-7955

Edward D. Bloom · Harris, Beach, Wilcox, Rubin and Levey · 130 East Main Street · Rochester, NY 14604 · 716-232-4440

Michael Buckley · Harter, Secrest & Emery · 700 Midtown Tower · Rochester, NY 14604 · 716-232-6500

John T. Fitzgerald, Jr. · Nixon, Hargrave, Devans & Doyle · Lincoln First Tower Rochester, NY 14603 · 716-546-8000

John L. Goldman · Underberg and Kessler · 1800 Lincoln First Tower · Rochester, NY 14604 · 716-258-2800

Alan Illig · Harter, Secrest & Emery · 700 Midtown Tower · Rochester, NY 14604 716-232-6500

George R. Parsons, Jr. · Nixon, Hargrave, Devans & Doyle · Lincoln First Tower · Rochester, NY 14603 · 716-546-8000

Jon L. Schumacher · Nixon, Hargrave, Devans & Doyle · Lincoln First Tower Rochester, NY 14603 · 716-546-8000

John E. Swett · Harter, Secrest & Emery · 700 Midtown Tower · Rochester, NY 14604 · 716-232-6500

John W. Tarbox · Harris, Beach, Wilcox, Rubin and Levey · 130 East Main Street Rochester, NY 14604 · 716-232-4440

Robert F. Baldwin, Jr. · Green & Seifter · One Lincoln Center, Ninth Floor Syracuse, NY 13202 · 315-422-1391

Arthur E. Bongiovanni · Bond, Schoeneck & King · One Lincoln Center, 18th Floor · Syracuse, NY 13202-1355 · 315-422-0121

Roger J. Edinger · Hiscock & Barclay · Financial Plaza · P.O. Box 4878 · Syracuse, NY 13221 · 315-422-2131

Robert J. Hughes, Jr. · Hancock & Estabrook · One Mony Plaza, 14th Floor · 100 Madison Street · P.O. Box 4976 · Syracuse, NY 13221-4976 · 315-471-3151

Harris Markhoff · Danziger & Markhoff · Centroplex, Suite 900 · 123 Main Street White Plains, NY 10601 · 914-948-1556

John G. McQuaid · McCarthy, Fingar, Donovan, Drazen & Smith · 11 Martine Avenue · White Plains, NY 10606 · 914-946-3700

Conrad Teitell · Prerau & Teitell · 50 Main Street, 12th Floor · White Plains, NY 10606 · 914-682-9300

NORTH CAROLINA

BANKRUPTCY LAW	519
USINESS LITIGATION	520
CORPORATE LAW	521
CRIMINAL DEFENSE	522
FAMILY LAW	524
LABOR AND EMPLOYMENT LAW	525
NATURAL RESOURCES AND ENVIRONMENTAL LAW	526
PERSONAL INJURY LITIGATION	527
REAL ESTATE LAW	529
TAX AND EMPLOYEE BENEFITS LAW	530
TRUSTS AND ESTATES	532

BANKRUPTCY LAW

J. Michael Booe · Petree Stockton & Robinson · 3500 One First Union Center 301 South College Street · P.O. Box 32397 · Charlotte, NC 28232-2397 · 704-372-9110

W. B. Hawfield, Jr. · Moore & Van Allen · 3000 NCNB Plaza · Charlotte, NC 28280 · 704-331-1000

Thomas B. Henson · Robinson, Bradshaw & Hinson · 1900 Independence Center 101 North Tryon Street · Charlotte, NC 28246 · 704-377-2536

Richard M. Hutson II · Mount, White, Hutson & Carden · 201 North Roxboro Street, Suite 200 · P.O. Box 1371 · Durham, NC 27702 · 919-683-1561

Richard A. Leippe · Smith Helms Mulliss & Moore · 101 West Friendly Avenue P.O. Box 21927 · Greensboro, NC 27420 · 919-378-5200

David F. Meschan · Tuggle Duggins Meschan & Elrod · 228 West Market Street P.O. Drawer X · Greensboro, NC 27402 · 919-378-1431

Trawick H. Stubbs, Jr. · Stubbs, Perdue, Chesnutt & Wheeler · 215 Broad Street P.O. Drawer 1564 · New Bern, NC 28560 · 919-633-2700

Gregory B. Crampton · Merriman, Nicholls & Crampton · 100 St. Albans Drive P.O. Box 18237 · Raleigh, NC 27619 · 919-781-1311

J. Larkin Pahl · Smith, Debnam, Hibbert & Pahl · 4700 New Bern Avenue · P.O. Drawer 26268 · Raleigh, NC 27611 · 919-831-2400

Stephen L. Beaman · 304 West Nash Street · P.O. Box 1907 · Wilson, NC 27894-1907 · 919-237-9020

James C. Frenzel · Womble Carlyle Sandridge & Rice · 2400 Wachovia Building 301 North Main Street · P.O. Drawer 84 · Winston-Salem, NC 27102-0084 919-721-3600

R. Bradford Leggett · Allman Spry Humphreys Leggett & Howington · Two Piedmont Plaza, Suite 500 · 2000 West First Street · P.O. Drawer 5129 · Winston-Salem, NC 27113-5129 · 919-722-2300

BUSINESS LITIGATION

E. Osborne Ayscue, Jr. · Smith Helms Mulliss & Moore · 227 North Tryon Street P.O. Box 31247 · Charlotte, NC 28231 · 704-343-200

Harry C. Hewson · Jones, Hewson & Woolard · 730 East Trade Street, Suite 1000 Charlotte, NC 28202 · 704-372-6541

A. Ward McKeithen · Robinson, Bradshaw & Hinson · 1900 Independence Center · 101 North Tryon Street · Charlotte, NC 28246 · 704-377-2536

William C. Raper · Womble Carlyle Sandridge & Rice · 3300 One First Union Center · 301 South College Street · Charlotte, NC 28202-6025 · 704-331-4900

Jack W. Floyd · Floyd, Greeson, Allen & Jacobs · 400 West Market Street, Suite 400 · P.O. Box 2460 · Greensboro, NC 27402 · 919-273-1797

Charles T. Hagan, Jr. · Adams, Kleemeier, Hagan, Hannah & Fouts · One Southern Life Center · P.O. Box 3463 · Greensboro, NC 27402 · 919-373-1600

Hubert Humphrey · Brooks, Pierce, McLendon, Humphrey & Leonard · 1400 Wachovia Building · 201 North Elm Street · P.O. Drawer U · Greensboro, NC 27402 · 919-373-8850

Charles E. Nichols · Nichols, Caffrey, Hill, Evans & Murrelle · 500 West Friendly Avenue · P.O. Box 989 · Greensboro, NC 27402 · 919-379-1390

McNeill Smith · Smith Helms Mulliss & Moore · 500 NCNB Building · 101 West Friendly Avenue · P.O. Box 21927 · Greensboro, NC 27420 · 919-378-1450

David W. Long · Poyner & Spruill · 3600 Glenwood Avenue · P.O. Box 10096 Raleigh, NC 27605-0096 · 919-783-6400

Howard E. Manning · Manning, Fulton & Skinner · 500 UCB Plaza · 3605 Glenwood Avenue · P.O. Box 20389 · Raleigh, NC 27619-0389 · 919-787-8880

H. Grady Barnhill, Jr. · Womble Carlyle Sandridge & Rice · 2400 Wachovia Building · 301 North Main Street · P.O. Drawer 84 · Winston-Salem, NC 27102-0084 · 919-721-3600

Jimmy H. Barnhill · Womble Carlyle Sandridge & Rice · 2400 Wachovia Building 301 North Main Street · P.O. Drawer 84 · Winston-Salem, NC 27102-0084 · 919-721-3600

J. Robert Elster · Petree Stockton & Robinson · 1001 West Fourth Street · P.O. Box 2860 · Winston-Salem, NC 27102 · 919-725-2351

Norwood Robinson · Petree Stockton & Robinson · 1001 West Fourth Street P.O. Box 2860 · Winston-Salem, NC 27102 · 919-725-2351

Ralph M. Stockton, Jr. · Petree Stockton & Robinson · 1001 West Fourth Street P.O. Box 2860 · Winston-Salem, NC 27102 · 919-725-2351

CORPORATE LAW

Larry J. Dagenhart · Smith Helms Mulliss & Moore · 227 North Tryon Street P.O. Box 31247 · Charlotte, NC 28231 · 704-372-9510

J. Carlton Fleming · Womble Carlyle Sandridge & Rice · 3300 One First Union Center · 301 South College Street · Charlotte, NC 28202-6025 · 704-331-4900

Russell M. Robinson II · Robinson, Bradshaw & Hinson · 1900 Independence Center · 101 North Tryon Street · Charlotte, NC 28246 · 704-377-2536

Clarence W. Walker · Kennedy Covington Lobdell & Hickman · 3300 NCNB Plaza · Charlotte, NC 28280 · 704-377-6000

Doris R. Bray · Schell, Bray, Aycock, Abel & Livingston · 201 North Elm Street, Suite 1520 · P.O. Box 21847 · Greensboro, NC 27420 · 919-370-8800

Braxton Schell · Schell, Bray, Aycock, Abel & Livingston · 201 North Elm Street, Suite 1520 · P.O. Box 21847 · Greensboro, NC 27420 · 919-370-8800

J. Troy Smith, Jr. · Ward and Smith · 1001 College Court · P.O. Box 867 · New Bern, NC 28560 · 919-633-1000

David L. Ward, Jr. · Ward and Smith · 1001 College Court · P.O. Box 867 · New Bern, NC 28560 · 919-633-1000

E. Lawrence Davis III · Womble Carlyle Sandridge & Rice · 901 Wachovia Building · P.O. Box 831 · Raleigh, NC 27602 · 919-828-7214

James K. Dorsett, Jr. · Smith, Anderson, Blount, Dorsett, Mitchell & Jernigan 1300 St. Mary's Street · P.O. Box 12807 · Raleigh, NC 27605 · 919-821-1220

Henry A. Mitchell, Jr. · Smith, Anderson, Blount, Dorsett, Mitchell & Jernigan 1300 St. Mary's Street · P.O. Box 12807 · Raleigh, NC 27605 · 919-821-1220

Linwood L. Davis · Womble Carlyle Sandridge & Rice · 2400 Wachovia Building 301 North Main Street · P.O. Drawer 84 · Winston-Salem, NC 27102-0084 919-721-3600

James S. Dockery, Jr. · Petree Stockton & Robinson · 1001 West Fourth Street P.O. Box 2860 · Winston-Salem, NC 27102 · 919-725-2351

John L. W. Garrou · Womble Carlyle Sandridge & Rice · 2400 Wachovia Building 301 North Main Street · P.O. Drawer 84 · Winston-Salem, NC 27102-0084 919-721-3600

CRIMINAL DEFENSE

Charles T. Browne · Bell and Browne · 151 North Fayetteville Street · Asheboro, NC 27203 · 919-625-2111

Allen A. Bailey · Bailey, Patterson, Caddell & Bailey · Equity Building, Suite One · 701 East Trade Street · Charlotte, NC 28202 · 704-333-8612

Martin L. Brackett, Jr. · Robinson, Bradshaw & Hinson · 1900 Independence Center · 101 North Tryon Street · Charlotte, NC 28246 · 704-377-2536

James E. Ferguson II · Ferguson, Stein, Watt, Wallas & Adkins · 700 East Stonewall Street · Charlotte, NC 28202 · 704-375-8461

James E. Walker · Kennedy Covington Lobdell & Hickman · 3300 NCNB Plaza Charlotte, NC 28280-8082 · 704-377-6000

Robert S. Cahoon · Cahoon & Swisher · 232 West Market Street · Greensboro, NC 27401 · 919-275-9867

Locke T. Clifford · McNairy, Clifford, Clendenin & Parks · 300 Southern National Bank Building · 127 North Greene Street · Greensboro, NC 27401 · 919-378-1212

William L. Osteen · Osteen & Adams · Gate City Savings & Loan Building, Suite 305 · 201 West Market Street · P.O. Box 2489 · Greensboro, NC 27402 · 919-274-2947

Percy L. Wall · Wall & Courtright · 440 West Market Street · P.O. Box 3483 Greensboro, NC 27402 · 919-275-7915

W. B. Jack Byerly, Jr. · Byerly & Byerly · 505 East Commerce Street · P.O. Box 2221 · High Point, NC 27261 · 919-883-9181

C. Richard Tate, Jr. · 115 West High Street · P.O. Box 2726 · High Point, NC 27261 · 919-885-0176

James R. Van Camp · Van Camp, Bryan, Webb & Hayes · The Theater Building, Third Floor · Village Green West · P.O. Box 1389 · Pinehurst, NC 28374 919-295-2525

Joseph B. Cheshire V · Purser, Cheshire, Parker & Hughes · 133 Fayetteville Street Mall · P.O. Box 1029 · Raleigh, NC 27602 · 919-833-3114

Russell W. DeMent, Jr. · DeMent, Askew, Gammon & Salisbury · Branch Bank Building, Suite 1513 · P.O. Box 711 · Raleigh, NC 27602 · 919-833-5555

Robert L. McMillan, Jr. · McMillan, Kimzey & Smith · 205 West Martin Street P.O. Box 150 · Raleigh, NC 27602 · 919-821-5124

Roger W. Smith · Tharrington, Smith & Hargrove · 209 Fayetteville Street Mall P.O. Box 1151 · Raleigh, NC 27602 · 919-821-4711

Wade M. Smith · Tharrington, Smith & Hargrove · 209 Fayetteville Street Mall · P.O. Box 1151 · Raleigh, NC 27602 · 919-821-4711

James L. Nelson · 124 Market Street · P.O. Box 1767 · Wilmington, NC 28402 · 919-763-7760

Fred G. Crumpler, Jr. · White and Crumpler · 11 West Fourth Street · Winston-Salem, NC 27101 · 919-725-1304

FAMILY LAW

Robert E. Riddle · Riddle, Kelly & Cagle · 35 North Market Street · P.O. Box 7206 · Asheville, NC 28801 · 704-258-2394

Thomas R. Cannon · Hamel, Helms, Cannon & Hamel · Two First Union Center, Suite 2300 · Charlotte, NC 28282 · 704-372-4884

William K. Diehl, Jr. · James, McElroy & Diehl · 600 South College Street, Suite 3000 · Charlotte, NC 28202 · 704-372-9870

Richard D. Stephens · Kennedy Covington Lobdell & Hickman · 3300 NCNB Plaza · Charlotte, NC 28280-8082 · 704-377-6000

James B. Maxwell · Maxwell, Martin, Freeman and Beason · 2741 University Drive · P.O. Drawer 8706 · Durham, NC 27707 · 919-493-6464

C. Richard Tate, Jr. · 115 West High Street · P.O. Box 2726 · High Point, NC 27261 · 919-885-0176

Lana S. Warlick · 410 New Bridge Street, Suite 1A · P.O. Box 1393 · Jacksonville, NC 28541-1393 · 919-347-4400

Robert L. Huffman · 340 West Morgan Street · P.O. Box 1008 · Monroe, NC 28110 · 704-283-1529

John Maclachlan Boxley · Boxley, Bolton & Garber · Nash Square Building · 227 West Martin Street · P.O. Drawer 1429 · Raleigh, NC 27602 · 919-832-3915

John H. Parker · Purser, Cheshire, Parker & Hughes · 133 Fayetteville Street Mall · P.O. Box 1029 · Raleigh, NC 27602 · 919-833-3114

J. Harold Tharrington · Tharrington, Smith & Hargrove · 209 Fayetteville Street Mall · P.O. Box 1151 · Raleigh, NC 27602 · 919-821-4711

J. Edgar Moore · Moore, Diedrick, Carlisle & Hester · Two Federal Square · 512 West Thomas Street · P.O. Box 2626 · Rocky Mount, NC 27802 · 919-977-1911

James L. Nelson · 124 Market Street · P.O. Box 1767 · Wilmington, NC 28402 · 919-763-7760

Fred G. Crumpler, Jr. · White and Crumpler · 11 West Fourth Street · Winston-Salem, NC 27101 · 919-725-1304

John F. Morrow · Morrow, Alexander, Tash, Long & Black · 3890 Vest Mill Road · P.O. Box 25226 · Winston-Salem, NC 27114 · 919-760-1400

LABOR AND EMPLOYMENT LAW

J. W. Alexander, Jr. · (Management) · Blakeney, Alexander and Machen · 3700 NCNB Plaza · Charlotte, NC 28280 · 704-372-3680

George Daly · (Individuals) · One North McDowell, Suite 226 · 101 North McDowell Street · Charlotte, NC 28204 · 704-333-5196

John J. Doyle, Jr. · (Management) · Weinstein & Sturges · 810 Baxter Street · Charlotte, NC 28202 · 704-372-4800

John O. Pollard · (Management) · Blakeney, Alexander and Machen · 3700 NCNB Plaza · Charlotte, NC 28280 · 704-372-3680

Jonathan Wallas · (Individuals) · Ferguson, Stein, Watt, Wallas & Adkins · 700 East Stonewall Street · Charlotte, NC 28202 · 704-375-8461

Thornton H. Brooks · (Management) · Brooks, Pierce, McLendon, Humphrey & Leonard · 1400 Wachovia Building · 201 North Elm Street · P.O. Drawer U · Greensboro, NC 27402 · 919-373-8850

R. D. Douglas, Jr. · (Management) · Douglas, Ravenel, Hardy, Crihfield & Moseley · 110 Commerce Place · P.O. Box 419 · Greensboro, NC 27401 · 919-378-0580

Martin N. Erwin · (Management) · Smith Helms Mulliss & Moore · 101 West Friendly Avenue · P.O. Box 21927 · Greensboro, NC 27420 · 919-378-1450

Jonathan Ross Harkavy · (Labor) · Smith, Patterson, Follin, Curtis, James & Harkavy · 101 South Elm Street · Greensboro, NC 27401 · 919-274-2992

Norman B. Smith · (Labor) · Smith, Patterson, Follin, Curtis, James & Harkavy · 101 South Elm Street · Greensboro, NC 27401 · 919-274-2992

Michael G. Okun · Smith, Patterson, Follin, Curtis, James & Harkavy · 206 New Bern Place · Raleigh, NC 27601 · 919-755-1812

Henry N. Patterson, Jr. · (Labor; Individuals) · Smith, Patterson, Follin, Curtis, James & Harkavy · 206 New Bern Place · Raleigh, NC 27601 · 919-755-1812

Robert A. Valois · (Management) · Maupin Taylor Ellis & Adams · Merrill Lynch Building · 3201 Glenwood Avenue · P.O. Drawer 19764 · Raleigh, NC 27619 · 919-781-6800

Frank P. Ward, Jr. · (Management) · Maupin Taylor Ellis & Adams · Merrill Lynch Building · 3201 Glenwood Avenue · P.O. Drawer 19764 · Raleigh, NC 27619 · 919-781-6800

Guy F. Driver, Jr. · (Management) · Womble Carlyle Sandridge & Rice · 2400 Wachovia Building · 301 North Main Street · P.O. Drawer 84 · Winston-Salem, NC 27102-0084 · 919-721-3600

David A. Irvin · (Management) · Womble Carlyle Sandridge & Rice · 2400 Wachovia Building · 301 North Main Street · P.O. Drawer 84 · Winston-Salem, NC 27102-0084 · 919-721-3600

W. Randolph Loftis, Jr. · Petree Stockton & Robinson · 1001 West Fourth Street · P.O. Box 2860 · Winston-Salem, NC 27102 · 919-725-2351

Charles F. Vance, Jr. · (Management) · Womble Carlyle Sandridge & Rice · 2400 Wachovia Building · 301 North Main Street · P.O. Drawer 84 · Winston-Salem, NC 27102-0084 · 919-721-3600

NATURAL RESOURCES AND ENVIRONMENTAL LAW

Harold N. Bynum · Smith Helms Mulliss & Moore · 101 West Friendly Avenue · P.O. Box 21927 · Greensboro, NC 27420 · 919-378-1450

George W. House · Brooks, Pierce, McLendon, Humphrey & Leonard · 1400 Wachovia Building · 201 North Elm Street · P.O. Drawer U · Greensboro, NC 27402 · 919-373-8850

William G. Ross, Jr. · Brooks, Pierce, McLendon, Humphrey & Leonard · 1400 Wachovia Building · 201 North Elm Street · P.O. Drawer U · Greensboro, NC 27402 · 919-373-8850

Charles D. Case · Moore & Van Allen · One Hanover Square, Suite 1700 · Raleigh, NC 27601 · 919-828-4481

Amos C. Dawson III · Maupin Taylor Ellis & Adams · Merrill Lynch Building 3201 Glenwood Avenue · P.O. Drawer 19764 · Raleigh, NC 27619 · 919-781-6800

H. Glenn T. Dunn · Poyner & Spruill · 3600 Glenwood Avenue · P.O. Box 10096 Raleigh, NC 27605-0096 · 919-783-6400

PERSONAL INJURY LITIGATION

Allen A. Bailey · (Plaintiffs) · Bailey, Patterson, Caddell & Bailey · Equity Building, Suite One · 701 East Trade Street · Charlotte, NC 28202 · 704-333-8612

James E. Ferguson II · (Plaintiffs) · Ferguson, Stein, Watt, Wallas & Adkins · 700 East Stonewall Street · Charlotte, NC 28202 · 704-375-8461

John G. Golding · (Defendants) · Golding, Crews & Meekins · Attorneys Building, Suite 400 · 806 East Trade Street · Charlotte, NC 28202 · 704-374-1600

Harry C. Hewson · (Defendants) · Jones, Hewson & Woolard · 1000 Law Building · Charlotte, NC 28202 · 704-372-6541

James B. Maxwell · (Plaintiffs) · Maxwell, Martin, Freeman and Beason · 2741 University Drive · P.O. Drawer 8706 · Durham, NC 27707 · 919-493-6464

W. Paul Pulley, Jr. · (Plaintiffs) · Pulley, Watson, King & Hofler · Brightleaf Square · P.O. Box 3600 · Durham, NC 27702 · 919-682-9691

Joe McLeod · (Plaintiffs) · McLeod, Senter & Winesette · 705 First Citizens Bank Building · P.O. Box 1539 · Fayetteville, NC 28302 · 919-323-1425

Tim L. Harris · (Plaintiffs) · Harris & Bumgardner · 233 West Main Avenue · P.O. Box 249 · Gastonia, NC 28053 · 704-864-3409

J. Donald Cowan, Jr. · (Defendants) · Smith Helms Mulliss & Moore · 101 West Friendly Avenue · P.O. Box 21927 · Greensboro, NC 27420 · 919-378-1450

Joseph E. Elrod III · (Defendants) · Tuggle Duggins Meschan & Elrod · 228 West Market Street · P.O. Drawer X · Greensboro, NC 27402 · 919-378-1431

Perry C. Henson · (Defendants) · Henson Henson Bayliss & Teague · 601 Wachovia Building · P.O. Box 3525 · Greensboro, NC 27402 · 919-275-0587

Charles E. Nichols · (Defendants) · Nichols, Caffrey, Hill, Evans & Murelle · 500 West Friendly Avenue · P.O. Box 989 · Greensboro, NC 27402 · 919-379-1390

McNeill Smith · (Defendants) · Smith Helms Mulliss & Moore · 500 NCNB Building · 101 West Friendly Avenue · P.O. Box 21927 · Greensboro, NC 27420 919-378-1450

Marvin K. Blount, Jr. · (Plaintiffs) · 400 West First Street · P.O. Drawer 58 Greenville, NC 27835-0058 · 919-752-6000

Arch K. Schoch, Jr. · (Plaintiffs) · Schoch, Schoch and Schoch · 310 South Main Street · P.O. Box 1893 · High Point, NC 27261 · 919-884-4151

John D. Warlick, Jr. · (Plaintiffs) · Ellis, Hooper, Warlick, Waters & Morgan 313 New Bridge Street · P.O. Drawer 1006 · Jacksonville, NC 28541-1006 919-455-3637

Thomas E. Harris · (Defendants) · Ward and Smith · 1001 College Court · P.O. Box 867 · New Bern, NC 28560 · 919-633-1000

James G. Billings · (Defendants) · Smith, Anderson, Blount, Dorsett, Mitchell & Jernigan · 1300 St. Mary's Street · P.O. Box 12807 · Raleigh, NC 27605 · 919-821-1220

Charles F. Blanchard · (Plaintiffs) · Blanchard, Twiggs, Abrams & Strickland 134 Fayetteville Street Mall · P.O. Drawer 30 · Raleigh, NC 27602 · 919-828-4357

James D. Blount, Jr. · (Defendants) · Smith, Anderson, Blount, Dorsett, Mitchell & Jernigan · 1300 St. Mary's Street · P.O. Box 12807 · Raleigh, NC 27605 919-821-1220

Robert M. Clay · (Defendants) · Patterson, Dilthey, Clay, Cranfill, Sumner & Hartzog · 225 Hillsborough Street, Suite 300 · P.O. Box 310 · Raleigh, NC 27602 919-821-7052

Ronald C. Dilthey · (Defendants) · Patterson, Dilthey, Clay, Cranfill, Sumner & Hartzog · 225 Hillsboro Street, Suite 300 · P.O. Box 310 · Raleigh, NC 27602 919-821-7052

John R. Edwards · (Plaintiffs) · Tharrington, Smith & Hargrove · 209 Fayetteville Street Mall · P.O. Box 1151 · Raleigh, NC 27602 · 919-821-4711

James C. Fuller, Jr. · (Plaintiffs) · Thorp, Fuller and Slifkin · 908 West Morgan Street · Raleigh, NC 27603 · 919-828-2467

William L. Thorp · (Plaintiffs) · Thorp, Fuller and Slifkin · 908 West Morgan Street · Raleigh, NC 27603 · 919-828-2467

Howard F. Twiggs · (Plaintiffs) · Blanchard, Twiggs, Abrams & Strickland · 134 Fayetteville Street Mall · P.O. Drawer 30 · Raleigh, NC 27602 · 919-828-4357

Joseph W. Yates III · (Defendants) · Yates, Fleishman, McLamb & Weyher Carolina Place, Suite 350 · 2626 Glenwood Avenue · P.O. Box 18037 · Raleigh, NC 27619 · 919-783-5300

Lonnie B. Williams · (Defendants) · Marshall, Williams, Gorham & Brawley · 14 South Fifth Street · P.O. Drawer 2088 · Wilmington, NC 28402-2088 · 919-763-9891

H. Grady Barnhill, Jr. · (Defendants) · Womble Carlyle Sandridge & Rice · 2400 Wachovia Building · 301 North Main Street · P.O. Drawer 84 · Winston-Salem, NC 27102-0084 · 919-721-3600

Jimmy H. Barnhill · (Defendants) · Womble Carlyle Sandridge & Rice · 2400 Wachovia Building · 301 North Main Street · P.O. Drawer 84 · Winston-Salem, NC 27102-0084 · 919-721-3600

Allan R. Gitter · (Defendants) · Womble Carlyle Sandridge & Rice · 2400 Wachovia Building · 301 North Main Street · P.O. Drawer 84 · Winston-Salem, NC 27102-0084 · 919-721-3600

William F. Maready · (Defendants) · Petree Stockton & Robinson · 1001 West Fourth Street · P.O. Box 2860 · Winston-Salem, NC 27102 · 919-725-2351

Ralph M. Stockton, Jr. · (Defendants) · Petree Stockton & Robinson · 1001 West Fourth Street · P.O. Box 2860 · Winston-Salem, NC 27102 · 919-725-2351

REAL ESTATE LAW

Alfred G. Adams · Van Winkle, Buck, Wall, Starnes and Davis · 11 North Market Street · P.O. Box 7376 · Asheville, NC 28802 · 704-258-2991

Ashley L. Hogewood, Jr. · Parker, Poe, Thompson, Bernstein, Gage & Preston 2600 Charlotte Plaza · Charlotte, NC 28244 · 704-372-9000

Bailey Patrick, Jr. · Perry, Patrick, Farmer & Michaux · 900 Baxter Street, Suite 300 · P.O. Box 35566 · Charlotte, NC 28235 · 704-372-1120

Robert E. Perry, Jr. · Perry, Patrick, Farmer & Michaux · 900 Baxter Street, Suite 300 · P.O. Box 35566 · Charlotte, NC 28235 · 704-372-1120

William P. Aycock II · Schell, Bray, Aycock, Abel & Livingston · 201 North Elm Street, Suite 1520 · P.O. Box 21847 · Greensboro, NC 27420 · 919-370-8800

Charles E. Melvin, Jr. · Smith Helms Mulliss & Moore · 500 NCNB Building 101 West Friendly Avenue · P.O. Box 21927 · Greensboro, NC 27420 · 919-378-1450

Thomas F. Adams, Jr. · Maupin Taylor Ellis & Adams · Merrill Lynch Building 3201 Glenwood Avenue · P.O. Drawer 19764 · Raleigh, NC 27619 · 919-781-6800

Charles L. Fulton · Manning, Fulton & Skinner · 3605 UCB Plaza · P.O. Box 20389 · Raleigh, NC 27619-0389 · 919-787-8880

Marshall B. Hartsfield · Poyner & Spruill · 3600 Glenwood Avenue · P.O. Box 10096 · Raleigh, NC 27605-0096 · 919-783-6400

James Lee Seay · Seay, Harvey, Titchener & Horne · 4934 Windy Hill Drive P.O. Box 18807 · Raleigh, NC 27619 · 919-876-4100

Frank M. Bell, Jr. · Bell, Davis & Pitt · 635 West Fourth Street, Suite 200 · P.O. Box 49 · Winston-Salem, NC 27102 · 919-722-3700

Leslie E. Browder · Womble Carlyle Sandridge & Rice · 2400 Wachovia Building 301 North Main Street · P.O. Drawer 84 · Winston-Salem, NC 27102-0084 919-721-3600

Richard E. Glaze, Sr. · Petree Stockton & Robinson · 1001 West Fourth Street P.O. Box 2860 · Winston-Salem, NC 27102 · 919-725-2351

TAX AND EMPLOYEE BENEFITS LAW

Barry B. Kempson · Van Winkle, Buck, Wall, Starnes and Davis · 18 Church Street · P.O. Box 7376 · Asheville, NC 28807 · 704-258-2991

Steve C. Horowitz · Weinstein & Sturges · 1100 South Tryon Street · Charlotte, NC 28203 · 704-372-4800

James E. Johnson, Jr. · 2400 NCNB Plaza · Charlotte, NC 28280 · 704-333-7177

Raleigh A. Shoemaker · (Employee Benefits) · Kennedy Covington Lobdell & Hickman · 3300 NCNB Plaza · Charlotte, NC 28280 · 704-377-6000

Richard E. Thigpen, Jr. · Poyner & Spruill · 128 South Tryon Street · Charlotte, NC 28202 · 704-342-5250

Joseph B. Alala, Jr. · Garland & Alala · 301 South York Street · P.O. Box 859 Gastonia, NC 28053 · 704-864-2634

Richard J. Tuggle · Tuggle Duggins Meschan & Elrod · 228 West Market Street P.O. Drawer X · Greensboro, NC 27402 · 919-378-1431

Jasper L. Cummings, Jr. · Womble Carlyle Sandridge & Rice · 800 Wachovia Building · P.O. Box 831 · Raleigh, NC 27602 · 919-828-7214

Thomas L. Norris, Jr. · (Employee Benefits) · Poyner & Spruill · 3600 Glenwood Avenue · P.O. Box 10096 · Raleigh, NC 27605-0096 · 919-783-6400

W. Gerald Thornton · Manning, Fulton & Skinner · 500 UCB Plaza · 3605 Glenwood Avenue · P.O. Box 20389 · Raleigh, NC 27619-0389 · 919-787-8880

William Allison Davis II · (Employee Benefits) · Womble Carlyle Sandridge & Rice · 2400 Wachovia Building · 301 North Main Street · P.O. Drawer 84 Winston-Salem, NC 27102-0084 · 919-721-3600

Murray C. Greason, Jr. · Womble Carlyle Sandridge & Rice · 2400 Wachovia Building · 301 North Main Street · P.O. Drawer 84 · Winston-Salem, NC 27102-0084 · 919-721-3600

Michael D. Gunter · (Employee Benefits) · Womble Carlyle Sandridge & Rice 2400 Wachovia Building · 301 North Main Street · P.O. Drawer 84 · Winston-Salem, NC 27102-0084 · 919-721-3600

R. Frank Murphy II · Petree Stockton & Robinson · 1001 West Fourth Street P.O. Box 2860 · Winston-Salem, NC 27102 · 919-725-2351

Robert C. Vaughn, Jr. · Petree Stockton & Robinson · 1001 West Fourth Street P.O. Box 2860 · Winston-Salem, NC 27102 · 919-725-2351

TRUSTS AND ESTATES

Barry B. Kempson · Van Winkle, Buck, Wall, Starnes and Davis · 11 North Market Street · P.O. Box 7376 · Asheville, NC 28802 · 704-258-2991

Brian F. D. Lavelle · Van Winkle, Buck, Wall, Starnes and Davis · 11 North Market Street · P.O. Box 7376 · Asheville, NC 28802 · 704-258-2991

William F. Drew, Jr. · Kennedy Covington Lobdell & Hickman · 3300 NCNB Plaza · Charlotte, NC 28280 · 704-377-6000

Mark B. Edwards · Poyner & Spruill · 128 South Tryon Street · Charlotte, NC 28202 · 704-342-5250

Neill G. McBryde · Smith Helms Mulliss & Moore · 227 North Tryon Street P.O. Box 31247 · Charlotte, NC 28231 · 704-372-9510

Robert B. Lloyd, Jr. · Block, Meyland & Lloyd · 500 West Friendly Avenue Building · P.O. Box 3365 · Greensboro, NC 27402 · 919-275-8615

David S. Evans · Ward and Smith · 1001 College Court · P.O. Box 867 · New Bern, NC 28560 · 919-633-1000

Curtis A. Twiddy · Poyner & Spruill · 3600 Glenwood Avenue · P.O. Box 10096 Raleigh, NC 27605-0096 · 919-783-6400

Jeff. D. Batts · 505 Sunset Avenue · P.O. Drawer 4847 · Rocky Mount, NC 27803 919-977-6450

Elizabeth L. Quick · Womble Carlyle Sandridge & Rice · 2400 Wachovia Building 301 North Main Street · P.O. Drawer 84 · Winston-Salem, NC 27102-0084 919-721-3600

Robert C. Vaughn, Jr. · Petree Stockton & Robinson · 1001 West Fourth Street P.O. Box 2860 · Winston-Salem, NC 27102 · 919-725-2351

NORTH DAKOTA

BANKRUPTCY LAW	533
BUSINESS LITIGATION	534
CORPORATE LAW	534
CRIMINAL DEFENSE	535
FAMILY LAW	535
LABOR AND EMPLOYMENT LAW	536
NATURAL RESOURCES AND ENVIRONMENTAL LAW	536
PERSONAL INJURY LITIGATION	537
REAL ESTATE LAW	538
TAX AND EMPLOYEE BENEFITS LAW	539
TRUSTS AND ESTATES	539

BANKRUPTCY LAW

Max D. Rosenberg · 400 East Broadway, Suite 401 · P.O. Box 1278 · Bismarck, ND 58502 · 701-222-3968

David T. DeMars · DeMars, Turman & Johnson · 210 Broadway Park Office Complex · 16 Broadway · Fargo, ND 58102 · 701-293-5592

John S. Foster · Vaaler, Gillig, Warcup, Woutat, Zimney & Foster · Metropolitan Building, Fifth Floor · 600 De Mers Avenue · P.O. Box 1617 · Grand Forks, ND 58206-1617 · 701-772-8111

Richard P. Olson · Olson, Sturdevant and Burns · First Avenue Building, Third Floor · P.O. Box 1925 · Minot, ND 58702-1925 · 701-839-1740

BUSINESS LITIGATION

Thomas A. Mayer · Fleck, Mather, Strutz & Mayer · Norwest Bank Building, Sixth Floor · 400 East Broadway · P.O. Box 2798 · Bismarck, ND 58502 · 701-223-6585

Kermit Edward Bye · Vogel, Brantner, Kelly, Knutson, Weir & Bye · 205 First Avenue North · P.O. Box 1389 · Fargo, ND 58107 · 701-237-6983

Timothy Q. Davies · Nilles, Hansen & Davies · 1800 Radisson Tower · P.O. Box 2626 · Fargo, ND 58108 · 701-237-5544

Charles A. Feste · Conmy, Feste, Bossart, Hubbard & Corwin · 400 Norwest Center · Fourth Street and Main Avenue · Fargo, ND 58126 · 701-293-9911

John S. Foster · Vaaler, Gillig, Warcup, Woutat, Zimney & Foster · Metropolitan Building, Fifth Floor · 600 De Mers Avenue · P.O. Box 1617 · Grand Forks, ND 58206-1617 · 701-772-8111

Garry A. Pearson · Pearson, Christensen & Fischer · 24 North Fourth Street P.O. Box 1075 · Grand Forks, ND 58206-1075 · 701-775-0521

Malcolm H. Brown · Bair, Brown & Kautzmann · 210 First Avenue, NW · P.O. Box 100 · Mandan, ND 58554-0100 · 701-663-6568

Richard P. Olson · Olson, Sturdevant and Burns · First Avenue Building, Third Floor · P.O. Box 1925 · Minot, ND 58702-1925 · 701-839-1740

CORPORATE LAW

Ernest R. Fleck · Fleck, Mather, Strutz & Mayer · Norwest Bank Building, Sixth Floor · 400 East Broadway · P.O. Box 2798 · Bismarck, ND 58502 · 701-223-6585

Lyle W. Kirmis · Zuger, Kirmis, Bolinske & Smith · Provident Life Building · 316 North Fifth Street · P.O. Box 1695 · Bismarck, ND 58501-1695 · 701-223-2711

William P. Pearce · (Utilities) · Pearce and Durick · 314 East Thayer Avenue, Third Floor · P.O. Box 400 · Bismarck, ND 58502 · 701-223-2890

R. W. Wheeler · (Utilities) · Wheeler, Wolf, Peterson, Schmitz, McDonald & Johnson · 220 North Fourth Street · P.O. Box 2056 · Bismarck, ND 58502-2056 701-223-5300

Kermit Edward Bye · Vogel, Brantner, Kelly, Knutson, Weir & Bye · 502 First Avenue North · P.O. Box 1389 · Fargo, ND 58107 · 701-237-6983

Charles A. Feste · Conmy, Feste, Bossart, Hubbard & Corwin · 400 Norwest Center · Fourth Street & Main Avenue · Fargo, ND 58126 · 701-293-9911

Russell F. Freeman · Nilles, Hansen & Davies · 1800 Radisson Tower · P.O. Box 2626 · Fargo, ND 58108 · 701-237-5544

Garry A. Pearson · Pearson, Christensen & Fischer · 24 North Fourth Street P.O. Box 1075 · Grand Forks, ND 58206-1075 · 701-775-0521

Malcolm H. Brown · Bair, Brown & Kautzmann · 210 First Avenue, NW · P.O. Box 100 · Mandan, ND 58554-0100 · 701-663-6568

Richard P. Olson · Olson, Sturdevant and Burns · First Avenue Building, Third Floor · P.O. Box 1925 · Minot, ND 58702-1925 · 701-839-1740

CRIMINAL DEFENSE

Irvin B. Nodland · Lundberg, Nodland, Lucas & Schulz · 425 North Fifth Street Bismarck, ND 58501 · 701-223-4022

Ralph A. Vinje · 523 Fourth Street · Bismarck, ND 58501 · 701-258-9475

Ronald A. Reichert · Freed, Dynes, Reichert & Buresh · 34 East First Street P.O. Drawer K · Dickinson, ND 58601 · 701-225-6711

Kenneth A. Olson · Lanier, Knox, Olson & Racek · 115 University Drive · P.O. Box 1007 · Fargo, ND 58107-1932 · 701-232-4437

William D. Yuill · Yuill, Wold, Johnson & Feder · Gate City Building, Suite 414 P.O. Box 1680 · Fargo, ND 58102 · 701-235-5515

Alan J. Larivee · 215 North Third Street, Suite 208B · Grand Forks, ND 58201 701-775-3921

FAMILY LAW

Carma Christensen · Christensen & Thompson · 1720 Burnt Boat Drive · Bismarck, ND 58502 · 701-223-9787

James R. Brothers · Schuster, Brothers & Beauchene · 124 North Eighth Street P.O. Box 2842 · Fargo, ND 58108-2842 · 701-293-7935

Robert A. Feder · Yuill, Wold, Johnson & Feder · Gate City Building, Suite 414 P.O. Box 1680 · Fargo, ND 58102 · 701-235-5515

Kenneth A. Olson · Lanier, Knox, Olson & Racek · 115 University Drive · P.O. Box 1007 · Fargo, ND 58107-1932 · 701-232-4437

William D. Yuill · Yuill, Wold, Johnson & Feder · Gate City Building, Suite 414 P.O. Box 1680 · Fargo, ND 58102 · 701-235-5515

Dwight C. H. Kautzmann · Bair, Brown & Kautzmann · 210 First Avenue, NW P.O. Box 100 · Mandan, ND 58554-0100 · 701-663-6568

LABOR AND EMPLOYMENT LAW

Patrick J. Ward · (Management) · Zuger, Kirmis, Bolinske & Smith · 316 North Fifth Street · P.O. Box 1695 · Bismarck, ND 58502 · 701-223-2711

Robert A. Feder · (Management) · Yuill, Wold, Johnson & Feder · Gate City Building, Suite 414 · P.O. Box 1680 · Fargo, ND 58102 · 701-235-5515

NATURAL RESOURCES AND ENVIRONMENTAL LAW

Ernest R. Fleck · Fleck, Mather, Strutz & Mayer · Norwest Bank Building, Sixth Floor · 400 East Broadway · P.O. Box 2798 · Bismarck, ND 58502 · 701-223-6585

Russell R. Mather · Fleck, Mather, Strutz & Mayer · Norwest Bank Building, Sixth Floor · 400 East Broadway · P.O. Box 2798 · Bismarck, ND 58502 · 701-223-6585

William P. Pearce · Pearce and Durick · 314 East Thayer Avenue, Third Floor · P.O. Box 400 · Bismarck, ND 58502 · 701-223-2890

John L. Sherman · Mackoff, Kellogg, Kirby & Kloster · 46 West Second Street P.O. Box 1097 · Dickinson, ND 58601 · 701-227-1841

Fred C. Rathert · Bjella Neff Rathert Wahl & Eiken · 111 East Broadway · P.O. Drawer 1526 · Williston, ND 58801 · 701-572-3794

PERSONAL INJURY LITIGATION

Leonard H. Bucklin · (Plaintiffs) · Norwest Bank Building, Suite 500 · P.O. Box 955 · Bismarck, ND 58502 · 701-258-8988

B. Timothy Durick · (Defendants) · Pearce & Durick · 314 East Thayer Avenue, Third Floor · P.O. Box 400 · Bismarck, ND 58502 · 701-223-2890

Irvin B. Nodland · (Plaintiffs) · Lundberg, Nodland, Lucas & Schulz · 425 North Fifth Street · Bismarck, ND 58501 · 701-223-4022

David L. Peterson · (Plaintiffs) · Wheeler, Wolf, Peterson, Schmitz, McDonald & Johnson · 220 North Fourth Street · P.O. Box 2056 · Bismarck, ND 58502-2056 701-223-5300

Orell D. Schmitz · (Plaintiffs) · Wheeler, Wolf, Peterson, Schmitz, McDonald & Johnson · 220 North Fourth Street · P.O. Box 2056 · Bismarck, ND 58502-2056 701-223-5300

William A. Strutz · (Defendants) · Fleck, Mather, Strutz & Mayer · Norwest Bank Bulding, Sixth Floor · 400 East Broadway · P.O. Box 2798 · Bismarck, ND 58502 · 701-223-6585

William P. Zuger · (Defendants) · Zuger, Kirmis, Bolinske & Smith · Provident Life Building · 316 North Fifth Street · P.O. Box 1695 · Bismarck, ND 58501-1695 · 701-223-2711

Paul G. Kloster · (Defendants) · Mackoff, Kellogg, Kirby & Kloster · 46 West Second Street · P.O. Box 1097 · Dickinson, ND 58601 · 701-227-1841

Ronald A. Reichert · (Plaintiffs) · Freed, Dynes, Reichert & Buresh · 34 East First Street · Drawer K · Dickinson, ND 58601 · 701-225-6711

David R. Bossart · (Plaintiffs) · Conmy, Feste, Bossart, Hubbard & Corwin · 400 Norwest Center · Fourth Street & Main Avenue · Fargo, ND 58126 · 701-293-9911

Lee Hagen · (Plaintiffs) · Pioneer Plaza, Suite 302 · 101 North 10th Street · P.O. Box 2982 · Fargo, ND 58108-2982 · 701-293-8425

Donald R. Hansen · (Defendants) · Nilles, Hansen & Davies · 1800 Radisson Tower · P.O. Box 2626 · Fargo, ND 58108 · 701-237-5544

Carlton J. Hunke · (Defendants) · Vogel, Brantner, Kelly, Knutson, Weir & Bye 502 First Avenue North · P.O. Box 1389 · Fargo, ND 58107 · 701-237-6983

Duane H. Ilvedson · (Defendants) · Nilles, Hansen & Davies · 1800 Radisson Tower · P.O. Box 2626 · Fargo, ND 58108 · 701-237-5544

John D. Kelly · (Defendants) · Vogel, Brantner, Kelly, Knutson, Weir & Bye · 502 First Avenue North · P.O. Box 1389 · Fargo, ND 58107 · 701-237-6983

Frank T. Knox · (Plaintiffs) · Lanier, Knox, Olson & Racek · 115 University Drive P.O. Box 1007 · Fargo, ND 58107-1932 · 701-232-4437

Jack G. Marcil · Serkland, Lundberg, Erickson, Marcil & McLean · 10 Roberts Street · P.O. Box 6017 · Fargo, ND 58108-6017 · 701-232-8957

Mart R. Vogel · (Defendants) · Vogel, Brantner, Kelly, Knutson, Weir & Bye · 502 First Avenue North · P.O. Box 1389 · Fargo, ND 58107 · 701-237-6983

Robert Vaaler · (Defendants) · Vaaler, Gillig, Warcup, Woutat, Zimney & Foster Metropolitan Building, Fifth Floor · 600 De Mers Avenue · P.O. Box 1617 · Grand Forks, ND 58206-1617 · 701-772-8111

Robert Vogel · (Plaintiffs) · 106 North Third Street, Suite M102 · P.O. Box 1376 Grand Forks, ND 58206-1376 · 701-775-3117

REAL ESTATE LAW

James D. Schlosser · 304 East Rosser Avenue · P.O. Box 2578 · Bismarck, ND 58502 · 701-258-8550

Paul M. Hubbard · Conmy, Feste, Bossart, Hubbard & Corwin · 400 Norwest Center · Fourth Street & Main Avenue · Fargo, ND 58126 · 701-293-9911

J. Philip Johnson · Yuill, Wold, Johnson & Feder · Gate City Building, Suite 414 P.O. Box 1680 · Fargo, ND 58102 · 701-235-5515

David F. Knutson · Vogel, Brantner, Kelly, Knutson, Weir & Bye · 502 First Avenue North · P.O. Box 1389 · Fargo, ND 58107 · 701-237-6983

Robert L. Stroup II · Nilles, Hansen & Davies · 1800 Radisson Tower · P.O. Box 2626 · Fargo, ND 58108 · 701-237-5544

Theodore M. Camrud · Degnan, McElroy, Lamb, Camrud, Maddock & Olson First National Bank Building, Fifth Floor · Grand Forks, ND 58201 · 701-775-5595

Donald A. Anderson · Anderson & Dobrovolny · 610 Midwest Federal Savings Bank Building · P.O. Box 997 · Minot, ND 58701 · 701-852-4105

TAX AND EMPLOYEE BENEFITS LAW

C. Nicholas Vogel · Vogel, Brantner, Kelly, Knutson, Weir & Bye · 205 First Avenue North · P.O. Box 1389 · Fargo, ND 58107 · 701-237-6983

Garry A. Pearson · Pearson, Christensen & Fischer · 24 North Fourth Street P.O. Box 1075 · Grand Forks, ND 58206-1075 · 701-775-0521

Robert J. Lamont · Lamont Law Office · 111 Eleventh Avenue, SW · P.O. Box 2226 · Minot, ND 58702 · 701-852-7002

TRUSTS AND ESTATES

Sean O. Smith · Tschider & Smith · 418 East Rosser Avenue · Bismarck, ND 58501 · 701-258-4000

C. Nicholas Vogel · Vogel, Brantner, Kelly, Knutson, Weir & Bye · 205 First Avenue North · P.O. Box 1389 · Fargo, ND 58107 · 701-237-6983

Garry A. Pearson · Pearson, Christensen & Fischer · 24 North Fourth Street P.O. Box 1075 · Grand Forks, ND 58206-1075 · 701-775-0521

Walfrid B. Hankla · McGee, Hankla, Backes & Wheeler · Norwest Bank Building, Suite 305 · P.O. Box 998 · Minot, ND 58702 · 701-852-2544

Robert J. Lamont · Lamont Law Office · 111 Eleventh Avenue, SW · P.O. Box 2226 · Minot, ND 58702 · 701-852-7002

OHIO

BANKRUPTCY LAW	540
BUSINESS LITIGATION	542
CORPORATE LAW	545
CRIMINAL DEFENSE	550
FAMILY LAW	552
LABOR AND EMPLOYMENT LAW	554
MARITIME LAW	558
NATURAL RESOURCES AND ENVIRONMENTAL LAW	558
PERSONAL INJURY LITIGATION	559
REAL ESTATE LAW	563
TAX AND EMPLOYEE BENEFITS LAW	566
TRUSTS AND ESTATES	570

BANKRUPTCY LAW

John J. Guy · Guy, Lammert & Towne · 2210 First National Tower · Akron, OH 44308-1449 · 216-535-2151

David M. Hunter · Brouse & McDowell · 500 First National Tower · Akron, OH 44308-1471 · 216-535-5711

John A. Schwemler · Brouse & McDowell · 500 First National Tower · Akron, OH 44308-1471 · 216-535-5711

Ronald N. Towne · Guy, Lammert & Towne · 2210 First National Tower · Akron, OH 44308-1449 · 216-535-2151

Stephen L. Black · Graydon, Head & Ritchey · 1900 Fifth Third Center · P.O. Box 6464 · Cincinnati, OH 45201 · 513-621-6464

Paul A. Nemann · Cohen, Todd, Kite & Stanford · 525 Vine Street, 16th Floor · Cincinnati, OH 45202 · 513-421-4020

Jay A. Rosenberg · Porter, Wright, Morris & Arthur · 250 East Fifth Street, Suite 2200 · Cincinnati, OH 45202-4166 · 513-381-4700

Peter J. Strauss · Graydon, Head & Ritchey · 1900 Fifth Third Center · P.O. Box 6464 · Cincinnati, OH 45201 · 513-621-6464

Richard A. Baumgart · Dettelbach and Sicherman · 1300 Ohio Savings Plaza · 1801 East Ninth Street · Cleveland, OH 44114-3169 · 216-696-6000

David G. Heiman · Jones, Day, Reavis & Pogue · North Point · 901 Lakeside Avenue · Cleveland, OH 44114 · 216-586-3939

G. Christopher Meyer · Squire, Sanders & Dempsey · 1800 Huntington Building · Cleveland, OH 44115 · 216-687-8500

Joseph Patchan · Baker & Hostetler · 3200 National City Center · Cleveland, OH 44114 · 216-621-0200

Lee D. Powar · Hahn Loeser & Parks · 800 National City East Sixth Building · Cleveland, OH 44114 · 216-621-0150

Marvin A. Sicherman · Dettelbach and Sicherman · 1300 Ohio Savings Plaza · 1801 East Ninth Street · Cleveland, OH 44114-3169 · 216-696-6000

Howard L. Sokolsky · Benesch, Friedlander, Coplan & Aronoff · 1100 Citizens Building · 850 Euclid Avenue · Cleveland, OH 44114 · 216-363-4500

Nick V. Cavalieri · Arter & Hadden · One Columbus, 21st Floor · 10 West Broad Street · Columbus, OH 43215 · 614-221-3155

R. P. Cunningham · Arter & Hadden · One Columbus, 21st Floor · 10 West Broad Street · Columbus, OH 43215 · 614-221-3155

John J. Dilenschneider · Smith & Schnacke · 41 South High Street, Suite 2250 · Columbus, OH 43215 · 614-224-6500

E. James Hopple · Schottenstein, Zox & Dunn · The Huntington Center, 26th Floor · 41 South High Street · Columbus, OH 43215 · 614-221-3211

William B. Logan, Jr. · Luper, Wolinetz, Sheriff & Neidenthal · 1200 LeVeque Tower · 50 West Broad Street · Columbus, OH 43215-3374 · 614-221-7663

Grady L. Pettigrew, Jr. · Arter & Hadden · One Columbus, 21st Floor · 10 West Broad Street · Columbus, OH 43215 · 614-221-3155

Jack R. Pigman · Porter, Wright, Morris & Arthur · 41 South High Street · Columbus, OH 43215 · 614-227-2000

Frederick R. Reed · Vorys, Sater, Seymour and Pease · 52 East Gay Street · P.O. Box 1008 · Columbus, OH 43216-1008 · 614-464-6400

Thomas C. Scott · Thompson, Hine and Flory · 100 East Broad Street · Columbus, OH 43215 · 614-461-6060

Robert J. Sidman · Vorys, Sater, Seymour and Pease · 52 East Gay Street · P.O. Box 1008 · Columbus, OH 43216-1008 · 614-464-6400

Robert W. Werth · Vorys, Sater, Seymour and Pease · 52 East Gay Street · P.O. Box 1008 · Columbus, OH 43215 · 614-464-6400

Dennis L. Patterson · Bogin & Patterson · 1200 Talbott Tower · 131 North Ludlow Street · Dayton, OH 45402 · 513-226-1200

H. Buswell Roberts, Jr. · Nathan & Roberts · 644 Spitzer Building · 520 Madison Avenue · Toledo, OH 43604-1302 · 419-255-3036

Joseph D. Shibley · Shibley & Shibley · 1400 National Bank Building · Toledo, OH 43604 · 419-248-2666

Michael A. Gallo · Nadler, Nadler & Bergman · 20 Federal Plaza West, Suite 600 Youngstown, OH 44503 · 216-744-0247

Myron J. Nadler · Nadler, Nadler & Bergman · 20 Federal Plaza West, Suite 600 Youngstown, OH 44503 · 216-744-0247

BUSINESS LITIGATION

Norman S. Carr · Roetzel & Andress · 75 East Market Street · Akron, OH 44308 216-376-2700

John W. Beatty · Dinsmore & Shohl · 2100 Fountain Square Plaza · 511 Walnut Street · P.O. Box 2547 · Cincinnati, OH 45202-3172 · 513-977-8200

Thomas S. Calder · Dinsmore & Shohl · 2100 Fountain Square Plaza · 511 Walnut Street · P.O. Box 2547 · Cincinnati, OH 45202-3172 · 513-977-8200

Murray S. Monroe · Taft, Stettinius & Hollister · 1800 First National Bank Center · Fountain Square · Cincinnati, OH 45202 · 513-381-2838

Robert G. Stachler · Taft, Stettinius & Hollister · 1800 First National Bank Center · Fountain Square · Cincinnati, OH 45202 · 513-381-2838

Jacob K. Stein · Paxton & Seasongood · 1700 Central Trust Tower · Cincinnati, OH 45202 · 513-352-6700

Glenn V. Whitaker · Graydon, Head & Ritchey · 1900 Fifth Third Center · P.O. Box 6464 · Cincinnati, OH 45201 · 513-621-6464

Richard Cusick · Calfee, Halter & Griswold · 1800 Society Building · East Ninth and Superior · Cleveland, OH 44114-2688 · 216-781-2166

William D. Ginn · Thompson, Hine and Flory · 1100 National City Bank Building 629 Euclid Avenue · Cleveland, OH 44114 · 216-566-5500

Daniel W. Hammer · Thompson, Hine and Flory · 1100 National City Bank Building · 629 Euclid Avenue · Cleveland, OH 44114 · 216-566-5500

Marvin L. Karp · Ulmer & Berne · 900 Bond Court Building · Cleveland, OH 44114 · 216-621-8400

Thomas S. Kilbane · Squire, Sanders & Dempsey · 1800 Huntington Building Cleveland, OH 44115 · 216-687-8500

H. Stephen Madsen · Baker & Hostetler · 3200 National City Center · Cleveland, OH 44114 · 216-621-0200

Patrick F. McCartan · Jones, Day, Reavis & Pogue · North Point · 901 Lakeside Avenue · Cleveland, OH 44114 · 216-586-3939

Gerald A. Messerman · Messerman & Messerman · 1525 Ohio Savings Plaza 1801 East Ninth Street · Cleveland, OH 44114 · 216-574-9990

Mark O'Neill · Weston, Hurd, Fallon, Paisley & Howley · 2500 Terminal Tower Cleveland, OH 44113-2241 · 216-241-6602

James M. Porter · Squire, Sanders & Dempsey · 1800 Huntington Building Cleveland, OH 44115 · 216-687-8500

John L. Strauch · Jones, Day, Reavis & Pogue · North Point · 901 Lakeside Avenue · Cleveland, OH 44114 · 216-586-3939

William H. Wallace · Thompson, Hine and Flory · 1100 National City Bank Building · 629 Euclid Avenue · Cleveland, OH 44114 · 216-566-5500

Alan L. Briggs · Squire, Sanders & Dempsey · 250 East Broad Street · Columbus, OH 43215-3753 · 614-365-2800

John J. Chester · Chester, Hoffman, Willcox and Saxbe · 17 South High Street, Suite 900 · Columbus, OH 43215 · 614-221-4000

David S. Cupps · Vorys, Sater, Seymour and Pease · 52 East Gay Street · P.O. Box 1008 · Columbus, OH 43216-1008 · 614-464-6400

Gerald L. Draper · Bricker & Eckler · 100 South Third Street · P.O. Box 100 Columbus, OH 43218 · 614-227-2300

Robert M. Duncan · Jones, Day, Reavis & Pogue · 1900 Huntington Center Columbus, OH 43215 · 614-469-3939

John C. Elam · Vorys, Sater, Seymour and Pease · 52 East Gay Street · P.O. Box 1008 · Columbus, OH 43216-1008 · 614-464-6400

George W. Hairston · Baker & Hostetler · 65 East State Street · Columbus, OH 43215 · 614-228-1541

Denis J. Murphy · Carlile Patchen Murphy & Allison · 366 East Broad Street Columbus, OH 43212 · 614-228-6135

Thomas E. Palmer · Squire, Sanders & Dempsey · 250 East Broad Street Columbus, OH 43215-3753 · 614-365-2800

James E. Pohlman · Porter, Wright, Morris & Arthur · 41 South High Street Columbus, OH 43215 · 614-227-2000

Thomas B. Ridgley · Vorys, Sater, Seymour and Pease · 52 East Gay Street · P.O. Box 1008 · Columbus, OH 43216-1008 · 614-464-6400

Edgar A. Strause · Vorys, Sater, Seymour and Pease · 52 East Gay Street · P.O. Box 1008 · Columbus, OH 43216-1008 · 614-464-6400

Duke W. Thomas · Vorys, Sater, Seymour and Pease · 52 East Gay Street · P.O. Box 1008 · Columbus, OH 43216-1008 · 614-464-6400

David J. Young · Squire, Sanders & Dempsey · 250 East Broad Street · Columbus, OH 43215-3753 · 614-365-2800

John W. Zeiger · Jones, Day, Reavis & Pogue · 1900 Huntington Center Columbus, OH 43215 · 614-469-3939

Charles J. Faruki · Smith & Schnacke · 2000 Courthouse Plaza, NE · P.O. Box 1817 · Dayton, OH 45401 · 513-443-6500

Armistead W. Gilliam, Jr. · Smith & Schnacke · 2000 Courthouse Plaza, NE P.O. Box 1817 · Dayton, OH 45401 · 513-443-6500

David C. Greer · Bieser, Greer & Landis · 400 Gem Plaza · Third and Main Streets · Dayton, OH 45402 · 513-223-3277

Roger J. Makley · Coolidge, Wall, Womsley & Lombard · 600 IBM Building · 33 West First Street · Dayton, OH 45402 · 513-223-8177

Robert G. Clayton, Jr. · Shumaker, Loop & Kendrick · North Courthouse Square 1000 Jackson · Toledo, OH 43624-1573 · 419-241-4201

Cary Rodman Cooper · Cooper, Straub, Walinski & Cramer · 900 Adams Street, Third Floor · P.O. Box 1568 · Toledo, OH 43603-1568 · 419-241-1200

John M. Curphey · Robison, Curphey & O'Connell · Four Seagate, Ninth Floor Toledo, OH 43604 · 419-249-7900

Jamille G. Jamra · Eastman & Smith · 800 United Savings Building · 240 Huron Street · Toledo, OH 43604-1141 · 419-241-6000

Richard M. Kerger · Marshall & Melhorn · Four Seagate, Eighth Floor · Toledo, OH 43604 · 419-249-7100

John G. Mattimoe · Marshall & Melhorn · Four Seagate, Eighth Floor · Toledo, OH 43604 · 419-249-7100

CORPORATE LAW

Richard A. Chenoweth · Buckingham, Doolittle & Burroughs · Akron Centre Plaza · 50 South Main Street · P.O. Box 1500 · Akron, OH 44309-1500 · 216-376-5300

Duane L. Isham · Roetzel & Andress · 75 East Market Street · Akron, OH 44308 216-376-2700

Robert P. Reffner · Brouse & McDowell · 500 First National Tower · Akron, OH 44308-1471 · 216-535-5711

Edmund J. Adams · Frost & Jacobs · 2500 Central Trust Center · 201 East Fourth Street · Cincinnati, OH 45202 · 513-651-6800

James M. Anderson · Taft, Stettinius & Hollister · 1800 First National Bank Center · Fountain Square · Cincinnati, OH 45202 · 513-381-2838

William T. Bahlman, Jr. · Paxton & Seasongood · 1700 Central Trust Tower · Cincinnati, OH 45202 · 513-352-6700

Dennis J. Barron · Frost & Jacobs · 2500 Central Trust Center · 201 East Fourth Street · Cincinnati, OH 45202 · 513-651-6800

James R. Bridgeland, Jr. · Taft, Stettinius & Hollister · 1800 First National Bank Center · Fountain Square · Cincinnati, OH 45202 · 513-381-2838

Nolan W. Carson · Dinsmore & Shohl · 2100 Fountain Square Plaza · 511 Walnut Street · P.O. Box 2547 · Cincinnati, OH 45202-3172 · 513-977-8200

Joseph H. Head, Jr. · Graydon, Head & Ritchey · 1900 Fifth Third Center · P.O. Box 6464 · Cincinnati, OH 45201 · 513-621-6464

Timothy E. Hoberg · Taft, Stettinius & Hollister · 1800 First National Bank Center · Fountain Square · Cincinnati, OH 45202 · 513-381-2838

Gary P. Kreider · Keating, Muething & Klekamp · Provident Tower, 18th Floor · One East Fourth Street · Cincinnati, OH 45202 · 513-579-6400

Charles D. Lindberg · Taft, Stettinius & Hollister · 1800 First National Bank Center · Fountain Square · Cincinnati, OH 45202 · 513-381-2838

Leonard S. Meranus · Paxton & Seasongood · 1700 Central Trust Tower · Cincinnati, OH 45202 · 513-352-6700

Murray S. Monroe · Taft, Stettinius & Hollister · 1800 First National Bank Center · Fountain Square · Cincinnati, OH 45202 · 513-381-2838

John L. Muething · Keating, Muething & Klekamp · Provident Tower, 18th Floor · One East Fourth Street · Cincinnati, OH 45202 · 513-579-6400

Charles G. Puchta · Frost & Jacobs · 2500 Central Trust Center · 201 East Fourth Street · Cincinnati, OH 45202 · 513-651-6800

Clifford A. Roe, Jr. · Dinsmore & Shohl · 2100 Fountain Square Plaza · 511 Walnut Street · P.O. Box 2547 · Cincinnati, OH 45202-3172 · 513-977-8200

Nelson Schwab, Jr. · Graydon, Head & Ritchey · 1900 Fifth Third Center · 511 Walnut Street · Cincinnati, OH 45201 · 513-621-6464

George N. Aronoff · Benesch, Friedlander, Coplan & Aronoff · 1100 Citizens Building · 850 Euclid Avenue · Cleveland, OH 44114 · 216-363-4500

Lawrence M. Bell · Benesch, Friedlander, Coplan & Aronoff · 1100 Citizens Building · 850 Euclid Avenue · Cleveland, OH 44114 · 216-363-4500

James H. Berick · Berick, Pearlman & Mills · 1350 Eaton Center · 1111 Superior Avenue · Cleveland, OH 44114 · 216-861-4900

Albert I. Borowitz · Jones, Day, Reavis & Pogue · North Point · 901 Lakeside Avenue · Cleveland, OH 44114 · 216-586-3939

John H. Burlingame · Baker & Hostetler · 3200 National City Center · Cleveland, OH 44114 · 216-621-0200

Paul B. Campbell · Squire, Sanders & Dempsey · 1800 Huntington Building Cleveland, OH 44115 · 216-687-8500

Joseph R. Cortese · Squire, Sanders & Dempsey · 1800 Huntington Building Cleveland, OH 44115 · 216-687-8500

John L. Dampeer · Thompson, Hine and Flory · 1100 National City Bank Building · 629 Euclid Avenue · Cleveland, OH 44114 · 216-566-5500

John D. Drinko · Baker & Hostetler · 3200 National City Center · Cleveland, OH 44114 · 216-621-0200

Daniel L. Ekelman · Calfee, Halter & Griswold · 1800 Society Building · East Ninth and Superior · Cleveland, OH 44114-2688 · 216-781-2166

John H. Gherlein · Thompson, Hine and Flory · 1100 National City Bank Building · 629 Euclid Avenue · Cleveland, OH 44114 · 216-566-5500

Bruce Griswold · Calfee, Halter & Griswold · 1800 Society Building · East Ninth and Superior · Cleveland, OH 44114-2688 · 216-781-2166

Donald W. Gruettner · Baker & Hostetler · 3200 National City Center · Cleveland, OH 44114 · 216-621-0200

David H. Gunning · Jones, Day, Reavis & Pogue · North Point · 901 Lakeside Avenue · Cleveland, OH 44114 · 216-586-3939

Alan L. Hyde · Thompson, Hine and Flory · 1100 National City Bank Building 629 Euclid Avenue · Cleveland, OH 44114 · 216-566-5500

Fred D. Kidder · Jones, Day, Reavis & Pogue · North Point · 901 Lakeside Avenue · Cleveland, OH 44114 · 216-586-3939

Robert G. Markey · Baker & Hostetler · 3200 National City Center · Cleveland, OH 44114 · 216-621-0200

William A. Papenbrock · Calfee, Halter & Griswold · 1800 Society Building East Ninth and Superior · Cleveland, OH 44114-2688 · 216-781-2166

Richard W. Pogue · Jones, Day, Reavis & Pogue · North Point · 901 Lakeside Avenue · Cleveland, OH 44114 · 216-586-3939

Carlton B. Schnell · Arter & Hadden · 1100 Huntington Building · Cleveland, OH 44115 · 216-696-1100

Wilton S. Sogg · Hahn Loeser & Parks · 800 National City East Sixth Building Cleveland, OH 44114 · 216-621-0150

William H. Steinbrink · Jones, Day, Reavis & Pogue · North Point · 901 Lakeside Avenue · Cleveland, OH 44114 · 216-586-3939

Richard E. Streeter · Thompson, Hine and Flory · 1100 National City Bank Building · 629 Euclid Avenue · Cleveland, OH 44114 · 216-566-5500

Leigh B. Trevor · Jones, Day, Reavis & Pogue · North Point · 901 Lakeside Avenue · Cleveland, OH 44114 · 216-586-3939

Owen F. Walker · Thompson, Hine and Flory · 1100 National City Bank Building 629 Euclid Avenue · Cleveland, OH 44114 · 216-566-5500

Richard T. Watson · Spieth, Bell, McCurdy & Newell · 2000 Huntington Building · Cleveland, OH 44115-1496 · 216-696-4700

William E. Arthur · Porter, Wright, Morris & Arthur · 41 South High Street Columbus, OH 43215 · 614-227-2000

John P. Beavers · Bricker & Eckler · 100 South Third Street · P.O. Box 100 Columbus, OH 43218-0100 · 614-227-2300

Charles F. Dugan II · Vorys, Sater, Seymour and Pease · 52 East Gay Street · P.O. Box 1008 · Columbus, OH 43216-1008 · 614-464-6400

J. Richard Emens · Emens, Hurd, Kegler & Ritter · Capitol Square · 65 East State Street · Columbus, OH 43215 · 614-462-5400

Philip C. Johnston · Vorys, Sater, Seymour and Pease · 52 East Gay Street · P.O. Box 1008 · Columbus, OH 43216-1008 · 614-464-6400

G. Robert Lucas II · Vorys, Sater, Seymour and Pease · 52 East Gay Street · P.O. Box 1008 · Columbus, OH 43216-1008 · 614-464-6400

Robert W. Minor · Vorys, Sater, Seymour and Pease · 52 East Gay Street · P.O. Box 1008 · Columbus, OH 43216-1008 · 614-464-6400

Michael E. Moritz · Baker & Hostetler · 65 East State Street · Columbus, OH 43215 · 614-228-1541

Frank R. Morris, Jr. · Porter, Wright, Morris & Arthur · 41 South High Street · Columbus, OH 43215 · 614-227-2000

Richard R. Murphey, Jr. · Squire, Sanders & Dempsey · BancOhio National Plaza · 155 East Broad Street · Columbus, OH 43125 · 614-365-2700

Edward A. Schrag, Jr. · Vorys, Sater, Seymour and Pease · 52 East Gay Street · P.O. Box 1008 · Columbus, OH 43216-1008 · 614-464-6400

Stanley Schwartz, Jr. · Schwartz, Kelm, Warren & Rubenstein · Huntington Center, 23rd Floor · 41 South High Street · Columbus, OH 43215-6188 · 614-224-3168

Roger R. Stinehart · Jones, Day, Reavis & Pogue · 1900 Huntington Center · Columbus, OH 43215 · 614-469-3939

Michael F. Sullivan · Bricker & Eckler · 100 South Third Street · P.O. Box 100 · Columbus, OH 43218 · 614-227-2300

John R. Thomas · Emens, Hurd, Kegler & Ritter · Capitol Square · 65 East State Street · Columbus, OH 43215 · 614-462-5400

James M. Tobin · Squire, Sanders & Dempsey · BancOhio National Plaza · 155 East Broad Street · Columbus, OH 43215 · 614-365-2700

Arthur I. Vorys · Vorys, Sater, Seymour and Pease · 52 East Gay Street · P.O. Box 1008 · Columbus, OH 43216-1008 · 614-464-6400

Richard J. Chernesky · Smith & Schnacke · 2000 Courthouse Plaza, NE · P.O. Box 1817 · Dayton, OH 45401 · 513-443-6500

Andrew K. Cherney · Smith & Schnacke · 2000 Courthouse Plaza, NE · P.O. Box 1817 · Dayton, OH 45401 · 513-443-6500

Stanley A. Freedman · Smith & Schnacke · 2000 Courthouse Plaza, NE · P.O. Box 1817 · Dayton, OH 45401 · 513-443-6500

J. Michael Herr · Smith & Schnacke · 2000 Courthouse Plaza, NE · P.O. Box 1817 · Dayton, OH 45401 · 513-443-6500

James J. Mulligan · Smith & Schnacke · 2000 Courthouse Plaza, NE · P.O. Box 1817 · Dayton, OH 45401 · 513-443-6500

Joseph M. Rigot · Smith & Schnacke · 2000 Courthouse Plaza, NE · P.O. Box 1817 · Dayton, OH 45401 · 513-443-6500

James W. Baehren · Fuller & Henry · One SeaGate, 17th Floor · P.O. Box 2088 Toledo, OH 43603-2088 · 419-247-2500

George L. Chapman · Shumaker, Loop & Kendrick · North Courthouse Square 1000 Jackson · Toledo, OH 43624-1573 · 419-241-4201

David A. Katz · Spengler, Nathanson, Heyman, McCarthy & Durfee · 1000 National Bank Building · Toledo, OH 43604 · 419-241-2201

James E. Kline · Shumaker, Loop & Kendrick · North Courthouse Square · 1000 Jackson · Toledo, OH 43624-1573 · 419-241-4201

David F. Waterman · Shumaker, Loop & Kendrick · North Courthouse Square 1000 Jackson · Toledo, OH 43624-1573 · 419-241-4201

James F. White, Jr. · Shumaker, Loop & Kendrick · North Courthouse Square 1000 Jackson · Toledo, OH 43624-1573 · 419-241-4201

CRIMINAL DEFENSE

James L. Burdon · Burdon & Merlitti · 73 East Mill Street · Akron, OH 44308 216-253-7171

Arnold Morelli · Bauer, Morelli & Heyd · 1029 Main Street · Cincinnati, OH 45202 · 513-241-3676

James N. Perry · 1804 Carew Tower · Cincinnati, OH 45202 · 513-621-0442

Martin S. Pinales · Sirkin, Pinales, Mezibov & Schwartz · 105 West Fourth Street, Suite 832 · Cincinnati, OH 45202 · 513-721-4876

Jack C. Rubenstein · Rubenstein and Rubenstein · 36 East Fourth Street · Cincinnati, OH 45202 · 513-241-7460

Elmer A. Giuliani · The Leader Building, Suite 410 · 526 Superior Avenue, NE · Cleveland, OH 44114 · 216-241-0520

Gerald S. Gold · Gold, Rotatori, Schwartz & Gibbons · 1500 Leader Building · 526 Superior Avenue, NE · Cleveland, OH 44114 · 216-696-6122

Gerald A. Messerman · Messerman & Messerman · 1525 Ohio Savings Plaza · 1801 East Ninth Street · Cleveland, OH 44114 · 216-574-9990

Jerome P. Milano · White and Milano · 1040 Standard Building · Cleveland, OH 44113 · 216-696-6996

George J. Moscarino · Jones, Day, Reavis & Pogue · North Point · 901 Lakeside Avenue · Cleveland, OH 44114 · 216-586-3939

Robert J. Rotatori · Gold, Rotatori, Schwartz & Gibbons · 1500 Leader Building · 526 Superior Avenue, NE · Cleveland, OH 44114 · 216-696-6122

James R. Willis · Willis & Blackwell · 1300 East Ninth Street · Cleveland, OH 44114 · 216-523-1100

Paul D. Cassidy · Cassidy & Meeks · 503 South High Street · Columbus, OH 43215 · 614-228-3569

R. William Meeks · Cassidy & Meeks · 503 South High Street · Columbus, OH 43215 · 614-228-3569

Thomas M. Tyack · Thomas M. Tyack & Associates · 536 South High Street · Columbus, OH 43215 · 614-221-1341

Jerry Weiner · Weiner, Ross & Associates · 19 West Beck Street · Columbus, OH 43215 · 614-224-1238

Samuel B. Weiner · 743 South Front Street · Columbus, OH 43206 · 614-443-6581

Harold E. Wonnell · 326 South High Street · Columbus, OH 43215 · 614-224-7291

Dennis A. Lieberman · Flanagan, Lieberman, Hoffman & Swaim · 318 West Fourth Street · Dayton, OH 45402 · 513-223-5200

Daniel J. O'Brien · Talbott Tower, Suite 202 · 131 North Ludlow Street · Dayton, OH 45402 · 513-228-6001

John H. Rion · John H. Rion & Associates · One First National Plaza · Dayton, OH 45402 · 513-223-9133

Roger L. Clark · Kimble, Stevens, Young, Clark & Rodeheffer · 622 Sixth Street Portsmouth, OH 45662 · 614-354-3214

Jack D. Young · Kimble, Stevens, Young, Clark & Rodeheffer · 622 Sixth Street Portsmouth, OH 45662 · 614-354-3214

John J. Callahan · Secor, Ide & Callahan · 1400 National Bank Building · Toledo, OH 43604 · 419-243-2101

William M. Connelly · Connelly, Soutar & Jackson · 2100 Ohio Citizens Bank Building · Toledo, OH 43604-1207 · 419-243-2100

Jon D. Richardson · Kaplan, Richardson and Rost · 524 Spitzer Building · Toledo, OH 43604 · 419-241-6168

R. Scott Krichbaum · 20 West Boardman Street · Youngstown, OH 44503 · 216-747-4481

Carmen A. Policy · Flask and Policy · 424 City Centre One · P.O. Box 837 · Youngstown, OH 44501-0837 · 216-746-3217

FAMILY LAW

Michael R. Barrett · Graydon, Head & Ritchey · 1900 Fifth Third Center · P.O. Box 6464 · Cincinnati, OH 45201 · 513-621-6464

Don C. Bolsinger · Bolsinger & Brinkman · 105 East Fourth Street, Suite 1520 Cincinnati, OH 45202 · 513-621-7878

Guy M. Hild · Katz, Teller, Brant & Hild · 1400 Tri-State Building · Cincinnati, OH 45202 · 513-721-4532

Bea V. Larsen · 1804 Carew Tower · Cincinnati, OH 45202 · 513-621-0442

Jerome S. Teller · Katz, Teller, Brant & Hild · 1400 Tri-State Building · Cincinnati, OH 45202 · 513-721-4532

Deborah Rowley Akers · Wolf & Akers · 1515 The East Ohio Building · 1717 East Ninth Street · Cleveland, OH 44114 · 216-623-9999

Joyce E. Barrett · 1370 Ontario Street · Cleveland, OH 44113 · 216-696-1545

James M. Wilsman · Hahn Loeser & Parks · 800 National City East Sixth Building · Cleveland, OH 44114 · 216-621-0150

Marshall J. Wolf · Wolf & Akers · 1515 The East Ohio Building · 1717 East Ninth Street · Cleveland, OH 44114 · 216-623-9999

Robert I. Zashin · Zashin, Rich, Sutula & Monastra · 250 Standard Building Cleveland, OH 44113 · 216-696-4441

John A. Carnahan · Arter & Hadden · One Columbus, 21st Floor · 10 West Broad Street · Columbus, OH 43215 · 614-221-3155

William S. Friedman · 519 South Fourth Street · Columbus, OH 43206 · 614-221-0090

Jeffrey A. Grossman · 523 South Third Street · Columbus, OH 43215-5763 · 614-221-7711

Harry Lewis · 625 City Park Avenue · Columbus, OH 43206 · 614-221-3938

Stanley Z. Greenberg · Rogers & Greenberg · 2160 Kettering Tower · Dayton, OH 45423 · 513-223-8171

Charles D. Lowe · Cowden, Pfarrer, Crew & Becker · 2580 Kettering Tower Dayton, OH 45423 · 513-223-6211

Jude T. Aubry · Aubry, Meyer, Yosses & Rudge · Lawyers Building · 329 Tenth Street · P.O. Box 2068 · Toledo, OH 43603-2068 · 419-241-4288

Peter L. Moran · Peppers, Moran & Sparrow · 626 Madison Avenue, Suite 300 Toledo, OH 43604 · 419-241-8171

Melvin G. Nusbaum · Lackey, Nusbaum, Harris, Reny & Torzewski · Two Maritime Plaza, Third Floor · Toledo, OH 43604 · 419-243-1105

Ron L. Rimelspach · Rimelspach, Gibson & Popil · 414 North Erie Street · Toledo, OH 43624 · 419-241-2153

Eugene B. Fox · 20 West Boardman Street · Youngstown, OH 44503 · 216-747-4481

LABOR AND EMPLOYMENT LAW

William B. Gore · (Labor) · Society Building, Suite 503 · 159 South Main Street · Akron, OH 44308 · 216-434-7167

Edward C. Kaminski · (Management) · Buckingham, Doolittle & Burroughs · Akron Centre Plaza · 50 South Main Street · P.O. Box 1500 · Akron, OH 44309-1500 · 216-376-5300

Kenneth R. Millisor · (Management) · Millisor & Nobil · 430 Quaker Square · Akron, OH 44308 · 216-253-5500

Dean E. Denlinger · (Management) · Denlinger, Rosenthal & Greenberg · 2310 First National Bank Center · 425 Walnut Street · Cincinnati, OH 45202 · 513-621-3440

Michael W. Hawkins · (Management) · Dinsmore & Shohl · 2100 Fountain Square Plaza · 511 Walnut Street · P.O. Box 2547 · Cincinnati, OH 45202-3172 · 513-977-8200

Hulse Hays, Jr. · (Management) · Taft, Stettinius & Hollister · 1800 First National Bank Center · Fountain Square · Cincinnati, OH 45202 · 513-381-2838

James B. Helmer, Jr. · (Individuals) · 2305 Central Trust Tower · One West Fourth Street · Cincinnati, OH 45202 · 513-421-2400

Thomas J. Kircher · (Labor) · Kircher and Phalen · 125 East Court Street, Suite 1000 · Cincinnati, OH 45202-1299 · 513-381-3525

James K. L. Lawrence · (Management) · Frost & Jacobs · 2500 Central Trust Center · 201 East Fifth Street · Cincinnati, OH 45202 · 513-651-6800

Alan J. Lips · (Management) · Taft, Stettinius & Hollister · 1800 First National Bank Center · Fountain Square · Cincinnati, OH 45202 · 513-381-2838

Marc D. Mezibov · (Individuals) · Sirkin, Pinales, Mezibov & Schwartz · 105 West Fourth Street, Suite 832 · Cincinnati, OH 45202 · 513-721-4876

Thomas F. Phalen, Jr. · (Labor) · Kircher and Phalen · 125 East Court Street, Suite 1000 · Cincinnati, OH 45202-1299 · 513-381-3525

James B. Robinson · (Labor) · Kircher and Phalen · 125 East Court Street, Suite 1000 · Cincinnati, OH 45202-1299 · 513-381-3525

Frank H. Stewart · (Management) · Taft, Stettinius & Hollister · 1800 First National Bank Center · Fountain Square · Cincinnati, OH 45202 · 513-381-2838

J. Mack Swigert · (Management) · Taft, Stettinius & Hollister · 1800 First National Bank Center · Fountain Square · Cincinnati, OH 45202 · 513-381-2838

Paul H. Tobias · (Individuals) · Tobias & Kraus · 911 Mercantile Library Building 414 Walnut Street · Cincinnati, OH 45202 · 513-241-8137

Alan S. Belkin · (Individuals) · Shapiro, Turoff, Gisser & Belkin · 1200 Standard Building · Cleveland, OH 44113 · 216-241-8080

Jeffrey A. Belkin · (Management) · Hahn, Loeser & Parks · 800 National City East Sixth Building · Cleveland, OH 44114 · 216-621-0150

Gerald B. Chattman · Chattman, Garfield, Friedlander & Paul · 400 Engineers Building · Cleveland, OH 44114 · 216-621-4422

Ronald L. Coleman · (Management) · Squire, Sanders & Dempsey · 1800 Huntington Building · Cleveland, OH 44115 · 216-687-8500

Robert P. Duvin · (Management) · Duvin, Cahn & Barnard · 1400 TransOhio Tower · 2000 East Ninth Street · Cleveland, OH 44115 · 216-696-7600

Arthur A. Kola · (Management) · Squire, Sanders & Dempsey · 1800 Huntington Building · Cleveland, OH 44115 · 216-687-8500

Robert L. Larson · (Management) · Thompson, Hine and Flory · 1100 National City Bank Building · 629 Euclid Avenue · Cleveland, OH 44114 · 216-566-5500

Joseph A. Rotolo · (Management) · Arter & Hadden · 1100 Huntington Building Cleveland, OH 44115 · 216-696-1100

Joseph S. Ruggie, Jr. · (Management) · Thompson, Hine and Flory · 1100 National City Bank Building · 629 Euclid Avenue · Cleveland, OH 44114 · 216-566-5500

Melvin S. Schwarzwald · (Labor; Individuals) · Schwarzwald, Robiner, Rock & Levin · 616 Bond Court · 1300 East Ninth Street · Cleveland, OH 44114 · 216-566-1600

Victor Strimbu, Jr. · (Management) · Baker & Hostetler · 3200 National City Center · Cleveland, OH 44114 · 216-621-0200

Richard V. Whelan, Jr. · (Management) · Thompson, Hine and Flory · 1100 National City Bank Building · 629 Euclid Avenue · Cleveland, OH 44114 216-566-5500

Frederick M. Gittes · (Individuals) · Spater, Gittes & Terzian · 723 Oak Street Columbus, OH 43205 · 614-221-1160

N. Victor Goodman · (Labor) · Benesch, Friedlander, Coplan & Aronoff · 88 East Broad Street · Columbus, OH 43215 · 614-223-9300

Stuart M. Gordon · (Management) · Porter, Wright, Morris & Arthur · 41 South High Street · Columbus, OH 43215 · 614-227-2000

Dennis D. Grant · (Management) · Arter & Hadden · One Columbus, 21st Floor 10 West Broad Street · Columbus, OH 43215 · 614-221-3155

Louis A. Jacobs · (Individuals) · 3040 Riverside Drive · Columbus, OH 43221 614-486-0407

Stewart R. Jaffy · (Labor) · Stewart Jaffy & Associates · 306 East Gay Street Columbus, OH 43215 · 614-228-6148

G. Roger King · (Management) · Bricker & Eckler · 100 South Third Street · P.O. Box 100 · Columbus, OH 43218 · 614-227-2300

Alvin J. McKenna · (Management) · Porter, Wright, Morris & Arthur · 41 South High Street · Columbus, OH 43215 · 614-227-2000

Charles D. Minor · (Management) · Vorys, Sater, Seymour and Pease · 52 East Gay Street · P.O. Box 1008 · Columbus, OH 43216-1008 · 614-464-6400

Andrew J. Ruzicho · (Individuals) · 3040 Riverside Drive · Columbus, OH 43221 614-486-0407

David M. Selcer · (Management) · Baker & Hostetler · 65 East State Street Columbus, OH 43215 · 614-228-1541

Bradd N. Siegel · (Management) · Porter, Wright, Morris & Arthur · 41 South High Street · Columbus, OH 43215 · 614-227-2000

Alexander M. Spater · (Individuals) · Spater, Gittes & Terzian · 723 Oak Street Columbus, OH 43205 · 614-221-1160

Barbara A. Terzian · (Individuals) · Spater, Gittes & Terzian · 723 Oak Street Columbus, OH 43205 · 614-221-1160

Robert J. Brown · (Management) · Smith & Schnacke · 2000 Courthouse Plaza, NE · P.O. Box 1817 · Dayton, OH 45401 · 513-443-6500

Sorrell Logothetis · (Labor; Individuals) · Logothetis and Pence · 111 West First Street, Suite 1100 · Dayton, OH 45402 · 513-461-5310

Leonard S. Sigall · (Labor) · 6470 East Main Street · Reynoldsburg, OH 43068 614-866-3731

Harland M. Britz · (Individuals) · Britz and Zemmelman · 414 North Erie Street, Suite 100 · Toledo, OH 43624-2399 · 419-242-7415

James F. Duggan · (Management) · Spengler, Nathanson, Heyman, McCarthy & Durfee · 1000 National Bank Building · Toledo, OH 43604 · 419-241-2201

Donald W. Fisher · (Labor) · 1320 National Bank Building · Toledo, OH 43604-1108 · 419-255-7368

Jack E. Gallon · (Labor) · Gallon, Kalniz & Iorio · 3161 North Republic Boulevard · Toledo, OH 43615 · 419-535-1976

Theodore M. Iorio · (Labor) · Gallon, Kalniz & Iorio · 3161 North Republic Boulevard · Toledo, OH 43615 · 419-535-1976

Justice G. Johnson, Jr. · (Management) · Marshall & Melhorn · Four Seagate, Eighth Floor · Toledo, OH 43604 · 419-249-7100

Patrick J. Johnson · (Management) · Eastman & Smith · 800 United Savings Building · 240 Huron Street · Toledo, OH 43604-1141 · 419-241-6000

Jeffrey Julius · (Labor) · Gallon, Kalniz & Iorio · 5550 West Central Avenue Toledo, OH 43615 · 419-535-1976

Gerald B. Lackey · (Labor) · Lackey, Nusbaum, Harris, Reny & Torzewski Two Maritime Plaza, Third Floor · Toledo, OH 43604 · 419-243-1105

John G. Mattimoe · (Management) · Marshall & Melhorn · Four Seagate, Eighth Floor · Toledo, OH 43604 · 419-249-7100

Donald M. Mewhort, Jr. · (Management) · Shumaker, Loop & Kendrick · North Courthouse Square · 1000 Jackson · Toledo, OH 43624-1573 · 419-241-4201

Rolf H. Scheidel · (Management) · Shumaker, Loop & Kendrick · North Courthouse Square · 1000 Jackson · Toledo, OH 43624-1573 · 419-241-4201

Anthony P. Sgambati II · (Labor) · Green, Haines, Sgambati, Murphy & Macala Dollar Bank Building, Fourth Floor · P.O. Box 849 · Youngstown, OH 44501 216-743-5101

MARITIME LAW

David G. Davies · Ray, Robinson, Hanninen & Carle · 1650 East Ohio Building 1717 East Ninth Street · Cleveland, OH 44114-2898 · 216-861-4533

Robert G. McCreary · Arter & Hadden · 1100 Huntington Building · Cleveland, OH 44115 · 216-696-1100

Thomas O. Murphy · Thompson, Hine and Flory · 1100 National City Bank Building · 629 Euclid Avenue · Cleveland, OH 44114 · 216-566-5500

NATURAL RESOURCES AND ENVIRONMENTAL LAW

William L. Caplan · Buckingham, Doolittle & Burroughs · Akron Centre Plaza 50 South Main Street · P.O. Box 1500 · Akron, OH 44309-1500 · 216-376-5300

Russell S. Frye · Smith & Schnacke · 2900 DuBois Tower · 511 Walnut Street · Cincinnati, OH 45202 · 513-443-6500

Thomas T. Terp · Taft, Stettinius & Hollister · 1800 First National Bank Center Fountain Square · Cincinnati, OH 45202 · 513-381-2838

G. David Van Epps · Frost & Jacobs · 2500 Central Trust Center · 201 East Fourth Street · Cincinnati, OH 45202 · 513-651-6800

Van Carson · Squire, Sanders & Dempsey · 1800 Huntington Building · Cleveland, OH 44115 · 216-687-8500

Michael A. Cyphert · Thompson, Hine and Flory · 1100 National City Bank Building · 629 Euclid Avenue · Cleveland, OH 44114 · 216-566-5500

William W. Falsgraf · Baker & Hostetler · 3200 National City Center · Cleveland, OH 44114 · 216-621-0200

James M. Friedman · Benesch, Friedlander, Coplan & Aronoff · 1100 Citizens Building · 850 Euclid Avenue · Cleveland, OH 44114 · 216-363-4500

Michael L. Hardy · Thompson, Hine and Flory · 1100 National City Bank Building · 629 Euclid Avenue · Cleveland, OH 44114 · 216-566-5500

Kenneth C. Moore · Squire, Sanders & Dempsey · 1800 Huntington Building · Cleveland, OH 44115 · 216-687-8500

John W. Edwards · (Coal) · Smith & Schnacke · 41 South High Street, Suite 2250 · Columbus, OH 43215 · 614-224-6500

J. Richard Emens · (Oil & Gas) · Emens, Hurd, Kegler & Ritter · Capitol Square · 65 East State Street · Columbus, OH 43215 · 614-462-5400

John W. Hoberg · Vorys, Sater, Seymour and Pease · 52 East Gay Street · P.O. Box 1008 · Columbus, OH 43216-1008 · 614-464-6400

J. Jeffrey McNealey · Porter, Wright, Morris & Arthur · 41 South High Street · Columbus, OH 43215 · 614-227-2000

Richard T. Sargeant · Eastman & Smith · 800 United Savings Building · 240 Huron Street · Toledo, OH 43604-1141 · 419-241-6000

Louis E. Tosi · Fuller & Henry · One SeaGate, 17th Floor · P.O. Box 2088 · Toledo, OH 43603-2088 · 419-247-2500

PERSONAL INJURY LITIGATION

K. Richard Aughenbaugh · (Defendants) · Roetzel & Andress · 75 East Market Street · Akron, OH 44308 · 216-376-2700

Orville L. Reed III · (Defendants) · Buckingham, Doolittle & Burroughs · Akron Centre Plaza · 50 South Main Street · P.O. Box 1500 · Akron, OH 44309-1500 · 216-376-5300

Timothy F. Scanlon · (Plaintiffs) · Scanlon & Gearinger · 1100 First National Tower · 106 South Main Street · Akron, OH 44308-1463 · 216-376-4558

Stanley M. Chesley · (Plaintiffs) · Waite, Schneider, Bayless & Chesley · 1513 Central Trust Tower · Fourth & Vine Streets · Cincinnati, OH 45202 · 513-621-0267

Clement J. DeMichelis · (Defendants) · McCaslin, Imbus & McCaslin · 1200 Gwynne Building · 602 Main Street · Cincinnati, OH 45202 · 513-421-4646

Louis F. Gilligan · Keating, Muething & Klekamp · Provident Tower, 18th Floor One East Fourth Street · Cincinnati, OH 45202 · 513-579-6400

Jacob K. Stein · (Defendants) · Paxton & Seasongood · 1700 Central Trust Tower Cincinnati, OH 45202 · 513-352-6700

Glenn V. Whitaker · (Plaintiffs) · Graydon, Head & Ritchey · 1900 Fifth Third Center · P.O. Box 6464 · Cincinnati, OH 45201 · 513-621-6464

Frank C. Woodside III · (Defendants) · Dinsmore & Shohl · 2100 Fountain Square Plaza · 511 Walnut Street · P.O. Box 2547 · Cincinnati, OH 45202-3172 513-977-8200

Charles F. Clarke · (Defendants) · Squire, Sanders & Dempsey · 1800 Huntington Building · Cleveland, OH 44115 · 216-687-8500

Burt J. Fulton · (Defendants) · Gallagher, Sharp, Fulton & Norman · Bulkley Building, Sixth Floor · 1501 Euclid Avenue · Cleveland, OH 44115 · 216-241-5310

Michael R. Gallagher · (Defendants) · Gallagher, Sharp, Fulton & Norman · Bulkley Building, Sixth Floor · 1501 Euclid Avenue · Cleveland, OH 44115 216-241-5310

Don C. Iler · (Plaintiffs) · 1640 Standard Building · Cleveland, OH 44113 · 216-696-5700

Charles Kampinski · (Plaintiffs) · 1530 Standard Building · 1370 Ontario Street Cleveland, OH 44113 · 216-781-4110

Robert Eric Kennedy · (Plaintiffs) · Weisman, Goldberg, Weisman & Kaufman 540 Leader Building · Cleveland, OH 44114 · 216-781-1111

Charles W. Kitchen · (Defendants) · Kitchen, Messner & Deery · Illuminating Building, Suite 1100 · 55 Public Square · Cleveland, OH 44113 · 216-241-5614

John D. Liber · (Plaintiffs) · Spangenberg, Shibley, Traci & Lancione · 1500 National City Bank Building · Cleveland, OH 44114-3062 · 216-696-3232

Robert C. Maynard · (Defendants) · Jacobson, Maynard, Tuschman & Kalur · 100 Erieview Plaza, 14th Floor · Cleveland, OH 44114 · 216-621-5400

Patrick F. McCartan · (Defendants) · Jones, Day, Reavis & Pogue · North Point · 901 Lakeside Avenue · Cleveland, OH 44114 · 216-586-3939

Harley J. McNeal · (Defendants) · McNeal, Schick, Archibald & Biro · Illuminating Building, 10th Floor · 55 Public Square · Cleveland, OH 44113 · 216-621-9870

Forrest A. Norman · (Defendants) · Gallagher, Sharp, Fulton & Norman · Bulkley Building, Sixth Floor · 1501 Euclid Avenue · Cleveland, OH 44115 · 216-241-5310

Marshall I. Nurenberg · (Plaintiffs) · Nurenberg, Plevin, Heller & McCarthy · Engineers Building, Seventh Floor · Cleveland, OH 44114 · 216-621-2300

Mark O'Neill · (Defendants) · Weston, Hurd, Fallon, Paisley & Howley · 2500 Terminal Tower · Cleveland, OH 44113-2241 · 216-241-6602

Louis Paisley · (Defendants) · Weston, Hurd, Fallon, Paisley & Howley · 2500 Terminal Tower · Cleveland, OH 44113-2241 · 216-241-6602

Keith E. Spero · (Plaintiffs) · Spero & Rosenfield · 113 St. Clair Avenue, Suite 500 · Cleveland, OH 44114-1211 · 216-771-1255

Lawrence E. Stewart · (Plaintiffs) · Stewart and DeChant · The Atrium Office Plaza, Suite 850 · 668 Euclid Avenue · Cleveland, OH 44114-3060 · 216-781-2258

Donald P. Traci · (Plaintiffs) · Spangenberg, Shibley, Traci & Lancione · 1500 National City Bank Building · Cleveland, OH 44114-3062 · 216-696-3232

Fred Weisman · (Plaintiffs) · Weisman, Goldberg, Weisman & Kaufman · 540 Leader Building · Cleveland, OH 44114 · 216-781-1111

Louis E. Gerber · (Defendants) · Arter & Hadden · One Columbus, 21st Floor · 10 West Broad Street · Columbus, OH 43215 · 614-221-3155

C. Richard Grieser · (Plaintiffs) · Grieser, Schafer, Blumenstiel & Slane · 261 West Johnstown Road · Columbus, OH 43230 · 614-475-9511

William L. Millard · (Defendants) · Lane, Alton & Horst · 175 South Third Street, Seventh Floor · Columbus, OH 43215 · 614-228-6885

Terrance M. Miller · (Defendants) · Porter, Wright, Morris & Arthur · 41 South High Street · Columbus, OH 43215 · 614-227-2000

James S. Monahan · (Defendants) · Bricker & Eckler · 100 South Third Street P.O. Box 100 · Columbus, OH 43218 · 614-227-2300

James S. Oliphant · (Defendants) · Porter, Wright, Morris & Arthur · 41 South High Street · Columbus, OH 43215 · 614-227-2000

James E. Pohlman · (Defendants) · Porter, Wright, Morris & Arthur · 41 South High Street · Columbus, OH 43215 · 614-227-2000

Alan T. Radnor · (Plaintiffs) · Vorys, Sater, Seymour and Pease · 52 East Gay Street · P.O. Box 1008 · Columbus, OH 43216-1008 · 614-464-6400

Frank A. Ray · (Plaintiffs) · 330 South High Street · Columbus, OH 43215-4510 614-221-7791

Hans Scherner · (Plaintiffs) · Scherner & Hanson · 130 Northwoods Boulevard Columbus, OH 43235 · 614-431-7200

Edgar A. Strause · (Defendants) · Vorys, Sater, Seymour and Pease · 52 East Gay Street · P.O. Box 1008 · Columbus, OH 43216-1008 · 614-464-6400

Thomas M. Tyack · (Plaintiffs) · Thomas M. Tyack & Associates · 536 South High Street · Columbus, OH 43215 · 614-221-1341

James J. Gilvary · (Defendants) · Smith & Schnacke · 2000 Courthouse Plaza, NE · P.O. Box 1817 · Dayton, OH 45401 · 513-443-6500

David C. Greer · (Defendants) · Bieser, Greer & Landis · 400 Gem Plaza · Third and Main Streets · Dayton, OH 45402 · 513-223-3277

Thomas E. Jenks · (Defendants) · Jenks, Surdyk & Cowdrey · 205 East First Street · Dayton, OH 45402 · 513-222-2333

Charles D. Lowe · (Plaintiffs) · Cowden, Pfarrer, Crew & Becker · 2580 Kettering Tower · Dayton, OH 45423 · 513-223-6211

Irving I. Saul · (Plaintiffs) · 113 Bethpolamy Court · Dayton, OH 45415 · 513-278-4858

Robert G. Clayton, Jr. · (Defendants) · Shumaker, Loop & Kendrick · North Courthouse Square · 1000 Jackson · Toledo, OH 43624-1573 · 419-241-9000

William M. Connelly · (Plaintiffs) · Connelly, Soutar & Jackson · 2100 Ohio Citizens Bank Building · Toledo, OH 43604 · 419-243-2100

John M. Curphey · (Defendants) · Robison, Curphey & O'Connell · Four SeaGate, Ninth Floor · Toledo, OH 43604 · 419-249-7900

John A. Harris III · (Plaintiffs) · Lackey, Nusbaum, Harris, Reny & Torzewski Two Maritime Plaza, Third Floor · Toledo, OH 43604 · 419-243-1105

James M. Tuschman · (Defendants) · Jacobson, Maynard, Tuschman & Kalur Four SeaGate, Ninth Floor · Toledo, OH 43604 · 419-249-7373

Martin W. Williams · (Plaintiffs) · Williams, Jilek and Lafferty · 500 Toledo Legal Building · 416 North Erie Street · Toledo, OH 43624-1696 · 419-241-2122

David C. Comstock · (Defendants) · Comstock, Springer & Wilson · 926 City Centre One · P.O. Box 6306 · Youngstown, OH 44501-6306 · 216-746-5643

Bernard J. Wilkes · (Defendants) · Wilkes & Wilkes · 824 City Centre One · P.O. Box 6305 · Youngstown, OH 44501 · 216-744-2168

REAL ESTATE LAW

John N. Teeple · Geiger, Teeple, Smith & Hahn · 404 Bank One Building · Alliance, OH 44601 · 216-821-1430

Edward D. Diller · Taft, Stettinius & Hollister · 1800 First National Bank Center · Fountain Square · Cincinnati, OH 45202 · 513-381-2838

Richard S. Roberts · Taft, Stettinius & Hollister · 1800 First National Bank Center · Fountain Square · Cincinnati, OH 45202 · 513-381-2838

Jay A. Rosenberg · Porter, Wright, Morris & Arthur · 250 East Fifth Street, Suite 4166 · Cincinnati, OH 45202 · 513-381-4700

Herbert B. Weiss · Smith & Schnacke · 2900 DuBois Tower · 511 Walnut Street · Cincinnati, OH 45202 · 513-443-6500

Jordan C. Band · Ulmer & Berne · 900 Bond Court Building · Cleveland, OH 44114 · 216-621-8400

George R. Barry · Squire, Sanders & Dempsey · 1800 Huntington Building · Cleveland, OH 44115 · 216-687-8500

Raymond J. Durn · Jones, Day, Reavis & Pogue · North Point · 901 Lakeside Avenue · Cleveland, OH 44114 · 216-586-3939

James J. Erb · Jones, Day, Reavis & Pogue · North Point · 901 Lakeside Avenue · Cleveland, OH 44114 · 216-586-3939

Bernard D. Goodman · Benesch, Friedlander, Coplan & Aronoff · 1100 Citizens Building · 850 Euclid Avenue · Cleveland, OH 44114 · 216-363-4500

Sidney B. Hopps · Squire, Sanders & Dempsey · 1800 Huntington Building · Cleveland, OH 44115 · 216-687-8500

Thomas A. Mason · Thompson, Hine and Flory · 1100 National City Bank Building · 629 Euclid Avenue · Cleveland, OH 44114 · 216-566-5500

James P. McAndrews · Benesch, Friedlander, Coplan & Aronoff · 1100 Citizens Building · 850 Euclid Avenue · Cleveland, OH 44114 · 216-363-4500

Albert P. Pickus · Squire, Sanders & Dempsey · 1800 Huntington Building · Cleveland, OH 44115 · 216-687-8500

Richard A. Rosner · Kahn, Kleinman, Yanowitz & Arnson · 1300 Bond Court Building · Cleveland, OH 44114-1546 · 216-696-3311

Lawrence C. Sherman · Kahn, Kleinman, Yanowitz & Arnson · 1300 Bond Court Building · Cleveland, OH 44114-1546 · 216-696-3311

Howard A. Steindler · Benesch, Friedlander, Coplan & Aronoff · 1100 Citizens Building · 850 Euclid Avenue · Cleveland, OH 44114 · 216-363-4500

George J. Umstead · Squire, Sanders & Dempsey · 1800 Huntington Building · Cleveland, OH 44115 · 216-687-8500

Lawrence H. Williams · Jones, Day, Reavis & Pogue · North Point · 901 Lakeside Avenue · Cleveland, OH 44114 · 216-586-3939

Stanley A. Williams · Arter & Hadden · 1100 Huntington Building · Cleveland, OH 44115 · 216-696-1100

David G. Baker · Bricker & Eckler · 100 South Third Street · P.O. Box 100 · Columbus, OH 43218 · 614-227-2300

Stephen R. Buchenroth · Vorys, Sater, Seymour and Pease · 52 East Gay Street P.O. Box 1008 · Columbus, OH 43216-1008 · 614-464-6400

James B. Cushman · Vorys, Sater, Seymour and Pease · 52 East Gay Street · P.O. Box 1008 · Columbus, OH 43216-1008 · 614-464-6400

Howard J. Haddow · Folkerth, O'Brien, Haddow & Davis · 230 East Town Street · Columbus, OH 43215-4656 · 614-228-2945

Richard G. Ison · Vorys, Sater, Seymour and Pease · 52 East Gay Street · P.O. Box 1008 · Columbus, OH 43216-1008 · 614-464-6400

Robert C. Kiger · Porter, Wright, Morris & Arthur · 41 South High Street Columbus, OH 43215 · 614-227-2000

Kenton L. Kuehnle · Thompson, Hine and Flory · 100 East Broad Street, 18th Floor · Columbus, OH 43215 · 614-461-6060

Richard L. Loveland · Loveland & Brosius · 50 West Broad Street, Suite 1016 Columbus, OH 43215 · 614-464-3563

Steven J. McCoy · Vorys, Sater, Seymour and Pease · 52 East Gay Street · P.O. Box 1008 · Columbus, OH 43216-1008 · 614-464-6400

Davis S. Sidor · Squire, Sanders & Dempsey · BancOhio National Plaza · 155 East Broad Street · Columbus, OH 43215 · 614-365-2700

Norman T. Smith · Porter, Wright, Morris & Arthur · 41 South High Street Columbus, OH 43215 · 614-227-2000

Robert M. Curry · Smith & Schnacke · 2000 Courthouse Plaza, NE · P.O. Box 1817 · Dayton, OH 45401 · 513-443-6500

J. Stephen Herbert · Coolidge, Wall, Womsley & Lombard · 600 IBM Building 33 West First Street · Dayton, OH 45402 · 513-223-8177

Richard H. Packard · Porter, Wright, Morris & Arthur · 2100 First National Bank Building · Dayton, OH 45402 · 513-228-2411

Edward L. Shank · Bieser, Greer & Landis · 400 Gem Plaza · Third and Main Streets · Dayton, OH 45402 · 513-223-3277

Robert L. Hausser · 406 Dime Bank Building · Marietta, OH 45750 · 614-373-1661

Jerome R. Parker · Gressley, Kaplin, Parker & Frederickson · 1600 Toledo Trust Building · 245 North Summit Street · Toledo, OH 43604-1539 · 419-244-8336

Joseph A. Rideout · Shumaker, Loop & Kendrick · North Courthouse Square 1000 Jackson · Toledo, OH 43624-1573 · 419-241-4201

Barton L. Wagenman · Shumaker, Loop & Kendrick · North Courthouse Square 1000 Jackson · Toledo, OH 43624-1573 · 419-241-4201

TAX AND EMPLOYEE BENEFITS LAW

Frank A. Lettieri · Amer Cunningham Brennan · Society Building, Sixth Floor Akron, OH 44308 · 216-762-2411

Robert W. Malone · Buckingham, Doolittle & Burroughs · 50 South Main Street Akron Centre Plaza · P.O Box 1500 · Akron, OH 44309-1500 · 216-376-5300

David H. Wilson · Buckingham, Doolittle & Burroughs · 50 South Main Street Akron Centre Plaza · P.O Box 1500 · Akron, OH 44309-1500 · 216-376-5300

Mark H. Berliant · Strauss & Troy · 2100 Central Trust Center · 201 East Fifth Street · Cincinnati, OH 45202 · 513-621-2120

Bart A. Brown, Jr. · Keating, Muething & Klekamp · Provident Tower, 18th Floor · One East Fourth Street · Cincinnati, OH 45202 · 513-579-6400

Scott B. Crooks · (Employee Benefits) · Smith & Schnacke · 2900 DuBois Tower 511 Walnut Street · Cincinnati, OH 45202 · 513-352-6500

Jerold A. Fink · (Employee Benefits) · Taft, Stettinius & Hollister · 1800 First National Bank Center · Fountain Square · Cincinnati, OH 45202 · 513-381-2838

William M. Freedman · (also Employee Benefits) · Dinsmore & Shohl · 2100 Fountain Square Plaza · 511 Walnut Street · P.O. Box 2547 · Cincinnati, OH 45202-3172 · 513-977-8200

Ronald E. Heinlen · Frost & Jacobs · 2500 Central Trust Center · 201 East Fifth Street · Cincinnati, OH 45202 · 513-651-6800

Stephen M. Nechemias · Taft, Stettinius & Hollister · 1800 First National Bank Center · Fountain Square · Cincinnati, OH 45202 · 513-381-2838

James J. Ryan · Taft, Stettinius & Hollister · 1800 First National Bank Center Fountain Square · Cincinnati, OH 45202 · 513-381-2838

Stephen J. Alfred · Squire, Sanders & Dempsey · 1800 Huntington Building · Cleveland, OH 44115 · 216-687-8500

Patrick J. Amer · Spieth, Bell, McCurdy & Newell · 2000 Huntington Building Cleveland, OH 44115-1496 · 216-696-4700

Malvin E. Bank · Thompson, Hine and Flory · 1100 National City Bank Building 629 Euclid Avenue · Cleveland, OH 44114 · 216-566-5500

Lewis T. Barr · Weston, Hurd, Fallon, Paisley & Howley · 2500 Terminal Tower Cleveland, OH 44113-2241 · 216-241-6602

Hugh Calkins · Jones, Day, Reavis & Pogue · North Point · 901 Lakeside Avenue Cleveland, OH 44114 · 216-586-3939

David Lyle Carpenter · Calfee, Halter & Griswold · 1800 Society Building · East Ninth and Superior · Cleveland, OH 44114-2688 · 216-781-2166

William H. Conner · Squire, Sanders & Dempsey · 1800 Huntington Building Cleveland, OH 44115 · 216-687-8500

Alan Doris · Benesch, Friedlander, Coplan & Aronoff · 1100 Citizens Building 850 Euclid Avenue · Cleveland, OH 44114 · 216-363-4500

Robert E. Glaser · Arter & Hadden · 1100 Huntington Building · Cleveland, OH 44115 · 216-696-1100

Thomas A. Jorgensen · (Employee Benefits) · Calfee, Halter & Griswold · 1800 Society Building · East Ninth and Superior · Cleveland, OH 44114-2688 · 216-781-2166

Stephen L. Kadish · Kadish & Bender · 2112 East Ohio Building · Cleveland, OH 44114 · 216-696-3030

Richard Katcher · Baker & Hostetler · 3200 National City Center · Cleveland, OH 44114 · 216-621-0200

Charles J. Kerester · Jones, Day, Reavis & Pogue · North Point · 901 Lakeside Avenue · Cleveland, OH 44114 · 216-586-3939

N. Herschel Koblenz · Hahn Loeser & Parks · 800 National City East Sixth Building · Cleveland, OH 44114 · 216-621-0150

Donald L. Korb · Thompson, Hine and Flory · 1100 National City Bank Building· 629 Euclid Avenue · Cleveland, OH 44114 · 216-566-5500

Herbert B. Levine · Ulmer & Berne · 900 Bond Court Building · Cleveland, OH 44114 · 216-621-8400

W. James Ollinger · (Employee Benefits) · Baker & Hostetler · 3200 National City Center · Cleveland, OH 44114 · 216-621-0200

Terrence G. Perris · Squire, Sanders & Dempsey · 1800 Huntington Building Cleveland, OH 44115 · 216-687-8500

Carlton B. Schnell · Arter & Hadden · 1100 Huntington Building · Cleveland, OH 44115 · 216-696-1100

William R. Stewart · Thompson, Hine and Flory · 1100 National City Bank Building · 629 Euclid Avenue · Cleveland, OH 44114 · 216-566-5500

William M. Toomajian · Baker & Hostetler · 3200 National City Center · Cleveland, OH 44114 · 216-621-0200

Kenneth E. Updegraft, Jr. · Jones, Day, Reavis & Pogue · North Point · 901 Lakeside Avenue · Cleveland, OH 44114 · 216-586-3939

Richard T. Watson · Spieth, Bell, McCurdy & Newell · 2000 Huntington Building · Cleveland, OH 44115-1496 · 216-696-4700

Jeffry L. Weiler · Benesch, Friedlander, Coplan & Aronoff · 1100 Citizens Building · 850 Euclid Avenue · Cleveland, OH 44114 · 216-363-4500

Jon M. Anderson · Porter, Wright, Morris & Arthur · 41 South High Street Columbus, OH 43215 · 614-227-2000

Kenneth D. Beck · Vorys, Sater, Seymour and Pease · 52 East Gay Street · P.O. Box 1008 · Columbus, OH 43216-1008 · 614-464-6400

Michael R. Becker · Isaac, Brant, Ledman & Becker · The Midland Building 250 East Broad Street · Columbus, OH 43215 · 614-221-2121

John A. Dunkel · Porter, Wright, Morris & Arthur · 41 South High Street Columbus, OH 43215 · 614-227-2000

William W. Ellis, Jr. · (also Employee Benefits) · Vorys, Sater, Seymour and Pease · 52 East Gay Street · P.O. Box 1008 · Columbus, OH 43216-1008 614-464-6400

Daniel M. Maher · (Employee Benefits) · Squire, Sanders & Dempsey · Banc Ohio National Plaza · 155 East Broad Street · Columbus, OH 43215 · 614-365-2700

Michael A. Mess · Bricker & Eckler · 100 South Third Street · P.O. Box 100 Columbus, OH 43218 · 614-227-2300

Richard R. Murphey, Jr. · Squire, Sanders & Dempsey · BancOhio National Plaza · 155 East Broad Street · Columbus, OH 43215 · 614-365-2700

Elbert R. Nester · (Employee Benefits) · Nester & Kovaks · 65 East State Street Columbus, OH 43215 · 614-461-9294

Paul D. Ritter, Jr. · (also Employee Benefits) · Emens, Hurd, Kegler & Ritter Capitol Square · 65 East State Street · Columbus, OH 43215 · 614-462-5400

Ronald L. Rowland · Vorys, Sater, Seymour and Pease · 52 East Gay Street · P.O. Box 1008 · Columbus, OH 43216-1008 · 614-464-6400

Fredric L. Smith · Squire, Sanders & Dempsey · BancOhio National Plaza · 155 East Broad Street · Columbus, OH 43215 · 614-365-2700

Richard R. Stedman · Vorys, Sater, Seymour and Pease · 52 East Gay Street P.O. Box 1008 · Columbus, OH 43216-1008 · 614-464-6400

John Terakedis, Jr. · (Employee Benefits) · Porter, Wright, Morris & Arthur · 41 South High Street · Columbus, OH 43215 · 614-227-2000

Ralph E. Heyman · Smith & Schnacke · 2000 Courthouse Plaza, NE · P.O. Box 1817 · Dayton, OH 45401 · 513-443-6500

Ronald A. Kladder · (Employee Benefits) · Smith & Schnacke · 2000 Courthouse Plaza, NE · P.O. Box 1817 · Dayton, OH 45401 · 513-443-6500

Bruce R. Lowry · Smith & Schnacke · 2000 Courthouse Plaza, NE · P.O. Box 1817 · Dayton, OH 45401 · 513-443-6500

Marc Gertner · (Employee Benefits) · Shumaker, Loop & Kendrick · North Courthouse Square · 1000 Jackson · Toledo, OH 43624-1573 · 419-241-4201

Frank D. Jacobs · Eastman & Smith · 800 United Savings Building · 240 Huron Street · Toledo, OH 43604-1141 · 419-241-6000

David F. Waterman · Shumaker, Loop & Kendrick · North Courthouse Square 1000 Jackson · Toledo, OH 43624-1573 · 419-241-4201

James F. White, Jr. · Shumaker, Loop & Kendrick · North Courthouse Square 1000 Jackson · Toledo, OH 43624-1573 · 419-241-4201

TRUSTS AND ESTATES

Patricia A. Pacenta · Buckingham, Doolittle & Burroughs · Akron Centre Plaza 50 South Main Street · P.O. Box 1500 · Akron, OH 44309-1500 · 216-376-5300

Michael L. Stark · Stark & Knoll · 1512 Ohio Edison Building · 76 South Main Street · Akron, OH 44308 · 216-376-3300

Cynthia F. Blank · Taft, Stettinius & Hollister · 1800 First National Bank Center Fountain Square · Cincinnati, OH 45202 · 513-381-2838

Joseph A. Brant · Katz, Teller, Brant & Hild · 1400 Tri-State Building · Cincinnati, OH 45202 · 513-721-4532

Wiley Dinsmore · Dinsmore & Shohl · 2100 Fountain Square Plaza · 511 Walnut Street · P.O. Box 2547 · Cincinnati, OH 45202-3172 · 513-977-8200

Jon Hoffheimer · 1006 Mercantile Library Building · 414 Walnut Street · Cincinnati, OH 45202 · 513-721-2180

Robert S. Marriott · Graydon, Head & Ritchey · 1900 Fifth Third Center · P.O. Box 6464 · Cincinnati, OH 45201 · 513-621-6464

T. Stephen Phillips · Frost & Jacobs · 2500 Central Trust Center · 201 East Fifth Street · Cincinnati, OH 45202 · 513-651-6800

James S. Wachs · Frost & Jacobs · 2500 Central Trust Center · 201 East Fifth Street · Cincinnati, OH 45202 · 513-651-6800

Oakley V. Andrews · Baker & Hostetler · 3200 National City Center · Cleveland, OH 44114 · 216-621-0200

Robert M. Brucken · Baker & Hostetler · 3200 National City Center · Cleveland, OH 44114 · 216-621-0200

J. Donald Cairns · Squire, Sanders & Dempsey · 1800 Huntington Building Cleveland, OH 44115 · 216-687-8500

Charles M. Driggs · Squire, Sanders & Dempsey · 1800 Huntington Building Cleveland, OH 44115 · 216-687-8500

Andrew L. Fabens III · Thompson, Hine and Flory · 1100 National City Bank Building · 629 Euclid Avenue · Cleveland, OH 44114 · 216-566-5500

Harold Fallon · Weston, Hurd, Fallon, Paisley & Howley · 2500 Terminal Tower Cleveland, OH 44113-2241 · 216-241-6602

Kenneth G. Hochman · Jones, Day, Reavis & Pogue · North Point · 901 Lakeside Avenue · Cleveland, OH 44114 · 216-586-3939

Leslie L. Knowlton · Arter & Hadden · 1100 Huntington Building · Cleveland, OH 44115 · 216-696-1100

Charles W. Landefeld · Arter & Hadden · 1100 Huntington Building · Cleveland, OH 44115 · 216-696-1100

Paul L. Millet · Millet & Sprague · Four Commerce Park Square, Suite 805 23200 Chagrin Boulevard · Cleveland, OH 44122 · 216-765-1188

Jerome D. Neifach · Arter & Hadden · 1100 Huntington Building · Cleveland, OH 44115 · 216-696-1100

Robert B. Nelson · Jones, Day, Reavis & Pogue · North Point · 901 Lakeside Avenue · Cleveland, OH 44114 · 216-586-3939

Sidney Nudelman · Hahn Loeser & Parks · 800 National City East Sixth Building Cleveland, OH 44114 · 216-621-0150

Lincoln Reavis · Spieth, Bell, McCurdy & Newell · 2000 Huntington Building Cleveland, OH 44115-1496 · 216-696-4700

Richard C. Renkert · Jones, Day, Reavis & Pogue · North Point · 901 Lakeside Avenue · Cleveland, OH 44114 · 216-586-3939

John E. Smeltz · Schneider, Smeltz, Huston & Ranney · 1525 National City Bank Building · Cleveland, OH 44114 · 216-696-4200

Leon A. Weiss · Reminger & Reminger · 113 St. Clair Building · Cleveland, OH 44114-1273 · 216-687-1311

Nelson E. Weiss · Burke, Haber & Berick · 300 National City Bank Building · 629 Euclid Avenue · Cleveland, OH 44114 · 216-771-2700

David C. Cummins · Bricker & Eckler · 100 South Third Street · P.O. Box 100 Columbus, OH 43218 · 614-227-2300

William W. Ellis, Jr. · Vorys, Sater, Seymour and Pease · 52 East Gay Street · P.O. Box 1008 · Columbus, OH 43216-1008 · 614-464-6400

Lawrence L. Fisher · Vorys, Sater, Seymour and Pease · 52 East Gay Street · P.O. Box 1008 · Columbus, OH 43216-1008 · 614-464-6400

Lloyd E. Fisher, Jr. · Porter, Wright, Morris & Arthur · 41 South High Street · Columbus, OH 43215 · 614-227-2000

Sol Morton Isaac · Isaac, Brant, Ledman & Becker · The Midland Building · 250 East Broad Street · Columbus, OH 43215 · 614-221-2121

Richard Heer Oman · Porter, Wright, Morris & Arthur · 41 South High Street · Columbus, OH 43215 · 614-227-2000

Marvin R. Pliskin · Squire, Sanders & Dempsey · BancOhio National Plaza · 155 East Broad Street · Columbus, OH 43215 · 614-365-2700

Robert K. Corwin · Altick & Corwin · 900 Talbott Tower · Dayton, OH 45402 · 513-223-1201

C. Terry Johnson · Smith & Schnacke · 2000 Courthouse Plaza, NE · P.O. Box 1817 · Dayton, OH 45401 · 513-443-6500

Crofford J. Macklin, Jr. · Smith & Schnacke · 2000 Courthouse Plaza, NE · P.O. Box 1817 · Dayton, OH 45401 · 513-443-6500

Donald G. Schweller · Pickrel, Schaeffer & Ebeling · 2700 Kettering Tower · Dayton, OH 45423 · 513-223-1130

Morton Bobowick · Eastman & Smith · 800 United Savings Building · 240 Huron Street · Toledo, OH 43604-1141 · 419-241-6000

Frank D. Jacobs · Eastman & Smith · 800 United Savings Building · 240 Huron Street · Toledo, OH 43604-1141 · 419-241-6000

Edward F. Weber · Marshall & Melhorn · Four Seagate, Eighth Floor · Toledo, OH 43604 · 419-249-7100

OKLAHOMA

BANKRUPTCY LAW	573
BUSINESS LITIGATION	575
CORPORATE LAW	577
CRIMINAL DEFENSE	579
FAMILY LAW	580
LABOR AND EMPLOYMENT LAW	580
NATURAL RESOURCES AND ENVIRONMENTAL LAW	582
PERSONAL INJURY LITIGATION	582
REAL ESTATE LAW	584
TAX AND EMPLOYEE BENEFITS LAW	585
TRUSTS AND ESTATES	587

BANKRUPTCY LAW

W. Rogers Abbott II · Abbott & Gordon · 500 Fidelity Plaza · Oklahoma City, OK 73102 · 405-232-2166

Richard R. Bailey · McClelland, Collins, Bailey, Bailey & Bellingham · Colcord Building, 11th Floor · 15 North Robinson · Oklahoma City, OK 73102 · 405-235-9371

Robert C. Bailey · McClelland, Collins, Bailey, Bailey & Bellingham · Colcord Building, 11th Floor · 15 North Robinson · Oklahoma City, OK 73102 · 405-235-9371

Gary A. Bryant · Mock, Schwabe, Waldo, Elder, Reeves & Bryant · One Leadership Square, 15th Floor · 211 North Robinson Avenue · Oklahoma City, OK 73102 · 405-235-5500

V. Burns Hargis · Reynolds, Ridings & Hargis · 2808 First National Center · Oklahoma City, OK 73102 · 405-232-8131

Kenneth I. Jones, Jr. · Jones, Blaney & Pringle · First City Place Building, 13th Floor · 204 North Robinson · P.O. Box 657 · Oklahoma City, OK 73101 · 405-235-8445

Jack L. Kinzie · Andrews Davis Legg Bixler Milsten and Murrah · 500 West Main Oklahoma City, OK 73102 · 405-272-9241

Michael Paul Kirschner · Hastie and Kirschner · 3000 First Oklahoma Tower 210 West Park Avenue · Oklahoma City, OK 73102 · 405-239-6404

David A. Kline · Kline & Kline · Kline Law Building · 720 Northeast 63rd Street Oklahoma City, OK 73105 · 405-848-4448

Timothy D. Kline · Kline & Kline · Kline Law Building · 720 Northeast 63rd Street · Oklahoma City, OK 73105 · 405-848-4448

Bruce McClelland · McClelland, Collins, Bailey, Bailey & Bellingham · Colcord Building, 11th Floor · 15 North Robinson · Oklahoma City, OK 73102 · 405-235-9371

D. Kent Meyers · Crowe & Dunlevy · 1800 Mid-America Tower · 20 North Broadway · Oklahoma City, OK 73102 · 405-235-7700

Ray G. Moss · Daugherty, Bradford, Fowler & Moss · 900 City Place · 204 North Robinson · Oklahoma City, OK 73102 · 405-232-0003

Don R. Nicholson II · Eagleton and Nicholson · Fidelity Plaza, Suite 310 · 201 West Robert S. Kerr Avenue · Oklahoma City, OK 73102 · 405-236-055-

Louis J. Price · McAfee & Taft · Two Leadership Square, 10th Floor · Oklahoma City, OK 73102 · 405-235-9621

Lynn A. Pringle · Jones, Blaney & Pringle · First City Place Building, 13th Floor 204 North Robinson · P.O. Box 657 · Oklahoma City, OK 73101 · 405-235-8445

Norman E. Reynolds · Reynolds, Ridings & Hargis · 2808 First National Center Oklahoma City, OK 73102 · 405-232-8131

G. Blaine Schwabe III · Mock, Schwabe, Waldo, Elder, Reeves & Bryant · One Leadership Square, 15th Floor · 211 North Robinson Avenue · Oklahoma City, OK 73102 · 405-235-5500

John W. Swinford, Jr. · Hastie and Kirschner · 3000 First Oklahoma Tower · 210 West Park Avenue · Oklahoma City, OK 73102 · 405-239-6404

Jerry Tubb · Fuller, Tubb & Pomeroy · 800 Fidelity Plaza · 201 Robert S. Kerr Avenue · Oklahoma City, OK 73102-4292 · 405-235-2575

Sam G. Bratton II · Doerner, Stuart, Saunders, Daniel & Anderson · 1000 Atlas Life Building · Tulsa, OK 74103 · 918-582-1211

Gary C. Clark · Baker, Hoster, McSpadden, Clark, Rasure & Slicker · 800 Kennedy Building · Tulsa, OK 74103 · 918-592-5555

Thomas E. English · English, Jones & Faulkner · 1700 Fourth National Bank Building · Tulsa, OK 74119 · 918-582-1564

Gary M. McDonald · Doerner, Stuart, Saunders, Daniel & Anderson · 1000 Atlas Life Building · Tulsa, OK 74103 · 918-582-1211

A. F. Ringold · Rosenstein, Fist & Ringold · 525 South Main, Suite 300 · Tulsa, OK 74103 · 918-585-9211

James R. Ryan · Conner & Winters · 2400 First National Tower · Tulsa, OK 74103 · 918-586-5711

BUSINESS LITIGATION

Burck Bailey · Fellers, Snider, Blankenship, Bailey & Tippens · 2400 First National Center · Oklahoma City, OK 73102 · 405-232-0621

Peter B. Bradford · Daugherty, Bradford, Fowler & Moss · 900 City Place · 204 North Robinson · Oklahoma City, OK 73102 · 405-232-0003

Andrew M. Coats · Crowe & Dunlevy · 1800 Mid-America Tower · 20 North Broadway · Oklahoma City, OK 73102 · 405-235-7700

Roy J. Davis · Andrews Davis Legg Bixler Milsten and Murrah · 500 West Main Oklahoma City, OK 73102 · 405-272-9241

John T. Edwards · Monnet, Hayes, Bullis, Thompson & Edwards · First National Center West, Suite 1719 · Oklahoma City, OK 73102 · 405-232-5481

Stephen P. Friot · Spradling, Alpern, Friot & Gum · Continental Savings Building, Suite 700 · 101 Park Avenue · Oklahoma City, OK 73102 · 405-272-0211

Robert H. Gilliland, Jr. · McAfee & Taft · Two Leadership Square, 10th Floor Oklahoma City, OK 73102 · 405-235-9621

James A. Kirk · Kirk & Chaney · Midland Center, Suite 1300 · Oklahoma City, OK 73102-6695 · 405-235-1333

James P. Linn · Linn & Helms · 1200 Fidelity Plaza · Robert S. Kerr at Robinson · Oklahoma City, OK 73102 · 405-239-6781

Kenneth N. McKinney · McKinney, Stringer & Webster · City Center Building, Eighth Floor · Main & Broadway · Oklahoma City, OK 73102 · 405-239-6444

Clyde A. Muchmore · Crowe & Dunlevy · 1800 Mid-America Tower · 20 North Broadway · Oklahoma City, OK 73102 · 405-235-7700

Jack L. (Drew) Neville, Jr. · Linn & Helms · 1200 Fidelity Plaza · Robert S. Kerr at Robinson Street · Oklahoma City, OK 73102 · 405-239-6781

Reid E. Robison · McAfee & Taft · Two Leadership Square, 10th Floor · Oklahoma City, OK 73102 · 405-235-9621

Patrick M. Ryan · Ryan, Holloman, Corbyn & Geister · 900 Robinson Renaissance · 119 North Robinson · Oklahoma City, OK 73102-4608 · 405-239-6041

Terry W. Tippens · Fellers, Snider, Blankenship, Bailey & Tippens · 2400 First National Center · Oklahoma City, OK 73102 · 405-232-0621

Harry A. Woods · Crowe & Dunlevy · 1800 Mid-America Tower · 20 North Broadway · Oklahoma City, OK 73102 · 405-235-7700

William C. Anderson · Doerner, Stuart, Saunders, Daniel & Anderson · 1000 Atlas Life Building · Tulsa, OK 74103 · 918-582-1211

John S. Athens · Conner & Winters · 2400 First National Tower · Tulsa, OK 74103 · 918-586-5711

B. Hayden Crawford · Crawford, Crowe & Bainbridge · 1714 First National Building · Tulsa, OK 74103 · 918-587-1128

Samuel P. Daniel, Jr. · Doerner, Stuart, Saunders, Daniel & Anderson · 1000 Atlas Life Building · Tulsa, OK 74103 · 918-582-1211

Sidney G. Dunagan · Gable & Gotwals · 2000 Fourth National Bank Building · Tulsa, OK 74119 · 918-582-9201

John M. Imel · Moyers, Martin, Santee, Imel & Tetrick · 320 South Boston Building, Suite 920 · Tulsa, OK 74103 · 918-582-5281

J. Warren Jackman · Pray, Walker, Jackman, Williamson & Marlar · ONEOK Plaza, Ninth Floor · Tulsa, OK 74103 · 918-584-4136

James L. Kincaid · Conner & Winters · 2400 First National Tower · Tulsa, OK 74103 · 918-586-5711

L. K. Smith · Boone, Smith, Davis & Hurst · 500 ONEOK Plaza · 100 West Fifth Street · Tulsa, OK 74103 · 918-587-0000

James M. Sturdivant · Gable & Gotwals · 2000 Fourth National Bank Building Tulsa, OK 74119 · 918-582-9201

Tom Hieronymus · Hieronymus, Hodgden & Meyer · 1002 Ninth Street · P.O. Box 529 · Woodward, OK 73802 · 405-256-5517

CORPORATE LAW

J. Edward Barth · Andrews Davis Legg Bixler Milsten and Murrah · 500 West Main · Oklahoma City, OK 73102 · 405-272-9241

Reford Bond · McAfee & Taft · Two Leadership Square, 10th Floor · Oklahoma City, OK 73102 · 405-235-9621

James F. Davis · Andrews, Davis, Legg, Bixler, Milsten and Murrah · 500 West Main · Oklahoma City, OK 73102 · 405-272-9241

Theodore M. Elam · McAfee & Taft · Two Leadership Square, 10th Floor Oklahoma City, OK 73102 · 405-235-9621

Irving L. Faught · Andrews, Davis, Legg, Bixler, Milsten and Murrah · 500 West Main · Oklahoma City, OK 73102 · 405-272-9241

James D. Fellers · Fellers, Snider, Blankenship, Bailey & Tippens · 2400 First National Center · Oklahoma City, OK 73102 · 405-232-0621

Lon Foster III · Crowe & Dunlevy · 1800 Mid-America Tower · 20 North Broadway · Oklahoma City, OK 73102 · 405-235-7700

Daniel J. Fowler · Daugherty, Bradford, Fowler & Moss · 900 First City Place 204 North Robinson · Oklahoma City, OK 73102 · 405-232-0003

Kent F. Frates · Frates & Farris · Colcord Building, Suite 610 · 15 North Robinson Oklahoma City, OK 73102 · 405-272-0616

Gary F. Fuller · McAfee & Taft · Two Leadership Square, 10th Floor · Oklahoma City, OK 73102 · 405-235-9621

James C. Gibbens · Crowe & Dunlevy · 1800 Mid-America Tower · 20 North Broadway · Oklahoma City, OK 73102 · 405-235-7700

James L. Hall, Jr. · Crowe & Dunlevy · 1800 Mid-America Tower · 20 North Broadway · Oklahoma City, OK 73102 · 405-235-7700

Charles B. Lutz, Jr. · Speck, Philbin, Fleig, Trudgeon & Lutz · 800 City Place 204 North Robinson · Oklahoma City, OK 73102 · 405-235-1603

John M. Mee · McAfee & Taft · Two Leadership Square, 10th Floor · Oklahoma City, OK 73102 · 405-235-9621

D. Kent Meyers · Crowe & Dunlevy · 1800 Mid-America Tower · 20 North Broadway · Oklahoma City, OK 73102 · 405-235-7700

D. Joe Rockett · Andrews Davis Legg Bixler Milsten and Murrah · 500 West Main Oklahoma City, OK 73102 · 405-272-9241

Michael M. Stewart · Crowe & Dunlevy · 1800 Mid-America Tower · 20 North Broadway · Oklahoma City, OK 73102 · 405-235-7700

Jerry Tubb · Fuller, Tubb & Pomeroy · 800 Fidelity Plaza · 201 Robert S. Kerr Avenue · Oklahoma City, OK 73102-4292 · 405-235-2575

John E. Barry · Conner & Winters · 2400 First National Tower · Tulsa, OK 74103 918-586-5711

Charles S. Chapel · Chapel, Wilkinson, Riggs & Abney · Frisco Building · 502 West Sixth Street · Tulsa, OK 74119 · 918-587-3161

Thomas D. Gable · Hall, Estill, Hardwick, Gable, Golden & Nelson · 4100 Bank of Oklahoma Tower · One Williams Center · Tulsa, OK 74172 · 918-588-2700

Thomas F. Golden · Hall, Estill, Hardwick, Gable, Golden & Nelson · 4100 Bank of Oklahoma Tower · One Williams Center · Tulsa, OK 74172 · 918-588-2700

John B. Johnson, Jr. · Gable & Gotwals · 2000 Fourth National Bank Building Tulsa, OK 74119 · 918-582-9201

Donald E. Pray · Pray, Walker, Jackman, Williamson & Marlar · ONEOK Plaza, Ninth Floor · Tulsa, OK 74103 · 918-584-4136

Dickson M. Saunders · Doerner, Stuart, Saunders, Daniel & Anderson · 1000 Atlas Life Building · Tulsa, OK 74103 · 918-582-1211

Patrick O. Waddel · Gable & Gotwals · 2000 Fourth National Bank Building · Tulsa, OK 74119 · 918-582-9201

CRIMINAL DEFENSE

Warren Gotcher · Gotcher, Brown & Bland · 209 East Wyandotte Street · P.O. Box 160 · McAlester, OK 74502 · 918-423-0412

Gene Stipe · Stipe, Gossett, Stipe, Harper, Estes, McCune & Parks · 323 East Carl Albert Parkway · P.O. Box 1368 · McAlester, OK 74501 · 918-423-0421

Burck Bailey · Fellers, Snider, Blankenship, Bailey & Tippens · 2400 First National Center · Oklahoma City, OK 73102 · 405-232-0621

James W. Bill Berry · Berry, Berry & Johnson · City Place, Suite 2500 · Oklahoma City, OK 73102 · 405-236-3167

Frank R. Courbois III · Courbois, Cox & Staggs · 2200 Classen Boulevard, Suite 2000 · Oklahoma City, OK 73106 · 405-235-7507

James P. Linn · Linn & Helms · 1200 Fidelity Plaza · Robert S. Kerr at Robinson · Oklahoma City, OK 73102 · 405-239-6781

D. C. Thomas · Thomas and Martin · Fidelity Plaza, Suite 504 · Oklahoma City, OK 73102 · 405-235-4300

Robert J. (Jim) Turner · Turner, Turner & Braun · 1319 Classen Drive · Oklahoma City, OK 73103 · 405-236-1646

Ronald H. Mook · 1560 East 21st Street, Suite 107 · Tulsa, OK 74114 · 918-583-7094

Larry L. Oliver · Larry L. Oliver & Associates · Oliver Building · 2211 East Skelly Drive · Tulsa, OK 74105-5913 · 918-745-6084

Patrick A. Williams · Williams & Savage · 324 Main Mall, Suite 600 · Tulsa, OK 74103 · 918-583-1338

FAMILY LAW

James W. Bill Berry · Berry, Berry & Johnson · First City Place, Suite 2500 Oklahoma City, OK 73102 · 405-236-3167

Arnold D. Fagin · Fagin, Lovell & Fagin · 531 Couch Drive · P.O. Box 26360 Oklahoma City, OK 73102 · 405-239-6771

Jon L. Hester · Jon L. Hester & Associates · 5400 Northwest Grand Boulevard, Suite 360 · Oklahoma City, OK 73112 · 405-947-8866

Philip F. Horning · Horning, Johnson, Grove, Moore & Hulett · City Place, Suite 1800 · Oklahoma City, OK 73102 · 405-232-3407

James A. Kirk · Kirk & Chaney · Midland Center, Suite 1300 · Oklahoma City, OK 73102-6695 · 405-235-1333

Robert J. (Jim) Turner · Turner, Turner & Braun · 1319 Classen Drive · Oklahoma City, OK 73103 · 405-236-1646

Samuel P. Daniel, Jr. · Doerner, Stuart, Saunders, Daniel & Anderson · 1000 Atlas Life Building · Tulsa, OK 74103 · 918-582-1211

William W. Hood, Jr. · Hood, Lindsey & Feamster · 1914 South Boston Avenue · Tulsa, OK 74119 · 918-583-5825

Arthur E. Rubin · James Gotwals & Associates · 525 South Main Street, Suite 1130 · Tulsa, OK 74103 · 918-599-7088

Don E. Williams · Naylor & Williams · 1701 South Boston Avenue · Tulsa, OK 74119 · 918-582-8000

LABOR AND EMPLOYMENT LAW

H. Leonard Court · (Management) · Crowe & Dunlevy · 1800 Mid-American Tower · 20 North Broadway · Oklahoma City, OK 73102 · 405-235-7700

Charles W. Ellis · (Management) · Lawrence, Ellis & Harmon · 602 Union Plaza 3030 Northwest Expressway · Oklahoma City, OK 73112 · 405-948-6000

Ben A. Goff · (Individuals) · 1212 Northwest 50th Street · Oklahoma City, OK 73118 · 405-843-8401

James L. Hall, Jr. · (Management) · Crowe & Dunlevy · 1800 Mid-American Tower · 20 North Broadway · Oklahoma City, OK 73102 · 405-235-7700

Mona S. Lambird · (Management) · Andrews Davis Legg Bixler Milsten and Murrah · 500 West Main · Oklahoma City, OK 73102 · 405-272-9241

George J. McCaffrey · (Labor; Individuals) · Lampkin, McCaffrey & Tawwater 245 Century Center · Oklahoma City, OK 73102 · 405-272-9611

James R. Moore · (Labor; Individuals) · Horning, Johnson, Grove, Moore & Hulett · First City Place, Suite 1800 · Oklahoma City, OK 73102 · 405-232-3407

Jerry D. Sokolosky · (Labor) · Abel, Musser, Sokolosky & Clark · One Leadership Square · 211 North Robinson, Suite 600 · Oklahoma City, OK 73102 · 405-239-7046

Peter T. Van Dyke · (Management) · Lytle Soule Curlee Harrington Chandler & Van Dyke · 1200 Robinson Renaissance · 119 North Robinson · Oklahoma City, OK 73102 · 405-235-7471

Thomas F. Birmingham · (Labor) · Ungerman, Conner & Little · Riverbridge Office Park, Suite 300 · 1323 East 71st Street · P.O. Box 2099 · Tulsa, OK 74101 918-495-0550

D. Gregory Bledsoe · (Individuals) · 1515 South Denver · Tulsa, OK 74119-3828 918-599-8118

Jon Patterson Bond · (Labor; Individuals) · Patterson Bond & Associates · 2626 East 21st Street, Suite Nine · Tulsa, OK 74114 · 918-743-4343

Louis W. Bullock · (Individuals) · Bullock and Bullock · 320 South Boston, Suite 718 · Tulsa, OK 74103 · 918-584-2001

J. Patrick Cremin · (Management) · Hall, Estill, Hardwick, Gable, Golden & Nelson · 4100 Bank of Oklahoma Tower · One Williams Center · Tulsa, OK 74172 918-588-2700

Lynn Paul Mattson · (Management) · Doerner, Stuart, Saunders, Daniel & Anderson · 1000 Atlas Life Building · Tulsa, OK 74103 · 918-582-1211

David E. Strecker · (Management) · Conner & Winters · 2400 First National Tower · Tulsa, OK 74103 · 918-586-5711

Maynard I. Ungerman · (Labor) · Ungerman, Conner & Little · Riverbridge Office Park, Suite 300 · 1323 East 71st Street · P.O. Box 2099 · Tulsa, OK 74101 · 918-495-0550

NATURAL RESOURCES AND ENVIRONMENTAL LAW

Stanley L. Cunningham · (Oil & Gas) · McAfee & Taft · Two Leadership Square, 10th Floor · Oklahoma City, OK 73102 · 405-235-9621

Philip D. Hart · (Oil & Gas) · McAfee & Taft · Two Leadership Square, 10th Floor · Oklahoma City, OK 73102 · 405-235-9621

William J. Legg · (Oil & Gas) · Andrews Davis Legg Bixler Milsten and Murrah · 500 West Main · Oklahoma City, OK 73102 · 405-272-9241

Barth P. Walker · (Oil & Gas) · Walker, Walker & Driskill · 3535 Northwest 58th Street, Suite 950 · Oklahoma City, OK 73112 · 405-943-9693

H. B. Watson, Jr. · (Oil & Gas) · Watson & McKenzie · 2900 Liberty Tower · 100 North Broadway · Oklahoma City, OK 73102 · 405-232-2501

James C. T. Hardwick · (Oil & Gas) · Hall, Estill, Hardwick, Gable, Collingsworth & Nelson · 4100 Bank of Oklahoma Tower · One Williams Center · Tulsa, OK 74172 · 918-588-2700

Joseph W. Morris · (Oil & Gas) · Gable & Gotwals · 2000 Fourth National Bank Building · 15 West Sixth Street · Tulsa, OK 74119 · 918-582-9201

W. Bland Williamson, Jr. · (Oil & Gas) · Pray, Walker, Jackman, Williamson & Marlar · ONEOK Plaza, Ninth Floor · Tulsa, OK 74103 · 918-584-4136

PERSONAL INJURY LITIGATION

Gene Stipe · (Plaintiffs) · Stipe, Gossett, Stipe, Harper, Estes, McCune & Parks · 323 East Carl Albert Parkway · P.O. Box 1368 · McAlester, OK 74502 · 918-423-0421

Ed Abel · (Plaintiffs) · Abel, Musser, Sokolosky & Clark · One Leadership Square · 211 North Robinson, Suite 600 · Oklahoma City, OK 73102 · 405-239-7046

Murray E. Abowitz · (Defendants) · Abowitz and Welch · 15 North Robinson, 10th Floor · P.O. Box 1937 · Oklahoma City, OK 73101 · 405-236-4645

Robert S. Baker · (Defendants) · Baker, Baker, Smith & Tait · 2140 Liberty Tower · Oklahoma City, OK 73102 · 405-232-3487

Howard K. Berry, Jr. · (Plaintiffs) · Berry & Berry · Berry Law Building · 1923 Classen Boulevard · Oklahoma City, OK 73106 · 405-524-0056

James W. Bill Berry · (Plaintiffs) · Berry, Berry & Johnson · City Place, Suite 2500 · Oklahoma City, OK 73102 · 405-236-3167

John R. Couch · (Defendants) · Pierce Couch Hendrickson Johnston & Baysinger · 1109 North Francis · P.O. Box 26350 · Oklahoma City, OK 73126 · 405-235-1611

James D. Foliart · (Defendants) · Foliart, Huff, Ottaway & Caldwell · First National Center, 20th Floor · Oklahoma City, OK 73102 · 405-232-4633

Calvin W. Hendrickson · (Defendants) · Pierce Couch Hendrickson Johnston & Baysinger · 1109 North Francis · P.O. Box 26350 · Oklahoma City, OK 73126 · 405-235-1611

Kenneth N. McKinney · (Defendants) · McKinney, Stringer & Webster · City Center Building, Eighth Floor · Main & Broadway · Oklahoma City, OK 73102 · 405-239-6444

Earl D. Mills · (Defendants) · Mills, Whitten, Mills, Mills & Hinkle · Two Leadership Square, Suite 810 · 211 North Robinson · Oklahoma City, OK 73102 · 405-239-2500

John W. Norman · (Plaintiffs) · 127 North 10th Street · Oklahoma City, OK 73103 · 405-272-0200

Patrick M. Ryan · Ryan, Holloman, Corbyn & Geister · 900 Robinson Renaissance · 119 North Robinson · Oklahoma City, OK 73102-4608 · 405-239-6041

George F. Short · (Defendants) · Short Barnes Wiggins Margo & Adler · 1400 American First Tower · Oklahoma City, OK 73102 · 405-232-1211

Kenneth R. Webster · McKinney, Stringer & Webster · City Center Building, Eighth Floor · Main & Broadway · Oklahoma City, OK 73102 · 405-239-6444

Joseph M. Best · (Defendants) · Best, Sharp, Sheridan & Stritzke · Kennedy Building, Suite 700 · 321 South Boston · Tulsa, OK 74103 · 918-582-8877

James E. Frasier · (Plaintiffs) · Frasier & Frasier · 1700 Southwest Boulevard, Suite 100 · Tulsa, OK 74127 · 918-584-4724

Richard D. Gibbon · (Defendants) · Gibbon, Gladd & Associates · 1611 South Harvard · Tulsa, OK 74112 · 918-745-0687

John A. Gladd · Gibbon, Gladd & Associates · 1611 South Harvard · Tulsa, OK 74112 · 918-745-0687

J. Warren Jackman · Pray, Walker, Jackman, Williamson & Marlar · ONEOK Plaza, Ninth Floor · Tulsa, OK 74103 · 918-584-4136

Alfred B. Knight · (Defendants) · Knight, Wagner, Stuart, Wilkerson & Lieber 233 West 11th · P.O. Box 1560 · Tulsa, OK 74101-1560 · 918-584-6457

James E. Poe · (Defendants) · Covington & Poe · Grantson Building, Suite 740 Tulsa, OK 74103 · 918-585-5537

REAL ESTATE LAW

Monty L. Bratcher · Bratcher & Teague · Herriman Building, Suite 500 · 923 North Robinson · Oklahoma City, OK 73102 · 405-272-0818

James C. Elder · Mock, Schwabe, Waldo, Elder, Reeves & Bryant · One Leadership Square, 15th Floor · 211 North Robinson Avenue · Oklahoma City, OK 73102 · 405-235-5500

James F. Hartmann, Jr. · Crowe & Dunlevy · 1800 Mid-America Tower · 20 North Broadway · Oklahoma City, OK 73102 · 405-235-7700

John D. Hastie · Hastie and Kirschner · 3000 First Oklahoma Tower · 210 West Park Avenue, Suite 3000 · Oklahoma City, OK 73102 · 405-239-6404

Frank D. Hill · McAfee & Taft · Two Leadership Square, 10th Floor · Oklahoma City, OK 73102 · 405-235-9621

Robert M. Johnson · Crowe & Dunlevy · 1800 Mid-America Tower · 20 North Broadway · Oklahoma City, OK 73102 · 405-235-7700

Warren E. Jones · Hastie and Kirschner · 3000 First Oklahoma Tower · 210 West Park Avenue, Suite 3000 · Oklahoma City, OK 73102 · 405-239-6404

Sally Mock · McAfee & Taft · Two Leadership Square, 10th Floor · Oklahoma City, OK 73102 · 405-235-9621

Henry P. Rheinberger · Crowe & Dunlevy · 1800 Mid-America Tower · 20 North Broadway · Oklahoma City, OK 73102 · 405-235-7700

Richard A. Riggs · McAfee & Taft · Two Leadership Square, 10th Floor · Oklahoma City, OK 73102 · 405-235-9621

Joe S. Rolston III · Elliott, Woodard, Rolston & Kelley · Lake Park Tower, Suite 201 · 6525 North Meridian · Oklahoma City, OK 73116 · 405-728-2242

John E. Sargent · McAfee & Taft · Two Leadership Square, 10th Floor · Oklahoma City, OK 73102 · 405-235-9621

John T. Spradling · Spradling, Alpern, Friot & Gum · Continental Savings Building, Suite 700 · 101 Park Avenue · Oklahoma City, OK 73102 · 405-272-0211

T. Scott Spradling · Spradling, Alpern, Friot & Gum · Continental Savings Building, Suite 700 · 101 Park Avenue · Oklahoma City, OK 73102 · 405-272-0211

Richard Cleverdon · Robert Parker & Associates · 2431 East 61st Street, Suite 100 · Tulsa, OK 74136 · 918-745-0792

Charles P. Gotwals, Jr. · Gable & Gotwals · 2000 Fourth National Bank Building · Tulsa, OK 74119 · 918-582-9201

Roy D. Johnsen · Epperson & Johnsen · 324 Main Mall, Suite 900 · Tulsa, OK 74103 · 918-585-5641

William B. Jones · Jones, Givens, Gotcher, Bogan & Hilborne · 3800 First National Tower · Tulsa, OK 74103 · 918-581-8200

TAX AND EMPLOYEE BENEFITS LAW

Len Cason · Hartzog Conger & Cason · 1800 Union Plaza · 3030 Northwest Expressway · Oklahoma City, OK 73112 · 405-947-1800

Gary F. Fuller · McAfee & Taft · Two Leadership Square, 10th Floor · Oklahoma City, OK 73102 · 405-235-9621

James H. Holloman, Jr. · (also Employee Benefits) · Ryan, Holloman, Corbyn & Geister · 900 Robinson Renaissance · 119 North Robinson · Oklahoma City, OK 73102-4608 · 405-239-6041

J. Dudley Hyde · (Employee Benefits) · McAfee & Taft · Two Leadership Square, 10th Floor · Oklahoma City, OK 73102 · 405-235-9621

Richard B. Kells, Jr. · Andrews Davis Legg Bixler Milsten and Murrah · 500 West Main · Oklahoma City, OK 73102 · 405-272-9241

Timothy M. Larason · Andrews Davis Legg Bixler Milsten and Murrah · 500 West Main · Oklahoma City, OK 73102 · 405-272-9241

Jean A. McDonald · (also Employee Benefits) · Crowe & Dunlevy · 1800 Mid-America Tower · 20 North Broadway · Oklahoma City, OK 73102 · 405-235-7700

Randall D. Mock · Mock, Schwabe, Waldo, Elder, Reeves & Bryant · One Leadership Square, 15th Floor · 211 North Robinson Avenue · Oklahoma City, OK 73102 · 405-235-5500

Jon H. Trudgeon · Speck, Philbin, Fleig, Trudgeon & Lutz · First City Place, Suite 800 · Oklahoma City, OK 73102 · 405-235-1603

E. John Eagleton · Houston and Klein · 320 South Boston, Suite 700 · Tulsa, OK 74103 · 918-583-2131

C. Robert Jones · (Employee Benefits) · Gable & Gotwals · 2000 Fourth National Bank Building · Tulsa, OK 74119 · 918-582-9201

David B. McKinney · Boesche, McDermott & Eskridge · ONEOK Plaza, Suite 800 · 100 West Fifth Street · Tulsa, OK 74103 · 918-583-1777

Gail R. Runnels · Holliman, Langholz, Runnels & Dorwart · Holarud Building, Suite 700 · 10 East Third Street · Tulsa, OK 74103-3695 · 918-584-1471

Varley H. Taylor, Jr. · (also Employee Benefits) · Doerner, Stuart, Saunders, Daniel & Anderson · 1000 Atlas Life Building · Tulsa, OK 74103 · 918-582-1211

John B. Turner · Doerner, Stuart, Saunders, Daniel & Anderson · 1000 Atlas Life Building · Tulsa, OK 74103 · 918-582-1211

Henry G. Will · (also Employee Benefits) · Conner & Winters · 2400 First National Tower · Tulsa, OK 74103 · 918-586-5711

Andrew M. Wolov · Hall, Estill, Hardwick, Gable, Golden & Nelson · 4100 Bank of Oklahoma Tower · One Williams Center · Tulsa, OK 74172 · 918-588-2700

TRUSTS AND ESTATES

James F. Davis · Andrews Davis Legg Bixler Milsten and Murrah · 500 West Main Oklahoma City, OK 73102 · 405-272-9241

Allen D. Evans · Crowe & Dunlevy · 1800 Mid-America Tower · 20 North Broadway · Oklahoma City, OK 73102 · 405-235-7700

Gary F. Fuller · McAfee & Taft · Two Leadership Square, 10th Floor · Oklahoma City, OK 73102 · 405-235-9621

James H. Holloman, Jr. · Ryan, Holloman, Corbyn & Geister · 900 Robinson Renaissance · 119 North Robinson · Oklahoma City, OK 73102-4608 · 405-239-6041

Richard B. Kells, Jr. · Andrews Davis Legg Bixler Milsten and Murrah · 500 West Main · Oklahoma City, OK 73102 · 405-272-9241

Randall D. Mock · Mock, Schwabe, Waldo, Elder, Reeves & Bryant · One Leadership Square, 15th Floor · 211 North Robinson Avenue · Oklahoma City, OK 73102 · 405-235-5500

Alan Newman · Hartzog Conger & Cason · 1800 Union Plaza · 3030 Northwest Expressway · Oklahoma City, OK 73112 · 405-947-1800

Cynda C. Ottaway · Crowe & Dunlevy · 1800 Mid-America Tower · 20 North Broadway · Oklahoma City, OK 73102 · 405-235-7700

Michael W. Thom · Thom & Hendrick · Union Bank Building, Suite 326 · 3030 Northwest Expressway · Oklahoma City, OK 73112 · 405-947-5551

W. Thomas Coffman · Gable & Gotwals · 2000 Fourth National Bank Building Tulsa, OK 74119 · 918-582-9201

John B. Johnson, Jr. · Gable & Gotwals · 2000 Fourth National Bank Building Tulsa, OK 74119 · 918-582-9201

Richard D. Jones · Gable & Gotwals · 2000 Fourth National Bank Building Tulsa, OK 74119 · 918-582-9201

Henry G. Will · Conner & Winters · 2400 First National Tower · Tulsa, OK 74103 918-586-5711

OREGON

BANKRUPTCY LAW	**588**
BUSINESS LITIGATION	**589**
CORPORATE LAW	**590**
CRIMINAL DEFENSE	**590**
FAMILY LAW	**591**
LABOR AND EMPLOYMENT LAW	**592**
MARITIME LAW	**593**
NATURAL RESOURCES AND ENVIRONMENTAL LAW	**593**
PERSONAL INJURY LITIGATION	**594**
REAL ESTATE LAW	**595**
TAX AND EMPLOYEE BENEFITS LAW	**596**
TRUSTS AND ESTATES	**597**

BANKRUPTCY LAW

Keith Y. Boyd · McGavic & Boyd · 700 Lawrence Street · Eugene, OR 97401 · 503-485-4555

Wilson C. Muhlheim · Hershner, Hunter, Moulton, Andrews & Neill · 180 East 11th Avenue · P.O. Box 1475 · Eugene, OR 97440 · 503-686-8511

Richard C. Josephson · Stoel, Rives, Boley, Jones & Grey · 900 Southwest Fifth Avenue, 23rd Floor · Portland, OR 97204-1268 · 503-224-3380

Albert N. Kennedy · Tonkon, Torp, Galen, Marmaduke & Booth · 1800 Orbanco Building · 1001 Southwest Fifth Avenue · Portland, OR 97204 · 503-221-1440

William M. McAllister · Stoel, Rives, Boley, Jones & Grey · 900 Southwest Fifth Avenue, 23rd Floor · Portland, OR 97204-1268 · 503-224-3380

Kevin D. Padrick · Miller, Nash, Wiener, Hager & Carlsen · 111 Southwest Fifth Avenue · Portland, OR 97204-3699 · 503-224-5858

Jerome B. Shank · Sussman, Shank, Wapnick, Caplan & Stiles · Orbanco Building, Suite 1111 · 1001 Southwest Fifth Avenue · Portland, OR 97204 · 503-227-1111

Leon Simson · Ransom, Blackman & Simson · 900 American Bank Building · 621 Southwest Morrison Street · Portland, OR 97205 · 503-228-0487

Norman Wapnick · Sussman, Shank, Wapnick, Caplan & Stiles · Orbanco Building, Suite 1111 · 1001 Southwest Fifth Avenue · Portland, OR 97204 · 503-227-1111

BUSINESS LITIGATION

Stanton F. Long · Harrang, Long, Watkinson & Arnold · 101 East Broadway, Suite 400 · P.O. Box 11620 · Eugene, OR 97440 · 503-485-0220

K. Patrick Neill · Hershner, Hunter, Moulton, Andrews & Neill · 180 East 11th Avenue · P.O. Box 1475 · Eugene, OR 97440 · 503-686-8511

William G. Wheatley · Jaqua, Wheatley, Gallagher & Holland · 825 East Park Street · Eugene, OR 97401 · 503-686-8485

James H. Clarke · (Appellate) · Spears, Lubersky, Bledsoe, Anderson, Young & Hilliard · 520 Southwest Yamhill Street, Suite 800 · Portland, OR 97204 · 503-226-6151

Barnes H. Ellis · Stoel, Rives, Boley, Jones & Grey · 900 Southwest Fifth Avenue, 23rd Floor · Portland, OR 97204 · 503-224-3380

John R. Faust, Jr. · (Appellate) · Schwabe, Williamson & Wyatt · Pacwest Center, Suites 1600-1800 · 1211 Southwest Fifth Avenue · Portland, OR 97204 · 503-222-9981

A. Allan Franzke · Schwabe, Williamson & Wyatt · Pacwest Center, Suites 1600-1800 · 1211 Southwest Fifth Avenue · Portland, OR 97204 · 503-222-9981

Wayne Hilliard · Spears, Lubersky, Bledsoe, Anderson, Young & Hilliard · 520 Southwest Yamhill Street, Suite 800 · Portland, OR 97204 · 503-226-6151

Jack L. Kennedy · Kennedy, King & Zimmer · 2600 Pacwest Center · 1211 Southwest Fifth Avenue · Portland, OR 97204 · 503-228-6191

Garr M. King · Kennedy, King & Zimmer · 2600 Pacwest Center · 1211 Southwest Fifth Avenue · Portland, OR 97204 · 503-228-6191

Wayne A. Williamson · Schwabe, Williamson & Wyatt · Pacwest Center, Suites 1600-1800 · 1211 Southwest Fifth Avenue · Portland, OR 97204 · 503-222-9981

CORPORATE LAW

John P. Bledsoe · Spears, Lubersky, Bledsoe, Anderson, Young & Hilliard · 520 Southwest Yamhill Street, Suite 800 · Portland, OR 97204 · 503-226-6151

Brian G. Booth · Tonkon, Torp, Galen, Marmaduke & Booth · 1800 Orbanco Building · 1001 Southwest Fifth Avenue · Portland, OR 97204 · 503-221-1440

Edward L. Epstein · Stoel, Rives, Boley, Jones & Grey · 900 Southwest Fifth Avenue, 23rd Floor · Portland, OR 97204 · 503-224-3380

David G. Hayhurst · Stoel, Rives, Boley, Jones & Grey · 900 Southwest Fifth Avenue, 23rd Floor · Portland, OR 97204 · 503-224-3380

Kenneth W. Hergenhan · Miller, Nash, Wiener, Hager & Carlsen · 111 Southwest Fifth Avenue · Portland, OR 97204-3699 · 503-224-5858

Henry H. Hewitt · Stoel, Rives, Boley, Jones & Grey · 900 Southwest Fifth Avenue, 23rd Floor · Portland, OR 97204 · 503-224-3380

Dexter E. Martin · Stoel, Rives, Boley, Jones & Grey · 900 Southwest Fifth Avenue, 23rd Floor · Portland, OR 97204 · 503-224-3380

Richard E. Roy · Stoel, Rives, Boley, Jones & Grey · 900 Southwest Fifth Avenue, 23rd Floor · Portland, OR 97204 · 503-224-3380

Robert A. Stout · Perkins Coie · U.S. Bancorp Tower, Suite 2500 · 111 Southwest Fifth Avenue · Portland, OR 97204 · 503-295-4400

CRIMINAL DEFENSE

Donald D. Diment, Jr. · Diment, Billings & Walker · 767 Willamette, Suite 208 Eugene, OR 97401 · 503-484-2422

Robert J. McCrea · 1147 High Street · Eugene, OR 97401 · 503-485-1182

Kenneth A. Morrow · Morrow Monks & Sharp · 310 East 11th Avenue · Eugene, OR 97401 · 503-345-2002

Wendell R. Birkland · Birkland & Houze · 1215 Orbanco Building · 1001 Southwest Fifth Avenue · Portland, OR 97204-1199 · 503-241-8601

Marc D. Blackman · Ransom, Blackman & Simson · 900 American Bank Building 621 Southwest Morrison Street · Portland, OR 97205 · 503-228-0487

Desmond D. Connall · Des Connall and Dan Lorenz · 1501 Southwest Harrison Street · Portland, OR 97201 · 503-227-2688

Ronald H. Hoevet · Hoevet, Snyder, Neuberger & Miller · 1400 Standard Insurance Center · 900 Southwest Fifth Avenue · Portland, OR 97204 · 503-228-0497

Stephen A. Houze · Birkland & Houze · 1215 Orbanco Building · 1001 Southwest Fifth Avenue · Portland, OR 97204-1199 · 503-241-8601

John S. Ransom · Ransom, Blackman & Simson · 900 American Bank Building 621 Southwest Morrison Street · Portland, OR 97205 · 503-228-0487

Norman Sepenuk · 1330 Bank of California Tower · 707 Southwest Washington Street · Portland, OR 97205 · 503-221-1633

FAMILY LAW

Ronald I. Gevurtz · Gevurtz, Menashe & Herbert · The 1515 Building, Suite 808 1515 Southwest Fifth Avenue · Portland, OR 97201 · 503-227-1515

Ira L. Gottlieb · Keller, Gottlieb & Gorin · 909 American Bank Building · 621 Southwest Morrison Street · Portland, OR 97205 · 503-224-7563

Jack L. Kennedy · Kennedy, King & Zimmer · 2600 Pacwest Center · 1211 Southwest Fifth Avenue · Portland, OR 97204 · 503-228-6191

Albert A. Menashe · Gevurtz, Menashe & Herbert · The 1515 Building, Suite 808 · 1515 Southwest Fifth Avenue · Portland, OR 97201 · 503-227-1515

William F. Schulte, Jr. · Holmes, DeFrancq & Schulte · The 811 Building, Fifth Floor · 811 Southwest Front Avenue · Portland, OR 97204 · 503-223-4131

Gary J. Zimmer · Kennedy, King & Zimmer · 2600 Pacwest Center · 1211 Southwest Fifth Avenue · Portland, OR 97204 · 503-228-6191

LABOR AND EMPLOYMENT LAW

Harlan Bernstein · (Labor; Individuals) · Jolles, Sokol & Bernstein · 721 Southwest Oak Street · Portland, OR 97205 · 503-228-6474

Garry R. Bullard · (Management) · Bullard, Korshoj, Smith & Jernstedt · 1515 Southwest Fifth Avenue, Suite 1000 · Portland, OR 97201 · 503-248-1134

Richard C. Busse, Jr. · (Individuals) · 621 Southwest Morrison Street, Suite 521 Portland, OR 97205 · 503-248-0504

Richard R. Carney · (Labor) · Carney, Buckley, Kasameyer & Hays · 1618 Southwest First Avenue · Portland, OR 97201 · 503-221-0611

Henry H. Drummonds · (Labor) · Durham, Drummonds, Smith & Wiser · 1020 Southwest Taylor Street · Portland, OR 97205 · 503-222-7130

Kenneth E. Jernstedt · (Management) · Bullard, Korshoj, Smith & Jernstedt 1515 Southwest Fifth Avenue, Suite 1000 · Portland, OR 97201 · 503-248-1134

Bernard Jolles · (Labor; Individuals) · Jolles, Sokol & Bernstein · 721 Southwest Oak Street · Portland, OR 97205 · 503-228-6474

Louis B. Livingston · (Management) · Miller, Nash, Wiener, Hager & Carlsen 111 Southwest Fifth Avenue · Portland, OR 97204-3699 · 503-224-5858

William F. Lubersky · (Management) · Spears, Lubersky, Bledsoe, Anderson, Young & Hilliard · 520 Southwest Yamhill Street, Suite 800 · Portland, OR 97204 503-226-6151

Donald S. Richardson · (Labor) · Carney, Buckley, Kasameyer & Hays · 1618 Southwest First Avenue · Portland, OR 97201 · 503-221-0611

Elden M. Rosenthal · (Individuals) · Rosenthal & Greene · 1907 Orbanco Building · 1001 Southwest Fifth Avenue · Portland, OR 97204 · 503-228-3015

Lewis K. Scott · (Management) · Spears, Lubersky, Bledsoe, Anderson, Young & Hilliard · 520 Southwest Yamhill Street, Suite 800 · Portland, OR 97204 · 503-226-6151

Lester V. Smith, Jr. · (Management) · Bullard, Korshoj, Smith & Jernstedt · 1515 Southwest Fifth Avenue, Suite 1000 · Portland, OR 97201 · 503-248-1134

MARITIME LAW

Dean D. Dechaine · Miller, Nash, Wiener, Hager & Carlsen · 111 Southwest Fifth Avenue · Portland, OR 97204-3699 · 503-224-5858

Kenneth E. Roberts · Schwabe, Williamson & Wyatt · Pacwest Center, Suites 1600-1800 · 1211 Southwest Fifth Avenue · Portland, OR 97204-3795 · 503-222-9981

Paul N. Wonacott · Wood, Tatum, Mosser, Brooke & Landis · 1001 Southwest Fifth Avenue, Suite 1300 · Portland, OR 97204 · 503-224-5430

NATURAL RESOURCES AND ENVIRONMENTAL LAW

John P. Bledsoe · (Timber) · Spears, Lubersky, Bledsoe, Anderson, Young & Hilliard · 520 Southwest Yamhill Street, Suite 800 · Portland, OR 97204 · 503-226-6151

David L. Blount · Adler & Blount · 540 Benjamin Franklin Plaza · One Southwest Columbia · Portland, OR 97258-2006 · 503-227-4420

John B. Crowell, Jr. · (Timber) · Spears, Lubersky, Bledsoe, Anderson, Young & Hilliard · 520 Southwest Yamhill Street, Suite 800 · Portland, OR 97204 503-226-6151

Jerry R. Fish · (Oil & Gas) · Stoel, Rives, Boley, Jones & Grey · 900 Southwest Fifth Avenue, 23rd Floor · Portland, OR 97204 · 503-224-3380

Kirk Johansen · (Timber) · Schwabe, Williamson & Wyatt · Pacwest Center, Suites 1600-1800 · 1211 Southwest Fifth Avenue · Portland, OR 97204-3795 503-222-9981

David P. Miller · (Timber) · Stoel, Rives, Boley, Jones & Grey · 900 Southwest Fifth Avenue, 23rd Floor · Portland, OR 97204 · 503-224-3380

Mark A. Norby · (Minerals) · Stoel, Rives, Boley, Jones & Grey · 900 Southwest Fifth Avenue, 23rd Floor · Portland, OR 97204 · 503-224-3380

James N. Westwood · (Timber) · Miller, Nash, Wiener, Hager & Carlsen · 111 Southwest Fifth Avenue · Portland, OR 97204-3699 · 503-224-5858

PERSONAL INJURY LITIGATION

Arthur C. Johnson · (Plaintiffs) · Johnson, Clifton, Larson & Eolin · Citizens Building, 10th Floor · 975 Oak Street · Eugene, OR 97401-3176 · 503-484-2434

William G. Wheatley · (Defendants) · Jaqua, Wheatley, Gallagher & Holland · 825 East Park · Eugene, OR 97401 · 503-686-8485

Richard P. Noble · (Plaintiffs) · One Centerpointe Drive, Suite 350 · Lake Oswego, OR 97035 · 503-620-3870

E. Richard Bodyfelt · (Defendants) · Bodyfelt, Mount, Stroup & Chamberlain · 300 Powers Building · 65 Southwest Yamhill Street · Portland, OR 97204 · 503-243-1022

A. Allan Franzke · (Defendants) · Schwabe, Williamson & Wyatt · Pacwest Center, Suites 1600-1800 · 1211 Southwest Fifth Avenue · Portland, OR 97204 · 503-222-9981

Burl L. Green · (Plaintiffs) · Hoevet, Snyder, Neuberger & Miller · 900 Southwest Fifth Avenue, Suite 1400 · Portland, OR 97204 · 503-228-0497

John E. Hart · (Defendants) · Schwabe, Williamson & Wyatt · Pacwest Center, Suites 1600-1800 · 1211 Southwest Fifth Avenue · Portland, OR 97204-3795 · 503-222-9981

Wayne Hilliard · (Defendants) · Spears, Lubersky, Bledsoe, Anderson, Young & Hilliard · 520 Southwest Yamhill Street, Suite 800 · Portland, OR 97204 · 503-226-6151

Jack L. Kennedy · (Defendants) · Kennedy, King & Zimmer · 2600 Pacwest Center · 1211 Southwest Fifth Avenue · Portland, OR 97204 · 503-228-6191

Dan O'Leary · (Plaintiffs) · Pozzi, Wilson, Atchison, O'Leary & Conboy · Standard Plaza, Suite 910 · 1100 Southwest Sixth Avenue · Portland, OR 97204 · 503-226-3232

Charles Paulson · (Plaintiffs) · 1905 Orbanco Building · 1001 Southwest Fifth Avenue · Portland, OR 97204 · 503-226-6361

Wayne A. Williamson · (Defendants) · Schwabe, Williamson & Wyatt · Pacwest Center, Suites 1600-1800 · 1211 Southwest Fifth Avenue · Portland, OR 97204 · 503-222-9981

REAL ESTATE LAW

Vernon D. Gleaves · Gleaves Swearingen Larson & Potter · 975 Oak Street, Eighth Floor · Eugene, OR 97401 · 503-686-8833

James P. Harrang · Harrang, Long, Watkinson & Arnold · 101 East Broadway, Suite 400 · P.O. Box 11620 · Eugene, OR 97440 · 503-485-0220

Arlen C. Swearingen · Gleaves Swearingen Larsen & Potter · 975 Oak Street, Eighth Floor · Eugene, OR 97401 · 503-686-8833

Robert S. Ball · Ball, Janik & Novack · One Main Place, Suite 1100 · 101 Southwest Main Street · Portland, OR 97204 · 503-228-2525

J. David Bennett · Copeland Landye Bennett and Wolf · 3500 First Interstate Tower · Portland, OR 97201 · 503-224-4100

Richard A. Cantlin · Miller, Nash, Wiener, Hager & Carlsen · 111 Southwest Fifth Avenue · Portland, OR 97204-3699 · 503-224-5858

Howard M. Feuerstein · Stoel, Rives, Boley, Jones & Grey · 900 Southwest Fifth Avenue, 23rd Floor · Portland, OR 97204 · 503-224-3380

Eugene L. Grant · Schwabe, Williamson & Wyatt · Pacwest Center, Suites 1600-1800 · 1211 Southwest Fifth Avenue · Portland, OR 97204 · 503-222-9981

Terry C. Hauck · Schwabe, Williamson & Wyatt · Pacwest Center, Suites 1600-1800 · 1211 Southwest Fifth Avenue · Portland, OR 97204 · 503-222-9981

Stephen Thomas Janik · Ball, Janik & Novack · One Main Place, Suite 1100 · 101 Southwest Main Street · Portland, OR 97204 · 503-228-2525

David P. Miller · Stoel, Rives, Boley, Jones & Grey · 900 Southwest Fifth Avenue, 23rd Floor · Portland, OR 97204 · 503-224-3380

Stanley M. Samuels · Preston, Thorgrimson, Ellis & Holman · 3200 U.S. Bancorp Tower · 111 Southwest Fifth Avenue · Portland, OR 97204-3635 · 503-228-3200

David P. Weiner · Samuels, Yoelin & Weiner · 200 Willamette Wharf · 4640 Southwest Macadam Avenue · Portland, OR 97201 · 503-226-2966

TAX AND EMPLOYEE BENEFITS LAW

Mark W. Perrin · Perrin, Gartland, Doyle & Nelson · 44 Club Road, Suite 200 · P.O. Box 11229 · Eugene, OR 97440 · 503-344-2174

Joyle C. Dahl · Schwabe, Williamson & Wyatt · Pacwest Center, Suites 1600-1800 · 1211 Southwest Fifth Avenue · Portland, OR 97204 · 503-222-9981

Thomas P. Deering · (Employee Benefits) · Stoel, Rives, Boley, Jones & Grey · 900 Southwest Fifth Avenue, 23rd Floor · Portland, OR 97204-1268 · 503-224-3380

John H. Doran · Spears, Lubersky, Bledsoe, Anderson, Young & Hilliard · 520 Southwest Yamhill Street, Suite 800 · Portland, OR 97204 · 503-226-6151

Charles P. Duffy · Duffy, Kekel, Jensen, Jones & Miller · 1404 Standard Plaza · 1100 Southwest Sixth Avenue · Portland, OR 97204 · 503-226-1371

Gerald A. Froebe · Miller, Nash, Wiener, Hager & Carlsen · 111 Southwest Fifth Avenue · Portland, OR 97204-3699 · 503-224-5858

Gersham Goldstein · Stoel, Rives, Boley, Jones & Grey · 900 Southwest Fifth Avenue, 23rd Floor · Portland, OR 97204-1268 · 503-224-3380

Joseph J. Hanna, Jr. · Hanna, Murphy, Jensen & Holloway · 2300 Pacwest Center · 1211 Southwest Fifth Avenue · Portland, OR 97204-3789 · 503-273-2300

Joel D. Kuntz · Stoel, Rives, Boley, Jones & Grey · 900 Southwest Fifth Avenue, 23rd Floor · Portland, OR 97204-1268 · 503-224-3380

Robert L. Weiss · Weiss, DesCamp & Botteri · 2300 U.S. Bancorp Tower · 111 Southwest Fifth Avenue · Portland, OR 97204 · 503-243-2300

Morton H. Zalutsky · (Employee Benefits) · Zalutsky, Klarquist & Johnson · 215 Southwest Washington Street, Third Floor · Portland, OR 97204 · 503-248-0300

TRUSTS AND ESTATES

David N. Andrews · Hershner, Hunter, Moulton, Andrews & Neill · 180 East 11th Avenue · P.O. Box 1475 · Eugene, OR 97440 · 503-686-8511

Nancy L. Cowgill · Stoel, Rives, Boley, Jones & Grey · 900 Southwest Fifth Avenue, 23rd Floor · Portland, OR 97204 · 503-224-3380

Robert D. Dayton · Schwabe, Williamson & Wyatt · Pacwest Center, Suites 1600-1800 · 1211 Southwest Fifth Avenue · Portland, OR 97204 · 503-222-9981

Joseph J. Hanna, Jr. · Hanna, Murphy, Jensen & Holloway · 2300 Pacwest Center · 1211 Southwest Fifth Avenue · Portland, OR 97204-3789 · 503-273-2300

David A. Kekel · Duffy, Kekel, Jensen, Jones & Miller · 1404 Standard Plaza 1100 Southwest Sixth Avenue · Portland, OR 97204 · 503-226-1371

Charles J. McMurchie · Stoel, Rives, Boley, Jones & Grey · 900 Southwest Fifth Avenue, 23rd Floor · Portland, OR 97204 · 503-224-3380

Conrad L. Moore · Miller, Nash, Wiener, Hager & Carlsen · 111 Southwest Fifth Avenue · Portland, OR 97204-3699 · 503-224-5858

Campbell Richardson · Stoel, Rives, Boley, Jones & Grey · 900 Southwest Fifth Avenue, 23rd Floor · Portland, OR 97204 · 503-224-3380

Daniel A. Ritter · Harland, Ritter, Saalfeld, Griggs & Gorsuch · 693 Chemeketa Street, NE · P.O. Box 470 · Salem, OR 97308 · 503-399-1070

PENNSYLVANIA

BANKRUPTCY LAW	598
BUSINESS LITIGATION	600
CORPORATE LAW	602
CRIMINAL DEFENSE	604
FAMILY LAW	605
LABOR AND EMPLOYMENT LAW	607
MARITIME LAW	612
NATURAL RESOURCES AND ENVIRONMENTAL LAW	612
PERSONAL INJURY LITIGATION	613
REAL ESTATE LAW	615
TAX AND EMPLOYEE BENEFITS LAW	618
TRUSTS AND ESTATES	620

BANKRUPTCY LAW

Robert L. Knupp · Knupp & Kodak · 407 North Front Street · P.O. Box 11848 · Harrisburg, PA 17108 · 717-238-7151

Edward W. Rothman · McNees, Wallace & Nurick · 100 Pine Street · P.O. Box 1166 · Harrisburg, PA 17108 · 717-232-8000

Neal D. Colton · Dechert Price & Rhoads · 3400 Centre Square West · 1500 Market Street · Philadelphia, PA 19102 · 215-981-2000

Nathan B. Feinstein · Dilworth, Paxson, Kalish & Kauffman · 2600 The Fidelity Building · Philadelphia, PA 19109-1094 · 215-875-7000

Leon S. Forman · Blank, Rome, Comisky & McCauley · Four Penn Center Plaza, 10th-13th Floors · Philadelphia, PA 19103 · 215-569-5500

Howard T. Glassman · Blank, Rome, Comisky & McCauley · Four Penn Center Plaza, 10th-13th Floors · Philadelphia, PA 19103 · 215-569-5500

Marvin Krasny · Wolf, Block, Schorr and Solis-Cohen · Packard Building, 12th Floor · Philadelphia, PA 19102 · 215-977-2000

Alexander N. Rubin, Jr. · Rubin, Quinn, Moss & Heaney · 1800 Penn Mutual Tower · 510 Walnut Street · Philadelphia, PA 19106 · 215-925-8300

Raymond L. Shapiro · Blank, Rome, Comisky & McCauley · Four Penn Center Plaza, 10th-13th Floors · Philadelphia, PA 19103 · 215-569-5500

David T. Sykes · Duane, Morris & Heckscher · One Franklin Plaza, Suite 1500 · Philadelphia, PA 19102 · 215-854-6300

Michael L. Temin · Wolf, Block, Schorr and Solis-Cohen · Packard Building, 12th Floor · Philadelphia, PA 19102 · 215-977-2000

Phillip E. Beard · Stonecipher, Cunningham, Beard & Schmitt · 125 First Avenue Building · Pittsburgh, PA 15222 · 412-391-8510

Douglas A. Campbell · Campbell & Levine · 3100 Grant Building · Pittsburgh, PA 15219 · 412-261-0310

George L. Cass · Buchanan Ingersoll · 600 Grant Street, 57th Floor · Pittsburgh, PA 15219 · 412-562-8800

Stanley E. Levine · Campbell & Levine · 3100 Grant Building · Pittsburgh, PA 15219 · 412-261-0310

M. Bruce McCullough · Buchanan Ingersoll · 600 Grant Street, 57th Floor · Pittsburgh, PA 15219 · 412-562-8800

David A. Murdoch · Kirkpatrick & Lockhart · 1500 Oliver Building · Pittsburgh, PA 15222 · 412-355-6500

Robert G. Sable · Lampl, Sable, Makoroff & Libenson · 710 Fifth Avenue, Suite 3000 · Pittsburgh, PA 15219-3088 · 412-471-4996

Bernhard Schaffler · Schaffler & Bohm · 967 Liberty Avenue · Pittsburgh, PA 15222 · 412-765-3888

Joseph E. Schmitt · Stonecipher, Cunningham, Beard & Schmitt · 125 First Avenue Building · Pittsburgh, PA 15222 · 412-391-8510

Paul M. Singer · Reed Smith Shaw & McClay · James H. Reed Building, Mellon Square · 435 Sixth Avenue · P.O. Box 2009 · Pittsburgh, PA 15230 · 412-288-3131

BUSINESS LITIGATION

John M. McLaughlin · Knox Graham McLaughlin Gornall and Sennett · 120 West 10th Street · Erie, PA 16501 · 814-459-2800

Thomas D. Caldwell, Jr. · Caldwell & Kearns · 3631 North Front Street · Harrisburg, PA 17110 · 717-232-7661

Ronald M. Katzman · Goldberg, Katzman & Shipman · 319 Market Street · P.O. Box 1268 · Harrisburg, PA 17108 · 717-234-4161

J. Thomas Menaker · McNees, Wallace & Nurick · 100 Pine Street · Harrisburg, PA 17108 · 717-232-8000

David Berger · Berger & Montague · 1622 Locust Street · Philadelphia, PA 19103 · 215-875-3000

Bernard M. Borish · Wolf, Block, Schorr and Solis-Cohen · Packard Building, 12th Floor · Philadelphia, PA 19102 · 215-977-2000

James D. Crawford · Schnader, Harrison, Segal & Lewis · 1600 Market Street, Suite 3600 · Philadelphia, PA 19103 · 215-751-2000

Alan J. Davis · Wolf, Block, Schorr and Solis-Cohen · Packard Building, 12th Floor · Philadelphia, PA 19102 · 215-977-2000

John G. Harkins, Jr. · Pepper, Hamilton & Scheetz · The Fidelity Building, 20th Floor · 123 South Broad Street · Philadelphia, PA 19109 · 215-893-3000

Lawrence T. Hoyle, Jr. · Hoyle, Morris & Kerr · One Liberty Place · 1650 Market Street · Philadelphia, PA 19103 · 215-981-5700

Arthur H. Kahn · Schnader, Harrison, Segal & Lewis · 1600 Market Street, Suite 3600 · Philadelphia, PA 19103 · 215-751-2000

Harold E. Kohn · Kohn, Savett, Klein & Graf · 2400 One Reading Center · 1101 Market Street · Philadelphia, PA 19107 · 215-238-1700

John H. Lewis, Jr. · Morgan, Lewis & Bockius · 2000 One Logan Square · Philadelphia, PA 19103 · 215-963-5000

Thomas A. Masterson · Morgan, Lewis & Bockius · 2000 One Logan Square · Philadelphia, PA 19103 · 215-963-5000

Henry T. Reath · Duane, Morris & Heckscher · One Franklin Plaza, Suite 1500 · Philadelphia, PA 19102 · 215-854-6300

Thomas B. Rutter · Rutter, Turner & Stein · Curtis Center · Independence Square West, Suite 750 · One Walnut Street · Philadelphia, PA 19106 · 215-925-9200

Robert S. Ryan · Drinker Biddle & Reath · 1100 Philadelphia National Bank Building · Broad & Chestnut Streets · Philadelphia, PA 19107 · 215-988-2700

Henry W. Sawyer III · Drinker Biddle & Reath · 1100 Philadelphia National Bank Building · Broad & Chestnut Streets · Philadelphia, PA 19107 · 215-988-2700

David J. Armstrong · Dickie, McCamey & Chilcote · Two PPG Place, Suite 400 · Pittsburgh, PA 15222-5402 · 412-281-7272

David B. Fawcett, Jr. · Dickie, McCamey & Chilcote · Two PPG Place, Suite 400 · Pittsburgh, PA 15222-5402 · 412-281-7272

J. Tomlinson Fort · Reed Smith Shaw & McClay · James H. Reed Building, Mellon Square · 435 Sixth Avenue · P.O. Box 2009 · Pittsburgh, PA 15230 · 412-288-3131

Joseph A. Katarincic · Kirkpatrick & Lockhart · 1500 Oliver Building · Pittsburgh, PA 15222 · 412-355-6500

Edwin L. Klett · Eckert, Seamans, Cherin & Mellott · 600 Grant Street, 42nd Floor · Pittsburgh, PA 15219 · 412-566-6000

Roslyn M. Litman · Litman Litman Harris Brown and Watzman · 1701 Grant Building · Pittsburgh, PA 15219-2377 · 412-456-2000

David L. McClenahan · Kirkpatrick & Lockhart · 1500 Oliver Building · Pittsburgh, PA 15222 · 412-355-6500

Cloyd R. Mellott · Eckert, Seamans, Cherin & Mellott · 600 Grant Street, 42nd Floor · Pittsburgh, PA 15219 · 412-566-6000

James D. Morton · Buchanan Ingersoll · 600 Grant Street, 57th Floor · Pittsburgh, PA 15219 · 412-562-8800

Charles Weiss · Thorp, Reed & Armstrong · One Riverfront Center · Pittsburgh, PA 15222 · 412-394-7711

CORPORATE LAW

William D. Boswell · Boswell, Tintner & Piccola · 315 North Front Street · Harrisburg, PA 17105 · 717-236-9377

Francis B. Haas, Jr. · McNees, Wallace & Nurick · 100 Pine Street · P.O. Box 1166 · Harrisburg, PA 17108 · 717-232-8000

Gerald K. Morrison · Rhoads & Sinon · 410 North Third Street · P.O. Box 1146 · Harrisburg, PA 17108 · 717-233-5731

Rod J. Pera · McNees, Wallace & Nurick · 100 Pine Street · P.O. Box 1166 · Harrisburg, PA 17108 · 717-232-8000

Henry W. Rhoads · Rhoads & Sinon · 410 North Third Street · P.O. Box 1146 · Harrisburg, PA 17108 · 717-233-5731

John J. Brennan · Dechert Price & Rhoads · 3400 Centre Square West · 1500 Market Street · Philadelphia, PA 19102 · 215-981-2000

J. Gordon Cooney · Schnader, Harrison, Segal & Lewis · 1600 Market Street, Suite 3600 · Philadelphia, PA 19103 · 215-751-2000

Park B. Dilks, Jr. · Morgan, Lewis & Bockius · 2000 One Logan Square · Philadelphia, PA 19103 · 215-963-5000

Vincent F. Garrity, Jr. · Duane, Morris & Heckscher · One Franklin Plaza, Suite 1500 · Philadelphia, PA 19102 · 215-854-6300

Stephen J. Harmelin · Dilworth, Paxson, Kalish & Kauffman · 2600 The Fidelity Building · Philadelphia, PA 19109-1094 · 215-875-7000

Thomas M. Hyndman, Jr. · Duane, Morris & Heckscher · One Franklin Plaza, Suite 1500 · Philadelphia, PA 19102 · 215-854-6300

William R. Klaus · Pepper, Hamilton & Scheetz · The Fidelity Building, 20th Floor · 123 South Broad Street · Philadelphia, PA 19109 · 215-893-3000

Frederick D. Lipman · Blank, Rome, Comisky & McCauley · Four Penn Center Plaza, 10th-13th Floors · Philadelphia, PA 19103 · 215-569-5500

David W. Maxey · Drinker Biddle & Reath · 1100 Philadelphia National Bank Building · Broad & Chestnut Streets · Philadelphia, PA 19107 · 215-988-2700

Duncan O. McKee · Ballard, Spahr, Andrews & Ingersoll · 30 South 17th Street, 20th Floor · Philadelphia, PA 19103 · 215-564-1800

Stephen R. Miller · Dechert Price & Rhoads · 3400 Centre Square West · 1500 Market Street · Philadelphia, PA 19102 · 215-981-2000

Carl W. Schneider · Wolf, Block, Schorr and Solis-Cohen · Packard Building, 12th Floor · Philadelphia, PA 19102 · 215-977-2000

Donald A. Scott · Morgan, Lewis & Bockius · 2000 One Logan Square · Philadelphia, PA 19103 · 215-963-5000

Robert E. Shields · Drinker Biddle & Reath · 1100 Philadelphia National Bank Building · Broad & Chestnut Streets · Philadelphia, PA 19107 · 215-988-2700

Robert Deland Williams · Dechert Price & Rhoads · 3400 Centre Square West 1500 Market Street · Philadelphia, PA 19102 · 215-981-2000

Barton J. Winokur · Dechert Price & Rhoads · 3400 Centre Square West · 1500 Market Street · Philadelphia, PA 19102 · 215-981-2000

Robert H. Young · Morgan, Lewis & Bockius · 2000 One Logan Square · Philadelphia, PA 19103 · 215-963-5000

William E. Zeiter · Morgan, Lewis & Bockius · 2000 One Logan Square · Philadelphia, PA 19103 · 215-963-5000

Carl F. Barger · Eckert, Seamans, Cherin & Mellott · 600 Grant Street, 42nd Floor · Pittsburgh, PA 15219 · 412-566-6000

Bruce D. Evans · Reed Smith Shaw & McClay · James H. Reed Building, Mellon Square · 435 Sixth Avenue · P.O. Box 2009 · Pittsburgh, PA 15230 · 412-288-3131

William P. Hackney · Reed Smith Shaw & McClay · James H. Reed Building, Mellon Square · 435 Sixth Avenue · P.O. Box 2009 · Pittsburgh, PA 15230 412-288-3131

James H. Hardie · Reed Smith Shaw & McClay · James H. Reed Building, Mellon Square · 435 Sixth Avenue · P.O. Box 2009 · Pittsburgh, PA 15230 412-288-3131

C. Kent May · Eckert, Seamans, Cherin & Mellott · 600 Grant Street, 42nd Floor · Pittsburgh, PA 15219 · 412-566-6000

Samuel K. McCune · Kirkpatrick & Lockhart · 1500 Oliver Building · Pittsburgh, PA 15222 · 412-355-6500

Michael C. McLean · Kirkpatrick & Lockhart · 1500 Oliver Building · Pittsburgh, PA 15222 · 412-355-6500

William R. Newlin · Buchanan Ingersoll · 600 Grant Street, 57th Floor · Pittsburgh, PA 15219 · 412-562-8800

John R. Previs · Buchanan Ingersoll · 600 Grant Street, 57th Floor · Pittsburgh, PA 15219 · 412-562-8800

William Dwight Sutton · Thorp, Reed & Armstrong · One Riverfront Center · Pittsburgh, PA 15222 · 412-394-7711

Thomas D. Wright · Eckert, Seamans, Cherin & Mellott · 600 Grant Street, 42nd Floor · Pittsburgh, PA 15219 · 412-566-6000

CRIMINAL DEFENSE

Arthur K. Dils · Dils, Dixon & Zulli · 101 South Second Street · Harrisburg, PA 17101 · 717-233-8743

Joshua D. Lock · 106 Walnut Street · P.O. Box 949 · Harrisburg, PA 17108 · 717-234-7025

William C. Costopoulos · Kollas, Costopoulos, Foster & Fields · 831 Market Street · P.O. Box 222 · Le Moyne, PA 17043 · 717-761-2121

John R. Carroll · Carroll & Carroll · 615 Chestnut Street · Philadelphia, PA 19106 · 215-925-4100

Thomas Colas Carroll · (Appellate) · Carroll & Carroll · 615 Chestnut Street · Philadelphia, PA 19106 · 215-925-4100

James D. Crawford · Schnader, Harrison, Segal & Lewis · 1600 Market Street, Suite 3600 · Philadelphia, PA 19103 · 215-751-2000

Donald J. Goldberg · 1310 Three Mellon Bank Center · Philadelphia, PA 19102 · 215-563-6345

Ronald F. Kidd · Duane, Morris & Heckscher · One Franklin Plaza, Suite 1500 Philadelphia, PA 19102 · 215-854-6300

A. Charles Peruto, Sr. · Peruto, Ryan & Vitullo · Washington West Building Northeast Corner Eighth & Locust Streets · Philadelphia, PA 19106 215-925-5800

Thomas B. Rutter · Rutter, Turner & Stein · Curtis Center · Independence Square West, Suite 750 · One Walnut Street · Philadelphia, PA 19106 215-925-9200

Stanford Shmukler · Packard Building, 24th Floor · 111 South 15th Street Philadelphia, PA 19102 · 215-751-9500

Richard A. Sprague · Sprague, Higgins & Creamer · The Wellington Building, Suite 400 · 135 South 19th Street · Philadelphia, PA 19103 · 215-561-7681

J. Clayton Undercofler III · Saul, Ewing, Remick & Saul · 3800 Centre Square West · Philadelphia, PA 19102 · 215-972-7777

David J. Armstrong · Dickie, McCamey & Chilcote · Two PPG Place, Suite 400 Pittsburgh, PA 15222-5402 · 412-281-7272

John L. Doherty · Manifesto, Doherty & Donahoe · 1550 Koppers Building Pittsburgh, PA 15219 · 412-471-8893

Harold Gondelman · 718 Fifth Avenue · Pittsburgh, PA 15219 · 412-765-2500

Stanley W. Greenfield · Greenfield & Associates · 728 Fifth Avenue · Pittsburgh, PA 15219 · 412-261-4466

Thomas A. Livingston · Livingston & Clark · The Colonial Building · 205 Ross Street · Pittsburgh, PA 15219 · 412-391-7686

William F. Manifesto · Manifesto, Doherty & Donahoe · 1550 Koppers Building Pittsburgh, PA 15219 · 412-471-8893

James K. O'Malley · The Colonial Building · 205 Ross Street · Pittsburgh, PA 15219 · 412-391-1148

Charles F. Scarlata · Scarlata & Plastino · 1550 Koppers Building · Pittsburgh, PA 15219 · 412-765-2855

Emmanuel H. Dimitriou · 522-24 Court Street · P.O. Box 677 · Reading, PA 19601 · 215-376-7466

FAMILY LAW

Sandra Schultz Newman · Astor, Weiss & Newman · Three Bala Plaza West, Suite 100 · P.O. Box 1665 · Bala Cynwyd, PA 19004 · 215-667-8660

Eric D. Turner · Astor, Weiss & Newman · Three Bala Plaza West, Suite 100 P.O. Box 1665 · Bala Cynwyd, PA 19004 · 215-667-8660

William L. Goldman · 90 East State Street · Doylestown, PA 18901 · 215-348-2605

Maria P. Cognetti · Killian & Gephart · 218 Pine Street · P.O. Box 886 · Harrisburg, PA 17108 · 717-232-1851

Bruce D. Desfor · Meyers, Desfor & Shollenberger · 410 North Second Street Harrisburg, PA 17101 · 717-236-9428

John C. Howett, Jr. · 132 Walnut Street · P.O. Box 810 · Harrisburg, PA 17108 717-234-2616

Bonnie D. Menaker · Hepford, Swartz, Menaker & Morgan · 111 North Front Street · P.O. Box 889 · Harrisburg, PA 17108-0889 · 717-234-4121

Neil Hurowitz · Valley View, Suite A-100 · 251 West DeKalb Pike · King of Prussia, PA 19406 · 215-265-7370

I. B. Sinclair · Sinclair, McErlean and Rubin · 20 West Third Street · Media, PA 19063 · 215-565-2500

Michael R. Sweeney · Kassab Cherry Archbold Ferrara and Mutzel · Lawyers-Title Building · 214 North Jackson Street · P.O. Box 626 · Media, PA 19063 215-565-3800

Mason Avrigian · Abrahams & Loewenstein · One Montgomery Plaza, Suite 700 Norristown, PA 19401-4814 · 215-277-7700

Emanuel A. Bertin · One Meetinghouse Place, Suite 102 · Norristown, PA 19401 215-277-1500

Jack A. Rounick · Pechner, Dorfman, Wolffe, Rounick & Cabot · 68 East Penn Street · Norristown, PA 19401 · 215-272-6666

Frederick Cohen · 900 Two Penn Center Plaza · Philadelphia, PA 19102 · 215-564-3395

Leonard Dubin · Blank, Rome, Comisky & McCauley · Four Penn Center Plaza, 10th-13th Floors · Philadelphia, PA 19103 · 215-569-5500

Michael E. Fingerman · Shainberg & Fingerman · 1500 Walnut Street, Suite 300 Philadelphia, PA 19102 · 215-546-9300

Saul Levit · Abrahams & Loewenstein · United Engineers Building, 14th Floor 30 South 17th Street · Philadelphia, PA 19103-4096 · 215-561-1030

Albert Momjian · Abrahams & Loewenstein · United Engineers Building, 14th Floor · 30 South 17th Street · Philadelphia, PA 19103-4096 · 215-561-1030

Norman Perlberger · Blank, Rome, Comisky & McCauley · Four Penn Center Plaza, 10th-13th Floors · Philadelphia, PA 19103 · 215-569-5500

Charles C. Shainberg · Shainberg & Fingerman · 1500 Walnut Street, Suite 300 Philadelphia, PA 19102 · 215-546-9300

Stewart B. Barmen · Rothman Gordon Foreman and Groudine · 300 Grant Building · Pittsburgh, PA 15219 · 412-281-0705

Chris F. Gillotti · Gillotti, Goldberg & Capristo · Grant Building, Suite 215 Pittsburgh, PA 15219 · 412-391-4242

Mark J. Goldberg · Gillotti, Goldberg & Capristo · Grant Building, Suite 215 Pittsburgh, PA 15219 · 412-391-4242

Harry J. Gruener · Raphael, Gruener and Raphael · Grant Building, 35th Floor Pittsburgh, PA 15219 · 412-471-8822

Patricia G. Miller · Reed Smith Shaw & McClay · James H. Reed Building, Mellon Square · 435 Sixth Avenue · P.O. Box 2009 · Pittsburgh, PA 15230 412-288-3131

Robert Raphael · Raphael, Gruener and Raphael · Grant Building, 35th Floor Pittsburgh, PA 15219 · 412-471-8822

Joanne Ross Wilder · Wilder & Mahood · 816 Frick Building · Pittsburgh, PA 15219 · 412-261-4040

LABOR AND EMPLOYMENT LAW

John S. Hayes · (Management) · Duane, Morris & Heckscher · 2851 West Emmaus Avenue · Allentown, PA 18103 · 215-791-3833

Irwin W. Aronson · (Labor) · Handler, Gerber, Johnston & Aronson · 132 State Street · Harrisburg, PA 17101 · 717-234-0770

Jerome H. Gerber · (Labor) · Handler, Gerber, Johnston & Aronson · 132 State Street · Harrisburg, PA 17101 · 717-234-0770

J. Thomas Menaker · (Management) · McNees, Wallace & Nurick · 100 Pine Street · P.O. Box 1166 · Harrisburg, PA 17108 · 717-232-8000

Ira H. Weinstock · (Labor) · 800 North Second Street, Suite 100 · Harrisburg, PA 17102 · 717-238-1657

Norman I. White · (Management) · McNees, Wallace & Nurick · 100 Pine Street P.O. Box 1166 · Harrisburg, PA 17108 · 717-232-8000

John J. McAleese, Jr. · (Management) · McAleese, McGoldrick & Susanin Executive Terrace, Suite 240 · 455 South Gulph Road · King of Prussia, PA 19406 215-337-4510

Frank H. Abbott · (Management) · Schnader, Harrison, Segal & Lewis · 1600 Market Street, Suite 3600 · Philadelphia, PA 19103 · 215-751-2000

Alice W. Ballard · (Individuals) · Samuel and Ballard · 225 South 15th Street, Suite 1700 · Philadelphia, PA 19102 · 215-893-9990

Warren J. Borish · (Labor) · Spear, Wilderman, Sigmond, Borish and Endy · 260 South Broad Street, Suite 1500 · Philadelphia, PA 19102 · 215-732-0101

Carter R. Buller · (Management) · Montgomery, McCracken, Walker & Rhoads Three Parkway, 20th Floor · Philadelphia, PA 19102 · 215-563-0650

Alfred J. D'Angelo, Jr. · (Management) · Pepper, Hamilton & Scheetz · The Fidelity Building, 20th Floor · 123 South Broad Street · Philadelphia, PA 19109 215-893-3000

Mark S. Dichter · (Management) · Morgan, Lewis & Bockius · 2000 One Logan Square · Philadelphia, PA 19103 · 215-963-5000

H. Thomas Felix II · (Management) · Sprecher, Felix, Visco, Hutchison & Young 2300 The Fidelity Building · 123 South Broad Street · Philadelphia, PA 19109 215-875-5100

Miriam L. Gafni · (Individuals) · Freedman and Lorry · Lafayette Building, Eighth Floor · Fifth and Chestnut Streets · Philadelphia, PA 19106 · 215-925-8400

David F. Girard-diCarlo · (Management) · Blank, Rome, Comisky & McCauley · Four Penn Central Plaza, 10th-13th Floors · Philadelphia, PA 19103 · 215-569-5500

Howard I. Hatoff · (Management) · Blank, Rome, Comisky & McCauley · Four Penn Central Plaza, 10th-13th Floors · Philadelphia, PA 19103 · 215-569-5500

Thomas W. Jennings · (Labor) · Sagot & Jennings · Public Ledger Building, Suite 1172 · Independence Square · Philadelphia, PA 19106 · 215-922-6700

Bernard N. Katz · (Labor) · Meranze and Katz · Lewis Tower Building, 12th Floor · Northeast Corner 15th & Locust Streets · Philadelphia, PA 19102 · 215-546-4183

Alan M. Lerner · (Management; Individuals) · Cohen, Shapiro, Polisher, Shiekman and Cohen · PSFS Building, 22nd Floor · 12 South 12th Street · Philadelphia, PA 19107-3981 · 215-922-1300

John Markle, Jr. · (Management) · Drinker Biddle & Reath · 1100 Philadelphia National Bank Building · Broad and Chestnut Streets · Philadelphia, PA 19107 · 215-988-2700

Richard H. Markowitz · (Labor) · Markowitz & Richman · 121 South Broad Street, 11th Floor · Philadelphia, PA 19107 · 215-875-3100

James A. Matthews, Jr. · (Management) · Morgan, Lewis & Bockius · 2000 One Logan Square · Philadelphia, PA 19103 · 215-963-5000

J. Anthony Messina · (Management) · Pepper, Hamilton & Scheetz · The Fidelity Building, 20th Floor · 123 South Broad Street · Philadelphia, PA 19109 · 215-893-3000

Mark P. Muller · (Labor) · Freedman and Lorry · Lafayette Building, Eighth Floor · Fifth and Chestnut Streets · Philadelphia, PA 19106 · 215-925-8400

John B. Nason III · (Management) · Duane, Morris & Heckscher · One Franklin Plaza, Suite 1500 · Philadelphia, PA 19102 · 215-854-6300

Timothy P. O'Reilly · (Management) · Morgan, Lewis & Bockius · 2000 One Logan Square · Philadelphia, PA 19103 · 215-963-5000

Harry Reagan · (Management) · Morgan, Lewis & Bockius · 2000 One Logan Square · Philadelphia, PA 19109 · 215-963-5000

Stephen C. Richman · (Labor) · Markowitz & Richman · 121 South Broad Street, 11th Floor · Philadelphia, PA 19107 · 215-875-3100

Richard B. Sigmond · (Labor) · Spear, Wilderman, Sigmond, Borish and Endy 260 South Broad Street, Suite 1500 · Philadelphia, PA 19102 · 215-732-0101

Robert E. Wachs · (Management) · Wolf, Block, Schorr and Solis-Cohen · Packard Building, 12th Floor · Philadelphia, PA 19102 · 215-977-2000

Martin Wald · (Management) · Schnader, Harrison, Segal & Lewis · 1600 Market Street, Suite 3600 · Philadelphia, PA 19103 · 215-751-2000

Steven R. Waxman · (Individuals) · Fox, Rothschild, O'Brien & Frankel · 2000 Market Street, 10th Floor · Philadelphia, PA 19103 · 215-299-2718

William A. Whiteside, Jr. · (Management) · Fox, Rothschild, O'Brien & Frankel 2000 Market Street, Ninth Floor · Philadelphia, PA 19103 · 215-299-2000

Deborah R. Willig · (Labor) · Kirschner, Walters & Willig · 1608 Walnut Street Philadelphia, PA 19103 · 215-893-9000

Joseph G. Armstrong III · (Management) · Reed Smith Shaw & McClay · James H. Reed Building, Mellon Square · 435 Sixth Avenue · P.O. Box 2009 · Pittsburgh, PA 15230 · 412-288-3131

William Bevan III · (Management) · Reed Smith Shaw & McClay · James H. Reed Building, Mellon Square · 435 Sixth Avenue · P.O. Box 2009 · Pittsburgh, PA 15230 · 412-288-3131

Aims C. Coney, Jr. · (Management) · Kirkpatrick & Lockhart · 1500 Oliver Building · Pittsburgh, PA 15222 · 412-355-6500

Walter P. DeForest III · (Management) · Reed Smith Shaw & McClay · James H. Reed Building, Mellon Square · 435 Sixth Avenue · P.O. Box 2009 · Pittsburgh, PA 15230 · 412-288-3131

John F. Dugan · (Management) · Kirkpatrick & Lockhart · 1500 Oliver Building Pittsburgh, PA 15222 · 412-355-6500

Lloyd F. Engle, Jr. · (Labor) · Kuhn, Engle and Stein · 1307 Manor Building · 564 Forbes Avenue · Pittsburgh, PA 15219 · 412-281-4555

Robert W. Hartland · (Management) · Reed Smith Shaw & McClay · James H. Reed Building, Mellon Square · 435 Sixth Avenue · P.O. Box 2009 · Pittsburgh, PA 15230 · 412-288-3131

James Q. Harty · (Management) · Reed Smith Shaw & McClay · James H. Reed Building, Mellon Square · 435 Sixth Avenue · P.O. Box 2009 · Pittsburgh, PA 15230 · 412-288-3131

Louis B. Kushner · (Labor) · Rothman Gordon Foreman and Groudine · 300 Grant Building · Pittsburgh, PA 15219 · 412-281-0705

William A. Meyer, Jr. · (Management) · Meyer, Unkovic & Scott · 1300 Oliver Building · Pittsburgh, PA 15222 · 412-456-2800

Joseph J. Pass, Jr. · (Labor) · Jubelirer, Pass & Intrieri · 219 Fort Pitt Boulevard Pittsburgh, PA 15222 · 412-281-3850

Patrick W. Ritchey · (Management) · Reed Smith Shaw & McClay · James H. Reed Building, Mellon Square · 435 Sixth Avenue · P.O. Box 2009 · Pittsburgh, PA 15230 · 412-288-3131

Leonard L. Scheinholtz · (Management) · Reed Smith Shaw & McClay · James H. Reed Building, Mellon Square · 435 Sixth Avenue · P.O. Box 2009 · Pittsburgh, PA 15230 · 412-288-3131

Stanford A. Segal · (Labor) · Gatz, Cohen, Segal & Koerner · 1708 Law & Finance Building · 429 Fourth Street · Pittsburgh, PA 15219 · 412-261-1380

Melvin P. Stein · (Labor) · Kuhn, Engle and Stein · 1307 Manor Building · 564 Forbes Avenue · Pittsburgh, PA 15219 · 412-281-4555

Hayes C. Stover · (Management) · Kirkpatrick & Lockhart · 1500 Oliver Building Pittsburgh, PA 15222 · 412-355-6500

John C. Unkovic · (Management) · Reed Smith Shaw & McClay · James H. Reed Building, Mellon Square · 435 Sixth Avenue · P.O. Box 2009 · Pittsburgh, PA 15230 · 412-288-3131

Charles R. Volk · (Management) · Volk, Frankovitch, Anetakis, Recht, Robertson & Hellerstedt · Three Gateway Center · Pittsburgh, PA 15222 · 412-392-2300

Scott F. Zimmerman · (Management) · Reed Smith Shaw & McClay · James H. Reed Building, Mellon Square · 435 Sixth Avenue · P.O. Box 2009 · Pittsburgh, PA 15230 · 412-288-3131

William R. Tait, Jr. · (Management) · McNerney, Page, Vanderlin & Hall · 433 Market Street · Williamsport, PA 17703 · 717-326-6555

MARITIME LAW

Henry C. Lucas III · Rawle & Henderson · 211 South Broad Street · Philadelphia, PA 19107 · 215-875-4000

Richard W. Palmer · Palmer Biezup & Henderson · Public Ledger Building, Suite 956 · Independence Square · Philadelphia, PA 19106 · 215-625-9900

NATURAL RESOURCES AND ENVIRONMENTAL LAW

Terry R. Bossert · McNees, Wallace & Nurick · 100 Pine Street · P.O. Box 1166 Harrisburg, PA 17108 · 717-232-8000

Eugene E. Dice · (Plaintiffs) · 1721 North Front Street, Suite 101 · Harrisburg, PA 17102 · 717-238-4256

John E. Childe, Jr. · (Plaintiffs) · 1389 Bradley Avenue · Hummelstown, PA 17036 · 717-566-5626

Robert L. Collings · Morgan, Lewis & Bockius · 2000 One Logan Square Philadelphia, PA 19103 · 215-963-5000

Marc E. Gold · Wolf, Block, Schorr and Solis-Cohen · Packard Building, 12th Floor · Philadelphia, PA 19102 · 215-977-2000

Donald K. Joseph · Wolf, Block, Schorr and Solis-Cohen · Packard Building, 12th Floor · Philadelphia, PA 19102 · 215-977-2000

Kenneth R. Myers · Morgan, Lewis & Bockius · 2000 One Logan Square Philadelphia, PA 19103 · 215-963-5000

Hershel J. Richman · Cohen, Shapiro, Polisher, Shiekman and Cohen · PSFS Building, 22nd Floor · 12 South 12th Street · Philadelphia, PA 19107-3981 215-922-1300

Bradford F. Whitman · Dechert Price & Rhoads · 3400 Centre Square West 1500 Market Street · Philadelphia, PA 19102 · 215-981-2000

Minturn T. Wright III · (Coal) · Dechert Price & Rhoads · 3400 Centre Square West · 1500 Market Street · Philadelphia, PA 19102 · 215-981-2000

Blair S. McMillin · Reed Smith Shaw & McClay · James H. Reed Building, Mellon Square · 435 Sixth Avenue · P.O. Box 2009 · Pittsburgh, PA 15230 412-288-3131

Harley N. Trice II · Reed Smith Shaw & McClay · James H. Reed Building, Mellon Square · 435 Sixth Avenue · P.O. Box 2009 · Pittsburgh, PA 15230 412-288-3131

Peter Greig Veeder · Thorp, Reed & Armstrong · One Riverfront Center Pittsburgh, PA 15222 · 412-394-7711

PERSONAL INJURY LITIGATION

Andrew J. Conner · Conner & Associates · 17 West 10th Street · Erie, PA 16501 814-453-3343

Richard C. Angino · (Plaintiffs) · Angino & Rovner · 4503 North Front Street Harrisburg, PA 17110-1799 · 717-238-6791

Thomas D. Caldwell, Jr. · (Defendants) · Caldwell & Kearns · 3631 North Front Street · Harrisburg, PA 17110 · 717-232-7661

James W. Evans · (Defendants) · Shearer, Mette, Evans & Woodside · 1801 North Front Street · P.O. Box 729 · Harrisburg, PA 17108-0729 · 717-232-5000

Joseph P. Hafer · (Defendants) · Thomas & Thomas · 212 Locust Street, Suite 500 · P.O. Box 999 · Harrisburg, PA 17108 · 717-255-7600

James E. Beasley · (Plaintiffs) · Beasley, Casey, Colleran, Erbstein, Thistle, Kline & Murphy · 21 South 12th Street, Fifth Floor · Philadelphia, PA 19107 215-665-1000

Perry S. Bechtle · (Defendants) · LaBrum and Doak · IVB Building, Seventh Floor · 1700 Market Street · Philadelphia, PA 19103 · 215-561-4400

Marshall A. Bernstein · (Plaintiffs) · Bernstein, Bernstein & Harrison · 1600 Market Street, Suite 2500 · Philadelphia, PA 19103 · 215-864-0770

Stephen M. Feldman · (Plaintiffs) · 1715 Rittenhouse Square · Philadelphia, PA 19103 · 215-546-2604

Joseph H. Foster · (Defendants) · White and Williams · 1234 Market Street, 17th Floor · Philadelphia, PA 19107 · 215-854-7000

James Lewis Griffith · (Defendants) · Griffith & Burr · 1608 Walnut Street, 14th Floor · Philaldephia, PA 19103 · 215-893-1234

Herbert F. Kolsby · (Plaintiffs) · Kolsby & Gordon · 243 South 10th Street · Philadelphia, PA 19107 · 215-627-6605

George J. Lavin, Jr. · (Defendants) · George J. Lavin, Jr. Associates · Penn Mutual Tower, 12th Floor · 510 Walnut Street · Philadelphia, PA 19106 · 215-627-0303

S. Gerald Litvin · (Plaintiffs) · Litvin, Blumberg, Matusow & Young · 210 West Washington Square, Fifth Floor · Philadelphia, PA 19106 · 215-925-4500

William J. O'Brien · (Defendants) · Conrad & O'Brien · The Drexel Building, Fourth Floor · 15th and Walnut Streets · Philadelphia, PA 19102 · 215-864-0810

Joseph V. Pinto · (Defendants) · White and Williams · 1234 Market Street, 17th Floor · Philadelphia, PA 19107 · 215-854-7000

Thomas B. Rutter · (Plaintiffs) · Rutter, Turner & Stein · Curtis Center · Independence Square West, Suite 750 · One Walnut Street · Philadelphia, PA 19106 · 215-925-9200

Daniel J. Ryan · (Defendants) · LaBrum and Doak · IVB Building, Seventh Floor · 1700 Market Street · Philadelphia, PA 19103-3997 · 215-561-4400

David S. Shrager · (Plaintiffs) · Shrager, McDaid & Loftus · Eight Penn Center Plaza, 17th Floor · 17th & John F. Kennedy Boulevard · Philadelphia, PA 19103 · 215-568-7771

David J. Armstrong · Dickie, McCamey & Chilcote · Two PPG Place, Suite 400 · Pittsburgh, PA 15222-5402 · 412-281-7272

Edward J. Balzarini, Sr. · (Plaintiffs) · Balzarini, Carey & Watson · 3303 Grant Building · Pittsburgh, PA 15219 · 412-471-1200

William R. Caroselli · (Plaintiffs) · Caroselli, Spagnolli & Beachler · 322 Boulevard of the Allies, Eighth Floor · Pittsburgh, PA 15222 · 412-391-9860

Thomas L. Cooper · (Plaintiffs) · Gilardi & Cooper · 808 Grant Building · Pittsburgh, PA 15219 · 412-391-9770

Carl A. Eck · (Defendants) · Meyer, Darragh, Buckler, Bebenek & Eck · 2000 The Frick Building · Pittsburgh, PA 15219 · 412-261-6600

David B. Fawcett, Jr. · (Defendants) · Dickie, McCamey & Chilcote · Two PPG Place, Suite 400 · Pittsburgh, PA 15222-5402 · 412-281-7272

Robert S. Grigsby · (Defendants) · Alder Cohen & Grigsby · 600 Grant Street, Fifth Floor · Pittsburgh, PA 15219 · 412-394-4900

Dennis C. Harrington · (Plaintiffs) · Harrington & Schweers · 100 Ross Street Pittsburgh, PA 15219 · 412-391-3477

Thomas Hollander · (Plaintiffs) · Evans, Ivory, Moses, Hollander & MacVay 1311 Frick Building · Pittsburgh, PA 15219 · 412-471-3740

Herman C. Kimpel · (Defendants) · Dickie, McCamey & Chilcote · Two PPG Place, Suite 400 · Pittsburgh, PA 15222-5402 · 412-281-7272

David H. Trushel · (Defendants) · Trushel, Klymm & Asti · 1207 Fifth Avenue Pittsburgh, PA 15219 · 412-232-3800

Joseph A. Quinn, Jr. · (Plaintiffs) · Hourigan, Kluger, Spohrer, Quinn & Myers 700 United Penn Bank Building · Wilkes Barre, PA 18701 · 717-825-9401

REAL ESTATE LAW

F. Richard Martsolf · Martsolf & Bratton · 125 State Street · Harrisburg, PA 17101 717-236-4241

Kenelm L. Shirk, Jr. · Shirk, Reist, Wagen, Seller and Shirk · 132 East Chestnut Street · P.O. Box 1552 · Lancaster, PA 17603 · 717-394-7247

David C. Auten · Reed Smith Shaw & McClay · 1600 Avenue of the Arts Building Broad & Chestnut Streets · Philadelphia, PA 19107 · 215-875-4300

Edward F. Beatty, Jr. · Saul, Ewing, Remick & Saul · 3800 Center Square West Philadelphia, PA 19102-2186 · 215-972-7777

Michael M. Dean · Wolf, Block, Schorr and Solis-Cohen · Packard Building, 12th Floor · Philadelphia, PA 19102 · 215-977-2000

Morris J. Dean · Blank, Rome, Comisky & McCauley · Four Penn Center Plaza, 10th-13th Floors · Philadelphia, PA 19103 · 215-569-5500

Alvin H. Dorsky · Wolf, Block, Schorr and Solis-Cohen · Packard Building, 12th Floor · Philadelphia, PA 19102 · 215-977-2000

Stuart F. Ebby · Toll, Ebby & Langer · 1760 Market Street, Sixth Floor Philadelphia, PA 19103 · 215-567-5770

Frank J. Ferro · Dechert Price & Rhoads · 3400 Centre Square West · 1500 Market Street · Philadelphia, PA 19102 · 215-981-2000

Marvin Garfinkel · Mesirov, Gelman, Jaffe, Cramer & Jamieson · 1500 The Fidelity Building · Philadelphia, PA 19109 · 215-893-5000

Ronald B. Glazer · Wolf, Block, Schorr and Solis-Cohen · Packard Building, 12th Floor · Philadelphia, PA 19102 · 215-977-2000

Morris C. Kellett · Dechert Price & Rhoads · 3400 Centre Square West · 1500 Market Street · Philadelphia, PA 19102 · 215-981-2000

David W. Maxey · Drinker Biddle & Reath · 1100 Philadelphia National Bank Building · Broad & Chestnut Streets · Philadelphia, PA 19107 · 215-988-2700

Henry F. Miller · Wolf, Block, Schorr and Solis-Cohen · Packard Building, 12th Floor · Philadelphia, PA 19102 · 215-977-2000

Harris Ominsky · Blank, Rome, Comisky & McCauley · Four Penn Center Plaza, 10th-13th Floors · Philadelphia, PA 19103 · 215-569-5500

Mitchell E. Panzer · Wolf, Block, Schorr and Solis-Cohen · Packard Building, 12th Floor · Philadelphia, PA 19102 · 215-977-2000

Julian P. Rackow · Blank, Rome, Comisky & McCauley · Four Penn Center Plaza, 10th-13th Floors · Philadelphia, PA 19103 · 215-569-5500

Kenneth I. Rosenberg · Mesirov, Gelman, Jaffe, Cramer & Jamieson · 1500 The Fidelity Building · Philadelphia, PA 19109 · 215-893-5000

Sanford M. Rosenbloom · Schnader, Harrison, Segal & Lewis · 1600 Market Street, Suite 3600 · Philadelphia, PA 19103 · 215-751-2000

James A. Rosenstein · Wolf, Block, Schorr and Solis-Cohen · Packard Building, 12th Floor · Philadelphia, PA 19102 · 215-977-2000

Robert M. Schwartz · White and Williams · 1234 Market Street, 17th Floor Philadelphia, PA 19107 · 215-854-7000

Robert M. Segal · Wolf, Block, Schorr and Solis-Cohen · Packard Building, 12th Floor · Philadelphia, PA 19102 · 215-977-2000

Russell W. Whitman · Dechert Price & Rhoads · 3400 Centre Square West · 1500 Market Street · Philadelphia, PA 19102 · 215-981-2000

Alan L. Ackerman · Berkman Ruslander Pohl Lieber & Engel · One Oxford Centre, 40th Floor · Pittsburgh, PA 15219-6498 · 412-392-2000

Alexander Black · Buchanan Ingersoll · 600 Grant Street, 57th Floor · Pittsburgh, PA 15219 · 412-562-8800

Raymond W. Cromer · Cromer, Reinbold & Lamb · 450 Porter Building · Pittsburgh, PA 15219 · 412-281-2738

Thomas J. Dempsey · 820 Frick Building · Pittsburgh, PA 15219 · 412-281-2442

Daniel B. Dixon · Rose, Schmidt, Hasley & DiSalle · 900 Oliver Building · Pittsburgh, PA 15222-5369 · 412-434-8600

Samuel L. Douglass · Rose, Schmidt, Hasley & DiSalle · 900 Oliver Building Pittsburgh, PA 15222-5369 · 412-434-8600

William J. Fahey · 706 Allegheny Building · Pittsburgh, PA 15219 · 412-281-7840

Vincent J. Grogan · Grogan, Graffam, McGinley & Lucchino · Three Gateway Center, 22nd Floor · Pittsburgh, PA 15222 · 412-471-5150

Calvin R. Harvey · Buchanan Ingersoll · 600 Grant Street, 57th Floor · Pittsburgh, PA 15219 · 412-562-8800

E. D. Hollinshead · Hollinshead and Mendelson · 230 Grant Building · Pittsburgh, PA 15219 · 412-355-7070

Leonard M. Mendelson · Hollinshead and Mendelson · 230 Grant Building Pittsburgh, PA 15219 · 412-355-7070

Regis D. Murrin · Reed Smith Shaw & McClay · James H. Reed Building, Mellon Square · 435 Sixth Avenue · P.O. Box 2009 · Pittsburgh, PA 15230 · 412-288-3131

Harvey E. Robins · Brennan, Robins & Daley · Commonwealth Building, 19th Floor · Pittsburgh, PA 15222 · 412-281-0776

Edward W. Seifert · Reed Smith Shaw & McClay · James H. Reed Building, Mellon Square · 435 Sixth Avenue · P.O. Box 2009 · Pittsburgh, PA 15230 · 412-288-3131

Herbert G. Sheinberg · Sheinberg & Hoover · 617 Grant Building · Pittsburgh, PA 15219 · 412-261-6300

William J. Staley · Tucker Arensberg · 1200 Pittsburgh National Building · Pittsburgh, PA 15222 · 412-566-1212

John H. White · Reed Smith Shaw & McClay · James H. Reed Building, Mellon Square · 435 Sixth Avenue · P.O. Box 2009 · Pittsburgh, PA 15230 · 412-288-3131

Nelson P. Young · Reed Smith Shaw & McClay · James H. Reed Building, Mellon Square · 435 Sixth Avenue · P.O. Box 2009 · Pittsburgh, PA 15230 · 412-288-3131

TAX AND EMPLOYEE BENEFITS LAW

Howell C. Mette · Shearer, Mette, Evans & Woodside · 1801 North Front Street · P.O. Box 729 · Harrisburg, PA 17108-0729 · 717-232-5000

Gerald K. Morrison · Rhoads & Sinon · 410 North Third Street · P.O. Box 1146 · Harrisburg, PA 17108 · 717-233-5731

John S. Oyler · McNees, Wallace & Nurick · 100 Pine Street · P.O. Box 1166 · Harrisburg, PA 17108 · 717-232-8000

Richard W. Stevenson · McNees, Wallace & Nurick · 100 Pine Street · P.O. Box 1166 · Harrisburg, PA 17108 · 717-232-8000

Anthony L. Bartolini · Dechert Price & Rhoads · 3400 Centre Square West · 1500 Market Street · Philadelphia, PA 19102 · 215-981-2000

John Marley Bernard · (Employee Benefits) · Ballard, Spahr, Andrews & Ingersoll · 30 South 17th Street, 20th Floor · Philadelphia, PA 19103 · 215-564-1800

Robert A. Bildersee · (Employee Benefits) · Morgan, Lewis & Bockius · 2000 One Logan Square · Philadelphia, PA 19103 · 215-963-5000

Sheldon M. Bonovitz · Duane, Morris & Heckscher · One Franklin Plaza, Suite 1500 · Philadelphia, PA 19102 · 215-854-6300

Christopher Branda, Jr. · Dechert Price & Rhoads · 3400 Centre Square West · 1500 Market Street · Philadelphia, PA 19102 · 215-981-2000

Robert D. Comfort · Morgan, Lewis & Bockius · 2000 One Logan Square · Philadelphia, PA 19103 · 215-963-5000

William M. Goldstein · Drinker Biddle & Reath · 1100 Philadelphia National Bank Building · Broad & Chestnut Streets · Philadelphia, PA 19107 215-988-2700

Selwyn A. Horvitz · Horvitz, Fisher, Miller & Sedlack · 1515 Locust Street, Suite 400 · Philadelphia, PA 19102 · 215-732-3232

Garry P. Jerome · (Employee Benefits) · Pepper, Hamilton & Scheetz · The Fidelity Building, 20th Floor · 123 South Broad Street · Philadelphia, PA 19109 215-893-3000

Paul S. Kimbol · (Employee Benefits) · Dechert Price & Rhoads · 3400 Centre Square West · 1500 Market Street · Philadelphia, PA 19102 · 215-981-2000

Charles G. Kopp · Wolf, Block, Schorr and Solis-Cohen · Packard Building, 12th Floor · Philadelphia, PA 19102 · 215-977-2000

Joseph E. Lundy · Ballard, Spahr, Andrews & Ingersoll · 30 South 17th Street, 20th Floor · Philadelphia, PA 19103 · 215-564-1800

William Scott Magargee III · (Employee Benefits) · Dechert Price & Rhoads · 3400 Centre Square West · 1500 Market Street · Philadelphia, PA 19102 215-981-2000

Robert E. McQuiston · Ballard, Spahr, Andrews & Ingersoll · 30 South 17th Street, 20th Floor · Philadelphia, PA 19103 · 215-564-1800

William A. Rosoff · Wolf, Block, Schorr and Solis-Cohen · Packard Building, 12th Floor · Philadelphia, PA 19102 · 215-977-2000

H. Peter Somers · Morgan, Lewis & Bockius · 2000 One Logan Square · Philadelphia, PA 19103 · 215-963-5000

Ronald M. Wiener · Wolf, Block, Schorr and Solis-Cohen · Packard Building, 12th Floor · Philadelphia, PA 19102 · 215-977-2000

Richard P. Wild · Dechert Price & Rhoads · 3400 Centre Square West · 1500 Market Street · Philadelphia, PA 19102 · 215-981-2000

Mervin M. Wilf · (also Employee Benefits) · Three Mellon Bank Center, Suite 1320 · Philadelphia, PA 19102 · 215-568-4842

Thomas D. Arbogast · Reed Smith Shaw & McClay · James H. Reed Building, Mellon Square · 435 Sixth Avenue · P.O. Box 2009 · Pittsburgh, PA 15230 412-288-3131

Edward A. Craig III · Kirkpatrick & Lockhart · 1500 Oliver Building · Pittsburgh, PA 15222 · 412-355-6500

Alan H. Finegold · Kirkpatrick & Lockhart · 1500 Oliver Building · Pittsburgh, PA 15222 · 412-355-6500

Robert A. Johnson · (Employee Benefits) · Buchanan Ingersoll · 600 Grant Street, 57th Floor · Pittsburgh, PA 15219 · 412-562-8800

David L. Ketter · Kirkpatrick & Lockhart · 1500 Oliver Building · Pittsburgh, PA 15222 · 412-355-6500

Marvin S. Lieber · Berkman Ruslander Pohl Lieber & Engel · One Oxford Centre, 40th Floor · Pittsburgh, PA 15219-6498 · 412-392-2000

Larry E. Phillips · Buchanan Ingersoll · 600 Grant Street, 57th Floor · Pittsburgh, PA 15219 · 412-562-8800

William H. Powderly III · (Employee Benefits) · Reed Smith Shaw & McClay James H. Reed Building, Mellon Square · 435 Sixth Avenue · P.O. Box 2009 Pittsburgh, PA 15230 · 412-288-3131

Charles J. Queenan, Jr. · Kirkpatrick & Lockhart · 1500 Oliver Building · Pittsburgh, PA 15222 · 412-355-6500

William Y. Rodewald · Buchanan Ingersoll · 600 Grant Street, 57th Floor · Pittsburgh, PA 15219 · 412-562-8800

Charles R. Smith, Jr. · (Employee Benefits) · Kirkpatrick & Lockhart · 1500 Oliver Building · Pittsburgh, PA 15222 · 412-355-6500

Robert B. Williams · Eckert, Seamans, Cherin & Mellot · 600 Grant Street, 42nd Floor · Pittsburgh, PA 15219 · 412-566-6000

Patrick J. Di Quinzio · 37 West Gay Street · Westchester, PA 19308 · 215-436-6535

TRUSTS AND ESTATES

Heath L. Allen · Keefer, Wood, Allen & Rahal · Walnut-Court Building · 210 Walnut Street · P.O. Box 11963 · Harrisburg, PA 17108-1963 · 717-255-8000

William D. Boswell · Boswell, Tintner & Piccola · 315 North Front Street · P.O. Box 3787 · Harrisburg, PA 17105 · 717-236-9377

Richard R. Lefever · McNees, Wallace & Nurick · 100 Pine Street · P.O. Box 1166 · Harrisburg, PA 17108 · 717-232-8000

Howell C. Mette · Shearer, Mette, Evans & Woodside · 1801 North Front Street P.O. Box 729 · Harrisburg, PA 17108-0729 · 717-232-5000

Henry W. Rhoads · Rhoads & Sinon · 410 North Third Street · P.O. Box 1146 Harrisburg, PA 17108 · 717-233-5731

Donald R. Waisel · McNees, Wallace & Nurick · 100 Pine Street · P.O. Box 1166 Harrisburg, PA 17108 · 717-232-8000

Paul E. Clouser · 4000 Vine Street · Middletown, PA 17057 · 717-944-0900

J. Brooke Aker · Smith, Aker, Grossman & Hollinger · 60 East Penn Street · P.O. Box 150 · Norristown, PA 19404 · 215-275-8200

Richard L. Grossman · Smith, Aker, Grossman & Hollinger · 60 East Penn Street P.O. Box 150 · Norristown, PA 19404 · 215-275-8200

James L. Hollinger · Smith, Aker, Grossman & Hollinger · 60 East Penn Street P.O. Box 150 · Norristown, PA 19404 · 215-275-8200

William C. Bullitt · Drinker Biddle & Reath · 1100 Philadelphia National Bank Building · Broad & Chestnut Streets · Philadelphia, PA 19107 · 215-988-2700

Bruce L. Castor · Ballard, Spahr, Andrews & Ingersoll · 30 South 17th Street, 20th Floor · Philadelphia, PA 19103 · 215-564-1800

William J. Daniel · Wolf, Block, Schorr and Solis-Cohen · Packard Building, 12th Floor · Philadelphia, PA 19103 · 215-977-2000

Robert I. Friedman · Wolf, Block, Schorr and Solis-Cohen · Packard Building, 12th Floor · Philadelphia, PA 19103 · 215-977-2000

Christopher H. Gadsden · Drinker Biddle & Reath · 1100 Philadelphia National Bank Building · Broad & Chestnut Streets · Philadelphia, PA 19107 · 215-988-2700

George J. Hauptfuhrer · Dechert Price & Rhoads · 3400 Centre Square West 1500 Market Street · Philadelphia, PA 19102 · 215-981-2000

Martin A. Heckscher · Duane, Morris & Heckscher · One Franklin Plaza, Suite1500 · Philadelphia, PA 19102 · 215-854-6300

H. Ober Hess · Ballard, Spahr, Andrews & Ingersoll · 30 South 17th Street, 20th Floor · Philadelphia, PA 19103 · 215-564-1800

Paul C. Heintz · Obermayer, Rebmann, Maxwell & Hippel · Packard Building, 14th Floor · Philadelphia, PA 19102 · 215-665-3000

David J. Kaufman · Wolf, Block, Schorr and Solis-Cohen · Packard Building, 12th Floor · Philadelphia, PA 19102 · 215-977-2000

James R. Ledwith · Pepper, Hamilton & Scheetz · The Fidelity Building, 20th Floor · 123 South Broad Street · Philadelphia, PA 19109-1083 · 215-893-3000

John J. Lombard, Jr. · Morgan, Lewis & Bockius · 2000 One Logan Square Philadelphia, PA 19103 · 215-963-5000

George H. Nofer · Schnader, Harrison, Segal & Lewis · 1600 Market Street, Suite 3600 · Philadelphia, PA 19103 · 215-751-2000

J. Pennington Straus · Schnader, Harrison, Segal & Lewis · 1600 Market Street, Suite 3600 · Philadelphia, PA 19103 · 215-751-2000

Regina O'Brien Thomas · Ballard, Spahr, Andrews & Ingersoll · 30 South 17th Street, 20th Floor · Philadelphia, PA 19103 · 215-564-1800

Minturn T. Wright III · Dechert Price & Rhoads · 3400 Centre Square West 1500 Market Street · Philadelphia, PA 19102 · 215-981-2000

Jack G. Armstrong · Buchanan Ingersoll · 600 Grant Street, 57th Floor · Pittsburgh, PA 15219 · 412-562-8800

G. Donald Gerlach · Reed, Smith, Shaw & McClay · James H. Reed Building, Mellon Square · 435 Sixth Avenue · P.O. Box 2009 · Pittsburgh, PA 15230 412-288-3131

William McC. Houston · Houston, Houston & Donnelly · 2510 Centre City Tower · 650 Smithfield Street · Pittsburgh, PA 15222 · 412-471-5828

W. Reid Lowe · Meyer, Unkovic & Scott · 1300 Oliver Building · Pittsburgh, PA 15222 · 412-456-2800

Stephen E. Nash · Meyer, Unkovic & Scott · 1300 Oliver Building · Pittsburgh, PA 15222 · 412-456-2800

K. Sidney Neuman · Buchanan Ingersoll · 600 Grant Street, 57th Floor · Pittsburgh, PA 15219 · 412-562-8800

James W. Ummer · Buchanan Ingersoll · 600 Grant Street, 57th Floor · Pittsburgh, PA 15219 · 412-562-8800

Robert B. Williams · Eckert, Seamans, Cherin & Mellott · 600 Grant Street, 42nd Floor · Pittsburgh, PA 15219 · 412-566-6000

S. Jonathan Emerson · Montgomery, McCracken, Walker & Rhoads · One Mennonite Church Road · Spring City, PA 19475 · 215-948-5566

RHODE ISLAND

BANKRUPTCY LAW	624
BUSINESS LITIGATION	624
CORPORATE LAW	625
CRIMINAL DEFENSE	626
FAMILY LAW	626
LABOR AND EMPLOYMENT LAW	627
NATURAL RESOURCES AND ENVIRONMENTAL LAW	627
PERSONAL INJURY LITIGATION	627
REAL ESTATE LAW	628
TAX AND EMPLOYEE BENEFITS LAW	629
TRUSTS AND ESTATES	629

BANKRUPTCY LAW

Allan M. Shine · Winograd, Shine & Zacks · 123 Dyer Street · Providence, RI 02903 · 401-273-8300

Michael A. Silverstein · Hinckley, Allen, Snyder & Conen · 1500 Fleet Center · Providence, RI 02903 · 401-274-2000

Edward J. Bertozzi, Jr. · Edwards & Angell · 2700 Hospital Trust Tower · Providence, RI 02903 · 401-274-9200

BUSINESS LITIGATION

John H. Blish · Blish & Cavanagh · Commerce Center · 30 Exchange Terrace · Providence, RI 02903 · 401-831-8900

Joseph V. Cavanagh, Jr. · Blish & Cavanagh · Commerce Center · 30 Exchange Terrace · Providence, RI 02903 · 401-831-8900

Michael P. DeFanti · Hinckley, Allen, Snyder & Conen · 1500 Fleet Center Providence, RI 02903 · 401-274-2000

Robert G. Flanders, Jr. · Flanders + Madeiros · One Turks Heap Place, Suite 700 · Providence, RI 02903 · 401-831-0700

Peter Lawson Kennedy · Adler Pollock & Sheehan · 2300 Hospital Trust Tower Providence, RI 02903 · 401-274-7200

Matthew F. Medeiros · Flanders + Madeiros · One Turks Heap Place, Suite 700 Providence, RI 02903 · 401-831-0700

George M. Vetter, Jr. · Vetter & White · 20 Washington Place · Providence, RI 02903 · 401-421-3060

Benjamin V. White III · Vetter & White · 20 Washington Place · Providence, RI 02903 · 401-421-3060

CORPORATE LAW

Stephen J. Carlotti · Hinckley, Allen, Snyder & Conen · 1500 Fleet Center Providence, RI 02903 · 401-274-2000

John F. Corrigan · Adler Pollock & Sheehan · 2300 Hospital Trust Tower Providence, RI 02903 · 401-274-7200

Robert Spink Davis · Edwards & Angell · 2700 Hospital Trust Tower · Providence, RI 02903 · 401-274-9200

Jacques V. Hopkins · Hinckley, Allen, Snyder & Conen · 1500 Fleet Center Providence, RI 02903 · 401-274-2000

James A. Jackson · Hinckley, Allen, Snyder & Conen · 1500 Fleet Center Providence, RI 02903 · 401-274-2000

V. Duncan Johnson · Edwards & Angell · 2700 Hospital Trust Tower · Providence, RI 02903 · 401-274-9200

Eustace T. Pliakas · Tillinghast, Collins & Graham · One Old Stone Square Providence, RI 02903 · 401-456-1200

James J. Skeffington · Edwards & Angell · 2700 Hospital Trust Tower · Providence, RI 02903 · 401-274-9200

Bentley Tobin · Hinckley, Allen, Snyder & Conen · 1500 Fleet Center · Providence, RI 02903 · 401-274-2000

Edwin G. Torrance · Hinckley, Allen, Snyder & Conen · 1500 Fleet Center Providence, RI 02903 · 401-274-2000

Joachim A. Weissfeld · Hinckley, Allen, Snyder & Conen · 1500 Fleet Center Providence, RI 02903 · 401-274-2000

CRIMINAL DEFENSE

Harold C. Arcaro, Jr. · Arcaro & Reilly · 1040 Fleet National Bank Building Providence, RI 02903 · 401-751-1040

Peter A. Di Biase · Toro Law Associates · 91 Friendship Street · Providence, RI 02903 · 401-351-7752

William A. Dimitri, Jr. · Jackvony & Dimitri · 733 Douglas Avenue · Providence, RI 02908 · 401-273-9092

John A. MacFadyen III · (Appellate) · 91 Friendship Street · Providence, RI 02903 · 401-521-4420

Eugene F. Toro · Toro Law Associates · 91 Friendship Street · Providence, RI 02903 · 401-351-7752

John Tramonti, Jr. · 808 Hospital Trust Building · Providence, RI 02903 · 401-751-5433

FAMILY LAW

Alfred Factor · Kirshenbaum and Kirshenbaum · 888 Reservoir Avenue · Cranston, RI 02910 · 401-946-3200

Joseph T. Houlihan · Corcoran, Peckham & Hayes · 61 Long Wharf · P.O. Box 389 · Newport, RI 02840 · 401-847-0872

Howard I. Lipsey · Lipsey & Skolnik · 369 South Main Street · Providence, RI 02903 · 401-351-7700

Jerry L. McIntyre · Edwards & Angell · 130 Bellevue Avenue · Newport, RI 02840 · 401-849-7800

LABOR AND EMPLOYMENT LAW

Patrick A. Liguori · (Management) · Adler Pollock & Sheehan · 2300 Hospital Trust Tower · Providence, RI 02903 · 401-274-7200

Raul L. Lovett · (Labor; Individuals) · Lovett, Schefrin & Gallogly · Two Thomas Street · Providence, RI 02903 · 401-863-8800

Thomas J. McAndrew · (Management) · 20 Washington Place · Providence, RI 02903 · 401-274-1144

Julius C. Michaelson · (Labor) · 321 South Main Street · Providence, RI 02903 401-277-9300

John J. Pendergast III · (Management) · Hinckley, Allen, Snyder & Conen 1500 Fleet Center · Providence, RI 02903 · 401-274-2000

William R. Powers III · (Management) · Powers, Harsch & Kinder · 20 Washington Place · Providence, RI 02903 · 401-421-2224

William J. Sheehan · (Labor; Management) · Adler Pollock & Sheehan · 2300 Hospital Trust Tower · Providence, RI 02903 · 401-274-7200

Richard A. Skolnik · (Labor) · Lipsey & Skolnik · 369 South Main Street · Providence, RI 02903 · 401-351-7700

NATURAL RESOURCES AND ENVIRONMENTAL LAW

Gregory L. Benik · Hinckley, Allen, Snyder & Conen · 1500 Fleet Center Providence, RI 02903 · 401-274-2000

PERSONAL INJURY LITIGATION

Leonard Decof · (Plaintiffs) · Decof & Grimm · One Smith Hill · Providence, RI 02903 · 401-272-1110

John F. Dolan · (Defendants) · Rice, Dolan & Kershaw · 101 Dyer Street, Suite 3-A · Providence, RI 02903 · 401-272-8800

Joseph A. Kelly · (Defendants) · Carroll, Kelly & Murphy · The Packet Building, Suite 200 · 155 South Main Street · Providence, RI 02903 · 401-331-7272

A. Lauriston Parks · (Defendants) · Hanson, Curran, Parks & Whitman · 1210 Turks Head Building · Providence, RI 02903-2274 · 401-421-2154

George M. Vetter, Jr. · (Defendants) · Vetter & White · 20 Washington Place Providence, RI 02903 · 401-421-3060

Max Wistow · (Plaintiffs) · Wistow & Barylick · Hanley Building · 56 Pine Street Providence, RI 02903 · 401-831-2700

REAL ESTATE LAW

E. Jerome Batty · Hinckley, Allen, Snyder & Conen · 1500 Fleet Center Providence, RI 02903 · 401-274-2000

Richard W. Billings · Hinckley, Allen, Snyder & Conen · 1500 Fleet Center Providence, RI 02903 · 401-274-2000

Michael R. Goldenberg · Goldenberg & Muri · 15 Westminster Street · Providence, RI 02903 · 401-421-7300

Timothy T. More · Edwards & Angell · 2700 Hospital Trust Tower · Providence, RI 02903 · 401-274-9200

Robert A. Pitassi · Licht & Semonoff · One Park Row · Providence, RI 02903 401-421-8030

Charles F. Rogers · Edwards & Angell · 2700 Hospital Trust Tower · Providence, RI 02903 · 401-274-9200

David J. Tracy · Hinckley, Allen, Snyder & Conen · 1500 Fleet Center · Providence, RI 02903 · 401-274-2000

TAX AND EMPLOYEE BENEFITS LAW

Harold C. Arcaro, Jr. · Arcaro & Reilly · 1040 Fleet National Bank Building Providence, RI 02903 · 401-751-1040

Edmund C. Bennett · Hinckley, Allen, Snyder & Conen · 1500 Fleet Center Providence, RI 02903 · 401-274-2000

Alfred S. Lombardi · Edwards & Angell · 2700 Hospital Trust Tower · Providence, RI 02903 · 401-274-9200

Frederick P. McClure · (Employee Benefits) · Hinckley, Allen, Snyder & Conen 1500 Fleet Center · Providence, RI 02903 · 401-274-2000

H. Peter Olsen · Hinckley, Allen, Snyder & Conen · 1500 Fleet Center · Providence, RI 02903 · 401-274-2000

John H. Reid III · (Employee Benefits) · Edwards & Angell · 2700 Hospital Trust Tower · Providence, RI 02903 · 401-274-9200

TRUSTS AND ESTATES

James H. Barnett · Edwards & Angell · 2700 Hospital Trust Tower · Providence, RI 02903 · 401-274-9200

Noel M. Field, Jr. · Hinckley, Allen, Snyder & Conen · 1500 Fleet Center Providence, RI 02903 · 401-274-2000

Mary Louise Kennedy · Edwards & Angell · 2700 Hospital Trust Tower · Providence, RI 02903 · 401-274-9200

Benjamin G. Paster · Adler Pollock & Sheehan · 2300 Hospital Trust Tower Providence, RI 02903 · 401-274-7200

Richard H. Pierce · Hinckley, Allen, Snyder & Conen · 1500 Fleet Center Providence, RI 02903 · 401-274-2000

Joachim A. Weissfeld · Hinckley, Allen, Snyder & Conen · 1500 Fleet Center Providence, RI 02903 · 401-274-2000

SOUTH CAROLINA

BANKRUPTCY LAW	630
BUSINESS LITIGATION	630
CORPORATE LAW	632
CRIMINAL DEFENSE	632
FAMILY LAW	633
LABOR AND EMPLOYMENT LAW	633
MARITIME LAW	633
NATURAL RESOURCES AND ENVIRONMENTAL LAW	634
PERSONAL INJURY LITIGATION	634
REAL ESTATE LAW	635
TAX AND EMPLOYEE BENEFITS LAW	636
TRUSTS AND ESTATES	636

BANKRUPTCY LAW

Gerald M. Finkel · Finkel, Georgaklis, Goldberg, Sheftman & Korn · 1331 Elmwood Avenue · P.O. Box 1799 · Columbia, SC 29202 · 803-765-2935

Donald H. Stubbs · Nelson, Mullins, Riley & Scarborough · Keenan Building, Third Floor · 130 Lady Street · P.O. Box 11070 · Columbia, SC 29211 · 803-799-2000

BUSINESS LITIGATION

Robert H. Hood · Robert H. Hood & Associates · 172 Meeting Street · P.O. Box 1508 · Charleston, SC 29402 · 803-577-4435

Joseph H. McGee · Buist, Moore, Smythe & McGee · Five Exchange Street · P.O. Box 999 · Charleston, SC 29402 · 803-722-8375

Morris D. Rosen · Rosen, Rosen & Hagood · 45 Broad Street · P.O. Box 1223 · Charleston, SC 29402 · 803-577-6726

Robert B. Wallace · Wallace and Tinkler · 129 Broad Street · P.O. Box 388 · Charleston, SC 29402 · 803-722-8313

Wilburn Brewer, Jr. · Nexsen Pruet Jacobs & Pollard · 1441 Main Street, 15th Floor · P.O. Drawer 2426 · Columbia, SC 29202 · 803-771-8900

Thomas E. McCutchen · Whaley, McCutchen, Blanton & Rhodes · 1414 Lady Street · P.O. Drawer 11209 · Columbia, SC 29211-1209 · 803-799-9791

Stephen G. Morrison · Nelson, Mullins, Riley & Scarborough · Keenan Building, Third Floor · 1330 Lady Street · P.O. Box 11070 · Columbia, SC 29211 · 803-799-2000

Edward W. Mullins, Jr. · Nelson, Mullins, Riley & Scarborough · Keenan Building, Third Floor · 1330 Lady Street · P.O. Box 11070 · Columbia, SC 29211 · 803-799-2000

William L. Pope · Robinson, McFadden & Moore · Jefferson Square, Suite 600 · 1801 Main Street · P.O. Box 944 · Columbia, SC 29202 · 803-779-8900

Saunders M. Bridges · Bridges and Orr · 318 West Palmetto Street · P.O. Box 130 · Florence, SC 29503 · 803-662-1418

Mark W. Buyck, Jr. · Willcox, Hardee, McLeod, Buyck, Baker & Williams · Willcox Building · 248 West Evans Street · P.O. Box 1909 · Florence, SC 29503 · 803-662-3258

Fletcher C. Mann · Leatherwood, Walker, Todd & Mann · 100 East Coffee Street · P.O. Box 87 · Greenville, SC 29602 · 803-242-6440

William Francis Marion, Sr. · Haynsworth, Marion, McKay & Guerard · Two Shelter Centre · 75 Beattie Place · P.O. Box 2048 · Greenville, SC 29602 · 803-240-3200

G. Dewey Oxner, Jr. · Haynsworth, Marion, McKay & Guerard · Two Shelter Centre · 75 Beattie Place · P.O. Box 2048 · Greenville, SC 29602 · 803-240-3200

J. D. Todd, Jr. · Leatherwood, Walker, Todd & Mann · 100 East Coffee Street · P.O. Box 87 · Greenville, SC 29602 · 803-242-6440

Wesley M. Walker · Leatherwood, Walker, Todd & Mann · 100 East Coffee Street · P.O. Box 87 · Greenville, SC 29602 · 803-242-6440

Thomas H. Pope · Pope and Hudgens · 1508 College Street · P.O. Box 190 · Newberry, SC 29108 · 803-276-2532

CORPORATE LAW

Augustine T. Smythe · Buist, Moore, Smythe & McGee · Five Exchange Street P.O. Box 999 · Charleston, SC 29402 · 803-722-8375

John W. Foster · McNair Law Firm · NCNB Tower, 18th Floor · 1301 Gervais Street · P.O. Box 11390 · Columbia, SC 29211 · 803-799-9800

Charles W. Knowlton · Sinkler & Boyd · The Palmetto Center, Suite 1200 · 1426 Main Street · P.O. Box 11889 · Columbia, SC 29211 · 803-779-3080

John H. Lumpkin, Jr. · McNair Law Firm · NCNB Tower, 18th Floor · 1301 Gervais Street · P.O. Box 11390 · Columbia, SC 29211 · 803-799-9800

Julian J. Nexsen · Nexsen Pruet Jacobs & Pollard · 1441 Main Street, 15th Floor P.O. Drawer 2426 · Columbia, SC 29202 · 803-771-8900

David W. Robinson II · Robinson, McFadden & Moore · Jefferson Square, Suite 600 · 1801 Main Street · P.O. Box 944 · Columbia, SC 29202 · 803-779-8900

David L. Freeman · Wyche, Burgess, Freeman & Parham · 44 East Camperdown Way · P.O. Box 10207 · Greenville, SC 29603 · 803-242-3131

Theodore B. Guerard · Haynsworth, Marion, McKay & Guerard · Two Shelter Centre · 75 Beattie Place · P.O. Box 2048 · Greenville, SC 29602 · 803-240-3200

David A. Quattlebaum III · Leatherwood, Walker, Todd & Mann · 100 East Coffee Street · P.O. Box 87 · Greenville, SC 29602 · 803-242-6440

CRIMINAL DEFENSE

Coming B. Gibbs, Jr. · Gibbs & Holmes · 171 Church Street, Suite 270 · P.O. Box 1512 · Charleston, SC 29402 · 803-722-0033

Gedney M. Howe III · Eight Chalmers Street · P.O. Box 1440 · Charleston, SC 29402 · 803-722-8048

Terrell L. Glenn · Glenn, Irvin, Murphy, Gray & Stepp · 1325 Laurel Street P.O. Box 1550 · Columbia, SC 29202 · 803-765-1100

FAMILY LAW

Robert B. Wallace · Wallace and Tinkler · 129 Broad Street · P.O. Box 388 Charleston, SC 29402 · 803-722-8313

Harvey L. Golden · 1712-1714 Main Street · Columbia, SC 29201 · 803-779-3700

Kermit S. King · 1426 Richland Street · P.O. Box 7667 · Columbia, SC 29202 803-779-3090

David H. Wilkins · Wilkins, Nelson, Kittredge & Simmons · 408 East North Street · Greenville, SC 29601 · 803-232-5629

LABOR AND EMPLOYMENT LAW

Homer L. Deakins, Jr. · (Management) · Ogletree, Deakins, Nash, Smoak and Stewart · 1000 East North Street · P.O. Box 2757 · Greenville, SC 29602 803-242-1410

Knox L. Haynsworth, Jr. · (Management) · Haynsworth, Baldwin, Miles, Johnson, Greaves and Edwards · 918 South Pleasantburg Drive · P.O. Box 10888 Greenville, SC 29603 · 803-271-7410

Robert T. Thompson, Sr. · (Management) · Thompson, Mann and Hutson · The Daniel Building, Suite 2200 · Greenville, SC 29602 · 803-242-3200

MARITIME LAW

Benj. Allston Moore, Jr. · Buist, Moore, Smythe & McGee · Five Exchange Street · P.O. Box 999 · Charleston, SC 29402 · 803-722-8375

Gordon D. Schreck · Buist, Moore, Smythe & McGee · Five Exchange Street P.O. Box 999 · Charleston, SC 29402 · 803-722-8375

NATURAL RESOURCES AND ENVIRONMENTAL LAW

William L. Want · 174 East Bay Street, Suite 202 · P.O. Box 1088 · Charleston, SC 29402 · 803-723-5148

PERSONAL INJURY LITIGATION

Robert H. Hood · (Defendants) · Robert H. Hood & Associates · 172 Meeting Street · P.O. Box 1508 · Charleston, SC 29402 · 803-577-4435

Arthur G. Howe · (Plaintiffs) · Uricchio, Howe & Krell · 171/2 Broad Street · P.O. Box 399 · Charleston, SC 29402 · 803-723-7491

Joseph H. McGee · (Defendants) · Buist, Moore, Smythe & McGee · Five Exchange Street · P.O. Box 999 · Charleston, SC 29402 · 803-722-8375

Morris D. Rosen · Rosen, Rosen & Hagood · 45 Broad Street · P.O. Box 893 Charleston, SC 29402 · 803-577-6726

Robert B. Wallace · (Plaintiffs) · Wallace and Tinkler · 129 Broad Street · P.O. Box 388 · Charleston, SC 29402 · 803-722-8313

Wilburn Brewer, Jr. · (Defendants) · Nexsen Pruet Jacobs & Pollard · 1441 Main Street, 15th Floor · P.O. Drawer 2426 · Columbia, SC 29202 · 803-771-8900

Terrell L. Glenn · Glenn, Irvin, Murphy, Gray & Stepp · 1325 Laurel Street P.O. Box 1550 · Columbia, SC 29202 · 803-765-1100

Thomas E. McCutchen · Whaley, McCutchen, Blanton & Rhodes · 1414 Lady Street · P.O. Drawer 11209 · Columbia, SC 29211-1209 · 803-799-9791

Stephen G. Morrison · (Defendants) · Nexsen Pruet Jacobs & Pollard · 1441 Main Street, 15th Floor · P.O. Drawer 2426 · Columbia, SC 29202 · 803-771-8900

Edward W. Mullins, Jr. · (Defendants) · Nelson, Mullins, Riley & Scarborough Keenan Building, Third Floor · 1330 Lady Street · P.O. Box 11070 · Columbia, SC 29211 · 803-799-2000

J. Kendall Few · (Plaintiffs) · 850 Wade Hampton Boulevard · P.O. Box 10085 Fed. Station · Greenville, SC 29603 · 803-232-6456

Richard J. Foster · (Plaintiffs) · Foster, Covington & Patrick · 117 Manly Street P.O. Box 2146 · Greenville, SC 29602 · 803-232-5662

Fletcher C. Mann · (Defendants) · Leatherwood, Walker, Todd & Mann · 100 East Coffee Street · P.O. Box 87 · Greenville, SC 29602 · 803-242-6440

William Francis Marion, Sr. · (Defendants) · Haynsworth, Marion, McKay & Guerard · Two Shelter Centre · 75 Beattie Place · P.O. Box 2048 · Greenville, SC 29602 · 803-240-3200

G. Dewey Oxner, Jr. · (Defendants) · Haynsworth, Marion, McKay & Guerard Two Shelter Centre · 75 Beattie Place · P.O. Box 2048 · Greenville, SC 29602 803-240-3200

J. D. Todd, Jr. · Leatherwood, Walker, Todd & Mann · 100 East Coffee Street P.O. Box 87 · Greenville, SC 29602 · 803-242-6440

Wesley M. Walker · (Defendants) · Leatherwood, Walker, Todd & Mann · 100 East Coffee Street · P.O. Box 87 · Greenville, SC 29602 · 803-242-6440

Thomas H. Pope, Jr. · (Defendants) · Pope and Hudgens · 1508 College Street P.O. Box 190 · Newberry, SC 29108 · 803-276-2532

William U. Gunn · (Defendants) · Holcombe, Bomar, Wynn and Gunn · Spartan Centre, Suite 201 · 101 West St. John Street · P.O. Drawer 1897 · Spartanburg, SC 29304 · 803-585-4273

REAL ESTATE LAW

Neil C. Robinson, Jr. · Robinson, Craver, Wall & Hastie · 134 Meeting Street P.O. Box 1860 · Charleston, SC 29402 · 803-577-9440

Rudolph C. Barnes, Sr. · Barnes, Alford, Stork & Johnson · 1613 Main Street P.O. Box 8448 · Columbia, SC 29202 · 803-799-1111

John H. Lumpkin, Jr. · McNair Law Firm · NCNB Tower, 18th Floor · 1301 Gervais Street · P.O. Box 11390 · Columbia, SC 29211 · 803-799-9800

Edward G. Menzie · Nexsen Pruet Jacobs & Pollard · 1441 Main Street, 15th Floor · P.O. Drawer 2426 · Columbia, SC 29202 · 803-771-8900

Ralston B. Vanzant II · Nelson, Mullins, Riley & Scarborough · Keenan Building, Third Floor · 1330 Lady Street · P.O. Box 11070 · Columbia, SC 29211 803-799-2000

Fred D. Cox, Jr. · Haynsworth, Marion, McKay & Guerard · Two Shelter Centre 75 Beattie Place · P.O. Box 2048 · Greenville, SC 29602 · 803-240-3200

TAX AND EMPLOYEE BENEFITS LAW

Scott Y. Barnes · Holmes & Thomson · 100 Broad Street · P.O. Box 858 · Charleston, SC 29402 · 803-722-1634

John C. Von Lehe, Jr. · Young, Clement, Rivers & Tisdale · 28 Broad Street P.O. Box 993 · Charleston, SC 29402 · 803-577-4000

J. Donald Dial, Jr. · Sinkler & Boyd · The Palmetto Center, Suite 1200 · 1426 Main Street · P.O. Box 11889 · Columbia, SC 29211 · 803-779-3080

Richard C. Handel · Nexsen Pruet Jacobs & Pollard · 1441 Main Street, 15th Floor · P.O. Drawer 2426 · Columbia, SC 29202 · 803-771-8900

Robert M. Nettles, Jr. · (Employee Benefits) · Sinkler & Boyd · The Palmetto Center, Suite 1200 · 1426 Main Street · P.O. Box 11889 · Columbia, SC 29211 803-779-3080

Robert Young · 1330 Richland Street · Columbia, SC 29201 · 803-254-2020

Daniel A. Collins · (Employee Benefits) · Haywood Commons, Suite 400 · 1212 Haywood Road · P.O. Box 25726 · Greenville, SC 29616 · 803-281-0284

David A. Merline · Merline & Thomas · 665 North Academy Street · P.O. Box 10796 · Greenville, SC 29603 · 803-242-4080

John R. Thomas · (Employee Benefits) · Merline & Thomas · 665 North Academy Street · P.O. Box 10796 · Greenville, SC 29603 · 803-242-4080

Johnnie M. Walters · Leatherwood, Walker, Todd & Mann · 100 East Coffee Street · P.O. Box 87 · Greenville, SC 29602 · 803-242-6440

TRUSTS AND ESTATES

Robert M. Kunes · Evans, Carter and Kunes · 151 Meeting Street, Suite 415 P.O. Box 369 · Charleston, SC 29402 · 803-577-2300

Robert M. Earle · Nexsen Pruet Jacobs & Pollard · 1441 Main Street, 15th Floor P.O. Drawer 2426 · Columbia, SC 29202 · 803-771-8900

Albert L. Moses · Sherrill & Townsend · 1337 Assembly Street · P.O. Drawer 447 Columbia, SC 29202 · 803-771-8880

Albert C. Todd III · Todd & Johnson · Standard Federal Savings & Loan Building, Suite 600 · 1136 Washington Street · P.O. Box 11262 · Columbia, SC 29211 803-252-1500

David A. Merline · Merline & Thomas · 665 North Academy Street · P.O. Box 10796 · Greenville, SC 29603 · 803-242-4080

William A. Ruth · Ruth, Clabaugh & Hack · One Sea Pine Circle · Hilton Head, SC 29928 · 803-785-4251

Robert P. Wilkins · 336 Old Chapin Road · P.O. Box 729 · Lexington, SC 29072 803-359-9940

James Carlisle Hardin III · Kennedy Covington Lobdell and Hickman · One Law Place, Suite 301 · P.O. Drawer 11429 · Rock Hill, SC 29731-1421 · 803-327-6171

James B. Drennan III · Drennan, Shelor, Cole & Evins · 126 Advent Street · P.O. Box 5446 · Spartanburg, SC 29304 · 803-585-5800

SOUTH DAKOTA

BANKRUPTCY LAW	638
BUSINESS LITIGATION	639
CORPORATE LAW	639
CRIMINAL DEFENSE	639
LABOR AND EMPLOYMENT LAW	640
NATURAL RESOURCES AND ENVIRONMENTAL LAW	640
PERSONAL INJURY LITIGATION	640
REAL ESTATE LAW	641
TAX AND EMPLOYEE BENEFITS LAW	642
TRUSTS AND ESTATES	642

BANKRUPTCY LAW

Brent A. Wilbur · May, Adam, Gerdes & Thompson · 503 South Pierre Street · P.O. Box 160 · Pierre, SD 57501-0160 · 605-224-8803

J. Bruce Blake · Law Center, Suite 201 · 505 West Ninth Street · Sioux Falls, SD 57104-3698 · 605-336-0948

Roger W. Damgaard · Woods, Fuller, Shultz & Smith · 310 South First Avenue · Sioux Falls, SD 57102 · 605-336-3890

Vance R. C. Goldammer · Boyce, Murphy, McDowell & Greenfield · Norwest Bank Building, Suite 505 · P.O. Box 5015 · Sioux Falls, SD 57117 · 605-336-2424

Robert E. Hayes · Davenport, Evans, Hurwitz & Smith · National Reserve Building · 513 South Main Avenue · Sioux Falls, SD 57102-0993 · 605-336-2880

BUSINESS LITIGATION

Ronald W. Banks · Banks & Johnson · 3202 West Main Street · Rapid City, SD 57702-2398 · 605-348-7300

Joseph M. Butler · Bangs, McCullen, Butler, Foye & Simmons · 818 St. Joseph Street · P.O. Box 2670 · Rapid City, SD 57709 · 605-343-1040

William G. Taylor, Jr. · Woods, Fuller, Shultz & Smith · 310 South First Avenue · Sioux Falls, SD 57102 · 605-336-3890

CORPORATE LAW

Thomas H. Foye · Bangs, McCullen, Butler, Foye & Simmons · 818 St. Joseph Street · P.O. Box 2670 · Rapid City, SD 57709 · 605-343-1040

Richard A. Cutler · Davenport, Evans, Hurwitz & Smith · National Reserve Building · 513 South Main Avenue · Sioux Falls, SD 57102-0993 · 605-336-2880

Vance R.C. Goldammer · Boyce, Murphy, McDowell & Greenfield · Norwest Bank Building, Suite 505 · P.O. Box 5015 · Sioux Falls, SD 57117 · 605-336-2424

David L. Knudson · Davenport, Evans, Hurwitz & Smith · National Reserve Building · 513 South Main Avenue · Sioux Falls, SD 57102-0993 · 605-336-2880

Jeremiah D. Murphy · Boyce, Murphy, McDowell & Greenfield · Norwest Bank Building, Suite 505 · P.O. Box 5015 · Sioux Falls, SD 57117 · 605-336-2424

William G. Taylor, Jr. · Woods, Fuller, Shultz & Smith · 310 South First Avenue · Sioux Falls, SD 57102 · 605-336-3890

CRIMINAL DEFENSE

Charles Rick Johnson · Johnson, Eklund & Davis · 405 Main Street · P.O. Box 149 · Gregory, SD 57533 · 605-835-8391

David Gienapp · Arneson, Issenhuth and Gienapp · 205 North Egan Avenue · Madison, SD 57042 · 605-256-9161

Gary C. Colbath · Banks, Johnson, Johnson, Colbath & Huffman · 3202 West Main Street · Rapid City, SD 57702-2398 · 605-348-7300

John E. Fitzgerald, Jr. · Nelson & Harding · 3685 Sturgis Road, Suite 101 · Rapid City, SD 57702-2346 · 605-348-7250

Sidney B. Strange · Strange & Palmer · 226 North Phillips Avenue · Sioux Falls, SD 57102 · 605-339-0780

LABOR AND EMPLOYMENT LAW

Ronald W. Banks (M) · Banks & Johnson · 3202 West Main Street · Rapid City, SD 57702-2398 · 605-348-7300

NATURAL RESOURCES AND ENVIRONMENTAL LAW

Max Main · Bennett & Main · 618 State Street · Belle Fourche, SD 57717 · 605-892-2011

Donn Bennett · Bennett & Main · 618 State Street · Belle Fourche, SD 57717 · 605-892-2011

Marvin D. Truhe · First Federal Plaza, Fifth Floor · Ninth and St. Joseph Streets P.O. Box 8106 · Rapid City, SD 57709 · 605-342-2800

PERSONAL INJURY LITIGATION

Charles Rick Johnson (P) · Johnson, Eklund & Davis · Johnson Building · 405 Main Street · P.O. Box 149 · Gregory, SD 57533 · 605-835-8391

Ronald W. Banks · Banks & Johnson · 3202 West Main · Rapid City, SD 57702-2398 · 605-348-7300

Joseph M. Butler · Bangs, McCullen, Butler, Foye & Simmons · 818 St. Joseph Street · P.O. Box 2670 · Rapid City, SD 57709 · 605-343-1040

William G. Porter (D) · Costello, Porter, Hill, Heisterkamp & Bushnell · 200 Security Building · 704 St. Joseph Street · P.O. Box 290 · Rapid City, SD 57709 605-343-2410

Carleton R. Hoy (D) · Hoy & Hoy · 401 South Second Avenue · Sioux Falls, SD 57102 · 605-336-2600

Gary J. Pashby (P) · Boyce, Murphy, McDowell & Greenfield · Norwest Bank Building, Suite 505 · P.O. Box 5015 · Sioux Falls, SD 57117 · 605-336-2424

John E. Simko (D) · Woods, Fuller, Shultz & Smith · 310 South First Avenue · Sioux Falls, SD 57102 · 605-336-3890

Deming Smith (D) Davenport, Evans, Hurwitz & Smith · National Reserve Building · 513 South Main Avenue · Sioux Falls, SD 57102-0993 · 605-336-2880

Arlo D. Sommervold (D) · Woods, Fuller, Shultz & Smith · 310 South First Avenue · Sioux Falls, SD 57102 · 605-336-3890

William F. Day, Jr. (D) · Day & Grossenburg · Fifth & Main Streets · P.O. Box 271 · Winner, SD 57580 · 605-842-1676

Steven M. Johnson (P) · Brady, Reade & Johnson · 200 West Third Street · P.O. Box 735 · Yankton, SD 57078 · 605-665-7468

REAL ESTATE LAW

Thomas C. Adam · May, Adam, Gerdes & Thompson · 503 South Pierre Street P.O. Box 160 · Pierre, SD 57501-0160 · 605-224-8803

Thomas H. Foye · Bangs, McCullen, Butler, Foye & Simmons · 818 St. Joseph Street · P.O. Box 2670 · Rapid City, SD 57709 · 605-343-1040

Charles L. Riter · Bangs, McCullen, Butler, Foye & Simmons · 818 St. Joseph Street · P.O. Box 2670 · Rapid City, SD 57709 · 605-343-1040

Richard A. Cutler · Davenport, Evans, Hurwitz & Smith · National Reserve Building · 513 South Main Avenue · Sioux Falls, SD 57102-0993 · 605-336-2880

Vance R. C. Goldammer · Boyce, Murphy, McDowell & Greenfield · Norwest Bank Building, Suite 505 · P.O. Box 5015 · Sioux Falls, SD 57117 · 605-336-2424

Russell R. Greenfield (P) · Boyce, Murphy, McDowell & Greenfield · Norwest Bank Building, Suite 505 · P.O. Box 5015 · Sioux Falls, SD 57117 · 605-336-2424

William G. Taylor, Jr. · Woods, Fuller, Shultz & Smith · 310 South First Avenue Sioux Falls, SD 57102 · 605-336-3890

TAX AND EMPLOYEE BENEFITS LAW

Thomas H. Foye · Bangs, McCullen, Butler, Foye & Simmons · 818 St. Joseph Street · P.O. Box 2670 · Rapid City, SD 57709 · 605-343-1040

Charles L. Riter · Bangs, McCullen, Butler, Foye & Simmons · 818 St. Joseph Street · P.O. Box 2670 · Rapid City, SD 57709 · 605-343-1040

Bradley C. Grossenburg · Woods, Fuller, Schultz & Smith · 310 South First Avenue · Sioux Falls, SD 57102 · 605-336-3890

David L. Knudson · Davenport, Evans, Hurwitz & Smith · National Reserve Building · 513 South Main Avenue · Sioux Falls, SD 57102-0993 · 605-336-2880

TRUSTS AND ESTATES

Thomas H. Foye · Bangs, McCullen, Butler, Foye & Simmons · 818 St. Joseph Street · P.O. Box 2670 · Rapid City, SD 57709 · 605-343-1040

Charles L. Riter · Bangs, McCullen, Butler, Foye & Simmons · 818 St. Joseph Street · P.O. Box 2670 · Rapid City, SD 57709 · 605-343-1040

Bradley C. Grossenburg · Woods, Fuller, Schultz & Smith · 310 South First Avenue · Sioux Falls, SD 57102 · 605-336-3890

Merle A. Johnson · Woods, Fuller, Schultz & Smith · 310 South First Avenue · Sioux Falls, SD 57102 · 605-336-3890

Richard Moe · May, Johnson, Dole & Becker · Western Surety Building, Suite 420 · 101 South Phillips Avenue · P.O. Box 1443 · Sioux Falls, SD 57101-1443 · 605-336-2565

Irving A. Hinderaker · Austin, Hinderaker, Hackett & Hopper · 25 First Avenue, SW · P.O. Box 966 · Watertown, SD 57201-0966 · 605-886-5823

TENNESSEE

BANKRUPTCY LAW	643
BUSINESS LITIGATION	644
CORPORATE LAW	646
CRIMINAL DEFENSE	648
FAMILY LAW	650
LABOR AND EMPLOYMENT LAW	651
NATURAL RESOURCES AND ENVIRONMENTAL LAW	652
PERSONAL INJURY LITIGATION	653
REAL ESTATE LAW	655
TAX AND EMPLOYEE BENEFITS LAW	656
TRUSTS AND ESTATES	658

BANKRUPTCY LAW

Lawrence R. Ahern III · Miller & Martin · Volunteer State Life Building, Suite 1000 · Chattanooga, TN 37402 · 615-756-6600

Thomas E. Ray · Ray & North · 914 First Tennessee Bank Building · Chattanooga, TN 37402 · 615-265-2641

Glenn C. Stophel · Stophel & Stophel · Maclellan Building, Third Floor · Chattanooga, TN 37402 · 615-756-2333

Kyle R. Weems · Weems & Wilson · 736 Georgia Avenue, Suite 404 · Chattanooga, TN 37402 · 615-266-2400

John A. Walker, Jr. · Walker & Walker · 715 First American Center · P.O. Box 2774 · Knoxville, TN 37901 · 615-523-0700

John David Blaylock · Udelsohn, Blaylock & Marlow · 44 North Second Street, Suite 700 · Memphis, TN 38103 · 901-527-7613

John R. Dunlap · Humphreys Dunlap & Wellford · First Tennessee Building, Suite 2200 · 165 Madison Avenue · Memphis, TN 38103 · 901-523-8088

Jack F. Marlow · Udelsohn, Blaylock & Marlow · 44 North Second Street, Suite 700 · Memphis, TN 38103 · 901-527-7613

John W. McQuiston II · Goodman, Glazer, Greener, Schneider & McQuiston · 1500 First Tennessee Bank Building · 165 Madison Avenue · Memphis, TN 38103-0001 · 901-525-4466

John L. Ryder · Apperson, Crump, Duzane & Maxwell · 100 North Main Building, Suite 2610 · Memphis, TN 38103 · 901-525-1711

Robert A. Udelsohn · Udelsohn, Blaylock & Marlow · 44 North Second Street, Suite 700 · Memphis, TN 38103 · 901-527-7613

John H. Bailey III · Bass, Berry & Sims · 2700 First American Center · Nashville, TN 37238 · 615-244-5370

Rhea G. Bucy · Gullett, Sanford, Robinson & Martin · Metropolitan Federal Building, Third Floor · 230 Fourth Avenue · P.O. Box 2757 · Nashville, TN 37219-0757 · 615-244-4994

C. Kinian Cosner, Jr. · Manier, Herod, Hollabaugh & Smith · 2200 One Nashville Place · Nashville, TN 37219 · 615-244-0030

Craig V. Gabbert, Jr. · Harwell Martin & Stegall · 172 Second Avenue North · Nashville, TN 37201 · 615-256-0500

Russell H. Hippe, Jr. · Trabue, Sturdivant & DeWitt · Life and Casualty Tower, 27th Floor · Nashville, TN 37219 · 615-244-9270

James R. Kelley · Dearborn & Ewing · One Commerce Place, Suite 1200 · Nashville, TN 37239 · 615-259-3560

Bradley A. MacLean · Farris, Warfield & Kanaday · Third National Financial Center, Suite 1900 · 424 Church Street · Nashville, TN 37219 · 615-244-5200

BUSINESS LITIGATION

Thomas Maxfield Bahner · Chambliss, Bahner, Crutchfield, Gaston & Irvine · Two Union Square, Suite 1000 · Chattanooga, TN 37402 · 615-756-3000

Charles J. Gearhiser · Gearhiser, Peters & Horton · 320 McCallie Avenue · Chattanooga, TN 37402 · 615-756-5171

Thomas O. Helton · Caldwell, Heggie & Helton · 450 Maclellan Building · 722 Chestnut Street · Chattanooga, TN 37402 · 615-756-2010

Ray H. Moseley · Hutcheson, Moseley, Pinchak, Powers & Disheroon · One Central Plaza, Suite 600 · Chattanooga, TN 37402 · 615-756-5600

Raymond R. Murphy, Jr. · Miller & Martin · Volunteer State Life Building, Suite 1000 · Chattanooga, TN 37402 · 615-756-6600

John R. Seymour · Caldwell, Heggie & Helton · 450 Maclellan Building · 722 Chestnut Street · Chattanooga, TN 37402 · 615-756-2010

J. Houston Gordon · Gordon, Forrester & Whitaker · Hotel Lindo Building, Suite 200 · 114 West Liberty Avenue · Covington, TN 38019 · 901-476-5229

Bernard E. Bernstein · Bernstein, Susano & Stair · First Tennessee Bank Building, Suite 600 · Knoxville, TN 37902 · 615-546-8030

Robert R. Campbell · Hodges, Doughty and Carson · 407 West Main Avenue · P.O. Box 869 · Knoxville, TN 37902 · 615-546-9611

Donald F. Paine · Paine, Swiney & Tarwater · 500 First American National Bank Center · 530 South Gay Street · P.O. Box 198 · Knoxville, TN 37901 · 615-525-0880

Leo Bearman, Jr. · Heiskell, Donelson, Bearman, Adams, Williams & Kirsch · First Tennessee Bank Building, 21st Floor · Memphis, TN 38103 · 901-526-2000

Lucius E. Burch, Jr. · Burch, Porter & Johnson · 130 North Court Avenue · Memphis, TN 38103 · 901-523-2311

James D. Causey · 208 Adams Avenue · Memphis, TN 38103 · 901-526-0206

Ronald Lee Gilman · Farris, Hancock, Gilman, Branan & Hellen · Morgan Keegan Tower, Suite 1400 · 50 North Front Street · Memphis, TN 38103 · 901-576-8200

Frank J. Glankler, Jr. · Glankler, Brown, Gilliland, Chase, Robinson & Raines · One Commerce Square, Suite 1700 · Memphis, TN 38103 · 901-525-1322

Thomas F. Johnston · Armstrong Allen Prewitt Gentry Johnston & Holmes · 1900 One Commerce Square · Memphis, TN 38103 · 901-523-8211

William F. Kirsch, Jr. · Heiskell, Donelson, Bearman, Adams, Williams & Kirsch · First Tennessee Bank Building, 21st Floor · Memphis, TN 38103 · 901-526-2000

James W. McDonnell, Jr. · Wildman, Harrold, Allen, Dixon & McDonnell · 67 Madison Avenue, 12th Floor · Memphis, TN 38103 · 901-521-1111

Thomas R. Prewitt · Armstrong Allen Prewitt Gentry Johnston & Holmes · 1900 One Commerce Square · Memphis, TN 38103 · 901-523-8211

Ames Davis · Waller Lansden Dortch & Davis · 2100 One Commerce Place · Nashville, TN 37239 · 615-244-6380

Ward DeWitt, Jr. · Trabue, Sturdivant & DeWitt · Life and Casualty Tower, 26th Floor · Nashville, TN 37219 · 615-244-9270

Thomas H. Peebles III · Trabue, Sturdivant & DeWitt · Life and Casualty Tower, 27th Floor · Nashville, TN 37219 · 615-244-9270

Wilson Sims · Bass, Berry & Sims · 2700 First American Center · Nashville, TN 37238 · 615-244-5370

Robert J. Walker · Bass, Berry & Sims · 2700 First American Center · Nashville, TN 37238 · 615-244-5370

William R. Willis, Jr. · Willis & Knight · 215 Second Avenue North · Nashville, TN 37201 · 615-259-9600

CORPORATE LAW

J. Guy Beatty, Jr. · Miller & Martin · Volunteer State Life Building, Suite 1000 Chattanooga, TN 37402 · 615-756-6600

Thomas A. Caldwell · Caldwell, Heggie & Helton · 450 Maclellan Building · 722 Chestnut Street · Chattanooga, TN 37402 · 615-756-2010

Joel W. Richardson, Jr. · Miller & Martin · Volunteer State Life Building, Suite 1000 · Chattanooga, TN 37402 · 615-756-6600

John C. Stophel · Stophel & Stophel · Maclellan Building, Third Floor · Chattanooga, TN 37402 · 615-756-2333

Robert Kirk Walker · Strang, Fletcher, Carriger, Walker, Hodge & Smith · 400 Krystal Building · One Union Square · Chattanooga, TN 37402 · 615-265-2000

Robert L. Crossley · Baker, Worthington, Crossley, Stansberry & Woolf · 900 Gay Street, SW, 22nd Floor · Knoxville, TN 37902 · 615-549-7000

E. Bruce Foster, Jr. · Frantz, McConnell & Seymour · Valley Fidelity Building, Suite 1001 · P.O. Box 39 · Knoxville, TN 37901 · 615-546-9321

Sam F. Fowler, Jr. · Wagner, Myers & Sanger · 1801 Plaza Tower · P.O. Box 1308 Knoxville, TN 37901-1308 · 615-525-4600

Jackson C. Kramer · Kramer, Rayson, McVeigh, Leake & Rodgers · Plaza Tower, Suite 2500 · P.O. Box 629 · Knoxville, TN 37901-0629 · 615-525-5134

Herbert S. Sanger, Jr. · Wagner, Myers & Sanger · 1801 Plaza Tower · P.O. Box 1308 · Knoxville, TN 37901-1308 · 615-525-4600

Arthur G. Seymour · Frantz, McConnell & Seymour · Valley Fidelity Building, Suite 1001 · P.O. Box 39 · Knoxville, TN 37901 · 615-546-9321

Richard H. Allen · Armstrong Allen Prewitt Gentry Johnston & Holmes · 1900 One Commerce Square · Memphis, TN 38103 · 901-523-8211

Robert Grattan Brown, Jr. · Glankler, Brown, Gilliland, Chase, Robinson & Raines · One Commerce Square, Suite 1700 · Memphis, TN 38103 · 901-525-1322

Samuel D. Chafetz · Waring Cox · 1300 Morgan Keegan Tower · Memphis, TN 38103 · 901-576-8000

Robert L. Cox · Waring Cox · 1300 Morgan Keegan Tower · Memphis, TN 38103 901-576-8000

Lewis R. Donelson III · Heiskell, Donelson, Bearman, Adams, Williams & Kirsch First Tennessee Bank Building, 21st Floor · Memphis, TN 38103 · 901-526-2000

Ronald Lee Gilman · Farris, Hancock, Gilman, Branan & Hellen · Morgan Keegan Tower, Suite 1400 · 50 North Front Street · Memphis, TN 38103 · 901-576-8200

Charles Forrest Newman · Burch, Porter & Johnson · 130 North Court Avenue Memphis, TN 38103 · 901-523-2311

S. Shepherd Tate · Martin, Tate, Morrow & Marston · The Falls Building, 11th Floor · 22 North Front Street · Memphis, TN 38103 · 901-522-9000

Charles T. Tuggle, Jr. · Heiskell, Donelson, Bearman, Adams, Williams & Kirsch First Tennessee Bank Building, 21st Floor · Memphis, TN 38103 · 901-526-2000

Alfred T. Adams, Jr. · Adams, Taylor, Philbin, Pigue and Marchetti · One Union Street · P.O. Box 3428 · Nashville, TN 37219-0428 · 615-244-5361

J. O. Bass, Jr. · Bass, Berry & Sims · 2700 First American Center · Nashville, TN 37238 · 615-244-5370

James H. Cheek III · Bass, Berry & Sims · 2700 First American Center · Nashville, TN 37238 · 615-244-5370

Thomas P. Kanaday, Jr. · Farris, Warfield & Kanaday · Third National Financial Center, Suite 1900 · 424 Church Street · Nashville, TN 37219 · 615-244-5200

James T. O'Hare · O'Hare, Sherrard & Roe · St. Cloud Corner, Fourth Floor · 500 Church Street · Nashville, TN 37219 · 615-742-4200

T. G. Pappas · Bass, Berry & Sims · 2700 First American Center · Nashville, TN 37238 · 615-244-5370

Thomas J. Sherrard III · O'Hare, Sherrard & Roe · St. Cloud Corner, Fourth Floor · 500 Church Street · Nashville, TN 37219 · 615-742-4200

Wilson Sims · Bass, Berry & Sims · 2700 First American Center · Nashville, TN 37238 · 615-244-5370

Robert D. Tuke · Farris, Warfield & Kanaday · Third National Financial Center, Suite 1900 · 424 Church Street · Nashville, TN 37219 · 615-244-5200

CRIMINAL DEFENSE

Leroy Phillips, Jr. · 312 Vine Street · Chattanooga, TN 37402 · 615-266-1211

Jerry H. Summers · Summers, McCrea & Wyatt · 500 Lindsay Street · Chattanooga, TN 37402 · 615-265-2385

Jerry C. Colley · Colley and Colley · 710 North Main Street · P.O. Box 1476 · Columbia, TN 38402-1476 · 615-388-8564

Charles W. B. Fels · Ritchie, Fels & Dillard · 606 West Main Avenue, Suite 300 P.O. Box 1126 · Knoxville, TN 37901-1126 · 615-637-0661

Robert W. Ritchie · Ritchie, Fels & Dillard · 606 West Main Avenue, Suite 300 P.O. Box 1126 · Knoxville, TN 37901-1126 · 615-637-0661

Hal Gerber · Gerber, Gerber & Agee · Cotton Exchange Building, Seventh Floor · 65 Union Avenue · Memphis, TN 38103 · 901-523-0019

Frank J. Glankler, Jr. · Glankler, Brown, Gilliland, Chase, Robinson & Raines · One Commerce Square, Suite 1700 · Memphis, TN 38103 · 901-525-1322

J. N. Raines · Glankler, Brown, Gilliland, Chase, Robinson & Raines · One Commerce Square, Suite 1700 · Memphis, TN 38103 · 901-525-1322

Lionel R. Barrett, Jr. · 207 Third Avenue North, Fifth Floor · Nashville, TN 37201 · 615-254-1471

Joe P. Binkley, Sr. · 174 Third Avenue North · Nashville, TN 37201 · 615-244-8630

Cecil D. Branstetter · Branstetter, Kilgore, Stranch & Jennings · 200 Church Street, Fourth Floor · Nashville, TN 37201 · 615-254-8801

E. E. Edwards III · Edwards & Spencer · 1707 Division Street · Nashville, TN 37203 · 615-254-3334

Aubrey B. Harwell, Jr. · Neal & Harwell · 2000 One Nashville Place · 150 Fourth Avenue North · Nashville, TN 37219-2417 · 615-244-1713

John J. Hollins · Hollins, Wagster & Yarbrough · Third National Bank Building, Eighth Floor · Nashville, TN 37219 · 615-256-6666

Alfred H. Knight · Willis & Knight · 215 Second Avenue North · Nashville, TN 37201 · 615-259-9600

James F. Neal · Neal & Harwell · 2000 One Nashville Place · 150 Fourth Avenue North · Nashville, TN 37219-2417 · 615-244-1713

James F. Sanders · Neal & Harwell · 2000 One Nashville Place · 150 Fourth Avenue North · Nashville, TN 37219-2417 · 615-244-1713

Vincent E. Wehby · Life & Casualty Tower, 12th Floor · Nashville, TN 37219 · 615-255-7534

Edward M. Yarbrough · Hollins, Wagster & Yarbrough · Third National Bank Building, Eighth Floor · Nashville, TN 37219 · 615-256-6666

Gordon W. Ball · Ball & Dunn · 306 East Main Street · Newport, TN 37821 · 615-623-6042

FAMILY LAW

Michael Ross Campbell · Campbell & Campbell · 1200 James Building · Chattanooga, TN 37402 · 615-266-1108

William H. Horton · Gearhiser, Peters & Horton · 320 McCallie Avenue · Chattanooga, TN 37402 · 615-756-5171

James C. Lee · 1200 James Building · Chattanooga, TN 37402 · 615-266-1108

James M. Hunter · Hunter & Hunter · 182 West Franklin Street · Gallatin, TN 37066 · 615-452-0437

James D. Causey · 208 Adams Avenue · Memphis, TN 38103 · 901-526-0206

David E. Caywood · Picard & Caywood · Sterick Building, Suite 2800 · Memphis, TN 38103 · 901-527-3561

James S. Cox · James S. Cox & Associates · 60 North Third Street · Memphis, TN 38103 · 901-575-2040

Hal Gerber · Gerber, Gerber & Agee · Cotton Exchange Building, Seventh Floor 65 Union Avenue · Memphis, TN 38103 · 901-523-0019

Lew Conner · Waller Lansden Dortch & Davis · 2100 One Commerce Place · Nashville, TN 37239 · 615-244-6380

Maclin P. Davis, Jr. · Waller Lansden Dortch & Davis · 2100 One Commerce Place · Nashville, TN 37239 · 615-244-6380

John J. Hollins · Hollins, Wagster & Yarbrough · Third National Bank Building, Eighth Floor · Nashville, TN 37219 · 615-256-6666

James G. Martin III · Farris, Warfield & Kanaday · Third National Financial Center, Suite 1900 · 424 Church Street · Nashville, TN 37219 · 615-244-5200

Jack Norman, Jr. · 213 Third Avenue North · Nashville, TN 37201 · 615-254-0656

Charles H. Warfield · Farris, Warfield & Kanaday · Third National Financial Center, Suite 1900 · 424 Church Street · Nashville, TN 37219 · 615-244-5200

LABOR AND EMPLOYMENT LAW

Hal F. S. Clements · (Management) · Miller & Martin · Volunteer Building, Suite 1000 · Chattanooga, TN 37402 · 615-899-3350

William P. Hutcheson · (Management) · Hutcheson, Moseley, Pinchak, Powers & Disheroon · One Central Plaza, Suite 600 · Chattanooga, TN 37402 · 615-756-5600

Ronald G. Ingham · (Management) · Miller & Martin · Volunteer Building, Suite 1000 · Chattanooga, TN 37402 · 615-899-3350

Frank P. Pinchak · (Management) · Hutcheson, Moseley, Pinchak, Powers & Disheroon · One Central Plaza, Suite 600 · Chattanooga, TN 37402 · 615-756-5600

Edwin O. Norris · (Management) · Hunter, Smith & Davis · 1212 North Eastman Road · P.O. Box 3740 · Kingsport, TN 37664 · 615-246-4186

Lewis R. Hagood · Arnett, Draper & Hagood · Plaza Tower, Suite 2300 · Knoxville, TN 37929-2300 · 615-546-7000

E. H. Rayson · (Management) · Kramer, Rayson, McVeigh, Leake & Rogers · Plaza Tower, Suite 2521 · P.O. Box 629 · Knoxville, TN 37901 · 615-525-5134

John B. Rayson · (Management) · Kramer, Rayson, McVeigh, Leake & Rogers · Plaza Tower, Suite 2521 · P.O. Box 629 · Knoxville, TN 37901 · 615-525-5134

Lynn A. Agee · (Labor) · Gerber, Gerber & Agee · Cotton Exchange Building, Seventh Floor · 65 Union Avenue · Memphis, TN 38103 · 901-523-0019

Allen S. Blair · (Labor) · Hanover, Walsh, Jalenak & Blair · 219 Adams Avenue Building · Memphis, TN 38103 · 901-526-0621

Donald A. Donati · (Individuals) · Donati & Associates · 329 Poplar Avenue · Memphis, TN 38105-4509 · 901-521-0570

Fletcher L. Hudson · (Management) · McKnight, Hudson, Lewis, Henderson & Clark · 1709 Kirby Parkway · P.O. Box 171375 · Memphis, TN 38187-1375 · 901-756-1550

Frederick J. Lewis · (Management) · McKnight, Hudson, Lewis, Henderson & Clark · 1709 Kirby Parkway · P.O. Box 171375 · Memphis, TN 38187-1375 · 901-756-1550

Dan M. Norwood · (Labor; Individuals) · Byrd, Cobb, Norwood, Lait, Dix & Babaoglu · 99 North Third Street · Memphis, TN 38103 · 901-523-0301

Arnold E. Perl · (Management) · Young & Perl · One Commerce Square, Suite 2380 · Memphis, TN 38103 · 901-525-2761

Samuel J. Weintraub · (Management) · Weintraub, Robinson, Weintraub & Stock · One Commerce Square, Suite 2560 · Memphis, TN 38103 · 901-526-0431

Robert L. Ballow · (Management) · King & Ballow · 1200 Noel Place · 200 Fourth Avenue North · Nashville, TN 37219 · 615-259-3456

George E. Barrett · (Labor) · Barrett, Bryan, Ray & Ross · 217 Second Avenue North · P.O. Box 2846 · Nashville, TN 37219 · 615-244-2202

Cecil D. Branstetter · (Labor) · Branstetter, Kilgore, Stranch & Jennings · 200 Church Street, Fourth Floor · Nashville, TN 37201 · 615-254-8801

Joseph Martin, Jr. · (Management) · Gullett, Sanford, Robinson & Martin · Metropolitan Federal Building, Third Floor · 230 Fourth Avenue North · P.O. Box 2757 · Nashville, TN 37219-0757 · 615-244-4994

Russell F. Morris, Jr. · (Management) · Bass, Berry & Sims · 2700 First American Center · Nashville, TN 37238 · 615-244-5370

William N. Ozier · (Management) · Bass, Berry & Sims · 2700 First American Center · Nashville, TN 37238 · 615-244-5370

James G. Stranch III · (Labor) · Branstetter, Kilgore, Stranch & Jennings · 200 Church Street, Fourth Floor · Nashville, TN 37201 · 615-254-8801

Charles Hampton White · (Management) · Cornelius & Collins · Third National Financial Center, 29th Floor · P.O. Box 2808 · Nashville, TN 37219 · 615-244-1440

NATURAL RESOURCES AND ENVIRONMENTAL LAW

James Gentry, Jr. · Gentry & Boehm · Dome Building, Suite 600 · Chattanooga, TN 37402 · 615-756-5020

Oscar C. Carr III · Glankler, Brown, Gilliland, Chase, Robinson & Raines · One Commerce Square, Suite 1700 · Memphis, TN 38103 · 901-525-1322

PERSONAL INJURY LITIGATION

Charles J. Gearhiser · Gearhiser, Peters & Horton · 320 McCallie Avenue · Chattanooga, TN 37402 · 615-756-5171

Paul R. Leitner · (Defendants) · Leitner, Warner, Moffitt, Williams, Dooley, Carpenter & Napolitan · Pioneer Building, Third Floor · Chattanooga, TN 37402 615-265-0214

Ray H. Moseley · (Defendants) · Hutcheson, Moseley, Pinchak, Powers & Disheroon · One Central Plaza, Suite 600 · Chattanooga, TN 37402 · 615-756-5600

Thomas H. O'Neal · (Plaintiffs) · O'Neal & Associates · 808 Maclellan Building · Chattanooga, TN 37402 · 615-756-5111

Jerry H. Summers · (Plaintiffs) · Summers, McCrea & Wyatt · 500 Lindsay Street · Chattanooga, TN 37402 · 615-265-2385

J. Houston Gordon · Gordon, Forrester & Whitaker · Hotel Lindo Building · 114 West Liberty Avenue, Suite 200 · Covington, TN 38019 · 901-476-5229

James M. Hunter · Hunter & Hunter · 182 West Franklin Street · Gallatin, TN 37066 · 615-452-0437

Robert R. Campbell · (Defendants) · Hodges, Doughty and Carson · 407 West Main Avenue · P.O. Box 869 · Knoxville, TN 37902 · 615-546-9611

Sidney W. Gilreath · (Plaintiffs) · Gilreath & Associates · 707 Gay Street, SW · P.O. Box 1270 · Knoxville, TN 37901 · 615-637-2442

Donald F. Paine · Paine, Swiney & Tarwater · 500 First American National Bank Center · 530 South Gay Street · P.O. Box 198 · Knoxville, TN 37901 · 615-525-0880

Don C. Stansberry, Jr. · (Defendants) · Baker, Worthington, Crossley, Stansberry & Woolf · 900 Gay Street, SW, 22nd Floor · Knoxville, TN 37902 · 615-549-7000

Louis C. Woolf · (Defendants) · Baker, Worthington, Crossley, Stansberry & Woolf · 900 Gay Street, SW, 22nd Floor · Knoxville, TN 37902 · 615-549-7000

Leo Bearman, Jr. · (Defendants) · Heiskell, Donelson, Bearman, Adams, Williams & Kirsch · First Tennessee Bank Building, 21st Floor · Memphis, TN 38103 · 901-526-2000

Lucius E. Burch, Jr. · Burch, Porter & Johnson · 130 North Court Avenue · Memphis, TN 38103 · 901-523-2311

James D. Causey · (Defendants) · 208 Adams Avenue · Memphis, TN 38103 · 901-526-0206

James S. Cox · (Plaintiffs) · James Cox & Associates · 60 North Third Street · Memphis, TN 38103 · 901-575-2040

Frank J. Glankler, Jr. · Glankler, Brown, Gilliland, Chase, Robinson & Raines One Commerce Square, Suite 1700 · Memphis, TN 38103 · 901-525-1322

Thomas R. Prewitt, Sr. · Armstrong Allen Prewitt Gentry Johnston & Holmes · 1900 One Commerce Square · Memphis, TN 38103 · 901-523-8211

Joe D. Spicer · (Defendants) · Spicer, Ridolphi, Flynn & Rudstrom · 109 Mid-America Mall, Suite 200 · Claridge House · Memphis, TN 38103-5072 · 901-523-1333

John J. Thomason · (Defendants) · Thomason, Hendrix, Harvey, Johnson, Mitchell, Blanchard & Adams · First American Bank Building, Ninth Floor · 44 North Second · Memphis, TN 38103 · 901-525-8721

Cecil D. Branstetter · (Plaintiffs) · Branstetter, Kilgore, Stranch & Jennings · 200 Church Street, Fourth Floor · Nashville, TN 37201 · 615-254-8801

Jack A. Butler · (Plaintiffs) · Butler, Lackey, Rogers & Snedeker · First American Center, 12th Floor · Nashville, TN 37238 · 615-244-5772

John T. Conners, Jr. · (Plaintiffs) · Boult, Cummings, Conners & Berry · 222 Third Avenue North · P.O. Box 198062 · Nashville, TN 37219 · 615-244-2582

Ward DeWitt, Jr. · (Defendants) · Trabue, Sturdivant & DeWitt · Life and Casualty Tower, 26th Floor · Nashville, TN 37219 · 615-244-9270

Douglas M. Fisher · (Defendants) · Howell, Fisher & Branham · Court Square Building · 300 James Robertson Parkway · Nashville, TN 37201 · 615-244-3370

James F. Neal · (Plaintiffs) · Neal & Harwell · 2000 One Nashville Place · 150 Fourth Avenue North · Nashville, TN 37219-2417 · 615-244-1713

Thomas H. Peebles III · Trabue, Sturdivant & DeWitt · Life and Casualty Tower, 26th Floor · Nashville, TN 37219 · 615-244-9270

William R. Willis, Jr. · Willis & Knight · 215 Second Avenue North · Nashville, TN 37201 · 615-259-9600

REAL ESTATE LAW

Steve A. Bovell · Shumacker & Thompson · First Tennessee Building, Fifth Floor · 701 Market Street · Chattanooga, TN 37402 · 615-265-2214

Richard D. Crotteau · Miller & Martin · Volunteer State Life Building, Suite 1000 · Chattanooga, TN 37402 · 615-756-6600

G. Richard Hostetter · Miller & Martin · Volunteer State Life Building, Suite 1000 · Chattanooga, TN 37402 · 615-756-6600

Henry M. Beaty, Jr. · 44 North Second Street, Suite 500 · Memphis, TN 38103 901-527-5636

C. Thomas Cates · Burch, Porter & Johnson · 6060 Poplar Avenue, Suite 411 · Memphis, TN 38119 · 901-763-1221

W. Emmett Marston · Martin, Tate, Morrow & Marston · The Falls Building, 11th Floor · 22 North Front Street · Memphis, TN 38103 · 901-522-9000

Wm. Rowlett Scott · Armstrong Allen Prewitt Gentry Johnston & Holmes · 1900 One Commerce Square · Memphis, TN 38103 · 901-523-8211

David G. Williams · Heiskell, Donelson, Bearman, Adams, Williams & Kirsch · First Tennessee Bank Building, 21st Floor · Memphis, TN 38103 · 901-526-2000

Alfred E. Abbey · Trabue, Sturdivant & DeWitt · Life and Casualty Tower, 27th Floor · Nashville, TN 37219 · 615-244-9270

Joseph N. Barker · Dearborn & Ewing · One Commerce Place, Suite 1200 · Nashville, TN 37239 · 615-259-3560

E. Warner Bass · Bass, Berry & Sims · 2700 First American Center · Nashville, TN 37238 · 615-244-5370

James I. Vance Berry · Boult, Cummings, Conners & Berry · 222 Third Avenue North · P.O. Box 198062 · Nashville, TN 37219 · 615-244-2582

Robert P. Thomas · Boult, Cummings, Conners & Berry · 222 Third Avenue North · P.O. Box 198062 · Nashville, TN 37219 · 615-244-2582

Charles K. Wray · Bass, Berry & Sims · 2700 First American Center · Nashville, TN 37238 · 615-244-5370

TAX AND EMPLOYEE BENEFITS LAW

Thomas A. Caldwell · Caldwell, Heggie & Helton · 450 Maclellan Building · 722 Chestnut Street · Chattanooga, TN 37402 · 615-756-2010

Wallace M. Davies · (Employee Benefits) · Miller & Martin · Volunteer State Life Building, Suite 1000 · Chattanooga, TN 37402 · 615-756-6600

Albert W. Secor · Hogshead Building, Suite Eight · 600 Georgia Avenue · Chattanooga, TN 37402 · 615-265-3433

John C. Stophel · Stophel & Stophel · Maclellan Building, Third Floor · Chattanooga, TN 37402 · 615-756-2333

William L. Taylor · Spears, Moore, Rebman & Williams · Blue Cross Building, Eighth Floor · Chattanooga, TN 37402 · 615-756-7000

Mack A. Gentry · Gentry, Tipton, Kaizer & Little · 2610 Plaza Tower · Knoxville, TN 37901 · 615-524-0313

H. Wynne James III · Heiskell, Donelson, Bearman, Adams, Williams & Kirsch Plaza Tower, Suite 600 · Knoxville, TN 37929 · 615-522-4400

Robert S. Marquis · (also Employee Benefits) · McCampbell & Young · 2021 Plaza Tower · P.O. Box 550 · Knoxville, TN 37901-0550 · 615-637-1440

William C. Myers, Jr. · Wagner, Myers & Sanger · 1801 Plaza Tower · P.O. Box 1308 · Knoxville, TN 37901-1308 · 615-525-4600

William P. Kenworthy · (Employee Benefits) · Heiskell, Donelson, Bearman, Adams, Williams & Kirsch · The Forum Building, Suite 308 · 6750 Poplar Avenue Memphis, TN 38138 · 901-755-6713

William H. Lawson, Jr. · Bogatin, Lawson & Chiapella · 245 Wagner Place, Suite 280 · Memphis, TN 38103 · 901-522-1234

B. Percy Magness · (Employee Benefits) · Thomason, Hendrix, Harvey, Johnson, Mitchell, Blanchard & Adams · First American Bank Building, Ninth Floor · 44 North Second Street · Memphis, TN 38103 · 901-525-8721

Shellie G. McCain, Jr. · Waring Cox · 1300 Morgan Keegan Tower · Memphis, TN 38103 · 901-576-8000

R. Michael Potter · Burch, Porter & Johnson · 130 North Court Avenue · Memphis, TN 38103 · 901-523-2311

Michael A. Robinson · Glankler, Brown, Gilliland, Chase, Robinson & Raines · One Commerce Square, Suite 1700 · Memphis, TN 38103 · 901-525-1322

D. Clayton Smith · Waring Cox · 1300 Morgan Keegan Tower · Memphis, TN 38103 · 901-576-8000

James W. Berry, Jr. · (Employee Benefits) · Bass, Berry & Sims · 2700 First American Center · Nashville, TN 37238 · 615-244-2370

W. W. Berry · Bass, Berry & Sims · 2700 First American Center · Nashville, TN 37238 · 615-244-2370

Ervin M. Entrekin · Tune, Entrekin & White · First American Center, 21st Floor Nashville, TN 37238 · 615-244-2770

James C. Gooch · Bass, Berry & Sims · 2700 First American Center · Nashville, TN 37238 · 615-244-2370

Michel G. Kaplan · Boult, Cummings, Conners & Berry · 222 Third Avenue North · P.O. Box 198062 · Nashville, TN 37219 · 615-244-2582

James D. Leckrone · Third National Bank Building, 18th Floor · Nashville, TN 37219 · 615-244-2191

H. Stennis Little, Jr. · Little & Weiss · 1900 First American Center · P.O. Box 80 Nashville, TN 37238 · 615-726-0994

James T. O'Hare · O'Hare, Sherrard & Roe · St. Cloud Corner, Fourth Floor · 500 Church Street · Nashville, TN 37219 · 615-742-4200

Larry T. Thrailkill · Boult, Cummings, Conners & Berry · 222 Third Avenue North · P.O. Box 198062 · Nashville, TN 37219 · 615-244-2582

Charles A. Trost · Waller Lansden Dortch & Davis · 2100 One Commerce Place Nashville, TN 37239 · 615-244-6380

Gary V. Webster · (Employee Benefits) · Manier, Herod, Hollabaugh & Smith · 2200 One Nashville Place · Nashville, TN 37219 · 615-244-0030

TRUSTS AND ESTATES

Thomas A. Caldwell · Caldwell, Heggie & Helton · 450 Maclellan Building · 722 Chestnut Street · Chattanooga, TN 37402 · 615-756-2010

Jon O. Fullerton · Caldwell, Heggie & Helton · 450 Maclellan Building · 722 Chestnut Street · Chattanooga, TN 37402 · 615-756-2010

Hunter D. Heggie · Caldwell, Heggie & Helton · 450 Maclellan Building · 722 Chestnut Street · Chattanooga, TN 37402 · 615-756-2010

Albert W. Secor · Hogshead Building, Suite Eight · 600 Georgia Avenue · Chattanooga, TN 37402 · 615-265-3433

Robert L. McMurray · Bell, Painter, McMurray, Callaway, Brown & Headrick · Merchants Bank Building · P.O. Box 1169 · Cleveland, TN 37364-1169 · 615-476-8541

Hope C. Evans · Wagner, Myers & Sanger · 1801 Plaza Tower · P.O. Box 1308 Knoxville, TN 37901-1308 · 615-525-4600

Mack A. Gentry · Gentry, Tipton, Kaizer & Little · 2610 Plaza Tower · P.O. Box 1275 · Knoxville, TN 37901 · 615-524-0313

Dan W. Holbrook · Egerton, McAfee, Armistead & Davis · 500 First American National Bank Center · P.O. Box 2047 · Knoxville, TN 37901 · 615-546-0500

Joe M. Duncan · Burch, Porter & Johnson · 130 North Court Avenue · Memphis, TN 38103 · 901-523-2311

Ronald Lee Gilman · Farris, Hancock, Gilman, Branan & Hellen · Morgan Keegan Tower, Suite 1400 · 50 North Front Street · Memphis, TN 38103 · 901-576-8200

W. Thomas Hutton · Martin, Tate, Morrow & Marston · The Falls Building, 11th Floor · 22 North Front Street · Memphis, TN 38103 · 901-522-9000

William H. Lawson, Jr. · Bogatin, Lawson & Chiapella · 245 Wagner Place, Suite 280 · Memphis, TN 38103 · 901-522-1234

Joseph Brent Walker · Armstrong Allen Prewitt Gentry Johnston & Holmes · 1900 One Commerce Square · Memphis, TN 38103 · 901-523-8211

W. W. Berry · Bass, Berry & Sims · 2700 First American Center · Nashville, TN 37238 · 615-244-5370

Ervin M. Entrekin · Tune, Entrekin & White · First American Center, 21st Floor · Nashville, TN 37238 · 615-244-2770

James C. Gooch · Bass, Berry & Sims · 2700 First American Center · Nashville, TN 37238 · 615-244-5370

Richard D. Holton · Holton & Walker · Third National Bank Building, 14th Floor · Nashville, TN 37219 · 615-256-3338

Michel G. Kaplan · Boult, Cummings, Conners & Berry · 222 Third Avenue North · P.O. Box 198062 · Nashville, TN 37219 · 615-244-2582

H. Stennis Little, Jr. · Little & Weiss · 1900 First American Center · P.O. Box 80 · Nashville, TN 37238 · 615-726-0994

James T. O'Hare · O'Hare, Sherrard & Roe · St. Cloud Corner, Fourth Floor · 500 Church Street · Nashville, TN 37219 · 615-742-4200

Jack Wright Robinson · Gullett, Sanford, Robinson & Martin · Metropolitan Federal Building, Third Floor · P.O. Box 2757 · 230 Fourth Avenue, North · Nashville, TN 37219-0757 · 615-244-4994

Charles A. Trost · Waller Lansden Dortch & Davis · 2100 One Commerce Place · Nashville, TN 37239 · 615-244-6380

TEXAS

BANKRUPTCY LAW	660
BUSINESS LITIGATION	662
CORPORATE LAW	668
CRIMINAL DEFENSE	675
FAMILY LAW	677
LABOR AND EMPLOYMENT LAW	679
MARITIME LAW	682
NATURAL RESOURCES AND ENVIRONMENTAL LAW	683
PERSONAL INJURY LITIGATION	684
REAL ESTATE LAW	689
TAX AND EMPLOYEE BENEFITS LAW	693
TRUSTS AND ESTATES	698

BANKRUPTCY LAW

Mina A. Clark · Haynes and Boone · 1600 One American Center · 600 Congress Avenue · Austin, TX 78701 · 512-397-2960

George E. Henderson · Fulbright & Jaworski · One American Center, Suite 2400 600 Congress Avenue · Austin, TX 78701 · 512-474-5201

Joseph D. Martinec · 1601 Rio Grande, Suite 451 · Austin, TX 78701 · 512-477-7599

Shelby A. Jordan · Harris, Browning, Jordan & Hyden · 1700 First City Bank Tower I · P.O. Drawer 1901 · Corpus Christi, TX 78403 · 512-883-1946

James A. Donohoe · Gardere & Wynne · 1500 Maxus Energy Tower · 717 North Harwood Street · Dallas, TX 75201 · 214-979-4500

Dean M. Gandy · Akin, Gump, Strauss, Hauer & Feld · 4100 First City Center · 1700 Pacific Avenue · Dallas, TX 75201-4618 · 214-969-2800

D. M. Lynn · Moore & Peterson · 2800 First City Center · Dallas, TX 75201-4621 · 214-754-4800

Mark E. MacDonald · Johnson & Swanson · Founders Square, Suite 100 · 900 Jackson Street · Dallas, TX 75202-4499 · 214-977-9000

Philip I. Palmer, Jr. · Palmer, Palmer & Coffee · One Main Place, Suite 1510 · Dallas, TX 75250 · 214-748-1211

Robin E. Phelan · Haynes and Boone · 3100 First RepublicBank Plaza · 901 Main Street · Dallas, TX 75202 · 214-670-0550

David R. Snodgrass · Gardere & Wynne · 1500 Maxus Energy Tower · 717 North Harwood Street · Dallas, TX 75201 · 214-979-4500

Daniel Clark Stewart · Winstead, McGuire, Sechrest & Minich · 5400 Renaissance Tower · 1201 Elm Street · Dallas, TX 75270 · 214-742-1700

Vernon O. Teofan · Jenkens & Gilchrist · 3200 First Interstate Tower · 1445 Ross Avenue · Dallas, TX 75202-2711 · 214-855-4500

Gerald P. Keith · Ginnings Birkelbach Keith & Delgado · American Bank of Commerce Building, Suite 700 · P.O. Box 54 · El Paso, TX 79940 · 915-532-5929

Larry C. Wood · Kemp, Smith, Duncan & Hammond · 2000 MBank Plaza · P.O. Drawer 2800 · El Paso, TX 79999 · 915-533-4424

John R. Blinn · Leonard Marsh Hurt Terry & Blinn · 301 Commerce Street, Suite 1100 · Fort Worth, TX 76102 · 817-332-6500

Theodore Mack · Wynn, Brown, Mack, Renfro & Thompson · 1800 First City Bank Tower · 201 Main Street · Fort Worth, TX 76102-3186 · 817-335-6261

Michael A. McConnell · Jackson & Walker · 2301 First City Bank Tower · 201 Main Street · Fort Worth, TX 76102 · 817-334-7200

D. Jansing Baker · Weil, Gotshal & Manges · 1600 Republic Bank Center · 700 Louisiana · Houston, TX 77002 · 713-546-5000

Thad Grundy · Hutcheson & Grundy · 3300 Citicorp Center · 1200 Smith Street · Houston, TX 77002-4579 · 713-951-2800

John L. King · Fulbright & Jaworski · Gulf Tower, 51st Floor · 1301 McKinney Street · Houston, TX 77010 · 713-651-5151

Robert C. Maley, Jr. · Sheinfeld, Maley & Kay · 3700 First City Tower · Houston, TX 77002 · 713-658-8881

Jarrel D. McDaniel · Vinson & Elkins · 3300 First City Tower · 1001 Fannin · Houston, TX 77002-6760 · 713-651-2222

Hugh M. Ray · Andrews & Kurth · 4200 Texas Commerce Tower · Houston, TX 77002 · 713-220-4200

Myron M. Sheinfeld · Sheinfeld, Maley & Kay · 3700 First City Tower · Houston, TX 77002 · 713-658-8881

Roderick G. Ayers, Jr. · Cox & Smith · 600 National Bank of Commerce Building · San Antonio, TX 78205 · 512-226-7000

Evelyn H. Biery · Fulbright & Jaworski · 2200 InterFirst Plaza · 300 Convent Street · San Antonio, TX 78205 · 512-224-5575

Claiborne B. Gregory, Jr. · Gresham, Davis, Gregory, Worthy & Moore · 1800 Frost Bank Tower · San Antonio, TX 78205 · 512-226-4157

Ronald Hornberger · Plunkett, Gibson & Allen · 600 InterFirst Financial Center · 6243 Northwest Expressway · P.O. Box BH002 · San Antonio, TX 78201 · 512-734-7092

William A. Jeffers, Jr. · Jeffers, Brook, Kreager & Gragg · 660 North Main Street, Suite 300 · San Antonio, TX 78205 · 512-227-3400

William H. Lemons III · Cox & Smith · 600 National Bank of Commerce Building · San Antonio, TX 78205 · 512-226-7000

John H. Tate II · Oppenheimer, Rosenberg, Kelleher & Wheatley · 711 Navarro, Sixth Floor · San Antonio, TX 78205 · 512-224-2000

BUSINESS LITIGATION

R. James George, Jr. · Graves, Dougherty, Hearon & Moody · 2300 Interfirst Tower · P.O. Box 98 · Austin, TX 78767 · 512-480-5600

Douglass D. Hearne · Hearne, Knolle, Lewallen, Livingston and Holcomb · 1500 Texas Commerce Bank Building · 700 Lavaca · P.O. Box 1687 · Austin, TX 78767 512-478-1500

Robert J. Hearon, Jr. · Graves, Dougherty, Hearon & Moody · 2300 Interfirst Tower · P.O. Box 98 · Austin, TX 78767 · 512-480-5600

Patton G. Lochridge · McGinnis, Lockridge & Kilgore · 1300 Capitol Center · 919 Congress Avenue · Austin, TX 78701 · 512-476-6982

Jack D. Maroney · Brown Maroney Rose Barber & Dye · 1400 One Congress Plaza · 111 Congress Avenue · Austin, TX 78701 · 512-472-5456

Richard T. McCarroll · Brown Maroney Rose Barber & Dye · 1400 One Congress Plaza · 111 Congress Avenue · Austin, TX 78701 · 512-472-5456

Robert C. McGinnis · McGinnis, Lochridge & Kilgore · 1300 Capitol Center · 919 Congress Avenue · Austin, TX 78701 · 512-476-6982

John J. McKetta III · Graves, Dougherty, Hearon & Moody · 2300 Interfirst Tower · P.O. Box 98 · Austin, TX 78767 · 512-480-5600

Paul J. Van Osselaer · Shapiro, Edens & Cook · 2200 One American Center · 600 Congress Avenue · Austin, TX 78701 · 512-499-3800

Thomas H. Watkins · Hilgers & Watkins · 98 San Jacinto Boulevard, Suite 1300 P.O. Box 2063 · Austin, TX 78768 · 512-476-4716

Cleve Bachman · Orgain, Bell & Tucker · 470 Orleans Street · Beaumont, TX 77701 · 409-838-6412

Otto J. Weber, Jr. · Mehaffy, Weber, Keith & Gonsoulin · InterFirst Tower · P.O. Box 16 · Beaumont, TX 77704 · 409-835-5011

James R. Harris · Harris, Browning, Jordan & Hyden · 1700 First City Bank Tower · P.O. Drawer 1901 · Corpus Christi, TX 78403 · 512-883-1946

Robert W. Johnson, Jr. · Matthews & Branscomb · 1800 First City Bank Tower 615 Upper North Broadway · P.O. Box 129 · Corpus Christi, TX 78477 · 512-888-9261

Glenn A. Sodd · Dawson & Sodd · Fifth and Main · P.O. Box 837 · Corsicana, TX 75110 · 214-872-3051

Louis P. Bickel · Akin, Gump, Strauss, Hauer & Feld · 4100 First City Center · 1700 Pacific Avenue · Dallas, TX 75201-4618 · 214-969-2800

George W. Bramblett, Jr. · Haynes and Boone · 3100 First RepublicBank Plaza 901 Main Street · Dallas, TX 75202 · 214-670-0550

George C. Chapman · Thompson & Knight · 3300 First City Center · 1700 Pacific Avenue · Dallas, TX 75201 · 214-969-1700

James E. Coleman, Jr. · Carrington, Coleman, Sloman & Blumenthal · 200 Crescent Court, Suite 1500 · Dallas, TX 75201 · 214-855-3000

J. Carlisle DeHay, Jr. · DeHay & Blanchard · 2500 South Tower · Plaza of the Americas · Dallas, TX 75201 · 214-953-1313

Ernest E. Figari, Jr. · Figari & Davenport · 4800 First RepublicBank Plaza · Dallas, TX 75202 · 214-939-2000

John A. Gilliam · Jenkens & Gilchrist · 3200 First Interstate Tower · 1445 Ross Avenue · Dallas, TX 75202-2711 · 214-855-4500

John H. Hall · Strasburger & Price · 4300 First RepublicBank Plaza · 901 Main Street · P.O. Box 50100 · Dallas, TX 75202 · 214-651-4300

Morris Harrell · Locke Purnell Rain Harrell · 2200 Ross Avenue, Suite 2200 · Dallas, TX 75201 · 214-740-8000

John L. Hauer · Akin, Gump, Strauss, Hauer & Feld · 4100 First City Center · 1700 Pacific Avenue · Dallas, TX 75201-4618 · 214-969-2800

David S. Kidder · Thompson & Knight · 3300 First City Center · 1700 Pacific Avenue · Dallas, TX 75201 · 214-969-1700

Thomas W. Luce III · Hughes & Luce · 2800 Momentum Place · 1717 Main Street · Dallas, TX 75201 · 214-939-5500

John H. McElhaney · Locke Purnell Rain Harrell · 2200 Ross Avenue, Suite 2200 Dallas, TX 75201 · 214-740-8000

Robert H. Mow, Jr. · Hughes & Luce · 2800 Momentum Place · 1717 Main Street Dallas, TX 75201 · 214-939-5500

Stanley E. Neely · Locke Purnell Rain Harrell · 2200 Ross Avenue, Suite 2200 · Dallas, TX 75201 · 214-740-8000

David R. Noteware · Thompson & Knight · 3300 First City Center · 1700 Pacific Avenue · Dallas, TX 75201 · 214-969-1700

Ronald L. Palmer · Baker & Botts · 800 Trammell Crow Center · 2001 Ross Avenue · Dallas, TX 75201 · 214-953-6500

Marvin S. Sloman · (Appellate) · Carrington, Coleman, Sloman & Blumenthal · 200 Crescent Court, Suite 1500 · Dallas, TX 75201 · 214-855-3000

Louis J. Weber, Jr. · Jenkens & Gilchrist · 3200 First Interstate Tower · 1445 Ross Avenue · Dallas, TX 75202-2711 · 214-855-4500

Fletcher L. Yarbrough · Carrington, Coleman, Sloman & Blumenthal · 200 Crescent Court, Suite 1500 · Dallas, TX 75201 · 214-855-3000

W. Royal Fergusen, Jr. · Kemp, Smith, Duncan & Hammond · 2000 MBank Plaza · P.O. Drawer 2800 · El Paso, TX 79999 · 915-533-4424

Richard G. Munzinger · Scott, Hulse, Marshall, Feuille, Finger & Thurmond · Texas Commerce Bank Building, 11th Floor · El Paso, TX 79901 · 915-533-2493

Sam Sparks · Grambling & Mounce · Texas Commerce Bank Building, Seventh Floor · El Paso, TX 79901 · 915-532-3911

R. David Broiles · Brown, Herman, Scott, Dean & Miles · Fort Worth Club Building, Suite 203 · Fort Worth, TX 76102 · 817-332-1391

Beale Dean · Brown, Herman, Scott, Dean & Miles · Fort Worth Club Building, Suite 203 · Fort Worth, TX 76102 · 817-332-1391

Kleber C. Miller · Shannon, Gracey, Ratliff & Miller · 2200 First City Bank Tower · 201 Main Street · Fort Worth, TX 76102 · 817-336-9333

Cecil E. Munn · Cantey & Hanger · 2100 InterFirst Tower · 801 Cherry Street · Fort Worth, TX 76102 · 817-877-2800

E. William Barnett · Baker & Botts · One Shell Plaza · Houston, TX 77002 · 713-229-1234

David J. Beck · Fulbright & Jaworski · Gulf Tower, 51st Floor · 1301 McKinney Street · Houston, TX 77010 · 713-651-5151

Richard H. Caldwell · Mayor, Day & Caldwell · 1900 RepublicBank Center · P.O. Box 61269 · Houston, TX 77208-1269 · 713-225-7000

Richard N. Carrell · Fulbright & Jaworski · Gulf Tower, 51st Floor · 1301 McKinney Street · Houston, TX 77010 · 713-651-5151

Ralph S. Carrigan · Baker & Botts · One Shell Plaza · Houston, TX 77002 · 713-229-1234

Finis E. Cowan · Baker & Botts · One Shell Plaza · Houston, TX 77002 · 713-229-1234

Alfred H. Ebert, Jr. · Andrews & Kurth · 4200 Texas Commerce Tower · Houston, TX 77002 · 713-220-4200

Robin C. Gibbs · Gibbs & Ratliff · 3400 InterFirst Plaza · 1100 Louisiana · Houston, TX 77002 · 713-650-8805

David T. Harvin · Vinson & Elkins · 3300 First City Tower · 1001 Fannin · Houston, TX 77002-6760 · 713-651-2222

David T. Hedges, Jr. · Vinson & Elkins · 3300 First City Tower · 1001 Fannin · Houston, TX 77002-6760 · 713-651-2222

Joseph D. Jamail · Jamail & Kolius · 3300 One Allen Center · Smith at Dallas Streets · Houston, TX 77002 · 713-651-3000

John L. Jeffers · Baker & Botts · One Shell Plaza · Houston, TX 77002 · 713-229-1234

Richard P. Keeton · Mayor, Day & Caldwell · 1900 RepublicBank Center · P.O. Box 61269 · Houston, TX 77208-1269 · 713-225-7000

Robert J. Malinak · Baker & Botts · One Shell Plaza · Houston, TX 77002 · 713-229-1234

John L. McConn, Jr. · McConn & Hardy · 6700 Texas Commerce Tower · 600 Travis Street · Houston, TX 77002 · 713-237-0222

Richard B. Miller · Miller, Bristow & Brown · 3900 Two Houston Center · Houston, TX 77010 · 713-759-1234

John L. Murchison, Jr. · Vinson & Elkins · 3300 First City Tower · 1001 Fannin · Houston, TX 77002-6760 · 713-651-2222

Harry M. Reasoner · Vinson & Elkins · 3300 First City Tower · 1001 Fannin · Houston, TX 77002-6760 · 713-651-2222

Joe H. Reynolds · Reynolds, Cunningham, Peterson & Cordell · 3300 First Interstate Bank Plaza · 1000 Louisiana · Houston, TX 77002-5087 · 713-951-9400

James B. Sales · Fulbright & Jaworski · Gulf Tower, 51st Floor · 1301 McKinney Street · Houston, TX 77010 · 713-651-5151

Stephen D. Susman · Susman, Godfrey & McGowan · 2400 First Interstate Bank Plaza · 1000 Louisiana · Houston, TX 77002 · 713-651-9366

G. Irvin Terrell · Baker & Botts · One Shell Plaza · Houston, TX 77002 · 713-229-1234

Rufus Wallingford · Fulbright & Jaworski · Gulf Tower, 51st Floor · 1301 McKinney Street · Houston, TX 77010 · 713-651-5151

Ewing Werlein, Jr. · Vinson & Elkins · 3300 First City Tower · 1001 Fannin · Houston, TX 77002-6760 · 713-651-2222

Walter E. Workman · Baker & Botts · One Shell Plaza · Houston, TX 77002 · 713-229-1234

W. O. Shafer · Shafer, Davis, McCollum, Ashley, O'Leary & Stoker · NCNB Texas Bank Building, Suite 201 · 700 North Grant Street · P.O. Drawer 1552 · Odessa, TX 79760 · 915-332-0893

Reese L. Harrison, Jr. · Oppenheimer, Rosenberg, Kelleher & Wheatley · 711 Navarro, Sixth Floor · San Antonio, TX 78205 · 512-224-2000

Jack Hebdon · Groce, Locke & Hebdon · 2000 Frost Bank Tower · San Antonio, TX 78205 · 512-225-3031

Ralph Langley · Foster, Lewis, Langley, Gardner & Banack · Frost Bank Tower, 16th Floor · San Antonio, TX 78205 · 512-226-3116

R. Laurence Macon · Cox & Smith · 600 National Bank of Commerce Building San Antonio, TX 78205 · 512-226-7000

George H. Spencer, Sr. · Clemens, Spencer, Welmaker & Finck · 1800 National Bank of Commerce Building · San Antonio, TX 78205 · 512-227-7121

Seagal V. Wheatley · Oppenheimer, Rosenberg, Kelleher & Wheatley · 711 Navarro, Sixth Floor · San Antonio, TX 78205 · 512-224-2000

CORPORATE LAW

Karen J. Bartoletti · Graves, Dougherty, Hearon & Moody · 2300 Interfirst Tower · P.O. Box 98 · Austin, TX 78767 · 512-480-5600

W. Amon Burton, Jr. · Jenkens & Gilchrist · 1306 Guadalupe · Austin, TX 78701 512-473-8903

J. Rowland Cook · Johnson & Swanson · 100 Congress Avenue, Suite 1400 · Austin, TX 78701 · 512-322-8000

C. Morris Davis · McGinnis, Lochridge & Kilgore · 1300 Capitol Center · 919 Congress Avenue · Austin, TX 78701 · 512-476-6982

Rod Edens, Jr. · Shapiro, Edens & Cook · 2200 One American Center · 600 Congress Avenue · Austin, TX 78701 · 512-499-3800

John E. Gangstad · Brown Maroney Rose Barber & Dye · 1400 One Congress Plaza · 111 Congress Avenue · Austin, TX 78701 · 512-472-5456

P. Michael Hebert · McGinnis, Lochridge & Kilgore · 1300 Capitol Center · 919 Congress Avenue · Austin, TX 78701 · 512-476-6982

R. Clarke Heidrick, Jr. · Graves, Dougherty, Hearon & Moody · 2300 Interfirst Tower · P.O. Box 98 · Austin, TX 78767 · 512-480-5600

Lloyd Lochridge · McGinnis, Lochridge & Kilgore · 1300 Capitol Center · 919 Congress Avenue · Austin, TX 78701 · 512-476-6982

Frank Oliver · McGinnis, Lochridge & Kilgore · 1300 Capitol Center · 919 Congress Avenue · Austin, TX 78701 · 512-476-6982

William R. Volk · Shapiro, Edens & Cook · 2200 One American Center · 600 Congress Avenue · Austin, TX 78701 · 512-499-3800

James A. Williams · Graves, Dougherty, Hearon & Moody · 2300 Interfirst Tower · P.O. Box 98 · Austin, TX 78767 · 512-480-5600

Charles W. Thomasson · Gary, Thomasson, Hall & Marks · 210 South Carancahua · P.O. Box 2888 · Corpus Christi, TX 78403 · 512-884-1961

Robert L. Blumenthal · Carrington, Coleman, Sloman & Blumenthal · 200 Crescent Court, Suite 1500 · Dallas, TX 75201 · 214-855-3000

Michael M. Boone · Haynes and Boone · 3100 First RepublicBank Plaza · 901 Main Street · Dallas, TX 75202 · 214-670-0550

Sam P. Burford, Jr. · Thompson & Knight · 3300 First City Center · 1700 Pacific Avenue · Dallas, TX 75201 · 214-969-1700

Dan Busbee · Locke Purnell Rain Harrell · 2200 Ross Avenue, Suite 2200 · Dallas, TX 75201 · 214-740-8000

Steven K. Cochran · Thompson & Knight · 3300 First City Center · 1700 Pacific Avenue · Dallas, TX 75201 · 214-969-1700

George W. Coleman · Jenkens & Gilchrist · 3200 First Interstate Tower · 1445 Ross Avenue · Dallas, TX 75202-2711 · 214-855-4500

John D. Curtis · Locke Purnell Rain Harrell · First RepublicBank Center, 3600 Tower II · 325 North St. Paul · Dallas, TX 75201 · 214-740-8000

Henry Gilchrist · Jenkens & Gilchrist · 3200 First Interstate Tower · 1445 Ross Avenue · Dallas, TX 75202-2711 · 214-855-4500

Campbell A. Griffin, Jr. · Vinson & Elkins · 3700 Trammell Crow Center · 2001 Ross Avenue · Dallas, TX 75201-2916 · 214-220-7700

Richard D. Haynes · Haynes and Boone · 3100 First RepublicBank Plaza · 901 Main Street · Dallas, TX 75202 · 214-670-0550

Daniel K. Hennessy · Hughes & Luce · 2800 Momentum Place · 1717 Main Street · Dallas, TX 75201 · 214-939-5500

James L. Irish III · Thompson & Knight · 3300 First City Center · 1700 Pacific Avenue · Dallas, TX 75201 · 214-969-1700

John T. Kipp · Gardere & Wynne · 1500 Maxus Energy Tower · 717 North Harwood Street · Dallas, TX 75201 · 214-979-4500

Harold F. Kleinman · Thompson & Knight · 3300 First City Center · 1700 Pacific Avenue · Dallas, TX 75201 · 214-969-1700

Jack M. Little · Thompson & Knight · 3300 First City Center · 1700 Pacific Avenue · Dallas, TX 75201 · 214-969-1700

Talbot Rain · Locke Purnell Rain Harrell · 2200 Ross Avenue, Suite 2200 · Dallas, TX 75201 · 214-740-8000

Larry L. Schoenbrun · Gardere & Wynne · 1500 Maxus Energy Tower · 717 North Harwood Street · Dallas, TX 75201 · 214-979-4500

Laurence D. Stuart, Jr. · Johnson & Swanson · Founders Square, Suite 100 · 900 Jackson Street · Dallas, TX 75202-4499 · 214-977-9000

Wallace M. Swanson · Johnson & Swanson · Founders Square, Suite 100 · 900 Jackson Street · Dallas, TX 75202-4499 · 214-977-9000

Jim A. Watson · Johnson & Swanson · Founders Square, Suite 100 · 900 Jackson Street · Dallas, TX 75202-4499 · 214-977-9000

Carl W. Wilson · Gardere & Wynne · 1500 Maxus Energy Tower · 717 North Harwood Street · Dallas, TX 75201 · 214-979-4500

Fletcher L. Yarbrough · Carrington, Coleman, Sloman, & Blumenthal · 200 Crescent Court, Suite 1500 · Dallas, TX 75201 · 214-855-3000

Barney T. Young · Locke Purnell Rain Harrell · 2200 Ross Avenue, Suite 2200 · Dallas, TX 75201 · 214-740-8000

Tad R. Smith · Kemp, Smith, Duncan & Hammond · 2000 MBank Plaza · P.O. Drawer 2800 · El Paso, TX 79999 · 915-533-4424

Mark L. Hart, Jr. · Kelly, Hart & Hallman · 2500 First City Bank Tower · 201 Main Street · Fort Worth, TX 76102 · 817-332-2500

Robert F. Watson · Law, Snakard & Gambill · 3200 Texas American Bank Building · Fort Worth, TX 76102 · 817-335-7373

Milton H. Anders · Vinson & Elkins · 3300 First City Tower · 1001 Fannin · Houston, TX 77002-6760 · 713-651-2222

Eric S. Anderson · Fulbright & Jaworski · Gulf Tower, 51st Floor · 1301 McKinney Street · Houston, TX 77010 · 713-651-5151

R. Dennis Anderson · Fulbright & Jaworski · Gulf Tower, 51st Floor · 1301 McKinney Street · Houston, TX 77010 · 713-651-5151

Robert J. Bachman · Vinson & Elkins · 3300 First City Tower · 1001 Fannin · Houston, TX 77002-6760 · 713-651-2222

Robert S. Baird · Vinson & Elkins · 3300 First City Tower · 1001 Fannin · Houston, TX 77002-6760 · 713-651-2222

Robert F. Barrett · Vinson & Elkins · 3300 First City Tower · 1001 Fannin · Houston, TX 77002-6760 · 713-651-2222

Douglas Y. Bech · Andrews & Kurth · 4200 Texas Commerce Tower · Houston, TX 77002 · 713-220-4200

Bruce R. Bilger · Vinson & Elkins · 3300 First City Tower · 1001 Fannin · Houston, TX 77002-6760 · 713-651-2222

John L. Bland · Bracewell & Patterson · 2900 South Tower, Pennzoil Place · Houston, TX 77002 · 713-223-2900

John H. Buck · Bracewell & Patterson · 2900 South Tower, Pennzoil Place · Houston, TX 77002 · 713-223-2900

David Alan Burns · Baker & Botts · One Shell Plaza · Houston, TX 77002 · 713-229-1234

John T. Cabaniss · Andrews & Kurth · 4200 Texas Commerce Tower · Houston, TX 77002 · 713-220-4200

Joseph A. Cialone II · Baker & Botts · One Shell Plaza · Houston, TX 77002 · 713-229-1234

Michael W. Conlon · Fulbright & Jaworski · Gulf Tower, 51st Floor · 1301 McKinney Street · Houston, TX 77010 · 713-651-5151

Rufus Cormier, Jr. · Baker & Botts · One Shell Plaza · Houston, TX 77002 · 713-229-1234

Alton F. Curry · Fulbright & Jaworski · Gulf Tower, 51st Floor · 1301 McKinney Street · Houston, TX 77010 · 713-651-5151

Christopher E. H. Dack · Fulbright & Jaworski · Gulf Tower, 51st Floor · 1301 McKinney Street · Houston, TX 77010 · 713-651-5151

John C. Dawson, Jr. · Vinson & Elkins · 3300 First City Tower · 1001 Fannin · Houston, TX 77002-6760 · 713-651-2222

Richard B. Dewey · Baker & Botts · One Shell Plaza · Houston, TX 77002 · 713-229-1234

Joseph C. Dilg · Vinson & Elkins · 3300 First City Tower · 1001 Fannin · Houston, TX 77002-6760 · 713-651-2222

James R. Doty · Baker & Botts · One Shell Plaza · Houston, TX 77002 · 713-229-1234

Michael P. Finch · Vinson & Elkins · 3300 First City Tower · 1001 Fannin · Houston, TX 77002-6760 · 713-651-2222

William T. Fleming, Jr. · Vinson & Elkins · 3300 First City Tower · 1001 Fannin Houston, TX 77002-6760 · 713-651-2222

Frank T. Garcia · Fulbright & Jaworski · Gulf Tower, 51st Floor · 1301 McKinney Street · Houston, TX 77010 · 713-651-5151

J. Patrick Garrett · Baker & Botts · One Shell Plaza · Houston, TX 77002 · 713-229-1234

Moulton Goodrum, Jr. · Baker & Botts · One Shell Plaza · Houston, TX 77002 713-229-1234

Charles R. Gregg · Hutcheson & Grundy · 3300 Citicorp Center · 1200 Smith Street · Houston, TX 77002-4579 · 713-951-2800

S. Tevis Grinstead · Vinson & Elkins · 3300 First City Tower · 1001 Fannin · Houston, TX 77002-6760 · 713-651-2222

Dewuse Guyton, Jr. · Butler & Binion · 1600 First Interstate Bank Plaza · Houston, TX 77002 · 713-237-3111

Ralph A. Harper · Vinson & Elkins · 3300 First City Tower · 1001 Fannin · Houston, TX 77002-6760 · 713-651-2222

Thomas L. Healey · Andrews & Kurth · 4200 Texas Commerce Tower · Houston, TX 77002 · 713-220-4200

Donald L. Howell · Vinson & Elkins · 3300 First City Tower · 1001 Fannin · Houston, TX 77002-6760 · 713-651-2222

John M. Huggins · Baker & Botts · One Shell Plaza · Houston, TX 77002 · 713-229-1234

Thad T. Hutcheson, Jr. · Baker & Botts · One Shell Plaza · Houston, TX 77002 713-229-1234

John L. Jeffers · Baker & Botts · One Shell Plaza · Houston, TX 77002 · 713-229-1234

J. Rolfe Johnson · Mayor, Day & Caldwell · 1900 RepublicBank Center · P.O. Box 61269 · Houston, TX 77208-1269 · 713-225-7000

William E. Joor III · Vinson & Elkins · 3300 First City Tower · 1001 Fannin · Houston, TX 77002-6760 · 713-651-2222

Wm. Franklin Kelly, Jr. · Vinson & Elkins · 3300 First City Tower · 1001 Fannin Houston, TX 77002-6760 · 713-651-2222

David R. Keyes · Vinson & Elkins · 3300 First City Tower · 1001 Fannin · Houston, TX 77002-6760 · 713-651-2222

Jerry V. Kyle · Andrews & Kurth · 4200 Texas Commerce Tower · Houston, TX 77002 · 713-220-4200

James L. Leader · Baker & Botts · One Shell Plaza · Houston, TX 77002 · 713-229-1234

Edgar J. Marston III · Bracewell & Patterson · 2900 South Tower, Pennzoil Place Houston, TX 77002 · 713-223-2900

Stephen A. Massad · Baker & Botts · One Shell Plaza · Houston, TX 77002 · 713-229-1234

Richard B. Mayor · Mayor, Day & Caldwell · 1900 RepublicBank Center · P.O. Box 61269 · Houston, TX 77208-1269 · 713-225-7000

Edward C. Norwood · Sewell & Riggs · 800 MCorp Plaza · 333 Clay Avenue · Houston, TX 77002-4086 · 713-652-8700

Dallas Parker · Baker, Brown, Sharman & Parker · Citicorp Center, Suite 3600 · 1200 Smith Street · Houston, TX 77002 · 713-654-8111

P. Dexter Peacock · Andrews & Kurth · 4200 Texas Commerce Tower · Houston, TX 77002 · 713-220-4200

T. William Porter · Porter & Clements · 3500 Republic Bank Center · Houston, TX 77002 · 713-226-0600

James D. Randall · Baker & Botts · One Shell Plaza · Houston, TX 77002 · 713-229-1234

Rush H. Record · Vinson & Elkins · 3300 First City Tower · 1001 Fannin · Houston, TX 77002-6760 · 713-651-2222

Arthur H. Rogers III · Fulbright & Jaworski · Gulf Tower, 51st Floor · 1301 McKinney Street · Houston, TX 77010 · 713-651-5151

Michael Q. Rosenwasser · Andrews & Kurth · 4200 Texas Commerce Tower · Houston, TX 77002 · 713-220-4200

Richard A. Royds · Bracewell & Patterson · 2900 South Tower, Pennzoil Place · Houston, TX 77002 · 713-223-2900

John M. Sanders · Fulbright & Jaworski · Gulf Tower, 51st Floor · 1301 McKinney Street · Houston, TX 77010 · 713-651-5151

George A. Shannon, Jr. · Shannon, Ustick, Tyler & Beller · One Shell Plaza, 50th Floor · Houston, TX 77002 · 713-227-6550

Charles H. Still · Fulbright & Jaworski · Gulf Tower, 51st Floor · 1301 McKinney Street · Houston, TX 77010 · 713-651-5151

Robert L. Stillwell · Baker & Botts · One Shell Plaza · Houston, TX 77002 · 713-229-1234

H. Don Teague · Vinson & Elkins · 3300 First City Tower · 1001 Fannin · Houston, TX 77002-6760 · 713-651-2222

John A. Watson · Fulbright & Jaworski · Gulf Tower, 51st Floor · 1301 McKinney Street · Houston, TX 77010 · 713-651-5151

John S. Watson · Vinson & Elkins · 3300 First City Tower · 1001 Fannin · Houston, TX 77002-6760 · 713-651-2222

Robert H. Whilden, Jr. · Vinson & Elkins · 3300 First City Tower · 1001 Fannin Houston, TX 77002-6760 · 713-651-2222

Jerry L. Wickliffe · Fulbright & Jaworski · Gulf Tower, 51st Floor · 1301 McKinney Street · Houston, TX 77010 · 713-651-5151

R. Daniel Witschey, Jr. · Bracewell & Patterson · 2900 South Tower, Pennzoil Place · Houston, TX 77002 · 713-223-2900

Howard Wolf · Fulbright & Jaworski · Gulf Tower, 51st Floor · 1301 McKinney Street · Houston, TX 77010 · 713-651-5151

Frank M. Wozencraft · Baker & Botts · One Shell Plaza · Houston, TX 77002 · 713-229-1234

Richard E. Goldsmith · Matthews & Branscomb · One Alamo Center, Suite 800 San Antonio, TX 78205 · 512-226-4211

J. David Oppenheimer · Oppenheimer, Rosenberg, Kelleher & Wheatley · 711 Navarro, Sixth Floor · San Antonio, TX 78205 · 512-224-2000

J. Burleson Smith · Cox & Smith · 600 National Bank of Commerce Building · San Antonio, TX 78205 · 512-226-7000

Dan G. Webster III · Cox & Smith · 600 National Bank of Commerce Building · San Antonio, TX 78205 · 512-226-7000

CRIMINAL DEFENSE

Charles R. Burton · Minton, Burton, Foster & Collins · 1100 Guadalupe Street · Austin, TX 78701 · 512-476-4873

Bill Fitzgerald · Fitzgerald, Meissner & Augustine · 1122 Colorado, Suite 2303 · Austin, TX 78701 · 512-474-4700

Frank Maloney · Maloney & Yeager · 505 West 12th Street · Austin, TX 78701 · 512-476-8700

Roy Q. Minton · Minton, Burton, Foster & Collins · 1100 Guadalupe Street · Austin, TX 78701 · 512-476-4873

Michael E. Tigar · University of Texas · 727 East 26th Street · Austin, TX 78705 · 512-471-5151

Joseph C. Hawthorn · Hawthorn & Black · 485 Milam · Beaumont, TX 77701 · 409-838-3969

Thomas G. Sharpe, Jr. · 107 East Price Road · P.O. Box 4648 · Brownsville, TX 78521 · 512-546-3783

J. A. Canales · Canales & Associates · 2601 Morgan Avenue · P.O. Box 5624 · Corpus Christi, TX 78405 · 512-883-0601

J. Douglas Tinker · Tinker, Tor & Brown · 622 South Tancahua Street · P.O. Box 276 · Corpus Christi, TX 78403 · 512-882-4378

Melvyn Carson Bruder · (Appellate) · 12221 Merit Drive, Suite 850 · Dallas, TX 75251 · 214-351-5597

Emmett Colvin · 701 Commerce Street · Dallas, TX 75202 · 214-744-5044

Michael P. Gibson · Burleson, Pate & Gibson · 2414 North Akard, Suite 700 · P.O. Box 190623 · Dallas, TX 75201 · 214-871-4900

George R. Milner, Jr. · Milner & Goranson · 714 Jackson Street, Suite 900 · Dallas, TX 75202 · 214-651-1121

Charles W. Tessmer · 1015 Elm Street · Dallas, TX 75202 · 214-748-3433

Joseph (Sib) Abraham, Jr. · Caples Building, Suite 505 · P.O. Box D · El Paso, TX 79951-0004 · 915-532-1601

Tim Evans · 115 West Second Street · Fort Worth, TX 76102 · 817-332-3822

Mike DeGeurin · Forman, DeGeurin & Nugent · 909 Fannin Street, Suite 590 · Houston, TX 77010 · 713-655-9000

Dick DeGuerin · DeGuerin & Dickson · The Republic Building, Seventh Floor 1018 Preston Avenue · Houston, TX 77002 · 713-223-5959

Richard Haynes · Haynes & Fullenweider · 4300 Scotland Street · Houston, TX 77007 · 713-868-1111

Michael Ramsey · Ramsey & Tyson · Old Cotton Exchange, Suite 200 · 202 Travis at Franklin Street · Houston, TX 77002 · 713-224-2001

Randolph Lee Schaffer · Schaffer, Lambright, Odom & Sparks · 1301 McKinney 3100 Gulf Tower · Houston, TX 77010 · 713-951-9555

Travis D. Shelton · Shelton & Jones · 1801 Avenue Q · Lubbock, TX 79401 · 806-763-5201

Warren Burnett · 307 Loop 338 East · Odessa, TX 79763 · 915-332-0106

Roy R. Barrera · Nicholas and Barrera · 424 East Nueva · San Antonio, TX 78205 512-224-5811

Charles D. Butts · 120 Villita Street · San Antonio, TX 78205 · 512-223-2941

Gerald H. Goldstein · Goldstein, Goldstein and Hilley · Tower Life Building, 29th Floor · San Antonio, TX 78205 · 512-226-1463

Jack Paul Leon · Leon & Bayless · 500 Lexington · San Antonio, TX 78215 · 512-223-4254

Anthony Nicholas · Nicholas and Barrera · 424 East Nueva by La Villita · San Antonio, TX 78205 · 512-224-5811

F. R. "Buck" Files, Jr. · Bain Files Allen and Caldwell · 109 West Ferguson Street P.O. Box 2013 · Tyler, TX 75710 · 214-595-3573

FAMILY LAW

Thomas L. Ausley · 3307 Northland Drive, Suite 420 · Mopac at Northland · Austin, TX 78731 · 512-454-8791

Jon N. Coffee · 200 East Sixth Street, Suite 301 · Austin, TX 78701 · 512-472-2272

Patricia A. English · Bankston, Wright & Greenhill · 1800 MBank Tower · 221 West Sixth Street · Austin, TX 78701 · 512-476-4600

Barbara Anne Kazen · Kazen & Price · 3001 Lake Austin Boulevard, Suite 205 · Austin, TX 78703-4204 · 512-476-7086

Dan R. Price · Kazen & Price · 3001 Lake Austin Boulevard, Suite 205 · Austin, TX 78703-4204 · 512-476-7086

Scott T. Cook · Scott T. Cook & Associates · 2820 South Padre Island Drive, Suite 290 · Corpus Christi, TX 78415 · 512-855-6655

Kenneth D. Fuller · Koons, Rasor, Fuller & McCurley · 2311 Cedar Springs Road, Suite 300 · Dallas, TX 75201 · 214-871-2727

William C. Koons · Koons, Rasor, Fuller & McCurley · 2311 Cedar Springs Road, Suite 300 · Dallas, TX 75201 · 214-871-2727

Thomas P. Goranson · 2750 One Dallas Centre · 350 North St. Paul Street · Dallas, TX 75201-4205 · 214-220-9033

Mike McCurley · Koons, Rasor, Fuller & McCurley · 2311 Cedar Springs Road, Suite 300 · Dallas, TX 75201 · 214-871-2727

Reba Graham Rasor · Koons, Rasor, Fuller & McCurley · 2311 Cedar Springs Road, Suite 300 · Dallas, TX 75201 · 214-871-2727

Charles H. Robertson · Robertson & Merrill · 705 Ross Avenue · Dallas, TX 75202 · 214-748-9211

Donald R. Smith · Law Offices of Donald R. Smith · 1616 Union Bank & Trust Tower · 5950 Berkshire Lane · Dallas, TX 75225 · 214-891-3201

Brian L. Webb · Webb & Kinser · 4620 Renaissance Tower · 1201 Elm Street · Dallas, TX 75270 · 214-744-4620

Curtis M. Loveless · Whitten & Loveless · 218 North Elm · P.O. Box 1566 · Denton, TX 76202 · 817-383-1618

Ann C. McClure · 6541 Vasco Way · El Paso, TX 79912 · 915-584-6033

David R. McClure · Schwartz, Earp, McClure, Cohen & Stewart · 609 Laurel Street · El Paso, TX 79903 · 915-542-1533

Larry H. Schwartz · Schwartz, Earp, McClure, Cohen & Stewart · 609 Laurel Street · El Paso, TX 79903 · 915-542-1533

James M. Loveless · 1300 Summit Avenue · Fort Worth, TX 76102 · 817-332-1334

Eugene A. Cook · Cook, Davis & McFall · Two Houston Center, Suite 2600 · 909 Fannin · Houston, TX 77010-1003 · 713-757-0440

Donn C. Fullenweider · Haynes & Fullenweider · 4300 Scotland Street · Houston, TX 77007 · 713-868-1111

Roy W. Moore · Gray & Moore · 1301 McKinney Street, Suite 3550 · Houston, TX 77010 · 713-651-9777

John F. Nichols · John F. Nichols and Associates · 1440 Lyric Centre · 440 Louisiana, Suite 1440 · Houston, TX 77002 · 713-227-7100

Robert J. Piro · Piro & Lilly · 4600 Allied Bank Plaza · Houston, TX 77002 · 713-658-9999

Donald R. Royall · The Royalls · 13430 Northwest Freeway, Suite 650 · Houston, TX 77040 · 713-462-6500

J. Lindsey Short, Jr. · Lindsey Short & Associates · 4600 Post Oak Place · Houston, TX 77027 · 713-626-0208

Harry L. Tindall · Tindall & Foster · 2801 Texas Commerce Tower · Houston, TX 77002 · 713-229-8733

Robert M. Welch, Jr. · Fulbright & Jaworski · Gulf Tower, 51st Floor · 1301 McKinney Street · Houston, TX 77010 · 713-651-5151

Thomas J. Purdom · Purdom Law Offices · 1801 Avenue Q · Lubbock, TX 79401 806-747-4653

William M. Boyd · Boyd, Veigel & Hance · 218 East Louisiana Street · McKinney, TX 75069 · 214-542-0191

Sam C. Bashara · Law Offices of Sam C. Bashara · 100 East Houston Street, Suite 800 · San Antonio, TX 78205 · 512-227-1496

John Compere · Shaddox, Compere, Gorham & Good · The North Frost Center, Suite 725 · 1250 North East Loop 410 · San Antonio, TX 78209 · 512-822-2018

Oliver S. Heard, Jr. · Heard, Groggan, Blair & Williams · 1019 Tower Life Building · San Antonio, TX 78205 · 512-225-6763

Richard R. Orsinger · Heard, Groggan, Blair & Williams · 1019 Tower Life Building · San Antonio, TX 78205 · 512-225-6763

James D. Stewart · Stewart, Hemmi & Pennypacker · Milam Building, 18th Floor San Antonio, TX 78205 · 512-225-4321

Jerry E. Bain · Bain Files Allen and Caldwell · 109 West Ferguson Street · P.O. Box 2013 · Tyler, TX 75710 · 214-595-3573

Coye Conner, Jr. · Connor, Gillen & Yarbrough · Tyler National Bank Building, Suite 211 · 3301 Golden Road · Tyler, TX 75701 · 214-595-0755

LABOR AND EMPLOYMENT LAW

Brian S. Greig · (Management) · Fulbright & Jaworski · One American Center, Suite 2400 · 600 Congress Avenue · Austin, TX 78701 · 512-474-5201

David R. Richards · (Labor; Individuals) · Richards, Wiseman & Durst · 600 West Seventh Street · Austin, TX 78701 · 512-479-5017

David Van Os · (Labor) · Fickman & Van Os · 900 Congress Avenue, Suite 400 P.O. Box 26946 · Austin, TX 78755 · 512-479-6155

Robert J. Hambright · (Management) · Orgain, Bell & Tucker · 470 Orleans Street · Beaumont, TX 77701 · 409-838-6412

G. William Baab · (Labor) · Mullinax, Wells, Baab & Cloutman · 3301 Elm Street Dallas, TX 75226 · 214-939-9222

Hershell L. Barnes · (Management) · Haynes and Boone · 3100 First RepublicBank Plaza · 901 Main Street · Dallas, TX 75202 · 214-670-0550

Allen Butler · (Management) · Clark, West, Keller, Butler & Ellis · 4800 Renaissance Tower · Dallas, TX 75270 · 214-741-1001

Bennett W. Cervin · (Management) · Thompson & Knight · 3300 First City Center · 1700 Pacific Avenue · Dallas, TX 75201 · 214-969-1700

Edward B. Cloutman III · (Labor; Individuals) · Mullinax, Wells, Baab & Cloutman · 3301 Elm Street · Dallas, TX 75226 · 214-939-9222

George C. Dunlap · (Management) · Strasburger & Price · 4300 First RepublicBank Plaza · 901 Main Street · P.O. Box 50100 · Dallas, TX 75202 · 214-651-4300

Stephen F. Fink · (Management) · Thompson & Knight · 3300 First City Center 1700 Pacific Avenue · Dallas, TX 75201 · 214-969-1700

James L. Hicks, Jr. · (Labor; Individuals) · Hicks, Gillespie, James, Rozen & Preston · 1420 West Mockingbird Lane · P.O. Box 47386 · Dallas, TX 75247-0386 214-630-8621

Phillip R. Jones · (Management) · Jenkens & Gilchrist · 3200 First Interstate Tower · 1445 Ross Avenue · Dallas, TX 75202-2711 · 214-855-4500

William L. Keller · (Management) · Clark, West, Keller, Butler & Ellis · 4949 Renaissance Tower · Dallas, TX 75270 · 214-741-1001

Robert G. Mebus · (Management) · Haynes and Boone · 3100 First RepublicBank Plaza · 901 Main Street · Dallas, TX 75202 · 214-670-0550

Marvin Menaker · (Labor) · Menaker & Huffman · 11311 North Central Expressway · Dallas, TX 75243 · 214-696-5441

Kenneth H. Molberg · (Individuals) · Wilson, Williams & Molberg · 2214 Main Dallas, TX 74201 · 214-748-5276

William C. Strock · (Management) · Haynes and Boone · 3100 First RepublicBank Plaza · 901 Main Street · Dallas, TX 75202 · 214-670-0550

L.N.D. Wells, Jr. · (Labor; Individuals) · Mullinax, Wells, Baab & Cloutman · 3301 Elm Street · Dallas, TX 75226 · 214-939-9222

Kenneth R. Carr · (Management) · Grambling & Mounce · Texas Commerce Bank Building, Seventh Floor · El Paso, TX 79901 · 915-532-3911

Charles C. High, Jr. · (Management) · Kemp, Smith, Duncan & Hammond · 2000 MBank Plaza · P.O. Drawer 2800 · El Paso, TX 79999 · 915-533-4424

Thomas A. Spieczny · (Labor) · 521 Texas Avenue · El Paso, TX 79901 · 915-533-5581

Robert S. Bambace · (Management) · Fulbright & Jaworski · Gulf Tower, 51st Floor · 1301 McKinney Street · Houston, TX 77010 · 713-651-5151

Richard R. Brann · (Management) · Baker & Botts · One Shell Plaza · Houston, TX 77002 · 713-229-1234

V. Reagan Burch · (Management) · Baker & Botts · One Shell Plaza · Houston, TX 77002 · 713-229-1234

Chris J. Dixie · (Labor) · Fickman & Van Os · 2100 Travis, Suite 727 · Houston, TX 77002 · 713-223-4444

Bruce A. Fickman · (Labor) · Fickman & Van Os · 2100 Travis, Suite 727 · Houston, TX 77002 · 713-223-4444

Patrick M. Flynn · (Labor) · Watson, Flynn & Bensik · 1225 North Loop West, Suite 800 · Houston, TX 77008 · 713-861-6163

A. J. Harper II · (Management) · Fulbright & Jaworski · Gulf Tower, 51st Floor 1301 McKinney Street · Houston, TX 77010 · 713-651-5151

W. Carl Jordan · Vinson & Elkins · 3300 First City Tower · 1001 Fannin · Houston, TX 77002-6760 · 713-651-2222

V. Scott Kneese · (Management) · Bracewell & Patterson · 2900 South Tower, Pennzoil Place · Houston, TX 77002 · 713-223-2900

Thomas M. Melo · (Management) · Bracewell & Patterson · 2900 South Tower, Pennzoil Place · Houston, TX 77002 · 713-223-2900

Stuart M. Nelkin · (Individuals) · Nelkin & Nelkin · 5417 Chaucer · P.O. Box 25303 · Houston, TX 77265 · 713-526-4500

L. Chapman Smith · (Management) · Baker & Botts · One Shell Plaza · Houston, TX 77002 · 713-229-1234

John H. Smither · (Management) · Vinson & Elkins · 3300 First City Tower · 1001 Fannin · Houston, TX 77002-6760 · 713-651-2222

Eliot P. Tucker · (Individuals) · Mandell & Wright · 712 Main Street, Suite 1600 Houston, TX 77002-3209 · 713-228-1521

James R. Watson, Jr. · (Labor) · Watson, Flynn & Bensik · 1225 North Loop West, Suite 800 · Houston, TX 77008 · 713-861-6163

J. Joe Harris · (Management) · Matthews & Branscomb · One Alamo Center, Suite 800 · San Antonio, TX 78205 · 512-226-4211

Frank Herrera, Jr. · (Labor) · Herrera & Vega · 115 Villita Street · San Antonio, TX 78205 · 512-224-1054

Shelton E. Padgett · (Management) · Kaufman, Becker, Clare and Padgett · 300 Convent Street, Suite 2300 · San Antonio, TX 78205 · 512-227-2000

Philip J. Pfeiffer · (Management) · Fulbright & Jaworski · 2200 InterFirst Plaza 300 Convent Street · San Antonio, TX 78205 · 512-224-5575

MARITIME LAW

Jack L. Allbritton · Fulbright & Jaworski · Gulf Tower, 51st Floor · 1301 McKinney Street · Houston, TX 77010 · 713-651-5151

Ed Bluestein, Jr. · Fulbright & Jaworski · Gulf Tower, 51st Floor · 1301 McKinney Street · Houston, TX 77010 · 713-651-5151

Joseph D. Cheavens · Baker & Botts · One Shell Plaza · Houston, TX 77002 · 713-229-1234

Theodore G. Dimitry · Vinson & Elkins · 3300 First City Tower · 1001 Fannin Houston, TX 77002-6760 · 713-651-2222

E. V. Greenwood · Hill, Rivkins, Carey, Loesberg, O'Brien & Mulroy · 712 Main Street, Suite 1515 · Houston, TX 77002 · 713-222-1515

Edward D. Vickery · Royston, Rayzor, Vickery & Williams · 2200 Texas Commerce Tower · Houston, TX 77002 · 713-224-8380

NATURAL RESOURCES AND ENVIRONMENTAL LAW

Jeff Civins · Vinson & Elkins · First City Centre · 816 Congress Avenue · Austin, TX 78701-2496 · 512-495-8400

Frank Douglass · (Oil & Gas) · Scott, Douglass & Luton · First City National Bank Building, 12th Floor · Austin, TX 78701 · 512-476-6337

Pamela M. Giblin · McGinnis, Lockridge & Kilgore · 1300 Capitol Center · 919 Congress Avenue · Austin, TX 78701 · 512-476-6982

R. Kinnan Golemon · Brown Maroney Rose Barber & Dye · 1400 One Congress Plaza · 111 Congress Avenue · Austin, TX 78701 · 512-472-5456

Robert C. McGinnis · (Oil & Gas) · McGinnis, Lochridge & Kilgore · 1300 Capitol Center · 919 Congress Avenue · Austin, TX 78701 · 512-476-6982

Dan Moody, Jr. · (Oil & Gas) · Graves, Dougherty, Hearon & Moody · 2300 Interfirst Tower · P.O. Box 98 · Austin, TX 78767 · 512-480-5600

Louis Seymour Zimmerman · (Oil & Gas) · Fulbright & Jaworski · One American Center, Suite 2400 · 600 Congress Avenue · Austin, TX 78701 · 512-474-5201

Linton E. Barbee · (Oil & Gas) · Hughes & Luce · 2800 Momentum Place · 1717 Main Street · Dallas, TX 75201 · 214-939-5500

Theodore R. Borrego · (Oil & Gas) · Johnson & Swanson · Founders Square, Suite 100 · 900 Jackson Street · Dallas, TX 75202-4499 · 214-977-9000

James B. Harris · Thompson & Knight · 3300 First City Center · 1700 Pacific Avenue · Dallas, TX 75201 · 214-969-1700

James C. Morriss III · Thompson & Knight · 3300 First City Center · 1700 Pacific Avenue · Dallas, TX 75201 · 214-969-1700

David J. Beck · Fulbright & Jaworski · Gulf Tower, 51st Floor · 1301 McKinney Street · Houston, TX 77010 · 713-651-5151

Charles L. Berry · Vinson & Elkins · 3300 First City Tower · 1001 Fannin · Houston, TX 77002-6760 · 713-651-2222

Larry B. Briggs · (Oil & Gas) · Deaton, Briggs & McCain · San Felipe Plaza, 40th Floor · 5847 San Felipe · Houston, TX 77057 · 713-780-1111

F. Walter Conrad, Jr. · Baker & Botts · One Shell Plaza · Houston, TX 77002 · 713-229-1234

Carol E. Dinkins · Vinson & Elkins · 3300 First City Tower · 1001 Fannin · Houston, TX 77002-6760 · 713-651-2222

William H. Drushel, Jr. · (Oil & Gas) · Vinson & Elkins · 3300 First City Tower · 1001 Fannin · Houston, TX 77002-6760 · 713-651-2222

Uriel E. Dutton · (Oil & Gas) · Fulbright & Jaworski · Gulf Tower, 51st Floor · 1301 McKinney Street · Houston, TX 77010 · 713-651-5151

Larry B. Feldcamp · Baker & Botts · One Shell Plaza · Houston, TX 77002 · 713-229-1234

John E. Kolb · (Oil & Gas) · Vinson & Elkins · 3300 First City Tower · 1001 Fannin · Houston, TX 77002-6760 · 713-651-2222

Norman D. Radford, Jr. · Vinson & Elkins · 3300 First City Tower · 1001 Fannin · Houston, TX 77002-6760 · 713-651-2222

Rush H. Record · (Oil & Gas) · Vinson & Elkins · 3300 First City Tower · 1001 Fannin · Houston, TX 77002-6760 · 713-651-2222

George L. Robertson · (Oil & Gas) · Butler & Binion · 1600 First Interstate Bank Plaza · Houston, TX 77002 · 713-237-3111

John S. Sellingsloh · (Oil & Gas) · Baker & Botts · One Shell Plaza · Houston, TX 77002 · 713-229-1234

William Byron White · (Oil & Gas) · Fulbright & Jaworski · Gulf Tower, 51st Floor · 1301 McKinney Street · Houston, TX 77010 · 713-651-5151

Richard T. Brady · (Oil & Gas) · Cox & Smith · 600 National Bank of Commerce Building · San Antonio, TX 78205 · 512-226-7000

Paul H. Smith · (Oil & Gas) · Cox & Smith · 600 National Bank of Commerce Building · San Antonio, TX 78205 · 512-226-7000

PERSONAL INJURY LITIGATION

L. Tonnett Byrd · (Plaintiffs) · Byrd, Davis and Eisenberg · 707 West 34th Street · Austin, TX 78705 · 512-454-3751

John H. Coates · (Defendants) · Clark, Thomas, Winters & Newton · Texas Commerce Bank Building, 12th Floor · P.O. Box 1148 · Austin, TX 78767 · 512-472-8800

Tom H. Davis · (Plaintiffs) · Byrd, Davis and Eisenberg · 707 West 34th Street · Austin, TX 78705 · 512-454-3751

Bob Gibbins · (Plaintiffs) · Gibbins, Bratton & Pan · 500 West 13th Street · Austin, TX 78701 · 512-474-2441

Mack Kidd · (Plaintiffs) · Kidd, Whitehurst, Harkness & Watson · Westgate Building, 24th Floor · P.O. Box 1802 · Austin, TX 78767 · 512-476-4346

Jack D. Maroney · (Defendants) · Brown Maroney Rose Barber & Dye · 1400 One Congress Plaza · 111 Congress Avenue · Austin, TX 78701 · 512-472-5456

Richard T. McCarroll · (Defendants) · Brown Maroney Rose Barber & Dye · 1400 One Congress Plaza · 111 Congress Avenue · Austin, TX 78701 · 512-472-5456

Charles (Lefty) Morris · (Plaintiffs) · Morris, Craven & Sulak · 2350 One American Center · 600 Congress Avenue · Austin, TX 78701 · 512-478-9535

Broadus A. Spivey · (Plaintiffs) · Spivey, Grigg, Kelly & Knisely · 111 West Sixth Street · P.O. Box 2011 · Austin, TX 78768 · 512-474-6061

T. B. Wright · (Defendants) · Bankston, Wright & Greenhill · 1800 MBank Tower 221 West Sixth Street · Austin, TX 78701 · 512-476-4600

Cleve Bachman · (Defendants) · Orgain, Bell & Tucker · 470 Orleans Street · Beaumont, TX 77701 · 409-838-6412

Gilbert I. Low · (Defendants) · Orgain, Bell & Tucker · 470 Orleans Street · Beaumont, TX 77701 · 409-838-6412

Otto J. Weber, Jr. · (Defendants) · Mehaffy, Weber, Keith & Gonsoulin · InterFirst Tower, Eighth Floor · P.O. Box 16 · Beaumont, TX 77704 · 409-835-5011

Guy H. Allison · 920 Leopard Street · Corpus Christi, TX 78401 · 512-884-1632

William R. Edwards · (Plaintiffs) · Edwards & Terry · Texas Commerce Plaza, Suite 1400 · P.O. Box 480 · Corpus Christi, TX 78470 · 512-883-0971

David L. Perry · (Plaintiffs) · David L. Perry & Associates · 2300 Texas Commerce Plaza · 802 North Carancahua · P.O. Drawer 1500 · Corpus Christi, TX 78403-1500 · 512-887-7500

Frank L. Branson · (Plaintiffs) · Law Offices of Frank L. Branson · Highland Park Place, Suite 1800 · 4514 Cole Avenue · Dallas, TX 75205 · 214-522-0200

Arlen (Spider) Bynum · (Defendants) · Law Offices of Arlen D. (Spider) Bynum Two Turtle Creek Village, Suite 820 · Dallas, TX 75219 · 214-559-0500

James E. Coleman, Jr. · (Defendants) · Carrington, Coleman, Solman & Blumenthal · 200 Crescent Court, Suite 1500 · Dallas, TX 75201 · 214-855-3000

Jim E. Cowles · (Defendants) · Cowles & Thompson · 4000 InterFirst Plaza · 901 Main Street · Dallas, TX 75202 · 214-670-1100

W. Richard Davis · (Defendants) · Strasburger & Price · 4300 InterFirst Plaza · 901 Main Street · P.O. Box 50100 · Dallas, TX 75202 · 214-651-4300

J. Carlisle DeHay, Jr. · (Defendants) · DeHay & Blanchard · 2500 South Tower Plaza of the Americas · Dallas, TX 75201 · 214-953-1313

John H. Hall · (Defendants) · Strasburger & Price · 4300 InterFirst Plaza · 901 Main Street · P.O. Box 50100 · Dallas, TX 75202 · 214-651-4300

Joe Hill Jones · (Plaintiffs) · Carter, Jones, Magee, Rudberg & Mayes · One Main Place, Suite 2400 · Dallas, TX 75250 · 214-742-6261

John L. Lancaster III · (Defendants) · Jackson & Walker · 6000 First RepublicBank Plaza · 901 Main Street · Dallas, TX 75250 · 214-953-6000

Fred Misko, Jr. · (Plaintiffs) · Misko & Howie · Trammell Crow Center, Suite 1100 · 2001 Ross Avenue · Dallas, TX 75201 · 214-969-0946

Ronald L. Palmer · (Defendants) · Baker & Botts · 800 Trammell Crow Center 2001 Ross Avenue · Dallas, TX 75201 · 214-953-6500

C. L. Mike Schmidt · Stradley, Schmidt, Stephens & Wright · Campbell Centre, Suite One · 8350 North Central Expressway · Dallas, TX 75206 · 214-696-4880

Fred S. Stradley · (Defendants) · Stradley, Schmidt, Stephens & Wright · Campbell Centre, Suite One · 8350 North Central Expressway · Dallas, TX 75206 · 214-696-4880

Windle Turley · (Plaintiffs) · Law Offices of Windle Turley · 1000 University Tower · 6440 North Central Expressway · Dallas, TX 75206 · 214-691-4025

Edwin E. Wright III · (Defendants) · Stradley, Schmidt, Stephens & Wright · Campbell Centre, Suite One · 8350 North Central Expressway · Dallas, TX 75206 · 214-696-4880

Raymond C. Caballero · (Plaintiffs) · Caballero & Panetta · 521 Texas Avenue · El Paso, TX 79901 · 915-542-4222

John A. Grambling · (Defendants) · Grambling & Mounce · Texas Commerce Bank Building, Seventh Floor · El Paso, TX 79901 · 915-532-3911

Sam Sparks · (Defendants) · Grambling & Mounce · Texas Commerce Bank Building, Seventh Floor · El Paso, TX 79901 · 915-532-3911

Beale Dean · (Defendants) · Brown, Herman, Scott, Dean & Miles · Fort Worth Club Building, Suite 203 · Fort Worth, TX 76102 · 817-332-1391

Richard L. Griffith · (Defendants) · Cantey & Hanger · 2100 First RepublicBank Tower · 801 Cherry Street · Fort Worth, TX 76102 · 817-877-2800

Kleber C. Miller · (Defendants) · Shannon, Gracey, Ratliff & Miller · 2200 First City Bank Tower · 201 Main Street · Fort Worth, TX 76102 · 817-336-9333

Warren Burnett · (Plaintiffs) · 1115 Twenty-First Street · Galveston, TX 77550 · 409-763-0124

J. Donald Bowen · (Plaintiffs) · Helm, Pletcher, Hogan, Bowen & Saunders · 2700 America Tower · 2929 Allen Parkway at Waugh · Houston, TX 77019-2120 · 713-522-4550

Richard H. Caldwell · (Defendants) · Mayor, Day & Caldwell · 1900 RepublicBank Center · P.O. Box 61269 · Houston, TX 77208-1269 · 713-225-7000

Lamberth S. Carsey · (Defendants) · Fulbright & Jaworski · Gulf Tower, 51st Floor · 1301 McKinney Street · Houston, TX 77010 · 713-651-5151

Wayne Fisher · (Plaintiffs) · Fisher, Gallagher, Perrin & Lewis · First Interstate Bank Plaza, 70th Floor · 1000 Louisiana · Houston, TX 77002 · 713-654-4433

Michael T. Gallagher · (Plaintiffs) · Fisher, Gallagher, Perrin & Lewis · First Interstate Bank Plaza, 70th Floor · 1000 Louisiana · Houston, TX 77002 · 713-654-4433

Charles W. Hurd · (Defendants) · Fulbright & Jaworski · Gulf Tower, 51st Floor · 1301 McKinney Street · Houston, TX 77010 · 713-651-5151

Joseph D. Jamail · (Plaintiffs) · Jamail & Kolius · 3300 One Allen Center · Smith at Dallas Streets · Houston, TX 77002 · 713-651-3000

Ronald D. Krist · (Plaintiffs) · Krist, Gunn, Weller, Neumann & Morrison · 17050 El Camino Real · Houston, TX 77058 · 713-488-2313

W. James Kronzer · 1001 Texas Street, Suite 1030 · Houston, TX 77002 · 713-236-1722

John L. McConn, Jr. · (Defendants) · McConn & Hardy · 6700 Texas Commerce Tower · 600 Travis Street · Houston, TX 77002 · 713-237-0222

Richard B. Miller · (Defendants) · Miller, Bristow & Brown · 3900 Two Houston Center · Houston, TX 77010 · 713-759-1234

Richard Warren Mithoff · (Plaintiffs) · Law Offices of Richard Warren Mithoff · 3450 One Allen Center, Penthouse · Houston, TX 77002 · 713-654-1122

Nick C. Nichols · (Plaintiffs) · Abraham, Watkins, Nichols, Ballard, Onstad & Friend · 800 Commerce Street · Houston, TX 77002 · 713-222-7211

Jim M. Perdue · (Plaintiffs) · Perdue, Turner & Berry · Lyric Office Centre, Suite 1900 · 440 Louisiana · Houston, TX 77002 · 713-227-1403

George E. Pletcher · (Plaintiffs) · Helm, Pletcher, Hogan, Bowen & Saunders · 2700 America Tower · 2929 Allen Parkway at Waugh · Houston, TX 77019-2120 713-522-4550

James B. Sales · (Defendants) · Fulbright & Jaworski · Gulf Tower, 51st Floor · 1301 McKinney Street · Houston, TX 77010 · 713-651-5151

Paul E. Stallings · (Defendants) · Vinson & Elkins · 3300 First City Tower · 1001 Fannin · Houston, TX 77002-6760 · 713-651-2222

Kenneth Tekell · (Defendants) · Tekell, Book, Matthews & Limmer · 3600 Two Houston Center · 909 Fannin Street · Houston, TX 77010 · 713-222-9542

Joe H. Tonahill · (Plaintiffs) · Tonahill, Hile, Leister & Jacobellis · 270 East Lamar · Jasper, TX 75951 · 409-384-2501

T. John Ward · (Defendants) · Sharp, Ward, Price & Searcy · MBank Building, Sixth Floor · P.O. Drawer 3106 · Longview, TX 75606 · 214-757-2880

F. Scott Baldwin · (Plaintiffs) · Baldwin & Baldwin · 115 North Wellington Street P.O. Drawer 1349 · Marshall, TX 75671 · 214-935-4131

Franklin Jones, Jr. · (Plaintiffs) · Jones, Jones, Curry & Roth · 201 West Houston Street · P.O. Drawer 1249 · Marshall, TX 75671-1249 · 214-938-4395

James L. Branton · (Plaintiffs) · Branton & Hall · 737 Travis Park Plaza Building San Antonio, TX 78205 · 512-224-4474

Franklin D. Houser · (Plaintiffs) · Tinsman & Houser · 1900 National Bank of Commerce Building · San Antonio, TX 78205 · 512-225-3121

Clarence Lyons · (Plaintiffs) · Southers & Lyons · 126 Villita Street · San Antonio, TX 78205 · 512-225-5251

George H. Spencer, Sr. · (Defendants) · Clemens, Spencer, Welmaker & Finck 1800 National Bank of Commerce Building · San Antonio, TX 78205 · 512-227-7121

Richard D. Cullen · (Defendants) · Cullen, Carsner & Cullen · 119 South Main Street · P.O. Box 2938 · Victoria, TX 77902 · 512-573-6318

Jack G. Banner · (Plaintiffs) · Banner, Dobbs & Briley · Hamilton Building, Suite 1200 · Wichita Falls, TX 76301 · 817-723-6644

REAL ESTATE LAW

David B. Armbrust · Armbrust & Brown · 2600 One American Center · 600 Congress Avenue · Austin, TX 78701 · 512-499-3600

Richard C. Baker · Brown Maroney Rose Barber & Dye · 1400 One Congress Plaza · 111 Congress Avenue · Austin, TX 78701 · 512-472-5456

Wm. Terry Bray · Graves, Dougherty, Hearon & Moody · 2300 Interfirst Tower P.O. Box 98 · Austin, TX 78767 · 512-480-5600

Michael L. Cook · Shapiro, Edens & Cook · 2200 One American Center · 600 Congress Avenue · Austin, TX 78701 · 512-499-3800

Robert W. Dupuy · Brown Maroney Rose Barber & Dye · 1400 One Congress Plaza · 111 Congress Avenue · Austin, TX 78701 · 512-472-5456

P. Michael Hebert · McGinnis, Lochridge & Kilgore · 1300 Capitol Center · 919 Congress Avenue · Austin, TX 78701 · 512-476-6982

Brian C. Rider · Brown Maroney Rose Barber & Dye · 1400 One Congress Plaza · 111 Congress Avenue · Austin, TX 78701 · 512-472-5456

Roy C. Snodgrass III · Shapiro, Edens & Cook · 2200 One American Center · 600 Congress Avenue · Austin, TX 78701 · 512-499-3800

Bickford G. Shaw · Shaw & Conoly · 5934 South Staples, Suite 200 · Corpus Christi, TX 78413 · 512-993-0201

Robert M. Allen · Clements, Allen & Bufkin · 6600 LBJ Freeway, Suite 4100 · Dallas, TX 75240 · 214-991-2600

Lawrence J. Brannian · Johnson & Swanson · Founders Square, Suite 100 · 900 Jackson Street · Dallas, TX 75202-4499 · 214-977-9000

Daniel K. Hennessey · Hughes & Luce · 2800 Momentum Place · 1717 Main Street · Dallas, TX 75201 · 214-939-5500

Steven R. Jenkins · Johnson & Swanson · Founders Square, Suite 100 · 900 Jackson Street · Dallas, TX 75202-4499 · 214-977-9000

John R. Johnson · Johnson & Swanson · Founders Square, Suite 100 · 900 Jackson Street · Dallas, TX 75202-4499 · 214-977-9000

Dan B. Miller · Jones, Day, Reavis & Pogue · 2300 Trammell Crow Center · 2001 Ross Avenue · P.O. Box 660623 · Dallas, TX 75266-0623 · 214-220-3939

Edward A. Peterson · Moore & Peterson · 2800 First City Center · Dallas, TX 75201-4621 · 214-754-4800

William D. Powell · Johnson, Bromberg & Leeds · 2600 Lincoln Plaza · Dallas, TX 75201 · 214-740-2600

Gary R. Rice · Payne & Vendig · 2355 Stemmons Freeway, Suite 10001 · Dallas, TX 75201 · 214-634-7656

Harry M. Roberts, Jr. · Thompson & Knight · 3300 First City Center · 1700 Pacific Avenue · Dallas, TX 75201 · 214-969-1700

James W. Rose · Thompson & Knight · 3300 First City Center · 1700 Pacific Avenue · Dallas, TX 75201 · 214-969-1700

William B. Sechrest · Winstead, McGuire, Sechrest & Minick · 5400 Renaissance Tower · 1201 Elm Street · Dallas, TX 75270 · 214-742-1700

Robert F. See, Jr. · Locke Purnell Rain Harrell · 2200 Ross Avenue, Suite 2200 · Dallas, TX 75201 · 214-740-8000

Philip B. Smith, Jr. · Locke Purnell Rain Harrell · 2200 Ross Avenue, Suite 2200 · Dallas, TX 75201 · 214-740-8000

Charles W. Spencer · Geary, Stahl & Spencer · 6400 First RepublicBank Plaza · 901 Main Street · Dallas, TX 75202 · 214-748-9901

William A. Thau · Jenkens & Gilchrist · 3200 First Interstate Tower · 1445 Ross Avenue · Dallas, TX 75202-2711 · 214-855-4500

James H. Wallenstein · Jenkens & Gilchrist · 3200 First Interstate Tower · 1445 Ross Avenue · Dallas, TX 75202-2711 · 214-855-4500

Philip D. Weller · Vinson & Elkins · 2020 Trammell Crow Center · 2001 Ross Avenue · Dallas, TX 75201-2916 · 214-220-7700

Ben B. West · Jackson & Walker · 6000 First RepublicBank Plaza · 901 Main Street · Dallas, TX 75250 · 214-953-6000

Robert E. Wilson · Haynes and Boone · 3100 First RepublicBank Plaza · 901 Main Street · Dallas, TX 75202 · 214-670-0550

Eldon L. Youngblood · Moore & Peterson · 2800 First City Center · Dallas, TX 75201-4621 · 214-754-4800

Marc P. Bernat · Potash, Bernat, Sipes & Bernat · 1424 First City National Bank Building · El Paso, TX 79901 · 915-532-1491

Raymond H. Marshall · Kemp, Smith, Duncan & Hammond · 2000 MBank Plaza P.O. Drawer 2800 · El Paso, TX 79999 · 915-533-4424

William J. Mounce · Grambling & Mounce · Texas Commerce Bank Building, Seventh Floor · El Paso, TX 79901 · 915-532-3911

Billie J. Ellis, Jr. · Kelly, Hart & Hallman · 2500 First City Bank Tower · 201 Main Street · Fort Worth, TX 76102 · 817-332-2500

William Kendall Adam · Fulbright & Jaworski · Gulf Tower, 51st Floor · 1301 McKinney Street · Houston, TX 77010 · 713-651-5151

Gus Block · Hirsch & Westheimer · 2500 RepublicBank Center · 700 Louisiana · Houston, TX 77002 · 713-223-5181

David Alan Burns · Baker & Botts · One Shell Plaza · Houston, TX 77002 · 713-229-1234

Bernard O. Dow · Dow, Cogburn & Friedman · Coastal Tower, Suite 2300 · Nine Greenway Plaza · Houston, TX 77046 · 713-626-5800

Melvin A. Dow · Dow, Cogburn & Friedman · Coastal Tower, Suite 2300 · Nine Greenway Plaza · Houston, TX 77046 · 713-626-5800

Fred H. Dunlop · Baker & Botts · One Shell Plaza · Houston, TX 77002 · 713-229-1234

Uriel E. Dutton · Fulbright & Jaworski · Gulf Tower, 51st Floor · 1301 McKinney Street · Houston, TX 77010 · 713-651-5151

Jack E. Fields · Andrews & Kurth · 4200 Texas Commerce Tower · Houston, TX 77002 · 713-220-4200

Abraham P. Friedman · Dow, Cogburn & Friedman · Coastal Tower, Suite 2300 · Nine Greenway Plaza · Houston, TX 77046 · 713-626-5870

Jesse B. Heath, Jr. · Mayor, Day & Caldwell · 1900 RepublicBank Center · P.O. Box 61269 · Houston, TX 77208-1269 · 713-225-7000

John S. Hollyfield · Fulbright & Jaworski · Gulf Tower, 51st Floor · 1301 McKinney Street · Houston, TX 77010 · 713-651-5151

Randall K. Howard · Sheinfeld, Maley & Kay · 3700 First City Tower · Houston, TX 77002 · 713-658-8881

M. Marvin Katz · De Lange, Hudspeth, Pitman & Katz · 2800 Summit Tower · 11 Greenway Plaza · Houston, TX 77046 · 713-871-9898

Darrell C. Morrow · Vinson & Elkins · 3300 First City Tower · 1001 Fannin · Houston, TX 77002-6760 · 713-651-2222

Carl G. Mueller, Jr. · Harpold, McDonald, Gitzgerald, Mueller & Hall · One Greenway Plaza, Suite 820 · Houston, TX 77046 · 713-626-8060

Lee D. Schlanger · Schlanger, Cook, Cohn, Mills & Grossberg · 5847 San Felipe, Suite 1700 · Houston, TX 77057 · 713-785-1700

John S. Sellingsloh · Baker & Botts · One Shell Plaza · Houston, TX 77002 · 713-229-1234

Joel I. Shannon · Andrews & Kurth · 4200 Texas Commerce Tower · Houston, TX 77002 · 713-220-4200

Frank F. Smith, Jr. · Vinson & Elkins · 3300 First City Tower · 1001 Fannin · Houston, TX 77002-6760 · 713-651-2222

Jack R. Sowell · Vinson & Elkins · 3300 First City Tower · 1001 Fannin · Houston, TX 77002-6760 · 713-651-2222

Sanford A. Weiner · Vinson & Elkins · 3300 First City Tower · 1001 Fannin · Houston, TX 77002-6760 · 713-651-2222

William Byron White · Fulbright & Jaworski · Gulf Tower, 51st Floor · 1301 McKinney Street · Houston, TX 77010 · 713-651-5151

Patricia G. Bridwell · Groce, Locke & Hebdon · 2000 Frost Bank Tower · San Antonio, TX 78205 · 512-225-3031

Norman S. Davis · Davis & Cedillo · Concord Plaza, Suite 400 · 200 Concord Plaza Drive · San Antonio, TX 78216 · 512-822-6666

Pat H. Gardner · Foster, Lewis, Langley, Gardner & Banack · Frost Bank Tower, 16th Floor · San Antonio, TX 78205 · 512-226-3116

Kenneth M. Gindy · Oppenheimer, Rosenberg, Kelleher & Wheatley · 711 Navarro, Sixth Floor · San Antonio, TX 78205 · 512-224-2000

Stanley D. Rosenberg · Oppenheimer, Rosenberg, Kelleher & Wheatley · 711 Navarro, Sixth Floor · San Antonio, TX 78205 · 512-224-2000

Paul H. Smith · Cox & Smith · 600 National Bank of Commerce Building · San Antonio, TX 78205 · 512-226-7000

David C. Spoor · Cox & Smith · 600 National Bank of Commerce Building · San Antonio, TX 78205 · 512-226-7000

Lewis T. Tarver, Jr. · Matthews & Branscomb · One Alamo Center · San Antonio, TX 78205 · 512-226-4211

TAX AND EMPLOYEE BENEFITS LAW

Thomas J. Brorby · Johnson & Swanson · 100 Congress Avenue, Suite 1400 · Austin, TX 78701 · 512-322-8000

Michael L. Cook · Shapiro, Edens & Cook · 2200 One American Center · 600 Congress Avenue · Austin, TX 78701 · 512-499-3800

J. Chrys Dougherty · Graves, Dougherty, Hearon & Moody · 2300 InterFirst Tower · P.O. Box 98 · Austin, TX 78767 · 512-480-5600

Denny O. Ingram · McGinnis, Lochridge & Kilgore · 1300 Capitol Center · 919 Congress Avenue · Austin, TX 78701 · 512-476-6982

David I. Kuperman · (also Employee Benefits) · Johnson & Swanson · 100 Congress Avenue, Suite 1400 · Austin, TX 78701 · 512-322-8000

Sander W. Shapiro · Shapiro, Edens & Cook · 2200 One American Center · 600 Congress Avenue · Austin, TX 78701 · 512-499-3800

Peter Winstead · Winstead, McGuire, Sechrest & Minick · 919 Congress Avenue, Suite 800 · Austin, TX 78701 · 512-370-2801

Harvie Branscomb, Jr. · Matthews & Branscomb · 1800 First City Bank Tower · Corpus Christi, TX 78477-0129 · 512-888-9261

Gerald W. Ostarch · Gary, Thomasson, Hall & Marks · 210 South Carancahua · P.O. Box 2888 · Corpus Christi, TX 78403 · 512-884-1961

Buford P. Berry · Thompson & Knight · 3300 First City Center · 1700 Pacific Avenue · Dallas, TX 75201 · 214-969-1700

Stuart M. Bumpas · (Employee Benefits) · Locke Purnell Rain Harrell · 2200 Ross Avenue, Suite 2200 · Dallas, TX 75201 · 214-740-8000

Robert Edwin Davis · Davis, Meadows, Owens, Collier & Zachry · 901 Main Street, Suite 3700 · Dallas, TX 75202 · 214-744-3700

Henry D. De Berry III · Johnson & Swanson · Founders Square, Suite 100 · 900 Jackson Street · Dallas, TX 75202-4499 · 214-977-9000

H. Gene Emery · Locke Purnell Rain Harrell · 2200 Ross Avenue, Suite 2200 · Dallas, TX 75201 · 214-740-8000

Richard A. Freling · Johnson & Swanson · Founders Square, Suite 100 · 900 Jackson Street · Dallas, TX 75202-4499 · 214-977-9000

Joseph J. French, Jr. · Locke Purnell Rain Harrell · 2200 Ross Avenue, Suite 2200 · Dallas, TX 75201 · 214-740-8000

W. John Glancy · Hughes & Luce · 2800 Momentum Place · 1717 Main Street · Dallas, TX 75201 · 214-939-5500

David G. Glickman · Johnson & Swanson · Founders Square, Suite 100 · 900 Jackson Street · Dallas, TX 75202-4499 · 214-977-9000

John Michael Holt · (Employee Benefits) · Thompson & Knight · 3300 First City Center · 1700 Pacific Avenue · Dallas, TX 75201 · 214-969-1700

Vester T. Hughes, Jr. · Hughes & Luce · 2800 Momentum Place · 1717 Main Street · Dallas, TX 75201 · 214-939-5500

William D. Jordan · Jackson & Walker · 6000 First RepublicBank Plaza · 901 Main Street · Dallas, TX 75250 · 214-953-6000

Cym H. Lowell · Johnson & Swanson · Founders Square, Suite 100 · 900 Jackson Street · Dallas, TX 75202-4499 · 214-977-9000

Richard A. Massman · Johnson & Swanson · Founders Square, Suite 100 · 900 Jackson Street · Dallas, TX 75202-4499 · 214-977-9000

William B. McClure, Jr. · (Employee Benefits) · Johnson & Swanson · Founders Square, Suite 100 · 900 Jackson Street · Dallas, TX 75202-4499 · 214-977-9000

P. M. McCullough · Thompson & Knight · 3300 First City Center · 1700 Pacific Avenue · Dallas, TX 75201 · 214-969-1700

Emily A. Parker · Thompson & Knight · 3300 First City Center · 1700 Pacific Avenue · Dallas, TX 75201 · 214-969-1700

Cecil A. Ray, Jr. · (Employee Benefits) · Hughes & Luce · 2800 Momentum Place · 1717 Main Street · Dallas, TX 75201 · 214-939-5500

Samuel G. Winstead · Jackson & Walker · 6000 First RepublicBank Plaza · 901 Main Street · Dallas, TX 75250 · 214-953-6000

Donald J. Zahn · Akin, Gump, Strauss, Hauer & Feld · 4100 First City Center · 1700 Pacific Avenue · Dallas, TX 75201-4618 · 214-969-2800

Hector Delgado · Ginnings Birkelbach Keith & Delgado · American Bank of Commerce Building, Suite 700 · P.O. Box 54 · El Paso, TX 79940 · 915-532-5929

R. Gordon Appleman · Thompson & Knight · 801 Cherry Street, Suite 1600 · Fort Worth, TX 76102 · 817-335-1700

Whitfield J. Collins · Cantey & Hanger · 2100 First RepublicBank Tower · 801 Cherry Street · Fort Worth, TX 76102 · 817-877-2800

Gary P. Amoan · (Employee Benefits) · Vinson & Elkins · 3300 First City Tower 1001 Fannin · Houston, TX 77002-6760 · 713-651-2222

Stanley C. Beyer · Baker & Botts · One Shell Plaza · Houston, TX 77002 · 713-229-1234

A. T. Blackshear, Jr. · Fulbright & Jaworski · Gulf Tower, 51st Floor · 1301 McKinney Street · Houston, TX 77010 · 713-651-5151

Richard P. Bogatto · (Employee Benefits) · Fulbright & Jaworski · Gulf Tower, 51st Floor · 1301 McKinney Street · Houston, TX 77010 · 713-651-5151

Gareth W. Cook · (Employee Benefits) · Vinson & Elkins · 3300 First City Tower 1001 Fannin · Houston, TX 77002-6760 · 713-651-2222

J. Cal Courtney, Jr. · (Employee Benefits) · Fulbright & Jaworski · Gulf Tower, 51st Floor · 1301 McKinney Street · Houston, TX 77010 · 713-651-5151

Thomas Crichton IV · Vinson & Elkins · 3300 First City Tower · 1001 Fannin · Houston, TX 77002-6760 · 713-651-2222

Sam G. Croom, Jr. · (Employee Benefits) · Baker & Botts · One Shell Plaza · Houston, TX 77002 · 713-229-1234

William C. Griffith · Baker & Botts · One Shell Plaza · Houston, TX 77002 · 713-229-1234

Charles W. Hall · Fulbright & Jaworski · Gulf Tower, 51st Floor · 1301 McKinney Street · Houston, TX 77010 · 713-651-5151

George H. Jewell · Baker & Botts · One Shell Plaza · Houston, TX 77002 · 713-229-1234

Carol H. Jewett · (Employee Benefits) · Vinson & Elkins · 3300 First City Tower 1001 Fannin · Houston, TX 77002-6760 · 713-651-2222

Lawrence Kalinec · Fulbright & Jaworski · Gulf Tower, 51st Floor · 1301 McKinney Street · Houston, TX 77010 · 713-651-5151

William M. Linden · Vinson & Elkins · 3300 First City Tower · 1001 Fannin · Houston, TX 77002-6760 · 713-651-2222

J. Holland McGuirt · (Employee Benefits) · Butler & Binion · 1600 First Interstate Bank Plaza · Houston, TX 77002 · 713-237-3111

John Edward Neslage · (Employee Benefits) · Baker & Botts · One Shell Plaza · Houston, TX 77002 · 713-229-1234

Edward C. Osterberg, Jr. · Vinson & Elkins · 3300 First City Tower · 1001 Fannin · Houston, TX 77002-6760 · 713-651-2222

James R. Raborn · (Employee Benefits) · Baker & Botts · One Shell Plaza · Houston, TX 77002 · 713-229-1234

Steven C. Salch · Fulbright & Jaworski · Gulf Tower, 51st Floor · 1301 McKinney Street · Houston, TX 77010 · 713-651-5151

Laurence D. Sikes, Jr. · Andrews & Kurth · 4200 Texas Commerce Tower · Houston, TX 77002 · 713-220-4200

Herbert D. Simons · Butler & Binion · 1600 First Interstate Bank Plaza · Houston, TX 77002 · 713-237-3111

Michael Dean Stewart · (Employee Benefits) · Urban & Coolidge · 1300 Post Oak Boulevard, Suite 700 · Houston, TX 77056 · 713-621-6160

C. W. Wellen · Fulbright & Jaworski · Gulf Tower, 51st Floor · 1301 McKinney Street · Houston, TX 77010 · 713-651-5151

Donald F. Wood · Vinson & Elkins · 3300 First City Tower · 1001 Fannin · Houston, TX 77002-6760 · 713-651-2222

Stanley L. Blend · Oppenheimer, Rosenberg, Kelleher & Wheatley · 711 Navarro, Sixth Floor · San Antonio, TX 78205 · 512-224-2000

R. James Curphy · Schoenbaum, Curphy & Scanlan · 1420 Alamo National Building · San Antonio, TX 78205 · 512-224-4491

Richard E. Goldsmith · Matthews & Branscomb · One Alamo Center, Suite 800 · San Antonio, TX 78205 · 512-226-4211

Richard Michael Green · (Employee Benefits) · Matthews & Branscomb · One Alamo Center, Suite 800 · San Antonio, TX 78205 · 512-226-4211

Farley P. Katz · Matthews & Branscomb · One Alamo Center · San Antonio, TX 78205 · 512-226-4211

William Scanlan, Jr. · (Employee Benefits) · Schoenbaum, Curphy & Scanlan · 1420 Alamo National Building · San Antonio, TX 78205 · 512-224-4491

Stanley Schoenbaum · Schoenbaum, Curphy & Scanlan · 1420 Alamo National Building · San Antonio, TX 78205 · 512-224-4491

Richard N. Weinstein · (also Employee Benefits) · Oppenheimer, Rosenberg, Kelleher & Wheatley · 711 Navarro, Sixth Floor · San Antonio, TX 78205 · 512-224-2000

W. Thomas Weir · Akin, Gump, Strauss, Hauer & Feld · 1500 InterFirst Plaza · 300 Convent Street · San Antonio, TX 78205 · 512-270-0800

TRUSTS AND ESTATES

J. Chrys Dougherty · Graves, Dougherty, Hearon & Moody · 2300 Interfirst Tower · P.O. Box 98 · Austin, TX 78767 · 512-480-5600

Alvin J. Golden · Johnson & Swanson · 100 Congress Avenue, Suite 1400 · Austin, TX 78701 · 512-322-8000

H. David Hughes · Brown Maroney Rose Barber & Dye · 1400 One Congress Plaza · 111 Congress Avenue · Austin, TX 78701 · 512-472-5456

Denny O. Ingram · McGinnis, Lochridge & Kilgore · 1300 Capitol Center · 900 Congress Avenue · Austin, TX 78701 · 512-476-6982

Duncan Elliott Osborne · Graves, Dougherty, Hearon & Moody · 2300 Interfirst Tower · P.O. Box 98 · Austin, TX 78767 · 512-480-5600

John L. Bell, Jr. · Mehaffy, Weber, Keith & Gonsoulin · Interfirst Tower, Eighth Floor · P.O. Box 16 · Beaumont, TX 77704 · 409-835-5011

Stephen R. Akers · Jenkens & Gilchrist · 3200 First Interstate Tower · 1445 Ross Avenue · Dallas, TX 75202-2711 · 214-855-4500

Barbara McComas Anderson · Locke Purnell Rain Harrell · 2200 Ross Avenue, Suite 2200 · Dallas, TX 75201 · 214-740-8000

R. W. Calloway · Turner, Rodgers & Calloway · 2700 First City Center · Dallas, TX 75201 · 214-969-7422

Thomas H. Cantrill · Jenkens & Gilchrist · 3200 First Interstate Tower · 1445 Ross Avenue · Dallas, TX 75202-2711 · 214-855-4500

Ronald R. Cresswell · Locke Purnell Rain Harrell · 2200 Ross Avenue, Suite 2200 · Dallas, TX 75201 · 214-740-8000

James J. Hartnett, Sr. · Law Offices of James J. Hartnett · 2800 MBank Building · Dallas, TX 75201 · 214-742-4655

Jack W. Hawkins · Gardere & Wynne · 1500 Maxus Energy Tower · 717 North Harwood Street · Dallas, TX 75201 · 214-979-4500

Jack M. Kinnebrew · Strasburger & Price · 4300 First RepublicBank Plaza · 901 Main Street · P.O. Box 50100 · Dallas, TX 75202 · 214-651-4300

Donald J. Malouf · Malouf Lynch Jackson Kessler & Collins · 8117 Preston Road, Suite 700 · Dallas, TX 75225 · 214-750-0722

P. M. McCullough · Thompson & Knight · 3300 First City Center · 1700 Pacific Avenue · Dallas, TX 75201 · 214-969-1700

Rust E. Reid · Thompson & Knight · 3300 First City Center · 1700 Pacific Avenue · Dallas, TX 75201 · 214-969-1700

Edward V. Smith III · Taylor & Mizell · 3000 Lincoln Plaza, L.B.5 · 500 North Akard · Dallas, TX 75201 · 214-954-3400

Donald A. Swanson, Jr. · Storey, Armstrong, Steger & Martin · 4600 First Interstate Bank Tower · 1445 Ross Avenue · Dallas, TX 75202 · 214-855-6800

Robert Hyer Thomas · Strasburger & Price · 4300 First RepublicBank Plaza · 901 Main Street · P.O. Box 50100 · Dallas, TX 75202 · 214-651-4300

Ronald M. Weiss · Carrington, Coleman, Sloman & Blumenthal · 200 Crescent Court, Suite 1500 · Dallas, TX 75201 · 214-855-3000

Edward B. Winn · Winn, Beaudry & Virden · 3330 Republic Bank Building · Dallas, TX 75201 · 214-969-0001

Richard H. Feuille · Scott, Hulse, Marshall, Feuille, Finger & Thurmond · Texas Commerce Bank Building, 11th Floor · El Paso, TX 79901 · 915-533-2493

Joseph P. Hammond · Kemp, Smith, Duncan & Hammond · 2000 MBank Plaza · P.O. Drawer 2800 · El Paso, TX 79999 · 915-533-4424

J. Sam Moore, Jr. · Scott, Hulse, Marshall, Feuille, Finger & Thurmond · Texas Commerce Bank Building, 11th Floor · El Paso, TX 79901 · 915-533-2493

Brainerd S. Parrish · Studdard, Melby, Schwartz & Parrish · Franklin Plaza, Third Floor · 415 North Mesa · El Paso, TX 79901 · 915-533-5938

R. Gordon Appleman · Thompson & Knight · 801 Cherry Street, Suite 1600 · Fort Worth, TX 76102 · 817-335-1700

Allan Howeth · Cantey & Hanger · 2100 First RepublicBank Tower · 801 Cherry Street · Fort Worth, TX 76102 · 817-877-2800

Rice M. Tilley, Jr. · Law, Snakard & Gambill · 3200 Texas American Bank Building · Fort Worth, TX 76102 · 817-335-7373

Preston Shirley · Mills, Shirley, Eckel & Bassett · 400 Washington Building · 2228 Mechanic Street · Galveston, TX 77550 · 409-763-2341

Frank L. Jennings · Jennings, Dies & Turner · 620 Fourth Street · P.O. Drawer 930 · Graham, TX 76046 · 817-549-3456

Thomas E. Berry · Baker & Botts · One Shell Plaza · Houston, TX 77002 · 713-229-1234

W. Fred Cameron · Fulbright & Jaworski · Gulf Tower, 51st Floor · 1301 McKinney Street · Houston, TX 77010 · 713-651-5151

S. Stacy Eastland · Baker & Botts · One Shell Plaza · Houston, TX 77002 · 713-229-1234

J. Thomas Eubank · Baker & Botts · One Shell Plaza · Houston, TX 77002 · 713-229-1234

Charles W. Giraud · Butler & Binion · 1600 First Interstate Bank Plaza · Houston, TX 77002 · 713-237-3111

L. Henry Gissel, Jr. · Fulbright & Jaworski · Gulf Tower, 51st Floor · 1301 McKinney Street · Houston, TX 77010 · 713-651-5151

Rodney C. Koenig · Fulbright & Jaworski · Gulf Tower, 51st Floor · 1301 McKinney Street · Houston, TX 77010 · 713-651-5151

R. Bruce LaBoon · Liddell, Sapp, Zivley, Hill & LaBoon · Texas Commerce Tower, 34th Floor · Houston, TX 77002 · 713-226-1200

Kent H. McMahan · Fulbright & Jaworski · Gulf Tower, 51st Floor · 1301 McKinney Street · Houston, TX 77010 · 713-651-5151

Harold L. Metts · Baker & Botts · One Shell Plaza · Houston, TX 77002 · 713-229-1234

William T. Miller · Andrews & Kurth · 4200 Texas Commerce Tower · Houston, TX 77002 · 713-220-4200

Charles A. Saunders, Jr. · Fulbright & Jaworski · Gulf Tower, 51st Floor · 1301 McKinney Street · Houston, TX 77010 · 713-651-5151

Walter P. Zivley · Liddell, Sapp, Zivley, Hill & LaBoon · Texas Commerce Tower, 34th Floor · Houston, TX 77002 · 713-226-1200

Arthur H. Bayern · Bayern, Paterson, Aycock & Amen · 1700 National Bank of Commerce Building · San Antonio, TX 78205 · 512-223-6306

Taylor S. Boone · Oppenheimer, Rosenberg, Kelleher & Wheatley · 711 Navarro, Sixth Floor · San Antonio, TX 78205 · 512-224-2000

Richard E. Goldsmith · Matthews & Branscomb · One Alamo Center, Suite 800 San Antonio, TX 78205 · 512-226-4211

Jesse H. Oppenheimer · Oppenheimer, Rosenberg, Kelleher & Wheatley · 711 Navarro, Sixth Floor · San Antonio, TX 78205 · 512-224-2000

Allan G. Paterson, Jr. · Bayern, Paterson, Aycock & Amen · 1700 National Bank of Commerce Building · San Antonio, TX 78205 · 512-223-6306

William Scanlan, Jr. · Schoenbaum, Curphy & Scanlan · 1420 Alamo National Building · San Antonio, TX 78205 · 512-224-4491

Jim D. Bowmer · Bowmer, Courtney, Burleson, Normand & Moore · First National Bank Building, Sixth Floor · P.O. Box 844 · Temple, TX 76503 · 817-778-1354

UTAH

BANKRUPTCY LAW	702
BUSINESS LITIGATION	703
CORPORATE LAW	703
CRIMINAL DEFENSE	704
FAMILY LAW	704
LABOR AND EMPLOYMENT LAW	705
NATURAL RESOURCES AND ENVIRONMENTAL LAW	706
PERSONAL INJURY LITIGATION	707
REAL ESTATE LAW	708
TAX AND EMPLOYEE BENEFITS LAW	708
TRUSTS AND ESTATES	709

BANKRUPTCY LAW

Peter W. Billings, Jr. · Fabian & Clendenin · 215 South State Street, 12th Floor · Salt Lake City, UT 84111-2309 · 801-531-8900

William G. Fowler · Van Cott, Bagley, Cornwall & McCarthy · 50 South Main Street, Suite 1600 · P.O. Box 45340 · Salt Lake City, UT 84145 · 801-532-3333

Ralph R. Mabey · LeBoeuf, Lamb, Leiby & MacRae · 1000 Kearns Building · 136 South Main · Salt Lake City, UT 84101 · 801-355-6900

Robert D. Merrill · Van Cott, Bagley, Cornwall & McCarthy · 50 South Main Street, Suite 1600 · P.O. Box 45340 · Salt Lake City, UT 84145 · 801-532-3333

Herschel J. Saperstein · Watkiss & Campbell · 310 South Main Street, Suite 1200 · Salt Lake City, UT 84101 · 801-363-3300

Alan L. Smith · LeBoeuf, Lamb, Leiby & MacRae · 1000 Kearns Building · 136 South Main · Salt Lake City, UT 84101 · 801-355-6900

BUSINESS LITIGATION

Daniel L. Berman · Berman & O'Rorke · 50 South Main Street, Suite 1250 · Salt Lake City, UT 84144 · 801-328-2200

Robert S. Campbell, Jr. · Watkiss & Campbell · 310 South Main Street, Suite 1200 · Salt Lake City, UT 84101 · 801-363-3300

Harold G. Christensen · Snow, Christensen & Martineau · 10 Exchange Place, 11th Floor · P.O. Box 45000 · Salt Lake City, UT 84145-4111 · 801-521-9000

Stephen G. Crockett · Kimball, Parr, Crockett & Waddoups · 185 South State Street, Suite 1300 · P.O. Box 11019 · Salt Lake City, UT 84147 · 801-532-7840

Richard W. Giauque · Giauque & Williams · 500 Kearns Building · 136 South Main Street · Salt Lake City, UT 84101 · 801-533-8383

Gordon L. Roberts · Parsons, Behle & Latimer · 185 South State Street, Suite 700 · P.O. Box 11895 · Salt Lake City, UT 84147-0898 · 801-532-1234

David K. Watkiss · Watkiss & Campbell · 310 South Main Street, Suite 1200 · Salt Lake City, UT 84101 · 801-363-3300

CORPORATE LAW

Don B. Allen · Ray, Quinney & Nebeker · Deseret Building, Suite 400 · 79 South Main Street · P.O. Box 45385 · Salt Lake City, UT 84145-0385 · 801-532-1500

Robert M. Anderson · Hansen & Anderson · 50 West Broadway, Suite 600 · Salt Lake City, UT 84144 · 801-532-7520

Peter W. Billings, Jr. · Fabian & Clendenin · 215 South State Street, 12th Floor · Salt Lake City, UT 84111-2309 · 801-531-8900

Edward W. Clyde · Clyde, Pratt & Snow · American Savings Plaza, Suite 200 · 77 West Second South · Salt Lake City, UT 84101 · 801-322-2516

Donald B. Holbrook · Jones, Waldo, Holbrook & McDonough · 1500 First Interstate Plaza · 170 South Main Street · Salt Lake City, UT 84101 · 801-521-3200

Wilford W. Kirton, Jr. · Kirton, McConkie & Bushnell · 330 South Third East · Salt Lake City, UT 84111 · 801-521-3680

James B. Lee · Parsons, Behle & Latimer · 185 South State Street, Suite 700 · P.O. Box 11898 · Salt Lake City, UT 84147 · 801-532-1234

Leonard J. Lewis · Van Cott, Bagley, Cornwall & McCarthy · 50 South Main Street, Suite 1600 · P.O. Box 45340 · Salt Lake City, UT 84145 · 801-532-3333

David E. Salisbury · Van Cott, Bagley, Cornwall & McCarthy · 50 South Main Street, Suite 1600 · P.O. Box 45340 · Salt Lake City, UT 84145-0898 · 801-532-3333

Alonzo W. Watson, Jr. · Ray, Quinney & Nebeker · 400 Deseret Building, Suite 400 · 79 South Main Street · P.O. Box 45385 · Salt Lake City, UT 84145-0385 · 801-532-1500

CRIMINAL DEFENSE

Brian R. Florence · Florence and Hutchison · 818 Twenty-Sixth Street · Ogden, UT 84401 · 801-399-9291

John Blair Hutchison · Florence and Hutchison · 818 Twenty-Sixth Street · Ogden, UT 84401 · 801-399-9291

D. Gilbert Athay · 72 East Fourth South, Suite 325 · Salt Lake City, UT 84111 801-363-7074

Sumner J. Hatch · Hatch & McCaughey · 72 East 400 South Street, Suite 330 · Salt Lake City, UT 84111 · 801-364-6474

Stephen R. McCaughey · Hatch & McCaughey · 72 East 400 South Street, Suite 330 · Salt Lake City, UT 84111 · 801-364-6474

G. Fred Metos · Yengich, Rich, Xaiz & Metos · 175 East 400 South, Suite 400 · Salt Lake City, UT 84111 · 801-355-0320

Ronald J. Yengich · Yengich, Rich, Xaiz & Metos · 175 East 400 South, Suite 400 Salt Lake City, UT 84111 · 801-355-0320

FAMILY LAW

Brian R. Florence · Florence and Hutchison · 818 Twenty-Sixth Street · Ogden, UT 84401 · 801-399-9291

James P. Cowley · Watkiss & Campbell · 310 South Main Street, Suite 1200 · Salt Lake City, UT 84101 · 801-363-3300

B. L. Dart · Dart, Adamson & Kasting · 310 South Main Street, Suite 1330 · Salt Lake City, UT 84101 · 801-521-6383

David S. Dolowitz · Cohne, Rappaport & Segal · 525 East First South, Suite 500 · P.O. Box 11008 · Salt Lake City, UT 84147-0008 · 801-532-2666

Frank J. Gustin · Gustin, Green, Stegall & Liapis · New York Building, Third Floor · 48 Post Office Place · Salt Lake City, UT 84101 · 801-532-6996

Kent M. Kasting · Dart, Adamson & Kasting · 310 South Main Street, Suite 1330 · Salt Lake City, UT 84101 · 801-521-6383

Clark W. Sessions · Sessions & Moore · First Federal Plaza, Suite 400 · 505 East 200 South · Salt Lake City, UT 84102 · 801-359-4100

LABOR AND EMPLOYMENT LAW

Stephen W. Cook · (Labor) · Cook & Wilde · Union Park Center, Suite 490 · 6925 Union Park Avenue · Midvale, UT 84047 · 801-255-6000

David A. Anderson · (Management) · Parsons, Behle & Latimer · 185 South State Street, Suite 700 · P.O. Box 11898 · Salt Lake City, UT 84147-0898 · 801-532-1234

Elizabeth Dunning · (Individuals) · Watkiss & Campbell · 310 South Main Street, Suite 1200 · Salt Lake City, UT 84101 · 801-363-3300

Nathan J. Fullmer · (Management) · McIntyre Building, Suite 800 · 68 South Main Street · Salt Lake City, UT 84101 · 801-531-8300

Gordon L. Roberts · (Management) · Parsons, Behle & Latimer · 185 South State Street, Suite 700 · P.O. Box 11898 · Salt Lake City, UT 84147-0898 · 801-532-1234

A. Wally Sandack · (Labor) · Sandack & Sandack · 370 East Fifth South Street · Salt Lake City, UT 84111 · 801-531-0555

Janet Hugie Smith · (Management) · Ray, Quinney & Nebeker · 400 Deseret Building, Suite 400 · 79 South Main Street · P.O. Box 45385 · Salt Lake City, UT 84145-0385 · 801-532-1500

Ronald F. Sysak · (Management) · Prince, Yeates & Geldzahler · City Centre Building, Ninth Floor · 175 East 400 South Street · Salt Lake City, UT 84111 · 801-524-1000

Keith E. Taylor · (Management) · Parsons, Behle & Latimer · 185 South State Street, Suite 700 · P.O. Box 11898 · Salt Lake City, UT 84147-0898 · 801-532-1234

Charles H. Thronson · (Management) · Parsons, Behle & Latimer · 185 South State Street, Suite 700 · P.O. Box 11898 · Salt Lake City, UT 84147-0898 · 801-532-1234

Robert M. Yeates · (Management) · Prince, Yeates & Geldzahler · City Centre Building, Ninth Floor · 175 East 400 South Street · Salt Lake City, UT 84111 · 801-524-1000

NATURAL RESOURCES AND ENVIRONMENTAL LAW

Stephen G. Boyden · (Indian Affairs) · 1100 South 1500 East · Salt Lake City, UT 84105 · 801-581-9305

Edward W. Clyde · (Oil & Gas; Water) · Clyde, Pratt & Snow · American Savings Plaza, Suite 200 · 77 West Second South · Salt Lake City, UT 84101 · 801-322-2516

Hugh C. Garner · (Oil & Gas) · 136 South Main Street, Suite 700 · Salt Lake City, UT 84101 · 801-532-5660

Patrick J. Garver · Parsons, Behle & Latimer · 185 South State Street, Suite 700 P.O. Box 11898 · Salt Lake City, UT 84147 · 801-532-1234

Oliver W. Gushee, Jr. · (Oil & Gas) · Pruitt, Gushee & Fletcher · Beneficial Life Tower, Suite 1850 · 36 South State Street · Salt Lake City, UT 84111 · 801-531-8446

James A. Holtkamp · Van Cott, Bagley, Cornwall & McCarthy · 50 South Main Street, Suite 1600 · P.O. Box 45340 · Salt Lake City, UT 84145 · 801-532-3333

Lee Kapaloski · (Land Planning; Water) · Parsons, Behle & Latimer · 185 South State Street, Suite 700 · P.O. Box 11898 · Salt Lake City, UT 84147 · 801-532-1234

James B. Lee · Parsons, Behle & Latimer · 185 South State Street, Suite 700 · P.O. Box 11898 · Salt Lake City, UT 84147 · 801-532-1234

William J. Lockhart · (Plaintiffs) · P.O. Box 8672 · Salt Lake City, UT 84108 · 801-581-8958

Joseph Novak · (Water) · Snow, Christensen & Martineau · 10 Exchange Place, 11th Floor · P.O. Box 45000 · Salt Lake City, UT 84145-4111 · 801-521-9000

Clayton J. Parr · Kimball, Parr, Crockett & Waddoups · 185 South State Street, Suite 1300 · P.O. Box 11019 · Salt Lake City, UT 84147 · 801-532-7840

Robert G. Pruitt, Jr. · (Oil & Gas) · Pruitt, Gushee & Fletcher · Beneficial Life Tower, Suite 1850 · 36 South State Street · Salt Lake City, UT 84111 · 801-531-8446

Richard K. Sager · Van Cott, Bagley, Cornwall & McCarthy · 50 South Main Street, Suite 1600 · P.O. Box 45340 · Salt Lake City, UT 84145 · 801-532-3333

PERSONAL INJURY LITIGATION

Richard W. Campbell · (Defendants) · Campbell and Neeley · 2485 Grant Avenue, Suite 200 · Ogden, UT 84401 · 801-621-3646

David S. Kunz · (Plaintiffs) · Kunz, Kunz & Hadley · Bank of Utah Building, Suite 300 · 2605 Washington Boulevard · Ogden, UT 84401 · 801-394-4573

Jackson B. Howard · (Plaintiffs) · Howard, Lewis & Petersen · Delphi Building 120 East 300 North Street · P.O. Box 778 · Provo, UT 84601 · 801-373-6345

Wayne L. Black · (Plaintiffs) · Black & Moore · 261 East Broadway, Suite 300 · Salt Lake City, UT 84111 · 801-363-2727

Harold G. Christensen · (Defendants) · Snow, Christensen & Martineau · 10 Exchange Place, 11th Floor · P.O. Box 45000 · Salt Lake City, UT 84145-4111 · 801-521-9000

Ray R. Christensen · (Defendants) · Christensen, Jensen & Powell · 175 South West Temple, Suite 510 · Salt Lake City, UT 84101 · 801-355-3431

Glenn C. Hanni · Strong & Hanni · Boston Building, Suite 600 · Nine Exchange Place · Salt Lake City, UT 84111 · 801-532-7080

W. Eugene Hansen · (Plaintiffs) · Hansen & Dewsnup · Beneficial Life Tower, Suite 2020 · 36 South State Street · Salt Lake City, UT 84111 · 801-533-0400

Carman E. Kipp · (Defendants) · Kipp and Christian · City Centre, Suite 330 · 175 East 400 South · Salt Lake City, UT 84111 · 801-521-3773

Stephen B. Nebeker · (Defendants) · Ray, Quinney & Nebeker · Deseret Building, Suite 400 · 79 South Main Street · P.O. Box 45385 · Salt Lake City, UT 84145-0385 · 801-532-1500

Gordon L. Roberts · (Plaintiffs) · Parsons, Behle & Latimer · 185 South State Street, Suite 700 · P.O. Box 11898 · Salt Lake City, UT 84147-0898 · 801-532-1234

David K. Watkiss, Sr. · Watkiss & Campbell · 310 South Main Street, Suite 1200 Salt Lake City, UT 84101 · 801-363-3300

W. Brent Wilcox · (Plaintiffs) · Giauque & Williams · 500 Kearns Building · 136 South Main · Salt Lake City, UT 84101 · 801-533-8383

REAL ESTATE LAW

Charles L. Maak · Maak & Maak · 185 South State Street, Suite 1300 · Salt Lake City, UT 84111 · 801-532-7840

Reed L. Martineau · Snow, Christensen & Martineau · 10 Exchange Place, 11th Floor · P.O. Box 45000 · Salt Lake City, UT 84145-4111 · 801-521-9000

Denis Roy Morrill · Prince, Yeates & Geldzahler · City Centre Building, Ninth Floor · 175 East 400 South Street · Salt Lake City, UT 84111 · 801-524-1000

TAX AND EMPLOYEE BENEFITS LAW

K. Jay Holdsworth · Holdsworth & Swenson · CSB Tower, Suite 1200 · 50 South Main · Salt Lake City, UT 84144 · 801-322-1100

Stanley D. Neeleman · Holme, Roberts & Owen · 50 South Main Street, Suite 900 · Salt Lake City, UT 84144 · 801-521-5800

David E. Salisbury · Van Cott, Bagley, Cornwall & McCarthy · 50 South Main Street, Suite 1600 · P.O. Box 45340 · Salt Lake City, UT 84145 · 801-532-3333

William Vogel · Watkiss & Campbell · 310 South Main Street, Suite 1200 · Salt Lake City, UT 84101 · 801-363-3300

TRUSTS AND ESTATES

Clark P. Giles · Ray, Quinney & Nebeker · Deseret Building, Suite 400 · 79 South Main Street · P.O. Box 45385 · Salt Lake City, UT 84145-0385 · 801-532-1500

K. Jay Holdsworth · Holdsworth & Swenson · CSB Tower, Suite 1200 · 50 South Main · Salt Lake City, UT 84144 · 801-322-1100

Stanley D. Neeleman · Holme, Roberts & Owen · 50 South Main Street, Suite 900 · Salt Lake City, UT 84144 · 801-521-5800

David E. Salisbury · Van Cott, Bagley, Cornwall & McCarthy · 50 South Main Street, Suite 1600 · P.O. Box 45340 · Salt Lake City, UT 84145 · 801-532-3333

William Vogel · Watkiss & Campbell · 310 South Main Street, Suite 1200 · Salt Lake City, UT 84101 · 801-363-3300

VERMONT

BANKRUPTCY LAW	710
BUSINESS LITIGATION	710
CORPORATE LAW	711
CRIMINAL DEFENSE	711
FAMILY LAW	712
NATURAL RESOURCES AND ENVIRONMENTAL LAW	712
PERSONAL INJURY LITIGATION	712
REAL ESTATE LAW	713
TAX AND EMPLOYEE BENEFITS LAW	714
TRUSTS AND ESTATES	714

BANKRUPTCY LAW

Douglas J. Wolinsky · Saxer, Anderson & Wolinsky · 200 Main Street · P.O. Box 1505 · Burlington, VT 05402-1505 · 802-658-2826

Jerome I. Meyers · Pine and Maple Streets · P.O. Box 919 · White River Junction, VT 05001 · 802-296-2100

BUSINESS LITIGATION

Richard E. Davis · 30 Washington Street · Barre, VT 05641 · 802-476-3123

William B. Gray · Sheehey, Brue, Gray & Furlong · 119 South Winooski Avenue · P.O. Box 66 · Burlington, VT 05402 · 802-864-9891

Robert B. Hemley · Gravel and Shea · 109 South Winooski Avenue · P.O. Box 1049 · Burlington, VT 05402-1049 · 802-658-0220

Fred I. Parker · Langrock Sperry Parker & Wool · 275 College Street · P.O. Box 721 · Burlington, VT 05402-0721 · 802-864-0217

Robert D. Rachlin · Downs Rachlin & Martin · 199 Main Street · P.O. Box 190 Burlington, VT 054012-0190 · 802-863-2375

John T. Sartore · Paul, Frank & Collins · One Church Street · P.O. Box 1307 Burlington, VT 05402-1307 · 802-658-2311

David L. Cleary · Miller, Cleary & Faignant · 36-38 Merchants Row · P.O. Box 6567 · Rutland, VT 05701 · 802-775-2521

CORPORATE LAW

Steven R. Crampton · Gravel and Shea · 109 South Winooski Avenue · P.O. Box 1049 · Burlington, VT 05402-1049 · 802-658-0220

Allen Martin · Downs Rachlin & Martin · 199 Main Street · P.O. Box 190 Burlington, VT 05402-0190 · 802-863-2375

Stewart H. McConaughy · (Utilities) · Gravel and Shea · 109 South Winooski Avenue · P.O. Box 1049 · Burlington, VT 05402-1049 · 802-658-0220

J. Paul Giuliani · McKee, Giuliani & Cleveland · 94 Main Street · P.O. Box F Montpelier, VT 05602 · 802-223-3479

Thomas M. Dowling · Ryan, Smith & Carbine · Mead Building · P.O. Box 310 Rutland, VT 05701 · 802-773-3344

John L. Primmer · Primmer & Piper · 12 Prospect Street · St. Johnsbury, VT 05819 · 802-748-5061

CRIMINAL DEFENSE

Richard E. Davis · 30 Washington Street · Barre, VT 05641 · 802-476-3123

Oreste V. Valsangiacomo, Jr. · Valsangiacomo, Detora & McQuesten · 162 North Main Street · P.O. Box 625 · Barre, VT 05641 · 802-476-4181

Robert B. Hemley · Gravel and Shea · 109 South Winooski Avenue · P.O. Box 1049 · Burlington, VT 05402-1049 · 802-658-0220

Jerome F. O'Neill · O'Neill and Crawford · One Lawson Lane · P.O. Box 5359 Burlington, VT 05402-5359 · 802-865-4700

Charles R. Tetzlaff · Latham, Eastman, Schweyer & Tetzlaff · 308 Main Street P.O. Box 568 · Burlington, VT 05402 · 802-863-2826

Peter F. Langrock · Langrock Sperry Parker & Wool · 15 South Pleasant Street P.O. Drawer 351 · Middlebury, VT 05753-0351 · 802-864-0217

William K. Sessions III · Sessions, Keiner, Newmont & Barnes · 72 Court Street Middlebury, VT 05753 · 802-388-4906

FAMILY LAW

Richard E. Davis · 30 Washington Street · Barre, VT 05641 · 802-476-3123

Fred I. Parker · Langrock Sperry Parker & Wool · 275 College Street · P.O. Box 721 · Burlington, VT 05402-0721 · 802-864-0217

Charles R. Tetzlaff · Latham, Eastman, Schweyer & Tetzlaff · 308 Main Street P.O. Box 568 · Burlington, VT 05402 · 802-863-2826

NATURAL RESOURCES AND ENVIRONMENTAL LAW

Raymond P. Perra · Weber, Perra & Wilson · 139 Main Street · Brattleboro, VT 05301 · 802-257-7161

John R. Ponsetto · Gravel and Shea · 109 South Winooski Avenue · P.O. Box 1049 · Burlington, VT 05402-1049 · 802-658-0220

Jonathan N. Brownell · Brownell & Moeser · 23 Mechanic Street · P.O. Box 200 Norwich, VT 05055 · 802-649-1200

PERSONAL INJURY LITIGATION

Richard E. Davis · (Plaintiffs) · 30 Washington Street · Barre, VT 05641 · 802-476-3123

Robert B. Hemley · Gravel and Shea · 109 South Winooski Avenue · P.O. Box 1049 · Burlington, VT 05402-1049 · 802-658-0220

Robert E. Manchester · (Plaintiffs) · One Lawson Lane, Suite Two · P.O. Box 1459 · Burlington, VT 05402-1459 · 802-658-7444

Fred I. Parker · (Plaintiffs) · Langrock Sperry Parker & Wool · 275 College Street P.O. Box 721 · Burlington, VT 05402-0721 · 802-864-0217

Robert D. Rachlin · Downs Rachlin & Martin · 100 Dorset Street · P.O. Box 190 Burlington, VT 05402-0190 · 802-863-2375

John T. Sartore · Paul, Frank & Collins · One Church Street · P.O. Box 1307 Burlington, VT 05402-1307 · 802-658-2311

Alan F. Sylvester · (Plaintiffs) · Sylvester & Maley · 78 Pine Street · P.O. Box 1053 · Burlington, VT 05401 · 802-864-5722

Peter F. Langrock · (Plaintiffs) · Langrock Sperry Parker & Wool · 15 South Pleasant Street · P.O. Drawer 351 · Middlebury, VT 05753-0351 · 802-388-6356

David L. Cleary · Miller, Cleary & Faignant · 36-38 Merchants Row · P.O. Box 6567 · Rutland, VT 05701 · 802-775-2521

REAL ESTATE LAW

Jonathan Bump · Fitts, Olson, Carnahan, Anderson and Bump · 16 High Street P.O. Box 801 · Brattleboro, VT 05301 · 802-254-2345

Peter M. Collins · Paul, Frank & Collins · One Church Street · P.O. Box 1307 Burlington, VT 05402-1307 · 802-658-2311

Stephen R. Crampton · Gravel and Shea · 109 South Winooski Avenue · P.O. Box 1049 · Burlington, VT 05402 · 802-658-0220

Carl H. Lisman · Lisman & Lisman · 84 Pine Street · P.O. Box 728 · Burlington, VT 05402-0728 · 802-864-5756

Mark L. Sperry III · Langrock Sperry Parker & Wool · 275 College Street · P.O. Box 721 · Burlington, VT 05402-0721 · 802-864-0217

Julian R. Goodrich · 26 State Street · P.O. Box 156 · Montpelier, VT 05602 802-223-1093

Jonathan N. Brownell · Brownell & Moeser · 23 Mechanic Street · P.O. Box 200 Norwich, VT 05055 · 802-649-1200

TAX AND EMPLOYEE BENEFITS LAW

Jon R. Eggleston · Miller, Eggleston & Rosenberg · 150 South Champlain Street · P.O. Box 1489 · Burlington, VT 05402-1489 · 802-864-0880

Charles T. Shea · Gravel and Shea · 109 South Winooski Avenue · P.O. Box 1049 · Burlington, VT 05402-1049 · 802-658-0220

Thomas M. Dowling · Ryan, Smith & Carbine · Mead Building · P.O. Box 310 · Rutland, VT 05701 · 802-773-3344

TRUSTS AND ESTATES

Harvey B. Otterman, Jr. · Otterman & Allen · 162 North Main Street · Barre, VT 05641 · 802-479-2552

Paul N. Olson · Fitts, Olson, Carnahan, Anderson and Bump · 16 High Street · P.O. Box 801 · Brattleboro, VT 05301 · 802-254-2345

Clarke A. Gravel · Gravel and Shea · 109 South Winooski Avenue · P.O. Box 1049 · Burlington, VT 05402 · 802-658-0220

William G. Post, Jr. · Gravel and Shea · 109 South Winooski Avenue · P.O. Box 1049 · Burlington, VT 05402-1049 · 802-658-0220

Christopher G. Stoneman · Downs Rachlin & Martin · 199 Main Street · P.O. Box 190 · Burlington, VT 054012-0190 · 802-863-2375

Austin B. Noble · Noble & Wilson · City Center · 89 Main Street · P.O. Box 159 · Montpelier, VT 05602 · 802-229-4914

Thomas M. Dowling · Ryan, Smith & Carbine · Mead Building · P.O. Box 310 · Rutland, VT 05701 · 802-773-3344

VIRGINIA

BANKRUPTCY LAW	715
BUSINESS LITIGATION	716
CORPORATE LAW	719
CRIMINAL DEFENSE	722
FAMILY LAW	723
LABOR AND EMPLOYMENT LAW	725
MARITIME LAW	727
NATURAL RESOURCES AND ENVIRONMENTAL LAW	727
PERSONAL INJURY LITIGATION	727
REAL ESTATE LAW	733
TAX AND EMPLOYEE BENEFITS LAW	735
TRUSTS AND ESTATES	736

BANKRUPTCY LAW

Richard A. Bartl · Tyler, Bartl, Burke & Albert · 300 North Washington Street, Suite 500 · Alexandria, VA 22314 · 703-549-5000

H. Bradley Evans, Jr. · Hazel, Thomas, Fiske, Beckhorn and Hanes · 510 King Street, Suite 200 · P.O. Box 820 · Alexandria, VA 22313-0820 · 703-836-8400

Robert O. Tyler · Tyler, Bartl, Burke & Albert · 300 North Washington Street, Suite 500 · Alexandria, VA 22314 · 703-549-5000

Stanley J. Samorajczyk · Hazel, Thomas, Fiske, Beckhorn and Hanes · 3110 Fairview Park Drive, Suite 1400 · P.O. Box 547 · Falls Church, VA 22042 · 703-641-4200

Jerrold G. Weinberg · Weinberg & Stein · 1825 Dominion Tower · 999 Waterside Drive · P.O. Box 3789 · Norfolk, VA 23514 · 804-627-1066

Frank J. Santoro · Marcus, Santoro & Kozak · 341 High Street · Portsmouth, VA 23705 · 804-393-2555

Benjamin C. Ackerly · Hunton & Williams · 707 East Main Street · P.O. Box 1535 · Richmond, VA 23212 · 804-788-8200

Harry Shaia, Jr. · Spinella, Owings & Shaia · 8550 Mayland Drive · Richmond, VA 23229 · 804-747-0920

M. Caldwell Butler · Woods, Rogers & Hazlegrove · 105 Franklin Road, SW P.O. Box 720 · Roanoke, VA 24004 · 703-982-4200

David H. Adams · Clark & Stant · 900 Sovran Bank Building · One Columbus Center · Virginia Beach, VA 23462 · 804-499-8800

BUSINESS LITIGATION

Edward B. Lowry · Michie, Hamlett, Donato & Lowry · 500 Court Square, Suite 300 · P.O. Box 298 · Charlottesville, VA 22902-0298 · 804-977-3390

Robert C. Wood III · Edmunds & Williams · 800 Main Street · P.O. Box 958 Lynchburg, VA 24505 · 804-846-9000

David McC. Estabrook · Cregger & Cregger · 6824 Elm Street · P.O. Box 459 McLean, VA 22101 · 703-790-1860

R. Terrence Ney · McGuire, Woods, Battle & Boothe · 8280 Greensboro Drive, Suite 900 · Tysons Corner · P.O. Box 9346 · McLean, VA 22102 · 703-356-2200

Lee A. Rau · Reed Smith Shaw & McClay · 8201 Greensboro Drive, Suite 820 McLean, VA 22102 · 703-556-8440

John S. Stump · McGuire, Woods, Battle & Boothe · 8280 Greensboro Drive, Suite 900 · Tysons Corner · P.O. Box 9346 · McLean, VA 22102 · 703-356-2200

Jack E. Greer · Williams, Worrell, Kelly, Greer & Frank · 600 Crestar Bank Building · P.O. Box 3416 · Norfolk, VA 23514 · 804-624-2600

Robert M. Hughes III · Hunton & Williams · First Virginia Bank Tower · 101 St. Paul's Boulevard · P.O. Box 3889 · Norfolk, VA 23514 · 804-625-5501

Robert R. MacMillan · Breeden, MacMillan & Green · 1700 First Virginia Bank Tower · 101 Saint Paul's Boulevard · Norfolk, VA 23510 · 804-622-1111

William T. Prince · Williams, Worrell, Kelly, Greer & Frank · 600 Crestar Bank Building · P.O. Box 3416 · Norfolk, VA 23514 · 804-624-2600

John M. Ryan · Vandeventer, Black, Meredith & Martin · 500 World Trade Center · Norfolk, VA 23510 · 804-622-4381

Conrad M. Shumadine · Willcox & Savage · 1800 Sovran Center · Norfolk, VA 23510-2197 · 804-628-5500

Gregory N. Stillman · Hunton & Williams · First Virginia Bank Tower · 101 St. Paul's Boulevard · P.O. Box 3889 · Norfolk, VA 23514 · 804-625-5501

Jerrold G. Weinberg · Weinberg & Stein · 1825 Dominion Tower · 999 Waterside Drive · P.O. Box 3789 · Norfolk, VA 23514 · 804-627-1066

Everette G. Allen, Jr. · Hirschler, Fleischer, Weinberg, Cox & Allen · Main Street Centre · 629 East Main Street · P.O. Box 1Q · Richmond, VA 23202 804-771-9500

Lewis Thomas Booker, Jr. · Hunton & Williams · 707 East Main Street · P.O. Box 1535 · Richmond, VA 23212 · 804-788-8200

J. Robert Brame III · McGuire, Woods, Battle & Boothe · One James Center Richmond, VA 23219 · 804-644-4131

Robert F. Brooks · Hunton & Williams · 707 East Main Street · P.O. Box 1535 Richmond, VA 23212 · 804-788-8200

R. Harvey Chappell, Jr. · Christian, Barton, Epps, Brent & Chappell · Mutual Building, 12th Floor · 909 East Main Street · Richmond, VA 23219 · 804-644-7851

William R. Cogar · Mays & Valentine · Sovran Center · 1111 East Main Street P.O. Box 1122 · Richmond, VA 23208 · 804-697-1200

James E. Farnham · Hunton & Williams · 707 East Main Street · P.O. Box 1535 Richmond, VA 23212 · 804-788-8200

J. Waller Harrison · McGuire, Woods, Battle & Boothe · One James Center Richmond, VA 23219 · 804-644-4131

John F. Kay, Jr. · Mays & Valentine · Sovran Center · 1111 East Main Street P.O. Box 1122 · Richmond, VA 23208 · 804-697-1200

William H. King, Jr. · McGuire, Woods, Battle & Boothe · One James Center Richmond, VA 23219 · 804-644-4131

Jack E. McClard · Hunton & Williams · 707 East Main Street · P.O. Box 1535 · Richmond, VA 23212 · 804-788-8200

Rosewell Page III · McGuire, Woods, Battle & Boothe · One James Center · Richmond, VA 23219 · 804-644-4131

Robert H. Patterson, Jr. · McGuire, Woods, Battle & Boothe · One James Center · Richmond, VA 23219 · 804-644-4131

Robert E. Payne · McGuire, Woods, Battle & Boothe · One James Center · Richmond, VA 23219 · 804-644-4131

Virginia W. Powell · Hunton & Williams · 707 East Main Street · P.O. Box 1535 · Richmond, VA 23212 · 804-788-8200

James C. Roberts · Mays & Valentine · Sovran Center · 1111 East Main Street · P.O. Box 1122 · Richmond, VA 23208 · 804-697-1200

James L. Sanderlin · McGuire, Woods, Battle & Boothe · One James Center · Richmond, VA 23219 · 804-644-4131

Alexander H. Slaughter · McGuire, Woods, Battle & Boothe · One James Center · Richmond, VA 23219 · 804-644-4131

Michael W. Smith · Christian, Barton, Epps, Brent & Chappell · Mutual Building, 12th Floor · 909 East Main Street · Richmond, VA 23219 · 804-644-7851

Joseph M. Spivey III · Hunton & Williams · 707 East Main Street · P.O. Box 1535 · Richmond, VA 23212 · 804-788-8200

Anthony F. Troy · Mays & Valentine · Sovran Center · 1111 East Main Street · P.O. Box 1122 · Richmond, VA 23208 · 804-697-1200

Anne Marie Whittemore · McGuire, Woods, Battle & Boothe · One James Center · Richmond, VA 23219 · 804-644-4131

Murray H. Wright · McGuire, Woods, Battle & Boothe · One James Center · Richmond, VA 23219 · 804-644-4131

William B. Poff · Woods, Rogers & Hazlegrove · 105 Franklin Road, SW · P.O. Box 720 · Roanoke, VA 24004 · 703-982-4200

William R. Rakes · Gentry, Locke, Rakes & Moore · 800 Colonial Plaza · P.O. Box 1018 · Roanoke, VA 24005 · 703-982-8000

Vernon M. Geddy, Jr. · McGuire, Woods, Battle & Boothe · 137 York Street · P.O. Box 379 · Williamsburg, VA 23185 · 804-229-2393

CORPORATE LAW

James B. Pittleman · Odin, Feldman & Pittleman · 10505 Judicial Drive · P.O. Box 367 · Fairfax, VA 22030-0367 · 703-385-7700

Jesse B. Wilson III · Miles & Stockbridge · 11350 Random Hills Road, Suite 500 · Fairfax, VA 22030 · 703-273-2440

Duane W. Beckhorn · Hazel, Thomas, Fiske, Beckhorn and Hanes · 3110 Fairview Park Drive, Suite 1400 · P.O. Box 547 · Falls Church, VA 22042 · 703-641-4200

Thomas C. Brown, Jr. · McGuire, Woods, Battle & Boothe · Tysons Corner · 8280 Greensboro Drive, Suite 900 · P.O. Box 9346 · McLean, VA 22102 · 703-356-2200

C. Thomas Hicks III · Shaw, Pittman, Potts & Trowbridge · 1501 Farm Credit Drive, Suite 4400 · McLean, VA 22102 · 703-790-7900

Arthur P. Scibelli · McGuire, Woods, Battle & Boothe · 8280 Greensboro Drive, Suite 900 · Tysons Corner · P.O. Box 9346 · McLean, VA 22102 · 703-356-2200

Leroy T. Canoles, Jr. · Kaufman & Canoles · Sovran Center · One Commercial Place · P.O. Box 3037 · Norfolk, VA 23514-3037 · 804-624-3000

Thomas G. Johnson, Jr. · Willcox & Savage · 1800 Sovran Center · Norfolk, VA 23510-2197 · 804-628-5500

Vincent J. Mastracco, Jr. · Kaufman & Canoles · Sovran Center · One Commercial Place · P.O. Box 3037 · Norfolk, VA 23514-3037 · 804-624-3000

Robert C. Nusbaum · Hofheimer, Nusbaum, McPhaul & Samuels · 1700 Dominion Tower · P.O. Box 3460 · Norfolk, VA 23514 · 804-622-3366

Toy D. Savage, Jr. · Willcox & Savage · 1800 Sovran Center · Norfolk, VA 23510-2197 · 804-628-5500

T. Howard Spainhour · McGuire, Woods, Battle & Boothe · World Trade Center, Suite 9000 · P.O. Box 3767 · Norfolk, VA 23514 · 804-627-7677

Guy K. Tower · Kaufman & Canoles · Sovran Center · One Commercial Place · P.O. Box 3037 · Norfolk, VA 23514-3037 · 804-624-3000

Thomas H. Willcox, Jr. · Willcox & Savage · 1800 Sovran Center · Norfolk, VA 23510-2197 · 804-628-5500

Albert J. Taylor, Jr. · Cooper and Davis · Central Fidelity Bank Building · High & Crawford Streets · P.O. Box 1475 · Portsmouth, VA 23705 · 804-397-3481

Evans B. Brasfield · (Utilities) · Hunton & Williams · 707 East Main Street · P.O. Box 1535 · Richmond, VA 23212 · 804-788-8200

Robert P. Buford · Hunton & Williams · 707 East Main Street · P.O. Box 1535 · Richmond, VA 23212 · 804-788-8200

Robert L. Burrus, Jr. · McGuire, Woods, Battle & Boothe · One James Center · Richmond, VA 23219 · 804-644-4131

Joseph C. Carter, Jr. · Hunton & Williams · 707 East Main Street · P.O. Box 1535 · Richmond, VA 23212 · 804-788-8200

Richard H. Catlett, Jr. · McGuire, Woods, Battle & Boothe · One James Center · Richmond, VA 23219 · 804-644-4131

Clifford A. Cutchins IV · McGuire, Woods, Battle & Boothe · One James Center · Richmond, VA 23219 · 804-644-4131

Marshall H. Earl, Jr. · McGuire, Woods, Battle & Boothe · One James Center · Richmond, VA 23219 · 804-644-4131

John W. Edmonds III · Mays & Valentine · Sovran Center · 1111 East Main Street · P.O. Box 1122 · Richmond, VA 23208 · 804-697-1200

George C. Freeman, Jr. · Hunton & Williams · 707 East Main Street · P.O. Box 1535 · Richmond, VA 23212 · 804-788-8200

Allen C. Goolsby III · Hunton & Williams · 707 East Main Street · P.O. Box 1535 · Richmond, VA 23212 · 804-788-8200

Leslie A. Grandis · McGuire, Woods, Battle & Boothe · One James Center · Richmond, VA 23219 · 804-644-4131

F. Claiborne Johnston, Jr. · Mays & Valentine · Sovran Center · 1111 East Main Street · P.O. Box 1122 · Richmond, VA 23208 · 804-697-1200

Stephen R. Larson · Christian, Barton, Epps, Brent & Chappell · Mutual Building, 12th Floor · 909 East Main Street · Richmond, VA 23219 · 804-644-7851

Michael W. Maupin · Hunton & Williams · 707 East Main Street · P.O. Box 1535 Richmond, VA 23212 · 804-788-8200

C. Cotesworth Pinckney · Mays & Valentine · Sovran Center · 1111 East Main Street · P.O. Box 1122 · Richmond, VA 23208 · 804-697-1200

Gordon F. Rainey, Jr. · Hunton & Williams · 707 East Main Street · P.O. Box 1535 · Richmond, VA 23212 · 804-788-8200

O. Randolph Rollins · McGuire, Woods, Battle & Boothe · One James Center Richmond, VA 23219 · 804-644-4131

Norman A. Scher · Hunton & Williams · 707 East Main Street · P.O. Box 1535 Richmond, Virginia 23212 · 804-788-8200

R. Gordon Smith · McGuire, Woods, Battle & Boothe · One James Center Richmond, VA 23219 · 804-644-4131

Randolph F. Totten · Hunton & Williams · 707 East Main Street · P.O. Box 1535 Richmond, VA 23212 · 804-788-8200

C. Porter Vaughan III · Hunton & Williams · 707 East Main Street · P.O. Box 1535 · Richmond, VA 23212 · 804-788-8200

Hugh V. White, Jr. · Hunton & Williams · 707 East Main Street · P.O. Box 1535 Richmond, VA 23212 · 804-788-8200

G. Franklin Flippin · Glenn, Flippin, Feldman & Darby · 200 First Campbell Square · P.O. Box 2887 · Roanoke, VA 24001 · 703-344-3000

Charles D. Fox III · Fox, Wooten & Hart · 707 Building, Suite 310 · P.O. Box 12247 · Roanoke, VA 24024 · 703-343-2451

Talfourd H. Kemper · Woods, Rogers & Hazlegrove · 105 Franklin Road, SW P.O. Box 720 · Roanoke, VA 24004 · 703-982-4200

Joel M. Birken · Rees, Broome & Diaz · 8133 Leesburg Pike, Suite 810 · Vienna, VA 22180 · 703-790-1911

Charles W. Best, Jr. · Kaufman & Canoles · 1104 Laskin Road · Virginia Beach, VA 23451 · 804-491-4000

Vernon M. Geddy, Jr. · McGuire, Woods, Battle & Boothe · 137 York Street · P.O. Box 379 · Williamsburg, VA 23185 · 804-229-2393

CRIMINAL DEFENSE

Blair D. Howard · Howard, Leino & Howard · 128 North Pitt Street · Alexandria, VA 22314 · 703-549-1188

J. Frederick Sinclair · Cohen, Dunn & Sinclair · 221 South Alfred Street · P.O. Box 117 · Alexandria, VA 22313-0117 · 703-836-9000

Frank W. Dunham, Jr. · Cohen, Gettings, Alper & Dunham · 1400 North Uhle Street, Suite 500 · Arlington, VA 20001 · 703-525-2260

Brian P. Gettings · Cohen, Gettings, Alper & Dunham · 1400 North Uhle Street, Suite 500 · Arlington, VA 20001 · 703-525-2260

Louis Koutoulakos · Varoutsos & Koutoulakos · 2009 North 14th Street, Suite 512 · Arlington, VA 22201 · 703-527-0124

Albert J. Ahern, Jr. · 5205 Leesburg Pike · Bailey's Crossroads, VA 22041 · 703-931-8400

John C. Lowe · Lowe and Jacobs · 300 Court Square · Charlottesville, VA 22901 · 804-296-8188

James R. McKenry · Heilig, McKenry, Fraim & Lollar · 700 Newtown Road, Suite 15 · Norfolk, VA 23502 · 804-461-2500

Stanley E. Sacks · Sacks & Sacks · Town Point Center, Suite 501 · 150 Bush Street · P.O. Box 3874 · Norfolk, VA 23514 · 804-623-2753

Dennis W. Dohnal · Bremner, Baber & Janus · Jefferson Bank Building, Suite 1500 · 701 East Franklin Street · P.O. Box 826 · Richmond, VA 23207 · 804-644-0721

Murray J. Janus · Bremner, Baber & Janus · Jefferson Bank Building, Suite 1500 · 701 East Franklin Street · P.O. Box 826 · Richmond, VA 23207 · 804-644-0721

Michael Morchower · Morchower, Luxton and Whaley · Nine East Franklin Street · Richmond, VA 23219 · 804-643-0147

Matthew N. Ott, Jr. · 106 East Cary Street · Richmond, VA 23219 · 804-783-8420

James C. Roberts · Mays & Valentine · Sovran Center · 1111 East Main Street P.O. Box 1122 · Richmond, VA 23208 · 804-697-1200

Robert F. Rider · Rider, Thomas, Cleveland, Ferris & Eakin · Southwest Virginia Savings and Loan Building · Campbell Avenue and Second Street, SW · Roanoke, VA 24011 · 703-343-0816

Samuel G. Wilson · Woods, Rogers & Hazelgrove · 105 Franklin Road, SW · P.O. Box 720 · Roanoke, VA 24004 · 703-982-4200

Richard G. Brydges · Brydges & Brydges · Professional Building · 1369 Laskin Road · P.O. Box 625 · Virginia Beach, VA 23451 · 804-428-6021

Wayne Lustig · Guy, Cromwell, Betz & Lustig · Pembroke One Building, Fifth Floor · Pembroke Office Park · 281 Independence Boulevard · Virginia Beach, VA 23462 · 804-499-8971

FAMILY LAW

James Ray Cottrell · Gannon, Cottrell & Ward · 411 North Washington Street P.O. Box 1286 · Alexandria, VA 22313 · 703-836-2770

Ilona Ely Freedman (Grenadier) · 649 South Washington Street · Alexandria, VA 22314 · 703-683-9000

Martin A. Gannon · Gannon, Cottrell & Ward · 411 North Washington Street P.O. Box 1286 · Alexandria, VA 22313 · 703-836-2770

Joanne Fogel Alper · Cohen, Gettings, Alper & Dunham · 1400 North Uhle Street, Suite 500 · Arlington, VA 20001 · 703-525-2260

L. Lee Bean · Bean, Kinney, Korman & Moore · 2000 North 14th Street, Suite 100 P.O. Box 749 · Arlington, VA 22216 · 703-525-4000

Betty A. Thompson · 1800 North Kent Street, Suite 1001 · Arlington, VA 22209 703-522-8100

Annie Lee Jacobs · Lowe and Jacobs · 100 Court Square · Charlottesville, VA 22901 · 804-296-8188

Ronald R. Tweel · Michie, Hamlett, Donato & Lowry · 500 Court Square, Suite 300 · P.O. Box 298 · Charlottesville, VA 22902-0298 · 804-977-3390

Richard J. Colten · Surovell, Jackson, Colten & Dugan · 4010 University Drive Fairfax, VA 22030 · 703-591-1300

Robert E. Shoun · 10521 Judicial Drive, Suite 200 · Fairfax, VA 22030 · 703-385-3000

Robert J. Surovell · Surovell, Jackson, Colten & Dugan · 4010 University Drive Fairfax, VA 22030 · 703-591-1300

Burke F. McCahill · Hanes, Sevila, Saunders & McCahill · 30 North King Street P.O. Box 678 · Leesburg, VA 22075 · 703-777-5700

William Rosenberger, Jr. · Central Fidelity Bank Building, Suite 1904 · P.O. Box 1328 · Lynchburg, VA 24505 · 804-845-2393

Jerrold G. Weinberg · Weinberg & Stein · 1825 Dominion Tower · 999 Waterside Drive · P.O. Box 3789 · Norfolk, VA 23514 · 804-627-1066

Morton B. Spero · 135 South Adams Street · Petersburg, VA 23803 · 804-733-0151

Donald K. Butler · Morano, Colan and Butler · 526 North Boulevard · Richmond, VA 23220 · 804-353-4931

Murray J. Janus · Bremner, Baber & Janus · Jefferson Bank Building, Suite 1500 701 East Franklin Street · P.O. Box 826 · Richmond, VA 23207 · 804-644-0721

Matthew N. Ott · 106 East Cary Street · Richmond, VA 23219 · 804-783-8420

James C. Roberts · Mays & Valentine · Sovran Center · 1111 East Main Street P.O. Box 1122 · Richmond, VA 23208 · 804-697-1200

G. Marshall Mundy · Mundy Rogers & Frith · Third Street & Woods Avenue, SW · P.O. Box 2240 · Roanoke, VA 24009 · 703-982-1351

Arthur E. Smith · 404 Shenandoah Building · 301 First Street, SW · Roanoke, VA 24011 · 703-344-2121

Joseph A. Condo · Rees, Broome & Diaz · 8133 Leesburg Pike, Suite 810 Vienna, VA 22180 · 703-790-1911

Barry Kantor · Christie, Held & Kantor · 209 Business Park Drive · Virginia Beach, VA 23462 · 804-499-9222

Wayne Lustig · Guy, Cromwell, Betz & Lustig · Pembroke One Building, Fifth Floor · Pembroke Office Park · 281 Independence Boulevard · Virginia Beach, VA 23462 · 804-499-8971

Grover C. Wright, Jr. · Beach Tower Building, Suite 303 · 3330 Pacific Avenue · Virginia Beach, VA 23451 · 804-428-2741

LABOR AND EMPLOYMENT LAW

Philip J. Hirschkop · (Individuals) · Hirschkop & Associates · 108 North Columbus Street · P.O. Box 1226 · Alexandria, VA 22313 · 703-836-6595

Jay T. Swett · (Management) · McGuire, Woods, Battle & Boothe · Court Square Building · P.O. Box 1288 · Charlottesville, VA 22902 · 804-977-2500

Thomas J. Cawley · (Management) · Hunton & Williams · 3050 Chain Bridge Road · Fairfaix, VA 22030 · 703-352-2200

Christine H. Perdue · (Management) · Hunton & Williams · 3050 Chain Bridge Road · Fairfaix, VA 22030 · 703-352-2200

James J. Vergara, Jr. · (Labor) · 100 Main Street Plaza · Hopewell, VA 23860 · 804-458-6394

Michael F. Marino · (Management) · McGuire, Woods, Battle & Boothe · 8280 Greensboro Drive, Suite 900 · Tysons Corner · P.O. Box 9346 · McLean, VA 22102 · 703-356-2200

Clifford R. Oviatt, Jr. · (Management) · McGuire, Woods, Battle & Boothe · 8280 Greensboro Drive, Suite 900 · Tysons Corner · P.O. Box 9346 · McLean, VA 22102 · 703-356-2200

Stanley G. Barr, Jr. · (Management) · Kaufman & Canoles · Sovran Center · One Commercial Place · P.O. Box 3037 · Norfolk, VA 23514-3037 · 804-624-3000

Henry E. Howell, Jr. · (Labor) · Howell, Daugherty, Brown & Lawrence · One East Plume Street · P.O. Box 3929 · Norfolk, VA 23514 · 804-623-7334

William E. Rachels, Jr. · (Management) · Willcox & Savage · 1800 Sovran Center · Norfolk, VA 23510-2197 · 804-628-5500

John M. Ryan · (Management) · Vandeventer, Black, Meredith & Martin · 500 World Trade Center · Norfolk, VA 23510 · 804-622-4381

Abram W. VanderMeer, Jr. · (Management) · Hunton & Williams · First Virginia Bank Tower · 101 St. Paul's Boulevard · P.O. Box 3889 · Norfolk, VA 23514 · 804-625-5501

Burt H. Whitt · (Management) · Kaufman & Canoles · Sovran Center · One Commercial Place · P.O. Box 3037 · Norfolk, VA 23514-3037 · 804-624-3000

John S. Barr · (Individuals) · Maloney, Yeatts & Barr · 600 Ross Building · 801 East Main Street · Richmond, VA 23219-2906 · 804-644-0313

J. Robert Brame III · (Management) · McGuire, Woods, Battle & Boothe · One James Center · Richmond, VA 23219 · 804-644-4131

Jack W. Burtch · (Individuals) · McSweeney, Burtch & Crump · Nine South 12th Street · P.O. Box 1463 · Richmond, VA 23212 · 804-643-5192

Jay J. Levit · (Labor) · Levit & Mann · 419 North Boulevard · Richmond, VA 23220 · 804-355-7766

Paul M. Thompson · (Management) · Hunton & Williams · 707 East Main Street · P.O. Box 1535 · Richmond, VA 23212 · 804-788-8200

William E. Twomey, Jr. · (Management) · McGuire, Woods, Battle & Boothe · One James Center · Richmond, VA 23219 · 804-644-4131

D. Eugene Webb, Jr. · (Management) · Mays & Valentine · Sovran Center · 111 East Main Street · P.O. Box 1122 · Richmond, VA 23208 · 804-697-1200

Hill B. Wellford, Jr. · (Management) · Hunton & Williams · 707 East Main Street · P.O. Box 1535 · Richmond, VA 23212 · 804-788-8200

W. Carter Younger · (Management) · McGuire, Woods, Battle & Boothe · One James Center · Richmond, VA 23219 · 804-644-4131

Bayard E. Harris · (Management) · Woods, Rogers & Hazlegrove · 105 Franklin Road, SW · P.O. Box 720 · Roanoke, VA 24004 · 703-982-4200

Donald Wise Huffman · (Individuals) · Bird, Kinder & Huffman · 126 Church Avenue, SW, Suite 200 · P.O. Box 2795 · Roanoke, VA 24001 · 703-982-1755

Clinton S. Morse · (Management) · Woods, Rogers & Hazlegrove · 105 Franklin Road, SW · P.O. Box 720 · Roanoke, VA 24004 · 703-982-4200

MARITIME LAW

Philip N. Davey · Hunton & Williams · First Virginia Bank Tower · 101 St. Paul's Boulevard · P.O. Box 3889 · Norfolk, VA 23514 · 804-625-5501

Robert M. Hughes III · Hunton & Williams · First Virginia Bank Tower · 101 St. Paul's Boulevard · P.O. Box 3889 · Norfolk, VA 23514 · 804-625-5501

Walter B. Martin, Jr. · Vandeventer, Black, Meredith & Martin · 500 World Trade Center · Norfolk, VA 23510 · 804-622-4381

A. Jackson Timms · Hunton & Williams · First Virginia Bank Tower · 101 St. Paul's Boulevard · P.O. Box 3889 · Norfolk, VA 23514 · 804-625-5501

Charles F. Tucker · Vandeventer, Black, Meredith & Martin · 500 World Trade Center · Norfolk, VA 23510 · 804-622-4381

Braden Vandeventer, Jr. · Vandeventer, Black, Meredith & Martin · 500 World Trade Center · Norfolk, VA 23510 · 804-622-4381

NATURAL RESOURCES AND ENVIRONMENTAL LAW

David E. Evans · McGuire, Woods, Battle & Boothe · One James Center · Richmond, VA 23219 · 804-644-4131

George Clemon Freeman, Jr. · Hunton & Williams · 707 East Main Street · P.O. Box 1535 · Richmond, VA 23212 · 804-788-8200

Jon J. Jewett III · McGuire, Woods, Battle & Boothe · One James Center · Richmond, VA 23219 · 804-644-4131

William L. Rosbe · Hunton & Williams · 707 East Main Street · P.O. Box 1535 · Richmond, VA 23212 · 804-788-8200

Turner T. Smith, Jr. · Hunton & Williams · 707 East Main Street · P.O. Box 1535 · Richmond, VA 23212 · 804-788-8200

PERSONAL INJURY LITIGATION

Fred C. Alexander, Jr. · (Defendants) · McGuire, Woods, Battle & Boothe · TransPotomac Plaza · 1199 North Fairfax Street · P.O. Box 1101 · Alexandria, VA 22313 · 703-549-5900

Thomas P. Mains, Jr. · (Plaintiffs) · Mains & Nichols · 1199 North Fairfax Street, Suite 800 · Alexandria, VA 22314 · 703-548-1112

Robert J. Arthur · Arthur and Speed · 5549 Lee Highway · Arlington, VA 22207 · 703-241-7171

Robert Custis Coleburn · (Defendants) · Simmonds, Coleburn & Towner · 2041 North 15th Street · P.O. Box 848 · Arlington, VA 22216 · 703-525-7700

Christopher K. Speed · (Plaintiffs) · Arthur and Speed · 5549 Lee Highway · Arlington, VA 22207 · 703-241-7171

Thomas E. Albro · (Plaintiffs) · Smith, Taggart, Gibson & Albro · 105-109 East High Street · P.O. Box 1585 · Charlottesville, VA 22902 · 804-977-4455

L. B. Chandler, Jr. · (Plaintiffs) · Chandler, Franklin & O'Bryan · 2564 Ivy Road · P.O. Box 6747 · Charlottesville, VA 22906 · 804-971-7273

Brian J. Donato · (Plaintiffs) · Michie, Hamlett, Donato & Lowry · 500 Court Square, Suite 300 · P.O. Box 298 · Charlottesville, VA 22902-0298 · 804-977-3390

John C. Lowe · (Plaintiffs) · Lowe and Jacobs · 300 Court Square · Charlottesville, VA 22901 · 804-296-8188

Bruce D. Rasmussen · (Plaintiffs) · Michie, Hamlett, Donato & Lowry · 500 Court Square, Suite 300 · P.O. Box 298 · Charlottesville, VA 22902-0298 · 804-977-3390

Jay T. Swett · (Defendants) · McGuire, Woods, Battle & Boothe · Court Square Building · P.O. Box 1288 · Charlottesville, VA 22902 · 804-977-2500

John W. Zunka · (Defendants) · Taylor & Zunka · 414 Park Street · P.O. Box 1567 · Charlottesville, VA 22902 · 804-977-0191

Charles E. Carter · (Plaintiffs) · Carter, Craig & Bass · 126 South Union Street · P.O. Box 601 · Danville, VA 24543 · 804-792-9311

James A. L. Daniel · (Defendants) · Meade, Tate & Daniel · 116 South Ridge Street · P.O. Box 720 · Danville, VA 24543 · 804-792-3911

Frank O. Meade · (Defendants) · Meade, Tate & Daniel · 116 South Ridge Street · P.O. Box 720 · Danville, VA 24543 · 804-792-3911

John J. Brandt · (Defendants) · Slenker, Brandt, Jennings & Johnston · 3026 Javier Road · Fairfax, VA 22031 · 703-849-8600

Joseph P. Dyer · (Defendants) · Siciliano, Ellis, Dyer & Boccarosse · 10521 Judicial Drive, Suite 300 · Fairfax, VA 22030 · 703-385-6692

Robert T. Hall · (Plaintiffs) · Hall, Markle & Sickels · 4010 University Drive Fairfax, VA 22030 · 703-591-8600

Richard H. Lewis · (Defendants) · Lewis, Tydings, Bryan & Trichilo · 4114 Leonard Drive · P.O. Box 250 · Fairfax, VA 22030 · 703-385-1000

Norman F. Slenker · (Defendants) · Slenker, Brandt, Jennings & Johnston · 3026 Javier Road · Fairfax, VA 22031 · 703-849-8600

William O. P. Snead III · (Plaintiffs) · 3923 Old Lee Highway · Fairfax, VA 22030 703-359-8111

Ronald D. Hodges · (Defendants) · Wharton, Aldhizer & Weaver · 100 South Mason Street · P.O. Box 809 · Harrisonburg, VA 22801 · 703-434-0316

Phillip C. Stone · (Defendants) · Wharton, Aldhizer & Weaver · 100 South Mason Street · P.O. Box 809 · Harrisonburg, VA 22801 · 703-434-0316

Thomas V. Monahan · Hall, Monahan, Engle, Mahan & Mitchell · Three East Market Street · P.O. Box 390 · Leesburg, VA 22075 · 703-777-1050

Henry M. Sackett III · (Defendants) · Edmunds & Williams · 800 Main Street P.O. Box 958 · Lynchburg, VA 24505 · 804-846-9000

S. J. Thompson, Jr. · (Defendants) · Caskie & Frost · 2306 Atherholt Road · P.O. Box 6360 · Lynchburg, VA 24505 · 804-846-2731

Thomas C. Palmer, Jr. · (Defendants) · Brault, Palmer, Grove and Zimmerman 8575-D Sudley Road · P.O. Box 534 · Manassas, VA 22110-0534 · 703-631-9727

J. Jay Corson IV · (Defendants) · McGuire, Woods, Battle & Boothe · 8280 Greensboro Drive, Suite 900 · Tysons Corner · P.O. Box 9346 · McLean, VA 22102 · 703-356-2200

Haynie Seay Trotter · McGuire, Woods, Battle & Boothe · 8280 Greensboro Drive, Suite 900 · Tysons Corner · P.O. Box 9346 · McLean, VA 22102 · 703-356-2200

Guy E. Daugherty · (Plaintiffs) · Howell, Daugherty, Brown & Lawrence · One East Plume Street · P.O. 3929 · Norfolk, VA 23514 · 804-623-7334

William B. Eley · (Defendants) · Willcox & Savage · 1800 Sovran Center · Norfolk, VA 23510-2197 · 804-628-5500

Richard S. Glasser · (Plaintiffs) · Glasser and Glasser · 125 St. Paul's Boulevard, Suite 400 · Norfolk, VA 23510 · 804-625-6787

Jack E. Greer · (Defendants) · Williams, Worrell, Kelly, Greer & Frank · 600 Crestar Bank Building · P.O. Box 3416 · Norfolk, VA 23514 · 804-624-2600

John A. Heilig · (Defendants) · Heilig, McKenry, Fraim & Lollar · 700 Newtown Road · Norfolk, VA 23502 · 804-461-2500

John M. Hollis · (Defendants) · Willcox & Savage · 1800 Sovran Center · Norfolk, VA 23510-2197 · 804-628-5500

Robert M. Hughes III · (Defendants) · Hunton & Williams · First Virginia Bank Tower · 101 St. Paul's Boulevard · P.O. Box 3889 · Norfolk, VA 23514 · 804-625-5501

William T. Prince · (Defendants) · Williams, Worrell, Kelly, Greer & Frank · 600 Crestar Bank Building · P.O. Box 3416 · Norfolk, VA 23514 · 804-624-2600

Stanley E. Sacks · (Plaintiffs) · Sacks & Sacks · Town Point Center, Suite 501 150 Bush Street · P.O. Box 3874 · Norfolk, VA 23514 · 804-623-2753

Charles F. Tucker · (Defendants) · Vandeventer, Black, Meredith & Martin · 500 World Trade Center · Norfolk, VA 23510 · 804-622-4381

J. Darrell Foster · (Plaintiffs) · Bangel, Bangel & Bangel · 505 Court Street · P.O. Box 760 · Portsmouth, VA 23705-0760 · 804-397-3471

Robert J. Ingram, Sr. · (Plaintiffs) · Gilmer, Sadler, Ingram, Sutherland & Hutton · Midtown Professional Building · 65 East Main Street · P.O. Box 878 Pulaski, VA 24301 · 703-980-1360

George E. Allen III · (Plaintiffs) · Allen, Allen, Allen & Allen · 1809 Staples Mill Road · P.O. Box 6855 · Richmond, VA 23230 · 804-359-9151

Lewis Thomas Booker, Jr. · (Defendants) · Hunton & Williams · 707 East Main Street · P.O. Box 1535 · Richmond, VA 23212 · 804-788-8200

Cary L. Branch · (Plaintiffs) · Allen, Allen, Allen & Allen · 1809 Staples Mill Road P.O. Box 6855 · Richmond, VA 23230 · 804-359-9151

Robert F. Brooks · (Defendants) · Hunton & Williams · 707 East Main Street P.O. Box 1535 · Richmond, VA 23212 · 804-788-8200

Frank N. Cowan · Cowan & Owen · 1930 Huguenot Road · P.O. Box 35655 Richmond, VA 23235-0655 · 804-320-8918

Emanuel Emroch · (Plaintiffs) · Emroch & Williamson · 6800 Paragon Place, Suite 233 · P.O. Box 8692 · Richmond, VA 23226 · 804-288-1661

J. Waller Harrison · (Defendants) · McGuire, Woods, Battle & Boothe · One James Center · Richmond, VA 23219 · 804-644-4131

John F. Kay, Jr. · (Defendants) · Mays & Valentine · Sovran Center · 1111 East Main Street · P.O. Box 1122 · Richmond, VA 23208 · 804-697-1200

William H. King, Jr. · (Defendants) · McGuire, Woods, Battle & Boothe · One James Center · Richmond, VA 23219 · 804-644-4131

David Craig Landin · (Defendants) · McGuire, Woods, Battle & Boothe · One James Center · Richmond, VA 23219 · 804-644-4131

Henry H. McVey III · (Defendants) · McGuire, Woods, Battle & Boothe · One James Center · Richmond, VA 23219 · 804-644-4131

Frank B. Miller III · (Defendants) · Sands, Anderson, Marks & Miller · 1400 Ross Building · 801 East Main Street · P.O. Box 1998 · Richmond, VA 23216-1998 804-648-1636

James W. Morris III · (Defendants) · Browder, Russell, Morris and Butcher · One James Center, Suite 1100 · 901 East Cary Street · Richmond, VA 23219 · 804-771-9300

John M. Oakey, Jr. · (Defendants) · McGuire, Woods, Battle & Boothe · One James Center · Richmond, VA 23219 · 804-644-4131

John H. O'Brion, Jr. · (Defendants) · Browder, Russell, Morris and Butcher One James Center, Suite 1100 · 901 East Cary Street · Richmond, VA 23219 804-771-9300

Albert M. Orgain IV · (Defendants) · Sands, Anderson, Marks & Miller · 1400 Ross Building · 801 East Main Street · P.O. Box 1998 · Richmond, VA 23216-1998 804-648-1636

Rosewell Page III · (Defendants) · McGuire, Woods, Battle & Boothe · One James Center · Richmond, VA 23219 · 804-644-4131

James C. Roberts · (Defendants) · Mays & Valentine · Sovran Center · 1111 East Main Street · P.O. Box 1122 · Richmond, VA 23208 · 804-697-1200

John B. Russell · (Defendants) · Browder, Russell, Morris and Butcher · One James Center, Suite 1100 · 901 East Cary Street · Richmond, VA 23219 · 804-771-9300

Joseph M. Spivey III · (Defendants) · Hunton & Williams · 707 East Main Street P.O. Box 1535 · Richmond, VA 23212 · 804-788-8200

Thomas W. Williamson, Jr. · (Plaintiffs) · Emroch & Williamson · 6800 Paragon Place, Suite 233 · P.O. Box 8692 · Richmond, VA 23226 · 804-288-1661

David B. Hart · (Defendants) · Fox, Wooten & Hart · 707 Building, Suite 310 P.O. Box 12247 · Roanoke, VA 24024 · 703-343-2451

James F. Johnson · (Defendants) · Johnson, Ayers & Matthews · Southwest Virginia Savings and Loan Building, Second Floor · Second Street and Campbell Avenue, SW · P.O. Box 2200 · Roanoke, VA 24009 · 703-982-3666

S. D. Roberts Moore · Gentry, Locke, Rakes & Moore · 800 Colonial Plaza · P.O. Box 1018 · Roanoke, VA 24005 · 703-982-8000

G. Marshall Mundy · (Plaintiffs) · Mundy Rogers & Frith · Third Street & Woods Avenue, SW · P.O. Box 2240 · Roanoke, VA 24009 · 703-982-1351

William B. Poff · (Defendants) · Woods, Rogers & Hazlegrove · 105 Franklin Road, SW · P.O. Box 720 · Roanoke, VA 24004 · 703-982-4200

George W. Wooten · (Defendants) · Fox, Wooten & Hart · 707 Building, Suite 310 · Roanoke, VA 24024 · 703-343-2451

Thomas L. Phillips · (Plaintiffs) · Phillips, Phillips & Phillips · Route Three P.O. Box 179-P · Rustburg, VA 24588 · 804-821-5022

Frank D. Harris · (Defendants) · Harris, Matthews & Warren · 115 West Danville Street · South Hill, VA 23970 · 804-447-3128

Colin J. S. Thomas, Jr. · Timberlake, Smith, Thomas & Moses · The Virginia Building · P.O. Box 2566 · Staunton, VA 24401 · 703-885-1517

John F. Gionfriddo · (Defendants) · 410 Pine Street, SE · Vienna, VA 22180 703-281-2855

Wayne Lustig · Guy, Cromwell, Betz & Lustig · Pembroke One Building, Fifth Floor · Pembroke Office Park · 281 Independence Boulevard · Virginia Beach, VA 23462 · 804-499-8971

Thomas V. Monahan · Hall, Monahan, Engle, Mahan & Mitchell · Nine East Boscawen Street · P.O. Box 848 · Winchester, VA 22601 · 703-662-3200

REAL ESTATE LAW

Fred S. Landess · McGuire, Woods, Battle & Boothe · Court Square Building P.O. Box 1288 · Charlottesville, VA 22902 · 804-977-2500

Gary C. McGee · McGuire, Woods, Battle & Boothe · Court Square Building P.O. Box 1288 · Charlottesville, VA 22902 · 804-977-2500

A. Hugo Blankingship, Jr. · Blankingship & Keith · 4020 University Drive Fairfax, VA 22030 · 703-691-1235

C. Christopher Giragosian · Hunton & Williams · 3050 Chain Bridge Road Fairfaix, VA 22030 · 703-352-2200

Henry C. Mackall · Mackall, Mackall, Walker & Gibb · 4031 Chain Bridge Road Fairfax, VA 22030 · 703-273-0320

Edgar Allen Prichard · McGuire, Woods, Battle & Boothe · 3950 Chain Bridge Road · P.O. Box 338 · Fairfax, VA 22030 · 703-359-1000

Grayson P. Hanes · 3110 Fairview Park Drive, Suite 1400 · P.O. Box 547 · Falls Church, VA 22042 · 703-641-4200

Minerva Wilson Andrews · McGuire, Woods, Battle & Boothe · 8280 Greensboro Drive, Suite 900 · Tysons Corner · P.O. Box 9346 · McLean, VA 22102 · 703-356-2200

R. Dennis McArver · McGuire, Woods, Battle & Boothe · 8280 Greensboro Drive, Suite 900 · Tysons Corner · P.O. Box 9346 · McLean, VA 22102 · 703-356-2200

Courtland L. Traver · McGuire, Woods, Battle & Boothe · 8280 Greensboro Drive, Suite 900 · Tysons Corner · P.O. Box 9346 · McLean, VA 22102 · 703-356-2200

Thomas G. Johnson, Jr. · Willcox & Savage · 1800 Sovran Center · Norfolk, VA 23510-2197 · 804-628-5500

John A. Scanelli · 1600 Crestar Bank Building · Five Main Plaza East · Norfolk, VA 23510 · 804-625-1411

Jay F. Wilks · Kaufman & Canoles · Sovran Center · One Commercial Place P.O. Box 3037 · Norfolk, VA 23514-3037 · 804-624-3000

Thomas H. Willcox, Jr. · Willcox & Savage · 1800 Sovran Center · Norfolk, VA 23510-2197 · 804-628-5500

Philip J. Bagley III · Mays & Valentine · Sovran Center · 1111 East Main Street P.O. Box 1122 · Richmond, VA 23208 · 804-697-1200

John W. Bates III · McGuire, Woods, Battle & Boothe · One James Center Richmond, VA 23219 · 804-644-4131

William F. Gieg · McGuire, Woods, Battle & Boothe · One James Center Richmond, VA 23219 · 804-644-4131

L. Charles Long, Jr. · Hirschler, Fleischer, Weinberg, Cox & Allen · Main Street Centre · 629 East Main Street · P.O. Box 1Q · Richmond, VA 23202 804-771-9500

Patrick J. Milmoe · Hunton & Williams · 707 East Main Street · P.O. Box 1535 Richmond, VA 23212 · 804-788-8200

Thomas L. Newton, Jr. · McGuire, Woods, Battle & Boothe · One James Center Richmond, VA 23219 · 804-644-4131

Jay M. Weinberg · Hirschler, Fleischer, Weinberg, Cox & Allen · Main Street Centre · 629 East Main Street · P.O. Box 1Q · Richmond, VA 23202 · 804-771-9500

Walter F. Witt, Jr. · Hunton & Williams · 707 East Main Street · P.O. Box 1535 Richmond, VA 23212 · 804-788-8200

W. Heywood Fralin · Jolly, Place, Fralin & Prillaman · 3912 Electric Road · P.O. Box 2865 · Roanoke, VA 24001 · 703-989-0000

Talfourd H. Kemper · Woods, Rogers & Hazlegrove · 105 Franklin Road, SW P.O. Box 720 · Roanoke, VA 24004 · 703-982-4200

Michael K. Smeltzer · Woods, Rogers & Hazlegrove · 105 Franklin Road, SW P.O. Box 720 · Roanoke, VA 24004 · 703-982-4200

TAX AND EMPLOYEE BENEFITS LAW

Philip Tierney · McGuire, Woods, Battle & Boothe · Trans Potomac Plaza · 1199 North Fairfax Street · P.O. Box 1101 · Alexandria, VA 22313 · 703-549-5900

Leigh B. Middleditch, Jr. · McGuire, Woods, Battle & Boothe · Court Square Building · P.O. Box 1288 · Charlottesville, VA 22902 · 804-977-2500

Robert E. Stroud · McGuire, Woods, Battle & Boothe · Court Square Building P.O. Box 1288 · Charlottesville, VA 22902 · 804-977-2500

James B. Pittleman · Odin, Feldman & Pittleman · 10505 Judicial Drive · P.O. Box 367 · Fairfax, VA 22030-0367 · 703-385-7700

Duane W. Beckhorn · Hazel, Thomas, Fiske, Beckhorn and Hanes · 3110 Fairview Park Drive, Suite 1400 · P.O. Box 547 · Falls Church, VA 22042 · 703-641-4200

Carrington Williams · McGuire, Woods, Battle & Boothe · 8280 Greensboro Drive, Suite 900 · Tysons Corner · P.O. Box 9346 · McLean, VA 22102 · 703-356-2200

Leroy T. Canoles, Jr. · Kaufman & Canoles · Sovran Center · One Commercial Place · P.O. Box 3037 · Norfolk, VA 23514-3037 · 804-624-3000

Allan G. Donn · Willcox & Savage · 1800 Sovran Center · Norfolk, VA 23510-2197 804-628-5500

Robert C. Nusbaum · Hofheimer, Nusbaum, McPhaul & Samuels · 1700 Dominion Tower · P.O. Box 3460 · Norfolk, VA 23514 · 804-622-3366

Toy D. Savage, Jr. · Willcox & Savage · 1800 Sovran Center · Norfolk, VA 23510-2197 · 804-628-5500

T. Howard Spainhour · McGuire, Woods, Battle & Boothe · World Trade Center, Suite 9000 · P.O. Box 3767 · Norfolk, VA 23514 · 804-627-7677

Albert J. Taylor, Jr. · Cooper and Davis · Central Fidelity Bank Building · High & Crawford Streets · P.O. Box 1475 · Portsmouth, VA 23705 · 804-397-3481

Carle E. Davis · McGuire, Woods, Battle & Boothe · One James Center · Richmond, VA 23219 · 804-644-4131

Thomas F. Dean · (Employee Benefits) · McGuire, Woods, Battle & Boothe · One James Center · Richmond, VA 23219 · 804-644-4131

W. Birch Douglass III · McGuire, Woods, Battle & Boothe · One James Center · Richmond, VA 23219 · 804-644-4131

Mark S. Dray · (Employee Benefits) · Hunton & Williams · 707 East Main Street · P.O. Box 1535 · Richmond, VA 23212 · 804-788-8200

Louis A. Mezzullo · (also Employee Benefits) · Mezzullo, McCandlish & Framme · 700 East Main Street, Suite 804 · Richmond, VA 23219 · 804-782-9250

Mims Maynard Powell · (Employee Benefits) · McGuire, Woods, Battle & Boothe · One James Center · Richmond, VA 23219 · 804-644-4131

Frank W. Rogers, Jr. · Woods, Rogers & Hazlegrove · 105 Franklin Road, SW · P.O. Box 720 · Roanoke, VA 24004 · 703-982-4200

Thomas R. Frantz · Clark & Stant · 900 Sovran Bank Building · One Columbus Center · Virginia Beach, VA 23462 · 804-499-8800

R. Braxton Hill III · Kaufman & Canoles · 1104 Laskin Road · P.O. Box 626 · Virginia Beach, VA 23451 · 804-491-4000

Lewis M. Costello · Costello, Dickinson, Johnston, Greenlee, Coleman & McLoughlin · 107 North Kent Street, Fourth Floor · P.O. Box 2740 · Winchester, VA 22601 · 703-665-0050

TRUSTS AND ESTATES

James G. Arthur · Fagelson, Schonberger, Payne and Arthur · 401 Wythe Street · P.O. Box 297 · Alexandria, VA 22314 · 703-548-8100

Philip Tierney · McGuire, Woods, Battle & Boothe · TransPotomac Plaza · 1199 North Fairfax Street · P.O. Box 1101 · Alexandria, VA 22313 · 703-549-5900

Patrick J. Vaughan · Adams, Porter & Radigan · 1415 North Court House Road · P.O. Box 549 · Arlington, VA 22216 · 703-525-7100

Lucius H. Bracey, Jr. · McGuire, Woods, Battle & Boothe · Court Square Building · P.O. Box 1288 · Charlottesville, VA 22902 · 804-977-2500

Dennis W. Good, Jr. · McGuire, Woods, Battle & Boothe · Court Square Building P.O. Box 1288 · Charlottesville, VA 22902 · 804-977-2500

Howard M. Zaritsky · Zaritsky & Zaritsky · 3040 Williams Drive, Suite 402 Fairfax, VA 22031 · 703-698-7540

George F. Albright, Jr. · Hazel, Thomas, Fiske, Beckhorn and Hanes · 3110 Fairview Park Drive, Suite 1400 · P.O. Box 547 · Falls Church, VA 22042 703-641-4200

Constantine L. Dimos · McGuire, Woods, Battle & Boothe · 8280 Greensboro Drive, Suite 900 · Tysons Corner · P.O. Box 9346 · McLean, VA 22102 · 703-356-2200

Leroy T. Canoles, Jr. · Kaufman & Canoles · Sovran Center · One Commercial Place · P.O. Box 3037 · Norfolk, VA 23514-3037 · 804-624-3000

Allan G. Donn · Willcox & Savage · 1800 Sovran Center · Norfolk, VA 23510-2197 804-628-5500

Robert C. Nusbaum · Hofheimer, Nusbaum, McPhaul & Samuels · 1700 Dominion Tower · P.O. Box 3460 · Norfolk, VA 23514 · 804-622-3366

Toy D. Savage, Jr. · Willcox & Savage · 1800 Sovran Center · Norfolk, VA 23510-2197 · 804-628-5500

T. Howard Spainhour · McGuire, Woods, Battle & Boothe · World Trade Center, Suite 9000 · P.O. Box 3767 · Norfolk, VA 23514 · 804-627-7677

Thomas H. Willcox, Jr. · Willcox & Savage · 1800 Sovran Center · Norfolk, VA 23510-2197 · 804-628-5500

Michael Armstrong · Mays & Valentine · Sovran Center · 1111 East Main Street P.O. Box 1122 · Richmond, VA 23208 · 804-697-1200

Dennis I. Belcher · McGuire, Woods, Battle & Boothe · One James Center Richmond, VA 23219 · 804-644-4131

Waller H. Horsley · Hunton & Williams · 707 East Main Street · P.O. Box 1535 Richmond, VA 23212 · 804-788-8200

Julious P. Smith, Jr. · Williams, Mullen & Christian · Central Fidelity Building · 1021 East Cary Street · P.O. Box 1320 · Richmond, VA 23210 · 804-643-1991

C. Daniel Stevens · Christian, Barton, Epps, Brent & Chappell · Mutual Building, 12th Floor · 909 East Main Street · Richmond, VA 23219 · 804-644-7851

Harry J. Warthen III · Hunton & Williams · 707 East Main Street · P.O. Box 1535 · Richmond, VA 23212 · 804-788-8200

Thomas S. Word, Jr. · McGuire, Woods, Battle & Boothe · One James Center · Richmond, VA 23219 · 804-644-4131

Frank W. Rogers, Jr. · Woods, Rogers & Hazlegrove · 105 Franklin Road, SW · P.O. Box 720 · Roanoke, VA 24004 · 703-982-4200

Thomas R. Frantz · Clark & Stant · 900 Sovran Bank Building · One Columbus Center · Virginia Beach, VA 23462 · 804-499-8800

R. Braxton Hill III · Kaufman & Canoles · 1104 Laskin Road · P.O. Box 626 · Virginia Beach, VA 23451 · 804-491-4000

Lewis M. Costello · Costello, Dickinson, Johnston, Greenlee, Coleman & McLoughlin · 107 North Kent Street, Fourth Floor · P.O. Box 2740 · Winchester, VA 22601 · 703-665-0050

WASHINGTON

BANKRUPTCY LAW	739
BUSINESS LITIGATION	740
CORPORATE LAW	742
CRIMINAL DEFENSE	745
FAMILY LAW	745
LABOR AND EMPLOYMENT LAW	746
MARITIME LAW	748
NATURAL RESOURCES AND ENVIRONMENTAL LAW	748
PERSONAL INJURY LITIGATION	749
REAL ESTATE LAW	751
TAX AND EMPLOYEE BENEFITS LAW	753
TRUSTS AND ESTATES	755

BANKRUPTCY LAW

Sheena Ramona Aebig · Shulkin, Hutton & Bucknell · Pacific Building, 11th Floor · Third & Columbia · Seattle, WA 98104 · 206-623-3515

Thomas N. Bucknell · Shulkin, Hutton & Bucknell · Pacific Building, 11th Floor · Third & Columbia · Seattle, WA 98104 · 206-623-3515

Gayle E. Bush · Culp, Guterson & Grader · One Union Square, 27th Floor · Seattle, WA 98101-3143 · 206-624-7141

Daniel M. Caine · Merkel Caine & Donohue · Columbia Center, 64th Floor · 701 Fifth Avenue · Seattle, WA 98104 · 206-386-5600

Jack J. Cullen · Hatch & Leslie · 2700 Columbia Seafirst Center · Seattle, WA 98104 · 206-622-0090

Charles R. Eckberg · Lane Powell Moss & Miller · 3800 Rainier Bank Tower 1301 Fifth Avenue · Seattle, WA 98101 · 206-223-7000

Willard Hatch · Hatch & Leslie · 2700 Columbia Seafirst Center · Seattle, WA 98104 · 206-622-0090

Arthur J. Hutton, Jr. · Shulkin, Hutton & Bucknell · Pacific Building, 11th Floor Third & Columbia · Seattle, WA 98104 · 206-623-3515

Dillon E. Jackson · Hatch & Leslie · 2700 Columbia Seafirst Center · Seattle, WA 98104 · 206-622-0090

Jerome Shulkin · Shulkin, Hutton & Bucknell · Pacific Building, 11th Floor Third & Columbia · Seattle, WA 98104 · 206-623-3515

Thomas G. Thorbeck · Davis, Wright & Jones · 2600 Century Square · 1501 Fourth Avenue · Seattle, WA 98101 · 206-622-3150

Thomas T. Bassett · Lukins & Annis · 1600 Washington Trust Financial Center West 717 Sprague Avenue · Spokane, WA 99204-0466 · 509-455-9555

John F. Bury · Murphy, Bantz & Bury · West 818 Riverside Avenue · Spokane, WA 99201 · 509-838-4458

Joseph A. Esposito · Esposito, Tombari & George · 960 Paulsen Building · Spokane, WA 99201 · 509-624-9219

Richard P. Guy · Winston & Cashatt · Seafirst Financial Center · Spokane, WA 99210 · 509-838-6131

Daniel O'Rourke · Southwell, O'Rourke, Jalbert & Kappelman · Paulsen Center, Suite 820 · West 421 Riverside Avenue · Spokane, WA 99201 · 509-624-0159

Charles F. Van Marter · Lukins & Annis · 1600 Washington Trust Financial Center · West 717 Sprague Avenue · Spokane, WA 99204-0466 · 509-455-9555

Frank L. Kurtz · Schwab, Kurtz & Hurley · 411 North Second Street · Yakima, WA 98901 · 509-248-4282

BUSINESS LITIGATION

J. David Andrews · Perkins Coie · 1201 Third Avenue, 40th Floor · Seattle, WA 98101 · 206-328-4000

Peter D. Byrnes · Byrnes & Keller · Key Tower, 38th Floor · 1000 Second Avenue · Seattle, WA 98104 · 206-622-2000

Thomas J. Greenan · Ferguson & Burdell · One Union Square, 29th Floor · Seattle, WA 98101 · 206-622-1711

William A. Helsell · Helsell, Fetterman, Martin, Todd & Hokanson · 1500 Washington Building · P.O. Box 21846 · Seattle, WA 98111 · 206-292-1144

Ronald E. McKinstry · Bogle & Gates · The Bank of California Center · Seattle, WA 98164 · 206-682-5151

Michael Mines · Betts, Patterson & Mines · The Financial Center, Suite 800 · 1215 Fourth Avenue · Seattle, WA 98161-1090 · 206-292-9988

Evan L. Schwab · Bogle & Gates · The Bank of California Center · Seattle, WA 98164 · 206-682-5151

Payton Smith · Davis, Wright & Jones · 2600 Century Square · 1501 Fourth Avenue · Seattle, WA 98101 · 206-622-3150

Fredric C. Tausend · Schweppe, Krug & Tausend · 800 Waterfront Place · 1011 Western Avenue · Seattle, WA 98104 · 206-223-1600

Paul J. Allison · Randall & Danskin · 1500 Seafirst Financial Center · West 601 Riverside · Spokane, WA 99201 · 509-747-2052

Eugene I. Annis · Lukins & Annis · 1600 Washington Trust Financial Center · West 717 Sprague Avenue · Spokane, WA 99204-0466 · 509-455-9555

Joseph P. Delay · Delay, Curran, Thompson & Pontarolo · West 601 Main Avenue · Spokane, WA 99201 · 509-455-9500

John G. Layman · Layman, Loft, Arpin & White · 820 Lincoln Building · Spokane, WA 99210 · 509-455-8883

William D. Symmes · Witherspoon, Kelley, Davenport & Toole · Old National Bank Building, 11th Floor · Spokane, WA 99201 · 509-624-5265

Robert H. Whaley · Winston & Cashatt · Seafirst Financial Center, Suite 1900 · West 601 Riverside Avenue · Spokane, WA 99201 · 509-838-6131

Albert R. Malanca · Gordon, Thomas, Honeywell, Malanca, Peterson & Daheim · 2200 First Interstate Plaza · Tacoma, WA 98402 · 206-572-5050

Warren R. Peterson · Gordon, Thomas, Honeywell, Malanca, Peterson & Daheim · 2200 First Interstate Plaza · Tacoma, WA 98402 · 206-572-5050

William J. Rush · Rush, Hannula & Harkins · 715 Tacoma Avenue South · Tacoma, WA 98402 · 206-383-5388

James A. Perkins · Bogle & Gates · 105 North Third Street · P.O. Box 550 · Yakima, WA 98907 · 509-457-1515

CORPORATE LAW

Richard S. Sprague · Bogle & Gates · 10900 Northeast Fourth Street, Suite 1500 · Bellevue, WA 98004 · 206-455-3940

Tom A. Alberg · Perkins Coie · 1201 Third Avenue, 40th Floor · Seattle, WA 98101 · 206-328-4000

C. Kent Carlson · Preston, Thorgrimson, Ellis & Holman · 5400 Columbia Seafirst Center · 701 Fifth Avenue · Seattle, WA 98104-7011 · 206-623-7580

Richard A. Clark · Stoel, Rives, Boley, Jones & Grey · One Union Square, 36th Floor · 600 University · Seattle, WA 98101 · 206-624-0900

John M. Davis · Davis, Wright & Jones · 2600 Century Square · 1501 Fourth Avenue · Seattle, WA 98101 · 206-622-3150

P. Cameron DeVore · Davis, Wright & Jones · 2600 Century Square · 1501 Fourth Avenue · Seattle, WA 98101 · 206-622-3150

Robert J. Diercks · Foster, Pepper & Shefelman · 1111 Third Avenue, 34th Floor · Seattle, WA 98101 · 206-447-4400

Richard B. Dodd · Shidler McBroom Gates & Lucas · 3500 First Interstate Center · Seattle, WA 98104 · 206-223-4600

Karl J. Ege · Bogle & Gates · The Bank of California Center · Seattle, WA 98164 · 206-682-5151

James R. Ellis · Preston, Thorgrimson, Ellis & Holman · 5400 Columbia Seafirst Center · 701 Fifth Avenue · Seattle, WA 98104-7011 · 206-623-7580

William H. Gates · Shidler McBroom Gates & Lucas · 3500 First Interstate Center · Seattle, WA 98104 · 206-223-4600

Robert Edward Giles · Perkins Coie · 1201 Third Avenue, 40th Floor · Seattle, WA 98101 · 206-328-4000

D. Wayne Gittinger · Lane Powell Moss & Miller · 3800 Rainier Bank Tower 1301 Fifth Avenue · Seattle, WA 98101 · 206-223-7000

Raymond W. Haman · Lane Powell Moss & Miller · 3800 Rainier Bank Tower 1301 Fifth Avenue · Seattle, WA 98101 · 206-223-7000

James M. Hilton · Perkins Coie · 1201 Third Avenue, 40th Floor · Seattle, WA 98101 · 206-328-4000

Robert D. Kaplan · Bogle & Gates · The Bank of California Center · Seattle, WA 98164 · 206-682-5151

Charles J. Katz, Jr. · Perkins Coie · 1201 Third Avenue, 40th Floor · Seattle, WA 98101 · 206-328-4000

Earl P. Lasher III · Lasher & Johnson · 6000 Westland Building · 100 South King Street · Seattle, WA 98104 · 206-624-1230

Kevin C. McMahon · Stoel, Rives, Boley, Jones & Grey · One Union Square, 36th Floor · 600 University · Seattle, WA 98101 · 206-624-0900

Michael E. Morgan · Lane Powell Moss & Miller · 3800 Rainier Bank Tower 1301 Fifth Avenue · Seattle, WA 98101 · 206-223-7000

J. Shan Mullin · Perkins Coie · 1201 Third Avenue, 40th Floor · Seattle, WA 98101 · 206-328-4000

Harold F. Olsen · Perkins Coie · 1201 Third Avenue, 40th Floor · Seattle, WA 98101 · 206-328-4000

Charles F. Osborn · Bogle & Gates · The Bank of California Center · Seattle, WA 98164 · 206-682-5151

William G. Pusch · Davis, Wright & Jones · 2600 Century Square · 1501 Fourth Avenue · Seattle, WA 98101 · 206-622-3150

Bruce M. Pym · Graham & Dunn · Rainier Bank Tower, 34th Floor · 1301 Fifth Avenue · Seattle, WA 98101 · 206-624-8300

Daniel B. Ritter · Davis, Wright & Jones · 2600 Century Square · 1501 Fourth Avenue · Seattle, WA 98101 · 206-622-3150

Michael E. Stansbury · Foster, Pepper & Shefelman · 1111 Third Avenue, 34th Floor · Seattle, WA 98101 · 206-447-4400

Irwin L. Treiger · Bogle & Gates · The Bank of California Center · Seattle, WA 98164 · 206-682-5151

Jerome D. Whalen · Foster, Pepper & Shefelman · 1111 Third Avenue, 34th Floor · Seattle, WA 98101 · 206-447-4400

Paul J. Allison · Randall & Danskin · 1500 Seafirst Financial Center · West 601 Riverside · Spokane, WA 99201 · 509-747-2052

Ned M. Barnes · Witherspoon, Kelley, Davenport & Toole · Old National Bank Building, 11th Floor · Spokane, WA 99201 · 509-624-5265

R. Calvin Cathcart · Lukins & Annis · 1600 Washington Trust Financial Center West 717 Sprague Avenue · Spokane, WA 99204-0466 · 509-455-9555

Patrick B. Cerutti · Underwood, Campbell, Brock & Cerutti · 1100 Seafirst Financial Center · West 601 Riverside Avenue · Spokane, WA 99201 · 509-455-8500

Lawrence R. Small · Paine, Hamblen, Coffin, Brooke & Miller · 1200 Washington Trust Financial Center · Spokane, WA 99204 · 509-455-6000

Charles F. Van Marter · Lukins & Annis · 1600 Washington Trust Financial Center · West 717 Sprague Avenue · Spokane, WA 99204-0466 · 509-455-9555

James J. Gallagher · Graham & Dunn · 1300 Tacoma Financial Center · 1145 Broadway Plaza · Tacoma, WA 98401 · 206-572-9294

Paul M. Larson · Bogle & Gates · 105 North Third Street · P.O. Box 550 Yakima, WA 98907 · 509-457-1515

Morris G. Shore · Velikanje, Moore & Shore · 405 East Lincoln Avenue · Yakima, WA 98901 · 509-248-6030

William L. Weigand, Jr. · Lyon, Beaulaurier, Weigand, Suko & Gustafson · 222 North Third Street · P.O. Box 1689 · Yakima, WA 98907 · 509-248-7220

CRIMINAL DEFENSE

Dan R. Dubitzky · 1011 Western Avenue, Suite 803 · Seattle, WA 98104 206-467-6709

Laurence B. Finegold · Finegold & Zulauf · Tower Building, 13th Floor · Seattle, WA 98101 · 206-682-9274

Murray B. Guterson · Culp, Guterson & Grader · One Union Square, 27th Floor Seattle, WA 98101 · 206-624-7141

Darrell D. Hallett · Chicoine & Hallett · Waterfront Place One, Suite 803 · 1011 Western Avenue · Seattle, WA 98104 · 206-223-0800

Richard A. Hansen · Allen & Hansen · 600 Pioneer Building · 600 First Avenue Seattle, WA 98104 · 206-447-9681

Peter K. Mair · Mair, Abercrombie, Camiel & Rummonds · 710 Cherry Street Seattle, WA 98104 · 206-624-1551

Katrina C. Pflaumer · 2300 Smith Tower · Seattle, WA 98104 · 206-622-5943

Anthony Savage · 615 Lyon Building · 607 Third Avenue · Seattle, WA 98104 206-682-1882

Irwin H. Schwartz · 710 Cherry Street · Seattle, WA 98104 · 206-623-5084

Carl Maxey · Maxey Law Offices · Maxey Building · West 1385 Broadway Spokane, WA 99201 · 509-326-0338

Mark E. Vovos · West 1309 Dean Avenue · Spokane, WA 99201 · 509-326-5220

FAMILY LAW

William L. Kinzel · Kinzel, Allen & Skone · The Redwood Building, Suite 206 845-106th Avenue Northeast · Bellevue, WA 98004 · 206-455-3333

John O. Burgess · Short, Cressman & Burgess · First Interstate Center, 30th Floor · 999 Third Avenue · Seattle, WA 98104 · 206-682-3333

Janet A. George · 5700 Columbia Center · 701 Fifth Avenue · Seattle, WA 98104 206-447-0717

Martin A. Godsil · Casey Pruzan & Kovarik · Pacific Building, 18th Floor · Third & Columbia · Seattle, WA 98104 · 206-623-3577

Lowell K. Halverson · Halverson & Strong · 900 Hoge Building · Seattle, WA 98104 · 206-623-1590

Bernice Jonson · Jonson, Hurley, Olson & Olson · 1734 Northwest Market Street Seattle, WA 98107 · 206-789-4700

Robert C. Mussehl · Mussehl, Rosenberg, Jeffers, Cotter & Wechsler · 1111 Third Avenue Building, Suite 1000 · Seattle, WA 98101-3202 · 206-292-9800

Carl Pruzan · Casey Pruzan & Kovarik · Pacific Building, 18th Floor · Third & Columbia · Seattle, WA 98104 · 206-623-3577

Richard H. Riddell · Riddell, Williams, Bullitt & Walkinshaw · 1001 Fourth Avenue Plaza, Suite 4400 · Seattle, WA 98154 · 206-624-3600

Gordon W. Wilcox · Riddell, Williams, Bullitt & Walkinshaw · 1001 Fourth Avenue Plaza, Suite 4400 · Seattle, WA 98154 · 206-624-3600

LABOR AND EMPLOYMENT LAW

Peter M. Anderson · (Management) · Bogle & Gates · The Bank of California Center · Seattle, WA 98164 · 206-682-5151

J. David Andrews · (Management) · Perkins Coie · 1201 Third Avenue, 40th Floor · Seattle, WA 98101 · 206-328-4000

John F. Aslin · (Management) · Perkins Coie · 1201 Third Avenue, 40th Floor Seattle, WA 98101 · 206-328-4000

Clemens H. Barnes · (Management) · Graham & Dunn · Rainier Bank Tower, 34th Floor · 1301 Fifth Avenue · Seattle, WA 98101 · 206-624-8300

John Burns · (Labor) · Hafer, Price, Rinehart & Schwerin · 2505 Third Avenue, Suite 309 · Seattle, WA 98121 · 206-728-7280

Carolyn Cairns · (Individuals) · 83 South King Street, Suite 715 · Seattle, WA 98104 · 206-464-1932

Michael E. Cavanaugh · (Management) · Bogle & Gates · The Bank of California Center · Seattle, WA 98164 · 206-682-5151

Bruce Michael Cross · (Management) · Perkins Coie · 1201 Third Avenue, 40th Floor · Seattle, WA 98101 · 206-328-4000

George H. Davies · (Labor) · Davies, Roberts & Reid · 101 Elliott Avenue West, Suite 550 · Seattle, WA 98119 · 206-285-3610

Patrick J. Donnelly · (Management) · 6120 Columbia Center · Seattle, WA 98104 206-386-5550

Kelby D. Fletcher · (Individuals) · Peterson, Bracelin, Young, Putra, Fletcher & Zeder · 2500 Smith Tower · Seattle, WA 98104 · 206-624-6800

Harold H. Green · (Individuals) · MacDonald, Hoague & Bayless · Hoge Building, 15th Floor · 701 Second Avenue · Seattle, WA 98104 · 206-622-1604

Hugh Hafer · (Labor) · Hafer, Price, Rinehart & Schwerin · 2505 Third Avenue, Suite 309 · Seattle, WA 98121 · 206-728-7280

Wayne W. Hansen · (Management) · Lane Powell Moss & Miller · 3800 Rainier Bank Tower · 1301 Fifth Avenue · Seattle, WA 98101 · 206-223-7000

Mark A. Hutcheson · (Management) · Davis, Wright & Jones · 2600 Century Square · 1501 Fourth Avenue · Seattle, WA 98101 · 206-622-3150

Thomas A. Lemly · (Management) · Davis, Wright & Jones · 2600 Century Square 1501 Fourth Avenue · Seattle, WA 98101 · 206-622-3150

Judith A. Lonnquist · (Individuals) · Hoge Building, Suite 1201 · 705 Second Avenue · Seattle, WA 98104 · 206-622-2086

James Markham Marshall · (Management) · Preston, Thorgrimson, Ellis & Holman · 701 Fifth Avenue · Seattle, WA 98104-7001 · 206-623-7580

Dustin C. McCreary · (Management) · Bogle & Gates · The Bank of California Center · Seattle, WA 98164 · 206-682-5151

Eugene R. Nielson · (Management) · Lane Powell Moss & Miller · 3800 Rainier Bank Tower · 1301 Fifth Avenue · Seattle, WA 98101 · 206-223-7000

John E. Rinehart, Jr. · (Labor) · Hafer, Price, Rinehart & Schwerin · 2505 Third Avenue, Suite 309 · Seattle, WA 98121 · 206-728-7280

William A. Roberts · (Labor) · Davies, Roberts & Reid · 101 Elliott Avenue West, Suite 550 · Seattle, WA 98119 · 206-285-3610

Jon Howard Rosen · (Labor; Individuals) · Frank & Rosen · 705 Second Avenue Seattle, WA 98104 · 206-682-6711

Jerome L. Rubin · (Management) · Schweppe, Krug & Tausend · 800 Waterfront Place · 1011 Western Avenue · Seattle, WA 98104 · 206-223-1600

Lawrence Schwerin · (Labor) · Hafer, Price, Rinehart & Schwerin · 2505 Third Avenue, Suite 309 · Seattle, WA 98121 · 206-728-7280

Sidney J. Strong · (Individuals) · Halverson & Strong · 900 Hoge Building Seattle, WA 98104 · 206-623-1590

Herman L. Wacker · (Management) · Riddell, Williams, Bullitt & Walkinshaw 1001 Fourth Avenue Plaza, Suite 4400 · Seattle, WA 98154 · 206-624-3600

Jerome F. McCarthy · (Management) · Gordon, Thomas, Honeywell, Malanca, Peterson & Daheim · 2200 First Interstate Plaza · Tacoma, WA 98402 · 206-572-5050

MARITIME LAW

David Danielson · Danielson Harrigan Smith & Tollefson · First Interstate Center, 44th Floor · 999 Third Avenue · Seattle, WA 98104 · 206-623-1700

Vincent R. Larson · Riddell, Williams, Bullitt & Walkinshaw · 1001 Fourth Avenue Plaza, Suite 4400 · Seattle, WA 98154 · 206-624-3600

Thomas J. McKey · Bogle & Gates · The Bank of California Center · Seattle, WA 98164 · 206-682-5151

NATURAL RESOURCES AND ENVIRONMENTAL LAW

J. Richard Aramburu · (Plaintiffs) · 505 Madison Street · Seattle, WA 98104 206-625-9515

Peter L. Buck · Buck & Gordon · Waterfront Place, Suite 902 · 1011 Western Avenue · Seattle, WA 98104 · 206-382-9540

Peter J. Eglick · (Plaintiffs) · 1411 Fourth Avenue · Seattle, WA 98101 · 206-464-1435

Jerome L. Hillis · Hillis, Clark, Martin & Peterson · 500 Galland Building · 1221 Second Avenue · Seattle, WA 98101 · 206-623-1745

James R. Moore · Perkins Coie · 1201 Third Avenue, 40th Floor · Seattle, WA 98101 · 206-328-4000

Ralph H. Palumbo · Heller, Ehrman, White & McAuliffe · Columbia SeaFirst Center, 61st Floor · 701 Fifth Avenue · Seattle, WA 98104 · 206-447-0900

William D. Ruckelshaus · Perkins Coie · 1201 Third Avenue, 40th Floor · Seattle, WA 98101 · 206-328-4000

Judith M. Runstad · Foster, Pepper & Shefelman · 1111 Third Avenue, 34th Floor · Seattle, WA 98101 · 206-447-4400

Daniel D. Syrdal · Heller, Ehrman, White & McAuliffe · Columbia SeaFirst Center, 61st Floor · 701 Fifth Avenue · Seattle, WA 98104 · 206-447-0900

John L. Neff · (Mining) · Neff, Nayes, Phillabaum & Harlow · SeaFirst Financial Center, Suite 1370 · West 601 Riverside Avenue · Spokane, WA 99201 · 509-838-6033

PERSONAL INJURY LITIGATION

Paul L. Stritmatter · (Plaintiffs) · Stritmatter, Kessler & McCauley · 407 Eighth Street · Hoquiam, WA 98550-3692 · 206-533-2710

Paul N. Luvera, Jr. · (Plaintiffs) · Paul N. Luvera, Jr. & Associates · 917 South Third Avenue · P.O. Box 427 · Mount Vernon, WA 98273-0427 · 206-336-6561

Craig P. Campbell · (Defendants) · Karr Tuttle Campbell · 1201 Third Avenue, Suite 2900 · Seattle, WA 98101-3028 · 206-223-1313

Thomas Chambers · (Plaintiffs) · 1400 Broadway · Seattle, WA 98122 · 206-328-5561

John Patrick Cook · (Defendants) · Lee, Smart, Cook, Martin & Patterson · 800 Washington Building · Fourth & Union · Seattle, WA 98101 · 206-624-7990

Joel D. Cunningham · (Defendants) · Williams, Kastner & Gibbs · 1400 Washington Building · P.O. Box 21926 · Seattle, WA 98111-0040 · 206-628-6600

William A. Helsell · (Defendants) · Helsell, Fetterman, Martin, Todd & Hokanson · 1500 Washington Building · P.O. Box 21846 · Seattle, WA 98111 · 206-292-1144

Lembhard G. Howell · (Plaintiffs) · Law Offices of Lembhard G. Howell · Arctic Building, Suite 800 · Seattle, WA 98104 · 206-623-5296

J. Murray Kleist · (Plaintiffs) · Schroeter, Goldmark & Bender · 540 Central Building · Third & Columbia · Seattle, WA 98104 · 206-622-8506

David L. Martin · (Defendants) · Lee, Smart, Cook, Martin & Patterson · 800 Washington Building · Fourth & Union · Seattle, WA 98101 · 206-624-7990

H. J. Merrick · (Defendants) · Merrick, Hofstedt & Lindsey · 710 Ninth Avenue · Seattle, WA 98104 · 206-682-0610

Jan Eric Peterson · (Plaintiffs) · Peterson, Bracelin, Young, Putra, Fletcher & Zeder · 2500 Smith Tower · Seattle, WA 98104 · 206-624-6800

Leonard W. Schroeter · (Plaintiffs) · Schroeter, Goldmark & Bender · 540 Central Building · Third & Columbia · Seattle, WA 98104 · 206-622-8506

Daniel F. Sullivan · (Plaintiffs) · Sullivan, Golden & Otorowski · Hoge Building, 10th Floor · 705 Second Avenue · Seattle, WA 98104 · 206-682-8813

Robert W. Thomas · (Defendants) · Lane Powell Moss & Miller · 3800 Rainier Bank Tower · 1301 Fifth Avenue · Seattle, WA 98101 · 206-223-7000

Eugene I. Annis · (Defendants) · Lukins & Annis · 1600 Washington Trust Financial Center · West 717 Sprague Avenue · Spokane, WA 99204-0466 · 509-455-9555

Daniel W. Keefe · (Defendants) · Keefe & King · West 601 Main Street, Suite 1102 · Spokane, WA 99201 · 509-624-8988

Daniel E. McKelvey, Jr. · (Plaintiffs) · McKelvey, Nelson & Fennessey · North 222 Wall Street, Suite 402 · Spokane, WA 99201 · 509-624-0888

Alvin A. Anderson · (Plaintiffs) · Anderson, Holman & Houghton · 950 Fawcett · Tacoma, WA 98402 · 206-627-1866

F. Ross Burgess · (Defendants) · Burgess, Kennedy, Fitzer & Strombom · 1551 Broadway, Suite 400 · Tacoma, WA 98402-3304 · 206-572-5324

John L. Messina · (Plaintiffs) · Messina & Duffy · 4002 Tacoma Mall Boulevard, Suite 200 · Tacoma, WA 98409 · 206-472-6000

Warren R. Peterson · (Defendants) · Gordon, Thomas, Honeywell, Malanca, Peterson & Daheim · 2200 First Interstate Plaza · Tacoma, WA 98402 · 206-572-5050

Jack G. Rosenow · (Defendants) · Rosenow, Hale & Johnson · Tacoma Mall Office Building, Suite 301 · Tacoma, WA 98409 · 206-473-0725

William J. Rush · Rush, Hannula & Harkins · 715 Tacoma Avenue South · Tacoma, WA 98402 · 206-383-5388

Dennis L. Fluegge · (Defendants) · Meyer & Fluegge · 230 South Second Street · P.O. Box 22680 · Yakima, WA 98907 · 509-575-8500

REAL ESTATE LAW

Richard U. Chapin · Ferguson & Burdell · 2100 Koll Center · 500 One-Hundred-Eighth Avenue NE · Bellevue, WA 98004 · 206-453-1711

Omar S. Parker, Jr. · Perkins Coie · One Bellevue Center, Suite 1800 · 411 One-Hundred-Eighth Avenue NE · Bellevue, WA 98004 · 206-328-4000

Richard S. Sprague · Bogle & Gates · 10900 Northeast Fourth Street, Suite 1500 · Bellvue, WA 98004 · 206-455-3940

Thaddas L. Alston · Alston, Courtnage, MacAulay & Proctor · 1000 Second Avenue, Suite 3900 · Seattle, WA 98104 · 206-623-7600

Timothy R. Clifford · Foster, Pepper & Shefelman · 1111 Third Avenue, 34th Floor · Seattle, WA 98101 · 206-447-4400

John A. Gose · Preston, Thorgrimson, Ellis & Holman · 5400 Columbia Seafirst Center · 701 Fifth Avenue · Seattle, WA 98104-7011 · 206-623-7580

Joel E. Haggard · 1515 IBM Building · 1200 Fifth Avenue · Seattle, WA 98101 · 206-682-5635

Jerome L. Hillis · Hillis, Clark, Martin & Peterson · 500 Galland Building · 1221 Second Avenue · Seattle, WA 98101 · 206-623-1745

Richard E. Keefe · Foster, Pepper & Shefelman · 1111 Third Avenue, 34th Floor · Seattle, WA 98101 · 206-447-4400

Edward W. Kuhrau · Perkins Coie · 1201 Third Avenue, 40th Floor · Seattle, WA 98101 · 206-328-4000

Richard E. McCann · Perkins Coie · 1201 Third Avenue, 40th Floor · Seattle, WA 98101 · 206-328-4000

Dennis E. McLean · Davis, Wright & Jones · 2600 Century Square · 1501 Fourth Avenue · Seattle, WA 98101 · 206-622-3150

Scott B. Osborne · Ferguson & Burdell · One Union Square, 29th Floor · Seattle, WA 98101 · 206-622-1711

John E. Phillips · Phillips & Wilson · Waterfront Place, Suite 920 · 1011 Western Avenue · Seattle, WA 98104 · 206-467-7766

Judith M. Runstad · Foster, Pepper & Riviera · 1111 Third Avenue Building, 34th Floor · Seattle, WA 98101 · 206-447-4400

Russell F. Tousley · Tousley Brain · 720 Olive Way, Suite 1700 · Seattle, WA 98101 · 206-624-5299

Jerome D. Whalen · Foster, Pepper & Shefelman · 1111 Third Avenue, 34th Floor · Seattle, WA 98101 · 206-447-4400

Paul J. Allison · Randall & Danskin · 1500 Seafirst Financial Center · West 601 Riverside · Spokane, WA 99201 · 509-747-2052

Ned M. Barnes · Witherspoon, Kelley, Davenport & Toole · Old National Bank Building, 11th Floor · Spokane, WA 99201 · 509-624-5265

Joseph P. Delay · Delay, Curran, Thompson & Pontarolo · West 601 Main Avenue · Spokane, WA 99210 · 509-455-9500

Stanley R. Schultz · Winston & Cashatt · Seafirst Financial Center, Suite 1900 West 601 Riverside Avenue · Spokane, WA 99201 · 509-838-6131

Edward F. Wroe · Lukins & Annis · 1600 Washington Trust Financial Center West 717 Sprague Avenue · Spokane, WA 99204-0466 · 509-455-9555

Dale L. Carlisle · Gordon, Thomas, Honeywell, Malanca, Peterson & Daheim 2200 First Interstate Plaza · Tacoma, WA 98402 · 206-572-5050

Warren J. Daheim · Gordon, Thomas, Honeywell, Malanca, Peterson & Daheim · 2200 First Interstate Plaza · Tacoma, WA 98402 · 206-572-5050

William F. Almon · Almon, Berg & Adams · 4112 Summitview Avenue, Suite B · P.O. Box 588 · Yakima, WA 98907-0588 · 509-965-5000

Thomas B. Grahn · Halverson & Applegate · 311 North Fourth Street · P.O. Box 526 · Yakima, WA 98907 · 509-575-6611

TAX AND EMPLOYEE BENEFITS LAW

Dwight J. Drake · Foster, Pepper & Shefelman · Rainier Bank Plaza, 15th Floor · 7770 One-Hundred-Eighth Avenue, NE · Bellevue, WA 98004 · 206-451-0500

William H. Burkhart · Preston, Thorgrimson, Ellis & Holman · 5400 Columbia Seafirst Center · 701 Fifth Avenue · Seattle, WA 98104-7011 · 206-623-7580

C. Kent Carlson · Preston, Thorgrimson, Ellis & Holman · 5400 Columbia Seafirst Center · 701 Fifth Avenue · Seattle, WA 98104-7011 · 206-623-7580

Donald C. Dahlgren · (Employee Benefits) · Dahlgren & Dauenhauer · 1702 Norton Building · Seattle, WA 98104 · 206-624-0450

Meade Emory · LeSourd & Patten · 2400 Columbia Seafirst Center · 701 Fifth Avenue · Seattle, WA 98104-7005 · 206-624-1040

Graham H. Fernald · Perkins Coie · 1201 Third Avenue, 40th Floor · Seattle, WA 98101 · 206-328-4000

G. Keith Grim · Lane Powell Moss & Miller · 3800 Rainier Bank Tower · 1301 Fifth Avenue · Seattle, WA 98101 · 206-223-7000

W. Michael Hafferty · Riddell, Williams, Bullitt & Walkinshaw · 1001 Fourth Avenue Plaza, Suite 4400 · Seattle, WA 98154 · 206-624-3600

Darrell D. Hallett · Chicoine & Hallett · Waterfront Place One, Suite 803 · 1011 Western Avenue · Seattle, WA 98104 · 206-223-0800

James M. Hilton · Perkins Coie · 1201 Third Avenue, 40th Floor · Seattle, WA 98101 · 206-328-4000

Roland L. Hjorth · Perkins Coie · 1201 Third Avenue, 40th Floor · Seattle, WA 98101 · 206-328-4000

Richard A. Hopp · (Employee Benefits) · Stoel, Rives, Boley, Jones & Grey · One Union Square, 36th Floor · 600 University · Seattle, WA 98101 · 206-624-0900

C. James Judson · Davis, Wright & Jones · 2600 Century Square · 1501 Fourth Avenue · Seattle, WA 98101 · 206-622-3150

Robert D. Kaplan · Bogle & Gates · The Bank of California Center · Seattle, WA 98164 · 206-682-5151

Patrick F. Kennedy · Foster, Pepper & Shefelman · 1111 Third Avenue, 34th Floor · Seattle, WA 98101 · 206-447-4400

Francis A. LeSourd · LeSourd & Patten · 2400 Columbia Seafirst Center · 701 Fifth Avenue · Seattle, WA 98104-7005 · 206-624-1040

Judd R. Marten · (Employee Benefits) · LeSourd & Patten · 2400 Columbia Seafirst Center · 701 Fifth Avenue · Seattle, WA 98104-7005 · 206-624-1040

Gerhardt Morrison · Bogle & Gates · The Bank of California Center · Seattle, WA 98164 · 206-682-5151

Anne L. Northrop · (Employee Benefits) · Davis, Wright & Jones · 2600 Century Square · 1501 Fourth Avenue · Seattle, WA 98101 · 206-622-3150

David F. P. O'Connor · Bogle & Gates · The Bank of California Center · Seattle, WA 98164 · 206-682-5151

Charles F. Osborn · Bogle & Gates · The Bank of California Center · Seattle, WA 98164 · 206-682-5151

John T. Piper · Bogle & Gates · The Bank of California Center · Seattle, WA 98164 · 206-682-5151

Samuel F. Saracino · Davis, Wright & Jones · 2600 Century Square · 1501 Fourth Avenue · Seattle, WA 98101 · 206-622-3150

Jon M. Schorr · Heller, Ehrman, White & McAuliffe · Columbia SeaFirst Center, 61st Floor · 701 Fifth Avenue · Seattle, WA 98104 · 206-447-0900

Lee Thorson · (Employee Benefits) · Lane Powell Moss & Miller · 3800 Rainier Bank Tower · 1301 Fifth Avenue · Seattle, WA 98101 · 206-223-7000

Irwin L. Treiger · Bogle & Gates · The Bank of California Center · Seattle, WA 98164 · 206-682-5151

Rodney J. Waldbaum · LeSourd & Patten · 2400 Columbia Seafirst Center · 701 Fifth Avenue · Seattle, WA 98104-7005 · 206-624-1040

Andrew H. Zuccotti · Stoel, Rives, Boley, Jones & Grey · One Union Square, 36th Floor · 600 University · Seattle, WA 98101 · 206-624-0900

James S. Black, Jr. · Lukins & Annis · 1600 Washington Trust Financial Center West 717 Sprague Avenue · Spokane, WA 99204-0466 · 509-455-9555

K. Thomas Connolly · (Employee Benefits) · Witherspoon, Kelley, Davenport & Toole · Old National Bank Building, 11th Floor · Spokane, WA 99201 · 509-624-5265

Scott B. Lukins · Lukins & Annis · 1600 Washington Trust Financial Center West 717 Sprague Avenue · Spokane, WA 99204-0466 · 509-455-9555

Gary C. Randall · Gonzaga Law School · 502 Boone Avenue East · Spokane, WA 99258 · 509-484-6481

James A. Furber · Gordon, Thomas, Honeywell, Malanca, Peterson & Daheim 2200 First Interstate Plaza · Tacoma, WA 98402 · 206-572-5050

TRUSTS AND ESTATES

Cleary S. Cone · Cone, Gilreath & Korte · 200 East Third Avenue · P.O. Box 499 Ellensburg, WA 98926 · 509-925-3191

Albert J. Schauble · Aitken, Schauble, Patrick, Neill & Charawell · 210 Old National Bank Building · P.O. Box 307 · Pullman, WA 99163 · 509-334-3505

Steven W. Andreasen · Davis, Wright & Jones · 2600 Century Square · 1501 Fourth Avenue · Seattle, WA 98101 · 206-622-3150

Janis A. Cunningham · Karr Tuttle Campbell · 1201 Third Avenue, Suite 2900 Seattle, WA 98101-3028 · 206-223-1313

Bruce P. Flynn · Karr Tuttle Campbell · 1201 Third Avenue, Suite 2900 · Seattle, WA 98101-3028 · 206-223-1313

Thomas C. Gores · Bogle & Gates · The Bank of California Center · Seattle, WA 98164 · 206-682-5151

Alan H. Kane · Preston, Thorgrimson, Ellis & Holman · 5400 Columbia Seafirst Senter · 701 Fifth Avenue · Seattle, WA 98104-7011 · 206-623-7580

Reginald S. Koehler III · Perkins Coie · 1201 Third Avenue, 40th Floor · Seattle, WA 98101 · 206-328-4000

Malcolm A. Moore · Davis, Wright & Jones · 2600 Century Square · 1501 Fourth Avenue · Seattle, WA 98101 · 206-622-3150

Robert S. Mucklestone · Perkins Coie · 1201 Third Avenue, 40th Floor · Seattle, WA 98101 · 206-328-4000

John R. Price · Perkins Coie · 1201 Third Avenue, 40th Floor · Seattle, WA 98101 206-328-4000

Kenneth L. Schubert, Jr. · Garvey, Schubert & Barer · Waterfront Place Building, 10th Floor · 1011 Western Avenue · Seattle, WA 98104 · 206-464-3939

John F. Sherwood · Lane Powell Moss & Miller · 3800 Rainier Bank Tower 1301 Fifth Avenue · Seattle, WA 98101 · 206-223-7000

Kimbrough Street · Davis, Wright & Jones · 2600 Century Square · 1501 Fourth Avenue · Seattle, WA 98101 · 206-622-3150

Evan O. Thomas III · Lane Powell Moss & Miller · 3800 Rainier Bank Tower 1301 Fifth Avenue · Seattle, WA 98101 · 206-223-7000

Scott B. Lukins · Lukins & Annis · 1600 Washington Trust Financial Center West 717 Sprague Avenue · Spokane, WA 99204-0466 · 509-455-9555

Donald K. Querna · Randall & Danskin · 1500 Seafirst Financial Center · West 601 Riverside Avenue · Spokane, WA 99201 · 509-747-2052

Allan H. Toole · Witherspoon, Kelley, Davenport & Toole · Old National Bank Building, 11th Floor · Spokane, WA 99201 · 509-624-5265

Roger H. Underwood · Underwood, Campbell, Brock & Cerutti · 1100 Seafirst Financial Center · West 601 Riverside Avenue · Spokane, WA 99201 · 509-455-8500

S. Alan Weaver · Eisenhower, Carlson, Newlands, Reha, Henriot & Quinn · First Interstate Plaza, Suite 1200 · Tacoma, WA 98402 · 206-572-4500

Herman H. Hayner · Minnick-Hayner · 249 West Adler Street · P.O. Box 1757 Walla Walla, WA 99362 · 509-527-3500

James K. Hayner · Minnick-Hayner · 249 West Adler Street · P.O. Box 1757 Walla Walla, WA 99362 · 509-527-3500

John M. Reese · Reese, Baffney, Schrag, Siegel & Hedine · Baker Building, Seventh Floor · Walla Walla, WA 99362 · 509-525-8130

George F. Velikanje · Velikanje, Moore & Shore · 405 East Lincoln Avenue Yakima, WA 98901 · 509-248-6030

WEST VIRGINIA

BANKRUPTCY LAW	758
BUSINESS LITIGATION	759
CORPORATE LAW	759
CRIMINAL DEFENSE	759
LABOR AND EMPLOYMENT LAW	760
NATURAL RESOURCES AND ENVIRONMENTAL LAW	760
PERSONAL INJURY LITIGATION	761
REAL ESTATE LAW	761
TAX AND EMPLOYEE BENEFITS LAW	762
TRUSTS AND ESTATES	762

BANKRUPTCY LAW

Thomas B. Bennett · Bowles, McDavid, Graff & Love · Commerce Square, 16th Floor · P.O. Box 1386 · Charleston, WV 25325-1386 · 304-347-1100

William W. Booker · Love, Wise & Woodroe · 1200 Charleston National Plaza P.O. Box 951 · Charleston, WV 25323 · 304-343-4841

William F. Dobbs, Jr. · Jackson & Kelly · 1600 Laidley Tower · P.O. Box 553 Charleston, WV 25322 · 304-340-1000

Thomas R. Goodwin · Goodwin & Goodwin · 1500 One Valley Square · Charleston, WV 25301 · 304-346-0321

Michael L. Bray · Steptoe & Johnson · Union National Center East, Sixth Floor P.O. Box 2190 · Clarksburg, WV 26302-2190 · 304-624-8000

BUSINESS LITIGATION

James K. Brown · Jackson & Kelly · 1600 Laidley Tower · P.O. Box 553 · Charleston, WV 25322 · 304-340-1000

John S. Haight · Kay, Casto & Chaney · 1600 Charleston National Plaza · P.O. Box 2031 · Charleston, WV 25327 · 304-345-8900

Herbert G. Underwood · Steptoe & Johnson · Union National Center East, Sixth Floor · P.O. Box 2190 · Clarksburg, WV 26302-2190 · 304-624-8000

John E. Jenkins, Jr. · Jenkins, Fenstermaker, Krieger, Kayes & Farrell · Coal Exchange Building, llth Floor · P.O. Drawer 2688 · Huntington, WV 25726 · 304-523-2100

CORPORATE LAW

James K. Brown · Jackson & Kelly · 1600 Laidley Tower · P.O. Box 553 · Charleston, WV 25322 · 304-340-1000

Thomas R. Goodwin · Goodwin & Goodwin · 1500 One Valley Square · Charleston, WV 25301 · 304-346-0321

John L. McClaugherty · Jackson & Kelly · 1600 Laidley Tower · P.O. Box 553 · Charleston, WV 25322 · 304-340-1000

Charles R. McElwee · Robinson & McElwee · 600 KB&T Center · 500 Virginia Street East · P.O. Box 1791 · Charleston, WV 25326 · 304-344-5800

John E. Jenkins, Jr. · Jenkins, Fenstermaker, Krieger, Kayes & Farrell · Coal Exchange Building, 11th Floor · P.O. Drawer 2688 · Huntington, WV 25726 · 304-523-2100

CRIMINAL DEFENSE

Arthur T. Ciccarello · Lewis, Ciccarello & Friedberg · Kanawha Valley Bank Building, Seventh Floor · One Valley Square · P.O. Box 1746 · Charleston, WV 25301 · 304-345-2000

Rudolph L. DiTrapano · DiTrapano & Jackson · 604-Virginia Street East · Charleston, WV 25301 · 304-342-0133

James B. McIntyre · McIntyre, Haviland & Jordan · 124 Capitol Street · Charleston, WV 25301 · 304-344-3652

LABOR AND EMPLOYMENT LAW

Grant Crandall · (Labor; Individuals) · Crandall & Pyles · 1021 Quarrier Street, Suite 414 · P.O. Box 3465 · Charleston, WV 25334 · 304-345-3080

James M. Haviland · (Labor) · McIntyre, Haviland & Jordan · 124 Capitol Street Charleston, WV 25301 · 304-344-3652

Stanley M. Hostler · (Labor) · Hostler & Segal · One Valley Square, 1030 · Charleston, WV 25301 · 304-344-9100

David D. Johnson, Jr. · (Management) · Jackson & Kelly · 1600 Laidley Tower P.O. Box 553 · Charleston, WV 25322 · 304-340-1000

Forrest H. Roles · (Management) · Smith, Heenan & Althen · One Valley Square, Suite 1380 · Charleston, WV 25301 · 304-342-8960

Robert M. Steptoe, Jr. · (Management) · Steptoe & Johnson · Union National Center East, Sixth Floor · Clarksburg, WV 26302-2190 · 304-624-8000

P. Thomas Krieger · (Management) · Jenkins, Fenstermaker, Krieger, Kayes & Farrell · Coal Exchange Building, 11th Floor · P.O. Drawer 2688 · Huntington, WV 25726 · 304-523-2100

Robert T. Goldenberg · (Labor) · Goldenberg, Goldenberg & Stealey · 205 Fourth Street · P.O. Box 1754 · Parkersburg, WV 26102 · 304-485-4516

NATURAL RESOURCES AND ENVIRONMENTAL LAW

M. Ann Bradley · Robinson & McElwee · 600 KB&T Center · 500 Virginia Street East · P.O. Box 1791 · Charleston, WV 25326 · 304-344-5800

David M. Flannery · Robinson & McElwee · 600 KB&T Center · 500 Virginia Street East · P.O. Box 1791 · Charleston, WV 25326 · 304-344-5800

Gregory R. Gorrell · Jackson & Kelly · 1600 Laidley Tower · P.O. Box 553 · Charleston, WV 25322 · 304-340-1000

F. Thomas Graff, Jr. · Bowles, McDavid, Graff & Love · Commerce Square, 16th Floor · P.O. Box 1386 · Charleston, WV 25325-1386 · 304-347-1100

J. Thomas Lane · Bowles, McDavid, Graff & Love · Commerce Square, 16th Floor · P.O. Box 1386 · Charleston, WV 25325-1386 · 304-347-1100

Patrick D. Deem · Steptoe & Johnson · Union National Center East, Sixth Floor P.O. Box 2190 · Clarksburg, WV 26302-2190 · 304-624-8000

PERSONAL INJURY LITIGATION

Rudolph L. DiTrapano · (Plaintiffs) · DiTrapano & Jackson · 604 Virginia Street East · Charleston, WV 25301 · 304-342-0133

John S. Haight · (Defendants) · Kay, Casto & Chaney · 1600 Charleston National Plaza · P.O. Box 2031 · Charleston, WV 25327 · 304-345-8900

Phillip Rodney Jackson · (Plaintiffs) · DiTrapano & Jackson · 604 Virginia Street East · Charleston, WV 25301 · 304-342-0133

Winfield T. Shaffer · (Defendants) · Jackson & Kelly · 1600 Laidley Tower · P.O. Box 553 · Charleston, WV 25322 · 304-340-1000

Herbert G. Underwood · (Defendants) · Steptoe & Johnson · Union National Center East, Sixth Floor · Clarksburg, WV 26302-2190 · 304-624-8000

Menis E. Ketchum · (Plaintiffs) · Greene, Ketchum, Bailey & Tweel · 419 Eleventh Street · Huntington, WV 25701 · 304-525-9115

REAL ESTATE LAW

Charles E. Barnett · Love, Wise & Woodroe · 1200 Charleston National Plaza P.O. Box 951 · Charleston, WV 25323 · 304-343-4841

George C. Leslie · Kay, Casto & Chaney · 1600 Charleston National Plaza · P.O. Box 2031 · Charleston, WV 25327 · 304-345-8900

Harvey Alan Siler · Jackson & Kelly · 1600 Laidley Tower · P.O. Box 553 · Charleston, WV 25322 · 304-340-1000

TAX AND EMPLOYEE BENEFITS LAW

Michael D. Foster · (Employee Benefits) · Jackson & Kelly · 1600 Laidley Tower · P.O. Box 553 · Charleston, WV 25322 · 304-340-1000

John T. Kay, Jr. · Kay, Casto & Chaney · 1600 Charleston National Plaza · P.O. Box 2031 · Charleston, WV 25327 · 304-345-8900

Charles W. Loeb · Payne, Loeb & Ray · 1210 One Valley Square · Charleston, WV 25301 · 304-342-1141

Louis S. Southworth II · Jackson & Kelly · 1600 Laidley Tower · P.O. Box 553 · Charleston, WV 25322 · 304-340-1000

Charles B. Stacy · Spilman, Thomas, Battle & Kostermeyer · 1200 KB&T Center · 500 Virginia Street East · P.O. Box 273 · Charleston, WV 25321 · 304-344-4081

TRUSTS AND ESTATES

Thomas G. Freeman II · Jackson & Kelly · 1600 Laidley Tower · P.O. Box 553 · Charleston, WV 25322 · 304-340-1000

Harry P. Henshaw III · 1726 Charleston National Plaza · Charleston, WV 25301 · 304-343-5613

Milton T. Herndon · Campbell, Woods, Bagley, Emerson, McNeer & Herndon · Charleston National Plaza, Suite 1400 · P.O. Box 2393 · Charleston, WV 25328-2393 · 304-346-2391

George C. Leslie · Kay, Casto & Chaney · 1600 Charleston National Plaza · P.O. Box 2031 · Charleston, WV 25327 · 304-345-8900

Charles W. Loeb · Payne, Loeb & Ray · 1210 One Valley Square · Charleston, WV 25301 · 304-342-1141

William H. Scharf · Bowles, McDavid, Graff & Love · Commerce Square, 16th Floor · P.O. Box 1386 · Charleston, WV 25325-1386 · 304-347-1100

Charles B. Stacy · Spilman, Thomas, Battle & Klostermeyer · 1200 KB&T Center · 500 Virginia Street East · P.O. Box 273 · Charleston, WV 25321 · 304-344-4081

WISCONSIN

BANKRUPTCY LAW	763
BUSINESS LITIGATION	764
CORPORATE LAW	765
CRIMINAL DEFENSE	768
FAMILY LAW	769
LABOR AND EMPLOYMENT LAW	770
NATURAL RESOURCES AND ENVIRONMENTAL LAW	773
PERSONAL INJURY LITIGATION	774
REAL ESTATE LAW	776
TAX AND EMPLOYEE BENEFITS LAW	777
TRUSTS AND ESTATES	778

BANKRUPTCY LAW

Denis P. Bartell · Ross & Stevens · First Wisconsin Plaza, Suite 801 · One South Pinckney Street · Madison, WI 53703 · 608-257-5353

Patricia M. Gibeault · Axley Brynelson · Two East Mifflin · P.O. Box 1767 Madison, WI 53701-1767 · 608-257-5661

Roy L. Prange, Jr. · Ross & Stevens · First Wisconsin Plaza, Suite 801 · One South Pinckney Street · Madison, WI 53703 · 608-257-5353

William J. Rameker · Murphy & Desmond · Two East Mifflin Street, Suite 800 P.O. Box 2038 · Madison, WI 53701-2038 · 608-257-7181

James D. Sweet · Murphy & Desmond · Two East Mifflin Street, Suite 800 · P.O. Box 2038 · Madison, WI 53701-2038 · 608-257-7181

David G. Walsh · Foley & Lardner · First Wisconsin Plaza, Seventh Floor · One South Pinckney Street · P.O. Box 1497 · Madison, WI 53701-1497 · 608-257-5035

Andrew M. Barnes · Quarles & Brady · 411 East Wisconsin Avenue · Milwaukee, WI 53202-4497 · 414-277-5000

Robert J. Berdan · Whyte & Hirschboeck · 2100 Marine Plaza · Milwaukee, WI 53202-4894 · 414-271-8210

Peter C. Blain · Reinhart, Boerner, Van Deuren, Norris & Rieselbach · 1800 Marine Plaza · Milwaukee, WI 53202-4884 · 414-271-1190

Richard H. Casper · Foley & Lardner · First Wisconsin Center · 777 East Wisconsin Avenue · Milwaukee, WI 53202-5367 · 414-271-2400

Robert A. DuPuy · Foley & Lardner · First Wisconsin Center · 777 East Wisconsin Avenue · Milwaukee, WI 53202-5367 · 414-271-2400

David A. Erne · Reinhart, Boerner, Van Deuren, Norris & Rieselbach · 1800 Marine Plaza · Milwaukee, WI 53202-4884 · 414-271-1190

Floyd A. Harris · Polacheck and Harris · 710 North Plankinton Avenue · Milwaukee, WI 53203 · 414-276-1941

R. Arthur Ludwig · Ludwig & Shlimovitz · 1568 North Farwell Avenue · Milwaukee, WI 53202 · 414-271-4550

K. Thor Lundgren · Michael, Best & Friedrich · 250 East Wisconsin Avenue Milwaukee, WI 53202-4286 · 414-271-6560

Paul S. Medved · Michael, Best & Friedrich · 250 East Wisconsin Avenue · Milwaukee, WI 53202-4286 · 414-271-6560

Jack U. Shlimovitz · Ludwig & Shlimovitz · 1568 North Farwell Avenue · Milwaukee, WI 53202 · 414-271-4550

Albert Solochek · Howard, Peterman, Solochek, Grodin & Nashban · 324 East Wisconsin Avenue · Milwaukee, WI 53202 · 414-272-0760

BUSINESS LITIGATION

Brian E. Butler · Stafford, Rosenbaum, Rieser & Hansen · Tenney Plaza, Suite 1000 · Three South Pinckney Street · P.O. Box 1784 · Madison, WI 53701 · 608-256-0226

Daniel W. Hildebrand · Ross & Stevens · First Wisconsin Plaza, Suite 801 · One South Pinckney Street · Madison, WI 53703 · 608-257-5353

John C. Mitby · Axley Brynelson · Two East Mifflin · P.O. Box 1767 · Madison, WI 53701-1767 · 608-257-5661

John S. Skilton · Foley & Lardner · First Wisconsin Plaza, Seventh Floor · One South Pinckney Street · P.O. Box 1497 · Madison, WI 53701-1497 · 608-257-5035

Robert V. Abendroth · Whyte & Hirschboeck · 2100 Marine Plaza · Milwaukee, WI 53202-4894 · 414-271-8210

David E. Beckwith · Foley & Lardner · First Wisconsin Center · 777 East Wisconsin Avenue · Milwaukee, WI 53202-5367 · 414-271-2400

James R. Clark · Foley & Lardner · First Wisconsin Center · 777 East Wisconsin Avenue · Milwaukee, WI 53202-5367 · 414-271-2400

Robert A. DuPuy · Foley & Lardner · First Wisconsin Center · 777 East Wisconsin Avenue · Milwaukee, WI 53202-5367 · 414-271-2400

Laurence C. Hammond, Jr. · Quarles & Brady · 411 East Wisconsin Avenue · Milwaukee, WI 53202-4497 · 414-277-5000

Maurice J. McSweeney · Foley & Lardner · First Wisconsin Center · 777 East Wisconsin Avenue · Milwaukee, WI 53202-5367 · 414-271-2400

Richard C. Ninneman · Whyte & Hirschboeck · 2100 Marine Plaza · Milwaukee, WI 53202-4894 · 414-271-8210

W. Stuart Parsons · Quarles & Brady · 411 East Wisconsin Avenue · Milwaukee, WI 53202-4497 · 414-277-5000

Thomas L. Shriner, Jr. · Foley & Lardner · First Wisconsin Center · 777 East Wisconsin Avenue · Milwaukee, WI 53202-5367 · 414-271-2400

Clay R. Williams · Gibbs, Roper, Loots & Williams · 735 North Water Street · Milwaukee, WI 53202 · 414-273-7010

CORPORATE LAW

Robert H. Consigny · Consigny, Andrews, Hemming & Grant · 303 East Court Street · P.O. Box 1449 · Janesville, WI 53547 · 608-754-3322

John Bosshard · Bosshard & Associates · 505 King Street · P.O. Box 966 · La Crosse, WI 54602-0966 · 608-782-1469

Jeffrey B. Bartell · Quarles & Brady · First Wisconsin Plaza · One South Pinckney Street · P.O. Box 2113 · Madison, WI 53701-2113 · 608-251-5000

Lawrence J. Bugge · Foley & Lardner · First Wisconsin Plaza, Seventh Floor One South Pinckney Street · P.O. Box 1497 · Madison, WI 53701-1497 · 608-257-5035

Joseph P. Hildebrandt · Foley & Lardner · First Wisconsin Plaza, Seventh Floor One South Pinckney Street · P.O. Box 1497 · Madison, WI 53701-1497 · 608-257-5035

John E. Knight · Boardman, Suhr, Curry & Field · One South Pinckney Street, Suite 410 · P.O. Box 927 · Madison, WI 53701-0927 · 608-257-9521

Tod B. Linstroth · Michael, Best & Friedrich · First Wisconsin Plaza · P.O. Box 1806 · Madison, WI 53701-1806 · 608-257-3501

Thomas G. Ragatz · Foley & Lardner · First Wisconsin Plaza, Seventh Floor One South Pinckney Street · P.O. Box 1497 · Madison, WI 53701-1497 · 608-257-5035

Jeremy C. Shea · Ross & Stevens · First Wisconsin Plaza, Suite 801 · One South Pinckney Street · Madison, WI 53703 · 608-257-5353

Seward Ritchey Stroud · Stroud, Stroud, Willink, Thompson & Howard · 25 West Main Street, Suite 300 · P.O. Box 2236 · Madison, WI 53701 · 608-257-2281

David G. Walsh · Foley & Lardner · First Wisconsin Plaza, Seventh Floor · One South Pinckney Street · P.O. Box 1497 · Madison, WI 53701-1497 · 608-257-5035

Thomas D. Zilavy · Ross & Stevens · First Wisconsin Plaza, Suite 801 · One South Pinckney Street · Madison, WI 53703 · 608-257-5353

William J. Abraham, Jr. · Foley & Lardner · First Wisconsin Center · 777 East Wisconsin Avenue · Milwaukee, WI 53202-5367 · 414-271-2400

A. William Asmuth, Jr. · Whyte & Hirschboeck · 2100 Marine Plaza · Milwaukee, WI 53202-4894 · 414-271-8210

Roger L. Boerner · Reinhart, Boerner, Van Deuren, Norris & Rieselbach · 1800 Marine Plaza · Milwaukee, WI 53202-4884 · 414-271-1190

Walter S. Davis · Davis & Kuelthau · 800 First Savings Plaza · 250 East Wisconsin Avenue · Milwaukee, WI 53202-4285 · 414-276-0200

Benjamin F. Garmer III · Foley & Lardner · First Wisconsin Center · 777 East Wisconsin Avenue · Milwaukee, WI 53202-5367 · 414-271-2400

Dudley J. Godfrey, Jr. · Godfrey & Kahn · 780 North Water Street · Milwaukee, WI 53202 · 414-273-3500

Conrad G. Goodkind · Quarles & Brady · 411 East Wisconsin Avenue · Milwaukee, WI 53202-4497 · 414-277-5000

Michael W. Grebe · Foley & Lardner · First Wisconsin Center · 777 East Wisconsin Avenue · Milwaukee, WI 53202-5367 · 414-271-2400

Robert J. Kalupa · Quarles & Brady · 411 East Wisconsin Avenue · Milwaukee, WI 53202-4497 · 414-277-5000

Bernard S. Kubale · Foley & Lardner · First Wisconsin Center · 777 East Wisconsin Avenue · Milwaukee, WI 53202-5367 · 414-271-2400

Roy C. LaBudde · Michael, Best & Friedrich · 250 East Wisconsin Avenue Milwaukee, WI 53202-4286 · 414-271-6560

Arthur H. Laun · Quarles & Brady · 411 East Wisconsin Avenue · Milwaukee, WI 53202-4497 · 414-277-5000

Robert J. Loots · Gibbs, Roper, Loots & Williams · 735 North Water Street Milwaukee, WI 53202 · 414-273-7010

John K. MacIver · Michael, Best & Friedrich · 250 East Wisconsin Avenue Milwaukee, WI 53202-4286 · 414-271-6560

Larry J. Martin · Quarles & Brady · 411 East Wisconsin Avenue · Milwaukee, WI 53202-4497 · 414-277-5000

Jere D. McGaffey · Foley & Lardner · First Wisconsin Center · 777 East Wisconsin Avenue · Milwaukee, WI 53202-5367 · 414-271-2400

Charles C. Mulcahy · Mulcahy & Wherry · 815 East Mason Street, Suite 1600 Milwaukee, WI 53202-4080 · 414-278-7110

Richard H. Norris III · Reinhart, Boerner, Van Deuren, Norris & Rieselbach 1800 Marine Plaza · Milwaukee, WI 53202-4884 · 414-271-1190

Frank J. Pelisek · Michael, Best & Friedrich · 250 East Wisconsin Avenue · Milwaukee, WI 53202-4286 · 414-271-6560

Wayne J. Roper · Gibbs, Roper, Loots & Williams · 735 North Water Street · Milwaukee, WI 53202 · 414-273-7010

Patrick M. Ryan · Quarles & Brady · 411 East Wisconsin Avenue · Milwaukee, WI 53202-4497 · 414-277-5000

Allen M. Taylor · Foley & Lardner · First Wisconsin Center · 777 East Wisconsin Avenue · Milwaukee, WI 53202-5367 · 414-271-2400

James Urdan · Quarles & Brady · 411 East Wisconsin Avenue · Milwaukee, WI 53202-4497 · 414-277-5000

Richard A. Van Deuren · Reinhart, Boerner, Van Deuren, Norris & Rieselbach · 1800 Marine Plaza · Milwaukee, WI 53202-4884 · 414-271-1190

Edwin P. Wiley · Foley & Lardner · First Wisconsin Center · 777 East Wisconsin Avenue · Milwaukee, WI 53202-5367 · 414-271-2400

Elwin J. Zarwell · Quarles & Brady · 411 East Wisconsin Avenue · Milwaukee, WI 53202-4497 · 414-277-5000

G. Lane Ware · Ruder, Ware, Michler & Forester · First American Center, Suite 700 · P.O. Box 8050 · Wausau, WI 54402-8050 · 715-845-4336

CRIMINAL DEFENSE

Sarah Furey Crandall · 330 East Wilson Street · Madison, WI 53703 · 608-255-6400

Charles W. Giesen · Giesen & Berman · 306 East Wilson Street · Madison, WI 53703 · 608-255-8200

Bruce J. Rosen · Fritschler, Pellino, Rosen & Mowris · 131 West Wilson Street · Madison, WI 53703 · 608-255-4501

Thomas E. Brown · Gimbel, Reilly, Guerin & Brown · One Plaza East, Suite 930 · 330 East Kilbourne Avenue · Milwaukee, WI 53202 · 414-271-1440

David J. Cannon · Michael, Best & Friedrich · 250 East Wisconsin Avenue · Milwaukee, WI 53202-4286 · 414-271-6560

Dennis P. Coffey · Coffey, Coffey & Geraghty · 3127 West Wisconsin Avenue · Milwaukee, WI 53208 · 414-344-5700

Francis R. Croak · Cook & Franke · 660 Building, Suite 401 · 660 East Mason Street · Milwaukee, WI 53202 · 414-271-5900

Franklyn M. Gimbel · Gimbel, Reilly, Guerin & Brown · One Plaza East, Suite 930 · 330 East Kilbourne Avenue · Milwaukee, WI 53202 · 414-271-1440

Stephen M. Glynn · Shellow, Shellow & Glynn · 222 East Mason Street · Milwaukee, WI 53202 · 414-271-8535

Robert J. Lerner · Perry, Lerner & Quindel · 823 North Cass Street · Milwaukee, WI 53202 · 414-272-7400

James M. Shellow · Shellow, Shellow & Glynn · 222 East Mason Street · Milwaukee, WI 53202 · 414-271-8535

Martin I. Hanson · Hanson, Gasiorkiewicz & Becker · 514 Wisconsin Avenue · P.O. Box 1875 · Racine, WI 53401 · 414-632-5550

FAMILY LAW

Kenneth H. Conway, Jr. · Conway, Conway & Gerhardt · 121 Fifth Street · Baraboo, WI 53913 · 608-356-9441

Donald A. Levy · Levy & Levy · N61 W6058 Columbia Road · Cedarburg, WI 53012 · 414-377-5555

J. Michael Jerry · Liebmann, Conway, Olejniczak & Jerry · 231 South Adams Street · P.O. Box 1241 · Green Bay, WI 54305 · 414-437-0476

Thomas W. Anderson · Anderson-Sumpter Law Offices · 5401 Sixtieth Street · Kenosha, WI 53142 · 414-654-0999

Steven A. Bach · Cullen, Weston, Pines & Bach · 20 North Carroll Street · Madison, WI 53703 · 608-251-0101

Allan R. Koritzinsky · Stolper, Koritzinsky, Brewster & Neider · 7617 Mineral Point Road · P.O. Box 5510 · Madison, WI 53703-0510 · 608-833-7617

Scott M. Cassidy · Margolis & Cassidy · 324 East Wisconsin Avenue · Milwaukee, WI 53202 · 414-272-5333

Robert E. Cook · Cook & Franke · 660 Building, Suite 401 · 660 East Mason Street · Milwaukee, WI 53202 · 414-271-5900

Leonard L. Loeb · Marine Plaza, Suite 1125 · 111 East Wisconsin Avenue · Milwaukee, WI 53202 · 414-272-5632

Marvin A. Margolis · Margolis & Cassidy · 324 East Wisconsin Avenue · Milwaukee, WI 53202 · 414-272-5333

Clifford K. Meldman · Meldman & Meldman · 5150 North Port Washington Road P.O. Box 17397 · Milwaukee, WI 53217 · 414-962-6299

Bruce M. Peckerman · Meldman & Meldman · 5150 North Port Washington Road · P.O. Box 17397 · Milwaukee, WI 53217 · 414-962-6299

James J. Podell · Podell & Podell · Security Savings Building, Suite 207 · 5555 North Port Washington Road · Milwaukee, WI 53217 · 414-961-0323

David L. Walther · Walther & Calvey · 602 East St. Paul Avenue · Milwaukee, WI 53202 · 414-273-4400

Gary L. Bakke · Bakke, Norman & Schumacher · 1200 Heritage Drive · P.O. Box 50 · New Richmond, WI 54017 · 715-246-3800

Gerald M. Crawford · Stewart, Peyton, Crawford, Crawford & Stutt · 840 Lake Avenue · Racine, WI 53403 · 414-634-6659

Herbert C. Humke · Hayes, Neumann, Humke, Moir & Van Akkeren · 607 Plaza 8, Suite 350 · Sheboygan, WI 53081 · 414-458-4654

Charles I. Phillips · Phillips & Davis · 358 West Main Street · Waukesha, WI 53186-4611 · 414-544-9998

William F. Alderson, Jr. · Schloemer, Schlaefer, Alderson, Seefeldt & Spella Sixth & Hickory Streets · P.O. Box 176 · West Bend, WI 53095 · 414-334-3471

LABOR AND EMPLOYMENT LAW

Dennis W. Rader · (Management) · Mulcahy & Wherry · 414 East Walnut Street P.O. Box 1103 · Green Bay, WI 54305-1103 · 414-435-4471

Michael H. Auen · (Management) · Foley & Lardner · First Wisconsin Plaza, Seventh Floor · One South Pinckney Street · P.O. Box 1497 · Madison, WI 53701-1497 · 608-257-5035

Charles Barnhill, Jr. · (Individuals) · Davis, Barnhill & Galland · Three South Pinckney Street, Suite 804 · Madison, WI 53703 · 608-255-5200

Lee Cullen · (Labor) · Cullen Weston Pines & Bach · 20 North Carroll Street Madison, WI 53703 · 608-251-0101

Bruce M. Davey · (Labor) · Lawton & Cates · 214 West Mifflin Street · Madison, WI 53703-2594 · 608-256-9031

Michael R. Fox · (Individuals) · Fox, Fox, Schaefer & Gingras · 44 East Mifflin Street · Madison, WI 53703 · 608-258-9588

Robert J. Gingras · (Individuals) · Fox, Fox, Schaefer & Gingras · 44 East Mifflin Street · Madison, WI 53703 · 608-258-9588

Robert C. Kelly · (Labor) · Kelly & Haus · 121 East Wilson Street · Madison, WI 53703 · 608-257-0420

Joseph A. Melli · (Management) · Melli, Walker, Pease & Ruhly · Insurance Building, Suite 600 · 119 Monona Avenue · P.O. Box 1664 · Madison, WI 53701 608-257-4812

Jeff Scott Olson · (Individuals) · Julian, Olson & Lasker · 330 East Wilson Street Madison, WI 53703 · 608-255-6400

James K. Pease, Jr. · (Management) · Melli, Walker, Pease & Ruhly · Insurance Building, Suite 600 · 119 Monona Avenue · P.O. Box 1664 · Madison, WI 53701 608-257-4812

James K. Ruhly · (Management) · Melli, Walker, Pease & Ruhly · Insurance Building, Suite 600 · 119 Monona Avenue · P.O. Box 1664 · Madison, WI 53701 608-257-4812

Jack D. Walker · (Management) · Melli, Walker, Pease & Ruhly · Insurance Building, Suite 600 · 119 Monona Avenue · P.O. Box 1664 · Madison, WI 53701 608-257-4812

Marshall R. Berkoff · (Management) · Michael, Best & Friedrich · 250 East Wisconsin Avenue · Milwaukee, WI 53202-4286 · 414-271-6560

Jacob L. Bernheim · (Management) · Michael, Best & Friedrich · 250 East Wisconsin Avenue · Milwaukee, WI 53202-4286 · 414-271-6560

John W. Brahm · (Management) · Foley & Lardner · First Wisconsin Center · 777 East Wisconsin Avenue · Milwaukee, WI 53202-5367 · 414-271-2400

Walter S. Davis · (Management) · Davis & Kuelthau · 800 First Savings Plaza 250 East Wisconsin Avenue · Milwaukee, WI 53202-4285 · 414-276-0200

Laurence E. Gooding, Jr. · (Management) · Quarles & Brady · 411 East Wisconsin Avenue · Milwaukee, WI 53202-4497 · 414-277-5000

George F. Graf · (Labor) · Zubrensky, Padden, Graf & Maloney · 828 North Broadway, Suite 410 · Milwaukee, WI 53202 · 414-276-4557

Timothy E. Hawks · (Labor) · Shneidman, Myers, Dowling & Blumenfeld · 700 West Michigan Avenue, Suite 500 · Milwaukee, WI 53233 · 414-271-8650

Walter F. Kelly · (Individuals) · Sutton & Kelly · 1409 East Capitol Drive · Milwaukee, WI 53211 · 414-961-0802

Kenneth R. Loebel · (Labor) · Habush, Habush & Davis · First Wisconsin Center, Suite 2200 · 777 East Wisconsin Avenue · Milwaukee, WI 53202 · 414-271-0900

James C. Mallatt · (Management) · Michael, Best & Friedrich · 250 East Wisconsin Avenue · Milwaukee, WI 53202-4286 · 414-271-6560

Gerry M. Miller · (Labor) · Previant, Goldberg, Uelmen, Gratz, Miller & Brueggeman · Office on the Square, Sixth Floor · 788 North Jefferson Street P.O. Box 92099 · Milwaukee, WI 53202 · 414-271-4500

Robert W. Mulcahy · (Management) · Mulcahy & Wherry · 815 East Mason Street, Suite 1600 · Milwaukee, WI 53202-4080 · 414-278-7110

Howard N. Myers · (Labor) · Shneidman, Myers, Dowling & Blumenfeld · 700 West Michigan Avenue, Suite 500 · Milwaukee, WI 53233 · 414-271-8650

Thomas E. Obenberger · (Management) · Michael, Best & Friedrich · 250 East Wisconsin Avenue · Milwaukee, WI 53202-4286 · 414-271-6560

David Previant · (Labor) · Previant, Goldberg, Uelmen, Gratz, Miller & Brueggeman · Office on the Square, Sixth Floor · 788 North Jefferson Street · P.O. Box 92099 · Milwaukee, WI 53202 · 414-271-4500

Barbara Zack Quindel · (Labor; Individuals) · Perry, Lerner & Quindel · 823 North Cass Street · Milwaukee, WI 53202 · 414-272-7400

John R. Sapp · (Management) · Michael, Best & Friedrich · 250 East Wisconsin Avenue · Milwaukee, WI 53202-4286 · 414-271-6560

Daniel L. Shneidman · (Labor) · Shneidman, Myers, Dowling & Blumenfield · 700 West Michigan Avenue, Suite 500 · Milwaukee, WI 53233 · 414-271-8650

Thomas W. Scrivner · (Management) · Michael, Best & Friedrich · 250 East Wisconsin Avenue · Milwaukee, WI 53202-4286 · 414-271-6560

David L. Uelmen · (Labor) · Previant, Goldberg, Uelmen, Gratz, Miller & Brueggeman · Office on the Square, Sixth Floor · 788 North Jefferson Street · P.O. Box 92099 · Milwaukee, WI 53202 · 414-271-4500

Roger E. Walsh · (Management) · Lindner & Marsack · 700 North Water Street, Eighth Floor · Milwaukee, WI 53202 · 414-273-3910

George K. Whyte, Jr. · (Management) · Quarles & Brady · 411 East Wisconsin Avenue · Milwaukee, WI 53202-4497 · 414-277-5000

Herbert P. Wiedemann · (Management) · Foley & Lardner · First Wisconsin Center · 777 East Wisconsin Avenue · Milwaukee, WI 53202-5367 · 414-271-2400

NATURAL RESOURCES AND ENVIRONMENTAL LAW

Henry J. Handzel, Jr. · Dewitt, Porter, Huggett, Schumacher & Morgan · Two East Mifflin Street, Suite 600 · Madison, WI 53703 · 608-255-8891

Richard S. Heymann · Foley & Lardner · First Wisconsin Plaza, Seventh Floor · One South Pinckney Street · P.O. Box 1497 · Madison, WI 53701-1497 · 608-257-5035

Richard J. Lewandowski · Dewitt, Porter, Huggett, Schumacher & Morgan · Two East Mifflin Street, Suite 600 · Madison, WI 53703 · 608-255-8891

Arthur J. Harrington · Godfrey & Kahn · 780 North Water Street · Milwaukee, WI 53202 · 414-273-3500

John L. Horwich · Reinhart, Boerner, Van Deuren, Norris & Rieselbach · 1800 Marine Plaza · Milwaukee, WI 53202-4884 · 414-271-1190

Charles Q. Kamps · Quarles & Brady · 411 East Wisconsin Avenue · Milwaukee, WI 53202-4497 · 414-277-5000

Raymond R. Krueger · Charne, Glassner, Tehan, Clancy & Taitelman · First Bank Building, Suite 800 · 211 West Wisconsin Avenue · Milwaukee, WI 53203-2377 · 414-273-2000

Mark A. Thimke · Foley & Lardner · First Wisconsin Center · 777 East Wisconsin Avenue · Milwaukee, WI 53202-5367 · 414-271-2400

Allen W. Williams, Jr. · Foley & Lardner · First Wisconsin Center · 777 East Wisconsin Avenue · Milwaukee, WI 53202-5367 · 414-271-2400

PERSONAL INJURY LITIGATION

James E. Garvey · (Defendants) · Garvey, Anderson, Kelly & Ryberg · 402 Graham Avenue · P.O. Box 187 · Eau Claire, WI 54702-0187 · 715-834-3425

Richard L. Cates · (Plaintiffs) · Lawton & Cates · 214 West Mifflin Street · Madison, WI 53703-2594 · 608-256-9031

Steven J. Caulum · (Defendants) · Bell, Metzner & Gierhart · 222 West Washington Avenue · P.O. Box 1807 · Madison, WI 53701 · 608-257-3764

Henry A. Field, Jr. · (Defendants) · Boardman, Suhr, Curry & Field · One South Pinckney Street, Suite 410 · P.O. Box 927 · Madison, WI 53701-0927 · 608-257-9521

Richard A. Hollern · (Defendants) · Stafford, Rosenbaum, Rieser & Hansen · Tenney Plaza, Suite 1000 · Three South Pinckney Street · P.O. Box 1784 · Madison, WI 53701 · 608-256-0226

Curtis M. Kirkhuff · (Plaintiffs) · Habush, Habush & Davis · 217 South Hamilton Street, Suite 500 · Madison, WI 53703 · 608-255-6663

William L. McCusker · (Plaintiffs) · McCusker and Robertson · Anchor Building, Suite 731 · 25 West Main Street · P.O. Box 1483 · Madison, WI 53703 · 608-256-1841

Carroll E. Metzner · (Defendants) · Bell, Metzner & Gierhart · 222 West Washington Avenue · P.O. Box 1807 · Madison, WI 53701 · 608-257-3764

John M. Moore · (Defendants) · Bell, Metzner & Gierhart · 222 West Washington Avenue · P.O. Box 1807 · Madison, WI 53701 · 608-257-3764

Gerald J. Bloch · (Plaintiffs) · Warshafsky, Rotter, Tarnoff, Gesler, Reinhardt & Bloch · 839 North Jefferson Street · Milwaukee, WI 53202 · 414-276-4970

Robert E. Cook · (Defendants) · Cook & Franke · 660 Building, Suite 401 · 660 East Mason Street · Milwaukee, WI 53202 · 414-271-5900

Kirk H. Frauen · (Defendants) · Borgelt, Powell, Peterson & Frauen · 735 North Water Street, 15th Floor · Milwaukee, WI 53202 · 414-276-3600

Alan E. Gesler · (Plaintiffs) · Warshafsky, Rotter, Tarnoff, Gesler, Reinhardt & Bloch · 839 North Jefferson Street · Milwaukee, WI 53202 · 414-276-4970

Robert L. Habush · (Plaintiffs) · Habush, Habush & Davis · First Wisconsin Center, Suite 2200 · 777 East Wisconsin Avenue · Milwaukee, WI 53202 · 414-271-0900

James J. Murphy · (Plaintiffs) · Gillick, Murphy, Gillick & Wicht · 330 East Kilbourne Avenue, Suite 1200 · Milwaukee, WI 53202 · 414-271-1011

James T. Murray · (Defendants) · Arnold, Murray, O'Neill & Schimmel · 312 East Wisconsin Avenue · Milwaukee, WI 53202 · 414-271-3282

James Peter O'Neill · (Defendants) · Arnold, Murray, O'Neill & Schimmel · 312 East Wisconsin Avenue · Milwaukee, WI 53202 · 414-271-3282

Donald R. Peterson · (Defendants) · Peterson, Johnson & Murray · 733 North Van Buren Street · Milwaukee, WI 53202 · 414-278-8800

John M. Swietlik · (Defendants) · Kasdorf, Lewis & Swietlik · 1551 South 108th Street · Milwaukee, WI 53214 · 414-257-1055

Ted M. Warshafsky · (Plaintiffs) · Warshafsky, Rotter, Tarnoff, Gesler, Reinhardt & Bloch · 839 North Jefferson Street · Milwaukee, WI 53202 · 414-276-4970

Einer Christensen · (Defendants) · Constantine, Christensen, Krohn & Kerscher · 723 Main Street · Racine, WI 53403 · 414-631-6140

Adrian P. Schoone · Schoone, Hankel, Ware & Fortune · Racine Professional Center · 1300 South Green Bay Road · P.O. Box 97 · Racine, WI 53406-0097 · 414-637-6791

REAL ESTATE LAW

John D. Kaiser · 1109 West MacArthur Avenue · P.O. Box 1028 · Eau Claire, WI 54702 · 715-832-1320

Lowell E. Sweet · Sweet & Leece · Inns of Court Building · 114 North Church Street · Elkhorn, WI 53121 · 414-723-5480

James J. Vance · Vance, Wilcox, Short & Ristow · 79 North Main Street · Fort Atkinson, WI 53538-1897 · 414-563-9523

Benjamin J. Abrohams · Foley & Lardner · First Wisconsin Center · 777 East Wisconsin Avenue · Milwaukee, WI 53202-5367 · 414-271-2400

Robert Bradley · Foley & Lardner · First Wisconsin Center · 777 East Wisconsin Avenue · Milwaukee, WI 53202-5367 · 414-271-2400

Gerald E. Connolly · Minahan & Peterson · 411 East Wisconsin Avenue, Suite 2200 · Milwaukee, WI 53202-4499 · 414-276-1400

Michael Hatch · Foley & Lardner · First Wisconsin Center · 777 East Wisconsin Avenue · Milwaukee, WI 53202-5367 · 414-271-2400

John L. Horwich · Reinhart, Boerner, Van Deuren, Norris & Rieselbach · 1800 Marine Plaza · Milwaukee, WI 53202-4884 · 414-271-1190

Lawrence J. Jost · Quarles & Brady · 411 East Wisconsin Avenue · Milwaukee, WI 53202-4497 · 414-277-5000

David S. Lott · Foley & Lardner · First Wisconsin Center · 777 East Wisconsin Avenue · Milwaukee, WI 53202-5367 · 414-271-2400

David L. Petersen · Quarles & Brady · 411 East Wisconsin Avenue · Milwaukee, WI 53202-4497 · 414-277-5000

Lyman A. Precourt · Foley & Lardner · First Wisconsin Center · 777 East Wisconsin Avenue · Milwaukee, WI 53202-5367 · 414-271-2400

Allen N. Rieselbach · Reinhart, Boerner, Van Deuren, Norris & Rieselbach · 1800 Marine Plaza · Milwaukee, WI 53202-4884 · 414-271-1190

TAX AND EMPLOYEE BENEFITS LAW

Thomas A. Hoffner · (Employee Benefits) · LaFollette & Sinykin · One East Main Street, Suite 500 · P.O. Box 2719 · Madison, WI 53701 · 608-257-3911

George R. Kamperschroer · (Employee Benefits) · Boardman, Suhr, Curry & Field · One South Pinckney Street, Suite 410 · P.O. Box 927 · Madison, WI 53701-0927 · 608-257-9521

Richard W. Pitzner · Murphy & Desmond · Two East Mifflin Street, Suite 800 P.O. Box 2038 · Madison, WI 53701-2038 · 608-257-7181

Thomas G. Ragatz · Foley & Lardner · First Wisconsin Plaza, Seventh Floor One South Pinckney Street · P.O. Box 1497 · Madison, WI 53701-1497 · 608-257-5035

John Rashke · (Employee Benefits) · Ross & Stevens · 402 Gammon Place, Suite 230 · Madison, WI 53719 · 608-833-2100

Leonard S. Sosnowski · Foley & Lardner · First Wisconsin Plaza · One South Pinckney Street · P.O. Box 1497 · Madison, WI 53701-1497 · 608-257-5035

Warren H. Stolper · Stolper, Koritzinsky, Brewster & Neider · 7617 Mineral Point Road · P.O. Box 5510 · Madison, WI 53705-0510 · 608-833-7617

Seward Ritchey Stroud · Stroud, Stroud, Willink, Thompson & Howard · 25 West Main Street, Suite 300 · P.O. Box 2236 · Madison, WI 53701 · 608-257-2281

Lloyd J. Dickinson · (Employee Benefits) · Reinhart, Boerner, Van Deuren, Norris & Rieselbach · 1800 Marine Plaza · Milwaukee, WI 53202-4884 · 414-271-1190

Thomas J. Donnelly · Quarles & Brady · 411 East Wisconsin Avenue · Milwaukee, WI 53202-4497 · 414-277-5000

Timothy C. Frautschi · Foley & Lardner · First Wisconsin Center · 777 East Wisconsin Avenue · Milwaukee, WI 53202-5367 · 414-271-2400

Richard S. Gallagher · Foley & Lardner · First Wisconsin Center · 777 East Wisconsin Avenue · Milwaukee, WI 53202-5367 · 414-271-2400

Dudley J. Godfrey, Jr. · Godfrey & Kahn · 780 North Water Street · Milwaukee, WI 53202 · 414-273-3500

John A. Hazelwood · Quarles & Brady · 411 East Wisconsin Avenue · Milwaukee, WI 53202-4497 · 414-277-5000

Kenneth C. Hunt · Godfrey & Kahn · 780 North Water Street · Milwaukee, WI 53202 · 414-273-3500

Gerald J. Kahn · Godfrey & Kahn · 780 North Water Street · Milwaukee, WI 53202 · 414-273-3500

Linda M. Laarman · (Employee Benefits) · Foley & Lardner · First Wisconsin Center · 777 East Wisconsin Avenue · Milwaukee, WI 53202-5367 · 414-271-2400

Jere D. McGaffey · Foley & Lardner · First Wisconsin Center · 777 East Wisconsin Avenue · Milwaukee, WI 53202-5367 · 414-271-2400

Robert E. Meldman · Mulcahy & Wherry · 815 East Mason Street, Suite 1600 Milwaukee, WI 53202-4080 · 414-278-7110

Greg W. Renz · (Employee Benefits) · Foley & Lardner · First Wisconsin Center 777 East Wisconsin Avenue · Milwaukee, WI 53202-5367 · 414-271-2400

Robert A. Schnur · Michael, Best & Friedrich · 250 East Wisconsin Avenue Milwaukee, WI 53202-4286 · 414-271-6560

Dale L. Sorden · Quarles & Brady · 411 East Wisconsin Avenue · Milwaukee, WI 53202-4497 · 414-277-5000

Robert M. Weiss · Weiss, Berzowski, Brady & Donahue · 700 North Water Street Milwaukee, WI 53202 · 414-276-5800

Richard C. Brodek · DeMark, Kolbe & Brodek · 6216 Washington Avenue Racine, WI 53406 · 414-886-9720

William F. Kolbe · DeMark, Kolbe & Brodek · 6216 Washington Avenue Racine, WI 53406 · 414-886-9720

TRUSTS AND ESTATES

J. Joseph Cummings · Bachman, Cummings & McIntyre · 211 East Franklin Street · P.O. Box 1155 · Appleton, WI 54912-1155 · 414-739-6356

Stephen R. Schrage · Hibbard, Schrage & Marjala · 204 East Grand Avenue · Eau Claire, WI 54701 · 715-832-3494

Robert H. Consigny · Consigny, Andrews, Hemming & Grant · 303 East Court Street · P.O. Box 1449 · Janesville, WI 53547 · 608-754-3322

James R. Cripe · Nowlan & Mouat · 100 South Main Street · P.O. Box 546 Janesville, WI 53547 · 608-755-4747

C. Vernon Howard · Stroud, Stroud, Willink, Thompson & Howard · 25 West Main Street, Suite 300 · P.O. Box 2236 · Madison, WI 53701 · 608-257-2281

Richard Z. Kabaker · Murphy & Desmond · Two East Mifflin Street, Suite 800 P.O. Box 2038 · Madison, WI 53701-2038 · 608-257-7181

Warren H. Stolper · Stolper, Koritzinsky, Brewster & Neider · 7617 Mineral Point Road · P.O. Box 5510 · Madison, WI 53705-0510 · 608-833-7617

Seward Ritchey Stroud · Stroud, Stroud, Willink, Thompson & Howard · 25 West Main Street, Suite 300 · P.O. Box 2236 · Madison, WI 53701 · 608-257-2281

Michael W. Wilcox · Quarles & Brady · First Wisconsin Plaza · One South Pinckney Street · P.O. Box 2113 · Madison, WI 53701-2113 · 608-251-5000

Robert J. Bonner · Foley & Lardner · First Wisconsin Center · 777 East Wisconsin Avenue · Milwaukee, WI 53202-5367 · 414-271-2400

Jackson M. Bruce, Jr. · Quarles & Brady · 411 East Wisconsin Avenue · Milwaukee, WI 53202-4497 · 414-277-5000

Keith A. Christiansen · Foley & Lardner · First Wisconsin Center · 777 East Wisconsin Avenue · Milwaukee, WI 53202-5367 · 414-271-2400

Thomas J. Drought · Cook & Franke · 660 Building, Suite 401 · 660 East Mason Street · Milwaukee, WI 53202 · 414-271-5900

Henry E. Fuldner · Godfrey & Kahn · 780 North Water Street · Milwaukee, WI 53202 · 414-273-3500

F. William Haberman · Michael, Best & Friedrich · 250 East Wisconsin Avenue · Milwaukee, WI 53202-4286 · 414-271-6560

John B. Haydon · Whyte & Hirschboeck · 2100 Marine Plaza · Milwaukee, WI 53202-4894 · 414-271-8210

David L. Kinnamon · Quarles & Brady · 411 East Wisconsin Avenue · Milwaukee, WI 53202-4497 · 414-277-5000

Roy C. LaBudde · Michael, Best & Friedrich · 250 East Wisconsin Avenue · Milwaukee, WI 53202-4286 · 414-271-6560

Robert J. Loots · Gibbs, Roper, Loots & Williams · 735 North Water Street · Milwaukee, WI 53202 · 414-273-7010

Arthur F. Lubke, Jr. · Reinhart, Boerner, Van Deuren, Norris & Rieselbach · 1800 Marine Plaza · Milwaukee, WI 53202-4884 · 414-271-1190

David L. MacGregor · Quarles & Brady · 411 East Wisconsin Avenue · Milwaukee, WI 53202-4497 · 414-277-5000

Harrold J. McComas · Foley & Lardner · First Wisconsin Center · 777 East Wisconsin Avenue · Milwaukee, WI 53202-5367 · 414-271-2400

Jere D. McGaffey · Foley & Lardner · First Wisconsin Center · 777 East Wisconsin Avenue · Milwaukee, WI 53202-5367 · 414-271-2400

Edwin Fitch Walmer · Foley & Lardner · First Wisconsin Center · 777 East Wisconsin Avenue · Milwaukee, WI 53202-5367 · 414-271-2400

Timothy M. Dempsey · Dempsey, Magnusen, Williamson & Lampe · First Wisconsin National Bank Building · P.O. Box 886 · Oshkosh, WI 54902 · 414-235-7300

Charles M. Constantine · Constantine, Christensen, Krohn & Kerscher · 723 Main Street · Racine, WI 53403 · 414-631-6140

Mark J. Bradley · Tuchscherer & Bradley · McClellan Place · P.O. Box 1185 · Wausau, WI 54402-1185 · 715-842-0907

C. Duane Patterson · Tinkham, Smith, Bliss, Patterson, Richards & Hessert · 630 Fourth Street · Wausau, WI 54402-1144 · 715-845-1151

WYOMING

BANKRUPTCY LAW	781
BUSINESS LITIGATION	781
CORPORATE LAW	782
CRIMINAL DEFENSE	783
LABOR AND EMPLOYMENT LAW	783
NATURAL RESOURCES AND ENVIRONMENTAL LAW	784
PERSONAL INJURY LITIGATION	784
REAL ESTATE LAW	785
TAX AND EMPLOYEE BENEFITS LAW	786
TRUSTS AND ESTATES	786

BANKRUPTCY LAW

Donn J. McCall · Brown & Drew · 111 West Second Street, Suite 500 · Casper, WY 82601 · 307-265-9210

Barry G. Williams · Williams, Porter, Day & Neville · Durbin Center, Suite 300 · 145 South Durbin Street · Casper, WY 82601 · 307-265-0700

Georg Jensen · 1613 Evans Avenue · Cheyenne, WY 82001 · 307-634-0991

BUSINESS LITIGATION

William S. Bon · Schwartz, Bon, McCrary & Walker · Consolidated Royalty Building, Suite 505 · Casper, WY 82601 · 307-235-6681

Richard E. Day · Williams, Porter, Day & Neville · Durbin Center, Suite 300 · 145 South Durbin Street · Casper, WY 82601 · 307-265-0700

William T. Schwartz · Schwartz, Bon, McCrary & Walker · Consolidated Royalty Building, Suite 505 · Casper, WY 82601 · 307-235-6681

James L. Applegate · Hirst & Applegate · 200 Boyd Building · P.O. Box 1083 Cheyenne, WY 82003-1083 · 307-632-0541

James E. Fitzgerald · 2108 Warren Avenue · Cheyenne, WY 82001 · 307-635-1108

Paul B. Godfrey · Godfrey, Sundahl & Jorgenson · 403 Rocky Mountain Plaza, Suite 403 · P.O. Box 328 · Cheyenne, WY 82001 · 307-632-6421

Marilyn S. Kite · Holland & Hart · 2020 Carey Avenue, Suite 500 · Cheyenne, WY 82001 · 307-632-2160

Carl L. Lathrop · Lathrop & Uchner · City Center Building, Suite 500 · 1920 Thomes Avenue · P.O. Box 4068 · Cheyenne, WY 82003-4068 · 307-632-0554

Edward P. Moriarity · Spence, Moriarity & Schuster · 265 West Pearl Street P.O. Box 548 · Jackson, WY 83001 · 307-733-7290

Gerald L. Spence · Spence, Moriarity & Schuster · 265 West Pearl Street · P.O. Box 548 · Jackson, WY 83001 · 307-733-7290

James L. Hettinger · Hettinger, Leedy & Vincent · Masonic Temple Building, Suite 214 · Riverton, WY 82501-4380 · 307-856-2239

Richard I. Leedy · Hettinger, Leedy & Vincent · Masonic Temple Building, Suite 214 · Riverton, WY 82501-4380 · 307-856-2239

Henry A. Burgess · Burgess & Davis · 40 South Main Street · P.O. Box 728 Sheridan, WY 82801 · 307-672-7491

CORPORATE LAW

William J. Kirven · Kirven & Kirven · 104 Fort Street · P.O. Box 640 · Buffalo, WY 82834 · 307-684-2248

Morris R. Massey · Brown & Drew · 111 West Second Street, Suite 500 · Casper, WY 82601 · 307-265-9210

William T. Schwartz · Schwartz, Bon, McCrary & Walker · Consolidated Royalty Building, Suite 505 · Casper, WY 82601 · 307-235-6681

Houston G. Williams · Williams, Porter, Day & Neville · Durbin Center, Suite 300 · 145 South Durbin Street · Casper, WY 82601 · 307-265-0700

Paul B. Godfrey · Godfrey, Sundahl & Jorgenson · 403 Rocky Mountain Plaza, Suite 403 · P.O. Box 328 · Cheyenne, WY 82001 · 307-632-6421

Carl L. Lathrop · Lathrop & Uchner · City Center Building, Suite 500 · 1920 Thomes Avenue · P.O. Box 4068 · Cheyenne, WY 82003-4068 · 307-632-0554

James L. Hettinger · Hettinger, Leedy & Vincent · Masonic Temple Building, Suite 214 · Riverton, WY 82501-4380 · 307-856-2239

Richard I. Leedy · Hettinger, Leedy & Vincent · Masonic Temple Building, Suite 214 · Riverton, WY 82501-4380 · 307-856-2239

Richard M. Davis, Jr. · Burgess & Davis · 40 South Main · P.O. Box 728 Sheridan, WY 82801 · 307-672-7491

CRIMINAL DEFENSE

James E. Fitzgerald · 2108 Warren Avenue · Cheyenne, WY 82001 · 307-635-1108

Terry W. Mackey · Rocky Mountain Plaza, Suite 709 · 2020 Carey Avenue, #111 Cheyenne, WY 82001 · 307-637-7841

Richard C. Wolf · Equality State Bank Building, Suite 300 · P.O. Box 491 Cheyenne, WY 82001 · 307-635-2876

Edward P. Moriarity · Spence, Moriarity & Schuster · 265 West Pearl Street P.O. Box 548 · Jackson, WY 83001 · 307-733-7290

Gerald L. Spence · Spence, Moriarity & Schuster · 265 West Pearl Street · P.O. Box 548 · Jackson, WY 83001 · 307-733-7290

LABOR AND EMPLOYMENT LAW

George M. Apostolos · Brown & Drew · 111 West Second Street, Suite 500 · Casper, WY 82601 · 307-265-9210

NATURAL RESOURCES AND ENVIRONMENTAL LAW

Morris R. Massey · Brown & Drew · 111 West Second Street, Suite 500 · Casper, WY 82601 · 307-265-9210

William T. Schwartz · Schwartz, Bon, McCrary & Walker · Consolidated Royalty Building, Suite 505 · Casper, WY 82601 · 307-235-6681

Houston G. Williams · Williams, Porter, Day & Neville · Durbin Center, Suite 300 · 145 South Durbin Street · Casper, WY 82601 · 307-265-0700

Charles G. Kepler · Simpson & Kepler · 1239 Rumsey Avenue, Suite 100 · P.O. Box 490 · Cody, WY 82414 · 307-587-4261

Paul B. Godfrey · Godfrey, Sundahl & Jorgenson · 403 Rocky Mountain Plaza, Suite 403 · P.O. Box 328 · Cheyenne, WY 82001 · 307-632-6421

Marilyn S. Kite · Holland & Hart · 2020 Carey Avenue, Suite 500 · Cheyenne, WY 82001 · 307-632-2160

Harry L. Harris · Harris and Harris · 927 Main Street · P.O. Box 130 · Evanston, WY 82930 · 307-789-3210

Henry A. Burgess · Burgess & Davis · 40 South Main Street · P.O. Box 728 · Sheridan, WY 82801 · 307-672-7491

Richard M. Davis, Jr. · Burgess & Davis · 40 South Main · P.O. Box 728 · Sheridan, WY 82801 · 307-672-7491

PERSONAL INJURY LITIGATION

William S. Bon · (Defendants) · Schwartz, Bon, McCrary & Walker · Consolidated Royalty Building, Suite 505 · 141 South Center Street · Casper, WY 82601 307-235-6681

Richard R. Bostwick · (Defendants) · Murane & Bostwick · 350 West A Street, Suite 100 · Casper, WY 82601 · 307-234-9345

Richard E. Day · (Defendants) · Williams, Porter, Day & Neville · Durbin Center, Suite 300 · 145 South Durbin Street · Casper, WY 82601 · 307-265-0700

J. E. Vlastos · (Defendants) · Vlastos, Brooks & Henley · First Wyoming Bank Building, Suite 320 · 300 South Wolcott Street · P.O. Box 10 · Casper, WY 82602 307-235-6613

James L. Applegate · (Defendants) · Hirst & Applegate · 200 Boyd Building · P.O. Box 1083 · Cheyenne, WY 82003-1083 · 307-632-0541

James E. Fitzgerald · (Plaintiffs) · 2108 Warren Avenue · Cheyenne, WY 82001 · 307-635-1108

Paul B. Godfrey · (Defendants) · Godfrey, Sundahl & Jorgenson · Rocky Mountain Plaza, Suite 403 · 2020 Carey Avenue · P.O. Box 328 · Cheyenne, WY 82001 · 307-632-6421

Carl L. Lathrop · (Defendants) · Lathrop & Uchner · City Center Building, Suite 500 · 1920 Thomes Avenue · P.O. Box 4068 · Cheyenne, WY 82003-4068 · 307-632-0554

Terry W. Mackey · (Plaintiffs) · Rocky Mountain Plaza, Suite 709 · 2020 Carey Avenue, #111 · Cheyenne, WY 82001 · 307-637-7841

Edward P. Moriarity · (Plaintiffs) · Spence, Moriarity & Schuster · 265 West Pearl Street · P.O. Box 548 · Jackson, WY 83001 · 307-733-7290

Gerald L. Spence · (Plaintiffs) · Spence, Moriarity & Schuster · 265 West Pearl Street · P.O. Box 548 · Jackson, WY 83001 · 307-733-7290

James L. Hettinger · Hettinger, Leedy & Vincent · Masonic Temple Building, Suite 214 · Riverton, WY 82501-4380 · 307-856-2239

John R. Hursh · (Plaintiffs) · Hursh, Miller & Fasse · 105-107 South Sixth Street East · P.O. Box 1783 · Riverton, WY 82501 · 307-856-4157

Richard I. Leedy · (Defendants) · Hettinger, Leedy & Vincent · Masonic Temple Building, Suite 214 · Riverton, WY 82501-4380 · 307-856-2239

Henry A. Burgess · (Defendants) · Burgess & Davis · 40 South Main Street · P.O. Box 728 · Sheridan, WY 82801 · 307-672-7491

REAL ESTATE LAW

William J. Kirven · Kirven & Kirven · 104 Fort Street · P.O. Box 640 · Buffalo, WY 82834 · 307-684-2248

Morris R. Massey · Brown & Drew · 111 West Second Street, Suite 500 · Casper, WY 82601 · 307-265-9210

William T. Schwartz · Schwartz, Bon, McCrary & Walker · Consolidated Royalty Building, Suite 505 · Casper, WY 82601 · 307-235-6681

Houston G. Williams · Williams, Porter, Day & Neville · Durbin Center, Suite 300 · 145 South Durbin Street · Casper, WY 82601 · 307-265-0700

Larry L. Jorgensen · Godfrey, Sundahl & Jorgenson · 403 Rocky Mountain Plaza, Suite 403 · P.O. Box 328 · Cheyenne, WY 82001 · 307-632-6421

Carl L. Lathrop · Lathrop & Uchner · City Center Building, Suite 500 · 1920 Thomes Avenue · P.O. Box 4068 · Cheyenne, WY 82003-4068 · 307-632-0554

Harry L. Harris · Harris and Harris · 927 Main Street · P.O. Box 130 · Evanston, WY 82930 · 307-789-3210

Thomas E. Lubnau · Lubnau Law Offices · 408 South Gillette Avenue · P.O. Box 1028 · Gillette, WY 82716 · 307-682-1313

Richard M. Davis, Jr. · Burgess & Davis · 40 South Main · P.O. Box 728 · Sheridan, WY 82801 · 307-672-7491

TAX AND EMPLOYEE BENEFITS LAW

Thomas N. Long · Hirst & Applegate · 200 Boyd Building · P.O. Box 1083 · Cheyenne, WY 82003-1083 · 307-632-0541

TRUSTS AND ESTATES

William J. Kirven · Kirven & Kirven · 104 Fort Street · P.O. Box 640 · Buffalo, WY 82834 · 307-684-2248

William T. Schwartz · Schwartz, Bon, McCrary & Walker · Consolidated Royalty Building, Suite 505 · 141 South Center Street · Casper, WY 82601 · 307-235-6681

Houston G. Williams · Williams, Porter, Day & Neville · Durbin Center, Suite 300 · 145 South Durbin Street · Casper, WY 82601 · 307-265-0700

Carl L. Lathrop · Lathrop & Uchner · City Center Building, Suite 500 · 1920 Thomes Avenue · P.O. Box 4068 · Cheyenne, WY 82003-4068 · 307-632-0554

Henry A. Burgess · Burgess & Davis · 40 South Main Street · P.O. Box 728 · Sheridan, WY 82801 · 307-672-7491